CODE OF FEDERA REGULATIONS

Title 23
Highways

Revised as of April 1, 2019

Containing a codification of documents
of general applicability and future effect

As of April 1, 2019

Published by the Office of the Federal Register
National Archives and Records Administration
as a Special Edition of the Federal Register

Table of Contents

Cite this Code: CFR

To cite the regulations in this volume use title, part and section number. Thus, 23 CFR 1.1 *refers to title 23, part 1, section 1.*

Explanation

The Code of Federal Regulations is a codification of the general and permanent rules published in the Federal Register by the Executive departments and agencies of the Federal Government. The Code is divided into 50 titles which represent broad areas subject to Federal regulation. Each title is divided into chapters which usually bear the name of the issuing agency. Each chapter is further subdivided into parts covering specific regulatory areas.

Each volume of the Code is revised at least once each calendar year and issued on a quarterly basis approximately as follows:

Title 1 through Title 16..........as of January 1
Title 17 through Title 27..........as of April 1
Title 28 through Title 41..........as of July 1
Title 42 through Title 50..........as of October 1

The appropriate revision date is printed on the cover of each volume.

LEGAL STATUS

The contents of the Federal Register are required to be judicially noticed (44 U.S.C. 1507). The Code of Federal Regulations is prima facie evidence of the text of the original documents (44 U.S.C. 1510).

HOW TO USE THE CODE OF FEDERAL REGULATIONS

The Code of Federal Regulations is kept up to date by the individual issues of the Federal Register. These two publications must be used together to determine the latest version of any given rule.

To determine whether a Code volume has been amended since its revision date (in this case, April 1, 2019), consult the "List of CFR Sections Affected (LSA)," which is issued monthly, and the "Cumulative List of Parts Affected," which appears in the Reader Aids section of the daily Federal Register. These two lists will identify the Federal Register page number of the latest amendment of any given rule.

EFFECTIVE AND EXPIRATION DATES

Each volume of the Code contains amendments published in the Federal Register since the last revision of that volume of the Code. Source citations for the regulations are referred to by volume number and page number of the Federal Register and date of publication. Publication dates and effective dates are usually not the same and care must be exercised by the user in determining the actual effective date. In instances where the effective date is beyond the cut-off date for the Code a note has been inserted to reflect the future effective date. In those instances where a regulation published in the Federal Register states a date certain for expiration, an appropriate note will be inserted following the text.

OMB CONTROL NUMBERS

The Paperwork Reduction Act of 1980 (Pub. L. 96–511) requires Federal agencies to display an OMB control number with their information collection request.

Many agencies have begun publishing numerous OMB control numbers as amendments to existing regulations in the CFR. These OMB numbers are placed as close as possible to the applicable recordkeeping or reporting requirements.

PAST PROVISIONS OF THE CODE

Provisions of the Code that are no longer in force and effect as of the revision date stated on the cover of each volume are not carried. Code users may find the text of provisions in effect on any given date in the past by using the appropriate List of CFR Sections Affected (LSA). For the convenience of the reader, a "List of CFR Sections Affected" is published at the end of each CFR volume. For changes to the Code prior to the LSA listings at the end of the volume, consult previous annual editions of the LSA. For changes to the Code prior to 2001, consult the List of CFR Sections Affected compilations, published for 1949-1963, 1964-1972, 1973-1985, and 1986-2000.

"[RESERVED]" TERMINOLOGY

The term "[Reserved]" is used as a place holder within the Code of Federal Regulations. An agency may add regulatory information at a "[Reserved]" location at any time. Occasionally "[Reserved]" is used editorially to indicate that a portion of the CFR was left vacant and not accidentally dropped due to a printing or computer error.

INCORPORATION BY REFERENCE

What is incorporation by reference? Incorporation by reference was established by statute and allows Federal agencies to meet the requirement to publish regulations in the Federal Register by referring to materials already published elsewhere. For an incorporation to be valid, the Director of the Federal Register must approve it. The legal effect of incorporation by reference is that the material is treated as if it were published in full in the Federal Register (5 U.S.C. 552(a)). This material, like any other properly issued regulation, has the force of law.

What is a proper incorporation by reference? The Director of the Federal Register will approve an incorporation by reference only when the requirements of 1 CFR part 51 are met. Some of the elements on which approval is based are:

(a) The incorporation will substantially reduce the volume of material published in the Federal Register.

(b) The matter incorporated is in fact available to the extent necessary to afford fairness and uniformity in the administrative process.

(c) The incorporating document is drafted and submitted for publication in accordance with 1 CFR part 51.

What if the material incorporated by reference cannot be found? If you have any problem locating or obtaining a copy of material listed as an approved incorporation by reference, please contact the agency that issued the regulation containing that incorporation. If, after contacting the agency, you find the material is not available, please notify the Director of the Federal Register, National Archives and Records Administration, 8601 Adelphi Road, College Park, MD 20740-6001, or call 202-741-6010.

CFR INDEXES AND TABULAR GUIDES

A subject index to the Code of Federal Regulations is contained in a separate volume, revised annually as of January 1, entitled CFR INDEX AND FINDING AIDS. This volume contains the Parallel Table of Authorities and Rules. A list of CFR titles, chapters, subchapters, and parts and an alphabetical list of agencies publishing in the CFR are also included in this volume.

An index to the text of "Title 3—The President" is carried within that volume.

The Federal Register Index is issued monthly in cumulative form. This index is based on a consolidation of the "Contents" entries in the daily Federal Register.

A List of CFR Sections Affected (LSA) is published monthly, keyed to the revision dates of the 50 CFR titles.

REPUBLICATION OF MATERIAL

There are no restrictions on the republication of material appearing in the Code of Federal Regulations.

INQUIRIES

For a legal interpretation or explanation of any regulation in this volume, contact the issuing agency. The issuing agency's name appears at the top of odd-numbered pages.

For inquiries concerning CFR reference assistance, call 202–741–6000 or write to the Director, Office of the Federal Register, National Archives and Records Administration, 8601 Adelphi Road, College Park, MD 20740-6001 or e-mail *fedreg.info@nara.gov.*

SALES

The Government Publishing Office (GPO) processes all sales and distribution of the CFR. For payment by credit card, call toll-free, 866-512-1800, or DC area, 202-512-1800, M-F 8 a.m. to 4 p.m. e.s.t. or fax your order to 202-512-2104, 24 hours a day. For payment by check, write to: US Government Publishing Office – New Orders, P.O. Box 979050, St. Louis, MO 63197-9000.

ELECTRONIC SERVICES

The full text of the Code of Federal Regulations, the LSA (List of CFR Sections Affected), The United States Government Manual, the Federal Register, Public Laws, Public Papers of the Presidents of the United States, Compilation of Presidential Documents and the Privacy Act Compilation are available in electronic format via *www.govinfo.gov.* For more information, contact the GPO Customer Contact Center, U.S. Government Publishing Office. Phone 202-512-1800, or 866-512-1800 (toll-free). E-mail, *ContactCenter@gpo.gov.*

The Office of the Federal Register also offers a free service on the National Archives and Records Administration's (NARA) World Wide Web site for public law numbers, Federal Register finding aids, and related information. Connect to NARA's web site at *www.archives.gov/federal-register.*

The e-CFR is a regularly updated, unofficial editorial compilation of CFR material and Federal Register amendments, produced by the Office of the Federal Register and the Government Publishing Office. It is available at *www.ecfr.gov.*

OLIVER A. POTTS,
Director,
Office of the Federal Register
April 1, 2019.

THIS TITLE

Title 23—HIGHWAYS is composed of one volume. The contents of this volume represent the current regulations of the National Highway Traffic Safety Administration and the Federal Highway Administration, Department of Transportation, issued under this title of the CFR as of April 1, 2019.

For this volume, Cheryl E. Sirofchuck was Chief Editor. The Code of Federal Regulations publication program is under the direction of John Hyrum Martinez, assisted by Stephen J. Frattini.

Title 23—Highways

Part

CHAPTER I—FEDERAL HIGHWAY ADMINISTRATION, DEPARTMENT OF TRANSPORTATION

SUBCHAPTER A—GENERAL MANAGEMENT AND ADMINISTRATION

PART 1—GENERAL

AUTHORITY: 23 U.S.C. 315; 49 CFR 1.48(b).

SOURCE: 25 FR 4162, May 11, 1960, unless otherwise noted.

§ 1.1 Purpose.

The purpose of the regulations in this part is to implement and carry out the provisions of Federal law relating to the administration of Federal aid for highways.

§ 1.2 Definitions.

(a) Terms defined in 23 U.S.C. 101(a), shall have the same meaning where used in the regulations in this part, except as modified herein.

(b) The following terms where used in the regulations in this part shall have the following meaning:

Administrator. The Federal Highway Administrator.

Advertising policy. The national policy relating to the regulation of outdoor advertising declared in title 23 U.S.C. 131.

Advertising standards. The "National Standards for Regulation by States of Outdoor Advertising Signs, Displays and Devices Adjacent to the National System of Interstate and Defense Highways" promulgated by the Secretary (part 20 of this chapter).

Federal laws. The provisions of title 23 U.S.C., and all other Federal laws, heretofore or hereafter enacted, relating to Federal aid for highways.

Latest available Federal census. The latest available Federal decennial census, except for the establishment of urban area.

Project. An undertaking by a State highway department for highway construction, including preliminary engineering, acquisition of rights-of-way and actual construction, or for highway planning and research, or for any other work or activity to carry out the provisions of the Federal laws for the administration of Federal aid for highways.

Secondary road plan. A plan for administration of Federal aid for highways on the Federal-aid secondary highway system pursuant to 23 U.S.C. 117.

Secretary. The Secretary of Transportation.

State. Any State of the United States, the District of Columbia and Puerto Rico.

Urban area. An area including and adjacent to a municipality or other urban place having a population of five thousand or more, as determined by the latest available published official Federal census, decennial or special, within boundaries to be fixed by a State highway department, subject to the approval of the Administrator.

[25 FR 4162, May 11, 1960, as amended at 35 FR 18719, Dec. 10, 1970]

§ 1.3 Federal-State cooperation; authority of State highway departments.

The Administrator shall cooperate with the States, through their respective State highway departments, in the construction of Federal-aid highways. Each State highway department, maintained in conformity with 23 U.S.C. 302, shall be authorized, by the laws of the State, to make final decisions for the State in all matters relating to, and to enter into, on behalf of the State, all contracts and agreements for projects and to take such other actions on behalf of the State as may be necessary to comply with the Federal laws and the regulations in this part.

§ 1.5 Information furnished by State highway departments.

At the request of the Administrator the State highway department shall furnish to him such information as the Administrator shall deem desirable in administering the Federal-aid highway program.

§ 1.7 Urban area boundaries.

Boundaries of an urban area shall be submitted by the State highway department and be approved by the Administrator prior to the inclusion in a program of any project wholly or partly in such area involving funds authorized for and limited to urban areas.

§ 1.8 [Reserved]

§ 1.9 Limitation on Federal participation.

(a) Federal-aid funds shall not participate in any cost which is not incurred in conformity with applicable Federal and State law, the regulations in this title, and policies and procedures prescribed by the Administrator. Federal funds shall not be paid on account of any cost incurred prior to authorization by the Administrator to the State highway department to proceed with the project or part thereof involving such cost.

(b) Notwithstanding the provisions of paragraph (a) of this section the Administrator may, upon the request of a State highway department, approve the participation of Federal-aid funds in a previously incurred cost if he finds:

(1) That his approval will not adversely affect the public,

(2) That the State highway department has acted in good faith, and that there has been no willful violation of Federal requirements,

(3) That there has been substantial compliance with all other requirements prescribed by the Administrator, and full compliance with requirements mandated by Federal statute,

(4) That the cost to the United States will not be in excess of the cost which it would have incurred had there been full compliance, and

(5) That the quality of work undertaken has not been impaired.

(c) Any request submitted under paragraph (b) of this section shall be accompanied by a detailed description of the relevant circumstances and facts, and shall explain the necessity for incurring the costs in question.

[38 FR 18368, July 10, 1973]

§ 1.11 Engineering services.

(a) *Federal participation.* Costs of engineering services performed by the State highway department or any instrumentality or entity referred to in paragraph (b) of this section may be eligible for Federal participation only to the extent that such costs are directly attributable and properly allocable to specific projects.

(b) *Governmental engineering organizations.* The State highway department may utilize, under its supervision, the services of well-qualified and suitably equipped engineering organizations of other governmental instrumentalities for making surveys, preparing plans, specifications and estimates, and for supervising the construction of any project.

(c) *Railroad and utility engineering organizations.* The State highway department may utilize, under its supervision, the services of well-qualified and suitably equipped engineering organizations of the affected railroad companies for railway-highway crossing projects and of the affected utility companies for projects involving utility installations.

(d) [Reserved]

(e) *Responsibility of the State highway department.* The State highway department is not relieved of its responsibilities under Federal law and the regulations in this part in the event it utilizes the services of any engineering organization under paragraphs (b), (c) or (d) of this section.

[25 FR 4162, May 11, 1960, as amended at 53 FR 18276, May 23, 1988; 57 FR 60728, Dec. 22, 1992; 66 FR 58666, Nov. 23, 2001]

§ 1.23 Rights-of-way.

(a) *Interest to be acquired.* The State shall acquire rights-of-way of such nature and extent as are adequate for the construction, operation and maintenance of a project.

(b) *Use for highway purposes.* Except as provided under paragraph (c) of this section, all real property, including air space, within the right-of-way boundaries of a project shall be devoted exclusively to public highway purposes. No project shall be accepted as complete until this requirement has been satisfied. The State highway department shall be responsible for preserving such right-of-way free of all public and private installations, facilities or encroachments, except (1) those approved under paragraph (c) of this section; (2) those which the Administrator approves as constituting a part of a highway or as necessary for its operation, use or maintenance for public highway purposes and (3) informational sites established and maintained in accordance with § 1.35 of the regulations in this part.

(c) *Other use or occupancy.* Subject to 23 U.S.C. 111, the temporary or permanent occupancy or use of right-of-way, including air space, for nonhighway purposes and the reservation of subsurface mineral rights within the boundaries of the rights-of-way of Federal-aid highways, may be approved by the Administrator, if he determines that such occupancy, use or reservation is in the public interest and will not impair the highway or interfere with the free and safe flow of traffic thereon.

§ 1.27 Maintenance.

The responsibility imposed upon the State highway department, pursuant to 23 U.S.C. 116, for the maintenance of projects shall be carried out in accordance with policies and procedures issued by the Administrator. The State highway department may provide for such maintenance by formal agreement with any adequately equipped county, municipality or other governmental instrumentality, but such an agreement shall not relieve the State highway department of its responsibility for such maintenance.

§ 1.28 Diversion of highway revenues.

(a) *Reduction in apportionment.* If the Secretary shall find that any State has diverted funds contrary to 23 U.S.C. 126, he shall take such action as he may deem necessary to comply with said provision of law by reducing the first Federal-aid apportionment of primary, secondary and urban funds made to the State after the date of such finding. In any such reduction, each of these funds shall be reduced in the same proportion.

(b) *Furnishing of information.* The Administrator may require any State to submit to him such information as he may deem necessary to assist the Secretary in carrying out the provisions of 23 U.S.C. 126 and paragraph (a) of this section.

§ 1.32 Issuance of directives.

(a) The Administrator shall promulgate and require the observance of policies and procedures, and may take other action as he deems appropriate or necessary for carrying out the provisions and purposes of Federal laws, the policies of the Federal Highway Administration, and the regulations of this part.

(b) The Administrator or his delegated representative, as appropriate, is authorized to issue the following type of directives:

(1) Federal Highway Administration Regulations are issued by the Administrator or his delegate, as necessary, to implement and carry out the provisions of title 23 U.S.C., relating to the administration of Federal aid for highways, direct Federal programs and State and community safety programs; and title 49 U.S.C., relating to motor carrier safety; and other applicable laws and programs under his jurisdiction.

(2) Notices are temporary issuances transmitting one-time or short-term instructions or information which is expected to remain in effect for less than 90 days or for a predetermined period of time normally not to exceed one year.

(3) Orders are directives limited in volume and contain permanent or longlasting policy, instructions, and procedures. FHWA Orders are to be used primarily as internal FHWA directives.

(4) Joint Interagency Orders and Notices are used by FHWA and the National Highway Traffic Safety Administration (NHTSA) to issue joint policies, procedures, and information pertaining to the joint administration of the State and Community Highway Safety Program. Where necessary, other joint directives may be issued with other modal administrations within the Department of Transportation.

(5) Manuals are generally designed for use in issuing permanent or long-lasting detailed policy and procedure. Some of the major manuals recognized by the FHWA Directives System follow:

(i) The Federal-Aid Highway Program Manual has been established to assemble and organize program material of the type previously contained in the Policy and Procedure and Instructional Memoranda which will continue in effect until specifically revoked or published in the new manual. Regulatory material is printed in italics in the manual and also appears in this code. Nonregulatory material is printed in delegate type.

(ii) The Administrative Manual covers all internal FHWA administrative support functions.

(iii) The Highway Planning Program Manual covers the methods and procedures necessary to conduct the highway planning functions.

(iv) The Research and Development Manual series entitled, "The Federally Coordinated Program of Research and Development in Highway Transportation" describes the FHWA research and development program.

(v) The External Audit Manual provides guidance to FHWA auditors in their review of State programs and processes.

(vi) The Civil Rights and Equal Opportunity Manual provides guidance to FHWA and State Civil Rights and Equal Employment Opportunity Officers.

(vii) The BMCS Operations Manual provides program guidance for all field employees assigned to the motor carrier safety program.

(viii) The Highway Safety Program Manual, issued jointly by FHWA and NHTSA, contains volumes relating to the joint administration of the program.

(6) Handbooks are internal operating instructions published in book form where, because of the program area covered, it is desirable to provide greater detail of administrative and technical instructions.

(7) Transmittals identify and explain the original issuance or page change, provide background information, and provide filing instructions for insertion of new pages and removal of changed pages, or both.

(49 U.S.C. 1655)

[39 FR 1512, Jan. 10, 1974]

§ 1.33 Conflicts of interest.

No official or employee of a State or any other governmental instrumentality who is authorized in his official capacity to negotiate, make, accept or approve, or to take part in negotiating, making, accepting or approving any contract or subcontract in connection with a project shall have, directly or indirectly, any financial or other personal interest in any such contract or subcontract. No engineer, attorney, appraiser, inspector or other person performing services for a State or a governmental instrumentality in connection with a project shall have, directly or indirectly, a financial or other personal interest, other than his employment or retention by a State or other governmental instrumentality, in any contract or subcontract in connection with such project. No officer or employee of such person retained by a State or other governmental instrumentality shall have, directly or indirectly, any financial or other personal interest in any real property acquired for a project unless such interest is openly disclosed upon the public records of the State highway department and of such other governmental instrumentality, and such officer, employee or person has not participated in such acquisition for and in behalf of the State. It shall be the responsibility of the State to enforce the requirements of this section.

§ 1.35 Bonus program.

(a) Any agreement entered into by a State pursuant to the provisions of section 12 of the Federal-Aid Highway Act of 1958, Pub. L. 85–381, 72 Stat. 95, as amended, shall provide for the control or regulation of outdoor advertising, consistent with the advertising policy and standards promulgated by the Administrator, in areas adjacent to the entire mileage of the Interstate System within that State, except such segments as may be excluded from the application of such policy and standards by section 12.

(b) Any such agreement for the control of advertising may provide for establishing publicly owned informational sites, whether publicly or privately operated, within the limits of or adjacent to the right-of-way of the Interstate System on condition that no such site shall be established or maintained except at locations and in accordance with plans, in furtherance of the advertising policy and standards, submitted to and approved by the Administrator.

(c) No advertising right in the acquisition of which Federal funds participated shall be disposed of without the prior approval of the Administrator.

[39 FR 28628, Aug. 9, 1974]

§ 1.36 Compliance with Federal laws and regulations.

If the Administrator determines that a State has violated or failed to comply with the Federal laws or the regulations in this part with respect to a project, he may withhold payment to the State of Federal funds on account of such project, withhold approval of further projects in the State, and take such other action that he deems appropriate under the circumstances, until compliance or remedial action has been accomplished by the State to the satisfaction of the Administrator.

SUBCHAPTER B—PAYMENT PROCEDURES

PART 140—REIMBURSEMENT

Subparts A–D [Reserved]

Subpart E—Administrative Settlement Costs—Contract Claims

AUTHORITY: 23 U.S.C. 101(e), 106, 109(e), 114(a), 120(g), 121, 122, 130, and 315; and 49 CFR 1.48(b).

Subparts A–D [Reserved]

Subpart E—Administrative Settlement Costs—Contract Claims

SOURCE: 44 FR 59233, Oct. 15, 1979, unless otherwise noted.

§ 140.501 Purpose.

This regulation establishes the criteria for eligibility for reimbursement of administrative settlement costs in defense of contract claims on projects performed by a State under Federal-aid procedures.

§ 140.503 Definition.

Administrative settlement costs are costs related to the defense and settlement of contract claims including, but not limited to, salaries of a contracting officer or his/her authorized representative, attorneys, and/or members of State boards of arbitration, appeals boards, or similar tribunals, which are allocable to the findings and determinations of contract claims, but not including administrative or overhead costs.

§ 140.505 Reimbursable costs.

(a) Federal funds may participate in administrative settlement costs which are:

(1) Incurred after notice of claim,

(2) Properly supported,

(3) Directly allocable to a specific Federal-aid or Federal project,

(4) For employment of special counsel for review and defense of contract claims, when

(i) Recommended by the State Attorney General or State Highway Agency (SHA) legal counsel and

(ii) Approved in advance by the FHWA Division Administrator, with advice of FHWA Regional Counsel, and

(5) For travel and transportation expenses, if in accord with established policy and practices.

(b) No reimbursement shall be made if it is determined by FHWA that there was negligence or wrongdoing of any kind by SHA officials with respect to the claim.

Subpart F—Reimbursement for Bond Issue Projects

SOURCE: 48 FR 54971, Dec. 8, 1983, unless otherwise noted.

§ 140.601 Purpose.

To prescribe policies and procedures for the use of Federal funds by State highway agencies (SHAs) to aid in the retirement of the principal and interest of bonds, pursuant to 23 U.S.C. 122 and the payment of interest on bonds of eligible Interstate projects.

§ 140.602 Requirements and conditions.

(a) An SHA that uses the proceeds of bonds issued by the State, a county, city or other political subdivision of the State, for the construction of projects on the Federal-aid primary or Interstate system, or extensions of any of the Federal-aid highway systems in urban areas, or for substitute highway projects approved under 23 U.S.C. 103(e)(4), may claim payment of any portion of such sums apportioned to it for expenditures on such system to aid in the retirement of the principal of bonds at their maturities, to the extent that the proceeds of bonds have actually been expended in the construction of projects.

(b) Any interest earned and payable on bonds, the proceeds of which were expended on Interstate projects after November 6, 1978, is an eligible cost of construction. The amount of interest eligible for participation will be based on (1) the date the proceeds were expended on the project, (2) amount expended, and (3) the date of conversion to a regularly funded project. As provided for in section 115(c), Pub. L. 95–599, November 6, 1978, interest on bonds issued in any fiscal year by a State after November 6, 1978, may be paid under the authority of 23 U.S.C. 122 only if such SHA was eligible to obligate Interstate Discretionary funds under the provisions of 23 U.S.C. 118(b) during such fiscal year, and the Administrator certifies that such eligible SHA has utilized, or will utilize to the fullest extent possible during such fiscal year, its authority to obligate funds under 23 U.S.C. 118(b).

(c) The Federal share payable at the time of conversion, as provided for in § 140.610 shall be the legal pro rata in effect at the time of execution of the project agreement for the bond issue project.

(d) The authorization of a bond issue project does not constitute a commitment of Federal funds until the project is converted to a regular Federal-aid project as provided for in § 140.610.

(e) Reimbursements for the redemption of bonds may not precede, by more than 60 days, the scheduled date of the retirement of the bonds.

(f) Federal funds are not eligible for payment into sinking funds created and maintained for the subsequent retirement of bonds.

§ 140.603 Programs.

Programs covering projects to be financed from the proceeds of bonds shall be prepared and submitted to FHWA. Project designations shall be the same as for regular Federal-aid projects except that the prefix letter "B" for bond issue shall be used as the first letter of each project designation, e.g., "BI" for Bond Issue Projects—Interstate.

§ 140.604 Reimbursable schedule.

Projects to be financed from other than Interstate funds shall be subject to a 36-month reimbursable schedule upon conversion to regular Federal-aid financing (See appendix). FHWA will consider requests for waiver of this provision at the time of conversion action. Waivers are subject to the availability of liquidating cash.

§ 140.605 Approval actions.

(a) Authorization to proceed with preliminary engineering and acquisition of rights-of-way shall be issued in the same manner as for regularly financed Federal-aid projects.

(b) Authorization of physical construction shall be given in the same manner as for regularly financed Federal-aid projects. The total cost and

Federal funds required, including interest, shall be indicated in the plans, specifications, and estimates.

(c) Projects subject to the reimbursable schedule shall be identified as an "E" project when the SHA is authorized to proceed with all or any phase of the work.

(d) Concurrence in the award of contracts shall be given.

§ 140.606 Project agreements.

Project Agreements, Form PR–2, shall be prepared and executed. Agreement provision 8 on the reverse side of Form PR–2[1] shall apply for bond issue projects.

§ 140.607 Construction.

Construction shall be supervised by the SHA in the same manner as for regularly financed Federal-aid projects. The FHWA will make construction inspections and reports.

§ 140.608 Reimbursable bond interest costs of Interstate projects.

(a) Bond interest earned on bonds actually retired may be reimbursed on the Federal pro rata basis applicable to such projects in accordance with § 140.602(b) and (c).

(b) No interest will be reimbursed for bonds issued after November 6, 1978, used to retire or otherwise refinance bonds issued prior to that date.

§ 140.609 Progress and final vouchers.

(a) Progress vouchers may be submitted for the Federal share of bonds retired or about to be retired, including eligible interest on Interstate Bond Issue Projects, the proceeds of which have actually been expended for the construction of the project.

(b) Upon completion of a bond issue project, a final voucher shall be submitted by the SHA. After final review, the SHA will be advised as to the total cost and Federal fund participation for the project.

§ 140.610 Conversion from bond issue to funded project status.

(a) At such time as the SHA elects to apply available apportioned Federal-aid funds to the retirement of bonds, including eligible interest earned and payable on Interstate Bond Projects, subject to available obligational authority, its claim shall be supported by appropriate certifications as follows:

I hereby certify that the following bonds, (list), the proceeds of which have been actually expended in the construction of bond issue projects authorized by title 23 U.S.C., section 122, (1) have been retired on ____, or (2) mature and are scheduled for retirement on ____, which is ___ days in advance of the maturity date of ____.

Eligible interest claimed on Interstate Bond Projects shall be shown for each bond and the certification shall include the statement:

I also certify that interest earned and paid or payable for each bond listed has been determined from the date on and after which the respective bond proceeds were actually expended on the project.

(b) The SHA's request for full conversion of a completed projects), or partial conversion of an active or completed project(s), may be made by letter, inclusive of the appropriate certification as described in § 140.610(a) making reference to any progress payments received or the final voucher(s) previously submitted and approved in accordance with § 140.609.

(c) Approval of the conversion action shall be by the Division Administrator.

(d) The SHA's request for partial conversion of an active or completed bond issue project shall provide for: (1) Conversion to funded project status of the portion to be financed out of the balance of currently available apportioned funds, and (2) retention of the unfunded portion of the project in the bond program.

(e) Where the SHA's request involves the partial conversion of a completed bond issue project, payment of the Federal funds made available under the conversion action shall be accomplished through use of Form PR–20, Voucher for Work Performed under Provisions of the Federal-aid and Federal Highway Acts, prepared in the division office and appropriately cross-referenced to the Bond Issue Project final voucher previously submitted and approved. The final voucher will be reduced by the amount of the approved reimbursement.

[1] The text of FHWA Form PR–2 is found in 23 CFR part 630, subpart C, appendix A.

§ 140.611 Determination of bond retirement.

Division Administrators shall be responsible for the prompt review of the SHA's records to determine that bonds issued to finance the projects and for which reimbursement has been made, including eligible bond interest expense, have been retired pursuant to the State's certification required by § 140.610(a), and that such action is documented in the project file.

§ 140.612 Cash management.

By July 1 of each year the SHA will provide FHWA with a schedule, including the anticipated claims for reimbursement, of bond projects to be converted during the next two fiscal years. The data will be used by FHWA in determining liquidating cash required to finance such conversions.

APPENDIX TO SUBPART F OF PART 140—REIMBURSABLE SCHEDULE FOR CONVERTED "E" (BOND ISSUE) PROJECTS (OTHER THAN INTERSTATE PROJECTS)

Time in months following conversion from "E" (bond issue) project to regular project	Cumulative amount reimbursable (percent of Federal funds obligated)
1	1
2	2
3	5
4	9
5	13
6	18
7	23
8	29
9	34
10	39
11	44
12	49
13	54
14	58
15	61
16	64
17	67
18	70
19	73
20	75
21	77
22	79
23	81
24	83
25	85
26	87
27	89
28	91
29	93
30	94
31	95
32	96
34	97
35	99
36	100

Subpart G [Reserved]

Subpart H—State Highway Agency Audit Expense

SOURCE: 49 FR 45578, Nov. 19, 1984, unless otherwise noted.

§ 140.801 Purpose.

To establish the reimbursement criteria for Federal participation in project related audit expenses.

§ 140.803 Policy.

Project related audits performed in accordance with generally accepted auditing standards (as modified by the Comptroller General of the United States) and applicable Federal laws and regulations are eligible for Federal participation. The State highway agency (SHA) may use other State, local public agency, and Federal audit organizations as well as licensed or certified public accounting firms to augment its audit force.

§ 140.805 Definitions.

(a) *Project related audits.* Audits which directly benefit Federal-aid highway projects. Audits performed in accordance with the requirements of 23 CFR part 12, audits of third party contract costs, and other audits providing assurance that a recipient has complied with FHWA regulations are all considered project related audits. Audits benefiting only nonfederal projects, those performed for SHA management use only, or those serving similar nonfederal purposes are not considered project related.

(b) *Third party contract costs.* Project related costs incurred by railroads, utilities, consultants, governmental instrumentalities, universities, nonprofit organizations, construction contractors (force account work), and organizations engaged in right-of-way studies, planning, research, or related activities where the terms of a proposal or contract (including lump sum) necessitate an audit. Construction contracts (except force account work) are not included in this group.

§ 140.807 Reimbursable costs.

(a) Federal funds may be used to reimburse an SHA for the following types of project related audit costs:

(1) Salaries, wages, and related costs paid to public employees in accordance with subpart G of this part,

(2) Payments by the SHA to any Federal, State, or local public agency audit organization, and

(3) Payments by the SHA to licensed or certified public accounting firms.

(b) Audit costs incurred by an SHA shall be equitably distributed to all benefiting parties. The portion of these costs allocated to the Federal-Aid Highway Program which are not directly related to a specific project or projects shall be equitably distributed, as a minimum, to the major FHWA funding categories in that State.

Subpart I—Reimbursement for Railroad Work

SOURCE: 40 FR 16057, Apr. 9, 1975, unless otherwise noted.

§ 140.900 Purpose.

The purpose of this subpart is to prescribe policies and procedures on reimbursement to the States for railroad work done on projects undertaken pursuant to the provisions of 23 CFR part 646, subpart B.

§ 140.902 Applicability.

This subpart, and all references hereinafter made to "projects," applies to Federal-aid projects involving railroad facilities, including projects for the elimination of hazards of railroad-highway crossings, and other projects which use railroad properties or which involve adjustments required by highway construction to either railroad facilities or facilities that are jointly owned or used by railroad and utility companies.

§ 140.904 Reimbursement basis.

(a) *General.* On projects involving the elimination of hazards of railroad-highway crossings, and on other projects where a railroad company is not obligated to move or to change its facilities at its own expense, reimbursement will be made for the costs incurred by the State in making changes to railroad facilities as required in connection with a Federal-aid highway project, in accordance with the provisions of this subpart.

(b) *Eligibility.* To be eligible, the costs must be:

(1) For work which is included in an approved statewide transportation improvement program.

(2) Incurred subsequent to the date of authorization by the Federal Highway Administration (FHWA),

(3) Incurred in accordance with the provisions of 23 CFR, part 646, subpart B, and

(4) Properly attributable to the project.

[40 FR 16057, Apr. 9, 1975, as amended at 53 FR 18276, May 23, 1988; 62 FR 45328, Aug. 27, 1997]

§ 140.906 Labor costs.

(a) *General.* (1) Salaries and wages, at actual or average rates, and related expenses paid by a company to individuals, for the time they are working on the project, are reimbursable when supported by adequate records. This shall include labor costs associated with preliminary engineering, construction engineering, right-of-way, and force account construction.

(2) Salaries and expenses paid to individuals who are normally part of the overhead organization of the company may be reimbursed for the time they are working directly on the project, such as for accounting and bill preparation, when supported by adequate records and when the work performed by such individuals is essential to the project and could not have been accomplished as economically by employees outside the overhead organization.

(3) Amounts paid to engineers, architects and others for services directly related to projects may be reimbursed.

(b) *Labor surcharges.* (1) Labor surcharges include worker compensation insurance, public liability and property damage insurance, and such fringe benefits as the company has established for the benefit of its employees. The cost of labor surcharges will be reimbursed at actual cost to the company or a company may, at its option, use an additive rate or other similar technique in lieu of actual costs provided that (i) the rate is based on historical cost data of the company, (ii) such rate is representative of actual costs incurred, (iii) the rate is adjusted at least annually taking into consideration known anticipated changes and correcting for any over or under applied costs for the preceding period, and (iv) the rate is approved by the SHA and FHWA.

(2) Where the company is a self-insurer there may be reimbursement:

(i) At experience rates properly developed from actual costs, not to exceed the rates of a regular insurance company for the class of employment covered, or

(ii) At the option of the company, a fixed rate of 8 percent of direct labor costs for worker compensation and public liability and property damage insurance together.

[40 FR 16057, Apr. 9, 1975, as amended at 47 FR 33955, Aug. 5, 1982; 56 FR 56578, Nov. 6, 1991]

§ 140.907 Overhead and indirect construction costs.

(a) A State may elect to reimburse the railroad company for its overhead and indirect construction costs.

(b) The FHWA will participate in these costs provided that:

(1) The costs are distributed to all applicable work orders and other functions on an equitable and uniform basis in accordance with generally accepted accounting principles;

(2) The costs included in the distribution are limited to costs actually incurred by the railroad;

(3) The costs are eligible in accordance with the Federal Acquisition Regulation (48 CFR), part 31, Contract Cost Principles and Procedures, relating to contracts with commercial organizations;

(4) The costs are considered reasonable;

(5) Records are readily available at a single location which adequately support the costs included in the distribution, the method used for distributing the costs, and the basis for determining additive rates;

(6) The rates are adjusted at least annually taking into consideration any overrecovery or underrecovery of costs; and

(7) The railroad maintains written procedures which assure proper control and distribution of the overhead and indirect construction costs.

[53 FR 18276, May 23, 1988]

§ 140.908 Materials and supplies.

(a) *Procurement.* Materials and supplies, if available, are to be furnished from company stock, except they may be obtained from other sources near the project site when available at less cost. Where not available from company stock, they may be purchased either under competitive bids or existing continuing contracts, under which the lowest available prices are developed. Minor quantities and proprietary products are excluded from these requirements. The company shall not be required to change its existing standards for materials used in permanent changes to its facilities.

(b) *Costs.* (1) Materials and supplies furnished from company stock shall be billed at current stock price of such new or used material at time of issue.

(2) Materials and supplies not furnished from company stock shall be billed at actual costs to the company delivered to the point of entry on the railroad company's line nearest the source of procurement.

(3) A reasonable cost of plant inspection and testing may be included in the costs of materials and supplies where such expense has been incurred. The computation of actual costs of materials and supplies shall include the deduction of all offered discounts, rebates and allowances.

(c) *Materials recovered.* (1) Materials recovered from temporary use and accepted for reuse by the company shall be credited to the project at prices charged to the job, less a consideration for loss in service life at 10 percent for rails, angle bars, tie plates and metal turnout materials and 15 percent for all other materials. Materials recovered from the permanent facility of the company that are accepted by the company for return to stock shall be credited to the project at current stock prices of such used material.

(2) Materials recovered and not accepted for reuse by the company, if determined to have a net sale value, shall be sold by the State or railroad following an opportunity for State inspection and appropriate solicitation for bids, to the highest bidder; or if the company practices a system of periodic disposal by sale, credit to the project shall be at the going prices supported by the records of the company. Where applicable, credit for materials recovered from the permanent facility in length or quantities in excess of that being placed should be reduced to reflect any increased cost of railroad operation resulting from the adjustment.

(d) *Removal costs.* Federal participation in the costs of removing, salvaging, transporting, and handling recovered materials will be limited to the value of materials recovered, except where FHWA approves additional measures for restoration of affected areas as required by the physical construction or by reason of safety or aesthetics.

(e) *Handling costs.* The actual and direct costs of handling and loading out of materials and supplies at and from company stores or material yards and of unloading and handling of recovered materials accepted by the company at its stores or material yards, are reimbursable. At the option of the company, 5 percent of the amounts billed for the materials and supplies which are issued from company stores and material yards will be reimbursable in lieu of actual costs.

(f) *Credit losses.* On projects where a company actually suffers loss by application of credits, the company shall have the opportunity of submitting a detailed statement of such loss as a basis for further adjustment.

§ 140.910 Equipment.

(a) *Company owned equipment.* Cost of company-owned equipment may be reimbursed for the average or actual cost of operation, light and running repairs, and depreciation, or at industry rates representative of actual costs as agreed to by the railroad, SHA, and FHWA. Reimbursement for company-owned vehicles may be made at average or actual costs or at rates of recorded use per mile which are representative of actual costs and agreed to by the company, SHA, and FHWA.

(b) *Other equipment.* Where company owned equipment is not available, reimbursement will be limited to the amount of rental paid (1) to the lowest qualified bidder, (2) under existing continuing contracts at reasonable cost, or (3) as an exception, by negotiation where (b) (1) and (2) are impractical due to project location or schedule.

[40 FR 16057, Apr. 9, 1975, as amended at 47 FR 33955, Aug. 5, 1982]

§ 140.912 Transportation.

(a) *Employees.* The company's cost of necessary employee transportation and subsistence directly attributable to the project, which is consistent with overall policy of the company, is reimbursable.

(b) *Materials, supplies, and equipment.* The most economical movement of materials, supplies and equipment to the project and necessary return to storage, including the associated costs of loading and unloading equipment, is reimbursable. Transportation by a railroad company over its own lines in a revenue train is reimbursable at average or actual costs, at rates which are representative of actual costs, or at rates which the company charges its customers for similar shipments provided the rate structure is documented and available to the public. These rates are to be agreed to by the company, SHA, and FHWA. No charge will be made for transportation by work train other than the operating expenses of the work train. When it is more practicable or more economical to move equipment on its own wheels, reimbursement may be made at average or actual costs or at rates which are representative of actual costs and are agreed to by the railroad, SHA, and FHWA.

[40 FR 16057, Apr. 9, 1975, as amended at 47 FR 33955, Aug. 5, 1982]

§ 140.914 Credits for improvements.

(a) Credit shall be made to the project for additions or improvements which provide for higher quality or increased service capability of the operating facility and which are provided solely for the benefit of the company.

(b) Where buildings and other depreciable structures of a company which are integral to operation of rail traffic must be replaced, credit shall be made to the project as set forth in 23 CFR 646.216(c)(2).

(c) No credit is required for additions or improvements which are:

(1) Necessitated by the requirements of the highway project.

(2) Replacements which, although not identical, are of equivalent standard.

(3) Replacements of devices or materials no longer regularly manufactured and the next highest grade or size is used.

(4) Required by governmental and appropriate regulatory commission requirements.

§ 140.916 Protection.

The cost of essential protective services which, in the opinion of a railroad company, are required to ensure safety to railroad operations during certain periods of the construction of a project, is reimbursable provided an item for such services is incorporated in the State-railroad agreement or in a work order issued by the State and approved by FHWA.

§ 140.918 Maintenance and extended construction.

The cost of maintenance and extended construction is reimbursable to the extent provided for in 23 CFR 646.216(f)(4), and where included in the State-Railroad Agreement or otherwise approved by the State and FHWA.

§ 140.920 Lump sum payments.

Where approved by FHWA, pursuant to 23 CFR 646.216(d)(3), reimbursement may be made as a lump sum payment, in lieu of actual costs.

§ 140.922 Billings.

(a) After the executed State-Railroad Agreement has been approved by FHWA, the company may be reimbursed on progress billings of incurred costs. Costs for materials stockpiled at the project site or specifically purchased and delivered to the company for use on the project may be reimbursed on progress billings following approval of the executed State-Railroad Agreement or the written agreement under 23 CFR 646.218(c).

(b) The company shall provide one final and complete billing of all incurred costs, or of the agreed-to lump sum, within one year following completion of the reimbursable railroad work. Otherwise, previous payments to the company may be considered final, except as agreed to between the SHA and the railroad.

(c) All company cost records and accounts relating to the project are subject to audit by representatives of the State and/or the Federal Government for a period of three years from the date final payment has been received by the company.

(d) A railroad company must advise the State promptly of any outstanding obligation of the State's contractor for services furnished by the company such as protective services.

[40 FR 16057, Apr. 9, 1975, as amended at 40 FR 29712, July 15, 1975; 62 FR 45328, Aug. 27, 1997]

PART 172—PROCUREMENT, MANAGEMENT, AND ADMINISTRATION OF ENGINEERING AND DESIGN RELATED SERVICES

Sec.

AUTHORITY: 23 U.S.C. 106, 112, 114(a), 302, 315, and 402; 40 U.S.C. 1101 *et seq.;* 48 CFR part 31; 49 CFR 1.48(b); and 2 CFR part 200.

SOURCE: 80 FR 29927, May 22, 2015, unless otherwise noted.

§ 172.1 Purpose and applicability.

This part prescribes the requirements for the procurement, management, and administration of engineering and design related services under 23 U.S.C. 112 and as supplemented by the Uniform

Administrative Requirements For Federal Awards rule. The Uniform Administrative Requirements, Cost Principles and Audit Requirements For Federal Awards rule (2 CFR part 200) shall apply except where inconsistent with the requirements of this part and other laws and regulations applicable to the Federal-aid highway program (FAHP). The requirements herein apply to federally funded contracts for engineering and design related services for projects subject to the provisions of 23 U.S.C. 112(a) (related to construction) and are issued to ensure that a qualified consultant is obtained through an equitable qualifications-based selection procurement process, that prescribed work is properly accomplished in a timely manner, and at fair and reasonable cost. State transportation agencies (STA) (or other recipients) shall ensure that subrecipients comply with the requirements of this part and the Uniform Administrative Requirements, Cost Principles and Audit Requirements For Federal Awards rule. Federally funded contracts for services not defined as engineering and design related, or for services not in furtherance of a highway construction project or activity subject to the provisions of 23 U.S.C. 112(a), are not subject to the requirements of this part and shall be procured and administered under the requirements of the Uniform Administrative Requirements, Cost Principles and Audit Requirements For Federal Awards rule and procedures applicable to such activities.

§ 172.3 Definitions.

As used in this part:

Audit means a formal examination, in accordance with professional standards, of a consultant's accounting systems, incurred cost records, and other cost presentations to test the reasonableness, allowability, and allocability of costs in accordance with the Federal cost principles (as specified in 48 CFR part 31).

Cognizant agency means any governmental agency that has performed an audit in accordance with generally accepted government auditing standards to test compliance with the requirements of the Federal cost principles (as specified in 48 CFR part 31) and issued an audit report of the consultant's indirect cost rate, or any described agency that has conducted a review of an audit report and related workpapers prepared by a certified public accountant and issued a letter of concurrence with the audited indirect cost rate(s). A cognizant agency may be any of the following:

(1) A Federal agency;

(2) A State transportation agency of the State where the consultant's accounting and financial records are located; or

(3) A State transportation agency to which cognizance for the particular indirect cost rate(s) of a consulting firm has been delegated or transferred in writing by the State transportation agency identified in paragraph (2) of this definition.

Competitive negotiation means qualifications-based selection procurement procedures complying with 40 U.S.C. 1101–1104, commonly referred to as the Brooks Act.

Consultant means the individual or firm providing engineering and design related services as a party to a contract with a recipient or subrecipient of Federal assistance (as defined in 2 CFR 200.86 or 2 CFR 200.93, respectively).

Contract means a written procurement contract or agreement between a contracting agency and consultant reimbursed under a FAHP grant or subgrant and includes any procurement subcontract under a contract.

Contracting agencies means a State transportation agency or a procuring agency of the State acting in conjunction with and at the direction of the State transportation agency, other recipients, and all subrecipients that are responsible for the procurement, management, and administration of engineering and design related services.

Contract modification means an agreement modifying the terms or conditions of an original or existing contract.

Engineering and design related services means:

(1) Program management, construction management, feasibility studies, preliminary engineering, design engineering, surveying, mapping, or architectural related services with respect

to a highway construction project subject to 23 U.S.C. 112(a) as defined in 23 U.S.C. 112(b)(2)(A); and

(2) Professional services of an architectural or engineering nature, as defined by State law, which are required to or may logically or justifiably be performed or approved by a person licensed, registered, or certified to provide the services with respect to a highway construction project subject to 23 U.S.C. 112(a) and as defined in 40 U.S.C. 1102(2).

Federal cost principles means the cost principles contained in 48 CFR part 31 of the Federal Acquisition Regulation for determination of allowable costs of commercial, for-profit entities.

Fixed fee means a sum expressed in U.S. dollars established to cover the consultant's profit and other business expenses not allowable or otherwise included as a direct or indirect cost.

Management support role means performing engineering management services or other services acting on the contracting agency's behalf, which are subject to review and oversight by agency officials, such as a program or project administration role typically performed by the contracting agency and necessary to fulfill the duties imposed by title 23 of the United States Code, other Federal and State laws, and applicable regulations.

Noncompetitive means the method of procurement of engineering and design related services when it is not feasible to award the contract using competitive negotiation or small purchase procurement methods.

One-year applicable accounting period means the annual accounting period for which financial statements are regularly prepared by the consultant.

Scope of work means all services, work activities, and actions required of the consultant by the obligations of the contract.

Small purchases means the method of procurement of engineering and design related services where an adequate number of qualified sources are reviewed and the total contract costs do not exceed an established simplified acquisition threshold.

State transportation agency (STA) means that department or agency maintained in conformity with 23 U.S.C. 302 and charged under State law with the responsibility for highway construction (as defined in 23 U.S.C. 101); and that is authorized by the laws of the State to make final decisions in all matters relating to, and to enter into, all contracts and agreements for projects and activities to fulfill the duties imposed by title 23 United States Code, title 23 Code of Federal Regulations, and other applicable Federal laws and regulations.

Subconsultant means the individual or firm contracted by a consultant to provide engineering and design related or other types of services that are part of the services which the consultant is under contract to provide to a recipient (as defined in 23 CFR 200.86) or subrecipient (as defined in 2 CFR 200.93) of Federal assistance.

§ 172.5 Program management and oversight.

(a) *STA responsibilities.* STAs or other recipients shall develop and sustain organizational capacity and provide the resources necessary for the procurement, management, and administration of engineering and design related consultant services, reimbursed in whole or in part with FAHP funding, as specified in 23 U.S.C. 302(a). Responsibilities shall include the following:

(1) Preparing and maintaining written policies and procedures for the procurement, management, and administration of engineering and design related consultant services in accordance with paragraph (c) of this section;

(2) Establishing a procedure for estimating the level of effort, schedule, and costs of needed consultant services and associated agency staffing and resources for management and oversight in support of project authorization requests submitted to FHWA for approval, as specified in 23 CFR 630.106;

(3) Procuring, managing, and administering engineering and design related consultant services in accordance with applicable Federal and State laws, regulations, and approved policies and procedures, as specified in 23 CFR 1.9(a); and

(4) Administering subawards in accordance with State laws and procedures as specified in 2 CFR part 1201, and the requirements of 23 U.S.C.

106(g)(4), and 2 CFR 200.331. Administering subawards includes providing oversight of the procurement, management, and administration of engineering and design related consultant services by subrecipients to ensure compliance with applicable Federal and State laws and regulations. Nothing in this part shall be taken as relieving the STA (or other recipient) of its responsibility under laws and regulations applicable to the FAHP for the work performed under any consultant agreement or contract entered into by a subrecipient.

(b) *Subrecipient responsibilities.* Subrecipients shall develop and sustain organizational capacity and provide the resources necessary for the procurement, management, and administration of engineering and design related consultant services, reimbursed in whole or in part with FAHP funding as specified in 23 U.S.C. 106(g)(4)(A). Responsibilities shall include the following:

(1) Adopting written policies and procedures prescribed by the awarding STA or other recipient for the procurement, management, and administration of engineering and design related consultant services in accordance with applicable Federal and State laws and regulations; or when not prescribed, shall include:

(i) Preparing and maintaining its own written policies and procedures in accordance with paragraph (c) of this section; or

(ii) Submitting documentation associated with each procurement and subsequent contract to the awarding STA or other grantee for review to assess compliance with applicable Federal and State laws, regulations, and the requirements of this part;

(2) Procuring, managing, and administering engineering and design related consultant services in accordance with applicable Federal and State laws, regulations, and approved policies and procedures, as specified in 23 CFR 1.9(a).

(c) *Written policies and procedures.* The contracting agency shall prepare and maintain written policies and procedures for the procurement, management, and administration of engineering and design related consultant services. The FHWA shall approve the written policies and procedures, including all revisions to such policies and procedures, of the STA or recipient to assess compliance with applicable requirements. The STA or other recipient shall approve the written policies and procedures, including all revisions to such policies and procedures, of a subrecipient to assess compliance with applicable requirements. These policies and procedures shall address, as appropriate for each method of procurement a contracting agency proposes to use, the following items to ensure compliance with Federal and State laws, regulations, and the requirements of this part:

(1) Preparing a scope of work and evaluation factors for the ranking/selection of a consultant;

(2) Soliciting interests, qualifications, or proposals from prospective consultants;

(3) Preventing, identifying, and mitigating conflicts of interest for employees of both the contracting agency and consultants and promptly disclosing in writing any potential conflict to the STA and FHWA, as specified in 2 CFR 200.112 and 23 CFR 1.33, and the requirements of this part.

(4) Verifying suspension and debarment actions and eligibility of consultants, as specified in 2 CFR part 1200 and 2 CFR part 180;

(5) Evaluating interests, qualifications, or proposals and the ranking/selection of a consultant;

(6) Determining, based upon State procedures and the size and complexity of a project, the need for additional discussions following RFP submission and evaluation;

(7) Preparing an independent agency estimate for use in negotiation with the selected consultant;

(8) Selecting appropriate contract type, payment method, and terms and incorporating required contract provisions, assurances, and certifications in accordance with § 172.9;

(9) Negotiating a contract with the selected consultant including instructions for proper disposal of concealed cost proposals of unsuccessful bidders;

(10) Establishing elements of contract costs, accepting indirect cost rate(s) for application to contracts, and

assuring consultant compliance with the Federal cost principles in accordance with §172.11;

(11) Ensuring consultant costs billed are allowable in accordance with the Federal cost principles and consistent with the contract terms as well as the acceptability and progress of the consultant's work;

(12) Monitoring the consultant's work and compliance with the terms, conditions, and specifications of the contract;

(13) Preparing a consultant's performance evaluation when services are completed and using such performance data in future evaluation and ranking of consultant to provide similar services;

(14) Closing-out a contract;

(15) Retaining supporting programmatic and contract records, as specified in 2 CFR 200.333 and the requirements of this part;

(16) Determining the extent to which the consultant, which is responsible for the professional quality, technical accuracy, and coordination of services, may be reasonably liable for costs resulting from errors and omissions in the work furnished under its contract;

(17) Assessing administrative, contractual, or legal remedies in instances where consultants violate or breach contract terms and conditions, and providing for such sanctions and penalties as may be appropriate; and

(18) Resolving disputes in the procurement, management, and administration of engineering and design related consultant services.

(d) A contracting agency may formally adopt, by statute or within approved written policies and procedures as specified in paragraph (c) of this section, any direct Federal Government or other contracting regulation, standard, or procedure provided its application does not conflict with the provisions of 23 U.S.C. 112, the requirements of this part, and other laws and regulations applicable to the FAHP.

(e) Notwithstanding paragraph (d) of this section, a contracting agency shall have a reasonable period of time, not to exceed 12 months from the effective date of this rule unless an extension is granted for unique or extenuating circumstances, to issue or update current written policies and procedures for review and approval in accordance with paragraph (c) of this section and consistent with the requirements of this part.

§172.7 Procurement methods and procedures.

(a) *Procurement methods.* The procurement of engineering and design related services funded by FAHP funds and related to a highway construction project subject to the provisions of 23 U.S.C. 112(a) shall be conducted in accordance with one of three methods: Competitive negotiation (qualifications-based selection) procurement, small purchases procurement for small dollar value contracts, and noncompetitive procurement where specific conditions exist allowing solicitation and negotiation to take place with a single consultant.

(1) *Competitive negotiation (qualifications-based selection).* Except as provided in paragraphs (a)(2) and (3) of this section, contracting agencies shall use the competitive negotiation method for the procurement of engineering and design related services when FAHP funds are involved in the contract, as specified in 23 U.S.C. 112(b)(2)(A). The solicitation, evaluation, ranking, selection, and negotiation shall comply with the qualifications-based selection procurement procedures for architectural and engineering services codified under 40 U.S.C. 1101–1104, commonly referred to as the Brooks Act. In accordance with the requirements of the Brooks Act, the following procedures shall apply to the competitive negotiation procurement method:

(i) *Solicitation.* The solicitation process shall be by public announcement, public advertisement, or any other public forum or method that assures qualified in-State and out-of-State consultants are given a fair opportunity to be considered for award of the contract. Procurement procedures may involve a single step process with issuance of a request for proposal (RFP) to all interested consultants or a multiphase process with issuance of a request for statements or letters of interest or qualifications (RFQ) whereby responding consultants are ranked based on qualifications and a RFP is then provided to three or more of the most highly qualified consultants. Minimum qualifications of consultants to perform services under general work categories or areas of expertise may also be assessed through a prequalification process whereby annual statements of qualifications and performance data are encouraged. Regardless of any process utilized for prequalification of consultants or for an initial assessment of a consultant's qualifications under a RFQ, a RFP specific to the project, task, or service is required for evaluation of a consultant's specific technical approach and qualifications.

(ii) *Request for proposal (RFP).* The RFP shall provide all information and requirements necessary for interested consultants to provide a response to the RFP and compete for the solicited services. The RFP shall:

(A) Provide a clear, accurate, and detailed description of the scope of work, technical requirements, and qualifications of consultants necessary for the services to be rendered. To the extent practicable, the scope of work should detail the purpose and description of the project, services to be performed, deliverables to be provided, estimated schedule for performance of the work, and applicable standards, specifications, and policies;

(B) Identify the requirements for any discussions that may be conducted with three or more of the most highly qualified consultants following submission and evaluation of proposals;

(C) Identify evaluation factors including their relative weight of importance in accordance with paragraph (a)(1)(iii) of this section;

(D) Specify the contract type and method(s) of payment anticipated to contract for the solicited services in accordance with § 172.9;

(E) Identify any special provisions or contract requirements associated with the solicited services;

(F) Require that submission of any requested cost proposals or elements of cost be in a concealed format and separate from technical/qualifications proposals, since these shall not be considered in the evaluation, ranking, and selection phase; and

(G) Provide an estimated schedule for the procurement process and establish a submittal deadline for responses to the RFP that provides sufficient time for interested consultants to receive notice, prepare, and submit a proposal, which except in unusual circumstances shall be not less than 14 calendar days from the date of issuance of the RFP.

(iii) *Evaluation factors.* (A) Criteria used for evaluation, ranking, and selection of consultants to perform engineering and design related services must assess the demonstrated competence and qualifications for the type of professional services solicited. These qualifications-based factors may include, but are not limited to, technical approach (e.g., project understanding, innovative concepts or alternatives, quality control procedures), work experience, specialized expertise, professional licensure, staff capabilities, workload capacity, and past performance.

(B) Price shall not be used as a factor in the evaluation, ranking, and selection phase. All price or cost related items which include, but are not limited to, cost proposals, direct salaries/ wage rates, indirect cost rates, and other direct costs are prohibited from being used as evaluation criteria.

(C) In-State or local preference shall not be used as a factor in the evaluation, ranking, and selection phase. State licensing laws are not preempted by this provision and professional licensure within a jurisdiction may be established as a requirement for the minimum qualifications and competence of a consultant to perform the solicited services.

(D) The following nonqualifications-based evaluation criteria are permitted under the specified conditions and provided the combined total of these criteria do not exceed a nominal value of 10 percent of the total evaluation criteria to maintain the integrity of a qualifications-based selection:

(*1*) A local presence may be used as a nominal evaluation factor where appropriate. This criteria shall not be based on political or jurisdictional boundaries and may be applied on a project-by-project basis for contracts where a need has been established for a consultant to provide a local presence, a local presence will add value to the quality and efficiency of the project, and application of this criteria leaves an appropriate number of qualified consultants, given the nature and size of the project. If a consultant from outside of the locality area indicates as part of a proposal that it will satisfy the criteria in some manner, such as establishing a local project office, that commitment shall be considered to have satisfied the local presence criteria.

(*2*) The participation of qualified and certified Disadvantaged Business Enterprise (DBE) subconsultants may be used as a nominal evaluation criterion where appropriate in accordance with 49 CFR part 26 and a contracting agency's FHWA-approved DBE program.

(iv) *Evaluation, ranking, and selection.* (A) The contracting agency shall evaluate consultant proposals based on the criteria established and published within the public solicitation.

(B) Although the contract will be with the consultant, proposal evaluations shall consider the qualifications of the consultant and any subconsultants identified within the proposal with respect to the scope of work and established criteria.

(C) The contracting agency shall specify in the RFP discussion requirements that shall follow submission and evaluation of proposals and based on the size and complexity of the project or as defined in contracting agency written policies and procedures, as specified in § 172.5(c). Discussions, as required by the RFP, may be written, by telephone, video conference, or by oral presentation/interview and shall be with at least three of the most highly qualified consultants to clarify the technical approach, qualifications, and capabilities provided in response to the RFP.

(D) From the proposal evaluation and any subsequent discussions which may have been conducted, the contracting agency shall rank, in order of preference, at least three consultants determined most highly qualified to perform the solicited services based on the established and published criteria. In instances where only two qualified consultants respond to the solicitation, the contracting agency may proceed with evaluation and selection if it is determined that the solicitation did not contain conditions or requirements that arbitrarily limited competition. Alternatively, a contracting agency may pursue procurement following the noncompetitive method when competition is determined to be inadequate and it is determined to not be feasible or practical to re-compete under a new solicitation as specified in paragraph (a)(3)(iii)(C) of this section.

(E) Notification must be provided to responding consultants of the final ranking of the three most highly qualified consultants.

(F) The contracting agency shall retain supporting documentation of the solicitation, proposal, evaluation, and selection of the consultant in accordance with this section and the provisions of 2 CFR 200.333.

(v) *Negotiation.* (A) The process for negotiation of the contract shall comply with the requirements codified in 40 U.S.C. 1104(b) for the order of negotiation.

(B) *Independent estimate.* Prior to receipt or review of the most highly qualified consultant's cost proposal, the contracting agency shall prepare a detailed independent estimate with an appropriate breakdown of the work or labor hours, types or classifications of labor required, other direct costs, and consultant's fixed fee for the defined scope of work. The independent estimate shall serve as the basis for negotiation.

(C) The contracting agency shall establish elements of contract costs (e.g., indirect cost rates, direct salary or wage rates, fixed fee, and other direct costs) separately in accordance with § 172.11. The use of the independent estimate and determination of cost allowance in accordance with § 172.11 shall ensure contracts for the consultant services are obtained at a fair and reasonable cost, as specified in 40 U.S.C. 1104(a).

(D) If concealed cost proposals were submitted in conjunction with technical/qualifications proposals, the contracting agency may consider only the cost proposal of the consultant with which negotiations are initiated. Due to the confidential nature of this data, as specified in 23 U.S.C. 112(b)(2)(E), concealed cost proposals of unsuccessful consultants may be disposed of in accordance with written policies and procedures established under § 172.5(c).

(E) The contracting agency shall retain documentation of negotiation activities and resources used in the analysis of costs to establish elements of the contract in accordance with the provisions of 2 CFR 200.333. This documentation shall include the consultant cost certification and documentation supporting the acceptance of the indirect cost rate to be applied to the contract, as specified in § 172.11(c).

(2) *Small purchases.* The contracting agency may use the State's small purchase procedures that reflect applicable State laws and regulations for the procurement of engineering and design related services provided the total contract costs do not exceed the Federal simplified acquisition threshold (as defined in 48 CFR 2.101). When a lower threshold for use of small purchase procedures is established in State law, regulation, or policy, the lower threshold shall apply to the use of FAHP funds. The following additional requirements shall apply to the small purchase procurement method:

(i) The scope of work, project phases, and contract requirements shall not be broken down into smaller components merely to permit the use of small purchase procedures.

(ii) A minimum of three consultants are required to satisfy the adequate number of qualified sources reviewed. In instances where only two qualified consultants respond to the solicitation, the contracting agency may proceed with evaluation and selection if it is determined that the solicitation did not contain conditions or requirements which arbitrarily limited competition. Alternatively, a contracting agency may pursue procurement following the noncompetitive method when competition is determined to be inadequate and it is determined to not be feasible or practical to re compete under a new solicitation as specified in § 172.7(a)(3)(iii)(C).

(iii) Contract costs may be negotiated in accordance with State small purchase procedures; however, the allowability of costs shall be determined in accordance with the Federal cost principles.

(iv) The full amount of any contract modification or amendment that would cause the total contract amount to exceed the established simplified acquisition threshold is ineligible for Federal-aid funding. The FHWA may withdraw all Federal-aid from a contract if it is modified or amended above the applicable established simplified acquisition threshold.

(3) *Noncompetitive.* The following requirements shall apply to the noncompetitive procurement method:

(i) A contracting agency may use its own noncompetitive procedures that reflect applicable State and local laws and regulations and conform to applicable Federal requirements.

(ii) A contracting agency shall establish a process to determine when noncompetitive procedures will be used and shall submit justification to, and receive approval from FHWA before using this form of contracting.

(iii) A contracting agency may award a contract by noncompetitive procedures under the following limited circumstances:

(A) The service is available only from a single source;

(B) There is an emergency which will not permit the time necessary to conduct competitive negotiations; or

(C) After solicitation of a number of sources, competition is determined to be inadequate.

(iv) Contract costs may be negotiated in accordance with contracting agency noncompetitive procedures; however, the allowability of costs shall be determined in accordance with the Federal cost principles.

(b) *Additional procurement requirements*—(1) *Uniform administrative requirements, cost principles and audit requirements for Federal awards.* (i) STAs or other recipients and their subrecipients shall comply with procurement requirements established in State and local laws, regulations, policies, and procedures that are not addressed by or are not in conflict with applicable Federal laws and regulations, as specified in 2 CFR part 1201.

(ii) When State and local procurement laws, regulations, policies, or procedures are in conflict with applicable Federal laws and regulations, a contracting agency shall comply with Federal requirements to be eligible for Federal-aid reimbursement of the associated costs of the services incurred following FHWA authorization, as specified in 2 CFR 200.102(c).

(2) *Disadvantaged Business Enterprise (DBE) program.* (i) A contracting agency shall give consideration to DBE consultants in the procurement of engineering and design related service contracts subject to 23 U.S.C. 112(b)(2) in accordance with 49 CFR part 26. When DBE program participation goals cannot be met through race-neutral measures, additional DBE participation on engineering and design related services contracts may be achieved in accordance with a contracting agency's FHWA approved DBE program through either:

(A) Use of an evaluation criterion in the qualifications-based selection of consultants, as specified in § 172.7(a)(1)(iii)(D); or

(B) Establishment of a contract participation goal.

(ii) The use of quotas or exclusive set-asides for DBE consultants is prohibited, as specified in 49 CFR 26.43.

(3) *Suspension and debarment.* A contracting agency shall verify suspension and debarment actions and eligibility status of consultants and subconsultants prior to entering into an agreement or contract in accordance with 2 CFR part 1200 and 2 CFR part 180.

(4) *Conflicts of interest.* (i) A contracting agency shall maintain a written code of standards of conduct governing the performance of their employees engaged in the award and administration of engineering and design related services contracts under this part and governing the conduct and roles of consultants in the performance of services under such contracts to prevent, identify, and mitigate conflicts of interest in accordance with 2 CFR 200.112, 23 CFR 1.33 and the provisions of this paragraph (b)(4).

(ii) No employee, officer, or agent of the contracting agency shall participate in selection, or in the award or administration of a contract supported by Federal-aid funds if a conflict of interest, real or apparent, would be involved. Such a conflict arises when there is a financial or other interest in the consultant selected for award by:

(A) The employee, officer, or agent;

(B) Any member of his or her immediate family;

(C) His or her partner; or

(D) An organization that employs or is about to employ any of the above.

(iii) The contracting agency's officers, employees, or agents shall neither solicit nor accept gratuities, favors, or anything of monetary value from consultants, potential consultants, or parties to subagreements. A contracting agency may establish dollar thresholds where the financial interest is not substantial or the gift is an unsolicited item of nominal value.

(iv) A contracting agency may provide additional prohibitions relative to real, apparent, or potential conflicts of interest.

(v) To the extent permitted by State or local law or regulations, the standards of conduct required by this paragraph shall provide for penalties, sanctions, or other disciplinary actions for violations of such standards by the contracting agency's officers, employees, or agents, or by consultants or their agents.

(vi) A contracting agency shall promptly disclose in writing any potential conflict of interest to FHWA.

(5) *Consultant services in management support roles.* (i) When FAHP funds participate in a consultant services contract, the contracting agency shall receive approval from FHWA, or the recipient as appropriate, before utilizing a consultant to act in a management support role for the contracting agency; unless an alternate approval procedure has been approved. Use of consultants in management support roles does not relieve the contracting agency of responsibilities associated with the use of FAHP funds, as specified in 23 U.S.C. 302(a) and 23 U.S.C. 106(g)(4) and should be limited to large projects or circumstances where unusual cost or time constraints exist, unique technical or managerial expertise is required, and/or an increase in contracting agency staff is not a viable option.

(ii) Management support roles may include, but are not limited to, providing oversight of an element of a highway program, function, or service on behalf of the contracting agency or may involve managing or providing oversight of a project, series of projects, or the work of other consultants and contractors on behalf of the contracting agency. Contracting agency written policies and procedures as specified in § 172.5(c) may further define allowable management roles and services a consultant may provide, specific approval responsibilities, and associated controls necessary to ensure compliance with Federal requirements.

(iii) Use of consultants or subconsultants in management support roles requires appropriate conflicts of interest standards as specified in paragraph (b)(4) of this section and adequate contracting agency staffing to administer and monitor the management consultant contract, as specified in § 172.9(d). A consultant serving in a management support role may be precluded from providing additional services on projects, activities, or contracts under its oversight due to potential conflicts of interest.

(iv) FAHP funds shall not participate in the costs of a consultant serving in a management support role where the consultant was not procured in accordance with Federal and State requirements, as specified in 23 CFR 1.9(a).

(v) Where benefiting more than a single Federal-aid project, allocability of consultant contract costs for services related to a management support role shall be distributed consistent with the cost principles applicable to the contracting agency, as specified in 2 CFR part 200, subpart E—Cost Principles.

§ 172.9 Contracts and administration.

(a) *Contract types.* The contracting agency shall use the following types of contracts:

(1) *Project-specific.* A contract between the contracting agency and consultant for the performance of services and defined scope of work related to a specific project or projects.

(2) *Multiphase.* A project-specific contract where the solicited services are divided into phases whereby the specific scope of work and associated costs may be negotiated and authorized by phase as the project progresses.

(3) *On-call or indefinite delivery/indefinite quantity (IDIQ).* A contract for the performance of services for a number of projects, under task or work orders issued on an as-needed or on-call basis, for an established contract period. The procurement of services to be performed under on-call or IDIQ contracts shall follow either competitive negotiation or small purchase procurement procedures, as specified in § 172.7. The solicitation and contract provisions shall address the following requirements:

(i) Specify a reasonable maximum length of contract period, including the number and period of any allowable contract extensions, which shall not exceed 5 years;

(ii) Specify a maximum total contract dollar amount that may be awarded under a contract;

(iii) Include a statement of work, requirements, specifications, or other description to define the general scope, complexity, and professional nature of the services; and

(iv) If multiple consultants are to be selected and multiple on-call or IDIQ contracts awarded through a single solicitation for specific services:

(A) Identify the number of consultants that may be selected or contracts that may be awarded from the solicitation; and

(B) Specify the procedures the contracting agency will use in competing and awarding task or work orders among the selected, qualified consultants. Task or work orders shall not be competed and awarded among the selected, qualified consultants on the basis of costs under on-call or IDIQ contracts for services procured with competitive negotiation procedures. Under competitive negotiation procurement, each specific task or work order shall be awarded to the selected, qualified consultants:

(*1*) Through an additional qualifications-based selection procedure, which may include, but does not require, a formal RFP in accordance with § 172.5(a)(1)(ii); or

(*2*) On a regional basis whereby the State is divided into regions and consultants are selected to provide on-call or IDIQ services for an assigned region(s) identified within the solicitation.

(b) *Payment methods.* (1) The method of payment to the consultant shall be set forth in the original solicitation, contract, and in any contract modification thereto. The methods of payment shall be: Lump sum, cost plus fixed fee, cost per unit of work, or specific rates of compensation. A single contract may contain different payment methods as appropriate for compensation of different elements of work.

(2) The cost plus a percentage of cost and percentage of construction cost methods of payment shall not be used.

(3) The lump sum payment method shall only be used when the contracting agency has established the extent, scope, complexity, character, and duration of the work to be required to a degree that fair and reasonable compensation, including a fixed fee, can be determined at the time of negotiation.

(4) When the method of payment is other than lump sum, the contract shall specify a maximum amount payable which shall not be exceeded unless adjusted by a contract modification.

(5) The specific rates of compensation payment method provides for reimbursement on the basis of direct labor hours at specified fixed hourly rates, including direct labor costs, indirect costs, and fee or profit, plus any other direct expenses or costs, subject to an agreement maximum amount. This payment method shall only be used when it is not possible at the time of procurement to estimate the extent or duration of the work or to estimate costs with any reasonable degree of accuracy. This specific rates of compensation payment method should be limited to contracts or components of contracts for specialized or support type services where the consultant is not in direct control of the number of hours worked, such as construction engineering and inspection. When using this payment method, the contracting agency shall manage and monitor the consultant's level of effort and classification of employees used to perform the contracted services.

(6) A contracting agency may withhold retainage from payments in accordance with prompt pay requirements, as specified in 49 CFR 26.29. When retainage is used, the terms and conditions of the contract shall clearly define agency requirements, including periodic reduction in retention and the conditions for release of retention.

(c) *Contract provisions.* (1) All contracts and subcontracts shall include the following provisions, either by reference or by physical incorporation into the language of each contract or subcontract, as applicable:

(i) Administrative, contractual, or legal remedies in instances where consultants violate or breach contract terms and conditions, and provide for such sanctions and penalties as may be appropriate;

(ii) Notice of contracting agency requirements and regulations pertaining to reporting;

(iii) Contracting agency requirements and regulations pertaining to copyrights and rights in data;

(iv) Access by recipient, the subrecipient, FHWA, the U.S. Department of Transportation's Inspector General, the Comptroller General of the United States, or any of their duly authorized representatives to any books, documents, papers, and records of the consultant which are directly pertinent to that specific contract for the purpose of making audit, examination, excerpts, and transcriptions;

(v) Retention of all required records for not less than 3 years after the contracting agency makes final payment and all other pending matters are closed;

(vi) Standard DOT Title VI Assurances (DOT Order 1050.2);

(vii) Disadvantaged Business Enterprise (DBE) assurance, as specified in 49 CFR 26.13(b);

(viii) Prompt pay requirements, as specified in 49 CFR 26.29;

(ix) Determination of allowable costs in accordance with the Federal cost principles;

(x) Contracting agency requirements pertaining to consultant errors and omissions;

(xi) Contracting agency requirements pertaining to conflicts of interest, as specified in 23 CFR 1.33 and the requirements of this part; and

(xii) A provision for termination for cause and termination for convenience by the contracting agency including the manner by which it will be effected and the basis for settlement.

(2) All contracts and subcontracts exceeding $100,000 shall contain, either by reference or by physical incorporation into the language of each contract, a provision for lobbying certification and disclosure, as specified in 49 CFR part 20.

(d) *Contract administration and monitoring*—(1) *Responsible charge.* A full-time, public employee of the contracting agency qualified to ensure that the work delivered under contract is complete, accurate, and consistent with the terms, conditions, and specifications of the contract shall be in responsible charge of each contract or project. While an independent consultant may be procured to serve in a program or project management support role, as specified in § 172.7(b)(5), or to provide technical assistance in review and acceptance of engineering and design related services performed and products developed by other consultants, the contracting agency shall designate a public employee as being in responsible charge. A public employee may serve in responsible charge of multiple projects and contracting agencies may use multiple public employees to fulfill monitoring responsibilities. The term responsible charge is intended to be applied only in the context defined within this regulation. It may or may not correspond to its usage in State laws regulating the licensure and/or conduct of professional engineers. The public employee's responsibilities shall include:

(i) Administering inherently governmental activities including, but not limited to, contract negotiation, contract payment, and evaluation of compliance, performance, and quality of services provided by consultant;

(ii) Being familiar with the contract requirements, scope of services to be performed, and products to be produced by the consultant;

(iii) Being familiar with the qualifications and responsibilities of the consultant's staff and evaluating any requested changes in key personnel;

(iv) Scheduling and attending progress and project review meetings, commensurate with the magnitude, complexity, and type of work, to ensure the work is progressing in accordance with established scope of work and schedule milestones;

(v) Ensuring consultant costs billed are allowable in accordance with the Federal cost principles and consistent with the contract terms as well as the acceptability and progress of the consultant's work;

(vi) Evaluating and participating in decisions for contract modifications; and

(vii) Documenting contract monitoring activities and maintaining supporting contract records, as specified in 2 CFR 200.333.

(2) *Performance evaluation.* The contracting agency shall prepare an evaluation summarizing the consultant's performance on a contract. The performance evaluation should include, but not be limited to, an assessment of the timely completion of work, adherence to contract scope and budget, and quality of the work conducted. The contracting agency shall provide the consultant a copy of the performance evaluation and an opportunity to provide written comments to be attached to the evaluation. The contracting agency should prepare additional interim performance evaluations based on the scope, complexity, and size of the contract as a means to provide feedback, foster communication, and achieve desired changes or improvements. Completed performance evaluations should be archived for consideration as an element of past performance in the future evaluation of the consultant to provide similar services.

(e) *Contract modification.* (1) Contract modifications are required for any amendments to the terms of the existing contract that change the cost of the contract; significantly change the character, scope, complexity, or duration of the work; or significantly change the conditions under which the work is required to be performed.

(2) A contract modification shall clearly define and document the changes made to the contract, establish the method of payment for any adjustments in contract costs, and be in compliance with the terms and conditions of the contract and original procurement.

(3) A contracting agency shall negotiate contract modifications following the same procedures as the negotiation of the original contract.

(4) A contracting agency may add to a contract only the type of services and work included within the scope of services of the original solicitation from which a qualifications-based selection was made.

(5) For any additional engineering and design related services outside of the scope of work established in the original request for proposal, a contracting agency shall:

(i) Procure the services under a new solicitation;

(ii) Perform the work itself using contracting agency staff; or

(iii) Use a different, existing contract under which the services would be within the scope of work.

(6) Overruns in the costs of the work shall not automatically warrant an increase in the fixed fee portion of a cost plus fixed fee reimbursed contract. Permitted changes to the scope of work or duration may warrant consideration for adjustment of the fixed fee portion of cost plus fixed fee or lump sum reimbursed contracts.

§ 172.11 Allowable costs and oversight.

(a) *Allowable costs.* (1) Costs or prices based on estimated costs for contracts shall be eligible for Federal-aid reimbursement only to the extent that costs incurred or cost estimates included in negotiated prices are allowable in accordance with the Federal cost principles.

(2) Consultants shall be responsible for accounting for costs appropriately and for maintaining records, including supporting documentation, adequate to demonstrate that costs claimed have been incurred, are allocable to the contract, and comply with Federal cost principles.

(b) *Elements of contract costs.* The following requirements shall apply to the establishment of the specified elements of contract costs:

(1) *Indirect cost rates.* (i) Indirect cost rates shall be updated on an annual basis in accordance with the consultant's annual accounting period and in compliance with the Federal cost principles.

(ii) Contracting agencies shall accept a consultant's or subconsultant's indirect cost rate(s) established for a 1-year applicable accounting period by a cognizant agency that has:

(A) Performed an audit in accordance with generally accepted government auditing standards to test compliance with the requirements of the Federal cost principles and issued an audit report of the consultant's indirect cost rate(s); or

(B) Conducted a review of an audit report and related workpapers prepared by a certified public accountant and issued a letter of concurrence with the related audited indirect cost rate(s).

(iii) When the indirect cost rate has not been established by a cognizant agency in accordance with paragraph (b)(1)(ii) of this section, a STA or other recipient shall perform an evaluation of a consultant's or subconsultant's indirect cost rate prior to acceptance and application of the rate to contracts administered by the recipient or its subrecipients. The evaluation performed by STAs or other recipients to establish or accept an indirect cost rate shall provide assurance of compliance with the Federal cost principles and may consist of one or more of the following:

(A) Performing an audit in accordance with generally accepted government auditing standards and issuing an audit report;

(B) Reviewing and accepting an audit report and related workpapers prepared by a certified public accountant or another STA;

(C) Establishing a provisional indirect cost rate for the specific contract and adjusting contract costs based upon an audited final rate at the completion of the contract; or

(D) Conducting other evaluations in accordance with a risk-based oversight process as specified in paragraph (c)(2) of this section and within the agency's approved written policies and procedures, as specified in § 172.5(c).

(iv) A lower indirect cost rate may be accepted for use on a contract if submitted voluntarily by a consultant; however, the consultant's offer of a lower indirect cost rate shall not be a condition or qualification to be considered for the work or contract award.

(v) Once accepted in accordance with paragraphs (b)(1)(ii) through (iv) of this section, contracting agencies shall apply such indirect cost rate for the purposes of contract estimation, negotiation, administration, reporting, and contract payment and the indirect cost rate shall not be limited by administrative or de facto ceilings of any kind.

(vi) A consultant's accepted indirect cost rate for its 1-year applicable accounting period shall be applied to contracts; however, once an indirect cost rate is established for a contract, it may be extended beyond the 1-year applicable period, through the duration of the specific contract, provided all concerned parties agree. Agreement to the extension of the 1-year applicable period shall not be a condition or qualification to be considered for the work or contract award.

(vii) *Disputed rates.* If an indirect cost rate established by a cognizant agency in paragraph (b)(1)(ii) of this section is in dispute, the contracting agency does not have to accept the rate. A contracting agency may perform its own audit or other evaluation of the consultant's indirect cost rate for application to the specific contract, until or unless the dispute is resolved. A contracting agency may alternatively negotiate a provisional indirect cost rate for the specific contract and adjust contract costs based upon an audited final rate. Only the consultant and the parties involved in performing the indirect cost audit may dispute the established indirect cost rate. If an error is discovered in the established indirect cost rate, the rate may be disputed by any prospective contracting agency.

(2) *Direct salary or wage rates.* (i) Compensation for each employee or classification of employee must be reasonable for the work performed in accordance with the Federal cost principles.

(ii) To provide for fair and reasonable compensation, considering the classification, experience, and responsibility of employees necessary to provide the desired engineering and design related services, contracting agencies may establish consultant direct salary or wage rate limitations or "benchmarks" based upon an objective assessment of the reasonableness of proposed rates performed in accordance with the reasonableness provisions of the Federal cost principles.

(iii) When an assessment of reasonableness in accordance with the Federal cost principles has not been performed, contracting agencies shall use and apply the consultant's actual direct salary or wage rates for estimation, negotiation, administration, and payment of contracts and contract modifications.

(3) *Fixed fee.* (i) The determination of the amount of fixed fee shall consider the scope, complexity, contract duration, degree of risk borne by the consultant, amount of subcontracting, and professional nature of the services as well as the size and type of contract.

(ii) The establishment of fixed fee shall be contract or task order specific.

(iii) Fixed fees in excess of 15 percent of the total direct labor and indirect costs of the contract may be justified only when exceptional circumstances exist.

(4) *Other direct costs.* A contracting agency shall use the Federal cost principles in determining the reasonableness, allowability, and allocability of other direct contract costs.

(c) *Oversight*—(1) *Agency controls.* Contracting agencies shall provide reasonable assurance that consultant costs on contracts reimbursed in whole or in part with FAHP funding are allowable in accordance with the Federal cost principles and consistent with the contract terms considering the contract type and payment method. Contracting agency written policies, procedures, contract documents, and other controls, as specified in §§ 172.5(c) and 172.9 shall address the establishment, acceptance, and administration of contract costs to assure compliance with the Federal cost principles and requirements of this section.

(2) *Risk-based analysis.* The STAs or other recipient may employ a risk-based oversight process to provide reasonable assurance of consultant compliance with Federal cost principles on FAHP funded contracts administered by the recipient or its subrecipients. If employed, this risk-based oversight process shall be incorporated into STA or other recipient written policies and procedures, as specified in § 172.5(c). In

addition to ensuring allowability of direct contract costs, the risk-based oversight process shall address the evaluation and acceptance of consultant and subconsultant indirect cost rates for application to contracts. A risk-based oversight process shall consist of the following:

(i) *Risk assessments.* Conducting and documenting an annual assessment of risks of noncompliance with the Federal cost principles per consultant doing business with the agency, considering the following factors:

(A) Consultant's contract volume within the State;

(B) Number of States in which the consultant operates;

(C) Experience of consultant with FAHP contracts;

(D) History and professional reputation of consultant;

(E) Audit history of consultant;

(F) Type and complexity of consultant accounting system;

(G) Size (number of employees or annual revenues) of consultant;

(H) Relevant experience of certified public accountant performing audit of consultant;

(I) Assessment of consultant's internal controls;

(J) Changes in consultant organizational structure; and

(K) Other factors as appropriate.

(ii) *Risk mitigation and evaluation procedures.* Allocating resources, as considered necessary based on the results of the annual risk assessment, to provide reasonable assurance of compliance with the Federal cost principles through application of the following types of risk mitigation and evaluation procedures appropriate to the consultant and circumstances:

(A) Audits performed in accordance with generally accepted government audit standards to test compliance with the requirements of the Federal cost principles;

(B) Certified public accountant or other STA workpaper reviews;

(C) Other analytical procedures;

(D) Consultant cost certifications in accordance with paragraph (c)(3) of this section; and

(E) Consultant and certified public accountant training on the Federal cost principles.

(iii) *Documentation.* Maintaining supporting documentation of the risk-based analysis procedures performed to support the allowability and acceptance of consultant costs on FAHP funded contracts.

(3) *Consultant cost certification.* (i) Indirect cost rate proposals for the consultant's 1-year applicable accounting period shall not be accepted and no agreement shall be made by a contracting agency to establish final indirect cost rates, unless the costs have been certified by an official of the consultant as being allowable in accordance with the Federal cost principles. The certification requirement shall apply to all indirect cost rate proposals submitted by consultants and subconsultants for acceptance by a STA or other recipient. Each consultant or subconsultant is responsible for certification of its own indirect cost rate and may not certify the rate of another firm.

(ii) The certifying official shall be an individual executive or financial officer of the consultant's organization at a level no lower than a Vice President or Chief Financial Officer, or equivalent, who has the authority to represent the financial information utilized to establish the indirect cost rate proposal submitted for acceptance.

(iii) The certification of final indirect costs shall read as follows:

Certificate of Final Indirect Costs

This is to certify that I have reviewed this proposal to establish final indirect cost rates and to the best of my knowledge and belief:

1. All costs included in this proposal (identify proposal and date) to establish final indirect cost rates for (identify period covered by rate) are allowable in accordance with the cost principles of the Federal Acquisition Regulation (FAR) of title 48, Code of Federal Regulations (CFR), part 31; and

2. This proposal does not include any costs which are expressly unallowable under applicable cost principles of the FAR of 48 CFR part 31.

Firm: __________

Signature: __________

Name of Certifying Official: __________

Title: __________

Date of Execution: __________

(4) *Sanctions and penalties.* Contracting agency written policies, procedures, and contract documents, as

specified in §§172.5(c) and 172.9(c), shall address the range of administrative, contractual, or legal remedies that may be assessed in accordance with Federal and State laws and regulations where consultants violate or breach contract terms and conditions. Where consultants knowingly charge unallowable costs to a FAHP funded contract:

(i) Contracting agencies shall pursue administrative, contractual, or legal remedies and provide for such sanctions and penalties as may be appropriate; and

(ii) Consultants are subject to suspension and debarment actions as specified in 2 CFR part 1200 and 2 CFR part 180, potential cause of action under the False Claims Act as specified in 32 U.S.C. 3729–3733, and prosecution for making a false statement as specified in 18 U.S.C. 1020.

(d) *Prenotification; confidentiality of data.* FHWA, recipients, and subrecipients of FAHP funds may share audit information in complying with the recipient's or subrecipient's acceptance of a consultant's indirect cost rates pursuant to 23 U.S.C. 112 and this part provided that the consultant is given notice of each use and transfer. Audit information shall not be provided to other consultants or any other government agency not sharing the cost data, or to any firm or government agency for purposes other than complying with the recipient's or subrecipient's acceptance of a consultant's indirect cost rates pursuant to 23 U.S.C. 112 and this part without the written permission of the affected consultants. If prohibited by law, such cost and rate data shall not be disclosed under any circumstance; however, should a release be required by law or court order, such release shall make note of the confidential nature of the data.

PART 180—CREDIT ASSISTANCE FOR SURFACE TRANSPORTATION PROJECTS

AUTHORITY: Secs. 1501 *et seq.*, Pub. L. 105–178, 112 Stat. 107, 241, as amended; 23 U.S.C. 181–189 and 315; 49 CFR 1.48.

SOURCE: 64 FR 29750, June 2, 1999, unless otherwise noted.

§ 180.1 Cross-reference to credit assistance.

The regulations in 49 CFR part 80 shall be followed in complying with the requirements of this part. Title 49 CFR part 80 implements the Transportation Infrastructure Finance and Innovation Act of 1998, secs. 1501 *et seq.*, Pub. L. 105–178, 112 Stat. 107, 241.

PART 190—INCENTIVE PAYMENTS FOR CONTROLLING OUTDOOR ADVERTISING ON THE INTERSTATE SYSTEM

AUTHORITY: 23 U.S.C. 131(j) and 315; 49 CFR 1.48(b).

SOURCE: 43 FR 42742, Sept. 21, 1978, unless otherwise noted.

§ 190.1 Purpose.

The purpose of this regulation is to prescribe project procedures for making the incentive payments authorized by 23 U.S.C. 131(j).

§ 190.3 Agreement to control advertising.

To qualify for the bonus payment, a State must have entered into an agreement with the Secretary to control outdoor advertising. It must fulfill, and must continue to fulfill its obligations under such agreement consistent with 23 CFR 750.101.

§ 190.5 Bonus project claims.

(a) The State may claim payment by submitting a form PR–20 voucher, supported by strip maps which identify advertising control limits and areas excluded from the claim and form FHWA–1175, for the one-half percent bonus claim.

(b) The bonus payment computation is based on projects or portions thereof for which (1) the section of highway on which the project is located has been opened to traffic, and (2) final payment has been made. A bonus project may cover an individual project, a part thereof, or a combination of projects, on a section of an Interstate route.

(c) The eligible system mileage to be shown for a bonus project is that on which advertising controls are in effect. The eligible system mileage reported in subsequent projects on the same Interstate route section should cover only the additional system mileage not previously reported. Eligible project cost is the total participating cost (State and Federal share of approved preliminary engineering (PE), right-of-way (R-O-W), and construction) exclusive of any ineligible costs. The amount of the bonus payment is to be based on the eligible total costs of the supporting projects included in each claim.

(d) Progress vouchers for route sections on which additional one-half percent bonus payments are to be claimed are to be so identified, and the final claim for each route section is to be identified as the final voucher.

§ 190.7 Processing of claims.

Audited and approved PR–20 vouchers with form FHWA–1175 shall be forwarded to the regional office for submission to the Finance Division, Washington Headquarters, for payment. The associated strip maps shall be retained with the division office copies of the PR–20 vouchers.

PART 192—DRUG OFFENDER'S DRIVER'S LICENSE SUSPENSION

Sec.

AUTHORITY: 23 U.S.C. 159 and 315.

SOURCE: 57 FR 35999, Aug. 12, 1992, unless otherwise noted. Redesignated at 60 FR 50100, Sept. 28, 1995.

§ 192.1 Scope.

This part prescribes the requirements necessary to implement 23 U.S.C. § 159, which encourages States to enact and enforce drug offender's driver's license suspensions.

§ 192.2 Purpose.

The purpose of this part is to specify the steps that States must take in order to avoid the withholding of Federal-aid highway funds for noncompliance with 23 U.S.C. 159.

§ 192.3 Definitions.

As used in this part:

(a) *Convicted* includes adjudicated under juvenile proceedings.

(b) *Driver's license* means a license issued by a State to any individual that authorizes the individual to operate a motor vehicle on highways.

(c) *Drug offense* means:

(1) The possession, distribution, manufacture, cultivation, sale, transfer, or the attempt or conspiracy to possess, distribute, manufacture, cultivate, sell, or transfer any substance the possession of which is prohibited under the Controlled Substances Act, or

(2) The operation of a motor vehicle under the influence of such a substance.

(d) *Substance the possession of which is prohibited under the Controlled Substances Act* or *substance* means a controlled or counterfeit chemical, as those terms are defined in subsections 102 (6) and (7) of the Comprehensive Drug Abuse Prevention and Control Act of 1970 (21 U.S.C. 802 (6) and (7) and listed in 21 CFR 1308.11–.15.

[57 FR 35999, Aug. 12, 1992; 58 FR 62415, Nov. 26, 1993; 59 FR 39256, Aug. 2, 1994]

§ 192.4 Adoption of drug offender's driver's license suspension.

(a) The Secretary shall withhold five percent of the amount required to be apportioned to any State under each of sections 104(b)(1), 104(b)(3), and 104(b)(5) of title 23 of the United States Code on the first day of fiscal years 1994 and 1995 if the States does not meet the requirements of this section on that date.

(b) The Secretary shall withhold ten percent of the amount required to be apportioned to any State under each of sections 104(b)(1), 104(b)(3), and 104(b)(5) of title 23 of the United States Code on the first day of fiscal year 1996 and any subsequent fiscal year if the State does not meet the requirements of this section on that date.

(c) A State meets the requirements of this section if:

(1) The State has enacted and is enforcing a law that requires in all circumstances, or requires in the absence of compelling circumstances warranting an exception:

(i) The revocation, or suspension for at least 6 months, of the driver's license of any individual who is convicted, after the enactment of such law, of

(A) Any violation of the Controlled Substances Act, or

(B) Any drug offense, and

(ii) A delay in the issuance or reinstatement of a driver's license to such an individual for at least 6 months after the individual otherwise would have been eligible to have a driver's license issued or reinstated if the individual does not have a driver's license, or the driver's license of the individual is suspended, at the time the individual is so convicted, or

(2) The Governor of the State:

(i) Submits to the Secretary no earlier than the adjournment sine die of the first regularly scheduled session of the State's legislature which begins after November 5, 1990, a written certification stating that he or she is opposed to the enactment or enforcement in the State of a law described in paragraph (c)(1) of this section relating to the revocation, suspension, issuance, or reinstatement of driver's licenses to convicted drug offenders; and

(ii) Submits to the Secretary a written certification that the legislature (including both Houses where applicable) has adopted a resolution expressing its opposition to a law described in paragraph (c)(1) of this section.

(d) A State that makes exceptions for compelling circumstances must do so in accordance with a State law, regulation, binding policy directive or Statewide published guidelines establishing the conditions for making such exceptions and in exceptional circumstances specific to the offender.

§ 192.5 Certification requirements.

(a) Each State shall certify to the Secretary of Transportation by April 1, 1993 and by January 1 of each subsequent year that it meets the requirements of 23 U.S.C. 159 and this regulation.

(b) If the State believes it meets the requirements of 23 U.S.C. 159 and this regulation on the basis that it has enacted and is enforcing a law that suspends or revokes the driver's license of drug offenders, the certification shall contain:

(1) A statement by the Governor of the State that the State has enacted and is enforcing a Drug Offender's Driver's License Suspension law that conforms to 23 U.S.C. 159(a)(3)(A). The certifying statement may be worded as follows: I, (Name of Governor), Governor of the (State or Commonwealth) of __________, do hereby certify that the (State or Commonwealth) of __________, has enacted is enforcing a Drug Offender's Driver's License Suspension law that conforms to section 23 U.S. C. 159(a)(3)(A).

(2) Until a State has been determined to be in compliance with the requirements of 23 U.S.C. 159 and this regulation, the certification shall include also:

(i) A copy of the State law, regulation, or binding policy directive implementing or interpreting such law or regulation relating to the suspension, revocation, issuance or reinstatement or driver's licenses of drug offenders, and

(ii) A statement describing the steps the State is taking to enforce its law with regard to within State convictions, out-of-State convictions, Federal convictions and juvenile adjudications. The statement shall demonstrate that, upon receiving notification that a State driver has been convicted of a within State, out-of-State or Federal conviction or juvenile adjudication, the State is revoking, suspending or delaying the issuance of that drug offender's driver's license; and that, when the State convicts an individual of a drug offense, it is notifying the appropriate State office or, if the offender is a non-resident driver, the appropriate office in the driver's home State. If the State is not yet making these notifications, the State may satisfy this element by submitting a plan describing the steps it is taking to establish notification procedures.

(c) If the State believes it meets the requirements of 23 U.S.C. 159(a)(3)(B) on the basis that it opposes a law that requires the suspension, revocation or delay in issuance or reinstatement of the driver's license of drug offenders that conforms to 23 U.S.C. 159(a)(3)(A), the certification shall contain:

(1) A statement by the Governor of the State that he or she is opposed to the enactment or enforcement of a law that conforms to 23 U.S.C. 159(a)(3)(A) and that the State legislature has adopted a resolution expressing its opposition to such a law. The certifying statement may be worded as follows: I, (Name of Governor), Governor of the (State or Commonwealth of __________, do hereby certify that I am opposed to the enactment or enforcement of a law that conforms to 23 U.S.C. 159(a)(3)(A) and that the legislature of the (State or Commonwealth) of __________, has adopted a resolution expressing its opposition to such a law.

(2) Until a State has been determined to be in compliance with the requirements of 23 U.S.C. 159(a)(3)(B) and this regulation, the certification shall include a copy of the resolution.

(d) The Governor each year shall submit the original and three copies of the certification to the local FHWA Division Administrator. The FHWA Division Administrator shall retain the original and forward one copy each to the FHWA Regional Administrator, FHWA Chief Counsel, and the Director of the Office of Highway Safety.

(e) Any changes to the original certification or supplemental information necessitated by the review of the certifications as they are forwarded, State legislative changes or changes in State enforcement activity (including failure to make progress in a plan previously submitted) shall be submitted in the same manner as the original.

[57 FR 35999, Aug. 12, 1992. Redesignated and amended at 60 FR 50100, Sept. 28, 1995]

§ 192.6 Period of availability of withheld funds.

(a) Funds withheld under § 1212.4 from apportionment to any State on or before September 30, 1995, will remain available for apportionment as follows:

(1) If the funds would have been apportioned under 23 U.S.C. 104(b)(5)(A) but for this section, the funds will remain available until the end of the fiscal year for which the funds are authorized to be appropriated.

(2) If the funds would have been apportioned under 23 U.S.C. 104(b)(5)(B) but for this section, the funds will remain available until the end of the second fiscal year following the fiscal year for which the funds are authorized to be appropriated.

(3) If the funds would have been apportioned under 23 U.S.C. 104(b)(1) or 104(b)(3) but for this section, the funds will remain available until the end of the third fiscal year following the fiscal year for which the funds are authorized to be appropriated.

(b) Funds withheld under § 1212.4 from apportionment to any State after September 30, 1995 will not be available for apportionment to the State.

§ 192.7 Apportionment of withheld funds after compliance.

Funds withheld under § 1212.4 from apportionment, which remain available for apportionment under § 1212.6(a), will be made available to any State that conforms to the requirements of § 1212.4 before the last day of the period of availability as defined in § 1212.6(a).

[57 FR 35999, Aug. 12, 1992, as amended at 59 FR 39256, Aug. 2, 1994]

§ 192.8 Period of availability of subsequently apportioned funds.

(a) Funds apportioned pursuant to § 1212.7 will remain available for expenditure as follows:

(1) Funds originally apportioned under 23 U.S.C. 104(b)(5)(A) will remain available until the end of the fiscal year succeeding the fiscal year in which the funds are apportioned.

(2) Funds originally apportioned under 23 U.S.C. 104(b)(1), 104(b)(2), 104(b)(5)(B), or 104(b)(6) will remain available until the end of the third fiscal year succeeding the fiscal year in which the funds are apportioned.

(b) Sums apportioned to a State pursuant to § 1212.7 and not obligated at the end of the periods defined in § 1212.8(a), shall lapse or, in the case of funds apportioned under 23 U.S.C. 104(b)(5), shall lapse and be made available by the Secretary for projects in accordance with 23 U.S.C. 118(b).

§ 192.9 Effect of noncompliance.

If a State has not met the requirements of 23 U.S.C. 159(a)(3) at the end of the period for which funds withheld under § 1212.4 are available for apportionment to a State under § 1212.6, then such funds shall lapse or, in the case of funds withheld from apportionment under 23 U.S.C. 104(b)(5), shall lapse and be made available by the Secretary for projects in accordance with 23 U.S.C. 118(b).

§ 192.10 Procedures affecting States in noncompliance.

(a) Each fiscal year, each State determined to be in noncompliance with 23 U.S.C. 159, based on FHWA's preliminary review of its statutes, will be advised of the funds expected to be withheld under § 1212.4 from apportionment, as part of the advance notice of apportionments required under 23 U.S.C. 104(e), normally not later than ninety days prior to final apportionment.

(b) If FHWA determines that the State is not in compliance with 23 U.S.C. 159 based on the agencies' preliminary review, the State may, within 30 days of its receipt of the advance notice of apportionments, submit documentation showing why it is in compliance. Documentation shall be submitted to the Federal Highway Administration, 1200 New Jersey Avenue, SE., Washington, DC 20590.

(c) Each fiscal year, each State determined not to be in compliance with 23 U.S.C. 159(a)(3), based on FHWA's final determination, will receive notice of the funds being withheld under § 1212.4 from apportionment, as part of the certification of apportionments required under 23 U.S.C. 104(e), which normally occurs on October 1 of each fiscal year.

[57 FR 35999, Aug. 12, 1992. Redesignated and amended at 60 FR 50100, Sept. 28, 1995; 74 FR 28442, June 16, 2009]

SUBCHAPTER C—CIVIL RIGHTS

PART 200—TITLE VI PROGRAM AND RELATED STATUTES—IMPLEMENTATION AND REVIEW PROCEDURES

AUTHORITY: Title VI of the Civil Rights Act of 1964, 42 U.S.C. 2000d to 2000d–4; Title VIII of the Civil Rights Act of 1968, 42 U.S.C. 3601–3619; 42 U.S.C. 4601 to 4655; 23 U.S.C. 109(h); 23 U.S.C. 324.

SOURCE: 41 FR 53982, Dec. 10, 1976, unless otherwise noted.

§ 200.1 Purpose.

To provide guidelines for: (a) Implementing the Federal Highway Administration (FHWA) Title VI compliance program under Title VI of the Civil Rights Act of 1964 and related civil rights laws and regulations, and (b) Conducting Title VI program compliance reviews relative to the Federal-aid highway program.

§ 200.3 Application of this part.

The provisions of this part are applicable to all elements of FHWA and provide requirements and guidelines for State highway agencies to implement the Title VI Program requirements. The related civil rights laws and regulations are listed under § 200.5(p) of this part. Title VI requirements for 23 U.S.C. 402 will be covered under a joint FHWA/NHTSA agreement.

§ 200.5 Definitions.

The following definitions shall apply for the purpose of this part:

(a) *Affirmative action.* A good faith effort to eliminate past and present discrimination in all federally assisted programs, and to ensure future nondiscriminatory practices.

(b) *Beneficiary.* Any person or group of persons (other than States) entitled to receive benefits, directly or indirectly, from any federally assisted program, *i.e.*, relocatees, impacted citizens, communities, etc.

(c) *Citizen participation.* An open process in which the rights of the community to be informed, to provide comments to the Government and to receive a response from the Government are met through a full opportunity to be involved and to express needs and goals.

(d) *Compliance.* That satisfactory condition existing when a recipient has effectively implemented all of the Title VI requirements or can demonstrate that every good faith effort toward achieving this end has been made.

(e) *Deficiency status.* The interim period during which the recipient State has been notified of deficiencies, has not voluntarily complied with Title VI Program guidelines, but has not been declared in noncompliance by the Secretary of Transportation.

(f) *Discrimination.* That act (or action) whether intentional or unintentional, through which a person in the United States, solely because of race, color, religion, sex, or national origin, has been otherwise subjected to unequal treatment under any program or activity receiving financial assistance from the Federal Highway Administration under title 23 U.S.C.

(g) *Facility.* Includes all, or any part of, structures, equipment or other real or personal property, or interests therein, and *the provision of facilities* includes the construction, expansion, renovation, remodeling, alternation or acquisition of facilities.

(h) *Federal assistance.* Includes:

(1) Grants and loans of Federal funds,

(2) The grant or donation of Federal property and interests in property,

(3) The detail of Federal personnel,

(4) The sale and lease of, and the permission to use (on other than a casual or transient basis), Federal property or any interest in such property without consideration or at a nominal consideration, or at a consideration which is reduced for the purpose of assisting the recipient, or in recognition of the public interest to be served by such sale or lease to the recipient, and

(5) Any Federal agreement, arrangement, or other contract which has, as one of its purposes, the provision of assistance.

(i) *Noncompliance.* A recipient has failed to meet prescribed requirements and has shown an apparent lack of good faith effort in implementing all of the Title VI requirements.

(j) *Persons.* Where designation of persons by race, color, or national origin is required, the following designations ordinarily may be used: "White not of Hispanic origin", "Black not of Hispanic origin", "Hispanic", "Asian or Pacific Islander", "American Indian or Alaskan Native." Additional subcategories based on national origin or primary language spoken may be used, where appropriate, on either a national or a regional basis.

(k) *Program.* Includes any highway, project, or activity for the provision of services, financial aid, or other benefits to individuals. This includes education or training, work opportunities, health, welfare, rehabilitation, housing, or other services, whether provided directly by the recipient of Federal financial assistance or provided by others through contracts or other arrangements with the recipient.

(l) *State highway agency.* That department, commission, board, or official of any State charged by its laws with the responsibility for highway construction. The term *State* would be considered equivalent to *State highway agency* if the context so implies.

(m) *Program area officials.* The officials in FHWA who are responsible for carrying out technical program responsibilities.

(n) *Recipient.* Any State, territory, possession, the District of Columbia, Puerto Rico, or any political subdivision, or instrumentality thereof, or any public or private agency, institution, or organization, or other entity, or any individual, in any State, territory, possession, the District of Columbia, or Puerto Rico, to whom Federal assistance is extended, either directly or through another recipient, for any program. Recipient includes any successor, assignee, or transferee thereof. The term *recipient* does not include any ultimate beneficiary under any such program.

(o) *Secretary.* The Secretary of Transportation as set forth in 49 CFR 21.17(g)(3) or the Federal Highway Administrator to whom the Secretary has delegated his authority in specific cases.

(p) *Title VI Program.* The system of requirements developed to implement Title VI of the Civil Rights Act of 1964. References in this part to Title VI requirements and regulations shall not be limited to only Title VI of the Civil Rights Act of 1964. Where appropriate, this term also refers to the civil rights provisions of other Federal statutes to the extent that they prohibit discrimination on the grounds of race, color, sex, or national origin in programs receiving Federal financial assistance of the type subject to Title VI itself. These Federal statutes are:

(1) Title VI of the Civil Rights Act of 1964, 42 U.S.C. 2000d-d4 (49 CFR part 21; the standard DOT Title VI assurances signed by each State pursuant to DOT Order 1050.2; Executive Order 11764; 28 CFR 50.3);

(2) Uniform Relocation Assistance and Real Property Acquisition Policies Act of 1970 (42 U.S.C. 4601–4655) (49 CFR part 25; Pub. L. 91–646);

(3) Title VIII of the Civil Rights Act of 1968, amended 1974 (42 U.S.C. 3601–3619);

(4) 23 U.S.C. 109(h);

(5) 23 U.S.C. 324;

(6) Subsequent Federal-Aid Highway Acts and related statutes.

§ 200.7 FHWA Title VI policy.

It is the policy of the FHWA to ensure compliance with Title VI of the Civil Rights Act of 1964; 49 CFR part 21; and related statutes and regulations.

§ 200.9 State highway agency responsibilities.

(a) State assurances in accordance with Title VI of the Civil Rights Act of 1964.

(1) Title 49, CFR part 21 (Department of Transportation Regulations for the implementation of Title VI of the Civil Rights Act of 1964) requires assurances from States that no person in the United States shall, on the grounds of race, color, or national origin, be excluded from participation in, be denied

the benefits of, or be otherwise subjected to discrimination under any program or activity for which the recipient receives Federal assistance from the Department of Transportation, including the Federal Highway Administration.

(2) Section 162a of the Federal-Aid Highway Act of 1973 (section 324, title 23 U.S.C.) requires that there be no discrimination on the ground of sex. The FHWA considers all assurances heretofore received to have been amended to include a prohibition against discrimination on the ground of sex. These assurances were signed by the 50 States, the District of Columbia, Puerto Rico, the Virgin Islands, Guam, and American Samoa. The State highway agency shall submit a certification to the FHWA indicating that the requirements of section 162a of the Federal-Aid Highway Act of 1973 have been added to its assurances.

(3) The State highway agency shall take affirmative action to correct any deficiencies found by the FHWA within a reasonable time period, not to exceed 90 days, in order to implement Title VI compliance in accordance with State-signed assurances and required guidelines. The head of the State highway agency shall be held responsible for implementing Title VI requirements.

(4) The State program area officials and Title VI Specialist shall conduct annual reviews of all pertinent program areas to determine the effectiveness of program area activities at all levels.

(b) *State actions.* (1) Establish a civil rights unit and designate a coordinator who has a responsible position in the organization and easy access to the head of the State highway agency. This unit shall contain a Title VI Equal Employment Opportunity Coordinator or a Title VI Specialist, who shall be responsible for initiating and monitoring Title VI activities and preparing required reports.

(2) Adequately staff the civil rights unit to effectively implement the State civil rights requirements.

(3) Develop procedures for prompt processing and disposition of Title VI and Title VIII complaints received directly by the State and not by FHWA. Complaints shall be investigated by State civil rights personnel trained in compliance investigations. Identify each complainant by race, color, sex, or national origin; the recipient; the nature of the complaint; the dates the complaint was filed and the investigation completed; the disposition; the date of the disposition; and other pertinent information. Each recipient (State) processing Title VI complaints shall be required to maintain a similar log. A copy of the complaint, together with a copy of the State's report of investigation, shall be forwarded to the FHWA division office within 60 days of the date the complaint was received by the State.

(4) Develop procedures for the collection of statistical data (race, color, religion, sex, and national origin) of participants in, and beneficiaries of State highway programs, *i.e.*, relocatees, impacted citizens and affected communities.

(5) Develop a program to conduct Title VI reviews of program areas.

(6) Conduct annual reviews of special emphasis program areas to determine the effectiveness or program area activities at all levels.

(7) Conduct Title VI reviews of cities, counties, consultant contractors, suppliers, universities, colleges, planning agencies, and other recipients of Federal-aid highway funds.

(8) Review State program directives in coordination with State program officials and, where applicable, include Title VI and related requirements.

(9) The State highway agency Title VI designee shall be responsible for conducting training programs on Title VI and related statutes for State program and civil rights officials.

(10) Prepare a yearly report of Title VI accomplishments for the past year and goals for the next year.

(11) Beginning October 1, 1976, each State highway agency shall annually submit an updated Title VI implementing plan to the Regional Federal Highway Administrator for approval or disapproval.

(12) Develop Title VI information for dissemination to the general public and, where appropriate, in languages other than English.

(13) Establishing procedures for pregrant and postgrant approval reviews of State programs and applicants for compliance with Title VI requirements; *i.e.*, highway location, design and relocation, and persons seeking contracts with the State.

(14) Establish procedures to identify and eliminate discrimination when found to exist.

(15) Establishing procedures for promptly resolving deficiency status and reducing to writing the remedial action agreed to be necessary, all within a period not to exceed 90 days.

§ 200.11 Procedures for processing Title VI reviews.

(a) If the regional Title VI review report contains deficiencies and recommended actions, the report shall be forwarded by the Regional Federal Highway Administrator to the Division Administrator, who will forward it with a cover letter to the State highway agency for corrective action.

(b) The division office, in coordination with the Regional Civil Rights Officer, shall schedule a meeting with the recipient, to be held not later than 30 days from receipt of the deficiency report.

(c) Recipients placed in a deficiency status shall be given a reasonable time, not to exceed 90 days after receipt of the deficiency letter, to voluntarily correct deficiencies.

(d) The Division Administrator shall seek the cooperation of the recipient in correcting deficiencies found during the review. The FHWA officials shall also provide the technical assistance and guidance needed to aid the recipient to comply voluntarily.

(e) When a recipient fails or refuses to voluntarily comply with requirements within the time frame allotted, the Division Administrator shall submit to the Regional Administrator two copies of the case file and a recommendation that the State be found in noncompliance.

(f) The Office of Civil Rights shall review the case file for a determination of concurrence or noncurrence with a recommendation to the Federal Highway Administrator. Should the Federal Highway Administrator concur with the recommendation, the file is referred to the Department of Transportation, Office of the Secretary, for appropriate action in accordance with 49 CFR.

PART 230—EXTERNAL PROGRAMS

Subpart A—Equal Employment Opportunity on Federal and Federal-Aid Construction Contracts (Including Supportive Services)

Subpart B—Supportive Services for Minority, Disadvantaged, and Women Business Enterprises

Subpart C—State Highway Agency Equal Employment Opportunity Programs

Subpart D—Construction Contract Equal Opportunity Compliance Procedures

AUTHORITY: 23 U.S.C. 101, 140, and 315; 42 U.S.C. 2000d *et seq.;* 49 CFR 1.48 and 60–1.

SOURCE: 40 FR 28053, July 3, 1975, unless otherwise noted.

Subpart A—Equal Employment Opportunity on Federal and Federal-Aid Construction Contracts (Including Supportive Services)

§ 230.101 Purpose.

The purpose of the regulations in this subpart is to prescribe the policies, procedures, and guides relative to the implementation of an equal employment opportunity program on Federal and Federal-aid highway construction contracts, except for those contracts awarded under 23 U.S.C. 117, and to the preparation and submission of reports pursuant thereto.

§ 230.103 Definitions.

For purposes of this subpart—

Administrator means the Federal Highway Administrator.

Areawide Plan means an affirmative action plan to increase minority utilization of crafts in a specified geographical area pursuant to Executive Order 11246, and taking the form of either a "Hometown" or an "Imposed" plan.

Bid conditions means contract requirements which have been issued by OFCC for purposes of implementing a Hometown Plan.

Division Administrator means the chief Federal Highway Administration (FHWA) official assigned to conduct FHWA business in a particular State, the District of Columbia, or the Commonwealth of Puerto Rico.

Division Equal Opportunity Officer means an individual with staff level responsibilities and necessary authority by which to operate as an Equal Opportunity Officer in a Division office. Normally the Equal Opportunity Officer will be a full-time civil rights specialist serving as staff assistant to the Division Administrator.

Hometown Plan means a voluntary areawide plan which was developed by representatives of affected groups (usually labor unions, minority organizations, and contractors), and subsequently approved by the Office of Federal Contract Compliance (OFCC), for purposes of implementing the equal employment opportunity requirements pursuant to Executive Order 11246, as amended.

Imposed Plan means an affirmative action requirement for a specified geographical area made mandatory by OFCC and, in some areas, by the courts.

Journeyman means a person who is capable of performing all the duties within a given job classification or craft.

State highway agency means that department, commission, board, or official of any State charged by its laws with the responsibility for highway construction. The term *State* should be considered equivalent to *State highway agency*.

Suggested minimum annual training goals means goals which have been assigned to each State highway agency annually for the purpose of specifying training positions on selected Federal-aid highway construction projects.

Supportive services means those services provided in connection with approved on-the-job training programs for highway construction workers and highway contractors which are designed to increase the overall effectiveness of training programs through the performance of functions determined to be necessary in connection with such programs, but which are not generally considered as comprising part of actual on-the-job craft training.

Trainee means a person who received on-the-job training, whether through an apprenticeship program or other programs approved or accepted by the FHWA.

[40 FR 28053, July 3, 1975, as amended at 41 FR 3080, Jan. 21, 1976]

§ 230.105 Applicability.

(a) *Federal-aid highway construction projects.* This subpart applies to all Federal-aid highway construction projects and to Appalachian highway construction projects and other State supervised cooperative highway construction projects except:

(1) Federal-aided highway construction projects being constructed pursuant to 23 U.S.C. 117; and

(2) Those projects located in areas where the Office of Federal Contract Compliance has implemented an "Imposed" or a "Hometown" Plan, except for those requirements pertaining to specific provisions involving on-the-job training and those provisions pertaining to supportive services and reporting requirements.

(b) *Direct Federal highway construction projects.* This subpart applies to all direct Federal highway construction projects except:

(1) For those provisions relating to the special requirements for the provision of supportive services; and

(2) For those provisions relating to implementation of specific equal employment opportunity requirements in areas where the Office of Federal Contract Compliance has implemented an "Imposed" or "Hometown" plan.

§ 230.107 Policy.

(a) *Direct Federal and Federal-aid highway construction projects.* It is the policy of the FHWA to require that all direct Federal and Federal-aid highway construction contracts include the same specific equal employment opportunity requirements. It is also the policy to require that all direct Federal and Federal-aid highway construction subcontracts of $10,000 or more (not including contracts for supplying materials) include these same requirements.

(b) *Federal-aid highway construction projects.* It is the policy of the FHWA to require full utilization of all available training and skill-improvement opportunities to assure the increased participation of minority groups and disadvantaged persons and women in all phases of the highway construction industry. Moreover, it is the policy of the Federal Highway Administration to encourage the provision of supportive services which will increase the effectiveness of approved on-the-job training programs conducted in connection with Federal-aid highway construction projects.

§ 230.109 Implementation of specific Equal Employment Opportunity requirements.

(a) *Federal-aid highway construction projects.* The special provisions set forth in appendix A shall be included in the advertised bidding proposal and made part of the contract for each contract and each covered Federal-aid highway construction subcontract.

(b) *Direct Federal highway construction projects.* Advertising, award and contract administration procedures for direct Federal highway construction contracts shall be as set forth in Federal Acquisition Regulations (48 CFR, chapter 1, section 22.803(c)). In order to obtain information required by 48 CFR, chapter 1, § 22.804–2(c), the following requirement shall be included at the end of the bid schedule in the proposal and contract assembly:

I expect to employ the following firms as subcontractors on this project: (Naming subcontractors at this time does not constitute a binding commitment on the bidder to retain such subcontractors, nor will failure to enter names affect the contract award):

Name ________________
Address ________________
Name ________________
Address ________________

[40 FR 28053, July 3, 1975, as amended at 51 FR 22800, June 23, 1986]

§ 230.111 Implementation of special requirements for the provision of on-the-job training.

(a) The State highway agency shall determine which Federal-aid highway construction contracts shall include the "Training Special Provisions" (appendix B) and the minimum number of trainees to be specified therein after giving appropriate consideration to the guidelines set forth in § 230.111(c). The "Training Special Provisions" shall supersede section 7(b) of the Special Provisions (appendix A) entitled "Specific Equal Employment Opportunity Responsibilities." Minor wording revisions will be required to the "Training Special Provisions" in areas having "Hometown" or "Imposed Plan" requirements.

(b) The Washington Headquarters shall establish and publish annually suggested minimum training goals. These goals will be based on the Federal-aid apportioned amounts and the minority population. A State will have achieved its goal if the total number of training slots on selected federally aided highway construction contracts which have been awarded during each 12-month period equals or exceeds the State's suggested minimum annual goal. In the event a State highway agency does not attain its goal during a calendar year, the State highway agency at the end of the calendar year shall inform the Administrator of the reasons for its inability to meet the suggested minimum number of training slots and the steps to be taken to achieve the goal during the next calendar year. The information is to be submitted not later than 30 days from the end of the calendar year and should be factual, and should not only indicate the situations occurring during the year but show the project conditions at least through the coming year. The final determination will be made on what training goals are considered to be realistic based on the information submitted by a State.

(c) The following guidelines shall be utilized by the State highway agency in selecting projects and determining the number of trainees to be provided training therein:

(1) Availability of minorities, women, and disadvantaged for training.

(2) The potential for effective training.

(3) Duration of the contract.

(4) Dollar value of the contract.

(5) Total normal work force that the average bidder could be expected to use.

(6) Geographic location.

(7) Type of work.

(8) The need for additional journeymen in the area.

(9) Recognition of the suggested minimum goal for the State.

(10) A satisfactory ratio of trainees to journeymen expected to be on the contractor's work force during normal operations (considered to fall between 1:10 and 1:4).

(d) Training programs which are established shall be approved only if they meet the standards set forth in appendix B with regard to:

(1) The primary objectives of training and upgrading minority group workers, women and disadvantaged persons.

(2) The development of full journeymen.

(3) The minimum length and type of training.

(4) The minimum wages of trainees.

(5) Trainees certifications.

(6) Keeping records and furnishing reports.

(e)(1) Training programs considered by a State highway agency to meet the standards under this directive shall be submitted to the FHWA division Administrator with a recommendation for approval.

(2) Employment pursuant to training programs approved by the FHWA division Administrator will be exempt from the minimum wage rate provisions of section 113 of title 23 U.S.C. Approval, however, shall not be given to training programs which provide for employment of trainees at wages less than those required by the Special Training Provisions. (Appendix B.)

(f)(1) Apprenticeship programs approved by the U.S. Department of Labor as of the date of proposed use by a Federal-aid highway contractor or subcontractor need not be formally approved by the State highway agency or the FHWA division Administrator. Such programs, including their minimum wage provisions, are acceptable for use, provided they are administered in a manner reasonably calculated to meet the equal employment opportunity obligations of the contractor.

(2) Other training programs approved by the U.S. Department of Labor as of the date of proposed use by a Federal-aid highway contractor or subcontractor are also acceptable for use without the formal approval of the State highway agency or the division Administrator provided:

(i) The U.S. Department of Labor has clearly approved the program aspects relating to equal employment opportunity and the payment of trainee wage rates in lieu of prevailing wage rates.

(ii) They are reasonably calculated to qualify the average trainees for journeyman status in the classification concerned by the end of the training period.

(iii) They are administered in a manner calculated to meet the equal employment obligations of the contractors.

(g) The State highway agencies have the option of permitting Federal-aid highway construction contractors to bid on training to be given under this directive. The following procedures are to be utilized by those State highway agencies that elect to provide a bid item for training:

(1) The number of training positions shall continue to be specified in the Special Training Provisions. Furthermore, this number should be converted into an estimated number of hours of training which is to be used in arriving at the total bid price for the training item. Increases and decreases from the estimated amounts would be handled as overruns or underruns;

(2) A section concerning the method of payment should be included in the Special Training Provisions. Some offsite training is permissible as long as the training is an integral part of an approved training program and does not comprise a substantial part of the overall training. Furthermore, the trainee must be concurrently employed on a federally aided highway construction project subject to the Special Training Provisions attached to this directive. Reimbursement for offsite training may only be made to the contractor where he does one or more of the following: Contributes to the cost of the training, provides the instruction to the trainee, or pays the trainee's wages during the offsite training period;

(3) A State highway agency may modify the special provisions to specify the numbers to be trained in specific job classifications;

(4) A State highway agency can specify training standards provided any prospective bidder can use them, the training standards are made known in the advertised specifications, and such standards are found acceptable by FHWA.

[40 FR 28053, July 3, 1975; 40 FR 57358, Dec. 9, 1975, as amended at 41 FR 3080, Jan. 21, 1976]

§ 230.113 Implementation of supportive services.

(a) The State highway agency shall establish procedures, subject to the availability of funds under 23 U.S.C. 140(b), for the provision of supportive services in support of training programs approved under this directive. Funds made available to implement this paragraph shall not be used to finance the training of State highway agency employees or to provide services in support of such training. State highway agencies are not required to match funds allocated to them under this section.

(b) In determining the types of supportive services to be provided which will increase the effectiveness of approved training programs. State highway agencies shall give preference to the following types of services in the order listed:

(1) Services related to recruiting, counseling, transportation, physical examinations, remedial training, with special emphasis upon increasing training opportunities for members of minority groups and women;

(2) Services in connection with the administration of on-the-job training programs being sponsored by individual or groups of contractors and/or minority groups and women's groups;

(3) Services designed to develop the capabilities of prospective trainees for undertaking on-the-job training;

(4) Services in connection with providing a continuation of training during periods of seasonal shutdown;

(5) Followup services to ascertain outcome of training being provided.

(c) State highway agencies which desire to provide or obtain supportive services other than those listed above shall submit their proposals to the Federal Highway Administration for approval. The proposal, together with recommendations of the division and regional offices shall be submitted to the Administrator for appropriate action.

(d) When the State highway agency provides supportive services by contract, formal advertising is not required by the FHWA, however, the State highway agency shall solicit proposals from such qualified sources as will assure the competitive nature of the procurement. The evaluation of proposals by the State highway agency must include consideration of the proposer's ability to effect a productive relationship with contractors, unions (if appropriate), minority and women groups, minority and women trainees, and other persons or organizations whose cooperation and assistance will contribute to the successful performance of the contract work.

(e) In the selection of contractors to provide supportive services, State highway agencies shall make conscientious efforts to search out and utilize the services of qualified minority or women organizations, or minority or women business enterprises.

(f) As a minimum, State highway agency contracts to obtain supportive services shall include the following provisions:

(1) A statement that a primary purpose of the supportive services is to increase the effectiveness of approved on-the-job training programs, particularly their effectiveness in providing meaningful training opportunities for minorities, women, and the disadvantaged on Federal-aid highway projects;

(2) A clear and complete statement of the services to be provided under the contract, such as services to construction contractors, subcontractors, and trainees, for recruiting, counseling, remedial educational training, assistance in the acquisition of tools, special equipment and transportation, followup procedures, etc.;

(3) The nondiscrimination provisions required by Title VI of the Civil Rights Act of 1964 as set forth in FHWA Form PR-1273, and a statement of nondiscrimination in employment because of race, color, religion, national origin or sex;

(4) The establishment of a definite perriod of contract performance together with, if appropriate, a schedule stating when specific supportive services are to be provided;

(5) Reporting requirements pursuant to which the State highway agency will receive monthly or quarterly reports containing sufficient statistical data and narrative content to enable evaluation of both progress and problems;

(6) A requirement that the contractor keep track of trainees receiving training on Federal-aid highway construction projects for up to 6 months during periods when their training is interrupted. Such contracts shall also require the contractor to conduct a 6 month followup review of the employment status of each graduate who completes an on-the-job training program on a Federal-aid highway construction project subsequent to the effective date of the contract for supportive services.

(7) The basis of payment;

(8) An estimated schedule for expenditures;

(9) The right of access to contractor and subcontractor records and the right to audit shall be granted to authorize State highway agency and FHWA officials;

(10) Noncollusion certification;

(11) A requirement that the contractor provide all information necessary to support progress payments if such are provided for in the contract;

(12) A termination clause.

(g) The State highway agency is to furnish copies of the reports received under paragraph (b)(5) of this section, to the division office.

[40 FR 28053, July 3, 1975, as amended at 41 FR 3080, Jan. 21, 1976]

§230.115 Special contract requirements for "Hometown" or "Imposed" Plan areas.

Direct Federal and Federal-aid contracts to be performed in "Hometown" or "Imposed" Plan areas will incorporate the special provision set forth in appendix G.

§ 230.117 Reimbursement procedures (Federal-aid highway construction projects only).

(a) *On-the-job special training provisions.* State highway agencies will be reimbursed on the same pro-rata basis as the construction costs of the Federal-aid project.

(b) *Supportive services.* (1) The State highway agency must keep a separate account of supportive services funds since they cannot be interchanged with regular Federal-aid funds. In addition, these funds may not be expended in a manner that would provide for duplicate payment of Federal or Federal-aid funds for the same service.

(2) Where a State highway agency does not obligate all its funds within the time specified in the particular year's allocation directive, the funds shall revert to the FHWA Headquarters Office to be made available for use by other State highway agencies, taking into consideration each State's need for and ability to use such funds.

§ 230.119 Monitoring of supportive services.

Supportive services procured by a State highway agency shall be monitored by both the State highway agency and the division office.

§ 230.121 Reports.

(a) Employment reports on Federal-aid highway construction contracts not subject to "Hometown" or "Imposed" plan requirements.

(1) Paragraph 10c of the special provisions (appendix A) sets forth specific reporting requirements. FHWA Form PR–1391, Federal-Aid Highway Construction Contractors Annual EEO Report, (appendix C) and FHWA Form PR 1392, Federal-Aid Highway Construction Summary of Employment Data (including minority breakdown) for all Federal-Aid Highway Projects for month ending July 31st, 19—, (appendix D) are to be used to fulfill these reporting requirements.

(2) Form PR 1391 is to be completed by each contractor and each subcontractor subject to this part for every month of July during which work is performed, and submitted to the State highway agency. A separate report is to be completed for each covered contract or subcontract. The employment data entered should reflect the work force on board during all or any part of the last payroll period preceding the end of the month. The State highway agency is to forward a single copy of each report to the FHWA division office.

(3) Form PR 1392 is to be completed by the State highway agencies, summarizing the reports on PR 1391 for the month of July received from all active contractors and subcontractors. Three (3) copies of completed Forms PR 1392 are to be forwarded to the division office.

(b) Employment reports on direct Federal highway construction contracts not subject to "Hometown" or "Imposed" plan requirements. Forms PR 1391 (appendix C) and PR 1392 (appendix D) shall be used for reporting purposes as prescribed in § 230.121(a).

(c) Employment reports on direct Federal and Federal-aid highway construction contracts subject to "Hometown" or "Imposed" plan requirements.

(1) Reporting requirements for direct Federal and Federal-aid highway construction projects located in areas where "Hometown" or "Imposed" plans are in effect shall be in accordance with those issued by the U.S. Department of Labor, Office of Federal Contract Compliance.

(2) In order that we may comply with the U.S. Senate Committee on Public Works' request that the Federal Highway Administration submit a report annually on the status of the equal employment opportunity program, Form PR 1391 is to be completed annually by each contractor and each subcontractor holding contracts or subcontracts exceeding $10,000 except as otherwise provided for under 23 U.S.C. 117. The employment data entered should reflect the work force on board during all or any part of the last payroll period preceding the end of the month of July.

(d) [Reserved]

(e) Reports on supportive services contracts. The State highway agency is to furnish copies of the reports received from supportive services contractors to the FHWA division office which will furnish a copy to the regional office.

[40 FR 28053, July 3, 1975, as amended at 43 FR 19386, May 5, 1978; 61 FR 14616, Apr. 3, 1996]

APPENDIX A TO SUBPART A OF PART 230—SPECIAL PROVISIONS

SPECIFIC EQUAL EMPLOYMENT OPPORTUNITY RESPONSIBILITIES

1. *General.* a. Equal employment opportunity requirements not to discriminate and to take affirmative action to assure equal employment opportunity as required by Executive Order 11246 and Executive Order 11375 are set forth in Required Contract, Provisions (Form PR–1273 or 1316, as appropriate) and these Special Provisions which are imposed pursuant to section 140 of title 23 U.S.C., as established by section 22 of the Federal-Aid Highway Act of 1968. The requirements set forth in these Special Provisions shall constitute the specific affirmative action requirements for project activities under this contract and supplement the equal employment opportunity requirements set forth in the Required Contract Provisions.

b. The contractor will work with the State highway agencies and the Federal Government in carrying out equal employment opportunity obligations and in their review of his/her activities under the contract.

c. The contractor and all his/her subcontractors holding subcontracts not including material suppliers, of $10,000 or more, will comply with the following minimum specific requirement activities of equal employment opportunity: (The equal employment opportunity requirements of Executive Order 11246, as set forth in volume 6, chapter 4, section 1, subsection 1 of the Federal-Aid Highway Program Manual, are applicable to material suppliers as well as contractors and subcontractors.) The contractor will include these requirements in every subcontract of $10,000 or more with such modification of language as is necessary to make them binding on the subcontractor.

2. *Equal Employment Opportunity Policy.* The contractor will accept as his operating policy the following statement which is designed to further the provision of equal employment opportunity to all persons without regard to their race, color, religion, sex, or national origin, and to promote the full realization of equal employment opportunity through a positive continuing program:

It is the policy of this Company to assure that applicants are employed, and that employees are treated during employment, without regard to their race, religion, sex, color, or national origin. Such action shall include: employment, upgrading, demotion, or transfer; recruitment or recruitment advertising; layoff or termination; rates of pay or other forms of compensation; and selection for training, including apprenticeship, preapprenticeship, and/or on-the-job training.

3. *Equal Employment Opportunity Officer.* The contractor will designate and make known to the State highway agency contracting officers and equal employment opportunity officer (hereinafter referred to as the EEO Officer) who will have the responsibility for and must be capable of effectively administering and promoting an active contractor program of equal employment opportunity and who must be assigned adequate authority and responsibility to do so.

4. *Dissemination of Policy.* a. All members of the contractor's staff who are authorized to hire, supervise, promote, and discharge employees, or who recommend such action, or who are substantially involved in such action, will be made fully cognizant of, and will implement, the contractor's equal employment opportunity policy and contractual responsibilities to provide equal employment opportunity in each grade and classification of employment. To ensure that the above agreement will be met, the following actions will be taken as a minimum:

(1) Periodic meetings of supervisory and personnel office employees will be conducted before the start of work and then not less often than once every six months, at which time the contractor's equal employment opportunity policy and its implementation will be reviewed and explained. The meetings will be conducted by the EEO Officer or other knowledgeable company official.

(2) All new supervisory or personnel office employees will be given a thorough indoctrination by the EEO Officer or other knowledgeable company official, covering all major aspects of the contractor's equal employment opportunity obligations within thirty days following their reporting for duty with the contractor.

(3) All personnel who are engaged in direct recruitment for the project will be instructed by the EEO Officer or appropriate company official in the contractor's procedures for locating and hiring minority group employees.

b. In order to make the contractor's equal employment opportunity policy known to all employees, prospective employees and potential sources of employees, *i.e.*, schools, employment agencies, labor unions (where appropriate), college placement officers, etc., the contractor will take the following actions:

(1) Notices and posters setting forth the contractor's equal employment opportunity

policy will be placed in areas readily accessible to employees, applicants for employment and potential employees.

(2) The contractor's equal employment opportunity policy and the procedures to implement such policy will be brought to the attention of employees by means of meetings, employee handbooks, or other appropriate means.

5. Recruitment. a. When advertising for employees, the contractor will include in all advertisements for employees the notation: "An Equal Opportunity Employer." All such advertisements will be published in newspapers or other publications having a large circulation among minority groups in the area from which the project work force would normally be derived.

b. The contractor will, unless precluded by a valid bargaining agreement, conduct systematic and direct recruitment through public and private employee referral sources likely to yield qualified minority group applicants, including, but not limited to, State employment agencies, schools, colleges and minority group organizations. To meet this requirement, the contractor will, through his EEO Officer, identify sources of potential minority group employees, and establish with such identified sources procedures whereby minority group applicants may be referred to the contractor for employment consideration.

In the event the contractor has a valid bargaining agreement providing for exclusive hiring hall referrals, he is expected to observe the provisions of that agreement to the extent that the system permits the contractor's compliance with equal employment opportunity contract provisions. (The U.S. Department of Labor has held that where implementation of such agreements have the effect of discriminating against minorities or women, or obligates the contractor to do the same, such implementation violates Executive Order 11246, as amended.)

c. The contractor will encourage his present employees to refer minority group applicants for employment by posting appropriate notices or bulletins in areas accessible to all such employees. In addition, information and procedures with regard to referring minority group applicants will be discussed with employees.

6. *Personnel Actions*. Wages, working conditions, and employee benefits shall be established and administered, and personnel actions of every type, including hiring, upgrading, promotion, transfer, demotion, layoff, and termination, shall be taken without regard to race, color, religion, sex, or national origin. The following procedures shall be followed:

a. The contractor will conduct periodic inspections of project sites to insure that working conditions and employee facilities do not indicate discriminatory treatment of project site personnel.

b. The contractor will periodically evaluate the spread of wages paid within each classification to determine any evidence of discriminatory wage practices.

c. The contractor will periodically review selected personnel actions in depth to determine whether there is evidence of discrimination. Where evidence is found, the contractor will promptly take corrective action. If the review indicates that the discrimination may extend beyond the actions reviewed, such corrective action shall include all affected persons.

d. The contractor will promptly investigate all complaints of alleged discrimination made to the contractor in connection with his obligations under this contract, will attempt to resolve such complaints, and will take appropriate corrective action within a reasonable time. If the investigation indicates that the discrimination may affect persons other than the complainant, such corrective action shall include such other persons. Upon completion of each investigation, the contractor will inform every complainant of all of his avenues of appeal.

7. *Training and Promotion*. a. The contractor will assist in locating, qualifying, and increasing the skills of minority group and women employees, and applicants for employment.

b. Consistent with the contractor's work force requirements and as permissible under Federal and State regulations, the contractor shall make full use of training programs, *i.e.*, apprenticeship, and on-the-job training programs for the geographical area of contract performance. Where feasible, 25 percent of apprentices or trainees in each occupation shall be in their first year of apprenticeship or training. In the event the Training Special Provision is provided under this contract, this subparagraph will be superseded as indicated in Attachment 2.

c. The contractor will advise employees and applicants for employment of available training programs and entrance requirements for each.

d. The contractor will periodically review the training and promotion potential of minority group and women employees and will encourage eligible employees to apply for such training and promotion.

8. *Unions*. If the contractor relies in whole or in part upon unions as a source of employees, the contractor will use his/her best efforts to obtain the cooperation of such unions to increase opportunities for minority groups and women within the unions, and to effect referrals by such unions of minority and female employees. Actions by the contractor either directly or through a contractor's association acting as agent will include the procedures set forth below:

a. The contractor will use best efforts to develop, in cooperation with the unions, joint training programs aimed toward qualifying more minority group members and women for membership in the unions and increasing the skills of minority group employees and women so that they may qualify for higher paying employment.

b. The contractor will use best efforts to incorporate an equal employment opportunity clause into each union agreement to the end that such union will be contractually bound to refer applicants without regard to their race, color, religion, sex, or national origin.

c. The contractor is to obtain information as to the referral practices and policies of the labor union except that to the extent such information is within the exclusive possession of the labor union and such labor union refuses to furnish such information to the contractor, the contractor shall so certify to the State highway department and shall set forth what efforts have been made to obtain such information.

d. In the event the union is unable to provide the contractor with a reasonable flow of minority and women referrals within the time limit set forth in the collective bargaining agreement, the contractor will, through independent recruitment efforts, fill the employment vacancies without regard to race, color, religion, sex, or national origin; making full efforts to obtain qualified and/or qualifiable minority group persons and women. (The U.S. Department of Labor has held that it shall be no excuse that the union with which the contractor has a collective bargaining agreement providing for exclusive referral failed to refer minority employees.) In the event the union referral practice prevents the contractor from meeting the obligations pursuant to Executive Order 11246, as amended, and these special provisions, such contractor shall immediately notify the State highway agency.

9. *Subcontracting*. a. The contractor will use his best efforts to solicit bids from and to utilize minority group subcontractors or subcontractors with meaningful minority group and female representation among their employees. Contractors shall obtain lists of minority-owned construction firms from State highway agency personnel.

b. The contractor will use his best efforts to ensure subcontractor compliance with their equal employment opportunity obligations.

10. *Records and Reports*. a. The contractor will keep such records as are necessary to determine compliance with the contractor's equal employment opportunity obligations. The records kept by the contractor will be designed to indicate:

(1) The number of minority and non-minority group members and women employed in each work classification on the project.

(2) The progress and efforts being made in cooperation with unions to increase employment opportunities for minorities and women (applicable only to contractors who rely in whole or in part on unions as a source of their work force),

(3) The progress and efforts being made in locating, hiring, training, qualifying, and upgrading minority and female employees, and

(4) The progress and efforts being made in securing the services of minority group subcontractors or subcontractors with meaningful minority and female representation among their employees.

b. All such records must be retained for a period of three years following completion of the contract work and shall be available at reasonable times and places for inspection by authorized representatives of the State highway agency and the Federal Highway Administration.

c. The contractors will submit an annual report to the State highway agency each July for the duration of the project, indicating the number of minority, women, and non-minority group employees currently engaged in each work classification required by the contract work. This information is to be reported on Form PR 1391. If on-the-job training is being required by "Training Special Provision", the contractor will be required to furnish Form FHWA 1409.

[40 FR 28053, July 3, 1975, as amended at 43 FR 19386, May 5, 1978. Correctly redesignated at 46 FR 21156, Apr. 9, 1981]

APPENDIX B TO SUBPART A OF PART 230—TRAINING SPECIAL PROVISIONS

This Training Special Provision supersedes subparagraph 7b of the Special Provision entitled "Specific Equal Employment Opportunity Responsibilities," (Attachment 1), and is in implementation of 23 U.S.C. 140(a).

As part of the contractor's equal employment opportunity affirmative action program training shall be provided as follows:

The contractor shall provide on-the-job training aimed at developing full journeymen in the type of trade or job classification involved.

The number of trainees to be trained under the special provisions will be ______ (amount to be filled in by State highway department).

In the event that a contractor subcontracts a portion of the contract work, he shall determine how many, if any, of the trainees are to be trained by the subcontractor, provided, however, that the contractor shall retain the primary responsibility for meeting the training requirements imposed by this special provision. The contractor shall also insure that this training special provision is made applicable to such subcontract. Where feasible, 25 percent of apprentices or trainees in each occupation shall be in their first year of apprenticeship or training.

The number of trainees shall be distributed among the work classifications on the basis of the contractor's needs and the availability of journeymen in the various classifications within a reasonable area of recruitment. Prior to commencing construction, the contractor shall submit to the State highway agency for approval the number of trainees to be trained in each selected classification and training program to be used. Furthermore, the contractor shall specify the starting time for training in each of the classifications. The contractor will be credited for each trainee employed by him on the contract work who is currently enrolled or becomes enrolled in an approved program and will be reimbursed for such trainees as provided hereinafter.

Training and upgrading of minorities and women toward journeymen status is a primary objective of this Training Special Provision. Accordingly, the contractor shall make every effort to enroll minority trainees and women (e.g., by conducting systematic and direct recruitment through public and private sources likely to yield minority and women trainees) to the extent that such persons are available within a reasonable area of recruitment. The contractor will be responsible for demonstrating the steps that he has taken in pursuance thereof, prior to a determination as to whether the contractor is in compliance with this Training Special Provision. This training commitment is not intended, and shall not be used, to discriminate against any applicant for training, whether a member of a minority group or not.

No employee shall be employed as a trainee in any classification in which he has successfully completed a training course leading to journeyman status or in which he has been employed as a journeyman. The contractor should satisfy this requirement by including appropriate questions in the employee application or by other suitable means. Regardless of the method used the contractor's records should document the findings in each case.

The minimum length and type of training for each classification will be as established in the training program selected by the contractor and approved by the State highway agency and the Federal Highway Administration. The State highway agency and the Federal Highway Administration shall approve a program if it is reasonably calculated to meet the equal employment opportunity obligations of the contractor and to qualify the average trainee for journeyman status in the classification concerned by the end of the training period. Furthermore, apprenticeship programs registered with the U.S. Department of Labor, Bureau of Apprenticeship and Training, or with a State apprenticeship agency recognized by the Bureau and training programs approved but not necessarily sponsored by the U.S. Department of Labor, Manpower Administration, Bureau of Apprenticeship and Training shall also be considered acceptable provided it is being administered in a manner consistent with the equal employment obligations of Federal-aid highway construction contracts. Approval or acceptance of a training program shall be obtained from the State prior to commencing work on the classification covered by the program. It is the intention of these provisions that training is to be provided in the construction crafts rather than clerk-typists or secretarial-type positions. Training is permissible in lower level management positions such as office engineers, estimators, timekeepers, etc., where the training is oriented toward construction applications. Training in the laborer classification may be permitted provided that significant and meaningful training is provided and approved by the division office. Some offsite training is permissible as long as the training is an integral part of an approved training program and does not comprise a significant part of the overall training.

Except as otherwise noted below, the contractor will be reimbursed 80 cents per hour of training given an employee on this contract in accordance with an approved training program. As approved by the engineer, reimbursement will be made for training persons in excess of the number specified herein. This reimbursement will be made even though the contractor receives additional training program funds from other sources, provided such other does not specifically prohibit the contractor from receiving other reimbursement. Reimbursement for offsite training indicated above may only be made to the contractor where he does one or more of the following and the trainees are concurrently employed on a Federal-aid project; contributes to the cost of the training, provides the instruction to the trainee or pays the trainee's wages during the offsite training period.

No payment shall be made to the contractor if either the failure to provide the required training, or the failure to hire the trainee as a journeyman, is caused by the contractor and evidences a lack of good faith on the part of the contractor in meeting the requirements of this Training Special Provision. It is normally expected that a trainee will begin his training on the project as soon as feasible after start of work utilizing the skill involved and remain on the project as long as training opportunities exist in his work classification or until he has completed his training program. It is not required that all trainees be on board for the entire length of the contract. A contractor will have fulfilled his responsibilities under this Training Special Provision if he has provided acceptable training to the number of trainees specified. The number trained shall be determined on the basis of the total number enrolled on the contract for a significant period.

Trainees will be paid at least 60 percent of the appropriate minimum journeyman's rate specified in the contract for the first half of the training period, 75 percent for the third quarter of the training period, and 90 percent for the last quarter of the training period, unless apprentices or trainees in an approved existing program are enrolled as trainees on this project. In that case, the appropriate rates approved by the Departments of Labor or Transportation in connection with the existing program shall apply to all trainees being trained for the same classification who are covered by this Training Special Provision.

The contractor shall furnish the trainee a copy of the program he will follow in providing the training. The contractor shall provide each trainee with a certification showing the type and length of training satisfactorily completed.

The contractor will provide for the maintenance of records and furnish periodic reports documenting his performance under this Training Special Provision.

[40 FR 28053, July 3, 1975. Correctly redesignated at 46 FR 21156, Apr. 9, 1981]

APPENDIX C TO SUBPART A OF PART 230—FEDERAL-AID HIGHWAY CONTRACTORS ANNUAL EEO REPORT (FORM PR–1391)

U.S. DEPARTMENT OF TRANSPORTATION
FEDERAL HIGHWAY ADMINISTRATION

FEDERAL-AID HIGHWAY CONSTRUCTION CONTRACTORS ANNUAL EEO REPORT

OMB NO 04 R2427
REPORT FOR
JULY __________ 19 ___

1. CHECK APPROPRIATE BLOCK ☐ CONTRACTOR ☐ SUBCONTRACTOR	2. NAME AND ADDRESS OF FIRM	3. FEDERAL AID PROJECT NUMBER	4. TYPE OF CONSTRUCTION

5. COUNTY AND STATE	6. PERCENT COMPLETE	7. BEGINNING CONSTR. DATE	8. DOLLAR AMOUNT OF CONTRACT	9. ESTIMATED PEAK EMPLOYMENT — MONTH AND YEAR (a)	NUMBER OF EMPLOYEES (b)

10. **EMPLOYMENT DATA**

JOB CATEGORIES	Table A: TOTAL EMPLOYEES		TOTAL MINORITIES		BLACK *Not of Hispanic Origin*		HISPANIC		AMERICAN INDIAN OR ALASKAN NATIVE		ASIAN OR PACIFIC ISLANDER		WHITE *Not of Hispanic Origin*		Table B: APPRENTICES		ON THE JOB TRAINEES	
	M	F	M	F	M	F	M	F	M	F	M	F	M	F	M	F	M	F
OFFICIALS *(Managers)*																		
SUPERVISORS																		
FOREMEN/WOMEN																		
CLERICAL																		
EQUIPMENT OPERATORS																		
MECHANICS																		
TRUCK DRIVERS																		
IRONWORKERS																		
CARPENTERS																		
CEMENT MASONS																		
ELECTRICIANS																		
PIPEFITTERS, PLUMBERS																		
PAINTERS																		
LABORERS, SEMI-SKILLED																		
LABORERS, UNSKILLED																		
TOTAL																		
Table C																		
APPRENTICES																		
ON THE JOB TRAINEES																		

11. PREPARED BY: *(Signature and Title of Contractors Representative)* DATE

12. REVIEWED BY: *(Signature and Title of State Highway Official)* DATE

This report is required by law and regulation (23 U.S.C. 140(a) and 23 CFR Part 230). Failure to report will result in noncompliance with this regulation.

Form PR-1391 PREVIOUS EDITIONS ARE OBSOLETE

APPENDIX D TO SUBPART A OF PART 230—FEDERAL-AID HIGHWAY CONSTRUCTION SUMMARY OF EMPLOYMENT DATA (FORM PR–1392)

DEPARTMENT OF TRANSPORTATION
FEDERAL HIGHWAY ADMINISTRATION

OMB NO. 04-R2427

FEDERAL-AID HIGHWAY CONSTRUCTION

SUMMARY OF EMPLOYMENT DATA (INCLUDING MINORITY BREAKDOWN) FOR ALL FEDERAL-AID HIGHWAY PROJECTS FOR MONTH ENDING JULY 31st, 19 ____

NOTE: See Instructions on REVERSE

STATE-REGION (5-8)	NUMBER OF PROJECTS (9-12)	TOTAL DOLLAR VALUE (13-23)
01		

EMPLOYMENT DATA

Table A

JOB CATEGORIES	TOTAL EMPLOYEES 9-13	14-18	TOTAL MINORITIES 19-23	24-28	BLACK *Not of Hispanic Origin* 29-33	34-38	HISPANIC 39-43	44-48	AMERICAN INDIAN OR ALASKAN NATIVE 49-53	54-58	ASIAN OR PACIFIC ISLANDER 59-63	64-68	WHITE *Not of Hispanic Origin* 69-73	74-78	APPRENTICES 79-83	84-88	ON THE JOB TRAINEES 89-93	94-98
	M	F	M	F	M	F	M	F	M	F	M	F	M	F	M	F	M	F
02 OFFICIALS (MANAGERS)																		
03 SUPERVISORS																		
04 FOREMEN/WOMEN																		
05 CLERICAL																		
06 EQUIPMENT OPERATORS																		
07 MECHANICS																		
08 TRUCK DRIVERS																		
09 IRONWORKERS																		
10 CARPENTERS																		
11 CEMENT MASONS																		
12 ELECTRICIANS																		
13 PIPEFITTERS, PLUMBERS																		
14 PAINTERS																		
15 LABORERS, SEMI-SKILLED																		
16 LABORERS, UNSKILLED																		
17 TOTAL																		

Table B

18 APPRENTICES														
19 ON THE JOB TRAINEES														

PREPARED BY (*Signature & Title*)	DATE	REVIEWED BY (*Signature & Title of State Hwy. Official*)	DATE

This report is required by law and regulation (23 U.S.C. 140(a) and 23 CFR Part 230). Failure to report will result in noncompliance with this regulation.

Form PR-1392
(Rev. 3-79)

PREVIOUS EDITIONS ARE OBSOLETE

GENERAL INFORMATION AND INSTRUCTIONS

This form is to be developed from the "Contractor's Annual EEO Report." This data is to be compiled by the State and submitted annually. It should reflect the total employment on all Federal-Aid Highway Projects in the State as of July 31st. The staffing figures to be reported should represent the project work force on board in all or any part of the last payroll period preceding the end of July. The staffing figures to be reported in Table A should include journey-level men and women, apprentices, and on-the-job trainees. Staffing figures to be reported in Table B should include only apprentices and on-the-job trainees as indicated.

Entries made for "Job Categories" are to be confined to the listing shown. Miscellaneous job classifications are to be incorporated in the most appropriate category listed on the form. All employees on projects should thus be accounted for.

This information will be useful in complying with the U.S. Senate Committee on Public Works request that the Federal Highway Administration submit a report annually on the status of the Equal Employment Opportunity Program, its effectiveness, and progress made by the States and the Administration in carrying out section 22(A) of the Federal-Aid Highway Act of 1968. In addition, the form should be used as a valuable tool for States to evaluate their own programs for ensuring equal opportunity.

It is requested that States submit this information annually to the FHWA Divisions no later than September 25.

Line 01—State & Region Code. Enter the 4-digit code from the list below.

State	Code	State	Code
Alabama	01–04	Montana	30–08
Alaska	02–10	Nebraska	31–07
Arizona	04–09	Nevada	32–09
Arkansas	05–06	New Hampshire	33–01
California	06–09	New Jersey	34–01
Colorado	08–08	New Mexico	35–06
Delaware	10–03	North Carolina	37–04
District of Columbia	11–03	North Dakota	38–08
Florida	12–04	Ohio	39–05
Georgia	13–04	Oklahoma	40–06
Hawaii	15–09	Oregon	41–10
Idaho	16–10	Pennsylvania	42–03
Illinois	17–05	Puerto Rico	43–01
Iowa	19–07	South Carolina	45–04
Kansas	20–07	South Dakota	46–08
Kentucky	21–04	Tennessee	47–04
Louisiana	22–06	Texas	48–06
Maine	23–01	Utah	49–08
Maryland	24–03	Vermont	50–01
Massachusetts	25–01	Virginia	51–03
Michigan	26–05	Washington	53–10
Minnesota	27–05	West Virginia	54–03
Mississippi	28–04	Wisconsin	55–05
Missouri	29–07	Wyoming	56–08

(23 U.S.C. sec. 140(a), 315, 49 CFR 1.48(b))

[44 FR 46832, Aug. 8, 1979. Correctly redesignated at 46 FR 21156, Apr. 9, 1981, and amended at 56 FR 4721, Feb. 6, 1991]

APPENDIXES E–F TO SUBPART A OF PART 230 [RESERVED]

APPENDIX G TO SUBPART A OF PART 230—SPECIAL REPORTING REQUIREMENTS FOR "HOMETOWN" OR "IMPOSED" PLAN AREAS

In addition to the reporting requirements set forth elsewhere in this contract the contractor and the subcontractors holding subcontracts, not including material suppliers, of $10,000 or more, shall submit for every month of July during which work is performed, employment data as contained under Form PR–1391 (appendix C to 23 CFR part 230) and in accordance with the instructions included thereon.

[40 FR 28053, July 3, 1975. Correctly redesignated at 46 FR 21156, Apr. 9, 1981]

Subpart B—Supportive Services for Minority, Disadvantaged, and Women Business Enterprises

SOURCE: 50 FR 51243, Dec. 16, 1985, unless otherwise noted.

§ 230.201 Purpose.

To prescribe the policies, procedures, and guidance to develop, conduct, and administer supportive services assistance programs for minority, disadvantaged, and women business enterprises.

§ 230.202 Definitions.

(a) *Minority Business Enterprise*, as used in this subpart, refers to all small businesses which participate in the Federal-aid highway program as a minority business enterprise (MBE), women business enterprise (WBE), or disadvantaged business enterprise (DBE), all defined under 49 CFR part 23. This expanded definition is used only in this subpart as a simplified way of defining the firms eligible to benefit from this supportive services program.

(b) *Supportive Services* means those services and activities provided in connection with minority business enterprise programs which are designed to increase the total number of minority businesses active in the highway program and contribute to the growth and eventual self-sufficiency of individual minority businesses so that such businesses may achieve proficiency to compete, on an equal basis, for contracts and subcontracts.

(c) *State highway agency* means that department, commission, board, or official of any State charged by its laws with the responsibility for highway construction. The term *State* is considered equivalent to *State highway agency* if the context so implies.

§ 230.203 Policy.

Based on the provisions of Pub. L. 97–424, dated January 6, 1983, it is the policy of the Federal Highway Administration (FHWA) to promote increased participation of minority business enterprises in Federal-aid highway contracts in part through the development and implementation of cost effective supportive services programs through the State highway agencies.

§ 230.204 Implementation of supportive services.

(a) Subject to the availability of funds under 23 U.S.C. 140(c), the State highway agency shall establish procedures to develop, conduct, and administer minority business enterprise training and assistance programs specifically for the benefit of women and minority businesses. Supportive services funds allocated to the States shall not be used to finance the training of State highway agency employees or to provide services in support of such training. State highway agencies are not required to match funds allocated to them under this section. Individual States are encouraged to be actively involved in the provision of supportive services. Such involvement can take the form of staff, funding, and/or direct assistance to augment the supportive services efforts financed by Federal-aid funds.

(b) State highway agencies shall give preference to the following types of services:

(1) Services relating to identification, prequalification, and certification assistance, with emphasis on increasing the total number of legitimate minority business enterprises participating in the Federal-aid highway program;

(2) Services in connection with estimating, bidding, and technical assistance designed to develop and improve the capabilities of minority businesses and assist them in achieving proficiency in the technical skills involved in highway construction;

(3) Services designed to develop and improve the immediate and long-term business management, recordkeeping, and financial accounting capabilities;

(4) Services to assist minority business enterprises to become eligible for and to obtain bonding and financial assistance;

(5) Services relating to verification procedures to ensure that only *bona fide* minority business enterprises are certified as eligible for participation in the Federal-aid highway program;

(6) Follow-up services to ascertain the outcome of training and assistance being provided; and

(7) Other services which contribute to long-term development, increased opportunities, and eventual self-sufficiency of minority business enterprises.

(c) A detailed work statement of the supportive services which the State highway agency considers to meet the guidance under this regulation and a program plan for meeting the requirements of paragraph (b) of this section and accomplishing other objectives shall be submitted to the FHWA for approval.

(d) State highway agencies which desire to provide or obtain services other than those listed in paragraph (b) of this section shall submit their proposals to the FHWA for approval.

(e) When the State highway agency provides supportive services by contract, formal advertising is not required by FHWA; however, the State highway agency shall solicit proposals from such qualified sources as will assure the competitive nature of the procurement. The evaluation of proposals by the State highway agency must include consideration of the proposer's ability to effect a productive relationship with majority and minority contractors, contractors' associations, minority groups, and other persons or organizations whose cooperation and assistance will increase the opportunities for minority business enterprises to compete for and perform contracts and subcontracts.

(f) In the selection of contractors to perform supportive services, State highway agencies shall make conscientious efforts to search out, and utilize the services of qualified minority or women organizations, or minority or women enterprises.

(g) As a minimum, State highway agency contracts to obtain supportive services shall include the following provisions:

(1) A statement that a primary purpose of the supportive services is to increase the total number of minority firms participating in the Federal-aid highway program and to contribute to the growth and eventual self-sufficiency of minority firms;

(2) A statement that supportive services shall be provided only to those minority business enterprises determined to be eligible for participation in the Federal-aid highway program in accordance with 49 CFR part 23 and have a work specialty related to the highway construction industry;

(3) A clear and complete statement of the services to be provided under the contract, such as technical assistance, managerial assistance, counseling, certification assistance, and follow-up procedures as set forth in § 230.204(b) of this part;

(4) The nondiscrimination provisions required by Title VI of the Civil Rights Act of 1964 as set forth in Form FHWA–1273, Required Contract Provisions, Federal-Aid Construction Contracts,[1] and a statement of nondiscrimination in employment because of race, color, religion, sex, or national origin;

(5) The establishment of a definite period of contract performance together with, if appropriate, a schedule stating when specific supportive services are to be provided;

(6) Monthly or quarterly reports to the State highway agency containing sufficient data and narrative content to enable evaluation of both progress and problems;

(7) The basis of payment;

(8) An estimated schedule for expenditures;

(9) The right of access to records and the right to audit shall be granted to authorize State highway agency and FHWA officials;

(10) Noncollusion certification;

(11) A requirement that the contractor provide all information necessary to support progress payments if such are provided for in the contract; and

(12) A termination clause.

(h) The State highway agency is to furnish copies of the reports received under paragraph (g)(6) of this section to the FHWA division office.

[50 FR 51243, Dec. 16, 1985, as amended at 52 FR 36922, Oct. 2, 1987]

§ 230.205 Supportive services funds obligation.

Supportive services funds shall be obligated in accordance with the procedures set forth in § 230.117(b) of this part. The point of obligation is defined as that time when the FHWA has approved a detailed work statement for the supportive services.

§ 230.206 Monitoring supportive services.

Supportive services programs shall be continually monitored and evaluated by the State highway agency so that needed improvements can be identified and instituted. This requires the documentation of valid effectiveness

[1] Form FHWA–1273 is available for inspection and copying at the locations given in 49 CFR part 7, appendix D, under Document Inspection Facilities, and at all State highway agencies.

measures by which the results of program efforts may be accurately assessed.

§ 230.207 Sources of assistance.

It is the policy of the FHWA that all potential sources of assistance to minority business enterprises be utilized. The State highway agency shall take actions to ensure that supportive services contracts reflect the availability of all sources of assistance in order to maximize resource utilization and avoid unnecessary duplication.

Subpart C—State Highway Agency Equal Employment Opportunity Programs

SOURCE: 41 FR 28270, July 9, 1976, unless otherwise noted.

§ 230.301 Purpose.

The purpose of the regulations in this subpart is to set forth Federal Highway Administration (FHWA) Federal-aid policy and FHWA and State responsibilities relative to a State highway agency's internal equal employment opportunity program and for assuring compliance with the equal employment opportunity requirements of federally-assisted highway construction contracts.

§ 230.303 Applicability.

The provisions of this subpart are applicable to all States that receive Federal financial assistance in connection with the Federal-aid highway program.

§ 230.305 Definitions.

As used in this subpart, the following definitions apply:

(a) *Affirmative Action Plan* means:

(1) With regard to State highway agency work forces, a written document detailing the positive action steps the State highway agency will take to assure internal equal employment opportunity (internal plan).

(2) With regard to Federal-aid construction contract work forces, the Federal equal employment opportunity bid conditions, to be enforced by a State highway agency in the plan areas established by the Secretary of Labor and FHWA special provisions in nonplan areas (external plan).

(b) *Equal employment opportunity program* means the total State highway agency program, including the affirmative action plans, for ensuring compliance with Federal requirements both in State highway agency internal employment and in employment on Federal-aid construction projects.

(c) *Minority groups*. An employee may be included in the minority group to which he or she appears to belong, or is regarded in the community as belonging. As defined by U.S. Federal agencies for employment purposes, minority group persons in the U.S. are identified as Blacks (not of Hispanic origin), Hispanics, Asian or Pacific Islanders, and American Indians or Alaskan Natives.

(d) *Racial/ethnic identification*. For the purpose of this regulation and any accompanying report requirements, an employee may be included in the group to which he or she appears to belong, identifies with, or is regarded in the community as belonging. However, no person should be counted in more than one racial/ethnic category. The following group categories will be used:

(1) The category *White (not of Hispanic origin):* All persons having origins in any of the original peoples of Europe, North Africa, the Middle East, or the Indian Subcontinent.

(2) The category *Black (not of Hispanic origin):* All persons having origins in any of the Black racial groups.

(3) The category *Hispanic:* All persons of Mexican, Puerto Rican, Cuban, Central or South American, or other Spanish culture or origin, regardless of race.

(4) The category *Asian or Pacific Islanders:* All persons having origins in any of the original peoples of the Far East, Southeast Asia, or the Pacific Islands. This area includes, for example, China, Japan, Korea, the Philippine Islands, and Samoa.

(5) The category *American Indian or Alaskan Native:* All persons having origins in any of the original peoples of North America.

(e) *State* means any of the 50 States of the United States, the District of Columbia, the Commonwealth of Puerto Rico, Guam, American Samoa, and the Virgin Islands.

(f) *State highway agency* means that department, commission, board, or official of any State charged by its laws with the responsibility for highway construction. The term *State* should be considered equivalent to *State highway agency* if the context so implies.

[41 FR 28270, July 9, 1976, as amended at 41 FR 46293, Oct. 20, 1976]

§ 230.307 Policy.

Every employee and representative of State highway agencies shall perform all official equal employment opportunity actions in an affirmative manner, and in full accord with applicable statutes, executive orders, regulations, and policies enunciated thereunder, to assure the equality of employment opportunity, without regard to race, color, religion, sex, or national origin both in its own work force and in the work forces of contractors, subcontractors, and material suppliers engaged in the performance of Federal-aid highway construction contracts.

§ 230.309 Program format.

It is essential that a standardized Federal approach be taken in assisting the States in development and implementation of EEO programs. The format set forth in appendix A provides that standardized approach. State equal employment opportunity programs that meet or exceed the prescribed standards will comply with basic FHWA requirements.

§ 230.311 State responsibilities.

(a) Each State highway agency shall prepare and submit an updated equal employment opportunity program, one year from the date of approval of the preceding program by the Federal Highway Administrator, over the signature of the head of the State highway agency, to the Federal Highway Administrator through the FHWA Division Administrator. The program shall consist of the following elements:

(1) The collection and analysis of internal employment data for its entire work force in the manner prescribed in part II, paragraph III of appendix A; and

(2) The equal employment opportunity program, including the internal affirmative action plan, in the format and manner set forth in appendix A.

(b) In preparation of the program required by § 230.311(a), the State highway agency shall consider and respond to written comments from FHWA regarding the preceding program.

§ 230.313 Approval procedure.

After reviewing the State highway agency equal employment opportunity program and the summary analysis and recommendations from the FHWA regional office, the Washington Headquarters Office of Civil Rights staff will recommend approval or disapproval of the program to the Federal Highway Administrator. The State highway agency will be advised of the Administrator's decision. Each program approval is effective for a period of one year from date of approval.

Appendix A to Subpart C of Part 230—State Highway Agency Equal Employment Opportunity Programs

Each State highway agency's (SHA) equal employment opportunity (EEO) program shall be in the format set forth herein and shall address Contractor Compliance (part I) and SHA Internal Employment (part II), including the organizational structure of the SHA total EEO Program (internal and external).

Part I—Contractor Compliance

I. *Organization and structure.* A. *Statehighway agency EEO Coordinator (External) and staff support.* 1. Describe the organizational location and responsibilities of the State highway agency EEO Coordinator. (Provided organization charts of the State highway agency and of the EEO staff.)

2. Indicate whether full or part-time; if part-time, indicate percentage of time devoted to EEO.

3. Indicate length of time in position, civil rights experience and training, and supervision.

4. Indicate whether compliance program is centralized or decentralized.

5. Identify EEO Coordinator's staff support (full- and part-time) by job title and indicate areas of their responsibilities.

6. Identify any other individuals in the central office having a responsibility for the implementation of this program and describe their respective roles and training received in program area.

B. *District or division personnel.* 1. Describe the responsibilities and duties of any district

EEO personnel. Identify to whom they report.

2. Explain whether district EEO personnel are full-time or have other responsibilities such as labor compliance or engineering.

3. Describe training provided for personnel having EEO compliance responsibility.

C. *Project personnel.* Describe the EEO role of project personnel.

II. *Compliance procedures.* A. *Applicable directives.* 1. FHWA Contract Compliance Procedures.

2. EEO Special Provisions (FHWA Federal-Aid Highway Program Manual, vol. 6, chap. 4, sec. 1, subsec. 2, Attachment 1)[1]

3. Training Special Provisions (FHWA Federal-Aid Highway Program Manual, vol. 6, chap. 4, sec. 1, subsec. 2, Attachment 2)[1]

4. FHWA Federal-Aid Highway Program Manual, vol. 6, chap. 4, sec. 1, subsec. 6 (Contract Procedures), and subsec. 8 (Minority Business Enterprise).[1]

B. *Implementation.* 1. Describe process (methods) of incorporating the above FHWA directives into the SHA compliance program.

2. Describe the methods used by the State to familiarize State compliance personnel with all FHWA contract compliance directives. Indicate frequency of work shops, training sessions, etc.

3. Describe the procedure for advising the contractor of the EEO contract requirements at any preconstruction conference held in connection with a Federal-aid contract.

III. *Accomplishments.* Describe accomplishments in the construction EEO compliance program during the past fiscal year.

A. *Regular project compliance review program.* This number should include at least all of the following items:

1. Number of compliance reviews conducted.

2. Number of contractors reviewed.

3. Number of contractors found in compliance.

4. Number of contractors found in noncompliance.

5. Number of show cause notices issued.

6. Number of show cause notices rescinded.

7. Number of show cause actions still under conciliation and unresolved.

8. Number of followup reviews conducted.

(NOTE: In addition to information requested in items 4–8 above, include a brief summary of total show cause and followup activities—findings and achievements.)

B. *Consolidated compliance reviews.* 1. Identify the target areas that have been reviewed since the inception of the consolidated compliance program. Briefly summarize total findings.

2. Identify any significant impact or effect of this program on contractor compliance.

C. *Home office reviews.* If the State conducts home office reviews, describe briefly the procedures followed by State.

D. *Major problems encountered.* Describe major problems encountered in connection with any review activities during the past fiscal year.

E. *Major breakthroughs.* Comment briefly on any major breakthrough or other accomplishment significant to the compliance review program.

IV. *Areawide plans/Hometown and Imposed (if applicable).* A. Provide overall analysis of the effectiveness of each areawide plan in the State.

B. Indicate by job titles the number of State personnel involved in the collection, consolidation, preparation, copying, reviewing, analysis, and transmittal of area plan reports (Contracting Activity and Post Contract Implementation). Estimate the amount of time (number of hours) spent collectively on this activity each month. How does the State use the plan report data?

C. Identify Office of Federal Contract Compliance Programs (OFCCP) area plan audits or compliance checks in which State personnel participated during the last fiscal year. On the average, how many hours have been spent on these audits and/or checks during the past fiscal year?

D. Describe the working relationship of State EEO compliance personnel with representatives of plan administrative committee(s).

E. Provide recommendations for improving the areawide plan program and the reporting system.

V. *Contract sanctions.* A. Describe the procedures used by the State to impose contract sanctions or institute legal proceedings.

B. Indicate the State or Federal laws which are applicable.

C. Does the State withhold a contractor's progress payments for failure to comply with EEO requirements? If so, identify contractors involved in such actions during the past fiscal year. If not, identify other actions taken.

VI. *Complaints.* A. Describe the State's procedures for handling discrimination complaints against contractors.

B. If complaints are referred to a State fair employment agency or similar agency, describe the referral procedure.

C. Identify the Federal-aid highway contractors that have had discrimination complaints filed against them during the past fiscal year and provide current status.

VII. *External training programs, including supportive services.* A. Describe the State's process for reviewing the work classifications of trainees to determine that there is a

[1] The Federal-Aid Highway Program Manual is available for inspection and copying at the Federal Highway Administration (FHWA), 1200 New Jersey Avenue, SE., Washington, DC 20590, or at FHWA offices listed in 49 CFR part 7, appendix D.

proper and reasonable distribution among appropriate craft.

B. Describe the State's procedures for identifying the number of minorities and women who have completed training programs.

C. Describe the extent of participation by women in construction training programs.

D. Describe the efforts made by the State to locate and use the services of qualified minority and female supportive service consultants. Indicate if the State's supportive service contractor is a minority or female owned enterprise.

E. Describe the extent to which reports from the supportive service contractors provide sufficient data to evaluate the status of training programs, with particular reference to minorities and women.

VIII. *Minority business enterprise program.* FHPM 6–4–1–8 sets forth the FHWA policy regarding the minority business enterprise program. The implementation of this program should be explained by responding to the following:

A. Describe the method used for listing of minority contractors capable of, or interested in, highway construction contracting or subcontracting. Describe the process used to circulate names of appropriate minority firms and associations to contractors obtaining contract proposals.

B. Describe the State's procedure for insuring that contractors take action to affirmatively solicit the interest, capability, and prices of potential minority subcontractors.

C. Describe the State's procedure for insuring that contractors have designated liaison officers to administer the minority business enterprise program in an effective manner. Specify resource material, including contracts, which the State provides to liaison officers.

D. Describe the action the State has taken to meet its goals for prequalification or licensing of minority business. Include dollar goals established for the year, and describe what criteria or formula the State has adopted for setting such goals. If it is different from the previous year, describe in detail.

E. Outline the State's procedure for evaluating its prequalification/licensing requirements.

F. Identify instances where the State has waived prequalification for subcontractors on Federal-aid construction work or for prime contractors on Federal-aid contracts with an estimated dollar value lower than $100,000.

G. Describe the State's methods of monitoring the progress and results of its minority business enterprise efforts.

IX. *Liaison.* Describe the liaison established by the State between public (State, county, and municipal) agencies and private organizations involved in EEO programs. How is the liaison maintained on a continuing basis?

X. *Innovative programs.* Identify any innovative EEO programs or management procedures initiated by the State and not previously covered.

PART II—STATE HIGHWAY AGENCY EMPLOYMENT

I. *General.* The State highway agency's (SHA) internal program is an integral part of the agency's total activities. It should include the involvement, commitment and support of executives, managers, supervisors and all other employees. For effective administration and implementation of the EEO Program, an affirmative action plan (AAP) is required. The scope of an EEO program and an AAP must be comprehensive, covering all elements of the agency's personnel management policies and practices. The major part of an AAP must be recognition and removal of any barriers to equal employment opportunity, identification of problem areas and of persons unfairly excluded or held back and action enabling them to compete for jobs on an equal basis. An effective AAP not only benefits those who have been denied equal employment opportunity but will also greatly benefit the organization which often has overlooked, screened out or underutilized the great reservoir of untapped human resources and skills, especially among women and minority groups.

Set forth are general guidelines designed to assist the State highway agencies in implementing internal programs, including the development and implementation of AAP's to ensure fair and equal treatment for all persons, regardless of race, color, religion, sex or national origin in all employment practices.

II. *Administration and implementation.* The head of each State highway agency is responsible for the overall administration of the internal EEO program, including the total integration of equal opportunity into all facets of personnel management. However, specific program responsibilities should be assigned for carrying out the program at all management levels.

To ensure effectiveness in the implementation of the internal EEO program, a specific and realistic AAP should be developed. It should include both short and long-range objectives, with priorities and target dates for achieving goals and measuring progress, according to the agency's individual need to overcome existing problems.

A. *State Highway Agency Affirmative Action Officer (internal).* 1. *Appointment of Affirmative Action Officer.* The head of the SHA should appoint a qualified Affirmative Action (AA) Officer (Internal EEO Officer) with responsibility and authority to implement the internal EEO program. In making the selection, the following factors should be considered:

a. The person appointed should have proven ability to accomplish major program goals.

b. Managing the internal EEO program requires a major time commitment; it cannot be added on to an existing full-time job.

c. Appointing qualified minority and/or female employees to head or staff the program may offer good role models for present and potential employees and add credibility to the programs involved. However, the most essential requirements for such position(s) are sensitivity to varied ways in which discrimination limits job opportunities, commitment to program goals and sufficient status and ability to work with others in the agency to achieve them.

2. *Responsibilities of the Affirmative Action Officer.* The responsibilities of the AA Officer should include, but not necessarily be limited to:

a. Developing the written AAP.

b. Publicizing its content internally and externally.

c. Assisting managers and supervisors in collecting and analyzing employment data, identifying problem areas, setting goals and timetables and developing programs to achieve goals. Programs should include specific remedies to eliminate any discriminatory practices discovered in the employment system.

d. Handling and processing formal discrimination complaints.

e. Designing, implementing and monitoring internal audit and reporting systems to measure program effectiveness and to determine where progress has been made and where further action is needed.

f. Reporting, at least quarterly, to the head of the SHA on progress and deficiencies of each unit in relation to agency goals.

g. In addition, consider the creation of:

(1) An EEO Advisory Committee, whose membership would include top management officials,

(2) An EEO Employee Committee, whose membership would include rank and file employees, with minority and female representatives from various job levels and departments to meet regularly with the AA officer, and

(3) An EEO Counseling Program to attempt informal resolution of discrimination complaints.

B. *Contents of an affirmative action plan.* The Affirmative Action Plan (AAP) is an integral part of the SHA's EEO program. Although the style and format of AAP's may vary from one SHA to another, the basic substance will generally be the same. The essence of the AAP should include, but not necessarily be limited to:

1. Inclusion of a strong agency policy statement of commitment to EEO.

2. Assignment of responsibility and authority for program to a qualified individual.

3. A survey of the labor market area in terms of population makeup, skills, and availability for employment.

4. Analyzing the present work force to identify jobs, departments and units where minorities and females are underutilized.

5. Setting specific, measurable, attainable hiring and promotion goals, with target dates, in each area of underutilization.

6. Making every manager and supervisor responsible and accountable for meeting these goals.

7. Reevaluating job descriptions and hiring criteria to assure that they reflect actual job needs.

8. Finding minorities and females who are qualified or qualifiable to fill jobs.

9. Getting minorities and females into upward mobility and relevant training programs where they have not had previous access.

10. Developing systems to monitor and measure progress regularly. If results are not satisfactory to meet goals, determine the reasons and make necessary changes.

11. Developing a procedure whereby employees and applicants may process allegations of discrimination to an impartial body without fear of reprisal.

C. *Implementation of an affirmative action plan.* The written AAP is the framework and management tool to be used at all organizational levels to actively implement, measure and evaluate program progress on the specific action items which represent EEO program problems or deficiencies. The presence of a written plan alone does not constitute an EEO program, nor is it, in itself, evidence of an ongoing program. As a minimum, the following specific actions should be taken.

1. *Issue written equal employment opportunity policy statement and affirmative action commitment.* To be effective, EEO policy provisions must be enforced by top management, and all employees must be made aware that EEO is basic agency policy. The head of the SHA (1) should issue a firm statement of personal commitment, legal obligation and the importance of EEO as an agency goal, and (2) assign specific responsibility and accountability to each executive, manager and supervisor.

The statement should include, but not necessarily be limited to, the following elements:

a. EEO for all persons, regardless of race, color, religion, sex or national origin as a fundamental agency policy.

b. Personal commitment to and support of EEO by the head of the SHA.

c. The requirement that special affirmative action be taken throughout the agency to overcome the effects of past discrimination.

d. The requirement that the EEO program be a goal setting program with measurement and evaluation factors similar to other major agency programs.

e. Equal opportunity in all employment practices, including (but not limited to) recruiting, hiring, transfers, promotions, training, compensation, benefits, recognition (awards), layoffs, and other terminations.

f. Responsibility for positive affirmative action in the discharge of EEO programs, including performance evaluations of managers and supervisors in such functions, will be expected of and shared by all management personnel.

g. Accountability for action or inaction in the area of EEO by management personnel.

2. *Publicize the affirmative action plan.* a. *Internally:* (1) Distribute written communications from the head of the SHA.

(2) Include the AAP and the EEO policy statement in agency operations manual.

(3) Hold individual meetings with managers and supervisors to discuss the program, their individual responsibilities and to review progress.

(4) Place Federal and State EEO posters on bulletin boards, near time clocks and in personnel offices.

(5) Publicize the AAP in the agency newsletters and other publications.

(6) Present and discuss the AAP as a part of employee orientation and all training programs.

(7) Invite employee organization representatives to cooperate and assist in developing and implementing the AAP.

b. *Externally:* Distribute the AAP to minority groups and women's organizations, community action groups, appropriate State agencies, professional organizations, etc.

3. *Develop and implement specific programs to eliminate discriminatory barriers and achieve goals.* a. *Job structuring and upward mobility:* The AAP should include specific provisions for:

(1) Periodic classification plan reviews to correct inaccurate position descriptions and to ensure that positions are allocated to the appropriate classification.

(2) Plans to ensure that all qualification requirements are closely job related.

(3) Efforts to restructure jobs and establish entry level and trainee positions to facilitate progression within occupational areas.

(4) Career counseling and guidance to employees.

(5) Creating career development plans for lower grade employees who are underutilized or who demonstrate potential for advancement.

(6) Widely publicizing upward mobility programs and opportunities within each work unit and within the total organizational structure.

b. *Recruitment and placement.* The AAP should include specific provisions for, but not necessarily limited to:

(1) Active recruitment efforts to support and supplement those of the central personnel agency or department, reaching all appropriate sources to obtain qualified employees on a nondiscriminatory basis.

(2) Maintaining contracts with organizations representing minority groups, women, professional societies, and other sources of candidates for technical, professional and management level positions.

(3) Ensuring that recruitment literature is relevant to all employees, including minority groups and women.

(4) Reviewing and monitoring recruitment and placement procedures so as to assure that no discriminatory practices exist.

(5) Cooperating with management and the central personnel agency on the review and validation of written tests and other selection devices.

(6) Analyzing the flow of applicants through the selection and appointment process, including an analytical review of reasons for rejections.

(7) Monitoring the placement of employees to ensure the assignment of work and workplace on a nondiscriminatory basis.

c. *Promotions.* The AAP should include specific provisions for, but not necessarily limited to:

1. Establishing an agency-wide merit promotion program, including a merit promotion plan, to provide equal opportunity for all persons based on merit and without regard to race, color, religion, sex or national origin.

2. Monitoring the operation of the merit promotion program, including a review of promotion actions, to assure that requirements procedures and practices support EEO program objectives and do not have a discriminatory impact in actual operation.

3. Establishing skills banks to match employee skills with available job advancement opportunities.

4. Evaluating promotion criteria (supervisory evaluations, oral interviews, written tests, qualification standards, etc.) and their use by selecting officials to identify and eliminate factors which may lead to improper "selection out" of employees or applicants, particularly minorities and women, who traditionally have not had access to better jobs. It may be appropriate to require selecting officials to submit a written justification when well qualified persons are passed over for upgrading or promotion.

5. Assuring that all job vacancies are posted conspicuously and that all employees are encouraged to bid on all jobs for which they feel they are qualified.

6. Publicizing the agency merit promotion program by highlighting breakthrough promotions, *i.e.*, advancement of minorities and women to key jobs, new career heights, etc.

d. *Training.* The AAP should include specific provisions for, but not necessarily limited to:

(1) Requiring managers and supervisors to participate in EEO seminars covering the AAP, the overall EEO program and the administration of the policies and procedures incorporated therein, and on Federal, State and local laws relating to EEO.

(2) Training in proper interviewing techniques of employees who conduct employment selection interviews.

(3) Training and education programs designed to provide opportunities for employees to advance in relation to the present and projected manpower needs of the agency and the employees' career goals.

(4) The review of profiles of training course participants to ensure that training opportunities are being offered to all eligible employees on an equal basis and to correct any inequities discovered.

e. *Layoffs, recalls, discharges, demotions, and disciplinary actions.* The standards for deciding when a person shall be terminated, demoted, disciplined, laid off or recalled should be the same for all employees, including minorities and females. Seemingly neutral practices should be reexamined to see if they have a disparate effect on such groups. For example, if more minorities and females are being laid off because they were the last hired, then, adjustments should be made to assure that the minority and female ratios do not decrease because of these actions.

(1) When employees, particularly minorities and females, are disciplined, laid off, discharged or downgraded, it is advisable that the actions be reviewed by the AA Officer before they become final.

(2) Any punitive action (*i.e.*, harassment, terminations, demotions), taken as a result of employees filing discrimination complaints, is illegal.

(3) The following records should be kept to monitor this area of the internal EEO program:

On all terminations, including layoffs and discharges: indicate total number, name, (home address and phone number), employment date, termination date, recall rights, sex, racial/ethnic identification (by job category), type of termination and reason for termination.

On all demotions: indicate total number, name, (home address and phone number), demotion date, sex, racial/ethnic identification (by job category), and reason for demotion.

On all recalls: indicate total number, name, (home address and phone number) recall date, sex, and racial/ethnic identification (by job category).

Exit interviews should be conducted with employees who leave the employment of the SHA.

f. *Other personnel actions.* The AAP should include specific provisions for, but not necessarily limited to:

(1) Assuring that information on EEO counseling and grievance procedures is easily available to all employees.

(2) A system for processing complaints alleging discrimination because of race, color, religion, sex or national origin to an impartial body.

(3) A system for processing grievances and appeals (*i.e.*, disciplinary actions, adverse actions, adverse action appeals, etc).

(4) Including in the performance appraisal system a factor to rate manager's and supervisors' performance in discharging the EEO program responsibilities assigned to them.

(5) Reviewing and monitoring the performance appraisal program periodically to determine its objectivity and effectiveness.

(6) Ensuring the equal availability of employee benefits to all employees.

4. *Program evaluation.* An internal reporting system to continually audit, monitor and evaluate programs is essential for a successful AAP. Therefore, a system providing for EEO goals, timetables, and periodic evaluations needs to be established and implemented. Consideration should be given to the following actions:

a. Defining the major objectives of EEO program evaluation.

b. The evaluation should be directed toward results accomplished, not only at efforts made.

c. The evaluation should focus attention on assessing the adequacy of problem identification in the AAP and the extent to which the specific action steps in the plan provide solutions.

d. The AAP should be reviewed and evaluated at least annually. The review and evaluation procedures should include, but not be limited to, the following:

(1) Each bureau, division or other major component of the agency should make annual and such other periodic reports as are needed to provide an accurate review of the operations of the AAP in that component.

(2) The AA Officer should make an annual report to the head of the SHA, containing the overall status of the program, results achieved toward established objectives, identity of any particular problems encountered and recommendations for corrective actions needed.

e. Specific, numerical goals and objectives should be established for the ensuing year. Goals should be developed for the SHA as a whole, as well as for each unit and each job category.

III. *Employment statistical data.* A. As a minimum, furnish the most recent data on the following:

1. The total population in the State,

2. The total labor market in State, with a breakdown by racial/ethnic identification and sex, and

3. An analysis of (1) and (2) above, in connection with the availability of personnel and jobs within SHA's.

B. State highway agencies shall use the EEO–4 Form in providing current work force data. This data shall reflect only State department of transportation/State highway department employment.

D. EMPLOYMENT DATA AS OF JUNE 30 5

(Do not include elected/appointed officials. Blanks will be counted as zero)

1. FULL TIME EMPLOYEES (Temporary employees not included)

JOB CATEGORIES	ANNUAL SALARY (In Thousands 000)	TOTAL (COLUMNS B-K)	MALE					FEMALE				
			NON-HISPANIC ORIGIN			ASIAN OR PACIFIC ISLANDER	AMERICAN INDIAN OR ALASKAN NATIVE	NON-HISPANIC ORIGIN			ASIAN OR PACIFIC ISLANDER	AMERICAN INDIAN OR ALASKAN NATIVE
			WHITE	BLACK	HISPANIC			WHITE	BLACK	HISPANIC		
		A	B	C	D	E	F	G	H	I	J	K
OFFICIALS/ ADMINISTRATORS	1. $ 0.1-3.9											
	2. 4.0-5.9											
	3. 6.0-7.9											
	4. 8.0-9.9											
	5. 10.0-12.9											
	6. 13.0-15.9											
	7. 16.0-24.9											
	8. 25.0 PLUS											
PROFESSIONALS	9. 0.1-3.9											
	10. 4.0-5.9											
	11. 6.0-7.9											
	12. 8.0-9.9											
	13. 10.0-12.9											
	14. 13.0-15.9											
	15. 16.0-24.9											
	16. 25.0 PLUS											
TECHNICIANS	17. 0.1-3.9											
	18. 4.0-5.9											
	19. 6.0-7.9											
	20. 8.0-9.9											
	21. 10.0-12.9											
	22. 13.0-15.9											
	23. 16.0-24.9											
	24. 25.0 PLUS											
PROTECTIVE SERVICE	25. 0.1-3.9											
	26. 4.0-5.9											
	27. 6.0-7.9											
	28. 8.0-9.9											
	29. 10.0-12.9											
	30. 13.0-15.9											
	31. 16.0-24.9											
	32. 25.0 PLUS											
PARA-PROFESSIONALS	33. 0.1-3.9											
	34. 4.0-5.9											
	35. 6.0-7.9											
	36. 8.0-9.9											
	37. 10.0-12.9											
	38. 13.0-15.9											
	39. 16.0-24.9											
	40. 25.0 PLUS											
OFFICE/ CLERICAL	41. 0.1-3.9											
	42. 4.0-5.9											
	43. 6.0-7.9											
	44. 8.0-9.9											
	45. 10.0-12.9											
	46. 13.0-15.9											
	47. 16.0-24.9											
	48. $ 25.0 PLUS											

EEOC FORM 164, APR. 76

6

D. EMPLOYMENT DATA AS OF JUNE 30 (Cont.)
(Do not include elected/appointed officials. Blanks will be counted as zero)

1. FULL TIME EMPLOYEES (Temporary employees not included)

JOB CATEGORIES	ANNUAL SALARY (In thousands 000)	TOTAL (COLUMNS B-K)	MALE					FEMALE				
			NON-HISPANIC ORIGIN		HISPANIC	ASIAN OR PACIFIC ISLANDER	AMERICAN INDIAN OR ALASKAN NATIVE	NON-HISPANIC ORIGIN		HISPANIC	ASIAN OR PACIFIC ISLANDER	AMERICAN INDIAN OR ALASKAN NATIVE
			WHITE	BLACK				WHITE	BLACK			
		A	B	C	D	E	F	G	H	I	J	K
SKILLED CRAFT	49. $ 0.1-3.9											
	50 4.0-5.9											
	51. 6.0-7.9											
	52. 8.0-9.9											
	53. 10.0-12.9											
	54. 13.0-15.9											
	55. 16.0-24.9											
	56. 25.0 PLUS											
SERVICE/ MAINTENANCE	57. 0.1-3.9											
	58. 4.0-5.9											
	59. 6.0-7.9											
	60. 8.0-9.9											
	61. 10.0-12.9											
	62. 13.0-15.9											
	63. 16.0-24.9											
	64. $ 25.0 PLUS											
65. TOTAL FULL TIME (LINES 1-64)												

2. OTHER THAN FULL TIME EMPLOYEES (Include temporary employees)

	A	B	C	D	E	F	G	H	I	J	K
66. OFFICIALS / ADMIN.											
67. PROFESSIONALS											
68. TECHNICIANS											
69. PROTECTIVE SERV.											
70. PARA-PROFESSIONAL											
71. OFFICE / CLERICAL											
72. SKILLED CRAFT											
73. SERV. / MAINT.											
74. TOTAL OTHER THAN FULL TIME (LINES 66-73)											

3. NEW HIRES DURING FISCAL YEAR Permanent full time only
JULY 1 - JUNE 30

	A	B	C	D	E	F	G	H	I	J	K
75. OFFICIALS / ADMIN.											
76. PROFESSIONALS											
77. TECHNICIANS											
78. PROTECTIVE SERV.											
79. PARA-PROFESSIONAL											
80. OFFICE / CLERICAL											
81. SKILLED CRAFT											
82. SERV. / MAINT.											
83. TOTAL NEW HIRES (LINES 75-82)											

[41 FR 28270, July 9, 1976, as amended at 41 FR 46294, Oct. 20, 1976; 74 FR 28442, June 16, 2009]

Subpart D—Construction Contract Equal Opportunity Compliance Procedures

SOURCE: 41 FR 34239, Aug. 13, 1976, unless otherwise noted.

§ 230.401 Purpose.

The purpose of the regulations in this subpart is to prescribe policies and procedures to standardize the implementation of the equal opportunity contract compliance program, including compliance reviews, consolidated compliance reviews, and the administration of areawide plans.

§ 230.403 Applicability.

The procedures set forth hereinafter apply to all nonexempt direct Federal and Federal-aid highway construction contracts and subcontracts, unless otherwise specified.

§ 230.405 Administrative responsibilities.

(a) *Federal Highway Administration (FHWA) responsibilities.* (1) The FHWA has the responsibility to ensure that contractors meet contractural equal opportunity requirements under E.O. 11246, as amended, and title 23 U.S.C., and to provide guidance and direction to States in the development and implementation of a program to assure compliance with equal opportunity requirements.

(2) The Federal Highway Administrator or a designee may inquire into the status of any matter affecting the FHWA equal opportunity program and, when considered necessary, assume jurisdiction over the matter, proceeding in coordination with the State concerned. This is without derogation of the authority of the Secretary of Transportation, Department of Transportation (DOT), the Director, DOT Departmental Office of Civil Rights (OCR) or the Director, Office of Federal Contract Compliance Programs (OFCCP), Department of Labor.

(3) Failure of the State highway agency (SHA) to discharge the responsibilities stated in § 230.405(b)(1) may result in DOT's taking any or all of the following actions (see appendix A to 23 CFR part 630, subpart C "Federal-aid project agreement"):

(i) Cancel, terminate, or suspend the Federal-aid project agreement in whole or in part;

(ii) Refrain from extending any further assistance to the SHA under the program with respect to which the failure or refusal occurred until satisfactory assurance of future compliance has been received from the SHA; and

(iii) Refer the case to an appropriate Federal agency for legal proceedings.

(4) Action by the DOT, with respect to noncompliant contractors, shall not relieve a SHA of its responsibilities in connection with these same matters; nor is such action by DOT a substitute for corrective action utilized by a State under applicable State laws or regulations.

(b) *State responsibilities.* (1) The SHA's, as contracting agencies, have a responsibility to assure compliance by contractors with the requirements of Federal-aid construction contracts, including the equal opportunity requirements, and to assist in and cooperate with FHWA programs to assure equal opportunity.

(2) The corrective action procedures outlined herein do not preclude normal contract administration procedures by the States to ensure the contractor's completion of specific contract equal opportunity requirements, as long as such procedures support, and sustain the objectives of E.O. 11246, as amended. The State shall inform FHWA of any actions taken against a contractor under normal State contract administration procedures, if that action is precipitated in whole or in part by noncompliance with equal opportunity contract requirements.

§ 230.407 Definitions.

For the purpose of this subpart, the following definitions shall apply, unless the context requires otherwise:

(a) *Actions*, identified by letter and number, shall refer to those items identified in the process flow chart. (Appendix D);

(b) *Affirmative Action Plan* means a written positive management tool of a total equal opportunity program indicating the action steps for all organizational levels of a contractor to initiate and measure equal opportunity program progress and effectiveness. (The Special Provisions [23 CFR part 230 A, appendix A] and areawide plans are Affirmative Action Plans.);

(c) *Affirmative Actions* means the efforts exerted towards achieving equal opportunity through positive, aggressive, and continuous result-oriented measures to correct past and present discriminatory practices and their effects on the conditions and privileges of employment. These measures include, but are not limited to, recruitment, hiring, promotion, upgrading, demotion, transfer, termination, compensation, and training;

(d) *Areawide Plan* means an Affirmative Action Plan approved by the Department of Labor to increase minority and female utilization in crafts of the construction industry in a specified geographical area pursuant to E.O. 11246, as amended, and taking the form of either a "Hometown" or an "Imposed" Plan.

(1) *Hometown Plan* means a voluntary areawide agreement usually developed by representatives of labor unions, minority organizations, and contractors, and approved by the OFCCP for the purpose of implementing the equal employment opportunity requirements pursuant to E.O. 11246, as amended;

(2) *Imposed Plan* means mandatory affirmative action requirements for a specified geographical area issued by OFCCP and, in some areas, by the courts;

(e) *Compliance Specialist* means a Federal or State employee regularly employed and experienced in civil rights policies, practices, procedures, and equal opportunity compliance review and evaluation functions;

(f) *Consolidated Compliance Review* means a review and evaluation of all significant construction employment in a specific geographical (target) area;

(g) *Construction* shall have the meanings set forth in 41 CFR 60–1.3(e) and 23 U.S.C. 101(a). References in both definitions to expenses or functions incidental to construction shall include preliminary engineering work in project development or engineering services performed by or for a SHA;

(h) *Corrective Action Plan* means a contractor's unequivocal written and signed commitment outlining actions taken or proposed, with time limits and goals, where appropriate to correct, compensate for, and remedy each violation of the equal opportunity requirements as specified in a list of deficiencies. (Sometimes called a conciliation agreement or a letter of commitment.);

(i) *Contractor* means, any person, corporation, partnership, or unincorporated association that holds a FHWA direct or federally assisted construction contract or subcontract regardless of tier;

(j) *Days* shall mean calendar days;

(k) *Discrimination* means a distinction in treatment based on race, color, religion, sex, or national origin;

(l) *Equal Employment Opportunity* means the absence of partiality or distinction in employment treatment, so that the right of all persons to work and advance on the basis of merit, ability, and potential is maintained;

(m) *Equal Opportunity Compliance Review* means an evaluation and determination of a nonexempt direct Federal or Federal-aid contractor's or subcontractor's compliance with equal opportunity requirements based on:

(1) *Project work force*—employees at the physical location of the construction activity;

(2) *Area work force*—employees at all Federal-aid, Federal, and non-Federal projects in a specific geographical area as determined under § 230.409 (b)(9); or

(3) *Home office work force*—employees at the physical location of the corporate, company, or other ownership headquarters or regional managerial, offices, including "white collar" personnel (managers, professionals, technicians, and clericals) and any maintenance or service personnel connected thereto;

(n) *Equal Opportunity Requirements* is a general term used throughout this document to mean all contract provisions relative to equal employment opportunity (EEO), subcontracting, and training;

(o) *Good Faith Effort* means affirmative action measures designed to implement the established objectives of an Affirmative Action Plan;

(p) *Show Cause Notice* means a written notification to a contractor based on the determination of the reviewer (or in appropriate cases by higher level authority) to be in noncompliance with the equal opportunity requirements. The notice informs the contractor of the specific basis for the determination and provides the opportunity, within 30 days from receipt, to present an explanation why sanctions should not be imposed;

(q) *State highway agency* (SHA) means that department, commission, board, or official of any State charged by its laws with the responsibility for highway construction. The term *State* should be considered equivalent to *State highway agency*. With regard to direct Federal contracts, references herein to SHA's shall be considered to refer to FHWA regional offices, as appropriate.

§ 230.409 Contract compliance review procedures.

(a) *General*. A compliance review consists of the following elements:

(1) Review Scheduling (Actions R–1 and R–2).

(2) Contractor Notification (Action R–3).

(3) Preliminary Analysis (Phase I) (Action R–4).

(4) Onsite Verification and Interviews (Phase II) (Action R–5).

(5) Exit Conference (Action R–6).

(6) Compliance Determination and Formal Notification (Actions R–8, R–9, R–10, R–11, R–12).

The compliance review procedure, as described herein and in appendix D provides for continual monitoring of the employment process. Monitoring officials at all levels shall analyze submissions from field offices to ensure proper completion of procedural requirements and to ascertain the effectiveness of program implementation.

(b) *Review scheduling. (Actions R–1 and R–2)*. Because construction work forces are not constant, particular attention should be paid to the proper scheduling of equal opportunity compliance reviews. Priority in scheduling equal opportunity compliance reviews shall be given to reviewing those contractor's work forces:

(1) Which hold the greatest potential for employment and promotion of minorities and women (particularly in higher skilled crafts or occupations);

(2) Working in areas which have significant minority and female labor forces within a reasonable recruitment area;

(3) Working on projects that include special training provisions; and

(4) Where compliance with equal opportunity requirements is questionable. (Based on previous PR–1391's (23 CFR part 230, subpart A, appendix C) Review Reports and Hometown Plan Reports).

In addition, the following considerations shall apply:

(5) Reviews specifically requested by the Washington Headquarters shall receive priority scheduling;

(6) Compliance Reviews in geographical areas covered by areawide plans would normally be reviewed under the Consolidated Compliance Review Procedures set forth in § 230.415.

(7) Reviews shall be conducted prior to or during peak employment periods.

(8) No compliance review shall be conducted that is based on a home office work force of less than 15 employees unless requested or approved by Washington Headquarters; and

(9) For compliance reviews based on an area work force (outside of areawide plan coverage), the Compliance Specialist shall define the applicable geographical area by considering:

(i) Union geographical boundaries;

(ii) The geographical area from which the contractor recruits employees, *i.e.*, reasonable recruitment area;

(iii) Standard Metropolitan Statistical Area (SMSA) or census tracts; and

(iv) The county in which the Federal or Federal-aid project(s) is located and adjacent counties.

(c) *Contractor notification (Action R–3)*. (1) The Compliance Specialist should usually provide written notification to the contractor of the pending compliance review at least 2 weeks prior to the onsite verification and interviews. This notification shall include the scheduled date(s), an outline of the mechanics and basis of the review, requisite interviews, and documents required.

(2) The contractor shall be requested to provide a meeting place on the day

of the visit either at the local office of the contractor or at the jobsite.

(3) The contractor shall be requested to supply all of the following information to the Compliance Specialist prior to the onsite verification and interviews.

(i) Current Form PR–1391 developed from the most recent payroll;

(ii) Copies of all current bargaining agreements;

(iii) Copies of purchase orders and subcontracts containing the EEO clause;

(iv) A list of recruitment sources available and utilized;

(v) A statement of the status of any action pertaining to employment practices taken by the Equal Employment Opportunity Commission (EEOC) or other Federal, State, or local agency regarding the contractor or any source of employees;

(vi) A list of promotions made during the past 6 months, to include race, national origin, and sex of employee, previous job held, job promoted into; and corresponding wage rates;

(vii) An annotated payroll to show job classification, race, national origin and sex;

(viii) A list of minority- or female-owned companies contacted as possible subcontractors, vendors, material suppliers, etc.; and

(ix) Any other necessary documents or statements requested by the Compliance Specialist for review prior to the actual onsite visit.

(4) For a project review, the prime contractor shall be held responsible for ensuring that all active subcontractors are present at the meeting and have supplied the documentation listed in § 230.409(c)(3).

(d) *Preliminary analysis (Phase I) (Action R–4)*. Before the onsite verification and interviews, the Compliance Specialist shall analyze the employment patterns, policies, practices, and programs of the contractor to determine whether or not problems exist by reviewing information relative to:

(1) The contractor's current work force;

(2) The contractor's relationship with referral sources, e.g., unions, employment agencies, community action agencies, minority and female organizations, etc.;

(3) The minority and female representation of sources;

(4) The availability of minorities and females with requisite skills in a reasonable recruitment area;

(5) Any pending EEOC or Department of Justice cases or local or State Fair Employment Agency cases which are relevant to the contractor and/or the referral sources; and

(6) The related projects (and/or contractor) files of FHWA regional or division and State Coordinator's offices to obtain current information relating to the status of the contractor's project(s), value, scheduled duration, written corrective action plans, PR–1391 or Manpower Utilization Reports, training requirements, previous compliance reviews, and other pertinent correspondence and/or reports.

(e) *Onsite verification and interviews (Phase II) (Action R–5)*. (1) Phase II of the review consists of the construction or home office site visit(s). During the initial meeting with the contractor, the following topics shall be discussed:

(i) Objectives of the visit;

(ii) The material submitted by the contractor, including the actual implementation of the employee referral source system and any discrepancies found in the material; and

(iii) Arrangements for the site tour(s) and employee interviews.

(2) The Compliance Specialist shall make a physical tour of the employment site(s) to determine that:

(i) EEO posters are displayed in conspicuous places in a legible fashion;

(ii) Facilities are provided on a nonsegregated basis (e.g. work areas, washroom, timeclocks, locker rooms, storage areas, parking lots, and drinking fountains);

(iii) Supervisory personnel have been oriented to the contractor's EEO commitments;

(iv) The employee referral source system is being implemented;

(v) Reported employment data is accurate;

(vi) Meetings have been held with employees to discuss EEO policy, particularly new employees; and

(vii) Employees are aware of their right to file complaints of discrimination.

(3) The Compliance Specialist should interview at least one minority, one nonminority, and one woman in each trade, classification, or occupation. The contractor's superintendent or home office manager should also be interviewed.

(4) The Compliance Specialist shall, on a sample basis, determine the union membership status of union employees on the site (e.g. whether they have permits, membership cards, or books, and in what category they are classified [e.g., A, B, or C]).

(5) The Compliance Specialist shall also determine the method utilized to place employees on the job and whether equal opportunity requirements have been followed.

(6) The Compliance Specialist shall determine, and the report shall indicate the following:

(i) Is there reasonable representation and utilization of minorities and women in each craft, classification or occupation? If not, what has the contractor done to increase recruitment, hiring, upgrading, and training of minorities and women?

(ii) What action is the contractor taking to meet the contractual requirement to provide equal employment opportunity?

(iii) Are the actions taken by the contractor acceptable? Could they reasonably be expected to result in increased utilization of minorities and women?

(iv) Is there impartiality in treatment of minorities and women?

(v) Are affirmative action measures of an isolated nature or are they continuing?

(vi) Have the contractor's efforts produced results?

(f) *Exit conference (Action R–6).* (1) During the exit conference with the contractor, the following topics shall be discussed:

(i) Any preliminary findings that, if not corrected immediately or not corrected by the adoption of an acceptable voluntary corrective action plan, would necessitate a determination of noncompliance;

(ii) The process and time in which the contractor shall be informed of the final determination (15 days following the onsite verification and interviews); and

(iii) Any other matters that would best be resolved before concluding the onsite portion of the review.

(2) Voluntary corrective action plans may be negotiated at the exit conference, so that within 15 days following the exit portion of the review, the Compliance Specialist shall prepare the review report and make a determination of either:

(i) Compliance, and so notify the contractor; or

(ii) Noncompliance, and issue a 30–day show cause notice.

The acceptance of a voluntary corrective action plan at the exit conference does not preclude a determination of noncompliance, particularly if deficiencies not addressed by the plan are uncovered during the final analysis and report writing. (Action R–7) A voluntary corrective action plan should be accepted with the understanding that it only address those problems uncovered prior to the exit conference.

(g) *Compliance determinations (Action R–8).* (1) The evidence obtained at the compliance review shall constitute a sufficient basis for an objective determination by the Compliance Specialist conducting the review of the contractor's compliance or noncompliance with contractual provisions pursuant to E.O. 11246, as amended, and FHWA EEO Special Provisions implementing the Federal-Aid Highway Act of 1968, where applicable.

(2) Compliance determinations on contractors working in a Hometown Plan Area shall reflect the status of those crafts covered by part II of the plan bid conditions. Findings regarding part I crafts shall be transmitted through channels to the Washington Headquarters, Office of Civil Rights.

(3) The compliance status of the contractor will usually be reflected by positive efforts in the following areas:

(i) The contractor's equal employment opportunity (EEO) policy;

(ii) Dissemination of the policy and education of supervisory employees concerning their responsibilities in implementing the EEO policy;

(iii) The authority and responsibilities of the EEO officer;

(iv) The contractor's recruitment activities, especially establishing minority and female recruitment and referral procedures;

(v) The extent of participation and minority and female utilization in FHWA training programs;

(vi) The contractor's review of personnel actions to ensure equal opportunities;

(vii) The contractor's participation in apprenticeship or other training;

(viii) The contractor's relationship (if any) with unions and minority and female union membership;

(ix) Effective measures to assure nonsegregated facilities, as required by contract provisions;

(x) The contractor's procedures for monitoring subcontractors and utilization of minority and female subcontractors and/or subcontractors with substantial minority and female employment; and

(xi) The adequacy of the contractor's records and reports.

(4) A contractor shall be considered to be in compliance (Action R–9) when the equal opportunity requirements have been effectively implemented, or there is evidence that every good faith effort has been made toward achieving this end. Efforts to acheive this goal shall be result-oriented, initiated and maintained in good faith, and emphasized as any other vital management function.

(5) A contractor shall be considered to be in noncompliance (Action R–10) when:

(i) The contractor has discriminated against applicants or employees with respect to the conditions or privileges of employment; or

(ii) The contractor fails to provide evidence of every good faith effort to provide equal opportunity.

(h) *Show cause procedures*—(1) *General.* Once the onsite verification and exit conference (Action R–5) have been completed and a compliance determination made, (Action R–8), the contractor shall be notified in writing of the compliance determination. (Action R–11 or R–12) This written notification shall be sent to the contractor within 15 days following the completion of the onsite verification and exit conference. If a contractor is found in noncompliance (Action R–10), action efforts to bring the contractor into compliance shall be initiated through the issuance of a show cause notice (Action R–12). The notice shall advise the contractor to show cause within 30 days why sanctions should not be imposed.

(2) *When a show cause notice is required.* A show cause notice shall be issued when a determination of noncompliance is made based upon:

(i) The findings of a compliance review;

(ii) The results of an investigation which verifies the existence of discrimination; or

(iii) Areawide plan reports that show an underutilization of minorities (based on criteria of U.S. Department of Labor's Optional Form 66 "Manpower Utilization Report") throughout the contractor's work force covered by part II of the plan bid conditions.

(3) *Responsibility for issuance.* (i) Show cause notices will normally be issued by SHA's to federally assisted contractors when the State has made a determination of noncompliance, or when FHWA has made such a determination and has requested the State to issue the notice.

(ii) When circumstances warrant, the Regional Federal Highway Administrator or a designee may exercise primary compliance responsibility by issuing the notice directly to the contractor.

(iii) The Regional Federal Highway Administrators in Regions 8, 10, and the Regional Engineer in Region 15, shall issue show cause notices to direct Federal contractors found in noncompliance.

(4) *Content of show cause notice.* The show cause notice must: (See sample—appendix A of this subpart)

(i) Notify the contractor of the determination of noncompliance;

(ii) Provide the basis for the determination of noncompliance;

(iii) Notify the contractor of the obligation to show cause within 30 days why formal proceedings should not be instituted;

(iv) Schedule (date, time, and place) a compliance conference to be held approximately 15 days from the contractor's receipt of the notice;

(v) Advise the contractor that the conference will be held to receive and discuss the acceptability of any proposed corrective action plan and/or correction of deficiencies; and

(vi) Advise the contractor of the availability and willingness of the Compliance Specialist to conciliate within the time limits of the show cause notice.

(5) *Preparing and processing the show cause notice.* (i) The State or FHWA official who conducted the investigation or review shall develop complete background data for the issuance of the show cause notice and submit the recommendation to the head of the SHA or the Regional Federal Highway Administrator, as appropriate.

(ii) The recommendation, background data, and final draft notice shall be reviewed by appropriate State or FHWA legal counsel.

(iii) Show cause notices issued by the SHA shall be issued by the head of that agency or a designee.

(iv) The notice shall be personally served to the contractor or delivered by certified mail, return receipt requested, with a certificate of service or the return receipt filed with the case record.

(v) The date of the contractor's receipt of the show cause notice shall begin the 30-day show cause period. (Action R–13).

(vi) The 30-day show cause notice shall be issued directly to the noncompliant contractor or subcontractor with an informational copy sent to any concerned prime contractors.

(6) *Conciliation efforts during show cause period.* (i) The Compliance Specialist is required to attempt conciliation with the contractor throughout the show cause time period. Conciliation and negotiation efforts shall be directed toward correcting contractor program deficiencies and initiating corrective action which will maintain and assure equal opportunity. Records shall be maintained in the State, FHWA division, or FHWA regional office's case files, as appropriate, indicating actions and reactions of the contractor, a brief synopsis of any meetings with the contractor, notes on verbal communication and written correspondence, requests for assistance or interpretations, and other relevant matters.

(ii) In instances where a contractor is determined to be in compliance after a show cause notice has been issued, the show cause notice will be recinded and the contractor formally notified (Action R–17). The FHWA Washington Headquarters, Office of Civil Rights, shall immediately be notified of any change in status.

(7) *Corrective action plans.* (i) When a contractor is required to show cause and the deficiencies cannot be corrected within the 30–day show cause period, a written corrective action plan may be accepted. The written corrective action plan shall specify clear unequivocal action by the contractor with time limits for completion. Token actions to correct cited deficiencies will not be accepted. (See Sample Corrective Action Plan—appendix B of this subpart)

(ii) When a contractor submits an acceptable written corrective action plan, the contractor shall be considered in compliance during the plan's effective implementation and submission of required progress reports. (Action R–15 and R–17).

(iii) When an acceptable corrective action plan is not agreed upon and the contractor does not otherwise show cause as required, the formal hearing process shall be recommended through appropriate channels by the compliance specialist immediately upon expiration of the 30–day show cause period. (Action R–16, R–18, R–19)

(iv) When a contractor, after having submitted an acceptable corrective action plan and being determined in compliance is subsequently determined to be in noncompliance based upon the contractor's failure to implement the corrective action plan, the formal hearing process must be recommended immediately. There are no provisions for reinstituting a show cause notice.

(v) When, however, a contractor operating under an acceptable corrective action plan carries out the provisions of the corrective action plan but the actions do not result in the necessary changes, the corrective action plan shall be immediately amended through negotiations. If, at this point, the contractor refuses to appropriately amend the corrective action plan, the formal hearing process shall be recommended immediately.

(vi) A contractor operating under an approved voluntary corrective action plan (*i.e.*, plan entered into prior to the issuance of a show cause) must be issued a 30–day show cause notice in the situations referred to in paragraphs (h) (7) (iv) and (v) of this section, *i.e.*, failure to implement an approved corrective action plan or failure of corrective actions to result in necessary changes.

(i) *Followup reviews.* (1) A followup review is an extension of the initial review process to verify the contractors performance of corrective action and to validate progress report information. Therefore, followup reviews shall only be conducted of those contractors where the initial review resulted in a finding of noncompliance and a show cause notice was issued.

(2) Followup reviews shall be reported as a narrative summary referencing the initial review report.

(j) *Hearing process.* (1) When such procedures as show cause issuance and conciliation conferences have been unsuccessful in bringing contractors into compliance within the prescribed 30 days, the reviewer (or other appropriate level) shall immediately recommend, through channels, that the Department of Transportation obtain approval from the Office of Federal Contract Compliance Programs for a formal hearing (Action R–19). The Contractor should be notified of this action.

(2) Recommendations to the Federal Highway Administrator for hearing approval shall be accompanied by full reports of findings and case files containing any related correspondence. The following items shall be included with the recommendation:

(i) Copies of all Federal and Federal-aid contracts and/or subcontracts to which the contractor is party;

(ii) Copies of any contractor or subcontractor certifications;

(iii) Copy of show cause notice;

(iv) Copies of any corrective action plans; and

(v) Copies of all pertinent Manpower Utilization Reports, if applicable.

(3) SHA's through FHWA regional and division offices, will be advised of decisions and directions affecting contractors by the FHWA Washington Headquarters, Office of Civil Rights, for the Department of Transportation.

(k) *Responsibility determinations.* (1) In instances where requests for formal hearings are pending OFCCP approval, the contractor may be declared a nonresponsible contractor for inability to comply with the equal opportunity requirements.

(2) SHA's shall refrain from entering into any contract or contract modification subject to E.O. 11246, as amended, with a contractor who has not demonstrated eligibility for Government contracts and federally assisted construction contracts pursuant to E.O. 11246, as amended.

§ 230.411 Guidance for conducting reviews.

(a) *Extensions of time.* Reasonable extensions of time limits set forth in these instructions may be authorized by the SHA's or the FHWA regional office, as appropriate. However, all extensions are subject to Washington Headquarters approval and should only be granted with this understanding. The Federal Highway Administrator shall be notified of all time extensions granted and the justification therefor. In sensitive or special interest cases, simultaneous transmittal of reports and other pertinent documents is authorized.

(b) *Contract completion.* Completion of a contract or seasonal shutdown shall not preclude completion of the administrative procedures outlined herein or the possible imposition of sanctions or debarment.

(c) *Home office reviews outside regions.* When contractor's home offices are located outside the FHWA region in which the particular contract is being performed, and it is determined that the contractors' home offices should be reviewed, requests for such reviews with accompanying justification shall be forwarded through appropriate channels to the Washington Headquarters, Office of Civil Rights. After approval, the Washington Headquarters, Office of Civil Rights, (OCR) shall request the appropriate region to conduct the home office review.

(d) *Employment of women.* Executive Order 11246, as amended, implementing rules and regulations regarding sex discrimination are outlined in 41 CFR part 60–20. It is the responsibility of the Compliance Specialist to ensure that contractors provide women full participation in their work forces.

(e) *Effect of exclusive referral agreements.* (1) The OFCCP has established the following criteria for determining compliance when an exclusive referral agreement is involved;

(i) It shall be no excuse that the union, with which the contractor has a collective bargaining agreement providing for exclusive referral, failed to refer minority or female employees.

(ii) Discrimination in referral for employment, even if pursuant to provisions of a collective bargaining agreement, is prohibited by the National Labor Relations Act and Title VII of the Civil Rights Act of 1964, as amended.

(iii) Contractors and subcontractors have a responsibility to provide equal opportunity if they want to participate in federally involved contracts. To the extent they have delegated the responsibility for some of their employment practices to some other organization or agency which prevents them from meeting their obligations, these contractors must be found in noncompliance.

(2) If the contractor indicates that union action or inaction is a proximate cause of the contractor's failure to provide equal opportunity, a finding of noncompliance will be made and a show cause notice issued, and:

(i) The contractor will be formally directed to comply with the equal opportunity requirements.

(ii) Reviews of other contractors with projects within the jurisdiction of the applicable union locals shall be scheduled.

(iii) If the reviews indicate a pattern and/or practice of discrimination on the part of specific union locals, each contractor in the area shall be informed of the criteria outlined in §230.411(e)(1) of this section. Furthermore, the FHWA Washington Headquarters, OCR, shall be provided with full documentary evidence to support the discriminatory pattern indicated.

(iv) In the event the union referral practices prevent the contractor from meeting the equal opportunity requirements pursuant to the E.O. 11246, as amended, such contractor shall immediately notify the SHA.

§230.413 Review reports.

(a) *General.* (1) The Compliance Specialist shall maintain detailed notes from the beginning of the review from which a comprehensive compliance review report can be developed.

(2) The completed compliance review report shall contain documentary evidence to support the determination of a contractor's or subcontractor's compliance status.

(3) Findings, conclusions, and recommendations shall be explicitly stated and, when necessary, supported by documentary evidence.

(4) The compliance review report shall contain at least the following information.[1] (Action R–20)

(i) Complete name and address of contractor.

(ii) Project(s) identification.

(iii) Basis for the review, *i.e.*, area work force, project work force, home office work force, and target area work force.

(iv) Identification of Federal or Federal-aid contract(s).

(v) Date of review.

(vi) Employment data by job craft, classification, or occupation by race and sex in accordance with (iii) above. This shall be the data verified during the onsite.

(vii) Identification of local unions involved with contractor, when applicable.

(viii) Determination of compliance status: compliance or noncompliance.

(ix) Copy of show cause notice or compliance notification sent to contractor.

---

[1] The Federal Highway Administration will accept completed Form FHWA–86 for the purpose. The form is available at the offices listed in 49 CFR part 7, appendix D.

(x) Name of the Compliance Specialist who conducted the review and whether that person is a State, division or regional Compliance Specialist.

(xi) Concurrences at appropriate levels.

(5) Each contractor (joint venture is one contractor) will be reported separately. When a project review is conducted, the reports should be attached, with the initial report being that of the prime contractor followed by the reports of each subcontractor.

(6) Each review level is responsible for ensuring that required information is contained in the report.

(7) When a project review is conducted, the project work force shall be reported. When an areawide review is conducted (all Federal-aid, Federal, and non-Federal projects in an area), then areawide work force shall be reported. When a home office review is conducted, only home office work force shall be reported. Other information required by regional offices shall be detached before forwarding the reports to the Washington Headquarters, OCR.

(8) The Washington Headquarters, OCR, shall be provided all of the following:

(i) The compliance review report required by § 230.413(a)(4).

(ii) Corrective action plans.

(iii) Show cause notices or compliance notifications.

(iv) Show cause recissions.

While other data and information should be kept by regional offices (including progress reports, correspondence, and similar review backup material), it should not be routinely forwarded to the Washington Headquarters, OCR.

(b) *Administrative requirements*—(1) *State conducted reviews.* (i) Within 15 days from the completion of the onsite verification and exit conference, the State Compliance Specialist will:

(A) Prepare the compliance review report, based on information obtained;

(B) Determine the contractor's compliance status;

(C) Notify the contractor of the compliance determination, *i.e.*, send the contractor either notification of compliance or show cause notice; and

(D) Forward three copies of the compliance review report, and the compliance notification or show cause notice to the FHWA division EEO Specialist.

(ii) Within 10 days of receipt, the FHWA division EEO Specialist shall:

(A) Analyze the State's report, ensure that it is complete and accurate;

(B) Resolve nonconcurrence, if any;

(C) Indicate concurrence, and, where appropriate, prepare comments; and

(D) Forward two copies of the compliance review report, and the compliance notification or show cause notice to the Regional Civil Rights Director.

(iii) Within 15 days of receipt, the FHWA Regional Civil Rights Director shall:

(A) Analyze the report, ensure that it is complete and accurate;

(B) Resolve nonconcurrence, if any;

(C) Indicate concurrence, and, where appropriate, prepare comments; and

(D) Forward one copy of the compliance review report, and the compliance notification or show cause notice to the Washington Headquarters, OCR.

(2) *FHWA division conducted reviews.* (i) Within 15 days from the completion of the onsite verification and exit conference, the division EEO Specialist shall:

(A) Prepare compliance review report, based on information obtained;

(B) Determine the contractor's compliance status;

(C) Notify the State to send the contractor the compliance determination, *i.e.*, either notification of compliance or show cause notice; and

(D) Forward two copies of the compliance review report and the compliance notification or show cause notice to the Regional Civil Rights Director.

(ii) Within 15 days of receipt, the FHWA Regional Civil Rights Director will take the steps outlined in § 230.413(b)(1)(iii).

(3) *FHWA region conducted reviews.* (i) Within 15 days from the completion of the onsite verification and exit conference the regional EEO Specialist shall:

(A) Prepare the compliance review report, based on information obtained;

(B) Determine the contractor's compliance status;

(C) Inform the appropriate division to notify the State to send the contractor the compliance determination *i.e.*, either notification of compliance or show cause notice; and

(D) Forward one copy of the compliance review report, and the compliance notification or show cause notice to the Washington Headquarters, OCR.

(4) Upon receipt of compliance review reports, the Washington Headquarters, OCR, shall review, resolve any nonconcurrences, and record them for the purpose of:

(i) Providing ongoing technical assistance to FHWA regional and division offices and SHA's;

(ii) Gathering a sufficient data base for program evaluation;

(iii) Ensuring uniform standards are being applied in the compliance review process;

(iv) Initiating appropriate changes in FHWA policy and implementing regulations; and

(v) Responding to requests from the General Accounting Office, Office of Management and Budget, Senate Subcommittee on Public Roads, and other agencies and organizations.

§ 230.415 Consolidated compliance reviews.

(a) *General.* Consolidated compliance reviews shall be implemented to determine employment opportunities on an areawide rather than an individual project basis. The consolidated compliance review approach shall be adopted and directed by either Headquarters, region, division, or SHA, however, consolidated reviews shall at all times remain a cooperative effort.

(b) OFCCP policy requires contracting agencies to ensure compliance, in hometown an imposed plan areas, on an areawide rather than a project basis. The consolidated compliance review approach facilitates implementation of this policy.

(c) *Methodology*—(1) *Selection of a target area.* In identifying the target area of a consolidated compliance review (e.g. SMSA, hometown or imposed plan area, a multicounty area, or an entire State), consideration shall at least be given to the following facts:

(i) Minority and female work force concentrations;

(ii) Suspected or alleged discrimination in union membership or referral practices by local unions involved in highway construction;

(iii) Present or potential problem areas;

(iv) The number of highway projects in the target area; and

(v) Hometown or imposed plan reports that indicate underutilization of minorities or females.

(2) *Determine the review period.* After the target area has been selected, the dates for the actual onsite reviews shall be established.

(3) *Obtain background information.* EEO–3's Local Union Reports, should be obtained from regional offices of the EEOC. Target area civilian labor force statistics providing percent minorities and percent females in the target area shall be obtained from State employment security agencies or similar State agencies.

(4) *Identify contractors.* Every nonexempt federally assisted or direct Federal contractor and subcontractor in the target area shall be identified. In order to establish areawide employment patterns in the target area, employment data is needed for all contractors and subcontractors in the area. However, only those contractors with significant work forces (working prior to peak and not recently reviewed) may need to be actually reviwed onsite. Accordingly, once all contractors are identified, those contractors which will actually be reviewed onsite shall be determined. Compliance determinations shall only reflect the status of crafts covered by part II of plan bid conditions. Employment data of crafts covered by part I of plan bid conditions shall be gathered and identified as such in the composite report, however, OFCCP has reserved the responsibility for compliance determinations on crafts covered by part I of the plan bid conditions.

(5) *Contractor notification.* Those contractors selected for onsite review shall be sent a notification letter as outlined in § 230.409(c) along with a request for current workforce data[2] for completion

[2]The Consolidated Workforce Questionnaire is convenient for the purpose and appears as attachment 4 to volume 2, chapter 2,

Continued

and submission at the onsite review. Those contractors in the target area not selected for onsite review shall also be requested to supply current workforce data as of the onsite review period, and shall return the data within 15 days following the onsite review period.

(6) *Onsite reviews.* Compliance reviews shall then be conducted in accordance with the requirements set forth in § 230.409. Reviewers may use Form FHWA–86, Compliance Data Report, if appropriate. It is of particular importance during the onsite reviews that the review team provide for adequate coordination of activities at every stage of the review process.

(7) *Compliance determinations.* Upon completion of the consolidated reviews, compliance determinations shall be made on each review by the reviewer. Individual show cause notices or compliance notifications shall be sent (as appropriate) to each reviewed contractor.

The compliance determination shall be based on the contractor's target area work force (Federal, Federal-aid and non-Federal), except when the target area is coincidental with hometown plan area, compliance determinations must not be based on that part of a contractor's work force covered by part I of the plan bid conditions, as previously set forth in this regulation. For example: ABC Contracting, Inc. employs carpenters, operating engineers, and cement masons. Carpenters and operating engineers are covered by part II of the plan bid conditions, however, cement masons are covered by part I of the plan bid conditions. The compliance determination must be based only on the contractor's utilization of carpenters and operating engineers.

(d) *Reporting*—(1) *Composite report.* A final composite report shall be submitted as a complete package to the Washington Headquarters, OCR, within 45 days after the review period and shall consist of the following:

(i) Compliance review report, for each contractor and subcontractor with accompanying show cause notice or compliance notification.

(ii) Work force data to show the aggregate employment of all contractors in the target area.

(iii) A narrative summary of findings and recommendations to include the following:

(A) A summary of highway construction employment in the target area by craft, race, and sex. This summary should explore possible patterns of discrimination or underutilization and possible causes, and should compare the utilization of minorities and females on contractor's work forces to the civilian labor force percent for minorities and females in the target area.

(B) If the target area is a plan area, a narrative summary of the plan's effectiveness with an identification of part I and part II crafts. This summary shall discuss possible differences in minority and female utilization between part I and part II crafts, documenting any inferences drawn from such comparisons.

(C) If applicable, discuss local labor unions' membership and/or referral practices that impact on the utilization of minorities and females in the target area. Complete and current copies of all collective bargaining agreements and copies of EEO–3, Local Union Reports, for all appropriate unions shall accompany the composite report.

(D) Any other appropriate data, analyses, or information deemed necessary for a complete picture of the areawide employment.

(E) Considering the information compiled from the summaries listed above, make concrete recommendations on possible avenues for correcting problems uncovered by the analyses.

(2) *Annual planning report.* The proper execution of consolidated compliance reviews necessitates scheduling, along with other fiscal program planning. The Washington Headquarters, OCR, shall be notified of all planned consolidated reviews by August 10 of each year and of any changes in the target area or review periods, as they become known. The annual consolidated planning report shall indicate:

(i) Selected target areas:

---

section 3 of the Federal-Aid Highway Program Manual, which is available at the offices listed in 49 CFR part 7, appendix D.

(ii) The basis for selection of each area; and

(iii) The anticipated review period (dates) for each target area.

APPENDIX A TO SUBPART D OF PART 230—SAMPLE SHOW CAUSE NOTICE

Certified Mail, Return Receipt Requested
Date
Contractor's Name
Address
City, State, and Zip Code.

DEAR CONTRACTOR: As a result of the review of your (Project Number) project located at (Project Location) conducted on (Date) by (Reviewing Agency), it is our determination that you are not in compliance with your equal opportunity requirements and that good faith efforts have not been made to meet your equal opportunity requirements in the following areas:

List of Deficiencies

1.

2.

3.

Your failure to take the contractually required affirmative action has contributed to the unacceptable level of minority and female employment in your operations, particularly in the semiskilled and skilled categories of employees.

The Department of Labor regulations (41 CFR 60) implementing Executive Order 11246, as amended, are applicable to your Federal-aid highway construction contract and are controlling in this matter (see Required Contract Provisions, Form PR–1273, Clause II). Section 60–1.20(b) of these regulations provides that when equal opportunity deficiencies exist, it is necessary that you make a commitment in writing to correct such deficiencies before you may be found in compliance. The commitment must include the specific action which you propose to take to correct each deficiency and the date of completion of such action. The time period allotted shall be no longer than the minimum period necessary to effect the necessary correction. In accordance with instructions issued by the Office of Federal Contract Compliance Programs (OFCCP), U.S. Department of Labor, your written commitment must also provide for the submission of monthly progress reports which shall include a head count of minority and female representation at each level of each trade and a list of minority employees.

You are specifically advised that making the commitment discussed above will not preclude a further determination of noncompliance upon a finding that the commitment is not sufficient to achieve compliance.

We will hold a compliance conference at ____________(Address) at ____________ (Time) on ____________(Date) for you to submit and discuss your written commitment. If your written commitment is acceptable and if the commitment is sufficient to achieve compliance, you will be found in compliance during the effective implementation of that commitment. You are cautioned, however, that our determination is subject to review by the Federal Highway Administration, the Department of Transportation, and OFCCP and may be disapproved if your written commitment is not considered sufficient to achieve compliance.

If you indicate either directly or by inaction that you do not wish to participate in the scheduled conference and do not otherwise show cause within 30 days from receipt of this notice why enforcement proceedings should not be instituted, this agency will commence enforcement proceedings under Executive Order 11246, as amended.

If your written commitment is accepted and it is subsequently found that you have failed to comply with its provisions, you will be advised of this determination and formal sanction proceedings will be instituted immediately.

In the event formal sanction proceedings are instituted and the final determination is that a violation of your equal opportunity contract requirements has taken place, any Federal-aid highway construction contracts or subcontracts which you hold may be canceled, terminated, or suspended, and you may be debarred from further such contracts or subcontracts. Such other sanctions as are authorized by Executive Order 11246, as amended, may also be imposed.

We encourage you to take whatever action is necessary to resolve this matter and are anxious to assist you in achieving compliance. Any questions concerning this notice should be addressed to (Name, Address, and Phone).

Sincerely yours,

[41 FR 34245, Aug. 13, 1976]

APPENDIX B TO SUBPART D OF PART 230—SAMPLE CORRECTIVE ACTION PLAN

Deficiency 1: Sources likely to yield minority employees have not been contacted for recruitment purposes.

Commitment: We have developed a system of written job applications at our home office which readily identifies minority applicants. In addition to this, as a minimum, we will contact the National Association for the Advancement of Colored People (NAACP), League of Latin American Citizens (LULAC), Urban League, and the Employment Security Office within 20 days to establish a referral system for minority group applicants and expand our recruitment base. We are in the process of identifying other community organizations and associations that may be able to provide minority applicants and will submit an updated listing of recruitment sources and evidence of contact by ________(Date).

Deficiency 2: There have been inadequate efforts to locate, qualify, and increase skills of minority and female employees and applicants for employment.

Commitment: We will set up an individual file for each apprentice or trainee by ________(Date) in order to carefully screen the progress, ensure that they are receiving the necessary training, and being promoted promptly upon completion of training requirements. We have established a goal of at least 50 percent of our apprentices and trainees will be minorities and 15 percent will be female. In addition to the commitment made to deficiency number 1, we will conduct a similar identification of organizations able to supply female applicants. Based on our projected personnel needs, we expect to have reached our 50 percent goal for apprentices and trainees by ________(Date).

Deficiency 3: Very little effort to assure subcontractors have meaningful minority group representation among their employees.

Commitment: In cooperation with the Regional Office of Minority Business Enterprise, Department of Commerce, and the local NAACP, we have identified seven minority-owned contractors that may be able to work on future contracts we may receive. These contractors (identified in the attached list) will be contacted prior to our bidding on all future contracts. In addition, we have scheduled a meeting with all subcontractors currently working on our contracts. This meeting will be held to inform the subcontractors of our intention to monitor their reports and require meaningful minority representation. This meeting will be held on ________(Date) and we will summarize the discussions and current posture of each subcontractor for your review by ________(Date) Additionally, as requested, we will submit a PR–1391 on ________(Date), ________(Date), ________(Date). Finally, we have committed ourselves to maintaining at least 20 percent minority and female representation in each trade during the time we are carrying out the above commitments. We plan to have completely implemented all the provisions of these commitments by ________(Date).

[41 FR 34245, Aug. 13, 1976]

Appendix C to Subpart D of Part 230—Sample Show Cause Rescission

Certified Mail, Return Receipt Requested
Date
Contractor
Address
City, State, and Zip Code

Dear Contractor: On ________, (Date) you received a 30-day show cause notice from this office for failing to implement the required contract requirements pertaining to equal employment opportunity.

Your corrective action plan, discussed and submitted at the compliance conference held on ________(Date), has been reviewed and determined to be acceptable. Your implementation of your corrective action plan shows that you are now taking the required affirmative action and can be considered in compliance with Executive Order 11246, as amended. If it should later be determined that your corrective action plan is not sufficient to achieve compliance, this Rescission shall not preclude a subsequent finding of noncompliance.

In view of the above, this letter is to inform you that the 30-day show cause notice of ________(Date) is hereby rescinded. You are further advised that if it is found that you have failed to comply with the provisions of your corrective action plan, formal sanction proceedings will be instituted immediately.

Sincerely,

Appendix D to Subpart D of Part 230—Equal Opportunity Compliance Review Process Flow Chart

EQUAL OPPORTUNITY COMPLIANCE REVIEW PROCESS FLOW CHART 46

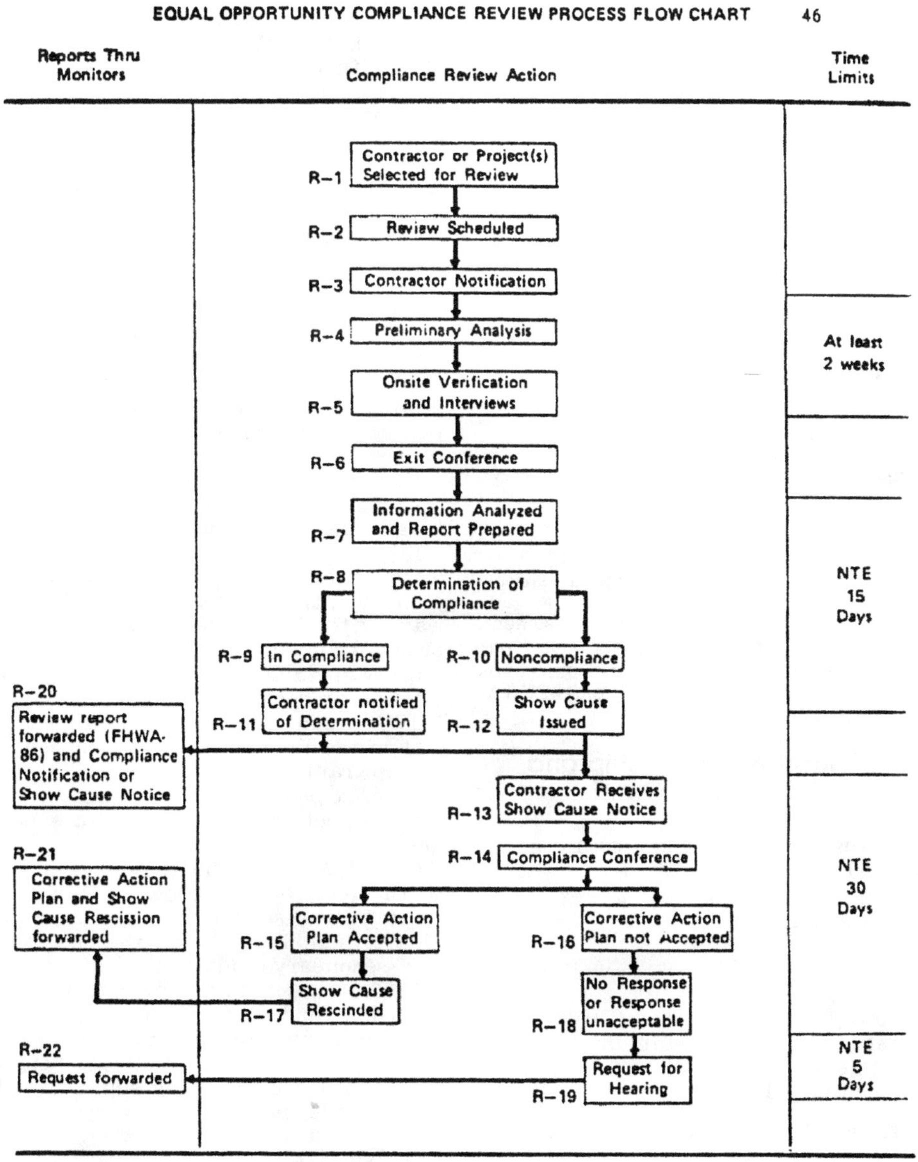

[41 FR 34245, Aug. 13, 1976]

SUBCHAPTER D—NATIONAL HIGHWAY INSTITUTE

PART 260—EDUCATION AND TRAINING PROGRAMS

Subpart A—Fellowship and Scholarship Grants

Subparts B–C [Reserved]

Subpart D—State Education and Training Programs

Subpart A—Fellowship and Scholarship Grants

AUTHORITY: 23 U.S.C. 307(a), 315, 321 and 403; and 49 CFR 1.48(b).

SOURCE: 43 FR 3558, Jan. 26, 1978, unless otherwise noted.

§ 260.101 Purpose.

To establish policy for the Federal Highway Administration (FHWA) Fellowship and Scholarship Programs as administered by the National Highway Institute (NHI).

§ 260.103 Definitions.

As used in this regulation, the following definitions apply:

(a) *Candidate.* One who meets the eligibility criteria set forth in § 260.107, and who has completed and submitted the necessary forms and documents in order to be considered for selection for a fellowship or scholarship.

(b) *Direct educational expenses.* Those expenses directly related to attending school including tuition, student fees, books, and expendable supplies but excluding travel expenses to and from the school.

(c) *Employing agency.* The agency for which the candidate works. This may be either a State or local highway/transportation agency or the FHWA.

(d) *Fellowship.* The grant presented to the recipient's school and administered by the school to assist the candidate financially during the period of graduate study.

(e) *Living stipend.* The portion of the fellowship or scholarship grant remaining after the direct educational expenses have been deducted.

(f) *Local highway/transportation agency.* The agency or metropolitan planning organization with the responsibility for initiating and carrying forward a highway program or public transportation program utilizing highways at the local level, usually the city or county level.

(g) *National Highway Institute (NHI).* The organization located within the FHWA responsible for the administration of the FHWA fellowship and scholarship grant programs.

(h) *Recipient.* The successful candidate receiving a fellowship or scholarship.

(i) *Scholarship.* The grant presented to the recipient's school and administered by the school to assist the candidate financially during the period of post-secondary study.

(j) *State highway/transportation agency.* The agency with the responsibility for initiating and carrying forward a highway program or public transportation program utilizing highways at the State level.

§ 260.105 Policy.

It is the policy of the FHWA to administer, through the NHI, fellowship and scholarship grant programs to assist State and local agencies and the FHWA in developing the expertise needed for the implementation of their highway programs and to assist in the development of more effective transportation programs at all levels of government. These programs shall provide financial support for up to 24 months of either full-time or part-time study in the field of highway transportation. The programs for each year shall be announced by FHWA notices.[1] These notices shall contain an application form and shall announce the number of grants to be awarded and their value.

[43 FR 3558, Jan. 26, 1978, as amended at 45 FR 67091, Oct. 9, 1980]

§260.107 Eligibility.

(a) Prior recipients of FHWA scholarships or fellowships are eligible if they will have completed all specific work commitments before beginining study under the programs for which applications are made.

(b) Candidates for the fellowship program shall have earned bachelor's or comparable college-level degrees prior to beginining advanced studies under the program.

(c) Candidates shall submit evidence of acceptance, or probable acceptance, for study in programs that will enhance their contributions to their employers. Evidence of probable acceptance may be a letter from the department chairman or other school official.

(d) Candidates shall agree to pursue certain minimum study loads as determined by the FHWA and designated in the FHWA notices announcing the programs each year.

(e) FHWA employees who receive awards will be required to execute continued service agreements, consistent with the Government Employees Training Act requirements, which obligate the employees to continue to work for the agency for three times the duration of the training received.

(f) Candidates who are students or employees of State or local highway/transportation agencies shall agree in writing to work on a full-time basis in public service with State or local highway/transportation agencies for a specified period of time after completing study under the program. The FHWA notices announcing the programs each year shall specify the time period of the work commitment.

(g) Candidates shall agree to respond to brief questionnaires designed to assist the NHI in program evaluation both during and following the study period.

(h) Recipients of awards for full-time shall agree to limit their part-time employment as stipulated in the FHWA notice announcing the programs.

(i) Candidates shall not profit financially from FHWA grants. Where acceptance of the living stipend portion of the grant would result in a profit to the candidate, as determined by comparing the candidate's regular full-time salary with the candidate's part-time salary and employer salary support plus living stipend, the grant amount will be reduced accordingly. In cases where a candidate must relocate and maintain two households, exceptions to this condition will be considered.

(j) Candidates shall be citizens, or shall declare their intent to become citizens of the United States.

§260.109 Selection.

(a) Candidates shall be rated by a selection panel appointed by the Director of the NHI. Members of the panel shall represent the highway transportation interests of government, industry, and the academic community. The factors considered by the selection panel are weighed in accordance with specific program objectives.

(b) The major factors to be considered by the panel are:

(1) Candidate's potential to contribute to a public agency's highway transportation program,

(2) Relevance of a candidate's study program to the objectives of the fellowship or scholarship program,

(3) Relevant experience, and

(4) Academic and professional achievements.

(c) Using ratings given by the selection panel, the Director of the NHI shall select candidates for awards and designate alternates.

(d) The FHWA may designate in the FHWA notices announcing the programs the maximum number of awards

[1] The Federal Highway Administration notices are available for inspection and copying as prescribed in 49 CFR part 7, appendix D.

that will be made to employees of any one agency.

§ 260.111 Responsibilities of educational institutions.

(a) The college or university chosen by the grant recipient shall enter into an appropriate agreement with the FHWA providing for the administration of the grant by the college or university.

(b) The college or university chosen by the recipient shall designate a faculty advisor prior to the commitment of funds by the FHWA. The faculty advisor will be requested to submit reports of the recipient's study progress following completion of each study period. These reports are oriented toward total program evaluation. To assure the recipient's rights to privacy, the FHWA will obtain appropriate advance concurrences from the recipient.

§ 260.113 Responsibilities of employing agencies.

(a) A candidate's employing agency is responsible for furnishing a statement of endorsement and information concerning the relevancy of the candidate's study to agency requirements. The agency is encouraged to identify educational and training priorities and to provide backup to support its priority candidates for these programs.

(b) Employing agencies are encouraged to give favorable consideration to the requests of candidates for educational leave and salary support for the study period to facilitate the candidates' applications. Agency decisions involving salary support and educational leave that will affect the acceptance of awards by recipients should be made at the earliest possible date to provide adequate time for the FHWA to select alternates to replace candidates that decline their awards.

(c) Agencies are responsible for negotiations with their candidates concerning conditions of reinstatement and the candidates' commitments to return to work.

(d) Employing agencies are encouraged to publicize the availability of these grants throughout the agencies, to implement procedures for internal evaluation of applications, and to forward the applications to the FHWA division office in their State.

(e) Employing agencies that choose to process their employees' applications are responsible for observing the cutoff date for the FHWA to receive applications. This date will be stipulated in the Notices announcing the program for each academic year.

§ 260.115 Equal opportunity.

(a) Consistent with the provisions of the Civil Rights Act of 1964 and Title VI, assurances executed by each State, 23 U.S.C. 324, and 29 U.S.C. 794, no applicant, including otherwise qualified handicapped individuals, shall on the grounds of race, color, religion, sex, national origin, or handicap, be excluded from participation in, be denied benefits of, or be otherwise subjected to discrimination under this program.

(b) In accordance with Executive Order 11141, no individual shall be denied benefits of this program because of age.

(c) Agencies should make information on this program available to all eligible employees, including otherwise qualified handicapped individuals, so as to assure nondiscrimination on the grounds of race, color, religion, sex, national origin, age, or handicap.

§ 260.117 Application procedures.

(a) The FHWA notices announcing each year's programs and containing the application form may be obtained from FHWA regional and division offices, State highway agencies, metropolitan planning organizations, Governors' highway safety representatives, Urban Mass Transportation Administration regional directors, major transit authorities and from colleges and universities. Forms may also be obtained from the NHI, HHI–3, FHWA, Washington, DC 20590.

(b) In order to become a candidate, the applicant shall complete and forward the application form according to the instructions in the FHWA notice announcing the programs. The cutoff date for submitting the application stipulated in the notices should be observed.

Subparts B–C [Reserved]

Subpart D—State Education and Training Programs

AUTHORITY: 23 U.S.C. 315, 321 (b) and (c); 49 CFR 1.48(b).

SOURCE: 43 FR 35477, Aug. 10, 1978, unless otherwise noted.

§ 260.401 Purpose.

To prescribe policy and implement procedures for the administration of Federal-aid funds for education and training of State and local highway department employees.

§ 260.403 Policy.

It is the policy of the Federal Highway Administration (FHWA) to provide continuing education of State and local highway agency employees engaged or to be engaged in Federal-aid highway work. To carry out this policy, States are encouraged to fully utilize the authority contained in 23 U.S.C. 321(b) and 321(c).

§ 260.405 Application and approval procedures.

The State may apply for education and training funds by submitting a signed agreement designating the desired Federal-aid funds, not to exceed the limits in 23 U.S.C. 321(b). The FHWA's approval of the agreement will constitute obligation of funds and authorization for work to proceed.

§ 260.407 Implementation and reimbursement.

(a) After execution of the fiscal agreement, the State may make grants and contracts with public and private agencies, institutions, individuals, and the National Highway Institute to provide highway-related training and education. The principal recipients of this training shall be employees who are engaged or likely to be engaged, in Federal-aid highway work.

(b) Claims for Federal-aid reimbursement of costs incurred may be submitted following established procedures to cover 75 percent of the cost of tuition and direct educational expenses (including incidental training, equipment, and program materials) exclusive of travel, subsistence, or salary of trainees.

(c) As provided in 23 U.S.C. 321(c), education and training for subject areas that are identified by the FHWA as Federal program responsibilities, shall be provided at no cost to State and local governments.

[43 FR 35477, Aug. 10, 1978, as amended at 45 FR 6378, Jan. 28, 1980; 53 FR 3745, Feb. 9, 1988]

APPENDIX A TO PART 260—REQUEST FOR USE OF FEDERAL-AID HIGHWAY FUNDS FOR EDUCATION OR TRAINING (FORM FHWA-1422)

U.S. DEPARTMENT OF TRANSPORTATION
FEDERAL HIGHWAY ADMINISTRATION

REQUEST FOR USE OF FEDERAL-AID HIGHWAY FUNDS FOR EDUCATION OR TRAINING

(NATIONAL HIGHWAY INSTITUTE)

1. STATE
2. DATE OF REQUEST
3. PROJECT NO.

4. NAME OF AGENCY SPONSORING COURSE
5. CO-SPONSOR *(If any)*

6. COURSE TITLE
7. DATE OF PROGRAM
7A. BEGINNING
7B. ENDING
8. ESTIMATED ATTENDANCE

9. PURPOSE AND EDUCATIONAL OBJECTIVES OF THE PROGRAM *(Be as Specific as Possible)*

10. PROPOSED COURSE OUTLINE *(Attach a copy of the course outline including a list of the subjects to be presented, the sequence of their presentation, the proposed speakers and the amount of time allotted to each subject. Also include the source material upon which the course is based, and the text books and collateral references to be used.)*

11. PROPOSED COURSE SCHEDULE. *(Provide information on the length of the course, including number of days, days of the week, and hours per day.)*

12, TOTAL HOURS OF INSTRUCTION

13. CRITERIA FOR ELIGIBILITY OF PARTICIPANTS *(Including organizational affiliation)*

14. WHERE WILL COURSE BE HELD?

15. IS THIS PROGRAM A REPEAT OF A COURSE PREVIOUSLY GIVEN? *(If yes fill-in 15A.)*
☐ YES ☐ NO
15A. WHEN WAS IT LAST HELD?

16. IS THIS PROGRAM RECURRING? *(If yes fill-in 16A.)*
☐ YES ☐ NO
16A. GIVE FREQUENCY
☐ SEMESTER ☐ QUARTER
☐ OTHER *(Specify)* ____________

17. NAME AND TITLE OF TECHNICAL DIRECTOR *(Responsible for technical content.)*

18. NAME AND TITLE OF COORDINATOR *(Responsible for arrangements)*

Form FHWA-1422
(Rev. 6-76)

PREVIOUS EDITIONS WILL NOT BE USED

EXPENDITURES	
19 ITEMS	AMOUNT
A. TEXT BOOKS	$
B. NOTEBOOKS AND SUPPLIES	$
C. PRINTING	$
D. COMMUNICATIONS	$
E. SECRETARIAL	$
F. AUDIO-VISUAL	$
G. PHOTOGRAPHS	$
H. BUSES	$
I. MEETING ROOM RENTAL	$
J. COSTS OF SPONSORING AGENCY'S STAFF TIME SPENT IN PREPARATION AND CONDUCT OF COURSE	$
K. COSTS OF CO-SPONSOR'S STAFF TIME SPENT IN PREPARATION AND CONDUCT OF COURSE	$
L. HONORARIA PAID TO OUTSIDE INSTRUCTOR	$
M. INCIDENTALS	$
N. OTHER ITEMS *(Specify)*	$
TOTAL ESTIMATED COSTS *(Excluding travel, subsistence and salaries of attendees)*	$
20. COST PER ATTENDEE	$
21. AMOUNT TO BE PAID OUT OF ½% FEDERAL-AID FUNDS	$
22. **REMARKS**	

23. APPROVAL	
REQUEST INITIATED BY *(State Representative, Name and Title)*	DATE
APPROVED *(Division Administrator, Federal Highway Administration)*	DATE

SUBCHAPTER E—PLANNING AND RESEARCH

PART 420—PLANNING AND RESEARCH PROGRAM ADMINISTRATION

Subpart A—Administration of FHWA Planning and Research Funds

Subpart B—Research, Development, and Technology Transfer Program Management

AUTHORITY: 23 U.S.C. 103(b)(6), 104(f), 115, 120, 133(b), 134(n), 303(g), 505, and 315; and 49 CFR 1.48(b).

SOURCE: 67 FR 47271, July 18, 2002, unless otherwise noted.

Subpart A—Administration of FHWA Planning and Research Funds

§ 420.101 What is the purpose of this part?

This part prescribes the Federal Highway Administration (FHWA) policies and procedures for the administration of activities undertaken by State departments of transportation (State DOTs) and their subrecipients, including metropolitan planning organizations (MPOs), with FHWA planning and research funds. Subpart A identifies the administrative requirements that apply to use of FHWA planning and research funds both for planning and for research, development, and technology transfer (RD&T) activities. Subpart B describes the policies and procedures that relate to the approval and authorization of RD&T work programs. The requirements in this part supplement those in 49 CFR part 18, Uniform Administrative Requirements for Grants and Cooperative Agreements to State and Local Governments and 49 CFR part 19, Uniform Administrative Requirements for Grants and Cooperative Agreements with Institutions of Higher Education, Hospitals and Other Non-Profit Organizations.

§ 420.103 How does the FHWA define the terms used in this part?

Unless otherwise specified in this part, the definitions in 23 U.S.C. 101(a) are applicable to this part. As used in this part:

FHWA planning and research funds include:

(1) State planning and research (SPR) funds (the two percent set aside of funds apportioned or allocated to a State DOT for activities authorized under 23 U.S.C. 505);

(2) Metropolitan planning (PL) funds (the one percent of funds authorized under 23 U.S.C. 104(f) to carry out the provisions of 23 U.S.C. 134);

(3) National highway system (NHS) funds authorized under 23 U.S.C. 104(b)(1) used for transportation planning in accordance with 23 U.S.C. 134

and 135, highway research and planning in accordance with 23 U.S.C. 505, highway-related technology transfer activities, or development and establishment of management systems under 23 U.S.C. 303;

(4) Surface transportation program (STP) funds authorized under 23 U.S.C. 104(b)(3) used for highway and transit research and development and technology transfer programs, surface transportation planning programs, or development and establishment of management systems under 23 U.S.C. 303; and

(5) Minimum guarantee (MG) funds authorized under 23 U.S.C. 505 used for transportation planning and research, development and technology transfer activities that are eligible under title 23, U.S.C.

Grant agreement means a legal instrument reflecting a relationship between an awarding agency and a recipient or subrecipient when the principal purpose of the relationship is to transfer a thing of value to the recipient or subrecipient to carry out a public purpose of support or stimulation authorized by a law instead of acquiring (by purchase, lease, or barter) property or services for the direct benefit or use of the awarding agency.

Metropolitan planning area means the geographic area in which the metropolitan transportation planning process required by 23 U.S.C. 134 and 49 U.S.C. 5303–5305 must be carried out.

Metropolitan planning organization (MPO) means the forum for cooperative transportation decisionmaking for a metropolitan planning area.

National Cooperative Highway Research Program (NCHRP) means the cooperative RD&T program directed toward solving problems of national or regional significance identified by State DOTs and the FHWA, and administered by the Transportation Research Board, National Academy of Sciences.

Procurement contract means a legal instrument reflecting a relationship between an awarding agency and a recipient or subrecipient when the principal purpose of the instrument is to acquire (by purchase, lease, or barter) property or services for the direct benefit or use of the awarding agency.

State Department of Transportation (State DOT) means that department, commission, board, or official of any State charged by its laws with the responsibility for highway construction.

Transportation management area (TMA) means an urbanized area with a population over 200,000 (as determined by the latest decennial census) and designated by the Secretary of Transportation or other area when TMA designation is requested by the Governor and the MPO (or affected local officials), and officially designated by the Secretary of Transportation.

Transportation pooled fund study means a planning, research, development, or technology transfer activity administered by the FHWA, a lead State DOT, or other organization that is supported by two or more participants and that addresses an issue of significant or widespread interest related to highway, public, or intermodal transportation. A transportation pooled fund study is intended to address a new area or provide information that will complement or advance previous investigations of the subject matter.

Work program means a periodic statement of proposed work, covering no less than one year, and estimated costs that documents eligible activities to be undertaken by State DOTs and/or their subrecipients with FHWA planning and research funds.

§420.105 What is the FHWA's policy on use of FHWA planning and research funds?

(a) If the FHWA determines that planning activities of national significance, identified in paragraph (b) of this section, and the requirements of 23 U.S.C. 134, 135, 303, and 505 are being adequately addressed, the FHWA will allow State DOTs and MPOs:

(1) Maximum possible flexibility in the use of FHWA planning and research funds to meet highway and local public transportation planning and RD&T needs at the national, State, and local levels while ensuring legal use of such funds and avoiding unnecessary duplication of efforts; and

(2) To determine which eligible planning and RD&T activities they desire

to support with FHWA planning and research funds and at what funding level.

(b) The State DOTs must provide data that support the FHWA's responsibilities to the Congress and to the public. These data include, but are not limited to, information required for: preparing proposed legislation and reports to the Congress; evaluating the extent, performance, condition, and use of the Nation's transportation systems; analyzing existing and proposed Federal-aid funding methods and levels and the assignment of user cost responsibility; maintaining a critical information base on fuel availability, use, and revenues generated; and calculating apportionment factors.

(c) The policy in paragraph (a) of this section does not remove the FHWA's responsibility and authority to determine which activities are eligible for funding. Activities proposed to be funded with FHWA planning and research funds by the State DOTs and their subrecipients shall be documented and submitted for FHWA approval and authorization as prescribed in §§ 420.111 and 420.113. (The information collection requirements in paragraph (b) of § 420.105 have been approved by the Office of Management and Budget (OMB) under control numbers 2125–0028 and 2125–0032.)

§ 420.107 What is the minimum required expenditure of State planning and research funds for research development and technology transfer?

(a) A State DOT must expend no less than 25 percent of its annual SPR funds on RD&T activities relating to highway, public transportation, and intermodal transportation systems in accordance with the provisions of 23 U.S.C. 505(b), unless a State DOT certifies, and the FHWA accepts the State DOT's certification, that total expenditures by the State DOT during the fiscal year for transportation planning under 23 U.S.C. 134 and 135 will exceed 75 percent of the amount apportioned for the fiscal year.

(b) Prior to submitting a request for an exception to the 25 percent requirement, the State DOT must ensure that:

(1) The additional planning activities are essential, and there are no other reasonable options available for funding these planning activities (including the use of NHS, STP, MG, or FTA State planning and research funds (49 U.S.C. 5313(b)) or by deferment of lower priority planning activities);

(2) The planning activities have a higher priority than RD&T activities in the overall needs of the State DOT for a given fiscal year; and

(3) The total level of effort by the State DOT in RD&T (using both Federal and State funds) is adequate.

(c) If the State DOT chooses to pursue an exception, it must send the request, along with supporting justification, to the FHWA Division Administrator for action by the FHWA Associate Administrator for Research, Development, and Technology. The Associate Administrator's decision will be based upon the following considerations:

(1) Whether the State DOT has a process for identifying RD&T needs and for implementing a viable RD&T program.

(2) Whether the State DOT is contributing to cooperative RD&T programs or activities, such as the National Cooperative Highway Research Program, the Transportation Research Board, and transportation pooled fund studies.

(3) Whether the State DOT is using SPR funds for technology transfer and for transit or intermodal research and development to help meet the 25 percent minimum requirement.

(4) Whether the State DOT can demonstrate that it will meet the requirement or substantially increase its RD&T expenditures over a multi-year period, if an exception is granted for the fiscal year.

(5) Whether Federal funds needed for planning exceed the 75 percent limit for the fiscal year and whether any unused planning funds are available from previous fiscal years.

(d) If the FHWA Associate Administrator for Research, Development, and Technology approves the State DOT's request for an exception, the exception is valid only for that fiscal year's funds. A new request must be submitted and approved for subsequent fiscal year funds.

§420.109 What are the requirements for distribution of metropolitan planning funds?

(a) The State DOTs shall make all PL funds authorized by 23 U.S.C. 104(f) available to the MPOs in accordance with a formula developed by the State DOT, in consultation with the MPOs, and approved by the FHWA Division Administrator. The formula may allow for a portion of the PL funds to be used by the State DOT, or other agency agreed to by the State DOT and the MPOs, for activities that benefit all MPOs in the State, but State DOTs shall not use any PL funds for grant or subgrant administration. The formula may also provide for a portion of the funds to be made available for discretionary grants to MPOs to supplement their annual amount received under the distribution formula.

(b) In developing the formula for distributing PL funds, the State DOT shall consider population, status of planning, attainment of air quality standards, metropolitan area transportation needs, and other factors necessary to provide for an appropriate distribution of funds to carry out the requirements of 23 U.S.C. 134 and other applicable requirements of Federal law.

(c) The State DOTs shall inform the MPOs and the FHWA Division Office of the amounts allocated to each MPO as soon as possible after PL funds have been apportioned by the FHWA to the State DOTs.

(d) If the State DOT, in a State receiving the minimum apportionment of PL funds under the provisions of 23 U.S.C. 104(f)(2), determines that the share of funds to be allocated to any MPO results in the MPO receiving more funds than necessary to carry out the provisions of 23 U.S.C. 134, the State DOT may, after considering the views of the affected MPO(s) and with the approval of the FHWA Division Administrator, use those funds for transportation planning outside of metropolitan planning areas.

(e) In accordance with the provisions of 23 U.S.C. 134(n), any PL funds not needed for carrying out the metropolitan planning provisions of 23 U.S.C. 134 in any State may be made available by the MPO(s) to the State DOT for funding statewide planning activities under 23 U.S.C. 135, subject to approval by the FHWA Division Administrator.

(f) Any State PL fund distribution formula that does not meet the requirements of paragraphs (a) and (b) of this section shall be brought into conformance with those requirements before distribution on any new apportionment of PL funds.

§420.111 What are the documentation requirements for use of FHWA planning and research funds?

(a) Proposed use of FHWA planning and research funds must be documented by the State DOTs and subrecipients in a work program, or other document that describes the work to be accomplished, that is acceptable to the FHWA Division Administrator. Statewide, metropolitan, other transportation planning activities, and transportation RD&T activities may be documented in separate programs, paired in various combinations, or brought together as a single work program. The expenditure of PL funds for transportation planning outside of metropolitan planning areas under §420.109(d) may be included in the work program for statewide transportation planning activities or in a separate work program submitted by the State DOT.

(b)(1) A work program(s) for transportation planning activities must include a description of work to be accomplished and cost estimates by activity or task. In addition, each work program must include a summary that shows:

(i) Federal share by type of fund;

(ii) Matching rate by type of fund;

(iii) State and/or local matching share; and

(iv) Other State or local funds.

(2) Additional information on metropolitan planning area work programs is contained in 23 CFR part 450. Additional information on RD&T work program content and format is contained in subpart B of this part.

(c) In areas not designated as TMAs, a simplified statement of work that describes who will perform the work and the work that will be accomplished using Federal funds may be used in lieu of a work program. If a simplified statement of work is used, it may be submitted separately or as part of the Statewide planning work program.

(d) The State DOTs that use separate Federal-aid projects in accordance with paragraph (a) of this section must submit an overall summary that identifies the amounts and sources of FHWA planning and research funds available, matching funds, and the amounts budgeted for each activity (e.g., statewide planning, RD&T, each metropolitan area, contributions to NCHRP and transportation pooled fund studies, etc.).

(e) The State DOTs and MPOs also are encouraged to include cost estimates for transportation planning, research, development, and technology transfer related activities funded with other Federal or State and/or local funds; particularly for producing the FHWA-required data specified in paragraph (b) of § 420.105, for planning for other transportation modes, and for air quality planning activities in areas designated as non-attainment for transportation-related pollutants in their work programs. The MPOs in TMAs must include such information in their work programs. (The information collection requirements in §§ 420.111 have been approved by the OMB and assigned control numbers 2125–0039 for States and 2132–0529 for MPOs.)

§ 420.113 What costs are eligible?

(a) Costs will be eligible for FHWA participation provided that the costs:

(1) Are for work performed for activities eligible under the section of title 23, U.S.C., applicable to the class of funds used for the activities;

(2) Are verifiable from the State DOT's or the subrecipient's records;

(3) Are necessary and reasonable for proper and efficient accomplishment of project objectives and meet the other criteria for allowable costs in the applicable cost principles cited in 49 CFR 18.22;

(4) Are included in the approved budget, or amendment thereto; and

(5) Were not incurred prior to FHWA authorization.

(b) Indirect costs of State DOTs and their subrecipients are allowable if supported by a cost allocation plan and indirect cost proposal prepared, submitted (if required), and approved by the cognizant or oversight agency in accordance with the OMB requirements applicable to the State DOT or subrecipient specified in 49 CFR 18.22(b).

§ 420.115 What are the FHWA approval and authorization requirements?

(a) The State DOT and its subrecipients must obtain approval and authorization to proceed prior to beginning work on activities to be undertaken with FHWA planning and research funds. Such approvals and authorizations should be based on final work programs or other documents that describe the work to be performed. The State DOT and its subrecipients also must obtain prior approval for budget and programmatic changes as specified in 49 CFR 18.30 or 49 CFR 19.25 and for those items of allowable costs which require approval in accordance with the cost principles specified in 49 CFR 18.22(b) applicable to the entity expending the funds.

(b) Authorization to proceed with the FHWA funded work in whole or in part is a contractual obligation of the Federal government pursuant to 23 U.S.C. 106 and requires that appropriate funds be available for the full Federal share of the cost of work authorized. Those State DOTs that do not have sufficient FHWA planning and research funds or obligation authority available to obligate the full Federal share of a work program or project may utilize the advance construction provisions of 23 U.S.C. 115(a) in accordance with the requirements of 23 CFR part 630, subpart G. The State DOTs that do not meet the advance construction provisions, or do not wish to utilize them, may request authorization to proceed with that portion of the work for which FHWA planning and research funds are available. In the latter case, authorization to proceed may be given for either selected work activities or for a portion of the program period, but such authorization does not constitute a commitment by the FHWA to fund the remaining portion of the work if additional funds do become available.

(c) A project agreement must be executed by the State DOT and the FHWA Division Office for each statewide transportation planning, metropolitan planning area, or RD&T work program, individual activity or study, or any combination administered as a single Federal-aid project. The project agreement may be executed concurrent with or after authorization has been given by the FHWA Division Administrator to proceed with the work in whole or in part. In the event that the project agreement is executed for only part of the work, the project agreement must be amended when authorization is given to proceed with additional work.

(The information collection requirements in §420.115(c) have been approved by the OMB and assigned control numbers 2125–0529)

§420.117 What are the program monitoring and reporting requirements?

(a) In accordance with 49 CFR 18.40, the State DOT shall monitor all activities performed by its staff or by subrecipients with FHWA planning and research funds to assure that the work is being managed and performed satisfactorily and that time schedules are being met.

(b)(1) The State DOT must submit performance and expenditure reports, including a report from each subrecipient, that contain as a minimum:

(i) Comparison of actual performance with established goals;

(ii) Progress in meeting schedules;

(iii) Status of expenditures in a format compatible with the work program, including a comparison of budgeted (approved) amounts and actual costs incurred;

(iv) Cost overruns or underruns;

(v) Approved work program revisions; and

(vi) Other pertinent supporting data.

(2) Additional information on reporting requirements for individual RD&T studies is contained in subpart B of this part.

(c) Reports required by paragraph (b) of this section shall be annual unless more frequent reporting is determined to be necessary by the FHWA Division Administrator. The FHWA may not require more frequent than quarterly reporting unless the criteria in 49 CFR 18.12 or 49 CFR 19.14 are met. Reports are due 90 days after the end of the reporting period for annual and final reports and no later than 30 days after the end of the reporting period for other reports.

(d) Events that have significant impact on the work must be reported as soon as they become known. The types of events or conditions that require reporting include: problems, delays, or adverse conditions that will materially affect the ability to attain program objectives. This disclosure must be accompanied by a statement of the action taken, or contemplated, and any Federal assistance needed to resolve the situation.

(e) Suitable reports that document the results of activities performed with FHWA planning and research funds must be prepared by the State DOT or subrecipient and submitted for approval by the FHWA Division Administrator prior to publication. The FHWA Division Administrator may waive this requirement for prior approval. The FHWA's approval of reports constitutes acceptance of such reports as evidence of work performed but does not imply endorsement of a report's findings or recommendations. Reports prepared for FHWA-funded work must include appropriate credit references and disclaimer statements. (The information collection requirements in §420.117 have been approved by the OMB and assigned control numbers 2125–0039 for States and 2132–0529 for MPOs.)

§420.119 What are the fiscal requirements?

(a) The maximum rate of Federal participation for FHWA planning and research funds shall be as prescribed in title 23, U.S.C., for the specific class of funds used (*i.e.*, SPR, PL, NHS, STP, or MG) except as specified in paragraph (d) of this section. The provisions of 49 CFR 18.24 or 49 CFR 19.23 are applicable to any necessary matching of FHWA planning and research funds.

(b) The value of third party in-kind contributions may be accepted as the match for FHWA planning and research funds, in accordance with the provisions of 49 CFR 18.24(a)(2) or 49 CFR 19.23(a) and may be on either a total planning work program basis or for specific line items or projects. The use of third party in-kind contributions must be identified in the original work program/scope of work and the grant/

subgrant agreement, or amendments thereto. The use of third-party in-kind contributions must be approved in advance by the FHWA Division Administrator and may not be made retroactive prior to approval of the work program/scope of work or an amendment thereto. The State DOT or subrecipient is responsible for ensuring that the following additional criteria are met:

(1) The third party performing the work agrees to allow the value of the work to be used as the match;

(2) The cost of the third party work is not paid for by other Federal funds or used as a match for other federally funded grants/subgrants;

(3) The work performed by the third party is an eligible transportation planning or RD&T related activity that benefits the federally funded work;

(4) The third party costs (*i.e.*, salaries, fringe benefits, etc.) are allowable under the applicable Office of Management and Budget (OMB) cost principles (*i.e.*, OMB Circular A–21, A–87, or A–122);[1]

(5) The third party work is performed during the period to which the matching requirement applies;

(6) The third party in-kind contributions are verifiable from the records of the State DOT or subrecipient and these records show how the value placed on third party in-kind contributions was derived; and

(7) If the total amount of third party expenditures at the end of the program period is not sufficient to match the total expenditure of Federal funds by the recipient/subrecipient, the recipient/subrecipient will need to make up any shortfall with its own funds.

(c) In accordance with the provisions of 23 U.S.C. 120(j), toll revenues that are generated and used by public, quasi-public, and private agencies to build, improve, or maintain highways, bridges, or tunnels that serve the public purpose of interstate commerce may be used as a credit for the non-Federal share of an FHWA planning and research funded project.

(d) In accordance with 23 U.S.C. 505(c) or 23 U.S.C. 104(f)(3), the requirement for matching SPR or PL funds may be waived if the FHWA determines the interests of the Federal-aid highway program would be best served. Waiver of the matching requirement is intended to encourage State DOTs and/or MPOs to pool SPR and/or PL funds to address national or regional high priority planning or RD&T problems that would benefit multiple States and/or MPOs. Requests for waiver of matching requirements must be submitted to the FHWA headquarters office for approval by the Associate Administrator for Planning and Environment (for planning activities) or the Associate Administrator for Research, Development, and Technology (for RD&T activities). The matching requirement may not be waived for NHS, STP, or MG funds.

(e) NHS, STP, or MG funds used for eligible planning and RD&T purposes must be identified separately from SPR or PL funds in the work program(s) and must be administered and accounted for separately for fiscal purposes. In accordance with the statewide and metropolitan planning process requirements for fiscally constrained transportation improvement program (TIPs) planning or RD&T activities funded with NHS, STP, or MG funds must be included in the Statewide and/or metropolitan TIP(s) unless the State DOT and MPO (for a metropolitan area) agree that they may be excluded from the TIP.

(f) Payment shall be made in accordance with the provisions of 49 CFR 18.21 or 49 CFR 19.22.

§ 420.121 What other requirements apply to the administration of FHWA planning and research funds?

(a) *Audits.* Audits of the State DOTs and their subrecipients shall be performed in accordance with OMB Circular A–133, Audits of States, Local Governments, and Non-Profit Organizations.[2] Audits of for-profit contractors are to be performed in accordance with State DOT or subrecipient contract administration procedures.

[1] OMB Circulars are available on the Internet at *http://www.whitehouse.gov/omb/circulars/index.html.*

[2] See footnote 1.

(b) *Copyrights.* The State DOTs and their subrecipients may copyright any books, publications, or other copyrightable materials developed in the course of the FHWA planning and research funded project. The FHWA reserves a royalty-free, nonexclusive and irrevocable right to reproduce, publish, or otherwise use, and to authorize others to use, the work for Government purposes.

(c) *Disadvantaged business enterprises.* The State DOTs must administer the transportation planning and RD&T program(s) consistent with their overall efforts to implement section 1001(b) of the Transportation Equity Act for the 21st Century (Pub. L. 105–178) and 49 CFR part 26 regarding disadvantaged business enterprises.

(d) *Drug free workplace.* In accordance with the provisions of 49 CFR part 29, subpart F, State DOTs must certify to the FHWA that they will provide a drug free workplace. This requirement may be satisfied through the annual certification for the Federal-aid highway program.

(e) *Equipment.* Acquisition, use, and disposition of equipment purchased with FHWA planning and research funds by the State DOTs must be in accordance with 49 CFR 18.32(b). Local government subrecipients of State DOTs must follow the procedures specified by the State DOT. Universities, hospitals, and other non-profit organizations must follow the procedures in 49 CFR 19.34.

(f) *Financial management systems.* The financial management systems of the State DOTs and their local government subrecipients must be in accordance with the provisions of 49 CFR 18.20(a). The financial management systems of universities, hospitals, and other non-profit organizations must be in accordance with 49 CFR 19.21.

(g) *Lobbying.* The provisions of 49 CFR part 20 regarding restrictions on influencing certain Federal activities are applicable to all tiers of recipients of FHWA planning and research funds.

(h) *Nondiscrimination.* The nondiscrimination provisions of 23 CFR parts 200 and 230 and 49 CFR part 21, with respect to Title VI of the Civil Rights Act of 1964 and the Civil Rights Restoration Act of 1987, apply to all programs and activities of recipients, subrecipients, and contractors receiving FHWA planning and research funds whether or not those programs or activities are federally funded.

(i) *Patents.* The State DOTs and their subrecipients are subject to the provisions of 37 CFR part 401 governing patents and inventions and must include or cite the standard patent rights clause at 37 CFR 401.14, except for §401.14(g), in all subgrants or contracts. In addition, State DOTs and their subrecipients must include the following clause, suitably modified to identify the parties, in all subgrants or contracts, regardless of tier, for experimental, developmental or research work: "The subgrantee or contractor will retain all rights provided for the State in this clause, and the State will not, as part of the consideration for awarding the subgrant or contract, obtain rights in the subgrantee's or contractor's subject inventions."

(j) *Procurement.* Procedures for the procurement of property and services with FHWA planning and research funds by the State DOTs must be in accordance with 49 CFR 18.36(a) and (i) and, if applicable, 18.36(t). Local government subrecipients of State DOTs must follow the procedures specified by the State DOT. Universities, hospitals, and other non-profit organizations must follow the procedures in 49 CFR 19.40 through 19.48. The State DOTs and their subrecipients must not use FHWA funds for procurements from persons (as defined in 49 CFR 29.105) who have been debarred or suspended in accordance with the provisions of 49 CFR part 29, subparts A through E.

(k) *Program income.* Program income, as defined in 49 CFR 18.25(b) or 49 CFR 19.24, must be shown and deducted from total expenditures to determine the Federal share to be reimbursed, unless the FHWA Division Administrator has given prior approval to use the program income to perform additional eligible work or as the non-Federal match.

(l) *Record retention.* Recordkeeping and retention requirements must be in accordance with 49 CFR 18.42 or 49 CFR 19.53.

(m) *Subgrants to local governments.* The State DOTs and subrecipients are responsible for administering FHWA planning and research funds passed through to MPOs and local governments, for ensuring that such funds are expended for eligible activities, and for ensuring that the funds are administered in accordance with this part, 49 CFR part 18, Uniform Administrative Requirements for Grants and Agreements to State and Local Governments, and applicable OMB cost principles. The State DOTs shall follow State laws and procedures when awarding and administering subgrants to MPOs and local governments and must ensure that the requirements of 49 CFR 18.37(a) have been satisfied.

(n) *Subgrants to universities, hospitals, and other non-profit organizations.* The State DOTs and subrecipients are responsible for ensuring that FHWA planning and research funds passed through to universities, hospitals, and other non-profit organizations are expended for eligible activities and for ensuring that the funds are administered in accordance with this part, 49 CFR part 19, Uniform Administrative Requirements for Grants and Agreements with Institutions of Higher Education, Hospitals, and Other Non-Profit Organizations, and applicable OMB cost principles.

(o) *Suspension and debarment.* (1) The State DOTs and their subrecipients shall not award grants or cooperative agreements to entities who are debarred or suspended, or otherwise excluded from or ineligible for participation in Federal assistance programs under Executive Order 12549 of February 18, 1986 (3 CFR, 1986 Comp., p. 189); and

(2) The State DOTs and their subrecipients shall comply with the provisions of 49 CFR part 29, subparts A through E, for procurements from persons (as defined in 49 CFR 29.105) who have been debarred or suspended.

(p) *Supplies.* Acquisition and disposition of supplies acquired by the State DOTs and their subrecipients with FHWA planning and research funds must be in accordance with 49 CFR 18.33 or 49 CFR 19.35.

Subpart B—Research, Development and Technology Transfer Program Management

§ 420.201 What is the purpose of this subpart?

The purpose of this subpart is to prescribe requirements for research, development, and technology transfer (RD&T) activities, programs, and studies undertaken by State DOTs and their subrecipients with FHWA planning and research funds.

§ 420.203 How does the FHWA define the terms used in this subpart?

Unless otherwise specified in this part, the definitions in 23 U.S.C. 101(a) and subpart A of this part, are applicable to this subpart. As used in this subpart:

Applied research means the study of phenomena to gain knowledge or understanding necessary for determining the means by which a recognized need may be met; the primary purpose of this kind of research is to answer a question or solve a problem.

Basic research means the study of phenomena, and of observable facts, without specific applications towards processes or products in mind; the primary purpose of this kind of research is to increase knowledge.

Development means the systematic use of the knowledge or understanding gained from research, directed toward the production of useful materials, devices, systems or methods, including design and development of prototypes and processes.

Final report means a report documenting a completed RD&T study or activity.

Intermodal RD&T means research, development, and technology transfer activities involving more than one mode of transportation, including transfer facilities between modes.

Peer exchange means a periodic review of a State DOT's RD&T program, or portion thereof, by representatives of other State DOT's, for the purpose of exchange of information or best practices. The State DOT may also invite the participation of the FHWA, and other Federal, State, regional or local transportation agencies, the Transportation Research Board, academic institutions, foundations or private firms that support transportation research, development or technology transfer activities.

RD&T activity means a basic or applied research project or study, development or technology transfer activity.

Research means a systematic study directed toward fuller scientific knowledge or understanding of the subject studied. Research can be basic or applied.

Technology transfer means those activities that lead to the adoption of a new technique or product by users and involves dissemination, demonstration, training, and other activities that lead to eventual innovation.

Transportation Research Information Services (TRIS) means the database produced and maintained by the Transportation Research Board and available online through the National Transportation Library. TRIS includes bibliographic records and abstracts of ongoing and completed RD&T activities. TRIS Online also includes links to the full text of public-domain documents.

§ 420.205 What is the FHWA's policy for research, development, and technology transfer funding?

(a) It is the FHWA's policy to administer the RD&T program activities utilizing FHWA planning and research funds consistent with the policy specified in § 420.105 and the following general principles in paragraphs (b) through (g) of this section.

(b) The State DOTs must provide information necessary for peer exchanges.

(c) The State DOTs are encouraged to develop, establish, and implement an RD&T program, funded with Federal and State DOT resources that anticipates and addresses transportation concerns before they become critical problems. Further, the State DOTs are encouraged to include in this program development and technology transfer programs to share the results of their own research efforts and promote the use of new technology.

(d) To promote effective use of available resources, the State DOTs are encouraged to cooperate with other State DOTs, the FHWA, and other appropriate agencies to achieve RD&T objectives established at the national level and to develop a technology transfer program to promote and use those results. This includes contributing to cooperative RD&T programs such as the NCHRP, the TRB, and transportation pooled fund studies as a means of addressing national and regional issues and as a means of leveraging funds.

(e) The State DOTs will be allowed the authority and flexibility to manage and direct their RD&T activities as presented in their work programs, and to initiate RD&T activities supported by FHWA planning and research funds, subject to the limitation of Federal funds and to compliance with program conditions set forth in subpart A of this part and § 420.207.

(f) The State DOTs will have primary responsibility for managing RD&T activities supported with FHWA planning and research funds carried out by other State agencies and organizations and for ensuring that such funds are expended for purposes consistent with this subpart.

(g) Each State DOT must develop, establish, and implement a management process that ensures effective use of available FHWA planning and research funds for RD&T activities on a statewide basis. Each State DOT is permitted to tailor its management process to meet State or local needs; however, the process must comply with the minimum requirements and conditions of this subpart.

(h) The State DOTs are encouraged to make effective use of the FHWA Division, Resource Center, and Headquarters office expertise in developing and carrying out their RD&T activities. Participation of the FHWA on advisory panels and in program exchange meetings is encouraged.

§ 420.207 What are the requirements for research, development, and technology transfer work programs?

(a) The State DOT's RD&T work program must, as a minimum, consist of a description of RD&T activities to be accomplished during the program period, estimated costs for each eligible activity, and a description of any cooperative activities including the State DOT's participation in any transportation pooled fund studies and the NCHRP. The State DOT's work program should include a list of the major items with a cost estimate for each item. The work program should also include any study funded under a previous work program until a final report has been completed for the study.

(b) The State DOT's RD&T work program must include financial summaries showing the funding levels and share (Federal, State, and other sources) for RD&T activities for the program year. State DOTs are encouraged to include any activity funded 100 percent with State or other funds for information purposes.

(c) Approval and authorization procedures in § 420.115 are applicable to the State DOT's RD&T work program.

§ 420.209 What are the conditions for approval?

(a) As a condition for approval of FHWA planning and research funds for RD&T activities, a State DOT must develop, establish, and implement a management process that identifies and results in implementation of RD&T activities expected to address high priority transportation issues. The management process must include:

(1) An interactive process for identification and prioritization of RD&T activities for inclusion in an RD&T work program;

(2) Use of all FHWA planning and research funds set aside for RD&T activities, either internally or for participation in transportation pooled fund studies or other cooperative RD&T programs, to the maximum extent possible;

(3) Procedures for tracking program activities, schedules, accomplishments, and fiscal commitments;

(4) Support and use of the TRIS database for program development, reporting of active RD&T activities, and input of the final report information;

(5) Procedures to determine the effectiveness of the State DOT's management process in implementing the RD&T program, to determine the utilization of the State DOT's RD&T outputs, and to facilitate peer exchanges of its RD&T Program on a periodic basis;

(6) Procedures for documenting RD&T activities through the preparation of final reports. As a minimum, the documentation must include the data collected, analyses performed, conclusions, and recommendations. The State DOT must actively implement appropriate research findings and should document benefits; and

(7) Participation in peer exchanges of its RD&T management process and of other State DOTs' programs on a periodic basis. To assist peer exchange teams in conducting an effective exchange, the State DOT must provide to them the information and documentation required to be collected and maintained under this subpart. Travel and other costs associated with the State DOT's peer exchange may be identified as a line item in the State DOT's work program and will be eligible for 100 percent Federal funding. The peer exchange team must prepare a written report of the exchange.

(b) Documentation that describes the State DOT's management process and the procedures for selecting and implementing RD&T activities must be developed by the State DOT and submitted to the FHWA Division office for approval. Significant changes in the management process also must be submitted by the State DOT to the FHWA for approval. The State DOT must make the documentation available, as necessary, to facilitate peer exchanges.

(c) The State DOT must include a certification that it is in full compliance with the requirements of this subpart in each RD&T work program. If the State DOT is unable to certify full compliance, the FHWA Division Administrator may grant conditional approval of the State DOT's work program. A conditional approval must cite those areas of the State DOT's management process that are deficient and require that the deficiencies be corrected within 6 months of conditional approval. The certification must consist of a statement signed by the Administrator, or an official designated by the Administrator, of the State DOT certifying as follows: "I (name of certifying official), (position title), of the State (Commonwealth) of _______, do hereby certify that the State (Commonwealth) is in compliance with all requirements of 23 U.S.C. 505 and its implementing regulations with respect to the research, development, and technology transfer program, and contemplate no changes in statutes, regulations, or administrative procedures which would affect such compliance.''

(d) The FHWA Division Administrator shall periodically review the State DOT's management process to determine if the State is in compliance with the requirements of this subpart. If the Division Administrator determines that a State DOT is not complying with the requirements of this subpart, or is not performing in accordance with its RD&T management process, the FHWA Division Administrator shall issue a written notice of proposed determination of noncompliance to the State DOT. The notice will set forth the reasons for the proposed determination and inform the State DOT that it may reply in writing within 30 calendar days from the date of the notice. The State DOT's reply should address the deficiencies cited in the notice and provide documentation as necessary. If the State DOT and the Division Administrator cannot resolve the differences set forth in the determination of nonconformity, the State DOT may appeal to the Federal Highway Administrator whose action shall constitute the final decision of the FHWA. An adverse decision shall result in immediate withdrawal of approval of FHWA planning and research funds for the State DOT's RD&T activities until the State DOT is in full compliance.

(The information collection requirements in §420.209 have been approved by the OMB and assigned control number 2125–0039)

PART 450—PLANNING ASSISTANCE AND STANDARDS

Subpart A—Transportation Planning and Programming Definitions

Sec.

Subpart B—Statewide and Nonmetropolitan Transportation Planning and Programming

Subpart C—Metropolitan Transportation Planning and Programming

AUTHORITY: 23 U.S.C. 134 and 135; 42 U.S.C. 7410 *et seq.*; 49 U.S.C. 5303 and 5304; 49 CFR 1.85 and 1.90.

SOURCE: 81 FR 34135, May 27, 2016, unless otherwise noted.

Subpart A—Transportation Planning and Programming Definitions

§ 450.100 Purpose.

The purpose of this subpart is to provide definitions for terms used in this part.

§ 450.102 Applicability.

The definitions in this subpart are applicable to this part, except as otherwise provided.

§ 450.104 Definitions.

Unless otherwise specified, the definitions in 23 U.S.C. 101(a) and 49 U.S.C. 5302 are applicable to this part.

Administrative modification means a minor revision to a long-range statewide or metropolitan transportation plan, Transportation Improvement Program (TIP), or Statewide Transportation Improvement Program (STIP) that includes minor changes to project/project phase costs, minor changes to funding sources of previously included projects, and minor changes to project/project phase initiation dates. An administrative modification is a revision that does not require public review and comment, a redemonstration of fiscal constraint, or a conformity determination (in nonattainment and maintenance areas).

Amendment means a revision to a long-range statewide or metropolitan transportation plan, TIP, or STIP that involves a major change to a project included in a metropolitan transportation plan, TIP, or STIP, including the addition or deletion of a project or a major change in project cost, project/project phase initiation dates, or a major change in design concept or design scope (e.g., changing project termini or the number of through traffic lanes or changing the number of stations in the case of fixed guideway transit projects). Changes to projects that are included only for illustrative purposes do not require an amendment. An amendment is a revision that requires public review and comment and a redemonstration of fiscal constraint. If an amendment involves "non-exempt" projects in nonattainment and maintenance areas, a conformity determination is required.

Asset management means a strategic and systematic process of operating, maintaining, and improving physical assets, with a focus on both engineering and economic analysis based upon quality information, to identify a structured sequence of maintenance, preservation, repair, rehabilitation, and replacement actions that will achieve and sustain a desired state of good repair over the lifecycle of the assets at minimum practicable cost.

Attainment area means any geographic area in which levels of a given criteria air pollutant (e.g., ozone, carbon monoxide, PM_{10}, $PM_{2.5}$, and nitrogen dioxide) meet the health-based National Ambient Air Quality Standards (NAAQS) for that pollutant. An area may be an attainment area for one pollutant and a nonattainment area for others. A "maintenance area" (see definition in this section) is not considered an attainment area for transportation planning purposes.

Available funds means funds derived from an existing source dedicated to or historically used for transportation purposes. For Federal funds, authorized and/or appropriated funds and the extrapolation of formula and discretionary funds at historic rates of increase are considered "available." A similar approach may be used for State and local funds that are dedicated to or historically used for transportation purposes.

Committed funds means funds that have been dedicated or obligated for transportation purposes. For State funds that are not dedicated to transportation purposes, only those funds over which the Governor has control may be considered "committed." Approval of a TIP by the Governor is considered a commitment of those funds over which the Governor has control. For local or private sources of funds not dedicated to or historically used for transportation purposes (including donations of property), a commitment in writing (e.g., letter of intent) by the responsible official or body having control of the funds may be considered a commitment. For projects involving 49 U.S.C. 5309 funding, execution of a Full Funding Grant Agreement (or equivalent) or an Expedited Grant Agreement (or equivalent) with the DOT shall be considered a multiyear commitment of Federal funds.

Conformity means a Clean Air Act (42 U.S.C. 7506(c)) requirement that ensures that Federal funding and approval are given to transportation plans, programs and projects that are consistent with the air quality goals established by a State Implementation Plan (SIP). Conformity to the purpose of the SIP means that transportation activities will not cause new air quality violations, worsen existing violations, or delay timely attainment of the NAAQS or any required interim emission reductions or other milestones in any nonattainment or maintenance area. The transportation conformity regulations (40 CFR part 93, subpart A) sets forth policy, criteria, and procedures for demonstrating and assuring conformity of transportation activities.

Conformity lapse means, pursuant to section 176(c) of the Clean Air Act (42 U.S.C. 7506(c)), as amended, that the conformity determination for a metropolitan transportation plan or TIP has expired and thus there is no currently conforming metropolitan transportation plan or TIP.

Congestion Management Process means a systematic approach required in transportation management areas (TMAs) that provides for effective management and operation, based on a cooperatively developed and implemented metropolitan-wide strategy, of new and existing transportation facilities eligible for funding under title 23 U.S.C., and title 49 U.S.C., through the use of travel demand reduction and operational management strategies.

Consideration means that one or more parties takes into account the opinions, action, and relevant information from other parties in making a decision or determining a course of action.

Consultation means that one or more parties confer with other identified parties in accordance with an established process and, prior to taking action(s), considers the views of the other parties and periodically informs them about action(s) taken. This definition does not apply to the "consultation" performed by the States and the Metropolitan Planning Organizations (MPOs) in comparing the long-range statewide transportation plan and the metropolitan transportation plan, respectively, to State and tribal conservation plans or maps or inventories of natural or historic resources (see section 450.216(j) and sections 450.324(g)(1) and (g)(2)).

Cooperation means that the parties involved in carrying out the transportation planning and programming processes work together to achieve a common goal or objective.

Coordinated public transit-human services transportation plan means a locally developed, coordinated transportation plan that identifies the transportation needs of individuals with disabilities, older adults, and people with low incomes, provides strategies for meeting those local needs, and prioritizes transportation services for funding and implementation.

Coordination means the cooperative development of plans, programs, and schedules among agencies and entities with legal standing and adjustment of such plans, programs, and schedules to achieve general consistency, as appropriate.

Design concept means the type of facility identified for a transportation improvement project (e.g., freeway, expressway, arterial highway, grade-separated highway, toll road, reserved right-of-way rail transit, mixed-traffic rail transit, or busway).

Design scope means the aspects that will affect the proposed facility's impact on the region, usually as they relate to vehicle or person carrying capacity and control (e.g., number of lanes or tracks to be constructed or added, length of project, signalization, safety features, access control including approximate number and location of interchanges, or preferential treatment for high-occupancy vehicles).

Designated recipient means an entity designated, in accordance with the planning process under 49 U.S.C. 5303 and 5304, by the Governor of a State, responsible local officials, and publicly owned operators of public transportation, to receive and apportion amounts under 49 U.S.C. 5336 that are attributable to urbanized areas of 200,000 or more in population, or a State or regional authority if the authority is responsible under the laws of a State for a capital project and for financing and directly providing public transportation.

Environmental mitigation activities means strategies, policies, programs, and actions that, over time, will serve to avoid, minimize, rectify, reduce or eliminate impacts to environmental resources associated with the implementation of a long-range statewide transportation plan or metropolitan transportation plan.

Expedited Grant Agreement (EGA) means a contract that defines the scope of a Small Starts project, the Federal financial contribution, and other terms and conditions, in accordance with 49 U.S.C. 5309(h)(7).

Federal land management agency means units of the Federal Government currently responsible for the administration of public lands (e.g., U.S. Forest Service, U.S. Fish and Wildlife Service, Bureau of Land Management, and the National Park Service).

Federally funded non-emergency transportation services means transportation services provided to the general public, including those with special transport needs, by public transit, private nonprofit service providers, and private third-party contractors to public agencies.

Financial plan means documentation required to be included with a metropolitan transportation plan and TIP (and optional for the long-range statewide transportation plan and STIP) that demonstrates the consistency between reasonably available and projected sources of Federal, State, local, and private revenues and the costs of implementing proposed transportation system improvements.

Financially constrained or Fiscal constraint means that the metropolitan transportation plan, TIP, and STIP includes sufficient financial information for demonstrating that projects in the metropolitan transportation plan, TIP, and STIP can be implemented using committed, available, or reasonably available revenue sources, with reasonable assurance that the federally supported transportation system is being adequately operated and maintained. For the TIP and the STIP, financial constraint/fiscal constraint applies to each program year. Additionally, projects in air quality nonattainment and maintenance areas can be included in the first 2 years of the TIP and STIP only if funds are "available" or "committed."

Freight shippers means any entity that routinely transport cargo from one location to another by providers of freight transportation services or by their own operations, involving one or more travel modes.

Full Funding Grant Agreement (FFGA) means an instrument that defines the scope of a project, the Federal financial contribution, and other terms and conditions for funding New Starts projects as required by 49 U.S.C. 5309(k)(2).

Governor means the Governor of any of the 50 States or the Commonwealth of Puerto Rico or the Mayor of the District of Columbia.

Highway Safety Improvement Program (HSIP) means a State safety program with the purpose to reduce fatalities and serious injuries on all public roads through the implementation of the provisions of 23 U.S.C. 130, 148, and 150 including the development of a Strategic Highway Safety Plan (SHSP), Railway-Highway Crossings Program, and program of highway safety improvement projects.

Illustrative project means an additional transportation project that may be included in a financial plan for a metropolitan transportation plan, TIP, or STIP if reasonable additional resources were to become available.

Indian Tribal government means a duly formed governing body for an Indian or Alaska Native tribe, band, nation, pueblo, village, or community that the Secretary of the Interior acknowledges to exist as an Indian Tribe pursuant to the Federally Recognized Indian Tribe List Act of 1994, Public Law 103–454.

Intelligent Transportation System (ITS) means electronics, photonics, communications, or information processing used singly or in combination to improve the efficiency or safety of a surface transportation system.

Interim metropolitan transportation plan means a transportation plan composed of projects eligible to proceed under a conformity lapse and otherwise meeting all other applicable provisions of this part, including approval by the MPO.

Interim Transportation Improvement Program (TIP) means a TIP composed of projects eligible to proceed under a conformity lapse and otherwise meeting all other applicable provisions of this part, including approval by the MPO and the Governor.

Long-range statewide transportation plan means the official, statewide, multimodal, transportation plan covering a period of no less than 20 years developed through the statewide transportation planning process.

Maintenance area means any geographic region of the United States that the Environmental Protection Agency (EPA) previously designated as a nonattainment area for one or more pollutants pursuant to the Clean Air Act Amendments of 1990, and subsequently redesignated as an attainment area subject to the requirement to develop a maintenance plan under section 175A of the Clean Air Act, as amended (42 U.S.C. 7505a).

Management system means a systematic process, designed to assist decision makers in selecting cost effective strategies/actions to improve the efficiency or safety of, and protect the investment in the nation's infrastructure. A management system can include: Identification of performance measures; data collection and analysis; determination of needs; evaluation and selection of appropriate strategies/actions to address the needs; and evaluation of the effectiveness of the implemented strategies/actions.

Metropolitan planning agreement means a written agreement between the MPO, the State(s), and the providers of public transportation serving the metropolitan planning area that describes how they will work cooperatively to meet their mutual responsibilities in carrying out the metropolitan transportation planning process.

Metropolitan planning area (MPA) means the geographic area determined by agreement between the MPO for the area and the Governor, in which the metropolitan transportation planning process is carried out.

Metropolitan Planning Organization (MPO) means the policy board of an organization created and designated to carry out the metropolitan transportation planning process.

Metropolitan transportation plan means the official multimodal transportation plan addressing no less than a 20-year planning horizon that the MPO develops, adopts, and updates through the metropolitan transportation planning process.

National Ambient Air Quality Standard (NAAQS) means those standards established pursuant to section 109 of the Clean Air Act (42 U.S.C. 7409).

Nonattainment area means any geographic region of the United States that EPA designates as a nonattainment area under section 107 of the Clean Air Act (42 U.S.C. 7407) for any pollutants for which an NAAQS exists.

Nonmetropolitan area means a geographic area outside a designated metropolitan planning area.

Nonmetropolitan local officials means elected and appointed officials of general purpose local government in a nonmetropolitan area with responsibility for transportation.

Obligated projects means strategies and projects funded under title 23 U.S.C. and title 49 U.S.C. Chapter 53 for which the State or designated recipient authorized and committed the supporting Federal funds in preceding or current program years, and authorized by the FHWA or awarded as a grant by the FTA.

Operational and management strategies means actions and strategies aimed at improving the performance of existing and planned transportation facilities to relieve congestion and maximize the safety and mobility of people and goods.

Performance measure refers to "Measure" as defined in 23 CFR 490.101.

Performance metric refers to "Metric" as defined in 23 CFR 490.101.

Performance target refers to "Target" as defined in 23 CFR 490.101.

Project selection means the procedures followed by MPOs, States, and public transportation operators to advance projects from the first 4 years of an approved TIP and/or STIP to implementation, in accordance with agreed upon procedures.

Provider of freight transportation services means any entity that transports or otherwise facilitates the movement of cargo from one location to another for others or for itself.

Public transportation agency safety plan means a comprehensive plan established by a State or recipient of funds under Title 49, Chapter 53 and in accordance with 49 U.S.C. 5329(d).

Public transportation operator means the public entity or government-approved authority that participates in the continuing, cooperative, and comprehensive transportation planning process in accordance with 23 U.S.C. 134 and 135 and 49 U.S.C. 5303 and 5304, and is a recipient of Federal funds under title 49 U.S.C. Chapter 53 for transportation by a conveyance that provides regular and continuing general or special transportation to the public, but does not include sightseeing, school bus, charter, certain types of shuttle service, intercity bus transportation, or intercity passenger rail transportation provided by Amtrak.

Regional ITS architecture means a regional framework for ensuring institutional agreement and technical integration for the implementation of ITS projects or groups of projects.

Regionally significant project means a transportation project (other than projects that may be grouped in the TIP and/or STIP or exempt projects as defined in EPA's transportation conformity regulations (40 CFR part 93, subpart A)) that is on a facility that serves regional transportation needs (such as access to and from the area outside the region; major activity centers in the region; major planned developments such as new retail malls, sports complexes, or employment centers; or transportation terminals) and would normally be included in the modeling of the metropolitan area's transportation network. At a minimum, this includes all principal arterial highways and all fixed guideway transit facilities that offer an alternative to regional highway travel.

Regional Transportation Planning Organization (RTPO) means a policy board of nonmetropolitan local officials or their designees created to carry out the regional transportation planning process.

Revision means a change to a long-range statewide or metropolitan transportation plan, TIP, or STIP that occurs between scheduled periodic updates. A major revision is an "amendment" while a minor revision is an "administrative modification."

Scenario planning means a planning process that evaluates the effects of alternative policies, plans and/or programs on the future of a community or region. This activity should provide information to decision makers as they develop the transportation plan.

State means any one of the 50 States, the District of Columbia, or Puerto Rico.

State Implementation Plan (SIP) means, as defined in section 302(q) of the Clean Air Act (CAA) (42 U.S.C. 7602(q)), the portion (or portions) of the implementation plan, or most recent revision thereof, which has been approved under section 110 of the CAA (42 U.S.C. 7410), or promulgated under section 110(c) of the CAA (42 U.S.C. 7410(c)), or promulgated or approved pursuant to regulations promulgated under section 301(d) of the CAA (42 U.S.C. 7601(d)) and which implements the relevant requirements of the CAA.

Statewide Transportation Improvement Program (STIP) means a statewide prioritized listing/program of transportation projects covering a period of 4 years that is consistent with the long-range statewide transportation plan, metropolitan transportation plans, and TIPs, and required for projects to be eligible for funding under title 23 U.S.C. and title 49 U.S.C. Chapter 53.

Strategic Highway Safety Plan means a comprehensive, multiyear, data-driven plan, developed by a State DOT in accordance with the 23 U.S.C. 148.

Transit Asset Management Plan means a plan that includes an inventory of capital assets, a condition assessment of inventoried assets, a decision support tool, and a prioritization of investments.

Transit Asset Management System means a strategic and systematic process of operating, maintaining, and improving public transportation capital assets effectively, throughout the life cycles of those assets.

Transportation Control Measure (TCM) means any measure that is specifically identified and committed to in the applicable SIP, including a substitute or additional TCM that is incorporated into the applicable SIP through the process established in CAA section 176(c)(8), that is either one of the types listed in section 108 of the CAA (42 U.S.C. 7408) or any other measure for the purpose of reducing emissions or concentrations of air pollutants from transportation sources by reducing vehicle use or changing traffic flow or congestion conditions. Notwithstanding the above, vehicle technology-based, fuel-based, and maintenance-based measures that control the emissions from vehicles under fixed traffic conditions are not TCMs.

Transportation improvement program (TIP) means a prioritized listing/program of transportation projects covering a period of 4 years that is developed and formally adopted by an MPO as part of the metropolitan transportation planning process, consistent with the metropolitan transportation plan, and required for projects to be eligible for funding under title 23 U.S.C. and title 49 U.S.C. chapter 53.

Transportation Management Area (TMA) means an urbanized area with a population over 200,000, as defined by the Bureau of the Census and designated by the Secretary of Transportation, or any additional area where TMA designation is requested by the Governor and the MPO and designated by the Secretary of Transportation.

Unified Planning Work Program (UPWP) means a statement of work identifying the planning priorities and activities to be carried out within a metropolitan planning area. At a minimum, a UPWP includes a description of the planning work and resulting products, who will perform the work, time frames for completing the work, the cost of the work, and the source(s) of funds.

Update means making current a long-range statewide transportation plan, metropolitan transportation plan, TIP, or STIP through a comprehensive review. Updates require public review and comment, a 20-year horizon for metropolitan transportation plans and long-range statewide transportation plans, a 4-year program period for TIPs and STIPs, demonstration of fiscal constraint (except for long-range statewide transportation plans), and a conformity determination (for metropolitan transportation plans and TIPs in nonattainment and maintenance areas).

Urbanized area (UZA) means a geographic area with a population of 50,000 or more, as designated by the Bureau of the Census.

Users of public transportation means any person, or groups representing such persons, who use transportation open to the general public, other than taxis and other privately funded and operated vehicles.

Visualization techniques means methods used by States and MPOs in the development of transportation plans and programs with the public, elected and appointed officials, and other stakeholders in a clear and easily accessible format such as GIS- or web-based surveys, inventories, maps, pictures, and/or displays identifying features such as roadway rights of way, transit, intermodal, and non-motorized transportation facilities, historic and cultural resources, natural resources, and environmentally sensitive areas, to promote improved understanding of existing or proposed transportation plans and programs.

[81 FR 34135, May 27, 2016, as amended at 81 FR 93469, Dec. 20, 2016; 82 FR 56542, Nov. 29, 2017]

Subpart B—Statewide and Nonmetropolitan Transportation Planning and Programming

§ 450.200 Purpose.

The purpose of this subpart is to implement the provisions of 23 U.S.C. 135, 23 U.S.C. 150, and 49 U.S.C. 5304, as amended, which require each State to carry out a continuing, cooperative, and comprehensive performance-based statewide multimodal transportation planning process, including the development of a long-range statewide transportation plan and STIP, that facilitates the safe and efficient management, operation, and development of surface transportation systems that will serve the mobility needs of people and freight (including accessible pedestrian walkways, bicycle transportation facilities, and intermodal facilities that support intercity transportation, including intercity bus facilities and commuter van pool providers) and that fosters economic growth and development within and between States and urbanized areas, and take into consideration resiliency needs while minimizing transportation-related fuel consumption and air pollution in all areas of the State, including those areas subject to the metropolitan transportation planning requirements of 23 U.S.C. 134 and 49 U.S.C. 5303.

§ 450.202 Applicability.

The provisions of this subpart are applicable to States and any other organizations or entities (e.g., MPOs, RTPOs and public transportation operators) that are responsible for satisfying the requirements for transportation plans and programs throughout the State pursuant to 23 U.S.C. 135 and 49 U.S.C. 5304.

§ 450.204 Definitions.

Except as otherwise provided in subpart A of this part, terms defined in 23 U.S.C. 101(a) and 49 U.S.C. 5302 are used in this subpart as so defined.

§ 450.206 Scope of the statewide and nonmetropolitan transportation planning process.

(a) Each State shall carry out a continuing, cooperative, and comprehensive statewide transportation planning process that provides for consideration and implementation of projects, strategies, and services that will address the following factors:

(1) Support the economic vitality of the United States, the States, metropolitan areas, and nonmetropolitan areas, especially by enabling global competitiveness, productivity, and efficiency;

(2) Increase the safety of the transportation system for motorized and non-motorized users;

(3) Increase the security of the transportation system for motorized and non-motorized users;

(4) Increase accessibility and mobility of people and freight;

(5) Protect and enhance the environment, promote energy conservation, improve the quality of life, and promote consistency between transportation improvements and State and local planned growth and economic development patterns;

(6) Enhance the integration and connectivity of the transportation system, across and between modes throughout the State, for people and freight;

(7) Promote efficient system management and operation;

(8) Emphasize the preservation of the existing transportation system;

(9) Improve the resiliency and reliability of the transportation system and reduce or mitigate stormwater impacts of surface transportation; and

(10) Enhance travel and tourism.

(b) Consideration of the planning factors in paragraph (a) of this section shall be reflected, as appropriate, in the statewide transportation planning process. The degree of consideration and analysis of the factors should be based on the scale and complexity of many issues, including transportation systems development, land use, employment, economic development, human and natural environment (including Section 4(f) properties as defined in 23 CFR 774.17), and housing and community development.

(c) *Performance-based approach.* (1) The statewide transportation planning process shall provide for the establishment and use of a performance-based approach to transportation decisionmaking to support the national goals described in 23 U.S.C. 150(b) and the general purposes described in 49 U.S.C. 5301.

(2) Each State shall select and establish performance targets in coordination with the relevant MPOs to ensure consistency to the maximum extent practicable. The targets shall address the performance areas described in 23 U.S.C. 150(c), and the measures established under 23 CFR part 490, where applicable, to use in tracking progress toward attainment of critical outcomes for the State. States shall establish performance targets that reflect the measures identified in 23 U.S.C. 150(c) not later than 1 year after the effective date of the DOT final rule on performance measures. Each State shall select and establish targets under this paragraph in accordance with the appropriate target setting framework established at 23 CFR part 490.

(3) In areas not represented by an MPO, the selection of public transportation performance targets by a State shall be coordinated, to the maximum extent practicable, with providers of public transportation to ensure consistency with the performance targets that public transportation providers establish under 49 U.S.C. 5326(c) and 49 U.S.C. 5329(d).

(4) A State shall integrate into the statewide transportation planning process, directly or by reference, the goals, objectives, performance measures, and targets described in this section, in other State transportation plans and transportation processes, as well as any plans developed pursuant to chapter 53 of title 49 by providers of public transportation in areas not represented by an MPO required as part of a performance-based program. Examples of such plans and processes include the HSIP, SHSP, the State Asset Management Plan for the National Highway System (NHS), the State Freight Plan (if the State has one), the Transit Asset Management Plan, and the Public Transportation Agency Safety Plan.

(5) A State shall consider the performance measures and targets established under this paragraph when developing policies, programs, and investment priorities reflected in the long-range statewide transportation plan and statewide transportation improvement program.

(d) The failure to consider any factor specified in paragraph (a) or (c) of this section shall not be subject to review by any court under title 23 U.S.C., 49 U.S.C. Chapter 53, subchapter II of title 5 U.S.C. Chapter 5, or title 5 U.S.C. Chapter 7 in any matter affecting a long-range statewide transportation plan, STIP, project or strategy, or the statewide transportation planning process findings.

(e) Funds provided under 23 U.S.C. 505 and 49 U.S.C. 5305(e) are available to the State to accomplish activities described in this subpart. At the State's option, funds provided under 23 U.S.C. 104(b)(2) and 49 U.S.C. 5307, 5310, and 5311 may also be used for statewide transportation planning. A State shall document statewide transportation planning activities performed with funds provided under title 23 U.S.C. and title 49 U.S.C. Chapter 53 in a statewide planning work program in accordance with the provisions of 23 CFR part 420. The work program should include a discussion of the transportation planning priorities facing the State.

§ 450.208 Coordination of planning process activities.

(a) In carrying out the statewide transportation planning process, each State shall, at a minimum:

(1) Coordinate planning carried out under this subpart with the metropolitan transportation planning activities carried out under subpart C of this part for metropolitan areas of the State. The State is encouraged to rely on information, studies, or analyses provided by MPOs for portions of the transportation system located in metropolitan planning areas;

(2) Coordinate planning carried out under this subpart with statewide trade and economic development planning activities and related multistate planning efforts;

(3) Consider the concerns of Federal land management agencies that have jurisdiction over land within the boundaries of the State;

(4) Cooperate with affected local elected and appointed officials with responsibilities for transportation, or, if applicable, through RTPOs described in

section 450.210(d) in nonmetropolitan areas;

(5) Consider the concerns of Indian Tribal governments that have jurisdiction over land within the boundaries of the State;

(6) Consider related planning activities being conducted outside of metropolitan planning areas and between States; and

(7) Coordinate data collection and analyses with MPOs and public transportation operators to support statewide transportation planning and programming priorities and decisions.

(b) The State air quality agency shall coordinate with the State department of transportation (State DOT) to develop the transportation portion of the State Implementation Plan (SIP) consistent with the Clean Air Act (42 U.S.C. 7401 *et seq.*).

(c) Two or more States may enter into agreements or compacts, not in conflict with any law of the United States, for cooperative efforts and mutual assistance in support of activities under this subpart related to interstate areas and localities in the States and establishing authorities the States consider desirable for making the agreements and compacts effective. The right to alter, amend, or repeal interstate compacts entered into under this part is expressly reserved.

(d) States may use any one or more of the management systems (in whole or in part) described in 23 CFR part 500.

(e) In carrying out the statewide transportation planning process, States should apply asset management principles and techniques consistent with the State Asset Management Plan for the NHS and the Transit Asset Management Plan, and Public Transportation Agency Safety Plan in establishing planning goals, defining STIP priorities, and assessing transportation investment decisions, including transportation system safety, operations, preservation, and maintenance.

(f) For non-NHS highways, States may apply principles and techniques consistent with other asset management plans to the transportation planning and programming processes, as appropriate.

(g) The statewide transportation planning process shall (to the maximum extent practicable) be consistent with the development of applicable regional intelligent transportation systems (ITS) architectures, as defined in 23 CFR part 940.

(h) Preparation of the coordinated public transit-human services transportation plan, as required by 49 U.S.C. 5310, should be coordinated and consistent with the statewide transportation planning process.

[81 FR 34135, May 27, 2016, as amended at 81 FR 93469, Dec. 20, 2016; 82 FR 56542, Nov. 29, 2017]

§450.210 Interested parties, public involvement, and consultation.

(a) In carrying out the statewide transportation planning process, including development of the long-range statewide transportation plan and the STIP, the State shall develop and use a documented public involvement process that provides opportunities for public review and comment at key decision points.

(1) The State's public involvement process at a minimum shall:

(i) Establish early and continuous public involvement opportunities that provide timely information about transportation issues and decisionmaking processes to individuals, affected public agencies, representatives of public transportation employees, public ports, freight shippers, private providers of transportation (including intercity bus operators), representatives of users of public transportation, representatives of users of pedestrian walkways and bicycle transportation facilities, representatives of the disabled, providers of freight transportation services, and other interested parties;

(ii) Provide reasonable public access to technical and policy information used in the development of the long-range statewide transportation plan and the STIP;

(iii) Provide adequate public notice of public involvement activities and time for public review and comment at key decision points, including a reasonable opportunity to comment on the proposed long-range statewide transportation plan and STIP;

(iv) To the maximum extent practicable, ensure that public meetings are held at convenient and accessible locations and times;

(v) To the maximum extent practicable, use visualization techniques to describe the proposed long-range statewide transportation plan and supporting studies;

(vi) To the maximum extent practicable, make public information available in electronically accessible format and means, such as the World Wide Web, as appropriate to afford reasonable opportunity for consideration of public information;

(vii) Demonstrate explicit consideration and response to public input during the development of the long-range statewide transportation plan and STIP;

(viii) Include a process for seeking out and considering the needs of those traditionally underserved by existing transportation systems, such as low-income and minority households, who may face challenges accessing employment and other services; and

(ix) Provide for the periodic review of the effectiveness of the public involvement process to ensure that the process provides full and open access to all interested parties and revise the process, as appropriate.

(2) The State shall provide for public comment on existing and proposed processes for public involvement in the development of the long-range statewide transportation plan and the STIP. At a minimum, the State shall allow 45 calendar days for public review and written comment before the procedures and any major revisions to existing procedures are adopted. The State shall provide copies of the approved public involvement process document(s) to the FHWA and the FTA for informational purposes.

(3) With respect to the setting of targets, nothing in this part precludes a State from considering comments made as part of the State's public involvement process.

(b) The State shall provide for nonmetropolitan local official participation in the development of the long-range statewide transportation plan and the STIP. The State shall have a documented process(es) for cooperating with nonmetropolitan local officials representing units of general purpose local government and/or local officials with responsibility for transportation that is separate and discrete from the public involvement process and provides an opportunity for their participation in the development of the long-range statewide transportation plan and the STIP. Although the FHWA and the FTA shall not review or approve this cooperative process(es), the State shall provide copies of the process document(s) to the FHWA and the FTA for informational purposes.

(1) At least once every 5 years, the State shall review and solicit comments from nonmetropolitan local officials and other interested parties for a period of not less than 60 calendar days regarding the effectiveness of the cooperative process and any proposed changes. The State shall direct a specific request for comments to the State association of counties, State municipal league, regional planning agencies, or directly to nonmetropolitan local officials.

(2) The State, at its discretion, is responsible for determining whether to adopt any proposed changes. If a proposed change is not adopted, the State shall make publicly available its reasons for not accepting the proposed change, including notification to nonmetropolitan local officials or their associations.

(c) For each area of the State under the jurisdiction of an Indian Tribal government, the State shall develop the long-range statewide transportation plan and STIP in consultation with the Tribal government and the Secretary of the Interior. States shall, to the extent practicable, develop a documented process(es) that outlines roles, responsibilities, and key decision points for consulting with Indian Tribal governments and Department of the Interior in the development of the long-range statewide transportation plan and the STIP.

(d) To carry out the transportation planning process required by this section, a Governor may establish and designate RTPOs to enhance the planning, coordination, and implementation of the long-range statewide transportation plan and STIP, with an emphasis on addressing the needs of nonmetropolitan areas of the State. In order to be treated as an RTPO for purposes of this Part, any existing regional planning organization must be established and designated as an RTPO under this section.

(1) Where established, an RTPO shall be a multijurisdictional organization of nonmetropolitan local officials or their designees who volunteer for such organization and representatives of local transportation systems who volunteer for such organization.

(2) An RTPO shall establish, at a minimum:

(i) A policy committee, the majority of which shall consist of nonmetropolitan local officials, or their designees, and, as appropriate, additional representatives from the State, private business, transportation service providers, economic development practitioners, and the public in the region; and

(ii) A fiscal and administrative agent, such as an existing regional planning and development organization, to provide professional planning, management, and administrative support.

(3) The duties of an RTPO shall include:

(i) Developing and maintaining, in cooperation with the State, regional long-range multimodal transportation plans;

(ii) Developing a regional TIP for consideration by the State;

(iii) Fostering the coordination of local planning, land use, and economic development plans with State, regional, and local transportation plans and programs;

(iv) Providing technical assistance to local officials;

(v) Participating in national, multistate, and State policy and planning development processes to ensure the regional and local input of nonmetropolitan areas;

(vi) Providing a forum for public participation in the statewide and regional transportation planning processes;

(vii) Considering and sharing plans and programs with neighboring RTPOs, MPOs, and, where appropriate, Indian Tribal Governments; and

(viii) Conducting other duties, as necessary, to support and enhance the statewide planning process under § 450.206.

(4) If a State chooses not to establish or designate an RTPO, the State shall consult with affected nonmetropolitan local officials to determine projects that may be of regional significance.

§ 450.212 Transportation planning studies and project development.

(a) Pursuant to section 1308 of the Transportation Equity Act for the 21st Century, TEA–21 (Pub. L. 105–178), a State(s), MPO(s), or public transportation operator(s) may undertake a multimodal, systems-level corridor or subarea planning study as part of the statewide transportation planning process. To the extent practicable, development of these transportation planning studies shall involve consultation with, or joint efforts among, the State(s), MPO(s), and/or public transportation operator(s). The results or decisions of these transportation planning studies may be used as part of the overall project development process consistent with the National Environmental Policy Act (NEPA) of 1969 (42 U.S.C. 4321 *et seq.*) and associated implementing regulations (23 CFR part 771 and 40 CFR parts 1500–1508). Specifically, these corridor or subarea studies may result in producing any of the following for a proposed transportation project:

(1) Purpose and need or goals and objective statement(s);

(2) General travel corridor and/or general mode(s) definition (e.g., highway, transit, or a highway/transit combination);

(3) Preliminary screening of alternatives and elimination of unreasonable alternatives;

(4) Basic description of the environmental setting; and/or

(5) Preliminary identification of environmental impacts and environmental mitigation.

(b) Publicly available documents or other source material produced by, or in support of, the transportation planning process described in this subpart may be incorporated directly or by reference into subsequent NEPA documents, in accordance with 40 CFR 1502.21, if:

(1) The NEPA lead agencies agree that such incorporation will aid in establishing or evaluating the purpose and need for the Federal action, reasonable alternatives, cumulative or other impacts on the human and natural environment, or mitigation of these impacts; and

(2) The systems-level, corridor, or subarea planning study is conducted with:

(i) Involvement of interested State, local, Tribal, and Federal agencies;

(ii) Public review;

(iii) Reasonable opportunity to comment during the statewide transportation planning process and development of the corridor or subarea planning study;

(iv) Documentation of relevant decisions in a form that is identifiable and available for review during the NEPA scoping process and can be appended to or referenced in the NEPA document; and

(v) The review of the FHWA and the FTA, as appropriate.

(c) By agreement of the NEPA lead agencies, the above integration may be accomplished through tiering (as described in 40 CFR 1502.20), incorporating the subarea or corridor planning study into the draft Environmental Impact Statement or Environmental Assessment, or other means that the NEPA lead agencies deem appropriate. Additional information to further explain the linkages between the transportation planning and project development/NEPA processes is contained in Appendix A to this part, including an explanation that is non-binding guidance material. The guidance in Appendix A applies only to paragraphs (a)–(c) in this section.

(d) In addition to the process for incorporation directly or by reference outlined in paragraph (b) of this section, an additional authority for integrating planning products into the environmental review process exists in 23 U.S.C. 168. As provided in 23 U.S.C. 168(f):

(1) The statutory authority in 23 U.S.C. 168 shall not be construed to limit in any way the continued use of processes established under other parts of this section or under an authority established outside this part, and the use of one of the processes in this section does not preclude the subsequent use of another process in this section or an authority outside of this part.

(2) The statute does not restrict the initiation of the environmental review process during planning.

§450.214 Development of programmatic mitigation plans.

(a) A State may utilize the optional framework in this section to develop programmatic mitigation plans as part of the statewide transportation planning process to address the potential environmental impacts of future transportation projects. The State in consultation with FHWA and/or FTA and with the agency or agencies with jurisdiction and special expertise over the resources being addressed in the plan, will determine:

(1) *Scope*. (i) A State may develop a programmatic mitigation plan on a local, regional, ecosystem, watershed, statewide or similar scale.

(ii) The plan may encompass multiple environmental resources within a defined geographic area(s) or may focus on a specific type(s) of resource(s) such as aquatic resources, parkland, or wildlife habitat.

(iii) The plan may address or consider impacts from all projects in a defined geographic area(s) or may focus on a specific type(s) of project(s).

(2) *Contents*. The programmatic mitigation plan may include:

(i) An assessment of the existing condition of natural and human environmental resources within the area covered by the plan, including an assessment of historic and recent trends and/or any potential threats to those resources.

(ii) An identification of economic, social, and natural and human environmental resources within the geographic area that may be impacted and considered for mitigation. Examples of these resources include wetlands, streams, rivers, stormwater, parklands, cultural resources, historic resources, farmlands, archeological resources, threatened or endangered species, and critical habitat. This may include the identification of areas of high conservation concern or value, and thus worthy of avoidance.

(iii) An inventory of existing or planned environmental resource banks for the impacted resource categories such as wetland, stream, stormwater, habitat, species, and an inventory of federally, State, or locally approved in-lieu-of-fee programs.

(iv) An assessment of potential opportunities to improve the overall quality of the identified environmental resources through strategic mitigation for impacts of transportation projects, which may include the prioritization of parcels or areas for acquisition and/or potential resource banking sites.

(v) An adoption or development of standard measures or operating procedures for mitigating certain types of impacts; establishment of parameters for determining or calculating appropriate mitigation for certain types of impacts, such as mitigation ratios, or criteria for determining appropriate mitigation sites.

(vi) Adaptive management procedures, such as protocols or procedures that involve monitoring actual impacts against predicted impacts over time and adjusting mitigation measures in response to information gathered through the monitoring.

(vii) Acknowledgment of specific statutory or regulatory requirements that must be satisfied when determining appropriate mitigation for certain types of resources.

(b) A State may adopt a programmatic mitigation plan developed pursuant to paragraph (a), or developed pursuant to an alternative process as provided for in paragraph (f) of this section through the following process:

(1) Consult with each agency with jurisdiction over the environmental resources considered in the programmatic mitigation plan;

(2) Make available a draft of the programmatic mitigation plan for review and comment by appropriate environmental resource agencies and the public;

(3) Consider comments received from such agencies and the public on the draft plan; and

(4) Address such comments in the final programmatic mitigation plan.

(c) A State may integrate a programmatic mitigation plan with other plans, including, watershed plans, ecosystem plans, species recovery plans, growth management plans, State Wildlife Action Plans, and land use plans.

(d) If a programmatic mitigation plan has been adopted pursuant to paragraph (b), any Federal agency responsible for environmental reviews, permits, or approvals for a transportation project shall give substantial weight to the recommendations in the programmatic mitigation plan when carrying out its responsibilities under the National Environmental Policy Act of 1969 (42 U.S.C. 4321 *et seq.*) (NEPA) or other Federal environmental law.

(e) Nothing in this section limits the use of programmatic approaches for reviews under NEPA.

(f) Nothing in this section prohibits the development, as part of or separate from the transportation planning process, of a programmatic mitigation plan independent of the framework described in paragraph (a) of this section. Further, nothing in this section prohibits the adoption of a programmatic mitigation plan in the statewide and nonmetropolitan transportation planning process that was developed under another authority, independent of the framework described in paragraph (a).

§ 450.216 Development and content of the long-range statewide transportation plan.

(a) The State shall develop a long-range statewide transportation plan, with a minimum 20-year forecast period at the time of adoption, that provides for the development and implementation of the multimodal transportation system for the State. The long-range statewide transportation plan shall consider and include, as applicable, elements and connections between public transportation, non-motorized modes, rail, commercial motor vehicle, waterway, and aviation facilities, particularly with respect to intercity travel.

(b) The long-range statewide transportation plan should include capital, operations and management strategies, investments, procedures, and other measures to ensure the preservation and most efficient use of the existing transportation system including consideration of the role that intercity buses may play in reducing congestion, pollution, and energy consumption in a cost-effective manner and strategies and investments that preserve and enhance intercity bus systems, including systems that are privately owned and operated. The long-range statewide transportation plan may consider projects and strategies that address areas or corridors where current or projected congestion threatens the efficient functioning of key elements of the State's transportation system.

(c) The long-range statewide transportation plan shall reference, summarize, or contain any applicable short-range planning studies; strategic planning and/or policy studies; transportation needs studies; management systems reports; emergency relief and disaster preparedness plans; and any statements of policies, goals, and objectives on issues (e.g., transportation, safety, economic development, social and environmental effects, or energy), as appropriate, that were relevant to the development of the long-range statewide transportation plan.

(d) The long-range statewide transportation plan should integrate the priorities, goals, countermeasures, strategies, or projects contained in the HSIP, including the SHSP, required under 23 U.S.C. 148, the Public Transportation Agency Safety Plan required under 49 U.S.C. 5329(d), or an Interim Agency Safety Plan in accordance with 49 CFR part 659, as in effect until completion of the Public Transportation Agency Safety Plan.

(e) The long-range statewide transportation plan should include a security element that incorporates or summarizes the priorities, goals, or projects set forth in other transit safety and security planning and review processes, plans, and programs, as appropriate.

(f) The statewide transportation plan shall include:

(1) A description of the performance measures and performance targets used in assessing the performance of the transportation system in accordance with §450.206(c); and

(2) A system performance report and subsequent updates evaluating the condition and performance of the transportation system with respect to the performance targets described in §450.206(c), including progress achieved by the MPO(s) in meeting the performance targets in comparison with system performance recorded in previous reports.

(g) Within each metropolitan area of the State, the State shall develop the long-range statewide transportation plan in cooperation with the affected MPOs.

(h) For nonmetropolitan areas, the State shall develop the long-range statewide transportation plan in cooperation with affected nonmetropolitan local officials with responsibility for transportation or, if applicable, through RTPOs described in §450.210(d) using the State's cooperative process(es) established under §450.210(b).

(i) For each area of the State under the jurisdiction of an Indian Tribal government, the State shall develop the long-range statewide transportation plan in consultation with the Tribal government and the Secretary of the Interior consistent with §450.210(c).

(j) The State shall develop the long-range statewide transportation plan, as appropriate, in consultation with State, Tribal, and local agencies responsible for land use management, natural resources, environmental protection, conservation, and historic preservation. This consultation shall involve comparison of transportation plans to State and Tribal conservation plans or maps, if available, and comparison of transportation plans to inventories of natural or historic resources, if available.

(k) A long-range statewide transportation plan shall include a discussion of potential environmental mitigation activities and potential areas to carry out these activities, including activities that may have the greatest potential to restore and maintain the environmental functions affected by the long-range statewide transportation plan. The discussion may focus on policies, programs, or strategies, rather than at the project level. The State shall develop the discussion in consultation with applicable Federal, State, regional, local and Tribal land management, wildlife, and regulatory agencies. The State may establish reasonable timeframes for performing this consultation.

(l) In developing and updating the long-range statewide transportation plan, the State shall provide:

(1) To nonmetropolitan local elected officials, or, if applicable, through RTPOs described in § 450.210(d), an opportunity to participate in accordance with § 450.216(h); and

(2) To individuals, affected public agencies, representatives of public transportation employees, public ports, freight shippers, private providers of transportation (including intercity bus operators, employer-based cash-out program, shuttle program, or telework program), representatives of users of public transportation, representatives of users of pedestrian walkways and bicycle transportation facilities, representatives of the disabled, providers of freight transportation services, and other interested parties with a reasonable opportunity to comment on the proposed long-range statewide transportation plan. In carrying out these requirements, the State shall use the public involvement process described under § 450.210(a).

(m) The long-range statewide transportation plan may include a financial plan that demonstrates how the adopted long-range statewide transportation plan can be implemented, indicates resources from public and private sources that are reasonably expected to be made available to carry out the plan, and recommends any additional financing strategies for needed projects and programs. In addition, for illustrative purposes, the financial plan may include additional projects that the State would include in the adopted long-range statewide transportation plan if additional resources beyond those identified in the financial plan were to become available. The financial plan may include an assessment of the appropriateness of innovative finance techniques (for example, tolling, pricing, bonding, public-private partnerships, or other strategies) as revenue sources.

(n) The State is not required to select any project from the illustrative list of additional projects included in the financial plan described in paragraph (m) of this section.

(o) The State shall publish or otherwise make available the long-range statewide transportation plan for public review, including (to the maximum extent practicable) in electronically accessible formats and means, such as the World Wide Web, as described in § 450.210(a).

(p) The State shall continually evaluate, revise, and periodically update the long-range statewide transportation plan, as appropriate, using the procedures in this section for development and establishment of the long-range statewide transportation plan.

(q) The State shall provide copies of any new or amended long-range statewide transportation plan documents to the FHWA and the FTA for informational purposes.

§ 450.218 Development and content of the statewide transportation improvement program (STIP).

(a) The State shall develop a statewide transportation improvement program (STIP) for all areas of the State. The STIP shall cover a period of no less than 4 years and shall be updated at least every 4 years, or more frequently if the Governor of the State elects a more frequent update cycle. However, if the STIP covers more than 4 years, the FHWA and the FTA will consider the projects in the additional years as informational. In case of difficulties developing a portion of the STIP for a particular area (e.g., metropolitan planning area, nonattainment or maintenance area, or Indian Tribal lands), the State may develop a partial STIP covering the rest of the State.

(b) For each metropolitan area in the State, the State shall develop the STIP in cooperation with the MPO designated for the metropolitan area. The State shall include each metropolitan TIP without change in the STIP, directly or by reference, after approval of the TIP by the MPO and the Governor. A metropolitan TIP in a nonattainment or maintenance area is subject to a FHWA/FTA conformity finding before inclusion in the STIP. In areas outside a metropolitan planning area but within an air quality nonattainment or maintenance area containing any part of a metropolitan area, projects must be included in the regional emissions analysis that supported the conformity determination of the associated metropolitan TIP before they are added to the STIP.

(c) For each nonmetropolitan area in the State, the State shall develop the STIP in cooperation with affected nonmetropolitan local officials with responsibility for transportation or, if applicable, through RTPOs described in §450.210(d) using the State's consultation process(es) established under §450.210(b).

(d) For each area of the State under the jurisdiction of an Indian Tribal government, the STIP shall be developed in consultation with the Tribal government and the Secretary of the Interior.

(e) Tribal Transportation Program, Federal Lands Transportation Program, and Federal Lands Access Program TIPs shall be included without change in the STIP, directly or by reference, once approved by the FHWA pursuant to 23 U.S.C. 201(c)(4).

(f) The Governor shall provide all interested parties with a reasonable opportunity to comment on the proposed STIP as required by §450.210(a).

(g) The STIP shall include capital and non-capital surface transportation projects (or phases of projects) within the boundaries of the State proposed for funding under title 23 U.S.C. and title 49 U.S.C. Chapter 53 (including transportation alternatives and associated transit improvements; Tribal Transportation Program projects, Federal Lands Transportation Program projects, and Federal Lands Access Program projects; HSIP projects; trails projects; and accessible pedestrian walkways and bicycle facilities), except the following that may be included:

(1) Safety projects funded under 23 U.S.C. 402 and 49 U.S.C. 31102;

(2) Metropolitan planning projects funded under 23 U.S.C. 104(d) and 49 U.S.C. 5305(d);

(3) State planning and research projects funded under 23 U.S.C. 505 and 49 U.S.C. 5305(e);

(4) State planning and research projects funded with Surface Transportation Program funds;

(5) Emergency relief projects (except those involving substantial functional, locational, or capacity changes);

(6) Research, development, demonstration, and deployment projects funded under 49 U.S.C. 5312, and technical assistance and standards development projects funded under 49 U.S.C. 5314;

(7) Project management oversight projects funded under 49 U.S.C. 5327; and

(8) State safety oversight programs funded under 49 U.S.C. 5329.

(h) The STIP shall contain all regionally significant projects requiring an action by the FHWA or the FTA whether or not the projects are to be funded with 23 U.S.C. Chapters 1 and 2 or title 49 U.S.C. Chapter 53 funds (e.g., addition of an interchange to the Interstate System with State, local, and/or private funds, and congressionally designated projects not funded under title 23 U.S.C. or title 49 U.S.C. Chapter 53). For informational and conformity purposes, the STIP shall include (if appropriate and included in any TIPs) all regionally significant projects proposed to be funded with Federal funds other than those administered by the FHWA or the FTA, as well as all regionally significant projects to be funded with non-Federal funds.

(i) The STIP shall include for each project or phase (e.g., preliminary engineering, environment/NEPA, right-of-way, design, or construction) the following:

(1) Sufficient descriptive material (*i.e.*, type of work, termini, and length) to identify the project or phase;

(2) Estimated total project cost or a project cost range, which may extend beyond the 4 years of the STIP;

(3) The amount of Federal funds proposed to be obligated during each program year. For the first year, this includes the proposed category of Federal funds and source(s) of non-Federal funds. For the second, third, and fourth years, this includes the likely category or possible categories of Federal funds and sources of non-Federal funds; and

(4) Identification of the agencies responsible for carrying out the project or phase.

(j) Projects that are not considered to be of appropriate scale for individual identification in a given program year may be grouped by function, work type, and/or geographic area using the applicable classifications under 23 CFR 771.117(c) and (d) and/or 40 CFR part 93. In nonattainment and maintenance areas, project classifications must be consistent with the "exempt project" classifications contained in the EPA's transportation conformity regulations (40 CFR part 93, subpart A). In addition, projects proposed for funding under title 23 U.S.C. Chapter 2 that are not regionally significant may be grouped in one line item or identified individually in the STIP.

(k) Each project or project phase included in the STIP shall be consistent with the long-range statewide transportation plan developed under § 450.216 and, in metropolitan planning areas, consistent with an approved metropolitan transportation plan developed under § 450.324.

(l) The STIP may include a financial plan that demonstrates how the approved STIP can be implemented, indicates resources from public and private sources that are reasonably expected to be available to carry out the STIP, and recommends any additional financing strategies for needed projects and programs. In addition, for illustrative purposes, the financial plan may include additional projects that would be included in the adopted STIP if reasonable additional resources beyond those identified in the financial plan were to become available. The State is not required to select any project from the illustrative list for implementation, and projects on the illustrative list cannot be advanced to implementation without an action by the FHWA and the FTA on the STIP. Revenue and cost estimates for the STIP must use an inflation rate to reflect "year of expenditure dollars," based on reasonable financial principles and information, developed cooperatively by the State, MPOs, and public transportation operators.

(m) In nonattainment and maintenance areas, projects included in the first 2 years of the STIP shall be limited to those for which funds are available or committed. Financial constraint of the STIP shall be demonstrated and maintained by year and shall include sufficient financial information to demonstrate which projects are to be implemented using current and/or reasonably available revenues, while federally supported facilities are being adequately operated and maintained. In the case of proposed funding sources, strategies for ensuring their availability shall be identified in the financial plan consistent with paragraph (l) of this section. For purposes of transportation operations and maintenance, the STIP shall include financial information containing system-level estimates of costs and revenue sources that are reasonably expected to be available to adequately operate and maintain Federal-aid highways (as defined by 23 U.S.C. 101(a)(5)) and public transportation (as defined by title 49 U.S.C. 5302).

(n) Projects in any of the first 4 years of the STIP may be advanced in place of another project in the first 4 years of the STIP, subject to the project selection requirements of § 450.222. In addition, subject to FHWA/FTA approval (see § 450.220), the State may revise the STIP at any time under procedures agreed to by the State, MPO(s), and public transportation operators consistent with the STIP development procedures established in this section, as well as the procedures for participation by interested parties (see § 450.210(a)). Changes that affect fiscal constraint must take place by amendment of the STIP.

(o) The STIP shall include a project, or an identified phase of a project, only if full funding can reasonably be anticipated to be available for the project within the time period contemplated for completion of the project.

(p) In cases where the FHWA and the FTA find a STIP to be fiscally constrained, and a revenue source is subsequently removed or substantially reduced (*i.e.*, by legislative or administrative actions), the FHWA and the FTA will not withdraw the original determination of fiscal constraint. However, in such cases, the FHWA and the FTA will not act on an updated or amended STIP that does not reflect the changed revenue situation.

(q) A STIP shall include, to the maximum extent practicable, a discussion of the anticipated effect of the STIP toward achieving the performance targets identified by the State in the statewide transportation plan or other State performance-based plan(s), linking investment priorities to those performance targets.

[81 FR 34135, May 27, 2016, as amended at 81 FR 93470, Dec. 20, 2016; 82 FR 56543, Nov. 29, 2017]

§450.220 Self-certifications, Federal findings, and Federal approvals.

(a) At least every 4 years, the State shall submit an updated STIP concurrently to the FHWA and the FTA for joint approval. The State must also submit STIP amendments to the FHWA and the FTA for joint approval. At the time the entire proposed STIP or STIP amendments are submitted to the FHWA and the FTA for joint approval, the State shall certify that the transportation planning process is being carried out in accordance with all applicable requirements of:

(1) 23 U.S.C. 134 and 135, 49 U.S.C. 5303 and 5304, and this part;

(2) Title VI of the Civil Rights Act of 1964, as amended (42 U.S.C. 2000d-1) and 49 CFR part 21;

(3) 49 U.S.C. 5332, prohibiting discrimination on the basis of race, color, creed, national origin, sex, or age in employment or business opportunity;

(4) Section 1101(b) of the FAST Act (Pub. L. 114–357) and 49 CFR part 26 regarding the involvement of disadvantaged business enterprises in DOT funded projects;

(5) 23 CFR part 230, regarding implementation of an equal employment opportunity program on Federal and Federal-aid highway construction contracts;

(6) The provisions of the Americans with Disabilities Act of 1990 (42 U.S.C. 12101 *et seq.*) and 49 CFR parts 27, 37, and 38;

(7) In States containing nonattainment and maintenance areas, sections 174 and 176(c) and (d) of the Clean Air Act, as amended (42 U.S.C. 7504, 7506(c) and (d)) and 40 CFR part 93;

(8) The Older Americans Act, as amended (42 U.S.C. 6101), prohibiting discrimination on the basis of age in programs or activities receiving Federal financial assistance;

(9) 23 U.S.C. 324, regarding the prohibition of discrimination based on gender; and

(10) Section 504 of the Rehabilitation Act of 1973 (29 U.S.C. 794) and 49 CFR part 27 regarding discrimination against individuals with disabilities.

(b) The FHWA and the FTA shall review the STIP or the amended STIP, and make a joint finding on the extent to which the STIP is based on a statewide transportation planning process that meets or substantially meets the requirements of 23 U.S.C. 134 and 135, 49 U.S.C. 5303 and 5304, and subparts A, B, and C of this part. Approval of the STIP by the FHWA and the FTA, in its entirety or in part, will be based upon the results of this joint finding.

(1) If the FHWA and the FTA determine that the STIP or amended STIP is based on a statewide transportation planning process that meets or substantially meets the requirements of 23 U.S.C. 135, 49 U.S.C. 5304, and this part, the FHWA and the FTA may jointly:

(i) Approve the entire STIP;

(ii) Approve the STIP subject to certain corrective actions by the State; or

(iii) Under special circumstances, approve a partial STIP covering only a portion of the State.

(2) If the FHWA and the FTA jointly determine and document in the planning finding that a submitted STIP or amended STIP does not substantially meet the requirements of 23 U.S.C. 135, 49 U.S.C. 5304, and this part for any identified categories of projects, the FHWA and the FTA will not approve the STIP.

(c) The approval period for a new or amended STIP shall not exceed 4 years. If a State demonstrates, in writing, that extenuating circumstances will delay the submittal of a new or amended STIP past its update deadline, the FHWA and the FTA will consider and take appropriate action on a request to extend the approval beyond 4 years for all or part of the STIP for a period not to exceed 180 calendar days. In these cases, priority consideration will be given to projects and strategies involving the operation and management of the multimodal transportation system. Where the request involves projects in a metropolitan planning area(s), the affected MPO(s) must concur in the request. If the delay was due to the development and approval of a metropolitan TIP(s), the affected MPO(s) must provide supporting information, in writing, for the request.

(d) Where necessary in order to maintain or establish highway and transit operations, the FHWA and the FTA may approve operating assistance for specific projects or programs, even though the projects or programs may not be included in an approved STIP.

§ 450.222 Project selection from the STIP.

(a) Except as provided in § 450.218(g) and § 450.220(d), only projects in a FHWA/FTA approved STIP are eligible for funds administered by the FHWA or the FTA.

(b) In metropolitan planning areas, transportation projects proposed for funds administered by the FHWA or the FTA shall be selected from the approved STIP in accordance with project selection procedures provided in § 450.332.

(c) In nonmetropolitan areas, with the exclusion of specific projects as described in this section, the State shall select projects from the approved STIP in cooperation with the affected nonmetropolitan local officials, or if applicable, through RTPOs described in § 450.210(e). The State shall select transportation projects undertaken on the NHS, under the Bridge and Interstate Maintenance programs in title 23 U.S.C. and under sections 5310 and 5311 of title 49 U.S.C. Chapter 53 from the approved STIP in consultation with the affected nonmetropolitan local officials with responsibility for transportation.

(d) Tribal Transportation Program, Federal Lands Transportation Program, and Federal Lands Access Program projects shall be selected from the approved STIP in accordance with the procedures developed pursuant to 23 U.S.C. 201, 202, 203, and 204.

(e) The projects in the first year of an approved STIP shall constitute an "agreed to" list of projects for subsequent scheduling and implementation. No further action under paragraphs (b) through (d) of this section is required for the implementing agency to proceed with these projects. If Federal funds available are significantly less than the authorized amounts, or where there is significant shifting of projects among years, § 450.332(a) provides for a revised list of "agreed to" projects to be developed upon the request of the State, MPO, or public transportation operator(s). If an implementing agency wishes to proceed with a project in the second, third, or fourth year of the STIP, the procedures in paragraphs (b) through (d) of this section or expedited procedures that provide for the advancement of projects from the second, third, or fourth years of the STIP may be used, if agreed to by all parties involved in the selection process.

§ 450.224 Applicability of NEPA to statewide transportation plans and programs.

Any decision by the Secretary concerning a long-range statewide transportation plan or STIP developed through the processes provided for in 23 U.S.C. 135, 49 U.S.C. 5304, and this subpart shall not be considered to be a Federal action subject to review under the National Environmental Policy Act of 1969 (42 U.S.C. 4321 *et seq.*).

§ 450.226 Phase-in of new requirements.

(a) Prior to May 27, 2018, a State may adopt a long-range statewide transportation plan that has been developed using the SAFETEA–LU requirements or the provisions and requirements of this part. On or after May 27, 2018, a State may only adopt a long-range statewide transportation plan that it has developed according to the provisions and requirements of this part.

(b) Prior to May 27, 2018 (2 years after the publication date of this rule), FHWA/FTA may approve a STIP update or amendment that has been developed using the SAFETEA–LU requirements or the provisions and requirements of this part. On or after May 27, 2018, FHWA/FTA may only approve a STIP update or amendment that a State has developed according to the provisions and requirements of this part, regardless of when the State developed the STIP.

(c) On and after May 27, 2018 (2 years after the publication date of this rule), the FHWA and the FTA will take action on an updated or amended STIP developed under the provisions of this part, even if the State has not yet adopted a new long-range statewide transportation plan under the provisions of this part, as long as the underlying transportation planning process is consistent with the requirements in the MAP–21.

(d) On or after May 27, 2018, a State may make an administrative modification to a STIP that conforms to either the SAFETEA–LU requirements or to the provisions and requirements of this part.

(e) Two years from the effective date of each rule establishing performance measures under 23 U.S.C. 150(c), 49 U.S.C. 5326, or 49 U.S.C. 5329, FHWA/FTA will only approve an updated or amended STIP that is based on a statewide transportation planning process that meets the performance-based planning requirements in this part and in such a rule.

(f) Prior to 2 years from the effective date of each rule establishing performance measures under 23 U.S.C. 150(c), 49 U.S.C. 5326, or 49 U.S.C. 5329, a State may adopt a long-range statewide transportation plan that it has developed using the SAFETEA–LU requirements or the performance-based provisions and requirements of this part and in such a rule. Two years on or after the effective date of each rule establishing performance measures under 23 U.S.C. 150(c), 49 U.S.C. 5326, or 49 U.S.C. 5329, a State may only adopt a long-range statewide transportation plan that it has developed according to the performance-based provisions and requirements of this part and in such a rule.

[81 FR 34135, May 27, 2016, as amended at 81 FR 93470, Dec. 20, 2016; 82 FR 56543, Nov. 29, 2017]

Subpart C—Metropolitan Transportation Planning and Programming

§ 450.300 Purpose.

The purposes of this subpart are to implement the provisions of 23 U.S.C. 134, 23 U.S.C. 150, and 49 U.S.C. 5303, as amended, which:

(a) Set forth the national policy that the MPO designated for each urbanized area is to carry out a continuing, cooperative, and comprehensive performance-based multimodal transportation planning process, including the development of a metropolitan transportation plan and a TIP, that encourages and promotes the safe and efficient development, management, and operation of surface transportation systems to serve the mobility needs of people and freight (including accessible pedestrian walkways, bicycle transportation facilities, and intermodal facilities that support intercity transportation, including intercity buses and intercity bus facilities and commuter vanpool providers) fosters economic growth and development, and takes into consideration resiliency needs, while minimizing transportation-related fuel consumption and air pollution; and

(b) Encourages continued development and improvement of metropolitan transportation planning processes guided by the planning factors set forth in 23 U.S.C. 134(h) and 49 U.S.C. 5303(h).

[81 FR 34135, May 27, 2016, as amended at 81 FR 93470, Dec. 20, 2016; 82 FR 56543, Nov. 29, 2017]

§ 450.302 Applicability.

The provisions of this subpart are applicable to organizations and entities responsible for the transportation planning and programming processes in metropolitan planning areas.

§ 450.304 Definitions.

Except as otherwise provided in subpart A of this part, terms defined in 23 U.S.C. 101(a) and 49 U.S.C. 5302 are used in this subpart as so defined.

§ 450.306 Scope of the metropolitan transportation planning process.

(a) To accomplish the objectives in § 450.300 and § 450.306(b), metropolitan planning organizations designated under § 450.310, in cooperation with the

State and public transportation operators, shall develop long-range transportation plans and TIPs through a performance-driven, outcome-based approach to planning for metropolitan areas of the State.

(b) The metropolitan transportation planning process shall be continuous, cooperative, and comprehensive, and provide for consideration and implementation of projects, strategies, and services that will address the following factors:

(1) Support the economic vitality of the metropolitan area, especially by enabling global competitiveness, productivity, and efficiency;

(2) Increase the safety of the transportation system for motorized and non-motorized users;

(3) Increase the security of the transportation system for motorized and non-motorized users;

(4) Increase accessibility and mobility of people and freight;

(5) Protect and enhance the environment, promote energy conservation, improve the quality of life, and promote consistency between transportation improvements and State and local planned growth and economic development patterns;

(6) Enhance the integration and connectivity of the transportation system, across and between modes, for people and freight;

(7) Promote efficient system management and operation;

(8) Emphasize the preservation of the existing transportation system;

(9) Improve the resiliency and reliability of the transportation system and reduce or mitigate stormwater impacts of surface transportation; and

(10) Enhance travel and tourism.

(c) Consideration of the planning factors in paragraph (b) of this section shall be reflected, as appropriate, in the metropolitan transportation planning process. The degree of consideration and analysis of the factors should be based on the scale and complexity of many issues, including transportation system development, land use, employment, economic development, human and natural environment (including Section 4(f) properties as defined in 23 CFR 774.17), and housing and community development.

(d) *Performance-based approach.* (1) The metropolitan transportation planning process shall provide for the establishment and use of a performance-based approach to transportation decisionmaking to support the national goals described in 23 U.S.C. 150(b) and the general purposes described in 49 U.S.C. 5301(c).

(2) *Establishment of performance targets by metropolitan planning organizations.* (i) Each metropolitan planning organization shall establish performance targets that address the performance measures or standards established under 23 CFR part 490 (where applicable), 49 U.S.C. 5326(c), and 49 U.S.C. 5329(d) to use in tracking progress toward attainment of critical outcomes for the region of the metropolitan planning organization.

(ii) The selection of targets that address performance measures described in 23 U.S.C. 150(c) shall be in accordance with the appropriate target setting framework established at 23 CFR part 490, and shall be coordinated with the relevant State(s) to ensure consistency, to the maximum extent practicable.

(iii) The selection of performance targets that address performance measures described in 49 U.S.C. 5326(c) and 49 U.S.C. 5329(d) shall be coordinated, to the maximum extent practicable, with public transportation providers to ensure consistency with the performance targets that public transportation providers establish under 49 U.S.C. 5326(c) and 49 U.S.C. 5329(d).

(3) Each MPO shall establish the performance targets under paragraph (d)(2) of this section not later than 180 days after the date on which the relevant State or provider of public transportation establishes the performance targets.

(4) An MPO shall integrate in the metropolitan transportation planning process, directly or by reference, the goals, objectives, performance measures, and targets described in other State transportation plans and transportation processes, as well as any plans developed under 49 U.S.C. chapter 53 by providers of public transportation, required as part of a performance-based program including:

(i) The State asset management plan for the NHS, as defined in 23 U.S.C. 119(e) and the Transit Asset Management Plan, as discussed in 49 U.S.C. 5326;

(ii) Applicable portions of the HSIP, including the SHSP, as specified in 23 U.S.C. 148;

(iii) The Public Transportation Agency Safety Plan in 49 U.S.C. 5329(d);

(iv) Other safety and security planning and review processes, plans, and programs, as appropriate;

(v) The Congestion Mitigation and Air Quality Improvement Program performance plan in 23 U.S.C. 149(l), as applicable;

(vi) Appropriate (metropolitan) portions of the State Freight Plan (MAP–21 section 1118);

(vii) The congestion management process, as defined in 23 CFR 450.322, if applicable; and

(viii) Other State transportation plans and transportation processes required as part of a performance-based program.

(e) The failure to consider any factor specified in paragraph (b) or (d) of this section shall not be reviewable by any court under title 23 U.S.C., 49 U.S.C. Chapter 53, subchapter II of title 5, U.S.C. Chapter 5, or title 5 U.S.C. Chapter 7 in any matter affecting a metropolitan transportation plan, TIP, a project or strategy, or the certification of a metropolitan transportation planning process.

(f) An MPO shall carry out the metropolitan transportation planning process in coordination with the statewide transportation planning process required by 23 U.S.C. 135 and 49 U.S.C. 5304.

(g) The metropolitan transportation planning process shall (to the maximum extent practicable) be consistent with the development of applicable regional intelligent transportation systems (ITS) architectures, as defined in 23 CFR part 940.

(h) Preparation of the coordinated public transit-human services transportation plan, as required by 49 U.S.C. 5310, should be coordinated and consistent with the metropolitan transportation planning process.

(i) In an urbanized area not designated as a TMA that is an air quality attainment area, the MPO(s) may propose and submit to the FHWA and the FTA for approval a procedure for developing an abbreviated metropolitan transportation plan and TIP. In developing proposed simplified planning procedures, consideration shall be given to whether the abbreviated metropolitan transportation plan and TIP will achieve the purposes of 23 U.S.C. 134, 49 U.S.C. 5303, and this part, taking into account the complexity of the transportation problems in the area. The MPO shall develop simplified procedures in cooperation with the State(s) and public transportation operator(s).

[81 FR 34135, May 27, 2016, as amended at 81 FR 93470, Dec. 20, 2016; 82 FR 56543, Nov. 29, 2017]

§ 450.308 Funding for transportation planning and unified planning work programs.

(a) Funds provided under 23 U.S.C. 104(d), 49 U.S.C. 5305(d), and 49 U.S.C. 5307, are available to MPOs to accomplish activities described in this subpart. At the State's option, funds provided under 23 U.S.C. 104(b)(2) and 23 U.S.C. 505 may also be provided to MPOs for metropolitan transportation planning. At the option of the State and operators of public transportation, funds provided under 49 U.S.C. 5305(e) may also be provided to MPOs for activities that support metropolitan transportation planning. In addition, an MPO serving an urbanized area with a population over 200,000, as designated by the Bureau of the Census, may at its discretion use funds sub-allocated under 23 U.S.C. 133(d)(4) for metropolitan transportation planning activities.

(b) An MPO shall document metropolitan transportation planning activities performed with funds provided under title 23 U.S.C. and title 49 U.S.C. Chapter 53 in a unified planning work program (UPWP) or simplified statement of work in accordance with the provisions of this section and 23 CFR part 420.

(c) Except as provided in paragraph (d) of this section, each MPO, in cooperation with the State(s) and public transportation operator(s), shall develop a UPWP that includes a discussion of the planning priorities facing the MPA. The UPWP shall identify work proposed for the next 1- or 2-year period by major activity and task (including activities that address the planning factors in § 450.306(b)), in sufficient detail to indicate who (e.g., MPO, State, public transportation operator, local government, or consultant) will perform the work, the schedule for completing the work, the resulting products, the proposed funding by activity/task, and a summary of the total amounts and sources of Federal and matching funds.

(d) With the prior approval of the State and the FHWA and the FTA, an MPO in an area not designated as a TMA may prepare a simplified statement of work, in cooperation with the State(s) and the public transportation operator(s), in lieu of a UPWP. A simplified statement of work shall include a description of the major activities to be performed during the next 1- or 2-year period, who (e.g., State, MPO, public transportation operator, local government, or consultant) will perform the work, the resulting products, and a summary of the total amounts and sources of Federal and matching funds. If a simplified statement of work is used, it may be submitted as part of the State's planning work program, in accordance with 23 CFR part 420.

(e) Arrangements may be made with the FHWA and the FTA to combine the UPWP or simplified statement of work with the work program(s) for other Federal planning funds.

(f) Administrative requirements for UPWPs and simplified statements of work are contained in 23 CFR part 420 and FTA Circular C8100, as amended (Program Guidance for Metropolitan Planning and State Planning and Research Program Grants).

§ 450.310 Metropolitan planning organization designation and redesignation.

(a) To carry out the metropolitan transportation planning process under this subpart, an MPO shall be designated for each urbanized area with a population of more than 50,000 individuals (as determined by the Bureau of the Census).

(b) MPO designation shall be made by agreement between the Governor and units of general purpose local government that together represent at least 75 percent of the affected population (including the largest incorporated city, based on population, as named by the Bureau of the Census) or in accordance with procedures established by applicable State or local law.

(c) The FHWA and the FTA shall identify as a TMA each urbanized area with a population of over 200,000 individuals, as defined by the Bureau of the Census. The FHWA and the FTA shall also designate any urbanized area as a TMA on the request of the Governor and the MPO designated for that area.

(d) TMA structure:

(1) Not later than October 1, 2014, each metropolitan planning organization that serves a designated TMA shall consist of:

(i) Local elected officials;

(ii) Officials of public agencies that administer or operate major modes of transportation in the metropolitan area, including representation by providers of public transportation; and

(iii) Appropriate State officials.

(2) An MPO may be restructured to meet the requirements of this paragraph (d) without undertaking a redesignation.

(3) *Representation.* (i) Designation or selection of officials or representatives under paragraph (d)(1) of this section shall be determined by the MPO according to the bylaws or enabling statute of the organization.

(ii) Subject to the bylaws or enabling statute of the MPO, a representative of a provider of public transportation may also serve as a representative of a local municipality.

(iii) An official described in paragraph (d)(1)(ii) shall have responsibilities, actions, duties, voting rights, and any other authority commensurate with other officials described in paragraph (d)(1) of this section.

(4) Nothing in this section shall be construed to interfere with the authority, under any State law in effect on December 18, 1991, of a public agency with multimodal transportation responsibilities—

(i) To develop the plans and TIPs for adoption by an MPO; and

(ii) To develop long-range capital plans, coordinate transit services and projects, and carry out other activities pursuant to State law.

(e) To the extent possible, only one MPO shall be designated for each urbanized area or group of contiguous urbanized areas. More than one MPO may be designated to serve an urbanized area only if the Governor(s) and the existing MPO, if applicable, determine that the size and complexity of the urbanized area-make designation of more than one MPO appropriate. In those cases where two or more MPOs serve the same urbanized area, the MPOs shall establish official, written agreements that clearly identify areas of coordination, and the division of transportation planning responsibilities among the MPOs.

(f) Nothing in this subpart shall be deemed to prohibit an MPO from using the staff resources of other agencies, non-profit organizations, or contractors to carry out selected elements of the metropolitan transportation planning process.

(g) An MPO designation shall remain in effect until an official redesignation has been made in accordance with this section.

(h) An existing MPO may be redesignated only by agreement between the Governor and units of general purpose local government that together represent at least 75 percent of the existing metropolitan planning area population (including the largest incorporated city, based on population, as named by the Bureau of the Census).

(i) For the purposes of redesignation, units of general purpose local government may be defined as elected officials from each unit of general purpose local government located within the metropolitan planning area served by the existing MPO.

(j) Redesignation of an MPO (in accordance with the provisions of this section) is required whenever the existing MPO proposes to make:

(1) A substantial change in the proportion of voting members on the existing MPO representing the largest incorporated city, other units of general purpose local government served by the MPO, and the State(s); or

(2) A substantial change in the decisionmaking authority or responsibility of the MPO, or in decisionmaking procedures established under MPO by-laws.

(k) Redesignation of an MPO serving a multistate metropolitan planning area requires agreement between the Governors of each State served by the existing MPO and units of general purpose local government that together represent at least 75 percent of the existing metropolitan planning area population (including the largest incorporated city, based on population, as named by the Bureau of the Census).

(l) The following changes to an MPO do not require a redesignation (as long as they do not trigger a substantial change as described in paragraph (j) of this section):

(1) The identification of a new urbanized area (as determined by the Bureau of the Census) within an existing metropolitan planning area;

(2) Adding members to the MPO that represent new units of general purpose local government resulting from expansion of the metropolitan planning area;

(3) Adding members to satisfy the specific membership requirements described in paragraph (d) of this section for an MPO that serves a TMA; or

(4) Periodic rotation of members representing units of general-purpose local government, as established under MPO by-laws.

(m) Each Governor with responsibility for a portion of a multistate metropolitan area and the appropriate MPOs shall, to the extent practicable, provide coordinated transportation planning for the entire MPA. The consent of Congress is granted to any two or more States to:

(1) Enter into agreements or compacts, not in conflict with any law of the United States, for cooperative efforts and mutual assistance in support of activities authorized under 23 U.S.C. 134 and 49 U.S.C. 5303 as the activities pertain to interstate areas and localities within the States; and

(2) Establish such agencies, joint or otherwise, as the States may determine desirable for making the agreements and compacts effective.

[81 FR 34135, May 27, 2016, as amended at 81 FR 93470, Dec. 20, 2016; 82 FR 56543, Nov. 29, 2017]

§ 450.312 Metropolitan Planning Area boundaries.

(a) The boundaries of a metropolitan planning area (MPA) shall be determined by agreement between the MPO and the Governor.

(1) At a minimum, the MPA boundaries shall encompass the entire existing urbanized area (as defined by the Bureau of the Census) plus the contiguous area expected to become urbanized within a 20-year forecast period for the metropolitan transportation plan.

(2) The MPA boundaries may be further expanded to encompass the entire metropolitan statistical area or combined statistical area, as defined by the Office of Management and Budget.

(b) An MPO that serves an urbanized area designated as a nonattainment area for ozone or carbon monoxide under the Clean Air Act (42 U.S.C. 7401 *et seq.*) as of August 10, 2005, shall retain the MPA boundary that existed on August 10, 2005. The MPA boundaries for such MPOs may only be adjusted by agreement of the Governor and the affected MPO in accordance with the redesignation procedures described in § 450.310(h). The MPA boundary for an MPO that serves an urbanized area designated as a nonattainment area for ozone or carbon monoxide under the Clean Air Act (42 U.S.C. 7401 *et seq.*) after August 10, 2005, may be established to coincide with the designated boundaries of the ozone and/or carbon monoxide nonattainment area, in accordance with the requirements in § 450.310(b).

(c) An MPA boundary may encompass more than one urbanized area.

(d) MPA boundaries may be established to coincide with the geography of regional economic development and growth forecasting areas.

(e) Identification of new urbanized areas within an existing metropolitan planning area by the Bureau of the Census shall not require redesignation of the existing MPO.

(f) Where the boundaries of the urbanized area or MPA extend across two or more States, the Governors with responsibility for a portion of the multistate area, the appropriate MPO(s), and the public transportation operator(s) are strongly encouraged to coordinate transportation planning for the entire multistate area.

(g) The MPA boundaries shall not overlap with each other.

(h) Where part of an urbanized area served by one MPO extends into an adjacent MPA, the MPOs shall, at a minimum, establish written agreements that clearly identify areas of coordination and the division of transportation planning responsibilities among and between the MPOs. Alternatively, the MPOs may adjust their existing boundaries so that the entire urbanized area lies within only one MPA. Boundary adjustments that change the composition of the MPO may require redesignation of one or more such MPOs.

(i) The MPO (in cooperation with the State and public transportation operator(s)) shall review the MPA boundaries after each Census to determine if existing MPA boundaries meet the minimum statutory requirements for new and updated urbanized area(s), and shall adjust them as necessary. As appropriate, additional adjustments should be made to reflect the most comprehensive boundary to foster an effective planning process that ensures connectivity between modes, improves access to modal systems, and promotes efficient overall transportation investment strategies.

(j) Following MPA boundary approval by the MPO and the Governor, the MPA boundary descriptions shall be provided for informational purposes to the FHWA and the FTA. The MPA boundary descriptions shall be submitted either as a geo-spatial database or described in sufficient detail to enable the boundaries to be accurately delineated on a map.

[82 FR 56543, Nov. 29, 2017]

§ 450.314 Metropolitan planning agreements.

(a) The MPO, the State(s), and the providers of public transportation shall cooperatively determine their mutual responsibilities in carrying out the metropolitan transportation planning process. These responsibilities shall be clearly identified in written agreements among the MPO, the State(s), and the providers of public transportation serving the MPA. To the extent possible, a single agreement between all responsible parties should be developed. The written agreement(s) shall include specific provisions for the development of financial plans that support the metropolitan transportation plan (see § 450.324) and the metropolitan TIP (see § 450.326), and development of the annual listing of obligated projects (see § 450.334).

(b) The MPO, the State(s), and the providers of public transportation should periodically review and update the agreement, as appropriate, to reflect effective changes.

(c) If the MPA does not include the entire nonattainment or maintenance area, there shall be a written agreement among the State department of transportation, State air quality agency, affected local agencies, and the MPO describing the process for cooperative planning and analysis of all projects outside the MPA within the nonattainment or maintenance area. The agreement must also indicate how the total transportation-related emissions for the nonattainment or maintenance area, including areas outside the MPA, will be treated for the purposes of determining conformity in accordance with the EPA's transportation conformity regulations (40 CFR part 93, subpart A). The agreement shall address policy mechanisms for resolving conflicts concerning transportation-related emissions that may arise between the MPA and the portion of the nonattainment or maintenance area outside the MPA.

(d) In nonattainment or maintenance areas, if the MPO is not the designated agency for air quality planning under section 174 of the Clean Air Act (42 U.S.C. 7504), there shall be a written agreement between the MPO and the designated air quality planning agency describing their respective roles and responsibilities for air quality related transportation planning.

(e) If more than one MPO has been designated to serve an urbanized area there shall be a written agreement among the MPOs, the State(s), and the public transportation operator(s) describing how the metropolitan transportation planning processes will be coordinated to assure the development of consistent metropolitan transportation plans and TIPs across the MPA boundaries, particularly in cases in which a proposed transportation investment extends across the boundaries of more than one MPA. If any part of the urbanized area is a nonattainment or maintenance area, the agreement also shall include State and local air quality agencies. The metropolitan transportation planning processes for affected MPOs should, to the maximum extent possible, reflect coordinated data collection, analysis, and planning assumptions across the MPAs. Alternatively, a single metropolitan transportation plan and/or TIP for the entire urbanized area may be developed jointly by the MPOs in cooperation with their respective planning partners. Coordination efforts and outcomes shall be documented in subsequent transmittals of the UPWP and other planning products, including the metropolitan transportation plan and TIP, to the State(s), the FHWA, and the FTA.

(f) Where the boundaries of the urbanized area or MPA extend across two or more States, the Governors with responsibility for a portion of the multistate area, the appropriate MPO(s), and the public transportation operator(s) shall coordinate transportation planning for the entire multistate area. States involved in such multistate transportation planning may:

(1) Enter into agreements or compacts, not in conflict with any law of the United States, for cooperative efforts and mutual assistance in support of activities authorized under this section as the activities pertain to interstate areas and localities within the States; and

(2) Establish such agencies, joint or otherwise, as the States may determine desirable for making the agreements and compacts effective.

(g) If part of an urbanized area that has been designated as a TMA overlaps into an adjacent MPA serving an urbanized area that is not designated as a TMA, the adjacent urbanized area shall not be treated as a TMA. However, a written agreement shall be established between the MPOs with MPA boundaries, including a portion of the TMA, which clearly identifies the roles and responsibilities of each MPO in meeting specific TMA requirements (e.g., congestion management process, Surface Transportation Program funds suballocated to the urbanized area over 200,000 population, and project selection).

(h)(1) The MPO(s), State(s), and the providers of public transportation shall jointly agree upon and develop specific written provisions for cooperatively developing and sharing information related to transportation performance data, the selection of performance targets, the reporting of performance targets, the reporting of performance to be used in tracking progress toward attainment of critical outcomes for the region of the MPO (see § 450.306(d)), and the collection of data for the State asset management plan for the NHS for each of the following circumstances:

(i) When one MPO serves an urbanized area;

(ii) When more than one MPO serves an urbanized area; and

(iii) When an urbanized area that has been designated as a TMA overlaps into an adjacent MPA serving an urbanized area that is not a TMA.

(2) These provisions shall be documented either:

(i) As part of the metropolitan planning agreements required under paragraphs (a), (e), and (g) of this section; or

(ii) Documented in some other means outside of the metropolitan planning agreements as determined cooperatively by the MPO(s), State(s), and providers of public transportation.

[82 FR 56544, Nov. 29, 2017]

§ 450.316 Interested parties, participation, and consultation.

(a) The MPO shall develop and use a documented participation plan that defines a process for providing individuals, affected public agencies, representatives of public transportation employees, public ports, freight shippers, providers of freight transportation services, private providers of transportation (including intercity bus operators, employer-based commuting programs, such as carpool program, vanpool program, transit benefit program, parking cash-out program, shuttle program, or telework program), representatives of users of public transportation, representatives of users of pedestrian walkways and bicycle transportation facilities, representatives of the disabled, and other interested parties with reasonable opportunities to be involved in the metropolitan transportation planning process.

(1) The MPO shall develop the participation plan in consultation with all interested parties and shall, at a minimum, describe explicit procedures, strategies, and desired outcomes for:

(i) Providing adequate public notice of public participation activities and time for public review and comment at key decision points, including a reasonable opportunity to comment on the proposed metropolitan transportation plan and the TIP;

(ii) Providing timely notice and reasonable access to information about transportation issues and processes;

(iii) Employing visualization techniques to describe metropolitan transportation plans and TIPs;

(iv) Making public information (technical information and meeting notices) available in electronically accessible formats and means, such as the World Wide Web;

(v) Holding any public meetings at convenient and accessible locations and times;

(vi) Demonstrating explicit consideration and response to public input received during the development of the metropolitan transportation plan and the TIP;

(vii) Seeking out and considering the needs of those traditionally underserved by existing transportation systems, such as low-income and minority households, who may face challenges accessing employment and other services;

(viii) Providing an additional opportunity for public comment, if the final metropolitan transportation plan or TIP differs significantly from the version that was made available for public comment by the MPO and raises new material issues that interested parties could not reasonably have foreseen from the public involvement efforts;

(ix) Coordinating with the statewide transportation planning public involvement and consultation processes under subpart B of this part; and

(x) Periodically reviewing the effectiveness of the procedures and strategies contained in the participation plan to ensure a full and open participation process.

(2) When significant written and oral comments are received on the draft metropolitan transportation plan and TIP (including the financial plans) as a result of the participation process in this section or the interagency consultation process required under the EPA transportation conformity regulations (40 CFR part 93, subpart A), a summary, analysis, and report on the disposition of comments shall be made as part of the final metropolitan transportation plan and TIP.

(3) A minimum public comment period of 45 calendar days shall be provided before the initial or revised participation plan is adopted by the MPO. Copies of the approved participation plan shall be provided to the FHWA and the FTA for informational purposes and shall be posted on the World Wide Web, to the maximum extent practicable.

(b) In developing metropolitan transportation plans and TIPs, the MPO should consult with agencies and officials responsible for other planning activities within the MPA that are affected by transportation (including State and local planned growth, economic development, tourism, natural disaster risk reduction, environmental protection, airport operations, or freight movements) or coordinate its planning process (to the maximum extent practicable) with such planning activities. In addition, the MPO shall develop the metropolitan transportation plans and TIPs with due consideration of other related planning activities within the metropolitan area, and the process shall provide for the design and delivery of transportation services within the area that are provided by:

(1) Recipients of assistance under title 49 U.S.C. Chapter 53;

(2) Governmental agencies and nonprofit organizations (including representatives of the agencies and organizations) that receive Federal assistance from a source other than the U.S. Department of Transportation to provide non-emergency transportation services; and

(3) Recipients of assistance under 23 U.S.C. 201–204.

(c) When the MPA includes Indian Tribal lands, the MPO shall appropriately involve the Indian Tribal government(s) in the development of the metropolitan transportation plan and the TIP.

(d) When the MPA includes Federal public lands, the MPO shall appropriately involve the Federal land management agencies in the development of the metropolitan transportation plan and the TIP.

(e) MPOs shall, to the extent practicable, develop a documented process(es) that outlines roles, responsibilities, and key decision points for consulting with other governments and agencies, as defined in paragraphs (b), (c), and (d) of this section, which may be included in the agreement(s) developed under §450.314.

[81 FR 34135, May 27, 2016, as amended at 81 FR 93473, Dec. 20, 2016; 82 FR 56544, Nov. 29, 2017]

§450.318 Transportation planning studies and project development.

(a) Pursuant to section 1308 of the Transportation Equity Act for the 21st Century, TEA–21 (Pub. L. 105–178), an MPO(s), State(s), or public transportation operator(s) may undertake a multimodal, systems-level corridor or subarea planning study as part of the metropolitan transportation planning process. To the extent practicable, development of these transportation planning studies shall involve consultation with, or joint efforts among, the MPO(s), State(s), and/or public transportation operator(s). The results or decisions of these transportation planning studies may be used as part of the overall project development process consistent with the National Environmental Policy Act (NEPA) of 1969 (42 U.S.C. 4321 *et seq.*) and associated implementing regulations (23 CFR part 771 and 40 CFR parts 1500–1508). Specifically, these corridor or subarea studies may result in producing any of the following for a proposed transportation project:

(1) Purpose and need or goals and objective statement(s);

(2) General travel corridor and/or general mode(s) definition (e.g., highway, transit, or a highway/transit combination);

(3) Preliminary screening of alternatives and elimination of unreasonable alternatives;

(4) Basic description of the environmental setting; and/or

(5) Preliminary identification of environmental impacts and environmental mitigation.

(b) Publicly available documents or other source material produced by, or in support of, the transportation planning process described in this subpart may be incorporated directly or by reference into subsequent NEPA documents, in accordance with 40 CFR 1502.21, if:

(1) The NEPA lead agencies agree that such incorporation will aid in establishing or evaluating the purpose and need for the Federal action, reasonable alternatives, cumulative or other impacts on the human and natural environment, or mitigation of these impacts; and

(2) The systems-level, corridor, or subarea planning study is conducted with:

(i) Involvement of interested State, local, Tribal, and Federal agencies;

(ii) Public review;

(iii) Reasonable opportunity to comment during the metropolitan transportation planning process and development of the corridor or subarea planning study;

(iv) Documentation of relevant decisions in a form that is identifiable and available for review during the NEPA scoping process and can be appended to or referenced in the NEPA document; and

(v) The review of the FHWA and the FTA, as appropriate.

(c) By agreement of the NEPA lead agencies, the above integration may be accomplished through tiering (as described in 40 CFR 1502.20), incorporating the subarea or corridor planning study into the draft Environmental Impact Statement (EIS) or Environmental Assessment, or other means that the NEPA lead agencies deem appropriate.

(d) Additional information to further explain the linkages between the transportation planning and project development/NEPA processes is contained in Appendix A to this part, including an explanation that it is non-binding guidance material. The guidance in Appendix A applies only to paragraphs (a)–(c) in this section.

(e) In addition to the process for incorporation directly or by reference outlined in paragraph (b) of this section, an additional authority for integrating planning products into the environmental review process exists in 23 U.S.C. 168. As provided in 23 U.S.C. 168(f):

(1) The statutory authority in 23 U.S.C. 168 shall not be construed to limit in any way the continued use of processes established under other parts of this section or under an authority established outside of this part, and the use of one of the processes in this section does not preclude the subsequent use of another process in this section or an authority outside of this part.

(2) The statute does not restrict the initiation of the environmental review process during planning.

§ 450.320 Development of programmatic mitigation plans.

(a) An MPO may utilize the optional framework in this section to develop programmatic mitigation plans as part of the metropolitan transportation planning process to address the potential environmental impacts of future transportation projects. The MPO, in consultation with the FHWA and/or the FTA and with the agency or agencies with jurisdiction and special expertise over the resources being addressed in the plan, will determine:

(1) *Scope.* (i) An MPO may develop a programmatic mitigation plan on a local, regional, ecosystem, watershed, statewide or similar scale.

(ii) The plan may encompass multiple environmental resources within a defined geographic area(s) or may focus on a specific type(s) of resource(s) such as aquatic resources, parkland, or wildlife habitat.

(iii) The plan may address or consider impacts from all projects in a defined geographic area(s) or may focus on a specific type(s) of project(s).

(2) *Contents*. The programmatic mitigation plan may include:

(i) An assessment of the existing condition of natural and human environmental resources within the area covered by the plan, including an assessment of historic and recent trends and/ or any potential threats to those resources.

(ii) An identification of economic, social, and natural and human environmental resources within the geographic area that may be impacted and considered for mitigation. Examples of these resources include wetlands, streams, rivers, stormwater, parklands, cultural resources, historic resources, farmlands, archeological resources, threatened or endangered species, and critical habitat. This may include the identification of areas of high conservation concern or value and thus worthy of avoidance.

(iii) An inventory of existing or planned environmental resource banks for the impacted resource categories such as wetland, stream, stormwater, habitat, species, and an inventory of federally, State, or locally approved in-lieu-of-fee programs.

(iv) An assessment of potential opportunities to improve the overall quality of the identified environmental resources through strategic mitigation for impacts of transportation projects which may include the prioritization of parcels or areas for acquisition and/or potential resource banking sites.

(v) An adoption or development of standard measures or operating procedures for mitigating certain types of impacts; establishment of parameters for determining or calculating appropriate mitigation for certain types of impacts, such as mitigation ratios, or criteria for determining appropriate mitigation sites.

(vi) Adaptive management procedures, such as protocols or procedures that involve monitoring actual impacts against predicted impacts over time and adjusting mitigation measures in response to information gathered through the monitoring.

(vii) Acknowledgement of specific statutory or regulatory requirements that must be satisfied when determining appropriate mitigation for certain types of resources.

(b) A MPO may adopt a programmatic mitigation plan developed pursuant to paragraph (a), or developed pursuant to an alternative process as provided for in paragraph (f) of this section through the following process:

(1) Consult with each agency with jurisdiction over the environmental resources considered in the programmatic mitigation plan;

(2) Make available a draft of the programmatic mitigation plan for review and comment by appropriate environmental resource agencies and the public;

(3) Consider comments received from such agencies and the public on the draft plan; and

(4) Address such comments in the final programmatic mitigation plan.

(c) A programmatic mitigation plan may be integrated with other plans, including watershed plans, ecosystem plans, species recovery plans, growth management plans, State Wildlife Action Plans, and land use plans.

(d) If a programmatic mitigation plan has been adopted pursuant to paragraph (b), any Federal agency responsible for environmental reviews, permits, or approvals for a transportation project shall give substantial weight to the recommendations in the programmatic mitigation plan when carrying out its responsibilities under the National Environmental Policy Act of 1969 (42 U.S.C. 4321 *et seq.*) (NEPA) or other Federal environmental law.

(e) Nothing in this section limits the use of programmatic approaches for reviews under NEPA.

(f) Nothing in this section prohibits the development, as part of or separate from the transportation planning process, of a programmatic mitigation plan independent of the framework described in paragraph (a) of this section. Further, nothing in this section prohibits the adoption of a programmatic mitigation plan in the metropolitan planning process that was developed under another authority, independent of the framework described in paragraph (a).

§ 450.322 Congestion management process in transportation management areas.

(a) The transportation planning process in a TMA shall address congestion management through a process that provides for safe and effective integrated management and operation of the multimodal transportation system, based on a cooperatively developed and implemented metropolitan-wide strategy, of new and existing transportation facilities eligible for funding under title 23 U.S.C. and title 49 U.S.C. Chapter 53 through the use of travel demand reduction (including intercity bus operators, employer-based commuting programs such as a carpool program, vanpool program, transit benefit program, parking cash-out program, shuttle program, or telework program), job access projects, and operational management strategies.

(b) The development of a congestion management process should result in multimodal system performance measures and strategies that can be reflected in the metropolitan transportation plan and the TIP.

(c) The level of system performance deemed acceptable by State and local transportation officials may vary by type of transportation facility, geographic location (metropolitan area or subarea), and/or time of day. In addition, consideration should be given to strategies that manage demand, reduce single occupant vehicle (SOV) travel, improve transportation system management and operations, and improve efficient service integration within and across modes, including highway, transit, passenger and freight rail operations, and non-motorized transport. Where the addition of general purpose lanes is determined to be an appropriate congestion management strategy, explicit consideration is to be given to the incorporation of appropriate features into the SOV project to facilitate future demand management strategies and operational improvements that will maintain the functional integrity and safety of those lanes.

(d) The congestion management process shall be developed, established, and implemented as part of the metropolitan transportation planning process that includes coordination with transportation system management and operations activities. The congestion management process shall include:

(1) Methods to monitor and evaluate the performance of the multimodal transportation system, identify the underlying causes of recurring and nonrecurring congestion, identify and evaluate alternative strategies, provide information supporting the implementation of actions, and evaluate the effectiveness of implemented actions;

(2) Definition of congestion management objectives and appropriate performance measures to assess the extent of congestion and support the evaluation of the effectiveness of congestion reduction and mobility enhancement strategies for the movement of people and goods. Since levels of acceptable system performance may vary among local communities, performance measures should be tailored to the specific needs of the area and established cooperatively by the State(s), affected MPO(s), and local officials in consultation with the operators of major modes of transportation in the coverage area, including providers of public transportation;

(3) Establishment of a coordinated program for data collection and system performance monitoring to define the extent and duration of congestion, to contribute in determining the causes of congestion, and evaluate the efficiency and effectiveness of implemented actions. To the extent possible, this data collection program should be coordinated with existing data sources (including archived operational/ITS data) and coordinated with operations managers in the metropolitan area;

(4) Identification and evaluation of the anticipated performance and expected benefits of appropriate congestion management strategies that will contribute to the more effective use and improved safety of existing and future transportation systems based on the established performance measures. The following categories of strategies, or combinations of strategies, are some examples of what should be appropriately considered for each area:

(i) Demand management measures, including growth management, and congestion pricing;

(ii) Traffic operational improvements;

(iii) Public transportation improvements;

(iv) ITS technologies as related to the regional ITS architecture; and

(v) Where necessary, additional system capacity.

(5) Identification of an implementation schedule, implementation responsibilities, and possible funding sources for each strategy (or combination of strategies) proposed for implementation; and

(6) Implementation of a process for periodic assessment of the effectiveness of implemented strategies, in terms of the area's established performance measures. The results of this evaluation shall be provided to decision makers and the public to provide guidance on selection of effective strategies for future implementation.

(e) In a TMA designated as nonattainment area for ozone or carbon monoxide pursuant to the Clean Air Act, Federal funds may not be programmed for any project that will result in a significant increase in the carrying capacity for SOVs (*i.e.*, a new general purpose highway on a new location or adding general purpose lanes, with the exception of safety improvements or the elimination of bottlenecks), unless the project is addressed through a congestion management process meeting the requirements of this section.

(f) In TMAs designated as nonattainment for ozone or carbon monoxide, the congestion management process shall provide an appropriate analysis of reasonable (including multimodal) travel demand reduction and operational management strategies for the corridor in which a project that will result in a significant increase in capacity for SOVs (as described in paragraph (d) of this section) is proposed to be advanced with Federal funds. If the analysis demonstrates that travel demand reduction and operational management strategies cannot fully satisfy the need for additional capacity in the corridor and additional SOV capacity is warranted, then the congestion management process shall identify all reasonable strategies to manage the SOV facility safely and effectively (or to facilitate its management in the future). Other travel demand reduction and operational management strategies appropriate for the corridor, but not appropriate for incorporation into the SOV facility itself, shall also be identified through the congestion management process. All identified reasonable travel demand reduction and operational management strategies shall be incorporated into the SOV project or committed to by the State and MPO for implementation.

(g) State laws, rules, or regulations pertaining to congestion management systems or programs may constitute the congestion management process, if the FHWA and the FTA find that the State laws, rules, or regulations are consistent with, and fulfill the intent of, the purposes of 23 U.S.C. 134 and 49 U.S.C. 5303.

(h) *Congestion management plan.* A MPO serving a TMA may develop a plan that includes projects and strategies that will be considered in the TIP of such MPO.

(1) Such plan shall:

(i) Develop regional goals to reduce vehicle miles traveled during peak commuting hours and improve transportation connections between areas with high job concentration and areas with high concentrations of low-income households;

(ii) Identify existing public transportation services, employer based commuter programs, and other existing transportation services that support access to jobs in the region; and

(iii) Identify proposed projects and programs to reduce congestion and increase job access opportunities.

(2) In developing the congestion management plan, an MPO shall consult with employers, private and nonprofit providers of public transportation, transportation management organizations, and organizations that provide job access reverse commute projects or job-related services to low-income individuals.

§ 450.324 Development and content of the metropolitan transportation plan.

(a) The metropolitan transportation planning process shall include the development of a transportation plan addressing no less than a 20-year planning horizon as of the effective date. In formulating the transportation plan, the MPO shall consider factors described in § 450.306 as the factors relate to a minimum 20-year forecast period. In nonattainment and maintenance areas, the effective date of the transportation plan shall be the date of a conformity determination issued by the FHWA and the FTA. In attainment areas, the effective date of the transportation plan shall be its date of adoption by the MPO.

(b) The transportation plan shall include both long-range and short-range strategies/actions that provide for the development of an integrated multimodal transportation system (including accessible pedestrian walkways and bicycle transportation facilities) to facilitate the safe and efficient movement of people and goods in addressing current and future transportation demand.

(c) The MPO shall review and update the transportation plan at least every 4 years in air quality nonattainment and maintenance areas and at least every 5 years in attainment areas to confirm the transportation plan's validity and consistency with current and forecasted transportation and land use conditions and trends and to extend the forecast period to at least a 20-year planning horizon. In addition, the MPO may revise the transportation plan at any time using the procedures in this section without a requirement to extend the horizon year. The MPO shall approve the transportation plan (and any revisions) and submit it for information purposes to the Governor. Copies of any updated or revised transportation plans must be provided to the FHWA and the FTA.

(d) In metropolitan areas that are in nonattainment for ozone or carbon monoxide, the MPO shall coordinate the development of the metropolitan transportation plan with the process for developing transportation control measures (TCMs) in a State Implementation Plan (SIP).

(e) The MPO, the State(s), and the public transportation operator(s) shall validate data used in preparing other existing modal plans for providing input to the transportation plan. In updating the transportation plan, the MPO shall base the update on the latest available estimates and assumptions for population, land use, travel, employment, congestion, and economic activity. The MPO shall approve transportation plan contents and supporting analyses produced by a transportation plan update.

(f) The metropolitan transportation plan shall, at a minimum, include:

(1) The current and projected transportation demand of persons and goods in the metropolitan planning area over the period of the transportation plan;

(2) Existing and proposed transportation facilities (including major roadways, public transportation facilities, intercity bus facilities, multimodal and intermodal facilities, nonmotorized transportation facilities (e.g., pedestrian walkways and bicycle facilities), and intermodal connectors) that should function as an integrated metropolitan transportation system, giving emphasis to those facilities that serve important national and regional transportation functions over the period of the transportation plan.

(3) A description of the performance measures and performance targets used in assessing the performance of the transportation system in accordance with § 450.306(d).

(4) A system performance report and subsequent updates evaluating the condition and performance of the transportation system with respect to the performance targets described in § 450.306(d), including—

(i) Progress achieved by the metropolitan planning organization in meeting the performance targets in comparison with system performance recorded in previous reports, including baseline data; and

(ii) For metropolitan planning organizations that voluntarily elect to develop multiple scenarios, an analysis of how the preferred scenario has improved the conditions and performance of the transportation system and how changes in local policies and investments have impacted the costs necessary to achieve the identified performance targets.

(5) Operational and management strategies to improve the performance of existing transportation facilities to relieve vehicular congestion and maximize the safety and mobility of people and goods;

(6) Consideration of the results of the congestion management process in TMAs that meet the requirements of this subpart, including the identification of SOV projects that result from a congestion management process in TMAs that are nonattainment for ozone or carbon monoxide.

(7) Assessment of capital investment and other strategies to preserve the existing and projected future metropolitan transportation infrastructure, provide for multimodal capacity increases based on regional priorities and needs, and reduce the vulnerability of the existing transportation infrastructure to natural disasters. The metropolitan transportation plan may consider projects and strategies that address areas or corridors where current or projected congestion threatens the efficient functioning of key elements of the metropolitan area's transportation system.

(8) Transportation and transit enhancement activities, including consideration of the role that intercity buses may play in reducing congestion, pollution, and energy consumption in a cost-effective manner and strategies and investments that preserve and enhance intercity bus systems, including systems that are privately owned and operated, and including transportation alternatives, as defined in 23 U.S.C. 101(a), and associated transit improvements, as described in 49 U.S.C. 5302(a), as appropriate;

(9) Design concept and design scope descriptions of all existing and proposed transportation facilities in sufficient detail, regardless of funding source, in nonattainment and maintenance areas for conformity determinations under the EPA's transportation conformity regulations (40 CFR part 93, subpart A). In all areas (regardless of air quality designation), all proposed improvements shall be described in sufficient detail to develop cost estimates;

(10) A discussion of types of potential environmental mitigation activities and potential areas to carry out these activities, including activities that may have the greatest potential to restore and maintain the environmental functions affected by the metropolitan transportation plan. The discussion may focus on policies, programs, or strategies, rather than at the project level. The MPO shall develop the discussion in consultation with applicable Federal, State, and Tribal land management, wildlife, and regulatory agencies. The MPO may establish reasonable timeframes for performing this consultation;

(11) A financial plan that demonstrates how the adopted transportation plan can be implemented.

(i) For purposes of transportation system operations and maintenance, the financial plan shall contain system-level estimates of costs and revenue sources that are reasonably expected to be available to adequately operate and maintain the Federal-aid highways (as defined by 23 U.S.C. 101(a)(5)) and public transportation (as defined by title 49 U.S.C. Chapter 53).

(ii) For the purpose of developing the metropolitan transportation plan, the MPO(s), public transportation operator(s), and State shall cooperatively develop estimates of funds that will be available to support metropolitan transportation plan implementation, as required under § 450.314(a). All necessary financial resources from public and private sources that are reasonably expected to be made available to carry out the transportation plan shall be identified.

(iii) The financial plan shall include recommendations on any additional financing strategies to fund projects and programs included in the metropolitan transportation plan. In the case of new funding sources, strategies for ensuring their availability shall be identified. The financial plan may include an assessment of the appropriateness of innovative finance techniques (for example, tolling, pricing, bonding, public private partnerships, or other strategies) as revenue sources for projects in the plan.

(iv) In developing the financial plan, the MPO shall take into account all projects and strategies proposed for funding under title 23 U.S.C., title 49 U.S.C. Chapter 53 or with other Federal funds; State assistance; local sources; and private participation. Revenue and cost estimates that support the metropolitan transportation plan must use an inflation rate(s) to reflect "year of expenditure dollars," based on reasonable financial principles and information, developed cooperatively by the MPO, State(s), and public transportation operator(s).

(v) For the outer years of the metropolitan transportation plan (*i.e.*, beyond the first 10 years), the financial plan may reflect aggregate cost ranges/cost bands, as long as the future funding source(s) is reasonably expected to be available to support the projected cost ranges/cost bands.

(vi) For nonattainment and maintenance areas, the financial plan shall address the specific financial strategies required to ensure the implementation of TCMs in the applicable SIP.

(vii) For illustrative purposes, the financial plan may include additional projects that would be included in the adopted transportation plan if additional resources beyond those identified in the financial plan were to become available.

(viii) In cases that the FHWA and the FTA find a metropolitan transportation plan to be fiscally constrained and a revenue source is subsequently removed or substantially reduced (*i.e.*, by legislative or administrative actions), the FHWA and the FTA will not withdraw the original determination of fiscal constraint; however, in such cases, the FHWA and the FTA will not act on an updated or amended metropolitan transportation plan that does not reflect the changed revenue situation.

(12) Pedestrian walkway and bicycle transportation facilities in accordance with 23 U.S.C. 217(g).

(g) The MPO shall consult, as appropriate, with State and local agencies responsible for land use management, natural resources, environmental protection, conservation, and historic preservation concerning the development of the transportation plan. The consultation shall involve, as appropriate:

(1) Comparison of transportation plans with State conservation plans or maps, if available; or

(2) Comparison of transportation plans to inventories of natural or historic resources, if available.

(h) The metropolitan transportation plan should integrate the priorities, goals, countermeasures, strategies, or projects for the metropolitan planning area contained in the HSIP, including the SHSP required under 23 U.S.C. 148, the Public Transportation Agency Safety Plan required under 49 U.S.C. 5329(d), or an Interim Agency Safety Plan in accordance with 49 CFR part 659, as in effect until completion of the Public Transportation Agency Safety Plan, and may incorporate or reference applicable emergency relief and disaster preparedness plans and strategies and policies that support homeland security, as appropriate, to safeguard the personal security of all motorized and non-motorized users.

(i) An MPO may, while fitting the needs and complexity of its community, voluntarily elect to develop multiple scenarios for consideration as part of the development of the metropolitan transportation plan.

(1) An MPO that chooses to develop multiple scenarios under this paragraph (i) is encouraged to consider:

(i) Potential regional investment strategies for the planning horizon;

(ii) Assumed distribution of population and employment;

(iii) A scenario that, to the maximum extent practicable, maintains baseline conditions for the performance areas identified in § 450.306(d) and measures established under 23 CFR part 490;

(iv) A scenario that improves the baseline conditions for as many of the performance measures identified in § 450.306(d) as possible;

(v) Revenue constrained scenarios based on the total revenues expected to be available over the forecast period of the plan; and

(vi) Estimated costs and potential revenues available to support each scenario.

(2) In addition to the performance areas identified in 23 U.S.C. 150(c), 49 U.S.C. 5326(c), and 5329(d), and the

measures established under 23 CFR part 490, MPOs may evaluate scenarios developed under this paragraph using locally developed measures.

(j) The MPO shall provide individuals, affected public agencies, representatives of public transportation employees, public ports, freight shippers, providers of freight transportation services, private providers of transportation (including intercity bus operators, employer-based commuting programs, such as carpool program, vanpool program, transit benefit program, parking cashout program, shuttle program, or telework program), representatives of users of public transportation, representatives of users of pedestrian walkways and bicycle transportation facilities, representatives of the disabled, and other interested parties with a reasonable opportunity to comment on the transportation plan using the participation plan developed under § 450.316(a).

(k) The MPO shall publish or otherwise make readily available the metropolitan transportation plan for public review, including (to the maximum extent practicable) in electronically accessible formats and means, such as the World Wide Web.

(l) A State or MPO is not required to select any project from the illustrative list of additional projects included in the financial plan under paragraph (f)(11) of this section.

(m) In nonattainment and maintenance areas for transportation-related pollutants, the MPO, as well as the FHWA and the FTA, must make a conformity determination on any updated or amended transportation plan in accordance with the Clean Air Act and the EPA transportation conformity regulations (40 CFR part 93, subpart A). A 12-month conformity lapse grace period will be implemented when an area misses an applicable deadline, in accordance with the Clean Air Act and the transportation conformity regulations (40 CFR part 93, subpart A). At the end of this 12-month grace period, the existing conformity determination will lapse. During a conformity lapse, MPOs can prepare an interim metropolitan transportation plan as a basis for advancing projects that are eligible to proceed under a conformity lapse. An interim metropolitan transportation plan consisting of eligible projects from, or consistent with, the most recent conforming transportation plan and TIP may proceed immediately without revisiting the requirements of this section, subject to interagency consultation defined in 40 CFR part 93, subpart A. An interim metropolitan transportation plan containing eligible projects that are not from, or consistent with, the most recent conforming transportation plan and TIP must meet all the requirements of this section.

[81 FR 34135, May 27, 2016, as amended at 81 FR 93473, Dec. 20, 2016; 82 FR 56544, Nov. 29, 2017]

§ 450.326 Development and content of the transportation improvement program (TIP).

(a) The MPO, in cooperation with the State(s) and any affected public transportation operator(s), shall develop a TIP for the metropolitan planning area. The TIP shall reflect the investment priorities established in the current metropolitan transportation plan and shall cover a period of no less than 4 years, be updated at least every 4 years, and be approved by the MPO and the Governor. However, if the TIP covers more than 4 years, the FHWA and the FTA will consider the projects in the additional years as informational. The MPO may update the TIP more frequently, but the cycle for updating the TIP must be compatible with the STIP development and approval process. The TIP expires when the FHWA/FTA approval of the STIP expires. Copies of any updated or revised TIPs must be provided to the FHWA and the FTA. In nonattainment and maintenance areas subject to transportation conformity requirements, the FHWA and the FTA, as well as the MPO, must make a conformity determination on any updated or amended TIP, in accordance with the Clean Air Act requirements and the EPA's transportation conformity regulations (40 CFR part 93, subpart A).

(b) The MPO shall provide all interested parties with a reasonable opportunity to comment on the proposed TIP as required by § 450.316(a). In addition, in nonattainment area TMAs, the

MPO shall provide at least one formal public meeting during the TIP development process, which should be addressed through the participation plan described in § 450.316(a). In addition, the MPO shall publish or otherwise make readily available the TIP for public review, including (to the maximum extent practicable) in electronically accessible formats and means, such as the World Wide Web, as described in § 450.316(a).

(c) The TIP shall be designed such that once implemented, it makes progress toward achieving the performance targets established under § 450.306(d).

(d) The TIP shall include, to the maximum extent practicable, a description of the anticipated effect of the TIP toward achieving the performance targets identified in the metropolitan transportation plan, linking investment priorities to those performance targets.

(e) The TIP shall include capital and non-capital surface transportation projects (or phases of projects) within the boundaries of the metropolitan planning area proposed for funding under 23 U.S.C. and 49 U.S.C. Chapter 53 (including transportation alternatives; associated transit improvements; Tribal Transportation Program, Federal Lands Transportation Program, and Federal Lands Access Program projects; HSIP projects; trails projects; accessible pedestrian walkways; and bicycle facilities), except the following that may be included:

(1) Safety projects funded under 23 U.S.C. 402 and 49 U.S.C. 31102;

(2) Metropolitan planning projects funded under 23 U.S.C. 104(d), and 49 U.S.C. 5305(d);

(3) State planning and research projects funded under 23 U.S.C. 505 and 49 U.S.C. 5305(e);

(4) At the discretion of the State and MPO, metropolitan planning projects funded with Surface Transportation Program funds;

(5) Emergency relief projects (except those involving substantial functional, locational, or capacity changes);

(6) National planning and research projects funded under 49 U.S.C. 5314; and

(7) Project management oversight projects funded under 49 U.S.C. 5327.

(f) The TIP shall contain all regionally significant projects requiring an action by the FHWA or the FTA whether or not the projects are to be funded under title 23 U.S.C. Chapters 1 and 2 or title 49 U.S.C. Chapter 53 (e.g., addition of an interchange to the Interstate System with State, local, and/or private funds and congressionally designated projects not funded under 23 U.S.C. or 49 U.S.C. Chapter 53). For public information and conformity purposes, the TIP shall include all regionally significant projects proposed to be funded with Federal funds other than those administered by the FHWA or the FTA, as well as all regionally significant projects to be funded with non-Federal funds.

(g) The TIP shall include, for each project or phase (e.g., preliminary engineering, environment/NEPA, right-of-way, design, or construction), the following:

(1) Sufficient descriptive material (*i.e.*, type of work, termini, and length) to identify the project or phase;

(2) Estimated total project cost, which may extend beyond the 4 years of the TIP;

(3) The amount of Federal funds proposed to be obligated during each program year for the project or phase (for the first year, this includes the proposed category of Federal funds and source(s) of non-Federal funds. For the second, third, and fourth years, this includes the likely category or possible categories of Federal funds and sources of non-Federal funds);

(4) Identification of the agencies responsible for carrying out the project or phase;

(5) In nonattainment and maintenance areas, identification of those projects that are identified as TCMs in the applicable SIP;

(6) In nonattainment and maintenance areas, included projects shall be specified in sufficient detail (design concept and scope) for air quality analysis in accordance with the EPA transportation conformity regulations (40 CFR part 93, subpart A); and

(7) In areas with Americans with Disabilities Act required paratransit and key station plans, identification of

those projects that will implement these plans.

(h) Projects that are not considered to be of appropriate scale for individual identification in a given program year may be grouped by function, work type, and/or geographic area using the applicable classifications under 23 CFR 771.117(c) and (d) and/or 40 CFR part 93. In nonattainment and maintenance areas, project classifications must be consistent with the "exempt project" classifications contained in the EPA transportation conformity regulations (40 CFR part 93, subpart A). In addition, projects proposed for funding under title 23 U.S.C. Chapter 2 that are not regionally significant may be grouped in one line item or identified individually in the TIP.

(i) Each project or project phase included in the TIP shall be consistent with the approved metropolitan transportation plan.

(j) The TIP shall include a financial plan that demonstrates how the approved TIP can be implemented, indicates resources from public and private sources that are reasonably expected to be made available to carry out the TIP, and recommends any additional financing strategies for needed projects and programs. In developing the TIP, the MPO, State(s), and public transportation operator(s) shall cooperatively develop estimates of funds that are reasonably expected to be available to support TIP implementation in accordance with § 450.314(a). Only projects for which construction or operating funds can reasonably be expected to be available may be included. In the case of new funding sources, strategies for ensuring their availability shall be identified. In developing the financial plan, the MPO shall take into account all projects and strategies funded under title 23 U.S.C., title 49 U.S.C. Chapter 53, and other Federal funds; and regionally significant projects that are not federally funded. For purposes of transportation operations and maintenance, the financial plan shall contain system-level estimates of costs and revenue sources that are reasonably expected to be available to adequately operate and maintain Federal-aid highways (as defined by 23 U.S.C. 101(a)(6)) and public transportation (as defined by title 49 U.S.C. Chapter 53). In addition, for illustrative purposes, the financial plan may include additional projects that would be included in the TIP if reasonable additional resources beyond those identified in the financial plan were to become available. Revenue and cost estimates for the TIP must use an inflation rate(s) to reflect "year of expenditure dollars," based on reasonable financial principles and information, developed cooperatively by the MPO, State(s), and public transportation operator(s).

(k) The TIP shall include a project, or a phase of a project, only if full funding can reasonably be anticipated to be available for the project within the time period contemplated for completion of the project. In nonattainment and maintenance areas, projects included in the first 2 years of the TIP shall be limited to those for which funds are available or committed. For the TIP, financial constraint shall be demonstrated and maintained by year and shall include sufficient financial information to demonstrate which projects are to be implemented using current and/or reasonably available revenues, while federally supported facilities are being adequately operated and maintained. In the case of proposed funding sources, strategies for ensuring their availability shall be identified in the financial plan consistent with paragraph (h) of this section. In nonattainment and maintenance areas, the TIP shall give priority to eligible TCMs identified in the approved SIP in accordance with the EPA transportation conformity regulations (40 CFR part 93, subpart A) and shall provide for their timely implementation.

(l) In cases that the FHWA and the FTA find a TIP to be fiscally constrained and a revenue source is subsequently removed or substantially reduced (*i.e.*, by legislative or administrative actions), the FHWA and the FTA will not withdraw the original determination of fiscal constraint. However, in such cases, the FHWA and the FTA will not act on an updated or amended TIP that does not reflect the changed revenue situation.

(m) Procedures or agreements that distribute suballocated Surface Transportation Program funds to individual jurisdictions or modes within the MPA by pre-determined percentages or formulas are inconsistent with the legislative provisions that require the MPO, in cooperation with the State and the public transportation operator, to develop a prioritized and financially constrained TIP and shall not be used unless they can be clearly shown to be based on considerations required to be addressed as part of the metropolitan transportation planning process.

(n) As a management tool for monitoring progress in implementing the transportation plan, the TIP should:

(1) Identify the criteria and process for prioritizing implementation of transportation plan elements (including multimodal trade-offs) for inclusion in the TIP and any changes in priorities from previous TIPs;

(2) List major projects from the previous TIP that were implemented and identify any significant delays in the planned implementation of major projects; and

(3) In nonattainment and maintenance areas, describe the progress in implementing any required TCMs, in accordance with 40 CFR part 93.

(o) In metropolitan nonattainment and maintenance areas, a 12-month conformity lapse grace period will be implemented when an area misses an applicable deadline, according to the Clean Air Act and the transportation conformity regulations (40 CFR part 93, subpart A). At the end of this 12-month grace period, the existing conformity determination will lapse. During a conformity lapse, MPOs may prepare an interim TIP as a basis for advancing projects that are eligible to proceed under a conformity lapse. An interim TIP consisting of eligible projects from, or consistent with, the most recent conforming metropolitan transportation plan and TIP may proceed immediately without revisiting the requirements of this section, subject to interagency consultation defined in 40 CFR part 93. An interim TIP containing eligible projects that are not from, or consistent with, the most recent conforming transportation plan and TIP must meet all the requirements of this section.

(p) Projects in any of the first 4 years of the TIP may be advanced in place of another project in the first 4 years of the TIP, subject to the project selection requirements of § 450.332. In addition, the MPO may revise the TIP at any time under procedures agreed to by the State, MPO, and public transportation operator(s) consistent with the TIP development procedures established in this section, as well as the procedures for the MPO participation plan (see § 450.316(a)) and FHWA/FTA actions on the TIP (see § 450.330).

[81 FR 34135, May 27, 2016, as amended at 81 FR 93473, Dec. 20, 2016; 82 FR 56545, Nov. 29, 2017]

§ 450.328 TIP revisions and relationship to the STIP.

(a) An MPO may revise the TIP at any time under procedures agreed to by the cooperating parties consistent with the procedures established in this part for its development and approval. In nonattainment or maintenance areas for transportation-related pollutants, if a TIP amendment involves non-exempt projects (per 40 CFR part 93), or is replaced with an updated TIP, the MPO and the FHWA and the FTA must make a new conformity determination. In all areas, changes that affect fiscal constraint must take place by amendment of the TIP. The MPO shall use public participation procedures consistent with § 450.316(a) in revising the TIP, except that these procedures are not required for administrative modifications.

(b) After approval by the MPO and the Governor, the State shall include the TIP without change, directly or by reference, in the STIP required under 23 U.S.C. 135. In nonattainment and maintenance areas, the FHWA and the FTA must make a conformity finding on the TIP before it is included in the STIP. A copy of the approved TIP shall be provided to the FHWA and the FTA.

(c) The State shall notify the MPO and Federal land management agencies when it has included a TIP including projects under the jurisdiction of these agencies in the STIP.

[81 FR 34135, May 27, 2016, as amended at 81 FR 93473, Dec. 20, 2016; 82 FR 56545, Nov. 29, 2017]

§ 450.330 TIP action by the FHWA and the FTA.

(a) The FHWA and the FTA shall jointly find that each metropolitan TIP is consistent with the metropolitan transportation plan produced by the continuing and comprehensive transportation process carried on cooperatively by the MPO, the State(s), and the public transportation operator(s) in accordance with 23 U.S.C. 134 and 49 U.S.C. 5303. This finding shall be based on the self-certification statement submitted by the State and MPO under § 450.336, a review of the metropolitan transportation plan by the FHWA and the FTA, and upon other reviews as deemed necessary by the FHWA and the FTA.

(b) In nonattainment and maintenance areas, the MPO, as well as the FHWA and the FTA, shall determine conformity of any updated or amended TIP, in accordance with 40 CFR part 93. After the FHWA and the FTA issue a conformity determination on the TIP, the TIP shall be incorporated, without change, into the STIP, directly or by reference.

(c) If an MPO has not updated the metropolitan transportation plan in accordance with the cycles defined in § 450.324(c), projects may only be advanced from a TIP that was approved and found to conform (in nonattainment and maintenance areas) prior to expiration of the metropolitan transportation plan and meets the TIP update requirements of § 450.326(a). Until the MPO approves (in attainment areas) or the FHWA and the FTA issue a conformity determination on (in nonattainment and maintenance areas) the updated metropolitan transportation plan, the MPO may not amend the TIP.

(d) In the case of extenuating circumstances, the FHWA and the FTA will consider and take appropriate action on requests to extend the STIP approval period for all or part of the TIP in accordance with § 450.220(b).

(e) If an illustrative project is included in the TIP, no Federal action may be taken on that project by the FHWA and the FTA until it is formally included in the financially constrained and conforming metropolitan transportation plan and TIP.

(f) Where necessary in order to maintain or establish operations, the FHWA and the FTA may approve highway and transit operating assistance for specific projects or programs, even though the projects or programs may not be included in an approved TIP.

[81 FR 34135, May 27, 2016, as amended at 81 FR 93473, Dec. 20, 2016; 82 FR 56545, Nov. 29, 2017]

§ 450.332 Project selection from the TIP.

(a) Once a TIP that meets the requirements of 23 U.S.C. 134(j), 49 U.S.C. 5303(j), and § 450.326 has been developed and approved, the first year of the TIP will constitute an "agreed to" list of projects for project selection purposes and no further project selection action is required for the implementing agency to proceed with projects, except where the appropriated Federal funds available to the metropolitan planning area are significantly less than the authorized amounts or where there are significant shifting of projects between years. In this case, the MPO, the State, and the public transportation operator(s) if requested by the MPO, the State, or the public transportation operator(s) shall jointly develop a revised "agreed to" list of projects. If the State or public transportation operator(s) wishes to proceed with a project in the second, third, or fourth year of the TIP, the specific project selection procedures stated in paragraphs (b) and (c) of this section must be used unless the MPO, the State, and the public transportation operator(s) jointly develop expedited project selection procedures to provide for the advancement of projects from the second, third, or fourth years of the TIP.

(b) In metropolitan areas not designated as TMAs, the State and/or the public transportation operator(s), in cooperation with the MPO shall select projects to be implemented using title 23 U.S.C. funds (other than Tribal Transportation Program, Federal Lands Transportation Program, and Federal Lands Access Program projects) or funds under title 49 U.S.C. Chapter 53, from the approved metropolitan TIP. Tribal Transportation

Program, Federal Lands Transportation Program, and Federal Lands Access Program projects shall be selected in accordance with procedures developed pursuant to 23 U.S.C. 201, 202, 203, and 204.

(c) In areas designated as TMAs, the MPO shall select all 23 U.S.C. and 49 U.S.C. Chapter 53 funded projects (excluding projects on the NHS and Tribal Transportation Program, Federal Lands Transportation Program, and Federal Lands Access Program) in consultation with the State and public transportation operator(s) from the approved TIP and in accordance with the priorities in the approved TIP. The State shall select projects on the NHS in cooperation with the MPO, from the approved TIP. Tribal Transportation Program, Federal Lands Transportation Program, and Federal Lands Access Program projects shall be selected in accordance with procedures developed pursuant to 23 U.S.C. 201, 202, 203, and 204.

(d) Except as provided in § 450.326(e) and § 450.330(f), projects not included in the federally approved STIP are not eligible for funding with funds under title 23 U.S.C. or 49 U.S.C. Chapter 53.

(e) In nonattainment and maintenance areas, priority shall be given to the timely implementation of TCMs contained in the applicable SIP in accordance with the EPA transportation conformity regulations (40 CFR part 93, subpart A).

[81 FR 34135, May 27, 2016, as amended at 81 FR 93473, Dec. 20, 2016; 82 FR 56545, Nov. 29, 2017]

§ 450.334 Annual listing of obligated projects.

(a) In metropolitan planning areas, on an annual basis, no later than 90 calendar days following the end of the program year, the State, public transportation operator(s), and the MPO shall cooperatively develop a listing of projects (including investments in pedestrian walkways and bicycle transportation facilities) for which funds under 23 U.S.C. or 49 U.S.C. Chapter 53 were obligated in the preceding program year.

(b) The listing shall be prepared in accordance with § 450.314(a) and shall include all federally funded projects authorized or revised to increase obligations in the preceding program year, and shall at a minimum include the TIP information under § 450.326(g)(1) and (4) and identify, for each project, the amount of Federal funds requested in the TIP, the Federal funding that was obligated during the preceding year, and the Federal funding remaining and available for subsequent years.

(c) The listing shall be published or otherwise made available in accordance with the MPO's public participation criteria for the TIP.

[81 FR 34135, May 27, 2016, as amended at 81 FR 93473, Dec. 20, 2016; 82 FR 56545, Nov. 29, 2017]

§ 450.336 Self-certifications and Federal certifications.

(a) For all MPAs, concurrent with the submittal of the entire proposed TIP to the FHWA and the FTA as part of the STIP approval, the State and the MPO shall certify at least every 4 years that the metropolitan transportation planning process is being carried out in accordance with all applicable requirements including:

(1) 23 U.S.C. 134, 49 U.S.C. 5303, and this subpart;

(2) In nonattainment and maintenance areas, sections 174 and 176(c) and (d) of the Clean Air Act, as amended (42 U.S.C. 7504, 7506(c) and (d)) and 40 CFR part 93;

(3) Title VI of the Civil Rights Act of 1964, as amended (42 U.S.C. 2000d–1) and 49 CFR part 21;

(4) 49 U.S.C. 5332, prohibiting discrimination on the basis of race, color, creed, national origin, sex, or age in employment or business opportunity;

(5) Section 1101(b) of the FAST Act (Pub. L. 114–357) and 49 CFR part 26 regarding the involvement of disadvantaged business enterprises in DOT funded projects;

(6) 23 CFR part 230, regarding the implementation of an equal employment opportunity program on Federal and Federal-aid highway construction contracts;

(7) The provisions of the Americans with Disabilities Act of 1990 (42 U.S.C. 12101 *et seq.*) and 49 CFR parts 27, 37, and 38;

(8) The Older Americans Act, as amended (42 U.S.C. 6101), prohibiting

discrimination on the basis of age in programs or activities receiving Federal financial assistance;

(9) Section 324 of title 23 U.S.C. regarding the prohibition of discrimination based on gender; and

(10) Section 504 of the Rehabilitation Act of 1973 (29 U.S.C. 794) and 49 CFR part 27 regarding discrimination against individuals with disabilities.

(b) In TMAs, the FHWA and the FTA jointly shall review and evaluate the transportation planning process for each TMA no less than once every 4 years to determine if the process meets the requirements of applicable provisions of Federal law and this subpart.

(1) After review and evaluation of the TMA planning process, the FHWA and FTA shall take one of the following actions:

(i) If the process meets the requirements of this part and the MPO and the Governor have approved a TIP, jointly certify the transportation planning process;

(ii) If the process substantially meets the requirements of this part and the MPO and the Governor have approved a TIP, jointly certify the transportation planning process subject to certain specified corrective actions being taken; or

(iii) If the process does not meet the requirements of this part, jointly certify the planning process as the basis for approval of only those categories of programs or projects that the FHWA and the FTA jointly determine, subject to certain specified corrective actions being taken.

(2) If, upon the review and evaluation conducted under paragraph (b)(1)(iii) of this section, the FHWA and the FTA do not certify the transportation planning process in a TMA, the Secretary may withhold up to 20 percent of the funds attributable to the metropolitan planning area of the MPO for projects funded under title 23 U.S.C. and title 49 U.S.C. Chapter 53 in addition to corrective actions and funding restrictions. The withheld funds shall be restored to the MPA when the metropolitan transportation planning process is certified by the FHWA and FTA, unless the funds have lapsed.

(3) A certification of the TMA planning process will remain in effect for 4 years unless a new certification determination is made sooner by the FHWA and the FTA or a shorter term is specified in the certification report.

(4) In conducting a certification review, the FHWA and the FTA shall provide opportunities for public involvement within the metropolitan planning area under review. The FHWA and the FTA shall consider the public input received in arriving at a decision on a certification action.

(5) The FHWA and the FTA shall notify the MPO(s), the State(s), and public transportation operator(s) of the actions taken under paragraphs (b)(1) and (b)(2) of this section. The FHWA and the FTA will update the certification status of the TMA when evidence of satisfactory completion of a corrective action(s) is provided to the FHWA and the FTA.

[81 FR 34135, May 27, 2016, as amended at 81 FR 93473, Dec. 20, 2016; 82 FR 56545, Nov. 29, 2017]

§ 450.338 Applicability of NEPA to metropolitan transportation plans and programs.

Any decision by the Secretary concerning a metropolitan transportation plan or TIP developed through the processes provided for in 23 U.S.C. 134, 49 U.S.C. 5303, and this subpart shall not be considered to be a Federal action subject to review under the National Environmental Policy Act of 1969 (42 U.S.C. 4321 *et seq.*).

§ 450.340 Phase-in of new requirements.

(a) Prior to May 27, 2018, an MPO may adopt a metropolitan transportation plan that has been developed using the SAFETEA–LU requirements or the provisions and requirements of this part. On or after May 27, 2018, an MPO may not adopt a metropolitan transportation plan that has not been developed according to the provisions and requirements of this part.

(b) Prior to May 27, 2018 (2 years after the publication date of this rule), FHWA/FTA may determine the conformity of, or approve as part of a STIP, a TIP that has been developed using SAFETEA–LU requirements or the provisions and requirements of this part. On or after May 27, 2018 (2 years after the publication date of this rule), FHWA/FTA may only determine the conformity of, or approve as part of a STIP, a TIP that has been developed according to the provisions and requirements of this part, regardless of when the MPO developed the TIP.

(c) On and after May 27, 2018 (2 years after the issuance date of this rule), the FHWA and the FTA will take action (*i.e.*, conformity determinations and STIP approvals) on an updated or amended TIP developed under the provisions of this part, even if the MPO has not yet adopted a new metropolitan transportation plan under the provisions of this part, as long as the underlying transportation planning process is consistent with the requirements in the MAP–21.

(d) On or after May 27, 2018 (2 years after the publication date of this rule), an MPO may make an administrative modification to a TIP that conforms to either the SAFETEA–LU or to the provisions and requirements of this part.

(e) Two years from the effective date of each rule establishing performance measures under 23 U.S.C. 150(c), 49 U.S.C. 5326, and 49 U.S.C. 5329 FHWA/FTA will only determine the conformity of, or approve as part of a STIP, a TIP that is based on a metropolitan transportation planning process that meets the performance based planning requirements in this part and in such a rule.

(f) Prior to 2 years from the effective date of each rule establishing performance measures under 23 U.S.C. 150(c), 49 U.S.C. 5326, or 49 U.S.C. 5329, an MPO may adopt a metropolitan transportation plan that has been developed using the SAFETEA–LU requirements or the performance-based planning requirements of this part and in such a rule. Two years on or after the effective date of each rule establishing performance measures under 23 U.S.C. 150(c), 49 U.S.C. 5326, or 49 U.S.C. 5329, an MPO may only adopt a metropolitan transportation plan that has been developed according to the performance-based provisions and requirements of this part and in such a rule.

(g) A newly designated TMA shall implement the congestion management process described in §450.322 within 18 months of designation.

[81 FR 34135, May 27, 2016, as amended at 81 FR 93473, Dec. 20, 2016; 82 FR 56545, Nov. 29, 2017]

Appendix A to Part 450—Linking the Transportation Planning and NEPA Processes

Background and Overview

This Appendix provides additional information to explain the linkage between the transportation planning and project development/National Environmental Policy Act (NEPA) processes. It is intended to be non-binding and should not be construed as a rule of general applicability.

For 40 years, the Congress has directed that federally funded highway and transit projects must flow from metropolitan and statewide transportation planning processes (pursuant to 23 U.S.C. 134–135 and 49 U.S.C. 5303–5306). Over the years, the Congress has refined and strengthened the transportation planning process as the foundation for project decisions, emphasizing public involvement, consideration of environmental and other factors, and a Federal role that oversees the transportation planning process but does not second-guess the content of transportation plans and programs.

Despite this statutory emphasis on transportation planning, the environmental analyses produced to meet the requirements of the NEPA of 1969 (42 U.S.C. 4231 *et seq.*) have often been conducted de novo, disconnected from the analyses used to develop long-range transportation plans, statewide and metropolitan Transportation Improvement Programs (STIPs/TIPs), or planning-level corridor/subarea/feasibility studies. When the NEPA and transportation planning processes are not well coordinated, the NEPA process may lead to the development of information that is more appropriately developed in the planning process, resulting in duplication of work and delays in transportation improvements.

The purpose of this Appendix is to change this culture, by supporting congressional intent that statewide and metropolitan transportation planning should be the foundation for highway and transit project decisions. This Appendix was crafted to recognize that transportation planning processes vary across the country. This document provides details on how information, analysis, and products from transportation planning can be incorporated into and relied upon in NEPA documents under existing laws, regardless of when the Notice of Intent has been published. This Appendix presents environmental review as a continuum of sequential study, refinement, and expansion performed in transportation planning and during project development/NEPA, with information developed and conclusions drawn in early stages utilized in subsequent (and more detailed) review stages.

The information below is intended for use by State departments of transportation (State DOTs), metropolitan planning organizations (MPOs), and public transportation operators to clarify the circumstances under which transportation planning level choices and analyses can be adopted or incorporated into the process required by NEPA. Additionally, the FHWA and the FTA will work with Federal environmental, regulatory, and resource agencies to incorporate the principles of this Appendix in their day-to-day NEPA policies and procedures related to their involvement in highway and transit projects.

This Appendix does not extend NEPA requirements to transportation plans and programs. The Transportation Efficiency Act for the 21st Century (TEA–21) and the Safe, Accountable, Flexible, Efficient Transportation Equity Act: A Legacy for Users (SAFETEA–LU) specifically exempted transportation plans and programs from NEPA review. Therefore, initiating the NEPA process as part of, or concurrently with, a transportation planning study does not subject transportation plans and programs to NEPA.

Implementation of this Appendix by States, MPOs, and public transportation operators is voluntary. The degree to which studies, analyses, or conclusions from the transportation planning process can be incorporated into the project development/NEPA processes will depend upon how well they meet certain standards established by NEPA regulations and guidance. While some transportation planning processes already meet these standards, others will need some modification.

The remainder of this Appendix document utilizes a "Question and Answer" format, organized into three primary categories ("Procedural Issues," "Substantive Issues," and "Administrative Issues").

I. Procedural Issues

1. In what format should the transportation planning information be included?

To be included in the NEPA process, work from the transportation planning process must be documented in a form that can be appended to the NEPA document or incorporated by reference. Documents may be incorporated by reference if they are readily available so as to not impede agency or public review of the action. Any document incorporated by reference must be "reasonably available for inspection by potentially interested persons within the time allowed for comment." Incorporated materials must be cited in the NEPA document and their contents briefly described, so that the reader understands why the document is cited and knows where to look for further information. To the extent possible, the documentation should be in a form such as official actions by the MPO, State DOT, or public transportation operator and/or correspondence within and among the organizations involved in the transportation planning process.

2. What is a reasonable level of detail for a planning product that is intended to be used in a NEPA document? How does this level of detail compare to what is considered a full NEPA analysis?

For purposes of transportation planning alone, a planning-level analysis does not need to rise to the level of detail required in the NEPA process. Rather, it needs to be accurate and up-to-date, and should adequately support recommended improvements in the statewide or metropolitan long-range transportation plan. The SAFETEA–LU requires transportation planning processes to focus on setting a context and following acceptable procedures. For example, the SAFETEA–LU requires a "discussion of the types of potential environmental mitigation activities" and potential areas for their implementation, rather than details on specific strategies. The SAFETEA–LU also emphasizes consultation with Federal, State, and Tribal land management, wildlife, and regulatory agencies.

However, the Environmental Assessment (EA) or Environmental Impact Statement (EIS) ultimately will be judged by the standards applicable under the NEPA regulations and guidance from the Council on Environmental Quality (CEQ). To the extent the information incorporated from the transportation planning process, standing alone, does not contain all of the information or analysis required by NEPA, then it will need to be supplemented by other information contained in the EIS or EA that would, in conjunction with the information from the plan, collectively meet the requirements of NEPA. The intent is not to require NEPA studies in the transportation planning process. As an option, the NEPA analyses prepared for project development can be integrated with transportation planning studies (see the response to Question 9 for additional information).

3. What type and extent of involvement from Federal, Tribal, State, and local environmental, regulatory, and resource agencies is needed in the transportation planning process in order for planning-level decisions to be more readily accepted in the NEPA process?

Sections 3005, 3006, and 6001 of the SAFETEA–LU established formal consultation requirements for MPOs and State DOTs to employ with environmental, regulatory, and resource agencies in the development of long-range transportation plans. For example, metropolitan transportation plans now "shall include a discussion of the types of potential environmental mitigation activities and potential areas to carry out these activities, including activities that may have the greatest potential to restore and maintain the environmental functions affected by the [transportation] plan," and that these planning-level discussions "shall be developed in consultation with Federal, State, and Tribal land management, wildlife, and regulatory agencies." In addition, MPOs "shall consult, as appropriate, with State and local agencies responsible for land use management, natural resources, environmental protection, conservation, and historic preservation concerning the development of a long-range transportation plan," and that this consultation "shall involve, as appropriate, comparison of transportation plans with State conservation plans or maps, if available, or comparison of transportation plans to inventories of natural or historic resources, if available." Similar SAFETEA–LU language addresses the development of the long-range statewide transportation plan, with the addition of Tribal conservation plans or maps to this planning-level "comparison."

In addition, section 6002 of the SAFETEA–LU established several mechanisms for increased efficiency in environmental reviews for project decision-making. For example, the term "lead agency" collectively means the U.S. Department of Transportation and a State or local governmental entity serving as a joint lead agency for the NEPA process. In addition, the lead agency is responsible for inviting and designating "participating agencies" (*i.e.*, other Federal or non-Federal agencies that may have an interest in the proposed project). Any Federal agency that is invited by the lead agency to participate in the environmental review process for a project shall be designated as a participating agency by the lead agency unless the invited agency informs the lead agency, in writing, by the deadline specified in the invitation that the invited agency:

(a) Has no jurisdiction or authority with respect to the project; (b) has no expertise or information relevant to the project; and (c) does not intend to submit comments on the project.

Past successful examples of using transportation planning products in NEPA analysis are based on early and continuous involvement of environmental, regulatory, and resource agencies. Without this early coordination, environmental, regulatory, and resource agencies are more likely to expect decisions made or analyses conducted in the transportation planning process to be revisited during the NEPA process. Early participation in transportation planning provides environmental, regulatory, and resource agencies better insight into the needs and objectives of the locality. Additionally, early participation provides an important opportunity for environmental, regulatory, and resource agency concerns to be identified and addressed early in the process, such as those related to permit applications. Moreover, Federal, Tribal, State, and local environmental, regulatory, and resource agencies are able to share data on particular resources, which can play a critical role in determining the feasibility of a transportation solution with respect to environmental impacts. The use of other agency planning outputs can result in a transportation project that could support multiple goals (transportation, environmental, and community). Further, planning decisions by these other agencies may have impacts on long-range transportation plans and/or the STIP/TIP, thereby providing important input to the transportation planning process and advancing integrated decision-making.

4. What is the procedure for using decisions or analyses from the transportation planning process?

The lead agencies jointly decide, and must agree, on what processes and consultation techniques are used to determine the transportation planning products that will be incorporated into the NEPA process. At a minimum, a robust scoping/early coordination process (which explains to Federal and State environmental, regulatory, and resource agencies and the public the information and/or analyses utilized to develop the planning products, how the purpose and need was developed and refined, and how the design concept and scope were determined) should play a critical role in leading to informed decisions by the lead agencies on the suitability of the transportation planning information, analyses, documents, and decisions for use in the NEPA process. As part of a rigorous scoping/early coordination process, the FHWA and the FTA should ensure that the transportation planning results are appropriately documented, shared, and used.

5. To what extent can the FHWA/FTA provide up-front assurance that decisions and additional investments made in the transportation planning process will allow planning-level decisions and analyses to be used in the NEPA process?

There are no guarantees. However, the potential is greatly improved for transportation planning processes that address the "3–C" planning principles (comprehensive, cooperative, and continuous); incorporate the intent of NEPA through the consideration of natural, physical, and social effects; involve environmental, regulatory, and resource agencies; thoroughly document the transportation planning process information, analysis, and decision; and vet the planning results through the applicable public involvement processes.

6. What considerations will the FHWA/FTA take into account in their review of transportation planning products for acceptance in project development/NEPA?

The FHWA and the FTA will give deference to decisions resulting from the transportation planning process if the FHWA and FTA determine that the planning process is consistent with the "3–C" planning principles and when the planning study process, alternatives considered, and resulting decisions have a rational basis that is thoroughly documented and vetted through the applicable public involvement processes. Moreover, any applicable program-specific requirements (e.g., those of the Congestion Mitigation and Air Quality Improvement Program or the FTA's Capital Investment Grant program) also must be met.

The NEPA requires that the FHWA and the FTA be able to stand behind the overall soundness and credibility of analyses conducted and decisions made during the transportation planning process if they are incorporated into a NEPA document. For example, if systems-level or other broad objectives or choices from the transportation plan are incorporated into the purpose and need statement for a NEPA document, the FHWA and the FTA should not revisit whether these are the best objectives or choices among other options. Rather, the FHWA and the FTA review would include making sure that objectives or choices derived from the transportation plan were: Based on transportation planning factors established by Federal law; reflect a credible and articulated planning rationale; founded on reliable data; and developed through transportation planning processes meeting FHWA and FTA statutory and regulatory requirements. In addition, the basis for the goals and choices must be documented and included in the NEPA document. The FHWA/FTA reviewers do not need to review whether assumptions or analytical methods used in the studies are the best available, but, instead, need to assure that such assumptions or analytical methods are reasonable, scientifically acceptable, and consistent with goals, objectives, and policies set forth in long-range transportation plans. This review would include determining whether: (a) Assumptions have a rational basis and are up-to-date and (b) data, analytical methods, and modeling techniques are reliable, defensible, reasonably current, and meet data quality requirements.

II. SUBSTANTIVE ISSUES

GENERAL ISSUES TO BE CONSIDERED

7. What should be considered in order to rely upon transportation planning studies in NEPA?

The following questions should be answered prior to accepting studies conducted during the transportation planning process for use in NEPA. While not a "checklist," these questions are intended to guide the practitioner's analysis of the planning products:

- How much time has passed since the planning studies and corresponding decisions were made?
- Were the future year policy assumptions used in the transportation planning process related to land use, economic development, transportation costs, and network expansion consistent with those to be used in the NEPA process?
- Is the information still relevant/valid?
- What changes have occurred in the area since the study was completed?
- Is the information in a format that can be appended to an environmental document or reformatted to do so?
- Are the analyses in a planning-level report or document based on data, analytical methods, and modeling techniques that are reliable, defensible, and consistent with those used in other regional transportation studies and project development activities?
- Were the FHWA and FTA, other agencies, and the public involved in the relevant planning analysis and the corresponding planning decisions?
- Were the planning products available to other agencies and the public during NEPA scoping?
- During NEPA scoping, was a clear connection between the decisions made in planning and those to be made during the project development stage explained to the public and others? What was the response?
- Are natural resource and land use plans being informed by transportation planning products, and vice versa?

PURPOSE AND NEED

8. How can transportation planning be used to shape a project's purpose and need in the NEPA process?

A sound transportation planning process is the primary source of the project purpose and need. Through transportation planning, State and local governments, with involvement of stakeholders and the public, establish a vision for the region's future transportation system, define transportation goals and objectives for realizing that vision, decide which needs to address, and determine the timeframe for addressing these issues. The transportation planning process also provides a potential forum to define a project's purpose and need by framing the scope of the problem to be addressed by a proposed project. This scope may be further refined during the transportation planning process as more information about the transportation need is collected and consultation with the public and other stakeholders clarifies other issues and goals for the region.

23 U.S.C. 139(f), as amended by the SAFETEA–LU Section 6002, provides additional focus regarding the definition of the purpose and need and objectives. For example, the lead agency, as early as practicable during the environmental review process, shall provide an opportunity for involvement by participating agencies and the public in defining the purpose and need for a project. The statement of purpose and need shall include a clear statement of the objectives that the proposed action is intended to achieve, which may include: (a) Achieving a transportation objective identified in an applicable statewide or metropolitan transportation plan; (b) supporting land use, economic development, or growth objectives established in applicable Federal, State, local, or Tribal plans; and (c) serving national defense, national security, or other national objectives, as established in Federal laws, plans, or policies.

The transportation planning process can be utilized to develop the purpose and need in the following ways:

(a) Goals and objectives from the transportation planning process may be part of the project's purpose and need statement;

(b) A general travel corridor or general mode or modes (e.g., highway, transit, or a highway/transit combination) resulting from planning analyses may be part of the project's purpose and need statement;

(c) If the financial plan for a metropolitan transportation plan indicates that funding for a specific project will require special funding sources (e.g., tolls or public-private financing), such information may be included in the purpose and need statement; or

(d) The results of analyses from management systems (e.g., congestion, pavement, bridge, and/or safety) may shape the purpose and need statement.

The use of these planning-level goals and choices must be appropriately explained during NEPA scoping and in the NEPA document.

Consistent with NEPA, the purpose and need statement should be a statement of a transportation problem, not a specific solution. However, the purpose and need statement should be specific enough to generate alternatives that may potentially yield real solutions to the problem at-hand. A purpose and need statement that yields only one alternative may indicate a purpose and need that is too narrowly defined.

Short of a fully integrated transportation decision-making process, many State DOTs develop information for their purpose and need statements when implementing interagency NEPA/Section 404 process merger agreements. These agreements may need to be expanded to include commitments to share and utilize transportation planning products when developing a project's purpose and need.

9. Under what conditions can the NEPA process be initiated in conjunction with transportation planning studies?

The NEPA process may be initiated in conjunction with transportation planning studies in a number of ways. A common method is the "tiered EIS," in which the first-tier EIS evaluates general travel corridors, modes, and/or packages of projects at a planning level of detail, leading to the refinement of purpose and need and, ideally, selection of the design concept and scope for a project or series of projects. Subsequently, second-tier NEPA review(s) of the resulting projects would be performed in the usual way. The first-tier EIS uses the NEPA process as a tool to involve environmental, regulatory, and resource agencies and the public in the planning decisions, as well as to ensure the appropriate consideration of environmental factors in these planning decisions.

Corridor or subarea analyses/studies are another option when the long-range transportation plan leaves open the possibility of multiple approaches to fulfill its goals and objectives. In such cases, the formal NEPA process could be initiated through publication of a NOI in conjunction with a corridor or subarea planning study.

ALTERNATIVES

10. In the context of this Appendix, what is the meaning of the term "alternatives"?

This Appendix uses the term "alternatives" as specified in the NEPA regulations (40 CFR 1502.14), where it is defined in its broadest sense to include everything from major modal alternatives and location alternatives to minor design changes that would mitigate adverse impacts. This Appendix does not use the term as it is used in many other contexts (e.g., "prudent and feasible alternatives" under Section 4(f) of the Department of Transportation Act or the "Least Environmentally Damaging Practicable Alternative" under the Clean Water Act.

11. Under what circumstances can alternatives be eliminated from detailed consideration during the NEPA process based on information and analysis from the transportation planning process?

There are two ways in which the transportation planning process can begin limiting the alternative solutions to be evaluated during the NEPA process: (a) Shaping the purpose and need for the project; or (b) evaluating alternatives during planning studies and eliminating some of the alternatives from detailed study in the NEPA process prior to its start. Each approach requires careful attention, and is summarized below.

(a) Shaping the Purpose and Need for the Project: The transportation planning process should shape the purpose and need and, thereby, the range of reasonable alternatives. With proper documentation and public involvement, a purpose and need derived from the planning process can legitimately narrow the alternatives analyzed in the NEPA process. See the response to Question 8 for further discussion on how the planning process can shape the purpose and need used in the NEPA process.

For example, the purpose and need may be shaped by the transportation planning process in a manner that consequently narrows the range of alternatives that must be considered in detail in the NEPA document when:

(1) The transportation planning process has selected a general travel corridor as best addressing identified transportation problems and the rationale for the determination in the planning document is reflected in the purpose and need statement of the subsequent NEPA document;

(2) The transportation planning process has selected a general mode (e.g., highway, transit, or a highway/transit combination) that accomplishes its goals and objectives, and these documented determinations are reflected in the purpose and need statement of the subsequent NEPA document; or

(3) The transportation planning process determines that the project needs to be funded by tolls or other non-traditional funding sources in order for the long-range transportation plan to be fiscally constrained or identifies goals and objectives that can only be met by toll roads or other non-traditional funding sources, and that determination of those goals and objectives is reflected in the purpose and need statement of the subsequent NEPA document.

(b) Evaluating and Eliminating Alternatives During the Transportation Planning Process: The evaluation and elimination of alternatives during the transportation planning process can be incorporated by reference into a NEPA document under certain circumstances. In these cases, the planning study becomes part of the NEPA process and provides a basis for screening out alternatives. As with any part of the NEPA process, the analysis of alternatives to be incorporated from the process must have a rational basis that has been thoroughly documented (including documentation of the necessary and appropriate vetting through the applicable public involvement processes). This record should be made available for public review during the NEPA scoping process.

See responses to Questions 4, 5, 6, and 7 for additional elements to consider with respect to acceptance of planning products for NEPA documentation and the response to Question 12 on the information or analysis from the transportation planning process necessary for supporting the elimination of an alternative(s) from detailed consideration in the NEPA process.

Development of planning Alternatives Analysis studies, required prior to MAP–21 for projects seeking funds through FTA's Capital Investment Grant program, are now optional, but may still be used to narrow the alternatives prior to the NEPA review, just as other planning studies may be used. In fact, through planning studies, FTA may be able to narrow the alternatives considered in detail in the NEPA document to the No-Build (No Action) alternative and the Locally Preferred Alternative. If the planning process has included the analysis and stakeholder involvement that would be undertaken in a first tier NEPA process, then the alternatives screening conducted in the transportation planning process may be incorporated by reference, described, and relied upon in the project-level NEPA document. At that point, the project-level NEPA analysis can focus on the remaining alternatives.

12. What information or analysis from the transportation planning process is needed in an EA or EIS to support the elimination of an alternative(s) from detailed consideration?

The section of the EA or EIS that discusses alternatives considered but eliminated from detailed consideration should:

(a) Identify any alternatives eliminated during the transportation planning process (this could include broad categories of alternatives, as when a long-range transportation plan selects a general travel corridor based on a corridor study, thereby eliminating all alternatives along other alignments);

(b) Briefly summarize the reasons for eliminating the alternative; and

(c) Include a summary of the analysis process that supports the elimination of alternatives (the summary should reference the relevant sections or pages of the analysis or study) and incorporate it by reference or append it to the NEPA document.

Any analyses or studies used to eliminate alternatives from detailed consideration should be made available to the public and participating agencies during the NEPA scoping process and should be reasonably available during comment periods.

Alternatives passed over during the transportation planning process because they are infeasible or do not meet the NEPA "purpose and need" can be omitted from the detailed analysis of alternatives in the NEPA document, as long as the rationale for elimination is explained in the NEPA document. Alternatives that remain "reasonable" after the planning-level analysis must be addressed in the EIS, even when they are not the preferred alternative. When the proposed action evaluated in an EA involves unresolved conflicts concerning alternative uses of available resources, NEPA requires that appropriate alternatives be studied, developed, and described.

AFFECTED ENVIRONMENT AND ENVIRONMENTAL CONSEQUENCES

13. What types of planning products provide analysis of the affected environment and environmental consequences that are useful in a project-level NEPA analysis and document?

The following planning products are valuable inputs to the discussion of the affected environment and environmental consequences (both its current state and future state in the absence of the proposed action) in the project-level NEPA analysis and document:

• Regional development and growth analyses;

• Local land use, growth management, or development plans; and

• Population and employment projections.

The following are types of information, analysis, and other products from the transportation planning process that can be used in the discussion of the affected environment and environmental consequences in an EA or EIS:

(a) Geographic information system (GIS) overlays showing the past, current, or predicted future conditions of the natural and built environments;

(b) Environmental scans that identify environmental resources and environmentally sensitive areas;

(c) Descriptions of airsheds and watersheds;

(d) Demographic trends and forecasts;

(e) Projections of future land use, natural resource conservation areas, and development; and

(f) The outputs of natural resource planning efforts, such as wildlife conservation plans, watershed plans, special area management plans, and multiple species habitat conservation plans.

However, in most cases, the assessment of the affected environment and environmental consequences conducted during the transportation planning process will not be detailed or current enough to meet NEPA standards and, thus, the inventory and evaluation of affected resources and the analysis of consequences of the alternatives will need to be supplemented with more refined analysis and possibly site-specific details during the NEPA process.

14. What information from the transportation planning process is useful in describing a baseline for the NEPA analysis of indirect and cumulative impacts?

Because the nature of the transportation planning process is to look broadly at future land use, development, population increases, and other growth factors, the planning analysis can provide the basis for the assessment of indirect and cumulative impacts required under NEPA. The consideration in the transportation planning process of development, growth, and consistency with local land use, growth management, or development plans, as well as population and employment projections, provides an overview of the multitude of factors in an area that are creating pressures not only on the transportation system, but on the natural ecosystem and important environmental and community resources. An analysis of all reasonably foreseeable actions in the area also should be a part of the transportation planning process. This planning-level information should be captured and utilized in the analysis of indirect and cumulative impacts during the NEPA process.

To be used in the analysis of indirect and cumulative impacts, such information should:

(a) Be sufficiently detailed that differences in consequences of alternatives can be readily identified;

(b) Be based on current data (e.g., data from the most recent Census) or be updated by additional information;

(c) Be based on reasonable assumptions that are clearly stated; and/or

(d) Rely on analytical methods and modeling techniques that are reliable, defensible, and reasonably current.

ENVIRONMENTAL MITIGATION

15. How can planning-level efforts best support advance mitigation, mitigation banking, and priorities for environmental mitigation investments?

A lesson learned from efforts to establish mitigation banks and advance mitigation agreements and alternative mitigation options is the importance of beginning interagency discussions during the transportation planning process. Development pressures, habitat alteration, complicated real estate transactions, and competition for potential mitigation sites by public and private project proponents can encumber the already difficult task of mitigating for "like" value and function and reinforce the need to examine mitigation strategies as early as possible.

Robust use of remote sensing, GIS, and decision support systems for evaluating conservation strategies are all contributing to the advancement of natural resource and environmental planning. The outputs from environmental planning can now better inform transportation planning processes, including the development of mitigation strategies, so that transportation and conservation goals can be optimally met. For example, long-range transportation plans can be screened to assess the effect of general travel corridors or density, on the viability of sensitive plant and animal species or habitats. This type of screening provides a basis for early collaboration among transportation and environmental staffs, the public, and regulatory agencies to explore areas where impacts must be avoided and identify areas for mitigation investments. This can lead to mitigation strategies that are both more economical and more effective from an environmental stewardship perspective than traditional project-specific mitigation measures.

III. ADMINISTRATIVE ISSUES

16. Are Federal funds eligible to pay for these additional, or more in depth, environmental studies in transportation planning?

Yes. For example, the following FHWA and FTA funds may be utilized for conducting environmental studies and analyses within transportation planning:

• FHWA planning and research funds, as defined under 23 CFR part 420 (e.g., Metropolitan Planning (PL), Statewide Planning and Research (SPR), National Highway System (NHS), STP, and Equity Bonus); and

• FTA planning and research funds (49 U.S.C. 5303), urban formula funds (49 U.S.C. 5307), and (in limited circumstances) transit capital investment funds (49 U.S.C. 5309).

The eligible transportation planning-related uses of these funds may include: (a) Conducting feasibility or subarea/corridor needs studies and (b) developing system-wide environmental information/inventories (e.g., wetland banking inventories or standards to identify historically significant sites). Particularly in the case of PL and SPR funds, the proposed expenditure must be closely related to the development of transportation plans and programs under 23 U.S.C. 134–135 and 49 U.S.C. 5303–5306.

For FHWA funding programs, once a general travel corridor or specific project has progressed to a point in the preliminary engineering/NEPA phase that clearly extends beyond transportation planning, additional in-depth environmental studies must be funded through the program category for which the ultimate project qualifies (e.g., NHS, STP, Interstate Maintenance, and/or Bridge), rather than PL or SPR funds.

Another source of funding is FHWA's Transportation Enhancement program, which may be used for activities such as: conducting archeological planning and research; developing inventories such as those for historic bridges and highways, and other surface transportation-related structures; conducting studies to determine the extent of water pollution due to highway runoff; and conducting studies to reduce vehicle-caused wildlife mortality while maintaining habitat connectivity.

The FHWA and the FTA encourage State DOTs, MPOs, and public transportation operators to seek partners for some of these studies from environmental, regulatory, and resource agencies, non-government organizations, and other government and private sector entities with similar data needs, or environmental interests. In some cases, these partners may contribute data and expertise to the studies, as well as funding.

17. What staffing or organizational arrangements may be helpful in allowing planning products to be accepted in the NEPA process?

Certain organizational and staffing arrangements may support a more integrated approach to the planning/NEPA decision-making continuum. In many cases, planning organizations do not have environmental expertise on staff or readily accessible. Likewise, the review and regulatory responsibilities of many environmental, regulatory, and resource agencies make involvement in the transportation planning process a challenge for staff resources. These challenges may be partially met by improved use of the outputs of each agency's planning resources and by augmenting their capabilities through greater use of GIS and remote sensing technologies (see *http://www.gis.fhwa.dot.gov/* for additional information on the use of GIS). Sharing databases and the planning products of local land use decision-makers and State and Federal environmental, regulatory, and resource agencies also provide efficiencies in acquiring and sharing the data and information needed for both transportation planning and NEPA work.

Additional opportunities such as shared staff, training across disciplines, and (in some cases) reorganizing to eliminate structural divisions between planning and NEPA practitioners may also need to be considered in order to better integrate NEPA considerations into transportation planning studies. The answers to the following two questions also contain useful information on training and staffing opportunities.

18. How have environmental, regulatory, and resource agency liaisons (Federally and State DOT funded positions) and partnership agreements been used to provide the expertise and interagency participation needed to enhance the consideration of environmental factors in the planning process?

For several years, States have utilized Federal and State transportation funds to support focused and accelerated project review by a variety of local, State, Tribal, and Federal agencies. While Section 1309(e) of the TEA–21 and its successor in SAFETEA–LU section 6002 speak specifically to transportation project streamlining, there are other authorities that have been used to fund positions, such as the Intergovernmental Cooperation Act (31 U.S.C. 6505). In addition, long-term, on-call consultant contracts can provide backfill support for staff that are detailed to other parts of an agency for temporary assignments. At last count (as of 2015), over 200 positions were being funded. Additional information on interagency funding agreements is available at: *http://environment.fhwa.dot.gov/strmlng/igdocs/index.htm.*

Moreover, every State has advanced a variety of stewardship and streamlining initiatives that necessitate early involvement of environmental, regulatory, and resource agencies in the project development process. Such process improvements have: addressed the exchange of data to support avoidance and impact analysis; established formal and informal consultation and review schedules; advanced mitigation strategies; and resulted in a variety of programmatic reviews. Interagency agreements and work plans have evolved to describe performance objectives, as well as specific roles and responsibilities related to new streamlining initiatives. Some States have improved collaboration and efficiency by co-locating environmental, regulatory, and resource and transportation agency staff.

19. What training opportunities are available to MPOs, State DOTs, public transportation operators and environmental, regulatory, and resource agencies to assist in their understanding of the transportation planning and NEPA processes?

Both the FHWA and the FTA offer a variety of transportation planning, public involvement, and NEPA courses through the National Highway Institute and/or the National Transit Institute. Of particular note is the Linking Planning and NEPA Workshop, which provides a forum and facilitated group discussion among and between State DOT; MPO; Federal, Tribal, and State environmental, regulatory, and resource agencies; and FHWA/FTA representatives (at both the executive and program manager levels) to develop a State-specific action plan that will provide for strengthened linkages between the transportation planning and NEPA processes.

Moreover, the U.S. Fish and Wildlife Service offers Green Infrastructure Workshops that are focused on integrating planning for natural resources (“green infrastructure”) with the development, economic, and other infrastructure needs of society (“gray infrastructure”).

Robust planning and multi-issue environmental screening requires input from a wide variety of disciplines, including information technology; transportation planning; the NEPA process; and regulatory, permitting, and environmental specialty areas (e.g., noise, air quality, and biology). Senior managers at transportation and partner agencies can arrange a variety of individual training programs to support learning curves and skill development that contribute to a strengthened link of the transportation planning and NEPA processes. Formal and informal mentoring on an intra-agency basis can be arranged. Employee exchanges within and between agencies can be periodically scheduled, and persons involved with professional leadership programs can seek temporary assignments with partner agencies.

IV. Additional Information on This Topic

Valuable sources of information are FHWA's environment Web site (*http://www.fhwa.dot.gov/environment/index.htm*) and FTA's environmental streamlining Web site (*http://www.environment.fta.dot.gov*). Another source of information and case studies is NCHRP Report 8–38 (Consideration of Environmental Factors in Transportation Systems Planning), which is available at *http://www4.trb.org/trb/crp.nsf/All?????38*. In addition, AASHTO's Center for Environmental Excellence Web site is continuously updated with news and links to information of interest to transportation and environmental professionals (*www.transportation.environment.org*).

PART 460—PUBLIC ROAD MILEAGE FOR APPORTIONMENT OF HIGHWAY SAFETY FUNDS

AUTHORITY: 23 U.S.C. 315, 402(c); 49 CFR 1.48.

SOURCE: 40 FR 44322, Sept. 26, 1975, unless otherwise noted.

§460.1 Purpose.

The purpose of this part is to prescribe the policies and procedures followed in identifying and reporting public road mileage for utilization in the statutory formula for the apportionment of highway safety funds under 23 U.S.C. 402(c).

§460.2 Definitions.

As used in this part:

(a) *Public road* means any road under the jurisdiction of and maintained by a public authority and open to public travel.

(b) *Public authority* means a Federal, State, county, town, or township, Indian tribe, municipal or other local government or instrumentality thereof, with authority to finance, build, operate or maintain toll or toll-free highway facilities.

(c) *Open to public travel* means that the road section is available, except during scheduled periods, extreme weather or emergency conditions, passable by four-wheel standard passenger cars, and open to the general public for use without restrictive gates, prohibitive signs, or regulation other than restrictions based on size, weight, or class of registration. Toll plazas of public toll roads are not considered restrictive gates.

(d) *Maintenance* means the preservation of the entire highway, including surfaces, shoulders, roadsides, structures, and such traffic control devices as are necessary for its safe and efficient utilization.

(e) *State* means any one of the 50 States, the District of Columbia, Puerto Rico, the Virgin Islands, Guam, American Samoa, and the Commonwealth of the Northern Mariana Islands. For the purpose of the application of 23 U.S.C. 402 on Indian reservations, *State* and *Governor of a State* include the Secretary of the Interior.

[40 FR 44322, Sept. 26, 1975, as amended at 76 FR 12849, Mar. 9, 2011]

§460.3 Procedures.

(a) *General requirements*. 23 U.S.C. 402(c) provides that funds authorized to carry out section 402 shall be apportioned according to a formula based on population and public road mileage of each State. Public road mileage shall be determined as of the end of the calendar year preceding the year in which the funds are apportioned and shall be certified to by the Governor of the State or his designee and subject to the approval of the Federal Highway Administrator.

(b) *State public road mileage*. Each State must annually submit a certification of public road mileage within the State to the Federal Highway Administration Division Administrator by the date specified by the Division Administrator. Public road mileage on Indian reservations within the State shall be identified and included in the State mileage and in computing the State's apportionment.

(c) *Indian reservation public road mileage*. The Secretary of the Interior or his designee will submit a certification of public road mileage within Indian reservations to the Federal Highway Administrator by June 1 of each year.

(d) *Action by the Federal Highway Administrator*. (1) The certification of Indian reservation public road mileage, and the State certifications of public road mileage together with comments thereon, will be reviewed by the Federal Highway Administrator. He will make a final determination of the public road mileage to be used as the basis for apportionment of funds under 23 U.S.C. 402(c). In any instance in which the Administrator's final determination differs from the public road mileage certified by a State or the Secretary of the Interior, the Administrator will advise the State or the Secretary of the Interior of his final determination and the reasons therefor.

(2) If a State fails to submit a certification of public road mileage as required by this part, the Federal Highway Administrator may make a determination of the State's public road mileage for the purpose of apportioning funds under 23 U.S.C. 402(c). The State's public road mileage determined by the Administrator under this subparagraph may not exceed 90 percent of the State's public road mileage utilized in determining the most recent apportionment of funds under 23 U.S.C. 402(c).

PART 470—HIGHWAY SYSTEMS

Subpart A—Federal-aid Highway Systems

Subparts B–C [Reserved]

AUTHORITY: 23 U.S.C. 103(b)(2), 103(c), 134, 135, and 315; and 49 CFR 1.48(b).

SOURCE: 40 FR 42344, Sept. 12, 1975, unless otherwise noted. Redesignated at 41 FR 51396, Nov. 22, 1976.

Subpart A—Federal-aid Highway Systems

SOURCE: 62 FR 33355, June 19, 1997, unless otherwise noted.

§470.101 Purpose.

This part sets forth policies and procedures relating to the identification of Federal-aid highways, the functional classification of roads and streets, the designation of urban area boundaries, and the designation of routes on the Federal-aid highway systems.

§470.103 Definitions.

Except as otherwise provided in this part, terms defined in 23 U.S.C. 101(a) are used in this part as so defined.

Consultation means that one party confers with another identified party and, prior to taking action(s), considers that party's views.

Cooperation means that the parties involved in carrying out the planning, programming and management systems processes work together to achieve a common goal or objective.

Coordination means the comparison of the transportation plans, programs, and schedules of one agency with related plans, programs, and schedules of other agencies or entities with legal standing, and adjustment of plans, programs, and schedules to achieve general consistency.

Federal-aid highway systems means the National Highway System and the Dwight D. Eisenhower National System of Interstate and Defense Highways (the "Interstate System").

Federal-aid highways means highways on the Federal-aid highway systems and all other public roads not classified as local roads or rural minor collectors.

Governor means the chief executive of the State and includes the Mayor of the District of Columbia.

Metropolitan planning organization (MPO) means the forum for cooperative transportation decisionmaking for the metropolitan planning area in which the metropolitan transportation planning process required by 23 U.S.C. 134 and 49 U.S.C. 5303–5305 must be carried out.

Responsible local officials means—

(1) In urbanized areas, principal elected officials of general purpose local governments acting through the Metropolitan Planning Organization designated by the Governor, or

(2) In rural areas and urban areas not within any urbanized area, principal

elected officials of general purpose local governments.

State means any one of the fifty States, the District of Columbia, Puerto Rico, or, for purposes of functional classification of highways, the Virgin Islands, American Samoa, Guam, or the Commonwealth of the Northern Marianas.

§470.105 Urban area boundaries and highway functional classification.

(a) *Urban area boundaries.* Routes on the Federal-aid highway systems may be designated in both rural and urban areas. Guidance for determining the boundaries of urbanized and nonurbanized urban areas is provided in the FHWA's Functional Classification Guidelines.[1]

(b) *Highway functional classification.* (1) The State transportation agency shall have the primary responsibility for developing and updating a statewide highway functional classification in rural and urban areas to determine functional usage of the existing roads and streets. Guidance criteria and procedures are provided in the FHWA's Functional Classification Guidelines. The State shall cooperate with responsible local officials, or appropriate Federal agency in the case of areas under Federal jurisdiction, in developing and updating the functional classification.

(2) The results of the functional classification shall be mapped and submitted to the Federal Highway Administration (FHWA) for approval and when approved shall serve as the official record for Federal-aid highways and the basis for designation of the National Highway System.

[62 FR 33355, June 19, 1997, as amended at 76 FR 6691, Feb. 8, 2011]

§470.107 Federal-aid highway systems.

(a) *Interstate System.* (1) The Dwight D. Eisenhower National System of Interstate and Defense Highways (Interstate System) shall consist of routes of highest importance to the Nation, built to the uniform geometric and construction standards of 23 U.S.C. 109(h), which connect, as directly as practicable, the principal metropolitan areas, cities, and industrial centers, including important routes into, through, and around urban areas, serve the national defense and, to the greatest extent possible, connect at suitable border points with routes of continental importance in Canada and Mexico.

(2) The portion of the Interstate System designated under 23 U.S.C. 103(c)(1)(D)(2) shall not exceed 69,230 kilometers (43,000 miles). Additional Interstate System segments are permitted under the provisions of 23 U.S.C. 103(c)(4) and section 1105(e)(5)(A) of the Intermodal Surface Transportation Efficiency Act of 1991 (ISTEA), Pub. L. 102–240, 105 Stat. 1914, as amended.

(b) *National Highway System.* (1) The National Highway System shall consist of interconnected urban and rural principal arterials and highways (including toll facilities) which serve major population centers, international border crossings, ports, airports, public transportation facilities, other intermodal transportation facilities and other major travel destinations; meet national defense requirements; and serve interstate and interregional travel. All routes on the Interstate System are a part of the National Highway System.

(2) The National Highway System shall not exceed 286,983 kilometers (178,250 miles).

(3) The National Highway System shall include the Strategic Highway Corridor Network (STRAHNET) and its highway connectors to major military installations, as designated by the Administrator in consultation with appropriate Federal agencies and the States. The STRAHNET includes highways which are important to the United States strategic defense policy and which provide defense access, continuity, and emergency capabilities for the movement of personnel, materials, and equipment in both peace time and war time.

(4) The National Highway System shall include all high priority corridors identified in section 1105(c) of the ISTEA.

[62 FR 33355, June 19, 1997, as amended at 76 FR 6691, Feb. 8, 2011]

[1] The Functional Classification Guidelines can be viewed at *http://www.fhwa.dot.gov/planning/fctoc.htm.*

§ 470.109 System procedures—General.

(a) The State transportation agency, in consultation with responsible local officials, shall have the responsibility for proposing to the Federal Highway Administration all official actions regarding the designation, or revision, of the Federal-aid highway systems.

(b) The routes of the Federal-aid highway systems shall be proposed by coordinated action of the State transportation agencies where the routes involve State-line connections.

(c) The designation of routes on the Federal-aid highway systems shall be in accordance with the planning process required, pursuant to the provisions at 23 U.S.C. 135, and, in urbanized areas, the provisions at 23 U.S.C. 134(a). The State shall cooperate with local and regional officials. In urbanized areas, the local officials shall act through the metropolitan planning organizations designated for such areas under 23 U.S.C. 134.

(d) In areas under Federal jurisdiction, the designation of routes on the Federal-aid highway systems shall be coordinated with the appropriate Federal agency.

§ 470.111 Interstate System procedures.

(a) Proposals for system actions on the Interstate System shall include a route description and a statement of justification. Proposals shall also include statements regarding coordination with adjoining States on State-line connections, with responsible local officials, and with officials of areas under Federal jurisdiction.

(b) Proposals for Interstate or future Interstate designation under 23 U.S.C. 103(c)(4)(A) or (B), as logical additions or connections, shall consider the criteria contained in appendix A of this subpart. For designation as a part of the Interstate system, 23 U.S.C. 103(c)(4)(A) requires that a highway meet all the standards of a highway on the Interstate System, be a logical addition or connection to the Interstate System, and have the affirmative recommendation of the State or States involved. For designation as a future part of the Interstate System, 23 U.S.C. 103(c)(4)(B) requires that a highway be a logical addition or connection to the Interstate System, have the affirmative recommendation of the State or States involved, and have the written agreement of the State or States involved that such highway will be constructed to meet all the standards of a highway on the Interstate System within twenty-five years of the date of the agreement between the FHWA Administrator and the State or States involved. Such highways must also be on the National Highway System.

(c) Routes proposed for Interstate designation under section 332(a)(2) of the NHS Designation Act of 1995 (NHS Act) shall be constructed to Interstate standards and connect to the Interstate System. Proposals shall consider the criteria contained in appendix B of this subpart.

(d) Proposals for Interstate route numbering shall be submitted by the State transportation agency to the Route Numbering Committee of the American Association of State Highway and Transportation Officials.

(e) Signing of corridors federally designated as future Interstate routes can follow the criteria contained in appendix C of this subpart. No law, rule, regulation, map, document, or other record of the United States, or of any State or political subdivision thereof, shall refer to any highway under 23 U.S.C. 103(c), nor shall any such highway be signed or marked, as a highway on the Interstate System until such time as such highway is constructed to the geometric and construction standards for the Interstate System and has been designated as a part of the Interstate System.

[62 FR 33355, June 19, 1997, as amended at 76 FR 6691, Feb. 8, 2011]

§ 470.113 National Highway System procedures.

(a) Proposals for system actions on the National Highway System shall include a route description, a statement of justification, and statements of coordination with adjoining States on State-line connections, with responsible local officials, and with officials of areas under Federal jurisdiction.

(b) Proposed modifications to the National Highway System shall enhance the national transportation characteristics of the National Highway System and shall follow the criteria listed in §470.107. Proposals shall also consider the criteria contained in appendix D of this subpart.

§470.115 Approval authority.

(a) The Federal Highway Administrator will approve Federal-aid highway system actions involving the designation, or revision, of routes on the Interstate System, including route numbers, future Interstate routes, and routes on the National Highway System.

(b) The Federal Highway Administrator will approve functional classification actions.

Appendix A to Subpart A of Part 470—Guidance Criteria for Evaluating Requests for Interstate System Designations Under 23 U.S.C. 103(c)(4)(A) and (B)

Section 103(c)(4)(A) and (B), of title 23, U.S.C., permits States to request the designation of National Highway System routes as parts or future parts of the Interstate System. The FHWA Administrator may approve such a request if the route is a logical addition or connection to the Interstate System and has been, or will be, constructed to meet Interstate standards. The following are the general criteria to be used to evaluate 23 U.S.C. 103(c) requests for Interstate System designations.

1. The proposed route should be of sufficient length to serve long-distance Interstate travel, such as connecting routes between principal metropolitan cities or industrial centers important to national defense and economic development.

2. The proposed route should not duplicate other Interstate routes. It should serve Interstate traffic movement not provided by another Interstate route.

3. The proposed route should directly serve major highway traffic generators. The term "major highway traffic generator" means either an urbanized area with a population over 100,000 or a similar major concentrated land use activity that produces and attracts long-distance Interstate and statewide travel of persons and goods. Typical examples of similar major concentrated land use activities would include a principal industrial complex, government center, military installation, or transportation terminal.

4. The proposed route should connect to the Interstate System at each end, with the exception of Interstate routes that connect with continental routes at an international border, or terminate in a "major highway traffic generator" that is not served by another Interstate route. In the latter case, the terminus of the Interstate route should connect to routes of the National Highway System that will adequately handle the traffic. The proposed route also must be functionally classified as a principal arterial and be a part of the National Highway System system.

5. The proposed route must meet all the current geometric and safety standards criteria as set forth in 23 CFR part 625 for highways on the Interstate System, or a formal agreement to construct the route to such standards within 25 years must be executed between the State(s) and the Federal Highway Administration. Any proposed exceptions to the standards shall be approved at the time of designation.

6. A route being proposed for designation under 23 U.S.C. 103(c)(4)(B) must have an approved final environmental document (including, if required, a 49 U.S.C. 303(c) [Section 4(f)] approval) covering the route and project action must be ready to proceed with design at the time of designation. Routes constructed to Interstate standards are not necessarily logical additions to the Interstate System unless they clearly meet all of the above criteria.

[40 FR 42344, Sept. 12, 1975. Redesignated at 41 FR 51396, Nov. 22, 1976, as amended at 76 FR 6692, Feb. 8, 2011]

Appendix B to Subpart A of Part 470—Designation of Segments of Section 332(a)(2) Corridors as Parts of the Interstate System

The following guidance is comparable to current procedures for Interstate System designation requests under 23 U.S.C. 103(c)(4)(A). All Interstate System additions must be approved by the Federal Highway Administrator. The provisions of section 332(a)(2) of the NHS Act have also been incorporated into the ISTEA as section 1105(e)(5)(A).

1. The request must be submitted through the appropriate FHWA Division Office to the Associate Administrator for Program Development (HEP–10). Comments and recommendations by the division and regional offices are requested.

2. The State DOT secretary (or equivalent) must request that the route segment be added to the Interstate System. The exact location and termini must be specified. If the route segment involves more than one State, each affected State must submit a separate request.

3. The request must provide information to support findings that the segment (a) is built to Interstate design standards and (b) connects to the existing Interstate System. The segment should be of sufficient length to

provide substantial service to the travelling public.

4. The request must also identify and justify any design exceptions for which approval is requested.

5. Proposed Interstate route numbering for the segment must be submitted to FHWA and the American Association of State Highway and Transportation Officials Route Numbering.

[40 FR 42344, Sept. 12, 1975. Redesignated at 41 FR 51396, Nov. 22, 1976, as amended at 76 FR 6692, Feb. 8, 2011]

APPENDIX C TO SUBPART A OF PART 470—POLICY FOR THE SIGNING AND NUMBERING OF FUTURE INTERSTATE CORRIDORS DESIGNATED BY SECTION 332 OF THE NHS DESIGNATION ACT OF 1995 OR DESIGNATED UNDER 23 U.S.C. 103(c)(4)(B)

POLICY

State transportation agencies are permitted to erect informational Interstate signs along a federally designated future Interstate corridor only after the specific route location has been established for the route to be constructed to Interstate design standards.

CONDITIONS

1. The corridor must have been designated a future part of the Interstate System under section 332(a)(2) of the NHS Designation Act of 1995 or 23 U.S.C. 103(c)(4)(B).

2. The specific route location to appropriate termini must have received Federal Highway (FHWA) environmental clearance. Where FHWA environmental clearance is not required or Interstate standards have been met, the route location must have been publicly announced by the State.

3. Numbering of future Interstate route segments must be coordinated with affected States and be approved by the American Association of State Highway and Transportation Officials and the FHWA at Headquarters. Short portions of a multistate corridor may require use of an interim 3-digit number.

4. The State shall coordinate the location and content of signing near the State line with the adjacent State.

5. Signing and other identification of a future Interstate route segment must not indicate, nor imply, that the route is on the Interstate System.

6. The FHWA Division Office must confirm in advance that the above conditions have been met and approve the general locations of signs.

SIGN DETAILS

1. Signs may not be used to give directions and should be away from directional signs, particularly at interchanges.

2. An Interstate shield may be located on a green informational sign of a few words. For example: Future Interstate Corridor or Future I–00 Corridor.

3. The Interstate shield may not include the word ''Interstate.''

4. The FHWA Division Office must approve the signs as to design, wording, and detailed location.

[40 FR 42344, Sept. 12, 1975. Redesignated at 41 FR 51396, Nov. 22, 1976, as amended at 76 FR 6692, Feb. 8, 2011]

APPENDIX D TO SUBPART A OF PART 470—GUIDANCE CRITERIA FOR EVALUATING REQUESTS FOR MODIFICATIONS TO THE NATIONAL HIGHWAY SYSTEM

Section 103(b), of title 23, U.S.C., allows the States to propose modifications to the National Highway System (NHS) and authorizes the Secretary to approve such modifications provided that they meet the criteria established for the NHS and enhance the characteristics of the NHS. In proposing modifications under 23 U.S.C. 103(b), the States must cooperate with local and regional officials. In urbanized areas, the local officials must act through the metropolitan planning organization (MPO) designated for such areas under 23 U.S.C. 134. The following guidance criteria should be used by the States to develop proposed modifications to the NHS.

1. Proposed additions to the NHS should be included in either an adopted State or metropolitan transportation plan or program.

2. Proposed additions should connect at each end with other routes on the NHS or serve a major traffic generator.

3. Proposals should be developed in consultation with local and regional officials.

4. Proposals to add routes to the NHS should include information on the type of traffic served (*i.e.*, percent of trucks, average trip length, local, commuter, interregional, interstate) by the route, the population centers or major traffic generators served by the route, and how this service compares with existing NHS routes.

5. Proposals should include information on existing and anticipated needs and any planned improvements to the route.

6. Proposals should include information concerning the possible effects of adding or deleting a route to or from the NHS might have on other existing NHS routes that are in close proximity.

7. Proposals to add routes to the NHS should include an assessment of whether modifications (adjustments or deletions) to

existing NHS routes, which provide similar service, may be appropriate.

8. Proposed modifications that might affect adjoining States should be developed in cooperation with those States.

9. Proposed modifications consisting of connections to major intermodal facilities should be developed using the criteria set forth below. These criteria were used for identifying initial NHS connections to major intermodal terminals. The primary criteria are based on annual passenger volumes, annual freight volumes, or daily vehicular traffic on one or more principal routes that serve the intermodal facility. The secondary criteria include factors which underscore the importance of an intermodal facility within a specific State.

PRIMARY CRITERIA

Commercial Aviation Airports

1. Passengers—scheduled commercial service with more than 250,000 annual enplanements.

2. Cargo—100 trucks per day in each direction on the principal connecting route, or 100,000 tons per year arriving or departing by highway mode.

Ports

1. Terminals that handle more than 50,000 TEUs (a volumetric measure of containerized cargo which stands for twenty-foot equivalent units) per year, or other units measured that would convert to more than 100 trucks per day in each direction. (Trucks are defined as large single-unit trucks or combination vehicles handling freight.)

2. Bulk commodity terminals that handle more than 500,000 tons per year by highway or 100 trucks per day in each direction on the principal connecting route. (If no individual terminal handles this amount of freight, but a cluster of terminals in close proximity to each other does, then the cluster of terminals could be considered in meeting the criteria. In such cases, the connecting route might terminate at a point where the traffic to several terminals begins to separate.)

3. Passengers—terminals that handle more than 250,000 passengers per year or 1,000 passengers per day for at least 90 days during the year.

Truck/Rail

1. 50,000 TEUs per year, or 100 trucks per day, in each direction on the principal connecting route, or other units measured that would convert to more than 100 trucks per day in each direction. (Trucks are defined as large single-unit trucks or combination vehicles carrying freight.)

Pipelines

1. 100 trucks per day in each direction on the principal connecting route.

Amtrak

1. 100,000 passengers per year (entrainments and detrainments). Joint Amtrak, intercity bus and public transit terminals should be considered based on the combined passenger volumes. Likewise, two or more separate facilities in close proximity should be considered based on combined passenger volumes.

Intercity Bus

1. 100,000 passengers per year (boardings and deboardings).

Public Transit

1. Stations with park and ride lots with more than 500 vehicle parking spaces, or 5,000 daily bus or rail passengers, with significant highway access (*i.e.*, a high percentage of the passengers arrive by cars and buses using a route that connects to another NHS route), or a major hub terminal that provides for the transfer of passengers among several bus routes. (These hubs should have a significant number of buses using a principal route connecting with the NHS.)

Ferries

1. Interstate/international—1,000 passengers per day for at least 90 days during the year. (A ferry which connects two terminals within the same metropolitan area should be considered as local, not interstate.)

2. Local—see public transit criteria above.

SECONDARY CRITERIA

Any of the following criteria could be used to justify an NHS connection to an intermodal terminal where there is a significant highway interface:

1. Intermodal terminals that handle more than 20 percent of passenger or freight volumes by mode within a State;

2. Intermodal terminals identified either in the Intermodal Management System or the State and metropolitan transportation plans as a major facility;

3. Significant investment in, or expansion of, an intermodal terminal; or

4. Connecting routes targeted by the State, MPO, or others for investment to address an existing, or anticipated, deficiency as a result of increased traffic.

PROXIMATE CONNECTIONS

Intermodal terminals, identified under the secondary criteria noted above, may not have sufficient highway traffic volumes to justify an NHS connection to the terminal. States and MPOs should fully consider whether a direct connection should be identified for such terminals, or whether being in the proximity (2 to 3 miles) of an NHS route is sufficient.

Subparts B–C [Reserved]

PART 490—NATIONAL PERFORMANCE MANAGEMENT MEASURES

Subpart A—General Information

Subpart B—National Performance Management Measures for the Highway Safety Improvement Program

Subpart C—National Performance Management Measures for the Assessing Pavement Condition

Subpart D—National Performance Management Measures for Assessing Bridge Condition

Subpart E—National Performance Management Measures To Assess Performance of the National Highway System

Subpart F—National Performance Management Measures To Assess Freight Movement on the Interstate System

Subpart G—National Performance Management Measure for Assessing the Congestion Mitigation and Air Quality Improvement Program—Traffic Congestion

Subpart H—National Performance Management Measures to Assess the Congestion Mitigation and Air Quality Improvement Program—On-Road Mobile Source Emissions

AUTHORITY: 23 U.S.C. 134, 135, 148(i) and 150; 49 CFR 1.85.

SOURCE: 81 FR 13913, Mar. 15, 2016, unless otherwise noted.

Subpart A—General Information

SOURCE: 82 FR 6031, Jan. 18, 2017, unless otherwise noted.

§490.101 Definitions.

Unless otherwise specified, the following definitions apply to this part:

American Community Survey (ACS) is a national level ongoing survey from the U.S. Census Bureau that includes data on jobs, occupations, educational attainment, transportations patterns, and other topics of the Nation's population.

Attainment area as used in this part is defined in §450.104 of this chapter, Transportation Planning and Programming Definitions.

Bridge as used in this part is defined in §650.305 of this chapter, the National Bridge Inspection Standards.

Criteria pollutant is any pollutant for which there is established a NAAQS at 40 CFR part 50. The transportation related criteria pollutants per 40 CFR 93.102(b)(1) are carbon monoxide, nitrogen dioxide, ozone, and particulate matter (PM_{10} and $PM_{2.5}$).

Full extent means continuous collection and evaluation of pavement condition data over the entire length of the roadway.

Highway Performance Monitoring System (HPMS) is a national level highway information system that includes data on the extent, condition, performance, use, and operating characteristics of the Nation's highways.

Mainline highways means the through travel lanes of any highway. Mainline highways specifically exclude ramps, shoulders, turn lanes, crossovers, rest areas, and other pavement surfaces that are not part of the roadway normally traveled by through traffic.

Maintenance area as used in this part is defined in §450.104 of this chapter, Transportation Planning and Programming Definitions. For the purposes of this part, areas that have reached the end of their 20-year maintenance period[1] are not considered as maintenance areas.

Measure means an expression based on a metric that is used to establish targets and to assess progress toward achieving the established targets (e.g., a measure for flight on-time performance is percent of flights that arrive on time, and a corresponding metric is an arithmetic difference between scheduled and actual arrival time for each flight).

Metric means a quantifiable indicator of performance or condition.

Metropolitan Planning Organization (MPO) as used in this part is defined in §450.104 of this chapter, Transportation Planning and Programming Definitions.

Metropolitan Planning Area as used in this part is defined in §450.104 of this chapter, Transportation Planning and Programming Definitions.

National Ambient Air Quality Standards (NAAQS) as used in this part is defined in §450.104 of this chapter, Transportation Planning and Programming Definitions.

National Bridge Inventory (NBI) is an FHWA database containing bridge information and inspection data for all highway bridges on public roads, on and off Federal-aid highways, including

[1] The maintenance period in CAA Section 175A (42 U.S.C. 7505a) requires the submittal of two maintenance plans totaling 20 years, unless the applicable implementation plan specifics a longer maintenance period. The end of the maintenance period is 20-years from the effective date of the re-designation to attainment and approval of the first 10-year maintenance plan.

tribally owned and federally owned bridges, that are subject to the National Bridge Inspection Standards (NBIS).

National Performance Management Research Data Set (NPMRDS) means a data set derived from vehicle/passenger probe data (sourced from Global Positioning Station (GPS), navigation units, cell phones) that includes average travel times representative of all traffic on each mainline highway segment of the National Highway System (NHS), and additional travel times representative of freight trucks for those segments that are on the Interstate System. The data set includes records that contain average travel times for every 15 minutes of every day (24 hours) of the year recorded and calculated for every travel time segment where probe data are available. The NPMRDS does not include any imputed travel time data.

Nonattainment area as used in this part is defined in § 450.104 of this chapter, Transportation Planning and Programming Definitions.

Non-SOV travel is defined as any travel mode other than driving alone in a motorized vehicle (*i.e.*, single occupancy vehicle or SOV travel), including travel avoided by telecommuting.

Non-urbanized area means a single geographic area that comprises all of the areas in the State that are not "urbanized areas" under 23 U.S.C. 101(a)(34).

Performance period means a determined time period during which condition/performance is measured and evaluated to: Assess condition/performance with respect to baseline condition/performance; and track progress toward the achievement of the targets that represent the intended condition/performance level at the midpoint and at the end of that time period. The term "performance period" applies to all measures in this part, except the measures for the Highway Safety Improvement Program (HSIP) in subpart B of this part. Each performance period covers a 4-year duration beginning on a specified date (provided in § 490.105).

Reporting segment means the length of roadway that the State Department of Transportation (DOT) and MPOs define for metric calculation and reporting and is comprised of one or more travel time segments.

Target means a quantifiable level of performance or condition, expressed as a value for the measure, to be achieved within a time period required by the Federal Highway Administration (FHWA).

Transportation Management Area (TMA) as used in this part is defined in § 450.104 of this chapter, Transportation Planning and Programming Definitions.

Travel time data set means either the NPMRDS or an equivalent data set that is used by State DOTs and MPOs as approved by FHWA, to carry out the requirements in subparts E, F, and G of this part.

Travel time reliability means the consistency or dependability of travel times from day to day or across different times of the day.

Travel time segment means a contiguous stretch of the NHS for which average travel time data are summarized in the travel time data set.

Truck freight bottleneck, as used in this part, is defined as a segment of roadway identified by the State DOT as having constraints that cause a significant impact on freight mobility and reliability. Bottlenecks may include highway sections that do not meet thresholds for freight reliability identified in § 490.613 or other locations identified by the State DOT. Causes may include recurring congestion, causing delays in freight movement, or roadway features that impact truck movements, such as steep grades, substandard vertical or horizontal clearances, weight restrictions, delays at border crossings or terminals, or truck operating restrictions.

§ 490.103 Data requirements.

(a) *In general.* Unless otherwise noted in paragraphs (b) through (g) of this section, the data requirements in this section apply to the measures identified in subparts C through H of this part. Additional data requirements for specific performance management measures are identified in 23 CFR sections—

(1) 490.309 for the condition of pavements on the Interstate System;

(2) 490.309 for the condition of pavements on the non-Interstate NHS;

(3) 490.409 for the condition of bridges on the NHS;

(4) 490.509 for the performance of the Interstate System;

(5) 490.509 for the performance of the non-Interstate NHS;

(6) 490.609 for the freight movement on the Interstate System;

(7) 490.709 for traffic congestion; and

(8) 490.809 for on-road mobile source emissions.

(b) *Urbanized area data.* The State DOTs shall submit urbanized area data, including boundaries of urbanized areas, in accordance with the HPMS Field Manual for the purpose of the additional targets for urbanized and non-urbanized areas in §490.105(e) and establishing and reporting on targets for the CMAQ Traffic Congestion measures in §490.707. The boundaries of urbanized areas shall be identified based on the most recent U.S. Decennial Census, unless FHWA approves adjustments to the urbanized area as provided by 23 U.S.C. 101(a)(34) and these adjustments are submitted to HPMS.

(c) *Nonattainment and maintenance areas data.* The State DOTs shall use the nonattainment and maintenance areas boundaries based on the effective date of U.S. Environmental Protection Agency (EPA) designations in 40 CFR part 81.

(d) *National Highway System data.* The State DOTs shall document and submit the extent of the NHS in accordance with the HPMS Field Manual.

(e) *Travel time data set.* Travel time data needed to calculate the measures in subparts E, F, and G of this part will come from the NPMRDS, unless the State DOT requests, and FHWA approves, the use of an equivalent data source(s) that meets the requirements of this section. The State DOT shall establish, in coordination with applicable MPOs, a single travel time data set (*i.e.*, NPMRDS or equivalent data set) that will be used to calculate the annual metrics in subparts E, F, and G of this part. The same data source shall be used for each calendar year. A State DOT and MPO(s) must use the same travel time data set for each reporting segment for the purposes of calculating the metrics and measures. The use of equivalent data source(s) shall comply with the following:

(1) State DOTs and MPOs shall use the same equivalent data source(s) for a calendar year;

(2) The State DOT shall request FHWA approval for the use of such equivalent data source(s) no later than October 1st before the beginning of the calendar year in which the data source would be used to calculate metrics and FHWA must approve the use of that data source prior to a State DOT and MPO(s)'s implementation and use of that data source;

(3) The State DOT shall make the equivalent data source(s) available to FHWA, on request;

(4) The State DOT shall maintain and use a documented data quality plan to routinely check the quality and accuracy of data contained within the equivalent data source(s); and

(5) If approved by FHWA, the equivalent data source(s) shall:

(i) Be used by both the State DOT and all MPOs within the State for all applicable travel time segments and be referenced by HPMS location referencing standards; and

(ii) In combination with or in place of NPMRDS data, include:

(A) Contiguous segments that cover the mainline highways full NHS, as defined in 23 U.S.C. 103, within the State and MPO boundary; and

(B) Average travel times for at least the same number of 15 minute intervals and the same locations that would be available in the NPMRDS;

(iii) Be populated with observed measured vehicle travel times and shall not be populated with travel times derived from imputed (historic travel times or other estimates) methods. Segment travel times may be derived from travel times reported over a longer time period of measurement (path processing or equivalent);

(iv) Include, for each segment at 15 minute intervals throughout the time periods specified in paragraphs (e)(5)(iv)(A) and (B) of this section for each day of the year, the average travel time, recorded to the nearest second, representative of at least one of the following:

(A) All traffic on each segment of the NHS (24 hours on Interstate; 6 a.m. to 8 p.m. for non-Interstate NHS); or

(B) Freight vehicle traffic on each segment of the Interstate System (24 hours);

(v) Include, for each segment, a recording of the time and date of each 15 minute travel time record;

(vi) Include the location (route, functional class, direction, State), length and begin and end points of each segment; and

(vii) Be available within 60 days of measurement.

(f) *Reporting segments.* State DOTs, in coordination with MPOs, shall define a single set of reporting segments of the Interstate System and non-Interstate NHS for the purpose of calculating the travel time-based measures specified in §§ 490.507, 490.607, and 490.707 in accordance with the following:

(1) Reporting segments shall be comprised of one or more contiguous Travel Time Segments of same travel direction. State DOTs have the option to accept the Travel Time Segments in the NPMRDS as the reporting segments;

(2) Reporting segments shall not exceed 1 mile in length in urbanized areas unless an individual Travel Time Segment is longer and 10 miles in length in non-urbanized areas unless an individual Travel Time Segment is longer;

(3) All reporting segments collectively shall be contiguous and cover the full extent of the directional mainline highways of the Interstate System and non-Interstate NHS required for reporting the measure; and

(4) The State DOT and applicable MPOs shall document, in manner that mutually agreed upon by all relevant parties, the coordination and agreement on the travel time data set and the defined reporting segments.

(g) *Posted speed limit.* State DOTs are encouraged to report the posted speed limits for the full extent of the NHS in their State via HPMS (HPMS Data Item "Speed_Limit").

§ 490.105 Establishment of performance targets.

(a) *In general.* State DOTs shall establish performance targets for all measures specified in paragraph (c) of this section for the respective target scope identified in paragraph (d) of this section with the requirements specified in paragraph (e) of this section. The MPOs shall establish performance targets for all measures specified in paragraph (c) of this section for respective target scope identified in paragraph (d) of this section with the requirements specified in paragraph (f) of this section.

(b) *Highway Safety Improvement Program measures.* State DOTs and MPOs shall establish performance targets for the Highway Safety Improvement Program (HSIP) measures in accordance with § 490.209.

(c) *Applicable measures.* State DOTs and MPOs that include, within their respective geographic boundaries, any portion of the applicable transportation network or area shall establish performance targets for the performance measures identified in 23 CFR sections—

(1) 490.307(a)(1) and (2) for the condition of pavements on the Interstate System;

(2) 490.307(a)(3) and (4) for the condition of pavements on the NHS (excluding the Interstate);

(3) 490.407(c)(1) and (2) for the condition of bridges on the NHS;

(4) 490.507(a)(1) and (2) for the NHS Travel Time Reliability;

(5) [Reserved]

(6) 490.607 for the freight movement on the Interstate System;

(7) 490.707(a) and (b) for traffic congestion; and

(8) 490.807 for on-road mobile source emissions.

(d) *Target scope.* Targets established by State DOTs and MPOs shall, regardless of ownership, represent the transportation network or geographic area, including bridges that cross State borders, that are applicable to the measures as specified in paragraphs (d)(1) and (2) of this section.

(1) State DOTs and MPOs shall establish statewide and metropolitan planning area wide targets, respectively, that represent the condition/performance of the transportation network or geographic area that are applicable to the measures, as specified in 23 CFR sections—

(i) 490.303 for the condition of pavements on the Interstate System measures specified in § 490.307(a)(1) and (2);

(ii) 490.303 for the condition of pavements on the NHS (excluding the Interstate) measures specified in § 490.307(a)(3) and (4);

(iii) 490.403 for the condition of bridges on the NHS measures specified in § 490.407(c)(1) and (2);

(iv) 490.503(a)(1) for the Travel Time Reliability measures specified in § 490.507(a)(1) and (2);

(v) [Reserved]

(vi) 490.603 for the Freight Reliability measure specified in § 490.607; and

(vii) 490.803 for the Total Emissions Reduction measure identified in § 490.807.

(2) State DOTs and MPOs shall establish a single urbanized area target that represents the performance of the transportation network in each applicable area for the CMAQ Traffic Congestion measures, as specified in § 490.703.

(3) For the purpose of target establishment in this section and reporting targets and progress evaluation in § 490.107, State DOTs shall describe the urbanized area boundaries within the State boundary in the Baseline Performance Period Report required by § 490.107(b)(1).

(e) *Establishment.* State DOTs shall establish targets for each of the performance measures identified in paragraph (c) of this section for respective target scope identified in paragraph (d) of this section as follows:

(1) *Schedule.* State DOTs shall establish targets not later than February 20, 2018, and for each performance period thereafter, in a manner that allows for the time needed to meet the requirements specified in this section and so that the final targets are submitted to FHWA by the due date provided in § 490.107(b).

(2) *Coordination.* State DOTs shall coordinate with relevant MPOs on the selection of targets in accordance with 23 U.S.C. 135(d)(2)(B)(i)(II) to ensure consistency, to the maximum extent practicable.

(3) *Additional targets for urbanized and non-urbanized areas.* In addition to statewide targets, described in paragraph (d)(1) of this section, State DOTs may, as appropriate, for each statewide target establish additional targets for portions of the State.

(i) State DOTs shall describe in the Baseline Performance Period Report required by § 490.107(b)(1) the boundaries used to establish each additional target.

(ii) State DOTs may select any number and combination of urbanized area boundaries and may also select a non-urbanized area boundary for the establishment of additional targets.

(iii) The boundaries used by the State DOT for additional targets shall be contained within the geographic boundary of the State.

(iv) State DOTs shall evaluate separately the progress of each additional target and report that progress as required under § 490.107(b)(2)(ii)(B) and (b)(3)(ii)(B).

(v) Additional targets for urbanized areas and the non-urbanized area are not applicable to the CMAQ Traffic Congestion measures and the Total Emissions Reduction measure in paragraphs (c)(7) and (8) of this section, respectively.

(4) *Time horizon for targets.* State DOTs shall establish targets for a performance period as follows:

(i) The performance period will begin on:

(A) January 1st of the year in which the Baseline Performance Period Report is due to FHWA and will extend for a duration of 4 years for the measures in paragraphs (c)(1) through (7) of this section; and

(B) October 1st of the year prior to which the Baseline Performance Report is due to FHWA and will extend for a duration of 4 years for the measure in paragraph (c)(8) of this section.

(ii) The midpoint of a performance period will occur 2 years after the beginning of a performance period described in paragraph (e)(4)(i) of this section.

(iii) Except as provided in paragraphs (e)(7) and (e)(8)(v) of this section, State DOTs shall establish 2-year targets that reflect the anticipated condition/performance level at the midpoint of each performance period for the measures in paragraphs (c)(1) through (7) of this section, and the anticipated cumulative emissions reduction to be reported for the first 2 years of a performance period by applicable criteria pollutant and precursor for the measure in paragraph (c)(8) of this section.

(iv) State DOTs shall establish 4-year targets that reflect the anticipated condition/performance level at the end of each performance period for the measures in paragraphs (c)(1) through (7) of this section, and the anticipated cumulative emissions reduction to be reported for the entire performance period by applicable criteria pollutant and precursor for the measure in paragraph (c)(8) of this section.

(5) *Reporting.* State DOTs shall report 2-year targets, 4-year targets, the basis for each established target, progress made toward the achievement of targets, and other requirements to FHWA in accordance with § 490.107. State DOTs shall provide relevant MPO(s) targets to FHWA, upon request, each time the relevant MPOs establish or adjust MPO targets, as described in paragraph (f) of this section.

(6) *Target adjustment.* State DOTs may adjust an established 4-year target in the Mid Performance Period Progress Report, as described in § 490.107(b)(2). State DOTs shall coordinate with relevant MPOs when adjusting their 4-year target(s). Any adjustments made to 4-year targets established for the CMAQ Traffic Congestion measures in paragraph (c)(7) of this section shall be agreed upon and made collectively by all State DOTs and MPOs that include any portion of the NHS in the respective urbanized area applicable to the measures.

(7) *Phase-in of new requirements for Interstate System pavement condition measures and the non-Interstate NHS Travel Time Reliability measures.* The following requirements apply only to the first performance period and to the measures in §§ 490.307(a)(1) and (2) and 490.507(a)(2):

(i) State DOTs shall establish their 4-year targets, required under paragraph (e)(4)(iv) of this section, and report these targets in their Baseline Performance Period Report, required under § 490.107(b)(1);

(ii) State DOTs shall not report 2-year targets, described in paragraph (e)(4)(iii) of this section, and baseline condition/performance in their Baseline Performance Period Report; and

(iii) State DOTs shall use the 2-year condition/performance in their Mid Performance Period Progress Report, described in § 490.107(b)(2)(ii)(A) as the baseline condition/performance. State DOTs may also adjust their 4-year targets, as appropriate.

(8) *Urbanized area specific targets.* The following requirements apply to establishing targets for the CMAQ Traffic Congestion measures in paragraph (c)(7) of this section, as their target scope provided in paragraph (d)(2) of this section:

(i) For the performance period that begins on January 1, 2018, State DOTs, with mainline highways on the NHS that cross any part of an urbanized area with a population more than 1 million within its geographic State boundary and that urbanized area contains any part of a nonattainment or maintenance area for any one of the criteria pollutants, as specified in § 490.703, shall establish targets for the CMAQ Traffic Congestion measures specified in § 490.707(a) and (b).

(ii) Beginning with the performance period that begins on January 1, 2022, and all subsequent performance periods thereafter, State DOTs, with mainline highways on the NHS that cross any part of an urbanized area with a population more than 200,000 within its geographic State boundary and that urbanized area contains any part of a nonattainment or maintenance area for any one of the criteria pollutants, as specified in § 490.703, shall establish targets for the CMAQ Traffic Congestion measures specified in § 490.707(a) and (b).

(iii) If required to establish targets for the CMAQ Traffic Congestion measures, as described in paragraphs (e)(8)(i) and/or (ii) of this section, State DOTs shall comply with the following:

(A) For each urbanized area, only one 2-year target and one 4-year target for the entire urbanized area shall be established regardless of roadway ownership.

(B) For each urbanized area, all State DOTs and MPOs that contain, within their respective boundaries, any portion of the NHS network in that urbanized area shall agree on one 2-year and one 4-year target for that urbanized area. In accordance with paragraphs (e)(5) and (f)(9) of this section, the targets reported by the State DOTs and MPOs for that urbanized area shall be identical.

(C) Except as provided in paragraphs (e)(8)(iii)(F) and (e)(8)(v) of this section, State DOTs shall meet all reporting requirements in § 490.107 for the entire performance period even if there is a change of population, NHS designation, or nonattainment/maintenance area designation during that performance period.

(D) The 1 million and 200,000 population thresholds, in paragraphs (e)(8)(i) and (ii) of this section, shall be determined based on the most recent annual population estimates published by the U.S. Census available 1 year before when the State DOT Baseline Performance Period Report is due to FHWA.

(E) NHS designations and urbanized areas, in paragraphs (e)(8)(i) and (ii) of this section, shall be determined from the data, contained in HPMS, 1 year before when the State DOT Baseline Performance Period Report is due to FHWA.

(F) The designation of nonattainment or maintenance areas, in paragraphs (e)(8)(i) and (ii) of this section, shall be determined based on the effective date of U.S. EPA's designation under the NAAQS in 40 CFR part 81, as of the date 1 year before the State DOT Baseline Performance Period Report is due to FHWA. The nonattainment and maintenance areas shall be revised if, on the date 1 year before the State DOT Mid Performance Period Progress Report in § 490.107(b)(2)(ii) is due to FHWA, the area is no longer in nonattainment or maintenance for a criteria pollutant included in § 490.703.

(iv) If a State DOT does not meet the criteria specified in paragraph (e)(8)(i) or (ii) of this section 1 year before when the State DOT Baseline Performance Period Report is due to FHWA, then that State DOT is not required to establish targets for the CMAQ Traffic Congestion measures for that performance period.

(v) If the urbanized area, in paragraph (e)(8)(i) or (ii) of this section, does not contain any part of a nonattainment or maintenance area for the applicable criteria pollutants, as specified in § 490.703, 1 year before the State DOT Mid Performance Period Progress Report is due to FHWA, as described in paragraph (e)(8)(iii)(F) of this section, then that State DOT is not required to meet the requirements in § 490.107 for the CMAQ Traffic Congestion measures for that urbanized area for the remainder of that performance period.

(vi) The following requirements apply only the Peak Hour Excessive Delay (PHED) measure in § 490.707(a) to assess CMAQ Traffic Congestion in to the first performance period:

(A) State DOTs shall establish their 4-year targets, required under paragraph (e)(4)(iv) of this section, and report these targets in their Baseline Performance Period Report, required under § 490.107(b)(1).

(B) State DOTs shall not report 2-year targets, described in paragraph (e)(4)(ii) of this section, and baseline condition/performance in their Baseline Performance Period Report.

(C) State DOTs shall use the 2-year condition/performance in their Mid Performance Period Progress Report, described in § 490.107(b)(2)(ii)(A) as the baseline condition/performance. The established baseline condition/performance shall be collectively developed and agreed upon with relevant MPOs.

(D) State DOTs may, as appropriate, adjust their 4-year target(s) in their Mid Performance Period Progress Report, described in § 490.107(b)(2)(ii)(A). Adjusted 4-year target(s) shall be developed and collectively agreed upon with relevant MPO(s), as described in paragraph (e)(6) of this section.

(E) State DOTs shall annually report metrics for all mainline highways on the NHS for all applicable urbanized area(s) throughout the performance period, as required in § 490.711(f).

(9) *Targets for Total Emissions Reduction measure.* The following requirements apply to establishing targets for the measures specified in paragraph (c)(8) of this section:

(i) The State DOTs shall establish statewide targets for the Total Emissions Reduction measure for all nonattainment and maintenance areas for all applicable criteria pollutants and precursors specified in § 490.803.

(ii) For all nonattainment and maintenance areas within the State geographic boundary, the State DOT shall establish separate statewide targets for each of the applicable criteria pollutants and precursors specified in § 490.803.

(iii) The established targets, as specified in paragraph (e)(4) of this section, shall reflect the anticipated cumulative emissions reduction to be reported in the CMAQ Public Access System required in § 490.809(a).

(iv) In addition to the statewide targets in paragraph (e)(9)(i) of this section, State DOTs may, as appropriate, establish additional targets for any number and combination of nonattainment and maintenance areas by applicable criteria pollutant within the geographic boundary of the State. If a State DOT establishes additional targets for nonattainment and maintenance areas, it shall report the targets in the Baseline Performance Period Report required by § 490.107(b)(1). State DOTs shall evaluate separately the progress of each of these additional targets and report that progress as required under § 490.107(b)(2)(ii)(B) and (b)(3)(ii)(B).

(v) The designation of nonattainment or maintenance areas shall be determined based on the effective date of U.S. EPA's designation under the NAAQS in 40 CFR part 81, as of the date 1 year before the State DOT Baseline Performance Period Report is due to FHWA. The nonattainment and maintenance areas shall be revised if, on the date 1 year before the State DOT Mid Performance Period Progress Report in § 490.107(b)(2)(ii) is due to FHWA, the area is no longer in nonattainment or maintenance for a criteria pollutant included in § 490.803.

(vi) Except as provided in paragraphs (e)(9)(vii) and (viii) of this section, the State DOT shall meet all reporting requirements in § 490.107 for the entire performance period even if there is a change of nonattainment or maintenance area during that performance period.

(vii) If a State geographic boundary does not contain any part of nonattainment or maintenance areas for applicable criteria pollutants and precursors, as specified in § 490.803, 1 year before the State DOT Baseline Performance Period Report is due to FHWA, then that State DOT is not required to establish targets for Total Emissions Reduction measures for that performance period.

(viii) If the State geographic boundary, in paragraph (e)(9)(ii) of this section, does not contain any part of the nonattainment or maintenance area for an applicable criteria pollutant or precursor, as specified in § 490.803, 1 year before the State DOT Mid Performance Period Progress Report is due to FHWA as described in paragraph (e)(9)(v) of this section, then that State DOT is not required to meet the requirements in § 490.107 for the Total Emissions Reduction measure for that applicable criteria pollutant or precursor for the remainder of that performance period.

(f) *MPO establishment.* The MPOs shall establish targets for each of the performance measures identified in paragraph (c) of this section for the respective target scope identified in paragraph (d) of this section as follows:

(1) *Schedule.* The MPOs shall establish targets no later than 180 days after the respective State DOT(s) establishes their targets, as provided in paragraph (e)(1) of this section.

(i) The MPOs shall establish 4-year targets, described in paragraph (e)(4)(iv) of this section, for all applicable measures, described in paragraphs (c) and (d) of this section.

(ii) Except as provided in paragraph (f)(5)(vi) of this section, the MPOs shall establish 2-year targets, described in paragraph (e)(4)(iii) of this section for the CMAQ Traffic Congestion and Total Emissions Reduction measures, described in paragraphs (c) and (d) of this section as their applicability criteria described in paragraphs (f)(5)(i) and (ii) and (f)(6)(iii) of this section, respectively.

(iii) If an MPO does not meet the criteria described in paragraph (f)(5)(i), (f)(5)(ii), or (f)(6)(iii) of this section, the

MPO is not required to establish 2-year target(s) for the corresponding measure(s).

(2) *Coordination.* The MPOs shall coordinate with relevant State DOT(s) on the selection of targets in accordance with 23 U.S.C. 134(h)(2)(B)(i)(II) to ensure consistency, to the maximum extent practicable.

(3) *Target establishment options.* For each performance measure identified in paragraph (c) of this section, except the CMAQ Traffic Congestion measures in paragraph (f)(5) of this section, and MPOs meeting the criteria under paragraph (f)(6)(iii) of this section for Total Emissions Reduction measure, the MPOs shall establish targets by either:

(i) Agreeing to plan and program projects so that they contribute toward the accomplishment of the relevant State DOT target for that performance measure; or

(ii) Committing to a quantifiable target for that performance measure for their metropolitan planning area.

(4) *MPOs serving a multistate planning area.* Except as provided in the CMAQ Traffic Congestion measures in paragraph (f)(5) of this section, and MPOs meeting the criteria under paragraph (f)(6)(iii) of this section, for Total Emissions Reduction measure, MPOs with planning areas extending across State boundaries shall follow these requirements for each performance measure identified in paragraph (c) of this section:

(i) For each measure, MPOs may choose different target establishment options, provided in paragraph (f)(3) of this section, for the portion of the planning area within each State.

(ii) If MPOs choose the option to agree to plan and program projects to contribute toward State DOT targets, in accordance with paragraph (f)(3)(i) of this section, for a measure, then they shall plan and program projects in support of State DOT targets for the portion of the planning area within each State.

(5) *Urbanized area specific targets.* The following requirements apply to establishing targets for the CMAQ Traffic Congestion measures in paragraph (c)(7) of this section, as their target scope provided in paragraph (d)(2) of this section:

(i) For the performance period that begins on January 1, 2018, MPOs shall establish targets for the CMAQ Traffic Congestion measures specified in §490.707(a) and (b) when mainline highways on the NHS within their metropolitan planning area boundary cross any part of an urbanized area with a population more than 1 million, and that portion of their metropolitan planning area boundary also contains any portion of a nonattainment or maintenance area for any one of the criteria pollutants, as specified in §490.703. If an MPO with mainline highways on the NHS within their metropolitan planning area boundary cross any part of an urbanized area with a population more than 1 million and that urbanized area contains any part of a nonattainment or maintenance area, for any one of the criteria pollutant as specified in §490.703, outside of its metropolitan planning area boundary, then that MPO should coordinate with relevant State DOT(s) and MPO(s) in the target establishment process for the CMAQ Traffic Congestion measures specified in §490.707.

(ii) Beginning with the performance period that begins on January 1, 2022, and all subsequent performance periods thereafter, MPOs shall establish targets for the CMAQ Traffic Congestion measures specified in §490.707(a) and (b) when mainline highways on the NHS within their metropolitan planning area boundary cross any part of an urbanized area with a population more than 200,000, and that portion of their metropolitan planning area boundary also contains any portion of a nonattainment or maintenance area for any one of the criteria pollutants, as specified in §490.703. If an MPO with mainline highways on the NHS within their metropolitan planning area boundary cross any part of an urbanized area with a population more than 200,000 and that urbanized area contains any part of a nonattainment or maintenance area, for any one of the criteria pollutant as specified in §490.703, outside of its metropolitan planning area boundary, then that MPO should coordinate with relevant State DOT(s) and MPO(s) in the target establishment process for the CMAQ

Traffic Congestion measures specified in § 490.707.

(iii) If required to establish a target for the CMAQ Traffic Congestion measures, as described in paragraphs (f)(5)(i) and/or (ii) of this section, MPOs shall comply with the following:

(A) For each urbanized area, only one 2-year target and one 4-year target for the entire urbanized area shall be established regardless of roadway ownership.

(B) For each urbanized area, all State DOTs and MPOs that contain, within their respective boundaries, any portion of the NHS network in that urbanized area shall agree on one 2-year and one 4-year target for that urbanized area. The targets reported, in accordance with paragraphs (e)(5) and (f)(9) of this section, by the State DOTs and MPOs for that urbanized area shall be identical.

(C) Except as provided in paragraphs (f)(5)(iii)(F) and (f)(5)(v) of this section, MPOs shall meet all reporting requirements in § 490.107(c) for the entire performance period even if there is a change of population, NHS designation, or nonattainment/maintenance area during that performance period.

(D) The 1 million and 200,000 population thresholds, in paragraph (f)(5)(i) and (ii) of this section, shall be determined based on the most recent annual population estimates published by the U.S. Census available 1 year before the State DOT Baseline Performance Period Report is due to FHWA.

(E) NHS designations and urbanized areas, in paragraphs (f)(5)(i) and (ii) of this section, shall be determined from the data, contained in HPMS, 1 year before State DOT Baseline Performance Period Report is due to FHWA.

(F) The designation of nonattainment or maintenance areas, in paragraph (f)(5)(i) and (ii) of this section, shall be determined based on the effective date of U.S. EPA's designation under the NAAQS in 40 CFR part 81, as of the date 1 year before the State DOT Baseline Performance Period Report is due to FHWA. The nonattainment and maintenance areas shall be revised if, on the date 1 year before the State DOT Mid Performance Period Progress Report in § 490.107(b)(2)(ii) is due to FHWA, the area is no longer in nonattainment or maintenance for a criteria pollutant included in § 490.703.

(iv) If an MPO does not meet the criteria specified in paragraph (f)(5)(i) or (ii) of this section at the time that is 1 year before when the State DOT Baseline Performance Period Report is due to FHWA, then that MPO is not required to establish targets for the CMAQ Traffic Congestion measure for that performance period.

(v) If the portion of the metropolitan planning area boundary within the urbanized area, in paragraph (f)(5)(i) or (ii) of this section, does not contain any part of a nonattainment or maintenance area for the applicable criteria pollutants, as specified in § 490.703, at the time that is 1 year before when the State DOT Mid Performance Period Progress Report is due to FHWA, as described in paragraph (f)(5)(iii)(F) of this section, then that MPO is not required to meet the requirements in § 490.107 for the CMAQ Traffic Congestion measures for that urbanized area for the remainder of that performance period.

(vi) The following requirements apply only to the first performance period and the PHED measure to assess traffic congestion in § 490.707(a):

(A) The MPOs shall not report 2-year targets, described in paragraph (f)(5)(iii)(A) of this section;

(B) The MPOs shall use the 2-year condition/performance in the State DOT Mid Performance Period Progress Report, described in § 490.107(b)(2)(ii)(A) as baseline condition/performance. The established baseline condition/performance shall be agreed upon and made collectively with relevant State DOTs; and

(C) The MPOs may, as appropriate, adjust their 4-year target(s). Adjusted 4-year target(s) shall be collectively developed and agreed upon with all relevant State DOT(s), as described in paragraph (f)(8) of this section.

(6) *Targets for the Total Emissions Reduction measure.* The following requirements apply to establishing targets for the measure in paragraph (c)(8) of this section:

(i) The MPO shall establish targets for each of the applicable criteria pollutants and precursors, specified in

§490.803, for which it is in nonattainment or maintenance, within its metropolitan planning area boundary.

(ii) The established targets, as specified in paragraph (e)(4) of this section, shall reflect the anticipated cumulative emissions reduction to be reported in the CMAQ Public Access System required in §490.809(a).

(iii) If any part of a designated nonattainment and maintenance area within the metropolitan planning area overlaps the boundary of an urbanized area with a population more than 1 million in population, as of 1 year before the State DOT Baseline Performance Period Report is due to FHWA, then that MPO shall establish both 2-year and 4-year targets for their metropolitan planning area. The population threshold shall be determined based on the most recent annual population estimates published by the U.S. Census available 1 year before the State DOT Baseline Performance Period Report is due to FHWA.

(iv) For the nonattainment and maintenance areas within the metropolitan planning area that do not meet the criteria in paragraph (f)(6)(iii) of this section, MPOs shall establish 4-year targets for their metropolitan planning area, as described in paragraph (f)(3) of this section.

(v) The designation of nonattainment or maintenance areas shall be determined based on the effective date of U.S. EPA's designation under the NAAQS in 40 CFR part 81, as of the date 1 year before the State DOT Baseline Performance Period Report is due to FHWA. The nonattainment and maintenance areas shall be revised if, on the date 1 year before the State DOT Mid Performance Period Progress Report in §490.107(b)(2)(ii) is due to FHWA, the area is no longer in nonattainment or maintenance for a criteria pollutant included in §490.803.

(vi) Except as provided in paragraphs (f)(6)(v) and (viii) of this section, MPOs shall meet all reporting requirements in §490.107(c) for the entire performance period even if there is a change of nonattainment or maintenance area or population during that performance period.

(vii) If a metropolitan planning area boundary does not contain any part of nonattainment or maintenance areas for applicable criteria pollutants 1 year before when the State DOT Baseline Performance Period Report is due to FHWA, then that MPO is not required to establish targets for the Total Emissions Reduction measure for that performance period.

(viii) If the metropolitan planning area boundary, in paragraph (f)(6)(i) of this section, does not contain any part of a nonattainment or maintenance area for the applicable criteria pollutants, as specified in §490.803, 1 year before the State DOT Mid Performance Period Progress Report is due to FHWA, as described in paragraph (f)(6)(v) of this section, then that MPO is not required to meet the requirements in §490.107 for the Total Emissions Reduction measure for that applicable criteria pollutant or precursor for the remainder of that performance period.

(7) *MPO response to State DOT target adjustment.* For the established targets in paragraph (f)(3) of this section, if the State DOT adjusts a 4-year target in the State DOT's Mid Performance Period Progress Report and if, for that respective target, the MPO established a target by supporting the State DOT target as allowed under paragraph (f)(3)(i) of this section, then the MPO shall, within 180 days, report to the State DOT whether it will either:

(i) Agree to plan a program of projects so that they contribute to the adjusted State DOT target for that performance measure; or

(ii) Commit to a new quantifiable target for that performance measure for its metropolitan planning area.

(8) *Target adjustment.* If the MPO establishes its target by committing to a quantifiable target, described in paragraph (f)(3)(ii) of this section or establishes target(s) for the Total Emissions Reduction measure required in paragraph (f)(6)(iii) of this section, then the MPOs may adjust its target(s) in a manner that is collectively developed, documented, and mutually agreed upon by the State DOT and MPO. Any adjustments made to 4-year targets, established for CMAQ Traffic Congestion measures in paragraph (f)(5)(i) or (ii) of this section, shall be collectively developed and agreed upon by all State

DOTs and MPOs that include any portion of the NHS in the respective urbanized area applicable to the measure.

(9) *Reporting.* The MPOs shall report targets and progress toward the achievement of their targets as specified in § 490.107(c). After the MPOs establish or adjust their targets, the relevant State DOT(s) must be able to provide these targets to FHWA upon request.

[82 FR 6031, Jan. 18, 2017, as amended at 83 FR 24936, May 31, 2018]

§ 490.107 Reporting on performance targets.

(a) *In general.* All State DOTs and MPOs shall report the information specified in this section for the targets required in § 490.105.

(1) All State DOTs and MPOs shall report in accordance with the schedule and content requirements under paragraphs (b) and (c) of this section, respectively.

(2) For the measures identified in § 490.207(a), all State DOTs and MPO shall report on performance in accordance with § 490.213.

(3) State DOTs shall report using an electronic template provided by FHWA.

(b) *State Biennial Performance Report.* State DOTs shall report to FHWA baseline condition/performance at the beginning of a performance period and progress achievement at both the midpoint and end of a performance period. State DOTs shall report at an ongoing 2-year frequency as specified in paragraphs (b)(1) through (3) of this section.

(1) *Baseline Performance Period Report*—(i) *Schedule.* State DOTs shall submit a Baseline Performance Period Report to FHWA by October 1st of the first year in a performance period. State DOTs shall submit their first Baseline Performance Period Report to FHWA by October 1, 2018, and subsequent Baseline Performance Period Reports to FHWA by October 1st every 4 years thereafter.

(ii) *Content.* The State DOT shall report the following information in each Baseline Performance Period Report:

(A) *Targets.* 2-year and 4-year targets for the performance period, as required in § 490.105(e), and a discussion, to the maximum extent practicable, of the basis for each established target;

(B) *Baseline condition/performance.* Baseline condition/performance derived from the latest data collected through the beginning date of the performance period specified in § 490.105(e)(4)(i) for each target, required under paragraph (b)(1)(ii)(A) of this section;

(C) *Relationship with other performance expectations.* A discussion, to the maximum extent practicable, on how the established targets in paragraph (b)(1)(ii)(A) of this section support expectations documented in longer range plans, such as the State asset management plan required by 23 U.S.C. 119(e) and the long-range statewide transportation plan provided in part 450 of this chapter;

(D) *Urbanized area boundaries and population data for targets.* For the purpose of establishing additional targets for urbanized and non-urbanized areas in § 490.105(e)(3) and the urbanized area specific targets in § 490.105(e)(8), State DOTs shall document the boundary extent for all applicable urbanized areas based on information in HPMS;

(E) *Congestion at truck freight bottlenecks.* The State DOT shall document the location of truck freight bottlenecks within the State, including those identified in the National Freight Strategic Plan. If a State has prepared a State Freight Plan under 49 U.S.C. 70202, within the last 2 years, then the State Freight Plan may serve as the basis for identifying truck freight bottlenecks;

(F) *Nonattainment and maintenance area for targets.* Where applicable, for the purpose of determining target scope in § 490.105(d) and any additional targets under § 490.105(e)(9)(iv), State DOTs shall describe the boundaries of U.S. EPA's designated nonattainment and maintenance areas, as described in §§ 490.103(c) and 490.105(e)(9)(v);

(G) *MPO CMAQ Performance Plan.* Where applicable, State DOTs shall include as an attachment the MPO CMAQ Performance Plan, described in paragraph (c)(3) of this section;

(H) [Reserved]

(I) *Data collection method for the Percent of Non-SOV Travel measure.* Where applicable, State DOTs shall report the data collection method that is used to determine the Percent of Non-SOV Travel measure, in §490.707(b), for each applicable urbanized area in the State, as provided in §490.709(f)(2).

(2) *Mid Performance Period Progress Report*—(i) *Schedule.* State DOTs shall submit a Mid Performance Period Progress Report to FHWA by October 1st of the third year in a performance period. State DOTs shall submit their first Mid Performance Period Progress Report to FHWA by October 1, 2020, and subsequent Mid Performance Period Progress Reports to FHWA by October 1st every 4 years thereafter.

(ii) *Content.* The State DOT shall report the following information in each Mid Performance Period Progress Report:

(A) *2-year condition/performance.* The actual condition/performance derived from the latest data collected through the midpoint of the performance period, specified in §490.105(e)(4), for each State DOT reported target required in paragraph (b)(1)(ii)(A) of this section;

(B) *2-year progress in achieving performance targets.* A discussion of the State DOT's progress toward achieving each established 2-year target in paragraph (b)(1)(ii)(A) of this section. The State DOT shall compare the actual 2-year condition/performance in paragraph (b)(2)(ii)(A) of this section, within the boundaries and limits documented in paragraphs (b)(1)(ii)(D) and (E) of this section, with the respective 2-year target and document in the discussion any reasons for differences in the actual and target values;

(C) *Investment strategy discussion.* A discussion on the effectiveness of the investment strategies developed and documented in the State asset management plan for the NHS required under 23 U.S.C. 119(e);

(D) *Congestion at truck freight bottlenecks.* Discussion on progress of the State DOT's efforts in addressing congestion at truck freight bottlenecks within the State, as described in paragraph (b)(1)(ii)(F) of this section, through comprehensive freight improvement efforts of State Freight Plan or MPO freight plans; the Statewide Transportation Improvement Program and Transportation Improvement Program; regional or corridor level efforts; other related planning efforts; and operational and capital activities targeted to improve freight movement on the Interstate System. If a State has prepared a State Freight Plan under 49 U.S.C. 70202 within the previous 2 years, then the State Freight Plan may serve as the basis for addressing congestion at truck freight bottlenecks. If the State Freight Plan has not been updated since the previous State Biennial Performance Report, then an updated analysis of congestion at truck freight bottlenecks must be completed;

(E) *Target adjustment discussion.* When applicable, a State DOT may submit an adjusted 4-year target to replace an established 4-year target in paragraph (b)(1)(ii)(A) of this section. If the State DOT adjusts its target, it shall include a discussion on the basis for the adjustment and how the adjusted target supports expectations documented in longer range plans, such as the State asset management plan and the long-range statewide transportation plan. The State DOT may only adjust a 4-year target at the midpoint and by reporting the change in the Mid Performance Period Progress Report;

(F) *2-year significant progress discussion for the National Highway Performance Program (NHPP) targets and the National Highway Freight Program (NHFP) target.* State DOTs shall discuss the progress they have made toward the achievement of all 2-year targets established for the NHPP measures in §490.105(c)(1) through (5) and the Freight Reliability measure in §490.105(c)(6). This discussion should document a summary of prior accomplishments and planned activities that will be conducted during the remainder of the performance period to make significant progress toward that achievement of 4-year targets for applicable measures;

(G) *Extenuating circumstances discussion on 2-year Targets.* When applicable, for 2-year targets for the NHPP or NHFP, a State DOT may include a discussion on the extenuating circumstance(s), described in §490.109(e)(5), beyond the State DOT's control that prevented the State DOT from making 2-year significant progress toward achieving NHPP or

NHFP target(s) in paragraph (b)(2)(ii)(F) of this section;

(H) *Applicable target achievement discussion.* If FHWA determined that a State DOT has not made significant progress toward the achievement of any 4-year NHPP or NHFP targets in the FHWA determination made after the State DOT submits the Full Performance Period Progress Report for the immediate prior performance period, then the State DOT shall include a description of the actions they will undertake to better achieve those targets as required under § 490.109(f). If FHWA determined under § 490.109(e) that the State DOT has made significant progress for immediate prior performance period's 4-year NHPP or NHFP targets, then the State DOT does not need to include this description for those targets;

(I) *MPO CMAQ Performance Plan.* Where applicable, State DOTs shall include as an attachment the MPO CMAQ Performance Plan, described in paragraph (c)(3) of this section; and

(J) [Reserved]

(3) *Full Performance Period Progress Report*—(i) *Schedule.* State DOTs shall submit a progress report on the full performance period to FHWA by October 1st of the first year following the reference performance period. State DOTs shall submit their first Full Performance Period Progress Report to FHWA by October 1, 2022, and subsequent Full Performance Period Progress Reports to FHWA by October 1st every 4 years thereafter.

(ii) *Content.* The State DOT shall report the following information for each Full Performance Period Progress Report:

(A) *4-year condition/performance.* The actual condition/performance derived from the latest data collected through the end of the performance period, specified in § 490.105(e)(4), for each State DOT reported target required in paragraph (b)(1)(ii)(A) of this section;

(B) *4-year progress in achieving performance targets.* A discussion of the State DOT's progress made toward achieving each established 4-year target in paragraph (b)(1)(ii)(A) or (b)(2)(ii)(E) of this section, when applicable. The State DOT shall compare the actual 4-year condition/performance in paragraph (b)(3)(ii)(A) of this section, within the boundaries and limits documented in paragraphs (b)(1)(ii)(D) and (E) of this section, with the respective 4-year target and document in the discussion any reasons for differences in the actual and target values;

(C) *Investment strategy discussion.* A discussion on the effectiveness of the investment strategies developed and documented in the State asset management plan for the NHS required under 23 U.S.C. 119(e);

(D) *Congestion at truck freight bottlenecks.* Discussion on progress of the State DOT's efforts in addressing congestion at truck freight bottlenecks within the State, as described in paragraphs (b)(1)(ii)(F) and (b)(2)(ii)(D) of this section;

(E) *4-year significant progress evaluation for applicable targets.* State DOTs shall discuss the progress they have made toward the achievement of all 4-year targets established for the NHPP measures in § 490.105(c)(1) through (5) and the Freight Reliability measure in § 490.105(c)(6). This discussion shall include a summary of accomplishments achieved during the performance period to demonstrate whether the State DOT has made significant progress toward achievement of 4-year targets for those measures;

(F) *Extenuating circumstances discussion on applicable targets.* When applicable, a State DOT may include discussion on the extenuating circumstance(s), described in § 490.109(e)(5), beyond the State DOT's control that prevented the State DOT from making a 4-year significant progress toward achieving NHPP or NHFP targets, described in paragraph (b)(3)(ii)(E) of this section;

(G) *Applicable target achievement discussion.* If FHWA determined that a State DOT has not made significant progress toward the achievement of any 2-year NHPP or NHFP targets in the biennial FHWA determination made after the State DOT submits the Mid Performance Period Progress Report for the performance period, then the State DOT shall include a description of the actions they will undertake to better achieve those targets as required under §490.109(f). If FHWA determined in §490.109(e) that the State DOT has made significant progress for the 2-year NHPP or NHFP targets for the performance period, then the State DOT does not need to include this description for those targets;

(H) *MPO CMAQ Performance Plan.* Where applicable, State DOTs shall include as an attachment the MPO CMAQ Performance Plan, described in paragraph (c)(3) of this section; and

(I) [Reserved]

(c) *MPO Report.* The MPOs shall establish targets in accordance with §490.105 and report targets and progress toward the achievement of their targets in a manner that is consistent with the following:

(1) The MPOs shall report their established targets to their respective State DOT in a manner that is documented and mutually agreed upon by both parties.

(2) The MPOs shall report baseline condition/performance and progress toward the achievement of their targets in the system performance report in the metropolitan transportation plan in accordance with part 450 of this chapter.

(3) The MPOs serving a TMA and meeting criteria, specified in §490.105(f)(6)(iii), shall develop a CMAQ performance plan as required by 23 U.S.C. 149(l). The CMAQ performance plan is not required when the MPO meets the criteria specified in §490.105(f)(6)(vii) or (viii).

(i) The CMAQ performance plan shall be submitted to FHWA by the State DOT, and be updated biennially on the same schedule as the State Biennial Performance Reports.

(ii) For the CMAQ Traffic Congestion and Total Emissions Reduction measures in subparts G and H of this part, the CMAQ performance plan submitted with the State DOT's Baseline Performance Period Report to FHWA shall include:

(A) The 2-year and 4-year targets for the CMAQ Traffic Congestion measures, identical to the relevant State DOT(s) reported target under paragraph (b)(1)(ii)(A) of this section, for each applicable urbanized area;

(B) The 2-year and 4-year targets for the Total Emissions Reduction measure for the performance period;

(C) Baseline condition/performance for each MPO reported CMAQ Traffic Congestion targets, identical to the relevant State DOT(s) reported baseline condition/performance under paragraph (b)(1)(ii)(B) of this section;

(D) Baseline condition/performance derived from the latest estimated cumulative emissions reductions from CMAQ projects for each MPO reported Total Emissions Reduction target; and

(E) A description of projects identified for CMAQ funding and how such projects will contribute to achieving the performance targets for these measures.

(iii) For the CMAQ Traffic Congestion and Total Emissions Reduction measures in subparts G and H of this part, the CMAQ performance plan submitted with the State DOT's Mid Performance Period Progress Report to FHWA shall include:

(A) 2-year condition/performance for the CMAQ Traffic Congestion measures, identical to the relevant State DOT(s) reported condition/performance under paragraph (b)(2)(ii)(A) of this section, for each applicable urbanized area;

(B) 2-year condition/performance derived from the latest estimated cumulative emissions reductions from CMAQ projects for each MPO reported Total Emissions Reduction target;

(C) An assessment of the progress of the projects identified in the CMAQ performance plan submitted with the Baseline Performance Period Report toward achieving the 2-year targets for these measures;

(D) When applicable, an adjusted 4-year target to replace an established 4-year target; and

(E) An update to the description of projects identified for CMAQ funding and how those updates will contribute to achieving the 4-year performance targets for these measures.

(iv) For the CMAQ Traffic Congestion and Total Emissions Reduction measures in subparts G and H of this part, the CMAQ performance plan submitted with the State DOT's Full Performance Period Progress Report to FHWA shall include:

(A) 4-year condition/performance for the CMAQ Traffic Congestion measures, identical to the relevant State DOT(s) reported condition/performance reported under paragraph (b)(3)(ii)(A) of this section, for each applicable urbanized area;

(B) 4-year condition/performance derived from the latest estimated cumulative emissions reductions from CMAQ projects for each MPO reported Total Emissions Reduction target; and

(C) An assessment of the progress of the projects identified in both paragraphs (c)(3)(ii)(C) and (c)(3)(iii)(D) of this section toward achieving the 4-year targets for these measures.

(4) [Reserved]

[82 FR 6031, Jan. 18, 2017, as amended at 83 FR 24936, May 31, 2018]

§ 490.109 Assessing significant progress toward achieving the performance targets for the National Highway Performance Program and the National Highway Freight Program.

(a) *In general.* The FHWA will assess each of the State DOT targets separately for the NHPP measures specified in § 490.105(c)(1) through (5) and the Freight Reliability measure specified in § 490.105(c)(6) to determine the significant progress made toward the achievement of those targets.

(b) *Frequency.* The FHWA will determine whether a State DOT has or has not made significant progress toward the achievement of applicable targets as described in paragraph (e) of this section at the midpoint and the end of each performance period.

(c) *Schedule.* The FHWA will determine significant progress toward the achievement of a State DOT's NHPP and NHFP targets after the State DOT submits the Mid Performance Period Progress Report for progress toward the achievement of 2-year targets, and again after the State DOT submits the Full Performance Period Progress Report for progress toward the achievement of 4-year targets. The FHWA will notify State DOTs of the outcome of the determination of the State DOT's ability to make significant progress toward the achievement of its NHPP and NHFP targets.

(d) *Source of data/information.* (1) The FHWA will use the following sources of information to assess NHPP target achievement and condition/performance progress:

(i) Data contained within the HPMS on June 15th of the year in which the significant progress determination is made that represents conditions from the prior year for targets established for Interstate System pavement condition measures, as specified in § 490.105(c)(1);

(ii) Data contained within the HPMS on August 15th of the year in which the significant progress determination is made that represents conditions from the prior year for targets established for non-Interstate NHS pavement condition measures, as specified in § 490.105(c)(2);

(iii) The most recently available data contained within the NBI as of June 15th of the year in which the significant progress determination is made for targets established for NHS bridge condition measures, as specified in § 490.105(c)(3);

(iv) Data contained within the HPMS on August 15th of the year in which the significant progress determination is made that represents performance from the prior year for targets established for the Travel Time Reliability measures, as specified in § 490.105(c)(4);

(v) [Reserved]

(vi) Baseline condition/performance data contained in HPMS and NBI of the year in which the Baseline Period Performance Report is due to FHWA that represents baseline conditions/performances for the performance period for the measures in § 490.105(c)(1) through (4).

(2) The FHWA will use the following sources of information to assess NHFP target achievement and condition/performance progress:

(i) Data contained within the HPMS on August 15th of the year in which the significant progress determination is made that represents performance from the prior year for targets established for the Freight Reliability measure, as specified in § 490.105(c)(6); and

(ii) Baseline condition/performance data contained in HPMS of the year in which the Baseline Period Performance Report is due to FHWA that represents baseline condition/performance for the performance period.

(e) *Significant progress determination for individual NHPP and NHFP targets*—(1) *In general.* The FHWA will biennially assess whether the State DOT has achieved or made significant progress toward each target established by the State DOT for the NHPP measures described in §490.105(c)(1) through (5) and the Freight Reliability measure described in §490.105(c)(6). The FHWA will assess the significant progress of each statewide target separately using the condition/performance data/information sources described in paragraph (d) of this section. The FHWA will not assess the progress achieved for any additional targets a State DOT may establish under §490.105(e)(3).

(2) *Significant progress toward individual NHPP and NHFP targets.* The FHWA will determine that a State DOT has made significant progress toward the achievement of each 2-year or 4-year applicable target if either:

(i) The actual condition/performance level is better than the baseline condition/performance; or

(ii) The actual condition/performance level is equal to or better than the established target.

(3) *Phase-in of new requirements.* The following requirements shall only apply to the first performance period and only to the Interstate System pavement condition targets and non-Interstate NHS Travel Time Reliability targets, described in §490.105(e)(7):

(i) At the midpoint of the first performance period, FHWA will not make a determination of significant progress toward the achievement of 2-year targets for Interstate System pavement condition measures:

(ii) The FHWA will classify the assessment of progress toward the achievement of targets in paragraph (e)(3)(i) of this section as "progress not determined" so that they will be excluded from the requirement under paragraph (e)(2) of this section; and

(iii) The FHWA will not make a determination of significant progress toward the achievement of 2-year targets for the Non-Interstate NHS Travel Time Reliability measure.

(4) *Insufficient data and/or information.* The FHWA will determine that a State DOT has not made significant progress toward the achievement of an individual NHPP or NHFP target if:

(i) A State DOT does not submit a required report, individual target, or other information as specified in §490.107 for the each of the measures in §490.105(c)(1) through (6);

(ii) The data contained in HPMS do not meet the requirements under §490.313(b)(4)(i) by the data extraction date specified in paragraph (d)(1) of this section for the each of the Interstate System pavement condition measures in §490.105(c)(1);

(iii) The data contained in HPMS do not meet the requirements under §490.313(b)(4)(i) by the data extraction date specified in paragraph (d)(2) of this section for the each of the non-Interstate NHS pavement condition measures in §490.105(c)(2);

(iv) A State DOT reported data are not cleared in the NBI by the data extraction date specified in paragraph (d)(3) of this section for the each of the NHS bridge condition measures in §490.105(c)(3); or

(v) The data were determined insufficient, as described in paragraphs (e)(4)(ii) through (iv) of this section, in the year in which the Baseline Period Performance Report is due to FHWA for the measures in §490.105(c)(1) through (3).

(5) *Extenuating circumstances.* The FHWA will consider extenuating circumstances documented by the State DOT in the assessment of progress toward the achievement of NHPP and NHFP targets in the relevant State Biennial Performance Report, provided in §490.107.

(i) The FHWA will classify the assessment of progress toward the achievement of an individual 2-year or 4-year target as "progress not determined" if the State DOT has provided an explanation of the extenuating circumstances beyond the control of the State DOT that prevented it from making significant progress toward the achievement of a 2-year or 4-year target and the State DOT has quantified the impacts on the condition/performance that resulted from the circumstances, which are:

(A) Natural or man-made disasters that caused delay in NHPP or NHFP project delivery, extenuating delay in data collection, and/or damage/loss of data system;

(B) Sudden discontinuation of Federal government furnished data due to natural and man-made disasters or sudden discontinuation of Federal government furnished data due to lack of funding; and/or

(C) New law and/or regulation directing State DOTs to change metric and/or measure calculation.

(ii) If the State DOT's explanation, described in paragraph (e)(5)(i) of this section, is accepted by FHWA, FHWA will classify the progress toward achieving the relevant target(s) as "progress not determined," and those targets will be excluded from the requirement in paragraph (e)(2) of this section.

(f) *Performance achievement.* (1) If FHWA determines that a State DOT has not made significant progress toward the achieving of NHPP targets, then the State DOT shall include as part of the next performance target report under 23 U.S.C. 150(e) [the Biennial Performance Report] a description of the actions the State DOT will undertake to achieve the targets related to the measure in which significant progress was not achieved as follows:

(i) If significant progress is not made for either target established for the Interstate System pavement condition measures, § 490.307(a)(1) and (2), then the State DOT shall document the actions it will take to achieve Interstate Pavement condition targets;

(ii) If significant progress is not made for either target established for the Non-Interstate System pavement condition measures, § 490.307(a)(3) and (4), then the State DOT shall document the actions it will take to to achieve Non-Interstate Pavement condition target;

(iii) If significant progress is not made for either target established for the NHS bridge condition measures, § 490.407(c)(1) and (2), then the State DOT shall document the actions it will take to to achieve NHS bridge condition target;

(iv) If significant progress is not made for either target established for the Travel Time Reliability measures, § 490.507(a)(1) and(2), then the State DOT shall document the actions it will take to achieve the NHS travel time targets; and

(v) [Reserved]

(2) If FHWA determines that a State DOT has not made significant progress toward achieving the target established for the Freight Reliability measure in § 490.607, then the State DOT shall include as part of the next performance target report under 23 U.S.C. 150(e) [the Biennial Performance Report] the following:

(i) An identification of significant freight system trends, needs, and issues within the State.

(ii) A description of the freight policies and strategies that will guide the freight-related transportation investments of the State.

(iii) An inventory of truck freight bottlenecks within the State and a description of the ways in which the State DOT is allocating funding under title 23 U.S.C. to improve those bottlenecks.

(A) The inventory of truck freight bottlenecks shall include the route and milepost location for each identified bottleneck, roadway section inventory data reported in HPMS, Average Annual Daily Traffic (AADT), Average Annual Daily Truck Traffic (AADTT), Travel-time data and measure of delay, such as travel time reliability, or Average Truck Speeds, capacity feature causing the bottleneck or any other constraints applicable to trucks, such as geometric constrains, weight limits or steep grades.

(B) For those facilities that are State-owned or operated, the description of the ways in which the State DOT is improving those bottlenecks shall include an identification of methods to address each bottleneck and improvement efforts planned or programed through the State Freight Plan or MPO freight plans; the Statewide Transportation Improvement Program and Transportation Improvement Program; regional or corridor level efforts; other related planning efforts; and operational and capital activities.

(iv) A description of the actions the State DOT will undertake to achieve the target established for the Freight Reliability measure in § 490.607.

(3) The State DOT should, within 6 months of the significant progress determination, amend its Biennial Performance Report to document the information specified in this paragraph to ensure actions are being taken to achieve targets.

[82 FR 6031, Jan. 18, 2017, as amended at 83 FR 24936, May 31, 2018]

§490.111 Incorporation by reference.

(a) Certain material is incorporated by reference into this part with the approval of the Director of the Federal Register under 5 U.S.C. 552(a) and 1 CFR part 51. To enforce any edition other than that specified in this section, FHWA must publish a notice of change in the FEDERAL REGISTER and the material must be available to the public. All approved material is available for inspection at the Federal Highway Administration, Office of Highway Policy Information (202–366–4631) 1200 New Jersey Avenue SE., Washington, DC 20590, *www.fhwa.dot.gov* and is available from the sources listed below. It is also available for inspection at the National Archives and Records Administration (NARA). For information on the availability of this material at NARA, call 202–741–6030 or go to *http://www.archives.gov/federal_register/code_of_federal_regulations/ibr_locations.html.*

(b) The Federal Highway Administration, 1200 New Jersey Avenue SE., Washington, DC 20590, *www.fhwa.dot.gov.*

(1) Highway Performance Monitoring System (HPMS) Field Manual, IBR approved for §§490.103, 490.309, 490.311, and 490.319.

(2) Recording and Coding Guide for the Structure Inventory and Appraisal of the Nation's Bridges, includes: Errata Sheet for Coding Guide 06/2011, Report No. FHWA–PD–96–001, December 1995, IBR approved for §§490.409 and 490.411.

(c) The American Association of State Highway and Transportation Officials, 444 North Capitol Street NW., Suite 249, Washington, DC 20001, (202) 624–5800, *www.transportation.org.*

(1) AASHTO Standard M328–14, Standard Specification for Transportation Materials and Methods of Sampling and Testing, Inertial Profiler, 2014, 34th/2014 Edition, IBR approved for §490.309.

(2) AASHTO Standard R57–14, Standard Specification for Transportation Materials and Methods of Sampling and Testing, Standard Practice for Operating Inertial Profiling Systems, 2014, 34th/2014 Edition, IBR approved for §490.309.

(3) AASHTO Standard R48–10 (2013), Standard Specification for Transportation Materials and Methods of Sampling and Testing, Standard Practice for Determining Rut Depth in Pavements, 2014, 34th/2014 Edition, IBR approved for §490.309.

(4) AASHTO Standard R36–13, Standard Specification for Transportation Materials and Methods of Sampling and Testing, Standard Practice for Evaluating Faulting of Concrete Pavements, 2014, 34th/2014 Edition, IBR approved for §490.309.

(5) AASHTO Standard R43–13, Standard Specification for Transportation Materials and Methods of Sampling and Testing, Standard Practice for Quantifying Roughness of Pavement, 2014, 34th/2014 Edition, IBR approved for §490.311.

Subpart B—National Performance Management Measures for the Highway Safety Improvement Program

§490.201 Purpose.

The purpose of this subpart is to implement the requirements of 23 U.S.C. 150(c)(4), which requires the Secretary of Transportation to establish performance measures for the purpose of carrying out the Highway Safety Improvement Program (HSIP) and for State departments of transportation (State DOTs) to use in assessing:

(a) Serious injuries and fatalities per vehicle miles traveled (VMT); and

(b) Number of serious injuries and fatalities.

§490.203 Applicability.

The performance measures are applicable to all public roads covered by the HSIP carried out under 23 U.S.C. 130 and 148.

§ 490.205 Definitions.

Unless otherwise specified, the following definitions apply in this subpart:

5-year rolling average means the average of 5 individual, consecutive annual points of data (e.g., the 5-year rolling average of the annual fatality rate).

Annual Report File (ARF) means FARS data that are published annually, but prior to Final FARS data.

Fatality Analysis Reporting System (FARS) means a nationwide census providing public yearly data regarding fatal injuries suffered in motor vehicle traffic crashes.

Final FARS means the FARS data that replace the ARF file and contain additional cases or updates to cases that became available after the ARF was released, and which are no longer subject to future changes.

KABCO means the coding convention system for injury classification established by the National Safety Council.

Number of fatalities means the total number of persons suffering fatal injuries in a motor vehicle traffic crash during a calendar year, based on the data reported by the FARS database.

Number of non-motorized fatalities means the total number of fatalities (as defined in this section) with the FARS person attribute codes: (5) Pedestrian, (6) Bicyclist, (7) Other Cyclist, and (8) Person on Personal Conveyance.

Number of non-motorized serious injuries means the total number of serious injuries (as defined in this section) where the injured person is, or is equivalent to, a pedestrian (2.2.36) or a pedalcylcist (2.2.39) as defined in the ANSI D16.1–2007 (incorporated by reference, see § 490.111).

Number of serious injuries means the total number of persons suffering at least one serious injury for each separate motor vehicle traffic crash during a calendar year, as reported by the State, where the crash involves a motor vehicle traveling on a public road, and the injury status is "suspected serious injury (A)" as described in MMUCC, (incorporated by reference, see § 490.111). For serious injury classifications that are not MMUCC compliant, the number of serious injuries means serious injuries that are converted to KABCO by use of conversion tables developed by the NHTSA.

Public road is as defined in 23 CFR 924.3.

Rate of fatalities means the ratio of the total number of fatalities (as defined in this section) to the number of vehicle miles traveled (VMT) (expressed in 100 million VMT) in a calendar year.

Rate of serious injuries means the ratio of the total number of serious injuries (as defined in this section) to the number of VMT (expressed in 100 million vehicle miles of travel) in a calendar year.

Serious injuries means:

(1) From April 14, 2016 to April 15, 2019, injuries classified as "A" on the KABCO scale through use of the conversion tables developed by NHTSA; and

(2) After April 15, 2019, "suspected serious injury (A)" as defined in the MMUCC.

§ 490.207 National performance management measures for the Highway Safety Improvement Program.

(a) There are five performance measures for the purpose of carrying out the HSIP. They are:

(1) Number of fatalities;

(2) Rate of fatalities;

(3) Number of serious injuries;

(4) Rate of serious injuries; and,

(5) Number of non-motorized fatalities and non-motorized serious injuries.

(b) Each performance measure is based on a 5-year rolling average. The performance measures are calculated as follows:

(1) The performance measure for the number of fatalities is the 5-year rolling average of the total number of fatalities for each State and shall be calculated by adding the number of fatalities for each of the most recent 5 consecutive years ending in the year for which the targets are established, dividing by 5, and rounding to the tenth decimal place. FARS ARF may be used if Final FARS is not available.

(2) The performance measure for the rate of fatalities is the 5-year rolling average of the State's fatality rate per VMT and shall be calculated by first calculating the number of fatalities per 100 million VMT for each of the most

recent 5 consecutive years ending in the year for which the targets are established, adding the results, dividing by 5, and rounding to the thousandth decimal place. The FARS ARF may be used if Final FARS is not available. State VMT data are derived from the HPMS. The Metropolitan Planning Organizations (MPO) VMT is estimated by the MPO. The sum of the fatality rates is divided by five and then rounded to the thousandth decimal place.

(3) The performance measure for the number of serious injuries is the 5-year rolling average of the total number of serious injuries for each State and shall be calculated by adding the number of serious injuries for each of the most recent 5 consecutive years ending in the year for which the targets are established, dividing by five, and rounding to the tenth decimal place.

(4) The performance measure for the rate of serious injuries is the 5-year rolling average of the State's serious injuries rate per VMT and shall be calculated by first calculating the number of serious injuries per 100 million VMT for each of the most recent 5 consecutive years ending in the year for which the targets are established, adding the results, dividing by five, and rounding to the thousandth decimal place. State VMT data are derived from the HPMS. The MPO VMT is estimated by the MPO.

(5) The performance measure for the number of Non-motorized Fatalities and Non-motorized Serious Injuries is the 5-year rolling average of the total number of non-motorized fatalities and non-motorized serious injuries for each State and shall be calculated by adding the number of non-motorized fatalities to the number non-motorized serious injuries for each of the most recent 5 consecutive years ending in the year for which the targets are established, dividing by five, and rounding to the tenth decimal place. FARS ARF may be used if Final FARS is not available.

(c) For purposes of calculating serious injuries in paragraphs (b)(3), (4), and (5) of this section:

(1) Before April 15, 2019, serious injuries may be determined by either of the following:

(i) Serious injuries coded (A) in the KABCO injury classification scale through use of the NHTSA serious injuries conversion tables; or

(ii) Using MMUCC (incorporated by reference, see § 490.111).

(2) By April 15, 2019, serious injuries shall be determined using MMUCC.

§ 490.209 Establishment of performance targets.

(a) State DOTs shall establish targets annually for each performance measure identified in § 490.207(a) in a manner that is consistent with the following:

(1) State DOT targets shall be identical to the targets established by the State Highway Safety Office for common performance measures reported in the State's Highway Safety Plan, subject to the requirements of 23 U.S.C. 402(k)(4), and as coordinated through the State Strategic Highway Safety Plan.

(2) State DOT targets shall represent performance outcomes anticipated for the calendar year following the HSIP annual report date, as provided in 23 CFR 924.15.

(3) State DOT performance targets shall represent the anticipated performance outcome for all public roadways within the State regardless of ownership or functional class.

(4) State DOT targets shall be reported in the HSIP annual report that is due after April 14, 2017, and in each subsequent HSIP annual report thereafter.

(5) The State DOT shall include, in the HSIP Report (see 23 CFR part 924), at a minimum, the most recent 5 years of serious injury data and non-motorized serious injury data. The serious injury data shall be either MMUCC compliant or converted to the KABCO system (A) for injury classification through use of the NHTSA conversion tables as required by § 490.207(c).

(6) Unless approved by FHWA and subject to § 490.209(a)(1), a State DOT shall not change one or more of its targets for a given year once it is submitted in the HSIP annual report.

(b) In addition to targets described in paragraph (a) of this section, State DOTs may, as appropriate, for each target in paragraph (a) establish additional targets for portions of the State.

(1) A State DOT shall declare and describe in the State HSIP annual report

required by § 490.213 the boundaries used to establish each additional target.

(2) State DOTs may select any number and combination of urbanized area boundaries and may also select a single non-urbanized area boundary for the establishment of additional targets.

(3) The boundaries used by the State DOT for additional targets shall be contained within the geographic boundary of the State.

(4) State DOTs shall evaluate separately the progress of each additional target and report that progress in the State HSIP annual report (see 23 CFR part 924).

(c) The Metropolitan Planning Organizations (MPO) shall establish performance targets for each of the measures identified in § 490.207(a), where applicable, in a manner that is consistent with the following:

(1) The MPOs shall establish targets not later than 180 days after the respective State DOT establishes and reports targets in the State HSIP annual report.

(2) The MPO target shall represent performance outcomes anticipated for the same calendar year as the State target.

(3) After the MPOs within each State establish the targets, the State DOT must be able to provide those targets to FHWA, upon request.

(4) For each performance measure, the MPOs shall establish a target by either:

(i) Agreeing to plan and program projects so that they contribute toward the accomplishment of the State DOT safety target for that performance measure; or

(ii) Committing to a quantifiable target for that performance measure for their metropolitan planning area.

(5) The MPOs that establish quantifiable fatality rate or serious injury rate targets shall report the VMT estimate used for such targets and the methodology used to develop the estimate. The methodology should be consistent with other Federal reporting requirements, if applicable.

(6) The MPO targets established under paragraph (c)(4) of this section specific to the metropolitan planning area shall represent the anticipated performance outcome for all public roadways within the metropolitan planning boundary regardless of ownership or functional class.

(d)(1) The State DOT and relevant MPOs shall coordinate on the establishment of targets in accordance with 23 CFR part 450 to ensure consistency, to the maximum extent practicable.

(2) The MPOs with multi-State boundaries that agree to plan and program projects to contribute toward State targets in accordance with paragraph (c)(4)(i) of this section shall plan and program safety projects in support of the State DOT targets for each area within each State (e.g., MPOs that extend into two States shall agree to plan and program projects to contribute toward two separate sets of targets (one set for each State)).

§ 490.211 Determining whether a State department of transportation has met or made significant progress toward meeting performance targets.

(a) The determination for having met or made significant progress toward meeting the performance targets under 23 U.S.C. 148(i) will be determined based on:

(1) The most recent available Final FARS data for the fatality number. The FARS ARF may be used if Final FARS is not available;

(2) The most recent available Final FARS and HPMS data for the fatality rate. The FARS ARF may be used if Final FARS is not available;

(3) The most recent available Final FARS data for the non-motorized fatality number. The FARS ARF may be used if Final FARS is not available;

(4) State reported data for the serious injuries number;

(5) State reported data and HPMS data for the serious injuries rate; and

(6) State reported data for the non-motorized serious injuries number.

(b) The State-reported serious injury data and non-motorized serious injury data will be taken from the HSIP report in accordance with 23 CFR part 924.

(c) The FHWA will evaluate whether a State DOT has met or made significant progress toward meeting performance targets.

(1) The FHWA will not evaluate any additional targets a State DOT may establish under § 490.209(b).

(2) A State DOT is determined to have met or made significant progress toward meeting its targets when at least four of the performance targets established under § 490.207(a) are:

(i) Met; or

(ii) The outcome for a performance measure is less than the 5-year rolling average data for the performance measure for the year prior to the establishment of the State's target. For example, of the State DOT's five performance targets, the State DOT is determined to have met or made significant progress toward meeting its targets if it met two targets and the outcome is less than the measure for the year prior to the establishment of the target for two other targets.

(d) If a State DOT has not met or made significant progress toward meeting performance targets in accordance with paragraph (c) of this section, the State DOT must comply with 23 U.S.C. 148(i) for the subsequent fiscal year.

(e) The FHWA will first evaluate whether a State DOT has met or made significant progress toward meeting performance targets after the calendar year following the year for which the first targets are established, and then annually thereafter.

§ 490.213 Reporting of targets for the Highway Safety Improvement Program.

(a) The targets established by the State DOT shall be reported to FHWA in the State's HSIP annual report in accordance with 23 CFR part 924.

(b) The MPOs shall annually report their established safety targets to their respective State DOT, in a manner that is documented and mutually agreed upon by both parties.

(c) The MPOs shall report baseline safety performance, VMT estimate and methodology if a quantifiable rate target was established, and progress toward the achievement of their targets in the system performance report in the metropolitan transportation plan in accordance with 23 CFR part 450. Safety performance and progress shall be reported based on the following data sources:

(1) The most recent available Final FARS data for the fatality number. The FARS ARF may be used if Final FARS is not available;

(2) The most recent available Final FARS and MPO VMT estimate for the fatality rate. The FARS ARF may be used if Final FARS is not available;

(3) The most recent available Final FARS data for the non-motorized fatality number. The FARS ARF may be used if Final FARS is not available;

(4) State reported data for the serious injuries number;

(5) State reported data and MPO VMT estimate for the serious injuries rate; and

(6) State reported data for the non-motorized serious injuries number.

Subpart C—National Performance Management Measures for the Assessing Pavement Condition

SOURCE: 82 FR 5962, Jan. 17, 2017, unless otherwise noted.

§ 490.301 Purpose.

The purpose of this subpart is to implement the following statutory requirements of 23 U.S.C. 150(c)(3) to:

(a) Establish measures for State DOTs and MPOs to assess the condition of pavements on the Interstate System;

(b) Establish measures for State DOTs and MPOs to assess the condition of pavements on the NHS (excluding the Interstate);

(c) Establish minimum levels for pavement condition on the Interstate System, only for purposes of carrying out 23 U.S.C. 119(f)(1);

(d) Establish data elements that are necessary to collect and maintain standardized data to carry out a performance-based approach; and

(e) Consider regional differences in establishing the minimum levels for pavement conditions on the Interstate System.

§ 490.303 Applicability.

The performance measures in this subpart are applicable to the mainline highways on the Interstate System and on the non-Interstate NHS.

§ 490.305 Definitions.

The following definitions are only applicable to this subpart, unless otherwise provided:

Asphalt pavements means pavements where the top-most surface is constructed with asphalt materials. These pavements are coded in the HPMS as having any one of the following Surface Types:

Code	Surface_type
2	Bituminous.
6	Asphalt-Concrete (AC) Overlay over Existing AC Pavement.
7	AC Overlay over Existing Jointed Concrete Pavement.
8	AC (Bituminous Overlay over Existing CRCP).

Continuously Reinforced Concrete Pavements (CRCP) means pavements where the top-most surface is constructed of reinforced Portland cement concrete with no joints. These pavements are coded in the HPMS as having the following Surface Type:

Code	Surface_type
5	CRCP—Continuously Reinforced Concrete Pavement.

Cracking means an unintentional break in the continuous surface of a pavement.

Cracking Percent means the percentage of pavement surface exhibiting cracking as follows:

(1) For asphalt pavements, Cracking Percent is the percentage of the area of the pavement section, exhibiting visible cracking.

(2) For jointed concrete pavements, Cracking Percent is the percentage of concrete slabs exhibiting cracking.

(3) For CRCP, the Cracking Percent is the percentage of pavement surface with longitudinal cracking and/or punchouts, spalling or other visible defects.

Faulting means a vertical misalignment of pavement joints in Portland Cement Concrete Pavements.

International Roughness Index (IRI) means a statistic used to estimate the amount of roughness in a measured longitudinal profile. The IRI is computed from a single longitudinal profile using a quarter-car simulation, as described in the report: "On the Calculation of IRI from Longitudinal Road Profile" (Sayers, M.W., Transportation Research Board 1501, Transportation Research Board, Washington, DC 1995).

Jointed concrete pavements means pavements where the top-most surface is constructed of Portland cement concrete with joints. It may be constructed of either reinforced or unreinforced (plain) concrete. It is coded in the HPMS as having any one of the following Surface Types:

Code	Surface_type
3	Jointed Plain Concrete Pavement (includes whitetopping).
4	Jointed Reinforced Concrete Pavement (includes whitetopping).
9	Unbonded Jointed Concrete Overlay on PCC Pavement.
10	Bonded PCC Overlay on PCC Pavement.

Pavement means any hard surfaced travel lanes of any highway.

Pavement section means a nominally 0.1 mile-long reported segment that defines the limits of pavement condition metrics required by FHWA.

Present Serviceability Rating (PSR) means an observation based system used to rate pavements.

Punchout means a distress specific to CRCP described as the area between two closely spaced transverse cracks and between a short longitudinal crack and the edge of the pavement (or a longitudinal joint) that is breaking up, spalling, or faulting.

Rutting means longitudinal surface depressions in the pavement derived from measurements of a profile transverse to the path of travel on a highway lane. It may have associated transverse displacement.

Sampling as applied to pavements, means measuring pavement conditions on a short section of pavement as a statistical representation for the entire section. Sampling is not to be used to measure or rate NHS pavement conditions.

§490.307 National performance management measures for assessing pavement condition.

(a) To carry out the NHPP, the performance measures for State DOTs to assess pavement condition are:

(1) Percentage of pavements of the Interstate System in Good condition;

(2) Percentage of pavements of the Interstate System in Poor condition;

(3) Percentage of pavements of the non-Interstate NHS in Good condition; and

(4) Percentage of pavements of the non-Interstate NHS in Poor condition.

(b) State DOTs will collect data using the methods described in §490.309 and will process this data to calculate individual pavement metrics for each section of pavement that will be reported to FHWA as described in §490.311. State DOTs and FHWA will use the reported pavement metrics to compute an overall performance of Good, Fair, or Poor, for each section of pavement as described in §490.313.

§490.309 Data requirements.

(a) The performance measures identified in §490.307 are to be computed using methods in §490.313 from the four condition metrics and three inventory data elements contained within the HPMS that shall be collected and reported following the HPMS Field Manual, which is incorporated by reference into this subpart (see §490.111). State DOTs shall report four condition metrics for each pavement section: IRI, rutting, faulting, and Cracking_Percent. State DOTs shall also report three inventory data elements as directed in the HPMS Field Manual: Through Lanes, Surface Type, and Structure Type. All pavement data collected after January 1, 2018 for Interstate highways and January 1, 2020 for non-Interstate National Highway System routes shall meet the requirements of this section.

(b) State DOTs shall collect data in accordance with the following relevant HPMS requirements to report IRI, rutting (asphalt pavements), faulting (jointed concrete pavements), and Cracking percent. State DOTs will be permitted to report present serviceability rating (PSR) for specific locations in accordance with the HPMS requirements as an alternative where posted speed limits are less than 40 miles per hour.

(1) For the Interstate System the following shall apply for all the pavement condition metrics:

(i) State DOTs shall collect data—

(A) From the full extent of the mainline highway;

(B) In the rightmost travel lane or one consistent lane for all data if the rightmost travel lane carries traffic that is not representative of the remainder of the lanes or is not readily accessible due to closure, excessive congestion, or other events impacting access;

(C) Continuously collected in a manner that will allow for reporting in nominally uniform pavement section lengths of 0.10 mile (528 feet); shorter pavement sections are permitted only at the beginning of a route, end of a route, at bridges, at locations where surface type changes or other locations where a pavement section length of 0.10 mile is not achievable; the maximum length of pavement sections shall not exceed 0.11 mile (580.8 feet);

(D) In at least one direction of travel; and

(E) On an annual frequency.

(ii) Estimating conditions from data samples of the full extent of the mainline highway is not permitted.

(iii) State DOTs may collect and report pavement condition data separately for each direction of divided highways on the Interstate System. Averaging across directions is not permitted. When pavement condition data is collected in one direction only, the measured conditions shall apply to all lanes in both directions for that pavement section for purposes of this part.

(iv) For the portions of the Interstate mainline highway pavements where posted speed limits are less than 40

MPH (e.g., border crossings, toll plazas), State DOTs may collect and report the Present Serviceability Rating (PSR) as an alternative to the IRI, Cracking_Percent, rutting, and faulting in this pavement section and shall follow the following requirements:

(A) The PSR shall be determined as a value from 0 to 5 per the procedures prescribed in the HPMS Field Manual;

(B) Alternative pavement condition methods may be allowed to estimate a PSR with prior approval from FHWA of the method of correlation between their condition determination and PSR as required in the HPMS Field Manual;

(C) The PSR data shall be continuously collected in a manner that will allow for reporting in uniform pavement section lengths of 0.10 mile (528 feet); shorter pavement sections are permitted only at the beginning of a route, end of a route, at bridges, at locations where surface type changes or other locations where a pavement section length of 0.10 mile is not achievable; the maximum length of pavement sections shall not exceed 0.11 mile (580.8 feet);

(D) The PSR data shall be collected in at least one direction of travel; and

(E) The PSR data shall be collected on an annual frequency.

(2) For the non-Interstate NHS the following shall apply:

(i) For the IRI metric, State DOTs shall collect and report data:

(A) From the full extent of the mainline highway;

(B) In the rightmost travel lane or one consistent lane for all data if the rightmost travel lane is not accessible;

(C) Continuously collected in a manner that will allow for reporting in uniform pavement section lengths of 0.10 mile (528 feet); shorter pavement sections are permitted only at the beginning of a route, end of a route, at bridges, at locations where surface type changes or other locations where a pavement section length of 0.10 mile is not achievable; the maximum length of pavement sections shall not exceed 0.11 mile (580.8 feet)

(D) In one direction of travel; and

(E) On a biennial frequency.

(F) Estimating IRI metrics from data samples of the full extent of the mainline will not be permitted.

(ii) For the Cracking percent, rutting and faulting metrics, State DOTs shall collect data—

(A) On the full extent (no sampling) of the mainline highway;

(B) In the rightmost travel lane or one consistent lane for all data if the rightmost travel lane is not accessible;

(C) Continuously collected in a manner that will allow for reporting in uniform pavement section lengths of 0.10 mile (528 feet); shorter pavement sections are permitted only at the beginning of a route, end of a route, at bridges, at locations where surface type changes or other locations where a pavement section length of 0.10 mile is not achievable; the maximum length of pavement sections shall not exceed 0.11 mile (580.8 feet)

(D) In one direction of travel; and

(E) On at least a biennial frequency.

(F) Estimating conditions from data samples of the full extent of the mainline highway will not be permitted.

(iii) For the portions of mainline highways where posted speed limits of less than 40 MPH, State DOTs may collect the Present Serviceability Rating (PSR) as an alternative to the IRI, Cracking_Percent, rutting, and faulting pavement condition metrics, in paragraphs (b)(2)(i) and (ii) of this section, and shall follow the following requirements:

(A) The PSR shall be determined as a 0 to 5 value per the procedures prescribed in the HPMS Field Manual;

(B) Alternative pavement condition methods may be allowed to estimate a PSR with prior approval from FHWA of the method of correlation between their condition determination and PSR as required in the HPMS Field Manual;

(C) The PSR data shall be continuously collected in a manner that will allow for reporting in uniform pavement section lengths of 0.10 mile (528 feet); shorter pavement sections are permitted only at the beginning of a route, end of a route, at bridges, at locations where surface type changes or other locations where a pavement section length of 0.10 mile is not achievable; the maximum length of pavement sections shall not exceed 0.11 mile (580.8 feet);

(D) The PSR data shall be collected in one direction of travel; and

(E) The PSR data shall be collected on at least a biennial frequency.

(3) Data collection methods for each of the condition metrics shall conform to the following:

(i) The device to collect data needed to calculate the IRI metric shall be in accordance with American Association of State Highway Transportation Officials (AASHTO) Standard M328–14, Standard Specification for Transportation Materials and Methods of Sampling and Testing, Standard Equipment Specification for Inertial Profiler (incorporated by reference, see §490.111).

(ii) The method to collect data needed to calculate the IRI metric shall be in accordance with AASHTO Standard R57–14, Standard Specification for Transportation Materials and Methods of Sampling and Testing, Standard Practice for Operating Inertial Profiling Systems (incorporated by reference, see §490.111).

(iii) For highways with a posted speed limit less than 40 miles per hour, an alternate method for estimation of IRI is permitted as described in §490.309(b)(1)(iv) or §490.309(b)(2)(iii) may be used in lieu of measuring IRI, cracking, rutting and faulting.

(iv) The method to collect data needed to determine the Cracking_Percent metric for all pavement types except CRCP shall be manual, semi-automated, or fully automated in accordance with the HPMS Field Manual (incorporated by reference, see 490.111).

(v) For CRCP the method to collect the data needed to determine the Cracking_Percent metric is described in the HPMS Field Manual (incorporated by reference, see §490.111) and includes longitudinal cracking and/or punchouts, spalling, or other visible defects.

(vi) For asphalt pavements, the method to collect data needed to determine the rutting metric shall either be:

(A) A 5-Point Collection of Rutting Data method in accordance with AASHTO Standard R48–10, Standard Specification for Transportation Materials and Methods of Sampling and Testing, Standard Practice for Determining Rut Depth in Pavements (incorporated by reference, see §490.111); or

(B) An Automated Transverse Profile Data method in accordance with the HPMS Field Manual (incorporated by reference, see §490.111).

(vii) For jointed concrete pavements, the method to collect data needed to determine the faulting metric shall be in accordance with AASHTO Standard R36–13, Standard Specification for Transportation Materials and Methods of Sampling and Testing, Standard Practice for Evaluating Faulting of Concrete Pavements (incorporated by reference, see §490.111).

(c) State DOTs shall collect data in accordance with the following relevant HPMS requirements to report Through Lanes, Surface Type, and Structure Type.

(1) State DOTs shall collect data:

(i) For the full extent of the mainline highway of the NHS;

(ii) In at least one direction of travel for the Interstate System and in one direction of travel for the non-Interstate NHS; and

(iii) On an annual frequency on the Interstate routes and on at least a biennial frequency on non-Interstate NHS routes.

(2) Estimating data elements from samples of the full extent of the mainline highway is not permitted.

§490.311 Calculation of pavement metrics.

(a) The condition metrics and inventory data elements needed to calculate the pavement performance measures shall be calculated in accordance with the HPMS Field Manual (incorporated by reference, see §490.111), except as noted below.

(b) State DOTs shall calculate metrics in accordance with the following relevant HPMS requirements.

(1) For all pavements, the IRI metric:

(i) Shall be computed from pavement profile data in accordance with AASHTO Standard R43–13, Standard Specification for Transportation Materials and Methods of Sampling and Testing, Standard Practice for Quantifying Roughness of Pavement, 2014, 34th/2014 Edition, AASHTO, 1–56051–606–4 (incorporated by reference, see §490.111);

(ii) Shall be reported for all pavements as the average value in inches per mile for each section; and

(iii) Shall not be estimated from a PSR or other observation-based method except where permitted in § 490.309(b)(3)(iii).

(2) For asphalt pavements—

(i) The Cracking_Percent metric shall be computed as the percentage of the total area containing visible cracks to the nearest whole percent in each section; and

(ii) The rutting metric shall be computed as the average depth of rutting, in inches to the nearest 0.01 inches, for the section.

(3) For CRCP, the Cracking_Percent metric shall be computed as the percentage of the area of the section to the nearest whole percent exhibiting longitudinal cracking, punchouts, spalling, or other visible defects. Transverse cracking shall not be considered in the Cracking_Percent metric.

(4) For jointed concrete pavements—

(i) The Cracking_Percent metric shall be computed as the percentage of slabs to the nearest whole percent within the section that exhibit cracking;

(ii) Partial slabs shall contribute to the section that contains the majority of the slab length; and

(iii) The faulting metric shall be computed as the average height, in inches to the nearest 0.01 inch, of faulting between pavement slabs for the section.

(5) For the mainline highways on the non-Interstate NHS with posted speed limits of less than 40 MPH—

(i) The present serviceability rating (PSR) may be used as an alternative to the IRI, Cracking_Percent, rutting, and faulting pavement condition metrics.

(ii) The PSR shall be determined as a 0 to 5 value per the procedures prescribed in the HPMS Field Manual.

(iii) Alternative pavement condition methods may be allowed to estimate a PSR with prior approval from FHWA of the method of correlation between their condition determination and PSR as required in the HPMS Field Manual.

(c) State DOTs shall report the four pavement metrics listed in § 490.309(a) as calculated following the requirements in paragraphs (a) and (b) of this section in accordance with the following relevant HPMS requirements:

(1) Pavement condition metrics shall be reported to the HPMS in uniform section lengths of 0.1 mile (528 feet); shorter sections are permitted only at the beginning of a route, the end of a route, at bridges, or other locations where a section length of 0.1 mile is not achievable; and the maximum length of sections shall not exceed 0.11 mile (580.8 feet)

(2) Each measured section shall have a single value for each of the relevant condition metrics. Sections where condition is estimated from PSR will have one value for the overall condition.

(3) The time and location reference shall be reported for each section as follows:

(i) The State_Code, Route_ID, Begin_Point, and End_Point shall be reported as specified in the HPMS field manual (incorporated by reference, see § 490.111) for each of the four condition metrics.

(ii) The Year_Record shall be reported as the four digit year for which the data represents for each of the four condition metrics; and

(iii) The Value_Date shall be reported as the month and year of data collection for each of the four condition metrics.

(4) Sections for the four condition metrics shall be reported to the HPMS for the Interstate System by April 15 of each year for the data collected during the previous calendar year.

(5) Sections for the four condition metrics shall be reported to the HPMS for the non-Interstate NHS by June 15 of each year for the data collected during the previous calendar year(s).

(d) The three inventory data elements, Through_Lanes, Surface_Type, and Structure Type shall be reported to the HPMS as directed in Chapter 4 of the HPMS Field Manual for the entire extent of the NHS.

(1) Section Lengths for the three inventory data items are not required to meet the 0.1 mile nominal length but may be any logical length as defined in the HPMS Field Manual.

(2) The three inventory data elements shall be reported to the HPMS

for the Interstate System by April 15 of each year.

(3) The three inventory data elements shall be reported to the HPMS for the non-Interstate NHS by June 15 of the each year that data reporting is required.

§ 490.313 Calculation of performance management measures.

(a) The pavement measures in § 490.307 shall be calculated in accordance with this section and used by State DOTs and MPOs to carry out the pavement condition related requirements of this part, and by FHWA to make the significant progress and minimum condition determinations specified in §§ 490.109 and 490.317, respectively.

(b) The performance measure for pavements shall be calculated based on the data collected in § 490.309 and pavement condition metrics computed in § 490.311. The performance measure for pavements shall be based on three condition ratings of Good, Fair, and Poor calculated for each pavement section. The ratings are determined as follows:

(1) IRI rating shall be determined for all pavement types using the following criteria. If an IRI value of a pavement section is:—

(i) Less than 95, the IRI rating for the pavement section is Good;

(ii) Between 95 and 170, the IRI rating for the pavement section is Fair; and

(iii) Greater than 170, the IRI rating for the pavement section is Poor.

(2) Cracking condition shall be determined using the following criteria:

(i) For asphalt pavement sections—

(A) If the Cracking_Percent value of a section is less than 5 percent, the cracking rating for the pavement section is Good;

(B) If the Cracking_Percent value of a section is equal to or greater than 5 percent and less than or equal to 20 percent the cracking rating for the pavement section is Fair; and

(C) If the Cracking_Percent value of a section is greater than 20 percent the cracking rating for the pavement section is Poor.

(ii) For jointed concrete pavement sections—

(A) If the Cracking_Percent value of a section is less than 5 percent, the cracking rating for the pavement section is Good;

(B) If the Cracking_Percent value of a section is equal to or greater than 5 percent and less than or equal to 15 percent the cracking rating for the pavement section is Fair; and

(C) If the Cracking_Percent value of a section is greater than 15 percent the cracking rating for the pavement section is Poor.

(iii) For CRCP sections:

(A) If the Cracking_Percent value of a section is less than 5 percent, the cracking rating for the pavement section is Good;

(B) If the Cracking_Percent value of a section is equal to or greater than 5 percent and less than or equal to 10 percent, the cracking rating for the pavement section is Fair; and

(C) If the Cracking_Percent value of a section is greater than 10 percent, the cracking rating for the pavement section is Poor.

(3) Rutting or faulting rating shall be determined using the following criteria.

(i) For asphalt pavement:

(A) If the rutting value of a section is less than 0.20 inches, the rutting rating for the pavement section is Good;

(B) If the rutting value of a section is equal to or greater than 0.20 inches and less than or equal to 0.40 inches, the rutting rating for the pavement section is Fair; and

(C) If the rutting value of a section in is greater than 0.40 inches, the rutting rating for the pavement section is Poor.

(ii) For jointed concrete pavement:

(A) If the faulting value of a section is less than 0.10 inches, the faulting rating for the pavement section is Good;

(B) If the faulting value of a section is equal to or greater than 0.10 inches and less than or equal to 0.15 inches, the faulting rating for the pavement section is Fair; and

(C) If the faulting value of a section is greater than 0.15 inches, the faulting rating for the pavement section is Poor.

(4) The FHWA will determine that a reported section in HPMS has a missing, invalid or unresolved data on the

dates specified in §490.317(b) for Interstate System and §490.109(d)(2) and (d)(4) for non-Interstate NHS, if a reported section does not meet any one of the data requirements specified in §§490.309 and 490.311(c) or that reported section does not provide sufficient data to determine its Overall Condition specified in paragraphs (c) through (f) of this section:

(i) Total mainline lane-miles of missing, invalid, or unresolved sections for Interstate System and non-Interstate NHS shall be limited to no more than 5 percent of the total lane miles less the sections excluded in §490.313(f)(1). For each pavement section without collected its condition metrics and inventory data, State DOTs shall note in the HPMS submittal with a specific code identified in the HPMS Field Manual (incorporated by reference, see §490.111) noting the reason it was not collected.

(ii) Calculation of overall pavement conditions in any State meeting the requirements of §490.309(b) shall be based only on sections containing data reported in the HPMS Submittal as of the submission dates required in §490.311(c)(4) and (5). State DOTs not meeting the requirements of §490.309(b) will be considered as not in compliance with §420.105(b) requiring State DOTs to submit data to the HPMS and not in compliance with §490.107 requiring reporting on performance targets. Failure to report data meeting the requirements of §490.309(b) by the submission dates for the Interstate System will be considered as not meeting the minimum requirements for pavement conditions on the Interstate System and that State DOT is subject to the penalties in §490.315.

(c) The Overall condition for asphalt and jointed concrete pavement sections shall be determined based on the ratings for IRI, Cracking_Percent, rutting and faulting, as described in paragraphs (b)(1), (b)(2), (b)(3) and (b)(4) of this section, respectively, for each section as follows:

(1) A pavement section shall be rated an overall condition of Good only if the section is exhibiting Good ratings for all three conditions (IRI, Cracking_Percent, and rutting or faulting);

(2) A pavement section shall be rated an overall condition of Poor if two or more of the three conditions are exhibiting Poor ratings (at least two ratings of Poor for IRI, Cracking_Percent, and rutting or faulting).

(3) A pavement section shall be rated an overall condition of Fair if it does not meet the criteria in paragraphs (c)(1) or (c)(2) of this section.

(4) For sections on roadways where the posted speed limit is less than 40 MPH and where the State DOT has reported PSR in lieu of the IRI, Cracking_Percent, rutting, and faulting metrics the PSR condition level shall be determined using the following criteria:

(i) If the PSR of a section is equal to or greater than 4.0 the PSR rating for the pavement section is Good;

(ii) If the PSR of a section is less than 4.0 and greater than 2.0 the PSR rating for the pavement section is Fair; and

(iii) If the PSR of a section is less than or equal to 2.0 the PSR rating for the pavement section is Poor.

(d) The Overall condition for CRCP sections shall be determined based on two ratings of IRI and Cracking_Percent, as described in paragraphs (b)(1) and (b)(2) of this section or based on PSR where appropriate as described in paragraph (c)(4) of this section, respectively, for each section as follows:

(1) A pavement section shall be rated an overall condition of Good only if the section is exhibiting Good ratings for both conditions (IRI and Cracking_Percent);

(2) A pavement section shall be rated an overall condition of Poor if it exhibits Poor ratings for both conditions (IRI and Cracking_Percent);

(3) A pavement section shall be rated an overall condition of Fair if it does not meet the criteria in paragraphs (d)(1) or (d)(2) of this section.

(4) For pavement sections that are on roadways with a posted speed limit of less than 40 MPH where the State DOT reported the PSR metric in lieu of the IRI, Cracking_Percent, faulting, and rutting metrics the pavement section shall be rated an overall condition equal to the PSR condition rating as described in section (c)(4) above

(e) State DOTs shall not be subject to paragraphs (c) and (d) of this section for Pavements on the until after the data collection cycle ending December 31, 2018, for Interstate highways and December 31, 2021, for the non-Interstate NHS. During this transition period, the Overall condition for all pavement types will be based on IRI rating, as described in paragraph (b)(1) of this section, or on PSR as described in paragraphs (c)(4) or (d)(4) of this section.

(f) The pavement condition measures in §490.307 shall be computed as described below. The measures shall be used for establishing targets in accordance with §490.105 and reporting the conditions of the pavements in the biennial performance reporting required in §490.107 as follows:

(1) Bridges shall be excluded prior to computing all pavement condition measures by removing the sections where the Structure_Type data item in the HPMS is coded as 1. Sections that have an unpaved surface or an "other" surface type (such as cobblestone, planks, brick) shall be excluded prior to computing all pavement condition measures by removing the sections where the Surface Type data item in the HPMS is coded as 1 or as 11.

(2) For §490.307(a)(1) the measure for percentage of lane-miles of the Interstate System in Good condition shall be computed to the one tenth of a percent as follows:

$$100 \times \frac{\sum_{g=1}^{Good}\{\langle End\_Point - Begin\_Point\rangle \times Through\_lanes\}_{section\ g}}{\sum_{t=1}^{Total}\{\langle End\_Point - Begin\_Point\rangle \times Through\_lanes\}_{section\ t}}$$

Where:

Good = total number of mainline highway Interstate System sections where the overall condition is Good;

g = a section's overall condition is determined Good per paragraphs (b) or (c) of this section;

t = an Interstate System section;

Total = total number of mainline highway Interstate System sections excluding bridges, unpaved surface and "other" surface types, and missing data sections, described in paragraph (f)(1) and (b)(4)(i) of this section.

Begin_Point = Begin Milepost of each section g or t;

End Point = End Milepost of each section g or t; and

Through_lanes = the number of lanes designated for through-traffic represented by a section g or t.

(3) For §490.307(a)(2) the measure for percentage of lane-miles of the Interstate System in Poor condition shall be computed to the one tenth of a percent as follows:

$$100 \times \frac{\sum_{p=1}^{Poor}\{\langle End\_Point - Begin\_Point\rangle \times Through\_lanes\}_{section\ p}}{\sum_{t=1}^{Total}\{\langle End\_Point - Begin\_Point\rangle \times Through\_lanes\}_{section\ t}}$$

Where:

Poor = total number of mainline highway Interstate System sections where the overall condition is Poor;

p = a section's overall condition is determined Poor per paragraphs (b) or (c) of this section;

t = an Interstate System section;

Total = total number of mainline highway Interstate System sections excluding bridges, unpaved surface and "other" surface types, and missing data sections, described in paragraph (f)(1) and (b)(4)(i) of this section;

Begin_Point = Begin Milepost of each section p or t;

End Point = End Milepost of each section p or t; and

Through_lanes = the number of lanes designated for through-traffic represented by a section p or t.

(4) For §490.307(a)(3) the measure for percentage of lane-miles of the non-Interstate NHS in Good condition in

§ 490.307(a)(3) shall be computed to the one tenth of a percent as follows:

$$100 \times \frac{\sum_{g=1}^{Good}\{\langle End\_Point - Begin\_Point\rangle \times Through\_lanes\}_{section\ g}}{\sum_{t=1}^{Total}\{\langle End\_Point - Begin\_Point\rangle \times Through\_lanes\}_{section\ t}}$$

Where:

Good = total number of mainline highway non-Interstate NHS sections where the overall condition is Good;

g = a section's overall condition is determined Good per paragraphs (b), (c) or (d) of this section;

t = a non-Interstate NHS section;

Total = total number of mainline highway non-Interstate NHS sections excluding bridges, unpaved surface and "other" surface types, and missing data sections, described in paragraph (f)(1) and (b)(4)(i) of this section;

Begin_Point = Begin Milepost of each section *g* or *t;*

End Point = End Milepost of each section *g* or *t;* and

Through_lanes = the number of lanes designated for through-traffic represented by a section *g* or *t*.

(5) For § 490.307(a)(4) the measure for percentage of lane-miles of the non-Interstate NHS in Poor condition in § 490.307(a)(4) shall be computed to the one tenth of a percent as follows:

$$100 \times \frac{\sum_{p=1}^{Poor}\{\langle End\_Point - Begin\_Point\rangle \times Through\_lanes\}_{section\ p}}{\sum_{t=1}^{Total}\{\langle End\_Point - Begin\_Point\rangle \times Through\_lanes\}_{section\ t}}$$

Where:

Poor = total number of mainline highway non-Interstate NHS sections where the overall condition is Poor;

p = a section's overall condition is determined Poor per paragraphs (b), (c) or (d) of this section;

t = a non-Interstate NHS section;

Total = total number of mainline highway non-Interstate NHS sections excluding bridges, unpaved surface and "other" surface types, and missing data sections, described in paragraph (f)(1) and (b)(4)(i) of this section;

Begin_Point = Begin Milepost of each section *p* or *t;*

End Point = End Milepost of each section *p* or *t;* and

Through_lanes = the number of lanes designated for through-traffic represented by a section *p* or *t*.

§ 490.315 Establishment of minimum level for condition of pavements.

(a) For the purposes of carrying out the requirements of 23 U.S.C. 119(f)(1), the percentage of lane-miles of Interstate System in Poor condition, as computed per § 490.313(e)(3), shall not exceed 5.0 percent except as noted in paragraph (b) of this section.

(b) For the purposes of carrying out the requirements of 23 U.S.C. 119(f)(1), the percentage of lane-miles of Interstate System in Poor condition within the State of Alaska, as computed per § 490.313(e)(3), shall not exceed 10.0 percent.

§ 490.317 Penalties for not maintaining minimum Interstate System pavement condition.

(a) The FHWA shall compute the Percentage of lane-miles of the Interstate System, excluding sections on bridges, in Poor Condition, in accordance with § 490.313(e)(3), for each State annually.

(b) Each year, FHWA shall extract data contained within the HPMS on June 15 that represents conditions from the prior calendar year for Interstate System pavement conditions to carry out paragraph (a) of this section, beginning with data collected during the 2018 calendar year.

(c) The FHWA shall determine if a State DOT is in compliance with § 490.315(a) or § 490.315(b) and 23 U.S.C. 119(f)(1) after the first full year of data collection for the Interstate System and each year thereafter.

(d) The FHWA will notify State DOTs of their compliance with 23 U.S.C. 119(f)(1) prior to October 1 of the year in which the determination was made.

(e) If FHWA determines through conduct of paragraph (d) of this section a State DOT to be out of compliance with 23 U.S.C. 119(f)(1) then the State DOT shall, during the following fiscal year:

(1) Obligate, from the amounts apportioned to the State DOT under 23 U.S.C. 104(b)(1) (for the NHPP), an amount that is not less than the amount of funds apportioned to the State for Federal fiscal year 2009 under the Interstate Maintenance program for the purposes described in 23 U.S.C. 119 (as in effect on the day before the date of enactment of the MAP–21), except that for each year after Federal fiscal year 2013, the amount required to be obligated under this clause shall be increased by 2 percent over the amount required to be obligated in the previous fiscal year; and

(2) Transfer, from the amounts apportioned to the State DOT under 23 U.S.C. 104(b)(2) (for the Surface Transportation Program) (other than amounts sub-allocated to metropolitan areas and other areas of the State under 23 U.S.C. 133(d)) to the apportionment of the State under 23 U.S.C. 104(b)(1), an amount equal to 10 percent of the amount of funds apportioned to the State for fiscal year 2009 under the Interstate Maintenance program for the purposes described in 23 U.S.C. 119 (as in effect on the day before the date of enactment of the MAP–21).

§490.319 Other requirements.

(a) In accordance with the HPMS Field Manual (incorporated by reference, see §490.111), each State DOT shall report the following to the HPMS no later than April 15 each year:

(1) The pavement condition metrics specified in §490.311 that are necessary to calculate the Interstate System condition measures identified in §§490.307(a)(1) and (a)(2) and;

(2) The data elements specified in §490.309(c) for the Interstate System

(b) In accordance with the HPMS Field Manual (incorporated by reference, see §490.111), each State DOT shall report to the HPMS no later than June 15 each year the pavement condition metrics specified in §490.311 that are necessary to calculate the non-Interstate NHS condition measures in §§490.307(a)(3) and (a)(4).

(c) Each State DOT shall develop and utilize a Data Quality Management Program, approved by FHWA that addresses the quality of all data collected, regardless of the method of acquisition, to report the pavement condition metrics, discussed in §490.311, and data elements discussed in §490.309(c).

(1) In a Data Quality Management Programs, State DOTs shall include, at a minimum, methods and processes for:

(i) Data collection equipment calibration and certification;

(ii) Certification process for persons performing manual data collection;

(iii) Data quality control measures to be conducted before data collection begins and periodically during the data collection program;

(iv) Data sampling, review and checking processes; and

(v) Error resolution procedures and data acceptance criteria.

(2) Not later than 1 year after the effective date of this regulation, State DOTs shall submit their Data Quality Management Program to FHWA for approval. Once FHWA approves a State DOT's Data Quality Management Program, the State DOT shall use that Program to collect and report data required by §§490.309 to 490.311. State DOTs also shall submit any proposed significant change to the Data Quality Management Program to FHWA for approval prior to implementing the change.

Subpart D—National Performance Management Measures for Assessing Bridge Condition

SOURCE: 82 FR 5968, Jan. 18, 2017, unless otherwise noted.

§490.401 Purpose.

The purpose of this subpart is to implement the requirements of 23 U.S.C. 150(c)(3)(A)(ii)(III), which requires the

Secretary of Transportation to establish performance measures for the purpose of carrying out the NHPP and for State DOTs and MPOs to use in assessing the condition of bridges carrying the NHS which includes on- and off-ramps connected to the NHS.

§ 490.403 Applicability.

The section is only applicable to bridges carrying the NHS, which includes on- and off-ramps connected to the NHS.

§ 490.405 Definitions.

The following definitions are only applicable to this subpart, unless otherwise provided:

Structurally deficient as used in §§ 490.411 and 490.413 is a classification given to a bridge which has any component in Poor or worse condition or the adequacy of the waterway opening provided by the bridge is determined to be insufficient to the point of causing overtopping with intolerable traffic interruptions. Beginning with calendar year 2018 and thereafter, *structurally deficient* as used in §§ 490.411 and 490.413 is a classification given to a bridge which has any component in Poor or worse condition.

§ 490.407 National performance management measures for assessing bridge condition.

(a) There are three classifications for the purpose of assessing bridge condition. They are:

(1) Percentage of NHS bridges classified as in Good condition;

(2) Percentage of NHS bridges classified as in Fair condition; and

(3) Percentage of NHS bridges classified as in Poor condition.

(b) [Reserved]

(c) To carry out the NHPP, two of the three classifications are performance measures for State DOTs to use to assess bridge condition on the NHS. They are:

(1) Percentage of NHS bridges classified as in Good condition; and

(2) Percentage of NHS bridges classified as in Poor condition.

(d) Determination of Good and Poor conditions are described in § 490.409.

§ 490.409 Calculation of National performance management measures for assessing bridge condition.

(a) The bridge measures in § 490.407 shall be calculated in accordance with this section and used by State DOTs and MPOs to carry out the bridge condition related requirements of this part and by FHWA to make the significant progress determination specified in § 490.109.

(b) The condition of bridges carrying the NHS, which includes on- and off-ramps connected to the NHS, shall be classified as Good, Fair, or Poor following the criteria specified in this paragraph. The assignment of a classification of Good, Fair, or Poor shall be based on the bridge's condition ratings for NBI Items 58—Deck, 59—Superstructure, 60—Substructure, and 62—Culverts. For the purposes of national performance measures under the NHPP, the method of assessment to determine the classification of a bridge will be the minimum of condition rating method (*i.e.*, the condition ratings for lowest rating of a bridge's 3 NBI Items, 58—Deck, 59—Superstructure, and 60—Substructure). For culverts, the rating of its NBI Item, 62—Culverts, will determine its classification. The bridges carrying the NHS which includes on- and off-ramps connected to the NHS will be classified as Good, Fair, or Poor based on the following criteria:

(1) *Good:* When the lowest rating of the 3 NBI items for a bridge (Items 58—Deck, 59—Superstructure, 60—Substructure) is 7, 8, or 9, the bridge will be classified as Good. When the rating of NBI item for a culvert (Item 62—Culverts) is 7, 8, or 9, the culvert will be classified as Good.

(2) *Fair:* When the lowest rating of the 3 NBI items for a bridge is 5 or 6, the bridge will be classified as Fair. When the rating of NBI item for a culvert is 5 or 6, the culvert will be classified as Fair.

(3) *Poor:* When the lowest rating of the 3 NBI items for a bridge is 4, 3, 2, 1, or 0, the bridge will be classified as Poor. When the rating of NBI item for a culvert is 4, 3, 2, 1, or 0, the culvert will be classified as Poor.

(c) The bridge measures specified in § 490.407(c) shall be calculated for the applicable bridges per paragraph (a) that pertain to each target established by the State DOT or MPO in §§490.105(e) and 490.105(f), respectively, as follows:

(1) For §490.407(c)(1), the measure for the percentage of bridges classified as in Good condition shall be computed and reported to the one tenth of a percent as follows:

$$100 \times \frac{\sum_{g=1}^{GOOD} [\text{Length} \times \text{Width}]_{\text{Bridge } g}}{\sum_{s=1}^{TOTAL} [\text{Length} \times \text{Width}]_{\text{Bridge } s}}$$

Where:

GOOD = total number of the applicable bridges, where their condition is Good per paragraph (b)(1) of this section;

g = a bridge determined to be in Good condition per paragraph (b)(1) of this section;

Length = corresponding value of NBI Item 49—Structure Length for every applicable bridge;

Width = corresponding value of NBI Item 52—Deck Width or value of Item 32 Approach Roadway Width for culverts where the roadway is on a fill [*i.e.*, traffic does not directly run on the top slab (or wearing surface) of the culvert] and the headwalls do not affect the flow of traffic for every applicable bridge.

s = an applicable bridge per paragraph (b) of this section; and

TOTAL = total number of the applicable bridges specified in paragraph (b) of this section.

(2) For §490.407(c)(2), the measure for the percentage of bridges classified as in Poor condition shall be computed and reported to the one tenth of a percent as follows:

$$100 \times \frac{\sum_{p=1}^{POOR} [\text{Length} \times \text{Width}]_{\text{Bridge } p}}{\sum_{s=1}^{TOTAL} [\text{Length} \times \text{Width}]_{\text{Bridge } s}}$$

Where:

POOR = total number of the applicable bridges, where their condition is Poor per paragraph (b)(3) of this section;

p = a bridge determined to be in Poor condition per paragraph (b)(3) of this section;

Length = corresponding value of NBI Item 49—Structure Length for every applicable bridge;

Width = corresponding value of NBI Item 52—Deck Width or value of Item 32 Approach Roadway Width for culverts where the roadway is on a fill [*i.e.*, traffic does not directly run on the top slab (or wearing surface) of the culvert] and the headwalls do not affect the flow of traffic for every applicable bridge.

s = an applicable bridge per paragraph (b) of this section; and

TOTAL = total number of the applicable bridges specified in paragraph (b) of this section.

(d) The measures identified in §490.407(c) shall be used to establish targets in accordance with §490.105 and report targets and conditions described in §490.107.

(e) The NBI Items included in this section are found in the Recording and Coding Guide for the Structure Inventory and Appraisal of the Nation's Bridges, which is incorporated by reference (see §490.111).

§490.411 Establishment of minimum level for condition for bridges.

(a) State DOTs will maintain bridges so that the percentage of the deck area of bridges classified as Structurally Deficient does not exceed 10.0 percent. This minimum condition level is applicable to bridges carrying the NHS, which includes on- and off-ramps connected to the NHS within a State, and bridges carrying the NHS that cross a State border.

(b) For the purposes of carrying out this section and §490.413, a bridge will be classified as Structurally Deficient when one of its NBI Items, 58—Deck,

59—Superstructure, 60—Substructure, or 62—Culverts, is 4 or less, or when one of its NBI Items, 67—Structural Evaluation or 71—Waterway Adequacy, is 2 or less. Beginning with calendar year 2018 and thereafter, a bridge will be classified as Structurally Deficient when one of its NBI Items, 58—Deck, 59—Superstructure, 60—Substructure, or 62—Culverts, is 4 or less.

(c) For all bridges carrying the NHS, which includes on- and off-ramps connected to the NHS and bridges carrying the NHS that cross a State border, FHWA shall calculate a ratio of the total deck area of all bridges classified as Structurally Deficient to the total deck area of all applicable bridges for each State. The percentage of deck area of bridges classified as Structurally Deficient shall be computed by FHWA to the one tenth of a percent as follows:

$$100 \times \frac{\sum_{SD=1}^{\text{Structurally Deficient}} [\text{Length} \times \text{Width}]_{\text{Bridge SD}}}{\sum_{s=1}^{\text{TOTAL}} [\text{Length} \times \text{Width}]_{\text{Bridge s}}}$$

Where:

Structurally Deficient = total number of the applicable bridges, where their classification is Structurally Deficient per this section and § 490.413;

SD = a bridge classified as Structurally Deficient per this section and § 490.413;

Length = corresponding value of NBI Item 49—Structure Length for every applicable bridge;

Width = corresponding value of NBI Item 52—Deck Width

Beginning with calendar year 2018 and thereafter, Width = corresponding value of NBI Item 52—Deck Width or value of Item 32 Approach Roadway Width for culverts where the roadway is on a fill [*i.e.*, traffic does not directly run on the top slab (or wearing surface) of the culvert] and the headwalls do not affect the flow of traffic for every applicable bridge.

s = an applicable bridge per this section and § 490.413; and

TOTAL = total number of the applicable bridges specified in this section and § 490.413.

(d) The FHWA will annually determine the percentage of the deck area of NHS bridges classified as Structurally Deficient for each State DOT and identify State DOTs that do not meet the minimum level of condition for NHS bridges based on data cleared in the NBI as of June 15 of each year. The FHWA will notify State DOTs of their compliance with 23 U.S.C. 119(f)(2) prior to October 1 of the year in which the determination was made.

(e) For the purposes of carrying out this section, State DOTs will annually submit their most current NBI data on highway bridges to FHWA no later than March 15 of each year.

(f) The NBI Items included in this section are found in the Recording and Coding Guide for the Structure Inventory and Appraisal of the Nation's Bridges, which is incorporated by reference (see § 490.111).

§ 490.413 Penalties for not maintaining bridge condition.

(a) If FHWA determines for the 3-year period preceding the date of the determination, that more than 10.0 percent of the total deck area of bridges in the State on the NHS is located on bridges that have been classified as Structurally Deficient, the following requirements will apply.

(1) During the fiscal year following the determination, the State DOT shall obligate and set aside in an amount equal to 50 percent of funds apportioned to such State for fiscal year 2009 to carry out 23 U.S.C. 144 (as in effect the day before enactment of MAP–21) from amounts apportioned to a State for a fiscal year under 23 U.S.C. 104(b)(1) only for eligible projects on bridges on the NHS.

(2) The set-aside and obligation requirement for bridges on the NHS in a State in paragraph (a) of this section for a fiscal year shall remain in effect for each subsequent fiscal year until such time as less than 10 percent of the total deck area of bridges in the State on the NHS is located on bridges that

have been classified as Structurally Deficient as determined by FHWA.

(b) The FHWA will make the first determination by October 1, 2016, and each fiscal year thereafter.

Subpart E—National Performance Management Measures To Assess Performance of the National Highway System

SOURCE: 82 FR 6042, Jan. 18, 2017, unless otherwise noted.

§490.501 Purpose.

The purpose of this subpart is to implement the requirements of 23 U.S.C. 150(c)(3)(A)(ii)(IV) and (V) to establish performance measures for State Departments of Transportation (State DOTs) and Metropolitan Planning Organizations (MPOs) to use to assess:

(a) Performance of the Interstate System; and

(b) Performance of the non-Interstate National Highway System (NHS).

§490.503 Applicability.

(a) The performance measures are applicable to those portions of the mainline highways on the NHS as provided in paragraphs (a)(1) and (2) of this section (and in more detail in §490.507):

(1) The Travel Time Reliability measures in §490.507(a) are applicable to all directional mainline highways on the Interstate System and non-Interstate NHS.

(2) [Reserved]

(b) [Reserved]

[82 FR 6031, Jan. 18, 2017, as amended at 83 FR 24936, May 31, 2018]

§490.505 Definitions.

All definitions in §490.101 apply to this subpart. Unless otherwise specified in this subpart, the following definitions apply to this subpart:

Level of Travel Time Reliability is a comparison, expressed as a ratio, of the 80th percentile travel time of a reporting segment to the "normal" (50th percentile) travel time of a reporting segment occurring throughout a full calendar year.

Normal Travel Time (or 50th percentile travel time) is the time of travel to traverse the full extent of a reporting segment which is greater than the time for 50 percent of the travel in a calendar year to traverse the same reporting segment.

Travel time cumulative probability distribution means a representation of all the travel times for a road segment during a defined reporting period (such as annually) presented in a percentile ranked order as provided in the travel time data set. The normal (50th percentile) and 80th percentile travel times used to compute the Travel Time Reliability measures may be identified by the travel time cumulative probability distribution.

[82 FR 6031, Jan. 18, 2017, as amended at 83 FR 24936, May 31, 2018]

§490.507 National performance management measures for system performance.

There are two performance measures to assess the performance of the Interstate System and the performance of the non-Interstate NHS for the purpose of carrying out the National Highway Performance Program (referred to collectively as the NHS Performance measures).

(a) Two measures are used to assess reliability (referred to collectively as the Travel Time Reliability measures). They are:

(1) Percent of the person-miles traveled on the Interstate that are reliable (referred to as the Interstate Travel Time Reliability measure); and

(2) Percent of person-miles traveled on the non-Interstate NHS that are reliable (referred to as the Non-Interstate Travel Time Reliability measure).

(b) [Reserved]

[82 FR 6031, Jan. 18, 2017, as amended at 83 FR 24936, May 31, 2018]

§490.509 Data requirements.

(a) Travel time data needed to calculate the Travel Time Reliability measures in §490.507(a) shall come from the travel time data set, as specified in §490.103(e).

(1) State DOTs, in coordination with MPOs, shall define reporting segments in accordance with §490.103(f). Reporting segments must be contiguous so that they cover the full extent of the

mainline highways of the NHS in the State.

(2) [Reserved]

(b) State DOTs shall not replace missing travel times when data are not available in the travel time data set (data not reported, or reported as "0" or null) as specified in § 490.511(b)(1)(v).

(c) AADT needed to calculate the Travel Time Reliability measures will be used, as reported to HPMS in June of the reporting year, to assign an annual volume to each reporting segment. Annual volume will be calculated as:

Annual Volume = AADT × 365 days

(d) The average occupancy factors for the State and/or metropolitan area (as applicable) needed to calculate Travel Time Reliability measures shall come from the most recently available data tables published by FHWA unless using other allowed data source(s).

(e) If an NHS roadway is closed, the State DOT is not required to include those time periods for those segments of road in the calculations required for the Level of Travel Time Reliability (LOTTR) metric (see § 490.511(a)(1)).

[82 FR 6031, Jan. 18, 2017, as amended at 83 FR 24936, May 31, 2018]

§ 490.511 Calculation of National Highway System performance metrics.

(a) Two performance metrics are required for the NHS Performance measures specified in § 490.507. These are:

(1) Level of Travel Time Reliability (LOTTR) for the Travel Time Reliability measures in § 490.507(a) (referred to as the LOTTR metric).

(2) [Reserved]

(b) The State DOT shall calculate the LOTTR metrics for each NHS reporting segment in accordance with the following:

(1) Data sets shall be created from the travel time data set to be used to calculate the LOTTR metrics. This data set shall include, for each reporting segment, a ranked list of average travel times for all traffic ("all vehicles" in NPMRDS nomenclature), to the nearest second, for 15 minute periods of a population that:

(i) Includes travel times occurring between the hours of 6 a.m. and 10 a.m. for every weekday (Monday–Friday) from January 1st through December 31st of the same year;

(ii) Includes travel times occurring between the hours of 10 a.m. and 4 p.m. for every weekday (Monday–Friday) from January 1st through December 31st of the same year;

(iii) Includes travel times occurring between the hours of 4 p.m. and 8 p.m. for every weekday (Monday–Friday) from January 1st through December 31st of the same year; and

(iv) Includes travel times occurring between the hours of 6: a.m. and 8: p.m. for every weekend day (Saturday–Sunday) from January 1st through December 31st of the same year.

(2) The Normal Travel Time (50th percentile) shall be determined from each data set defined under paragraph (b)(1) of this section as the time in which 50 percent of the times in the data set are shorter in duration and 50 percent are longer in duration. The 80th percentile travel time shall be determined for each data set defined under paragraph (b)(1) of this section as the time in which 80 percent of the times in the data set are shorter in duration and 20 percent are longer in duration. Both the Normal and 80th percentile travel times can be determined by plotting the data on a travel time cumulative probability distribution graph or using the percentile functions available in spreadsheet and other analytical tools.

(3) Four LOTTR metrics shall be calculated for each reporting segment; one for each data set defined under paragraph (b)(1) of this section as the 80th percentile travel time divided by the 50th percentile travel time and rounded to the nearest hundredth.

(c)-(d) [Reserved]

(e) Starting in 2018 and annually thereafter, State DOTs shall report the LOTTR metrics, defined in paragraph (b) of this section, in accordance with HPMS Field Manual by June 15th of each year for the previous year's measures.

(1) Metrics are reported to HPMS by reporting segment. All reporting segments where the NPMRDS is used shall be referenced by NPMRDS TMC(s) or HPMS section(s). If a State DOT elects to use, in part or in whole, the equivalent data set, all reporting segment

shall be referenced by HPMS section(s); and

(2) The LOTTR metric (to the nearest hundredths) for each of the four time periods identified in paragraphs (b)(1)(i) through (iv) of this section: the corresponding 80th percentile travel times (to the nearest second), the corresponding Normal (50th percentile) Travel Times (to the nearest second), and directional AADTs. If a State DOT does not elect to use FHWA supplied occupancy factor, as provided in §490.507(d), that State DOT shall report vehicle occupancy factor (to the nearest tenth) to HPMS.

(f) [Reserved]

[82 FR 6031, Jan. 18, 2017, as amended at 83 FR 24936, May 31, 2018]

§490.513 Calculation of National Highway System performance measures.

(a) The NHS Performance measures in §490.507 shall be calculated in accordance with this section by State DOTs and MPOs to carry out the Interstate System and non-Interstate NHS performance-related requirements of this part, and by FHWA to make the significant progress determinations specified in §490.109 and to report on system performance.

(b) The Interstate Travel Time Reliability measure specified in §490.507(a)(1) shall be computed to the nearest tenth of a percent as follows:

$$100 \times \frac{\sum_{i=1}^{R} SL_i \times AV_i \times OF_j}{\sum_{i=1}^{T} SL_i \times AV_i \times OF_j}$$

Where:

R = total number of Interstate System reporting segments that are exhibiting an LOTTR below 1.50 during all of the time periods identified in §490.511(b)(1)(i) through (iv);

I = Interstate System reporting segment "i";

SL_i = length, to the nearest thousandth of a mile, of Interstate System reporting segment "i";

AV_i = total annual traffic volume to the nearest single vehicle, of the Interstate System reporting segment "i";

J = geographic area in which the reporting segment "i" is located where a unique occupancy factor has been determined;

OF_i = occupancy factor for vehicles on the NHS within a specified geographic area within the State/Metropolitan planning area; and

T = total number of Interstate System reporting segments.

(c) The Non-Interstate Travel Time Reliability measure specified in §490.507(a)(2) shall be computed to the nearest tenth of a percent as follows:

$$100 \times \frac{\sum_{i=1}^{R} SL_i \times AV_i \times OF_j}{\sum_{i=1}^{T} SL_i \times AV_i \times OF_j}$$

Where:

R = total number of non-Interstate NHS reporting segments that are exhibiting an LOTTR below 1.50 during all of the time periods identified in §490.511(b)(1)(i) through (iv);

i = non-Interstate NHS reporting segment "i";

SL_i = length, to the nearest thousandth of a mile, of non-Interstate NHS reporting segment "i";

AV_i = total annual traffic volume to the nearest 1 vehicle, of the Interstate System reporting segment "i";

j = geographic area in which the reporting segment "i" is located where a unique occupancy factor has been determined;

OF_j = occupancy factor for vehicles on the NHS within a specified geographic area within the State/Metropolitan planning area; and

T = total number of non-Interstate NHS reporting segments.

[82 FR 6031, Jan. 18, 2017, as amended at 83 FR 24936, May 31, 2018]

Subpart F—National Performance Management Measures To Assess Freight Movement on the Interstate System

SOURCE: 82 FR 6044, Jan. 18, 2017, unless otherwise noted.

§ 490.601 Purpose.

The purpose of this subpart is to implement the requirements of 23 U.S.C. 150(c)(6) to establish performance measures for State Departments of Transportation (State DOTs) and the Metropolitan Planning Organizations (MPOs) to use to assess the national freight movement on the Interstate System.

§ 490.603 Applicability.

The performance measures to assess the national freight movement are applicable to the Interstate System.

§ 490.605 Definitions.

The definitions in § 490.101 apply to this subpart.

§ 490.607 National performance management measures to assess freight movement on the Interstate System.

The performance measure to assess freight movement on the Interstate System is the: Truck Travel Time Reliability (TTTR) Index (referred to as the Freight Reliability measure).

§ 490.609 Data requirements.

(a) Travel time data needed to calculate the Freight Reliability measure in § 490.607 shall come from the travel time data set, as specified in § 490.103(e).

(b) State DOTs, in coordination with MPOs, shall define reporting segments in accordance with § 490.103(f). Reporting segments must be contiguous so that they cover the full extent of the directional mainline highways of the Interstate in the State.

(c) When truck travel times are not available in the travel time data set (data not reported, or reported as "0" or null) as specified in § 490.611(a)(1)(ii) for a given 15 minute interval, State DOTs shall replace the missing travel time with an observed travel time that represents all traffic on the roadway during the same 15 minute interval ("all vehicles" in NPMRDS nomenclature).

(d) If an NHS roadway is closed, the State DOT is not required to include those time periods for those segments of road in the calculations required for the Freight Reliability metric/measure.

§ 490.611 Calculation of Truck Travel Time Reliability metrics.

(a) The State DOT shall calculate the TTTR Index metric (referred to as the TTTR metric) for each Interstate System reporting segment in accordance with the following:

(1) A truck travel time data set shall be created from the travel time data set to be used to calculate the TTTR metric. This data set shall include, for each reporting segment, a ranked list of average truck travel times, to the nearest second, for 15 minute periods of a 24-hour period for an entire calendar year that:

(i) Includes "AM Peak" travel times occurring between the hours of 6 a.m. and 10 a.m. for every weekday (Monday –Friday) from January 1st through December 31st of the same year;

(ii) Includes "Mid Day" travel times occurring between the hours of 10 a.m. and 4 p.m. for every weekday (Monday-Friday) from January 1st through December 31st of the same year;

(iii) Includes "PM Peak" travel times occurring between the hours of 4 p.m. and 8 p.m. for every weekday (Monday-Friday) from January 1st through December 31st of the same year;

(iv) Includes "Overnight" travel times occurring between the hours of 8 p.m. and 6 a.m. for every day (Sunday-Saturday) from January 1st through December 31st of the same year; and

(v) Includes "Weekend" travel times occurring between the hours of 6 a.m. and 8 p.m. for every weekend day (Saturday-Sunday) from January 1st through December 31st of the same year.

(2) The Normal Truck Travel Time (50th percentile) shall be determined from each of the truck travel time data sets defined under paragraph (a)(1) of this section as the time in which 50 percent of the times in the data set are shorter in duration and 50 percent are longer in duration. The 95th percentile truck travel time shall be determined from each of the truck travel time data sets defined under paragraph (a)(1) of this section as the time in which 95 percent of the times in the data set are shorter in duration. Both the Normal and 95th percentile truck travel times can be determined by plotting the data on a travel time cumulative probability distribution graph or using the percentile functions available in spreadsheet and other analytical tools.

(3) Five TTTR metrics shall be calculated for each reporting segment; one for each data set defined under paragraph (a)(1) of this section as the 95th percentile travel time divided by the Normal Truck Travel Time and rounded to the nearest hundredth.

(b) Starting in 2018 and annually thereafter, State DOTs shall report the TTTR metrics, as defined in this section, in accordance with the HPMS Field Manual by June 15th of each year for the previous year's Freight Reliability measures.

(1) All metrics shall be reported to HPMS by reporting segments. When the NPMRDS is used metrics shall be referenced by NPMRDS TMC(s) or HPMS section(s). If a State DOT elects to use, in part or in whole, the equivalent data set, all reporting segment shall be referenced by HPMS section(s).

(2) The TTTR metric shall be reported to HPMS for each reporting segment (to the nearest hundredths) for each of the five time periods identified in paragraphs (a)(1)(i) through (v) of this section; the corresponding 95th percentile travel times (to the nearest second) and the corresponding normal (50th percentile) travel times (to the nearest second).

§ 490.613 Calculation of Freight Reliability measure.

(a) The performance for freight movement on the Interstate in § 490.607 (the Freight Reliability measure) shall be calculated in accordance with this section by State DOTs and MPOs to carry out the freight movement on the Interstate System related requirements of this part, and by FHWA to make the significant progress determinations specified in § 490.109 and to report on freight performance of the Interstate System.

(b) The Freight Reliability measure shall be computed to the nearest hundredth as follows:

$$\frac{\sum_{i=1}^{T}(SL_i \times \max TTTR_i)}{\sum_{i=1}^{T}(SL_i)}$$

Where:

i = An Interstate System reporting segment;

$\max TTTR_i$ = The maximum TTTR of the five time periods in paragraphs (a)(1)(i) through (v) of § 490.611, to the nearest hundredth, of Interstate System reporting segment "i";

SL_i = Segment length, to the nearest thousandth of a mile, of Interstate System reporting segment "i"; and

T= A total number of Interstate System reporting segments.

Subpart G—National Performance Management Measure for Assessing the Congestion Mitigation and Air Quality Improvement Program—Traffic Congestion

SOURCE: 82 FR 6045, Jan. 18, 2017, unless otherwise noted.

§ 490.701 Purpose.

The purpose of this subpart is to implement the requirements of 23 U.S.C. 150(c)(5)(A) to establish performance measures for State DOTs and the MPOs to use in assessing CMAQ Traffic Congestion for the purpose of carrying out the CMAQ program.

§ 490.703 Applicability.

The CMAQ Traffic Congestion performance measures are applicable to all urbanized areas that include NHS mileage and with a population over 1 million for the first performance period and in urbanized areas with a population over 200,000 for the second and all other performance periods, that are, in all or part, designated as nonattainment or maintenance areas for ozone (O_3), carbon monoxide (CO), or particulate matter (PM_{10} and $PM_{2.5}$) National Ambient Air Quality Standards (NAAQS).

§ 490.705 Definitions.

All definitions in § 490.101 apply to this subpart. Unless otherwise specified, the following definitions apply in this subpart:

Excessive delay means the extra amount of time spent in congested conditions defined by speed thresholds that are lower than a normal delay threshold. For the purposes of this rule, the speed threshold is 20 miles per hour (mph) or 60 percent of the posted speed limit, whichever is greater.

Peak Period is defined as weekdays from 6 a.m. to 10 a.m. and either 3 p.m. to 7 p.m. or 4 p.m. to 8 p.m. State DOTs and MPOs may choose whether to use 3 p.m. to 7 p.m. or 4 p.m. to 8 p.m.

§ 490.707 National performance management measures for traffic congestion.

There are two performance measures to assess traffic congestion for the purpose of carrying out the CMAQ program (referred to collectively as the CMAQ Traffic Congestion measures. They are:

(a) Annual Hours of Peak Hour Excessive Delay (PHED) Per Capita (referred to as the PHED measure); and

(b) Percent of Non-SOV Travel.

§ 490.709 Data requirements.

(a) Travel time data needed to calculate the PHED measure in § 490.707(a) shall come from the travel time data set, as specified in § 490.103(e).

(b) State DOTs, in coordination with MPOs, shall define reporting segments in accordance with § 490.103(f). Reporting segments must be contiguous so that they cover the full extent of the directional mainline highways of the NHS in the urbanized area(s).

(c) State DOTs shall develop hourly traffic volume data for each reporting segment as follows:

(1) State DOTs shall measure or estimate hourly traffic volumes for Peak Periods on each weekday of the reporting year by using either paragraph (c)(1)(i) or (ii) of this section.

(i) State DOTs may use hourly traffic volume counts collected by continuous count stations and apply them to multiple reporting segments; or

(ii) State DOTs may use Annual Average Daily Traffic (AADT) reported to the HPMS to estimate hourly traffic volumes when no hourly volume counts exist. In these cases the AADT data used should be the most recently available, but not more than 2 years older than the reporting period (e.g., if reporting for calendar year 2018, AADT should be from 2016 or 2017) and should be split to represent the appropriate direction of travel of the reporting segment.

(2) State DOTs shall assign hourly traffic volumes to each reporting segment by hour (e.g., between 8 a.m. and 8:59 a.m.).

(3) State DOTs shall report the methodology they use to develop hourly traffic volume estimates to FHWA no later than 60 days before the submittal of the first Baseline Performance Period Report.

(4) If a State DOT elects to change the methodology it reported under paragraph (c)(3) of this section, then the State DOT shall submit the changed methodology no later than 60 days before the submittal of next State Biennial Performance Report required in § 490.107(b).

(5) If an NHS roadway is closed, the State DOT is not required to include those time periods for the segment of road in the calculation required for this metric and measure.

(d) State DOTs shall develop annual vehicle classification data for each reporting segment using data as follows:

(1) State DOTs shall measure or estimate the percentage of cars, buses, and trucks, relative to total AADT for each segment using either paragraph (d)(1)(i) or (ii) of this section.

(i) State DOTs may use annual traffic volume counts collected by continuous count stations to estimate the annual percent share of traffic volumes for cars, buses, and trucks for each segment; or

(ii) State DOTs may use AADT reported to the HPMS to estimate the annual percent share of traffic volumes for cars, buses, and trucks, where:

(A) Buses = value in HPMS Data Item "AADT_Single_Unit";

(B) Trucks = value in HPMS Data Item "AADT_Combination"; and

(C) Cars = subtract values for Buses and Trucks from the value in HPMS Data Item "AADT".

(iii) If a State DOT uses the data reported to the HPMS in paragraph (d)(1)(ii) of this section, then the data values should be split to represent the appropriate direction of travel of the reporting segment.

(2) State DOTs shall report the methodology they use to develop annual percent share of traffic volume by vehicle class to FHWA no later than 60 days before the submittal of the first Baseline Performance Period Report.

(3) If a State DOT elects to change the methodology it reported under paragraph (d)(2) of this section, then the State DOT shall submit the changed methodology no later than 60 days before the submittal of next State Biennial Performance Report required in §490.107(b).

(e) State DOTs shall develop annual average vehicle occupancy (AVO) factors for cars, buses, and trucks in applicable urbanized areas using either method under paragraph (e)(1)(i) or (ii) of this section.

(1) State DOTs shall measure or estimate annual vehicle occupancy factors for cars, buses, and trucks in applicable urbanized areas.

(i) State DOTs shall use estimated annual vehicle occupancy factors for cars, buses, and trucks in urbanized areas provided by FHWA; and/or

(ii) State DOTs may use an alternative estimate of annual vehicle occupancy factors for a specific reporting segment(s) for cars, buses, and trucks in urbanized areas, provided that it is more specific than the data provided by FHWA.

(f) All State DOTs and MPOs contributing to the unified target for the applicable area as specified in §490.105(d)(2) shall agree to using one of the methods specified in paragraph (f)(1)(i), (ii), or (iii) of this section to identify the data that will be used to determine the Percent of Non-SOV Travel for the applicable urbanized area.

(1) The data to determine the Percent of Non-SOV Travel measure shall be developed using any one of the following methods.

(i) *Method A—American Community Survey.* Populations by predominant travel to commute to work may be identified from Table DP03 of the American Community Survey using the totals by transportation mode listed within the "Commuting to Work" subject heading under the "Estimate" column of the table. The "5 Year Estimate" DP03 table using a geographic filter that represents the applicable "Urban Area" shall be used to identify these populations. The Percent of Non-SOV Travel measure shall be developed from the most recent data as of August 15th of the year in which the State Biennial Performance Report is due to FHWA.

(ii) *Method B—local survey.* The Percent of Non-SOV Travel may be estimated from a local survey focused on either work travel or household travel for the area and conducted as recently as 2 years before the beginning of the performance period. The survey method shall estimate travel mode choice for the full urbanized area using industry accepted methodologies and approaches resulting in a margin of error that is acceptable to industry standards, allow for updates on at least a biennial frequency, and distinguish non-SOV travel occurring in the area as a percent of all work or household travel.

(iii) *Method C—system use measurement.* The volume of travel using surface modes of transportation may be estimated from measurements of actual use of each transportation mode. Sample or continuous measurements may be used to count the number of travelers using different surface modes of transportation. The method used to count travelers shall estimate the total volume of annual travel for the full urbanized area within a margin of error that is acceptable to industry standards and allows for updates on at least a biennial frequency. The method shall include sufficient information to calculate the amount of non-SOV travel occurring in the area as a percentage of all surface transportation travel. State DOTs are encouraged to report use counts to FHWA that are not included in currently available national data sources.

(2) State DOTs shall report the data collection method that is used to determine the Percent of Non-SOV Travel measure for each applicable urbanized area in the State to FHWA in their first Baseline Performance Period Report required in § 490.107(b)(1). The State DOT shall include sufficient detail to understand how the data are collected if either Method B or Method C are used for the urbanized area. This method shall be used for the full performance period for each applicable urbanized area.

(3) If State DOTs and MPOs that contribute to an applicable urbanized area elect to change the data collection method reported under paragraph (f)(2) of this section, then each respective State DOT shall report this change in their next Baseline Performance Report required in § 490.107(b)(1). The new method reported as a requirement of this paragraph shall not be used until the beginning of the next performance period for the Baseline Performance Report in which the method was reported to be changed.

(g) Populations of urbanized areas shall be as identified based on the most recent annual estimates published by the U.S. Census available 1 year before the State DOT Baseline Performance Period Report is due to FHWA to identify applicability of the CMAQ Traffic Congestion measures in § 490.707(a) and (b) for each performance period, as described in § 490.105(e)(8)(iii)(D) and (f)(5)(iii)(D). For computing the PHED measure in § 490.713(b), the most recent annual population estimate published by the U.S. Census, at the time when the State DOT Biennial Performance Period Report is due to FHWA shall be used.

(h) Nonattainment and maintenance area determinations for the CMAQ Traffic Congestion measures:

(1) The CMAQ Traffic Congestion measures apply to nonattainment and maintenance areas. Such areas shall be identified based on the effective date of U.S. EPA's designations under the NAAQS in 40 CFR part 81, as of the date 1 year before the State DOT Baseline Performance Period Report is due to FHWA.

(2) The nonattainment and maintenance areas to which the CMAQ Traffic Congestion measures applies shall be revised if, on the date 1 year before the State DOT Mid Performance Period Progress Report is due to FHWA, the area is no longer in nonattainment or maintenance for a criteria pollutant included in § 490.703.

§ 490.711 Calculation of Peak Hour Excessive Delay metric.

(a) The performance metric required to calculate the measure specified in § 490.707(a) is Total Peak Hour Excessive Delay (person-hours)(referred to as the PHED metric). The following paragraphs explain how to calculate this PHED metric.

(b) State DOTs shall use the following data to calculate the PHED metric:

(1) Travel times of all traffic ("all vehicles" in NPMRDS nomenclature) during each 15 minute interval for all applicable reporting segments in the travel time data set occurring for peak periods from January 1st through December 31st of the same year;

(2) The length of each applicable reporting segment, reported as required under § 490.709(b);

(3) Hourly volume estimation for all days and for all reporting segments where excessive delay is measured, as specified in § 490.709(c);

(4) Annual vehicle classification data for all days and for all reporting segments where excessive delay is measured, as specified in § 490.709(d); and

(5) Annual vehicle occupancy factors for cars, buses, and trucks for all days and for all reporting segments where excessive delay is measured, as specified in § 490.709(e).

(c) The State DOT shall calculate the "excessive delay threshold travel time" for all applicable travel time segments as follows:

$$Excessive\ Delay\ Threshold\ Travel\ Time_s = \left(\frac{Travel\ Time\ Segment\ Length_s}{Threshold\ Speed_s}\right) \times 3{,}600$$

Where:

Excessive Delay Threshold Travel $Time_s$ = the time of travel, to the nearest whole second, to traverse the Travel Time Segment at which any longer measured travel times would result in excessive delay for the travel time segment "";

Travel Time Segment $Length_s$ = total length of travel time segment to the nearest thousandth of a mile for travel time reporting segment ""; and

Threshold $Speed_s$ = the speed of travel at which any slower measured speeds would result in excessive delay for travel time reporting segment "." As defined in §490.705, the speed threshold is 20 miles per hour (mph) or 60 percent of the posted speed limit travel time reporting segment "s," whichever is greater.

(d) State DOTs shall determine the "excessive delay" for each 15 minute bin of each reporting segment for every hour and every day in a calendar year as follows:

(1) The travel time segment delay (RSD) shall be calculated to the nearest whole second as follow:

$RSD_{s,b}$ – *Excessive Delay Threshold Travel* $Time_s$ and $RSD_{s,b} \leq 900$ *seconds*

Where:

$RSD_{s,b}$ = travel time segment delay, calculated to the nearest whole second, for a 15-minute bin "b" of travel time reporting segment "s" for in a day in a calendar year. $RSD(s)_b$ not to exceed 900 seconds;

Travel $time_{s,b}$ = a measured travel time, to the nearest second, for 15-minute time bin "b" recorded for travel time reporting segment "s";

Excessive Delay Threshold Travel $Time_s$ = The maximum amount of time, to the nearest second, for a vehicle to traverse through travel time segment "s" before excessive delay would occur, as specified in paragraph (c) of this section;

b = a 15-minute bin of a travel time reporting segment "s"; and

s = a travel time reporting segment.

(2) Excessive delay, the additional amount of time to traverse a travel time segment in a 15-minute bin as compared to the time needed to traverse the travel time segment when traveling at the excessive delay travel speed threshold, shall be calculated to the nearest thousandths of an hour as follows:

$$Excessive\ Delay_{s,b} = \begin{cases} \dfrac{RSD_{s,b}}{3{,}600}\ when\ RSD_{s,b} \geq 0 \\ or \\ 0\ when\ RSD_{s,b} < 0 \end{cases}$$

Where:

Excessive $Delay_{s,b}$ = excessive delay, calculated to the nearest thousandths of an hour, for 15-minute bin "b" of travel time reporting segment "s";

$RSD_{s,b}$ = the calculated travel time reporting segment delay for fifteen minute bin "b" of a travel time reporting segment "s," as described in paragraph (d)(1) of this section;

b = a fifteen minute bin of a travel time reporting segment "s"; and

s = a travel time reporting segment.

(e) State DOTs shall use the hourly traffic volumes as described in

§ 490.709(c) to calculate the PHED metric for each reporting segment as follows:

$$Total\ Excessive\ Delay_s = AVO \times \sum_{d=1}^{TD}\left\{\sum_{h=1}^{TH}\left[\sum_{b=1}^{TB}\left(Excessive\ Delay_{s,b,h,d} \times \left(\frac{hourly\ volume}{4}\right)_{s,h,d}\right)_b\right]_h\right\}_d$$

Where:

Total Excessive Delay$_s$ (in person-hours) = the sum of the excessive delay, to the nearest thousandths, for all traffic traveling through single travel time reporting segment "s" on NHS within an urbanized area, specified in § 490.703, accumulated over the full reporting year;

AVO = Average Vehicle Occupancy;

s = a travel time reporting segment;

d = a day of the reporting year;

TD = total number of days in the reporting year;

h = single hour interval of the day where the first hour interval is 12 a.m. to 12:59 a.m.;

TH = total number of hour intervals in day "h";

b = 15-minute bin for hour interval "h";

TB = total number of 15-minute bins where travel times are recorded in the travel time data set for hour interval "h";

Excessive Delay$_{s,b,h,d}$ = calculated excessive travel time, in hundredths of an hour, for 15 minute bin (), hour interval (h), day (d), and travel time segment (s), as described in paragraph (d)(2) of this section; and

$$\left(\frac{\text{hourly volume}}{4}\right)_{s,hd}$$

Where the equation equals hourly traffic volume, to the nearest tenth, for hour interval "h" and day "d" that corresponds to 15-minute bin "b" and travel time reporting segment "s" divided by 4. For example, the 9 a.m. to 9:15 a.m. minute bin would be assigned one fourth of the hourly traffic volume for the 9 a.m. to 9:59 a.m. hour on the roadway in which travel time segment is included;

$AVO = (P_C \times AVO_C) + (P_B \times AVO_B) + (P_T \times AVO_T)$

Where:

P_C = the percent of cars as a share of total AADT on the segment as specified in § 490.709(d);

P_B = the percent of buses as a share of total AADT on the segment as specified in § 490.709(d);

P_T = the percent of trucks as a share of total AADT on the segment as specified in § 490.709(d);

AVO_C = the average vehicle occupancy of cars as specified in §490.709(e);
AVO_B = the average vehicle occupancy of buses as specified in §490.709(e); and
AVO_T = the average vehicle occupancy of trucks as specified in §490.709(e).

(f) Starting in 2018 and annually thereafter, State DOTs shall report the PHED metric (to the nearest one hundredth hour) in accordance with HPMS Field Manual by June 15th of each year for the previous year's PHED measures. The PHED metric shall be reported for each reporting segment. All reporting segments of the NPMRDS shall be referenced by NPMRDS TMC or HPMS section(s). If a State DOT elects to use, in part or in whole, the equivalent data set, all reporting segments shall be referenced by HPMS sections.

§490.713 Calculation of Traffic Congestion measures.

(a) The performance measures in §490.707 shall be computed in accordance with this section by State DOTs and MPOs to carry out CMAQ traffic congestion performance-related requirements of this part and by FHWA to report on traffic congestion performance.

(b) The performance measure for CMAQ traffic congestion specified in §490.707, Annual Hours of Peak Hour Excessive Delay Per Capita (the PHED measure), shall be computed to the nearest tenth, and by summing the PHED metrics of all reporting segments in each of the urbanized area, specified in §490.703, and dividing it by the population of the urbanized area to produce the PHED measure. The equation for calculating the PHED measure is as follows:

$$\textit{Annual Hours of Peak Hour Excessive Delay per Capita} = \frac{\sum_{s=1}^{T} \textit{Total Excessive Delay}_s}{\textit{Total Population}}$$

Where:
Annual Hours of Peak Hour Excessive Delay per Capita = the cumulative hours of excessive delay, to the nearest tenth, experienced by all people traveling through all reporting segments during peak hours in the applicable urbanized area for the full reporting calendar year;
s = travel time reporting segment within an urbanized area, specified in §490.703;
T = total number of travel time reporting segments in the applicable urbanized area;
Total Population = total hours of excessive delay in §490.711(e) for all people traveling through travel time reporting segment "s" during a calendar year (as defined in §490.711(f)); and
Total Population = the total population in the applicable urbanized area from the most recent annual population published by the U.S. Census at the time that the State Biennial Performance Period Report is due to FHWA.

(c) Calculation for the PHED measure, described in paragraph (b) of this section, and target establishment for the measure shall be phased-in under the requirements in §490.105(e)(8)(vi) and (f)(5)(vi).

(d) The performance measure for CMAQ traffic congestion specified in §490.707(b), Percent of Non-SOV Travel, shall be computed as specified in paragraphs (d)(1) through (3) of this section corresponding to the method reported by the State DOT to collect travel data for the applicable area under §490.709(f)(2).

(1) *Method A—American Community Survey*. The Percent of Non-SOV Travel shall be calculated to the nearest tenth of a percent using the following formula:

Percent of Non-SOV Travel = 100% − % SOV

Where:
Percent of Non-SOV Travel = percent of commuting working population, to the nearest tenth of a percent, that predominantly do not commute by driving alone

in a car, van, or truck, including travel avoided by telecommuting; and

% SOV = percent estimate for "Car, truck, or van—drive alone".

(2) *Method B—local survey.* The Percent of Non-SOV Travel shall be calculated using the data derived from local survey results as specified in §490.709(f)(1)(ii). The Percent of Non-SOV Travel measure shall be calculated to represent travel that is not occurring by driving alone in a motorized vehicle, including travel avoided by telecommuting, as a percentage of all surface transportation occurring in the applicable area. The Percent of Non-SOV Travel measure shall be calculated to the nearest tenth of a percent.

(3) *Method C—system use measurement.* The Percent of Non-SOV Travel shall be calculated to the nearest tenth of a percent from the data collected from system use measurements as specified in §490.709(f)(1)(iii) using the general form of the following formula:

$$Percent\ of\ Non-SOV\ Travel = 100 \times \left(\frac{Volume_{non-sov}}{(Volume_{non-sov}) + (Volume_{sov})}\right)$$

Where:

Percent of Non-SOV Travel = percentage of travel, to the nearest tenth of a percent, that is not occurring by driving alone in a motorized vehicle, including travel avoided by telecommuting

$Volume_{non\text{-}SOV}$ *Volume* = Annual volume of person travel occurring while driving alone in a motorized vehicle; and

$Volume_{SOV}$ = Annual volume of person travel occurring on modes other than driving alone in a motorized vehicle, calculated as:

$$\sum_{m=1}^{t} Volume_m$$

Where:

m = travel mode (modes other than driving alone in a motorized vehicle, including travel avoided by telecommuting);

$Volume_m$ = annual volume of person travel for each mode, "m"; and

t = total number of modes that are not driving alone in a motorized vehicle.

Subpart H—National Performance Management Measures to Assess the Congestion Mitigation and Air Quality Improvement Program—On-Road Mobile Source Emissions

SOURCE: 82 FR 6049, Jan. 18, 2017, unless otherwise noted.

§490.801 Purpose.

The purpose of this subpart is to implement the requirements of 23 U.S.C. 150(c)(5)(B) to establish performance measures for State DOTs and the MPOs to use in assessing on-road mobile source emissions.

§490.803 Applicability.

(a) The on-road mobile source emissions performance measure (called the Total Emissions Reduction- see §490.807) is applicable to all States and MPOs with projects financed with funds from the 23 U.S.C. 149 CMAQ program apportioned to State DOTs for areas designated as nonattainment or maintenance for ozone (O_3), carbon monoxide (CO), or particulate matter (PM_{10} and $PM_{2.5}$) National Ambient Air Quality Standards (NAAQS).

(b) This performance measure does not apply to States and MPOs that do not contain any portions of nonattainment or maintenance areas for the criteria pollutants identified in paragraph (a) of this section.

§490.805 Definitions.

All definitions in §490.101 apply to this subpart. Unless otherwise specified in this subpart, the following definitions apply in this subpart:

On-road mobile source means, within this part, emissions created by all projects and sources financed with funds from the 23 U.S.C. 149 CMAQ program.

§490.807 National performance management measure for assessing on-road mobile source emissions for the purposes of the Congestion Mitigation and Air Quality Improvement Program.

The performance measure for the purpose of carrying out the CMAQ Program and for State DOTs to use to assess on-road mobile source emissions is "Total Emissions Reduction," which is the 2-year and 4-year cumulative reported emission reductions, for all projects funded by CMAQ funds, of each criteria pollutant and applicable precursors ($PM_{2.5}$, PM_{10}, CO, VOC, and NOx) under the CMAQ program for which the area is designated nonattainment or maintenance.

§490.809 Data requirements.

(a) The data needed to calculate the Total Emission Reduction measure shall come from the CMAQ Public Access System and includes:

(1) The applicable nonattainment or maintenance area;

(2) The applicable MPO; and

(3) The emissions reduction estimated for each CMAQ funded project for each of the applicable criteria pollutants and their precursors for which the area is nonattainment or maintenance.

(b) The State DOT shall:

(1) Enter project information into the CMAQ project tracking system for each CMAQ project funded in the previous fiscal year by March 1st of the following fiscal year; and

(2) Extract the data necessary to calculate the Total Emissions Reduction measures as it appears in the CMAQ Public Access System on July 1st for projects obligated in the prior fiscal year.

(c) Nonattainment and maintenance area determinations for the CMAQ Total Emissions Reduction measure:

(1) The CMAQ Total Emissions Reduction measure applies to nonattainment and maintenance areas. Such areas shall be identified based on the effective date of U.S. EPA's designations under the NAAQS in 40 CFR part 81, as of the date 1 year before the State DOT Baseline Performance Period Report is due to FHWA.

(2) The nonattainment and maintenance areas to which the Total Emissions Reduction measure applies shall be revised if, on the date 1 year before the State DOT Mid Performance Period Progress Report is due to FHWA, the area is no longer in nonattainment or maintenance for a pollutant included in §490.803.

§490.811 Calculation of Total Emissions Reduction measure.

(a) The Total Emission Reductions performance measure specified in §490.807 shall be calculated in accordance with this section by State DOTs and MPOs to carry out CMAQ on-road mobile source emissions performance-related requirements of this part.

(b) The Total Emission Reductions measure for each of the criteria pollutant or applicable precursor for all projects reported to the CMAQ Public Access System shall be calculated to the nearest one thousandths, as follows:

$$\textit{Total Emission Reduction}_p = \sum_{i=1}^{T} \textit{Daily Kilograms of Emission Reductions}_{p,i}$$

Where:

i = applicable projects reported in the CMAQ Public Access System for the first 2 Federal fiscal years of a performance period and for the entire performance period, as described in in §490.105(e)(4)(i)(B);

p = criteria pollutant or applicable precursor: $PM_{2.5}$, PM_{10}, CO, VOC, or NOx;

Daily Kilograms of Emission $\text{Reductions}_{p,i}$ = total daily kilograms, to the nearest one thousandths, of reduced emissions for a criteria pollutant or an applicable precursor "p" in the in the first year the project is obligated;

T = total number of applicable projects reported to the CMAQ Public Access System for the first 2 Federal fiscal years of a performance period and for the entire performance period, as described in § 490.105(e)(4)(i)(B); and

Total Emission $Reduction_p$ = cumulative reductions in emissions over 2 and 4 Federal fiscal years, total daily kilograms, to the nearest one thousandths, of reduced emissions for criteria pollutant or precursor "p."

SUBCHAPTER F—TRANSPORTATION INFRASTRUCTURE MANAGEMENT

PART 500—MANAGEMENT AND MONITORING SYSTEMS

Subpart A—Management systems

Subpart B—Traffic Monitoring System

AUTHORITY: 23 U.S.C. 134, 135, 303, and 315; 49 U.S.C. 5303–5305; 23 CFR 1.32; and 49 CFR 1.48 and 1.51.

SOURCE: 61 FR 67170, Dec. 19, 1996, unless otherwise noted.

Subpart A—Management Systems

§ 500.101 Purpose.

The purpose of this part is to implement the requirements of 23 U.S.C. 303(a) which directs the Secretary of Transportation (the Secretary) to issue regulations for State development, establishment, and implementation of systems for managing highway pavement of Federal-aid highways (PMS), bridges on and off Federal-aid highways (BMS), highway safety (SMS), traffic congestion (CMS), public transportation facilities and equipment (PTMS), and intermodal transportation facilities and systems (IMS). This regulation also implements 23 U.S.C. 303(b) which directs the Secretary to issue guidelines and requirements for State development, establishment, and implementation of a traffic monitoring system for highways and public transportation facilities and equipment (TMS).

§ 500.102 Policy.

(a) Federal, State, and local governments are under increasing pressure to balance their budgets and, at the same time, respond to public demands for quality services. Along with the need to invest in America's future, this leaves transportation agencies with the task of trying to manage current transportation systems as cost-effectively as possible to meet evolving, as well as backlog needs. The use of existing or new transportation management systems provides a framework for cost-effective decision making that emphasizes enhanced service at reduced public and private life-cycle cost. The primary outcome of transportation management systems is improved system performance and safety. The Federal Highway Administration (FHWA) and the Federal Transit Administration (FTA) strongly encourage implementation of transportation management systems consistent with State, metropolitan planning organization, transit operator, or local government needs.

(b) Whether the systems are developed under the provisions of this part or under a State's own procedures, the following categories of FHWA administered funds may be used for development, establishment, and implementation of any of the management systems and the traffic monitoring system: National highway system; surface transportation program; State planning and research and metropolitan planning funds (including the optional use of minimum allocation funds authorized under 23 U.S.C. 157(c) and restoration funds authorized under § 202(f) of the National Highway System Designation Act of 1995 (Pub.L. 104–59) for carrying out the provisions of 23 U.S.C. 307(c)(1) and 23 U.S.C. 134(a)); congestion mitigation and air quality improvement program funds for those management systems that can be shown to contribute to the attainment of a national ambient air quality standard; and apportioned bridge funds for development and establishment of the bridge management system. The following categories of FTA administered funds may be used for development, establishment, and implementation of the CMS, PTMS, IMS, and TMS: Metropolitan planning; State planning and research, and formula transit funds.

§ 500.103 Definitions.

Unless otherwise specified in this part, the definitions in 23 U.S.C. 101(a) are applicable to this part. As used in this part:

Federal-aid highways means those highways eligible for assistance under title 23, U.S.C., except those functionally classified as local or rural minor collectors.

Metropolitan planning organization (MPO) means the forum for cooperative transportation decision making for a metropolitan planning area.

National Highway System (NHS) means the system of highways designated and approved in accordance with the provisions of 23 U.S.C. 103(b).

State means any one of the fifty States, the District of Columbia, or Puerto Rico.

Transportation management area (TMA) means an urbanized area with a population over 200,000 (as determined by the latest decennial census) or other area when TMA designation is requested by the Governor and the MPO (or affected local officials), and officially designated by the Administrators of the FHWA and the FTA. The TMA designation applies to the entire metropolitan planning area(s).

§ 500.104 State option.

Except as specified in § 500.105 (a) and (b), a State may elect at any time not to implement any one or more of the management systems required under 23 U.S.C. 303, in whole or in part.

§ 500.105 Requirements.

(a) The metropolitan transportation planning process (23 U.S.C. 134 and 49 U.S.C. 5303–5005) in TMAs shall include a CMS that meets the requirements of § 500.109 of this regulation.

(b) States shall develop, establish, and implement a TMS that meets the requirements of subpart B of this regulation.

(c) Any of the management systems that the State chooses to implement under 23 U.S.C. 303 and this regulation shall be developed in cooperation with MPOs in metropolitan areas, affected agencies receiving assistance under the Federal Transit Act (49 U.S.C., Chapter 53), and other agencies (including private owners and operators) that have responsibility for operation of the affected transportation systems or facilities.

(d) The results (e.g., policies, programs, projects, etc.) of any of the management systems that a State chooses to develop under 23 U.S.C. 303 and this regulation shall be considered in the development of metropolitan and statewide transportation plans and improvement programs and in making project selection decisions under title 23, U.S.C., and under the Federal Transit Act. Plans and programs adopted after September 30, 1997, shall demonstrate compliance with this requirement.

§ 500.106 PMS.

An effective PMS for Federal-aid highways is a systematic process that provides information for use in implementing cost-effective pavement reconstruction, rehabilitation, and preventative maintenance programs and that results in pavements designed to accommodate current and forecasted traffic in a safe, durable, and cost-effective manner. The PMS should be based on the "AASHTO Guidelines for Pavement Management Systems."[1]

§ 500.107 BMS.

An effective BMS for bridges on and off Federal-aid highways that should be based on the "AASHTO Guidelines for Bridge Management Systems"[2] and

[1] *AASHTO Guidelines for Pavement Management Systems*, July 1990, can be purchased from the American Association of State Highway and Transportation Officials, 444 N. Capitol Street, NW., Suite 249, Washington, D.C. 20001. Available for inspection as prescribed in 49 CFR part 7, appendix D.

[2] *AASHTO Guidelines for Bridge Management Systems*, 1992, can be purchased from the American Association of State Highway and Transportation Officials, 444 N. Capitol Street, NW., Suite 249, Washington, D.C.

that supplies analyses and summaries of data, uses mathematical models to make forecasts and recommendations, and provides the means by which alternative policies and programs may be efficiently considered. An effective BMS should include, as a minimum, formal procedures for:

(a) Collecting, processing, and updating data;

(b) Predicting deterioration;

(c) Identifying alternative actions;

(d) Predicting costs;

(e) Determining optimal policies;

(f) Performing short- and long-term budget forecasting; and

(g) Recommending programs and schedules for implementation within policy and budget constraints.

§ 500.108 SMS.

An SMS is a systematic process with the goal of reducing the number and severity of traffic crashes by ensuring that all opportunities to improve highway safety are identified, considered, implemented as appropriate, and evaluated in all phases of highway planning, design, construction, maintenance, and operation and by providing information for selecting and implementing effective highway safety strategies and projects. The development of the SMS may be based on the guidance in "Safety Management Systems: Good Practices for Development and Implementation."[3] An effective SMS should include, at a minimum:

(a) Communication, coordination, and cooperation among the organizations responsible for the roadway, human, and vehicle safety elements;

(b) A focal point for coordination of the development, establishment, and implementation of the SMS among the agencies responsible for these major safety elements;

(c) Establishment of short- and long-term highway safety goals to address identified safety problems;

(d) Collection, analysis, and linkage of highway safety data;

(e) Identification of the safety responsibilities of units and positions;

(f) Public information and education activities; and

(g) Identification of skills, resources, and training needs to implement highway safety programs.

§ 500.109 CMS.

(a) For purposes of this part, congestion means the level at which transportation system performance is unacceptable due to excessive travel times and delays. Congestion management means the application of strategies to improve system performance and reliability by reducing the adverse impacts of congestion on the movement of people and goods in a region. A congestion management system or process is a systematic and regionally accepted approach for managing congestion that provides accurate, up-to-date information on transportation system operations and performance and assesses alternative strategies for congestion management that meet State and local needs.

(b) The development of a congestion management system or process should result in performance measures and strategies that can be integrated into transportation plans and programs. The level of system performance deemed acceptable by State and local officials may vary by type of transportation facility, geographic location (metropolitan area or subarea and/or non-metropolitan area), and/or time of day. In both metropolitan and non-metropolitan areas, consideration needs to be given to strategies that manage demand, reduce single occupant vehicle (SOV) travel, and improve transportation system management and operations. Where the addition of general purpose lanes is determined to be an appropriate congestion management strategy, explicit consideration is to be given to the incorporation of appropriate features into the SOV project to facilitate future demand management strategies and operational improvements that will maintain the functional integrity of those lanes.

[72 FR 7285, Feb. 14, 2007]

20001. Available for inspection as prescribed in 49 CFR part 7, appendix D.

[3] *Safety Management Systems: Good Practices for Development and Implementation*, FHWA and NHTSA, May 1996. Available for inspection and copying as prescribed in 49 CFR part 7, appendix D.

§ 500.110 PTMS.

An effective PTMS for public transportation facilities (e.g., maintenance facilities, stations, terminals, transit related structures), equipment, and rolling stock is a systematic process that collects and analyzes information on the condition and cost of transit assets on a continual basis, identifies needs, and enables decision makers to select cost-effective strategies for providing and maintaining transit assets in serviceable condition. The PTMS should cover public transportation systems operated by the State, local jurisdictions, public transportation agencies and authorities, and private (for profit and non-profit) transit operators receiving funds under the Federal Transit Act and include, at a minimum:

(a) Development of transit asset condition measures and standards;

(b) An inventory of the transit assets including age, condition, remaining useful life, and replacement cost; and

(c) Identification, evaluation, and implementation of appropriate strategies and projects.

§ 500.111 IMS.

An effective IMS for intermodal facilities and systems provides efficient, safe, and convenient movement of people and goods through integration of transportation facilities and systems and improvement in the coordination in planning, and implementation of air, water, and the various land-based transportation facilities and systems. An IMS should include, at a minimum:

(a) Establishment of performance measures;

(b) Identification of key linkages between one or more modes of transportation, where the performance or use of one mode will affect another;

(c) Definition of strategies for improving the effectiveness of these modal interactions; and

(d) Evaluation and implementation of these strategies to enhance the overall performance of the transportation system.

Subpart B—Traffic Monitoring System

§ 500.201 Purpose.

The purpose of this subpart is to set forth requirements for development, establishment, implementation, and continued operation of a traffic monitoring system for highways and public transportation facilities and equipment (TMS) in each State in accordance with the provisions of 23 U.S.C. 303 and subpart A of this part.

§ 500.202 TMS definitions.

Unless otherwise specified in this part, the definitions in 23 U.S.C. 101(a) and § 500.103 are applicable to this subpart. As used in this part:

Highway traffic data means data used to develop estimates of the amount of person or vehicular travel, vehicle usage, or vehicle characteristics associated with a system of highways or with a particular location on a highway. These types of data support the estimation of the number of vehicles traversing a section of highway or system of highways during a prescribed time period (traffic volume), the portion of such vehicles that may be of a particular type (vehicle classification), the weights of such vehicles including the weight of each axle and associated distances between axles on a vehicle (vehicle weight), or the average number of persons being transported in a vehicle (vehicle occupancy).

Traffic monitoring system means a systematic process for the collection, analysis, summary, and retention of highway and transit related person and vehicular traffic data.

Transit traffic data means person and vehicular data for public transportation on public highways and streets and the number of vehicles and ridership for dedicated transit rights-of-way (e.g., rail and busways), at the maximum load points for the peak period in the peak direction and for the daily time period.

§ 500.203 TMS general requirements.

(a) Each State shall develop, establish, and implement, on a continuing basis, a TMS to be used for obtaining highway traffic data when:

(1) The data are supplied to the U.S. Department of Transportation (U.S. DOT);

(2) The data are used in support of transportation management systems;

(3) The data are used in support of studies or systems which are the responsibility of the U.S. DOT;

(4) The collection of the data is supported by the use of Federal funds provided from programs of the U.S. DOT;

(5) The data are used in the apportionment or allocation of Federal funds by the U.S. DOT;

(6) The data are used in the design or construction of an FHWA funded project; or

(7) The data are required as part of a federally mandated program of the U.S. DOT.

(b) The TMS for highway traffic data should be based on the concepts described in the American Association of State Highway and Transportation Officials (AASHTO) "AASHTO Guidelines for Traffic Data Programs"[4] and the FHWA "Traffic Monitoring Guide (TMG),"[5] and shall be consistent with the FHWA "Highway Performance Monitoring System Field Manual."[6]

(c) The TMS shall cover all public roads except those functionally classified as local or rural minor collector or those that are federally owned. Coverage of federally owned public roads shall be determined cooperatively by the State, the FHWA, and the agencies that own the roads.

(d) The State's TMS shall apply to the activities of local governments and other public or private non-State government entities collecting highway traffic data within the State if the collected data are to be used for any of the purposes enumerated in §500.203(a) of this subpart.

(e) Procedures other than those referenced in this subpart may be used if the alternative procedures are documented by the State to furnish the precision levels as defined for the various purposes enumerated in §500.203(a) of this subpart and are found acceptable by the FHWA.

(f) Nothing in this subpart shall prohibit the collection of additional highway traffic data if such data are needed in the administration or management of a highway activity or are needed in the design of a highway project.

(g) Transit traffic data shall be collected in cooperation with MPOs and transit operators.

(h) The TMS for highways and public transportation facilities and equipment shall be fully operational and in use by October 1, 1997.

§500.204 TMS components for highway traffic data.

(a) *General.* Each State's TMS, including those using alternative procedures, shall address the components in paragraphs (b) through (h) of this section.

(b) *Precision of reported data.* Traffic data supplied for the purposes identified in §500.203(a) of this subpart shall be to the statistical precision applicable at the time of the data's collection as specified by the data users at various levels of government. A State's TMS shall meet the statistical precisions established by FHWA for the HPMS.

(c) *Continuous counter operations.* Within each State, there shall be sufficient continuous counters of traffic volumes, vehicle classification, and vehicle weight to provide estimates of changes in highway travel patterns and to provide for the development of day-of-week, seasonal, axle correction, growth factors, or other comparable factors approved by the FHWA that support the development of traffic estimates to meet the statistical precision requirements of the data uses identified in §500.203(a) of this subpart. As appropriate, sufficient continuous

[4] AASHTO Guidelines for Traffic Data Programs, 1992, ISBN 1-56051-054-4, can be purchased from the American Association of State Highway and Transportation Officials, 444 N. Capitol Street, NW., Suite 249, Washington, D.C. 20001. Available for inspection as prescribed in 49 CFR part 7, appendix D.

[5] Traffic Monitoring Guide, DOT/FHWA, publication No. FHWA-PL-95-031, February 1995. Available for inspection and copying as prescribed in 49 CFR part 7, appendix D.

[6] Highway Performance Monitoring System (HPMS) Field Manual for the Continuing Analytical and Statistical Data Base, DOT/FHWA, August 30, 1993 (FHWA Order M5600.1B). Available for inspection and copying as prescribed in 49 CFR part 7, appendix D.

counts of vehicle classification and vehicle weight should be available to address traffic data program needs.

(d) *Short term traffic monitoring.* (1) Count data for traffic volumes collected in the field shall be adjusted to reflect annual average conditions. The estimation of annual average daily traffic will be through the appropriate application of only the following: Seasonal factors, day-of-week factors, and, when necessary, axle correction and growth factors or other comparable factors approved by the FHWA. Count data that have not been adjusted to represent annual average conditions will be noted as being unadjusted when they are reported. The duration and frequency of such monitoring shall comply to the data needs identified in § 500.203(a) of this subpart.

(2) Vehicle classification activities on the National Highway System (NHS), shall be sufficient to assure that, on a cycle of no greater than three years, every major system segment (*i.e.*, segments between interchanges or intersections of principal arterials of the NHS with other principal arterials of the NHS) will be monitored to provide information on the numbers of single-trailer combination trucks, multiple-trailer combination trucks, two-axle four-tire vehicles, buses and the total number of vehicles operating on an average day. If it is determined that two or more continuous major system segments have both similar traffic volumes and distributions of the vehicle types identified above, a single monitoring session will be sufficient to monitor these segments.

(e) *Vehicle occupancy monitoring.* As deemed appropriate to support the data uses identified in § 500.203(a) of this subpart, data will be collected on the average number of persons per automobile, light two-axle truck, and bus. The duration, geographic extent, and level of detail shall be consistent with the intended use of the data, as cooperatively agreed to by the organizations that will use the data and the organizations that will collect the data. Such vehicle occupancy data shall be reviewed at least every three years and updated as necessary. Acceptable data collection methods include roadside monitoring, traveler surveys, the use of administrative records (e.g., accident reports or reports developed in support of public transportation programs), or any other method mutually acceptable to the responsible organizations and the FHWA.

(f) *Field operations.* (1) Each State's TMS for highway traffic data shall include the testing of equipment used in the collection of the data. This testing shall be based on documented procedures developed by the State. This documentation will describe the test procedure as well as the frequency of testing. Standards of the American Society for Testing and Materials or guidance from the AASHTO may be used. Only equipment passing the test procedures will be used for the collection of data for the purposes identified in § 500.203(a) of this subpart.

(2) Documentation of field operations shall include the number of counts, the period of monitoring, the cycle of monitoring, and the spatial and temporal distribution of count sites. Copies of the State's documentation shall be provided to the FHWA Division Administrator when it is initially developed and after each revision.

(g) *Source data retention.* For estimates of traffic or travel, the value or values collected during a monitoring session, as well as information on the date(s) and hour(s) of monitoring, will remain available until the traffic or travel estimates based on the count session are updated. Data shall be available in formats that conform to those in the version of the TMG current at the time of data collection or as then amended by the FHWA.

(h) *Office factoring procedures.* (1) Factors to adjust data from short term monitoring sessions to estimates of average daily conditions shall be used to adjust for month, day of week, axle correction, and growth or other comparable factors approved by the FHWA. These factors will be reviewed annually and updated at least every three years.

(2) The procedures used by a State to edit and adjust highway traffic data collected from short term counts at field locations to estimates of average traffic volume shall be documented. The documentation shall include the factors discussed in paragraph (d)(1) of this section. The documentation shall remain available as long as the traffic

or travel estimates discussed in paragraph (g) of this section remain current. Copies of the State's documentation shall be provided to the FHWA Division Administrator when it is initially developed and after each revision.

PART 505—PROJECTS OF NATIONAL AND REGIONAL SIGNIFICANCE EVALUATION AND RATING

AUTHORITY: Section 1301 of the Safe, Accountable, Flexible, Efficient Transportation Equity Act: A Legacy for Users (Pub. L. 109–59; 119 Stat. 1144); 23 U.S.C. 315; 49 CFR 1.48.

SOURCE: 73 FR 63370, Oct. 24, 2008, unless otherwise noted.

§ 505.1 Purpose.

The purpose of this part is to establish evaluation, rating, and selection guidelines for funding proposed Projects of National and Regional Significance (PNRS).

§ 505.3 Policy.

A Project of National and Regional Significance should quantitatively improve the throughput or provide long term congestion relief for passenger or freight movement for a part of the transportation network and clearly connect this improvement to sustainable economic productivity for the nation or the region in which it is located.

§ 505.5 Definitions.

Unless otherwise specified in this part, the definitions contained in 23 U.S.C. 101(a) are applicable to this part. In addition, the following definitions apply:

Applicant means either:

(1) A State Transportation Department, or

(2) A group of State Transportation Departments, with one State acting as the project lead.

Eligible project means any surface transportation project or set of integrated surface transportation projects closely related in the function they perform eligible for Federal assistance under title 23, United States Code, including public or private rail facilities providing benefits to highway users, surface transportation infrastructure modifications to facilitate intermodal interchange, transfer, and access into and out of ports and other activities eligible under such title.

Eligible project costs means the costs pertaining to an eligible project for:

(1) Development phase activities, including planning, feasibility analysis, revenue forecasting, environmental review, preliminary engineering and design work, and other preconstruction activities;

(2) Construction, reconstruction, rehabilitation, and acquisition of real property (including land related to the project and improvements to land), environmental mitigation, construction contingencies, acquisition of equipment, and operational improvements; and

(3) all debt financing costs authorized by 23 U.S.C. 122.

Full Funding Grant Agreement (FFGA) means the agreement used to provide Federal financial assistance under title 23, United States Code, for Projects of National and Regional Significance. An FFGA defines the scope of the project, establishes the maximum amount of Government financial assistance for the project, covers the period of time for completion of the project, facilitates the efficient management of the project in accordance with applicable Federal statutes, regulations, and policy, including oversight roles and responsibilities, and other terms and conditions.

§ 505.7 Eligibility.

To be eligible for assistance under this program:

(a) A project meeting the definition of an eligible project under 505.5 of this section located fully within one State shall have eligible project costs that are quantified in the project proposal as equal to or exceeding the lesser of:

(1) $500,000,000; or

(2) 75 percent of the amount of Federal highway assistance funds apportioned for the most recently completed fiscal year to the State in which the project is located.

(b) A multi-State project meeting the definition of an eligible project under 505.5 of this section shall have eligible project costs that are quantified in the project proposal as equal to or exceeding the lesser of:

(1) $500,000,000; or

(2) 75 percent of the amount of Federal highway assistance funds apportioned for the most recently completed fiscal year to the State in which the project is located that has the largest apportionment.

§ 505.9 Criteria for grants.

(a) The Secretary will approve a grant for a Project of National and Regional Significance project only if the Secretary determines, based upon information submitted by the applicant, that the project:

(1) Is based on the results of preliminary engineering;

(2) Is supported by an acceptable degree of non-Federal financial commitments, including evidence of stable and dependable financing sources to construct, maintain, and operate the infrastructure facility. In evaluating a non-Federal financial commitment, the Secretary shall require that:

(i) The proposed project plan provides for the availability of contingency amounts that the Secretary determines to be reasonable to cover unanticipated cost increases; and

(ii) Each proposed non-Federal source of capital and operating financing is stable, reliable, and available within the proposed project timetable. In assessing the stability, reliability, and availability of proposed sources of non-Federal financing, the Secretary will consider:

(A) Existing financial commitments;

(B) The degree to which financing sources are dedicated to the purposes proposed;

(C) Any debt obligation that exists or is proposed by the recipient for the proposed project; and

(D) The extent to which the project has a non-Federal financial commitment that exceeds the required non-Federal share of the cost of the project.

(3) Emerges from the metropolitan and Statewide planning process, consistent with 23 CFR Part 450;

(4) Is justified based on the ability of the project:

(i) To generate national and/or regional economic benefits, as evidenced by, but not limited to:

(A) The creation of jobs, expansion of business opportunities, and impacts to the gross domestic product due to quantitatively increased throughput;

(B) The amount and importance of freight and passenger travel served; and

(C) The demographic and economic characteristics of the area served.

(ii) To allocate public and private costs commensurate with the share of public and private benefits and risks;

(iii) To generate long-term congestion relief that impacts the State, the region, and the Nation, as evidenced by, but not limited to:

(A) Congestion levels, delay and consequences of delay;

(B) Efficiency and effectiveness of congestion mitigation; and

(C) Travel time reliability.

(iv) To improve transportation safety, including reducing transportation accidents, injuries, and fatalities, as evidenced by, but not limited to, number, rate and consequences of crashes, injuries and fatalities in the affected region and corridor;

(v) To otherwise enhance the national transportation system by improving throughput; and

(vi) To garner support for non-Federal financial commitments and provide evidence of stable and dependable financing sources to construct, maintain, and operate the infrastructure facility.

(b) In selecting projects under this section, the Secretary will consider the extent to which the project:

(1) Leverages Federal investment by encouraging non-Federal contributions to the project, including contributions from public-private partnerships;

(2) Uses new technologies, including intelligent transportation systems,

that enhance the efficiency of the project;

(3) Helps maintain or protect the environment; and

(4) Demonstrates that the proposed project cannot be readily and efficiently realized without Federal support and participation.

(c) All information submitted as part of or in support of an application shall use publicly available data or data that can be made public and methodologies that are accepted by industry practice and standards.

(d) Measures for the selection criteria shall include projections for both the build and no-build scenarios.

(e) PNRS solicitations or guidance documents will contain, as needed, additional specific information regarding measures, weighting, and use of these criteria.

(f) All proposed PNRS projects are required to comply with the requirements of 23 U.S.C. 106(h) regardless of whether the project meets project cost threshold for classification as a major project.

§505.11 Project evaluation and rating.

(a) The Secretary shall evaluate and rate each proposed project as "highly recommended," "recommended," or "not recommended" based on the criteria in section 505.9 of this part. Individual ratings of "highly recommended," "recommended," or "not recommended" will be conducted for each of the selection criteria.

(b) In response to a PNRS project solicitation a State may submit a project for a non-binding preliminary rating and evaluation at any point in the project development after the project's concept plan is developed.

(c) Non-binding preliminary rating and evaluation will be reported in the appendix of the Secretary's Annual Report on PNRS.

(d) A rating and evaluation will be considered complete and listed in the Secretary's Annual Report on PNRS only after preliminary engineering is completed.

(e) The rating and evaluation for a proposed project will remain valid until the closing date of the next PNRS solicitation.

§505.13 Federal Government's share of project cost.

(a) Based on engineering studies, studies of economic feasibility, and information on the expected use of equipment or facilities, the Secretary shall estimate the project's eligible costs.

(b) A FFGA for the project shall not exceed 80 percent of the eligible project cost. A refund or reduction of the remainder may only be made if a refund of a proportional amount of the grant of the Federal Government is made at the same time.

§505.15 Full funding grant agreement.

(a) A proposed project may not be funded under this program unless the Secretary finds that the project meets the requirements of this part and there is a reasonable likelihood that the project will continue to meet such requirements.

(b) A project financed under this section shall be carried out through a FFGA. The Secretary shall enter into a FFGA based on the evaluations and ratings required herein, and in accordance with the terms specified in section 1301(g)(2) of the Safe, Accountable, Flexible, Efficient Transportation Equity Act: A Legacy for Users, (Pub. L. 109–59; 119 Stat. 1144).

(c) A FFGA will be entered into only after the project has commitments for non-Federal funding in place and all other requirements are met.

(d) A State may request the use of Advanced Construction for the project and subsequently convert those funds to an eligible Federal-aid funding category or to PNRS funding as part of the FFGA.

§505.17 Applicability of Title 23, U.S. Code.

Funds made available to carry out this section shall be available for obligation in the same manner as if such funds were apportioned under chapter 1 of title 23, United States Code; except that such funds shall not be transferable to other agencies and shall remain available until expended and the Federal share of the cost of a Project of National and Regional Significance shall be as provided in section 505.13.

PART 511—REAL-TIME SYSTEM MANAGEMENT INFORMATION PROGRAM

AUTHORITY: Section 1201, Pub. L. 109–59; 23 U.S.C. 315; 23 U.S.C. 120; 49 CFR 1.48.

SOURCE: 75 FR 68427, Nov. 8, 2010, unless otherwise noted.

Subparts A–B [Reserved]

Subpart C—Real-Time System Management Information Program

§ 511.301 Purpose.

The purpose of this part is to establish the provisions and parameters for the Real-Time System Management Information Program. These provisions implement Subsections 1201(a)(1), (a)(2), and (c)(1) of the Safe, Accountable, Flexible, Efficient Transportation Equity Act: A Legacy for Users (SAFETEA-LU) (Pub. L. 109–59; 119 Stat. 1144), pertaining to Congestion Relief.

§ 511.303 Definitions.

Unless otherwise specified in this part, the definitions in 23 U.S.C. 101(a) are applicable to this subpart. As used in this part:

Accuracy means the measure or degree of agreement between a data value or set of values and a source assumed to be correct.

Availability means the degree to which data values are present in the attributes (e.g., speed and travel time are attributes of traffic) that require them. Availability is typically described in terms of percentages or number of data values.

Congestion means the level at which transportation system performance is unacceptable due to excessive travel times and delays.

Data quality means the fitness of data for all purposes that require such data.

Full construction activities mean roadway construction or maintenance activities that affect travel conditions by closing and reopening roadways or lanes.

Metropolitan areas means the geographic areas designated as Metropolitan Statistical Areas by the Office of Management and Budget in the Executive Office of the President with a population exceeding 1,000,000 inhabitants.

Real-time information program means the program by which States gather and make available the data for traffic and travel conditions. Such means may involve State-only activity (including cooperative activities engaging multiple State agencies), State partnership with commercial providers of value-added information products, or other effective means that enable the State to satisfy the provisions for traffic and travel time conditions reporting stated in this section.

Routes of significance are non-Interstate roadways in metropolitan areas that are designated by States as meriting the collection and provision of information related to traffic and travel conditions. Factors to be considered in designating routes of significance include roadway safety (e.g., crash rate, routes affected by environmental events), public safety (e.g., routes used for evacuations), economic productivity, severity and frequency of congestion, and utility of the highway to serve as a diversion route for congestion locations. All public roadways including arterial highways, toll facilities and other facilities that apply end user pricing mechanisms shall be considered when designating routes of significance. In identifying these routes, States shall apply the collaborative practices and procedures that are used for compliance with 23 CFR part 940 and 23 CFR part 420.

Statewide incident reporting system means a statewide system for facilitating the real-time electronic reporting of surface transportation incidents to a central location for use in monitoring the event, providing accurate traveler information, and responding to the incident as appropriate. This definition is consistent with Public Law 109–59; 119 Stat. 1144, Section 1201(f).

Timeliness means the degree to which data values or a set of values are provided at the time required or specified.

Traffic and travel conditions means the characteristics that the traveling public experiences. Traffic and travel conditions include, but are not limited to, the following characteristics:

(1) Road or lane closures because of construction, traffic incidents, or other events;

(2) Roadway weather or other environmental conditions restricting or adversely affecting travel; and

(3) Travel times or speeds on limited access roadways in metropolitan areas that experience recurring congestion.

Validity means the degree to which data values fall within the respective domain of acceptable values.

Value-added information products means crafted products intended for commercial use, for sale to a customer base, or for other commercial enterprise purposes. These products may be derived from information gathered by States and may be created from other party or proprietary sources. These products may be created using the unique means of the value-added information provider.

§511.305 Policy.

This part establishes the provisions and parameters for the Real-Time System Management Information Program for State DOTs, other responsible agencies, and partnerships with other commercial entities in establishing real-time information programs that provide accessibility to traffic and travel conditions information by other public agencies, the traveling public, and by other parties who may deliver value-added information products.

§511.307 Eligibility for Federal funding.

(a) Subject to project approval by the Secretary, a State may obligate funds apportioned to the State under Title 23 U.S.C. sections 104(b)(1), also known as National Highway System funds, 104(b)(2), also known as CMAQ Improvement funds, and 104(b)(3), also known as STP funds, for activities relating to the planning, deployment and operation, including preventative maintenance, of real-time monitoring elements that advance the goals and purposes of the Real-Time System Management Information Program. The SPC funds, apportioned according to 23 U.S.C. 505(a), may be applied to the development and implementation of a real-time information program.

(b) Those project applications to establish a real-time information program solely for Interstate System highways are entitled to a Federal share of 90 percent of the total project cost, pursuant to 23 U.S.C. 120(a). Those project applications to establish a real-time information program for non-Interstate highways are entitled to a Federal share of 80 percent of the total project cost, as per 23 U.S.C. 120(b).

§511.309 Provisions for traffic and travel conditions reporting.

(a) Minimum requirements for traffic and travel conditions made available by real-time information programs are:

(1) *Construction activities.* The timeliness for the availability of information about full construction activities that close or reopen roadways or lanes will be 20 minutes or less from the time of the closure for highways outside of Metropolitan Areas. For roadways within Metropolitan Areas, the timeliness for the availability of information about full construction activities that close or reopen roadways or lanes will be 10 minutes or less from the time of the closure or reopening. Short-term or intermittent lane closures of limited duration that are less than the required reporting times are not included as a minimum requirement under this section.

(2) *Roadway or lane blocking incidents.* The timeliness for the availability of information related to roadway or lane blocking traffic incidents will be 20

minutes or less from the time that the incident is verified for highways outside of Metropolitan Areas. For roadways within Metropolitan Areas, the timeliness for the availability of information related to roadway or lane blocking traffic incidents will be 10 minutes or less from the time that the incident is verified.

(3) *Roadway weather observations.* The timeliness for the availability of information about hazardous driving conditions and roadway or lane closures or blockages because of adverse weather conditions will be 20 minutes or less from the time the hazardous conditions, blockage, or closure is observed.

(4) *Travel time information.* The timeliness for the availability of travel time information along limited access roadway segments within Metropolitan Areas, as defined under this subpart, will be 10 minutes or less from the time that the travel time calculation is completed.

(5) *Information accuracy.* The designed accuracy for a real-time information program shall be 85 percent accurate at a minimum, or have a maximum error rate of 15 percent.

(6) *Information availability.* The designed availability for a real-time information program shall be 90 percent available at a minimum.

(b) Real-time information programs may be established using legacy monitoring mechanisms applied to the highways, using a statewide incident reporting system, using new monitoring mechanisms applied to the highways, using value-added information products, or using a combination of monitoring mechanisms and value-added information products.

§ 511.311 Real-time information program establishment.

(a) *Requirement.* States shall establish real-time information programs that are consistent with the parameters defined under § 511.309. The real-time information program shall be established to take advantage of the existing traffic and travel condition monitoring capabilities, and build upon them where applicable. The real-time information program shall include traffic and travel condition information for, as a minimum, all the Interstate highways operated by the State. In addition, the real-time information program shall complement current transportation performance reporting systems by making it easier to gather or enhance required information.

(b) *Data quality.* States shall develop the methods by which data quality can be ensured to the data consumers. The criteria for defining the validity of traffic and travel conditions made available from real-time information programs shall be established by the States in collaboration with their partners for establishing the programs. States shall receive FHWA's concurrence that the selected methods provide reasonable checks of the quality of the information made available by the real-time information program. In requesting FHWA's concurrence, the State shall demonstrate to FHWA how the selected methods gauge the accuracy and availability of the real-time information and the remedial actions if the information quality falls below the levels described in § 511.309(a)(5) and § 511.309(a)(6).

(c) *Participation.* The establishment, or the enhancement, of a real-time information program should include participation from the following agencies: Highway agencies; public safety agencies (e.g., police, fire, emergency/medical); transit operators; and other operating agencies necessary to sustain mobility through the region and/or the metropolitan area. Nothing in this subpart is intended to alter the existing relationships among State, regional, and local agencies.

(d) *Update of Regional ITS Architecture.* All States and regions that have created a Regional ITS Architecture in accordance with Section 940 in Title 23 CFR shall evaluate their Regional ITS Architectures to determine whether the Regional ITS Architectures explicitly address real-time highway and transit information needs and the methods needed to meet such needs. Traffic and travel conditions monitoring needs for all Interstate system highways shall be considered. If necessary, the Regional ITS Architectures shall be updated to address coverage, monitoring systems, data fusion and archiving, and accessibility to highway and transit information for other

States and for value added information product providers. The Regional ITS Architecture shall feature the components and functionality of the real-time information program.

(e) *Effective date.* Establishment of the real-time information program for traffic and travel conditions on the Interstate system highways shall be completed no later than November 8, 2014.

§511.313 Metropolitan Area real-time information program supplement.

(a) *Applicability.* Metropolitan Areas as defined under this subpart.

(b) *Requirement.* Metropolitan Areas shall establish a real-time information program for traffic and travel conditions reporting with the same provisions described in §511.311.

(c) *Routes of significance.* States shall designate metropolitan areas, non-Interstate highways that are routes of significance as defined under this subpart. In identifying the metropolitan routes of significance, States shall collaborate with local or regional agencies using existing coordination methods. Nothing in this subpart is intended to alter the existing relationships among State, regional, and local agencies.

(d) *Effective date.* Establishment of the real-time information program for traffic and travel conditions reporting along the Metropolitan Area Interstate system highways shall be completed no later than November 8, 2014. Establishment of the real-time information program for traffic and travel conditions reporting along the State-designated metropolitan area routes of significance shall be completed no later than November 8, 2016.

§511.315 Program administration.

Compliance with this subpart will be monitored under Federal-aid oversight procedures as provided under 23 U.S.C. 106 and 133, 23 CFR 1.36, and 23 CFR 940.13.

PART 515—ASSET MANAGEMENT PLANS

Sec.

AUTHORITY: Sec. 1106 and 1203 of Pub. L. 112–141, 126 Stat. 405; 23 U.S.C. 109, 119(e), 144, 150(c), and 315; 49 CFR 1.85(a).

SOURCE: 81 FR 73263, Oct. 24, 2016, unless otherwise noted.

§515.1 Purpose.

The purpose of this part is to:

(a) Establish the processes that a State transportation department (State DOT) must use to develop its asset management plan, as required under 23 U.S.C. 119(e)(8);

(b) Establish the minimum requirements that apply to the development of an asset management plan;

(c) Describe the penalties for a State DOT's failure to develop and implement an asset management plan in accordance with 23 U.S.C. 119 and this part;

(d) Set forth the minimum standards for a State DOT to use in developing and operating highway bridge and pavement management systems under 23 U.S.C. 150(c)(3)(A)(i).

§515.3 Applicability and effective date.

This part applies to all State DOTs. The effective date for the requirements in this part is October 2, 2017.

§515.5 Definitions.

As used in this part:

Asset means all physical highway infrastructure located within the right-of-way corridor of a highway. The term *asset* includes all components necessary for the operation of a highway including pavements, highway bridges, tunnels, signs, ancillary structures, and other physical components of a highway.

Asset class means assets with the same characteristics and function (e.g., bridges, culverts, tunnels, pavements, or guardrail) that are a subset of a group or collection of assets that serve a common function (e.g., roadway system, safety, Intelligent Transportation (IT), signs, or lighting).

Asset condition means the actual physical condition of an asset.

Asset management means a strategic and systematic process of operating, maintaining, and improving physical assets, with a focus on both engineering and economic analysis based upon quality information, to identify a structured sequence of maintenance, preservation, repair, rehabilitation, and replacement actions that will achieve and sustain a desired state of good repair over the life cycle of the assets at minimum practicable cost.

Asset management plan means a document that describes how a State DOT will carry out asset management as defined in this section. This includes how the State DOT will make risk-based decisions from a long-term assessment of the National Highway System (NHS), and other public roads included in the plan at the option of the State DOT, as it relates to managing its physical assets and laying out a set of investment strategies to address the condition and system performance gaps. This document describes how the highway network system will be managed to achieve State DOT targets for asset condition and system performance effectiveness while managing the risks, in a financially responsible manner, at a minimum practicable cost over the life cycle of its assets. The term *asset management plan* under this part is the risk-based asset management plan that is required under 23 U.S.C. 119(e) and is intended to carry out asset management as defined in 23 U.S.C. 101(a)(2).

Asset sub-group means a specialized group of assets within an asset class with the same characteristics and function (e.g., concrete pavements or asphalt pavements.)

Bridge as used in this part, is defined in 23 CFR 650.305, the National Bridge Inspection Standards.

Critical infrastructure means those facilities the incapacity or failure of which would have a debilitating impact on national or regional economic security, national or regional energy security, national or regional public health or safety, or any combination of those matters.

Financial plan means a long-term plan spanning 10 years or longer, presenting a State DOT's estimates of projected available financial resources and predicted expenditures in major asset categories that can be used to achieve State DOT targets for asset condition during the plan period, and highlighting how resources are expected to be allocated based on asset strategies, needs, shortfalls, and agency policies.

Investment strategy means a set of strategies that result from evaluating various levels of funding to achieve State DOT targets for asset condition and system performance effectiveness at a minimum practicable cost while managing risks.

Life-cycle cost means the cost of managing an asset class or asset sub-group for its whole life, from initial construction to its replacement.

Life-cycle planning means a process to estimate the cost of managing an asset class, or asset sub-group over its whole life with consideration for minimizing cost while preserving or improving the condition.

Minimum practicable cost means lowest feasible cost to achieve the objective.

NHS pavements and bridges and NHS pavement and bridge assets mean Interstate System pavements (inclusion of ramps that are not part of the roadway normally traveled by through traffic is optional); NHS pavements (excluding the Interstate System) (inclusion of ramps that are not part of the roadway normally traveled by through traffic is optional); and NHS bridges carrying the NHS (including bridges that are part of the ramps connecting to the NHS).

Performance of the NHS refers to the effectiveness of the NHS in providing for the safe and efficient movement of people and goods where that performance can be affected by physical assets. This term does not include the performance measures established for performance of the Interstate System and performance of the NHS (excluding the Interstate System) under 23 U.S.C. 150(c)(3)(ii)(A)(IV)–(V).

Performance gap means the gaps between the current asset condition and State DOT targets for asset condition, and the gaps in system performance effectiveness that are best addressed by improving the physical assets.

Risk means the positive or negative effects of uncertainty or variability upon agency objectives.

Risk management means the processes and framework for managing potential risks, including identifying, analyzing, evaluating, and addressing the risks to assets and system performance.

Statewide Transportation Improvement Program (STIP) has the same meaning as defined in §450.104 of this title.

Work type means initial construction, maintenance, preservation, rehabilitation, and reconstruction.

§515.7 Process for establishing the asset management plan.

A State shall develop a risk-based asset management plan that describes how the NHS will be managed to achieve system performance effectiveness and State DOT targets for asset condition, while managing the risks, in a financially responsible manner, at a minimum practicable cost over the life cycle of its assets. The State DOT shall develop and use, at a minimum the following processes to prepare its asset management plan:

(a) A State DOT shall establish a process for conducting performance gap analysis to identify deficiencies hindering progress toward improving or preserving the NHS and achieving and sustaining the desired state of good repair. At a minimum, the State DOT's process shall address the following in the gap analysis:

(1) The State DOT targets for asset condition of NHS pavements and bridges as established by the State DOT under 23 U.S.C. 150(d) once promulgated.

(2) The gaps, if any, in the performance-of the NHS that affect NHS pavements and bridges regardless of their physical condition; and

(3) Alternative strategies to close or address the identified gaps.

(b) A State DOT shall establish a process for conducting life-cycle planning for an asset class or asset sub-group at the network level (network to be defined by the State DOT). As a State DOT develops its life-cycle planning process, the State DOT should include future changes in demand; information on current and future environmental conditions including extreme weather events, climate change, and seismic activity; and other factors that could impact whole of life costs of assets. The State DOT may propose excluding one or more asset sub-groups from its life-cycle planning if the State DOT can demonstrate to FHWA the exclusion of the asset sub-group would have no material adverse effect on the development of sound investment strategies due to the limited number of assets in the asset sub-group, the low level of cost associated with managing the assets in that asset sub-group, or other justifiable reasons. A life-cycle planning process shall, at a minimum, include the following:

(1) The State DOT targets for asset condition for each asset class or asset sub-group;

(2) Identification of deterioration models for each asset class or asset sub-group, provided that identification of deterioration models for assets other than NHS pavements and bridges is optional;

(3) Potential work types across the whole life of each asset class or asset sub-group with their relative unit cost; and

(4) A strategy for managing each asset class or asset sub-group by minimizing its life-cycle costs, while achieving the State DOT targets for asset condition for NHS pavements and bridges under 23 U.S.C. 150(d).

(c) A State DOT shall establish a process for developing a risk management plan. This process shall, at a minimum, produce the following information:

(1) Identification of risks that can affect condition of NHS pavements and bridges and the performance of the NHS, including risks associated with current and future environmental conditions, such as extreme weather events, climate change, seismic activity, and risks related to recurring damage and costs as identified through the evaluation of facilities repeated damaged by emergency events carried out under part 667 of this title. Examples of other risk categories include financial risks such as budget uncertainty; operational risks such as asset failure; and strategic risks such as environmental compliance.

(2) An assessment of the identified risks in terms of the likelihood of their occurrence and their impact and consequence if they do occur;

(3) An evaluation and prioritization of the identified risks;

(4) A mitigation plan for addressing the top priority risks;

(5) An approach for monitoring the top priority risks; and

(6) A summary of the evaluations of facilities repeatedly damaged by emergency events carried out under part 667 of this title that discusses, at a minimum, the results relating to the State's NHS pavements and bridges.

(d) A State DOT shall establish a process for the development of a financial plan that identifies annual costs over a minimum period of 10 years. The financial plan process shall, at a minimum, produce:

(1) The estimated cost of expected future work to implement investment

strategies contained in the asset management plan, by State fiscal year and work type;

(2) The estimated funding levels that are expected to be reasonably available, by fiscal year, to address the costs of future work types. State DOTs may estimate the amount of available future funding using historical values where the future funding amount is uncertain;

(3) Identification of anticipated funding sources; and

(4) An estimate of the value of the agency's NHS pavement and bridge assets and the needed investment on an annual basis to maintain the value of these assets.

(e) A State DOT shall establish a process for developing investment strategies meeting the requirements in § 515.9(f). This process must result in a description of how the investment strategies are influenced, at a minimum, by the following:

(1) Performance gap analysis required under paragraph (a) of this section;

(2) Life-cycle planning for asset classes or asset sub-groups resulting from the process required under paragraph (b) of this section;

(3) Risk management analysis resulting from the process required under paragraph (c) of this section; and

(4) Anticipated available funding and estimated cost of expected future work types associated with various candidate strategies based on the financial plan required by paragraph (d) of this section.

(f) The processes established by State DOTs shall include a provision for the State DOT to obtain necessary data from other NHS owners in a collaborative and coordinated effort.

(g) States DOTs shall use the best available data to develop their asset management plans. Pursuant to 23 U.S.C. 150(c)(3)(A)(i), each State DOT shall use bridge and pavement management systems meeting the requirements of § 515.17 to analyze the condition of NHS pavements and bridges for the purpose of developing and implementing the asset management plan required under this part. The use of these or other management systems for other assets that the State DOT elects to include in the asset management plan is optional (e.g., Sign Management Systems, etc.).

§ 515.9 Asset management plan requirements.

(a) A State DOT shall develop and implement an asset management plan to improve or preserve the condition of the assets and improve the performance of the NHS in accordance with the requirements of this part. Asset management plans must describe how the State DOT will carry out asset management as defined in § 515.5.

(b) An asset management plan shall include, at a minimum, a summary listing of NHS pavement and bridge assets, regardless of ownership.

(c) In addition to the assets specified in paragraph (b) of this section, State DOTs are encouraged, but not required, to include all other NHS infrastructure assets within the right-of-way corridor and assets on other public roads. Examples of other NHS infrastructure assets include tunnels, ancillary structures, and signs. Examples of other public roads include non-NHS Federal-aid highways. If a State DOT decides to include other NHS assets in its asset management plan, or to include assets on other public roads, the State DOT, at a minimum, shall evaluate and manage those assets consistent with paragraph (l) of this section.

(d) The minimum content for an asset management plan under this part includes a discussion of each element in this paragraph (d).

(1) Asset management objectives. The objectives should align with the State DOT's mission. The objectives must be consistent with the purpose of asset management, which is to achieve and sustain the desired state of good repair over the life cycle of the assets at a minimum practicable cost.

(2) Asset management measures and State DOT targets for asset condition, including those established pursuant to 23 U.S.C. 150, for NHS pavements and bridges. The plan must include measures and associated targets the State DOT can use in assessing the condition of the assets and performance of the highway system as it relates to those assets. The measures and targets must be consistent with the State DOT's asset management objectives. The

State DOT must include the measures established under 23 U.S.C. 150(c)(3)(A)(ii)(I)–(III), once promulgated in 23 CFR part 490, for the condition of NHS pavements and bridges. The State DOT also must include the targets the State DOT has established for the measures required by 23 U.S.C. 150(c)(3)(A)(ii)(I)–(III), once promulgated, and report on such targets in accordance with 23 CFR part 490. The State DOT may include measures and targets for NHS pavements and bridges that the State DOT established through pre-existing management efforts or develops through new efforts if the State DOT wishes to use such additional measures and targets to supplement information derived from the pavement and bridge measures and targets required under 23 U.S.C. 150.

(3) A summary description of the condition of NHS pavements and bridges, regardless of ownership. The summary must include a description of the condition of those assets based on the performance measures established under 23 U.S.C. 150(c)(3)(A)(ii) for condition, once promulgated. The description of condition should be informed by evaluations required under part 667 of this title of facilities repeated damaged by emergency events.

(4) Performance gap identification.

(5) Life-cycle planning.

(6) Risk management analysis, including the results for NHS pavements and bridges, of the periodic evaluations under part 667 of this title of facilities repeated damaged by emergency event.

(7) Financial plan.

(8) Investment strategies.

(e) An asset management plan shall cover, at a minimum, a 10-year period.

(f) An asset management plan shall discuss how the plan's investment strategies collectively would make or support progress toward:

(1) Achieving and sustaining a desired state of good repair over the life cycle of the assets,

(2) Improving or preserving the condition of the assets and the performance of the NHS relating to physical assets,

(3) Achieving the State DOT targets for asset condition and performance of the NHS in accordance with 23 U.S.C. 150(d), and

(4) Achieving the national goals identified in 23 U.S.C. 150(b).

(g) A State DOT must include in its plan a description of how the analyses required by State processes developed in accordance with §515.7 (such as analyses pertaining to life cycle planning, risk management, and performance gaps) support the State DOT's asset management plan investment strategies.

(h) A State DOT shall integrate its asset management plan into its transportation planning processes that lead to the STIP, to support its efforts to achieve the goals in paragraphs (f)(1) through (4) of this section.

(i) A State DOT is required to make its asset management plan available to the public, and is encouraged to do so in a format that is easily accessible.

(j) Inclusion of performance measures and State DOT targets for NHS pavements and bridges established pursuant to 23 U.S.C. 150 in the asset management plan does not relieve the State DOT of any performance management requirements, including 23 U.S.C. 150(e) reporting, established in other parts of this title.

(k) The head of the State DOT shall approve the asset management plan.

(l) If the State DOT elects to include other NHS infrastructure assets or other public roads assets in its asset management plan, the State at a minimum shall address the following, using a level of effort consistent with the State DOT's needs and resources:

(1) Summary listing of assets, including a description of asset condition;

(2) Asset management measures and State DOT targets for asset condition;

(3) Performance gap analysis;

(4) Life-cycle planning;

(5) Risk analysis, including summaries of evaluations carried out under part 667 of this title for the assets, if available, and consideration of those evaluations;

(6) Financial plan; and

(7) Investment strategies.

(m) The asset management plan of a State may include consideration of critical infrastructure from among those facilities in the State that are eligible under 23 U.S.C. 119(c).

§ 515.11 Deadlines and phase-in of asset management plan development.

(a) *Deadlines.* (1) Not later than April 30, 2018, the State DOT shall submit to FHWA a State-approved initial asset management plan meeting the requirements in paragraph (b) of this section. The FHWA will review the processes described in the initial plan and make a process certification decision as provided in § 515.13(a).

(2) Not later than June 30, 2019, the State DOT shall submit a State-approved asset management plan meeting all the requirements of 23 U.S.C. 119 and this part, including paragraph (c) of this section, together with documentation demonstrating implementation of the asset management plan. The FWHA will determine whether the State DOT's plan and implementation meet the requirements of 23 U.S.C. 119 and this part as provided in § 515.13(b).

(b) The initial plan shall describe the State DOT's processes for developing its risk-based asset management plan, including the policies, procedures, documentation, and implementation approach that satisfy the requirements of this part. The plan also must contain measures and targets for assets covered by the plan. The investment strategies required by § 515.7(e) and 515.9((d)(8) must support progress toward the achievement of the national goals identified in 23 U.S.C. 150(b). The initial plan must include and address the State DOT's 23 U.S.C. 150(d) targets for NHS pavements and bridges only if the first target-setting deadline established in 23 CFR part 490 for NHS pavements and bridges is a date more than 6 months before the initial plan submission deadline in paragraph (a)(1). The initial asset management plan may exclude one or more of the necessary analyses with respect to the following required asset management processes:

(1) Life-cycle planning required under § 515.7(a)(2);

(2) The risk management analysis required under § 515.7(a)(3); and

(3) Financial plan under § 515.7(a)(4).

(c) The State-approved asset management plan submitted not later than June 30, 2019, shall include all required analyses, performed using FHWA-certified processes, and the section 150 measures and State DOT targets for the NHS pavements and bridges. The plan must meet all requirements in §§ 515.7 and 515.9. This includes investment strategies that are developed based on the analyses from all processes required under § 515.7, and meet the requirements in 23 U.S.C. 119(e)(2).

§ 515.13 Process certification and recertification, and annual plan consistency review.

(a) *Process certification and recertification under 23 U.S.C. 119(e)(6).* Not later than 90 days after the date on which the FHWA receives a State DOT's processes and request for certification or recertification, the FHWA shall decide whether the State DOT's processes for developing its asset management plan meet the requirements of this part. The FHWA will treat the State DOT's submission of an initial State-approved asset management plan under § 515.11(b) as the State DOT's request for the first certification of the State's DOT's plan development processes under 23 U.S.C. 119(e)(6). As provided in paragraph (c) of this section, State DOT shall update and resubmit its asset management plan development processes to the FHWA for a new process certification at least every 4 years.

(1) If FHWA determines that the processes used by a State DOT to develop and maintain the asset management plan do not meet the requirements established under this part, FHWA will send the State DOT a written notice of the denial of certification or recertification, including a listing of the specific requirement deficiencies.

(2) Upon receiving a notice of denial of certification or recertification, the State DOT shall have 90 days from receipt of the notice to address the deficiencies identified in the notice and resubmit the State DOT's processes to FHWA for review and certification. The FHWA may extend the State DOT's 90-day period to cure deficiencies upon request. During the cure period established, all penalties and other legal impacts of a denial of certification shall be stayed as provided in 23 U.S.C. 119(e)(6)(C)(i).

(3) If FHWA finds that a State DOT's asset management processes substantially meet the requirements of this part except for minor deficiencies, FHWA may certify or recertify the State DOT's processes as being in compliance, but the State DOT must take actions to correct the minor deficiencies within 90 days of receipt of the notification of certification. The State shall notify FHWA, in writing, when corrective actions are completed.

(b) *Annual determination of consistency under 23 U.S.C. 119(e)(5).* Not later than August 31, 2019, and not later than July 31 in each year thereafter, FHWA will notify the State DOT whether the State DOT has developed and implemented an asset management plan consistent with 23 U.S.C. 119. The notice will be in writing and, in the case of a negative determination, will specify the deficiencies the State DOT needs to address. In making the annual consistency determination, the FHWA will consider the most recent asset management plan submitted by the State DOT, as well as any documentation submitted by the State DOT to demonstrate implementation of the plan. The FHWA determination is only as to the consistency of the State DOT asset management plan and State DOT implementation of that plan with applicable requirements, and is not an approval or disapproval of strategies or other decisions contained in the plan. With respect to any assets the State DOT may elect to include in its plan in addition to NHS pavement and bridge assets, the FHWA consistency determination will consider only whether the State DOT has complied with §515.9(l) with respect to such discretionary assets.

(1) *Plan development.* The FHWA will review the State DOT's asset management plan to ensure that it was developed with certified processes, includes the required content, and is consistent with other applicable requirements in this part.

(2) *Plan implementation.* The State DOT must demonstrate implementation of an asset management plan that meets the requirements of 23 U.S.C. 119 and this part. Each State DOT may determine the most suitable approach for demonstrating implementation of its asset management plan, so long as the information is current, documented, and verifiable. The submission must show the State DOT is using the investment strategies in its plan to make progress toward achievement of its targets for asset condition and performance of the NHS and to support progress toward the national goals identified in 23 U.S.C. 150(b). The State DOT must submit its implementation documentation not less than 30 days prior to the deadline for the FHWA consistency determination.

(i) FHWA considers the best evidence of plan implementation to be that, for the 12 months preceding the consistency determination, the State DOT funding allocations are reasonably consistent with the investment strategies in the State DOT's asset management plan. This demonstration takes into account the alignment between the actual and planned levels of investment for various work types (*i.e.*, initial construction, maintenance, preservation, rehabilitation and reconstruction).

(ii) FHWA may find a State DOT has implemented its asset management plan even if the State has deviated from the investment strategies included in the asset management plan, if the State DOT shows the deviation was necessary due to extenuating circumstances beyond the State DOT's reasonable control.

(3) *Opportunity to cure deficiencies.* In the event FHWA notifies a State DOT of a negative consistency determination, the State DOT has 30 days to address the deficiencies. The State DOT may submit additional information showing the FHWA negative determination was in error, or to demonstrate the State DOT has taken corrective action that resolves the deficiencies specified in FHWA's negative determination.

(c) *Updates and other amendments to plans and development processes.* A State DOT must update its asset management plan and asset management plan development processes at least every 4 years, beginning on the date of the initial FHWA certification of the State DOT's processes under paragraph (a) of this section. Whenever the State DOT updates or otherwise amends its asset management plan or its asset management plan development processes, the State DOT must submit the amended plan or processes to the FHWA for a new process certification and consistency determination at least 30 days prior to the deadline for the next FHWA consistency determination under paragraph (b) of this section. Minor technical corrections and revisions with no foreseeable material impact on the accuracy and validity of the processes, analyses, or investment strategies in the plan do not constitute amendments and do not require submission to FHWA.

§ 515.15 Penalties

(a) Beginning on October 1, 2019, and in each fiscal year thereafter, if a State DOT has not developed and implemented an asset management plan consistent with the requirements of 23 U.S.C. 119 and this part, the maximum Federal share for National Highway Performance Program projects and activities carried out by the State in that fiscal year shall be reduced to 65 percent for that fiscal year.

(b)(1) Except as provided in paragraph (b)(2) of this section, if the State DOT has not developed and implemented an asset management plan that is consistent with the requirements of 23 U.S.C. 119 and this part and established the performance targets for NHS pavements and bridges required under 23 U.S.C. 150(d) by the date that is 18 months after the effective date of the 23 U.S.C. 150(c) final rule for NHS pavements and bridges, the FHWA will not approve any further projects using National Highway Performance Program funds. Such suspension of funding approvals will terminate once the State DOT has developed and implemented an asset management plan that is consistent with the requirements of 23 U.S.C. 119 and this part and established its performance targets for NHS pavements and bridges required under 23 U.S.C. 150(d).

(2) The FHWA may extend this deadline if FHWA determines that the State DOT has made a good faith effort to develop and implement an asset management plan and establish the performance targets for NHS pavements and bridges required under 23 U.S.C. 150(d).

§ 515.17 Minimum standards for developing and operating bridge and pavement management systems

Pursuant to 23 U.S.C.150(c)(3)(A)(i), this section establishes the minimum standards States must use for developing and operating bridge and pavement management systems. State DOT bridge and pavement management systems are not subject to FHWA certification under § 515.13. Bridge and pavement management systems shall include, at a minimum, documented procedures for:

(a) Collecting, processing, storing, and updating inventory and condition data for all NHS pavement and bridge assets.

(b) Forecasting deterioration for all NHS pavement and bridge assets;

(c) Determining the benefit-cost over the life cycle of assets to evaluate alternative actions (including no action decisions), for managing the condition of NHS pavement and bridge assets;

(d) Identifying short- and long-term budget needs for managing the condition of all NHS pavement and bridge assets;

(e) Determining the strategies for identifying potential NHS pavement and bridge projects that maximize overall program benefits within the financial constraints.; and

(f) Recommending programs and implementation schedules to manage the condition of NHS pavement and bridge assets within policy and budget constraints.

§ 515.19 Organizational integration of asset management.

(a) The purpose of this section is to describe how a State DOT may integrate asset management into its organizational mission, culture and capabilities at all levels. The activities described in paragraphs (b) through (d) of this section are not requirements.

(b) A State DOT should establish organizational strategic goals and include the goals in its organizational strategic implementation plans with an explanation as to how asset management will help it to achieve those goals.

(c) A State DOT should conduct a periodic self-assessment of the agency's capabilities to conduct asset management, as well as its current efforts in implementing an asset management plan. The self-assessment should consider, at a minimum, the adequacy of the State DOT's strategic goals and policies with respect to asset management, whether asset management is considered in the agency's planning and programming of resources, including development of the STIP; whether the agency is implementing appropriate program delivery processes, such as consideration of alternative project delivery mechanisms, effective program management, and cost tracking and estimating; and whether the agency is implementing adequate data collection and analysis policies to support an effective asset management program.

(d) Based on the results of the self-assessment, the State DOT should conduct a gap analysis to determine which areas of its asset management process require improvement. In conducting a gap analysis, the State DOT should:

(1) Determine the level of organizational performance effort needed to achieve the objectives of asset management;

(2) Determine the performance gaps between the existing level of performance effort and the needed level of performance effort; and

(3) Develop strategies to close the identified organizational performance gaps and define the period of time over which the gap is to be closed.

SUBCHAPTER G—ENGINEERING AND TRAFFIC OPERATIONS

PART 620—ENGINEERING

AUTHORITY: 23 U.S.C. 315 and 318; 49 CFR 1.48, 23 CFR 1.32.

SOURCE: 39 FR 33311, Sept. 17, 1974, unless otherwise noted.

Subpart A—Highway Improvements in the Vicinity of Airports

SOURCE: 39 FR 35145, Sept. 30, 1974, unless otherwise noted.

§ 620.101 Purpose.

The purpose of this section is to implement title 23 U.S.C., section 318 which requires coordination of airport and highway developments to insure (a) that airway-highway clearances are adequate for the safe movement of air and highway traffic, and (b) that the expenditure of public funds for airport and highway improvements is in the public interest.

§ 620.102 Applicability.

The requirements of this section apply to all projects on which Federal-aid highway funds are to be expended and to both civil and military airports.

§ 620.103 Policy.

(a) Federal-aid highway funds shall not participate in the costs of reconstruction or relocation of any highway to which this section applies unless the Federal Highway Administration (FHWA) and State officials, in cooperation with the Federal Aviation Administration (FAA) or appropriate military authority, or in the case of privately owned airports, the owner of that airport, determine that the location or extension of the airport in question and the consequent relocation or reconstruction of the highway is in the public interest.

(b) In addition to complying with 23 U.S.C. 318 and insuring the prudent use of public funds, it is the policy of FHWA to provide a high degree of safety in the location, design, construction and operation of highways and airports.

(c) Federal-aid funds shall not participate in projects where substandard clearances are created or will continue to exist.

§ 620.104 Standards.

A finding of public interest by FHWA will be based on compliance with airway-highway clearances which conform to FAA standards for aeronautical safety.

Subpart B—Relinquishment of Highway Facilities

SOURCE: 39 FR 33311, Sept. 17, 1974, unless otherwise noted.

§ 620.201 Purpose.

To prescribe Federal Highway Administration (FHWA) procedures relating to relinquishment of highway facilities.

§ 620.202 Applicability.

The provisions of this subpart apply to highway facilities where Federal-aid funds have participated in either right-of-way or physical construction costs of a project. The provisions of this subpart apply only to relinquishment of facilities for continued highway purposes. Other real property disposals and modifications or disposal of access rights are governed by the requirements of 23 CFR part 710.

[64 FR 71289, Dec. 21, 1999]

§ 620.203 Procedures.

(a) After final acceptance of a project on the Federal-aid primary, urban, or secondary system or after the date that the plans, specifications and estimates (PS&E) for the physical construction on the right-of-way for a Federal-aid Interstate project have been approved by the FHWA, relinquishment of the right-of-way or any change made in control of access shall be in accordance with the provisions of this section. For the purposes of this section, final acceptance for a project involving physical construction is the date of the acceptance of the physical construction by the FHWA and for right-of-way projects, the date the division engineer determines to be the date of the completion of the acquisition of the right-of-way shown on the final plans.

(b) Other than a conveyance made as part of a concession agreement as defined in section 710.703, for purposes of this section, *relinquishment* is defined as the conveyance of a portion of a highway right-of-way or facility by a State highway agency (SHA) to another Government agency for highway use.

(c) The following facilities may be relinquished in accordance with paragraph 203(f):

(1) Sections of a State highway which have been superseded by construction on new location and removed from the Federal-aid system and the replaced section thereof is approved by the FHWA as the new location of the Federal-aid route. Federal-aid funds may not participate in rehabilitation work performed for the purpose of placing the superseded section of the highway in a condition acceptable to the local authority. The relinquishment of any Interstate mileage shall be submitted to the Federal Highway Administrator as a special case for prior approval.

(2) Sections of reconstructed local facilities that are located outside the control of access lines, such as turnarounds of severed local roads or streets adjacent to the Federal-aid project's right-of-way, and local roads and streets crossing over or under said project that have been adjusted in grade and/or alignment, including new right-of-way required for adjustments. Eligibility for Federal-aid participation in the costs of the foregoing adjustments is as determined at the time of PS&E approval under policies of the FHWA.

(3) Frontage roads or portions thereof that are constructed generally parallel to and outside the control of access lines of a Federal-aid project for the purpose of permitting access to private properties rather than to serve as extensions of ramps to connect said Federal-aid project with the nearest crossroad or street.

(d) The following facilities may be relinquished only with the approval of the Federal Highway Administrator in accordance with paragraph 203(g).

(1) Frontage roads or portions thereof located outside the access control lines of a Federal-aid project that are constructed to service (in lieu of or in addition to the purposes outlined under paragraph (c)(3) of this section) as connections between ramps to or from the Federal-aid project and existing public roads or streets.

(2) Ramps constructed to serve as connections for interchange of traffic between the Federal-aid project and local roads or streets.

(e) Where a frontage road is not on an approved Federal-aid system title to the right-of-way may be acquired initially in the name of the political subdivision which is to assume control thus eliminating the necessity of a formal transfer later. Such procedure would be subject to prior FHWA approval and would be limited to those facilities which meet the criteria set forth in paragraphs (c) (2) and (3) of this section.

(f) Upon presentation by a State that it intends to relinquish facilities such as described in paragraph (c) (1), (2) or (3) of this section to local authorities, the division engineer of the FHWA shall have appropriate field and office examination made thereof to assure that such relinquishments are in accordance with the provisions of the cited paragraphs. Relinquishments of the types described in paragraph (c) (1), (2) or (3) of this section may be made on an individual basis or on a project or route basis subject to the following conditions and understandings:

(1) Immediately following action by the State in approving a relinquishment, it shall furnish to the Division Administrator for record purposes a

copy of a suitable map or maps identified by the Federal-aid project number, with the facilities to be relinquished and the date of such relinquishment action clearly delineated thereon.

(2) If it is found at any time after relinquishment that a relinquished facility is in fact required for the safe and proper operation of the Federal-aid highway, the State shall take immediate action to restore such facility to its jurisdiction without cost to Federal-aid highway funds.

(3) If it is found at any time that a relinquished frontage road or portion thereof or any part of the right-of-way therefor has been abandoned by local governmental authority and a showing cannot be made that such abandoned facility is no longer required as a public road, it is to be understood that the Federal Highway Administrator may cause to be withheld from Federal-aid highway funds due to the State an amount equal to the Federal-aid participation in the abandoned facility.

(4) In no case shall any relinquishment include any portion of the right-of-way within the access control lines as shown on the plans for a Federal-aid project approved by the FHWA, without the prior approval of the Federal Highway Administrator.

(5) There cannot be additional Federal-aid participation in future construction or reconstruction on any relinquished "off the Federal-aid system" facility unless the underlying reason for such future work is caused by future improvement of the associated Federal-aid highway.

(g) In the event that a State desires to apply for approval by the Federal Highway Administrator for the relinquishment of a facility such as described in paragraph (d) (1) and (2) of this section, the facts pertinent to such proposal are to be presented to the division engineer of the FHWA. The division engineer shall have appropriate review made of such presentation and forward the material presented by the State together with his findings thereon through the Regional Federal Highway Administrator for consideration by the Federal Highway Administrator and determination of action to be taken.

(h) No change may be made in control of access, without the joint determination and approval of the SHA and FHWA. This would not prevent the relinquishment of title, without prior approval of the FHWA, of a segment of the right-of-way provided there is an abandonment of a section of highway inclusive of such segment.

(i) Relinquishments must be justified by the State's finding concurred in by the FHWA, that:

(1) The subject land will not be needed for Federal-aid highway purposes in the foreseeable future;

(2) That the right-of-way being retained is adequate under present day standards for the facility involved;

(3) That the release will not adversely affect the Federal-aid highway facility or the traffic thereon;

(4) That the lands to be relinquished are not suitable for retention in order to restore, preserve, or improve the scenic beauty adjacent to the highway consonant with the intent of 23 U.S.C. 319 and Pub. L. 89–285, Title III, sections 302–305 (Highway Beautification Act of 1965).

(j) If a relinquishment is to a Federal, State, or local government agency for highway purposes, there need not be a charge to the said agency, nor in such event any credit to Federal funds. If for any reason there is a charge, the STD may retain the Federal share of the proceeds if used for projects eligible under title 23 of the United States Code.

[39 FR 33311, Sept. 17, 1974, as amended at 64 FR 71289, Dec. 21, 1999; 73 FR 77502, Dec. 19, 2008]

PART 625—DESIGN STANDARDS FOR HIGHWAYS

AUTHORITY: 23 U.S.C. 109, 315, and 402; Sec. 1073 of Pub. L. 102–240, 105 Stat. 1914, 2012; 49 CFR 1.48(b) and (n).

SOURCE: 62 FR 15397, Apr. 1, 1997, unless otherwise noted.

§625.1 Purpose.

To designate those standards, policies, and standard specifications that are acceptable to the Federal Highway Administration (FHWA) for application in the geometric and structural design of highways.

§625.2 Policy.

(a) Plans and specifications for proposed National Highway System (NHS) projects shall provide for a facility that will—

(1) Adequately serve the existing and planned future traffic of the highway in a manner that is conducive to safety, durability, and economy of maintenance; and

(2) Be designed and constructed in accordance with criteria best suited to accomplish the objectives described in paragraph (a)(1) of this section and to conform to the particular needs of each locality.

(b) Resurfacing, restoration, and rehabilitation (RRR) projects, other than those on the Interstate system and other freeways, shall be constructed in accordance with standards which preserve and extend the service life of highways and enhance highway safety. Resurfacing, restoration, and rehabilitation work includes placement of additional surface material and/or other work necessary to return an existing roadway, including shoulders, bridges, the roadside, and appurtenances to a condition of structural or functional adequacy.

(c) An important goal of the FHWA is to provide the highest practical and feasible level of safety for people and property associated with the Nation's highway transportation systems and to reduce highway hazards and the resulting number and severity of accidents on all the Nation's highways.

§625.3 Application.

(a) *Applicable Standards.* (1) Design and construction standards for new construction, reconstruction, resurfacing (except for maintenance resurfacing), restoration, or rehabilitation of a highway on the NHS (other than a highway also on the Interstate System or other freeway) shall be those approved by the Secretary in cooperation with the State highway departments. These standards may take into account, in addition to the criteria described in §625.2(a), the following:

(i) The constructed and natural environment of the area;

(ii) The environmental, scenic, aesthetic, historic, community, and preservation impacts of the activity; and

(iii) Access for other modes of transportation.

(2) Federal-aid projects not on the NHS are to be designed, constructed, operated, and maintained in accordance with State laws, regulations, directives, safety standards, design standards, and construction standards.

(b) The standards, policies, and standard specifications cited in §625.4 of this part contain specific criteria and controls for the design of NHS projects. Deviations from specific minimum values therein are to be handled in accordance with procedures in paragraph (f) of this section. If there is a conflict between criteria in the documents enumerated in §625.4 of this part, the latest listed standard, policy, or standard specification will govern.

(c) Application of FHWA regulations, although cited in §625.4 of this part as standards, policies, and standard specifications, shall be as set forth therein.

(d) This regulation establishes Federal standards for work on the NHS regardless of funding source.

(e) The Division Administrator shall determine the applicability of the roadway geometric design standards to traffic engineering, safety, and preventive maintenance projects which include very minor or no roadway work. Formal findings of applicability are expected only as needed to resolve controversies.

(f) *Exceptions.* (1) Approval within the delegated authority provided by FHWA Order M1100.1A may be given on a project basis to designs which do not conform to the minimum criteria as set forth in the standards, policies, and standard specifications for:

(i) Experimental features on projects; and

(ii) Projects where conditions warrant that exceptions be made.

(2) The determination to approve a project design that does not conform to the minimum criteria is to be made only after due consideration is given to

all project conditions such as maximum service and safety benefits for the dollar invested, compatibility with adjacent sections of roadway and the probable time before reconstruction of the section due to increased traffic demands or changed conditions.

§ 625.4 Standards, policies, and standard specifications.

(a) *Roadway and appurtenances.* (1) A Policy on Geometric Design of Highways and Streets, AASHTO, 2011 (incorporated by reference; see § 625.4(d)).

(2) A Policy on Design Standards—Interstate System, AASHTO (paragraph (d) of this section).

(3) The geometric design standards for resurfacing, restoration, and rehabilitation (RRR) projects on NHS highways other than freeways shall be the procedures and the design or design criteria established for individual projects, groups of projects, or all nonfreeway RRR projects in a State, and as approved by the FHWA. The other geometric design standards in this section do not apply to RRR projects on NHS highways other than freeways, except as adopted on an individual State basis. The RRR design standards shall reflect the consideration of the traffic, safety, economic, physical, community, and environmental needs of the projects.

(4) Location and Hydraulic Design of Encroachments on Flood Plains, refer to 23 CFR part 650, subpart A.

(5) Procedures for Abatement of Highway Traffic Noise and Construction Noise, refer to 23 CFR part 772.

(6) Accommodation of Utilities, refer to 23 CFR part 645, subpart B.

(7) Pavement Design, refer to 23 CFR part 626.

(b) *Bridges and structures.* (1) For existing bridges originally designed to any edition of the AASHTO Standard Specifications for Highway Bridges, modifications may be designed to the Standard Specifications for Highway Bridges, 17th Edition, AASHTO, 2002 (incorporated by reference; see § 625.4(d)), or to the standards and specifications that are listed in § 625.4(b).

(2) AASHTO LRFD Bridge Construction Specifications (paragraph (d) of this section).

(3) AASHTO LRFD Bridge Design Specifications (paragraph (d) of this section).

(4) AASHTO LRFD Movable Highway Bridge Design Specifications (paragraph (d) of this section).

(5) AASHTO/AWS D1.5M/D1.5 Bridge Welding Code (paragraph (d) of this section).

(6) D1.4/D1.4M: 2011Structural Welding Code-Reinforcing Steel, American Welding Society, 2011 (incorporated by reference; see § 625.4(d)).

(7) Standard Specifications for Structural Supports for Highway Signs, Luminaires, and Traffic Signals, (paragraph (d) of this section); or LRFD Specifications for Structural Supports for Highway Signs, Luminaires, and Traffic Signals (paragraph (d) of this section).

(8) Navigational Clearances for Bridges, refer to 23 CFR part 650, subpart H.

(c) *Materials.* (1) General Materials Requirements, refer to 23 CFR part 635, subpart D.

(2) Transportation Materials, AASHTO (paragraph (d) of this section).

(3) Quality Assurance Procedures for Construction, refer to 23 CFR part 637, subpart B.

(d) *Documents incorporated by reference.* The standards required in this section are incorporated by reference into this section with the approval of the Director of the Federal Register under 5 U.S.C. 552(a) and 1 CFR part 51. All approved material is available for inspection at U.S. Department of Transportation's National Transportation Library at 1200 New Jersey Avenue SE, Washington, DC 20590; (800) 853–1351 and is available from the sources indicated below. It is also available for inspection at the National Archives and Records Administration (NARA). For information on the availability of this material at NARA, call 202–741–6030 or go to *www.archives.gov/federal-register/cfr/ibr-locations.html.*

(1) American Association of State Highway and Transportation Officials (AASHTO), Suite 249, 444 North Capitol Street NW., Washington, DC 20001; *www.transportation.org;* or (202) 624–5800.

(i) A Policy on Geometric Design of Highways and Streets, 6th Edition, 2011.

(ii) A Policy on Design Standards—Interstate System, May 2016.

(iii) Standard Specifications for Highway Bridges, 17th Edition, 2002

(iv) AASHTO–LRFD Bridge Construction Specifications, 4th Edition, copyright 2017.

(v) AASHTO LRFD–8, LRFD Bridge Design Specifications, 8th Edition, 2017.

(vi) AASHTO LRFD Movable Highway Bridge Design Specifications, 2nd Edition, 2007, with:

(A) Interim Revisions, 2008,

(B) Interim Revisions, 2010,

(C) Interim Revisions, 2011,

(D) Interim Revisions, 2012,

(E) Interim Revisions, 2014, and

(F) Interim Revisions, 2015.

(vii) AASHTO/AWS D1.5M/D1.5: 2015–AMD1, Bridge Welding Code, Amendment: Second Printing December 12, 2016; with

(A) AASHTO BWC–7–I1–OL, 2018 Interim Revisions to AASHTO/AWS D1.5M/D1.5: 2015 Bridge Welding Code, 7th Edition, copyright 2017.

(B) [Reserved]

(viii) AASHTO LTS–6, Standard Specifications for Structural Supports for Highway Signs, Luminaires, and Traffic Signals, 6th Edition, copyright 2013, with:

(A) AASHTO LTS–6–I1, 2015 Interim Revisions to Standard Specifications for Structural Supports for Highway Signs, Luminaires, and Traffic Signals, copyright 2014.

(B) [Reserved]

(ix) AASHTO LRFDLTS–1, LRFD Specifications for Structural Supports for Highway Signs, Luminaires, and Traffic Signals, 1st Edition, copyright 2015, with:

(A) AASHTO LRFDLTS–1–I1–OL, 2017 Interim Revisions to LRFD Specifications for Structural Supports for Highway Signs, Luminaires, and Traffic Signals, copyright 2016, and

(B) AASHTO LRFDLTS–1–I2–OL, 2018 Interim Revisions to LRFD Specifications for Structural Supports for Highway Signs, Luminaires, and Traffic Signals, copyright 2017.

(x) 2017 Edition of Transportation Materials, Parts 1–3, copyright 2017.

(2) American Welding Society (AWS), 8669 NW 36 Street, #130 Miami, FL 33166–6672; *www.aws.org*; or (800) 443–9353 or (305) 443–9353.

(i) D1.4/D1.4M: 2011 Structural Welding Code—Reinforcing Steel, 2011.

(ii) [Reserved]

(e) The FHWA supports using, as design resources to achieve context sensitive designs, guides that national organizations develop from peer-reviewed research, or equivalent guides that are developed in cooperation with State or local officials, when such guides are not in conflict with Federal laws and regulations.

[62 FR 15397, Apr. 1, 1997, as amended at 67 FR 6395, Feb. 12, 2002; 69 FR 18803, Apr. 9, 2004; 71 FR 26414, May 5, 2006; 74 FR 28442, June 16, 2009; 80 FR 61307, Oct. 13, 2015; 83 FR 54880, Nov. 1, 2018]

PART 626—PAVEMENT POLICY

AUTHORITY: 23 U.S.C. 101(e), 109, and 315; 49 CFR 1.48(b)

SOURCE: 61 FR 67174, Dec. 19, 1996, unless otherwise noted.

§626.1 Purpose.

To set forth pavement design policy for Federal-aid highway projects.

§626.2 Definitions.

Unless otherwise specified in this part, the definitions in 23 U.S.C. 101(a) are applicable to this part. As used in this part:

Pavement design means a project level activity where detailed engineering and economic considerations are given to alternative combinations of subbase, base, and surface materials which will provide adequate load carrying capacity. Factors which are considered include: Materials, traffic, climate, maintenance, drainage, and life-cycle costs.

§626.3 Policy.

Pavement shall be designed to accommodate current and predicted traffic needs in a safe, durable, and cost effective manner.

PART 627—VALUE ENGINEERING

AUTHORITY: 23 U.S.C. 106(e), 106(g), 106(h), 112(a) and (b), 302, 315; and 49 CFR part 18.

SOURCE: 79 FR 52975, Sept. 5, 2014, unless otherwise noted.

§ 627.1 Purpose and applicability.

(a) The purpose of this part is to prescribe the programs, policies and procedures for the integration of value engineering (VE) into the planning and development of all applicable Federal-aid highway projects.

(b) Each State transportation agency (STA) shall establish and sustain a VE program. This program shall establish the policies and procedures under which VE analyses are identified, conducted and approved VE recommendations implemented on applicable projects (as defined in § 627.5 of this part). These policies and procedures should also identify when a VE analysis is encouraged on all other projects where there is a high potential to realize the benefits of a VE analysis.

(c) The STAs shall establish the policies, procedures, functions, and capacity to monitor, assess, and report on the performance of the VE program, along with the VE analyses that are conducted and Value Engineering Change Proposals (VECP) that are accepted. The STAs shall ensure that its sub-recipients conduct VE analyses in compliance with this part.

§ 627.3 Definitions.

The following terms used in this part are defined as follows:

(a) *Bridge project.* A bridge project shall include any project where the primary purpose is to construct, reconstruct, rehabilitate, resurface, or restore a bridge.

(b) *Final design.* Any design activities following preliminary design and expressly includes the preparation of final construction plans and detailed specifications for the performance of construction work.

(c) *Project.* The term "project" means any undertaking eligible for assistance under title 23 of the United States Code. The limits of a project are defined as the logical termini in the environmental document and may consist of several contracts, or phases of a project or contract, which may be implemented over several years.

(d) *Total project costs.* The estimated costs of all work to be conducted on a project including the environment, design, right-of-way, utilities and construction phases.

(e) *Value Engineering (VE) analysis.* The systematic process of reviewing and assessing a project by a multidisciplinary team not directly involved in the planning and development phases of a specific project that follows the VE Job Plan and is conducted to provide recommendations for:

(1) Providing the needed functions, considering community and environmental commitments, safety, reliability, efficiency, and overall lifecycle cost (as defined in 23 U.S.C. 106(f)(2));

(2) Optimizing the value and quality of the project; and

(3) Reducing the time to develop and deliver the project.

(f) *Value Engineering (VE) Job Plan.* A systematic and structured action plan for conducting and documenting the results of the VE analysis. While each VE analysis shall address each phase in the VE Job Plan, the level of analysis conducted and effort expended for each phase may be scaled to meet the needs of each individual project. The VE Job Plan shall include and document the following seven phases:

(1) Information Phase: Gather project information including project commitments and constraints.

(2) Function Analysis Phase: Analyze the project to understand the required functions.

(3) Creative Phase: Generate ideas on ways to accomplish the required functions which improve the project's performance, enhance its quality, and lower project costs.

(4) Evaluation Phase: Evaluate and select feasible ideas for development.

(5) Development Phase: Develop the selected alternatives into fully supported recommendations.

(6) Presentation Phase: Present the VE recommendation to the project stakeholders.

(7) Resolution Phase: Evaluate, resolve, document and implement all approved recommendations.

(g) *Value Engineering Change Proposal (VECP).* A construction contract change proposal submitted by the construction contractor based on a VECP provision in the contract. These proposals may improve the project's performance, value and/or quality, lower construction costs, or shorten the delivery time, while considering their impacts on the project's overall life-cycle cost and other applicable factors.

§627.5 Applicable projects.

(a) A VE analysis shall be conducted prior to the completion of final design on each applicable project that utilizes Federal-aid highway funding, and all approved recommendations shall be included in the project's plans, specifications and estimates prior to authorizing the project for construction (as specified in 23 CFR 630.205).

(b) Applicable projects requiring a VE analysis shall include the following:

(1) Each project located on the National Highway System (NHS) (as specified in 23 U.S.C. 103) with an estimated total project cost of $50 million or more that utilizes Federal-aid highway funding;

(2) Each bridge project located on the NHS with an estimated total project cost of $40 million or more that utilizes Federal-aid highway funding;

(3) Any major project (as defined in 23 U.S.C. 106(h)), located on or off of the NHS, that utilizes Federal-aid highway funding in any contract or phase comprising the major project;

(4) Any project where a VE analysis has not been conducted and a change is made to the project's scope or design between the final design and the construction letting which results in an increase in the project's total cost exceeding the thresholds identified in paragraphs (b)(1), (2) or (3) of this section; and

(5) Any other project FHWA determines to be appropriate that utilizes Federal-aid highway program funding.

(c) An additional VE analysis is not required if, after conducting a VE analysis required under this part, the project is subsequently split into smaller projects in the design phase or the project is programmed to be completed by the letting of multiple construction projects. However, the STA may not avoid the requirement to conduct a VE analysis on an applicable project by splitting the project into smaller projects, or programming multiple design or construction projects.

(d) The STA's VE Program's policies and procedures should identify when VE analyses are to be considered or conducted for projects falling below the required thresholds identified in paragraph (b) of this section in the planning and development of transportation projects where there is a high potential for the project to benefit from a VE analysis. While not required, FHWA encourages STAs to consider the following projects that may benefit from a VE analysis:

(1) Complex projects on or off the NHS that have a total project cost of $25 million or more;

(2) Complex Bridge Projects on or off the NHS with an estimated total project cost of $20 million or more;

(3) Design-build projects on or off the NHS with an estimated cost of $25 million or more; and

(4) Any other complex, difficult or high cost project as determined by the STA.

(e) A VE analysis is not required for projects delivered using the design-build method of construction. While not required, FHWA encourages STAs and local public authorities to conduct a VE analysis on design-build projects that meet the requirements identified in paragraph (b) of this section.

(f) A VE analysis is required on projects delivered using the Construction Manager/General Contractor (CM/GC) method of contracting, if the project meets the requirements identified in paragraph (b) of this section.

§627.7 VE programs.

(a) The STA shall establish and sustain a VE program under which VE analyses are identified, conducted and approved VE recommendations implemented on all applicable projects (as defined in § 627.5). The STA's VE program shall:

(1) Establish and document VE program policies and procedures that ensure the required VE analysis is conducted on all applicable projects, and encourage conducting VE analyses on other projects that have the potential to benefit from this analysis;

(2) Ensure the VE analysis is conducted and all approved recommendations are implemented and documented in a final VE report prior to the project being authorized to proceed to a construction letting;

(3) Monitor and assess the VE Program, and disseminate an annual report to the FHWA consisting of a summary of all approved recommendations implemented on applicable projects requiring a VE analysis, the accepted VECPs, and VE program functions and activities;

(4) Establish and document policies, procedures, and contract provisions that identify when VECP's may be used; identify the analysis, documentation, basis, and process for evaluating and accepting a VECP; and determine how the net savings of each VECP may be shared between the agency and contractor;

(5) Establish and document policies, procedures, and controls to ensure a VE analysis is conducted and all approved recommendations are implemented for all applicable projects administered by local public agencies; and ensure the results of these analyses are included in the VE program monitoring and reporting; and

(6) Provide for the review of any project where a delay occurs between when the final plans are completed and the project advances to a letting for construction to determine if a change has occurred to the project's scope or design where a VE analysis would be required to be conducted (as specified in § 625.5(b)).

(b) STAs shall ensure the required VE analysis has been performed on each applicable project including those administered by subrecipients, and shall ensure approved recommendations are implemented into the project's plans, specifications, and estimates prior to the project being authorized for construction (as specified in 23 CFR 630.205).

(c) STAs shall designate a VE Program Coordinator to promote and advance VE program activities and functions. The VE Coordinator's responsibilities should include establishing and maintaining the STA's VE policies and procedures; facilitating VE training; ensuring VE analyses are conducted on applicable projects; monitoring, assessing, and reporting on the VE analyses conducted and VE program; participating in periodic VE program and project reviews; submitting the required annual VE report to the FHWA; and supporting the other elements of the VE program.

§ 627.9 Conducting a VE analysis.

(a) A VE analysis should be conducted as early as practicable in the planning or development of a project, preferably before the completion of the project's preliminary design. At a minimum, the VE analysis shall be conducted prior to completing the project's final design.

(b) The VE analysis should be closely coordinated with other project development activities to minimize the impact approved recommendations might have on previous agency, community, or environmental commitments; the project's scope or schedule; and the use of innovative technologies, materials, methods, plans or construction provisions.

(c) When the STA or local public agency chooses to conduct a VE analysis for a project utilizing the design-build project delivery method, the VE analysis should be performed prior to the release of the final Request for Proposals or other applicable solicitation documents.

(d) For projects delivered using the CM/GC contracting method, a VE analysis is not required prior to the preparation and release of the RFP for the CM/GC contract. The VE analysis is required to be completed and approved recommendations incorporated into the project plans prior to requesting a construction price proposal from the CM/GC contractor.

(e) STAs shall ensure the VE analysis meets the following requirements:

(1) Uses a multidisciplinary team not directly involved in the planning or design of the project, with at least one individual who has training and experience with leading VE analyses;

(2) Develops and implements the VE Job Plan;

(3) Produces a formal written report outlining, at a minimum:

(i) Project information;

(ii) Identification of the VE analysis team;

(iii) Background and supporting documentation, such as information obtained from other analyses conducted on the project (e.g., environmental, safety, traffic operations, constructability);

(iv) Documentation of the stages of the VE Job Plan which would include documentation of the life-cycle costs that were analyzed;

(v) Summarization of the analysis conducted;

(vi) Documentation of the proposed recommendations and approvals received at the time the report is finalized; and

(vii) The formal written report shall be retained for at least 3 years after the completion of the project.

(f) For bridge projects, in addition to the requirements in subsection (e), the VE analyses shall:

(1) Include bridge substructure and superstructure requirements that consider alternative construction materials; and

(2) Be conducted based on:

(i) An engineering and economic assessment, taking into consideration acceptable designs for bridges; and

(ii) An analysis of life-cycle costs and duration of project construction.

(g) STAs and local public agencies may employ qualified consultants (as defined in 23 CFR 172.3) to conduct a VE analysis. The consultant shall possess training and experience with leading VE analyses. A consulting firm or individual shall not be used to conduct or support a VE analysis if they have a conflict of interest (as specified in 23 CFR 1.33).

(h) STAs, and local public agencies are encouraged to use a VECP clause (or other such clauses under a different name) in an applicable project's contract, allowing the construction contractor to propose changes to the project's plans, specifications, or other contract documents. Whenever such clauses are used, the STA and local authority will consider changes that could improve the project's performance, value and quality, shorten the delivery time, or lower construction costs, while considering impacts on the project's overall life-cycle cost and other applicable factors. The basis for a STA or local authority to consider a VECP is the analysis and documentation supporting the proposed benefits that would result from implementing the proposed change in the project's contract or project plans.

(i) Proposals to accelerate construction after the award of the contract will not be considered a VECP and will not be eligible for Federal-aid highway program funding participation. Where it is necessary to accelerate construction, STAs and local public agencies are encouraged to use the appropriate incentive or disincentive clauses so that all proposers will take this into account when preparing their bids or price proposals.

PART 630—PRECONSTRUCTION PROCEDURES

Subpart A—Project Authorization and Agreements

Sec.

Subpart B—Plans, Specifications, and Estimates

Subpart C [Reserved]

Subpart D—Geodetic Markers

Subparts E–F [Reserved]

AUTHORITY: 23 U.S.C. 106, 109, 112, 115, 315, 320, and 402(a); Sec. 1501 and 1503 of Pub. L. 109–59, 119 Stat. 1144; Pub. L. 105–178, 112 Stat. 193; Pub. L. 104–59, 109 Stat. 582; Pub. L. 97–424, 96 Stat. 2106; Pub. L. 90–495, 82 Stat. 828; Pub. L. 85–767, 72 Stat. 896; Pub. L. 84–627, 70 Stat. 380; 23 CFR 1.32 and 49 CFR 1.48(b), and Pub. L. 112–141, 126 Stat. 405, section 1303.

Subpart A—Project Authorization and Agreements

SOURCE: 66 FR 23847, May 10, 2001, unless otherwise noted.

§ 630.102 Purpose.

The purpose of this subpart is to prescribe policies for authorizing Federal-aid projects through execution of the project agreement required by 23 U.S.C. 106(a)(2).

§ 630.104 Applicability.

(a) This subpart is applicable to all Federal-aid projects unless specifically exempted.

(b) Other projects which involve special procedures are to be approved, or authorized as set out in the implementing instructions or regulations for those projects.

§ 630.106 Authorization to proceed.

(a)(1) The State transportation department (STD) must obtain an authorization to proceed from the FHWA before beginning work on any Federal-aid project. The STD may request an authorization to proceed in writing or by electronic mail for a project or a group of projects.

(2) The FHWA will issue the authorization to proceed either through or after the execution of a formal project agreement with the State. The agreement can be executed only after applicable prerequisite requirements of Federal laws and implementing regulations and directives are satisfied. Except as provided in paragraphs (c)(1) through (c)(4) of this section, the FHWA will obligate Federal funds in the project or group of projects upon execution of the project agreement.

(3) The State's request that Federal funds be obligated shall be supported by a documented cost estimate that is based on the State's best estimate of costs.

(4) The State shall maintain a process to adjust project cost estimates. For example, the process would require a review of the project cost estimate when the bid is approved, a project phase is completed, a design change is approved, etc. Specifically, the State shall revise the Federal funds obligated within 90 days after it has determined that the estimated Federal share of project costs has decreased by $250,000 or more.

(5) The State shall review, on a quarterly basis, inactive projects (for the purposes of this subpart an "inactive project" means a project for which no expenditures have been charged against Federal funds for the past 12 months) with unexpended Federal obligations

and shall revise the Federal funds obligated for a project within 90 days to reflect the current cost estimate, based on the following criteria:

(i) Projects inactive for the past 12 months with unexpended balances more than $500,000,

(ii) Projects inactive for the past 24 months with unexpended balances of $50,000 to $500,000, and

(iii) Projects inactive for the past 36 months with unexpended balances less than $50,000.

(6) If the State fails to comply with the requirements of paragraphs (a)(3), (4), or (5) of this section, then the FHWA shall revise the obligations or take such other action as authorized by 23 CFR 1.36. The FHWA shall advise the State of its proposed actions and provide the State with the opportunity to respond before actions are taken. The FHWA shall not adjust obligations without a State's consent during the August redistribution process, August 1 to September 30.

(7) For design-build projects, the execution or modification of the project agreement for final design and physical construction, and authorization to proceed, shall not occur until after the completion of the NEPA process. However, preliminary design (as defined in 23 CFR 636.103) and preliminary engineering may be authorized in accordance with this section.

(8) For Construction Manager/General Contractor projects, the execution or modification of the project agreement for preconstruction services associated with final design and for construction services, and authorization to proceed with such services, shall not occur until after the completion of the NEPA process. However, preconstruction services associated with preliminary design may be authorized in accordance with this section.

(b) Federal funds shall not participate in costs incurred prior to the date of a project agreement except as provided by 23 CFR 1.9(b).

(c) The execution of the project agreement shall be deemed a contractual obligation of the Federal government under 23 U.S.C. 106 and shall require that appropriate funds be available at the time of authorization for the agreed Federal share, either pro rata or lump sum, of the cost of eligible work to be incurred by the State except as follows:

(1) Advance construction projects authorized under 23 U.S.C. 115.

(2) Projects for preliminary studies for the portion of the preliminary engineering and right-of-way (ROW) phase(s) through the selection of a location.

(3) Projects for ROW acquisition in hardship and protective buying situations through the selection of a particular location. This includes ROW acquisition within a potential highway corridor under consideration where necessary to preserve the corridor for future highway purposes. Authorization of work under this paragraph shall be in accord with the provisions of 23 CFR part 710.

(4) In special cases where the Federal Highway Administrator determines it to be in the best interest of the Federal-aid highway program.

(d) For projects authorized to proceed under paragraphs (c)(1) through (c)(4) of this section, the executed project agreement shall contain the following statement: "Authorization to proceed is not a commitment or obligation to provide Federal funds for that portion of the undertaking not fully funded herein."

(e) For projects authorized under paragraphs (c)(2) and (c)(3) of this section, subsequent authorizations beyond the location stage shall not be given until appropriate available funds have been obligated to cover eligible costs of the work covered by the previous authorization.

(f)(1) The Federal-aid share of eligible project costs shall be established at the time the project agreement is executed in one of the following manners:

(i) Pro rata, with the agreement stating the Federal share as a specified percentage; or

(ii) Lump sum, with the agreement stating that Federal funds are limited to a specified dollar amount not to exceed the legal pro rata.

(2) The pro-rata or lump sum share may be adjusted before or shortly after contract award to reflect any substantive change in the bids received as compared to the STD's estimated cost

of the project at the time of FHWA authorization, provided that Federal funds are available.

(3) Federal participation is limited to the agreed Federal share of eligible costs actually incurred by the State, not to exceed the maximum permitted by enabling legislation.

(g) The State may contribute more than the normal non-Federal share of title 23, U.S.C. projects. In general, financing proposals that result in only minimal amounts of Federal funds in projects should be avoided unless they are based on sound project management decisions.

(h)(1) Donations of cash, land, material or services may be credited to the State's non-Federal share of the participating project work in accordance with title 23, U.S.C., and implementing regulations.

(2) Contributions may not exceed the total costs incurred by the State on the project. Cash contributions from all sources plus the Federal funds may not exceed the total cost of the project.

[66 FR 23847, May 10, 2001, as amended at 71 FR 4995, Jan. 31, 2006; 72 FR 45336, Aug. 14, 2007; 81 FR 86942, Dec. 2, 2016]

§ 630.108 Preparation of agreement.

(a) The STD shall prepare a project agreement for each Federal-aid project.

(b) The STD may develop the project agreement in a format acceptable to both the STD and the FHWA provided the following are included:

(1) A description of each project location including State and project termini;

(2) The Federal-aid project number;

(3) The work covered by the agreement;

(4) The total project cost and amount of Federal funds under agreement;

(5) The Federal-aid share of eligible project costs expressed as either a pro rata percentage or a lump sum as set forth in § 630.106(f)(1);

(6) A statement that the State accepts and will comply with the agreement provisions set forth in § 630.112;

(7) A statement that the State stipulates that its signature on the project agreement constitutes the making of the certifications set for in § 630.112; and

(8) Signatures of officials from both the State and the FHWA, and the date executed.

(c) The project agreement should also document, by comment, instances where:

(1) The State is applying amounts of credits from special accounts (such as the 23 U.S.C. 120(j) toll credits, 23 U.S.C. 144(n) off-system bridge credits and 23 U.S.C. 323 land value credits) to cover all or a portion of the normal percent non-Federal share of the project;

(2) The project involves other arrangements affecting Federal funding or non-Federal matching provisions, including tapered match, donations, or use of other Federal agency funds, if known at the time the project agreement is executed; and

(3) The State is claiming finance related costs for bond and other debt instrument financing (such as payments to States under 23 U.S.C. 122).

(d) The STD may use an electronic version of the agreement as provided by the FHWA.

(Approved by the Office of Management and Budget under control number 2125–0529)

§ 630.110 Modification of original agreement.

(a) When changes are needed to the original project agreement, a modification of agreement shall be prepared. Agreements should not be modified to replace one Federal fund category with another unless specifically authorized by statute.

(b) The STD may develop the modification of project agreement in a format acceptable to both the STD and the FHWA provided the following are included:

(1) The Federal-aid project number and State;

(2) A sequential number identifying the modification;

(3) A reference to the date of the original project agreement to be modified;

(4) The original total project cost and the original amount of Federal funds under agreement;

(5) The revised total project cost and the revised amount of Federal funds under agreement;

(6) The reason for the modifications; and,

(7) Signatures of officials from both the State and the FHWA and date executed.

(c) The STD may use an electronic version of the modification of project agreement as provided by the FHWA.

§ 630.112 Agreement provisions.

(a) The State, through its transportation department, accepts and agrees to comply with the applicable terms and conditions set forth in title 23, U.S.C., the regulations issued pursuant thereto, the policies and procedures promulgated by the FHWA relative to the designated project covered by the agreement, and all other applicable Federal laws and regulations.

(b) Federal funds obligated for the project must not exceed the amount agreed to on the project agreement, the balance of the estimated total cost being an obligation of the State. Such obligation of Federal funds extends only to project costs incurred by the State after the execution of a formal project agreement with the FHWA.

(c) The State must stipulate that as a condition to payment of the Federal funds obligated, it accepts and will comply with the following applicable provisions:

(1) *Project for acquisition of rights-of-way.* In the event that actual construction of a road on this right-of-way is not undertaken by the close of the twentieth fiscal year following the fiscal year in which the project is authorized, the STD will repay to the FHWA the sum or sums of Federal funds paid to the transportation department under the terms of the agreement. The State may request a time extension beyond the 20-year limit with no repayment of Federal funds, and the FHWA may approve this request if it is considered reasonable.

(2) *Preliminary engineering project.* In the event that right-of-way acquisition for, or actual construction of, the road for which this preliminary engineering is undertaken is not started by the close of the tenth fiscal year following the fiscal year in which the project is authorized, the STD will repay to the FHWA the sum or sums of Federal funds paid to the transportation department under the terms of the agreement. The State may request a time extension for any preliminary engineering project beyond the 10-year limit with no repayment of Federal funds, and the FHWA may approve this request if it is considered reasonable.

(3) *Drug-free workplace certification.* By signing the project agreement, the STD agrees to provide a drug-free workplace as required by 49 CFR part 29, subpart F. In signing the project agreement, the State is providing the certification required in appendix C to 49 CFR part 29, unless the State provides an annual certification.

(4) *Suspension and debarment certification.* By signing the project agreement, the STD agrees to fulfill the responsibility imposed by 49 CFR 29.510 regarding debarment, suspension, and other responsibility matters. In signing the project agreement, the State is providing the certification for its principals required in appendix A to 49 CFR part 29.

(5) *Lobbying certification.* By signing the project agreement, the STD agrees to abide by the lobbying restrictions set forth in 49 CFR part 20. In signing the project agreement, the State is providing the certification required in appendix A to 49 CFR part 20.

Subpart B—Plans, Specifications, and Estimates

SOURCE: 43 FR 58564, Dec. 15, 1978, unless otherwise noted.

§ 630.201 Purpose.

The purpose of this subpart is to prescribe Federal Highway Administration (FHWA) procedures relating to the preparation, submission, and approval of plans, specifications and estimates (PS&E), and supporting documents for Federal-aid projects.

§ 630.203 Applicability.

The provisions of this regulation apply to all highway construction projects financed in whole or in part with Federal-aid highway funds and to be undertaken by a State or political subdivision.

[69 FR 7118, Feb. 13, 2004]

§ 630.205 Preparation, submission, and approval.

(a) The contents and number of copies of the PS&E assembly shall be determined by the FHWA.

(b) Plans and specifications shall describe the location and design features and the construction requirements in sufficient detail to facilitate the construction, the contract control and the estimation of construction costs of the project. The estimate shall reflect the anticipated cost of the project in sufficient detail to provide an initial prediction of the financial obligations to be incurred by the State and FHWA and to permit an effectice review and comparison of the bids received.

(c) PS&E assemblies for Federal-aid highway projects shall be submitted to the FHWA for approval.

(d) The State highway agency (SHA) shall be advised of approval of the PS&E by the FHWA.

(e) No project or part thereof for actual construction shall be advertised for contract nor work commenced by force account until the PS&E has been approved by the FHWA and the SHA has been so notified.

Subpart C [Reserved]

Subpart D—Geodetic Markers

SOURCE: 39 FR 26414, July 19, 1974, unless otherwise noted.

§ 630.401 Purpose.

The purpose of this subpart is to prescribe procedures for conducting geodetic control surveys when participation with Federal-aid highway funds in the cost thereof is proposed and to encourage inter-agency cooperation in setting station markers, surveying to measure their position, and preserving the control so established.

§ 630.402 Policy.

(a) Geodetic surveys along Federal-aid highway routes may be programmed as Federal-aid highway projects.

(b) All geodetic survey work performed as a Federal-aid highway project will conform to National Ocean Survey (NOS) specifications. NOS will, as the representative of FHWA, be responsible for the inspection and verification of the work to ascertain that the specifications for the work have been met. Final project acceptance by FHWA will be predicated on a finding of acceptability by NOS.

§ 630.403 Initiation of projects.

All projects shall be coordinated by the FHWA Division Administrator, the State highway department and the National Ocean Survey.

§ 630.404 Standards.

(a) Highway purposes may best be served by the establishment of station markings for horizontal control along Federal-aid highway routes at spacings of three to eight kilometers (about 2 to 5 miles) and station markers for vertical control of spacings no closer than one kilometer. These requirements may be waived only with the approval of the Administrator.

(b) Projects should be of sufficient scope to permit efficient use of field parties. Projects should extend at least 30 kilometers. Projects may be coordinated with adjoining States to attain greater efficiency.

(c) Where geodetic station markers cannot be established inititally at points readily accessible from the Federal-aid route, or where unavoidable circumstances result in their being established within construction limits, supplemental projects may later be approved to set and survey markers at satisfactory permanent points, preferably within the right-of-way but at points where their use does not introduce traffic hazards.

Subparts E–F [Reserved]

Subpart G—Advance Construction of Federal-Aid Projects

SOURCE: 60 FR 36993, July 19, 1995, unless otherwise noted.

§ 630.701 Purpose.

The purpose of this subpart is to prescribe procedures for advancing the construction of Federal-aid highway projects without obligating Federal funds apportioned or allocated to the State.

§630.703 Eligibility.

(a) The State Department of Transportation (DOT) may proceed with a project authorized in accordance with title 23, United States Code:

(1) Without the use of Federal funds; and

(2) In accordance with all procedures and requirements applicable to the project other than those procedures and requirements that limit the State to implementation of a project—

(i) With the aid of Federal funds previously apportioned or allocated to the State; or

(ii) With obligation authority previously allocated to the State.

(b) The FHWA, on the request of a State and execution of a project agreement, may obligate all or a portion of the Federal share of a project authorized to proceed under this section from any category of funds for which the project is eligible.

[73 FR 50196, Aug. 26, 2008]

§630.705 Procedures.

(a) An advance construction project shall meet the same requirements and be processed in the same manner as a regular Federal-aid project, except,

(1) The FHWA authorization does not constitute any commitment of Federal funds on the project, and

(2) The FHWA shall not reimburse the State until the project is converted under §630.709.

(b) Project numbers shall be identified by the letters "AC" preceding the regular project number prefix.

[60 FR 36993, July 19, 1995, as amended at 68 FR 60033, Oct. 21, 2003]

§630.707 [Reserved]

§630.709 Conversion to a regular Federal-aid project.

(a) The State Department of Transportation may submit a written request to the FHWA that a project be converted to a regular Federal-aid project at any time provided that sufficient Federal-aid funds and obligation authority are available.

(b) Subsequent to FHWA approval the State Department of Transportation may claim reimbursement for the Federal share of project costs incurred, provided the project agreement has been executed. If the State Department of Transportation has previously submitted a final voucher, the FHWA will process the voucher for payment.

[60 FR 36993, July 19, 1995, as amended at 73 FR 50196, Aug. 26, 2008]

Subpart H—Bridges on Federal Dams

SOURCE: 39 FR 36474, Oct. 10, 1974, unless otherwise noted.

§630.801 Purpose.

The purpose of this subpart is to prescribe procedures for the construction and financing, by an agency of the Federal Government, of public highway bridges over dams constructed and owned by or for the United States.

§630.802 Applicability.

A proposed bridge over a dam, together with the approach roads to connect the bridge with existing public highways, must be eligible for inclusion in the Federal-aid highway system, if not already a part thereof.

§630.803 Procedures.

A State's application to qualify a project under this subpart will include:

(a) A certification that the bridge is economically desirable and needed as a link in the Federal-aid highway system.

(b) A statement showing the source and availability of funds to be used in construction of the roadway approaches.

(c) A statement of any obligation on the part of the agency constructing the dam to provide such bridge or approach roads to satisfy a legal liability incurred independently of this subpart.

Subpart I [Reserved]

Subpart J—Work Zone Safety and Mobility

SOURCE: 69 FR 54569, Sept. 9, 2004, unless otherwise noted.

§630.1002 Purpose.

Work zones directly impact the safety and mobility of road users and highway workers. These safety and mobility impacts are exacerbated by an aging highway infrastructure and growing congestion in many locations. Addressing these safety and mobility issues requires considerations that start early in project development and continue through project completion. Part 6 of the Manual On Uniform Traffic Control Devices (MUTCD)[1] sets forth basic principles and prescribes standards for the design, application, installation, and maintenance of traffic control devices for highway and street construction, maintenance operation, and utility work. In addition to the provisions in the MUTCD, there are other actions that could be taken to further help mitigate the safety and mobility impacts of work zones. This subpart establishes requirements and provides guidance for systematically addressing the safety and mobility impacts of work zones, and developing strategies to help manage these impacts on all Federal-aid highway projects.

§630.1004 Definitions and explanation of terms.

As used in this subpart:

Highway workers include, but are not limited to, personnel of the contractor, subcontractor, DOT, utilities, and law enforcement, performing work within the right-of-way of a transportation facility.

Mobility is the ability to move from place to place and is significantly dependent on the availability of transportation facilities and on system operating conditions. With specific reference to work zones, mobility pertains to moving road users efficiently through or around a work zone area with a minimum delay compared to baseline travel when no work zone is present, while not compromising the safety of highway workers or road users. The commonly used performance measures for the assessment of mobility include delay, speed, travel time and queue lengths.

Safety is a representation of the level of exposure to potential hazards for users of transportation facilities and highway workers. With specific reference to work zones, safety refers to minimizing potential hazards to road users in the vicinity of a work zone and highway workers at the work zone interface with traffic. The commonly used measures for highway safety are the number of crashes or the consequences of crashes (fatalities and injuries) at a given location or along a section of highway during a period of time. Highway worker safety in work zones refers to the safety of workers at the work zone interface with traffic and the impacts of the work zone design on worker safety. The number of worker fatalities and injuries at a given location or along a section of highway, during a period of time are commonly used measures for highway worker safety.

Work zone[2] is an area of a highway with construction, maintenance, or utility work activities. A work zone is typically marked by signs, channelizing devices, barriers, pavement markings, and/or work vehicles. It extends from the first warning sign or high-intensity rotating, flashing, oscillating, or strobe lights on a vehicle to the END ROAD WORK sign or the last temporary traffic control (TTC) device.

Work zone crash[3] means a traffic crash in which the first harmful event

---

[1] The MUTCD is approved by the FHWA and recognized as the national standard for traffic control on all public roads. It is incorporated by reference into the Code of Federal Regulations at 23 CFR part 655. It is available on the FHWA's Web site at *http://mutcd.fhwa.dot.gov* and is available for inspection and copying at the FHWA Washington, DC Headquarters and all FHWA Division Offices as prescribed at 49 CFR part 7.

[2] MUTCD, Part 6, "Temporary Traffic Control," Section 6C.02, "Temporary Traffic Control Zones."

[3] "Model Minimum Uniform Crash Criteria Guideline" (MMUCC), 2d Ed. (Electronic), 2003, produced by National Center for Statistics and Analysis, National Highway Traffic Safety Administration (NHTSA). Telephone 1–(800)–934–8517. Available at the URL: *http://www-nrd.nhtsa.dot.gov*. The NHTSA, the FHWA, the Federal Motor Carrier Safety Administration (FMCSA), and the Governors Highway Safety Association (GHSA) sponsored the development of the MMUCC Guideline which recommends voluntary implementation of the 111 MMUCC data elements and

occurs within the boundaries of a work zone or on an approach to or exit from a work zone, resulting from an activity, behavior, or control related to the movement of the traffic units through the work zone. This includes crashes occurring on approach to, exiting from or adjacent to work zones that are related to the work zone.

Work zone impacts refer to work zone-induced deviations from the normal range of transportation system safety and mobility. The extent of the work zone impacts may vary based on factors such as, road classification, area type (urban, suburban, and rural), traffic and travel characteristics, type of work being performed, time of day/night, and complexity of the project. These impacts may extend beyond the physical location of the work zone itself, and may occur on the roadway on which the work is being performed, as well as other highway corridors, other modes of transportation, and/or the regional transportation network.

§630.1006 Work zone safety and mobility policy.

Each State shall implement a policy for the systematic consideration and management of work zone impacts on all Federal-aid highway projects. This policy shall address work zone impacts throughout the various stages of the project development and implementation process. This policy may take the form of processes, procedures, and/or guidance, and may vary based on the characteristics and expected work zone impacts of individual projects or classes of projects. The States should institute this policy using a multi-disciplinary team and in partnership with the FHWA. The States are encouraged to implement this policy for non-Federal-aid projects as well.

§630.1008 State-level processes and procedures.

(a) This section consists of State-level processes and procedures for States to implement and sustain their respective work zone safety and mobility policies. State-level processes and procedures, data and information resources, training, and periodic evaluation enable a systematic approach for addressing and managing the safety and mobility impacts of work zones.

(b) *Work zone assessment and management procedures.* States should develop and implement systematic procedures to assess work zone impacts in project development, and to manage safety and mobility during project implementation. The scope of these procedures shall be based on the project characteristics.

(c) *Work zone data.* States shall use field observations, available work zone crash data, and operational information to manage work zone impacts for specific projects during implementation. States shall continually pursue improvement of work zone safety and mobility by analyzing work zone crash and operational data from multiple projects to improve State processes and procedures. States should maintain elements of the data and information resources that are necessary to support these activities.

(d) *Training.* States shall require that personnel involved in the development, design, implementation, operation, inspection, and enforcement of work zone related transportation management and traffic control be trained, appropriate to the job decisions each individual is required to make. States shall require periodic training updates that reflect changing industry practices and State processes and procedures.

(e) *Process review.* In order to assess the effectiveness of work zone safety and mobility procedures, the States shall perform a process review at least every two years. This review may include the evaluation of work zone data at the State level, and/or review of randomly selected projects throughout their jurisdictions. Appropriate personnel who represent the project development stages and the different offices within the State, and the FHWA should participate in this review. Other non-State stakeholders may also be included in this review, as appropriate. The results of the review are intended to lead to improvements in work zone

serves as a reporting threshold that includes all persons (injured and uninjured) in crashes statewide involving death, personal injury, or property damage of $1,000 or more. The Guideline is a tool to strengthen existing State crash data systems.

processes and procedures, data and information resources, and training programs so as to enhance efforts to address safety and mobility on current and future projects.

§ 630.1010 Significant projects.

(a) A significant project is one that, alone or in combination with other concurrent projects nearby is anticipated to cause sustained work zone impacts (as defined in § 630.1004) that are greater than what is considered tolerable based on State policy and/or engineering judgment.

(b) The applicability of the provisions in §§ 630.1012(b)(2) and 630.1012(b)(3) is dependent upon whether a project is determined to be significant. The State shall identify upcoming projects that are expected to be significant. This identification of significant projects should be done as early as possible in the project delivery and development process, and in cooperation with the FHWA. The State's work zone policy provisions, the project's characteristics, and the magnitude and extent of the anticipated work zone impacts should be considered when determining if a project is significant or not.

(c) All Interstate system projects within the boundaries of a designated Transportation Management Area (TMA) that occupy a location for more than three days with either intermittent or continuous lane closures shall be considered as significant projects.

(d) For an Interstate system project or categories of Interstate system projects that are classified as significant through the application of the provisions in § 630.1010(c), but in the judgment of the State they do not cause sustained work zone impacts, the State may request from the FHWA, an exception to §§ 630.1012(b)(2) and 630.1012(b)(3). Exceptions to these provisions may be granted by the FHWA based on the State's ability to show that the specific Interstate system project or categories of Interstate system projects do not have sustained work zone impacts.

§ 630.1012 Project-level procedures.

(a) This section provides guidance and establishes procedures for States to manage the work zone impacts of individual projects.

(b) *Transportation Management Plan (TMP).* A TMP consists of strategies to manage the work zone impacts of a project. Its scope, content, and degree of detail may vary based upon the State's work zone policy, and the State's understanding of the expected work zone impacts of the project. For significant projects (as defined in § 630.1010), the State shall develop a TMP that consists of a Temporary Traffic Control (TTC) plan and addresses both Transportation Operations (TO) and Public Information (PI) components. For individual projects or classes of projects that the State determines to have less than significant work zone impacts, the TMP may consist only of a TTC plan. States are encouraged to consider TO and PI issues for all projects.

(1) A TTC plan describes TTC measures to be used for facilitating road users through a work zone or an incident area. The TTC plan plays a vital role in providing continuity of reasonably safe and efficient road user flow and highway worker safety when a work zone, incident, or other event temporarily disrupts normal road user flow. The TTC plan shall be consistent with the provisions under Part 6 of the MUTCD and with the work zone hardware recommendations in Chapter 9 of the American Association of State Highway and Transportation Officials (AASHTO) Roadside Design Guide. Chapter 9 of the AASHTO Roadside Design Guide: "Traffic Barriers, Traffic Control Devices, and Other Safety Features for Work Zones" 2002, is incorporated by reference in accordance with 5 U.S.C. 552(a) and 1 CFR part 51 and is on file at the National Archives and Record Administration (NARA). For information on the availability of this material at NARA call (202) 741–6030, or go to *http://www.archives.gov/federal_register/code_of_federal_regulations/ibr_locations.html.* The entire document is available for purchase from the American Association of State Highway and Transportation Officials (AASHTO), 444 North Capitol Street, NW., Suite 249, Washington, DC 20001 or

at the URL: *http://www.aashto.org/bookstore.* It is available for inspection from the FHWA Washington Headquarters and all Division Offices as listed in 49 CFR part 7. In developing and implementing the TTC plan, pre-existing roadside safety hardware shall be maintained at an equivalent or better level than existed prior to project implementation. The scope of the TTC plan is determined by the project characteristics, and the traffic safety and control requirements identified by the State for that project. The TTC plan shall either be a reference to specific TTC elements in the MUTCD, approved standard TTC plans, State transportation department TTC manual, or be designed specifically for the project.

(2) The TO component of the TMP shall include the identification of strategies that will be used to mitigate impacts of the work zone on the operation and management of the transportation system within the work zone impact area. Typical TO strategies may include, but are not limited to, demand management, corridor/network management, safety management and enforcement, and work zone traffic management. The scope of the TO component should be determined by the project characteristics, and the transportation operations and safety strategies identified by the State.

(3) The PI component of the TMP shall include communications strategies that seek to inform affected road users, the general public, area residences and businesses, and appropriate public entities about the project, the expected work zone impacts, and the changing conditions on the project. This may include traveler information strategies. The scope of the PI component should be determined by the project characteristics and the public information and outreach strategies identified by the State. Public information should be provided through methods best suited for the project, and may include, but not be limited to, information on the project characteristics, expected impacts, closure details, and commuter alternatives.

(4) States should develop and implement the TMP in sustained consultation with stakeholders (e.g., other transportation agencies, railroad agencies/operators, transit providers, freight movers, utility suppliers, police, fire, emergency medical services, schools, business communities, and regional transportation management centers).

(c) The Plans, Specifications, and Estimates (PS&Es) shall include either a TMP or provisions for contractors to develop a TMP at the most appropriate project phase as applicable to the State's chosen contracting methodology for the project. A contractor developed TMP shall be subject to the approval of the State, and shall not be implemented before it is approved by the State.

(d) The PS&Es shall include appropriate pay item provisions for implementing the TMP, either through method or performance based specifications.

(1) For method-based specifications individual pay items, lump sum payment, or a combination thereof may be used.

(2) For performance based specifications, applicable performance criteria and standards may be used (e.g., safety performance criteria such as number of crashes within the work zone; mobility performance criteria such as travel time through the work zone, delay, queue length, traffic volume; incident response and clearance criteria; work duration criteria).

(e) *Responsible persons.* The State and the contractor shall each designate a trained person, as specified in § 630.1008(d), at the project level who has the primary responsibility and sufficient authority for implementing the TMP and other safety and mobility aspects of the project.

§ 630.1014 Implementation.

Each State shall work in partnership with the FHWA in the implementation of its policies and procedures to improve work zone safety and mobility. At a minimum, this shall involve an FHWA review of conformance of the State's policies and procedures with this regulation and reassessment of the State's implementation of its procedures at appropriate intervals. Each State is encouraged to address implementation of this regulation in its stewardship agreement with the FHWA.

§ 630.1016 Compliance date.

States shall comply with all the provisions of this rule no later than October 12, 2007. For projects that are in the later stages of development at or about the compliance date, and if it is determined that the delivery of those projects would be significantly impacted as a result of this rule's provisions, States may request variances for those projects from the FHWA, on a project-by-project basis.

Subpart K—Temporary Traffic Control Devices

AUTHORITY: 23 U.S.C. 109(c) and 112; Sec. 1110 of Pub. L. 109–59; 23 CFR 1.32; and 49 CFR 1.48(b).

SOURCE: 72 FR 68489, Dec. 5, 2007, unless otherwise noted.

§ 630.1102 Purpose.

To decrease the likelihood of highway work zone fatalities and injuries to workers and road users by establishing minimum requirements and providing guidance for the use of positive protection devices between the work space and motorized traffic, installation and maintenance of temporary traffic control devices, and use of uniformed law enforcement officers during construction, utility, and maintenance operations, and by requiring contract pay items to ensure the availability of funds for these provisions. This subpart is applicable to all Federal-aid highway projects, and its application is encouraged on other highway projects as well.

§ 630.1104 Definitions.

For the purposes of this subpart, the following definitions apply:

Agency means a State or local highway agency or authority that receives Federal-aid highway funding.

Exposure Control Measures means traffic management strategies to avoid work zone crashes involving workers and motorized traffic by eliminating or reducing traffic through the work zone, or diverting traffic away from the work space.

Federal-aid Highway Project means highway construction, maintenance, and utility projects funded in whole or in part with Federal-aid funds.

Motorized Traffic means the motorized traveling public. This term does not include motorized construction or maintenance vehicles and equipment within the work space.

Other Traffic Control Measures means all strategies and temporary traffic controls other than Positive Protection Devices and Exposure Control Measures, but including uniformed law enforcement officers, used to reduce the risk of work zone crashes involving motorized traffic.

Positive Protection Devices means devices that contain and/or redirect vehicles and meet the crashworthiness evaluation criteria contained in National Cooperative Highway Research Program (NCHRP) Report 350, Recommended Procedures for the Safety Performance Evaluation of Highway Features, 1993, Transportation Research Board, National Research Council. The Director of the Federal Register approves this incorporation by reference in accordance with 5 U.S.C. 552(a) and 1 CFR part 51. This document is available for inspection and copying at FHWA, 1200 New Jersey Avenue, SE., Washington, DC 20590, as provided in 49 CFR part 7. You may also inspect a copy at the National Archives and Records Administration (NARA). For information on the availability of this material at NARA, call (202) 741 6030, or go to: *http://www.archives.gov/federal_register/code_of_federal_regulations/ibr_locations.html.*

Work Zone Safety Management means the entire range of traffic management and control and highway safety strategies and devices used to avoid crashes in work zones that can lead to worker and road user injuries and fatalities, including Positive Protection Devices, Exposure Control Measures, and Other Traffic Control Measures.

§ 630.1106 Policy and procedures for work zone safety management.

(a) Each agency's policy and processes, procedures, and/or guidance for the systematic consideration and management of work zone impacts, to be established in accordance with 23 CFR 630.1006, shall include the consideration and management of road user and worker safety on Federal-aid highway projects. These processes, procedures, and/or guidance, to be developed in partnership with the FHWA, shall address the use of Positive Protection Devices to prevent the intrusion of motorized traffic into the work space and other potentially hazardous areas in the work zone; Exposure Control Measures to avoid or minimize worker exposure to motorized traffic and road user exposure to work activities; Other Traffic Control Measures including uniformed law enforcement officers to minimize work zone crashes; and the safe entry/exit of work vehicles onto/from the travel lanes. Each of these strategies should be used to the extent that they are possible, practical, and adequate to manage work zone exposure and reduce the risks of crashes resulting in fatalities or injuries to workers and road users.

(b) Agency processes, procedures, and/or guidance should be based on consideration of standards and/or guidance contained in the Manual on Uniform Traffic Control Devices (MUTCD) and the AASHTO Roadside Design Guide, as well as project characteristics and factors. The strategies and devices to be used may be determined by a project-specific engineering study, or determined from agency guidelines that define strategies and approaches to be used based on project and highway characteristics and factors. The types of measures and strategies to be used are not mutually exclusive, and should be considered in combination as appropriate based on characteristics and factors such as those listed below:

(1) Project scope and duration;

(2) Anticipated traffic speeds through the work zone;

(3) Anticipated traffic volume;

(4) Vehicle mix;

(5) Type of work (as related to worker exposure and crash risks);

(6) Distance between traffic and workers, and extent of worker exposure;

(7) Escape paths available for workers to avoid a vehicle intrusion into the work space;

(8) Time of day (e.g., night work);

(9) Work area restrictions (including impact on worker exposure);

(10) Consequences from/to road users resulting from roadway departure;

(11) Potential hazard to workers and road users presented by device itself and during device placement and removal;

(12) Geometrics that may increase crash risks (e.g., poor sight distance, sharp curves);

(13) Access to/from work space;

(14) Roadway classification; and

(15) Impacts on project cost and duration.

(c) Uniformed Law Enforcement Policy. Each agency, in partnership with the FHWA, shall develop a policy addressing the use of uniformed law enforcement on Federal-aid highway projects. The policy may consist of processes, procedures, and/or guidance. The processes, procedures, and/or guidance should address the following:

(1) Basic interagency agreements between the highway agency and appropriate law enforcement agencies to address work zone enforcement needs;

(2) Interaction between highway and law-enforcement agency during project planning and development;

(3) Conditions where law enforcement involvement in work zone traffic control may be needed or beneficial, and criteria to determine the project-specific need for law enforcement;

(4) General nature of law enforcement services to be provided, and procedures to determine project-specific services;

(5) Appropriate work zone safety and mobility training for the officers, consistent with the training requirements in 23 CFR 630.1008(d);

(6) Procedures for interagency and project-level communications between highway agency and law enforcement personnel; and

(7) Reimbursement agreements for law enforcement service.

§ 630.1108 Work zone safety management measures and strategies.

(a) *Positive Protection Devices.* The need for longitudinal traffic barrier and other positive protection devices shall be based on an engineering study. The engineering study may be used to develop positive protection guidelines for the agency, or to determine the measures to be applied on an individual project. The engineering study should be based on consideration of the factors and characteristics described in section 630.1106(b). At a minimum, positive protection devices shall be considered in work zone situations that place workers at increased risk from motorized traffic, and where positive protection devices offer the highest potential for increased safety for workers and road users, such as:

(1) Work zones that provide workers no means of escape from motorized traffic (e.g., tunnels, bridges, etc.);

(2) Long duration work zones (e.g., two weeks or more) resulting in substantial worker exposure to motorized traffic;

(3) Projects with high anticipated operating speeds (e.g., 45 mph or greater), especially when combined with high traffic volumes;

(4) Work operations that place workers close to travel lanes open to traffic; and

(5) Roadside hazards, such as drop-offs or unfinished bridge decks, that will remain in place overnight or longer.

(b) *Exposure Control Measures.* Exposure Control Measures should be considered where appropriate to avoid or minimize worker exposure to motorized traffic and exposure of road users to work activities, while also providing adequate consideration to the potential impacts on mobility. A wide range of measures may be appropriate for use on individual projects, such as:

(1) Full road closures;

(2) Ramp closures;

(3) Median crossovers;

(4) Full or partial detours or diversions;

(5) Protection of work zone setup and removal operations using rolling road blocks;

(6) Performing work at night or during off-peak periods when traffic volumes are lower; and

(7) Accelerated construction techniques.

(c) *Other Traffic Control Measures.* Other Traffic Control Measures should be given appropriate consideration for use in work zones to reduce work zone crashes and risks and consequences of motorized traffic intrusion into the work space. These measures, which are not mutually exclusive and should be considered in combination as appropriate, include a wide range of other traffic control measures such as:

(1) Effective, credible signing;

(2) Changeable message signs;

(3) Arrow panels;

(4) Warning flags and lights on signs;

(5) Longitudinal and lateral buffer space;

(6) Trained flaggers and spotters;

(7) Enhanced flagger station setups;

(8) Intrusion alarms;

(9) Rumble strips;

(10) Pace or pilot vehicle;

(11) High quality work zone pavement markings and removal of misleading markings;

(12) Channelizing device spacing reduction;

(13) Longitudinal channelizing barricades;

(14) Work zone speed management (including changes to the regulatory speed and/or variable speed limits);

(15) Law enforcement;

(16) Automated speed enforcement (where permitted by State/local laws);

(17) Drone radar;

(18) Worker and work vehicle/equipment visibility;

(19) Worker training;

(20) Public information and traveler information; and

(21) Temporary traffic signals.

(d) *Uniformed Law Enforcement Officers.* (1) A number of conditions may indicate the need for or benefit of uniformed law enforcement in work zones. The presence of a uniformed law enforcement officer and marked law enforcement vehicle in view of motorized traffic on a highway project can affect driver behavior, helping to maintain appropriate speeds and improve driver alertness through the work zone. However, such law enforcement presence is not a substitute for the temporary traffic control devices required by Part 6 of the MUTCD. In general, the need for law enforcement is greatest on projects with high traffic speeds and volumes, and where the work zone is expected to result in substantial disruption to or changes in normal traffic flow patterns. Specific project conditions should be examined to determine the need for or potential benefit of law enforcement, such as the following:

(i) Frequent worker presence adjacent to high-speed traffic without positive protection devices;

(ii) Traffic control setup or removal that presents significant risks to workers and road users;

(iii) Complex or very short term changes in traffic patterns with significant potential for road user confusion or worker risk from traffic exposure;

(iv) Night work operations that create substantial traffic safety risks for workers and road users;

(v) Existing traffic conditions and crash histories that indicate a potential for substantial safety and congestion impacts related to the work zone activity, and that may be mitigated by improved driver behavior and awareness of the work zone;

(vi) Work zone operations that require brief stoppage of all traffic in one or both directions;

(vii) High-speed roadways where unexpected or sudden traffic queuing is anticipated, especially if the queue forms a considerable distance in advance of the work zone or immediately adjacent to the work space; and

(viii) Other work site conditions where traffic presents a high risk for workers and road users, such that the risk may be reduced by improving road user behavior and awareness.

(2) Costs associated with the provision of uniformed law enforcement to help protect workers and road users, and to maintain safe and efficient travel through highway work zones, are eligible for Federal-aid participation. Federal-aid eligibility excludes law enforcement activities that would normally be expected in and around highway problem areas requiring routine or ongoing law enforcement traffic control and enforcement activities. Payment for the services of uniformed law enforcement in work zones may be included in the construction contract, or be provided by direct reimbursement from the highway agency to the law enforcement agency. When payment is included through the construction contract, the contractor will be responsible for reimbursing the law enforcement agency, and in turn will recover those costs through contract pay items. Direct interagency reimbursement may be made on a project-specific basis, or on a program-wide basis that considers the overall level of services to be provided by the law enforcement agency. Contract pay items for law enforcement service may be either unit price or lump sum items. Unit price items should be utilized when the highway agency can estimate and control the quantity of law enforcement services required on the project. The use of lump sum payment should be limited to situations where the quantity of services is directly affected by the contractor's choice of project scheduling and chosen manner of staging and performing the work. Innovative payment items may also be considered when they offer an advantage to both the highway agency and the contractor. When reimbursement to the law enforcement agency is made by interagency transfer of funds, the highway agency should establish a program-level or project-level budget that is adequate to meet anticipated program or project needs, and include provisions to address unplanned needs and other contingencies.

(e) *Work Vehicles and Equipment.* In addition to addressing risks to workers and road users from motorized traffic, the agency processes, procedures, and/or guidance established in accordance with 23 CFR 630.1006 should also address safe means for work vehicles and equipment to enter and exit traffic lanes and for delivery of construction materials to the work space, based on individual project characteristics and factors.

(f) *Payment for Traffic Control.* Consistent with the requirements of 23 CFR 630.1012, Project-level Procedures, project plans, specifications and estimates (PS&Es) shall include appropriate pay item provisions for implementing the project Transportation Management Plan (TMP), which includes a Temporary Traffic Control (TTC) plan, either through method or performance based specifications. Pay item provisions include, but are not limited to, the following:

(1) Payment for work zone traffic control features and operations shall not be incidental to the contract, or included in payment for other items of

work not related to traffic control and safety;

(2) As a minimum, separate pay items shall be provided for major categories of traffic control devices, safety features, and work zone safety activities, including but not limited to positive protection devices, and uniformed law enforcement activities when funded through the project;

(3) For method based specifications, the specifications and other PS&E documents should provide sufficient details such that the quantity and types of devices and the overall effort required to implement and maintain the TMP can be determined;

(4) For method-based specifications, unit price pay items, lump sum pay items, or a combination thereof may be used;

(5) Lump sum payment should be limited to items for which an estimate of the actual quantity required is provided in the PS&E or for items where the actual quantity required is dependent upon the contractor's choice of work scheduling and methodology;

(6) For Lump Sum items, a contingency provision should be included such that additional payment is provided if the quantity or nature of the required work changes, either an increase or decrease, due to circumstances beyond the control of the contractor;

(7) Unit price payment should be provided for those items over which the contractor has little or no control over the quantity, and no firm estimate of quantities is provided in the PS&Es, but over which the highway agency has control of the actual quantity to be required during the project;

(8) Specifications should clearly indicate how placement, movement/relocation, and maintenance of traffic control devices and safety features will be compensated; and

(9) The specifications should include provisions to require and enforce contractor compliance with the contract provisions relative to implementation and maintenance of the project TMP and related traffic control items. Enforcement provisions may include remedies such as liquidated damages, work suspensions, or withholding payment for noncompliance.

§ 630.1110 Maintenance of temporary traffic control devices.

To provide for the continued effectiveness of temporary traffic control devices, each agency shall develop and implement quality guidelines to help maintain the quality and adequacy of the temporary traffic control devices for the duration of the project. Agencies may choose to adopt existing quality guidelines such as those developed by the American Traffic Safety Services Association (ATSSA) or other state highway agencies.[1] A level of inspection necessary to provide ongoing compliance with the quality guidelines shall be provided.

PART 633—REQUIRED CONTRACT PROVISIONS

Subpart A—Federal-Aid Construction Contracts (Other Than Appalachian Contracts)

Subpart B—Federal-Aid Contracts (Appalachian Contracts)

[1] The American Traffic Safety Services Association's (ATSSA) Quality Guidelines for Work Zone Traffic Control Devices uses photos and written descriptions to help judge when a traffic control device has outlived its usefulness. These guidelines are available for purchase from ATSSA through the following URL: *http://www.atssa.com/store/bc_item_detail.jsp?productId=1.* Similar guidelines are available from various State highway agencies. The Illinois Department of Transportation "Quality Standards for Work Zone Traffic Control Devices" is available online at *http://dot.state.il.us/workzone/wztcd2004r.pdf.* The Minnesota Department of Transportation "Quality Standards—Methods to determine whether the various traffic control devices are Acceptable, Marginal, or Unacceptable" is available online at *http://www.dot.state.mn.us/trafficeng/otepubl/fieldmanual2007/FM–2007–QualityStandards.pdf.*

Subpart A—Federal-Aid Construction Contracts (Other Than Appalachian Contracts)

AUTHORITY: 23 U.S.C. 114 and 315; 49 CFR 1.48.

SOURCE: 52 FR 36920, Oct. 2, 1987, unless otherwise noted.

§ 633.101 Purpose.

To prescribe for Federal-aid highway proposals and construction contracts the method for inclusion of required contract provisions of existing regulations which cover employment, nonsegregated facilities, record of materials and supplies, subletting or assigning the contract, safety, false statements concerning highway projects, termination of a contract, and implementation of the Clean Air Act and the Federal Water Pollution Control Act, and other provisions as shall from time-to-time be required by law and regulation as conditions of Federal assistance.

§ 633.102 Applicability.

(a) The required contract provisions and the required proposal notices apply to all Federal-aid construction contracts other than Appalachian construction contracts.

(b) Form FHWA-1273, "Required Contract Provisions, Federal-aid Construction Contracts," contains required contract provisions and required proposal notices that are required by regulations promulgated by the FHWA or other Federal agencies. The required contract provisions of Form FHWA-1273 shall be physically incorporated in each Federal-aid highway construction contract other than Appalachian construction contracts (see § 633.104 for availability of form).

(c) [Reserved]

(d) The required contract provisions contained in Form FHWA-1273 shall apply to all work performed on the contract by the contractor's own organization and to all work performed on the contract by piecework, station work, or by subcontract.

(e) The contractor shall insert in each subcontract, except as excluded by law or regulation, the required contract provisions contained in Form FHWA-1273 and further require their inclusion in any lower tier subcontract that may in turn be made. The required contract provisions of Form FHWA-1273 shall not be incorporated by reference in any case. The prime contractor shall be responsible for compliance by any subcontractor or lower tier subcontractor with the requirements contained in the provisions of Form FHWA-1273.

(f) The State highway agency (SHA) shall include the notices concerning certification of nonsegregated facilities and implementation of the Clean Air Act and Federal Water Pollution Control Act, pursuant to 40 CFR part 15, in all bidding proposals for Federal-aid highway construction projects. As the notices are reproduced in Form FHWA-1273, the SHA may include Form FHWA-1273 in its entirety to meet this requirement.

[52 FR 36920, Oct. 2, 1987, as amended at 69 FR 7118, Feb. 13, 2004]

§ 633.103 Regulatory authority.

All required contract provisions contained in Form FHWA-1273 are requirements of regulations promulgated by the FHWA or other Federal agencies. The authority for each provision will be cited in the text of Form FHWA-1273.

§ 633.104 Availability.

(a) Form FHWA-1273 will be maintained by the FHWA and as regulatory revisions occur, the form will be updated.

(b) Current copies of Form FHWA–1273, Required Contract Provisions, will be made available to the SHAs by the FHWA.

Subpart B—Federal-Aid Contracts (Appalachian Contracts)

AUTHORITY: 40 U.S.C. App. 201, 402; 23 U.S.C. 315; 49 CFR 1.48(b)(35).

SOURCE: 39 FR 35146, Sept. 30, 1974, unless otherwise noted.

§ 633.201 Purpose.

The purpose of the regulations in this subpart is to establish policies and outline procedures for administering projects and funds for the Appalachian Development Highway System and Appalachian local access roads.

§ 633.202 Definitions.

(a) The word *Commission* means the Appalachian Regional Commission (ARC) established by the Appalachian Regional Development Act of 1965, as amended (Act).

(b) The term *division administrator*'' means the chief Federal Highway Administration (FHWA) official assigned to conduct FHWA business in a particular State.

[39 FR 35156, Sept. 30, 1974, as amended at 40 FR 49084, Oct. 21, 1975; 41 FR 8769, Mar. 1, 1976]

§ 633.203 Applicability of existing laws, regulations, and directives.

The provisions of title 23 U.S.C., that are applicable to the construction and maintenance of Federal-aid primary and secondary highways, and which the Secretary of Transportation determines are not inconsistent with the Act, shall apply, respectively, to the development highway system and the local access roads. In addition, the Regulations for the Administration of Federal-aid for Highways (title 23, Code of Federal Regulations) and directives implementing applicable provisions of title 23 U.S.C., where not inconsistent with the Act, shall be applicable to such projects.

§ 633.204 Fiscal allocation and obligations.

(a) Federal assistance to any project under the Act shall be as determined by the Commission, but in no event shall such Federal assistance exceed 70 per centum of the cost of such a project.

(b) The division administrator's authorization to proceed with the proposed work shall establish obligation of Federal funds with regard to a particular project.

[39 FR 35156, Sept. 30, 1974, as amended at 40 FR 49084, Oct. 21, 1975; 41 FR 8769, Mar. 1, 1976]

§ 633.205 Prefinancing.

(a) Under the provisions of subsection 201(h) of the Act, projects located on the Appalachian Development Highway System including preliminary engineering, right-of-way, and/or construction may be programed and advanced with interim State financing.

(b) Program approvals, plans, specifications, and estimates (PS&E) approval, authorizations to proceed, concurrence in award of contracts, and all other notifications to the State of advancement of a project shall include the statement, ''There is no commitment or obligation on the part of the United States to provide funds for this highway improvement. However, this project is eligible for Federal reimbursement when sufficient funds are available from the amounts allocated by the Appalachian Regional Commission.''

§ 633.206 Project agreements.

(a) Project agreements executed for projects under the Appalachian program shall contain the following paragraphs:

(1) ''For projects constructed under section 201 of the Appalachian Regional Development Act of 1965, as amended, the State highway department agrees to comply with all applicable provisions of said Act, regulations issued thereunder, and policies and procedures promulgated by the Appalachian Regional Commission, and the Federal Highway Administration. Inasmuch as a primary objective of the Appalachian Regional Development Act of 1965 is to

provide employment, the State highway department further agrees that in addition to the other applicable provisions of title 49, Code of Federal Regulations, part 21, § 21.5(c)(1), and paragraphs (2)(iii) and (2)(v) of appendix C thereof, shall be applicable to all employment practices in connection with this project, and to the State's employment practices with respect to those employees connected with the Appalachian Highway Program."

(2) "For projects constructed on a section of an Appalachian development route not already on the Federal-aid Primary System, the State highway department agrees to add the section to the Federal-aid Primary System prior to, or upon completion of, construction accomplished with Appalachian funds."

(b) For prefinanced projects, the following additional provision shall be incorporated into the project agreement: "Project for Construction on the Appalachian Development Highway System in Advance of the Appropriation of Funds. This project, to be constructed pursuant to subsection 201(h) of the Appalachian Regional Development Act Amendments of 1967, will be constructed in accordance with all procedures and requirements and standards applicable to projects on the Appalachian Development Highway System financed with the aid of Appalachian funds. No obligation of Appalachian funds is created by this agreement, its purpose and intent being to provide that, upon application by the State highway department, and approval thereof by the Federal Highway Administration, any Appalachian development highway funds made available to the State by the Appalachian Regional Commission subsequent to the date of this agreement may be used to reimburse the State for the Federal share of the cost of work done on the project."

§ 633.207 Construction labor and materials.

(a) Construction and materials shall be in accordance with the State highway department standard construction specifications approved for use on Federal-aid primary projects and special provisions and supplemental specifications amendatory thereto approved for use on the specific projects.

(b) The provisions of 23 U.S.C. 324 and of title VI of the Civil Rights Act of 1964 (78 Stat. 252; 42 U.S.C. 2000d–2000d-4) and the implementing regulations in 49 CFR part 21, including the provisions of § 21.5(c)(1), and paragraphs (2)(iii) and (2)(v) of appendix C thereof relative to employment practices, shall be applicable to all types of contracts listed in appendix A.

(c) The "Required Contract Provisions, Appalachian Development Highway System and Local Access Roads Construction Contracts," Form PR-1316 (appendix B), shall be included in all construction contracts awarded under the Act.

(d) The required contract provisions set forth in Form PR-1317 (appendix C) shall be included in all types of contracts described in appendix A, other than construction contracts.

(e) In the design and construction of highways and roads under the Act, the State may give special preference to the use of mineral resource materials native to the Appalachian region. The provisions of § 635.409 of this chapter shall not apply to projects under the Act to the extent such provisions are inconsistent with sections 201(d) and (e) of the Act.

[39 FR 35146, Sept. 30, 1974, as amended at 40 FR 49084, Oct. 21, 1975; 41 FR 36204, Aug. 27, 1976]

§ 633.208 Maintenance.

Maintenance of all highway projects constructed under the Act, whether on the development system or local access roads, shall be the responsibility of the State. The State may arrange for maintenance of such roads or portions thereof, by agreement with a local governmental unit.

§ 633.209 Notices to prospective Federal-aid construction contractors.

The State highway department shall include the notices set forth in appendix D in all future bidding proposals for Appalachian Development System and Appalachian local access roads construction contracts.

§ 633.210 Termination of contract.

All contracts exceeding $2,500 shall contain suitable provisions for termination by the State, including the manner in which the termination will be effected and the basis for settlement. In addition, such contracts shall describe conditions under which the contract may be terminated for default as well as conditions where the contract may be terminated because of circumstances beyond the control of the contractor.

§ 633.211 Implementation of the Clean Air Act and the Federal Water Pollution Control Act.

Pursuant to regulations of the Environmental Protection Agency (40 CFR part 15) implementing requirements with respect to the Clean Air Act and the Federal Water Pollution Control Act are included in appendix B to this part.

[40 FR 49084, Oct. 21, 1975]

Appendix A to Subpart B of Part 633—Types of Contracts to Which the Civil Rights Act of 1964 Is Applicable

Section 324 of title 23 U.S.C., the Civil Rights Act of 1964, and the implementing regulations of the Department of Transportation (49 CFR part 21), including the provisions of paragraphs (2)(iii) and (2)(v) of appendix C thereof relative to employment practices, are applicable to the following types of contracts awarded by State highway departments, contractors, and first tier subcontractors, including those who supply materials and lease equipment:

1. Construction.
2. Planning.
3. Research.
4. Highway Safety.
5. Engineering.
6. Property Management.
7. Fee contracts and other commitments with persons for services incidental to the acquisition of right-of-way including, but not limited to:

a. Advertising contracts.

b. Agreements for economic studies.

c. Contracts for surveys and plats.

d. Contracts for abstracts of title certificates and title insurance.

e. Contracts for appraisal services and expert witness fees.

f. Contracts to negotiate for the acquisition of right-of-way.

g. Contracts for disposal of improvements and property management services.

h. Contracts for employment of fee attorneys for right-of-way procurement, or preparation and trial of condemnation cases.

i. Contracts for escrow and closing services.

[40 FR 49084, Oct. 21, 1975]

Appendix B to Subpart B of Part 633—Required Contract Provisions, Appalachian Development Highway System and Local Access Roads Construction Contracts

I. *Application.*

1. These contract provisions shall apply to all work performed on the contract by the contractor with his own organization and with the assistance of workmen under his immediate superintendence and to all work performed on the contract by piecework, station work, or by subcontract.

2. Except as otherwise provided in sections II, III, and IV hereof, the contractor shall insert in each of his subcontracts all of the stipulations contained in these Required Contract Provisions and also a clause requiring his subcontractors to include these Required Contract Provisions in any lower tier subcontracts which they may enter into, together with a clause requiring the inclusion of these provisions in any further subcontracts that may in turn be made. The Required Contract Provisions shall in no instance be incorporated by reference.

3. A breach of any of the stipulations contained in these Required Contract Provisions may be grounds for termination of the contract.

4. A breach of the following clauses may also be grounds for debarment as provided in 29 CFR 5.6(b):

Section 1, paragraph 2.

Section VI, paragraphs 1, 2, 3, 5 and 8a.

Section VII, paragraphs 1, 5a, 5b and 5d.

II. *Employment preference.*

1. During the performance of this contract, the contractor undertaking to do work which is, or reasonably may be, done as onsite work, shall give preference to qualified persons who regularly reside in the labor area as designated by the United States Department of Labor wherein the contract

work is situated, or the subregion, or the Appalachian counties of the State wherein the contract work is situated, except:

a. To the extent that qualified persons regularly residing in the area are not available.

b. For the reasonable needs of the contractor to employ supervisory or specially experienced personnel necessary to assure an efficient execution of the contract work.

c. For the obligation of the contractor to offer employment to present or former employees as the result of a lawful collective bargaining contract, provided that the number of nonresident persons employed under this subparagraph 1c shall not exceed 20 percent of the total number of employees employed by the contractor on the contract work, except as provided in subparagraph 4 below.

2. The contractor shall place a job order with the State Employment Service indicating (a) the classifications of laborers, mechanics and other employees he anticipates will be required to perform the contract work, (b) the number of employees required in each classification, (c) the date on which he estimates such employees will be required, and (d) any other pertinent information required by the State Employment Service to complete the job order form. The job order may be placed with the State Employment Service in writing or by telephone. If during the course of the contract work, the information submitted by the contractor in the original job order is substantially modified, he shall promptly notify the State Employment Service.

3. The contractor shall give full consideration to all qualified job applicants referred to him by the State Employment Service. The contractor is not required to grant employment to any job applicants who, in his opinion, are not qualified to perform the classification of work required.

4. If, within one week following the placing of a job order by the contractor with the State Employment Service, the State Employment Service is unable to refer any qualified job applicants to the contractor, or less than the number requested, the State Employment Service will forward a certificate to the contractor indicating the unavailability of applicants. Such certificate shall be made a part of the contractor's permanent project records. Upon receipt of this certificate, the contractor may employ persons who do not normally reside in the labor area to fill the positions covered by the certificate, notwithstanding the provisions of subparagraph 1c above.

5. The contractor shall include the provisions of section II-1 through II-4 in every subcontract for work which is, or reasonably may be, done as on-site work.

III. *Equal opportunity: employment practices.*

During the performance of this contract, the contractor agrees as follows:

a. The contractor will not discriminate against any employee or applicant for employment because of race, color, religion, sex, or national origin. The contractor will take affirmative action to ensure that applicants are employed, and that employees are treated during employment without regard to their race, color, religion, sex, or national origin. Such action shall include, but not be limited to the following: Employment, upgrading, demotion or transfer; recruitment or recruitment advertising; layoffs or termination; rates of pay or other forms of compensation; and selection of training, including apprenticeship. The contractor agrees to post in conspicuous places, available to employees and applicants for employment, notices to be provided by the State highway department setting forth the provisions of this nondiscrimination clause.

b. The contractor will, in all solicitations or advertisements for employees placed by or on behalf of the contractor, state that all qualified applicants will receive consideration for employment without regard to race, color, religion, sex, or national origin.

c. The contractor will send to each labor union or representative of workers with which he has a collective bargaining agreement or other contract or understanding, a notice to be provided by the State highway department advising the said labor union or workers' representative of the contractor's commitments under this section III and shall post copies of the notice in conspicuous places available to employees and applicants for employment.

d. The contractor will comply with all provisions of Executive Order 11246 of September 24, 1965, and of the rules, regulations and relevant orders of the Secretary of Labor.

e. The contractor will furnish all information and reports required by Executive Order 11246 of September 24, 1965, and by rules, regulations and orders of the Secretary of Labor or pursuant thereto, and will permit access to his books, records and accounts by the Federal Highway Administration and the Secretary of Labor for purposes of investigation to ascertain compliance with such rules, regulations and orders.

f. In the event of the contractor's noncompliance with the nondiscrimination clauses of this contract or with any of the said rules, regulations or orders, this contract may be canceled, terminated or suspended in whole or in part and the contractor may be declared ineligible for further Government contracts or federally-assisted construction contracts in accordance with procedures authorized in Executive Order 11246 of September 24, 1965, and such other sanctions may be imposed and remedies invoked as provided in Executive Order 11246 of

September 24, 1965, or by rule, regulation or order of the Secretary of Labor, or as otherwise provided by law.

g. The contractor will include the provisions of this section III in every subcontract or purchase order unless exempted by rules, regulations or orders of the Secretary of Labor issued pursuant to section 204 of Executive Order 11246 of September 24, 1965, so that such provisions will be binding upon each subcontractor or vendor. The contractor will take such action with respect to any subcontract or purchase order as the State Highway Department or the Federal Highway Administration may direct as a means of enforcing such provisions including sanctions for noncompliance: *Provided, however,* That in the event a contractor becomes involved in, or is threatened with litigation with a subcontractor or vendor as a result of such direction by the Federal Highway Administration, the contractor may request the United States to enter into such litigation to protect the interests of the United States.

IV. *Equal opportunity selection of subcontractors, procurement of materials, and leasing of equipment.*

During the performance of this contract, the contractor, for itself, its assignees and successors in interest (hereinafter referred to as the *contractor), agrees as follows:*

1. *Compliance with regulations.* The contractor shall comply with the provisions of 23 U.S.C. 324 and with the regulations relative to nondiscrimination in Federally-assisted programs of the Department of Transportation (hereinafter, "DOT") title 49, Code of Federal Regulations, part 21, as they may be amended from time to time (hereinafter referred to as the Regulations), which are herein incorporated by reference and made a part of this contract.

2. *Nondiscrimination.* The contractor, with regard to the work performed by it during the contract, shall not discriminate on the grounds of race, color, sex, or national origin in the selection and retention of subcontractors, including procurements of materials and leases of equipments. The contractor shall not participate either directly or indirectly in the discrimination prohibited by section 21.5 of the Regulations, including employment practices.

3. *Solicitations for subcontracts including procurement of materials and equipment.* In all solicitations either by competitive bidding or negotiation made by the contractor for work to be performed under a subcontract, including procurements of materials or leases of equipment, each potential subcontractor or supplier, shall be notified by the contractor of the contractor's obligations under this contract and the Regulations relative to nondiscrimination on the grounds of race, color, sex, or national origin.

4. *Information and reports.* The contractor shall provide all information and reports required by the Regulations, or directives issued pursuant thereto, and shall permit access to its books, records, accounts, other sources of information, and its facilities as may be determined by the State highway department or the Federal Highway Administration to be pertinent to ascertain compliance with such Regulations, orders and instructions. Where any information required of a contractor is in the exclusive possession of another who fails or refuses to furnish this information, the contractor shall so certify to the State highway department, or the Federal Highway Administration, as appropriate, and shall set forth what efforts it has made to obtain the information.

5. *Sanctions for noncompliance.* In the event of the contractor's noncompliance with the nondiscrimination provisions of this contract, the State highway department shall impose such contract sanctions as it or the Federal Highway Administration may determine to be appropriate, including, but not limited to:

a. Withholding of payments to the contractor under the contract until the contractor complies, and/or

b. Cancellation, termination or suspension of the contract, in whole or in part.

6. *Incorporation of provisions.* The contractor will include the provisions of paragraphs (1) through (6) in every subcontract, including procurements of materials and leases of equipment, unless exempt by the Regulations, or directives issued pursuant thereto. The contractor shall take such action with respect to any subcontract or procurement, as the State highway department or the Federal Highway Administration may direct as a means of enforcing such provisions including sanctions for noncompliance: *Provided, however,* That, in the event a contractor becomes involved in, or is threatened with, litigation with a subcontractor or supplier, as a result of such direction, the contractor may request the State to enter into such litigation to protect the interests of the State, and, in addition, the contractor may request the United States to enter into such litigation to protect the interests of the United States.

V. *Nonsegregated facilities.*

(Applicable to Federal-aid construction contracts and related subcontracts exceeding $10,000 which are not exempt from the Equal Opportunity clause.)

By submission of this bid, the execution of this contract or subcontract, or the consummation of this material supply agreement, as appropriate, the bidder, Federal-aid construction contractor, subcontractor, or material supplier, as appropriate, certifies that he does not maintain or provide for his employees any segregated facilities at any of his establishments, and that he does not permit his employees to perform their services at any location, under his control, where segregated facilities are maintained. He certifies further that he will not maintain or provide for his employees any segregated facilities at any of his establishments, and that he will not permit his employees to perform their services at any location, under his control, where segregated facilities are maintained. He agrees that a breach of this certification is a violation of the Equal Opportunity clause in this contract. As used in this certification, the term *segregated facilities* means any waiting rooms, work areas, restrooms and washrooms, restaurants and other eating areas, timeclocks, locker rooms and other storage or dressing areas, parking lots, drinking fountains, recreation or entertainment areas, transportation, and housing facilities provided for employees which are segregated by explicit directive or are in fact segregated on the basis of race, creed, color, or national origin, because of habit, local custom, or otherwise. He agrees that (except where he has obtained identical certifications from proposed subcontractors and material suppliers for specific time periods), he will obtain identical certifications from proposed subcontractors or material suppliers prior to the award of subcontracts or the consummation of material supply agreements, exceeding $10,000 which are not exempt from the provisions of the Equal Opportunity clause, and that he will retain such certification in his files.

VI. *Payment of predetermined minimum wages.*

1. *General.* All mechanics and laborers employed or working upon the site of the work will be paid unconditionally and not less than once a week, and without subsequent deduction or rebate on any account, except such payroll deductions as are permitted by regulations issued by the Secretary of Labor under the Copeland Act (29 CFR part 3), the full amounts due at time of payment computed at wage rates not less than those contained in the wage determination decision of the Secretary of Labor which is attached hereto and made a part thereof, regardless of any contractual relationship which may be alleged to exist between the contractor and such laborers and mechanics; and the wage determination decision shall be posted by the contractor at the site of the work in a prominent place where it can be easily seen by the workers. For the purpose of this clause, contributions made or costs reasonably anticipated under section 1(b)(2) of the Davis-Bacon Act on behalf of laborers or mechanics are considered wages paid to such laborers or mechanics, subject to the provisions of section VI, paragraph 3b, hereof. Also for the purpose of this clause, regular contributions made or costs incurred for more than a weekly period under plans, funds, or programs, but covering the particular weekly period, are deemed to be constructively made or incurred during such weekly period.

2. *Classifications*—a. The State highway department contracting officer shall require that any class of laborers or mechanics which is not listed in the wage determination and which is to be employed under the contract, shall be classified or reclassified conformably to the wage determination, and a report of the action taken shall be sent by the State highway department contracting officer to the Secretary of Labor.

b. In the event the interested parties cannot agree on the proper classification or reclassification of a particular class of laborers and mechanics to be used, the question accompanied by the recommendation of the State highway department contracting officer shall be referred to the Secretary for final determination.

3. *Payment of fringe benefits*—a. The State highway department contracting officer shall require, whenever the minimum wage rate prescribed in the contract for a class of laborers or mechanics includes a fringe benefit which is not expressed as an hourly wage rate and the contractor is obligated to pay a cash equivalent of such a fringe benefit, an hourly cash equivalent thereof to be established. In the event the interested parties cannot agree upon a cash equivalent of the fringe benefits, the question, accompanied by the recommendation of the contracting officer, shall be referred to the Secretary of Labor for determination.

b. If the contractor does not make payments to a trustee or other third person, he may consider as part of the wage of any laborer or mechanic the amount of any costs reasonably anticipated in providing benefits under a plan or program of a type expressly listed in the wage determination decision of the Secretary of Labor which is part of this contract: *Provided, however,* The Secretary of Labor has found, upon the written request of the contractor, that the applicable standards of the Davis-Bacon Act have been met. The Secretary of Labor may require the contractor to set aside in a separate account assets for the meeting of obligations under the plan or program.

4. *Payment of excess wages.* While the wage rates shown are the minimum rates required by the contract to be paid during its life, this is not a representation that labor can be obtained at these rates. No increase in the contract price shall be allowed or authorized on account of the payment of wage rates in excess of those listed herein.

5. *Apprentices and trainees (Programs of Department of Labor).* a. Apprentices will be permitted to work at less than the predetermined rate for the work they performed when they are employed and individually

registered in a bona fide apprenticeship program registered with the U.S. Department of Labor, Manpower Administration, Bureau of Apprenticeship and Training, or with a State Apprenticeship Agency recognized by the Bureau, or if a person is employed in his first 90 days of probationary employment as an apprentice in such an apprenticeship program, who is not individually registered in the program, but who has been certified by the Bureau of Apprenticeship and Training or a State Apprenticeship Agency (where appropriate) to be eligible for probationary employment as an apprentice. The allowable ratio of apprentices to journeymen in any craft classification shall not be greater than the ratio permitted to the contractor as to his entire work force under the registered program. Any employee listed on a payroll at an apprentice wage rate, who is not a trainee as defined in 29 CFR 5.2(c)(2) or is not registered or otherwise employed as stated above, shall be paid the wage rate determined by the Secretary of Labor for the classification of work he actually performed. The contractor or subcontractor will be required to furnish to the State highway department or to a representative of the Wage-Hour Division of the U.S. Department of Labor written evidence of the registration of his program and apprentices as well as the appropriate ratios and wage rates (expressed in percentages of the journeyman hourly rates), for the area of construction prior to using any apprentices on the contract work. The wage rate paid apprentices shall be not less than the appropriate percentage of the journeyman's rate contained in the applicable wage determination.

b. Trainees, except as provided in 29 CFR 5.15, will not be permitted to work at less than the predetermined rate for the work performed unless they are employed pursuant to and individually registered in a program which has received prior approval, evidenced by formal certification, by the U.S. Department of Labor, Manpower Administration, Bureau of Apprenticeship and Training. The ratio of trainees to journeymen shall not be greater than permitted under the plan approved by the Bureau of Apprenticeship and Training. Every trainee must be paid at not less than the rate specified in the approved program for his level of progress. Any employee listed on the payroll at a trainee rate who is not registered and participating in a training plan approved by the Bureau of Apprenticeship and Training shall be paid not less than the wage rate determined by the Secretary of Labor for the classification of work he actually performed. The contractor or subcontractor will be required to furnish the State highway department or a representative of the Wage-Hour Division of the U.S. Department of Labor written evidence of the certification of his program, the registration of the trainees, and the ratios and wage rates prescribed in that program. In the event the Bureau of Apprenticeship and Training withdraws approval of a training program, the contractor will no longer be permitted to utilize trainees at less than the applicable predetermined rate for the work performed until an acceptable program is approved.

c. The utilization of apprentices, trainees and journeymen shall be in conformity with the equal employment opportunity requirements of Executive Order 11246, as amended, and 29 CFR part 30.

6. *Apprentices and trainees (Programs of Department of Transportation).* Apprentices and trainees working under apprenticeship and skill training programs which have been certified by the Secretary of Transportation as promoting equal opportunity in connection with Federal-aid highway construction programs are not subject to the requirements of section VI, paragraph 5 above. The straight time hourly wage rates for apprentices and trainees under such programs will be established by the particular programs.

7. *Withholding for unpaid wages.* The State highway department contracting officer may withhold or cause to be withheld from the contractor so much of the accrued payments or advances as may be considered necessary to pay laborers, mechanics, (including apprentices and trainees) watchmen, or guards employed by the contractor or any subcontractor on the work the full amount of wages required by the contract. In the event of failure to pay any laborer, mechanic, (including apprentices and trainees) watchman or guard employed or working on the site of the work, all or part of the wages required by the contract, the State highway department contracting officer may, after written notice to the contractor, take such action as may be necessary to cause the suspension of any further payment, advance, or guarantee of funds until such violations have ceased.

8. *Overtime requirements.* a. No contractor or subcontractor contracting for any part of the contract work which may require or involve the employment of laborers, mechanics, watchmen or guards (including apprentices and trainees described in paragraphs 5 and 6 above) shall require or permit any laborer, mechanic, watchman or guard in any workweek in which he is employed on such work, to work in excess of eight hours in any calendar day or in excess of forty hours in such workweek unless such laborer, mechanic, watchman or guard receives compensation at a rate not less than one and one-half times his basic rate of pay for all hours worked in excess of eight hours in any calendar day or in excess of forty hours in such workweek, as the case may be.

b. In the event of any violation of paragraph 8a, the contractor and any subcontractor responsible therefor shall be liable to any affected employee for his unpaid wages.

In addition, such contractor and subcontractor shall be liable to the United States for liquidated damages. Such liquidated damages shall be computed with respect to each individual laborer, mechanic, watchman or guard employed in violation of paragraph 8a, in the sum of $10 for each calendar day on which such employee was required or permitted to work in excess of eight hours or in excess of the standard workweek of forty hours without payment of the overtime wages required by paragraph 8a.

c. The State highway department contracting officer may withhold or cause to be withheld, from any moneys payable on account of work performed by the contractor or subcontractor, such sums as may administratively be determined to be necessary to satisfy any liabilities of such contractor or subcontractor for liquidated damages as provided in paragraph 8b.

VII. *Statements and payrolls.*

1. *Compliance with Copeland Regulations (29 CFR part 3).* The contractor shall comply with the Copeland Regulations (29 CFR part 3) of the Secretary of Labor which are herein incorporated by reference.

2. *Weekly statement.* Each contractor or subcontractor shall furnish each week a statement to the State highway department resident engineer with respect to the wages paid each of its employees, including apprentices and trainees described in section VI, paragraphs 5 and 6, and watchmen and guards on work covered by the Copeland Regulations during the preceding weekly payroll period. The statement shall be executed by the contractor or subcontractor or by an authorized officer or employee of the contractor or subcontractor who supervises the payment of wages. Contractors and subcontractors must use the certification set forth on U.S. Department of Labor Form WH–348, or the same certification appearing on the reverse of Optional U.S. Department of Labor Form WH–347, or on any form with identical wording.

3. *Final labor summary.* The contractor and each subcontractor shall furnish, upon the completion of the contract, a summary of all employment, indicating for the completed project the total hours worked and the total amount earned. This data shall be submitted to the State highway department resident engineer on Form PR–47 together with the data required in section VIII, hereof, relative to materials and supplies.

4. *Final certificate.* Upon completion of the contract, the contractor shall submit to the State highway department contracting officer, for transmission to the Federal Highway Administration with the voucher for final payment for any work performed under the contract, a certificate concerning wages and classifications for laborers, mechanics, watchmen and guards employed on the project, in the following form:

* * * * *

The undersigned, contractor on

(Project No.)

hereby certifies that all laborers, mechanics, apprentices, trainees, watchmen and guards employed by him or by any subcontractor performing work under the contract on the project have been paid wages at rates not less than those required by the contract provisions, and that the work performed by each such laborer, mechanic, apprentice or trainee conformed to the classifications set forth in the contract or training program provisions applicable to the wage rate paid.

Signature and title ____________________

* * * * *

5. *Payrolls and payroll records*—a. Payrolls and basic records relating thereto will be maintained during the course of the work and preserved for a period of three years thereafter for all laborers, mechanics, apprentices, trainees, watchmen and guards working at the site of the work.

b. The payroll records shall contain the name, social security number and address of each such employee, his correct classification, rates of pay (including rates of contributions or costs anticipated of the types described in section 1(b)(2) of the Davis-Bacon Act), daily and weekly number of hours worked, deductions made and actual wages paid. Whenever the Secretary of Labor, pursuant to section VI, paragraph 3.b., has found that the wages of any laborer or mechanic include the amount of any costs reasonably anticipated in providing benefits under a plan or program described in section I(b)(2)(B) of the Davis-Bacon Act, the contractor shall maintain records which show that the commitment to provide such benefits is enforceable, that the plan or program is financially responsible, and that the plan or program has been communicated in writing to the laborers or mechanics affected, and records which show the costs anticipated or the actual cost incurred in providing such benefits.

c. The payrolls shall contain the following information:

1. The employee's full name, address and social security number and a notation indicating whether the employee does, or does not, normally reside in the labor area as defined in section II, paragraph 1.a. (The employee's full name and social security number need only appear on the first payroll on which his name appears. The employee's address need only be shown on the first submitted payroll on which the employee's

name appears, unless a change of address necessitates a submittal to reflect the new address.)

2. The employee's classification.

3. Entries indicating the employee's basic hourly wage rate and, where applicable, the overtime hourly wage rate. The payroll should indicate separately the amounts of employee and employer contributions to fringe benefits funds and/or programs. Any fringe benefits paid to the employee in cash must be indicated. There is no prescribed or mandatory form for showing the above information on payrolls.

4. The employee's daily and weekly hours worked in each classification, including actual overtime hours worked (not adjusted).

5. The itemized deductions made and

6. The net wages paid.

d. The contractor will submit weekly a copy of all payrolls to the State highway department resident engineer. The copy shall be accompanied by a statement signed by the employer or his agent indicating that the payrolls are correct and complete, that the wage rates contained therein are not less than those determined by the Secretary of Labor and the classifications set forth for each laborer or mechanic conform with the work he performed. Submission of a weekly statement which is required under this contract by section VII, paragraph 2, and the Copeland Regulations of the Secretary of Labor (29 CFR part 3) and the filing with the initial payroll or any subsequent payroll of a copy of any findings by the Secretary of Labor pursuant to section VI, paragraph 3b, shall satisfy this requirement. The prime contractor shall be responsible for the submission of copies of payrolls of all subcontractors. The contractor will make the records required under the labor standards clauses of the contract available for inspection by authorized representatives of the State highway department, the Federal Highway Administration and the Department of Labor, and will permit such representatives to interview employees during working hours on the job.

e. The wages of labor shall be paid in legal tender of the United States, except that this condition will be considered satisfied if payment is made by negotiable check, on a solvent bank, which may be cashed readily by the employee in the local community for the full amount, without discount or collection charges of any kind. Where checks are used for payment, the contractor shall make all necessary arrangements for them to be cashed and shall given information regarding such arrangements.

f. No fee of any kind shall be asked or accepted by the contractor or any of his agents from any person as a condition of employment on the project.

g. No laborers shall be charged for any tools used in performing their respective duties except for reasonably avoidable loss or damage thereto.

h. Every employee on the work covered by this contract shall be permitted to lodge, board and trade where and with whom he elects and neither the contractor nor his agents, nor his employees shall, directly or indirectly, require as a condition of employment that an employee shall lodge, board or trade at a particular place or with a particular person.

i. No charge shall be made for any transportation furnished by the contractor, or his agents, to any person employed on the work.

j. No individual shall be employed as a laborer or mechanic on this contract except on a wage basis, but this shall not be construed to prohibit the rental of teams, trucks, or other equipment from individuals.

VIII. *Record of materials, supplies and labor.*

1. The contractor shall maintain a record of the total cost of all materials and supplies purchased for and incorporated in the work, and also of the quantities of those specific materials and supplies listed on Form PR–47 and in the units shown. Upon completion of the contract, this record, together with the final labor summary required in section VII, paragraph 3, hereof, shall be transmitted to the State highway department resident engineer for the project on Form PR–47 in accordance with instructions attached thereto, which will be furnished for this purpose upon request. The quantities for the listed items shall be reported separately for roadway and for structures over 20 feet long as measured along the centerline of the roadway.

2. The contractor shall become familiar with the list of specific materials and supplies contained in Form PR–47 prior to the commencement of work under this contract. Any additional materials information required will be solicited through revisions of Form PR–47 with attendant explanations.

3. Where subcontracts are involved the contractor shall submit either a single report covering work both by himself and all his subcontractors, or he may submit separate reports for himself and for each of his subcontractors.

IX. *Subletting or assigning the contract.*

1. The contractor shall perform with his own organization contract work amounting to not less than 50 percent of the original total contract price, except that any items designated by the State as *Specialty Items* may be performed by subcontract and the amount of any such *Specialty Items* so performed may be deducted from the original total contract price before computing the amount of work required to be performed by the contractor with his own organization.

a. *His own organization* shall be construed to include only workmen employed and paid directly by the prime contractor and equipment owned or rented by him, with or without operators.

b. *Specialty items* shall be construed to be limited to work that requires highly specialized knowledge, craftsmanship or equipment not ordinarily available in contracting organizations qualified to bid on the contract as a whole and in general are to be limited to minor components of the overall contract.

2. In addition to the 50 percent requirements set forth in paragraph 1 above, the contractor shall furnish (a) a competent superintendent or foreman who is employed by him, who has full authority to direct performance of the work in accordance with the contract requirements, and who is in charge of all construction operations (regardless of who performs the work), and (b) such other of his own organizational capability and responsibility (supervision, management, and engineering services) as the State highway department contracting officer determines is necessary to assure the performance of the contract.

3. The contract amount upon which the 50 percent requirement set forth in paragraph 1 is computed includes the cost of materials and manufactured products which are to be purchased or produced by the contractor under the contract provisions.

4. Any items that have been selected as *Specialty Items* for the contract are listed as such in the Special Provisions, bid schedule, or elsewhere in the contract documents.

5. No portion of the contract shall be sublet, assigned or otherwise disposed of except with the written consent of the State highway department contracting officer, or his authorized representative, and such consent when given shall not be construed to relieve the contractor of any responsibility for the fulfillment of the contract. Request for permission to sublet, assign or otherwise dispose of any portion of the contract shall be in writing and accompanied by (a) a showing that the organization which will perform the work is particularly experienced and equipped for such work, and (b) an assurance by the contractor that the labor standards provisions set forth in thiscontract shall apply to labor performed on all work encompassed by the request.

X. *Safety: Accident prevention.*

In the performance of this contract, the contractor shall comply with all applicable Federal, State and local laws governing safety, health and sanitation. The contractor shall provide all safeguards, safety devices and protective equipment and take any other needed actions, on his own responsibility, or as the State highway department contracting officer may determine, reasonably necessary to protect the life and health of employees on the job and the safety of the public and to protect property in connection with the performance of the work covered by the contract.

It is a condition of this contract, and shall be made a condition of each subcontract entered into pursuant to this contract, that the contractor and any subcontractor shall not require any laborer or mechanic employed in performance of the contract to work in surroundings or under working conditions which are unsanitary, hazardous, or dangerous to his health or safety, as determined under construction safety and health standards (title 29, Code of Federal Regulations, part 1926, formerly part 1518, as revised from time to time), promulgated by the United States Secretary of Labor, in accordance with section 107 of the Contract Work Hours and Safety Standards Act (83 Stat. 96).

XI. *False statements concerning highway projects.*

In order to assure high quality and durable construction in conformity with approved plans and specifications and a high degree of reliability on statements and representations made by engineers, contractors, suppliers, and workers on Federal-aid highway projects, it is essential that all persons concerned with the project perform their functions as carefully, thoroughly and honestly as possible. Willfull falsification, distortion, or misrepresentation with respect to any facts related to the project is a violation of Federal law. To prevent any misunderstanding regarding the seriousness of these and similar acts, the following notice shall be posted on each Federal-aid highway project in one or more places where it is readily available to all personnel concerned with the project:

* * * * *

NOTICE TO ALL PERSONNEL ENGAGED ON FEDERAL-AID HIGHWAY PROJECTS

Title 18 U.S.C., section 1020, reads as follows:

"Whoever, being an officer, agent, or employee of the United States, or of any State or Territory, or whoever, whether a person, association, firm, or corporation, knowingly makes any false statement, false representation, or false report as to the character, quality, quantity, or cost of the material used or to be used, or the quantity or quality of the work performed or to be performed or the costs thereof in connection with the submission of plans, maps, specifications, contracts, or costs of construction of any highway or related project submitted for approval to the Secretary of Transportation; or

"Whoever knowingly makes any false statement, false representation, false report, or false claim with respect to the character, quality, quantity, or cost of any work performed or to be performed, or materials furnished or to be furnished, in connection with the construction of any highway or related project approved by the Secretary of Transportation; or

"Whoever knowingly makes any false statement or false representation as to a material fact in any statement, certificate, or report submitted pursuant to provisions of the Federal-Aid Road Act approved July 1, 1916 (39 Stat. 355), as amended and supplemented;

"Shall be fined not more than $10,000 or imprisoned not more than five years, or both."

XII. *Implementation of Clean Air Act and Federal Water Pollution Control Act (applicable to contracts and subcontracts which exceed $100,000).*

1. The contractor stipulates that any facility to be utilized in the performance of this contract, unless such contract is exempt under the Clean Air Act, as amended (42 U.S.C. 1857 *et seq.*, as amended by Pub. L. 91–604), and under the Federal Water Pollution Control Act, as amended (33 U.S.C. 1251 *et seq.*, as amended by Pub. L. 92–500), Executive Order 11738, and regulations in implementation thereof (40 CFR part 15), is listed not on the date of contract award, on the U.S. Environmental Protection Agency (EPA) List of Violating Facilities Pursuant to 40 CFR part 15.20.

2. The contractor agrees to comply with all the requirements of section 114 of the Clean Air Act and section 308 of the Federal Water Pollution Control Act and all regulations and guidelines listed thereunder.

3. The contractor shall promptly notify the State highway department of the receipt of any communication from the Director, Office of Federal Activities, EPA, indicating that a facility to be utilized for the contract is under consideration to be listed on the EPA List of Violating Facilities.

4. The contractor agrees to include or cause to be included the requirements of subparagraphs 1 through 4 of this paragraph XII in every subcontract which exceeds $100,000, and further agrees to take such action as Government may direct as a means of enforcing such requirements.

[40 FR 49084, Oct. 21, 1975]

APPENDIX C TO SUBPART B OF PART 633—ADDITIONAL REQUIRED CONTRACT PROVISIONS, APPALACHIAN DEVELOPMENT HIGHWAY SYSTEM AND LOCAL ACCESS ROADS CONTRACTS OTHER THAN CONSTRUCTION CONTRACTS

EQUAL OPPORTUNITY: EMPLOYMENT PRACTICES AND SELECTION OF SUBCONTRACTORS, SUPPLIERS OF MATERIALS, AND LESSORS OF EQUIPMENT

During the performance of this contract, the contractor agrees as follows:

1. *Compliance with regulations.*

The contractor will comply with the provisions of 23 U.S.C. 324 and with the Regulations of the Department of Transportation relative to nondiscrimination in Federally-assisted programs of the Department of Transportation (Title 49, Code of Federal Regulations, part 21, hereinafter referred to as the regulations), which are herein incorporated by reference and made a part of this contract.

2. *Employment practices*

a. The contractor will not discriminate against any employee or applicant for employment because of race, color, sex, or national origin. The contractor will take affirmative action to ensure that applicants are employed, and that employees are treated during employment without regard to their race, color, sex, or national origin. Such action shall include, but not be limited to the following: recruitment or recruitment advertising, hiring, firing, upgrading, promotion, demotion, transfer, layoff, termination, rates of pay or other forms of compensation or benefits, selection for training or apprenticeship, use of facilities and treatment of employees. The contractor agrees to post in conspicuous places, available to employees and applicants for employment, notices setting forth the provisions of this employment practices clause.

b. The contractor will, in all solicitations or advertisements for employees placed by or on behalf of the contractor, state that all qualified applicants will receive consideration for employment without regard to race, color, sex, or national origin.

c. The contractor will send to each labor union or representative of workers with which he has a collective bargaining agreement or other contract or understanding, a notice advising the said labor union or workers representative of the contractor's commitments under the employment practices provision, and shall post copies of the notice in conspicuous places available to employees and applicants for employment.

3. *Selection of subcontractors, procurement of materials and leasing of equipment.*

a. The contractor, with regard to the work performed by him after award and prior to completion of the contract work, will not discriminate on the ground of race, color, sex, or national origin in the selection and retention of subcontractors, including procurements of materials and leases of equipment. The contractor will not participate either directly or indirectly in the discrimination prohibited by Section 21.5 of the Regulations.

b. In all solicitations either by competitive bidding or negotiation made by the contractor for work to be performed under a subcontract, including procurements of materials or leases of equipment, each potential subcontractor, supplier, or lessor shall be notified by the contractor of the contractor's obligations under this contract and the Regulations relative to nondiscrimination on the ground of race, color, sex, or national origin.

4. *Information and reports.*

The contractor will provide all information and reports required by the Regulations, or orders and instructions issued pursuant thereto, and will permit access to its books, records, accounts, other sources of information, and its facilities as may be determined by the State highway department or the Federal Highway Administration to be pertinent to ascertain compliance with such Regulations, orders and instructions. Where any information required of a contractor is in the exclusive possession of another who fails or refuses to furnish this information, the contractor shall so certify to the State highway department, or the Federal Highway Administration as appropriate, and shall set forth what efforts it has made to obtain the information.

5. *Incorporation of provisions.*

The contractor will include these additional required contract provisions in every subcontract, including procurements of materials and leases of equipment, unless exempt by the Regulations or orders, or instructions issued pursuant thereto. The contractor will take such action with respect to any subcontract, procurement, or lease as the State highway department or the Federal Highway Administration may direct as a means of enforcing such provisions including sanctions for non-compliance: *Provided, however*, That, in the event a contractor becomes involved in, or is threatened with, litigation with a subcontractor, supplier, or lessor as a result of such directed action, the contractor may request the State to enter into such litigation to protect the interest of the State, and, in addition, the contractor may request the United States to enter into such litigation to protect the interest of the United States.

6. *Sanctions for noncompliance.*

In the event of the contractor's noncompliance with sections 1 through 5 above, the State highway department shall impose such contract sanctions as it or the Federal Highway Administration may determine to be appropriate, including but not limited to.

a. Withholding of payments to the contractor under the contract until the contractor complies, and/or

b. Cancellation, termination or suspension of the contract in whole or in part.

[40 FR 49088, Oct. 21, 1975]

Appendix D to Subpart B of Part 633—Federal-Aid Proposal Notices

Notices to Prospective Federal-Aid Construction Contractors

I. *Certification of nonsegregated facilities.*

(a) A Certification of Nonsegregated Facilities, as required by the May 9, 1967, Order of the Secretary of Labor (32 FR 7439, May 19, 1967) on Elimination of Segregated Facilities (is included in the proposal and must be submitted prior to the award of a Federal-aid highway construction contract exceeding $10,000 which is not exempt from the provisions of the Equal Opportunity clause).

(b) Bidders are cautioned as follows: By signing this bid, the bidder will be deemed to have signed and agreed to the provisions of the "Certification of Nonsegregated Facilities" in this proposal. This certification provides that the bidder does not maintain or provide for his employees facilities which are segregated on a basis of race, creed, color, or national origin, whether such facilities are segregated by directive or on a de facto basis. The certification also provides that the bidder will not maintain such segregated facilities.

(c) Bidders receiving Federal-aid highway construction contract awards exceeding $10,000 which are not exempt from the provisions of the Equal Opportunity clause, will be required to provide for the forwarding of the following notice to prospective subcontractors for construction contracts and material suppliers where the subcontracts or material supply agreements exceed $10,000 and are not exempt from the provisions of the Equal Opportunity clause.

Notice to Prospective Subcontractors and Material Suppliers of Requirement for Certification of Nonsegregated Facilities

(a) A Certification of Nonsegregated Facilities is required by the May 9, 1967, Order of the Secretary of Labor (32 FR 7431, May 19, 1967) on Elimination of Segregated Facilities, which is included in the proposal, or attached hereto, must be submitted by each subcontractor and material supplier prior to the award of the subcontract or consummation of a material supply agreement if such subcontract or agreement exceeds $10,000 and is not exempt from the provisions of the Equal Opportunity clause.

(b) Subcontractors and material suppliers are cautioned as follows: By signing the subcontract or entering into a material supply agreement, the subcontractor or material supplier will be deemed to have signed and agreed to the provisions of the "Certification of Nonsegregated Facilities" in the subcontract or material supply agreement. This certification provides that the subcontractor or material supplier does not maintain or provide for his employees facilities which are segregated on the basis of race, creed, color, or national origin, whether such facilities are segregated by directive or on a de facto basis. The certification also provides that the subcontractor or material supplier will not maintain such segregated facilities.

(c) Subcontractors or material suppliers receiving subcontract awards or material supply agreements exceeding $10,000 which are not exempt from the provisions of the Equal Opportunity clause will be required to provide for the forwarding of this notice to prospective subcontractors for construction contracts and material suppliers where the subcontracts or material supply agreements exceed $10,000 and are not exempt from the provisions of the Equal Opportunity clause.

II. *Implementation of Clean Air Act.*

(a) By signing this bid, the bidder will be deemed to have stipulated as follows:

(1) That any facility to be utilized in the performance of this contract, unless such contract is exempt under the Clean Air Act, as amended (42 U.S.C. 1857 *et seq.*, as by Pub. L. 91–604), Executive order 11738, and regulations in implementation thereof (40 CFR part 15, is not listed on the U.S. Environmental Protection Agency (EPA) List of Violating Facilities pursuant to 40 CFR 15.20.

(2) That the State highway department shall be promptly notified prior to contract award of the receipt by the bidder of any communication from the Director, Office of Federal Activities, EPA, indicating that a facility to be utilized for the contract is under consideration to be listed on the EPA List of Violating Facilities.

PART 635—CONSTRUCTION AND MAINTENANCE

Subpart A—Contract Procedures

Sec.

Subpart B—Force Account Construction

Subpart C—Physical Construction Authorization

Subpart D—General Material Requirements

Subpart E—Construction Manager/General Contractor (CM/GC) Contracting

AUTHORITY: Sections 1525 and 1303 of Pub. L. 112–141, Sec. 1503 of Pub. L. 109–59, 119 Stat. 1144; 23 U.S.C. 101 (note), 109, 112, 113, 114, 116, 119, 128, and 315; 31 U.S.C. 6505; 42 U.S.C. 3334, 4601 *et seq.;* Sec. 1041(a), Pub. L. 102–240, 105 Stat. 1914; 23 CFR 1.32; 49 CFR 1.85(a)(1).

EDITORIAL NOTE: Nomenclature changes to part 635 appear at 67 FR 75924, Dec. 10, 2002.

Subpart A—Contract Procedures

SOURCE: 56 FR 37004, Aug. 2, 1991, unless otherwise noted.

§635.101 Purpose.

To prescribe policies, requirements, and procedures relating to Federal-aid highway projects, from the time of authorization to proceed to the construction stage, to the time of final acceptance by the Federal Highway Administration (FHWA).

§635.102 Definitions.

As used in this subpart:

Administrator means the Federal Highway Administrator.

Calendar day means each day shown on the calendar but, if another definition is set forth in the State contract specifications, that definition will apply.

Construction Manager/General Contractor (CM/GC) project means a project to be delivered using a two-phase contract with a construction manager or general contractor for services during both the preconstruction and construction phases of a project.

Contract time means the number of workdays or calendar days specified in a contract for completion of the contract work. The term includes authorized time extensions.

Design-build project means a project to be developed using one or more design-build contracts.

Division Administrator means the chief FHWA official assigned to conduct business in a particular State. A State is as defined in 23 U.S.C. 101.

Force account means a basis of payment for the direct performance of highway construction work with payment based on the actual cost of labor, equipment, and materials furnished and consideration for overhead and profit.

Formal approval means approval in writing or the electronic transmission of such approval.

Incentive/disincentive for early completion as used in this subpart, describes a contract provision which compensates the contractor a certain amount of money for each day identified critical work is completed ahead of schedule and assesses a deduction for each day the contractor overruns the incentive/disincentive time. Its use is primarily intended for those critical projects where traffic inconvenience and delays are to be held to a minimum. The amounts are based upon estimates of such items as traffic safety, traffic maintenance, and road user delay costs.

Liquidated damages means the daily amount set forth in the contract to be deducted from the contract price to cover additional costs incurred by a State transportation department because of the contractor's failure to complete the contract work within the number of calendar days or workdays specified. The term may also mean the total of all daily amounts deducted under the terms of a particular contract.

Local public agency means any city, county, township, municipality, or other political subdivision that may be empowered to cooperate with the State transportation department in highway matters.

Major change or major extra work means a change which will significantly affect the cost of the project to the Federal Government or alter the termini, character or scope of the work.

Materially unbalanced bid means a bid which generates a reasonable doubt that award to the bidder submitting a mathematically unbalanced bid will result in the lowest ultimate cost to the Federal Government.

Mathematically unbalanced bid means a bid containing lump sum or unit bid items which do not reflect reasonable actual costs plus a reasonable proportionate share of the bidder's anticipated profit, overhead costs, and other indirect costs.

Public agency means any organization with administrative or functional responsibilities which are directly or indirectly affiliated with a governmental body of any nation, State, or local jurisdiction.

Publicly owned equipment means equipment previously purchased or otherwise acquired by the public agency involved primarily for use in its own operations.

Specialty items means work items identified in the contract which are not normally associated with highway construction and require highly specialized knowledge, abilities or equipment not ordinarily available in the type of contracting organizations qualified and expected to bid on the contract; in general, these items are to be limited to minor components of the overall contract.

State transportation department (STD) means that department, commission, board, or official of any State charged by its laws with the responsibility for highway construction. The term "State" should be considered equivalent to "State transportation department" if the context so implies.

Workday means a calendar day during which construction operations could proceed for a major part of a shift, normally excluding Saturdays, Sundays, and State-recognized legal holidays.

[62 FR 6873, Feb. 14, 1997, as amended at 67 FR 75924, Dec. 10, 2002; 81 FR 86942, Dec. 2, 2016]

§635.103 Applicability.

The policies, requirements, and procedures prescribed in this subpart shall apply to all Federal-aid highway projects.

[69 FR 7118, Feb. 13, 2004]

§635.104 Method of construction.

(a) Actual construction work shall be performed by contract awarded by competitive bidding; unless, as provided in §635.104(b), the STD demonstrates to the satisfaction of the Division Administrator that some other method is more cost effective or that an emergency exists. The STD shall assure opportunity for free, open, and competitive bidding, including adequate publicity of the advertisements or calls for bids. The advertising or calling for bids and the award of contracts shall comply with the procedures and requirements set forth in §§635.112 and 635.114.

(b) Approval by the Division Administrator for construction by a method other than competitive bidding shall be requested by the State in accordance with subpart B of part 635 of this chapter. Before such finding is made, the STD shall determine that the organization to undertake the work is so staffed and equipped as to perform such work satisfactorily and cost effectively.

(c) In the case of a design-build project, the requirements of 23 CFR part 636 and the appropriate provisions pertaining to design-build contracting in this part will apply. However, no justification of cost effectiveness is necessary in selecting projects for the design-build delivery method.

(d) In the case of a CM/GC project, the requirements of subpart E and the appropriate provisions pertaining to the CM/GC method of contracting in this part will apply. However, no justification of cost effectiveness is necessary in selecting projects for the CM/GC delivery method.

[56 FR 37004, Aug. 2, 1991, as amended at 67 FR 75925, Dec. 10, 2002; 81 FR 86942, Dec. 2, 2016]

§635.105 Supervising agency.

(a) The STD has responsibility for the construction of all Federal-aid projects, and is not relieved of such responsibility by authorizing performance of the work by a local public agency or other Federal agency. The STD shall be responsible for insuring that such projects receive adequate supervision and inspection to insure that projects are completed in conformance with approved plans and specifications.

(b) Although the STD may employ a consultant to provide construction engineering services, such as inspection or survey work on a project, the STD shall provide a full-time employed State engineer to be in responsible charge of the project.

(c) When a project is located on a street or highway over which the STD does not have legal jurisdiction, or when special conditions warrant, the

STD, while not relieved of overall project responsibility, may arrange for the local public agency having jurisdiction over such street or highway to perform the work with its own forces or by contract; provided the following conditions are met and the Division Administrator approves the arrangements in advance.

(1) In the case of force account work, there is full compliance with subpart B of this part.

(2) When the work is to be performed under a contract awarded by a local public agency, all Federal requirements including those prescribed in this subpart shall be met.

(3) The local public agency is adequately staffed and suitably equipped to undertake and satisfactorily complete the work; and

(4) In those instances where a local public agency elects to use consultants for construction engineering services, the local public agency shall provide a full-time employee of the agency to be in responsible charge of the project.

§ 635.106 Use of publicly owned equipment.

(a) Publicly owned equipment should not normally compete with privately owned equipment on a project to be let to contract. There may be exceptional cases, however, in which the use of equipment of the State or local public agency for highway construction purposes may be warranted or justified. A proposal by any STD for the use of publicly owned equipment on such a project must be supported by a showing that it would clearly be cost effective to do so under the conditions peculiar to the individual project or locality.

(b) Where publicly owned equipment is to be made available in connection with construction work to be let to contract, Federal funds may participate in the cost of such work provided the following conditions are met:

(1) The proposed use of such equipment is clearly set forth in the Plans, Specifications and Estimate (PS&E) submitted to the Division Administrator for approval.

(2) The advertised specifications specify the items of publicly owned equipment available for use by the successful bidder, the rates to be charged, and the points of availability or delivery of the equipment; and

(3) The advertised specifications include a notification that the successful bidder has the option either of renting part or all of such equipment from the State or local public agency or otherwise providing the equipment necessary for the performance of the contract work.

(c) In the rental of publicly owned equipment to contractors, the State or local public agency shall not profit at the expense of Federal funds.

(d) Unforeseeable conditions may make it necessary to provide publicly owned equipment to the contractor at rental rates agreed to between the contractor and the State or local public agency after the work has started. Any such arrangement shall not form the basis for any increase in the cost of the project on which Federal funds are to participate.

(e) When publicly owned equipment is used on projects constructed on a force account basis, costs may be determined by agreed unit prices or on an actual cost basis. When agreed unit prices are applied the equipment need not be itemized nor rental rates shown in the estimate. However, if such work is to be performed on an actual cost basis, the STD shall submit to the Division Administrator for approval the schedule of rates proposed to be charged, exclusive of profit, for the publicly owned equipment made available for use.

§ 635.107 Participation by disadvantaged business enterprises.

(a) The STD shall schedule contract lettings in a balanced program providing contracts of such size and character as to assure an opportunity for all sizes of contracting organizations to compete. In accordance with Title VI of the Civil Rights Act of 1964, subsequent Federal-aid Highway Acts, and 49 CFR part 26, the STD shall ensure equal opportunity for disadvantaged business enterprises (DBEs) participating in the Federal-aid highway program.

(b) In the case of a design-build or CM/GC project funded with title 23 funds, the requirements of 49 CFR part

26 and the State's approved DBE plan apply.

[67 FR 75925, Dec. 10, 2002, as amended at 81 FR 86942, Dec. 2, 2016]

§ 635.108 Health and safety.

Contracts for projects shall include provisions designed:

(a) To insure full compliance with all applicable Federal, State, and local laws governing safety, health and sanitation; and

(b) To require that the contractor shall provide all safeguards, safety devices, and protective equipment and shall take any other actions reasonably necessary to protect the life and health of persons working at the site of the project and the safety of the public and to protect property in connection with the performance of the work covered by the contract.

§ 635.109 Standardized changed condition clauses.

(a) Except as provided in paragraph (b) of this section, the following changed conditions contract clauses shall be made part of, and incorporated in, each highway construction project, including construction services contracts of CM/GC projects, approved under 23 U.S.C. 106:

(1) *Differing site conditions.* (i) During the progress of the work, if subsurface or latent physical conditions are encountered at the site differing materially from those indicated in the contract or if unknown physical conditions of an unusual nature, differing materially from those ordinarily encountered and generally recognized as inherent in the work provided for in the contract, are encountered at the site, the party discovering such conditions shall promptly notify the other party in writing of the specific differing conditions before the site is disturbed and before the affected work is performed.

(ii) Upon written notification, the engineer will investigate the conditions, and if it is determined that the conditions materially differ and cause an increase or decrease in the cost or time required for the performance of any work under the contract, an adjustment, excluding anticipated profits, will be made and the contract modified in writing accordingly. The engineer will notify the contractor of the determination whether or not an adjustment of the contract is warranted.

(iii) No contract adjustment which results in a benefit to the contractor will be allowed unless the contractor has provided the required written notice.

(iv) No contract adjustment will be allowed under this clause for any effects caused on unchanged work. (This provision may be omitted by the STD's at their option.)

(2) *Suspensions of work ordered by the engineer.* (i) If the performance of all or any portion of the work is suspended or delayed by the engineer in writing for an unreasonable period of time (not originally anticipated, customary, or inherent to the construction industry) and the contractor believes that additional compensation and/or contract time is due as a result of such suspension or delay, the contractor shall submit to the engineer in writing a request for adjustment within 7 calendar days of receipt of the notice to resume work. The request shall set forth the reasons and support for such adjustment.

(ii) Upon receipt, the engineer will evaluate the contractor's request. If the engineer agrees that the cost and/or time required for the performance of the contract has increased as a result of such suspension and the suspension was caused by conditions beyond the control of and not the fault of the contractor, its suppliers, or subcontractors at any approved tier, and not caused by weather, the engineer will make an adjustment (excluding profit) and modify the contract in writing accordingly. The contractor will be notified of the engineer's determination whether or not an adjustment of the contract is warranted.

(iii) No contract adjustment will be allowed unless the contractor has submitted the request for adjustment within the time prescribed.

(iv) No contract adjustment will be allowed under this clause to the extent that performance would have been suspended or delayed by any other cause, or for which an adjustment is provided or excluded under any other term or condition of this contract.

(3) *Significant changes in the character of work.* (i) The engineer reserves the right to make, in writing, at any time during the work, such changes in quantities and such alterations in the work as are necessary to satisfactorily complete the project. Such changes in quantities and alterations shall not invalidate the contract nor release the surety, and the contractor agrees to perform the work as altered.

(ii) If the alterations or changes in quantities significantly change the character of the work under the contract, whether such alterations or changes are in themselves significant changes to the character of the work or by affecting other work cause such other work to become significantly different in character, an adjustment, excluding anticipated profit, will be made to the contract. The basis for the adjustment shall be agreed upon prior to the performance of the work. If a basis cannot be agreed upon, then an adjustment will be made either for or against the contractor in such amount as the engineer may determine to be fair and equitable.

(iii) If the alterations or changes in quantities do not significantly change the character of the work to be performed under the contract, the altered work will be paid for as provided elsewhere in the contract.

(iv) The term "significant change" shall be construed to apply only to the following circumstances:

(A) When the character of the work as altered differs materially in kind or nature from that involved or included in the original proposed construction; or

(B) When a major item of work, as defined elsewhere in the contract, is increased in excess of 125 percent or decreased below 75 percent of the original contract quantity. Any allowance for an increase in quantity shall apply only to that portion in excess of 125 percent of original contract item quantity, or in case of a decrease below 75 percent, to the actual amount of work performed.

(b) The provisions of this section shall be governed by the following:

(1) Where State statute does not permit one or more of the contract clauses included in paragraph (a) of this section, the State statute shall prevail and such clause or clauses need not be made applicable to Federal-aid highway contracts.

(2) Where the State transportation department has developed and implemented one or more of the contract clauses included in paragraph (a) of this section, such clause or clauses, as developed by the State transportation department may be included in Federal-aid highway contracts in lieu of the corresponding clause or clauses in paragraph (a) of this section. The State's action must be pursuant to a specific State statute requiring differing contract conditions clauses. Such State developed clause or clauses, however, must be in conformance with 23 U.S.C., 23 CFR and other applicable Federal statutes and regulations as appropriate and shall be subject to the Division Administrator's approval as part of the PS&E.

(c) In the case of a design-build project, STDs are strongly encouraged to use "suspensions of work ordered by the engineer" clauses, and may consider "differing site condition" clauses and "significant changes in the character of work" clauses which are appropriate for the risk and responsibilities that are shared with the design-builder.

[56 FR 37004, Aug. 2, 1991; 57 FR 10062, Mar. 23, 1992, as amended at 67 FR 75925, Dec. 10, 2002; 81 FR 86943, Dec. 2, 2016]

§635.110 Licensing and qualification of contractors.

(a) The procedures and requirements a STD proposes to use for qualifying and licensing contractors, who may bid for, be awarded, or perform Federal-aid highway contracts, shall be submitted to the Division Administrator for advance approval. Only those procedures and requirements so approved shall be effective with respect to Federal-aid highway projects. Any changes in approved procedures and requirements shall likewise be subject to approval by the Division Administrator.

(b) No procedure or requirement for bonding, insurance, prequalification, qualification, or licensing of contractors shall be approved which, in the judgment of the Division Administrator, may operate to restrict competition, to prevent submission of a bid by, or to prohibit the consideration of a bid submitted by, any responsible contractor, whether resident or nonresident of the State wherein the work is to be performed.

(c) No contractor shall be required by law, regulation, or practice to obtain a license before submission of a bid or before the bid may be considered for award of a contract. This, however, is not intended to preclude requirements for the licensing of a contractor upon or subsequent to the award of the contract if such requirements are consistent with competitive bidding. Prequalification of contractors may be required as a condition for submission of a bid or award of contract only if the period between the date of issuing a call for bids and the date of opening of bids affords sufficient time to enable a bidder to obtain the required prequalification rating.

(d) Requirements for the prequalification, qualification or licensing of contractors, that operate to govern the amount of work that may be bid upon by, or may be awarded to, a contractor, shall be approved only if based upon a full and appropriate evaluation of the contractor's capability to perform the work.

(e) Contractors who are currently suspended, debarred or voluntarily excluded under 49 CFR part 29 or otherwise determined to be ineligible, shall be prohibited from participating in the Federal-aid highway program.

(f) In the case of design-build and CM/GC projects, the STDs may use their own bonding, insurance, licensing, qualification or prequalification procedure for any phase of procurement.

(1) The STDs may not impose statutory or administrative requirements which provide an in-State or local geographical preference in the solicitation, licensing, qualification, pre-qualification, short listing or selection process. The geographic location of a firm's office may not be one of the selection criteria. However, the STDs may require the successful design-builder to establish a local office after the award of contract.

(2) If required by State statute, local statute, or administrative policy, the STDs may require prequalification for construction contractors. The STDs may require offerors to demonstrate the ability of their engineering staff to become licensed in that State as a condition of responsiveness; however, licensing procedures may not serve as a barrier for the consideration of otherwise responsive proposals. The STDs may require compliance with appropriate State or local licensing practices as a condition of contract award.

[56 FR 37004, Aug. 2, 1991, as amended at 67 FR 75925, Dec. 10, 2002; 81 FR 86943, Dec. 2, 2016]

§ 635.111 Tied bids.

(a) The STD may tie or permit the tying of Federal-aid highway projects or Federal-aid and State-financed highway projects for bidding purposes where it appears that by so doing more favorable bids may be received. To avoid discrimination against contractors desiring to bid upon a lesser amount of work than that included in the tied combinations, provisions should be made to permit bidding separately on the individual projects whenever they are of such character as to be suitable for bidding independently.

(b) When Federal-aid and State-financed highway projects are tied or permitted to be tied together for bidding purposes, the bid schedule shall set forth the quantities separately for the Federal-aid work and the State-financed work. All proposals submitted for the tied projects must contain separate bid prices for each project individually. Federal participation in the cost of the work shall be on the basis of the lowest overall responsive bid proposal unless the analysis of bids reveals that mathematical unbalancing has caused an unsupported shift of cost liability to the Federal-aid work. If such a finding is made, Federal participation shall be based on the unit prices represented in the proposal by the individual contractor who would be the lowest responsive and responsible bidder if only the Federal-aid project were considered.

(c) Federal-aid highway projects and State-financed highway projects may be combined in one contract if the conditions of the projects are so similar that the unit costs on the Federal-aid projects should not be increased by such combinations of projects. In such cases, like quantities should be combined in the proposal to avoid the possibility of unbalancing of bids in favor of either of the projects in the combination.

§635.112 Advertising for bids and proposals.

(a) No work shall be undertaken on any Federal-aid project, nor shall any project be advertised for bids, prior to authorization by the Division Administrator.

(b) The advertisement and approved plans and specifications shall be available to bidders a minimum of 3 weeks prior to opening of bids except that shorter periods may be approved by the Division Administrator in special cases when justified.

(c) The STD shall obtain the approval of the Division Administrator prior to issuing any addenda which contain a major change to the approved plans or specifications during the advertising period. Minor addenda need not receive prior approval but should be identified by the STD at the time of or prior to requesting FHWA concurrence in award. The STD shall provide assurance that all bidders have received all issued addenda.

(d) Nondiscriminatory bidding procedures shall be afforded to all qualified bidders regardless of National, State or local boundaries and without regard to race, color, religion, sex, national origin, age, or handicap. If any provisions of State laws, specifications, regulations, or policies may operate in any manner contrary to Federal requirements, including title VI of the Civil Rights Act of 1964, to prevent submission of a bid, or prohibit consideration of a bid submitted by any responsible bidder appropriately qualified in accordance with §635.110, such provisions shall not be applicable to Federal-aid projects. Where such nonapplicable provisions exist, notices of advertising, specifications, special provisions or other governing documents shall include a positive statement to advise prospective bidders of those provisions that are not applicable.

(e) Except in the case of a concession agreement, as defined in section 710.703 of this title, no public agency shall be permitted to bid in competition or to enter into subcontracts with private contractors.

(f) The STD shall include a noncollusion provision substantially as follows in the bidding documents:

> Each bidder shall file a statement executed by, or on behalf of the person, firm, association, or corporation submitting the bid certifying that such person, firm, association, or corporation has not, either directly or indirectly, entered into any agreement, participated in any collusion, or otherwise taken any action, in restraint of free competitive bidding in connection with the submitted bid. Failure to submit the executed statement as part of the bidding documents will make the bid nonresponsive and not eligible for award consideration.

(1) The required form for the statement will be provided by the State to each prospective bidder.

(2) The statement shall either be in the form of an affidavit executed and sworn to by the bidder before a person who is authorized by the laws of the State to administer oaths or in the form of an unsworn declaration executed under penalty of perjury of the laws of the United States.

(g) The STD shall include the lobbying certification requirement pursuant to 49 CFR part 20 and the requirements of 49 CFR part 29 regarding suspension and debarment certification in the bidding documents.

(h) The STD shall clearly identify in the bidding documents those requirements which the bidder must assure are complied with to make the bid responsive. Failure to comply with these identified bidding requirements shall make the bid nonresponsive and not eligible for award consideration.

(i) In the case of a design-build project, the following requirements apply:

(1) When a Request for Proposals document is issued after the NEPA process is complete, the FHWA Division Administrator's approval of the Request for Proposals document will constitute the FHWA's project authorization and

the FHWA's approval of the STD's request to release the document. This approval will carry the same significance as plan, specification and estimate approval on a design-bid-build Federal-aid project.

(2) Where a Request for Proposals document is issued prior to the completion of the NEPA process, the FHWA's approval of the document will only constitute the FHWA's approval of the STD's request to release the document.

(3) The STD may decide the appropriate solicitation schedule for all design-build requests. This includes all project advertising, the release of the Request for Qualifications document, the release of the Request for Proposals document and all deadlines for the receipt of qualification statements and proposals. Typical advertising periods range from six to ten weeks and can be longer for large, complicated projects.

(4) The STD must obtain the approval of the Division Administrator prior to issuing addenda which result in major changes to the Request for Proposals document. Minor addenda need not receive prior approval but may be identified by the STD at the time of or prior to requesting the FHWA's concurrence in award. The STD must provide assurance that all offerors have received all issued addenda.

(j) In the case of a CM/GC project, the FHWA Division Administrator's approval of the solicitation document will constitute the FHWA's approval to use the CM/GC contracting method and approval to release the solicitation document. The STD must obtain the approval of the FHWA Division Administrator before issuing addenda which result in major changes to the solicitation document.

[56 FR 37004, Aug. 2, 1991, as amended at 67 FR 75925, Dec. 10, 2002; 72 FR 45336, Aug. 14, 2007; 73 FR 77502, Dec. 19, 2008; 81 FR 86943, Dec. 2, 2016]

§635.113 Bid opening and bid tabulations.

(a) All bids received in accordance with the terms of the advertisement shall be publicly opened and announced either item by item or by total amount. If any bid received is not read aloud, the name of the bidder and the reason for not reading the bid aloud shall be publicly announced at the letting. Negotiation with contractors, during the period following the opening of bids and before the award of the contract shall not be permitted.

(b) The STD shall prepare and forward tabulations of bids to the Division Administrator. These tabulations shall be certified by a responsible STD official and shall show:

(1) Bid item details for at least the low three acceptable bids and

(2) The total amounts of all other acceptable bids.

(c) In the case of a design-build project, the following requirements apply:

(1) All proposals received must be opened and reviewed in accordance with the terms of the solicitation. The STD must use its own procedures for the following:

(i) The process of handling proposals and information;

(ii) The review and evaluation of proposals;

(iii) The submission, modification, revision and withdrawal of proposals; and

(iv) The announcement of the successful offeror.

(2) The STD must submit a post-award tabulation of proposal prices to the FHWA Division Administrator. The tabulation of price proposal information may include detailed pricing information when available or lump sum price information if itemized prices are not used.

(d) In the case of a CM/GC project, the requirements of this section do not apply. See subpart E of this part for approval procedures.

[56 FR 37004, Aug. 2, 1991, as amended at 67 FR 75925, Dec. 10, 2002; 81 FR 86943, Dec. 2, 2016]

§635.114 Award of contract and concurrence in award.

(a) Federal-aid contracts shall be awarded only on the basis of the lowest responsive bid submitted by a bidder meeting the criteria of responsibility as may have been established by the STD in accordance with §635.110. Award shall be within the time established by the STD and subject to the prior concurrence of the Division Administrator.

(b) The STD shall formally request concurrence by the Division Administrator in the award of all Federal-aid contracts. Concurrence in award by the Division Administrator is a prerequisite to Federal participation in construction costs and is considered as authority to proceed with construction, unless specifically stated otherwise. Concurrence in award shall be formally approved and shall only be given after receipt and review of the tabulation of bids.

(c) Following the opening of bids, the STD shall examine the unit bid prices of the apparent low bid for reasonable conformance with the engineer's estimated prices. A bid with extreme variations from the engineer's estimate, or where obvious unbalancing of unit prices has occurred, shall be thoroughly evaluated.

(d) Where obvious unbalanced bid items exist, the STD's decision to award or reject a bid shall be supported by written justification. A bid found to be mathematically unbalanced, but not found to be materially unbalanced, may be awarded.

(e) When a low bid is determined to be both mathematically and materially unbalanced, the Division Administrator will take appropriate steps to protect the Federal interest. This action may be concurrence in a STD decision not to award the contract. If, however, the STD decides to proceed with the award and requests FHWA concurrence, the Division Administrator's action may range from nonconcurrence to concurrence with contingency conditions limiting Federal participation.

(f) If the STD determines that the lowest bid is not responsive or the bidder is not responsible, it shall so notify and obtain the Division Administrator's concurrence before making an award to the next lowest bidder.

(g) If the STD rejects or declines to read or consider a low bid on the grounds that it is not responsive because of noncompliance with a requirement which was not clearly identified in the bidding documents, it shall submit justification for its action. If such justification is not considered by the Division Administrator to be sufficient, concurrence will not be given to award to another bidder on the contract at the same letting.

(h) Any proposal by the STD to reject all bids received for a Federal-aid contract shall be submitted to the Division Administrator for concurrence, accompanied by adequate justification.

(i) In the event the low bidder selected by the STD for contract award forfeits the bid guarantee, the STD may dispose of the amounts of such forfeited guarantees in accordance with its normal practices.

(j) A copy of the executed contract between the STD and the construction contractor should be furnished to the Division Administrator as soon as practicable after execution.

(k) In the case of a design-build project, the following requirements apply: Design-build contracts shall be awarded in accordance with the Request for Proposals document. *See* 23 CFR Part 636, Design-build Contracting, for details.

(l) In the case of a CM/GC project, the CM/GC contract shall be awarded in accordance with the solicitation document. See subpart E for CM/GC project approval procedures.

[56 FR 37004, Aug. 2, 1991, as amended at 67 FR 75925, Dec. 10, 2002; 81 FR 86943, Dec. 2, 2016]

§635.115 Agreement estimate.

(a) Following the award of contract, an agreement estimate based on the contract unit prices and estimated quantities shall be prepared by the STD and submitted to the Division Administrator as soon as practicable for use in the preparation of the project agreement. The agreement estimate shall also include the actual or best estimated costs of any other items to be included in the project agreement.

(b) An agreement estimate shall be submitted by the STD for each force account project (see 23 CFR part 635, subpart B) when the plans and specifications are submitted to the Division Administrator for approval. It shall normally be based on the estimated quantities and the unit prices agreed upon in advance between the STD and the Division Administrator, whether the work is to be done by the STD or by a local public agency. Such agreed unit prices shall constitute a commitment as the basis for Federal participation in the cost of the project. The unit prices shall be based upon the estimated actual cost of performing the work but shall in no case exceed unit prices currently being obtained by competitive bidding on comparable highway construction work in the same general locality. In special cases involving unusual circumstances, the estimate may be based upon the estimated costs for labor, materials, equipment rentals, and supervision to complete the work rather than upon agreed unit prices. This paragraph shall not be applicable to agreement estimates for railroad and utility force account work.

§ 635.116 Subcontracting and contractor responsibilities.

(a) Contracts for projects shall specify the minimum percentage of work that a contractor must perform with its own organization. This percentage shall be not less than 30 percent of the total original contract price excluding any identified specialty items. Specialty items may be performed by subcontract and the amount of any such specialty items so performed may be deducted from the total original contract before computing the amount of work required to be performed by the contractor's own organization. The contract amount upon which the above requirement is computed includes the cost of materials and manufactured products which are to be purchased or produced by the contractor under the contract provisions.

(b) The STD shall not permit any of the contract work to be performed under a subcontract, unless such arrangement has been authorized by the STD in writing. Prior to authorizing a subcontract, the STD shall assure that each subcontract is evidenced in writing and that it contains all pertinent provisions and requirements of the prime contract. The Division Administrator may permit the STD to satisfy the subcontract assurance requirements by concurrence in a STD process which requires the contractor to certify that each subcontract arrangement will be in the form of a written agreement containing all the requirements and pertinent provisions of the prime contract. Prior to the Division Administrator's concurrence, the STD must demonstrate that it has an acceptable plan for monitoring such certifications.

(c) To assure that all work (including subcontract work) is performed in accordance with the contract requirements, the contractor shall be required to furnish:

(1) A competent superintendent or supervisor who is employed by the firm, has full authority to direct performance of the work in accordance with the contract requirements, and is in charge of all construction operations (regardless of who performs the work), and;

(2) Such other of its own organizational resources (supervision, management, and engineering services) as the STD contracting officer determines are necessary to assure the performance of the contract.

(d) In the case of a design-build project, the following requirements apply:

(1) The provisions of paragraph (a) of this section are not applicable to design-build contracts;

(2) At their discretion, the STDs may establish a minimum percentage of work that must be done by the design-builder. For the purpose of this section, the term design-builder may include any firms that are equity participants in the design-builder, their sister and parent companies, and their wholly owned subsidiaries;

(3) No procedure, requirement or preference shall be imposed which prescribes minimum subcontracting requirements or goals (other than those necessary to meet the Disadvantaged Business Enterprise program requirements of 49 CFR part 26).

[56 FR 37004, Aug. 2, 1991, as amended at 67 FR 75925, Dec. 10, 2002]

§ 635.117 Labor and employment.

(a) No construction work shall be performed by convict labor at the work site or within the limits of any Federal-aid highway construction project from the time of award of the contract or the start of work on force account until final acceptance of the work by the STD unless it is labor performed by convicts who are on parole, supervised release, or probation.

(b) No procedures or requirement shall be imposed by any State which will operate to discriminate against the employment of labor from any other State, possession or territory of the United States, in the construction of a Federal-aid project.

(c) The selection of labor to be employed by the contractor on any Federal-aid project shall be by the contractor without regard to race, color, religion, sex, national origin, age, or handicap and in accordance with 23 CFR part 230, 41 CFR part 60 and Exec. Order No. 11246 (Sept. 24, 1965), 3 CFR 339 (1964–1965), as amended.

(d) Pursuant to 23 U.S.C. 140(d), it is permissible for STD's to implement procedures or requirements which will extend preferential employment to Indians living on or near a reservation on eligible projects as defined in paragraph (e) of this section. Indian preference shall be applied without regard to tribal affiliation or place of enrollment. In no instance should a contractor be compelled to layoff or terminate a permanent core-crew employee to meet a preference goal.

(e) Projects eligible for Indian employment preference consideration are projects located on roads within or providing access to an Indian reservation or other Indian lands as defined under the term "Indian Reservation Roads" in 23 U.S.C. 101 and regulations issued thereunder. The terminus of a road "providing access to" is that point at which it intersects with a road functionally classified as a collector or higher classification (outside the reservation boundary) in both urban and rural areas. In the case of an Interstate highway, the terminus is the first interchange outside the reservation.

(f) The advertisement or call for bids on any contract for the construction of a project located on the Federal-aid system either shall include the minimum wage rates determined by the Secretary of Labor to be prevailing on the same type of work on similar construction in the immediate locality or shall provide that such rates are set out in the bidding documents and shall further specify that such rates are a part of the contract covering the project.

§635.118 Payroll and weekly statements.

For all projects, copies of payrolls and statements of wages paid, filed with the State as set forth in the required contract provisions for the project, are to be retained by the STD for the time period pursuant to 49 CFR part 18 for review as needed by the Federal Highway Administration, the Department of Labor, the General Accounting Office, or other agencies.

§635.119 False statements.

The following notice shall be posted on each Federal-aid highway project in one or more places where it is readily available to and viewable by all personnel concerned with the project:

NOTICE TO ALL PERSONNEL ENGAGED ON FEDERAL-AID HIGHWAY PROJECTS

United States Code, title 18, section 1020, reads as follows:

Whoever, being an officer, agent, or employee of the United States, or of any State or Territory, or whoever, whether a person, association, firm, or corporation, knowingly makes any false statement, false representation, or false report as to the character, quality, quantity, or cost of the material used or to be used, or the quantity or quality of the work performed or to be performed, or the costs thereof in connection with the submission of plans, maps, specifications, contracts, or costs of construction of any highway or related project submitted for approval to the Secretary of Transportation; or

Whoever, knowingly makes any false statement, false representation, false report, or false claim with respect to the character, quality, quantity, or cost of any work performed or to be performed, or materials furnished or to be furnished, in connection with the construction of any highway or related project approved by the Secretary of Transportation; or

Whoever, knowingly makes any false statement or false representation as to a material fact in any statement, certificate, or report submitted pursuant to the provisions of the Federal-aid Road Act approved July 11, 1916 (39 Stat. 355), as amended and supplemented,

Shall be fined not more than $10,000 or imprisoned not more than five years, or both.

§635.120 Changes and extra work.

(a) Following authorization to proceed with a project, all major changes in the plans and contract provisions and all major extra work shall have formal approval by the Division Administrator in advance of their effective dates. However, when emergency or unusual conditions justify, the Division Administrator may give tentative advance approval orally to such changes or extra work and ratify such approval with formal approval as soon thereafter as practicable.

(b) For non-major changes and non-major extra work, formal approval is necessary but such approval may be given retroactively at the discretion of the Division Administrator. The STD should establish and document with the Division Administrator's concurrence specific parameters as to what constitutes a non-major change and non-major extra work.

(c) Changes in contract time, as related to contract changes or extra work, should be submitted at the same time as the respective work change for approval by the Division Administrator.

(d) In establishing the method of payment for contract changes or extra work orders, force account procedures shall only be used when strictly necessary, such as when agreement cannot be reached with the contractor on the price of a new work item, or when the extent of work is unknown or is of such character that a price cannot be determined to a reasonable degree of accuracy. The reason or reasons for using force account procedures shall be documented.

(e) The STD shall perform and adequately document a cost analysis of each negotiated contract change or negotiated extra work order. The method and degree of the cost analysis shall be subject to the approval of the Division Administrator.

(f) Proposed changes and extra work involved in nonparticipating operations that may affect the design or participating construction features of a project, shall be subject to review and concurrence by the Division Administrator.

§ 635.121 Contract time and contract time extensions.

(a) The STD should have adequate written procedures for the determination of contract time. These procedures should be submitted for approval to the Division Administrator within 6 months of the effective date of this Final Rule.

(b) Contract time extensions granted by a STD shall be subject to the concurrence of the Division Administrator and will be considered in determining the amount of Federal participation. Contract time extensions submitted for approval to the Division Administrator, shall be fully justified and adequately documented.

§ 635.122 Participation in progress payments.

(a) Federal funds will participate in the costs to the STD of construction accomplished as the work progresses, based on a request for reimbursement submitted by State transportation departments. When the contract provisions provide for payment for stockpiled materials, the amount of the reimbursement request upon which participation is based may include the appropriate value of approved specification materials delivered by the contractor at the project site or at another designated location in the vicinity of such construction, provided that:

(1) The material conforms with the requirements of the plans and specifications.

(2) The material is supported by a paid invoice or a receipt for delivery of materials. If supported by a receipt of delivery of materials, the contractor must furnish the paid invoice within a reasonable time after receiving payment from the STD; and

(3) The quantity of a stockpiled material eligible for Federal participation in any case shall not exceed the total estimated quantity required to complete the project. The value of the stockpiled material shall not exceed the appropriate portion of the value of the contract item or items in which such materials are to be incorporated.

(b) The materials may be stockpiled by the contractor at a location not in the vicinity of the project, if the STD determines that because of required fabrication at an off-site location, it is not feasible or practicable to stockpile the materials in the vicinity of the project.

(c) In the case of a design-build project, the STD must define its procedures for making progress payments on lump sum contracts in the Request for Proposal document.

(d) In the case of a CM/GC project, the STD must define its procedures for making construction phase progress payments in either the solicitation or the construction services contract documents.

[56 FR 37004, Aug. 2, 1991, as amended at 67 FR 75925, Dec. 10, 2002; 81 FR 86943, Dec. 2, 2016]

§635.123 Determination and documentation of pay quantities.

(a) The STD shall have procedures in effect which will provide adequate assurance that the quantities of completed work are determined accurately and on a uniform basis throughout the State. All such determinations and all related source documents upon which payment is based shall be made a matter of record.

(b) Initial source documents pertaining to the determination of pay quantities are among those records and documents which must be retained pursuant to 49 CFR part 18.

§635.124 Participation in contract claim awards and settlements.

(a) The eligibility for and extent of Federal-aid participation up to the Federal statutory share in a contract claim award made by a State to a Federal-aid contractor on the basis of an arbitration or mediation proceeding, administrative board determination, court judgment, negotiated settlement, or other contract claim settlement shall be determined on a case-by-case basis. Federal funds will participate to the extent that any contract adjustments made are supported, and have a basis in terms of the contract and applicable State law, as fairly construed. Further, the basis for the adjustment and contractor compensation shall be in accord with prevailing principles of public contract law.

(b) The FHWA shall be made aware by the STD of the details of the claim at an early stage so that coordination of efforts can be satisfactorily accomplished. It is expected that STDs will diligently pursue the satisfactory resolution of claims within a reasonable period of time. Claims arising on exempt non-NHS projects should be processed in accordance with the State's approved Stewardship Plan.

(c) When requesting Federal participation, the STD shall set forth in writing the legal and contractual basis for the claim, together with the cost data and other facts supporting the award or settlement. Federal-aid participation in such instances shall be supported by a STD audit of the actual costs incurred by the contractor unless waived by the FHWA as unwarranted. Where difficult, complex, or novel legal issues appear in the claim, such that evaluation of legal controversies is critical to consideration of the award or settlement, the STD shall include in its submission a legal opinion from its counsel setting forth the basis for determining the extent of the liability under local law, with a level of detail commensurate with the magnitude and complexity of the issues involved.

(d) In those cases where the STD receives an adverse decision in an amount more than the STD was able to support prior to the decision or settles a claim in an amount more than the STD can support, the FHWA will participate up to the appropriate Federal matching share, to the extent that it involves a Federal-aid participating portion of the contract, provided that:

(1) The FHWA was consulted and concurred in the proposed course of action;

(2) All appropriate courses of action had been considered; and

(3) The STD pursued the case diligently and in a professional manner.

(e) Federal funds will not participate:

(1) If it has been determined that STD employees, officers, or agents acted with gross negligence, or participated in intentional acts or omissions, fraud, or other acts not consistent with usual State practices in project design, plan preparation, contract administration, or other activities which gave rise to the claim;

(2) In such cost items as consequential or punitive damages, anticipated profit, or any award or payment of attorney's fees paid by a State to an opposing party in litigation; and

(3) In tort, inverse condemnation, or other claims erroneously styled as claims "under a contract."

(f) Payment of interest associated with a claim will be eligible for participation provided that the payment to the contractor for interest is allowable by State statute or specification and the costs are not a result of delays caused by dilatory action of the State or the contractor. The interest rates must not exceed the rate provided for by the State statute or specification.

(g) In cases where STD's affirmatively recover compensatory damages through contract claims, cross-claims, or counter claims from contractors, subcontractors, or their agents on projects on which there was Federal-aid participation, the Federal share of such recovery shall be equivalent to the Federal share of the project or projects involved. Such recovery shall be credited to the project or projects from which the claim or claims arose.

[56 FR 37004, Aug. 2, 1991, as amended at 62 FR 6873, Feb. 14, 1997; 69 FR 7118, Feb. 13, 2004]

§635.125 Termination of contract.

(a) All contracts exceeding $10,000 shall contain suitable provisions for termination by the State, including the manner by which the termination will be effected and the basis for settlement. In addition, such contracts shall describe conditions under which the contract may be terminated for default as well as conditions where the contract may be terminated because of circumstances beyond the control of the contractor.

(b) The STD prior to termination of a Federal-aid contract shall consult with and receive the concurrence of the Division Administrator. The extent of Federal-aid participation in contract termination costs, including final settlement, will depend upon the merits of the individual case. However, under no circumstances shall Federal funds participate in anticipated profit on work not performed.

(c) Except as provided for in paragraph (e) of this section, normal Federal-aid plans, specifications, and estimates, advertising, and award procedures are to be followed when a STD awards the contract for completion of a terminated Federal-aid contract.

(d) When a STD awards the contract for completion of a Federal-aid contract previously terminated for default, the construction amount eligible for Federal participation on the project should not exceed whichever amount is the lesser, either:

(1) The amount representing the payments made under the original contract plus payments made under the new contract; or

(2) The amount representing what the cost would have been if the construction had been completed as contemplated by the plans and specifications under the original contract.

(e) If the surety awards a contract for completion of a defaulted Federal-aid contract or completes it by some other acceptable means, the FHWA will consider the terms of the original contract to be in effect and that the work will be completed in accordance with the approved plans and specifications included therein. No further FHWA approval or concurrence action will therefore be needed in connection with any defaulted Federal-aid contract awarded by a surety. Under this procedure, the construction amount eligible for Federal participation on the project should not exceed the amount representing what the cost would have been if the construction had been completed as contemplated by the plans and specifications under the original contract.

§635.126 [Reserved]

§635.127 Agreement provisions regarding overruns in contract time.

(a) Each State transportation department (STD) shall establish specific liquidated damages rates applicable to projects in that State. The rates may be project-specific or may be in the form of a table or schedule developed for a range of project costs and/or project types. These rates shall, as a minimum, be established to cover the estimated average daily construction engineering (CE) costs associated with the type of work encountered on the project. The amounts shall be assessed by means of deductions, for each calendar day or workday overrun in contract time, from payments otherwise due to the contractor for performance in accordance with the contract terms.

(b) The rates established shall be subject to FHWA approval either on a project-by-project basis, in the case of project-specific rates, or on a periodic basis after initial approval where a rate table or schedule is used. In the latter case, the STD shall periodically review its cost data to ascertain if the rate table/schedule closely approximates, at a minimum, the actual average daily CE costs associated with the type and size of the projects in the State. Where rate schedules or other means are already included in the STD specifications or standard special provisions, verification by the STD that the amounts are adequate shall be submitted to the FHWA for review and approval. After initial approval by the FHWA of the rates, the STD shall review the rates at least every 2 years and provide updated rates, when necessary, for FHWA approval. If updated rates are not warranted, justification of this fact is to be sent to the FHWA for review and acceptance.

(c) The STD may, with FHWA concurrence, include additional amounts as liquidated damages in each contract to cover other anticipated costs of project related delays or inconveniences to the STD or the public. Costs resulting from winter shutdowns, retaining detours for an extended time, additional demurrage, or similar costs as well as road user delay costs may be included.

(d) In addition to the liquidated damages provisions, the STD may also include incentive/disincentive for early completion provisions in the contract. The incentive/disincentive amounts shall be shown separately from the liquidated damages amounts.

(e) Where there has been an overrun in contract time, the following principles shall apply in determining the cost of a project that is eligible for Federal-aid reimbursement:

(1) A proportional share, as used in this section, is the ratio of the final contract construction costs eligible for Federal participation to the final total contract construction costs of the project.

(2) Where CE costs are claimed as a participating item based upon actual expenses incurred or where CE costs are not claimed as a participating item, and where the liquidated damages rates cover only CE expenses, the total CE costs for the project shall be reduced by the assessed liquidated damages amounts prior to figuring any Federal pro rata share payable. If the amount of liquidated damages assessed is more than the actual CE totals for the project, a proportional share of the excess shall be deducted from the federally participating contract construction cost before determining the final Federal share.

(3) Where the STD is being reimbursed for CE costs on the basis of an approved percentage of the participating construction cost, the total contract construction amount that would be eligible for Federal participation shall be reduced by a proportional share of the total liquidated damages amounts assessed on the project.

(4) Where liquidated damages include extra anticipated non-CE costs due to contractor caused delays, the amount assessed shall be used to pay for the actual non-CE expenses incurred by the STD, and, if a Federal participating item(s) is involved, to reduce the Federal share payable for that item(s). If the amount assessed is more than the actual expenses incurred by the STD, a proportional share of the excess shall be deducted from the federally participating contract construction cost of the project before the Federal share is figured.

(f) When provisions for incentive/disincentive for early completion are used in the contract, a proportion of the increased project costs due to any incentive payments to the contractor shall be added to the federally participating contract construction cost before calculating the Federal share. When the disincentive provision is applicable, a proportion of the amount assessed the contractor shall be deducted from the federally participating contract construction cost before the Federal share calculation. Proportions are to be calculated in the same manner as set forth in paragraph (e)(1) of this section.

[52 FR 31390, Aug. 20, 1987. Redesignated at 62 FR 6872, Feb. 14, 1997]

Subpart B—Force Account Construction

§ 635.201 Purpose.

The purpose of this subpart is to prescribe procedures in accordance with 23 U.S.C. 112(b) for a State transportation department to request approval that highway construction work be performed by some method other than contract awarded by competitive bidding.

[48 FR 22912, May 23, 1983]

§ 635.202 Applicability.

This subpart applies to all Federal-aid and other highway construction projects financed in whole or in part with Federal funds and to be constructed by a State transportation department or a subdivision thereof in pursuant of agreements between any other State transportation department and the Federal Highway Administration (FHWA).

[69 FR 7119, Feb. 13, 2004]

§ 635.203 Definitions.

The following definitions shall apply for the purpose of this subpart:

(a) A *State transportation department* is that department, commission, board, or official of any State charged by its laws with the responsibility for highway construction. The term *State* should be considered equivalent to *State transportation department* if the context so implies.

(b) Except as provided for as emergency repair work in § 668.105(i) and in § 635.204(b), the term *some other method* of construction as used in 23 U.S.C. 112(b) shall mean the *force account* method of construction as defined herein. In the unlikely event that circumstances are considered to justify a negotiated contract or another unusual method of construction, the policies and procedures prescribed herein for force account work will apply.

(c) The term *force account* shall mean the direct performance of highway construction work by a State transportation department, a county, a railroad, or a public utility company by use of labor, equipment, materials, and supplies furnished by them and used under their direct control.

(d) The term *county* shall mean any county, township, municipality or other political subdivision that may be empowered to cooperate with the State transportation department in highway matters.

(e) The term *cost effective* shall mean the efficient use of labor, equipment, materials and supplies to assure the lowest overall cost.

(f) For the purpose of this part, an *emergency* shall be deemed to exist when emergency repair work as provided for in § 668.105(i) is necessary or when a major element or segment of the highway system has failed and the situation is such that competitive bidding is not possible or is impractical because immediate action is necessary to:

(1) Minimize the extent of the damage,

(2) Protect remaining facilities, or

(3) Restore essential travel.

This definition of *emergency* has no applicability to the Emergency Relief Program of 23 CFR part 668.

[39 FR 35158, Sept. 30, 1974, as amended at 48 FR 22912, May 23, 1983; 52 FR 45172, Nov. 25, 1987]

§ 635.204 Determination of more cost effective method or an emergency.

(a) Congress has expressly provided that the contract method based on competitive bidding shall be used by a State transportation department or county for performance of highway work financed with the aid of Federal funds unless the State transportation department demonstrates, to the satisfaction of the Secretary, that some other method is more cost effective or that an emergency exists.

(b) When a State transportation department determines it necessary due to an emergency to undertake a federally financed highway construction project by force account or negotiated contract method, it shall submit a request to the Division Administrator identifying and describing the project, the kinds of work to be performed, the method to be used, the estimated costs, the estimated Federal Funds to be provided, and the reason or reasons that an emergency exists.

(c) Except as provided in paragraph (b) of this section, when a State transportation department desires that highway construction work financed with the aid of Federal funds, other than the kinds of work designated under §635.205(b), be undertaken by force account, it shall submit a request to the Division Administrator identifying and describing the project and the kind of work to be performed, the estimated costs, the estimated Federal funds to be provided, and the reason or reasons that force account for such project is considered cost effective.

(d) The Division Administrator shall notify the State transportation department in writing of his/her determination.

[52 FR 45172, Nov. 25, 1987]

§635.205 Finding of cost effectiveness.

(a) It may be found cost effective for a State transportation department or county to undertake a federally financed highway construction project by force account when a situation exists in which the rights or resposibilities of the community at large are so affected as to require some special course of action, including situations where there is a lack of bids or the bids received are unreasonable.

(b) Pursuant to authority in 23 U.S.C. 112(b), it is hereby determined that by reason of the inherent nature of the operations involved, it is cost effective to perform by force account the adjustment of railroad or utility facilities and similar types of facilities owned or operated by a public agency, a railroad, or a utility company provided that the organization is qualified to perform the work in a satisfactory manner. The installation of new facilities shall be undertaken by competitive bidding except as provided in §635.204(c). Adjustment of railroad facilities shall include minor work on the railroad's operating facilities routinely performed by the railroad with its own forces such as the installation of grade crossing warning devices, crossing surfaces, and minor track and signal work. Adjustment of utility facilities shall include minor work on the utility's existing facilities routinely performed by the utility with its own forces and includes minor installations of new facilities to provide power, minor lighting, telephone, water and similar utility service to a rest area, weigh-station, movable bridge, or other highway appurtenance, provided such installation cannot feasibly be done as incidental to a major installation project such as an extensive highway lighting system.

[52 FR 45173, Nov. 25, 1987]

Subpart C—Physical Construction Authorization

SOURCE: 40 FR 17251, Apr. 18, 1975, unless otherwise noted.

§635.301 Purpose.

To prescribe the policies and procedures under which a State transportation department may be authorized to advance a Federal-aid highway project to the physical construction stage.

§635.303 Applicability.

The provisions of this subpart are applicable to all Federal-aid highway construction projects.

[69 FR 7119, Feb. 13, 2004]

§635.305 Physical construction.

For purposes of this subpart the physical construction of a project is considered to consist of the actual construction of the highway itself with its appurtenant facilities. It includes any removal, adjustment or demolition of buildings or major obstructions, and utility or railroad work that is a part of the contract for the physical construction.

§635.307 Coordination.

(a) The right-of-way clearance, utility, and railroad work are to be so coordinated with the physical construction that no unnecessary delay or cost for the physical construction will occur.

(b) All right-of-way clearance, utility, and railroad work performed separately from the contract for the physical construction of the project are to be accomplished in accordance with provisions of the following:

(1) 23 CFR part 140, subpart I;

(2) 23 CFR part 646, subpart B;

(3) 23 CFR 710.403; and

(4) 23 CFR part 645, subpart A.

[40 FR 17251, Apr. 18, 1975, as amended at 40 FR 25585, June 17, 1975; 64 FR 71289, Dec. 21, 1999]

§ 635.309 Authorization.

Authorization to advertise the physical construction for bids or to proceed with force account construction thereof shall normally be issued as soon as, but not until, all of the following conditions have been met:

(a) The plans, specifications, and estimates (PS&E) have been approved.

(b) A statement is received from the State, either separately or combined with the information required by paragraph (c) of this section, that either all right-of-way (ROW) clearance, utility, and railroad work has been completed or that all necessary arrangements have been made for it to be undertaken and completed as required for proper coordination with the physical construction schedules. Where it is determined that the completion of such work in advance of the highway construction is not feasible or practical due to economy, special operational problems or the like, there shall be appropriate notification provided in the bid proposals identifying the ROW clearance, utility, and railroad work which is to be underway concurrently with the highway construction.

(c) Except as otherwise provided for design-build projects in § 710.309 of this chapter and paragraph (p) of this section, a statement is received from the State certifying that all individuals and families have been relocated to decent, safe, and sanitary housing or that the State has made available to relocatees adequate replacement housing in accordance with the provisions of the 49 CFR part 24 and that one of the following has application:

(1) All necessary ROW, including control of access rights when pertinent, have been acquired including legal and physical possession. Trial or appeal of cases may be pending in court but legal possession has been obtained. There may be some improvements remaining on the ROW but all occupants have vacated the lands and improvements and the State has physical possession and the right to remove, salvage, or demolish these improvements and enter on all land.

(2) Although all necessary ROW have not been fully acquired, the right to occupy and to use all ROW required for the proper execution of the project has been acquired. Trial or appeal of some parcels may be pending in court and on other parcels full legal possession has not been obtained but right of entry has been obtained, the occupants of all lands and improvements have vacated and the State has physical possession and right to remove, salvage, or demolish these improvements.

(3) The acquisition or right of occupancy and use of a few remaining parcels is not complete, but all occupants of the residences on such parcels have had replacement housing made available to them in accordance with 49 CFR 24.204. Under these circumstances, the State may request the Federal Highway Administration (FHWA) to authorize actions based on a conditional certification as provided in this paragraph.

(i) The State may request approval for the advertisement for bids based on a conditional certification. The FHWA will approve the request unless it finds that it will not be in the public interest to proceed with the bidding before acquisition activities are complete.

(ii) The State may request approval for physical construction under a contract or through force account work based on a conditional certification. The FHWA will approve the request only if FHWA finds there are exceptional circumstances that make it in the public interest to proceed with construction before acquisition activities are complete.

(iii) Whenever a conditional certification is used, the State shall ensure that occupants of residences, businesses, farms, or non-profit organizations who have not yet moved from the

ROW are protected against unnecessary inconvenience and disproportionate injury or any action coercive in nature.

(iv) When the State requests authorization under a conditional certification to advertise for bids or to proceed with physical construction where acquisition or right of occupancy and use of a few parcels has not been obtained, full explanation and reasons therefor, including identification of each such parcel, will be set forth in the State's request along with a realistic date when physical occupancy and use is anticipated as well as substantiation that such date is realistic. Appropriate notification must be provided in the request for bids, identifying all locations where right of occupancy and use has not been obtained. Prior to the State issuing a notice to proceed with construction to the contractor, the State shall provide an updated notification to FHWA identifying all locations where right of occupancy and use has not been obtained along with a realistic date when physical occupancy and use is anticipated.

(v) Participation of title 23 funds in construction delay claims resulting from unavailable parcels shall be determined in accordance with §635.124. The FHWA will determine the extent of title 23 participation in costs related to construction delay claims resulting from unavailable parcels where FHWA determines the State did not follow approved processes and procedures.

(d) The State transportation department (SDOT), in accordance with 23 CFR 771.111(h), has submitted public hearing transcripts, certifications and reports pursuant to 23 U.S.C. 128.

(e) An affirmative finding of cost effectiveness or that an emergency exists has been made as required by 23 U.S.C. 112, when construction by some method other than contract based on competitive bidding is contemplated.

(f) Minimum wage rates determined by the Department of Labor in accordance with the provisions of 23 U.S.C. 113, are in effect and will not expire before the end of the period within which it can reasonably be expected that the contract will be awarded.

(g) A statement has been received that ROW has been acquired or will be acquired in accordance with 49 CFR part 24 and part 710 of this chapter, or that acquisition of ROW is not required.

(h) A statement has been received that the steps relative to relocation advisory assistance and payments as required by 49 CFR part 24 have been taken, or that they are not required.

(i) The FHWA has determined that appropriate measures have been included in the PS&E in keeping with approved guidelines, for minimizing possible soil erosion and water pollution as a result of highway construction operations.

(j) The FHWA has determined that requirements of 23 CFR part 771 have been fulfilled and appropriate measures have been included in the PS&E to ensure that conditions and commitments made in the development of the project to mitigate environmental harm will be met.

(k) Where utility facilities are to use and occupy the right-of-way, the State has demonstrated to the satisfaction of the FHWA that the provisions of §645.119(b) of this chapter have been fulfilled.

(l) The FHWA has verified the fact that adequate replacement housing is in place and has been made available to all affected persons.

(m) Where applicable, area wide agency review has been accomplished as required by 42 U.S.C. 3334 and 4231 through 4233.

(n) The FHWA has determined that the PS&E provide for the erection of only those information signs and traffic control devices that conform to the standards developed by the Secretary of Transportation or mandates of Federal law and do not include promotional or other informational signs regarding such matters as identification of public officials, contractors, organizational affiliations, and related logos and symbols.

(o) The FHWA has determined that, where applicable, provisions are included in the PS&E that require the erection of funding source signs, for the life of the construction project, in accordance with section 154 of the Surface Transportation and Uniform Relocation Assistance and Real Property Acquisition Policies Act of 1970, as amended (Pub. L. 91–646, 84 Stat. 1894; primarily codified in 42 U.S.C. 4601 *et seq.*;) (Uniform Act).

(p) In the case of a design-build or CM/GC project, the following certification requirements apply

(1) The FHWA's project authorization for final design and physical construction will not be issued until the following conditions have been met:

(i) All projects must conform with the statewide and metropolitan transportation planning requirements (23 CFR part 450).

(ii) All projects in air quality nonattainment and maintenance areas must meet all transportation conformity requirements (40 CFR parts 51 and 93).

(iii) The NEPA review process has been concluded. (*See* § 636.109 of this chapter).

(iv) The Request for Proposals document has been approved.

(v) A statement is received from the SDOT that either all ROW, utility, and railroad work has been completed or that all necessary arrangements will be made for the completion of ROW, utility, and railroad work.

(vi) If the STD elects to include right-of-way, utility, and/or railroad services as part of the design-builder's or CM/GC contractor's scope of work, then the applicable design-build Request for Proposals document, or the CM/GC solicitation document must include:

(2) During a conformity lapse, an Early Acquisition Project carried out in accordance with § 710.501 of this chapter or a design-build project (including ROW acquisition activities) may continue if, prior to the conformity lapse, the National Environmental Policy Act (NEPA) (42 U.S.C. 4321, *et seq.*) process was completed and the project has not changed significantly in design scope, FHWA authorized the early acquisition or design-build project, and the project met transportation conformity requirements (40 CFR parts 51 and 93).

(3) Changes to the design-build or CM/GC project concept and scope may require a modification of the transportation plan and transportation improvement program. The project sponsor must comply with the metropolitan and statewide transportation planning requirements in 23 CFR part 450 and the transportation conformity requirements (40 CFR parts 51 and 93) in air quality nonattainment and maintenance areas, and provide appropriate approval notification to the design builder or the CM/GC contractor for such changes.

[81 FR 57728, Aug. 23, 2016, as amended at 81 FR 86943, Dec. 2, 2016]

Subpart D—General Material Requirements

SOURCE: 41 FR 36204, Aug. 27, 1976, unless otherwise noted.

§ 635.401 Purpose.

The purpose of this subpart is to prescribe requirements and procedures relating to product and material selection and use on Federal-aid highway projects.

§ 635.403 Definitions.

As used in this subpart, the following terms have the meanings indicated:

(a) *FHWA Division Administrator* means the chief Federal Highway Administration (FHWA) official assigned to conduct business in a particular State;

(b) *Material* means any tangible substance incorporated into a Federal-aid highway project;

(c) *PS&E* means plans, specifications, and estimates;

(d) *Special provisions* means additions and revisions to the standard and supplemental specifications applicable to an individual project;

(e) *Standard specifications* means a compilation in book form of specifications approved for general application and repetitive use;

(f) *State* has the meaning set forth in 23 U.S.C. 101;

(g) *State transportation department* means that department, commission, board, or official of any State charged by its laws with the responsibility for highway construction;

(h) *Supplemental specifications* means approved additions and revisions to the standard specifications.

§ 635.405 Applicability.

The requirements and procedures prescribed in this subpart apply to all contracts relating to Federal-aid highway projects.

[69 FR 7119, Feb. 13, 2004]

§ 635.407 Use of materials made available by a public agency.

(a) Contracts for highway projects shall require the contractor to furnish all materials to be incorporated in the work and shall permit the contractor to select the sources from which the materials are to be obtained. Exception to this requirement may be made when there is a definite finding by the State transportation department and concurred in by the FHWA Division Administrator, that it is in the public interest to require the contractor to use material furnished by the State transportation department or from sources designated by the State transportation department. In cases such as this, the FHWA does not expect mutual sharing of costs unless the State transportation department receives a related credit from another agency or political subdivision of the State. Where such a credit does accrue to the State transportation department, it shall be applied to the Federal-aid project involved. The designation of a mandatory material source may be permitted based on environmental considerations, provided the environment would be substantially enhanced without excessive cost. Otherwise, if a State transportation department proposal to designate a material source for mandatory use would result in higher project costs, Federal-aid funds shall not participate in the increase even if the designation would conserve other public funds.

(b) The provisions of paragraph (a) of this section will not preclude the designation in the plans and specifications of sources of local natural materials, such as borrow aggregates, that have been investigated by the State transportation department and found to contain materials meeting specification requirements. The use of materials from such designated sources shall not be mandatory unless there is a finding of public interest as stated in paragraph (a) of this section.

(c) Federal funds may participate in the cost of specifications materials made available by a public agency when they have been actually incorporated in accepted items of work, or in the cost of such materials meeting the criteria and stockpiled at the locations specified in § 635.114 of this chapter.

(d) To be eligible for Federal participation in its cost, any material, other than local natural materials, to be purchased by the State transportation department and furnished to the contractor for mandatory use in the project, must have been acquired on the basis of competitive bidding, except when there is a finding of public interest justifying the use of another method of acquisition. The location and unit price at which such material will be available to the contractor must be stated in the special provisions for the benefit of all prospective bidders. The unit cost eligible for Federation participation will be limited to the unit cost of such material to the State transportation department.

(e) When the State transportation department or another public agency owns or has control over the source of a local natural material the unit price at which such material will be made available to the contractor must be stated in the plans or special provisions. Federal participation will be limited to (1) the cost of the material to the State transportation department or other public agency; or (2) the fair and reasonable value of the material, whichever is less. Special cases may arise that will justify Federal participation on a basis other than that set forth above. Such cases should be fully documented and receive advance approval by the FHWA Division Administrator.

(f) Costs incurred by the State transportation department or other public agency for acquiring a designated source or the right to take materials from it will not be eligible for Federal participation if the source is not used by the contractor.

(g) The contract provisions for one or a combination of Federal-aid projects shall not specify a mandatory site for the disposal of surplus excavated materials unless there is a finding by the State transportation department with the concurrence of the FHWA Division Administrator that such placement is the most economical except that the designation of a mandatory site may be permitted based on environmental considerations, provided the environment would be substantially enhanced without excessive cost.

§ 635.409 Restrictions upon materials.

No requirement shall be imposed and no procedure shall be enforced by any State transportation department in connection with a project which may operate:

(a) To require the use of or provide a price differential in favor of articles or materials produced within the State, or otherwise to prohibit, restrict or discriminate against the use of articles or materials shipped from or prepared, made or produced in any State, territory or possession of the United States; or

(b) To prohibit, restrict or otherwise discriminate against the use of articles or materials of foreign origin to any greater extent than is permissible under policies of the Department of Transportation as evidenced by requirements and procedures prescribed by the FHWA Administrator to carry out such policies.

§ 635.410 Buy America requirements.

(a) The provisions of this section shall prevail and be given precedence over any requirements of this subpart which are contrary to this section. However, nothing in this section shall be construed to be contrary to the requirements of § 635.409(a) of this subpart.

(b) No Federal-aid highway construction project is to be authorized for advertisement or otherwise authorized to proceed unless at least one of the following requirements is met:

(1) The project either: (i) Includes no permanently incorporated steel or iron materials, or (ii) if steel or iron materials are to be used, all manufacturing processes, including application of a coating, for these materials must occur in the United States. Coating includes all processes which protect or enhance the value of the material to which the coating is applied.

(2) The State has standard contract provisions that require the use of domestic materials and products, including steel and iron materials, to the same or greater extent as the provisions set forth in this section.

(3) The State elects to include alternate bid provisions for foreign and domestic steel and iron materials which comply with the following requirements. Any procedure for obtaining alternate bids based on furnishing foreign steel and iron materials which is acceptable to the Division Administrator may be used. The contract provisions must (i) require all bidders to submit a bid based on furnishing domestic steel and iron materials, and (ii) clearly state that the contract will be awarded to the bidder who submits the lowest total bid based on furnishing domestic steel and iron materials unless such total bid exceeds the lowest total bid based on furnishing foreign steel and iron materials by more than 25 percent.

(4) When steel and iron materials are used in a project, the requirements of this section do not prevent a minimal use of foreign steel and iron materials, if the cost of such materials used does not exceed one-tenth of one percent (0.1 percent) of the total contract cost or $2,500, whichever is greater. For purposes of this paragraph, the cost is that shown to be the value of the steel and iron products as they are delivered to the project.

(c)(1) A State may request a waiver of the provisions of this section if;

(i) The application of those provisions would be inconsistent with the public interest; or

(ii) Steel and iron materials/products are not produced in the United States in sufficient and reasonably available quantities which are of a satisfactory quality.

(2) A request for waiver, accompanied by supporting information, must be submitted in writing to the Regional Federal Highway Administrator (RFHWA) through the FHWA Division Administrator. A request must be submitted sufficiently in advance of the need for the waiver in order to allow time for proper review and action on

the request. The RFHWA will have approval authority on the request.

(3) Requests for waivers may be made for specific projects, or for certain materials or products in specific geographic areas, or for combinations of both, depending on the circumstances.

(4) The denial of the request by the RFHWA may be appealed by the State to the Federal Highway Administrator (Administrator), whose action on the request shall be considered administratively final.

(5) A request for a waiver which involves nationwide public interest or availability issues or more than one FHWA region may be submitted by the RFHWA to the Administrator for action.

(6) A request for waiver and an appeal from a denial of a request must include facts and justification to support the granting of the waiver. The FHWA response to a request or appeal will be in writing and made available to the public upon request. Any request for a nationwide waiver and FHWA's action on such a request may be published in the FEDERAL REGISTER for public comment.

(7) In determining whether the waivers described in paragraph (c)(1) of this section will be granted, the FHWA will consider all appropriate factors including, but not limited to, cost, administrative burden, and delay that would be imposed if the provision were not waived.

(d) Standard State and Federal-aid contract procedures may be used to assure compliance with the requirements of this section.

[48 FR 53104, Nov. 25, 1983, as amended at 49 FR 18821, May 3, 1984; 58 FR 38975, July 21, 1993]

§635.411 Material or product selection.

(a) Federal funds shall not participate, directly or indirectly, in payment for any premium or royalty on any patented or proprietary material, specification, or process specifically set forth in the plans and specifications for a project, unless:

(1) Such patented or proprietary item is purchased or obtained through competitive bidding with equally suitable unpatented items; or

(2) The State transportation department certifies either that such patented or proprietary item is essential for synchronization with existing highway facilities, or that no equally suitable alternate exists; or

(3) Such patented or proprietary item is used for research or for a distinctive type of construction on relatively short sections of road for experimental purposes.

(b) When there is available for purchase more than one nonpatented, nonproprietary material, semifinished or finished article or product that will fulfill the requirements for an item of work of a project and these available materials or products are judged to be of satisfactory quality and equally acceptable on the basis of engineering analysis and the anticipated prices for the related item(s) of work are estimated to be approximately the same, the PS&E for the project shall either contain or include by reference the specifications for each such material or product that is considered acceptable for incorporation in the work. If the State transportation department wishes to substitute some other acceptable material or product for the material or product designated by the successful bidder or bid as the lowest alternate, and such substitution results in an increase in costs, there will not be Federal-aid participation in any increase in costs.

(c) A State transportation department may require a specific material or product when there are other acceptable materials and products, when such specific choice is approved by the Division Administrator as being in the public interest. When the Division Administrator's approval is not obtained, the item will be nonparticipating unless bidding procedures are used that establish the unit price of each acceptable alternative. In this case Federal-aid participation will be based on the lowest price so established.

(d) Reference in specifications and on plans to single trade name materials will not be approved on Federal-aid contracts.

(e) In the case of a design-build project, the following requirements apply: Federal funds shall not participate, directly or indirectly, in payment for any premium or royalty on any patented or proprietary material, specification, or process specifically set forth in the Request for Proposals document unless the conditions of paragraph (a) of this section are applicable.

(f) State transportation departments (State DOTs) shall have the autonomy to determine culvert and storm sewer material types to be included in the construction of a project on a Federal-aid highway.

[41 FR 36204, Aug. 27, 1976, as amended at 67 FR 75926, Dec. 10, 2002; 71 FR 66454, Nov. 15, 2006; 78 FR 5717, Jan. 28, 2013]

§ 635.413 Guaranty and warranty clauses.

The STD may include warranty provisions in National Highway System (NHS) construction contracts in accordance with the following:

(a) Warranty provisions shall be for a specific construction product or feature. Items of maintenance not eligible for Federal participation shall not be covered.

(b) All warranty requirements and subsequent revisions shall be submitted to the Division Administrator for advance approval.

(c) No warranty requirement shall be approved which, in the judgment of the Division Administrator, may place an undue obligation on the contractor for items over which the contractor has no control.

(d) A STD may follow its own procedures regarding the inclusion of warranty provisions in non-NHS Federal-aid contracts.

(e) In the case of a design-build project, the following requirements will apply instead of paragraphs (a) through (d) of this section.

(1) General project warranties may be used on NHS projects, provided:

(i) The term of the warranty is short (generally one to two years); however, projects developed under a public-private agreement may include warranties that are appropriate for the term of the contract or agreement.

(ii) The warranty is not the sole means of acceptance;

(iii) The warranty must not include items of routine maintenance which are not eligible for Federal participation; and,

(iv) The warranty may include the quality of workmanship, materials and other specific tasks identified in the contract.

(2) Performance warranties for specific products on NHS projects may be used at the STD's discretion. If performance warranties are used, detailed performance criteria must be provided in the Request for Proposal document.

(3) The STD may follow its own procedures regarding the inclusion of warranty provisions on non-NHS Federal-aid design-build contracts.

(4) For best value selections, the STD may allow proposers to submit alternate warranty proposals that improve upon the warranty terms in the RFP document. Such alternate warranty proposals must be in addition to the base proposal that responds to the RFP requirements.

[60 FR 44274, Aug. 25, 1995, as amended at 67 FR 75926, Dec. 10, 2002; 72 FR 45336, Aug. 14, 2007]

§ 635.417 Convict produced materials.

(a) Materials produced after July 1, 1991, by convict labor may only be incorporated in a Federal-aid highway construction project if such materials have been:

(1) Produced by convicts who are on parole, supervised release, or probation from a prison or

(2) Produced in a qualified prison facility and the cumulative annual production amount of such materials for use in Federal-aid highway construction does not exceed the amount of such materials produced in such facility for use in Federal-aid highway construction during the 12-month period ending July 1, 1987.

(b) *Qualified prison facility* means any prison facility in which convicts, during the 12-month period ending July 1, 1987, produced materials for use in Federal-aid highway construction projects.

[53 FR 1923, Jan. 25, 1988, as amended at 58 FR 38975, July 21, 1993]

Subpart E—Construction Manager/General Contractor (CM/GC) Contracting

SOURCE: 81 FR 86943, Dec. 2, 2016, unless otherwise noted.

§ 635.501 Purpose.

The regulations in this subpart prescribe policies, requirements, and procedures relating to the use of the CM/GC method of contracting on Federal-aid projects.

§ 635.502 Definitions.

As used in this subpart:

Agreed price means the price agreed to by the Construction Manager/General Contractor (CM/GC) contractor and the contracting agency to provide construction services for a specific scope and schedule.

CM/GC contractor means the entity that has been awarded a two-phase contract for a CM/GC project and is responsible for providing preconstruction services under the first phase and, if a price agreement is reached, construction services under the second phase of such contract.

CM/GC project means a project to be delivered using a two-phase contract with a CM/GC contractor for services during the preconstruction and, if there is an agreed price, construction phases of a project.

Construction services means the physical construction work undertaken by a CM/GC contractor to construct a project or a portion of the project (including early work packages). Construction services include all costs to perform, supervise, and administer physical construction work. Construction services may be authorized as a single contract for the project, or through a combination of contracts covering portions of the CM/GC project.

Contracting agency means the State Transportation Agency (STA), and any State or local government agency, public-private partnership, or Indian tribe (as defined in 2 CFR 200.54) that is the acting under the supervision of the STA and is awarding and administering a CM/GC contract.

Division Administrator means the chief FHWA official assigned to conduct business in a particular State.

Early work package means a portion or phase of physical construction work (including but not limited to site preparation, structure demolition, hazardous material abatement/treatment/removal, early material acquisition/fabrication contracts, or any action that materially affects the objective consideration of alternatives in the NEPA review process) that is procured after NEPA is complete but before all design work for the project is complete. Contracting agencies may procure an early work package when construction risks have been addressed (both agency and CM/GC contractor risks) and the scope of work is defined sufficiently for the contracting agency and the CM/GC contractor to reasonably determine price. The requirements in § 635.506 (including § 635.506(d)(2)) and § 635.507 apply to procuring an early work package and FHWA authorization for an early work package.

Final design has the same meaning as defined in § 636.103 of this chapter.

NEPA process means the environmental review required under the National Environmental Policy Act (NEPA) of 1969 (42 U.S.C. 4321 *et seq.*), applicable portions of the NEPA implementing regulations at 40 CFR parts 1500–1508, and part 771 of this chapter.

Preconstruction services means consulting to provide a contracting agency and its designer with information regarding the impacts of design on the physical construction of the project, including but not limited to: Scheduling, work sequencing, cost engineering, constructability, cost estimating, and risk identification. Under a preconstruction services contract, the CM/GC contractor may provide consulting services during both preliminary and, subject to provisions in this subpart, final design. Such services may include on-site material sampling and data collection to assist the contacting agency's design team in its preliminary design work, but do not include design and engineering-related services as defined in § 172.3 of this chapter. The services may include the preparation of plans typically developed by a construction contractor during the construction phase (such as preliminary staging or preliminary falsework plans) when needed for the NEPA process. However, services involving plans or submittals that are considered elements of final design and not needed for the NEPA process (such as shop drawings or fabrication plans) is not allowed, even on an at-risk basis, prior to the completion of the NEPA review process.

Preliminary design has the same meaning as defined in section 636.103 of this title.

Solicitation document means the document used by the contracting agency to advertise the CM/GC project and request expressions of interest, statements of qualifications, proposals, or offers.

State transportation agency (STA) has the same meaning as the term State transportation department (STD) under § 635.102 of this chapter.

§ 635.503 Applicability.

The provisions of this subpart apply to all Federal-aid projects within the right-of-way of a public highway, those projects required by law to be treated as if located on a Federal-aid highway, and other projects which are linked to such projects (*i.e.*, the project would not exist without another Federal-aid highway project) that are to be delivered using the CM/GC contractor method.

§ 635.504 CM/GC Requirements.

(a) *In general.* A contracting agency may award a two-phase contract to a CM/GC contractor for preconstruction and construction services. The first phase of this contract is the preconstruction services phase. The second phase is the construction services phase. The construction services phase may occur under one contract or under multiple contracts covering portions of the project, including early work packages.

(b) *Procurement requirements.* (1) The contracting agency may procure the CM/GC contract using applicable State or local competitive selection procurement procedures as long as those procedures do not serve as a barrier to free and open competition or conflict with applicable Federal laws and regulations.

(2) Contracting agency procedures may use any of the following solicitation options in procuring a CM/GC contract: Letters of interest, requests for qualifications, interviews, request for proposals or other solicitation procedures provided by applicable State law, regulation or policy. Single-phase or multiple-phase selection procedures may also be used.

(3) Contracting agency procedures shall require, at a minimum, that a CM/GC contract be advertised through solicitation documents that:

(i) Clearly define the scope of services being requested;

(ii) List evaluation factors and significant subfactors and their relative importance in evaluating proposals;

(iii) List all required deliverables;

(iv) Identify whether interviews will be conducted before establishing the final rank (however, the contracting agency may reserve the right to make a final determination whether interviews are needed based on responses to the solicitation); and

(v) Include or reference sample contract form(s).

(4) If interviews are used in the selection process, the contracting agency must offer the opportunity for an interview to all short listed firms (or firms that submitted responsive proposals, if a short list is not used). Also, if interviews are used, then the contracting agency must not engage in conduct that favors one firm over another and must not disclose a firm's offer to another firm.

(5) A contracting agency may award a CM/GC contract based on qualifications, experience, best value, or any other combination of factors considered appropriate by the contracting agency and the Division Administrator and which are clearly specified in the solicitation documents.

(6) In the event that the contracting agency is unwilling or unable to enter into a contract with the CM/GC contractor for the construction services phase of the project (including any early work package), after the concurrence of the Division Administrator, the contracting agency may initiate a new procurement process meeting the requirements of subpart A of this part, or of another approved method for the affected portion of the construction work. If Federal-aid participation is being requested in the cost of construction, the contracting agency must request FHWA's approval before advertising for bids or proposals in accordance with § 635.112 and part 636 of this chapter. When the contracting agency

makes a decision to initiate a new procurement, the contracting agency may determine that the CM/GC contractor is likely to have a competitive advantage that could adversely affect fair and open competition and not allow the CM/GC contractor to submit competitive bids.

(c) *FHWA approval of CM/GC procedures.* (1) The STA must submit its proposed CM/GC procurement procedures to the FHWA Division Administrator for review and approval. Any changes in approved procedures and requirements shall also be subject to approval by the Division Administrator. Other contracting agencies may follow STA approved procedures, or their own procedures if approved by both the STA and FHWA.

(2) The Division Administrator may approve procedures that conform to the requirements of this subpart and which do not, in the opinion of the Division Administrator, operate to restrict competition. The Division Administrator's approval of CM/GC procurement procedures may not be delegated or assigned to the STA.

(d) *Subcontracting.* Consistent with §635.116(a), contracts for construction services must specify a minimum percentage of work (no less than 30 percent of the total cost of all construction services performed under the CM/GC contract, excluding specialty work) that a contractor must perform with its own forces. If required by State law, regulation, or administrative policy, the contracting agency may require the CM/GC contractor to competitively let and award subcontracts for construction services to the lowest responsive bidder.

(e) *Payment methods.* (1) The method of payment to the CM/GC contractor shall be set forth in the original solicitation documents, contract, and any contract modification or change order thereto. A single contract may contain different payment methods as appropriate for compensation of different elements of work.

(2) The methods of payment for preconstruction services shall be: Lump sum, cost plus fixed fee, cost per unit of work, specific rates of compensation, or other comparable payment method permitted in State law and regulation. When compensation is based on actual costs, an approved indirect cost rate must be used. The cost plus a percentage of cost and percentage of construction cost methods of payment shall not be used.

(3) The method of payment for construction services may include any method of payment authorized by State law (including, but not limited to, lump sum, unit price, and target price). The cost plus a percentage of cost and percentage of construction cost methods of payment shall not be used.

§635.505 Relationship to the NEPA process.

(a) In procuring a CM/GC contract before the completion of the NEPA process, the contracting agency may:

(1) Issue solicitation documents;

(2) Proceed with the award of a CM/GC contract providing for preconstruction services and an option to enter into a future contract for construction services once the NEPA review process is complete;

(3) Issue notices to proceed to the CM/GC contractor for preconstruction services, excluding final design-related activities; and

(4) Issue a notice-to-proceed to a consultant design firm for the preliminary design and any work related to preliminary design of the project to the extent that those actions do not limit any reasonable range of alternatives.

(b) The contracting agency shall not initiate construction activities (even on an at-risk basis) or allow such activities to proceed prior to the completion of the NEPA process. The contracting agency shall not perform or contract for construction services (including early work packages of any kind) prior to the completion of the NEPA process.

(c) A contracting agency may proceed, solely at the risk and expense of the contracting agency, with design activities at any level of detail, including final design and preconstruction services associated with final design, for a CM/GC project before completion of the NEPA process without affecting subsequent approvals required for the project. However, FHWA shall not authorize final design activities and preconstruction services associated with final design, and such activities shall not be eligible for Federal funding as provided in § 635.506(c), until after the completion the NEPA process. A contracting agency may use a CM/GC contractor for preconstruction services associated with at-risk final design only if the contracting agency has a procedure for segregating the costs of the CM/GC contractor's at-risk work from preconstruction services eligible for reimbursement during the NEPA process. If a contracting agency decides to perform at-risk final design, it must notify FHWA of its decision to do so before undertaking such activities.

(d) The CM/GC contract must include termination provisions in the event the environmental review process does not result in the selection of a build alternative. This termination provision is in addition to the termination for cause or convenience clause required by Appendix II to 2 CFR part 200.

(e) If the contracting agency expects to use information from the CM/GC contractor in the NEPA review for the project, then the contracting agency is responsible for ensuring its CM/GC contract gives the contracting agency the right to obtain, as needed, technical information on all alternatives analyzed in the NEPA review.

(f) The CM/GC contract must include appropriate provisions ensuring no commitments are made to any alternative during the NEPA process, and that the comparative merits of all alternatives identified and considered during the NEPA process, including the no-build alternative, will be evaluated and fairly considered.

(g) The CM/GC contractor must not prepare NEPA documentation or have any decisionmaking responsibility with respect to the NEPA process. However, the CM/GC contractor may be requested to provide information about the project and possible mitigation actions, including constructability information, and its work product may be considered in the NEPA analysis and included in the record.

(h) Any contract for construction services under a CM/GC contract must include appropriate provisions ensuring that all environmental and mitigation measures identified in the NEPA documentation and committed to in the NEPA determination for the selected alternative will be implemented, excepting only measures the contracting agency expressly describes in the CM/GC contract as excluded because they are the responsibility of others.

§ 635.506 Project approvals and authorizations.

(a) *In general.* (1) Under 23 U.S.C. 106(c), the States may assume certain FHWA responsibilities for project design, plans, specifications, estimates, contract awards, and inspections. Any individual State's assumption of FHWA responsibilities for approvals and determinations for CM/GC projects, as described in this subpart, will be addressed in the State's FHWA/STA Stewardship and Oversight Agreement. The State may not further delegate or assign those responsibilities. If an STA assumes responsibility for an FHWA approval or determination contained in this subpart, the STA will include documentation in the project file sufficient to substantiate its actions and to support any request for authorization of funds. The STA will provide FHWA with the documentation upon request.

(2) States cannot assume FHWA review or approval responsibilities for §§ 635.504(c) (review and approval of CM/GC procurement procedures) or 635.506(c) (FHWA post-NEPA review of at-risk final design costs for eligibility).

(3) In accordance with 23 U.S.C. 106(c), States may assume FHWA review or approval responsibilities for §§ 635.504(b)(6) (approval of bidding), 635.504(e)(3) (approval of indirect cost rate), 635.506(b) (approval of preconstruction price and cost/price analysis), 635.506(d)(2) (approval of price estimate for entire project), 635.506(d)(4) (approval of construction price analysis for each construction services contract), and 635.506(e) (approval of preconstruction services and construction services contract awards) for CM/GC projects on the National Highway System, including projects on the Interstate System, and must assume such responsibilities for projects

off the National Highway System unless the State determines such assumption is not appropriate.

(b) *Preconstruction services approvals and authorization.* (1) If the contracting agency wishes Federal participation in the cost of the CM/GC contractor's preconstruction services, it must request FHWA's authorization of preliminary engineering before incurring such costs, except as provided by section 1440 of the Fixing America's Surface Transportation Act, Pub. L. 114–357 (December 1, 2015).

(2) Before authorizing pre-construction services by the CM/GC contractor, the Division Administrator must review and approve the contracting agency's cost or price analysis for the preconstruction services procurement (including contract modifications). A cost or price analysis is encouraged but not required for procurements less than the simplified acquisition threshold in 2 CFR 200.88. The requirements of this paragraph apply when the contracting agency is requesting Federal assistance in the cost of preconstruction services.

(c) *Final design during NEPA process.* (1) If the contracting agency proceeds with final design activities, including CM/GC preconstruction services associated with final design activities, at its own expense before the completion of the NEPA process, then those activities for the selected alternative may be eligible for Federal reimbursement after the completion of the NEPA process so long as the Division Administrator finds that the contracting agency's final design-related activities:

(i) Did not limit the identification and fair evaluation of a reasonable range of alternatives for the proposed project;

(ii) Did not result in an irrevocable commitment by the contracting agency to the selection of a particular alternative;

(iii) Did not have an adverse environmental impact; and

(iv) Are necessary and reasonable and adequately documented.

(2) If, during the NEPA process, the Division Administrator finds the final design work limits the fair evaluation of alternatives, irrevocably commits the contracting agency to the selection of any alternative, or causes an adverse environmental impact, then the Division Administrator shall require the contracting agency to take any necessary action to ensure the integrity of the NEPA process regardless of whether or not the contracting agency wishes to receive Federal reimbursement for such activities.

(d) *Construction services approvals and authorizations.* (1) Subject to the requirements in § 635.505, the contracting agency may request Federal participation in the construction services costs associated with a CM/GC construction project, or portion of a project (including an early work package). In such cases, FHWA's construction contracting requirements will apply to all of the CM/GC project's construction contracts if any portion (including an early work package) of the CM/GC project construction is funded with title 23 funds. Any expenses incurred for construction services before FHWA authorization shall not be eligible for reimbursement except as may be determined in accordance with § 1.9 of this chapter.

(2) The Division Administrator must approve the price estimate for construction costs for the entire project before authorization of construction services (including authorization of an early work package).

(3) The contracting agency must perform a price analysis for any contract (or contract modification) that establishes or revises the scope, schedule or price for the construction of the CM/GC project or a portion of the project (including an early work package). The price analysis must compare the agreed price with the contracting agency's engineer's estimate or an independent cost estimate (if required by the contracting agency). A price analysis is encouraged but not required for procurements less than the simplified acquisition threshold in 2 CFR 200.88.

(4) The Division Administrator must review and approve the contracting agency's price analysis and agreed price for the construction services of a CM/GC project or a portion of the project (including an early work package) before authorization of construction services.

(5) Where the contracting agency and the CM/GC contractor agree on a price for construction services that is approved under paragraph (d)(4) of this section, FHWA's authorization of construction services will be based on the approved agreed price for the project or portion of the project. The authorization may include authorization of an early work package, including the advanced acquisition of materials consistent with § 635.122 and this subpart. In the event that construction materials are acquired for a CM/GC project but not installed in the CM/GC project, the cost of such material will not be eligible for Federal-aid participation. In accordance with § 635.507 and 2 CFR part 200, FHWA may deny eligibility for part or all of an early work package if such work is not needed for, or used for, the project.

(e) *Contract award.* The award of a Federal-aid CM/GC contract for preconstruction services and the award of contract(s) for construction services require prior concurrence from the Division Administrator. The concurrence is a prerequisite to authorization of preconstruction and construction services (including authorization for an early work package). Concurrence in the CM/GC contract award for construction services constitutes approval of the agreed price, scope, and schedule for the work under that contract. Where the contracting agency has established a Disadvantaged Business Enterprise (DBE) contract goal for the CM/GC construction services contract, the initial proposal for CM/GC construction services must include the DBE documentation required by 49 CFR 26.53(b)(2), or it must include a contractually binding commitment to meet the DBE contract goal, with the information required by 49 CFR 26.53(b)(2) provided before the contracting agency awards the contract for construction services. A copy of the executed contract between the contracting agency and the CM/GC contractor, including any contract for construction services, shall be furnished to the Division Administrator as soon as practical after execution. If the contracting agency decides not to proceed with the award of a CM/GC construction services contract, then it must notify the FHWA Division Administrator as provided in § 635.504(b)(6).

§ 635.507 Cost eligibility.

(a) Costs, or prices based on estimated costs, under a CM/GC contract shall be eligible for Federal-aid reimbursement only to the extent that costs incurred, or cost estimates included in negotiated prices, are allowable in accordance with the Federal cost principles (as specified in 2 CFR part 200, subpart E). Contracting agencies must perform a cost or price analysis in connection with procurement actions, including contract modifications, in accordance with 2 CFR 200.323(a) and this subpart.

(1) For preconstruction services, to the extent that actual costs or cost estimates are included in negotiated prices that will be used for cost reimbursement, the costs must comply with the Federal cost principles to be eligible for participation.

(2) For construction services, the price analysis must confirm the agreed price is reasonable in order to satisfy cost eligibility requirements (see § 635.506(d)(3)). The FHWA will rely on an approved price analysis when authorizing funds for construction.

(b) *Indirect cost rates.* Where preconstruction service payments are based on actual costs the CM/GC contractor must provide an indirect cost rate established in accordance with the Federal cost principles (as specified in 2 CFR part 200 subpart E).

(c) *Cost certification.* (1) If the CM/GC contractor presents an indirect cost rate established in accordance with the Federal cost principles (as specified in 2 CFR part 200 subpart E), it shall include a certification by an official of the CM/GC contractor that all costs are allowable in accordance with the Federal cost principles.

(2) An official of the CM/GC contractor shall be an individual executive or financial officer of the CM/GC contractor's organization, at a level no lower than a Vice President or Chief Financial Officer, or equivalent, who has the authority to make representations about the financial information utilized to establish the indirect cost rate proposal submitted.

(3) The certification of final indirect costs shall read as follows:

Certificate of Final Indirect Costs

This is to certify that I have reviewed this proposal to establish final indirect cost rates and to the best of my knowledge and belief:

1. All costs included in this proposal (identify proposal and date) to establish final indirect cost rates for (identify period covered by rate) are allowable in accordance with the cost principles in 2 CFR part 200 subpart E; and

2. This proposal does not include any costs which are expressly unallowable under applicable cost principles of 2 CFR part 200 subpart E.

PART 636—DESIGN-BUILD CONTRACTING

Subpart A—General

Sec.

Subpart B—Selection Procedures, Award Criteria

Subpart C—Proposal Evaluation Factors

Subpart D—Exchanges

Subpart E—Discussions, Proposal Revisions and Source Selection

AUTHORITY: Sec. 1503 of Pub. L. 109–59, 119 Stat. 1144; Sec. 1307 of Pub. L. 105–178, 112 Stat. 107; 23 U.S.C. 101, 109, 112, 113, 114, 115, 119, 128, and 315; 49 CFR 1.48(b).

SOURCE: 67 FR 75926, Dec. 10, 2002, unless otherwise noted.

Subpart A—General

§636.101 What does this part do?

This part describes the FHWA's policies and procedures for approving design-build projects financed under title 23, United States Code (U.S.C.). This part satisfies the requirement of section 1307(c) of the Transportation Equity Act for the 21st Century (TEA–21), enacted on June 9, 1998. The contracting procedures of this part apply to all design-build project funded under title 23, U.S.C.

§636.102 Does this part apply to me?

(a) This part uses a plain language format to make the rule easier for the general public and business community to use. The section headings and text, often in the form of questions and answers, must be read together.

(b) Unless otherwise noted, the pronoun "you" means the primary recipient of Federal-aid highway funds, the State Transportation Department (STD). Where the STD has an agreement with a local public agency (or other governmental agency) to administer a Federal-aid design-build project, the term "you" will also apply to that contracting agency.

§636.103 What are the definitions of terms used in this part?

Unless otherwise specified in this part, the definitions in 23 U.S.C. 101(a) are applicable to this part. Also, the following definitions are used:

Adjusted low bid means a form of best value selection in which qualitative aspects are scored on a 0 to 100 scale expressed as a decimal; price is then divided by qualitative score to yield an "adjusted bid" or "price per quality point." Award is made to offeror with the lowest adjusted bid.

Best value selection means any selection process in which proposals contain both price and qualitative components and award is based upon a combination of price and qualitative considerations.

Clarifications means a written or oral exchange of information which takes place after the receipt of proposals when award without discussions is contemplated. The purpose of clarifications is to address minor or clerical revisions in a proposal.

Communications are exchanges, between the contracting agency and offerors, after receipt of proposals, which lead to the establishment of the competitive range.

Competitive acquisition means an acquisition process which is designed to foster an impartial and comprehensive evaluation of offerors' proposals, leading to the selection of the proposal representing the best value to the contracting agency.

Competitive range means a list of the most highly rated proposals based on the initial proposal rankings. It is based on the rating of each proposal against all evaluation criteria.

Contracting agency means the public agency awarding and administering a design-build contract. The contracting agency may be the STD or another State or local public agency.

Deficiency means a material failure of a proposal to meet a contracting agency requirement or a combination of significant weaknesses in a proposal that increases the risk of unsuccessful contract performance to an unacceptable level.

Design-bid-build means the traditional project delivery method where design and construction are sequential steps in the project development process.

Design-build contract means an agreement that provides for design and construction of improvements by a contractor or private developer. The term encompasses design-build-maintain, design-build-operate, design-build-finance and other contracts that include services in addition to design and construction. Franchise and concession agreements are included in the term if they provide for the franchisee or concessionaire to develop the project which is the subject of the agreement.

Design-builder means the entity contractually responsible for delivering the project design and construction.

Discussions mean written or oral exchanges that take place after the establishment of the competitive range with the intent of allowing the offerors to revise their proposals.

Final design means any design activities following preliminary design and expressly includes the preparation of final construction plans and detailed specifications for the performance of construction work.

Fixed price/best design means a form of best value selection in which contract price is established by the owner and stated in the Request for Proposals document. Design solutions and other qualitative factors are evaluated and rated, with award going to the firm offering the best qualitative proposal for the established price.

Intelligent Transportation System (ITS) services means services which provide for the acquisition of technologies or systems of technologies (e.g., computer hardware or software, traffic control devices, communications link, fare payment system, automatic vehicle location system, etc.) that provide or contribute to the provision of one or more ITS user services as defined in the National ITS Architecture.

Modified design-build means a variation of design-build in which the contracting agency furnishes offerors with partially complete plans. The design-builders role is generally limited to the completion of the design and construction of the project.

Organizational conflict of interest means that because of other activities or relationships with other persons, a person is unable or potentially unable to render impartial assistance or advice to the owner, or the person's objectivity in performing the contract work is or might be otherwise impaired, or a person has an unfair competitive advantage.

Preliminary design defines the general project location and design concepts. It includes, but is not limited to, preliminary engineering and other activities and analyses, such as environmental assessments, topographic surveys, metes and bounds surveys, geotechnical investigations, hydrologic analysis, hydraulic analysis, utility engineering, traffic studies, financial plans, revenue estimates, hazardous materials assessments, general estimates of the types and quantities of materials, and other work needed to establish parameters for the final design. Prior to completion of the NEPA review process, any such preliminary engineering and other activities and analyses must not materially affect the objective consideration of alternatives in the NEPA review process.

Prequalification means the contracting agency's process for determining whether a firm is fundamentally qualified to compete for a certain project or class of projects. The prequalification process may be based on financial, management and other types of qualitative data. Prequalification should be distinguished from short listing.

Price proposal means the price submitted by the offeror to provide the required design and construction services.

Price reasonableness means the determination that the price of the work for any project or series of projects is not excessive and is a fair and reasonable price for the services to be performed.

Proposal modification means a change made to a proposal before the solicitation closing date and time, or made in response to an amendment, or made to correct a mistake at any time before award.

Proposal revision means a change to a proposal made after the solicitation closing date, at the request of or as allowed by a contracting officer, as the result of negotiations.

Public-private agreement means an agreement between a public agency and a private party involving design and construction of transportation improvements by the private party to be paid for in whole or in part by Federal-aid highway funds. The agreement may also provide for project financing, at-risk equity investment, operations, or maintenance of the project.

Qualified project means any design-build project (including intermodal projects) funded under Title 23, United States Code, which meets the requirements of this part and for which the contracting agency deems to be appropriate on the basis of project delivery time, cost, construction schedule, or quality.

Request for Proposals (RFP) means the document that describes the procurement process, forms the basis for the final proposals and may potentially become an element in the contract.

Request for Qualification (RFQ) means the document issued by the owner in Phase I of the two-phased selection process. It typically describes the project in enough detail to let potential offerors determine if they wish to compete and forms the basis for requesting qualifications submissions from which the most highly qualified offerors can be identified.

Short listing means the narrowing of the field of offerors through the selection of the most qualified offerors who have responded to an RFQ.

Single-phase selection process means a procurement process where price and/or technical proposals are submitted in response to an RFP. Short listing is not used.

Solicitation means a public notification of an owner's need for information, qualifications, or proposals related to identified services.

Stipend means a monetary amount sometimes paid to unsuccessful offerors.

Technical proposal means that portion of a design-build proposal which contains design solutions and other qualitative factors that are provided in response to the RFP document.

Tradeoff means an analysis technique involving a comparison of price and non-price factors to determine the best value when considering the selection of other than the lowest priced proposal.

Two-phase selection process means a procurement process in which the first phase consists of short listing (based on qualifications submitted in response to an RFQ) and the second phase consists of the submission of price and technical proposals in response to an RFP.

Weakness means a flaw in the proposal that increases the risk of unsuccessful contract performance. A significant weakness in the proposal is a flaw that appreciably increases the risk of unsuccessful contract performance.

Weighted criteria process means a form of best value selection in which maximum point values are pre-established for qualitative and price components, and award is based upon high total points earned by the offerors.

[67 FR 75926, Dec. 10, 2002, as amended at 72 FR 45336, Aug. 14, 2007]

§ 636.104 Does this part apply to all Federal-aid design-build projects?

The provisions of this part apply to all Federal-aid design-build projects within the highway right-of-way or linked to a Federal-aid highway project (*i.e.*, the project would not exist without another Federal-aid highway project). Projects that are not located within the highway right-of-way, and not linked to a Federal-aid highway project may utilize State-approved procedures.

§ 636.105 Is the FHWA requiring the use of design-build?

No, the FHWA is neither requiring nor promoting the use of the design-build contracting method. The design-build contracting technique is optional.

§636.106 [Reserved]

§636.107 May contracting agencies use geographic preference in Federal-aid design-build or public-private partnership projects?

No. Contracting agencies must not use geographic preferences (including contractual provisions, preferences or incentives for hiring, contracting, proposing, or bidding) on Federal-aid highway projects, even though the contracting agency may be subject to statutorily or administratively imposed in-State or local geographical preferences in the evaluation and award of such projects.

[72 FR 45336, Aug. 14, 2007]

§636.108 [Reserved]

§636.109 How does the NEPA process relate to the design-build procurement process?

The purpose of this section is to ensure that there is an objective NEPA process, that public officials and citizens have the necessary environmental impact information for federally funded actions before actions are taken, and that design-build proposers do not assume an unnecessary amount of risk in the event the NEPA process results in a significant change in the proposal, and that the amount payable by the contracting agency to the design-builder does not include significant contingency as the result of risk placed on the design-builder associated with significant changes in the project definition arising out of the NEPA process. Therefore, with respect to the design-build procurement process:

(a) The contracting agency may:

(1) Issue an RFQ prior to the conclusion of the NEPA process as long as the RFQ informs proposers of the general status of NEPA review;

(2) Issue an RFP after the conclusion of the NEPA process;

(3) Issue an RFP prior to the conclusion of the NEPA process as long as the RFP informs proposers of the general status of the NEPA process and that no commitment will be made as to any alternative under evaluation in the NEPA process, including the no-build alternative;

(4) Proceed with the award of a design-build contract prior to the conclusion of the NEPA process;

(5) Issue notice to proceed with preliminary design pursuant to a design-build contract that has been awarded prior to the completion of the NEPA process; and

(6) Allow a design-builder to proceed with final design and construction for any projects, or portions thereof, for which the NEPA process has been completed.

(b) If the contracting agency proceeds to award a design-build contract prior to the conclusion of the NEPA process, then:

(1) The contracting agency may permit the design-builder to proceed with preliminary design;

(2) The contracting agency may permit any design and engineering activities to be undertaken for the purposes of defining the project alternatives and completing the NEPA alternatives analysis and review process; complying with other related environmental laws and regulations; supporting agency coordination, public involvement, permit applications, or development of mitigation plans; or developing the design of the preferred alternative to a higher level of detail when the lead agencies agree that it is warranted in accordance with 23 U.S.C. 139(f)(4)(D);

(3) The design-build contract must include appropriate provisions preventing the design-builder from proceeding with final design activities and physical construction prior to the completion of the NEPA process (contract hold points or another method of issuing multi-step approvals must be used);

(4) The design-build contract must include appropriate provisions ensuring that no commitments are made to any alternative being evaluated in the NEPA process and that the comparative merits of all alternatives presented in the NEPA document, including the no-build alternative, will be evaluated and fairly considered;

(5) The design-build contract must include appropriate provisions ensuring that all environmental and mitigation

measures identified in the NEPA document will be implemented;

(6) The design-builder must not prepare the NEPA document or have any decisionmaking responsibility with respect to the NEPA process;

(7) Any consultants who prepare the NEPA document must be selected by and subject to the exclusive direction and control of the contracting agency;

(8) The design-builder may be requested to provide information about the project and possible mitigation actions, and its work product may be considered in the NEPA analysis and included in the record; and

(9) The design-build contract must include termination provisions in the event that the no-build alternative is selected.

(c) The contracting agency must receive prior FHWA concurrence before issuing the RFP, awarding a design-build contract and proceeding with preliminary design work under the design-build contract. Should the contracting agency proceed with any of the activities specified in this section before the completion of the NEPA process (with the exception of preliminary design, as provided in paragraph (d) of this section), the FHWA's concurrence merely constitutes the FHWA approval that any such activities complies with Federal requirements and does not constitute project authorization or obligate Federal funds.

(d) The FHWA's authorization and obligation of preliminary engineering and other preconstruction funds prior to the completion of the NEPA process is limited to preliminary design and such additional activities as may be necessary to complete the NEPA process. After the completion of the NEPA process, the FHWA may issue an authorization to proceed with final design and construction and obligate Federal funds for such purposes.

[72 FR 45337, Aug. 14, 2007]

§ 636.110 What procedures may be used for solicitations and receipt of proposals?

You may use your own procedures for the solicitation and receipt of proposals and information including the following:

(a) Exchanges with industry before receipt of proposals;

(b) RFQ, RFP and contract format;

(c) Solicitation schedules;

(d) Lists of forms, documents, exhibits, and other attachments;

(e) Representations and instructions;

(f) Advertisement and amendments;

(g) Handling proposals and information; and

(h) Submission, modification, revisions and withdrawal of proposals.

§ 636.111 Can oral presentations be used during the procurement process?

(a) Yes, the use of oral presentations as a substitute for portions of a written proposal can be effective in streamlining the source selection process. Oral presentations may occur at any time in the acquisition process, however, you must comply with the appropriate State procurement integrity standards.

(b) Oral presentations may substitute for, or augment, written information. You must maintain a record of oral presentations to document what information you relied upon in making the source selection decision. You may decide the appropriate method and level of detail for the record (e.g., videotaping, audio tape recording, written record, contracting agency notes, copies of offeror briefing slides or presentation notes). A copy of the record should be placed in the contract file and may be provided to offerors upon request.

§ 636.112 May stipends be used?

At your discretion, you may elect to pay a stipend to unsuccessful offerors who have submitted responsive proposals. The decision to do so should be based on your analysis of the estimated proposal development costs and the anticipated degree of competition during the procurement process.

§ 636.113 Is the stipend amount eligible for Federal participation?

(a) Yes, stipends are eligible for Federal-aid participation. Stipends are recommended on large projects where there is substantial opportunity for innovation and the cost of submitting a proposal is significant. On such projects, stipends are used to:

(1) Encourage competition;

(2) Compensate unsuccessful offerors for a portion of their costs (usually one-third to one-half of the estimated proposal development cost); and

(3) Ensure that smaller companies are not put at a competitive disadvantage.

(b) Unless prohibited by State law, you may retain the right to use ideas from unsuccessful offerors if they accept stipends. If stipends are used, the RFP should describe the process for distributing the stipend to qualifying offerors. The acceptance of any stipend must be optional on the part of the unsuccessful offeror to the design-build proposal.

(c) If you intend to incorporate the ideas from unsuccessful offerors into the same contract on which they unsuccessfully submitted a proposal, you must clearly provide notice of your intent to do so in the RFP.

[67 FR 75926, Dec. 10, 2002, as amended at 73 FR 77502, Dec. 19, 2008]

§ 636.114 What factors should be considered in risk allocation?

(a) You may consider, identify, and allocate the risks in the RFP document and define these risks in the contract. Risk should be allocated with consideration given to the party who is in the best position to manage and control a given risk or the impact of a given risk.

(b) Risk allocation will vary according to the type of project and location, however, the following factors should be considered:

(1) Governmental risks, including the potential for delays, modifications, withdrawal, scope changes, or additions that result from multi-level Federal, State, and local participation and sponsorship;

(2) Regulatory compliance risks, including environmental and third-party issues, such as permitting, railroad, and utility company risks;

(3) Construction phase risks, including differing site conditions, traffic control, interim drainage, public access, weather issues, and schedule;

(4) Post-construction risks, including public liability and meeting stipulated performance standards; and

(5) Right-of-way risks including acquisition costs, appraisals, relocation delays, condemnation proceedings, including court costs and others.

§ 636.115 May I meet with industry to gather information concerning the appropriate risk allocation strategies?

(a) Yes, information exchange at an early project stage is encouraged if it facilitates your understanding of the capabilities of potential offerors. However, any exchange of information must be consistent with State procurement integrity requirements. Interested parties include potential offerors, end users, acquisition and supporting personnel, and others involved in the conduct or outcome of the acquisition.

(b) The purpose of exchanging information is to improve the understanding of your requirements and industry capabilities, thereby allowing potential offerors to judge whether or how they can satisfy your requirements, and enhancing your ability to obtain quality supplies and services, including construction, at reasonable prices, and increase efficiency in proposal preparation, proposal evaluation, negotiation, and contract award.

(c) An early exchange of information can identify and resolve concerns regarding the acquisition strategy, including proposed contract type, terms and conditions, and acquisition planning schedules. This also includes the feasibility of the requirement, including performance requirements, statements of work, and data requirements; the suitability of the proposal instructions and evaluation criteria, including the approach for assessing past performance information; the availability of reference documents; and any other industry concerns or questions. Some techniques to promote early exchanges of information are as follows:

(1) Industry or small business conferences;

(2) Public hearings;

(3) Market research;

(4) One-on-one meetings with potential offerors (any meetings that are substantially involved with potential

contract terms and conditions should include the contracting officer; also see paragraph (e) of this section regarding restrictions on disclosure of information);

(5) Presolicitation notices;

(6) Draft RFPs;

(7) Request for Information (RFI) ;

(8) Presolicitation or preproposal conferences; and

(9) Site visits.

(d) RFIs may be used when you do not intend to award a contract, but want to obtain price, delivery, other market information, or capabilities for planning purposes. Responses to these notices are not offers and cannot be accepted to form a binding contract. There is no required format for an RFI.

(e) When specific information about a proposed acquisition that would be necessary for the preparation of proposals is disclosed to one or more potential offerors, that information shall be made available to all potential offerors as soon as practicable, but no later than the next general release of information, in order to avoid creating an unfair competitive advantage. Information provided to a particular offeror in response to that offeror's request must not be disclosed if doing so would reveal the potential offeror's confidential business strategy. When a presolicitation or preproposal conference is conducted, materials distributed at the conference should be made available to all potential offerors, upon request.

§636.116 What organizational conflict of interest requirements apply to design-build projects?

(a) State statutes or policies concerning organizational conflict of interest should be specified or referenced in the design-build RFQ or RFP document as well as any contract for engineering services, inspection or technical support in the administration of the design-build contract. All design-build solicitations should address the following situations as appropriate:

(1) Consultants and/or sub-consultants who assist the owner in the preparation of a RFP document will not be allowed to participate as an offeror or join a team submitting a proposal in response to the RFP. However, a contracting agency may determine there is not an organizational conflict of interest for a consultant or sub-consultant where:

(i) The role of the consultant or sub-consultant was limited to provision of preliminary design, reports, or similar "low-level" documents that will be incorporated into the RFP, and did not include assistance in development of instructions to offerors or evaluation criteria, or

(ii) Where all documents and reports delivered to the agency by the consultant or sub-consultant are made available to all offerors.

(2) All solicitations for design-build contracts, including related contracts for inspection, administration or auditing services, must include a provision which:

(i) Directs offerors attention to this subpart;

(ii) States the nature of the potential conflict as seen by the owner;

(iii) States the nature of the proposed restraint or restrictions (and duration) upon future contracting activities, if appropriate;

(iv) Depending on the nature of the acquisition, states whether or not the terms of any proposed clause and the application of this subpart to the contract are subject to negotiation; and

(v) Requires offerors to provide information concerning potential organizational conflicts of interest in their proposals. The apparent successful offerors must disclose all relevant facts concerning any past, present or currently planned interests which may present an organizational conflict of interest. Such firms must state how their interests, or those of their chief executives, directors, key project personnel, or any proposed consultant, contractor or subcontractor may result, or could be viewed as, an organizational conflict of interest. The information may be in the form of a disclosure statement or a certification.

(3) Based upon a review of the information submitted, the owner should make a written determination of whether the offeror's interests create an actual or potential organizational conflict of interest and identify any actions that must be taken to avoid, neutralize, or mitigate such conflict. The

owner should award the contract to the apparent successful offeror unless an organizational conflict of interest is determined to exist that cannot be avoided, neutralized, or mitigated.

(b) The organizational conflict of interest provisions in this subpart provide minimum standards for STDs to identify, mitigate or eliminate apparent or actual organizational conflicts of interest. To the extent that State-developed organizational conflict of interest standards are more stringent than that contained in this subpart, the State standards prevail.

(c) If the NEPA process has been completed prior to issuing the RFP, the contracting agency may allow a consultant or subconsultant who prepared the NEPA document to submit a proposal in response to the RFP.

(d) If the NEPA process has not been completed prior to issuing the RFP, the contracting agency may allow a subconsultant to the preparer of the NEPA document to participate as an offeror or join a team submitting a proposal in response to the RFP only if the contracting agency releases such subconsultant from further responsibilities with respect to the preparation of the NEPA document.

[67 FR 75926, Dec. 10, 2002, as amended at 72 FR 45337, Aug. 14, 2007]

§636.117 What conflict of interest standards apply to individuals who serve as selection team members for the owner?

State laws and procedures governing improper business practices and personal conflicts of interest will apply to the owner's selection team members. In the absence of such State provisions, the requirements of 48 CFR Part 3, Improper Business Practices and Personal Conflicts of Interest, will apply to selection team members.

§636.118 Is team switching allowed after contract award?

Where the offeror's qualifications are a major factor in the selection of the successful design-builder, team member switching (adding or switching team members) is discouraged after contract award. However, the owner may use its discretion in reviewing team changes or team enhancement requests on a case-by-case basis. Specific project rules related to changes in team members or changes in personnel within teams should be explicitly stated by the STD in all project solicitations.

§636.119 How does this part apply to a project developed under a public-private partnership?

(a) In order for a project being developed under a public-private agreement to be eligible for Federal-aid funding (including traditional Federal-aid funds, direct loans, loan guarantees, lines of credit, or some other form of credit assistance), the contracting agency must have awarded the contract to the public-private entity through a competitive process that complies with applicable State and local laws.

(b) If a contracting agency wishes to utilize traditional Federal-aid funds in a project under a public-private agreement, the applicability of Federal-aid procurement procedures will depend on the nature of the public-private agreement.

(1) If the public-private agreement establishes price, then all subsequent contracts executed by the developer are considered to be subcontracts and are not subject to Federal-aid procurement requirements.

(2) If the public-private agreement does not establish price, the developer is considered to be an agent of the owner, and the developer must follow the appropriate Federal-aid procurement requirements (23 CFR part 172 for engineering service contracts, 23 CFR part 635 for construction contracts and the requirements of this part for design-build contracts) for all prime contracts (not subcontracts).

(c) The STD must ensure such public-private projects comply with all non-procurement requirements of 23 U. S. Code, regardless of the form of the FHWA funding (traditional Federal-aid funding or credit assistance). This includes compliance with all FHWA policies such as environmental and right-of-way requirements and compliance with such construction contracting requirements as Buy America, Davis-

Bacon minimum wage rate requirements, for federally funded construction or design-build contracts under the public-private agreement.

[67 FR 75926, Dec. 10, 2002, as amended at 72 FR 45337, Aug. 14, 2007]

Subpart B—Selection Procedures, Award Criteria

§ 636.201 What selection procedures and award criteria may be used?

You should consider using two-phase selection procedures for all design-build projects. However, if you do not believe two-phase selection procedures are appropriate for your project (based on the criteria in § 636.202), you may use a single phase selection procedure or the modified-design-build contracting method. The following procedures are available:

Selection procedure	Criteria for using a selection procedure	Award criteria options
(a) Two-Phase Selection Procedures (RFQ followed by RFP).	§ 636.202	Lowest price, Adjusted low-bid (price per quality point), meets criteria/low bid, weighted criteria process, fixed price/best design, best value.
(b) Single Phase (RFP).	Project not meeting the criteria in § 636.202.	All of the award criteria in item (a) of this table.
(c) Modified Design-Build (may be one or two phases).	Any project	Lowest price technically acceptable.

§ 636.202 When are two-phase design-build selection procedures appropriate?

You may consider the following criteria in deciding whether two-phase selection procedures are appropriate. A negative response may indicate that two-phase selection procedures are not appropriate.

(a) Are three or more offers anticipated?

(b) Will offerors be expected to perform substantial design work before developing price proposals?

(c) Will offerors incur a substantial expense in preparing proposals?

(d) Have you identified and analyzed other contributing factors, including:

(1) The extent to which you have defined the project requirements?

(2) The time constraints for delivery of the project?

(3) The capability and experience of potential contractors?

(4) Your capability to manage the two-phase selection process?

(5) Other criteria that you may consider appropriate?

§ 636.203 What are the elements of two-phase selection procedures for competitive proposals?

The first phase consists of short listing based on a RFQ. The second phase consists of the receipt and evaluation of price and technical proposals in response to a RFP.

§ 636.204 What items may be included in a phase-one solicitation?

You may consider including the following items in any phase-one solicitation:

(a) The scope of work;

(b) The phase-one evaluation factors and their relative weights, including:

(1) Technical approach (but not detailed design or technical information);

(2) Technical qualifications, such as—

(i) Specialized experience and technical competence;

(ii) Capability to perform (including key personnel); and

(iii) Past performance of the members of the offeror's team (including the architect-engineer and construction members);

(3) Other appropriate factors (excluding cost or price related factors, which are not permitted in phase-one);

(c) Phase-two evaluation factors; and

(d) A statement of the maximum number of offerors that will be short listed to submit phase-two proposals.

§ 636.205 Can past performance be used as an evaluation criteria?

(a) Yes, past performance information is one indicator of an offeror's ability to perform the contract successfully. Past performance information may be used as an evaluation criteria in either phase-one or phase-two solicitations. If you elect to use past performance criteria, the currency and relevance of the information, source of the information, context of the data, and general trends in contractor's performance may be considered.

(b) Describe your approach for evaluating past performance in the solicitation, including your policy for evaluating offerors with no relevant performance history. You should provide offerors an opportunity to identify past or current contracts (including Federal, State, and local government and private) for efforts similar to the current solicitation.

(c) If you elect to request past performance information, the solicitation should also authorize offerors to provide information on problems encountered on the identified contracts and the offeror's corrective actions. You may consider this information, as well as information obtained from any other sources, when evaluating the offeror's past performance. You may use your discretion in determining the relevance of similar past performance information.

(d) The evaluation should take into account past performance information regarding predecessor companies, key personnel who have relevant experience, or subcontractors that will perform major or critical aspects of the requirement when such information is relevant to the current acquisition.

§636.206 How do I evaluate offerors who do not have a record of relevant past performance?

In the case of an offeror without a record of relevant past performance or for whom information on past performance is not available, the offeror may not be evaluated favorably or unfavorably on past performance.

§636.207 Is there a limit on short listed firms?

Normally, three to five firms are short listed, however, the maximum number specified shall not exceed five unless you determine, for that particular solicitation, that a number greater than five is in your interest and is consistent with the purposes and objectives of two-phase design-build contracting.

§636.208 May I use my existing prequalification procedures with design-build contracts?

Yes, you may use your existing prequalification procedures for either construction or engineering design firms as a supplement to the procedures in this part.

§636.209 What items must be included in a phase-two solicitation?

(a) You must include the requirements for technical proposals and price proposals in the phase-two solicitation. All factors and significant subfactors that will affect contract award and their relative importance must be stated clearly in the solicitation. Use your own procedures for the solicitation as long as it complies the requirements of this part.

(b)(1) At your discretion, you may allow proposers to submit alternative technical concepts (ATCs) in their proposals if:

(i) The ATCs:

(A) Provide an equal or better solution; and

(B) Do not conflict with criteria agreed upon in the environmental decisionmaking process; and

(ii) The RFP document clearly describes your:

(A) Requirements for ATC content, submission, and review;

(B) Procedures for confidential meetings (if used); and

(C) Methods for evaluating ATCs in the proposal review process.

(2) You must maintain the confidentiality of ATCs, except to the extent that disclosure is necessary to maintain compliance with Federal or State permitting and other legal requirements necessary for the delivery of the project. When disclosure is necessary, you must revise the RFP documents by releasing the minimal amount of information necessary to ensure:

(i) Compliance with Federal or State permitting and other legal requirements; and

(ii) All proposers are aware of the revised RFP requirements.

[67 FR 75926, Dec. 10, 2002, as amended at 79 FR 8266, Feb. 12, 2014]

§ 636.210 What requirements apply to projects which use the modified design-build procedure?

(a) Modified design-build selection procedures (lowest price technically acceptable source selection process) may be used for any project.

(b) The solicitation must clearly state the following:

(1) The identification of evaluation factors and significant subfactors that establish the requirements of acceptability.

(2) That award will be made on the basis of the lowest evaluated price of proposals meeting or exceeding the acceptability standards for non-cost factors.

(c) The contracting agency may forgo a short listing process and advertise for the receipt of proposals from all responsible offerors. The contract is then awarded to the lowest responsive bidder.

(d) Tradeoffs are not permitted, however, you may incorporate cost-plus-time bidding procedures (A + B bidding), lane rental, or other cost-based provisions in such contracts.

(e) Proposals are evaluated for acceptability but not ranked using the non-cost/price factors.

(f) Exchanges may occur (see subpart D of this part).

§ 636.211 When and how should tradeoffs be used?

(a) At your discretion, you may consider the tradeoff technique when it is desirable to award to other than the lowest priced offeror or other than the highest technically rated offeror.

(b) If you use a tradeoff technique, the following apply:

(1) All evaluation factors and significant subfactors that will affect contract award and their relative importance must be clearly stated in the solicitation; and

(2) The solicitation must also state, at a minimum, whether all evaluation factors other than cost or price, when combined, are—

(i) Significantly more important than cost or price; or

(ii) Approximately equal to cost or price; or

(iii) Significantly less important than cost or price.

[67 FR 75926, Dec. 10, 2002; 68 FR 7922, Feb. 19, 2003]

§ 636.212 To what extent must tradeoff decisions be documented?

When tradeoffs are performed, the source selection records must include the following:

(a) An assessment of each offeror's ability to accomplish the technical requirements; and

(b) A summary, matrix, or quantitative ranking, along with appropriate supporting narrative, of each technical proposal using the evaluation factors.

Subpart C—Proposal Evaluation Factors

§ 636.301 How should proposal evaluation factors be selected?

(a) The proposal evaluation factors and significant subfactors should be tailored to the acquisition.

(b) Evaluation factors and significant subfactors should:

(1) Represent the key areas of importance and emphasis to be considered in the source selection decision; and

(2) Support meaningful comparison and discrimination between and among competing proposals.

§ 636.302 Are there any limitations on the selection and use of proposal evaluation factors?

(a) The selection of the evaluation factors, significant subfactors and their relative importance are within your broad discretion subject to the following requirements:

(1) You must evaluate price in every source selection where construction is a significant component of the scope of work. However, where the contracting agency elects to release the final RFP and award the design-build contract before the conclusion of the NEPA process (see § 636.109), then the following requirements apply:

(i) It is not necessary to evaluate the total contract price;

(ii) Price must be considered to the extent the contract requires the contracting agency to make any payments to the design-builder for any work performed prior to the completion of the NEPA process and the contracting agency wishes to use Federal-aid highway funds for those activities;

(iii) The evaluation of proposals and award of the contract may be based on qualitative considerations;

(iv) If the contracting agency wishes to use Federal-aid highway funds for final design and construction, the subsequent approval of final design and construction activities will be contingent upon a finding of price reasonableness by the contracting agency;

(v) The determination of price reasonableness for any design-build project funded with Federal-aid highway funds shall be based on at least one of the following methods:

(A) Compliance with the applicable procurement requirements for part 172, 635, or 636, where the contractor providing the final design or construction services, or both, is a person or entity other than the design-builder;

(B) A negotiated price determined on an open-book basis by both the design-builder and contracting agency; or

(C) An independent estimate by the contracting agency based on the price of similar work;

(vi) The contracting agency's finding of price reasonableness is subject to FHWA concurrence.

(2) You must evaluate the quality of the product or service through consideration of one or more non-price evaluation factors. These factors may include (but are not limited to) such criteria as:

(i) Compliance with solicitation requirements;

(ii) Completion schedule (contractual incentives and disincentives for early completion may be used where appropriate); or

(iii) Technical solutions.

(3) At your discretion, you may evaluate past performance, technical experience and management experience (subject to § 636.303(b)).

(b) All factors and significant subfactors that will affect contract award and their relative importance must be stated clearly in the solicitation.

[67 FR 75926, Dec. 10, 2002, as amended at 72 FR 45338, Aug. 14, 2007]

§ 636.303 May pre-qualification standards be used as proposal evaluation criteria in the RFP?

(a) If you use a prequalification procedure or a two-phase selection procedure to develop a short list of qualified offerors, then pre-qualification criteria should not be included as proposal evaluation criteria.

(b) The proposal evaluation criteria should be limited to the quality, quantity, value and timeliness of the product or service being proposed. However, there may be circumstances where it is appropriate to include prequalification standards as proposal evaluation criteria. Such instances include situations where:

(1) The scope of work involves very specialized technical expertise or specialized financial qualifications; or

(2) Where prequalification procedures or two-phase selection procedures are not used (short listing is not performed).

§ 636.304 What process may be used to rate and score proposals?

(a) Proposal evaluation is an assessment of the offeror's proposal and ability to perform the prospective contract successfully. You must evaluate proposals solely on the factors and subfactors specified in the solicitation.

(b) You may conduct evaluations using any rating method or combination of methods including color or adjectival ratings, numerical weights, and ordinal rankings. The relative strengths, deficiencies, significant weaknesses, and risks supporting proposal evaluation must be documented in the contract file.

§ 636.305 Can price information be provided to analysts who are reviewing technical proposals?

Normally, technical and price proposals are reviewed independently by separate evaluation teams. However, there may be occasions where the same experts needed to review the technical proposals are also needed in the review of the price proposals. This may occur where a limited amount of technical expertise is available to review proposals. Price information may be provided to such technical experts in accordance with your procedures.

Subpart D—Exchanges

§ 636.401 What types of information exchange may take place prior to the release of the RFP document?

Verbal or written information exchanges (such as in the first-phase of a two-phase selection procedure) must be consistent with State and/or local procurement integrity requirements. See § 636.115(a) for additional details.

§ 636.402 What types of information exchange may take place after the release of the RFP document?

Certain types of information exchange may be desirable at different points after the release of the RFP document. The following table summarizes the types of communications that will be discussed in this subpart. These communication methods are optional.

Type of information exchange	When	Purpose	Parties involved
(a) Clarifications	After receipt of proposals	Used when award without discussions is contemplated. Used to clarify certain aspects of a proposal (resolve minor errors, clerical errors, obtain additional past performance information, etc.).	Any offeror whose proposal is not clear to the contracting agency.
(b) Communications	After receipt of proposals, prior to the establishment of the competitive range.	Used to address issues which might prevent a proposal from being placed in the competitive range.	Only those offerors whose exclusion from, or inclusion in, the competitive range is uncertain. All offerors whose past performance information is the determining factor preventing them from being placed in the competitive range.
(c) Discussions (see Subpart E of this part).	After receipt of proposals and after the determination of the competitive range.	Enhance contracting agency understanding of proposals and offerors understanding of scope of work. Facilitate the evaluation process.	Must be held with all offerors in the competitive range.

§ 636.403 What information may be exchanged with a clarification?

(a) You may wish to clarify any aspect of proposals which would enhance your understanding of an offeror's proposal. This includes such information as an offeror's past performance or information regarding adverse past performance to which the offeror has not previously had an opportunity to respond. Clarification exchanges are discretionary. They do not have to be held with any specific number of offerors and do not have to address specific issues.

(b) You may wish to clarify and revise the RFP document through an addenda process in response to questions from potential offerors.

§ 636.404 Can a competitive range be used to limit competition?

If the solicitation notifies offerors that the competitive range can be limited for purposes of efficiency, you may limit the number of proposals to the greatest number that will permit an efficient competition. However, you must provide written notice to any offeror whose proposal is no longer considered to be included in the competitive range. Offerors excluded or otherwise eliminated from the competitive range may request a debriefing. Debriefings may be conducted in accordance with your procedures as long as you comply with § 636.514.

§ 636.405 After developing a short list, can I still establish a competitive range?

Yes, if you have developed a short list of firms, you may still establish a competitive range. The short list is based on qualifications criteria. The competitive range is based on the rating of technical and price proposals.

§ 636.406 Are communications allowed prior to establishing the competitive range?

Yes, prior to establishing the competitive range, you may conduct communications to:

(a) Enhance your understanding of proposals;

(b) Allow reasonable interpretation of the proposal; or

(c) Facilitate your evaluation process.

§ 636.407 Am I limited in holding communications with certain firms?

Yes, if you establish a competitive range, you must do the following:

(a) Hold communications with offerors whose past performance information is the determining factor preventing them from being placed within the competitive range;

(b) Address adverse past performance information to which an offeror has not had a prior opportunity to respond; and

(c) Hold communications only with those offerors whose exclusion from, or inclusion in, the competitive range is uncertain.

§ 636.408 Can communications be used to cure proposal deficiencies?

(a) No, communications must not be used to:

(1) Cure proposal deficiencies or material omissions;

(2) Materially alter the technical or cost elements of the proposal; and/or

(3) Otherwise revise the proposal.

(b) Communications may be considered in rating proposals for the purpose of establishing the competitive range.

§ 636.409 Can offerors revise their proposals during communications?

(a) No, communications shall not provide an opportunity for an offeror to revise its proposal, but may address the following:

(1) Ambiguities in the proposal or other concerns (e.g., perceived deficiencies, weaknesses, errors, omissions, or mistakes); and

(2) Information relating to relevant past performance.

(b) Communications must address adverse past performance information to which the offeror has not previously had an opportunity to comment.

Subpart E—Discussions, Proposal Revisions and Source Selection

§ 636.501 What issues may be addressed in discussions?

In a competitive acquisition, discussions may include bargaining. The term bargaining may include: persuasion, alteration of assumptions and positions, give-and-take, and may apply to price, schedule, technical requirements, type of contract, or other terms of a proposed contract.

§ 636.502 Why should I use discussions?

You should use discussions to maximize your ability to obtain the best value, based on the requirements and the evaluation factors set forth in the solicitation.

§ 636.503 Must I notify offerors of my intent to use/not use discussions?

Yes, in competitive acquisitions, the solicitation must notify offerors of your intent. You should either:

(a) Notify offerors that discussions may or may not be held depending on the quality of the proposals received (except clarifications may be used as described in § 636.401). Therefore, the offeror's initial proposal should contain the offeror's best terms from a cost or price and technical standpoint; or

(b) Notify offerors of your intent to establish a competitive range and hold discussions.

§ 636.504 If the solicitation indicated my intent was to award contract without discussions, but circumstances change, may I still hold discussions?

Yes, you may still elect to hold discussions when circumstances dictate, as long as the rationale for doing so is documented in the contract file. Such circumstances might include situations where all proposals received have deficiencies, when fair and reasonable prices are not offered, or when the cost or price offered is not affordable.

§ 636.505 Must a contracting agency establish a competitive range if it intends to have discussions with offerors?

Yes, if discussions are held, they must be conducted with all offerors in the competitive range. If you wish to hold discussions and do not formally establish a competitive range, then you must hold discussions with all responsive offerors.

§ 636.506 What issues must be covered in discussions?

(a) Discussions should be tailored to each offeror's proposal. Discussions must cover significant weaknesses, deficiencies, and other aspects of a proposal (such as cost or price, technical approach, past performance, and terms and conditions) that could be altered or explained to enhance materially the proposal's potential for award. You may use your judgment in setting limits for the scope and extent of discussions.

(b) In situations where the solicitation stated that evaluation credit would be given for technical solutions exceeding any mandatory minimums, you may hold discussions regarding increased performance beyond any mandatory minimums, and you may suggest to offerors that have exceeded any mandatory minimums (in ways that are not integral to the design), that their proposals would be more competitive if the excesses were removed and the offered price decreased.

§ 636.507 What subjects are prohibited in discussions, communications and clarifications with offerors?

You may not engage in conduct that:

(a) Favors one offeror over another;

(b) Reveals an offeror's technical solution, including unique technology, innovative and unique uses of commercial items, or any information that would compromise an offeror's intellectual property to another offeror;

(c) Reveals an offerors price without that offeror's permission;

(d) Reveals the names of individuals providing reference information about an offeror's past performance; or

(e) Knowingly furnish source selection information which could be in violation of State procurement integrity standards.

§ 636.508 Can price or cost be an issue in discussions?

You may inform an offeror that its price is considered to be too high, or too low, and reveal the results of the analysis supporting that conclusion. At your discretion, you may indicate to all offerors your estimated cost for the project.

§ 636.509 Can offerors revise their proposals as a result of discussions?

(a) Yes, you may request or allow proposal revisions to clarify and document understandings reached during discussions. At the conclusion of discussions, each offeror shall be given an opportunity to submit a final proposal revision.

(b) You must establish a common cut-off date only for receipt of final proposal revisions. Requests for final proposal revisions shall advise offerors that the final proposal revisions shall be in writing and that the contracting agency intends to make award without obtaining further revisions.

§ 636.510 Can the competitive range be further defined once discussions have begun?

Yes, you may further narrow the competitive range if an offeror originally in the competitive range is no longer considered to be among the most highly rated offerors being considered for award. That offeror may be eliminated from the competitive range whether or not all material aspects of the proposal have been discussed, or whether or not the offeror has been afforded an opportunity to submit a proposal revision. You must provide an offeror excluded from the competitive range with a written determination and notice that proposal revisions will not be considered.

§ 636.511 Can there be more than one round of discussions?

Yes, but only at the conclusion of discussions will the offerors be requested to submit a final proposal revision, also called best and final offer (BAFO). Thus, regardless of the length or number of discussions, there will be only one request for a revised proposal (*i.e.*, only one BAFO).

§ 636.512 What is the basis for the source selection decision?

(a) You must base the source selection decision on a comparative assessment of proposals against all selection criteria in the solicitation. While you may use reports and analyses prepared by others, the source selection decision shall represent your independent judgment.

(b) The source selection decision shall be documented, and the documentation shall include the rationale for any business judgments and tradeoffs made or relied on, including benefits associated with additional costs. Although the rationale for the selection decision must be documented, that documentation need not quantify the tradeoffs that led to the decision.

§ 636.513 Are limited negotiations allowed prior to contract execution?

(a) Yes, after the source selection but prior to contract execution, you may conduct limited negotiations with the selected design-builder to clarify any remaining issues regarding scope, schedule, financing or any other information provided by that offeror. You must comply with the provisions of §636.507 in the exchange of this information.

(b) Limited negotiations conducted under this section may include negotiations necessary to incorporate the ideas and concepts from unsuccessful offerors into the contract if a stipend is offered by the contracting agency and accepted by the unsuccessful offeror and if the requirements of section 636.113 are met.

[67 FR 75926, Dec. 10, 2002, as amended at 73 FR 77502, Dec. 19, 2008]

§ 636.514 How may I provide notifications and debriefings?

You may provide pre-award or post-award notifications in accordance with State approved procedures. If an offeror requests a debriefing, you may provide pre-award or post-award debriefings in accordance with State approved procedures.

PART 637—CONSTRUCTION INSPECTION AND APPROVAL

AUTHORITY: Sec. 1307, Pub. L. 105–178, 112 Stat. 107; 23 U.S.C. 109, 114, and 315; 49 CFR 1.48(b).

SOURCE: 60 FR 33717, June 29, 1995, unless otherwise noted.

EDITORIAL NOTE: Nomenclature changes to part 637 appear at 67 FR 75934, Dec. 10, 2002.

Subpart A [Reserved]

Subpart B—Quality Assurance Procedures for Construction

§ 637.201 Purpose.

To prescribe policies, procedures, and guidelines to assure the quality of materials and construction in all Federal-aid highway projects on the National Highway System.

§ 637.203 Definitions.

Acceptance program. All factors that comprise the State transportation department's (STD) determination of the quality of the product as specified in the contract requirements. These factors include verification sampling, testing, and inspection and may include results of quality control sampling and testing.

Independent assurance program. Activities that are an unbiased and independent evaluation of all the sampling and testing procedures used in the acceptance program. Test procedures used in the acceptance program which are performed in the STD's central laboratory would not be covered by an independent assurance program.

Proficiency samples. Homogeneous samples that are distributed and tested by two or more laboratories. The test results are compared to assure that the laboratories are obtaining the same results.

Qualified laboratories. Laboratories that are capable as defined by appropriate programs established by each STD. As a minimum, the qualification program shall include provisions for checking test equipment and the laboratory shall keep records of calibration checks.

Qualified sampling and testing personnel. Personnel who are capable as defined by appropriate programs established by each STD.

Quality assurance. All those planned and systematic actions necessary to provide confidence that a product or service will satisfy given requirements for quality.

Quality control. All contractor/vendor operational techniques and activities that are performed or conducted to fulfill the contract requirements.

Random sample. A sample drawn from a lot in which each increment in the lot has an equal probability of being chosen.

Vendor. A supplier of project-produced material that is not the contractor.

Verification sampling and testing. Sampling and testing performed to validate the quality of the product.

§ 637.205 Policy.

(a) *Quality assurance program.* Each STD shall develop a quality assurance program which will assure that the materials and workmanship incorporated into each Federal-aid highway construction project on the NHS are in conformity with the requirements of the approved plans and specifications, including approved changes. The program must meet the criteria in § 637.207 and be approved by the FHWA.

(b) *STD capabilities.* The STD shall maintain an adequate, qualified staff to administer its quality assurance program. The State shall also maintain a central laboratory. The State's central laboratory shall meet the requirements in § 637.209(a)(2).

(c) *Independent assurance program.* Independent assurance samples and tests or other procedures shall be performed by qualified sampling and testing personnel employed by the STD or its designated agent.

(d) *Verification sampling and testing.* The verification sampling and testing are to be performed by qualified testing personnel employed by the STD or its designated agent, excluding the contractor and vendor.

(e) *Random samples.* All samples used for quality control and verification sampling and testing shall be random samples.

§ 637.207 Quality assurance program.

(a) Each STD's quality assurance program shall provide for an acceptance program and an independent assurance (IA) program consisting of the following:

(1) Acceptance program.

(i) Each STD's acceptance program shall consist of the following:

(A) Frequency guide schedules for verification sampling and testing which will give general guidance to personnel responsible for the program and allow adaptation to specific project conditions and needs.

(B) Identification of the specific location in the construction or production operation at which verification sampling and testing is to be accomplished.

(C) Identification of the specific attributes to be inspected which reflect the quality of the finished product.

(ii) Quality control sampling and testing results may be used as part of the acceptance decision provided that:

(A) The sampling and testing has been performed by qualified laboratories and qualified sampling and testing personnel.

(B) The quality of the material has been validated by the verification sampling and testing. The verification testing shall be performed on samples that are taken independently of the quality control samples.

(C) The quality control sampling and testing is evaluated by an IA program.

(iii) If the results from the quality control sampling and testing are used in the acceptance program, the STD shall establish a dispute resolution system. The dispute resolution system shall address the resolution of discrepancies occurring between the verification sampling and testing and the quality control sampling and testing. The dispute resolution system may be administered entirely within the STD.

(iv) In the case of a design-build project on the National Highway System, warranties may be used where appropriate. See 23 CFR 635.413(e) for specific requirements.

(2) The IA program shall evaluate the qualified sampling and testing personnel and the testing equipment. The program shall cover sampling procedures, testing procedures, and testing equipment. Each IA program shall include a schedule of frequency for IA evaluation. The schedule may be established based on either a project basis or a system basis. The frequency can be based on either a unit of production or on a unit of time.

(i) The testing equipment shall be evaluated by using one or more of the following: Calibration checks, split samples, or proficiency samples.

(ii) Testing personnel shall be evaluated by observations and split samples or proficiency samples.

(iii) A prompt comparison and documentation shall be made of test results obtained by the tester being evaluated and the IA tester. The STD shall develop guidelines including tolerance limits for the comparison of test results.

(iv) If the STD uses the system approach to the IA program, the STD shall provide an annual report to the FHWA summarizing the results of the IA program.

(3) The preparation of a materials certification, conforming in substance to appendix A of this subpart, shall be submitted to the FHWA Division Administrator for each construction project which is subject to FHWA construction oversight activities.

(b) In the case of a design-build project funded under title 23, U.S. Code, the STD's quality assurance program should consider the specific contractual needs of the design-build project. All provisions of paragraph (a) of this section are applicable to design-build projects. In addition, the quality assurance program may include the following:

(1) Reliance on a combination of contractual provisions and acceptance methods;

(2) Reliance on quality control sampling and testing as part of the acceptance decision, provided that adequate verification of the design-builder's quality control sampling and testing is performed to ensure that the design-builder is providing the quality of materials and construction required by the contract documents.

(3) Contractual provisions which require the operation of the completed facility for a specific time period.

[60 FR 33717, June 29, 1995, as amended at 67 FR 75934, Dec. 10, 2002]

§ 637.209 Laboratory and sampling and testing personnel qualifications.

(a) Laboratories.

(1) After June 29, 2000, all contractor, vendor, and STD testing used in the acceptance decision shall be performed by qualified laboratories.

(2) After June 30, 1997, each STD shall have its central laboratory accredited by the AASHTO Accreditation Program or a comparable laboratory accreditation program approved by the FHWA.

(3) After June 29, 2000, any non-STD designated laboratory which performs IA sampling and testing shall be accredited in the testing to be performed by the AASHTO Accreditation Program or a comparable laboratory accreditation program approved by the FHWA.

(4) After June 29, 2000, any non-STD laboratory that is used in dispute resolution sampling and testing shall be accredited in the testing to be performed by the AASHTO Accreditation Program or a comparable laboratory accreditation program approved by the FHWA.

(5) After September 24, 2009, laboratories that perform crash testing for acceptance of roadside hardware by the FHWA shall be accredited by a laboratory accreditation body that is recognized by the National Cooperation for Laboratory Accreditation (NACLA), is a signatory to the Asia Pacific Laboratory Accreditation Cooperation (APLAC) Mutual Recognition Arrangement (MRA), is a signatory to the

International Laboratory Accreditation Cooperation (ILAC) Mutual Recognition Arrangement (MRA), or another accreditation body acceptable to FHWA.

(b) Sampling and testing personnel. After June 29, 2000, all sampling and testing data to be used in the acceptance decision or the IA program shall be executed by qualified sampling and testing personnel.

(c) Conflict of interest. In order to avoid an appearance of a conflict of interest, any qualified non-STD laboratory shall perform only one of the following types of testing on the same project: Verification testing, quality control testing, IA testing, or dispute resolution testing.

[60 FR 33717, June 29, 1995, as amended at 72 FR 54212, Sept. 24, 2007]

APPENDIX A TO SUBPART B OF PART 637—GUIDE LETTER OF CERTIFICATION BY STATE ENGINEER

Date ____________________

Project No. ____________________

This is to certify that:

The results of the tests used in the acceptance program indicate that the materials incorporated in the construction work, and the construction operations controlled by sampling and testing, were in conformity with the approved plans and specifications. (The following sentence should be added if the IA testing frequencies are based on project quantities. All independent assurance samples and tests are within tolerance limits of the samples and tests that are used in the acceptance program.)

Exceptions to the plans and specifications are explained on the back hereof (or on attached sheet).

____

Director of STD Laboratory or other appropriate STD Official.

PART 645—UTILITIES

Subpart A—Utility Relocations, Adjustments, and Reimbursement

Subpart B—Accommodation of Utilities

AUTHORITY: 23 U.S.C. 101, 109, 111, 116, 123, and 315; 23 CFR 1.23 and 1.27; 49 CFR 1.48(b); and E.O. 11990, 42 26961 (May 24, 1977).

EDITORIAL NOTE: Nomenclature changes to part 645 appear at 65 FR 70311, Nov. 22, 2000.

Subpart A—Utility Relocations, Adjustments, and Reimbursement

SOURCE: 50 FR 20345, May 15, 1985, unless otherwise noted.

§ 645.101 Purpose.

To prescribe the policies, procedures, and reimbursement provisions for the adjustment and relocation of utility facilities on Federal-aid and direct Federal projects.

§ 645.103 Applicability.

(a) The provisions of this regulation apply to reimbursement claimed by a State transportation department (STD) for costs incurred under an approved and properly executed transportation department (TD)/utility agreement and for payment of costs incurred under all Federal Highway Administration (FHWA)/utility agreements.

(b) Procedures on the accommodation of utilities are set forth in 23 CFR part 645, subpart B, Accommodation of Utilities.

(c) When the lines or facilities to be relocated or adjusted due to highway construction are privately owned, located on the owner's land, devoted exclusively to private use and not directly or indirectly serving the public, the provisions of the FHWA's right-of-way procedures in 23 CFR 710.203, apply. When applicable, under the foregoing conditions, the provisions of this regulation may be used as a guide to establish a cost-to-cure.

(d) The FHWA's reimbursement to the STD will be governed by State law (or State regulation) or the provisions of this regulation, whichever is more restrictive. When State law or regulation differs from this regulation, a determination shall be made by the STD subject to the concurrence of the FHWA as to which standards will govern, and the record documented accordingly, for each relocation encountered.

(e) For direct Federal projects, all references herein to the STD or TD are inapplicable, and it is intended that the FHWA be considered in the relative position of the STD or TD.

[50 FR 20345, May 15, 1985, as amended at 64 FR 71289, Dec. 21, 1999]

§ 645.105 Definitions.

For the purposes of this regulation, the following definitions shall apply:

Authorization—for Federal-aid projects authorization to the STD by the FHWA, or for direct Federal projects authorization to the utility by the FHWA, to proceed with any phase of a project. The date of authorization establishes the date of eligibility for Federal funds to participate in the costs incurred on that phase of work.

Betterment—any upgrading of the facility being relocated that is not attributable to the highway construction and is made solely for the benefit of and at the election of the utility.

Cost of relocation—the entire amount paid by or on behalf of the utility properly attributable to the relocation after deducting from that amount any increase in value of the new facility, and any salvage derived from the old facility.

Cost of Removal—the amount expended to remove utility property including the cost of demolishing, dismantling, removing, transporting, or otherwise disposing of utility property and of cleaning up to leave the site in a neat and presentable condition.

Cost of salvage—the amount expended to restore salvaged utility property to usable condition after its removal.

Direct Federal projects—highway projects such as projects under the Federal Lands Highways Program which are under the direct administration of the FHWA.

Indirect or overhead costs—those costs which are not readily identifiable with one specific task, job, or work order. Such costs may include indirect labor, social security taxes, insurance, stores expense, and general office expenses. Costs of this nature generally are distributed or allocated to the applicable job or work orders, other accounts and other functions to which they relate. Distribution and allocation is made on a uniform basis which is reasonable, equitable, and in accordance with generally accepted cost accounting practices.

Relocation—the adjustment of utility facilities required by the highway project. It includes removing and reinstalling the facility, including necessary temporary facilities, acquiring necessary right-of-way on the new location, moving, rearranging or changing the type of existing facilities and taking any necessary safety and protective measures. It shall also mean constructing a replacement facility that is both functionally equivalent to the existing facility and necessary for continuous operation of the utility service, the project economy, or sequence of highway construction.

Salvage value—the amount received from the sale of utility property that has been removed or the amount at which the recovered material is charged to the utility's accounts, if retained for reuse.

State transportation department—the transportation department of one of the 50 States, the District of Columbia, or Puerto Rico.

Transportation department(TD)—that department, commission, board, or official of any State or political subdivison thereof, charged by its law with the responsibility for highway administration.

Use and occupancy agreement—the document (written agreement or permit) by which the TD approves the use and occupancy of highway right-of-way by utility facilities or private lines.

Utility—a privately, publicly, or cooperatively owned line, facility or system for producing, transmitting, or distributing communications, cable television, power, electricity, light, heat, gas, oil, crude products, water, steam, waste, storm water not connected with highway drainage, or any other similar commodity, including any fire or police signal system or street lighting system, which directly or indirectly serves the public. The term utility shall also mean the utility company inclusive of any wholly owned or controlled subsidiary.

Work order system—a procedure for accumulating and recording into separate accounts of a utility all costs to the utility in connection with any change in its system or plant.

[50 FR 20345, May 15, 1985, as amended at 65 FR 70311, Nov. 22, 2000]

§ 645.107 Eligibility.

(a) When requested by the STD, Federal funds may participate, subject to the provisions of § 645.103(d) of this part and at the pro rata share applicable, in an amount actually paid by an TD for the costs of utility relocations. Federal funds may participate in safety corrective measures made under the provisions of § 645.107(k) of this part. Federal funds may also participate for relocations necessitated by the actual construction of highway project made under one or more of the following conditions when:

(1) The STD certifies that the utility has the right of occupancy in its existing location because it holds the fee, an easement, or other real property interest, the damaging or taking of which is compensable in eminent domain,

(2) The utility occupies privately or publicly owned land, including public road or street right-of-way, and the STD certifies that the payment by the TD is made pursuant to a law authorizing such payment in conformance with the provisions of 23 U.S.C. 123, and/or

(3) The utility occupies publicy owned land, including public road and street right-of-way, and is owned by a public agency or political subdivision of the State, and is not required by law or agreement to move at its own expense, and the STD certifies that the TD has the legal authority or obligation to make such payments.

(b) On projects which the STD has the authority to participate in project costs, Federal funds may not participate in payments made by a political subdivision for relocation of utility facilities, other than those proposed under the provisions of § 645.107(k) of this part, when State law prohibits the STD from making payment for relocation of utility facilities.

(c) On projects which the STD does not have the authority to participate in project costs, Federal funds may participate in payments made by a political subdivision for relocation of utility facilities necessitated by the actual construction of a highway project when the STD certifies that such payment is based upon the provisions of § 645.107(a) of this part and does not violate the terms of a use and occupancy agreement, or legal contract, between the utility and the TD or for utility safety corrective measures under the provisions of § 645.107(k) of this part.

(d) Federal funds are not eligible to participate in any costs for which the utility contributes or repays the TD, except for utilities owned by the political subdivision on projects which qualify under the provisions of § 645.107(c) of this part in which case the costs of the utility are considered to be costs of the TD.

(e) The FHWA may deny Federal fund participation in any payments made by a TD for the relocation of utility facilities when such payments do not constitute a suitable basis for Federal fund participation under the provisions of title 23 U.S.C.

(f) The rights of any public agency or political subdivision of a State under contract, franchise, or other instrument or agreement with the utility, pertaining to the utility's use and occupancy of publicly owned land, including public road and street right-of-way, shall be considered the rights of the STD in the absence of State law to the contrary.

(g) In lieu of the individual certifications required by § 645.107(a) and (c), the STD may file a statement with the FHWA setting forth the conditions under which the STD will make payments for the relocation of utility facilities. The FHWA may approve Federal fund participation in utility relocations proposed by the STD under the conditions of the statement when the

FHWA has made an affirmative finding that such statement and conditions form a suitable basis for Federal fund participation under the provisions of 23 U.S.C. 123.

(h) Federal funds may not participate in the cost of relocations of utility facilities made solely for the benefit or convenience of a utility, its contractor, or a highway contractor.

(i) When the advance installation of new utility facilities crossing or otherwise occupying the proposed right-of-way of a planned highway project is underway, or scheduled to be underway, prior to the time such right-of-way is purchased by or under control of the TD, arrangements should be made for such facilities to be installed in a manner that will meet the requirements of the planned highway project. Federal funds are eligible to participate in the additional cost incurred by the utility that are attributable to, and in accommodation of, the highway project provided such costs are incurred subsequent to authorization of the work by the FHWA. Subject to the other provisions of this regulation, Federal participation may be approved under the foregoing circumstances when it is demonstrated that the action taken is necessary to protect the public interest and the adjustment of the facility is necessary by reason of the actual construction of the highway project.

(j) Federal funds are eligible to participate in the costs of preliminary engineering and allied services for utilities, the acquisition of replacement right-of-way for utilities, and the physical construction work associated with utility relocations. Such costs must be incurred by or on behalf of a utility after the date the work is included in an approved program and after the FHWA has authorized the STD to proceed in accordance with 23 CFR part 630, subpart A, Federal-Aid Programs Approval and Project Authorization.

(k) Federal funds may participate in projects solely for the purpose of implementing safety corrective measures to reduce the roadside hazards of utility facilities to the highway user. Safety corrective measures should be developed in accordance with the provisions of 23 CFR 645.209(k).

(Information collection requirements in paragraph (g) were approved by the Office of Management and Budget under control number 2125–0515)

[50 FR 20345, May 15, 1985, as amended at 53 FR 24932, July 1, 1988]

§645.109 Preliminary engineering.

(a) As mutually agreed to by the TD and utility, and subject to the provisions of paragraph (b) of this section, preliminary engineering activities associated with utility relocation work may be done by:

(1) The TD's or utility's engineering forces;

(2) An engineering consultant selected by the TD, after consultation with the utility, the contract to be administered by the TD; or,

(3) An engineering consultant selected by the utility, with the approval of the TD, the contract to be administered by the utility.

(b) When a utility is not adequately staffed to pursue the necessary preliminary engineering and related work for the utility relocation, Federal funds may participate in the amount paid to engineers, architects, and others for required engineering and allied services provided such amounts are not based on a percentage of the cost of relocation. When Federal participation is requested by the STD in the cost of such services, the utility and its consultant shall agree in writing as to the services to be provided and the fees and arrangements for the services. Federal funds may participate in the cost of such services performed under existing written continuing contracts when it is demonstrated that such work is performed regularly for the utility in its own work and that the costs are reasonable.

(c) The procedures in 23 CFR part 172, Administration of Engineering and Design Related Service Contracts, may be used as a guide for reviewing proposed consultant contracts.

[50 FR 20345, May 15, 1985, as amended at 60 FR 34850, July 5, 1995; 65 FR 70311, Nov. 22, 2000]

§ 645.111 Right-of-way.

(a) Federal participation may be approved for the cost of replacement right-of-way provided:

(1) The utility has the right of occupancy in its existing location beause it holds the fee, an easement, or another real property interest, the damaging or taking of which is compensable in eminent domain, or the acquisition is made in the interest of project economy or is necessary to meet the requirements of the highway project, and

(2) There will be no charge to the project for that portion of the utility's existing right-of-way being transferred to the TD for highway purposes.

(b) The utility shall determine and make a written valuation of the replacement right-of-way that it acquires in order to justify amounts paid for such right-of-way. This written valuation shall be accomplished prior to negotiation for acquisition.

(c) Acquisition of replacement right-of-way by the TD on behalf of a utility or acquisition of nonoperating real property from a utility shall be in accordance with the Uniform Relocation Assistance and Real Property Acquisition Policies Act of 1970 (42 U.S.C. 4601 *et seq.*) and applicable right-of-way procedures in 23 CFR 710.203.

(d) When the utility has the right-of-occupancy in its existing location because it holds the fee, an easement, or another real property interest, and it is not necessary by reason of the highway construction to adjust or replace the facilities located thereon, the taking of and damage to the utility's real property, including the disposal or removal of such facilities, may be considered a right-of-way transaction in accordance with provisions of the applicable right-of-way procedures in 23 CFR 710.203.

[50 FR 20345, May 15, 1985, as amended at 64 FR 71289, Dec. 21, 1999]

§ 645.113 Agreements and authorizations.

(a) On Federal-aid and direct Federal projects involving utility relocations, the utility and the TD shall agree in writing on their separate responsibilities for financing and accomplishing the relocation work. When Federal participation is requested, the agreement shall incorporate this regulation by reference and designate the method to be used for performing the work (by contract or force account) and for developing relocation costs. The method proposed by the utility for developing relocation costs must be acceptable to both the TD and the FHWA. The preferred method for the development of relocation costs by a utility is on the basis of actual direct and related indirect costs accumulated in accordance with a work order accounting procedure prescribed by the applicable Federal or State regulatory body.

(b) When applicable, the written agreement shall specify the terms and amounts of any contribution or repayments made or to be made by the utility to the TD in connection with payments by the TD to the utility under the provisions of § 645.107 of this regulation.

(c) The agreement shall be supported by plans, specifications when required, and itemized cost estimates of the work agreed upon, including appropriate credits to the project, and shall be sufficiently informative and complete to provide the TD and the FHWA with a clear description of the work required.

(d) When the relocation involves both work to be done at the TD's expense and work to be done at the expense of the utility, the written agreement shall state the share to be borne by each party.

(e) In the event there are changes in the scope of work, extra work or major changes in the planned work covered by the approved agreement, plans, and estimates, Federal participation shall be limited to costs covered by a modification of the agreement, a written change, or extra work order approved by the TD and the FHWA.

(f) When proposed utility relocation and adjustment work on a project for a specific utility company can be clearly defined and the cost can be accurately estimated, the FHWA may approve an agreement between the TD and the utility company for a lump-sum payment without later confirmation by audit of actual costs.

(g) Except as otherwise provided by § 645.113(h), authorization by the FHWA to the STD to proceed with the physical relocation of a utility's facilities may be given after:

(1) The utility relocation work, or the right-of-way, or physical construction phase of the highway construction work is included in an approved Statewide transportation improvement program,

(2) The appropriate environmental evaluation and public hearing procedures required by 23 CFR part 771, Environmental Impact and Related Procedures, have been satisfied.

(3) The FHWA has reviewed and approved the plans, estimates, and proposed or executed agreements for the utility work and is furnished a schedule for accomplishing the work.

(h) The FHWA may authorize the physical relocation of utility facilities before the requirements of §645.113(g)(2) are satisfied when the relocation or adjustment of utility facilities meets the requirements of §645.107(i) of this regulation.

(i) Whenever the FHWA has authorized right-of-way acquisition under the hardship and protective buying provisions of 23 CFR 710.503, the FHWA may authorize the physical relocation of utility facilities located in whole or in part on such right-of-way.

(j) When all efforts by the TD and utility fail to bring about written agreement of their separate responsibilities under the provisions of this regulation, the STD shall submit its proposal and a full report of the circumstances to the FHWA. Conditional authorizations for the relocation work to proceed may be given by the FHWA to the STD with the understanding that Federal funds will not be paid for work done by the utility until the STD proposal has been approved by the FHWA.

(k) The FHWA will consider for approval any special procedure under State law, or appropriate administrative or judicial order, or under blanket master agreements with the utilities, that will fully accomplish all of the foregoing objectives and accelerate the advancement of the construction and completion of projects.

[50 FR 20345, May 15, 1985, as amended at 60 FR 34850, July 5, 1995; 64 FR 71289, Dec. 21, 1999; 65 FR 70311, Nov. 22, 2000]

§645.115 Construction.

(a) Part 635, subpart B, of this title, Force Account Construction (justification required for force account work), states that it is cost-effective for certain utility adjustments to be performed by a utility with its own forces and equipment, provided the utility is qualified to perform the work in a satisfactory manner. This cost-effectiveness finding covers minor work on the utility's existing facilities routinely performed by the utility with its own forces. When the utility is not adequately staffed and equipped to perform such work with its own forces and equipment at a time convenient to and in coordination with the associated highway construction, such work may be done by:

(1) A contract awarded by the TD or utility to the lowest qualified bidder based on appropriate solicitation,

(2) Inclusion as part of the TD's highway construction contract let by the TD as agreed to by the utility,

(3) An existing continuing contract, provided the costs are reasonable, or

(4) A contract for low-cost incidental work, such as tree trimming and the like, awarded by the TD or utility without competitive bidding, provided the costs are reasonable.

(b) When it has been determined under part 635, subpart B, that the force account method is not the most cost-effective means for accomplishing the utility adjustment, such work is to be done under competitive bid contracts as described in §645.115(a) (1) and (2) or under an existing continuing contract provided it can be demonstrated this is the most cost-effective method.

(c) Costs for labor, materials, equipment, and other services furnished by the utility shall be billed by the utility directly to the TD. The special provisions of contracts let by the utility or the TD shall be explicit in this respect. The costs of force account work performed for the utility by the TD and of contract work performed for the utility under a contract let by the TD shall be reported separately from the costs of other force account and contract items on the highway project.

§ 645.117 Cost development and reimbursement.

(a) *Developing and recording costs.* (1) All utility relocation costs shall be recorded by means of work orders in accordance with an approved work order system except when another method of developing and recording costs, such as lump-sum agreement, has been approved by the TD and the FHWA. Except for work done under contracts, the individual and total costs properly reported and recorded in the utility's accounts in accordance with the approved method for developing such costs, or the lump-sum agreement, shall constitute the maximum amount on which Federal participation may be based.

(2) Each utility shall keep its work order system or other approved accounting procedure in such a manner as to show the nature of each addition to or retirement from a facility, the total costs thereof, and the source or sources of cost. Separate work orders may be issued for additions and retirements. Retirements, however, may be included with the construction work order provided that all items relating to retirements shall be kept separately from those relating to construction.

(3) The STD may develop, or work in concert with utility companies to develop, other acceptable costing methods, such as unit costs, to estimate and reimburse utility relocation expenditures. Such other methods shall be founded in generally accepted industry practices and be reasonably supported by recent actual expenditures. Unit costs should be developed periodically and supported annually by a maintained data base of relocation expenses. Development of any alternate costing method should consider the factors listed in paragraphs (b) through (g) of this section. Streamlining of the cost development and reimbursement procedures is encouraged so long as adequate accountability for Federal expenditures is maintained. Concurrence by the FHWA is required for any costing method used other than actual cost.

(b) *Direct labor costs.* (1) Salaries and wages, at actual or average rates, and related expenses paid by the utility to individuals for the time worked on the project are reimbursable when supported by adequate records. This includes labor associated with preliminary engineering, construction engineering, right-of-way, and force account construction.

(2) Salaries and expenses paid to individuals who are normally part of the overhead organization of the utility may be reimbursed for the time worked directly on the project when supported by adequate records and when the work performed by such individuals is essential to the project and could not have been accomplished as economically by employees outside the overhead organization.

(3) Amounts paid to engineers, architects and others for services directly related to projects may be reimbursed.

(c) *Labor surcharges.* (1) Labor surcharges include worker compensation insurance, public liability and property damage insurance, and such fringe benefits as the utility has established for the benefit of its employees. The cost of labor surcharges will be reimbursed at actual cost to the utility, or, at the option of the utility, average rates which are representative of actual costs may be used in lieu of actual costs if approved by the STD and the FHWA. These average rates should be adjusted at least once annually to take into account known anticipated changes and correction for any over or under applied costs for the preceding period.

(2) When the utility is a self-insurer, there may be reimbursement at experience rates properly developed from actual costs. The rates cannot exceed the rates of a regular insurance company for the class of employment covered.

(d) *Overhead and indirect construction costs.* (1) Overhead and indirect construction costs not charged directly to work order or construction accounts may be allocated to the relocation provided the allocation is made on an equitable basis. All costs included in the allocation shall be eligible for Federal reimbursement, reasonable, actually incurred by the utility, and consistent with the provisions of 48 CFR part 31.

(2) Costs not eligible for Federal reimbursement include, but are not limited to, the costs associated with advertising, sales promotion, interest on borrowings, the issuance of stock, bad

debts, uncollectible accounts receivable, contributions, donations, entertainment, fines, penalties, lobbying, and research programs.

(3) The records supporting the entries for overhead and indirect construction costs shall show the total amount, rate, and allocation basis for each additive, and are subject to audit by representatives of the State and Federal Government.

(e) *Material and supply costs.* (1) Materials and supplies, if available, are to be furnished from company stock except that they may be obtained from other sources near the project site when available at a lower cost. When not available from company stock, they may be purchased either under competitive bids or existing continuing contracts under which the lowest available prices are developed. Minor quantities of materials and supplies and proprietary products routinely used in the utility's operation and essential for the maintenance of system compatibility may be excluded from these requirements. The utility shall not be required to change its existing standards for materials used in permanent changes to its facilities. Costs shall be determined as follows:

(i) Materials and supplies furnished from company stock shall be billed at the current stock prices for such new or used materials at time of issue.

(ii) Materials and supplies not furnished from company stock shall be billed at actual costs to the utility delivered to the project site.

(iii) A reasonable cost for plant inspection and testing may be included in the costs of materials and supplies when such expense has been incurred. The computation of actual costs of materials and supplies shall include the deduction of all offered discounts, rebates, and allowances.

(iv) The cost of rehabilitating rather than replacing existing utility facilities to meet the requirements of a project is reimbursable, provided this cost does not exceed replacement costs.

(2) Materials recovered from temporary use and accepted for reuse by the utility shall be credited to the project at prices charged to the job, less a considertion for loss in service life at 10 percent. Materials recovered from the permanent facility of the utility that are accepted by the utility for return to stock shall be credited to the project at the current stock prices of such used materials. Materials recovered and not accepted for reuse by the utility, if determined to have a net sale value, shall be sold to the highest bidder by the TD or utility following an opportunity for TD inspection and appropriate solicitation for bids. If the utility practices a system of periodic disposal by sale, credit to the project shall be at the going prices supported by records of the utility.

(3) Federal participation may be approved for the total cost of removal when either such removal is required by the highway construction or the existing facilities cannot be abandoned in place for aesthetic or safety reasons. When the utility facilities can be abandoned in place but the utility or highway constructor elects to remove and recover the materials, Federal funds shall not participate in removal costs which exceed the value of the materials recovered.

(4) The actual and direct costs of handling and loading materials and supplies at company stores or material yards, and of unloading and handling recovered materials accepted by the utility at its stores or material yards are reimbursable. In lieu of actual costs, average rates which are representative of actual costs may be used if approved by the STD and the FHWA. These average rates should be adjusted at least once annually to take into account known anticipated changes and correction for any over or under applied costs for the preceding period. At the option of the utility, 5 percent of the amounts billed for the materials and supplies issued from company stores and material yards or the value of recovered materials will be reimbursed in lieu of actual or average costs for handling.

(f) *Equipment costs.* The average or actual costs of operation, minor maintenance, and depreciation of utility-owned equipment may be reimbursed. Reimbursement for utility-owned vehicles may be made at average or actual costs. When utility-owned equipment is not available, reimbursement will be limited to the amount of rental paid (1) to the lowest qualified bidder, (2) under existing continuing contracts at reasonable costs, or (3) as an exception by negotiation when paragraph (f) (1) and (2) of this section are impractical due to project location or schedule.

(g) *Transportation costs.* (1) The utility's cost, consistent with its overall policy, of necessary employee transportation and subsistence directly attributable to the project is reimbursable.

(2) Reasonable cost for the movement of materials, supplies, and equipment to the project and necessary return to storage including the associated cost of loading and unloading equipment is reimbursable.

(h) *Credits.* (1) Credit to the highway project will be required for the cost of any betterments to the facility being replaced or adjusted, and for the salvage value of the materials removed.

(2) Credit to the highway project will be required for the accrued depreciation of a utility facility being replaced, such as a building, pumping station, filtration plant, power plant, substation, or any other similar operational unit. Such accrued depreciation is that amount based on the ratio between the period of actual length of service and total life expectancy applied to the original cost. Credit for accrued depreciation shall not be required for a segment of the utility's service, distribution, or transmission lines.

(3) No betterment credit is required for additions or improvements which are:

(i) Required by the highway project,

(ii) Replacement devices or materials that are of equivalent standards although not identical,

(iii) Replacement of devices or materials no longer regularly manufactured with next highest grade or size,

(iv) Required by law under governmental and appropriate regulatory commission code, or

(v) Required by current design practices regularly followed by the company in its own work, and there is a direct benefit to the highway project.

(4) When the facilities, including equipment and operating facilities, described in §645.117(h)(2) are not being replaced, but are being rehabilitated and/or moved, as necessitated by the highway project, no credit for accrued depreciation is needed.

(5) In no event will the total of all credits required under the provisions of this regulation exceed the total costs of adjustment exclusive of the cost of additions or improvements necessitated by the highway construction.

(i) *Billings.* (1) After the executed TD/utility agreement has been approved by the FHWA, the utility may be reimbursed through the STD by progress billings for costs incurred. Cost for materials stockpiled at the project site or specifically purchased and delivered to the utility for use on the project may also be reimbursed on progress billings following approval of the executed TD/utility agreement.

(2) The utility shall provide one final and complete billing of all costs incurred, or of the agreed-to lump-sum, within one year following completion of the utility relocation work, otherwise previous payments to the utility may be considered final, except as agreed to between the STD and the utility. Billings received from utilities more than one year following completion of the utility relocation work may be paid if the STD so desires, and Federal-aid highway funds may participate in these payments.

(3) All utility cost records and accounts relating to the project are subject to audit by representatives of the State and Federal Government for a period of 3 years from the date final payment has been received by the utility.

(Information collection requirements in paragraph (i) were approved by the Office of Management and Budget under control number 2125–0159)

[50 FR 20345, May 15, 1985, as amended at 60 FR 34850, July 5, 1995; 65 FR 70311, Nov. 22, 2000]

§645.119 Alternate procedure.

(a) This alternate procedure is provided to simplify the processing of utility relocations or adjustments under the provisions of this regulation. Under this procedure, except as otherwise provided in paragraph (b) of this section, the STD is to act in the relative position of the FHWA for reviewing and approving the arrangements, fees, estimates, plans, agreements, and other related matters required by this regulation as prerequisites for authorizing the utility to proceed with and complete the work.

(b) The scope of the STD's approval authority under the alternate procedure includes all actions necessary to advance and complete all types of utility work under the provisions of this regulation except in the following instances:

(1) Utility relocations and adjustments involving major transfer, production, and storage facilities such as generating plants, power feed stations, pumping stations and reservoirs.

(2) Utility relocations falling within the scope of §645.113 (h), (i), and (j), and §645.107(i) of this regulation.

(c) To adopt the alternate procedure, the STD must file a formal application for approval by the FHWA. The application must include the following:

(1) The STD's written policies and procedures for administering and processing Federal-aid utility adjustments. Those policies and procedures must make adequate provisions with respect to the following:

(i) Compliance with the requirements of this regulation, except as otherwise provided by §645.119(b), and the provisions of 23 CFR part 645, subpart B, Accommodation of Utilities.

(ii) Advance utility liaison, planning, and coordination measures for providing adequate lead time and early scheduling of utility relocation to minimize interference with the planned highway construction.

(iii) Appropriate administrative, legal, and engineering review and coordination procedures as needed to establish the legal basis of the TD's payment; the extent of eligibility of the work under State and Federal laws and regulations; the more restrictive payment standards under §645.103(d) of this regulation; the necessity of the proposed utility work and its compatibility with proposed highway improvements; and the uniform treatment of all utility matters and actions, consistent with sound management practices.

(iv) Documentation of actions taken in compliance with STD policies and the provisions of this regulation, shall be retained by the STD.

(2) A statement signed by the chief administrative officer of the STD certifying that:

(i) Federal-aid utility relocations will be processed in accordance with the applicable provisions of this regulation, and the STD's utility policies and procedures submitted under §645.119(c)(1).

(ii) Reimbursement will be requested only for those costs properly attributable to the proposed highway construction and eligible for participation under the provisions of this regulation.

(d) The STD's application and any changes to it will be submitted to the FHWA for review and approval.

(e) After the alternate procedure has been approved, the FHWA may authorize the STD to proceed with utility relocation on a project in accordance with the certification, subject to the following conditions:

(1) The utility work must be included in an approved program.

(2) The STD must submit a request in writing for such authorization. The request shall include a list of the utility relocations to be processed under the alternate procedure, along with the best available estimate of the total costs involved.

(f) The FHWA may suspend approval of the alternate procedure when any FHWA review discloses noncompliance with the certification. Federal funds will not participate in relocation costs incurred that do not comply with the requirements under §645.119(c)(1).

(Information collection requirements in paragraph (c) were approved by the Office of Management and Budget under control number 2125–0533)

[50 FR 20345, May 15, 1985, as amended at 65 FR 70311, Nov. 22, 2000]

Subpart B—Accommodation of Utilities

SOURCE: 50 FR 20354, May 15, 1985, unless otherwise noted.

§645.201 Purpose.

To prescribe policies and procedures for accommodating utility facilities and private lines on the right-of-way of Federal-aid or direct Federal highway projects.

§ 645.203 Applicability.

This subpart applies to:

(a) New utility installations within the right-of-way of Federal-aid or direct Federal highway projects,

(b) Existing utility facilities which are to be retained, relocated, or adjusted within the right-of-way of active projects under development or construction when Federal-aid or direct Federal highway funds are either being or have been used on the involved highway facility. When existing utility installations are to remain in place without adjustments on such projects the transportation department and utility are to enter into an appropriate agreement as discussed in § 645.213 of this part,

(c) Existing utility facilities which are to be adjusted or relocated under the provisions of § 645.209(k), and

(d) Private lines which may be permitted to cross the right-of-way of a Federal-aid or direct Federal highway project pursuant to State law and regulations and the provisions of this subpart. Longitudinal use of such right-of-way by private lines is to be handled under the provisions of 23 CFR 1.23(c).

§ 645.205 Policy.

(a) Pursuant to the provisions of 23 CFR 1.23, it is in the public interest for utility facilities to be accommodated on the right-of-way of a Federal-aid or direct Federal highway project when such use and occupancy of the highway right-of-way do not adversely affect highway or traffic safety, or otherwise impair the highway or its aesthetic quality, and do not conflict with the provisions of Federal, State or local laws or regulations.

(b) Since by tradition and practice highway and utility facilities frequently coexist within common right-of-way or along the same transportation corridors, it is essential in such situations that these public service facilities be compatibly designed and operated. In the design of new highway facilities consideration should be given to utility service needs of the area traversed if such service is to be provided from utility facilities on or near the highway. Similarly the potential impact on the highway and its users should be considered in the design and location of utility facilities on or along highway right-of-way. Efficient, effective and safe joint highway and utility development of transportation corridors is important along high speed and high volume roads, such as major arterials and freeways, particularly those approaching metropolitan areas where space is increasingly limited. Joint highway and utility planning and development efforts are encouraged on Federal-aid highway projects.

(c) The manner is which utilities cross or otherwise occupy the right-of-way of a direct Federal or Federal-aid highway project can materially affect the highway, its safe operation, aesthetic quality, and maintenance. Therefore, it is necessary that such use and occupancy, where authorized, be regulated by transportation departments in a manner which preserves the operational safety and the functional and aesthetic quality of the highway facility. This subpart shall not be construed to alter the basic legal authority of utilities to install their facilities on public highways pursuant to law or franchise and reasonable regulation by transportation departments with respect to location and manner of installation.

(d) When utilities cross or otherwise occupy the right-of-way of a direct Federal or Federal-aid highway project on Federal lands, and when the right-of-way grant is for highway purposes only, the utility must also obtain and comply with the terms of a right-of-way or other occupancy permit for the Federal agency having jurisdiction over the underlying land.

[50 FR 20354, May 15, 1985, as amended at 53 FR 2833, Feb. 2, 1988]

§ 645.207 Definitions.

For the purpose of this regulation, the following definitions shall apply:

Aesthetic quality—those desirable characteristics in the appearance of the highway and its environment, such as harmony between or blending of natural and manufactured objects in the environment, continuity of visual form without distracting interruptions, and simplicity of designs which are desirably functional in shape but without clutter.

Border area—the area between the traveled way and the right-of-way line.

Clear roadside policy—that policy employed by a transportation department to provide a clear zone in order to increase safety, improve traffic operations, and enhance the aesthetic quality of highways by designing, constructing and maintaining highway roadsides as wide, flat, and rounded as practical and as free as practical from natural or manufactured hazards such as trees, drainage structures, nonyielding sign supports, highway lighting supports, and utility poles and other ground-mounted structures. The policy should address the removal of roadside obstacles which are likely to be associated with accident or injury to the highway user, or when such obstacles are essential, the policy should provide for appropriate countermeasures to reduce hazards. Countermeasures include placing utility facilities at locations which protect out-of-control vehicles, using breakaway features, using impact attenuation devices, or shielding. In all cases full consideration shall be given to sound engineering principles and economic factors.

Clear zone—the total roadside border area starting at the edge of the traveled way, available for safe use by errant vehicles. This area may consist of a shoulder, a recoverable slope, a non-recoverable slope, and/or the area at the toe of a non-recoverable slope available for safe use by an errant vehicle. The desired width is dependent upon the traffic volumes and speeds, and on the roadside geometry. The current edition of the AASHTO "Roadside Design Guide" should be used as a guide for establishing clear zones for various types of highways and operating conditions. This publication is available for inspection and copying from the FHWA Washington Headquarters and all FHWA Division Offices as prescribed in 49 CFR part 7. Copies of current AASHTO publications are available for purchase from the American Association of State Highway and Transportation Officials, Suite 225, 444 North Capitol Street, NW., Washington, D.C. 20001, or electronically at *http://www.aashto.org*.

Direct Federal highway projects—those active or completed highway projects such as projects under the Federal Lands Highways Program which are under the direct administration of the Federal Highway Administration (FHWA)

Federal-aid highway projects—those active or completed highway projects administered by or through a State transportation department which involve or have involved the use of Federal-aid highway funds for the development, acquisition of right-of-way, construction or improvement of the highway or related facilities, including highway beautification projects under 23 U.S.C. 319, Landscaping and Scenic Enhancement.

Freeway—a divided arterial highway with full control of access.

Highway—any public way for vehicular travel, including the entire area within the right-of-way and related facilities constructed or improved in whole or in part with Federal-aid or direct Federal highway funds.

Transportation department—that department, agency, commission, board, or official of any State or political subdivision thereof, charged by its law with the responsibility for highway administration.

Private lines—privately owned facilities which convey or transmit the commodities outlined in the definition of *utility facility* of this section, but devoted exclusively to private use.

Right-of-way—real property, or interests therein, acquired, dedicated or reserved for the construction, operation, and maintenance of a highway in which Federal-aid or direct Federal highway funds are or have been involved in any stage of development. Lands acquired under 23 U.S.C. 319 shall be considered to be highway right-of-way.

State transportation department—the transportation department of one of the 50 States, the District of Columbia, or Puerto Rico.

Use and occupancy agreement—the document (written agreement or permit) by which the transportation department approves the use and occupancy of highway right-of-way by utility facilities or private lines.

Utility facility—privately, publicly or cooperatively owned line, facility, or system for producing, transmitting, or distributing communications, cable television, power, electricity, light, heat, gas, oil, crude products, water, steam, waste, storm water not connected with highway drainage, or any other similar commodity, including any fire or police signal system or street lighting system, which directly or indirectly serves the public. The term utility shall also mean the utility company inclusive of any substantially owned or controlled subsidiary. For the purposes of this part, the term includes those utility-type facilities which are owned or leased by a government agency for its own use, or otherwise dedicated solely to governmental use. The term utility includes those facilities used solely by the utility which are a part of its operating plant.

[50 FR 20345, May 15, 1985, as amended at 51 FR 16834, May 7, 1986; 53 FR 2833, Feb. 2, 1988; 55 FR 25828, June 25, 1990; 60 FR 34850, July 5, 1995; 61 FR 12022, Mar. 25, 1996; 65 FR 70311, Nov. 22, 2000]

§ 645.209 General requirements.

(a) *Safety.* Highway safety and traffic safety are of paramount, but not of sole, importance when accommodating utility facilities within highway right-of-way. Utilities provide an essential public service to the general public. Traditionally, as a matter of sound economic public policy and law, utilities have used public road right-of-way for transmitting and distributing their services. The lack of sufficient right-of-way width to accommodate utilities outside the desirable clear zone, in and of itself, is not a valid reason to preclude utilities from occupying the highway right-of-way. However, due to the nature and volume of highway traffic, the effect of such joint use on the traveling public must be carefully considered by transportation departments before approval of utility use of the right-of-way of Federal-aid or direct Federal highway projects is given. Adjustments in the operating characteristics of the utility or the highway or other special efforts may be necessary to increase the compatibility of utility-highway joint use. The possibility of this joint use should be a consideration in establishing right-of-way requirements for highway projects. In any event, the design, location, and manner in which utilities use and occupy the right-of-way of Federal-aid or direct Federal highway projects must conform to the clear roadside policies for the highway involved and otherwise provide for a safe traveling environment as required by 23 U.S.C. 109(l)(1).

(b) *New above ground installations.* On Federal-aid or direct Federal highway projects, new above ground utility installations, where permitted, shall be located as far from the traveled way as possible, preferably along the right-of-way line. No new above ground utility installations are to be allowed within the established clear zone of the highway unless a determination has been made by the transportation department that placement underground is not technically feasible or is unreasonably costly and there are no feasible alternate locations. In exceptional situations when it is essential to locate such above ground utility facilities within the established clear zone of the highway, appropriate countermeasures to reduce hazards shall be used. Countermeasures include placing utility facilities at locations which protect or minimize exposure to out-of-control vehicles, using breakaway features, using impact attenuation devices, using delineation, or shielding.

(c) *Installations within freeways.* (1) Each State transportation department shall submit an accommodation plan in accordance with §§645.211 and 645.215 which addresses how the State transportation department will consider applications for longitudinal utility installations within the access control lines of a freeway. This includes utility installations within interchange areas which must be constructed or serviced by direct access from the main lanes or ramps. If a State transportation department elects to permit such use, the plan must address how the State transportation department will oversee such use consistent with this subpart, Title 23 U.S.C., and the safe and efficient use of the highways.

(2) Any accommodation plan shall assure that installations satisfy the following criteria:

(i) The effects utility installations will have on highway and traffic safety will be ascertained, since in no case shall any use be permitted which would adversely affect safety.

(ii) The direct and indirect environmental and economic effects of any loss of productive agricultural land or any productivity of any agricultural land which would result from the disapproval of the use of such right-of-way for accommodation of such utility facility will be evaluated.

(iii) These environmental and economic effects together with any interference with or impairment of the use of the highway in such right-of-way which would result from the use of such right-of-way for the accommodation of such utility facility will be considered.

(iv) [Reserved]

(v) A utility strip will be established along the outer edge of the right-of-way by locating a utility access control line between the proposed utility installation and the through roadway and ramps. Existing fences should be retained and, except along sections of freeways having frontage roads, planned fences should be located at the freeway right-of-way line. The State or political subdivision is to retain control of the utility strip right-of-way including its use by utility facilities. Service connections to adjacent properties shall not be permitted from within the utility strip.

(3) Nothing in this part shall be construed as prohibiting a transportation department from adopting a more restrictive policy than that contained herein with regard to longitudinal utility installations along freeway right-of-way and access for constructing and/or for servicing such installations.

(d) *Uniform policies and procedures.* For a transportation department to fulfill its responsibilities to control utility use of Federal-aid highway right-of-way within the State and its political subdivisions, it must exercise or cause to be exercised, adequate regulation over such use and occupancy through the establishment and enforcement of reasonably uniform policies and procedures for utility accommodation.

(e) *Private lines.* Because there are circumstances when private lines may be allowed to cross or otherwise occupy the right-of-way of Federal-aid projects, transportation departments shall establish uniform policies for properly controlling such permitted use. When permitted, private lines must conform to the provisions of this part and the provisions of 23 CFR 1.23(c) for longitudinal installations.

(f) *Direct Federal highway projects.* On direct Federal highway projects, the FHWA will apply, or cause to be applied, utility and private line accommodation policies similar to those required on Federal-aid highway projects. When appropriate, agreements will be entered into between the FHWA and the transportation department or other government agencies to ensure adequate control and regulation of use by utilities and private lines of the right-of-way on direct Federal highway projects.

(g) *Projects where state lacks authority.* On Federal-aid highway projects where the State transportation department does not have legal authority to regulate highway use by utilities and private lines, the State transportation department must enter into formal agreements with those local officials who have such authority. The agreements must provide for a degree of protection to the highway at least equal to the protection provided by the State transportation department's utility accommodation policy approved under the provisions of § 645.215(b) of this part. The project agreement between the State transportation department and the FHWA on all such Federal-aid highway projects shall contain a special provision incorporating the formal agreements with the responsible local officials.

(h) *Scenic areas.* New utility installations, including those needed for highway purposes, such as for highway lighting or to serve a weigh station, rest area or recreation area, are not permitted on highway right-of-way or other lands which are acquired or improved with Federal-aid or direct Federal highway funds and are located within or adjacent to areas of scenic enhancement and natural beauty. Such areas include public park and recreational lands, wildlife and waterfowl refuges, historic sites as described in 23 U.S.C. 138, scenic strips, overlooks, rest areas and landscaped areas. The State transportation department may permit exceptions provided the following conditions are met:

(1) New underground or aerial installations may be permitted only when they do not require extensive removal or alteration of trees or terrain features visible to the highway user or impair the aesthetic quality of the lands being traversed.

(2) Aerial installations may be permitted only when:

(i) Other locations are not available or are unusually difficult and costly, or are less desirable from the standpoint of aesthetic quality,

(ii) Placement underground is not technically feasible or is unreasonably costly, and

(iii) The proposed installation will be made at a location, and will employ suitable designs and materials, which give the greatest weight to the aesthetic qualities of the area being traversed. Suitable designs include, but are not limited to, self-supporting armless, single-pole construction with vertical configuration of conductors and cable.

(3) For new utility installations within freeways, the provisions of paragraph (c) of this section must also be satisfied.

(i) *Joint use agreements.* When the utility has a compensable interest in the land occupied by its facilities and such land is to be jointly occupied and used for highway and utility purposes, the transportation department and utility shall agree in writing as to the obligations and responsibilities of each party. Such joint-use agreements shall incorporate the conditions of occupancy for each party, including the rights vested in the transportation department and the rights and privileges retained by the utility. In any event, the interest to be acquired by or vested in the transportation department in any portion of the right-of-way of a Federal-aid or direct Federal highway project to be vacated, used or occupied by utilities or private lines, shall be adequate for the construction, safe operation, and maintenance of the highway project.

(j) *Traffic control plan.* Whenever a utility installation, adjustment or maintenance activity will affect the movement of traffic or traffic safety, the utility shall implement a traffic control plan and utilize traffic control devices as necessary to ensure the safe and expeditious movement of traffic around the work site and the safety of the utility work force in accordance with procedures established by the transportation department. The traffic control plan and the application of traffic control devices shall conform to the standards set forth in the current edition of the "Manual on Uniform Traffic Control Devices" (MUTCD) and 23 CFR part 630, subpart J. This publication is available for inspection and copying from the FHWA Washington Headquarters and all FHWA Division Offices as prescribed in 49 CFR part 7.

(k) *Corrective measures.* When the transportation department determines that existing utility facilities are likely to be associated with injury or accident to the highway user, as indicated by accident history or safety studies, the transportation department shall initiate or cause to be initiated in consultation with the affected utilities, corrective measures to provide for a safer traffic environment. The corrective measures may include changes to utility or highway facilities and should be prioritized to maximum safety benefits in the most cost-effective manner. The scheduling of utility safety improvements should take into consideration planned utility replacement or upgrading schedules, accident potential, and the availability of resources. It is expected that the requirements of this paragraph will result in an orderly and positive process to address the identified utility hazard problems in a timely and reasonable manner with due regard to the effect of the corrective measures on both the utility consumer and the road user. The type of corrective measures are not prescribed. Any requests received involving Federal participation in the cost of adjusting or relocating utility facilities pursuant to this paragrpah shall be subject to the provisions of 23 CFR part 645, subpart A, Utility Relocations, Adjustments and Reimbursement, and 23 CFR part 924, Highway Safety Improvement Program.

(l) *Wetlands.* The installation of privately owned lines or conduits on the right-of-way of Federal-aid or direct Federal highway projects for the purpose of draining adjacent wetlands onto the highway right-of-way is considered to be inconsistent with Executive Order 11990, Protection of Wetlands, dated May 24, 1977, and shall be prohibited.

(m) *Utility determination.* In determining whether a proposed installation is a utility or not, the most important consideration is how the STD views it under its own State laws and/or regulations.

[50 FR 20354, May 15, 1985, as amended at 53 FR 2833, Feb. 2, 1988; 60 FR 34851, July 5, 1995; 65 FR 70311, Nov. 22, 2000]

§ 645.211 State transportation department accommodation policies.

The FHWA should use the current editions of the AASHTO publications, "A Guide for Accommodating Utilities Within Highway Right-of-Way" and "Roadside Design Guide" to assist in the evaluation of adequacy of STD utility accommodation policies. These publications are available for inspection from the FHWA Washington Headquarters and all FHWA Division Offices as prescribed in 49 CFR part 7. Copies of current AASHTO publications are available for purchase from the American Association of State Highway and Transportation Officials, Suite 225, 444 North Capitol Street NW., Washington, DC 20001, or electronically at *http://www.aashto.org.* At a minimum, such policies shall make adequate provisions with respect to the following:

(a) Utilities must be accommodated and maintained in a manner which will not impair the highway or adversely affect highway or traffic safety. Uniform procedures controlling the manner, nature and extent of such utility use shall be established.

(b) Consideration shall be given to the effect of utility installations in regard to safety, aesthetic quality, and the costs or difficulty of highway and utility construction and maintenance.

(c) The State transportation department's standards for regulating the use and occupancy of highway right-of-way by utilities must include, but are not limited to, the following:

(1) The horizontal and vertical location requirements and clearances for the various types of utilities must be clearly stated. These must be adequate to ensure compliance with the clear roadside policies for the particular highway involved.

(2) The applicable provisions of government or industry codes required by law or regulation must be set forth or appropriately referenced, including highway design standards or other measures which the State transportation department deems necessary to provide adequate protection to the highway, its safe operation, aesthetic quality, and maintenance.

(3) Specifications for and methods of installation; requirements for preservation and restoration of highway facilities, appurtenances, and natural features and vegetation on the right-of-way; and limitations on the utility's activities within the right-of-way including installation within areas set forth by § 645.209(h) of this part should be prescribed as necessary to protect highway interests.

(4) Measures necessary to protect traffic and its safe operation during and after installation of facilities, including control-of-access restrictions, provisions for rerouting or detouring traffic, traffic control measures to be employed, procedures for utility traffic control plans, limitations on vehicle parking and materials storage, protection of open excavations, and the like must be provided.

(5) A State transportation department may deny a utility's request to occupy highway right-of-way based on State law, regulation, or ordinances or the State transportation department's policy. However, in any case where the provisions of this part are to be cited as the basis for disapproving a utility's request to use and occupy highway right-of-way, measures must be provided to evaluate the direct and indirect environmental and economic effects of any loss of productive agricultural land or any impairment of the productivity of any agricultural land that would result from the disapproval. The environmental and economic effects on productive agricultural land together with the possible interference with or impairment of the use of the highway and the effect on highway

safety must be considered in the decision to disapprove any proposal by a utility to use such highway right-of-way.

(d) Compliance with applicable State laws and approved State transportation department utility accommodation policies must be assured. The responsible State transportation department's file must contain evidence of the written arrangements which set forth the terms under which utility facilities are to cross or otherwise occupy highway right-of-way. All utility installations made on highway right-of-way shall be subject to written approval by the State transportation department. However, such approval will not be required where so provided in the use and occupancy agreement for such matters as utility facility maintenance, installation of service connections on highways other than freeways, or emergency operations.

(e) The State transportation department shall set forth in its utility accommodation plan detailed procedures, criteria, and standards it will use to evaluate and approve individual applications of utilities on freeways under the provisions of § 645.209(c) of this part. The State transportation department also may develop such procedures, criteria and standards by class of utility. In defining utility classes, consideration may be given to distinguishing utility services by type, nature or function and their potential impact on the highway and its user.

(f) The means and authority for enforcing the control of access restrictions applicable to utility use of controlled access highway facilities should be clearly set forth in the State transportation department plan.

(Information collection requirements in paragraphs (a), (b) and (c) were approved under control number 2125–0522, and paragraph (d) under control number 2125–0514)

[50 FR 20354, May 15, 1985, as amended at 53 FR 2834, Feb. 2, 1988; 55 FR 25828, June 25, 1990; 65 FR 70312, Nov. 22, 2000]

§ 645.213 Use and occupancy agreements (permits).

The written arrangements, generally in the form of use and occupancy agreements setting forth the terms under which the utility is to cross or otherwise occupy the highway right-of-way, must include or incorporate by reference:

(a) The transportation department standards for accommodating utilities. Since all of the standards will not be applicable to each individual utility installation, the use and occupancy agreement must, as a minimum, describe the requirements for location, construction, protection of traffic, maintenance, access restriction, and any special conditions applicable to each installation.

(b) A general description of the size, type, nature, and extent of the utility facilities being located within the highway right-of-way.

(c) Adequate drawings or sketches showing the existing and/or proposed location of the utility facilities within the highway right-of-way with respect to the existing and/or planned highway improvements, the traveled way, the right-of-way lines and, where applicable, the control of access lines and approved access points.

(d) The extent of liability and responsibilities associated with future adjustment of the utilities to accommodate highway improvements.

(e) The action to be taken in case of noncompliance with the transportation department's requirements.

(f) Other provisions as deemed necessary to comply with laws and regulations.

(Approved by the Office of Management and Budget under control number 2125–0522)

§ 645.215 Approvals.

(a) Each State transportation department shall submit a statement to the FHWA on the authority of utilities to use and occupy the right-of-way of State highways, the State transportation department's power to regulate such use, and the policies the State transportation department employs or proposes to employ for accommodating utilities within the right-of-way Federal-aid highways under its jurisdiction. Statements previously submitted and approved by the FHWA need not be resubmitted provided the statement adequately addresses the requirements of this part. When revisions are deemed necessary the changes to the previously approved statement may be submitted separately to the FHWA for approval. The State transportation department shall include similar information on the use and occupancy of such highways by private lines where permitted. The State shall identify those areas, if any, of Federal-aid highways within its borders where the State transportation department is without legal authority to regulate use by utilities. The statement shall address the nature of the formal agreements with local officials required by §645.209(g) of this part. It is expected that the statements required by this part or necessary revisions to previously submitted and approved statements will be submitted to FHWA within 1 year of the effective date of this regulation.

(b) Upon determination by the FHWA that a State transportation department's policies satisfy the provisions of 23 U.S.C. 109, 111, and 116, and 23 CFR 1.23 and 1.27, and meet the requirements of this regulation, the FHWA will approve their use on Federal-aid highway projects in that State

(c) Any changes, additions or deletions the State transportation department proposes to the approved policies are subject to FHWA approval.

(d) When a utility files a notice or makes an individual application or request to a STD to use or occupy the right-of-way of a Federal-aid highway project, the STD is not required to submit the matter to the FHWA for prior concurrence, except when the proposed installation is not in accordance with this regulation or with the STD's utility accommodation policy approved by the FHWA for use on Federal-aid highway projects.

(e) The State transportation department's practices under the policies or agreements approved under §645.215(b) of this part shall be periodically reviewed by the FHWA.

(Information collection requirements in paragraph (a) were approved by the Office of Management and Budget under control number 2125–0514)

[50 FR 20354, May 15, 1985, as amended at 53 FR 2834, Feb. 2, 1988; 60 FR 34851, July 5, 1995; 65 FR 70312, Nov. 22, 2000]

PART 646—RAILROADS

Subpart A—Railroad-Highway Insurance Protection

Subpart B—Railroad-Highway Projects

AUTHORITY: 23 U.S.C. 109(e), 120(c), 130, 133(d)(1), and 315; 49 CFR 1.48(b).

Subpart A—Railroad-Highway Insurance Protection

SOURCE: 39 FR 36474, Oct. 10, 1974, unless otherwise noted.

§646.101 Purpose.

The purpose of this part is to prescribe provisions under which Federal funds may be applied to the costs of public liability and property damage insurance obtained by contractors (a) for their own operations, and (b) on behalf of railroads on or about whose right-of-way the contractors are required to work in the construction of highway projects financed in whole or in part with Federal funds.

§646.103 Application.

(a) This part applies:

(1) To a contractors' legal liability for bodily injury to, or death of, persons and for injury to, or destruction of, property.

(2) To the liability which may attach to railroads for bodily injury to, or death of, persons and for injury to, or destruction of, property.

(3) To damage to property owned by or in the care, custody or control of the railroads, both as such liability or damage may arise out of the contractor's operations, or may result from work performed by railroads at or about railroad rights-of-way in connection with projects financed in whole or in part with Federal funds.

(b) Where the highway construction is under the direct supervision of the Federal Highway Administration (FHWA), all references herein to the State shall be considered as references to the FHWA.

§ 646.105 Contractor's public liability and property damage insurance.

(a) Contractors may be subject to liability with respect to bodily injury to or death of persons, and injury to, or destruction of property, which may be suffered by persons other than their own employees as a result of their operations in connection with construction of highway projects located in whole or in part within railroad right-of-way and financed in whole or in part with Federal funds. Protection to cover such liability of contractors shall be furnished under regular contractors' public liability and property damage insurance policies issued in the names of the contractors. Such policies shall be so written as to furnish protection to contractors respecting their operations in performing work covered by their contract.

(b) Where a contractor sublets a part of the work on any project to a subcontractor, the contractor shall be required to secure insurance protection in his own behalf under contractor's public liability and property damage insurance policies to cover any liability imposed on him by law for damages because of bodily injury to, or death of, persons and injury to, or destruction of, property as a result of work undertaken by such subcontractors. In addition, the contractor shall provide for and on behalf of any such subcontractors protection to cover like liability imposed upon the latter as a result of their operations by means of separate and individual contractor's public liability and property damage policies; or, in the alternative, each subcontractor shall provide satisfactory insurance on his own behalf to cover his individual operations.

(c) The contractor shall furnish to the State highway department evidence satisfactory to such department and to the FHWA that the insurance coverages required herein have been provided. The contractor shall also furnish a copy of such evidence to the railroad or railroads involved. The insurance specified shall be kept in force until all work required to be performed shall have been satisfactorily completed and accepted in accordance with the contract under which the construction work is undertaken.

§ 646.107 Railroad protective insurance.

In connection with highway projects for the elimination of hazards of railroad-highway crossings and other highway construction projects located in whole or in part within railroad right-of-way, railroad protective liability insurance shall be purchased on behalf of the railroad by the contractor. The standards for railroad protective insurance established by §§ 646.109 through 646.111 shall be adhered to insofar as the insurance laws of the State will permit.

[39 FR 36474, Oct. 10, 1974, as amended at 47 FR 33955, Aug. 5, 1982]

§ 646.109 Types of coverage.

(a) Coverage shall be limited to damage suffered by the railroad on account of occurrences arising out of the work of the contractor on or about the railroad right-of-way, independent of the railroad's general supervision or control, except as noted in § 646.109(b)(4).

(b) Coverage shall include:

(1) Death of or bodily injury to passengers of the railroad and employees of the railroad not covered by State workmen's compensation laws;

(2) Personal property owned by or in the care, custody or control of the railroads;

(3) The contractor, or any of his agents or employees who suffer bodily injury or death as the result of acts of

the railroad or its agents, regardless of the negligence of the railroad;

(4) Negligence of only the following classes of railroad employees:

(i) Any supervisory employee of the railroad at the job site;

(ii) Any employee of the railroad while operating, attached to, or engaged on, work trains or other railroad equipment at the job site which are assigned exclusively to the contractor; or

(iii) Any employee of the railroad not within (b)(4) (i) or (ii) who is specifically loaned or assigned to the work of the contractor for prevention of accidents or protection of property, the cost of whose services is borne specifically by the contractor or governmental authority.

§ 646.111 Amount of coverage.

(a) The maximum dollar amounts of coverage to be reimbursed from Federal funds with respect to bodily injury, death and property damage is limited to a combined amount of $2 million per occurrence with an aggregate of $6 million applying separately to each annual period except as provided in paragraph (b) of this section.

(b) In cases involving real and demonstrable danger of appreciably higher risks, higher dollar amounts of coverage for which premiums will be reimbursable from Federal funds shall be allowed. These larger amounts will depend on circumstances and shall be written for the individual project in accordance with standard underwriting practices upon approval of the FHWA.

[39 FR 36474, Oct. 10, 1974, as amended at 47 FR 33955, Aug. 5, 1982]

Subpart B—Railroad-Highway Projects

SOURCE: 40 FR 16059, Apr. 9, 1975, unless otherwise noted.

§ 646.200 Purpose and applicability.

(a) The purpose of this subpart is to prescribe policies and procedures for advancing Federal-aid projects involving railroad facilities.

(b) This subpart, and all references hereinafter made to *projects*, applies to Federal-aid projects involving railroad facilities, including projects for the elimination of hazards of railroad-highway crossings, and other projects which use railroad properties or which involve adjustments required by highway construction to either railroad facilities or facilities that are jointly owned or used by railroad and utility companies.

(c) Additional instructions for projects involving the elimination of hazards of railroad/highway grade crossings pursuant to 23 U.S.C. 130 are set forth in 23 CFR part 924.

(d) Procedures on reimbursement for projects undertaken pursuant to this subpart are set forth in 23 CFR part 140, subpart I.

(e) Procedures on insurance required of contractors working on or about railroad right-of-way are set forth in 23 CFR part 646, subpart A.

[40 FR 16059, Apr. 9, 1975, as amended at 45 FR 20795, Mar. 31, 1980; 62 FR 45328, Aug. 27, 1997]

§ 646.202 [Reserved]

§ 646.204 Definitions.

For the purposes of this subpart, the following definitions apply:

Active warning devices means those traffic control devices activated by the approach or presence of a train, such as flashing light signals, automatic gates and similar devices, as well as manually operated devices and crossing watchmen, all of which display to motorists positive warning of the approach or presence of a train.

Company shall mean any railroad or utility company including any wholly owned or controlled subsidiary thereof.

Construction shall mean the actual physical construction to improve or eliminate a railroad-highway grade crossing or accomplish other railroad involved work.

A diagnostic team means a group of knowledgeable representatives of the parties of interest in a railroad-highway crossing or a group of crossings.

Main line railroad track means a track of a principal line of a railroad, including extensions through yards, upon which trains are operated by timetable or train order or both, or the use of which is governed by block signals or by centralized traffic control.

Passive warning devices means those types of traffic control devices, including signs, markings and other devices, located at or in advance of grade crossings to indicate the presence of a crossing but which do not change aspect upon the approach or presence of a train.

Preliminary engineering shall mean the work necessary to produce construction plans, specifications, and estimates to the degree of completeness required for undertaking construction thereunder, including locating, surveying, designing, and related work.

Railroad shall mean all rail carriers, publicly-owned, private, and common carriers, including line haul freight and passenger railroads, switching and terminal railroads and passenger carrying railroads such as rapid transit, commuter and street railroads.

Utility shall mean the lines and facilities for producing, transmitting or distributing communications, power, electricity, light, heat, gas, oil, water, steam, sewer and similar commodities.

[40 FR 16059, Apr. 9, 1975, as amended at 62 FR 45328, Aug. 27, 1997]

§ 646.206 Types of projects.

(a) Projects for the elimination of hazards, to both vehicles and pedestrians, of railroad-highway crossings may include but are not limited to:

(1) Grade crossing elimination;

(2) Reconstruction of existing grade separations; and

(3) Grade crossing improvements.

(b) Other railroad-highway projects are those which use railroad properties or involve adjustments to railroad facilities required by highway construction but do not involve the elimination of hazards of railroad-highway crossings. Also included are adjustments to facilities that are jointly owned or used by railroad and utility companies.

§ 646.208 Funding.

(a) Railroad/highway crossing projects may be funded through the Federal-aid funding source appropriate for the involved project.

(b) Projects for the elimination of hazards at railroad/highway crossings may, at the option of the State, be funded with the funds provided by 23 U.S.C. 133(d)(1).

[62 FR 45328, Aug. 27, 1997]

§ 646.210 Classification of projects and railroad share of the cost.

(a) State laws requiring railroads to share in the cost of work for the elimination of hazards at railroad-highway crossings shall not apply to Federal-aid projects.

(b) Pursuant to 23 U.S.C. 130(b), and 49 CFR 1.48:

(1) Projects for grade crossing improvements are deemed to be of no ascertainable net benefit to the railroads and there shall be no required railroad share of the costs.

(2) Projects for the reconstruction of existing grade separations are deemed to generally be of no ascertainable net benefit to the railroad and there shall be no required railroad share of the costs, unless the railroad has a specific contractual obligation with the State or its political subdivision to share in the costs.

(3) On projects for the elimination of existing grade crossings at which active warning devices are in place or ordered to be installed by a State regulatory agency, the railroad share of the project costs shall be 5 percent.

(4) On projects for the elimination of existing grade crossings at which active warning devices are not in place and have not been ordered installed by a State regulatory agency, or on projects which do not eliminate an existing crossing, there shall be no required railroad share of the project cost.

(c) The required railroad share of the cost under § 646.210(b)(3) shall be based on the costs for preliminary engineering, right-of-way and construction within the limits described below:

(1) Where a grade crossing is eliminated by grade separation, the structure and approaches required to transition to a theoretical highway profile which would have been constructed if there were no railroad present, for the number of lanes on the existing highway and in accordance with the current design standards of the State highway agency.

(2) Where another facility, such as a highway or waterway, requiring a

bridge structure is located within the limits of a grade separation project, the estimated cost of a theoretical structure and approaches as described in §646.210(c)(1) to eliminate the railroad-highway grade crossing without considering the presence of the waterway or other highway.

(3) Where a grade crossing is eliminated by railroad or highway relocation, the actual cost of the relocation project, the estimated cost of the relocation project, or the estimated cost of a structure and approaches as described in §646.210(c)(1), whichever is less.

(d) Railroads may voluntarily contribute a greater share of project costs than is required. Also, other parties may voluntarily assume the railroad's share.

§646.212 Federal share.

(a) *General.* (1) Federal funds are not eligible to participate in costs incurred solely for the benefit of the railroad.

(2) At grade separations Federal funds are eligible to participate in costs to provide space for more tracks than are in place when the railroad establishes to the satisfaction of the State highway agency and FHWA that it has a definite demand and plans for installation of the additional tracks within a reasonable time.

(3) The Federal share of the cost of a grade separation project shall be based on the cost to provide horizontal and/or vertical clearances used by the railroad in its normal practice subject to limitations as shown in the appendix or as required by a State regulatory agency.

(b) The Federal share of railroad/highway crossing projects may be:

(1) Regular pro rata sharing as provided by 23 U.S.C. 120(a) and 120(b).

(2) One hundred percent Federal share, as provided by 23 U.S.C. 120(c).

(3) Ninety percent Federal share for funds made available through 23 U.S.C. 133(d)(1).

[40 FR 16059, Apr. 9, 1975, as amended at 47 FR 33955, Aug. 5, 1982; 53 FR 32218, Aug. 24, 1988; 62 FR 45328, Aug. 27, 1997]

§646.214 Design.

(a) *General.* (1) Facilities that are the responsibility of the railroad for maintenance and operation shall conform to the specifications and design standards used by the railroad in its normal practice, subject to approval by the State highway agency and FHWA.

(2) Facilities that are the responsibility of the highway agency for maintenance and operation shall conform to the specifications and design standards and guides used by the highway agency in its normal practice for Federal-aid projects.

(b) *Grade crossing improvements.* (1) All traffic control devices proposed shall comply with the latest edition of the Manual on Uniform Traffic Control Devices for Streets and Highways supplemented to the extent applicable by State standards.

(2) Pursuant to 23 U.S.C. 109(e), where a railroad-highway grade crossing is located within the limits of or near the terminus of a Federal-aid highway project for construction of a new highway or improvement of the existing roadway, the crossing shall not be opened for unrestricted use by traffic or the project accepted by FHWA until adequate warning devices for the crossing are installed and functioning properly.

(3)(i) *Adequate warning devices,* under §646.214(b)(2) or on any project where Federal-aid funds participate in the installation of the devices are to include automatic gates with flashing light signals when one or more of the following conditions exist:

(A) Multiple main line railroad tracks.

(B) Multiple tracks at or in the vicinity of the crossing which may be occupied by a train or locomotive so as to obscure the movement of another train approaching the crossing.

(C) High Speed train operation combined with limited sight distance at either single or multiple track crossings.

(D) A combination of high speeds and moderately high volumes of highway and railroad traffic.

(E) Either a high volume of vehicular traffic, high number of train movements, substantial numbers of schoolbuses or trucks carrying hazardous materials, unusually restricted sight distance, continuing accident occurrences, or any combination of these conditions.

(F) A diagnostic team recommends them.

(ii) In individual cases where a diagnostic team justifies that gates are not appropriate, FHWA may find that the above requirements are not applicable.

(4) For crossings where the requirements of § 646.214(b)(3) are not applicable, the type of warning device to be installed, whether the determination is made by a State regulatory agency, State highway agency, and/or the railroad, is subject to the approval of FHWA.

(c) *Grade crossing elimination.* All crossings of railroads and highways at grade shall be eliminated where there is full control of access on the highway (a freeway) regardless of the volume of railroad or highway traffic.

[40 FR 16059, Apr. 9, 1975, as amended at 47 FR 33955, Aug. 5, 1982; 62 FR 45328, Aug. 27, 1997]

§ 646.216 General procedures.

(a) *General.* Unless specifically modified herein, applicable Federal-aid procedures govern projects undertaken pursuant to this subpart.

(b) *Preliminary engineering and engineering services.* (1) As mutually agreed to by the State highway agency and railroad, and subject to the provisions of § 646.216(b)(2), preliminary engineering work on railroad-highway projects may be accomplished by one of the following methods:

(i) The State or railroad's engineering forces;

(ii) An engineering consultant selected by the State after consultation with the railroad, and with the State administering the contract; or

(iii) An engineering consultant selected by the railroad, with the approval of the State and with the railroad administering the contract.

(2) Where a railroad is not adequately staffed, Federal-aid funds may participate in the amounts paid to engineering consultants and others for required services, provided such amounts are not based on a percentage of the cost of construction, either under contracts for individual projects or under existing written continuing contracts where such work is regularly performed for the railroad in its own work under such contracts at reasonable costs.

(c) *Rights-of-way.* (1) Acquisition of right-of-way by a State highway agency on behalf of a railroad or acquisition of nonoperating real property from a railroad shall be in accordance with the Uniform Relocation Assistance and Real Property Acquisition Policies Act of 1970 (42 U.S.C. 4601 *et seq.*) and applicable FHWA right-of-way procedures in 23 CFR, chapter I, subchapter H. On projects for the elimination of hazards of railroad-highway crossings by the relocation of railroads, acquisition or replacement right-of-way by a railroad shall be in accordance with 42 U.S.C. 4601 *et seq.*

(2) Where buildings and other depreciable structures of the railroad (such as signal towers, passenger stations, depots, and other buildings, and equipment housings) which are integral to operation of railroad traffic are wholly or partly affected by a highway project, the costs of work necessary to functionally restore such facilities are eligible for participation. However, when replacement of such facilities is necessary, credits shall be made to the cost of the project for:

(i) Accrued depreciation, which is that amount based on the ratio between the period of actual length of service and total life expectancy applied to the original cost.

(ii) Additions or improvements which provide higher quality or increased service capability of the facility and which are provided solely for the benefit of the railroad.

(iii) Actual salvage value of the material recovered from the facility being replaced. Total credits to a project shall not be required in excess of the replacement cost of the facility.

(3) Where Federal funds participate in the cost of replacement right-of-way, there will be no charge to the project for the railroad's existing right-of-way being transferred to the State highway agency except when the value of the right-of-way being taken exceeds the value of the replacement right-of-way.

(d) *State-railroad agreements.* (1) Where construction of a Federal-aid project requires use of railroad properties or adjustments to railroad facilities, there shall be an agreement in writing between the State highway agency and the railroad company.

(2) The written agreement between the State and the railroad shall, as a minimum include the following, where applicable:

(i) The provisions of this subpart and of 23 CFR part 140, subpart I, incorporated by reference.

(ii) A detailed statement of the work to be performed by each party.

(iii) Method of payment (either actual cost or lump sum),

(iv) For projects which are not for the elimination of hazards of railroad-highway crossings, the extent to which the railroad is obligated to move or adjust its facilities at its own expense,

(v) The railroad's share of the project cost,

(vi) An itemized estimate of the cost of the work to be performed by the railroad,

(vii) Method to be used for performing the work, either by railroad forces or by contract,

(viii) Maintenance responsibility,

(ix) Form, duration, and amounts of any needed insurance,

(x) Appropriate reference to or identification of plans and specifications,

(xi) Statements defining the conditions under which the railroad will provide or require protective services during performance of the work, the type of protective services and the method of reimbursement to the railroad, and

(xii) Provisions regarding inspection of any recovered materials.

(3) On work to be performed by the railroad with its own forces and where the State highway agency and railroad agree, subject to approval by FHWA, an agreement providing for a lump sum payment in lieu of later determination of actual costs may be used for any of the following:

(i) Installation or improvement of grade crossing warning devices and/or grade crossing surfaces, regardless of cost, or

(ii) Any other eligible work where the estimated cost to the State of the proposed railroad work does not exceed $100,000 or

(iii) Where FHWA finds that the circumstances are such that this method of developing costs would be in the best interest of the public.

(4) Where the lump sum method of payment is used, periodic reviews and analyses of the railroad's methods and cost data used to develop lump sum estimates will be made.

(5) Master agreements between a State and a railroad on an areawide or statewide basis may be used. These agreements would contain the specifications, regulations, and provisions required in conjunction with work performed on all projects. Supporting data for each project or group of projects must, when combined with the master agreement by reference, satisfy the provisions of §646.216(d)(2).

(6) Official orders issued by regulatory agencies will be accepted in lieu of State-railroad agreements only where, together with supplementary written understandings between the State and the railroad, they include the items required by §646.216(d)(2).

(7) In extraordinary cases where FHWA finds that the circumstances are such that requiring such agreement or order would not be in the best interest of the public, projects may be approved for construction with the aid of Federal funds, provided satisfactory commitments have been made with respect to construction, maintenance and the railroad share of project costs.

(e) *Authorizations.* (1) The costs of preliminary engineering, right-of-way acquisition, and construction incurred after the date each phase of the work is included in an approved statewide transportation improvement program and authorized by the FHWA are eligible for Federal-aid participation. Preliminary engineering and right-of-way acquisition costs which are otherwise eligible, but incurred by a railroad prior to authorization by the FHWA, although not reimbursable, may be included as part of the railroad share of project cost where such a share is required.

(2) Prior to issuance of authorization by FHWA either to advertise the physical construction for bids or to proceed with force account construction for railroad work or for other construction affected by railroad work, the following must be accomplished:

(i) The plans, specifications and estimates must be approved by FHWA.

(ii) A proposed agreement between the State and railroad must be found satisfactory by FHWA. Before Federal funds may be used to reimburse the State for railroad costs the executed agreement must be approved by FHWA. However, cost for materials stockpiled at the project site or specifically purchased and delivered to the company for use on the project may be reimbursed on progress billings prior to the approval of the executed State-Railroad Agreement in accordance with 23 CFR 140.922(a) and § 646.218 of this part.

(iii) Adequate provisions must be made for any needed easements, right-of-way, temporary crossings for construction purposes or other property interests.

(iv) The pertinent portions of the State-railroad agreement applicable to any protective services required during performance of the work must be included in the project specifications and special provisions for any construction contract.

(3) In unusual cases, pending compliance with § 646.216(e)(2)(ii), (iii) and (iv), authorization may be given by FHWA to advertise for bids for highway construction under conditions where a railroad grants a right-of-entry to its property as necessary to prosecute the physical construction.

(f) *Construction.* (1) Construction may be accomplished by:

(i) Railroad force account,

(ii) Contracting with the lowest qualified bidder based on appropriate solicitation,

(iii) Existing continuing contracts at reasonable costs, or

(iv) Contract without competitive bidding, for minor work, at reasonable costs.

(2) Reimbursement will not be made for any increased costs due to changes in plans:

(i) For the convenience of the contractor, or

(ii) Not approved by the State and FHWA.

(3) The State and FHWA shall be afforded a reasonable opportunity to inspect materials recovered by the railroad prior to disposal by sale or scrap. This requirement will be satisfied by the railroad giving written notice, or oral notice with prompt written confirmation, to the State of the time and place where the materials will be available for inspection. The giving of notice is the responsibility of the railroad, and it may be held accountable for full value of materials disposed of without notice.

(4) In addition to normal construction costs, the following construction costs are eligible for participation with Federal-aid funds when approved by the State and FHWA:

(i) The cost of maintaining temporary facilities of a railroad company required by and during the highway construction to the extent that such costs exceed the documented normal cost of maintaining the permanent facilities.

(ii) The cost of stage or extended construction involving grade corrections and/or slope stabilization for permanent tracks of a railroad which are required to be relocated on new grade by the highway construction. Stage or extended construction will be approved by FHWA only when documentation submitted by the State establishes the proposed method of construction to be the only practical method and that the cost of the extended construction within the period specified is estimated to be less than the cost of any practicable alternate procedure.

(iii) The cost of restoring the company's service by adustments of existing facilities away from the project site, in lieu of and not to exceed the cost of replacing, adjusting or relocating facilities at the project site.

(iv) The cost of an addition or improvement to an existing railroad facility which is required by the highway construction.

[40 FR 16059, Apr. 9, 1975, as amended at 40 FR 29712, July 15, 1975; 47 FR 33956, Aug. 5, 1982; 62 FR 45328, Aug. 27, 1997]

§ 646.218 Simplified procedure for accelerating grade crossing improvements.

(a) The procedure set forth in this section is encouraged for use in simplifying and accelerating the processing of single or multiple grade crossing improvements.

(b) Eligible preliminary engineering costs may include those incurred in selecting crossings to be improved, determining the type of improvement for each crossing, estimating the cost and preparing the required agreement.

(c) The written agreement between a State and a railroad shall contain as a minimum:

(1) Identification of each crossing location.

(2) Description of improvement and estimate of cost for each crossing location.

(3) Estimated schedule for completion of work at each location.

(d) Following programming, authorization and approval of the agreement under § 646.218(c), FHWA may authorize construction, including acquisition of warning device materials, with the condition that work at any particular location will not be undertaken until the proposed or executed State-railroad agreement under § 646.216(d)(2) is found satisfactory by FHWA and the final plans, specifications, and estimates are approved and with the condition that only material actually incorporated into the project will be eligible for Federal participation.

(e) Work programmed and authorized under this simplified procedure should include only that which can reasonably be expected to reach the construction stage within one year and be completed within two years after the initial authorization date.

§ 646.220 Alternate Federal-State procedure.

(a) On other than Interstate projects, an alternate procedure may be used, at the election of the State, for processing certain types of railroad-highway work. Under this procedure, the State highway agency will act in the relative position of FHWA for reviewing and approving projects.

(b) The scope of the State's approval authority under the alternate procedure includes all actions necessary to advance and complete the following types of railroad-highway work:

(1) All types of grade crossing improvements under § 646.206(a)(3).

(2) Minor adjustments to railroad facilities under § 646.206(b).

(c) The following types of work are to be reviewed and approved in the normal manner, as prescribed elsewhere in this subpart.

(1) All projects under § 646.206(a) (1) and (2).

(2) Major adjustments to railroad facilities under § 646.206(b).

(d) Any State wishing to adopt the alternate procedure may file a formal application for approval by FHWA. The application must include the following:

(1) The State's written policies and procedures for administering and processing Federal-aid railroad-highway work, which make adequate provisions with respect to all of the following:

(i) Compliance with the provisions of title 23 U.S.C., title 23 CFR, and other applicable Federal laws and Executive Orders.

(ii) Compliance with this subpart and 23 CFR part 140, subpart I and 23 CFR part 172.

(iii) For grade crossing safety improvements, compliance with the requirements of 23 CFR part 924.

(2) A statement signed by the Chief Administrative Officer of the State highway agency certifying that:

(i) The work will be done in accordance with the applicable provisions of the State's policies and procedures submitted under § 646.220(d)(1), and

(ii) Reimbursement will be requested in only those costs properly attributable to the highway construction and eligible for Federal fund participation.

(e) When FHWA has approved the alternate procedure, it may authorize the State to proceed in accordance with the State's certification, subject to the following conditions:

(1) The work has been programmed.

(2) The State submits in writing a request for such authorization which shall include a list of the improvements or adjustments to be processed under the alternate procedure, along with the best available estimate of cost.

(f) The FHWA Regional Administrator may suspend approval of the certified procedure, where FHWA reviews disclose noncompliance with the certification. Federal-aid funds will not be eligible to participate in costs that do not qualify under §646.220(d)(1).

[40 FR 16059, Apr. 9, 1975; 40 FR 29712, July 15, 1975; 40 FR 31211, July 25, 1975; 42 FR 30835, June 17, 1977, as amended at 45 FR 20795, Mar. 31, 1980]

APPENDIX TO SUBPART B OF PART 646—HORIZONTAL AND VERTICAL CLEARANCE PROVISIONS FOR OVERPASS AND UNDERPASS STRUCTURES

The following implements provisions of 23 CFR 646.212(a)(3).

a. *Lateral Geometrics*

A cross section with a horizontal distance of 6.1 meters, measured at right angles from the centerline of track at the top of rails, to the face of the embankment slope, may be approved. The 6.1-meters distance may be increased at individual structure locations as appropriate to provide for drainage if justified by a hydraulic analysis or to allow adequate room to accommodate special conditions, such as where heavy and drifting snow is a problem. The railroad must demonstrate that this is its normal practice to address these special conditions in the manner proposed. Additionally, this distance may also be increased up to 2.5 meters as may be necessary for off-track maintenance equipment, provided adequate horizontal clearance is not available in adjacent spans and where justified by the presence of an existing maintenance road or by evidence of future need for such equipment. All piers should be placed at least 2.8 meters horizontally from the centerline of the track and preferably beyond the drainage ditch. For multiple track facilities, all dimensions apply to the centerline of the outside track.

Any increase above the 6.1-meters horizontal clearance distance must be required by specific site conditions and be justified by the railroad to the satisfaction of the State highway agency (SHA) and the FHWA.

b. *Vertical Clearance*

A vertical clearance of 7.1 meters above the top of rails, which includes an allowance for future ballasting of the railroad tracks, may be approved. Vertical clearance greater than 7.1 meters may be approved when the State regulatory agency having jurisdiction over such matters requires a vertical clearance in excess of 7.1 meters or on a site by site basis where justified by the railroad to the satisfaction of the SHA and the FHWA. A railroad's justification for increased vertical clearance should be based on an analysis of engineering, operational and/or economic conditions at a specific structure location.

Federal-aid highway funds are also eligible to participate in the cost of providing vertical clearance greater than 7.1 meters where a railroad establishes to the satisfaction of a SHA and the FHWA that it has a definite formal plan for electrification of its rail system where the proposed grade separation project is located. The plan must cover a logical independent segment of the rail system and be approved by the railroad's corporate headquarters. For 25 kv line, a vertical clearance of 7.4 meters may be approved. For 50 kv line, a vertical clearance of 8.0 meters may be approved.

A railroad's justification to support its plan for electrification shall include maps and plans or drawings showing those lines to be electrified; actions taken by its corporate headquarters committing it to electrification including a proposed schedule; and actions initiated or completed to date implementing its electrification plan such as a showing of the amounts of funds and identification of structures, if any, where the railroad has expended its own funds to provide added clearance for the proposed electrification. If available, the railroad's justification should include information on its contemplated treatment of existing grade separations along the section of its rail system proposed for electrification.

The cost of reconstructing or modifying any existing railroad-highway grade separation structures solely to accommodate electrification will not be eligible for Federal-aid highway fund participation.

c. *Railroad Structure Width*

Two and eight tenths meters of structure width outside of the centerline of the outside tracks may be approved for a structure carrying railroad tracks. Greater structure width may be approved when in accordance with standards established and used by the affected railroad in its normal practice.

In order to maintain continuity of off-track equipment roadways at structures carrying tracks over limited access highways, consideration should be given at the preliminary design stage to the feasibility of using public road crossings for this purpose. Where not feasible, an additional structure width of 2.5 meters may be approved if designed for off-track equipment only.

[53 FR 32218, Aug. 24, 1988, as amended at 62 FR 45328, Aug. 27, 1997]

PART 650—BRIDGES, STRUCTURES, AND HYDRAULICS

Subpart A—Location and Hydraulic Design of Encroachments on Flood Plains

Sec.

Subpart B—Erosion and Sediment Control on Highway Construction Projects

Subpart C—National Bridge Inspection Standards

Subpart D—Highway Bridge Replacement and Rehabilitation Program

Subpart E—National Tunnel Inspection Standards

Subpart F [Reserved]

Subpart G—Discretionary Bridge Candidate Rating Factor

Subpart H—Navigational Clearances for Bridges

AUTHORITY: 23 U.S.C. 119, 144, and 315.

Subpart A—Location and Hydraulic Design of Encroachments on Flood Plains

SOURCE: 44 FR 67580, Nov. 26, 1979, unless otherwise noted.

§650.101 Purpose.

To prescribe Federal Highway Administration (FHWA) policies and procedures for the location and hydraulic design of highway encroachments on flood plains, including direct Federal highway projects administered by the FHWA.

§650.103 Policy.

It is the policy of the FHWA:

(a) To encourage a broad and unified effort to prevent uneconomic, hazardous or incompatible use and development of the Nation's flood plains,

(b) To avoid longitudinal encroachments, where practicable,

(c) To avoid significant encroachments, where practicable,

(d) To minimize impacts of highway agency actions which adversely affect base flood plains,

(e) To restore and preserve the natural and beneficial flood-plain values that are adversely impacted by highway agency actions,

(f) To avoid support of incompatible flood-plain development,

(g) To be consistent with the intent of the Standards and Criteria of the National Flood Insurance Program, where appropriate, and

(h) To incorporate "A Unified National Program for Floodplain Management" of the Water Resources Council into FHWA procedures.

§ 650.105 Definitions.

(a) *Action* shall mean any highway construction, reconstruction, rehabilitation, repair, or improvement undertaken with Federal or Federal-aid highway funds or FHWA approval.

(b) *Base flood* shall mean the flood or tide having a 1-percent chance of being exceeded in any given year.

(c) *Base flood plain* shall mean the area subject to flooding by the base flood.

(d) *Design Flood* shall mean the peak discharge, volume if appropriate, stage or wave crest elevation of the flood associated with the probability of exceedance selected for the design of a highway encroachment. By definition, the highway will not be inundated from the stage of the design flood.

(e) *Encroachment* shall mean an action within the limits of the base flood plain.

(f) *Floodproof* shall mean to design and construct individual buildings, facilities, and their sites to protect against structural failure, to keep water out or to reduce the effects of water entry.

(g) *Freeboard* shall mean the vertical clearance of the lowest structural member of the bridge superstructure above the water surface elevation of the overtopping flood.

(h) *Minimize* shall mean to reduce to the smallest practicable amount or degree.

(i) *Natural and beneficial flood-plain values* shall include but are not limited to fish, wildlife, plants, open space, natural beauty, scientific study, outdoor recreation, agriculture, aquaculture, forestry, natural moderation of floods, water quality maintenance, and groundwater recharge.

(j) *Overtopping flood* shall mean the flood described by the probability of exceedance and water surface elevation at which flow occurs over the highway, over the watershed divide, or through structure(s) provided for emergency relief.

(k) *Practicable* shall mean capable of being done within reasonable natural, social, or economic constraints.

(l) *Preserve* shall mean to avoid modification to the functions of the natural flood-plain environment or to maintain it as closely as practicable in its natural state.

(m) *Regulatory floodway* shall mean the flood-plain area that is reserved in an open manner by Federal, State or local requirements, *i.e.*, unconfined or unobstructed either horizontally or vertically, to provide for the discharge of the base flood so that the cumulative increase in water surface elevation is no more than a designated amount (not to exceed 1 foot as established by the Federal Emergency Management Agency (FEMA) for administering the National Flood Insurance Program).

(n) *Restore* shall mean to reestablish a setting or environment in which the functions of the natural and beneficial flood-plain values adversely impacted by the highway agency action can again operate.

(o) *Risk* shall mean the consequences associated with the probability of flooding attributable to an encroachment. It shall include the potential for property loss and hazard to life during the service life of the highway.

(p) *Risk analysis* shall mean an economic comparison of design alternatives using expected total costs (construction costs plus risk costs) to determine the alternative with the least total expected cost to the public. It shall include probable flood-related costs during the service life of the facility for highway operation, maintenance, and repair, for highway-aggravated flood damage to other property, and for additional or interrupted highway travel.

(q) *Significant encroachment* shall mean a highway encroachment and any direct support of likely base flood-plain development that would involve one or more of the following construction-or flood-related impacts:

(1) A significant potential for interruption or termination of a transportation facility which is needed for emergency vehicles or provides a community's only evacuation route.

(2) A significant risk, or

(3) A significant adverse impact on natural and beneficial flood-plain values.

(r) *Support base flood-plain development* shall mean to encourage, allow, serve, or otherwise facilitate additional base flood-plain development. Direct support results from an encroachment, while indirect support results from an action out of the base flood plain.

§650.107 Applicability.

(a) The provisions of this regulation shall apply to all encroachments and to all actions which affect base flood plains, except for repairs made with emergency funds (23 CFR part 668) during or immediately following a disaster.

(b) The provisions of this regulation shall not apply to or alter approvals or authorizations which were given by FHWA pursuant to regulations or directives in effect before the effective date of this regulation.

§650.109 Public involvement.

Procedures which have been established to meet the public involvement requirements of 23 CFR part 771 shall be used to provide opportunity for early public review and comment on alternatives which contain encroachments.

[53 FR 11065, Apr. 5, 1988]

§650.111 Location hydraulic studies.

(a) National Flood Insurance Program (NFIP) maps or information developed by the highway agency, if NFIP maps are not available, shall be used to determine whether a highway location alternative will include an encroachment.

(b) Location studies shall include evaluation and discussion of the practicability of alternatives to any longitudinal encroachments.

(c) Location studies shall include discussion of the following items, commensurate with the significance of the risk or environmental impact, for all alternatives containing encroachments and for those actions which would support base flood-plain development:

(1) The risks associated with implementation of the action,

(2) The impacts on natural and beneficial flood-plain values,

(3) The support of probable incompatible flood-plain development,

(4) The measures to minimize flood-plain impacts associated with the action, and

(5) The measures to restore and preserve the natural and beneficial flood-plain values impacted by the action.

(d) Location studies shall include evaluation and discussion of the practicability of alternatives to any significant encroachments or any support of incompatible flood-plain development.

(e) The studies required by §650.111 (c) and (d) shall be summarized in environmental review documents prepared pursuant to 23 CFR part 771.

(f) Local, State, and Federal water resources and flood-plain management agencies should be consulted to determine if the proposed highway action is consistent with existing watershed and flood-plain management programs and to obtain current information on development and proposed actions in the affected watersheds.

§650.113 Only practicable alternative finding.

(a) A proposed action which includes a significant encroachment shall not be approved unless the FHWA finds that the proposed significant encroachment is the only practicable alternative. This finding shall be included in the final environmental document (final environmental impact statement or finding of no significant impact) and shall be supported by the following information:

(1) The reasons why the proposed action must be located in the flood plain,

(2) The alternatives considered and why they were not practicable, and

(3) A statement indicating whether the action conforms to applicable State or local flood-plain protection standards.

(b) [Reserved]

[44 FR 67580, Nov. 26, 1979, as amended at 48 FR 29274, June 24, 1983]

§650.115 Design standards.

(a) The design selected for an encroachment shall be supported by analyses of design alternatives with consideration given to capital costs and risks, and to other economic, engineering, social and environmental concerns.

(1) Consideration of capital costs and risks shall include, as appropriate, a risk analysis or assessment which includes:

(i) The overtopping flood or the base flood, whichever is greater, or

(ii) The greatest flood which must flow through the highway drainage structure(s), where overtopping is not practicable. The greatest flood used in the analysis is subject to state-of-the-art capability to estimate the exceedance probability.

(2) The design flood for encroachments by through lanes of Interstate highways shall not be less than the flood with a 2-percent chance of being exceeded in any given year. No minimum design flood is specified for Interstate highway ramps and frontage roads or for other highways.

(3) Freeboard shall be provided, where practicable, to protect bridge structures from debris- and scour-related failure.

(4) The effect of existing flood control channels, levees, and reservoirs shall be considered in estimating the peak discharge and stage for all floods considered in the design.

(5) The design of encroachments shall be consistent with standards established by the FEMA, State, and local governmental agencies for the administration of the National Flood Insurance Program for:

(i) All direct Federal highway actions, unless the standards are demonstrably inappropriate, and

(ii) Federal-aid highway actions where a regulatory floodway has been designated or where studies are underway to establish a regulatory floodway.

(b) Rest area buildings and related water supply and waste treatment facilities shall be located outside the base flood plain, where practicable. Rest area buildings which are located on the base flood plain shall be floodproofed against damage from the base flood.

(c) Where highway fills are to be used as dams to permanently impound water more than 50 acre-feet (6.17×10^4 cubic metres) in volume or 25 feet (7.6 metres) deep, the hydrologic, hydraulic, and structural design of the fill and appurtenant spillways shall have the approval of the State or Federal agency responsible for the safety of dams or like structures within the State, prior to authorization by the Division Administrator to advertise for bids for construction.

§ 650.117 Content of design studies.

(a) The detail of studies shall be commensurate with the risk associated with the encroachment and with other economic, engineering, social or environmental concerns.

(b) Studies by highway agencies shall contain:

(1) The hydrologic and hydraulic data and design computations,

(2) The analysis required by § 650.115(a), and

(3) For proposed direct Federal highway actions, the reasons, when applicable, why FEMA criteria (44 CFR 60.3, formerly 24 CFR 1910.3) are demonstrably inappropriate.

(c) For encroachment locations, project plans shall show:

(1) The magnitude, approximate probability of exceedance and, at appropriate locations, the water surface elevations associated with the overtopping flood or the flood of § 650.115(a)(1)(ii), and

(2) The magnitude and water surface elevation of the base flood, if larger than the overtopping flood.

Subpart B—Erosion and Sediment Control on Highway Construction Projects

SOURCE: 59 FR 37939, July 26, 1994, unless otherwise noted.

§ 650.201 Purpose.

The purpose of this subpart is to prescribe policies and procedures for the control of erosion, abatement of water pollution, and prevention of damage by sediment deposition from all construction projects funded under title 23, United States Code.

§ 650.203 Policy.

It is the policy of the Federal Highway Administration (FHWA) that all highways funded in whole or in part under title 23, United States Code, shall be located, designed, constructed and operated according to standards that will minimize erosion and sediment damage to the highway and adjacent properties and abate pollution of surface and ground water resources. Guidance for the development of standards used to minimize erosion and sediment damage is referenced in §650.211 of this part.

§650.205 Definitions.

Erosion control measures and practices are actions that are taken to inhibit the dislodging and transporting of soil particles by water or wind, including actions that limit the area of exposed soil and minimize the time the soil is exposed.

Permanent erosion and sediment control measures and practices are installations and design features of a construction project which remain in place and in service after completion of the project.

Pollutants are substances, including sediment, which cause deterioration of water quality when added to surface or ground waters in sufficient quantity.

Sediment control measures and practices are actions taken to control the deposition of sediments resulting from surface runoff.

Temporary erosion and sediment control measures and practices are actions taken on an interim basis during construction to minimize the disturbance, transportation, and unwanted deposition of sediment.

§650.207 Plans, specifications and estimates.

(a) Emphasis shall be placed on erosion control in the preparation of plans, specifications and estimates.

(b) All reasonable steps shall be taken to insure that highway project designs for the control of erosion and sedimentation and the protection of water quality comply with applicable standards and regulations of other agencies.

[39 FR 36332, Oct. 9, 1974]

§650.209 Construction.

(a) Permanent erosion and sediment control measures and practices shall be established and implemented at the earliest practicable time consistent with good construction and management practices.

(b) Implementation of temporary erosion and sediment control measures and practices shall be coordinated with permanent measures to assure economical, effective, and continuous control throughout construction.

(c) Erosion and sediment control measures and practices shall be monitored and maintained or revised to insure that they are fulfilling their intended function during the construction of the project.

(d) Federal-aid funds shall not be used in erosion and sediment control actions made necessary because of contractor oversight, carelessness, or failure to implement sufficient control measures.

(e) Pollutants used during highway construction or operation and material from sediment traps shall not be stockpiled or disposed of in a manner which makes them susceptible to being washed into any watercourse by runoff or high water. No pollutants shall be deposited or disposed of in watercourses.

§650.211 Guidelines.

(a) The FHWA adopts the AASHTO Highway Drainage Guidelines, Volume III, "Erosion and Sediment Control in Highway Construction," 1992,[1] as guidelines to be followed on all construction projects funded under title 23, United States Code. These guidelines are not intended to preempt any requirements made by or under State law if such requirements are more stringent.

(b) Each State highway agency should apply the guidelines referenced in paragraph (a) of this section or apply its own guidelines, if these guidelines are more stringent, to develop standards and practices for the control of erosion and sediment on Federal-aid construction projects. These specific standards and practices may reference

[1] This document is available for inspection from the FHWA headquarters and field offices as prescribed by 49 CFR part 7, appendix D. It may be purchased from the American Association of State Highway and Transportation Officials offices at Suite 225, 444 North Capitol Street, NW., Washington, DC 20001.

available resources, such as the procedures presented in the AASHTO "Model Drainage Manual," 1991.[2]

(c) Consistent with the requirements of section 6217(g) of the Coastal Zone Act Reauthorization Amendments of 1990 (Pub. L. 101–508, 104 Stat. 1388–299), highway construction projects funded under title 23, United States Code, and located in the coastal zone management areas of States with coastal zone management programs approved by the United States Department of Commerce, National Oceanic and Atmospheric Administration, should utilize "Guidance Specifying Management Measures for Sources of Nonpoint Source Pollution in Coastal Waters," 84–B–92–002, U.S. EPA, January 1993.[3] State highway agencies should refer to this Environmental Protection Agency guidance document for the design of projects within coastal zone management areas.

Subpart C—National Bridge Inspection Standards

SOURCE: 69 FR 74436, Dec. 14, 2004, unless otherwise noted.

§ 650.301 Purpose.

This subpart sets the national standards for the proper safety inspection and evaluation of all highway bridges in accordance with 23 U.S.C. 151.

§ 650.303 Applicability.

The National Bridge Inspection Standards (NBIS) in this subpart apply to all structures defined as highway bridges located on all public roads.

§ 650.305 Definitions.

Terms used in this subpart are defined as follows:

American Association of State Highway and Transportation Officials (AASHTO) Manual. "The Manual for Bridge Evaluation," First Edition, 2008, published by the American Association of State Highway and Transportation Officials (incorporated by reference, *see* § 650.317).

Bridge. A structure including supports erected over a depression or an obstruction, such as water, highway, or railway, and having a track or passageway for carrying traffic or other moving loads, and having an opening measured along the center of the roadway of more than 20 feet between undercopings of abutments or spring lines of arches, or extreme ends of openings for multiple boxes; it may also include multiple pipes, where the clear distance between openings is less than half of the smaller contiguous opening.

Bridge inspection experience. Active participation in bridge inspections in accordance with the NBIS, in either a field inspection, supervisory, or management role. A combination of bridge design, bridge maintenance, bridge construction and bridge inspection experience, with the predominant amount in bridge inspection, is acceptable.

Bridge inspection refresher training. The National Highway Institute "Bridge Inspection Refresher Training Course"[1] or other State, local, or federally developed instruction aimed to improve quality of inspections, introduce new techniques, and maintain the consistency of the inspection program.

Bridge Inspector's Reference Manual (BIRM). A comprehensive FHWA manual on programs, procedures and techniques for inspecting and evaluating a variety of in-service highway bridges. This manual may be purchased from the U.S. Government Printing Office, Washington, DC 20402 and from National Technical Information Service, Springfield, Virginia 22161, and is available at the following URL: *http://www.fhwa.dot.gov/bridge/bripub.htm.*

Complex bridge. Movable, suspension, cable stayed, and other bridges with unusual characteristics.

[2] This document is available for inspection from the FHWA headquarters and field offices as prescribed by 49 CFR part 7, appendix D. It may be purchased from the American Association of State Highway and Transportation Officials offices at Suite 225, 444 North Capitol Street, NW., Washington, DC 20001.

[3] This document is available for inspection and copying as prescribed by 49 CFR part 7, appendix D.

[1] The National Highway Institute training may be found at the following URL: *http://www.nhi.fhwa.dot.gov./*

Comprehensive bridge inspection training. Training that covers all aspects of bridge inspection and enables inspectors to relate conditions observed on a bridge to established criteria (see the Bridge Inspector's Reference Manual for the recommended material to be covered in a comprehensive training course).

Critical finding. A structural or safety related deficiency that requires immediate follow-up inspection or action.

Damage inspection. This is an unscheduled inspection to assess structural damage resulting from environmental factors or human actions.

Fracture critical member (FCM). A steel member in tension, or with a tension element, whose failure would probably cause a portion of or the entire bridge to collapse.

Fracture critical member inspection. A hands-on inspection of a fracture critical member or member components that may include visual and other nondestructive evaluation.

Hands-on. Inspection within arms length of the component. Inspection uses visual techniques that may be supplemented by nondestructive testing.

Highway. The term "highway" is defined in 23 U.S.C. 101(a)(11).

In-depth inspection. A close-up, inspection of one or more members above or below the water level to identify any deficiencies not readily detectable using routine inspection procedures; hands-on inspection may be necessary at some locations.

Initial inspection. The first inspection of a bridge as it becomes a part of the bridge file to provide all Structure Inventory and Appraisal (SI&A) data and other relevant data and to determine baseline structural conditions.

Legal load. The maximum legal load for each vehicle configuration permitted by law for the State in which the bridge is located.

Load rating. The determination of the live load carrying capacity of a bridge using bridge plans and supplemented by information gathered from a field inspection.

National Institute for Certification in Engineering Technologies (NICET). The NICET provides nationally applicable voluntary certification programs covering several broad engineering technology fields and a number of specialized subfields. For information on the NICET program certification contact: National Institute for Certification in Engineering Technologies, 1420 King Street, Alexandria, VA 22314–2794.

Operating rating. The maximum permissible live load to which the structure may be subjected for the load configuration used in the rating.

Professional engineer (PE). An individual, who has fulfilled education and experience requirements and passed rigorous exams that, under State licensure laws, permits them to offer engineering services directly to the public. Engineering licensure laws vary from State to State, but, in general, to become a PE an individual must be a graduate of an engineering program accredited by the Accreditation Board for Engineering and Technology, pass the Fundamentals of Engineering exam, gain four years of experience working under a PE, and pass the Principles of Practice of Engineering exam.

Program manager. The individual in charge of the program, that has been assigned or delegated the duties and responsibilities for bridge inspection, reporting, and inventory. The program manager provides overall leadership and is available to inspection team leaders to provide guidance.

Public road. The term "public road" is defined in 23 U.S.C. 101(a)(27).

Quality assurance (QA). The use of sampling and other measures to assure the adequacy of quality control procedures in order to verify or measure the quality level of the entire bridge inspection and load rating program.

Quality control (QC). Procedures that are intended to maintain the quality of a bridge inspection and load rating at or above a specified level.

Routine inspection. Regularly scheduled inspection consisting of observations and/or measurements needed to determine the physical and functional condition of the bridge, to identify any changes from initial or previously recorded conditions, and to ensure that the structure continues to satisfy present service requirements.

Routine permit load. A live load, which has a gross weight, axle weight or distance between axles not conforming with State statutes for legally configured vehicles, authorized for unlimited trips over an extended period of time to move alongside other heavy vehicles on a regular basis.

Scour. Erosion of streambed or bank material due to flowing water; often considered as being localized around piers and abutments of bridges.

Scour critical bridge. A bridge with a foundation element that has been determined to be unstable for the observed or evaluated scour condition.

Special inspection. An inspection scheduled at the discretion of the bridge owner, used to monitor a particular known or suspected deficiency.

State transportation department. The term "State transportation department" is defined in 23 U.S.C. 101(a)(34).

Team leader. Individual in charge of an inspection team responsible for planning, preparing, and performing field inspection of the bridge.

Underwater diver bridge inspection training. Training that covers all aspects of underwater bridge inspection and enables inspectors to relate the conditions of underwater bridge elements to established criteria (see the Bridge Inspector's Reference Manual section on underwater inspection for the recommended material to be covered in an underwater diver bridge inspection training course).

Underwater inspection. Inspection of the underwater portion of a bridge substructure and the surrounding channel, which cannot be inspected visually at low water by wading or probing, generally requiring diving or other appropriate techniques.

[69 FR 74436, Dec. 14, 2004, as amended at 74 FR 68379, Dec. 24, 2009]

§ 650.307 Bridge inspection organization.

(a) Each State transportation department must inspect, or cause to be inspected, all highway bridges located on public roads that are fully or partially located within the State's boundaries, except for bridges that are owned by Federal agencies.

(b) Federal agencies must inspect, or cause to be inspected, all highway bridges located on public roads that are fully or partially located within the respective agency responsibility or jurisdiction.

(c) Each State transportation department or Federal agency must include a bridge inspection organization that is responsible for the following:

(1) Statewide or Federal agencywide bridge inspection policies and procedures, quality assurance and quality control, and preparation and maintenance of a bridge inventory.

(2) Bridge inspections, reports, load ratings and other requirements of these standards.

(d) Functions identified in paragraphs (c)(1) and (2) of this section may be delegated, but such delegation does not relieve the State transportation department or Federal agency of any of its responsibilities under this subpart.

(e) The State transportation department or Federal agency bridge inspection organization must have a program manager with the qualifications defined in § 650.309(a), who has been delegated responsibility for paragraphs (c)(1) and (2) of this section.

§ 650.309 Qualifications of personnel.

(a) A program manager must, at a minimum:

(1) Be a registered professional engineer, or have ten years bridge inspection experience; and

(2) Successfully complete a Federal Highway Administration (FHWA) approved comprehensive bridge inspection training course.

(b) There are five ways to qualify as a team leader. A team leader must, at a minimum:

(1) Have the qualifications specified in paragraph (a) of this section; or

(2) Have five years bridge inspection experience and have successfully completed an FHWA approved comprehensive bridge inspection training course; or

(3) Be certified as a Level III or IV Bridge Safety Inspector under the National Society of Professional Engineer's program for National Certification in Engineering Technologies (NICET) and have successfully completed an FHWA approved comprehensive bridge inspection training course, or

(4) Have all of the following:

(i) A bachelor's degree in engineering from a college or university accredited by or determined as substantially equivalent by the Accreditation Board for Engineering and Technology;

(ii) Successfully passed the National Council of Examiners for Engineering and Surveying Fundamentals of Engineering examination;

(iii) Two years of bridge inspection experience; and

(iv) Successfully completed an FHWA approved comprehensive bridge inspection training course, or

(5) Have all of the following:

(i) An associate's degree in engineering or engineering technology from a college or university accredited by or determined as substantially equivalent by the Accreditation Board for Engineering and Technology;

(ii) Four years of bridge inspection experience; and

(iii) Successfully completed an FHWA approved comprehensive bridge inspection training course.

(c) The individual charged with the overall responsibility for load rating bridges must be a registered professional engineer.

(d) An underwater bridge inspection diver must complete an FHWA approved comprehensive bridge inspection training course or other FHWA approved underwater diver bridge inspection training course.

§ 650.311 Inspection frequency.

(a) *Routine inspections.* (1) Inspect each bridge at regular intervals not to exceed twenty-four months.

(2) Certain bridges require inspection at less than twenty-four-month intervals. Establish criteria to determine the level and frequency to which these bridges are inspected considering such factors as age, traffic characteristics, and known deficiencies.

(3) Certain bridges may be inspected at greater than twenty-four month intervals, not to exceed forty-eight-months, with written FHWA approval. This may be appropriate when past inspection findings and analysis justifies the increased inspection interval.

(b) *Underwater inspections.* (1) Inspect underwater structural elements at regular intervals not to exceed sixty months.

(2) Certain underwater structural elements require inspection at less than sixty-month intervals. Establish criteria to determine the level and frequency to which these members are inspected considering such factors as construction material, environment, age, scour characteristics, condition rating from past inspections and known deficiencies.

(3) Certain underwater structural elements may be inspected at greater than sixty-month intervals, not to exceed seventy-two months, with written FHWA approval. This may be appropriate when past inspection findings and analysis justifies the increased inspection interval.

(c) *Fracture critical member (FCM) inspections.* (1) Inspect FCMs at intervals not to exceed twenty-four months.

(2) Certain FCMs require inspection at less than twenty-four-month intervals. Establish criteria to determine the level and frequency to which these members are inspected considering such factors as age, traffic characteristics, and known deficiencies.

(d) Damage, in-depth, and special inspections. Establish criteria to determine the level and frequency of these inspections.

§ 650.313 Inspection procedures.

(a) Inspect each bridge in accordance with the inspection procedures in the AASHTO Manual (incorporated by reference, *see* § 650.317).

(b) Provide at least one team leader, who meets the minimum qualifications stated in § 650.309, at the bridge at all times during each initial, routine, in-depth, fracture critical member and underwater inspection.

(c) Rate each bridge as to its safe load-carrying capacity in accordance with the AASHTO Manual (incorporated by reference, *see* § 650.317). Post or restrict the bridge in accordance with the AASHTO Manual or in accordance with State law, when the maximum unrestricted legal loads or State routine permit loads exceed that allowed under the operating rating or equivalent rating factor.

(d) Prepare bridge files as described in the AASHTO Manual (incorporated by reference, *see* § 650.317). Maintain reports on the results of bridge inspections together with notations of any action taken to address the findings of such inspections. Maintain relevant maintenance and inspection data to allow assessment of current bridge condition. Record the findings and results of bridge inspections on standard State or Federal agency forms.

(e) Identify bridges with FCMs, bridges requiring underwater inspection, and bridges that are scour critical.

(1) Bridges with fracture critical members. In the inspection records, identify the location of FCMs and describe the FCM inspection frequency and procedures. Inspect FCMs according to these procedures.

(2) Bridges requiring underwater inspections. Identify the location of underwater elements and include a description of the underwater elements, the inspection frequency and the procedures in the inspection records for each bridge requiring underwater inspection. Inspect those elements requiring underwater inspections according to these procedures.

(3) Bridges that are scour critical. Prepare a plan of action to monitor known and potential deficiencies and to address critical findings. Monitor bridges that are scour critical in accordance with the plan.

(f) *Complex bridges.* Identify specialized inspection procedures, and additional inspector training and experience required to inspect complex bridges. Inspect complex bridges according to those procedures.

(g) *Quality control and quality assurance.* Assure systematic quality control (QC) and quality assurance (QA) procedures are used to maintain a high degree of accuracy and consistency in the inspection program. Include periodic field review of inspection teams, periodic bridge inspection refresher training for program managers and team leaders, and independent review of inspection reports and computations.

(h) *Follow-up on critical findings.* Establish a statewide or Federal agency wide procedure to assure that critical findings are addressed in a timely manner. Periodically notify the FHWA of the actions taken to resolve or monitor critical findings.

§ 650.315 Inventory.

(a) Each State or Federal agency must prepare and maintain an inventory of all bridges subject to the NBIS. Certain Structure Inventory and Appraisal (SI&A) data must be collected and retained by the State or Federal agency for collection by the FHWA as requested. A tabulation of this data is contained in the SI&A sheet distributed by the FHWA as part of the "Recording and Coding Guide for the Structure Inventory and Appraisal of the Nation's Bridges," (December 1995) together with subsequent interim changes or the most recent version. Report the data using FHWA established procedures as outlined in the "Recording and Coding Guide for the Structure Inventory and Appraisal of the Nation's Bridges."

(b) For routine, in-depth, fracture critical member, underwater, damage and special inspections enter the SI&A data into the State or Federal agency inventory within 90 days of the date of inspection for State or Federal agency bridges and within 180 days of the date of inspection for all other bridges.

(c) For existing bridge modifications that alter previously recorded data and for new bridges, enter the SI&A data into the State or Federal agency inventory within 90 days after the completion of the work for State or Federal agency bridges and within 180 days after the completion of the work for all other bridges.

(d) For changes in load restriction or closure status, enter the SI&A data into the State or Federal agency inventory within 90 days after the change in status of the structure for State or Federal agency bridges and within 180 days after the change in status of the structure for all other bridges.

§ 650.317 Reference manuals.

(a) The materials listed in this subpart are incorporated by reference in the corresponding sections noted. These incorporations by reference were approved by the Director of the Federal Register in accordance with 5 U.S.C. 552(a) and 1 CFR part 51. These materials are incorporated as they exist on the date of the approval, and notice of any change in these documents will be published in the FEDERAL REGISTER. The materials are available for purchase at the address listed below, and are available for inspection at the National Archives and Records Administration (NARA). These materials may also be reviewed at the Department of Transportation Library, 1200 New Jersey Avenue, SE., Washington, DC 20590, (202) 366–0761. For information on the availability of these materials at NARA call (202) 741–6030, or go to the following URL: *http://www.archives.gov/federal_register/code_of_federal_regulations/ibr_locations.html*. In the event there is a conflict between the standards in this subpart and any of these materials, the standards in this subpart will apply.

(b) The following materials are available for purchase from the American Association of State Highway and Transportation Officials, Suite 249, 444 N. Capitol Street, NW., Washington, DC 20001, (202) 624–5800. The materials may also be ordered via the AASHTO bookstore located at the following URL: *http://www.transportation.org*.

(1) The Manual for Bridge Evaluation, First Edition, 2008, AASHTO, incorporation by reference approved for §§ 650.305 and 650.313.

(2) [Reserved]

[74 FR 68379, Dec. 24, 2009]

Subpart D—Highway Bridge Replacement and Rehabilitation Program

SOURCE: 44 FR 15665, Mar. 15, 1979, unless otherwise noted.

§ 650.401 Purpose.

The purpose of this regulation is to prescribe policies and outline procedures for administering the Highway Bridge Replacement and Rehabilitation Program in accordance with 23 U.S.C. 144.

§ 650.403 Definition of terms.

As used in this regulation:

(a) *Bridge*. A structure, including supports, erected over a depression or an obstruction, such as water, a highway, or a railway, having a track or passageway for carrying traffic or other moving loads, and having an opening measured along the center of the roadway of more than 20 feet between undercopings of abutments or spring lines of arches, or extreme ends of the openings for multiple boxes; it may include multiple pipes where the clear distance between openings is less than half of the smaller contiguous opening.

(b) *Sufficiency rating*. The numerical rating of a bridge based on its structural adequacy and safety, essentiality for public use, and its serviceability and functional obsolescence.

(c) *Rehabilitation*. The major work required to restore the structural integrity of a bridge as well as work necessary to correct major safety defects.

§ 650.405 Eligible projects.

(a) *General*. Deficient highway bridges on all public roads may be eligible for replacement or rehabilitation.

(b) *Types of projects which are eligible*. The following types of work are eligible for participation in the Highway Bridge Replacement and Rehabilitation Program (HBRRP), hereinafter known as the bridge program.

(1) *Replacement*. Total replacement of a structurally deficient or functionally obsolete bridge with a new facility constructed in the same general traffic corridor. A nominal amount of approach work, sufficient to connect the new facility to the existing roadway or to return the gradeline to an attainable touchdown point in accordance with good design practice is also eligible. The replacement structure must meet the current geometric, construction and structural standards required for the types and volume of projected traffic on the facility over its design life.

(2) *Rehabilitation*. The project requirements necessary to perform the major work required to restore the structural integrity of a bridge as well as work necessary to correct major safety defects are eligible except as noted under ineligible work. Bridges to be rehabilitated both on or off the F-A System shall, as a minimum, conform with the provisions of 23 CFR part 625, Design Standards for Federal-aid Highways, for the class of highway on which the bridge is a part.

(c) *Ineligible work.* Except as otherwise prescribed by the Administrator, the costs of long approach fills, causeways, connecting roadways, interchanges, ramps, and other extensive earth structures, when constructed beyond the attainable touchdown point, are not eligible under the bridge program.

§ 650.407 Application for bridge replacement or rehabilitation.

(a) Agencies participate in the bridge program by conducting bridge inspections and submitting Structure Inventory and Appraisal (SI&A) sheet inspection data. Federal and local governments supply SI&A sheet data to the State agency for review and processing. The State is responsible for submitting the six computer card format or tapes containing all public road SI&A sheet bridge information through the Division Administrator of the Federal Highway Administration (FHWA) for processing. These requirements are prescribed in 23 CFR 650.309 and 650.311, the National Bridge Inspection Standards.

(b) Inventory data may be submitted as available and shall be submitted at such additional times as the FHWA may request.

(c) Inventory data on bridges that have been strengthened or repaired to eliminate deficiencies, or those that have been replaced or rehabilitated using bridge replacement and/or other funds, must be revised in the inventory through data submission.

(d) The Secretary may, at the request of a State, inventory bridges, on and off the Federal-aid system, for historic significance.

[44 FR 15665, Mar. 15, 1979, as amended at 44 FR 72112, Dec. 13, 1979]

§ 650.409 Evaluation of bridge inventory.

(a) *Sufficiency rating of bridges.* Upon receipt and evaluation of the bridge inventory, a sufficiency rating will be assigned to each bridge by the Secretary in accordance with the approved AASHTO[1] sufficiency rating formula. The sufficiency rating will be used as a basis for establishing eligibility and priority for replacement or rehabilitation of bridges; in general the lower the rating, the higher the priority.

(b) *Selection of bridges for inclusion in State program.* After evaluation of the inventory and assignment of sufficiency ratings, the Secretary will provide the State with a selection list of bridges within the State that are eligible for the bridge program. From that list or from previously furnished selection lists, the State may select bridge projects.

§ 650.411 Procedures for bridge replacement and rehabilitation projects.

(a) Consideration shall be given to projects which will remove from service highway bridges most in danger of failure.

(b) *Submission and approval of projects.* (1) Bridge replacement or rehabilitation projects shall be submitted by the State to the Secretary in accordance with 23 CFR part 630, subpart A Federal-Aid Programs, Approval and Authorization.

(2) Funds apportioned to a State shall be made available throughout each State on a fair and equitable basis.

(c)(1) Each approved project will be designed, constructed, and inspected for acceptance in the same manner as other projects on the system on which the project is located. It shall be the responsibility of the State agency to properly maintain, or cause to be properly maintained, any project constructed under this bridge program. The State highway agency shall enter into a formal agreement for maintenance with appropriate local government officials in cases where an eligible project is located within and is under the legal authority of such a local government.

(2) Whenever a deficient bridge is replaced or its deficiency alleviated by a new bridge under the bridge program, the deficient bridge shall either be dismantled or demolished or its use limited to the type and volume of traffic

[1] American Association of State Highway and Transporation Officials, Suite 225, 444 North Capitol Street, NW, Washington, DC 20001.

the structure can safely service over its remaining life. For example, if the only deficiency of the existing structure is inadequate roadway width and the combination of the new and existing structure can be made to meet current standards for the volume of traffic the facility will carry over its design life, the existing bridge may remain in place and be incorporated into the system.

[44 FR 15665, Mar. 15, 1979, as amended at 44 FR 72112, Dec. 13, 1979]

§ 650.413 Funding.

(a) Funds authorized for carrying out the Highway Bridge Replacement and Rehabilitation Program are available for obligation at the beginning of the fiscal year for which authorized and remain available for expenditure for the same period as funds apportioned for projects on the Federal-aid primary system.

(b) The Federal share payable on account of any project carried out under 23 U.S.C. 144 shall be 80 percent of the eligible cost.

(c) Not less than 15 percent nor more than 35 percent of the apportioned funds shall be expended for projects located on public roads, other than those on a Federal-aid system. The Secretary after consultation with State and local officials may, with respect to a State, reduce the requirement for expenditure for bridges not on a Federal-aid system when he determines that such State has inadequate needs to justify such expenditure.

§ 650.415 Reports.

The Secretary must report annually to the Congress on projects approved and current inventories together with recommendations for further improvements.

Subpart E—National Tunnel Inspection Standards

SOURCE: 80 FR 41368, July 14, 2015, unless otherwise noted.

§ 650.501 Purpose.

This subpart sets the national minimum standards for the proper safety inspection and evaluation of all highway tunnels in accordance with 23 U.S.C. 144(h) and the requirements for preparing and maintaining an inventory in accordance with 23 U.S.C. 144(b).

§ 650.503 Applicability.

The National Tunnel Inspection Standards (NTIS) in this subpart apply to all structures defined as highway tunnels on all public roads, on and off Federal-aid highways, including tribally and federally owned tunnels.

§ 650.505 Definitions.

The following terms used in this subpart are defined as follows:

American Association of State Highway and Transportation Officials (AASHTO) Manual for Bridge Evaluation. The term "AASHTO Manual for Bridge Evaluation" means the "Manual for Bridge Evaluation", incorporated by reference in § 650.517.

At-grade roadway. The term "at-grade roadway" means paved or unpaved travel ways within the tunnel that carry vehicular traffic and are not suspended or supported by a structural system.

Bridge inspection experience. The term "bridge inspection experience" has the same meaning as in § 650.305.

Complex tunnel. The term "complex tunnel" means a tunnel characterized by advanced or unique structural elements or functional systems.

Comprehensive tunnel inspection training. The term "comprehensive tunnel inspection training" means the FHWA-approved training that covers all aspects of tunnel inspection and enables inspectors to relate conditions observed in a tunnel to established criteria.

Critical finding. The term "critical finding" has the same meaning as in § 650.305.

Damage inspection. The term "damage inspection" has the same meaning as in § 650.305.

End-of-course assessment. The term "end-of-course assessment" means a comprehensive examination given to students after the completion of a training course.

Federal-aid highway. The term "Federal-aid highway" has the same meaning as in 23 U.S.C. 101(a)(5).

Functional systems. The term "functional systems" means non-structural systems, such as electrical, mechanical, fire suppression, ventilation, lighting, communications, monitoring, drainage, traffic signals, emergency response (including egress, refuge room spacing, or carbon monoxide detection), or traffic safety components.

Hands-on inspection. The term "hands-on inspection" has the same meaning as in §650.305.

Highway. The term "highway" has the same meaning as in 23 U.S.C. 101(a)(11).

In-depth inspection. The term "in-depth inspection" means a close-up inspection of one, several, or all tunnel structural elements or functional systems to identify any deficiencies not readily detectable using routine inspection procedures. In-depth inspections may occur more or less frequently than routine inspections, as outlined in the tunnel-specific inspection procedures.

Initial inspection. The term "initial inspection" means the first inspection of a tunnel to provide all inventory, appraisal, and other data necessary to determine the baseline condition of the structural elements and functional systems.

Inspection Date. The term "Inspection Date" means the date established by the Program Manager on which a regularly scheduled routine inspection begins for a tunnel.

Legal load. The terms "legal load means the maximum legal load for each vehicle configuration permitted by law for the State in which the tunnel is located.

Load rating. The term "load rating" means the determination of the safe vehicular live load carrying capacity within or above the tunnel using structural plans, and information gathered from an inspection. The results of the load rating may include the need for load posting.

Operating rating. The term "operating rating" has the same meaning as in §650.305.

Portal. The term "portal" means the entrance and exit of the tunnel exposed to the environment; portals may include bare rock, constructed tunnel entrance structures, or buildings.

Procedures. The term "procedures" means the written documentation of policies, methods, considerations, criteria, and other conditions that direct the actions of personnel so that a desired end result is achieved consistently.

Professional Engineer (P.E.). The term "Professional Engineer (P.E.)" means an individual who has fulfilled education and experience requirements and passed examinations that, under State licensure laws, permits the individual to offer engineering services within areas of expertise directly to the public.

Program Manager. The term "Program Manager" means the individual in charge of the inspection program who has been assigned or delegated the duties and responsibilities for tunnel inspection, reporting, and inventory. The Program Manager provides overall leadership and guidance to inspection Team Leaders and load raters.

Public road. The term "public road" has the same meaning as in 23 U.S.C. 101(a)(21).

Quality assurance (QA). The term "quality assurance (QA)" means the use of sampling and other measures to ensure the adequacy of quality control procedures in order to verify or measure the quality of the entire tunnel inspection and load rating program.

Quality control (QC). The term "quality control (QC)" means the procedures that are intended to maintain the quality of a tunnel inspection and load rating at or above a specified level.

Routine inspection. The term "routine inspection" means a regularly scheduled comprehensive inspection encompassing all tunnel structural elements and functional systems and consisting of observations and measurements needed to determine the physical and functional condition of the tunnel, to identify any changes from initial or previously recorded conditions, and to ensure that tunnel components continue to satisfy present service requirements.

Routine permit load. The term "routine permit load" means a vehicular load that has a gross weight, axle weight, or distance between axles not conforming with State laws for legally configured vehicles, and is authorized for unlimited trips over an extended period of time to move alongside other heavy vehicles on a regular basis.

Special inspection. The term "special inspection" means an inspection, scheduled at the discretion of the tunnel owner, used to monitor a particular known or suspected deficiency.

State transportation department (State DOT). The term "State transportation department (State DOT)" has the same meaning as in 23 U.S.C. 101(a)(28).

Team Leader. The term "Team Leader" means the on-site individual in charge of an inspection team responsible for planning, preparing, performing, and reporting on tunnel inspections.

Tunnel. The term "tunnel" means an enclosed roadway for motor vehicle traffic with vehicle access limited to portals, regardless of type of structure or method of construction, that requires, based on the owner's determination, special design considerations that may include lighting, ventilation, fire protection systems, and emergency egress capacity. The terms "tunnel" does not include bridges or culverts inspected under the National Bridge Inspection Standards (subpart C of this part).

Tunnel inspection experience. The term "tunnel inspection experience" means active participation in the performance of tunnel inspections in accordance with the National Tunnel Inspection Standards, in either a field inspection, supervisory, or management role.

Tunnel inspection refresher training. The term "tunnel inspection refresher training" means an FHWA-approved training course that aims to improve the quality of tunnel inspections, introduce new techniques, and maintain the consistency of the tunnel inspection program.

Tunnel Operations, Maintenance, Inspection and Evaluation (TOMIE) Manual. The term "Tunnel Operations, Maintenance, Inspection and Evaluation (TOMIE) Manual" means the "Tunnel Operations, Maintenance, Inspection and Evaluation (TOMIE) Manual" (incorporated by reference, *see* § 650.517).

Tunnel-specific inspection procedures. The term "tunnel-specific inspection procedures" means the written documentation of the directions necessary to plan for, and conduct an inspection. Directions include coverage of inspection methods, frequency of each method, inspection equipment, access equipment, identification of tunnel elements, components and functional systems, traffic coordination, and specialized qualifications for inspecting personnel.

§ 650.507 Tunnel inspection organization responsibilities.

(a) Each State DOT shall inspect, or cause to be inspected, all highway tunnels located on public roads, on and off Federal-aid highways, that are fully or partially located within the State's boundaries, except for tunnels that are owned by Federal agencies or tribal governments.

(b) Each Federal agency shall inspect, or cause to be inspected, all highway tunnels located on public roads, on and off Federal-aid highways, that are fully or partially located within the respective agency's responsibility or jurisdiction.

(c) Each tribal government shall inspect, or cause to be inspected, all highway tunnels located on public roads, on and off Federal-aid highways, that are fully or partially located within the respective tribal government's responsibility or jurisdiction.

(d) Where a tunnel is jointly owned, all bordering States, Federal agencies, and tribal governments with ownership interests should determine through a joint formal written agreement the inspection responsibilities of each State, Federal agency, and tribal government.

(e) Each State that contains one or more tunnels subject to these regulations, or Federal agency or tribal government with a tunnel under its jurisdiction, shall include a tunnel inspection organization that is responsible for all of the following:

(1) Statewide, Federal agency-wide, or tribal government-wide tunnel inspection policies and procedures (both general and tunnel-specific), quality control and quality assurance procedures, and preparation and maintenance of a tunnel inventory.

(2) Tunnel inspections, written reports, load ratings, management of

critical findings, and other requirements of these standards.

(3) Maintaining a registry of nationally certified tunnel inspectors that work in their State or for their Federal agency or tribal government that includes, at a minimum, a method to positively identify each inspector, documentation that the inspector's training requirements are up-to-date, the inspector's current contact information, and detailed information about any adverse action that may affect the good standing of the inspector.

(4) A process, developed under the direction of a Professional Engineer and approved by FHWA, to determine when an inspection Team Leader's qualifications must meet § 650.509(b)(4) in order to adequately and appropriately lead an inspection of a complex tunnel or a tunnel with distinctive features or functions. At a minimum, the process shall consider a tunnel's type of construction, functional systems, history of performance, and physical and operational conditions.

(f) A State DOT, Federal agency, or tribal government may delegate functions identified in paragraphs (e)(1), (2), and (3) of this section through a formal written agreement, but such delegation does not relieve the State DOT, Federal agency, or tribal government of any of its responsibilities under this subpart.

(g) The State DOT, Federal agency, or tribal government tunnel inspection organization shall have a Program Manager with the qualifications listed in § 650.509(a), who has been delegated responsibility for paragraphs (e)(1), (2), and (3) of this section.

§ 650.509 Qualifications of personnel.

(a) A Program Manager shall, at a minimum:

(1) Be a registered Professional Engineer, or have 10 years of tunnel or bridge inspection experience;

(2) Be a nationally certified tunnel inspector;

(3) Satisfy the requirements of paragraphs (a)(1) and (2) of this section by August 13, 2017; and

(4) Be able to determine when a Team Leader's qualifications must meet the requirements of paragraph (b)(1)(i) of this section in accordance with the FHWA approved process developed in accordance with § 650.507(e)(4).

(b) A Team Leader shall, at a minimum:

(1) Meet at least one of the four qualifications listed in paragraphs (b)(1)(i) through (iv) of this section:

(i) Be a registered professional engineer and have six months of tunnel or bridge inspection experience.

(ii) Have 5 years of tunnel or bridge inspection experience.

(iii) Have all of the following:

(A) A bachelor's degree in engineering or engineering technology from a college or university accredited or determined as substantially equivalent by the Accreditation Board for Engineering and Technology.

(B) Successfully passed the National Council of Examiners for Engineering and Surveying Fundamentals of Engineering examination.

(C) Two (2) years of tunnel or bridge inspection experience.

(iv) Have all of the following:

(A) An associate's degree in engineering or engineering technology from a college or university accredited or determined as substantially equivalent by the Accreditation Board for Engineering and Technology.

(B) Four years of tunnel or bridge inspection experience.

(2) Be a nationally certified tunnel inspector.

(3) Provide documentation supporting the satisfaction of paragraphs (b)(1) and (2) of this section to the Program Manager of each State DOT, Federal agency, or tribal government for which they are performing tunnel inspections.

(4) Be a registered Professional Engineer and have six months of tunnel or bridge inspection experience if the Program Manager determines through the approved process developed under § 650.507(e)(4) that the tunnel being inspected is complex or has distinctive features or functions that warrant this level of qualifications.

(c) Load ratings shall be performed by, or under the direct supervision of, a registered Professional Engineer.

(d) Each State DOT, Federal agency, and tribal government shall determine inspection personnel qualifications for damage, cursory, and special inspections.

(e) A nationally certified tunnel inspector shall:

(1) Complete an FHWA-approved comprehensive tunnel inspection training course and score 70 percent or greater on an end-of-course assessment;

(2) Complete a cumulative total of 18 hours of FHWA-approved tunnel inspection refresher training over each 60 month period; and

(3) Maintain documentation supporting the satisfaction of paragraphs (e)(1) and (2) of this section, and, upon request, provide documentation of their training status and current contact information to the Tunnel Inspection Organization of each State DOT, Federal agency, or tribal government for which they will be performing tunnel inspections.

(f) Acceptable tunnel inspection training includes the following:

(1) *National Highway Institute training.* NHI courses on comprehensive tunnel inspection training.

(2) *FHWA approval of alternate training.* A State DOT, Federal agency, or tribal government may submit to FHWA a training course as an alternative to the NHI course. The FHWA shall approve alternative course materials and end-of-course assessments for national consistency and certification purposes. The Program Manager shall review the approved alternative training course every 5 years to ensure the material is current. Updates to approved course materials and end-of-course assessments shall be resubmitted to FHWA for approval.

(g) In evaluating the tunnel inspection experience requirements under paragraphs (a) and (b) of this section, a combination of tunnel design, tunnel maintenance, tunnel construction, and tunnel inspection experience, with the predominant amount in tunnel inspection, is acceptable. Also, the following criteria should be considered:

(1) The relevance of the individual's actual experience, including the extent to which the experience has enabled the individual to develop the skills needed to properly lead a tunnel safety inspection.

(2) The individual's exposure to the problems or deficiencies common in the types of tunnels being inspected by the individual.

(3) The individual's understanding of the specific data collection needs and requirements.

§650.511 Inspection interval.

(a) *Initial inspection.* A State DOT, Federal agency, or tribal government tunnel inspection organization shall conduct, or cause to be conducted, an initial inspection for each tunnel described in §650.503 as follows:

(1) For existing tunnels, conduct a routine inspection of each tunnel according to the inspection guidance provided in the Tunnel Operations, Maintenance, Inspection and Evaluation (TOMIE) Manual (incorporated by reference, *see* §650.517) by August 13, 2017.

(2) For tunnels completed after these regulations take effect, the initial routine inspection shall be conducted after all construction is completed and prior to opening to traffic, according to the inspection guidance provided in the Tunnel Operations, Maintenance, Inspection and Evaluation (TOMIE) Manual (incorporated by reference, *see* §650.517).

(b) *Routine inspections.* A State DOT, Federal agency, or tribal government tunnel inspection organization shall conduct, or cause to be conducted, routine inspections for each tunnel described in §650.503 as follows:

(1) Establish for each tunnel the NTIS routine Inspection Date in a month and year (MM/DD/YYYY) format. This date should only be modified by the Program Manager in rare circumstances.

(2) Inspect each tunnel at regular 24-month intervals.

(3) For tunnels needing inspection more frequently than 24-month intervals, establish criteria to determine the level and frequency to which these tunnels are inspected, based on a risk analysis approach that considers such factors as tunnel age, traffic characteristics, geotechnical conditions, and known deficiencies.

(4) Certain tunnels may be inspected at regular intervals up to 48 months. Inspecting a tunnel at an increased interval may be appropriate when past

inspection findings and analysis justifies the increased inspection interval. At a minimum, the following criteria shall be used to determine the level and frequency of inspection based on an assessed lower risk: Tunnel age, time from last major rehabilitation, tunnel complexity, traffic characteristics, geotechnical conditions, functional systems, and known deficiencies. A written request that justifies a regular routine inspection interval between 24 and 48 months shall be submitted to FHWA for review and comment prior to the extended interval being implemented.

(5) Inspect each tunnel in accordance with the established interval. The acceptable tolerance for inspection interval is within 2 months before or after the Inspection Date established in paragraph (b)(1) of this section in order to maintain that date. The actual month, day, and year of the inspection are to be reported in the National Tunnel Inventory.

(c) *Damage, in-depth, and special inspections.* The Program Manager shall establish criteria to determine the level and frequency of damage, in-depth, and special inspections. Damage, in-depth, and special inspections may use non-destructive testing or other methods not used during routine inspections at an interval established by the Program Manager. In-depth inspections should be scheduled for complex tunnels and for certain structural elements and functional systems when necessary to fully ascertain the condition of the element or system; hands-on inspection may be necessary at some locations.

§ 650.513 Inspection procedures.

Each State DOT, Federal agency, or tribal government tunnel inspection organization, to carry out its inspection responsibilities, shall perform or cause to be performed all of the following:

(a) Inspect tunnel structural elements and functional systems in accordance with the inspection guidance provided in the Tunnel Operations, Maintenance, Inspection and Evaluation (TOMIE) Manual (incorporated by reference, *see* § 650.517).

(b) Provide at least one Team Leader, who meets the minimum qualifications stated in § 650.509, at the tunnel at all times during each initial, routine, and in-depth inspection. The State DOT, Federal agency, or tribal government shall report the nationally certified tunnel inspector identification for each Team Leader that is wholly or partly responsible for a tunnel inspection must be reported to the National Tunnel Inventory.

(c) Prepare and document tunnel-specific inspection procedures for each tunnel inspected and inventoried that shall:

(1) Take into account the design assumptions and the tunnel complexity; and

(2) Identify the—

(i) Tunnel structural elements and functional systems to be inspected;

(ii) Methods of inspection to be used;

(iii) Frequency of inspection for each method; and

(iv) Inspection equipment, access equipment, and traffic coordination needed.

(d) Establish requirements for functional system testing, direct observation of critical system checks, and testing documentation.

(e) For complex tunnels, identify specialized inspection procedures and additional inspector training and experience required to inspect complex tunnels. Inspect complex tunnels according to the specialized inspection procedures.

(f) Conduct tunnel inspections with qualified staff not associated with the operation or maintenance of the tunnel structure or functional systems.

(g) Rate each tunnel's safe vehicular load-carrying capacity in accordance with the Sections 6 or 8, AASHTO Manual for Bridge Evaluation (incorporated by reference, *see* § 650.517). A State DOT, Federal agency, or tribal government shall conduct a load rating evaluation as soon as practical, but not later than three months after the completion of the inspection, if a change in condition is identified. Post or restrict the highways in or over the tunnel in accordance with Section 6, AASHTO Manual for Bridge Evaluation (incorporated by reference, *see* § 650.517), or in accordance with State law, when the maximum unrestricted legal loads or State routine permit loads exceed those allowed under the operating rating or equivalent rating factor. Postings shall be made as soon as possible but not later than 30 days after a valid load rating determines a need for such posting. At-grade roadways in tunnels are exempt from load rating. A State DOT, Federal agency, or tribal government, shall maintain load rating calculations or input files with a summary of results as a part of the tunnel record.

(h) Prepare tunnel inspection documentation as described in the Tunnel Operations, Maintenance, Inspection and Evaluation (TOMIE) Manual (incorporated by reference, *see* §650.517), and maintain written reports or electronic files on the results of tunnel inspections, together with notations of any action taken to address the findings of such inspections. Maintain relevant maintenance and inspection data to allow assessment of current tunnel condition. At a minimum, information collected will include data regarding basic tunnel information (e.g., tunnel location, posted speed, inspection reports, repair recommendations, and repair and rehabilitation work completed), tunnel and roadway geometrics, interior tunnel structural features, portal structure features, and tunnel systems information. When available, tunnel data collected shall include diagrams, photos, condition of each structural and functional system component, notations of any action taken to address the findings of such inspections, and the national tunnel inspector certification registry identification for each Team Leader responsible in whole or in part for the inspection.

(i) Use systematic quality control and quality assurance procedures to maintain a high degree of accuracy and consistency in the inspection program. Include periodic field review of inspection teams, data quality checks, and independent review of inspection reports and computations.

(j) Establish a Statewide, Federal agency-wide, or tribal government-wide procedure to ensure that critical findings are addressed in a timely manner. Notify FHWA within 24 hours of any critical finding and the activities taken, underway, or planned to resolve or monitor the critical finding. Update FHWA regularly or as requested on the status of each critical finding until it is resolved. Annually provide a written report to FHWA with a summary of the current status of the resolutions for each critical finding identified within that year or unresolved from a previous year.

(k) Provide information at least annually, or more frequently upon request, in cooperation with any FHWA review of State DOT, Federal agency, or tribal government compliance with the NTIS. The FHWA will assess annually State DOT compliance using statistical assessments and well-defined measures based on the requirements of this subpart.

§650.515 Inventory.

(a) *Preliminary inventory.* Each State, Federal agency, or tribal government shall collect and submit the inventory data items described in the Specifications for the National Tunnel Inventory (incorporated by reference, *see* §650.517) for all tunnels subject to the NTIS by December 11, 2015.

(b) *National Tunnel Inventory.* Each State, Federal agency, or tribal government shall prepare, maintain, and make available to FHWA upon request, an inventory of all highway tunnels subject to the NTIS that includes the preliminary inventory information submitted in paragraph (a) of this section, reflects the findings of the most recent tunnel inspection conducted, and is consistent and coordinated with the Specifications for the National Tunnel Inventory.

(c) *Data entry for inspections.* For all inspections, each State DOT, Federal agency, or tribal government shall enter the appropriate tunnel inspection data into its inventory within 3 months after the completion of the inspection.

(d) *Data entry for tunnel modifications and new tunnels.* For modifications to existing tunnels that alter previously recorded data and new tunnels, each State DOT, Federal agency, or tribal government shall enter the appropriate data into its inventory within 3 months after the completion of the work.

(e) *Data entry for tunnel load restriction and closure changes.* For changes in traffic load restriction or closure status, each State DOT, Federal agency, or tribal government shall enter the data into its inventory within 3 months after the change in status of the tunnel.

§ 650.517 Incorporation by reference.

(a) Certain material is incorporated by reference into this part with the approval of the Director of the Federal Register under 5 U.S.C. 552(a) and 1 CFR part 51. To enforce any edition other than that specified in this section, the FHWA must publish notice of change in the FEDERAL REGISTER and the material must be available to the public. All approved material is available for inspection at 1200 New Jersey Avenue SE., Washington, DC 20590. For questions regarding the availability of this material at FHWA, call the FHWA Regulations Officer, Office of the Chief Counsel, HCC–10, 202–366–0761. This material is also available for inspection at the National Archives and Records Administration (NARA). For information on the availability of this material at NARA, call 202–741–6030 or go to *http://www.archives.gov/federal_register/code_of_federal_regulations/ibr_locations.html.*

(b) American Association of State Highway and Transportation Officials (AASHTO), Suite 249, 444 N. Capitol Street NW., Washington, DC 20001, 800–231–3475, *https://bookstore.transportation.org.*

(1) "The Manual of Bridge Evaluation," Section 6 "Load Rating" and Section 8 "Nondestructive Load Testing," Second Edition, 2011, copyright 2011, incorporation by reference approved for §§ 650.505 and 650.513(a).

(2) 2011 Interim Revisions to "The Manual of Bridge Evaluation," Section 6 "Load Rating," Second Edition, 2010, copyright 2011, incorporation by reference approved for §§ 650.505 and 650.513(a).

(3) 2013 Interim Revisions to "The Manual of Bridge Evaluation," Section 6 "Load Rating," Second Edition, 2010, copyright 2013, incorporation by reference approved for §§ 650.505 and 650.513(a).

(4) 2014 Interim Revisions to "The Manual of Bridge Evaluation," Section 6 "Load Rating," Second Edition, 2010, copyright 2013, incorporation by reference approved for §§ 650.505 and 650.513(a).

(5) 2015 Interim Revisions to "The Manual of Bridge Evaluation," Section 6 "Load Rating," Second Edition, 2010, copyright 2014, incorporation by reference approved for §§ 650.505 and 650.513(a).

(c) Office of Bridges and Structures, Federal Highway Administration, U.S. Department of Transportation, 1200 New Jersey Avenue SE., Washington, DC 20590.

(1) FHWA–HIF–15–005, "Tunnel Operations, Maintenance, Inspection and Evaluation (TOMIE) Manual," 2015 edition, available in electronic format at *http://www.fhwa.dot.gov/bridge/inspection/tunnel/.* Incorporation by reference approved for §§ 650.505, 650.511(a), and 650.513(a) and (h).

(2) FHWA–HIF–15–006, "Specifications for National Tunnel Inventory," 2015 edition, available in electronic format at *http://www.fhwa.dot.gov/bridge/inspection/tunnel/.* Incorporation by reference approved for § 650.515(a) and (b).

Subpart F [Reserved]

Subpart G—Discretionary Bridge Candidate Rating Factor

SOURCE: 48 FR 52296, Nov. 17, 1983, unless otherwise noted.

§ 650.701 Purpose.

The purpose of this regulation is to describe a rating factor used as part of a selection process of allocation of discretionary bridge funds made available to the Secretary of Transportation under 23 U.S.C. 144.

§ 650.703 Eligible projects.

(a) Deficient highway bridges on Federal-aid highway system roads may be eligible for allocation of discretionary bridge funds to the same extent as they are for bridge funds apportioned under 23 U.S.C. 144, provided that the total project cost for a discretionary bridge candidate is at least $10 million or twice the amont of 23 U.S.C. 144 funds apportioned to the State during the fiscal year for which funding for the candidate bridge is requested.

(b) After November 14, 2002 only candidate bridges not previously selected with a computed rating factor of 100 or less and ready to begin construction in the fiscal year in which funds are available for obligation will be eligible for consideration.

(c) Projects from States that have transferred Highway Bridge Replacement and Rehabilitation funds to other funding categories will not be eligible for funding the following fiscal year.

[48 FR 52296, Nov. 17, 1983, as amended at 67 FR 63542, Oct. 15, 2002]

§650.705 Application for discretionary bridge funds.

Each year through its field offices, the FHWA will issue an annual call for discretionary bridge candidate submittals including updates of previously submitted but not selected projects. Each State is responsible for submitting such data as required for candidate bridges. Data requested will include structure number, funds needed by fiscal year, total project cost, current average daily truck traffic and a narrative describing the existing bridge, the proposed new or rehabilitated bridge and other relevant factors which the State believes may warrant special consideration.

§650.707 Rating factor.

(a) The following formula is to be used in the selection process for ranking discretionary bridge candidates.

$$\text{Rating Factor (RF)} = \frac{\text{SR}}{\text{N}} \times \frac{\text{TPC}}{\text{ADT}'} \times \left[1 + \frac{\text{Unobligated HBRRP Balance}}{\text{Total HBRRP Funds Received}}\right]$$

The lower the rating factor, the higher the priority for selection and funding.

(b) The terms in the rating factor are defined as follows:

(1) SR is Sufficiency Rating computed as illustrated in appendix A of the Recording and Coding Guide for the Structure Inventory and Appraisal of the Nation's Bridges, USDOT/FHWA (latest edition); (If SR is less than 1.0, use SR = 1.0);

(2) ADT is Average Daily Traffic in thousands taking the most current value from the national bridge inventory data;

(3) ADTT is Average Daily Truck Traffic in thousands (Pick up trucks and light delivery trucks not included). For load posted bridges, the ADTT furnished should be that which would use the bridge if traffic were not restricted. The ADTT should be the annual average volume, not peak or seasonal;

(4) N is National Highway System Status. N = 1 if not on the National Highway System. N = 1.5 if bridge carries a National Highway System road;

(5) The last term of the rating factor expression includes the State's unobligated balance of funds received under 23 U.S.C. 144 as of June 30 preceding the date of calculation, and the total funds received under 23 U.S.C. 144 for the last four fiscal years ending with the most recent fiscal year of the FHWA's annual call for discretionary bridge candidate submittals; (if unobligated HBRRP balance is less than $10 million, use zero balance);

(6) TPC is Total Project Cost in millions of dollars;

(7) HBRRP is Highway Bridge Replacement and Rehabilitation Program;

(8) ADT′ is ADT plus ADTT.

(c) In order to balance the relative importance of candidate bridges with very low (less than one) sufficiency ratings and very low ADT's against candidate bridges with high ADT's, the minimum sufficiency rating used will be 1.0. If the computed sufficiency rating for a candidate bridge is less than 1.0, use 1.0 in the rating factor formula.

(d) If the unobligated balance of HBRRP funds for the State is less than $10 million, the HBRRP modifier is 1.0. This will limit the effect of the modifier on those States with small apportionments or those who may be accumulating funds to finance a major bridge.

[48 FR 52296, Nov. 17, 1983; 48 FR 53407, Nov. 28, 1983, as amended at 67 FR 63542, Oct. 15, 2002]

§ 650.709 Special considerations.

(a) The selection process for new discretionary bridge projects will be based upon the rating factor priority ranking. However, although not specifically included in the rating factor formula, special consideration will be given to bridges that are closed to all traffic or that have a load restriction of less than 10 tons. Consideration will also be given to bridges with other unique situations, and to bridge candidates in States that have not previously been allocated discretionary bridge funds. In addition, consideration will be given to candidates that receive additional funds or contributions from local, State, county, or private sources, but not from Federal sources which reduce the total Federal cost or Federal share of the project. These funds or contributions may be used to reduce the total project cost for use in the rating factor formula.

(b) The need to administer the program from a balanced national perspective requires that the special cases set forth in paragraph (a) of this section and other unique situations be considered in the discretionary bridge candidate evaluation process.

(c) Priority consideration will be given to the continuation and completion of projects previously begun with discretionary bridge funds which will be ready to begin construction in the fiscal year in which funds are available for obligation.

[48 FR 52296, Nov. 17, 1983, as amended at 67 FR 63543, Oct. 15, 2002]

Subpart H—Navigational Clearances for Bridges

SOURCE: 52 FR 28139, July 28, 1987, unless otherwise noted.

§ 650.801 Purpose.

The purpose of this regulation is to establish policy and to set forth coordination procedures for Federal-aid highway bridges which require navigational clearances.

§ 650.803 Policy.

It is the policy of FHWA:

(a) To provide clearances which meet the reasonable needs of navigation and provide for cost-effective highway operations,

(b) To provide fixed bridges wherever practicable, and

(c) To consider appropriate pier protection and vehicular protective and warning systems on bridges subject to ship collisions.

§ 650.805 Bridges not requiring a USCG permit.

(a) The FHWA has the responsibility under 23 U.S.C. 144(h) to determine that a USCG permit is not required for bridge construction. This determination shall be made at an early stage of project development so that any necessary coordination can be accomplished during environmental processing.

(b) A USCG permit shall not be required if the FHWA determines that the proposed construction, reconstruction, rehabilitation, or replacement of the federally aided or assisted bridge is over waters (1) which are not used or are not susceptible to use in their natural condition or by reasonable improvement as a means to transport interstate or foreign commerce and (2) which are (i) not tidal, or (ii) if tidal, used only by recreational boating, fishing, and other small vessels less than 21 feet in length.

(c) The highway agency (HA) shall assess the need for a USCG permit or navigation lights or signals for proposed bridges. The HA shall consult the appropriate District Offices of the U.S. Army Corps of Engineers if the susceptibility to improvement for navigation of the water of concern is unknown and shall consult the USCG if the types of vessels using the waterway are unknown.

(d) For bridge crossings of waterways with navigational traffic where the HA believes that a USCG permit may not be required, the HA shall provide supporting information early in the environmental analysis stage of project development to enable the FHWA to make a determination that a USCG permit is not required and that proposed navigational clearances are reasonable.

(e) Since construction in waters exempt from a USCG permit may be subject to other USCG authorizations, such as approval of navigation lights and signals and timely notice to local mariners of waterway changes, the USCG should be notified whenever the proposed action may substantially affect local navigation.

§ 650.807 Bridges requiring a USCG permit.

(a) The USCG has the responsibility (1) to determine whether a USCG permit is required for the improvement or construction of a bridge over navigable waters except for the exemption exercised by FHWA in § 650.805 and (2) to approve the bridge location, alignment and appropriate navigational clearances in all bridge permit applications.

(b) A USCG permit shall be required when a bridge crosses waters which are: (1) tidal and used by recreational boating, fishing, and other small vessels 21 feet or greater in length or (2) used or susceptible to use in their natural condition or by reasonable improvement as a means to transport interstate or foreign commerce. If it is determined that a USCG permit is required, the project shall be processed in accordance with the following procedures.

(c) The HA shall initiate coordination with the USCG at an early stage of project development and provide opportunity for the USCG to be involved throughout the environmental review process in accordance with 23 CFR part 771. The FHWA and Coast Guard have developed internal guidelines which set forth coordination procedures that both agencies have found useful in streamlining and expediting the permit approval process. These guidelines include (1) USCG/FHWA Procedures for Handling Projects which Require a USCG Permit[1] and (2) the USCG/FHWA Memorandum of Understanding on Coordinating The Preparation and Processing of Environmental Projects.[2]

(d) The HA shall accomplish sufficient preliminary design and consultation during the environmental phase of project development to investigate bridge concepts, including the feasibility of any proposed movable bridges, the horizontal and vertical clearances that may be required, and other location considerations which may affect navigation. At least one fixed bridge alternative shall be included with any proposal for a movable bridge to provide a comparative analysis of engineering, social, economic and environmental benefit and impacts.

(e) The HA shall consider hydraulic, safety, environmental and navigational needs along with highway costs when designing a proposed navigable waterway crossing.

(f) For bridges where the risk of ship collision is significant, HA's shall consider, in addition to USCG requirements, the need for pier protection and warning systems as outlined in FHWA Technical Advisory 5140.19, Pier Protection and Warning Systems for Bridges Subject to Ship Collisions, dated February 11, 1983.

(g) Special navigational clearances shall normally not be provided for accommodation of floating construction equipment of any type that is not required for navigation channel maintenance. If the navigational clearances are influenced by the needs of such equipment, the USCG should be consulted to determine the appropriate clearances to be provided.

(h) For projects which require FHWA approval of plans, specifications and estimates, preliminary bridge plans shall be approved at the appropriate level by FHWA for structural concepts,

---

[1] This document is an internal directive in the USCG Bridge Administration Manual, Enclosure 1a, COMDT INST M16590.5, change 2 dated Dec. 1, 1983. It is available for inspection and copying from the U.S. Coast Guard or the Federal Highway Administration as prescribed in 49 CFR part 7, appendices B and D.

[2] FHWA Notice 6640.22 dated July 17, 1981, is available for inspection and copying as prescribed in 49 CFR part 7, appendix D.

hydraulics, and navigational clearances prior to submission of the permit application.

(i) If the HA bid plans contain alternative designs for the same configuration (fixed or movable), the permit application shall be prepared in sufficient detail so that all alternatives can be evaluated by the USCG. If appropriate, the USCG will issue a permit for all alternatives. Within 30 days after award of the construction contract, the USCG shall be notified by the HA of the alternate which was selected. The USCG procedure for evaluating permit applications which contain alternates is presented in its Bridge Administration Manual (COMDT INST M16590.5).[3] The FHWA policy on alternates, Alternate Design for Bridges; Policy Statement, was published at 48 FR 21409 on May 12, 1983.

§ 650.809 Movable span bridges.

A fixed bridge shall be selected wherever practicable. If there are social, economic, environmental or engineering reasons which favor the selection of a movable bridge, a cost benefit analysis to support the need for the movable bridge shall he prepared as a part of the preliminary plans.

PART 652—PEDESTRIAN AND BICYCLE ACCOMMODATIONS AND PROJECTS

AUTHORITY: 23 U.S.C. 109, 217, 315, 402(b)(1)(F); 49 CFR 1.48(b).

SOURCE: 49 FR 10662, Mar. 22, 1984, unless otherwise noted.

§ 652.1 Purpose.

To provide policies and procedures relating to the provision of pedestrian and bicycle accommodations on Federal-aid projects, and Federal participation in the cost of these accommodations and projects.

§ 652.3 Definitions.

(a) *Bicycle.* A vehicle having two tandem wheels, propelled solely by human power, upon which any person or persons may ride.

(b) *Bikeway.* Any road, path, or way which in some manner is specifically designated as being open to bicycle travel, regardless of whether such facilities are designated for the exclusive use of bicycles or are to be shared with other transportation modes.

(c) *Bicycle path (bike path).* A bikeway physically separated from motorized vehicular traffic by an open space or barrier and either within the highway right-of-way or within an independent right-of-way.

(d) *Bicycle lane (bike lane).* A portion of a roadway which has been designated by striping, signing and pavement markings for the preferential or exclusive use of bicyclists.

(e) *Bicycle route (bike route).* A segment of a system of bikeways designated by the jurisdiction having authority with appropriate directional and informational markers, with or without a specific bicycle route number.

(f) *Shared roadway.* Any roadway upon which a bicycle lane is not designated and which may be legally used by bicycles regardless of whether such facility is specifically designated as a bikeway.

(g) *Pedestrian walkway or walkway.* A continuous way designated for pedestrians and separated from the through lanes for motor vehicles by space or barrier.

(h) *Highway construction project.* A project financed in whole or in part with Federal-aid or Federal funds for the construction, reconstruction or improvement of a highway or portions thereof, including bridges and tunnels.

(i) *Independent bicycle construction project (independent bicycle project).* A project designation used to distinguish a bicycle facility constructed independently and primarily for use by bicyclists from an improvement included as an incidental part of a highway construction project.

[3] United States Coast Guard internal directives are available for inspection and copying as prescribed in 49 CFR part 7, appendix B.

(j) *Independent pedestrian walkway construction project (independent walkway project).* A project designation used to distinguish a walkway constructed independently and solely as a pedestrian walkway project from a pedestrian improvement included as an incidental part of a highway construction project.

(k) *Incidental bicycle or pedestrian walkway construction project (incidental feature).* One constructed as an incidental part of a highway construction project.

(l) *Nonconstruction bicycle project.* A bicycle project not involving physical construction which enhances the safe use of bicycles for transportation purposes.

(m) *Snowmobile.* A motorized vehicle solely designed to operate on snow or ice.

§652.5 Policy.

The safe accommodation of pedestrians and bicyclists should be given full consideration during the development of Federal-aid highway projects, and during the construction of such projects. The special needs for the elderly and the handicapped shall be considered in all Federal-aid projects that include pedestrian facilities. Where current or anticipated pedestrian and/or bicycle traffic presents a potential conflict with motor vehicle traffic, every effort shall be made to minimize the detrimental effects on all highway users who share the facility. On highways without full control of access where a bridge deck is being replaced or rehabilitated, and where bicycles are permitted to operate at each end, the bridge shall be reconstructed so that bicycles can be safely accommodated when it can be done at a reasonable cost. Consultation with local groups of organized bicyclists is to be encouraged in the development of bicycle projects.

§652.7 Eligibility.

(a) Independent bicycle projects, incidental bicycle projects, and nonconstruction bicycle projects must be principally for transportation rather than recreational use and must meet the project conditions for authorization where applicable.

(b) The implementation of pedestrian and bicycle accommodations may be authorized for Federal-aid participation as either incidental features of highways or as independent projects where all of the following conditions are satisfied.

(1) The safety of the motorist, bicyclist, and/or pedestrian will be enhanced by the project.

(2) The project is initiated or supported by the appropriate State highway agency(ies) and/or the Federal land management agency. Projects are to be located and designed pursuant to an overall plan, which provides due consideration for safety and contiguous routes.

(3) A public agency has formally agreed to:

(i) Accept the responsibility for the operation and maintenance of the facility,

(ii) Ban all motorized vehicles other than maintenance vehicles, or snowmobiles where permitted by State or local regulations, from pedestrian walkways and bicycle paths, and

(iii) Ban parking, except in the case of emergency, from bicycle lanes that are contiguous to traffic lanes.

(4) The estimated cost of the project is consistent with the anticipated benefits to the community.

(5) The project will be designed in substantial conformity with the latest official design criteria. (See §652.13.)

[49 FR 10662, Mar. 22, 1984; 49 FR 14729, Apr. 13, 1984]

§652.9 Federal participation.

(a) Independent walkway projects, independent bicycle projects and nonconstruction bicycle projects shall be financed with 100 percent Federal-aid primary, secondary or urban highway funds, provided the total amount obligated for all such projects in any one State in any fiscal year does not exceed $4.5 million of Federal-aid funds or a lesser amount apportioned by the Federal Highway Administrator to avoid exceeding the annual $45 million cost limitation on these projects for all States in a fiscal year. The Federal Highway Administrator may, upon application, waive this limitation for a State for any fiscal year. This limitation also applies to projects funded under § 652.9(d). This limitation does not apply to projects of the type described in § 652.9(c). The FHWA Offices of Direct Federal Programs and Engineering will coordinate projects of the type described in § 652.9(d) to ensure that the annual cost limitations will not be exceeded.

(b) Specific eligibility requirements for Federal-aid participation in independent and nonconstruction projects are:

(1) An independent walkway project must be constructed on highway right-of-way or easement, or right-of-way acquired for this purpose. Independent walkway projects may be constructed separately or in conjunction with a Federal-aid highway construction project. Where an independent walkway project is located away from the Federal-aid highway right-of-way, it must serve pedestrians who would normally desire to use the Federal-aid route.

(2) An independent bicycle project may include the acquisition of land needed for the facility, or such projects may be constructed on existing highway right-of-way or easement acquired for this purpose. Independent bicycle projects may include construction of bicycle lanes, paths, shelters, bicycle parking facilities and other roadway and bridge work necessary to accommodate bicyclists.

(3) Nonconstruction bicycle projects must be related to the safe use of bicycles for transportation, and may include safety educational material and route maps for safe bicycle transportation purposes. Nonconstruction bicycle projects shall not include salaries for administration, law enforcement, maintenance and similar items required to operate transportation networks and programs, but may include cost of staff or consultants for development of specific nonconstruction projects.

(c) Bicycle and pedestrian accommodations may also be constructed as incidental features of highway construction projects. These incidental features may be financed with the same type of Federal-aid funds, including funds of the type described in § 652.9(d) (except Interstate construction funds) and at the same Federal share payable as a basic highway project. These accommodations are not subject to the funding limitations for independent walkway, independent bicycle and nonconstruction bicycle projects. In the case of the Interstate construction projects, Federal-aid Interstate construction funds may only be used to replace existing facilities that would be interrupted by construction of the project, or to mitigate specific environmental impacts. Interstate 4R funds provided by 23 U.S.C. 104(b)(5)(B) may be used only for incidental features. As incidental features, these accommodations must be part of a highway improvement and must be located within the right-of-way of the highway, including land acquired under 23 U.S.C. 319 (Scenic Enhancement Program).

(d) Funds authorized for Federal lands highways (forest highways, public lands highways, park roads, parkways, and Indian reservation roads which are public roads), forest development roads and trails (*i.e.*, roads or trails under the jurisdiction of the Forest Service), and public lands development roads and trails (*i.e.*, roads or trails which the Secretary of the Interior determines are of primary importance for the development, protection, administration, and utilization of public lands and resources under his/her control), may be used for independent bicycle routes and independent walkway projects. These funds may not be used for nonconstruction bicycle projects.

§ 652.11 Planning.

Federally aided bicycle and pedestrian projects implemented within urbanized areas must be included in the transportation improvement program/annual (or biennial) element unless excluded by agreement between the State and the metropolitan planning organization.

§ 652.13 Design and construction criteria.

(a) The American Association of State Highway and Transportation Officials' "Guide for Development of New Bicycle Facilities, 1981" (AASHTO Guide) or equivalent guides developed in cooperation with State or local officials and acceptable to the division office of the FHWA, shall be used as standards for the construction and design of bicycle routes. Copies of the AASHTO Guide may be obtained from the American Association of State Highway and Transportation Officials, 444 North Capitol Street, NW., Suite 225, Washington, DC 20001.

(b) Curb cuts and other provisions as may be appropriate for the handicapped are required on all Federal and Federal-aid projects involving the provision of curbs or sidewalks at all pedestrian crosswalks.

PART 655—TRAFFIC OPERATIONS

Subparts A–E [Reserved]

Subpart F—Traffic Control Devices on Federal-Aid and Other Streets and Highways

Subpart G [Reserved]

AUTHORITY: 23 U.S.C. 101(a), 104, 109(d), 114(a), 217, 315, and 402(a); 23 CFR 1.32; and 49 CFR 1.48(b).

Subparts A–E [Reserved]

Subpart F—Traffic Control Devices on Federal-Aid and Other Streets and Highways

SOURCE: 48 FR 46776, Oct. 14, 1983, unless otherwise noted.

§ 655.601 Purpose.

To prescribe the policies and procedures of the Federal Highway Administration (FHWA) to obtain basic uniformity of traffic control devices on all streets and highways in accordance with the following references that are approved by the FHWA for application on Federal-aid projects:

(a) MUTCD.

(b) AASHTO Guide to Metric Conversion.

(c) AASHTO Traffic Engineering Metric Conversion Factors.

(d) The standards required in this section are incorporated by reference into this section in accordance with 5 U.S.C. 552(a) and 1 CFR part 51. To enforce any edition other than that specified in this section, the FHWA must publish notice of change in the FEDERAL REGISTER and the material must be available to the public. All approved material is available for inspection at the Federal Highway Administration, Office of Transportation Operations, 1200 New Jersey Avenue SE., Washington, DC 20590, (202) 366–8043 and is available from the sources listed below. It is also available for inspection at the National Archives and Records Administration (NARA). For information on the availability of this material at NARA call (202) 741–6030, or go to *http://www.archives.gov/federal-register/cfr/index.html.*

(1) AASHTO, American Association of State Highway and Transportation Officials, Suite 249, 444 North Capitol Street NW., Washington, DC 20001

(i) AASHTO Guide to Metric Conversion, 1993;

(ii) AASHTO, Traffic Engineering Metric Conversion Factors, 1993—Addendum to the Guide to Metric Conversion, October 1993.

(2) FHWA, Federal Highway Administration, 1200 New Jersey Avenue SE., Washington, DC 20590, telephone (202) 366–1993, also available at *http://mutcd.fhwa.dot.gov.*

(i) Manual on Uniform Traffic Control Devices for Streets and Highways (MUTCD), 2009 Edition, including Revisions No. 1 and No. 2, FHWA, dated May 2012.

(ii) [Reserved]

[77 FR 28466, May 14, 2012]

§ 655.602 Definitions.

The terms used herein are defined in accordance with definitions and usages contained in the MUTCD and 23 U.S.C. 101(a).

§ 655.603 Standards.

(a) *National MUTCD.* The MUTCD approved by the Federal Highway Administrator is the national standard for all traffic control devices installed on any street, highway, or bicycle trail open to public travel in accordance with 23 U.S.C. 109(d) and 402(a). For the purpose of MUTCD applicability, open to public travel includes toll roads and roads within shopping centers, airports, sports arenas, and other similar business and/or recreation facilities that are privately owned but where the public is allowed to travel without access restrictions. Except for gated toll roads, roads within private gated properties where access is restricted at all times are not included in this definition. Parking areas, driving aisles within parking areas, and private highway-rail grade crossings are also not included in this definition.

(b) *State or other Federal MUTCD.* (1) Where State or other Federal agency MUTCDs or supplements are required, they shall be in substantial conformance with the National MUTCD. Substantial conformance means that the State MUTCD or supplement shall conform as a minimum to the standard statements included in the National MUTCD. The FHWA Division Administrators and Associate Administrator for the Federal Lands Highway Program may grant exceptions in cases where a State MUTCD or supplement cannot conform to standard statements in the National MUTCD because of the requirements of a specific State law that was in effect prior to the effective date of this final rule, provided that the Division Administrator or Associate Administrator determines based on information available and documentation received from the State that the non-conformance does not create a safety concern. The guidance statements contained in the National MUTCD shall also be in the State Manual or supplement unless the reason for not including it is satisfactorily explained based on engineering judgment, specific conflicting State law, or a documented engineering study. The FHWA Division Administrators shall approve the State MUTCDs and supplements that are in substantial conformance with the National MUTCD. The FHWA AssociateAdministrator of the Federal Lands Highway Program shall approve other Federal land management agencies MUTCDs and supplements that are in substantial conformance with the National MUTCD. The FHWA Division Administrators and the FHWA Associate Administrators for the Federal Lands Highway Program have the flexibility to determine on a case-by-case basis the degree of variation allowed.

(2) States and other Federal agencies are encouraged to adopt the National MUTCD in its entirety as their official Manual on Uniform Traffic Control Devices.

(3) States and other Federal agencies shall adopt changes issued by the FHWA to the National MUTCD within two years from the effective date of the final rule. For those States that automatically adopt the MUTCD immediately upon the effective date of the latest edition or revision of the MUTCD, the FHWA Division Administrators have the flexibility to allow these States to install certain devices from existing inventory or previously approved construction plans that comply with the previous MUTCD during the two-year adoption period.

(c) *Color specifications.* Color determinations and specifications of sign and pavement marking materials shall conform to requirements of the FHWA Color Tolerance Charts.[1] An alternate method of determining the color of retroreflective sign material is provided in the appendix.

(d) *Compliance*—(1) *Existing highways.* Each State, in cooperation with its political subdivisions, and Federal agency shall have a program as required by 23 U.S.C. 402(a), which shall include provisions for the systematic upgrading of substandard traffic control devices and for the installation of needed devices to achieve conformity with the MUTCD. The FHWA may establish target dates of achieving compliance with changes to specific devices in the MUTCD.

[1] Available for inspection from the Office of Traffic Operations, Federal Highway Administration, 1200 New Jersey Avenue, SE., Washington, DC.

(2) *New or reconstructed highways.* Federal-aid projects for the construction, reconstruction, resurfacing, restoration, or rehabilitation of streets and highways shall not be opened to the public for unrestricted use until all appropriate traffic control devices, either temporary or permanent, are installed and functioning properly. Both temporary and permanent devices shall conform to the MUTCD.

(3) *Construction area activities.* All traffic control devices installed in construction areas using Federal-aid funds shall conform to the MUTCD. Traffic control plans for handling traffic and pedestrians in construction zones and for protection of workers shall conform to the requirements of 23 CFR part 630, subpart J, Traffic Safety in Highway and Street Work Zones.

[48 FR 46776, Oct. 14, 1983, as amended at 51 FR 16834, May 7, 1986; 68 FR 14139, Mar. 24, 2003; 71 FR 75115, Dec. 14, 2006; 74 FR 28442, June 16, 2009; 74 FR 66861, Dec. 16, 2009]

§ 655.604 Achieving basic uniformity.

(a) *Programs.* Programs for the orderly and systematic upgrading of existing traffic control devices or the installation of needed traffic control devices on or off the Federal-aid system should be based on inventories made in accordance with the Highway Safety Program Guideline 21, "Roadway Safety." These inventories provide the information necessary for programming traffic control device upgrading projects.

(b) *Inventory.* An inventory of all traffic control devices is recommended in the Highway Safety Program Guideline 21, "Roadway Safety." Highway planning and research funds and highway related safety grant program funds may be used in statewide or systemwide studies or inventories. Also, metropolitan planning (PL) funds may be used in urbanized areas provided the activity is included in an approved unified work program.

[48 FR 46776, Oct. 14, 1983, as amended at 71 FR 75115, Dec. 14, 2006]

§ 655.605 Project procedures.

(a) *Federal-aid highways.* Federal-aid projects involving the installation of traffic control devices shall follow procedures as established in 23 CFR part 630, subpart A, Federal-Aid Programs Approval and Project Authorization. Simplified and timesaving procedures are to be used to the extent permitted by existing policy.

(b) *Off-system highways.* Certain federally funded programs are available for installation of traffic control devices on streets and highways that are not on the Federal-aid system. The procedures used in these programs may vary from project to project but, essentially, the guidelines set forth herein should be used.

§ 655.606 Higher cost materials.

The use of signing, pavement marking, and signal materials (or equipment) having distinctive performance characteristics, but costing more than other materials (or equipment) commonly used may be approved by the FHWA Division Administrator when the specific use proposed is considered to be in the public interest.

§ 655.607 Funding.

(a) *Federal-aid highways.* (1) Funds apportioned or allocated under 23 U.S.C. 104(b) are eligible to participate in projects to install traffic control devices in accordance with the MUTCD on newly constructed, reconstructed, resurfaced, restored, or rehabilitated highways, or on existing highways when this work is classified as construction in accordance with 23 U.S.C. 101(a). Federal-aid highway funds for eligible pavement markings and traffic control signalization may amount to 100 percent of the construction cost. Federal-aid highway funds apportioned or allocated under other sections of 23 U.S.C. are eligible for participation in improvements conforming to the MUTCD in accordance with the provisions of applicable program regulations and directives.

(2) Traffic control devices are eligible, in keeping with paragraph (a)(1) of this section, provided that the work is classified as construction in accordance with 23 U.S.C. 101(a) and the State or local agency has a policy acceptable to the FHWA Division Administrator for selecting traffic control devices material or equipment based on items such as cost, traffic volumes, safety, and expected service life. The State's

policy should provide for cost-effective selection of materials which will provide for substantial service life taking into account expected and necessary routine maintenance. For these purposes, effectiveness would normally be measured in terms of durability, service life and/or performance of the material. Specific projects including material or equipment selection shall be developed in accordance with this policy. Proposed work may be approved on a project-by-project basis when the work is (i) clearly warranted, (ii) on a Federal-aid system, (iii) clearly identified by site, (iv) substantial in nature, and (v) of sufficient magnitude at any given location to warrant Federal-aid participation as a construction item.

(3) The method of accomplishing the work will be in accordance with 23 CFR part 635, subpart A, Contract Procedures.

(b) *Off-system highways.* Certain Federal-aid highway funds are eligible to participate in traffic control device improvement projects on off-system highways. In addition, Federal-aid highway funds apportioned or allocated in 23 U.S.C. are eligible for the installation of traffic control devices on any public road not on the Federal-aid system when the installation is directly related to a traffic improvement project on a Federal-aid system route.

APPENDIX TO SUBPART F OF PART 655—ALTERNATE METHOD OF DETERMINING THE COLOR OF RETROREFLECTIVE SIGN MATERIALS AND PAVEMENT MARKING MATERIALS

1. Although the FHWA Color Tolerance Charts depreciate the use of spectrophotometers or accurate tristimulus colorimeters for measuring the daytime color of retroreflective materials, recent testing has determined that 0/45 or 45/0 spectroradiometers and tristimulus colorimeters have proved that the measurements can be considered reliable and may be used.

2. The daytime color of non-fluorescent retroreflective materials may be measured in accordance with ASTM Test Method E1349, "Standard Test Method for Reflectance Factor and Color by Spectrophotometry Using Bidirectional Geometry" or ASTM Test Method E 1347 (Replaces E97), "Standard Test Method for Color and Color-Difference Measurement by Tristimulus (Filter) Colorimetry." The latter test method specified bidirectional geometry for the measurement of retroreflective materials. The geometric conditions to be used in both test methods are 0/45 or 45/0 circumferential illumination or viewing. Uniplanar geometry is not recommended for material types IV or higher (designated microprismatic). The CIE standard illuminant used in computing the colorimetric coordinates shall be D_{65} and the 2 Degree Standard CIE observer shall be used.

3. For fluorescent retroreflective materials ASTM E991 may be used to determine the chromaticity provided that the D_{65} illumination meets the requirements of E 991. This practice, however, allows only the total luminous factor to be measured. The fluorescent luminous factor must be determined using bispectral fluorescent colorimetry. Commercial instruments are available which allow such determination. Some testing laboratories are also equipped to perform these measurements.

4. For nighttime measurements CIE Standard Illuminant A shall be used in computing the colorimetric coordinates and the 2 Degree Standard CIE Observer shall be used.

5. Average performance sheeting is identified as Types I and II sheeting and high performance sheeting is identified as Type III. Super-high intensity sheeting is identified as Types V, VI, and VII in ASTM D 4956.

6. The following nine tables depict the 1931 CIE Chromaticity Diagram x and y coordinates for the corner points defining the recommended color boxes in the diagram and the daytime luminance factors for those colors. Lines drawn between these corner points specify the limits of the chromaticity allowed in the 1931 Chromaticity Diagram. Color coordinates of samples that lie within these lines are acceptable. For blue and green colors the spectrum locus is the defining limit between the corner points located on the spectrum locus:

TABLE 1 TO APPENDIX TO PART 655, SUBPART F—DAYTIME COLOR SPECIFICATION LIMITS FOR RETROREFLECTIVE MATERIAL WITH CIE 2° STANDARD OBSERVER AND 45/0 (0/45) GEOMETRY AND CIE STANDARD ILLUMINANT D_{65}.

Color	Chromaticity Coordinates							
	1		2		3		4	
	x	y	x	y	y	x	x	y
White	0.303	0.300	0.368	0.366	0.340	0.393	0.274	0.329
Red	0.648	0.351	0.735	0.265	0.629	0.281	0.565	0.346
Orange	0.558	0.352	0.636	0.364	0.570	0.429	0.506	0.404
Brown	0.430	0.340	0.430	0.390	0.518	0.434	0.570	0.382
Yellow	0.498	0.412	0.557	0.442	0.479	0.520	0.438	0.472
Green	0.026	0.399	0.166	0.364	0.286	0.446	0.207	0.771
Blue	0.078	0.171	0.150	0.220	0.210	0.160	0.137	0.038
Light Blue	0.180	0.260	0.240	0.300	0.270	0.260	0.230	0.200
Purple	0.302	0.064	0.310	0.210	0.380	0.255	0.468	0.140

TABLE 1A TO APPENDIX TO PART 655, SUBPART F—DAYTIME LUMINANCE FACTORS (%) FOR RETROREFLECTIVE MATERIAL WITH CIE 2° STANDARD OBSERVER AND 45/0 (0/45) GEOMETRY AND CIE STANDARD ILLUMINANT D_{65}.

Color	Daytime Luminance Factor (Y %) by ASTM Type					
	Types I, II, III and VI		Types IV, VII, and VIII		Type V	
	Minimum	Maximum	Minimum	Maximum	Minimum	Maximum
White	27	....	40	....	15	....
Red	2.5	12	3.0	15	2.5	11
Orange	14	30	12	30	7.0	25
Brown	4.0	9.0	1.0	6.0	1.0	9.0
Yellow	15	45	24	45	12	30
Green	3.0	9.0	3.0	12	2.5	11
Blue	1.0	10	1.0	10	1.0	10
Light Blue	12	40	18	40	8.0	25
Purple	2.0	10	2.0	10	2.0	10

TABLE 2 TO APPENDIX TO PART 655, SUBPART F—NIGHTTIME COLOR SPECIFICATION LIMITS FOR RETROREFLECTIVE MATERIAL WITH CIE 2° STANDARD OBSERVER AND OBSERVATION ANGLE OF 0.33°, ENTRANCE ANGLE OF + 5° AND CIE STANDARD ILLUMINANT A.

Color	Chromaticity Coordinates							
	1		2		3		4	
	x	*y*	*x*	*y*	*x*	*y*	*x*	*y*
White	0.475	0.452	0.360	0.415	0.392	0.370	0.515	0.409
Red	0.650	0.348	0.620	0.348	0.712	0.2550	0.735	0.265
Orange	0.595	0.405	0.565	0.405	0.613	0.355	0.643	0.355
Brown	0.595	0.405	0.540	0.405	0.570	0.365	0.643	0.355
Yellow	0.513	0.487	0.500	0.4700	0.545	0.425	0.572	0.425
Green	0.007	0.570	0.200	0.500	0.322	0.590	0.193	0.782
Blue	0.033	0.370	0.180	0.370	0.230	0.240	0.091	0.133
Purple	0.355	0.088	0.385	0.288	0.500	0.350	0.635	0.221
Light Blue	Chromaticity coordinates are yet to be determined.							

NOTE: Materials used as High-Conspicuity, Retroreflective Traffic Signage Materials shall meet the requirements for Daytime Color Specification Limits, Daytime Luminance Factors and Nighttime Color Specification Limits for Fluorescent Retroreflective Material, as described in Tables 3, 3a, and 4, throughout the service life of the sign.

TABLE 3 TO APPENDIX TO PART 655, SUBPART F—DAYTIME COLOR SPECIFICATION LIMITS FOR FLUORESCENT RETROREFLECTIVE MATERIAL WITH CIE 2° STANDARD OBSERVER AND 45/0 (0/45) GEOMETRY AND CIE STANDARD ILLUMINANT D_{65}.

Color	Chromaticity Coordinates							
	1		2		3		4	
	x	y	x	y	x	y	x	y
Fluorescent Orange	0.583	0.416	0.535	0.400	0.595	0.351	0.645	0.355
Fluorescent Yellow	0.479	0.520	0.446	0.483	0.512	0.421	0.557	0.442
Fluorescent Yellow-Green	0.387	0.610	0.369	.546	.428	.496	0.460	0.540
Fluorescent Green	0.210	0.770	0.232	0.656	0.320	0.590	0.320	0.675
Fluorescent Pink	0.450	0.270	0.590	0.350	0.644	0.290	0.536	0.230
Fluorescent Red	0.666	0.334	0.613	0.333	0.671	0.275	9.735	0.265

TABLE 3A TO APPENDIX TO PART 655, SUBPART F—DAYTIME LUMINANCE FACTORS (%) FOR FLUORESCENT RETROREFLECTIVE MATERIAL WITH CIE 2° STANDARD OBSERVER AND 45/0 (0/45) GEOMETRY AND CIE STANDARD ILLUMINANT D_{65}.

Color	Luminance Factor Limits (Y)		
	Min	Max	Y_F*
Fluorescent Orange	25	None	15
Fluorescent Yellow	45	None	20
Fluorescent Yellow-Green	60	None	20
Fluorescent Green	20	30	12
Fluorescent Pink	25	None	15
Fluorescent Red	20	30	15

*Fluorescence luminance factors (YF) are typical values, and are provided for quality assurance purposes only. YF shall not be used as a measure of performance during service.

TABLE 4 TO APPENDIX TO PART 655, SUBPART F—NIGHTTIME COLOR SPECIFICATION LIMITS FOR FLUORESCENT RETROREFLECTIVE MATERIAL WITH CIE 2° STANDARD OBSERVER AND OBSERVATION ANGLE OF 0.33°, ENTRANCE ANGLE OF + 5° AND CIE STANDARD ILLUMINANT A.

Color	Chromaticity Coordinates							
	1		2		3		4	
	x	y	x	y	x	y	x	y
Fluorescent Orange	0.625	0.375	0.589	0.376	0.636	0.330	0.669	0.331
Fluorescent Yellow	0.554	0.445	0.526	0.437	0.569	0.394	0.610	0.390
Fluorescent Yellow-Green	0.480	0.520	0.473	0.490	0.523	0.440	0.550	0.449
Fluorescent Green	0.007	0.570	0.200	0.500	0.322	0.590	0.193	0.782
Fluorescent Red	0.680	0.320	0.645	0.320	0.712	0.253	0.735	0.265

TABLE 5 TO APPENDIX TO PART 655, SUBPART F—DAYTIME COLOR SPECIFICATION LIMITS FOR RETROREFLECTIVE PAVEMENT MARKING MATERIAL WITH CIE 2° STANDARD OBSERVER AND 45/0 (0/45) GEOMETRY AND CIE STANDARD ILLUMINANT D_{65}.

Color	Chromaticity Coordinates							
	1		2		3		4	
	x	y	x	y	x	y	x	y
White	0.355	0.355	0.305	0.305	0.285	0.325	0.335	0.375
Yellow	0.560	0.440	0.490	0.510	0.420	0.440	0.460	0.400
Red	0.480	0.300	0.690	0.315	0.620	0.380	0.480	0.360
Blue	0.105	0.100	0.220	0.180	0.200	0.260	0.060	0.220
Purple	0.300	0.064	0.309	0.260	0.362	0.295	0.475	0.144

TABLE 5A TO APPENDIX TO PART 655, SUBPART F—DAYTIME LUMINANCE FACTORS (%) FOR RETROREFLECTIVE PAVEMENT MARKING MATERIAL WITH CIE 2° STANDARD OBSERVER AND 45/0 (0/45) GEOMETRY AND CIE STANDARD ILLUMINANT D_{65}.

Color	Luminance Factor (Y%)	
	Minimum	Maximum
White	35	
Yellow	25	
Red	6	15
Blue	5	14
Purple	5	15

TABLE 6 TO APPENDIX TO PART 655, SUBPART F—NIGHTIME COLOR SPECIFICATION LIMITS FOR RETROREFLECTIVE PAVEMENT MARKING MATERIAL WITH CIE 2° STANDARD OBSERVER, OBSERVATION ANGLE OF 1.05°, ENTRANCE ANGLE OF + 88.76° AND CIE STANDARD ILLUMINANT A.

Color	Chromaticity Coordinates							
	1		2		3		4	
	x	y	x	y	x	y	x	y
White	0.480	0.410	0.430	0.380	0.405	0.405	0.455	0.435
Yellow	0.575	0.425	0.508	0.415	0.473	0.453	0.510	0.490
Purple	0.338	0.080	0.425	0.365	0.470	0.385	0.635	0.221

NOTE: Luminance factors for retroreflective pavement marking materials are for materials as they are intended to be used. For paint products, that means inclusion of glass beads and/or other retroreflective components.

[67 FR 49572, July 31, 2002, as amended at 67 FR 70163, Nov. 21, 2002; 68 FR 65582, 65583, Nov. 20, 2003; 74 FR 66862, 66863, Dec. 16, 2009]

EDITORIAL NOTE: At 74 FR 66862, Dec. 16, 2009, the appendix to subpart F was amended in Table 3 by revising the daytime chromaticity coordinates for the color Fluorescent Pink; however, the amendment could not be incorporated due to inaccurate amendatory instruction.

Subpart G [Reserved]

PART 656—CARPOOL AND VANPOOL PROJECTS

AUTHORITY: 23 U.S.C. 146 and 315; sec. 126 of the Surface Transportation Assistance Act of 1978, Pub. L. 95–599, 92 Stat. 2689; 49 CFR 1.48(b).

SOURCE: 47 FR 43024, Sept. 30, 1982, unless otherwise noted.

§ 656.1 Purpose.

The purpose of this regulation is to prescribe policies and general procedures for administering a program of ridesharing projects using Federal-aid primary, secondary, and urban system funds.

§ 656.3 Policy.

Section 126(d) of the Surface Transportation Assistance Act of 1978 declares that special effort should be made to promote commuter modes of transportation which conserve energy, reduce pollution, and reduce traffic congestion.

§ 656.5 Eligibility.

(a) Projects which promote ridesharing programs need not be located on but must serve a Federal-aid system to be eligible for Federal-aid primary, secondary, or urban system funds depending on the system served. The Federal share payable will be in accordance with the provisions of 23 U.S.C. 120. Except for paragraph (c)(3) of this section, for all purposes of this regulation the term *carpool* includes *vanpool*.

(b) Projects shall not be approved under this regulation if they will have an adverse effect on any mass transportation system.

(c) The following types of projects and work are considered eligible under this program:

(1) Systems, whether manual or computerized, for locating potential participants in carpools and informing them of the opportunities for participation. Eligible costs for such systems may include costs of use or rental of computer hardware, costs of software, and installation costs (including both labor and other related items).

(2) Specialized procedures to provide carpooling opportunities to elderly or handicapped persons.

(3) The costs of acquiring vanpool vehicles and actual financial losses that occur when the operation of any vanpool is aborted before the scheduled termination date for the reason, concurred in by the State, that its continuation is no longer productive. The cost of acquiring a vanpool vehicle is eligible under the following conditions:

(i) The vanpool vehicle is a four-wheeled vehicle manufactured for use on public highways for transportation of 7–15 passengers (no passenger cars which do not meet the 7–15 criteria and no buses); and

(ii) Provision is made for repayment of the acquisition cost to the project within the passenger-service life of the vehicle. Repayment may be accomplished through the charging of a reasonable user fee based on an estimated number of riders per vehicle and the cost of reasonable vehicle depreciation, operation, and maintenance. Repayment is not required under the following conditions:

(A) When vehicles are purchased as demonstrator vans for use as a marketing device. Vehicles procured for this purpose should be used to promote the vanpool concept among employees, employers, and other groups by allowing potential riders and sponsors to examine commuter vans; or

(B) When vehicles are purchased for use on a trial commuting basis to enable people to experience vanpooling first hand. The trial period must be limited to a maximum of 2 months. That part of the user fee normally collected to cover the capital or ownership cost of the van would be eligible for reimbursement as a promotional cost during the limited trial period. As with established vanpool service, all vehicle operating costs must be borne by the user(s) during the trial period.

(4) Work necessary to designate existing highway lanes as preferential carpool lanes or bus and carpool lanes. Eligible work may include preliminary engineering to determine traffic flow and design criteria, signing, pavement markings, traffic control devices, and minor physical modifications to permit the use of designated lanes as preferential carpool lanes or bus and carpool lanes. Such improvements on any public road may be approved if such projects facilitate more efficient use of any Federal-aid highway. Eligible costs may also include costs of initial inspection or monitoring of use, including special equipment, to ensure that the high occupancy vehicle (HOV) lanes designation is effective and that the project is fully developed and operating properly. While no fixed time limit is being arbitrarily prescribed for the inspection and monitoring period, it is intended that this activity be conducted as soon as possible to evaluate the effectiveness of the project and does not extend indefinitely nor become a part of routine facility operations.

(5) Signing of and modifications to existing facilities to provide preferential parking for carpools inside or outside the central business district. Eligible costs may include trail blazers, on-site signs designating highway interchange areas or other existing publicly or privately owned facilities as preferential parking for carpool participants, and initial or renewal costs for leasing parking space or acquisition or easements or restrictions, as, for example, at shopping centers and public or private parking facilities. The lease or acquisition cost may be computed on the demonstrated reduction in the overall number of vehicles using the designated portion of a commercial facility, but not on a reduction of the per-vehicle user charge for parking.

(6) Construction of carpool parking facilities outside the central business district. Eligible costs may include acquisition of land and normal construction activities, including installation of lighting and fencing, trail blazers, on-site signing, and passenger shelters. Such facilities need not be located in conjunction with any existing or planned mass transportation service,

but should be designed so that the facility could accommodate mass transportation in the event such service may be developed. Except for the requirement of the availability of mass/public transportation facilities, fringe parking construction under this section shall be subject to the provisions of 23 CFR part 810.106.

(7) Reasonable public information and promotion expenses, including personnel costs, incurred in connection with any of the other eligible items mentioned herein.

§ 656.7 Determination of an exception.

(a) The FHWA has determined under provisions of 23 U.S.C. 146(b) that an exceptional situation exists in regard to the funding of carpools so as to allow the State to contribute as its share of the non-Federal match essential project-related work and services performed by local agencies and private organizations when approved and authorized in accordance with regular Federal-aid procedures. The cost of such work must be properly valued, supportable and verifiable in order for inclusion as an eligible project cost. Examples of such contributed work and services include: public service announcements, computer services, and project-related staff time for administration by employees of public and private organizations.

(b) This determination is based on: (1) The nature of carpool projects to provide a variety of services to the public; (2) the fact that carpool projects are labor intensive and require professional and specialized technical skills; (3) the extensive use of joint public and private endeavors; and (4) the fact that project costs involve the acquisition of capital equipment as opposed to construction of fixed items.

(c) This exception is limited to carpool projects and therefore is not applicable to other Federal-aid projects. The exception does not affect or replace the standard Federal-aid funding procedures or real property acquisition procedures and requirements, part 712, The Acquisition Function.

PART 657—CERTIFICATION OF SIZE AND WEIGHT ENFORCEMENT

AUTHORITY: 23 U.S.C. 127, 141 and 315; 49 U.S.C. 31111, 31113 and 31114; sec. 1023, Pub. L. 102–240, 105 Stat. 1914; and 49 CFR 1.48(b)(19), (b)(23), (c)(1) and (c)(19).

SOURCE: 45 FR 52368, Aug. 7, 1980; 62 FR 62261, Nov. 21, 1997, unless otherwise noted.

NOTE: The recordkeeping requirements contained in this part have been approved by the Office of Management and Budget under control number 2125–0034.

§ 657.1 Purpose.

To prescribe requirements for administering a program of vehicle size and weight enforcement on the Interstate System, and those routes which, prior to October 1, 1991, were designated as part of the Federal-aid primary, Federal-aid secondary, or Federal-aid urban systems, including the required annual certification by the State.

[72 FR 7747, Feb. 20, 2007]

§ 657.3 Definitions.

Unless otherwise specified in this part, the definitions in 23 U.S.C. 101(a) are applicable to this part. As used in this part:

Enforcing or *Enforcement* means all actions by the State to obtain compliance with size and weight requirements by all vehicles operating on the Interstate System and those roads which, prior to October 1, 1991, were designated as part of the Federal-aid Primary, Federal-aid Secondary, or Federal-aid Urban Systems.

Urbanized area means an area with a population of 50,000 or more.

[72 FR 7747, Feb. 20, 2007]

§ 657.5 Policy.

Federal Highway Administration (FHWA) policy is that each State enforce vehicle size and weight laws to assure that violations are discouraged and that vehicles traversing the highway system do not exceed the limits specified by law. These size and weight limits are based upon design specifications and safety considerations, and enforcement shall be developed and maintained both to prevent premature deterioration of the highway pavement and structures and to provide a safe driving environment.

§ 657.7 Objective.

The objective of this regulation is the development and operation by each State of an enforcement process which identifies vehicles of excessive size and weight and provides a systematic approach to eliminate violations and thus improve conditions.

§ 657.9 Formulation of a plan for enforcement.

(a) Each State shall develop a plan for the maintenance of an effective enforcement process. The plan shall describe the procedures, resources, and facilities which the State intends to devote to the enforcement of its vehicle size and weight laws. Each State plan must be accepted by the FHWA and will then serve as a basis by which the annual certification of enforcement will be judged for adequacy.

(b) The plan shall discuss the following subjects:

(1) *Facilities and resources.* (i) No program shall be approved which does not utilize a combination of at least two of the following listed devices to deter evasion of size and weight measurement in sufficient quantity to cover the FA system: fixed platform scales; portable wheel weigher scales; semiportable or ramp scales; WIM equipment.

(ii) Staff assigned to the program, identified by specific agency. Where more than one State agency has weight enforcement responsibility, the lead agency should be indicated.

(2) *Practices and procedures.* (i) Proposed plan of operation, including geographical coverage and hours of operation in general terms.

(ii) Policy and practices with respect to overweight violators, including off-loading requirements for divisible loads. In those States in which off-loading is mandatory by law, an administrative variance from the legal requirement shall be fully explained. In those States in which off-loading is permissive administrative guidelines shall be included.

(iii) Policy and practices with respect to penalties, including those for repeated violations. Administrative directives, booklets or other written criteria shall be made part of the plan submission.

(iv) Policy and practices with respect to special permits for overweight. Administrative directives, booklets or other written criteria shall be made part of the plan submission.

(3) *Updating.* Modification and/or additions to the plan based on experience and new developments in the enforcement program. It is recognized that the plan is not static and that changes may be required to meet changing needs.

§ 657.11 Evaluation of operations.

(a) The State shall submit its enforcement plan or annual update to the FHWA Division Office by July 1 of each year. However, if a State's legislative or budgetary cycle is not consonant with that date, the FHWA and the State may jointly select an alternate date. In any event, a State must have an approved plan in effect by October 1 of each year. Failure of a State to submit or update a plan will result in the State being unable to certify in accordance with § 657.13 for the period to be covered by the plan.

(b) The FHWA shall review the State's operation under the accepted plan on a continuing basis and shall prepare an evaluation report annually. The State will be advised of the results of the evaluation and of any needed changes in the plan itself or in its implementation. Copies of the evaluation reports and subsequent modifications resulting from the evaluation shall be forwarded to the FHWA's Office of Operations.

[59 FR 30418, June 13, 1994, as amended at 72 FR 7747, Feb. 20, 2007]

§657.13 Certification requirement.

Each State shall certify to the Federal Highway Administrator, before January 1 of each year, that it is enforcing all State laws respecting maximum vehicle size and weight permitted on what, prior to October 1, 1991, were the Federal-aid Primary, Secondary, and Urban Systems, including the Interstate System, in accordance with 23 U.S.C. 127. The States must also certify that they are enforcing and complying with the ISTEA freeze on the use of LCV's and other multi-unit vehicles. The certification shall be supported by information on activities and results achieved during the preceding 12-month period ending on September 30 of each year.

[59 FR 30418, June 13, 1994]

§657.15 Certification content.

The certification shall consist of the following elements and each element shall be addressed even though the response is negative:

(a) A statement by the Governor of the State, or an official designated by the Governor, that the State's vehicle weight laws and regulations governing use of the Interstate System conform to 23 U.S.C. 127.

(b) A statement by the Governor of the State, or an official designated by the Governor, that all State size and weight limits are being enforced on the Interstate System and those routes which, prior to October 1, 1991, were designated as part of the Federal-aid Primary, Urban, and Secondary Systems, and that the State is enforcing and complying with the provisions of 23 U.S.C. 127(d) and 49 U.S.C. 31112. Urbanized areas not subject to State jurisdiction shall be identified. The statement shall include an analysis of enforcement efforts in such areas.

(c) Except for Alaska and Puerto Rico, the certifying statements required by paragraphs (a) and (b) of this section shall be worded as follows (the statements for Alaska and Puerto Rico do not have to reference 23 U.S.C. 127(d) in (c)(2), or include paragraph (c)(3) of this section):

I, (*name of certifying official*), (*position title*), of the State of __________ do hereby certify:

(1) That all State laws and regulations governing vehicle size and weight are being enforced on those highways which, prior to October 1, 1991, were designated as part of the Federal-aid Primary, Federal-aid Secondary, or Federal-aid Urban Systems;

(2) That the State is enforcing the freeze provisions of the Intermodal Surface Transportation Efficiency Act of 1991 (23 U.S.C. 127(d) and 49 U.S.C. 31112); and

(3) That all State laws governing vehicle weight on the Interstate System are consistent with 23 U.S.C. 127 (a) and (b).

(d) If this statement is made by an official other than the Governor, a copy of the document designating the official, signed by the Governor, shall also be included in the certification made under this part.

(e) A copy of any State law or regulation pertaining to vehicle sizes and weights adopted since the State's last certification and an analysis of the changes made.

(f) A report of State size and weight enforcement efforts during the period covered by the certification which addresses the following:

(1) Actual operations as compared with those forecast by the plan submitted earlier, with particular attention to changes in or deviations from the operations proposed.

(2) Impacts of the process as actually applied, in terms of changes in the number of oversize and/or overweight vehicles.

(3) *Measures of activity*—(i) *Vehicles weighed*. Separate totals shall be reported for the annual number of vehicles weighed on fixed scales, on semiportable scales, on portable scales, and on WIM when used for enforcement.

(ii) *Penalties*. Penalties reported shall include the number of citations or civil assessments issued for violations of each of the following: Axle, gross and bridge formula weight limits. The number of vehicles whose loads are either shifted or offloaded must also be reported.

(iii) *Permits*. The number of permits issued for overweight loads shall be reported. The reported numbers shall specify permits for divisible and non-divisible loads and whether issued on a trip or annual basis.

[59 FR 30418, June 13, 1994, as amended at 62 FR 10181, Mar. 5, 1997; 72 FR 7747, Feb. 20, 2007]

§ 657.17 Certification submittal.

(a) The Governor, or an official designated by the Governor, shall submit the certification to the FHWA division office prior to January 1 of each year.

(b) The FHWA division office shall forward the original certification to the FHWA's Office of Operations and one copy to the Office of Chief Counsel. Copies of appropriate evaluations and/or comments shall accompany any transmittal.

[72 FR 7747, Feb. 20, 2007]

§ 657.19 Effect of failure to certify or to enforce State laws adequately.

If a State fails to certify as required by this regulation or if the Secretary determines that a State is not adequately enforcing all State laws respecting maximum vehicle sizes and weights on the Interstate System and those routes which, prior to October 1, 1991, were designated as part of the Federal-aid primary, Federal-aid secondary or Federal-aid urban systems, notwithstanding the State's certification, the Federal-aid funds for the National Highway System apportioned to the State for the next fiscal year shall be reduced by an amount equal to 10 percent of the amount which would otherwise be apportioned to the State under 23 U.S.C. 104, and/or by the amount required pursuant to 23 U.S.C. 127.

[72 FR 7747, Feb. 20, 2007]

§ 657.21 Procedure for reduction of funds.

(a) If it appears to the Federal Highway Administrator that a State has not submitted a certification conforming to the requirements of this regulation, or that the State is not adequately enforcing State laws respecting maximum vehicle size and weight, including laws applicable to vehicles using the Interstate System with weights or widths in excess of those provided under 23 U.S.C. 127, the Federal Highway Administrator shall make in writing a proposed determination of nonconformity, and shall notify the Governor of the State of the proposed determination by certified mail. The notice shall state the reasons for the proposed determination and inform the State that it may, within 30 days from the date of the notice, request a hearing to show cause why it should not be found in nonconformity. If the State informs the Administrator before the end of this 30-day period that it wishes to attempt to resolve the matter informally, the Administrator may extend the time for requesting a hearing. In the event of a request for informal resolution, the State and the Administrator (or designee) shall promptly schedule a meeting to resolve the matter.

(b) In all instances where the State proceeds on the basis of informal resolution, a transcript of the conference will be made and furnished to the State by the FHWA.

(1) The State may offer any information which it considers helpful to a resolution of the matter, and the scope of review at the conference will include, but not be limited to, legislative actions, including those proposed to remedy deficiencies, budgetary considerations, judicial actions, and proposals for specific actions which will be implemented to bring the State into compliance.

(2) The information produced at the conference may constitute an explanation and offer of settlement and the Administrator will make a determination on the basis of the certification, record of the conference, and other information submitted by the State. The Administrator's final decision together with a copy of the transcript of the conference will be furnished to the State.

(3) If the Administrator does not accept an offer of settlement made pursuant to paragraph (b)(2) of this section, the State retains the right to request a hearing on the record pursuant to paragraph (d) of this section, except in the case of a violation of section 127.

(c) If the State does not request a hearing in a timely fashion as provided in paragraph (a) of this section, the Federal Highway Administrator shall forward the proposed determination of nonconformity to the Secretary. Upon approval of the proposed determination by the Secretary, the fund reduction specified by § 657.19 shall be effected.

(d) If the State requests a hearing, the Secretary shall expeditiously convene a hearing on the record, which shall be conducted according to the provisions of the Administrative Procedure Act, 5 U.S.C. 555 *et seq.* Based on the record of the proceeding, the Secretary shall determine whether the State is in nonconformity with this regulation. If the Secretary determines that the State is in nonconformity, the fund reduction specified by section 567.19 shall be effected.

(e) The Secretary may reserve 10 percent of a State's apportionment of funds under 23 U.S.C. 104 pending a final administrative determination under this regulation to prevent the apportionment to the State of funds which would be affected by a determination of nonconformity.

(f) Funds withheld pursuant to a final administrative determination under this regulation shall be reapportioned to all other eligible States one year from the date of this determination, unless before this time the Secretary determines, on the basis of information submitted by the State and the FHWA, that the State has come into conformity with this regulation. If the Secretary determines that the State has come into conformity, the withheld funds shall be released to the State.

(g) The reapportionment of funds under paragraph (e) of this section shall be stayed during the pendency of any judicial review of the Secretary's final administrative determination of nonconformity.

Appendix to Part 657—Guidelines To Be Used in Developing Enforcement Plans and Certification Evaluation

A. Facilities and Equipment

1. Permanent Scales

a. Number

b. Location (a map appropriately coded is suggested)

c. Public-private (if any)

2. Weigh-in-motion (WIM)

a. Number

b. Location (notation on above map is suggested)

3. Semi-portable scales

a. Type and number

b. If used in sets, the number comprising a set

4. Portable Scales

a. Type and number

b. If used in sets, the number comprising a set

B. Resources

1. Agencies involved (*i.e.*, highway agency, State police, motor vehicle department, etc.)

2. Personnel—numbers from respective agencies assigned to weight enforcement

3. Funding

a. Facilities

b. Personnel

C. Practices

1. Proposed schedule of operation of fixed scale locations in general terms

2. Proposed schedule of deployment of portable scale equipment in general terms

3. Proposed schedule of deployment of semi-portable equipment in general terms

4. Strategy for prevention of bypassing of fixed weighing facility location

5. Proposed action for implementation of off-loading, if applicable

D. Goals

1. Short term—the year beginning October 1 following submission of a vehicle size and weight enforcement plan

2. Medium term—2-4 years after submission of the enforcement plan

3. Long term—5 years beyond the submission of the enforcement plan

4. Provision for annual review and update of vehicle size and weight enforcement plan

E. Evaluation

The evaluation of an existing plan, in comparison to goals for strengthening the enforcement program, is a difficult task, especially since there is very limited experience nationwide.

The FHWA plans to approach this objective through a continued cooperative effort with State and other enforcement agencies by gathering useful information and experience on elements of enforcement practices that produce positive results.

It is not considered practicable at this time to establish objective minimums, such as the number of vehicles to be weighed by each State, as a requirement for satisfactory compliance. However, the States will want to know as many specifics as possible about what measuring tools will be used to evaluate their annual certifications for adequacy.

The above discussion goes to the heart of the question concerning numerical criteria. The assumption that a certain number of weighings will provide a maximum or even satisfactory deterrent is not supportable.

The enforcement of vehicle size and weight laws requires that vehicles be weighed but it does not logically follow that the more vehicles weighed, the more effective the enforcement program, especially if the vehicles are weighed at a limited number of fixed locations. A "numbers game" does not necessarily provide a deterrent to deliberate overloading. Consistent, vigorous enforcement activities, the certainty of apprehension and of penalty, the adequacy of the penalty, even the publicity given these factors, may be greater deterrents than the number of weighings alone.

In recognizing that all States are unique in character, there are some similarities between certain States and useful perspectives may be obtained by relating their program elements. Some comparative factors are:

1. Truck registration (excluding pickups and panels)
2. Population
3. Average Daily Traffic (ADT) for trucks on FA highways
4. To total mileage of Federal-aid highways
5. Geographic location of the State
6. Annual truck miles traveled in State
7. Number of truck terminals (over 6 doors)
8. Vehicle miles of intrastate truck traffic

Quantities relating to the above items can become factors that in the aggregate are descriptive of a State's characteristics and can identify States that are similar from a trucking operation viewpoint. This is especially applicable for States within the same area.

After States with similar truck traffic operations have been identified in a regional area, another important variable must be considered: the type of weighing equipment that has been or is proposed for predominant use in the States. When data become available on the number of trucks weighed by each type of scale (fixed, portable, semi-portable, etc.) some indicators will be developed to relate one State's effort to those of other States. The measures of activity that are a part of each certification submitted will provide a basis for the development of more precise numerical criteria by which an enforcement plan and its activities can be judged for adequacy.

Previous certifications have provided information from which the following gross scale capabilities have been derived.

Potential Weighing Capacities

1. Permanent scales 60 veh/hr.
2. Weigh-in-motion scales 100 veh/hr.
3. Semi-portable scales 25 veh/hr.
4. Portable scales 3 veh/hr.

To meet the mandates of Federal and other laws regarding truck size and weight enforcement, the FHWA desires to become a resource for all States in achieving a successful exchange of useful information. Some States are more advanced in their enforcement activities. Some have special experience with portable, semi-portable, fixed, or weighing-in-motion devices. Others have operated permanent scales in combination with concentrated safety inspection programs. The FHWA is interested in information on individual State experiences in these specialized areas as part of initial plan submissions. If such information has recently been furnished to the Washington Headquarters, an appropriate cross reference should be included on the submission.

It is the policy of the FHWA to avoid red tape, and information volunteered by the States will be of assistance in meeting many needs. The ultimate goal in developing information through the evaluation process is to assemble criteria for a model enforcement program.

PART 658—TRUCK SIZE AND WEIGHT, ROUTE DESIGNATIONS—LENGTH, WIDTH AND WEIGHT LIMITATIONS

Sec.

AUTHORITY: 23 U.S.C. 127 and 315; 49 U.S.C. 31111, 31112, and 31114; sec. 347, Pub. L. 108–7, 117 Stat. 419; sec, 756, Pub. L. 109–58, 119 Stat. 829; sec. 1309, Pub. L. 109–59, 119 Stat. 1219; sec. 115, Pub. L. 109–115, 119 Stat. 2408; 49 CFR 1.48(b)(19) and (c)(19).

SOURCE: 49 FR 23315, June 5, 1984, unless otherwise noted.

§658.1 Purpose.

The purpose of this part is to identify a National Network of highways available to vehicles authorized by provisions of the Surface Transportation Assistance Act of 1982 (STAA) as amended, and to prescribe national policies that govern truck and bus size and weight.

[59 FR 30419, June 13, 1994]

§658.3 Policy statement.

The Federal Highway Administration's (FHWA) policy is to provide a safe and efficient National Network of highways that can safely and efficiently accommodate the large vehicles authorized by the STAA. This network includes the Interstate System plus other qualifying Federal-aid Primary System Highways.

§658.5 Definitions.

Automobile transporters. Any vehicle combination designed and used specifically for the transport of assembled highway vehicles, including truck camper units.

Beverage semitrailer. A van-type, drop-frame semitrailer designed and used specifically for the transport and delivery of bottled or canned beverages (*i.e.*, liquids for drinking, including water) which has side-only access for loading and unloading this commodity. Semitrailer has the same meaning as in 49 CFR 390.5.

Boat transporters. Any vehicle combination designed and used specifically to transport assembled boats and boat hulls. Boats may be partially disassembled to facilitate transporting.

Bridge gross weight formula. The standard specifying the relationship between axle (or groups of axles) spacing and the gross weight that (those) axle(s) may carry expressed by the formula:

$$W = 500\left(\frac{LN}{N-1} + 12N + 36\right)$$

where W = overall gross weight on any group of two or more consecutive axles to the nearest 500 pounds, L = distance in feet between the extreme of any group of two or more consecutive axles, and N = number of axles in the group under consideration.

Cargo-carrying unit. As used in this part, cargo-carrying unit means any portion of a commercial motor vehicle (CMV) combination (other than a truck tractor) used for the carrying of cargo, including a trailer, semitrailer, or the cargo-carrying section of a single-unit truck. The length of the cargo carrying units of a CMV with two or more such units is measured from the front of the first unit to the rear of the last [including the hitch(es) between the units].

Commercial motor vehicle. For purposes of this regulation, a motor vehicle designed or regularly used to carry freight, merchandise, or more than ten passengers, whether loaded or empty, including buses, but not including vehicles used for vanpools, or recreational vehicles operating under their own power.

Drive-away saddlemount vehicle transporter combination. The term drive-away saddlemount vehicle transporter combination means a vehicle combination designed and specifically used to tow up to 3 trucks or truck tractors, each connected by a saddle to the frame or fifth wheel of the forward vehicle of the truck tractor in front of it. Such combinations may include up to one fullmount.

Dromedary unit. A box, deck, or plate mounted behind the cab and forward of the fifth wheel on the frame of the power unit of a truck tractor-semitrailer combination.

Federal-aid Primary System. The Federal-aid Highway System of rural arterials and their extensions into or through urban areas in existence on June 1, 1991, as described in 23 U.S.C. 103(b) in effect at that time.

Fullmount. A fullmount is a smaller vehicle mounted completely on the frame of either the first or last vehicle in a saddlemount combination.

Interstate System. The National System of Interstate and Defense Highways described in sections 103(e) and 139(a) of Title 23, U.S.C. For the purpose of this regulation this system includes toll roads designated as Interstate.

Length exclusive devices. Devices excluded from the measurement of vehicle length. Such devices shall not be designed or used to carry cargo.

Longer combination vehicle (LCV). As used in this part, longer combination vehicle means any combination of a truck tractor and two or more trailers or semitrailers which operates on the Interstate System at a gross vehicle weight greater than 80,000 pounds.

Maxi-cube vehicle. A maxi-cube vehicle is a combination vehicle consisting of a power unit and a trailing unit, both of which are designed to carry cargo. The power unit is a nonarticulated truck with one or more drive axles that carries either a detachable or a permanently attached cargo box. The trailing unit is a trailer or semitrailer with a cargo box so designed that the power unit may be loaded and unloaded through the trailing unit. Neither cargo box shall exceed 34 feet in length, excluding drawbar or hitching device; the distance from the front of the first to the rear of the second cargo box shall not exceed 60 feet, including the space between the cargo boxes; and the overall length of the combination vehicle shall not exceed 65 feet, including the space between the cargo boxes.

Motor carrier of passengers. As used in this part, a motor carrier of passengers is a common, contract, or private carrier using a bus to provide commercial transportation of passengers. Bus has the same meaning as in 49 CFR 390.5.

National Network (NN). The composite of the individual network of highways from each State on which vehicles authorized by the provisions of the STAA are allowed to operate. The network in each State includes the Interstate System, exclusive of those portions excepted under § 658.11(f) or deleted under § 658.11(d), and those portions of the Federal-aid Primary System in existence on June 1, 1991, set out by the FHWA in appendix A to this part.

Nondivisible load or vehicle.

(1) As used in this part, *nondivisible* means any load or vehicle exceeding applicable length or weight limits which, if separated into smaller loads or vehicles, would:

(i) Compromise the intended use of the vehicle, *i.e.*, make it unable to perform the function for which it was intended;

(ii) Destroy the value of the load or vehicle, *i.e.*, make it unusable for its intended purpose; or

(iii) Require more than 8 workhours to dismantle using appropriate equipment. The applicant for a nondivisible load permit has the burden of proof as to the number of workhours required to dismantle the load.

(2) A State may treat as nondivisible loads or vehicles: emergency response vehicles, including those loaded with salt, sand, chemicals or a combination thereof, with or without a plow or blade attached in front, and being used for the purpose of spreading the material on highways that are or may become slick or icy; casks designed for the transport of spent nuclear materials; and military vehicles transporting marked military equipment or materiel.

Over-the-road bus. The term over-the-road bus means a bus characterized by an elevated passenger deck located over a baggage compartment, and typically operating on the Interstate System or roads previously designated as making up the Federal-aid Primary System.

Saddlemount combination. A saddlemount combination is a combination of vehicles in which a truck or truck tractor tows one or more trucks or truck tractors, each connected by a saddle to the frame or fifth wheel of the vehicle in front of it. The saddle is a mechanism that connects the front axle of the towed vehicle to the frame or fifth wheel of the vehicle in front and functions like a fifth wheel kingpin connection. When two vehicles are towed in this manner the combination is called a double saddlemount combination. When three vehicles are towed in this manner, the combination is called a triple saddlemount combination.

Single axle weight. The total weight transmitted to the road by all wheels whose centers may be included between two parallel transverse vertical planes 40 inches apart, extending across the full width of the vehicle. The Federal single axle weight limit on the Interstate System is 20,000 pounds.

Special mobile equipment. Every self-propelled vehicle not designed or used primarily for the transportation of persons or property and incidentally operated or moved over the highways, including military equipment, farm equipment, implements of husbandry, road construction or maintenance machinery, and emergency apparatus which includes fire and police emergency equipment. This list is partial and not exclusive of such other vehicles as may fall within the general terms of this definition.

Stinger-steered combination. A truck tractor semitrailer wherein the fifth wheel is located on a drop frame located behind and below the rear-most axle of the power unit.

Tandem axle weight. The total weight transmitted to the road by two or more consecutive axles whose centers may be included between parallel transverse vertical planes spaced more than 40 inches and not more than 96 inches apart, extending across the full width of the vehicle. The Federal tandem axle weight limit on the Interstate System is 34,000 pounds.

Terminal. The term *terminal* as used in this regulation means, at a minimum, any location where:

Freight either originates, terminates, or is handled in the transportation process; or

Commercial motor carriers maintain operating facilities.

Tractor or Truck tractor. The noncargo carrying power unit that operates in combination with a semitrailer or trailer, except that a truck tractor and semitrailer engaged in the transportation of automobiles may transport motor vehicles on part of the power unit, and a truck tractor equipped with a dromedary unit operating in combination with a semitrailer transporting Class 1 explosives and/or any munitions related security material as specified by the U.S. Department of Defense in compliance with 49 CFR 177.835 may use the dromedary unit to carry a portion of the cargo.

Truck-tractor semitrailer-semitrailer. In a truck-tractor semitrailer-semitrailer combination vehicle, the two trailing units are connected with a "B-train" assembly. The B-train assembly is a rigid frame extension attached to the rear frame of a first semitrailer which allows for a fifth wheel connection point for the second semitrailer. This combination has one less articulation point than the conventional "A dolly" connected truck-tractor semitrailer-trailer combination.

Truck-trailer boat transporter. A boat transporter combination consisting of a straight truck towing a trailer using typically a ball and socket connection. The trailer axle(s) is located substantially at the trailer center of gravity (rather than the rear of the trailer) but so as to maintain a downward force on the trailer tongue.

Width exclusive devices. Devices excluded from the measurement of vehicle width. Such devices shall not be designed or used to carry cargo.

[49 FR 23315, June 5, 1984]

EDITORIAL NOTE: For FEDERAL REGISTER citations affecting §658.5, see the List of CFR Sections Affected, which appears in the Finding Aids section of the printed volume and at *www.govinfo.gov.*

§658.7 Applicability.

Except as limited in §658.17(a) the provisions of this part are applicable to the National Network and reasonable access thereto. However, nothing in this regulation shall be construed to prevent any State from applying any weight and size limits to other highways, except when such limits would deny reasonable access to the National Network.

§658.9 National Network criteria.

(a) The National Network listed in the appendix to this part is available for use by commerical motor vehicles of the dimensions and configurations described in §§658.13 and 658.15.

(b) For those States with detailed lists of individual routes in the appendix, the routes have been designated on the basis of their general adherence to the following criteria.

(1) The route is a geometrically typical component of the Federal-Aid Primary System, serving to link principal cities and densely developed portions of the States.

(2) The route is a high volume route utilized extensively by large vehicles for interstate commerce.

(3) The route does not have any restrictions precluding use by conventional combination vehicles.

(4) The route has adequate geometrics to support safe operations, considering sight distance, severity and length of grades, pavement width, horizontal curvature, shoulder width, bridge clearances and load limits, traffic volumes and vehicle mix, and intersection geometry.

(5) The route consists of lanes designed to be a width of 12 feet or more or is otherwise consistent with highway safety.

(6) The route does not have any unusual characteristics causing current or anticipated safety problems.

(c) For those States where State law provides that STAA authorized vehicles may use all or most of the Federal-Aid Primary system, the National Network is no more restrictive than such law. The appendix contains a narrative summary of the National Network in those States.

[49 FR 23315, June 5, 1984, as amended at 53 FR 12148, Apr. 13, 1988]

§ 658.11 Additions, deletions, exceptions, and restrictions.

To ensure that the National Network remains substantially intact, FHWA retains the authority to rule upon all requested additions to and deletions from the National Network as well as requests for the imposition of certain restrictions. FHWA approval or disapproval will constitute the final decision of the U.S. Department of Transportation.

(a) *Additions.* (1) Requests for additions to the National Network, including justification, shall have the endorsement of the Governor or the Governor's authorized representative, and be submitted in writing to the appropriate FHWA Division Office. Proposals for addition of routes to the National Network shall be accompanied by an analysis of suitability based on the criteria in § 658.9.

(2) Proposals for additions that meet the criteria of § 658.9 and have the endorsement of the Governor or the Governor's authorized representative will be published in the FEDERAL REGISTER for public comment as a notice of proposed rulemaking (NPRM), and if found acceptable, as a final rule.

(b) *Deletions—Federal-aid primary—other than interstate.* Changed conditions or additional information may require the deletion of a designated route or a portion thereof. The deletion of any route or route segment shall require FHWA approval. Requests for deletion of routes from the National Network, including the reason(s) for the deletion, shall be submitted in writing to the appropriate FHWA Division Office. These requests shall be assessed on the basis of the criteria of § 658.9. FHWA proposed deletions will be published in the FEDERAL REGISTER as a Notice of Proposed Rulemaking (NPRM).

(c) *Requests for deletion—Federal-aid primary—other than interstate.* Requests for deletion should include the following information, where appropriate:

(1) Did the route segment prior to designation carry combination vehicles or 102-inch buses?

(2) Were truck restrictions in effect on the segment on January 6, 1983? If so, what types of restrictions?

(3) What is the safety record of the segment, including current or anticipated safety problems? Specifically, is the route experiencing above normal accident rates and/or accident severities? Does analysis of the accident problem indicate that the addition of larger trucks have aggravated existing accident problems?

(4) What are the geometric, structural or traffic operations features that might preclude safe, efficient operation? Specifically describe lane widths, sight distance, severity and length of grades, horizontal curvature, shoulder width, narrow bridges, bridge clearances and load limits, traffic volumes and vehicle mix, intersection geometrics and vulnerability of roadside hardware.

(5) Is there a reasonable alternate route available?

(6) Are there operational restrictions that might be implemented in lieu of deletion?

(d) *Deletions and use restrictions—Federal-aid interstate.* (1) The deletion of, or imposition of use restrictions on, any specific segment of the Interstate

Highway System on the National Network, except as otherwise provided in this part, must be approved by the FHWA. Such action will be initiated on the FHWA's own initiative or on the request of the Governor or the Governor's authorized representative of the State in which the Interstate segment is located. Requests from the Governor or the Governor's authorized representative shall be submitted along with justification for the deletion or restriction, in writing, to the appropriate FHWA Division Office for transmittal to Washington Headquarters.

(2) The justification accompanying a request shall be based on the following:

(i) Analysis of evidence of safety problems supporting the deletion or restriction as identified in §658.11(c).

(ii) Analysis of the impact on interstate commerce.

(iii) Analysis and recommendation of any alternative routes that can safely accommodate commercial motor vehicles of the dimensions and configurations described in §§658.13 and 658.15 and serve the area in which such segment is located.

(iv) Evidence of consultation with the local governments in which the segment is located as well as the Governor or the Governor's authorized representative of any adjacent State that might be directly affected by such a deletion or restriction.

(3) Actions to ban all commercial vehicles on portions of the Interstate System not excepted under §658.11(f) are considered deletions subject to the requirements of subsection (d) of this section.

(4) Reasonable restrictions on the use of Interstate routes on the National Network by STAA-authorized vehicles related to specific travel lanes of multi-lane facilities, construction zones, adverse weather conditions or structural or clearance deficiencies are not subject to the requirements of paragraph (d) of this section.

(5) Proposed deletions or restrictions will be published in the FEDERAL REGISTER as an NPRM, except in the case of an emergency deletion as prescribed in §658.11(e). The FHWA will consider the factors set out in paragraph (d)(2) of this section and the comments of interested parties. Any approval of deletion or restriction will be published as a final rule. A deletion of or restriction on a segment for reasons ascribable to dimensions of commercial motor vehicles described in either §658.13 or §658.15 shall result in a deletion or restriction for the purposes of both §§658.13 and 658.15.

(e) *Emergency deletions.* FHWA has the authority to delete any route from the National Network, on an emergency basis, for safety considerations. Emergency deletions are not considered final, and will be published in the FEDERAL REGISTER for notice and comment.

(f) *Exceptions.* Those portions of the Interstate System which were open to traffic and on which all commercial motor vehicles were banned on January 6, 1983, are not included in the National Network.

(g) *Restrictions—Federal-aid primary—other than interstate.* (1) Reasonable restrictions on the use of non-Interstate Federal-aid Primary routes on the National Network by STAA-authorized vehicles may be imposed during certain peak hours of travel or on specific travel lanes of multi-lane facilities. Restrictions related to construction zones, seasonal operation, adverse weather conditions or structural or clearance deficiencies may be imposed.

(2) All restrictions on the use of the National Network based on hours of use by vehicles authorized by the STAA require prior FHWA approval. Requests for such restrictions on the National Network shall be submitted in writing to the appropriate FHWA Division Office. Approval of requests for restrictions will be contingent on the ability to justify significant negative impact on safety, the environment and/or operational efficiency.

[49 FR 23315, June 5, 1984, as amended at 53 FR 12148, Apr. 13, 1988]

§658.13 Length.

(a) The length provisions of the STAA apply only to the following types of vehicle combinations:

(1) Truck tractor-semitrailer

(2) Truck tractor-semitrailer-trailer.

The length provisions apply only when these combinations are in use on the

National Network or in transit between these highways and terminals or service locations pursuant to § 658.19.

(b) The length provisions referred to in paragraph (a) of this section include the following:

(1) No State shall impose a length limitation of less than 48 feet on a semitrailer operating in a truck tractor-semitrailer combination.

(2) No State shall impose a length limitation of less than 28 feet on any semitrailer or trailer operating in a truck tractor-semitrailer-trailer combination.

(3) No State shall impose an overall length limitation on commercial vehicles operating in truck tractor-semitrailer or truck tractor-semitrailer-trailer combinations.

(4) No State shall prohibit commercial motor vehicles operating in truck tractor-semitrailer-trailer combinations.

(5) No State shall prohibit the operation of semitrailers or trailers which are 28½ feet long when operating in a truck tractor-semitrailer-trailer combination if such a trailer or semitrailer was in actual and lawful operation on December 1, 1982, and such combination had an overall length not exceeding 65 feet.

(c) State maximum length limits for semitrailers operating in a truck tractor-semitrailer combination and semitrailers and trailers operating in a truck tractor-semitrailer-trailer combination are subject to the following:

(1) No State shall prohibit the use of trailers or semitrailers of such dimensions as those that were in actual and lawful use in such State on December 1, 1982, as set out in appendix B of this part.

(2) If on December 1, 1982, State length limitations on a semitrailer were described in terms of the distance from the kingpin to rearmost axle, or end of semitrailer, the operation of any semitrailer that complies with that limitation must be allowed.

(d) No State shall impose a limit of less than 45 feet on the length of any bus on the NN.

(e) *Specialized equipment*—(1) *Automobile transporters*. (i) Automobile transporters are considered to be specialized equipment. As provided in § 658.5, automobile transporters may carry vehicles on the power unit behind the cab and on an over-cab rack. No State shall impose an overall length limitation of less than 65 feet on traditional automobile transporters (5th wheel located on tractor frame over rear axle(s)), including "low boys," or less than 75 feet on stinger-steered automobile transporters. Paragraph (c) requires the States to allow operation of vehicles with the dimensions that were legal in the State on December 1, 1982.

(ii) All length provisions regarding automobile transporters are exclusive of front and rear cargo overhang. No State shall impose a front overhang limitation of less than 3 feet or a rear overhang limitation of less than 4 feet. Extendable ramps or "flippers" on automobile transporters that are used to achieve the allowable 3-foot front and 4-foot rear cargo overhangs are excluded from the measurement of vehicle length, but must be retracted when not supporting vehicles.

(iii) Drive-away saddlemount vehicle transporter combinations are considered to be specialized equipment. No State shall impose an overall length limit of less or more than 97 feet on such combinations. This provision applies to drive-away saddlemount combinations with up to three saddlemounted vehicles. Such combinations may include one fullmount. Saddlemount combinations must also comply with the applicable motor carrier safety regulations at 49 CFR parts 390–399.

(2) *Boat transporters*. (i) Boat transporters are considered to be specialized equipment. As provided for automobile transporters in § 658.5, boat transporters may carry boats on the power unit so long as the length and width restrictions of the vehicles and load are not exceeded. No State shall impose an overall length limitation of less than 65 feet on traditional boat transporters (fifth wheel located on tractor frame over rear axle(s), including "low boys," or less than 75 feet on stinger-steered boat transporters. In addition, no State shall impose an overall length limitation of less than 65 feet on truck-trailer boat transporters. Paragraph (c) of this section requires the States to

allow operation of vehicles with the dimensions that were legal in the State on December 1, 1982.

(ii) All length provisions regarding boat transporters are exclusive of front and rear overhang. Further, no State shall impose a front overhang limitation of less than three (3) feet nor a rearmost overhang limitation of less than four (4) feet.

(3) *Truck-tractor semitrailer-semitrailer.* (i) Truck-tractor semitrailer-semitrailer combination vehicles are considered to be specialized equipment. No State shall impose a length limitation of less than 28 feet on any semitrailer or 28½ feet if the semitrailer was in legal operation on December 1, 1982, operating in a truck-tractor semitrailer-semitrailer combination. No State shall impose an overall length limitation on a truck-tractor semitrailer-semitrailer combination when each semitrailer length is 28 feet, or 28½ feet if grandfathered.

(ii) The B-train assembly is excluded from the measurement of trailer length when used between the first and second trailer of a truck-tractor semitrailer-semitrailer combination vehicle. However, when there is no semitrailer mounted to the B-train assembly, it will be included in the length measurement of the semitrailer, the length limitation in this case being 48 feet, or longer if grandfathered.

(4) *Maxi-cube vehicle.* No State shall impose a length limit on a maxi-cube vehicle, as defined in §658.5 of this part, of less than 34 feet on either cargo box, excluding drawbar or hitching device; 60 feet on the distance from the front of the first to the rear of the second cargo box, including the space between the cargo boxes; or 65 feet on the overall length of the combination, including the space between the cargo boxes. The measurement for compliance with the 60- and 65-foot distance shall include the actual distance between cargo boxes, measured along the centerline of the drawbar or hitching device. For maxi-cubes with an adjustable length drawbar or hitching device, the 60- and 65-foot distances shall be measured with a drawbar spacing of not more than 27 inches. The drawbar may be temporarily extended beyond that distance to maneuver or load the vehicle.

(5) *Beverage semitrailer.* (i) A beverage semitrailer is specialized equipment if it has an upper coupler plate that extends beyond the front of the semitrailer, but not beyond its swing radius, as measured from the center line of the kingpin to a front corner of the semitrailer, which cannot be used for carrying cargo other than the structure of the semitrailer, and with the center line of the kingpin not more than 28 feet from the rear of the semitrailer (exclusive of rear-mounted devices not measured in determining semitrailer length). No State shall impose an overall length limit on such vehicles when operating in a truck tractor-beverage semitrailer or truck tractor-beverage semitrailer-beverage trailer combination on the NN.

(ii) The beverage trailer referred to in paragraph (e)(5)(i) of this section means a beverage semitrailer and converter dolly. Converter dolly has the same meaning as in 49 CFR 393.5.

(iii) Truck tractor-beverage semitrailer combinations shall have the same access to points of loading and unloading as 28-foot semitrailers (28.5-foot where allowed by §658.13) in 23 CFR 658.19.

(6) *Munitions carriers using dromedary equipment.* A truck tractor equipped with a dromedary unit operating in combination with a semitrailer is considered to be specialized equipment, providing the combination is transporting Class 1 explosives and/or any munitions related security material as specified by the U.S. Department of Defense in compliance with 49 CFR 177.835. No State shall impose an overall length limitation of less than 75 feet on the combination while in operation.

(f) A truck tractor containing a dromedary box, deck, or plate in legal operation on December 1, 1982, shall be permitted to continue to operate, notwithstanding its cargo carrying capacity, throughout its useful life. Proof of such legal operation on December 1, 1982, shall rest upon the operator of the equipment.

(g) No State shall impose a limitation of less than 46 feet on the distance from the kingpin to the center of the rear axle on trailers or semitrailers used exclusively or primarily to transport vehicles in connection with motorsports competition events.

(h) Truck-tractors, pulling 2 trailers or semitrailers, used to transport custom harvester equipment during harvest months within the State of Nebraska may not exceed 81 feet 6 inches.

[49 FR 23315, June 5, 1984, as amended at 53 FR 2597, 2599, Jan. 29, 1988; 53 FR 25485, July 7, 1988; 53 FR 48636, Dec. 2, 1988; 55 FR 4998, Feb. 13, 1990; 55 FR 32399, Aug. 9, 1990; 59 FR 30419, June 13, 1994; 62 FR 10181, Mar. 5, 1997; 63 FR 70653, Dec. 22, 1998; 67 FR 15109, Mar. 29, 2002; 68 FR 37968, June 26, 2003; 72 FR 7748, Feb. 20, 2007]

§ 658.15 Width.

(a) No State shall impose a width limitation of more or less than 102 inches, or its approximate metric equivalent, 2.6 meters (102.36 inches) on a vehicle operating on the National Network, except for the State of Hawaii, which is allowed to keep the State's 108-inch width maximum by virtue of section 416(a) of the STAA.

(b) The provisions of paragraph (a) of this section do not apply to special mobile equipment as defined in § 658.5.

(c) Notwithstanding the provisions of this section or any other provision of law, a State may grant special use permits to motor vehicles, including manufactured housing, that exceed 102 inches in width.

[49 FR 23315, June 5, 1984, as amended at 59 FR 30419, June 13, 1994; 67 FR 15110, Mar. 29, 2002; 72 FR 7748, Feb. 20, 2007]

§ 658.16 Exclusions from length and width determinations.

(a) Vehicle components not excluded by law or regulation shall be included in the measurement of the length and width of commercial motor vehicles.

(b) The following shall be excluded from either the measured length or width of commercial motor vehicles, as applicable:

(1) Rear view mirrors, turn signal lamps, handholds for cab entry/egress, splash and spray suppressant devices, load induced tire bulge;

(2) All non-property-carrying devices, or components thereof—

(i) At the front of a semitrailer or trailer, or

(ii) That do not extend more than 3 inches beyond each side or the rear of the vehicle, or

(iii) That do not extend more than 24 inches beyond the rear of the vehicle and are needed for loading or unloading, or

(vi) Listed in appendix D to this part;

(3) Resilient bumpers that do not extend more than 6 inches beyond the front or rear of the vehicle;

(4) Aerodynamic devices that extend a maximum of 5 feet beyond the rear of the vehicle, provided such devices have neither the strength, rigidity nor mass to damage a vehicle, or injure a passenger in a vehicle, that strikes a trailer so equipped from the rear, and provided also that they do not obscure tail lamps, turn signals, marker lamps, identification lamps, or any other required safety devices, such as hazardous materials placards or conspicuity markings; and

(5) A fixed step up to 3 inches deep at the front of an existing automobile transporter until April 29, 2005. It will be the responsibility of the operator of the unit to prove that the step existed prior to April 29, 2002. Such proof can be in the form of a work order for equipment modification, a receipt for purchase and installation of the piece, or any similar type of documentation. However, after April 29, 2005, the step shall no longer be excluded from a vehicle's length.

(c) Each exclusion allowance is specific and may not be combined with other excluded devices.

(d) Measurements are to be made from a point on one side or end of a commercial motor vehicle to the same point on the opposite side or end of the vehicle.

[67 FR 15110, Mar. 29, 2002]

§ 658.17 Weight.

(a) The provisions of the section are applicable to the National System of Interstate and Defense Highways and reasonable access thereto.

(b) The maximum gross vehicle weight shall be 80,000 pounds except where lower gross vehicle weight is dictated by the bridge formula.

(c) The maximum gross weight upon any one axle, including any one axle of a group of axles, or a vehicle is 20,000 pounds.

(d) The maximum gross weight on tandem axles is 34,000 pounds.

(e) No vehicle or combination of vehicles shall be moved or operated on any Interstate highway when the gross weight on two or more consecutive axles exceeds the limitations prescribed by the following formula, referred to as the Bridge Gross Weight Formula:

$$W = 500\left(\frac{LN}{N-1} + 12N + 36\right)$$

except that two consecutive sets of tandem axles may carry a gross load of 34,000 pounds each if the overall distance between the first and last axle is 36 feet or more. In no case shall the total gross weight of a vehicle exceed 80,000 pounds.

(f) Except as provided herein, States may not enforce on the Interstate System vehicle weight limits of less than 20,000 pounds on a single axle, 34,000 pounds on a tandem axle, or the weights derived from the Bridge Formula, up to a maximum of 80,000 pounds, including all enforcement tolerances. States may not limit tire loads to less than 500 pounds per inch of tire or tread width, except that such limits may not be applied to tires on the steering axle. States may not limit steering axle weights to less than 20,000 pounds or the axle rating established by the manufacturer, whichever is lower.

(g) The weights in paragraphs (b), (c), (d), and (e) of this section shall be inclusive of all tolerances, enforcement or otherwise, with the exception of a scale allowance factor when using portable scales (wheel-load weighers). The current accuracy of such scales is generally within 2 or 3 percent of actual weight, but in no case shall an allowance in excess of 5 percent be applied. Penalty or fine schedules which impose no fine up to a specified threshold, *i.e.*, 1,000 pounds, will be considered as tolerance provisions not authorized by 23 U.S.C. 127.

(h) States may issue special permits without regard to the axle, gross, or Federal Bridge Formula requirements for nondivisible vehicles or loads.

(i) The provisions of paragraphs (b), (c), and (d) of this section shall not apply to single-, or tandem-axle weights, or gross weights legally authorized under State law on July 1, 1956. The group of axles requirement established in this section shall not apply to vehicles legally grandfathered under State groups of axles tables or formulas on January 4, 1975. Grandfathered weight limits are vested on the date specified by Congress and remain available to a State even if it chooses to adopt a lower weight limit for a time.

(j) The provisions of paragraphs (c) through (e) of this section shall not apply to the operation on Interstate Route 68 in Allegany and Garrett Counties, Maryland, of any specialized vehicle equipped with a steering axle and a tridem axle and used for hauling coal, logs, and pulpwood if such vehicle is of a type of vehicle as was operating in such counties on U.S. Routes 40 or 48 for such purposes on August 1, 1991.

(k) Any over-the-road bus, or any vehicle which is regularly and exclusively used as an intrastate public agency transit passenger bus, is excluded from the axle weight limits in paragraphs (c) through (e) of this section until October 1, 2009. Any State that has enforced, in the period beginning October 6, 1992, and ending November 30, 2005, a single axle weight limitation of 20,000 pounds or greater but less than 24,000 pounds may not enforce a single axle weight limit on these vehicles of less than 24,000 lbs.

(m) The provisions of paragraphs (b) through (e) of this section shall not apply to the operation, on I–99 between Bedford and Bald Eagle, Pennsylvania, of any vehicle that could legally operate on this highway section before December 29, 1995.

(n) Any vehicle subject to this subpart that utilizes an auxiliary power or idle reduction technology unit in order to promote reduction of fuel use and emissions because of engine idling, may be allowed up to an additional 400 lbs. total in gross, axle, tandem, or bridge formula weight limits.

(1) To be eligible for this exception, the operator of the vehicle must be able to prove:

(i) By written certification, the weight of the APU; and

(ii) By demonstration or certification, that the idle reduction technology is fully functional at all times.

(2) Certification of the weight of the APU must be available to law enforcement officers if the vehicle is found in violation of applicable weight laws. The additional weight allowed cannot exceed 400 lbs. or the weight certified, whichever is less.

[49 FR 23315, June 5, 1984, as amended at 59 FR 30420, June 13, 1994; 60 FR 15214, Mar. 22, 1995; 62 FR 10181, Mar. 5, 1997; 63 FR 70653, Dec. 22, 1998; 72 FR 7748, Feb. 20, 2007]

§ 658.19 Reasonable access.

(a) No State may enact or enforce any law denying reasonable access to vehicles with dimensions authorized by the STAA between the NN and terminals and facilities for food, fuel, repairs, and rest. In addition, no State may enact or enforce any law denying reasonable access between the NN and points of loading and unloading to household goods carriers, motor carriers of passengers, and any truck tractor-semitrailer combination in which the semitrailer has a length not to exceed 28 feet (28.5 feet where allowed pursuant to § 658.13(b)(5) of this part) and which generally operates as part of a vehicle combination described in §§ 658.13(b)(5) and 658.15(a) of this part.

(b) All States shall make available to commercial motor vehicle operators information regarding their reasonable access provisions to and from the National Network.

(c) Nothing in this section shall be construed as preventing any State or local government from imposing any reasonable restriction, based on safety considerations, on access to points of loading and unloading by any truck tractor-semitrailer combination in which the semitrailer has a length not to exceed 28½ feet and which generally operates as part of a vehicle combination described in §§ 658.13(b)(5) and 658.15(a).

(d) No State may enact or enforce any law denying access within 1 road-mile from the National Network using the most reasonable and practicable route available except for specific safety reasons on individual routes.

(e) Approval of access for specific vehicles on any individual route applies to all vehicles of the same type regardless of ownership. Distinctions between vehicle types shall be based only on significant, substantial differences in their operating characteristics.

(f) Blanket restrictions on 102-inch wide vehicles may not be imposed.

(g) Vehicle dimension limits shall not be more restrictive than Federal requirements.

(h) States shall ensure compliance with the requirements of this section for roads under the jurisdiction of local units of government.

(i)(1) Except in those States in which State law authorizes the operation of STAA-dimensioned vehicles on all public roads and highways, all States shall have an access review process that provides for the review of requests for access from the National Network.

(2) State access review processes shall provide for:

(i) One or more of the following:

(A) An analysis of the proposed access routes using observations or other data obtained from the operation of test vehicles over the routes;

(B) An analysis of the proposed access routes by application of vehicle templates to plans of the routes;

(C) A general provision for allowing access, without requiring a request, for commercial motor vehicles with semitrailers with a kingpin distance of 41 feet or less (measured from the kingpin to the center of the rear axle, if single, or the center of a group of rear axles). State safety analyses may be conducted on individual routes if warranted; and

(ii) All of the following:

(A) The denial of access to terminals and services only on the basis of safety and engineering analysis of the access route.

(B) The automatic approval of an access request if not acted upon within 90 days of receipt by the State. This provision shall become effective no later than 12 months following the effective date of this rule unless an extension is requested by the State and approved by FHWA.

(C) The denial of access for any 102-inch wide vehicles only on the basis of the characteristics of specific routes, in particular significant deficiencies in lane width.

(j)(1) Each State shall submit its access provisions to FHWA for approval within 6 months after June 1, 1990. In those States in which State law authorizes the operation of STAA-dimensioned vehicles on all public roads and highways, no submission or approval under this paragraph is required. If, in the future, such a State changes its authorizing legislation and restricts the operation of STAA-dimensioned vehicles, then compliance with these provisions will be necessary.

(2) The FHWA will review the access provisions as submitted by each State subject to the provisions in paragraph (j)(1) and approve those that are in compliance with the requirements of this section. The FHWA may, at a State's request, approve State provisions that differ from the requirements of this section if FHWA determines that they provide reasonable access for STAA-dimensioned vehicles and do not impose an unreasonable burden on motor freight carriers, shippers and receivers and service facility operators.

(3) Any State that does not have FHWA approved access provisions in effect within 1 year after June 1, 1990 shall follow the requirements and the criteria set forth in this section and section 658.5 and 658.19 for determining access for STAA-dimensioned vehicles to terminals and services. The FHWA may approve a State's request for a time extension if it is received by FHWA at least 1 month before the end of the 1 year period.

[53 FR 12149, Apr. 13, 1988, as amended at 55 FR 22763, June 1, 1990; 59 FR 30420, June 13, 1994]

§ 658.21 Identification of National Network.

(a) To identify the National Network, a State may sign the routes or provide maps of lists of highways describing the National Network.

(b) Exceptional local conditions on the National Network shall be signed. All signs shall conform to the Manual on Uniform Traffic Control Devices. Exceptional conditions shall include but not be limited to:

(1) Operational restrictions designed to maximize the efficiency of the total traffic flow, such as time of day prohibitions, or lane use controls.

(2) Geometric and structural restrictions, such as vertical clearances, posted weight limits on bridges, or restrictions caused by construction operations.

(3) Detours from urban Interstate routes to bypass of circumferential routes for commercial motor vehicles not destined for the urban area to be bypassed.

§ 658.23 LCV freeze; cargo-carrying unit freeze.

(a)(1) Except as otherwise provided in this section and except for tow trucks with vehicles in tow, a State may allow the operation of LCV's on the Interstate System only as listed in appendix C to this part.

(2) Except as otherwise provided in this section, a State may not allow the operation on the NN of any CMV combination with two or more cargo-carrying units (not including the truck tractor) whose cargo-carrying units exceed:

(i) The maximum combination trailer, semitrailer, or other type of length limitation authorized by State law or regulation of that State on or before June 1, 1991; or

(ii) The length of the cargo-carrying units of those CMV combinations, by specific configuration, in actual, lawful operation on a regular or periodic basis (including continuing seasonal operation) in that State on or before June 1, 1991, as listed in appendix C to this part.

(b) Notwithstanding paragraph (a)(2) of this section, the following CMV combinations with two or more cargo-carrying units may operate on the NN.

(1) Truck tractor-semitrailer-trailer and truck tractor-semitrailer-semitrailer combinations with a maximum length of the individual cargo units of 28.5 feet or less.

(2) Vehicles described in § 658.13(e) and (g).

(3) Truck-trailer and truck-semitrailer combinations with an overall length of 65 feet or less.

(4) Maxi-cubes.

(5) Tow trucks with vehicles in tow.

(c) For specific safety purposes and road construction, a State may make minor adjustments of a temporary and emergency nature to route designation and vehicle operating restrictions applicable to combinations subject to 23 U.S.C. 127(d) and 49 U.S.C. 31112 and in effect on June 1, 1991 (July 6, 1991, for Alaska). Minor adjustments which last 30 days or less may be made without notifying the FHWA. Minor adjustments which exceed 30 days require approval of the FHWA. When such adjustments are needed, a State must submit to the FHWA, by the end of the 30th day, a written description of the emergency, the date on which it began, and the date on which it is expected to conclude. If the adjustment involves alternate route designations, the State shall describe the new route on which vehicles otherwise subject to the freeze imposed by 23 U.S.C. 127(d) and 49 U.S.C. 31112 are allowed to operate. To the extent possible, the geometric and pavement design characteristics of the alternate route should be equivalent to those of the highway section which is temporarily unavailable. If the adjustment involves vehicle operating restrictions, the State shall list the restrictions that have been removed or modified. If the adjustment is approved, the FHWA will publish the notice of adjustment, with an expiration date, in the FEDERAL REGISTER. Requests for extension of time beyond the originally established conclusion date shall be subject to the same approval and publications process as the original request. If upon consultation with the FHWA a decision is reached that minor adjustments made by a State are not legitimately attributable to road or bridge construction or safety, the FHWA will inform the State, and the original conditions of the freeze must be reimposed immediately. Failure to do so may subject the State to a penalty pursuant to 23 U.S.C. 141.

(d) A State may issue a permit authorizing a CMV to transport an overlength nondivisible load on two or more cargo-carrying units on the NN without regard to the restrictions in §658.23(a)(2).

(e) States further restricting or prohibiting the operation of vehicles subject to 23 U.S.C. 127(d) and 49 U.S.C. 31112 after June 1, 1991, shall notify the FHWA within 30 days after the restriction is effective. The FHWA will publish the restriction in the FEDERAL REGISTER as an amendment to appendix C to this part. Failure to provide such notification may subject the State to a penalty pursuant to 23 U.S.C. 141.

(f) The Federal Highway Administrator, on his or her own motion or upon a request by any person (including a State), shall review the information set forth in appendix C to this part. If the Administrator determines there is cause to believe that a mistake was made in the accuracy of the information contained in appendix C to this part, the Administrator shall commence a proceeding to determine whether the information published should be corrected. If the Administrator determines that there is a mistake in the accuracy of the information contained in appendix C to this part, the Administrator shall publish in the FEDERAL REGISTER the appropriate corrections to reflect that determination.

[59 FR 30420, June 13, 1994, as amended at 60 FR 15214, Mar. 22, 1995; 62 FR 10181, Mar. 5, 1997; 72 FR 7748, Feb. 20, 2007]

APPENDIX A TO PART 658—NATIONAL NETWORK—FEDERALLY-DESIGNATED ROUTES

[The federally-designated routes on the National Network consist of the Interstate System, except as noted, and the following additional highways.]

Route	From	To
Alabama		
US 43	I–65 N. of Mobile	Sunflower.
US 43	AL 5 near Russellville.	TN State Line.
US 72	MS State Line	CR 33 Hollywood.
US 72 Alt	US 72 Tuscumbia	US 72/231/431 Huntsville.
US 78	End of 4-lane W. of AL 5 Jasper.	I–59 Birmingham.
US 80	AL 14 W. Int. Selma	US 82 Montgomery.
US 82	Coker W. of I–59	Eoline W. of AL 5.
US 82	AL 206 Prattville	US 231 N. Int. Montgomery.
US 84	AL 92 E. of Daleville (via AL 210 Dothan Cir.).	End of 4-lane E. of Dothan.
US 98	I–10 Daphne	End of 4-lane near Fairhope.
US 231	FL State Line (via AL 210 Dothan Circle.).	End of 4-lane N. of Wetumpka.
US 231	Arab	TN State Line.
US 280	US 31 Mountain Brook.	AL 22 Alexander City.
US 280	I–85 Opelika	GA State Line Phenix City.
US 431	AL 210 Dothan	AL 173 Headland.

[The federally-designated routes on the National Network consist of the Interstate System, except as noted, and the following additional highways.]

Route	From	To
US 431	I–20 Anniston	AL 79 N. Int. Columbus City (via I–59—AL 77 Gadsden).
US 431	CR 8 New Hope	TN State Line.
AL 21	US 31 Atmore	I–65 N. of Atmore.
AL 21	US 431 Anniston	Jacksonville.
AL 67	I–65 Priceville	US 72 Alt. W. of Decatur.
AL 79	I–59 Birmingham	Pinson.
AL 152	US 231 N. Int. Montgomery.	I–65 N. Int. Montgomery.
AL 210	Dothan Circle (Beltway).	
AL 248	US 84 Enterprise	Ft. Rucker.
AL 249	Ft. Rucker	US 231.
Alaska		
AK 1	Potter Weigh Station Anchorage.	AK 3 Palmer.
AK 2	AK 3 Fairbanks	Milepost 1412 Delta Junction.
AK 3	AK 1 Palmer	AK 2 Fairbanks.

Note: Routes added to the Interstate System under 23 U.S.C. 139(c) are included only to the extent designated above.

Route	From	To
Arizona		
US 60	I–10 Brenda	I–17 Phoenix.
US 60	AZ 87 Mesa	AZ 70 Globe.
US 60	AZ 260 E. Int. Show Low.	NM State Line.
US 64	US 160 Teec Nos Pos.	NM State Line.
US 70	US 60 Globe	NM State Line.
US 80	AZ 92 Bisbee	NM State Line.
US 89	I–10 Tucson	US 60 Florence Junction.
US 89	AZ 69 Prescott	I–40 Ash Fork.
US 89	I–40 Flagstaff	UT State Line.
US 95	Mexican Border	I–8 Yuma.
US 160	US 89 Tuba City	NM State Line.
US 163	US 160 Kayenta	UT State Line.
US 666	I–10 Bowie	US 70 Safford.
US 666	US 60 Springerville	I–40 Sanders.
US 666	Mexican Border	US 80 Douglas.
AZ 69	US 89 Prescott	I–17 Cordes Junction.
AZ 77	US 60 Show Low	I–40 Holbrook.
AZ 84	I–10 Picacho	AZ 87 E. of Eloy.
AZ 85	I–8 Gila Bend (via I–8B).	I–10 Buckeye (via AZ 85 Spur).
AZ 87	AZ 84 E. of Eloy	AZ 387 W. of Coolidge.
AZ 87	AZ 587 Chandler	US 60 Mesa.
AZ 90	I–10 Benson	AZ 92 Sierra Vista.
AZ 169	AZ 69 Dewey	I–17 S. of Camp Verde.
AZ 189	Mexican Border	I–19 Nogales.
AZ 287	AZ 87 Coolidge	US 89 Florence.
AZ 360	I–10 Phoenix	AZ 87 Mesa.
AZ 387	I–10 Exit 185	AZ 87 W. of Coolidge.
AZ 587 (Old AZ 93).	I–10 Exit 175	AZ 87 Chandler.

[The federally-designated routes on the National Network consist of the Interstate System, except as noted, and the following additional highways.]

Arkansas

No additional routes have been federally designated; under State law STAA-dimensioned commercial vehicles may legally operate on all highways which, prior to June 1, 1991, were designated as Federal-aid primary highways.

Route	From	To
California		
I–80 Bus. Loop (US 50–CA 51).	I–80 W. Sacramento	I–80 near Watt Ave., Sacramento.
US 6	US 395 Bishop	NV State Line.
US 50	I–80 W. of Sacramento.	Sly Park Rd. Pollock Pines.
US 95	I–40 near Needles	NV State Line.
US 101	I–5 Los Angeles	I–80 San Francisco.
US 395	I–15 S. of Victorville	NV State Line.
CA 2	I–5	I–210 Los Angeles.
CA 10 (San Bern. Fwy.).	US 101	I–5 Los Angeles.
CA 14	I–5 near San Fernando.	US 395 Ridgecrest.
CA 15	I–5	I–805 San Diego.
CA 22	I–405 Seal Beach	CA 55 Orange.
CA 24	I–580 Oakland	I–680 Walnut Creek.
CA 52	I–5	I–805 San Diego.
CA 55	I–405 Costa Mesa	CA 91 Anaheim.
CA 57	I–5 Santa Ana	I–210 Pomona.
CA 58	CA 99 Bakersfield	I–15 Barstow.
CA 60	I–10 Los Angeles	I–10 Beaumont.
CA 71	I–210	CA 60 Pomona.
CA 78	I–5 Carlsbad	I–15 Escondido.
CA 85	I–280 near San Jose	CA 101 Mountain View.
CA 91	I–110 Los Angeles	I–215/CA 60 Riverside.
CA 92	I–280 San Mateo	I–880 Hayward.
CA 94	I–5	CA 125 San Diego.
CA 99	I–5 Wheeler Ridge	I–80 Bus. Loop/US 50 Sacramento.
CA 110	I–10	US 101 Los Angeles.
CA 118	I–405 Los Angeles	I–210 San Fernando.
CA 125	CA 94	I–8 La Mesa.
CA 133	I–405	I–5 near El Toro.
CA 134	US 101 Los Angeles	I–210 Pasadena.
CA 163	I–8	I–15 San Diego.
CA 170	US 101	I–5 Los Angeles.
CA 198	I–5 Coalinga	CA 99 Visalia.
CA 215	I–15 N. of Temecula	CA 60 Riverside.
CA 905 (Old CA 117).	I–5	I–805 San Diego.

Note: I–580 Oakland—All vehicles over 4½ tons (except passenger buses and stages) are prohibited on MacArthur Freeway between Grand Avenue and the north city limits of San Leandro. (Excepted under 23 CFR 658.11(f)).

Colorado

No additional routes have been federally designated; under State law STAA-dimensioned commercial vehicles may legally operate on all highways which, prior to June 1, 1991, were designated as Federal-aid primary highways.

Route	From	To
Connecticut		
CT 2	Columbus Blvd. Hartford.	I–395 Norwich.
CT 8	I–95 Bridgeport	US 44 Winsted.
CT 9	I–95 Old Saybrook	I–91 Cromwell.

[The federally-designated routes on the National Network consist of the Interstate System, except as noted, and the following additional highways.]

Route	From	To
CT 20	CT 401 Bradley Intl. Airport, Windsor Locks.	I–91 Windsor.
CT 401	CT 20 Windsor Locks	Bradley Intl. Airport Access Rd., Windsor Lks.
Delaware		
US 13	MD State Line	I–495 S. Int. Wilmington.
US 40	MD State Line	I–295/US 13 Wilmington.
US 113	MD State Line	US 13 Dover.
US 301	MD State Line	I–295/US 13 Wilmington.
District of Columbia		
Anacostia Fwy/Ken. Ave.	I–295	MD State Line Cheverly MD

Note: I–66—There is a 24 hour total truck ban on the Theodore Roosevelt Memorial Bridge and its approaches. (Excepted under 23 CFR 658.11(f).)

Route	From	To
Florida		
US 27	FL Turnpike Ext	FL 84 Andytown.
US 27	South Bay	I–75 Ocala.
US 301	SR 24 Waldo	I–10.
FL 24	SR 331 Gainesville	US 301 Waldo.
FL 85	FL 397 Valparaiso	I–10 near Crestview.
FL 202	I–95 Jacksonville	FL A–1–A.
FL 263	US 90 W. of Tallahassee.	I–10.
FL 331	I–75 S. of Gainesville	FL 24.
FL 397	Entrance Eglin AFB	FL 85 Valparaiso.
FL 528–FL 407.	I–4 Orlando	Cape Canaveral.
20th St. Expwy.	1–95 Jacksonville	Adams St. near Matthews Bridge.
FL Turnpike	S. End of Homestead Extension.	I–75 Wildwood.
Georgia		
US 19	FL State Line	US 82 Albany.
US 23/GA 365.	I–985 near Gainesville.	US 441 near Cornelia.
US 25	I–16	N. of Statesboro.
US 27	GA 53 Rome	US 278 Cedartown.
US 27	FL State Line	GA 38 Bainbridge.
US 27 Alternate GA 85.	I–185 Columbus	Ellerslie.
US 29	US 78 W. Interchange.	US 129/441 E. Interchange Athens.
US 41	I–75 W. of Morrow	Near Barnesville.
US 41	GA 5 Connector	County Road 633 Emerson.
US 76	I–75 Dalton	US 411 Chatsworth.
US 78–US 29	GA 138 Monroe	US 29 W. Interchange Athens.
US 78/GA 410.	Valleybrook Rd. Scottsdale.	GA 10 Stone Mountain.
US 78/GA 10	Stone Mountain Freeway.	Monroe Bypass.
US 80/GA 22	AL State Line	GA 85 Columbus.
US 82/GA 520.	Dawson	I–95 Exit 6 Brunswick.
US 84/GA 38	Alabama State Line	I–75.
US 84/GA 38	GA 520 Waycross	GA 32 Patterson.
US 129	I–16	Gray.
US 129	GA 247 Connector Warner Robins.	I–75 Macon.
US 129/GA 11.	I–85	I–985.
US 280/GA 520.	Alabama State Line	Dawson.
US 319/GA 35.	US 19/GA 300 Thomasville.	US 82/GA 520 Tifton.
US 411–US 41.	US 27 Rome	I–75 near Emerson.
US 441/GA 31.	US 82/GA 520 Pearson.	GA 135 Douglas.
US 441/GA 24.	I–20	GA 22 Milledgeville.
US 441/GA 15.	Athens Bypass	I–85.
GA 2	US 27 Fort Oglethorpe..	I–75.
GA 5 Connector.	I–75	US 41.
GA 6	I–20	GA 6 Bypass near Dallas.
GA 6 Bypass	E. of Dallas	W. of Dallas.
GA 10 Loop	E. and S. Bypass in Athens.	
GA 14 Spur	US 29/Welcome All Road.	I–85/285 S. Interchange Atlanta.
GA 21	I–95 Monteith	GA 204 Savannah.
GA 25	GA 520	GA 25 Spur.
GA 25 Spur	US 17 N. of Brunswick.	I–95 Exit 8.
GA 53	Rome	I–75 Calhoun.
GA 61	I–20	GA 166 near Carrollton.
GA 85	Fayetteville	I–75.
GA 138	I–20 Conyers	US 78 Monroe.
GA 166	GA 61	End of 4-lane section of W. GA 1 Carrollton.
GA 247C	I–75	GA 247 Warner Robins.
GA 300	US 82 Albany	I–75 near Cordele.
GA 316	I–85	US 29.
GA 400	I–285 near Atlanta	GA 60.
GA 515	I–575	Blairsville.
GA 520	I–95	GA 25.

Note: Atlanta area—Interstate highways within the I–285 beltway are not available to through trucks with more than 6 wheels because of construction.

Route	From	To
Hawaii		
HI 61	HI 98 (Vineyard Boulevard).	Kawainui Bridge Kailua.
HI 63	HI 92 (Nimitz Hwy.)	HI 83 (Kahekili Hwy.).
HI 64	Sand Island Park	HI 92 (Nimitz Hwy.).
HI 72	61 Kailua/Waimanalo Junction.	Ainakoa.
HI 78	H–1 Middle St	HI 99 (Kamehameha Hwy.) Aiea.
HI 83	HI 99 Weed Junction	HI 61 (Kalanianaole Hwy).
HI 92	Pearl Harbor/Main Gate.	Kalakaua Avenue.
HI 93	Beginning of H–1	Makaha Bridge.
HI 95	H–1	Barbers Point Harbor.

[The federally-designated routes on the National Network consist of the Interstate System, except as noted, and the following additional highways.]

Route	From	To
HI 99	Pearl Harbor Int.	HI 83 Weed Junction.
Idaho		
I–15B	I–15/US 26 S. of Idaho Falls.	US 26 N. Int. Idaho Falls.
US 2	Dover	US 95 Sandpoint.
US 2	US 95 Bonners Ferry	MT State Line.
US 20/26	OR State Line	I–84 W. Caldwell Int. Caldwell
US 20	I–84 Mountain Home	MT State Line.
US 26	I–84 Bliss	I–15 Blackfoot.
US 30	US 95 Fruitland	ID 72 New Plymouth.
US 30	I–15 McCammon	WY State Line.
US 89	UT State Line	US 30 Montpelier.
US 91	UT State Line	I–15 Virginia.
US 93	NV State Line	Arco.
US 95	OR State Line S. of Marsing.	OR State Line Weiser (via US 95 Spur).
US 95	Grangeville	Moscow.
US 95	I–90 Coeur D'Alene	US 2 Bonners Ferry.
ID 16	ID 44 Star	Emmett.
ID 28	ID 33 Mud Lake	US 93 Salmon.
ID 33	ID 28 Mud Lake	US 20 Rexburg
ID 44	I–84 Caldwe1l	ID 55 Eagle.
ID 51	NV State Line	I–84 Mountain Home.
ID 53	WA State Line	US 95 Garwood.
ID 55	US 95 Marsing	I–84 Nampa.
ID 55	US 20/26 S. of Eagle	ID 44 Eagle.
ID 75	US 93 Shoshone	Ketchum.
ID 87	US 20 N. of Macks Inn.	MT State Line.
Illinois		
US 20	US 20 BR W. of Rockford.	I–39 Rockford.
US 36	IL 100 NW. of Winchester.	I–55 Springfield.
US 50	US 50 BR E. of Lawrenceville.	IN State Line.
US 51	US 51 BR S. of Decatur.	I–72 Decatur.
US 67	IL 92 Rock Island	IA State Line.
IL 6	I–74/474 Peoria	IL 88 N. of Peoria.
IL 53	Army Trail Rd. Addison.	IL 68 Arlington Heights.
IL 92	I–280 Rock Island	US 67 Rock Island.
IL 336	IL 57 Fall Creek	US 24 NE. of Quincy.
IL 394	IL 1 Goodenow	I–80/94/294 S. Holland.
IL Toll Hwys	All Routes.	

Indiana

No additional routes have been federally designated; under State law STAA-dimensioned commercial vehicles may legally operate on all highways which, prior to June 1, 1991, were designated as Federal-aid primary highways.

Iowa

Note: Iowa State law allows STAA-dimensioned vehicles to operate on all highways in the State. The routes shown below were incorporated into the NN by the FHWA in 1984.

Route	From	To
US 6	NE State Line	I–80 Council Bluffs.
US 6	IA 48 Lewis	I–80 N. of Wilton.
US 6	IA 130 Davenport	I–74.
US 18	WCL Rock Valley	WI State Line.
US 20	I–29 Sioux City	IL State Line.
US 30	Missouri River Bridge (NE).	IL State Line Clinton.
US 34	Missouri River Bridge (NE).	IL State Line Burlington.
US 52	US 61 Dubuque	IA 386 N. Int. Sageville.
US 52	IA 3 Luxemburg	US 18 E. Int.
US 52	ECL Calmar	Burr Oak.
US 59	IA 2 Shenandoah	IA 184.
US 59	IA 92 Carson	US 6 N. Int.
US 59	IA 83 Avoca	US 30 Denison.
US 59	US 20 Holstein	IA 3.
US 59	IA 10 E. Int. W. of Sutherland.	US 18 Sanborn.
US 61	Des Moines River Bridge (MO) Keokuk.	WI State Line.
US 63	MO State Line	IA 146 New Sharon.
US 63	I–80 Malcom	NCL Chester.
US 65	US 34 N. Int. Lucas	IA 117/330.
US 65	US 30 Colo	Sheffield.
US 65	SCL Mason City	IA 105 Northwood.
US 67	IL State Line Davenport.	4.64 Miles N. of Clinton.
US 69	SCL Lamoni	I–35.
US 69	US 6/65 Des Moines	IA 105 Lake Mills.
US 71	MO State Line	IA 196 Ulmer.
US 71	US 20 Early	MN State Line.
US 75	I–29 N. Int. Sioux City.	IA 9 E. Int.
US 77	NE State Line	I–29 Sioux City.
US 136	Des Moines River Bridge (MO).	Mississippi River Bridge Keokuk.
US 151	I–80 E. of Williamsburg.	US 61 S. Int.
US 169	SCL Arispe	IA 92 Winterset.
US 169	SCL Desoto	I–80.
US 169	US 6 Adel	IA 141 Perry.
US 169	US 30 Beaver	IA 3.
US 169	US 18 Algona	IA 9 W. Int. Swea City.
US 218	US 136 Keokuk	IA 92 Ainsworth.
US 218	IA 22 Riverside	IA 227.
IA 1	IA 16 N. Int	IA 78 W. Int. Richland.
IA 1	IA 92 N. Int	IA 22 Kalona.
IA 1	US 6/218 N. Int. Iowa City.	I–80 Iowa City.
IA 1	SCL Martelle	US 151.
IA 2	NE State Line	IA 25 W. of Mt. Ayr.
IA 2	Decatur Co. Line	Mississippi River Bridge (IL) Ft. Madison.
IA 3	SD State Line	IA 12 N. Int. Akron.
IA 3	US 75 Le Mars	IA 7.
IA 3	IA 17 E. Int. Goldfield	IA 13 W. Int.
IA 4	IA 3 Pocahontas	US 18 E. Int.
IA 4	SCL Wallingford	IA 9 Estherville.
IA 5	IA 2 Centerville	I–35.
IA 7	IA 3	US 71 N. Int. Storm Lake.
IA 7	Barnum	US 20 Fort Dodge.
IA 8	US 63 Traer	US 218.
IA 9	IA 60	IA 26 Lansing.
IA 10	US 59 E. Int	ECL Sutherland.
IA 12	US 20	NCL Sioux City.
IA 13	US 30 Bertram	US 52.
IA 14	IA 92/5	NCL Newton.
IA 14	US 30 Marshalltown	US 20 S. Int.

[The federally-designated routes on the National Network consist of the Interstate System, except as noted, and the following additional highways.]

Route	From	To
IA 15	US 18 Whittemore	IA 9 W. Int.
IA 16	NCL Eldon	IA 1 N. Int.
IA 16	Denmark	US 61 Wever.
IA 17	IA 141 Granger	IA 3 E. Int.
IA 21	SCL What Cheer	IA 412 Waterloo.
IA 22	WCL Wellman	IA 70 W. Int.
IA 23	US 63 Ottumwa	IA 137 Eddyville.
IA 25	IA 2	IA 92 Greenfield.
IA 25	IA 925 W. Int	IA 44 Guthrie Center.
IA 26	IA 9 Lansing	New Albin.
IA 28	IA 92	US 6 Des Moines.
IA 31	SCL Correctionville	US 59.
IA 37	WCL Earling	US 59.
IA 38	US 61 Muscatine	I–80.
IA 38	SCL Tipton	US 30 E. Int.
IA 39	US 59 Denison	Deloit.
IA 44	US 71 Hamlin	IA 141.
IA 46	IA 5	IA 163 Des Moines.
IA 48	US 59 Shenandoah	NCL Essex.
IA 48	US 34 Red Oak	US 6.
IA 49	SCL Lenox	US 34.
IA 51	US 18 Postville	IA 9.
IA 55	Seymour	IA 2.
IA 60	US 75 Lemars	MN State Line.
IA 62	US 61 Maquoketa	US 52 Bellevue.
IA 64	US 151 Anamosa	US 61.
IA 70	Columbus City	IA 22 W. Int.
IA 77	IA 92	Keota.
IA 78	IA 149	IA 249 Winfield.
IA 78	WCL Morning Sun	US 61.
IA 83	S. of Walnut	US 6 Atlantic.
IA 85	US 63 Montezuma	IA 21.
IA 86	US 71	IA 9 Montgomery.
IA 92	NE State Line	IA 48 Griswold.
IA 92	WCL Fontanelle	IA 1 N. Int.
IA 92	IA 1 S. Int	Cotter.
IA 93	WCL Sumner	IA 150 Fayette.
IA 94	I–380 Cedar Rapids	Palo.
IA 96	Gladbrook	US 63 Traer.
IA 99	Toolesboro	US 61 Wapello.
IA 100	IA 151 Cedar Rapids	I–380.
IA 103	US 218	US 61 Fort Madison.
IA 105	US 69 Lake Mills	US 218 St. Ansgar.
IA 107	SCL Thornton	US 18 Clear Lake.
IA 110	US 20	IA 7 Storm Lake.
IA 111	US 18 Britt	Woden.
IA 117	IA 163 Prairie City	US 65.
IA 127	IA 183 S. Int	US 30 Logan.
IA 130	US 61/67 Davenport	I–80.
IA 133	US 30	Nevada.
IA 136	ECL Delmar	WCL Lost Nation.
IA 136	SCL Worthington	US 52/IA 3 Luxemburg.
IA 137	IA 5 Albia	IA 23.
IA 141	I–29	US 30/59 Denison.
IA 141	WCL Manning	US 169.
IA 141	IA 210 Woodward	I–35 Urbandale.
IA 144	IA 141 Perry	US 30 Grand Junction.
IA 145	I–29	ECL Thurman.
IA 146	US 63 New Sharon	Dunbar.
IA 148	IA 2 Bedford	US 34.
IA 148	IA 951 Carbon	I–80.
IA 149	US 63	IA 78 Martinsburg.
IA 149	SCL Williamsburg	I–80.
IA 150	US 218 Vinton	IA 283.
IA 150	US 20	US 18 West Union.
IA 150 (Old)	I–380 Center Point	IA 150.
IA 157	US 63	Lime Springs.
IA 160	US 69/IA 415	I–35 Ankeny.
IA 163	US 65 Des Moines	IA 92 Oskaloosa.

[The federally-designated routes on the National Network consist of the Interstate System, except as noted, and the following additional highways.]

Route	From	To
IA 173	IA 83 Atlantic	I–80.
IA 175	NE State Line	ECL Onawa.
IA 175	US 71 S. Int	ECL Lake City.
IA 175	Gowrie	ECL Dayton.
IA 175	WCL Stratford	ECL Radcliffe.
IA 175	US 65 N. Int	US 63 Voorhies.
IA 181	Melcher-Dallas	IA 5/92.
IA 183	IA 127 N. Int	NCL Pisgah.
IA 184	WCL Randolph	US 59.
IA 192	I–29/80	I–29 Council Bluffs.
IA 196	US 71	US 20 Sac City.
IA 210	IA 141	NCL Woodward.
IA 210	IA 17 N. Int	ECL Slater.
IA 215	Union	IA 175 Eldora.
IA 221	I–35	Roland.
IA 227	US 218	Stacyville.
IA 244	I–80	IA 191 Neola.
IA 249	IA 78	Winfield.
IA 272	Elma	US 63.
IA 273	WCL Drakesville	US 63.
IA 276	US 71	IA 327 Orleans.
IA 279	US 30	Atkins.
IA 281	WCL Fairbank	IA 150.
IA 283	Brandon	IA 150.
IA 287	US 30	Newhall.
IA 300	Modale	I–29.
IA 316	IA 5 Pleasantville	NCL Runnells.
IA 330	US 65	US 30 Marshalltown.
IA 363	IA 101	Urbana.
IA 401	US 6	Johnston.
IA 405	Lone Tree	IA 22.
IA 406	US 34	US 61 Burlington.
IA 415	US 6 Des Moines	IA 160.
IA 927	IA 38 Wilton	1–280 Davenport.
IA 928	US 20/IA 17	US 20 Williams.
IA 930	US 30	Ames.
IA 939	IA 150 Independence	IA 187.
IA 964	IA 5/92	IA 975/14 Knoxville.
IA 967	US 20	Farley.
IA 975	IA 5/92	IA 964/14 Knoxville.
University Ave.	US 20 SW. of Cedar Falls.	US 218 Cedar Falls.

Kansas

No additional routes have been federally designated; under State law STAA-dimensioned commercial vehicles may legally operate on all highways which, prior to June 1, 1991, were designated as Federal-aid primary highways.

Kentucky

Route	From	To
I–471 Connector.	US 27 Highland Heights.	I–275/471 Interchange.
US 23	Virginia State Line	US 119 near Jenkins.
US 23	US 119 N. of Pikeville.	S. end U.S. Grant Bridge South Portsmouth.
US 23 Spur	US 60 Ashland (via 13th St. Bridge).	Ohio State Line.
US 25/421	Int. US 25/US 421 S. of Richmond.	KY 876 Richmond.
US 25/421	KY 418 (via KY 4)	Nandino Blvd., Lexington.
US 25E	Virginia State Line	I–75 Exit 29 N. of Corbin.
US 27	Tennessee State Line (via KY 4 Lexington).	Ohio State Line.
US 31W	Tennessee State Line.	KY 255 Park City.

[The federally-designated routes on the National Network consist of the Interstate System, except as noted, and the following additional highways.]

Route	From	To
US 31W	Byp US 31W N. of Elizabethtown.	I–264 Exit 8 Louisville.
US 31W Byp	Western Kentucky Parkway Exit 136.	US 31W N. of Elizabethtown.
US 41	Pennyrile Parkway Henderson.	Indiana State Line.
US 41	Tennessee State Line.	Pennyrile Parkway near SCL Hopkinsville.
US 45	Jackson Purchase Parkway N. of Mayfield.	US 60 Paducah.
US 60	US 45 Paducah	Int. US 60/62 Paducah.
US 60	US 60 Byp W. of Owensboro.	KY 69 Hawesville.
US 60	KY 144 Garrett	US 31W S. of Muldraugh.
US 60	Int. US 421/KY 676 Frankfort (via KY 4 Lexington).	I–75 Exit 110 Lexington.
US 60	KY 180 Cannonsburg	US 23 Ashland.
US 60 Byp	US 60 W. of Owensboro.	US 60 E. of Owensboro.
US 62	I–24 Exit 7 Paducah (via US 60 Paducah).	US 68.
US 62/68	Washington	Ohio State Line.
US 68	US 62	I–24 Exit 16.
US 68	I–24 Exit 65 E. of Cadiz (via US 41 Hopkinsville).	Green River Parkway Exit 5 Bowling Green.
US 68	US 27 Paris (via Paris Byp).	Int. US 62/68 Washington.
US 119	KY 15 E. of Whitesburg.	US 23 near Jenkins.
US 119	US 25E S. of Pineville.	US 421 Harlan.
US 119	US 23 N. of Pikeville	KY 1441.
US 127	KY 22 Owenton	KY 35 Bromley.
US 127	US 127 Byp N. of Danville (via US 68 Harrosdburg).	US 60 Frankfort (via Lawrenceburg Byp.).
US 127 Byp	US 127 S. of Danville	US 127 N. of Danville.
US 127 Byp	US 127 S. of Lawrenceburg.	US 127 N. of Lawrenceburg.
US 150	US 62 Bardstown (via US 68 Perryville, the Danville Byp, and the Stanford Byp).	US 27 N. of Stanford.
US 150 Byp	US 127 S. of Danville	US 150 E. of Danville.
US 150 Byp	US 150 N. of Stanford.	US 27 N. of Stanford.
US 231	US 60 Byp Owensboro.	Indiana State Line.
US 421	0.1 mile S. of Harlan Appalachian Regional Hospital.	US 119.
US 421	Int. US 60/460 Frankfort.	US 127 Wilkinson Blvd./Owenton Rd. Interchange Frankfort.
US 431	US 60 Byp Owensboro.	US 60 (4th St.) Owensboro.
US 460	I–64 Exit 110 N. of Mt. Sterling.	KY 686 Mt. Sterling.
US 460	E. end Mountain Pkwy. Extension.	US 23 W. of Paintsville.
US 641	Tennessee State Line.	KY 348 Benton.
KY 4	US 27 S. Lexington	Entire Circle of Lexington.
KY 11	KY 3170 Lewisburg	US 62/68 Maysville.
KY 15	US 119 Whitesburg (via KY 7 Isom).	KY 15 Spur/KY 191 Campton.
KY 15 Spur	KY 15/191 Campton	Mountain Parkway Exit 43.
KY 21	I–75 Exit 76 W. of Berea.	US 25 Berea.
KY 35	US 127 Bromley	I–71 Exit 57.
KY 55	Cumberland Parkway Exit 49 Columbia.	US 150 Springfield.
KY 61	Peytonsburg	KY 90 Burkesville
KY 69	US 60 Hawesville	Indiana State Line.
KY 70/90	I–65 Exit 53	US 31E Glasgow.
KY 79	KY 1051 Brandenburg.	Indiana State Line.
KY 80	KY 80 Byp. E. of Somerset.	US 25 N. of London.
KY 80	KY 15 N. of Hazard	US 23 Watergap.
KY 80/US 421.	S. ramps Daniel Boone Parkway Exit 20.	2nd Street Manchester.
KY 80 Byp	US 27 Somerset	KY 80 E. of Somerset.
KY 90	KY 61 Burkesville	US 27 Burnside.
KY 114	US 460 E. of Salyersville.	US 23/460 S. of Prestonburg.
KY 118	Int. US 421/KY 80 Hyden.	Daniel Boone Parkway Exit 44.
KY 144	KY 448	US 60 Garrett.
KY 151	US 127 N. of Lawrenceburg.	I–64 Exit 48.
KY 180	I–64 Exit 185	Int. US 60/KY 180 Cannonsburg.
KY 192	I–75 Exit 38	Daniel Boone Parkway E. of London.
KY 259	Western Kentucky Parkway Exit 107.	US 62 Leitchfield.
KY 418	US 25/421 Lexington	I–75 Exit 104.
KY 446	US 31W Bowling Green.	I–65 Exit 28.
KY 448	KY 144	KY 1051 Brandenburg.
KY 555	US 150 Springfield	Bluegrass Parkway Exit 42.
KY 676	US 127 Frankfort	US 60/421 Frankfort.
KY 686	US 460 Mt. Sterling	KY 11 S. of Mt. Sterling.
KY 876	I–75 Exit 87 Richmond.	KY 52.
KY 922	KY 4 Lexington	I–64/75 Exit 115.
KY 1051	KY 448 S. of Brandenburg.	KY 79.
KY 1682	US 68 W. of Hopkinsville.	Pennyrile Parkway Exit 12 NCL Hopkinsville.
KY 1958	KY 627 S. of Winchester.	I–64 Exit 94 Winchester.
Audubon Parkway.	Pennyrile Parkway Exit 77 Henderson.	US 60 Byp Owensboro.
Blue Grass Parkway.	I–65 Exit 93 E. of Elizabethtown.	US 60 E. of Versailles.
Cumberland Parkway.	I–65 Exit 43 N. of Hays.	US 27 Somerset.
Daniel Boone Parkway.	US 25 N. of London	KY 15 N. of Hazard.
Green River Parkway.	I–65 Exit 20 S.E. of Bowling Green.	US 60 Byp Owensboro.

[The federally-designated routes on the National Network consist of the Interstate System, except as noted, and the following additional highways.]

Route	From	To
Jackson Purchase Parkway.	Tennessee State Line.	I–24 Exit 25 E. of Calvert City.
Mountain Parkway and Mountain Parkway Extension.	I–64 Exit 98 E. of Winchester.	US 460 Salyersville.
Pennyrile Parkway.	US 41 Alt. Hopkinsville.	US 41 Henderson.
Western Kentucky Parkway.	I–24 Exit 42 S. of Eddyville.	I–65 Exit 91 S. of Elizabethtown.

Note: US 23 crosses the Ohio River between South Portsmouth, KY and Portsmouth, OH via the U.S. Grant Bridge. Although the state line is near the Ohio shoreline, putting most of the bridge in Kentucky, the terminal point for US 23 is listed as the south end of the bridge because the bridge is maintained by the Ohio DOT.

Louisiana

No additional routes have been federally designated; under State law STAA-dimensioned commercial vehicles may legally operate on all highways which, prior to June 1, 1991, were designated as Federal-aid primary highways.

Maine

Route	From	To
US 1	I–95 Brunswick	Old US 1 (Vicinity of Congress St.) Bath.
Scarboro Connector.	I–295 South Portland	US 1 Scarborough.
South Portland Spur.	I–95 South Portland	US 1 South Portland.

Maryland

Route	From	To
US 13	VA State Line	DE State Line.
US 15	US 40/340 Frederick	MD 26 Frederick.
US 40	US 15/340 Frederick	I–70/270 Frederick.
US 48	WV State Line	I–70 Hancock.
US 50	MD 201/Kenilworth Ave. Cheverly.	US 13 Salisbury.
US 301	VA State Line	DE State Line.
US 340	MD 67 Weverton	US 15/40 Frederick.
MD 3	US 50/301 Bowie	I–695/MD 695 Glen Burnie.
MD 4	I–95 Forestville	US 301 Upper Marlboro.
MD 10	MD 648 Glen Burnie	MD 695 Glen Burnie.
MD 100	MD 3	MD 607 Jacobsville.
MD 201 (Kenilw. Ave.).	D.C. Line	US 50 Cheverly.
MD 295	I–695 Linthicum	I–95 Baltimore.
MD 695	I–695/MD 3 Glen Burnie.	I–95/695 Kenwood.
MD 702	Old Eastern Avenue	MD 695 Essex.

Note: I–895 Baltimore—Widths over 96 inches and tandem trailers may be prohibited on the Harbor Tunnel Thruway because of construction.

Massachusetts

Route	From	To
US 3	I–95 Burlington	NH State Line.
MA 2	I–190 Leominister	I–495 Littleton.
MA 24	I–195 Fall River	I–93 Randolph.
MA 140	I–195 New Bedford	MA 24 Taunton.

[The federally-designated routes on the National Network consist of the Interstate System, except as noted, and the following additional highways.]

Note: I–93 Boston—Restrictions may be applied, when necessary, to portions of I–93 affected by reconstruction of the Central Artery (I–93) and construction of the Third Harbor Tunnel (I–90).

Michigan

Route	From	To
I–75 Conn	US 24BR Pontiac	I–75.
US 2	WI State Line Ironwood.	WI State Line S. of Crystal Falls.
US 2	WI State Line Iron Mountain.	I–75 St. Ignace.
US 8	US 2 Norway	WI State Line.
US 10	Ludington	I–75 Bay City.
US 12	IN State Line	I–94 W. Jct. Ypsilanti.
US 23	OH State Line	I–75 Mackinaw City.
US 24	OH State Line	MI 15 Waterford.
US 24BR	US 24 S. of Pontiac	MI 1 Pontiac.
US 27	IN State Line	I–75 S. of Grayling.
US 31	IN State Line	I–75 Mackinaw City.
US 33	IN State Line	US 12 Niles.
US 41	WI State Line	Houghton.
US 45	WI State Line	MI 26 Rockland.
US 127	OH State Line	I–69/US 27 N. of Lansing.
US 131	IN State Line	US 31 Petoskey.
US 141	WI State Line S. of Crystal Falls.	US 41/MI 28.
US 223	US 23	US 12/127 Somerset.
MI 10	I–375 Detroit	Orchard Lake Road.
MI 13	I–69 Lennon	I–75 Saginaw (via MI 81).
MI 13	I–75 Kawkawlin (via I–75 Conn.).	US 23 Standish.
MI 14	I–94 Ann Arbor	I–96/275 Plymouth.
MI 15	US 24 Clarkston	MI 25 Bay City.
MI 18	US 10	MI 61 Gladwin.
MI 20	US 31 New Era	MI 37 White Cloud.
MI 20	US 27 Mt. Pleasant	US 10 Midland.
MI 21	I–96 near Grand Rapids.	I–69 Flint.
MI 24	I–75 Auburn Hills (via I–75 Conn.).	I–69 Lapeer.
MI 24	MI 46	MI 81 Caro.
MI 26	US 45 Rockland	MI 38.
MI 27	I–75	US 23 Cheboygan.
MI 28	US 2 Wakefield	I–75.
MI 32	Hillman	Alpena.
MI 33	Mio	Fairview.
MI 35	US 2/41 Escanaba	US 2/41 Gladstone.
MI 36	US 127 Mason	Dansville.
MI 37	MI 55	US 31/MI 72 Traverse City.
MI 37	I–96 Grand Rapids	MI 46 Kent City.
MI 38	US 45 Ontonagon	US 41 Baraga.
MI 39	I–75 Lincoln Park	MI 10 Southfield.
MI 40	MI 89 Allegan	US 31BR/I–196BL Holland.
MI 43	MI 37 Hastings	US 127 Lansing.
MI 46	US 131 Howard City	MI 25 Port Sanilac.
MI 47	I–675 Saginaw (via MI 58).	US 10.
MI 50	MI 43/66 Woodbury	MI 99 Eaton Rapids.
MI 50	US 127 S. Jct	I–75 Monroe.
MI 51	US 12 Niles	I–94.
MI 52	OH State Line	US 12 Clinton.
MI 52	I–96 Webberville	MI 46 W. of Saginaw.
MI 53	MI 3 Detroit	MI 25 Port Austin.
MI 55	US 31 Manistee	I–75.
MI 55	MI 65	US 23 Tawas City.

[The federally-designated routes on the National Network consist of the Interstate System, except as noted, and the following additional highways.]

Route	From	To
MI 57	US 131 N. of Rockford.	US 27.
MI 57	MI 52 Chesaning	I–75 Clio.
MI 59	US 24 BR Pontiac	I–94.
MI 60	MI 62 Cassopolis	I–69/US 27.
MI 61	MI 115	US 27 Harrison.
MI 61	MI 18 Gladwin	US 23 Standish.
MI 63	US 31 Scottdale	I–196.
MI 65	US 23 Omer	MI 55.
MI 65	MI 72 Curran	MI 32.
MI 65	Posen	US 23 N. of Posen.
MI 66	IN State Line	US 12 Sturgis.
MI 66	Battle Creek	MI 78.
MI 66	MI 43/50 Woodbury	MI 46 Edmore.
MI 67	US 41 Trenary	MI 94 Chatham.
MI 68	US 31/131 Petoskey	US 23 Rogers City.
MI 69	US 2/141 Crystal Falls.	MI 95 Sagola.
MI 72	US 31/MI 37 Traverse City.	US 23 Harrisville.
MI 77	US 2	MI 28 Seney.
MI 78	MI 66	I–69 Olivet.
MI 81	MI 24 Caro	MI 53.
MI 82	MI 37 S. Jct. Newago	US 131.
MI 83	Frankenmuth	I–75.
MI 84	I–75	MI 25 Bay City.
MI 89	MI 40 Allegan	US 131.
MI 94	US 41	MI 28 Munising.
MI 95	US 2 Iron Mountain	US 41/MI 28.
MI 104	US 31 Grand Haven	I–96.
MI 115	US 27	MI 22 Frankfort.
MI 117	US 2 Engadine	MI 28.
MI 123	I–75 N. of St. Ignace	MI 28.
MI 142	MI 25 Bay Port	MI 53.
MI 205	IN State Line	US 12 W. of Union.
Minnesota		
US 2	ND State Line E. Grand Forks.	I–35 Duluth.
US 10	CH 11 E. of Moorhead.	I–694 Arden Hills.
US 12	US 59 Holloway	I–94 Minneapolis.
US 14	US 75 Lake Benton	US 52 Rochester.
US 52	I–90 S. of Rochester	MN 110 Inver Grove Hts.
US 53	I–35/535 Duluth	US 169 S. Int. Virginia.
US 59	I–90 Worthington	MN 30 S. Int. Slayton.
US 59	MN 7 Appleton	US 12 Holloway.
US 59	I–94 N. Int. Fergus Falls.	MN 175 Lake Bronson.
US 61	WI State Line	MN 60 Wabasha.
US 61	MN 55 Hastings	I–94 St. Paul.
US 61	I–35 Duluth	CH 2 Two Harbors.
US 63	I–90 Rochester	US 52 Rochester.
US 63	MN 58 Red Wing	WI State Line.
US 71	IA State Line	MN 34 Park Rapids.
US 75	I–90	US 2 Crookston.
US 75	MN 175 Hallock	Canadian Border.
US 169	I–90 Blue Earth	US 212 Chanhassen.
US 169	I–94 Brooklyn Park	MN 23 Milaca.
US 169	US 2 Grand Rapids	US 53 S. Int. Virginia.
US 212	SD State Line	MN 62 Edina.
US 218	I–90 Austin	US 14 Owatonna.
MN 1	ND State Line	US 59/MN 32 Thief River Falls.
MN 3	MN 110 Inver Grove Hts.	I–94 St. Paul.
MN 5	MN 22 Gaylord	US 212.
MN 7	US 75 near Odessa	MN 100 St. Louis Park.
MN 9	US 12 Benson	US 59 Morris.
MN 11	MN 32 Greenbush	MN 72 Baudette.
MN 13	I–90	MN 14 Waseca.
MN 15	I–90 Fairmont	MN 60.
MN 15	US 14 New Ulm	MN 19 Winthrop.
MN 19	US 59 Marshall	MN 22 Gaylord.
MN 22	MN 109 Wells	US 14/MN 60 Mankato.
MN 22	US 212 Glencoe	US 12 Litchfield.
MN 23	US 75 Pipestone	I–35 near Hinckley.
MN 24	I–94 Clearwater	US 10 Clear Lake.
MN 25	I–94 Monticello	US 10 Big Lake.
MN 27	MN 29 Alexandria	MN 127 Osakis.
MN 27	US 71 N. Int. Long Prairie.	US 10 Little Falls.
MN 28	SD State Line Browns Valley.	I–94/US 71 Sauk Centre.
MN 29	I–94 Alexandria	MN 27 Alexandria.
MN 30	US 75 Pipestone	US 59 S. Int. Slayton.
MN 32	US 59/MN 1 Thief River Falls.	MN 11 Greenbush.
MN 33	I–35 Cloquet	US 53 Independence.
MN 34	US 71 Park Rapids	MN 371 Walker.
MN 36	I–35W Roseville	MN 95 Oak Park Hts.
MN 43	I–90 Wilson	US 61 Winona.
MN 55	MN 28 Glenwood	7th St. N., W. Int. Minneapolis.
MN 55	I–94 E. Int. Minneapolis.	MN 3 Inver Grove Hts.
MN 60	IA State Line Bigelow	US 14/169 Mankato.
MN 62	US 212 Edina	MN 100 Edina.
MN 65	I–694 Fridley	MN 23 Mora.
MN 68	US 75 Canby	MN 19 Marshall.
MN 101	I–94 Rogers	US 10 Elk River.
MN 109	I–90 Alden	MN 22 Wells.
MN 175	US 75 Hallock	US 59.
MN 210	ND State Line Breckenridge.	US 59 W. Int. Fergus Falls.
MN 210	US 10 Motley	I–35 Carlton.
MN 371	US 10 Little Falls	US 2 Cass Lake.

NOTE: I–35E St. Paul—The parkway segment of I–35E from 7th Street to I–94 is not available to trucks because of reduced design standards.

Mississippi

No additional routes have been federally designated; under State law STAA-dimensioned commercial vehicles may legally operate on all highways which, prior to June 1, 1991, were designated as Federal-aid primary highways.

Missouri

Route	From	To
US 24	I–435 Kansas City	US 65 Waverly.
US 24	US 36 E. Jct. W. of Hannibal.	IL State Line.
US 36	KS State Line St. Joseph.	IL State Line Hannibal.
US 40	I–70 Wentzville	I–270 W. of St. Louis.
US 50	I–470 Exit 7 Kansas City.	I–44 Exit 247 Union.
US 54	US 54BR Lake Ozark	IL State Line.
US 59	KS State Line	I–229 St. Joseph.
US 60	OK State Line	US 71 Neosho.
US 60	MO 37 Monett	US 63 Cabool.

[The federally-designated routes on the National Network consist of the Interstate System, except as noted, and the following additional highways.]

Route	From	To
US 60	2 Mi. E. of E. Jct. MO 21 Ellsinore.	I–55/57 Sikeston.
US 61	I–70 Wentzville	IA State Line.
US 63	AR State Line Thayer	IA State Line.
US 65	AR State Line Ridgedale.	IA State Line.
US 67	AR State Line	I–55 Exit 174 Crystal City.
US 67	MO 367 N. of St. Louis.	IL State Line.
US 71	AR State Line	I–435/470 Kansas City.
US 71	I–29 Exit 53 N. of St. Joseph.	US 136 Maryville.
US 71 Alt	I–44 E. of Joplin	US 71 Carthage.
US 136	NE State Line	I–29 Exit 110 Rock Port.
US 166	KS State Line	I–44 SW. of Joplin.
US 169	I–29 Kansas City	MO 152 Kansas City.
US 412	AR State Line	I–55 Exit 19 Hayti.
MO 5	AR State Line	US 60 Mansfield.
MO 7	US 71 Harrisonville	MO 13 Clinton.
MO 13	I–44 Springfield	US 24 Lexington.
MO 25	US 412 near Kennett	US 60 Dexter.
MO 37	MO 76 Cassville	US 60 Monett.
MO 47	US 50 Union	MO 100 Washington.
MO 84	AR State Line	US 412 near Kennett.
MO 100	MO 47 Washington	I–44 SE. of Washington.
MO 171	KS State Line/KS 57	US 71 Webb City.
MO 367	I–270 N. of St. Louis	US 67 N. of St. Louis.

Montana

No additional routes have been federally designated; under State law STAA-dimensioned commercial vehicles may legally operate on all highways which, prior to June 1, 1991, were designated as Federal-aid primary highways.

Nebraska

No additional routes have been federally designated; under State law STAA-dimensioned commercial vehicles may legally operate on all highways which, prior to June 1, 1991, were designated as Federal-aid primary highways.

Nevada

No additional routes have been federally designated; under State law STAA-dimensioned commercial vehicles may legally operate on all highways which, prior to June 1, 1991, were designated as Federal-aid primary highways.

New Hampshire

Route	From	To
US 3	MA State Line	NH 101A Nashua.
US 4/ Spaulding Tpk.	I–95 Portsmouth	Exit 6 E. of Durham.

New Jersey

Route	From	To
US 130	US 322 Bridgeport	I–295 Logan Township.
US 130	I–295/NJ 44 West Deptford.	I–295 West Deptford.
US 322	PA State Line	US 130 Bridgeport.
NJ 42	Atlantic City Expwy. Turnersville.	I–295 Bellmawr.

[The federally-designated routes on the National Network consist of the Interstate System, except as noted, and the following additional highways.]

Route	From	To
NJ 81	I–95 Elizabeth	US 1/9 Newark Intl. Airport.
NJ 440	I–287/I–95 Edison	NY State Line Outerbridge Crossing.

Note: I–95—The following two sections of the New Jersey Turnpike are available to STAA-dimensioned vehicles. They were added to the Interstate System on March 3, 1983, but are not signed as Interstate.

Route	From	To
PA Tpk. Connector.	PA State Line	Exit 6 Mansfield.
NJ Tpk.	Exit 6 Mansfield	Exit 10 Edison.

New Mexico

Route	From	To
US 56	I–25 Springer	OK State Line.
US 60	AZ State Line	I–25 Socorro.
US 62	US 285 Carlsbad	Tx State Line.
US 64	AZ State Line	NM 516 Farmington.
US 70	AZ State Line	I–10 Lordsburg.
US 70	I–10 Las Cruces	U.S. 54 Tularosa.
US 70	US 285 Roswell	U.S. 84 Clovis.
NM 80	AZ State Line	I–10 Road Forks.
US 84	Tx State Line Clovis	CO State Line.
US 87	US 56 Clayton	Tx State Line.
US 160	Az State Line (Four Corners).	CO State Line.
US 285	Tx State Line s. of Carlsbad.	CO State Line.
US 491	1–40 Gallup	CO State Line.
NM 516	U.S. 64 Farmington	U.S. 550 Aztec.
US 550	NM 516 Aztec	CO State Line.

New York

Route	From	To
US 15	Presho Int	NY 17 Corning.
US 20	NY 75 Mt. Vernon	Howard Rd. Mt. Vernon.
US 219	NY 39 Springville	I–90 S. of Exit 55.
NY 5	NY 174 Camillus	NY 695 Fairmont.
NY 5	ECL Schenectady	I–87 Colonie.
NY 5	NY 179 Woodlawn Beach.	NY 75 Mt. Vernon.
NY 7	Schenectady/Albany Co. Line.	I–87 Colonie.
NY 8	CR 9/Main St. Sauquoit.	I–790 Utica.
NY 12	I–790 Utica	Putnam Road Trenton.
NY 17	Exit 24 Allegany	I–87 Exit 16 Harriman.
NY 17	NJ State Line	I–87 Exit 15 Suffern.
NY 33	Michigan Ave. Buffalo.	Greater Buffalo Intl. Airport.
NY 49	NY 365 Rome	NY 291 near Oriskany.
NY 104	Maplewood Dr. Rochester.	Monroe/Wayne Co. Line.
NY 179	NY 5 Woodlawn Beach.	I–90 Exit 56 Windom.
NY 198	I–190 Exit N11	NY 33 Buffalo.
NY 254	I–87 Glens Falls	0.3 Miles E. of US 9.
NY 365	I–90 Exit 33	NY 49 Rome.
NY 390	I–390/490 Rochester	NY 18 North Greece.
NY 400	I–90 Exit 54	NY 16 South Wales.
NY 481	I–81 North Syracuse	NY 3 Fulton.
NY 590	I–490/590 Rochester	NY 104 Irondequoit.
NY 690	I–90/690 Lakeland	NY 370 Baldwinsville.
NY 695	NY 5 Fairmont	I–690 Solvay.

[The federally-designated routes on the National Network consist of the Interstate System, except as noted, and the following additional highways.]

Route	From	To
Berkshire Conn. (NY 912M).	I–87 Exit 21A S. of Albany.	I–90 Exit B1.
Inner Loop (NY 940T).	I–490 W. Int. Rochester.	I–490 E. Int. Rochester.
Walden Avenue (NY 952Q).	I–90 Exit 52	NY 277 Cheektowaga.
Sheridan Boulevard (NY 895).	I–278 Bruckner Expressway.	I–95 Cross Bronx Expressway.
North Carolina		
I–40 Conn	US 19/23/74 Clyde	I–40 W. of Clyde.
I–95 BR	I–95 S. of Fayetteville.	I–95 N. of Fayetteville.
US 1	US 74 Rockingham	I–85 near Henderson.
US 15	US 401 Laurinburg	US 1 Aberdeen.
US 15	US 1 Northview	US 64 Pittsboro.
US 17	SC State Line	US 74/76 W. of Wilmington.
US 17	SR 1409 E. of Wilmington.	VA State Line.
US 19/US 23	I–240 Asheville	N. Int. Mars Hill.
US 23	US 441 Franklin	US 74 Dillsboro.
US 25	SC State Line	I–26 East Flat Rock.
US 25/US 70	US 19/23 Weaverville	US 25/70 Bypass Marshall.
US 29	US 52 Lexington	VA State Line.
US 52	NC 24/27 Albemarle	VA State Line.
US 64	I–40 Morganton	US 321 Lenoir.
US 64	US 29 Lexington	US 15 Pittsboro.
US 64	US 1/70/401 Raleigh	US 17 Williamston.
US 70	I–77 Statesville	I–85 Salisbury (via US 601).
US 70	I–85 Durham	US 70A W. of Smithfield.
US 70A	US 70 W. of Smithfield.	US 70 Princeton.
US 70	US 70A Princeton	Beaufort.
US 74	TN State Line	I–40 Conn. Clyde.
US 74	US 221 Rutherfordton.	I–85 Kings Mountain.
US 74 (See Note Below).	I–277 Charlotte	US 17 W. Int. Wilmington.
US 74	I–26 EXIT 36	US 74 ALT: near Forest City.
US 76	US 17/74 W. Int. Wilmington.	SR 1409 E. of Wilmington.
US 158	I–40 Winston-Salem	US 29 Reidsville.
US 158	I–85 Henderson	US 258 Murfreesboro.
US 220	US 74 Rockingham	VA State Line.
US 221	US 74 Rutherfordton	I–40 Glenwood.
US 258	NC 24 N. Int. Richlands.	US 64 Tarboro.
US 258	US 158 Murfreesboro	VA State Line.
US 264	US 64 Zebulon	US 17 Washington.
US 301	I–95 Kenly	NC 4 Battleboro.
US 321	SC State Line	I–85 Gastonia.
US 321	I–40 Hickory	NC 18/90 Lenoir.
US 401	SC State Line	I–40 Raleigh.
US 421	Carolina Beach	I–95 Dunn.
US 421	US 1 Sanford	US 64 Siler City.
US 421	I–40 Winston-Salem	Wilkesboro.
US 521	SC State Line	I–77 Charlotte.
US 601	SC State Line	US 74 Monroe.
NC 4	I–95 Gold Rock	US 301 Battleboro.

[The federally-designated routes on the National Network consist of the Interstate System, except as noted, and the following additional highways.]

Route	From	To
NC 11	US 70 Kinston	US 264 Greenville.
NC 24	US 74 Charlotte	US 52 Albemarle.
NC 24	NC 87 Spout Springs	I–95 Fayetteville.
NC 24	US 421 Clinton	US 70 Mansfield.
NC 49	I–85 Charlotte	US 64 Asheboro.
NC 87	NC 24/27 Spout Springs.	US 1 Sanford.
SR 1409	US 76 E. of Wilmington.	US 17.
SR 1728	I–40 W. of Raleigh	US 1/Wade Ave. Raleigh.
SR 1959–SR 2028.	US 70 Bethesda	I–40 S. of Durham.

Note: US 74 Charlotte—STAA-dimensioned vehicles are subject to State restrictions on US 74 in Charlotte because of narrow lane widths.

Route	From	To
North Dakota		
US 2	MT State Line	MN State Line Grand Forks.
US 10	I–94 W. Fargo	MN State Line.
US 12	MT State Line Marmarth.	SD State Line.
US 52	I–94 Jamestown	Canadian Border.
US 81	I–29 Manvel	I–29 Joliette.
US 83	SD State Line	Canadian Border Westhope.
US 85	SD State Line	Canadian Border Fortuna.
US 281	SD State Line Ellendale.	Canadian Border.
ND 1	ND 11 Ludden	ND 13 S. Jct.
ND 5	MT State Line	US 85 Fortuna.
ND 11	US 281 Ellendale	ND 1 Ludden.
ND 13	ND 1 S. Jct	MN State Line.
ND 32	West Junction of ND Highway 13.	1–94.
ND 68	MT State Line	US 85 Alexander.
ND 200	MT State Line	US 85 Alexander.

Ohio

No additional routes have been federally designated; under State law STAA-dimensioned commercial vehicles may legally operate on all highways which, prior to June 1, 1991, were designated as Federal-aid primary highways.

Oklahoma

No additional routes have been federally designated; STAA-dimensioned commercial vehicles may legally operate on all Federal-aid Primary highways under State law.

Route	From	To
Oregon		
US 20	OR 34 W. Int. Philomath.	ECL Sweet Home.
US 20	OR 126 Sisters	ID State Line Nyssa.
US 26	US 101 Cannon Beach Junction.	OR 126 Prineville.
US 30	US 101 Astoria	I–405 Portland.
US 30 BR	OR 201 Ontario	ID State Line.
US 95	NV State Line	ID State Line.
US 95 Spur	OR 201	ID State Line Weiser, ID.
US 97	CA State Line	WA State Line.
US 101	SCL Port Orford	OR 126 Florence.
US 101	US 20 Newport	OR 18 Otis.
US 101	OR 6 Tillamook	WA State Line.
US 197	I–84 The Dalles	WA State Line.

[The federally-designated routes on the National Network consist of the Interstate System, except as noted, and the following additional highways.]

Route	From	To
US 199	CA State Line	OR 99 Grants Pass.
US 395	CA State Line	US 26 John Day.
US 395	I–84 Stanfield	US 730 near Umatilla.
US 730	I–84 Boardman	WA State Line.
OR 6	US 101 Tillamook	US 26 Near Banks.
OR 8	OR 47 Forest Grove	OR 217 Beaverton.
OR 11	I–84 Pendelton	WA State Line.
OR 18	US 101 Otis	OR 99W Dayton.
OR 19	OR 206 Condon	I–84 Arlington.
OR 22	OR 18 near Willamina.	US 20 Santiam Junction.
OR 31	US 97 La Pine	US 395 Valley Falls.
OR 34	OR 99W Corvallis	US 20 Lebanon.
OR 35	US 26 Government Camp.	I–84 Hood River.
OR 38	US 101 Reedsport	I–5 Anlauf.
OR 39	CA State Line	OR 140 E. of Klamath Falls.
OR 42	US 101 Coos Bay	OR 42S Coquille.
OR 47	OR 8 Forest Grove	US 26 N. of Banks.
OR 58	I–5 Eugene	US 97 near Chemult.
OR 62	Medford	OR 140 White City.
OR 78	Burns	US 95 Burns Junction.
OR 99	I–5 E. of Rogue River.	I–5 Grants Pass.
OR 99	I–5 Eugene	OR 99W/E Junction City.
OR 99E	OR 99/99W Junction City.	I–5 Albany.
OR 99E	I–5 Salem	I–5 Portland.
OR 99W	OR 99/99E Junction City.	I–5 Portland.
OR 126	US 101 Florence	US 26 Prineville.
OR 138	OR 38 Elkton	I–5 near Sutherlin.
OR 140	OR 62 White City	OR 39 E. of Klamath Falls.
OR 201	US 26 Cairo	US 95 Spur near Weiser, ID.
OR 207	US 730 Cold Springs Jct.	OR 74 S. Int. Heppner.
OR 212	OR 224 E. Int. near Rock Ck. Corner.	US 26 near Boring.
OR 214	I–5 Woodburn	OR 213 Silverton.
OR 217	US 26 Beaverton	I–5 Tigard.
OR 223	Kings Valley Hwy. in Dallas.	OR 99W Rickreall.
OR 224	OR 99E Milwaukie	OR 212 E. Int. near Rock Ck. Corner
Pennsylvania		
US 1	US 13 Morrisville	NJ State Line.
US 6	Conneaut Lake Borough.	End of 4-lane Bypass NE. of Meadville.
US 11	Turnpike Int. 16	US 15 Harrisburg.
US 13	US 1 Morrisville	Turnpike Int. 29.
US 15	Turnpike Int. 17	US 11 Harrisburg Expwy.
US 15	PA 642 West Milton	White Deer Int.
US 15	I–180/US 220 Williamsport.	End of lim. acc. Williamsport.
US 20	PA 89 North East	I–90 Int. 12.
US 22	WV State Line	I–79 Int. 15 Carnegie.
US 22	I–78 Fogelsville	NJ State Line.
US 30	End of lim. acc. W. of Greensburg.	End of lim. acc. E. of Greensburg.
US 30	PA 462 W. of York	PA 462 E. of Lancaster.

[The federally-designated routes on the National Network consist of the Interstate System, except as noted, and the following additional highways.]

Route	From	To
US 119	End of lim. acc. S. of Uniontown.	US 30 Greensburg.
US 202	DE State Line	I–76 Int. 26 King of Prussia.
US 209	PA 33 Snydersville	I–80 Stroudsburg.
US 219	PA 601 N. of Somerset.	US 422 W. Int.
US 219	South Bradford Int	NY State Line.
US 220	Turnpike Int. 11	King.
US 220	End of lim. acc. Linden.	I–180/US 15 Williamsport.
US 220	PA 199 S. of Athens	NY State Line NY 17.
US 222	US 422 N. Int. Reading.	PA 61 S. of Tuckerton.
US 222	US 30 Lancaster	Turnpike Int. 21.
US 322	NJ State Line (Comm. Barry Br.).	I–95 Chester.
US 322	I–83/283	US 422/PA 39 Hershey.
US 422	US 322/PA 39 Hershey.	Hockersville Rd. Hershey.
US 422	US 422 Bus. Reiffton	US 422 Bus. Wyomissing.
PA 3	US 202	Garrett Rd. Upper Darby.
PA 9	Turnpike Int. 25	I–81 Int. 58 N. of Scranton.
PA 28	PA 8	Creighton.
PA 33	US 22 Easton	I–80.
PA 42	I–80 Int. 34	US 11 Bloomsburg.
PA 51	US 119 Uniontown	Monongahela Riv. Elizabeth.
PA 54	I–80 Int. 33	US 11 Danville.
PA 60	PA 51 Beaver Falls	US 22.
PA 60–US 422.	I–80 Int. 1	1 Mile E. of PA 65 New Castle.
PA 61	US 222 S. of Tuckerton.	I–78 Int. 9.
PA 93	I–81 Int. 41	PA 924 Hazelton.
PA 114	US 11 Hogestown	I–81 Int. 18.
PA 132	I–95 Cornwells Heights.	Turnpike Int. 28 (via US 1 Connection).
PA 283	I–283 Int. 2	US 30 Lancaster.
PA 924	I–81 Int. 40	PA 93 Hazelton.
Airport Access (SR 3032).	PA 283	Harrisburg International Airport.
Harrisburg Exp. (Sr 2022).	US 11/15	I–83 Int. 20.
Reading Outer Loop (SR 3055).	PA 183 Leinbachs	US 222.
Puerto Rico		
PR 1	PR 2 Ponce	PR 52 Ponce.
PR 2	PR 22 San Juan	PR 1 Ponce.
PR 3	N. Ent. Roosevelt Roads Naval Sta..	PR 26 Carolina.
PR 18	PR 52 San Juan	PR 22 San Juan.
PR 22	PR 26 San Juan	PR 165 Toa Baja.
PR 26	PR 22 San Juan	PR 3 Carolina.
PR 30	PR 52 Caguas	PR 3 Humacao.
PR 52	PR 1 Ponce	PR 18 San Juan.
PR 165	PR 22 Toa Baja	PR 2 Toa Baja.

[The federally-designated routes on the National Network consist of the Interstate System, except as noted, and the following additional highways.]

Route	From	To
Note: Routes added to the Interstate System under 23 U.S.C. 139(c) are included only to the extent designated above.		
Rhode Island		
RI 10	RI 195 Providence	I–95 Cranston.
RI 37	I–295 Cranston	I–95 near Lincoln Park.
RI 146	I–95 Providence	I–295 N. of Lime Rock.
RI 195	I–295 Johnston	RI 10 Providence.
South Carolina		
US 15/401	NC State Line	US 52 Society Hill.
US 17	I–95 Pocotaligo	US 21 Gardens Corner.
US 17	I–26 Charleston	NC State Line.
US 21	US 17 Gardens Corner.	SC 170 Beaufort.
US 25	NC State Line	US 78 North Augusta (via Greenwood Bypass).
US 52	US 15/401 Society Hill.	End of 4-ln. div. N. of urban limits of Kingstree.
US 52	US 17 A1t. S. Int. Moncks Corner.	I–26 Exit 208 N. Charleston connector.
US 76	US 52 Florence	SC 576 Marion.
US 76	SC 277 Columbia	I–126 Columbia.
US 78	GA State Line	I–95 St. George.
US 78	I–26 Exit 205 N. Charleston.	US 52 N. Charleston.
US 123	Bibb St. Westminister	US 25 Greenville.
US 21/178 Bypass.	US 601 Orangeburg	Orangeburg.
US276	I–385 Simpsonville	I–85 Greenville.
US 301	US 321 Ulmer	I–95 Santee.
US 321	I–26 S. of Columbia	I–95 Hardeeville.
US 378	SC 262 Columbia	US 501 Conway.
US 501	SC 576 Marion	US 17 Myrtle Beach.
US 601	NC State Line	SC 151 Pageland.
US 601	I–26 Jamison	US 21/178 Bypass Orangeburg.
SC 72	US 25 Byp. Greenwood.	I–77 Exit 61 (via SC 72 Byp.-US 21 BR-US 21 Rock Hill).
SC 121	SC 72 Whitmire	US 25 Trenton.
SC 151	US 601 Pageland	US 52 Darlington.
SC 2 77	I–77 Columbia	US 76 Columbia.
SC 576	US 76 Marion	US 501 Marion.
South Dakota		
No additional routes have been federally designated; under State law STAA-dimensioned commercial vehicles may legally operate on all highways which, prior to June 1, 1991, were designated as Federal-aid primary highways.		
Tennessee		
US 25E	I–81	VA State Line Cumberland Gap.
US 27	End of I–124 Chattanooga.	US 127 Chattanooga.
US 27	TN 153 Chattanooga	KY State Line Winfield.
US 43	AL State Line St. Joseph.	US 64 Lawrenceburg.
US 45	MS State Line	US 45 Bypass S. Int. Jackson.
US 45 Bypass-US 45W.	US 45 S. Int. Jackson.	US 51 Union City.
US 51	TN 300 Memphis	KY State Line Jackson Purchase Pkwy.
US 64	I–40 E. Int. Memphis	I–24 Monteagle.
US 70 Alt	US 79 Atwood	TN 22 Huntingdon.
US 70	TN 22 Huntingdon	TN 96 Dickson.
US 70	TN 155 Nashville	US 127 Crossville.
US 70S	TN 102 Smyrna	US 70/TN 111 Sparta.
US 72	AL State Line	I–24 Kimball.
US 74	I–75 Cleveland	NC State Line Isabella.
US 79	I–40 Memphis	KY State Line US 41 Guthrie.
US 127	US 27 Chattanooga	TN 27 W. Int.
US 127	TN 28 Dunlap	KY State Line Static.
US 231	AL State Line S. of Fayetteville.	KY State Line N. of Westmoreland.
US 412	I–40 Jackson	US 51 Dyersburg.
US 641	I–40 near Natchez Trace State Park.	KY State Line N. of Paris.
TN 96	US 70 Dickson	I–40 E. of Dickson.
TN 153	I–75 Chattanooga	US 27 Chattanooga.
TN 155	I–40 Nashville	I–65 N. of Nashville.
TN 300	I–40 Memphis	US 51 Memphis.
Texas		
No additional routes have been federally designated; under State law STAA-dimensioned commercial vehicles may legally operate on all highways which, prior to June 1, 1991, were designated as Federal-aid primary highways.		
Utah		
No additional routes have been federally designated; under State law STAA-dimensioned commercial vehicles may legally operate on all highways which, prior to June 1, 1991, were designated as Federal-aid primary highways.		
Vermont		
US 4	NY State Line	ECL Rutland.
US 7	End of 4-lane divided hwy. Wallingford.	US 4 N. Int. Rutland.
VT 9	I–91 Int. 3 N. of Brattleboro.	NH State Line.
Virginia		
US 11	I–81 Exit 195	0.16 Mi. N. of VA 645 Rockbridge Co.
US 11	VA 220 Alt. N. Int	2.15 Mi. S. of VA 220 Alt. N. Int. Cloverdale.
US 11	VA 100 Dublin	VA 643 S. of Dublin.
US 11	1.52 Mi. N. of VA 75	US 19 N. Int. Abingdon.
US 13	MD State Line	I–64 Exit 282 Norfolk.
US 17	US 29 Opal	VA 2/US 17 BR New Post.
US 17	VA 134 York County	I–64 Exit 258 Newport News.
US 17	BR/SCL Fredericksburg.	US 17 New Post VA 2.

[The federally-designated routes on the National Network consist of the Interstate System, except as noted, and the following additional highways.]

Route	From	To
US 19	I–81 Exit 14 (via VA 140) Abington.	US 460 N. Int./VA 720 Bluefield.
US 23	TN State Line	US 58 Alt. Big Stone Gap.
US 23	0.33 Mi. N. of US 23 BR Norton.	KY State Line.
US 25E	TN State Line	KY State Line.
US 29	NC State Line	I–66 Exit 43 Gainesville.
US 33	N. Carlton Street Harrisonburg.	US 340 Elkton.
US 33	I–295 Exit 49	0.96 Mi. W. of I–295 Hanover County.
US 50	VA 259 Gore	VA 37 Frederick County.
US 50	Apple Blossom Loop Road Winchester.	I–81 Exit 313 Winchester.
US 58	VA 721 W. of Martinsville.	US 220 BR N. Int. Martinsville.
US 58	S. Fairy Street Martinsville.	WCL Emporia.
US 58	0.6 Mi. E. of ECL Emporia.	VA 35 S. Int. Courtland.
US 58	US 58 BR E. of Courtland.	US 13/I–264 Bowers Hill.
US 58 Alt	US 23 Norton	US 19 Hansonville.
US 58 Alt	0.4 Mi. W. of US 11	I–81 Exit 17 Abington.
US 58 BR	VA 35 Courtland	US 58 E. of Courtland.
US 58	W. Int. VA 337 Claremont St. Norfolk.	US 460/St. Paul's Blvd. Norfolk.
US 60	0.03 Mi. West of VA 887 Chesterfield County.	US 522 Powhatan.
US 220	NC State Line	I–581 Roanoke.
US 220	I–81 Exit 150	SCL Fincastle.
US 220 BR	US 220 S. Int.	0.16 Mi. N. of VA 825 S. of Martinsville.
US 220 BR	US 58 N. Int. Martinsville.	US 220 N. Int. Bassett Forks.
US 250	US 340 E. Int. Waynesboro.	VA 254 Waynesboro.
US 250	I–81 Exit 222	VA 261 Statler Blvd. Staunton.
US 258	NC State Line	US 58 Franklin.
US 258	VA 10 Benns Church	VA 143 Jefferson Ave. Newport News.
US 301	VA 1250 S. of I–295	I–295 Exit 41 Hanover County.
US 301	US 301 BR N. Int. Bowling Green.	MD State Line.
US 340/522	I–66 Exit 6 Front Royal.	2.85 Mi. N. of I–66.
US 340	VA 7 Berryville	WV State Line.
US 360	US 58 South Boston	VA 150 Chesterfield County.
US 360	I–64 Exit 192 Richmond.	VA 617 Village.
US 460	VA 67 W. Int. Raven	US 19 Claypool Hill.
US 460	VA 720 Bluefield	WV State Line at Bluefield.
US 460	WV State Line at Glen Lyn.	I–81 Exit 118 Christiansburg.
US 460	I–581 Roanoke	0.08 Mi. E. of VA 1512 Lynchburg.
US 460	US 29 Lynchburg	1 Mi. W. of VA 24 Appomattox County.

[The federally-designated routes on the National Network consist of the Interstate System, except as noted, and the following additional highways.]

Route	From	To
US 460	0.64 Mi. E. of VA 707 Appomattox County.	I–85 Exit 61 Petersburg.
US 460	I–95 Exit 50 Petersburg.	US 58 Suffolk.
US 501	VA 360 S. Int. Halifax	US 58 South Boston.
US 522	0.6 Mi. S. of US 50	US 50 Frederick County.
US 522	VA 37 Frederick County.	1.07 Mi. N. of VA 705 Cross Junction.
VA 3	US 1 Fredericksburg	VA 20 Wilderness.
VA 7	I–81 Exit 315 Winchester.	0.68 Mi. W. of WCL Round Hill.
VA 10	US 58 Suffolk	VA 666 Smithfield.
VA 10	ECL Hopewell	0.37 Mi. W. of W. Int. VA 156 Hopewell.
VA 10	US 1 Chesterfield County.	VA 827 W. of Hopewell.
VA 20	I–64 Exit 121	Carlton Rd. Charlottesville.
VA 30	I–95 Exit 98 Doswell	US 1.
VA 33	I–64 Exit 220	VA 30 E. Int. West Point.
VA 36	I–95 Exit 52 Petersburg.	VA 156 Hopewell.
VA 37	I–81 Exit 310 S. of Winchester.	I–81 Exit 317 (via US 11) N. of Winchester.
VA 42	VA 257 S. Int. Bridgewater.	VA 290 Dayton.
VA 57	VA 753 Bassett	US 220 Bassett Forks.
VA 86	US 29 Danville	NC State Line.
VA 100	I–81 Exit 98	US 11 Dublin.
VA 105	US 60 Newport News	I–64 Exit 250.
VA 114	US 460 Christiansburg.	0.09 Mi. E. of VA 750 Montgomery County.
VA 156	VA 10 W. Int. Hopewell.	VA 36 Hopewell.
VA 199	US 60 Williamsburg	I–64 Exit 242.
VA 207	I–95 Exit 104	0.2 Mi. S. of VA 619 Milford.
VA 220 Alt	US 11 N. Int. N. of Cloverdale.	I–81 Exit 150/US 220.
VA 277	I–81 Exit 307 Stephens City.	1.6 MI. E. of I–81 Exit 307.
VA 419	I–81 Exit 141 Salem	Midland Ave. Salem.
VA 624	I–64 Exit 96	Old SCL Waynesboro.
Commonwealth Blvd. in Martinsville.	Market Street	N. Fairy Street.

[The federally-designated routes on the National Network consist of the Interstate System, except as noted, and the following additional highways.]

Route	From	To

Note 1: I–66 Washington, DC, area—There is a 24-hour total truck ban on I–66 from I–495 Capital Beltway to the District of Columbia. (Excepted under 23 CFR 658.11(f)).

Note 2: I–264 Norfolk—Truck widths are limited to 96 inches for the westbound tube of the Elizabeth River Downtown Tunnel from Norfolk to Portsmouth because of clearance deficiencies.

Washington

No additional routes have been federally designated; under State law STAA-dimensioned commercial vehicles may legally operate on all highways which, prior to June 1, 1991, were designated as Federal-aid primary highways.

West Virginia

Route	From	To
US 19	I–77 Bradley	I–79 Gassaway.
US 35	WV 34 Winfield	OH State Line.
US 48	I–79 Morgantown	MD State Line.
US 50	I–77 Parkersburg	I–79 Clarksburg.
US 460	VA State Line Bluefield.	VA State Line Kelleysville.
WV 34	I–64 Putnam Co	US 35 Winfield.

Wisconsin

Route	From	To
US 2	I–535/US 53 Superior	MI State Line Hurley.
US 2	MI State Line W. of Florence.	MI State Line E. of Florence.
US 8	US 63 Turtle Lake	MI State Line Norway MI.
US 10	US 53 Osseo	I–43 Manitowoc.
US 12	I–94/CH "EE" W. of Eau Claire.	US 53 Eau Claire.
US 12	I–90/94 Lake Delton	End of 4-lane S. of W. Baraboo.
US 12	WI 67 S. Jct. Elkhorn	IL State Line Genoa City.
US 14	US 51 N. of Janesville.	I–90 Janesville.
US 14	WI 11/89 N. of Darien.	I–43 Darien.
US 18	IA State Line Prairie Du Chien.	I–90 Madison.
US 41	National Ave. Milwaukee.	Garfield Ave. Milwaukee.
US 41	107th St. Milwaukee	MI State Line Marinette.
US 45	IL State Line Bristol	WI 28 Kewaskum.
US 45	WI 29 Wittenberg	MI State Line Land O'Lakes.
US 51	SCL Janesville	US 14 Janesville.
US 51	WI 78 N. of Portage	US 2 Hurley.
US 53	US 14/61 La Crosse	US 10 Osseo.
US 53	I–94 Eau Claire	I–535/US 2 Superior.
US 61	IA State Line Dubugue IA.	MN State Line La Crosse (via WI 129 Lancaster Byp.).
US 63	MN State Line Red Wing MN.	US 2 W. of Ashland.
US 141	US 41 Abrams	US 8 Pembine.
US 151	IA State Line Dubugue IA.	US 18 E. of Dodgeville.
US 151	I–90/94 Madison	US 41 Fond Du Lac.
WI 11	IA State Line Dubuque IA.	US 51 Janesville.
WI 11	I–90 Janesville	US 14/WI 89 N. of Darien.
WI 11	I–43 Elkhorn	WI 31 Racine.
WI 13	WI 21 Friendship	US 2 Ashland.
WI 16	WI 78 Portage	I–94 Waukesha.
WI 17	US 8 Rhinelander	US 45 Eagle River.
WI 20	I–94 Racine	WI 31 Racine.
WI 21	WI 27 Sparta	US 41 Oshkosh.
WI 23	WI 32 N. of Sheboygan Falls.	Taylor Dr. Sheboygan.
WI 26	I–94 Johnson Creek	WI 16 Watertown.
WI 26	US 151 Waupun	US 41 SW. of Oshkosh.
WI 27	US 14/61 Westby	US 10 Fairchild.
WI 28	US 41 Theresa	US 45 Kewaskum.
WI 29	I–94 Elk Mound	US 53 Chippewa Falls.
WI 29	WI 124 S. of Chippewa Falls.	US 41 Green Bay.
WI 30	US 151 Madison	I–90/94 Madison.
WI 31	WI 11 Racine	WI 20 Racine.
WI 32	WI 29 W. of Green Bay.	Gillett.
WI 34	WI 13 Wisconsin Rapids.	US 51 Knowlton.
WI 42	I–43 Manitowoc	WI 57 SW. of Sturgeon Bay.
WI 47	US 10 Appleton	WI 29 Bonduel.
WI 50	I–94 Kenosha	45th Ave. Kenosha.
WI 54	WI 13 Wisconsin Rapids.	US 51 Plover.
WI 57	I–43 Green Bay	Sturgeon Bay.
WI 69	WI 11 Monroe	CH "PB" Paoli.
WI 73	US 51 Plainfield	WI 54 Wisconsin Rapids.
WI 78	I–90/94 S. of Portage	US 51 N. of portage.
WI 80	WI 21 Necedah	WI 13 Pittsville.
WI 119	I–94 Milwaukee	WI 38 Milwaukee.
WI 124	US 53 N. of Eau Claire.	WI 29 S. of Chippewa Falls.
WI 139	US 8 Cavour, Forest Co.	Long Lake.
WI 145	Broadway Milwaukee	US 41/45 Milwaukee.
WI 172	US 41 Ashwaubenon	CH "x" S. of Green Bay.
CH "PB"	WI 69 Paoli	US 18/151 E. of Verona.

Wyoming

No additional routes have been federally designated; under State law STAA-dimensioned commercial vehicles may legally operate on all highways which, prior to June 1, 1991, were designated as Federal-aid primary highways.

Note: Information on additional highways on which STAA-dimensioned vehicles may legally operate may be obtained from the respective State highway agencies.

[55 FR 17953, Apr. 30, 1990; 55 FR 19145, May 8, 1990, as amended at 59 FR 30421, June 13, 1994; 59 FR 36053, July 15, 1994; 60 FR 15214, Mar. 22, 1995; 60 FR 16571, Mar. 31, 1995; 62 FR 30758, June 5, 1997; 63 FR 70653, Dec. 22, 1998; 63 FR 71748, Dec. 30, 1998; 72 FR 7748, Feb. 20, 2007; 83 FR 30335, June 28, 2018]

APPENDIX B TO PART 658—GRANDFATHERED SEMITRAILER LENGTHS

State	Feet and inches
Alabama	53–6
Alaska	48–0
Arizona	57–6
Arkansas	53–6
California	[1] 48–0
Colorado	57–4
Connecticut	48–0
Delaware	53–0
District of Columbia	48–0
Florida	48–0
Georgia	48–0
Hawaii	48–0
Idaho	48–0
Illinois	53–0
Indiana	[2] 48–6
Iowa	53–0
Kansas	57–6
Kentucky	53–0
Louisiana	59–6
Maine	48–0
Maryland	48–0
Massachusetts	48–0
Michigan	48–0
Minnesota	48–0
Mississippi	53–0
Missouri	53–0
Montana	53–0
Nebraska	53–0
Nevada	53–0
New Hampshire	48–0
New Jersey	48–0
New Mexico	57–6
New York	48–0
North Carolina	48–0
North Dakota	53–0
Ohio	53–0
Oklahoma	59–6
Oregon	53–0
Pennsylvania	53–0
Puerto Rico	48–0
Rhode Island	48–6
South Carolina	48–0
South Dakota	53–0
Tennessee	50–0
Texas	59–0
Utah	48–0
Vermont	48–0
Virginia	48–0
Washington	48–0
West Virginia	48–0
Wisconsin	[3] 48–0
Wyoming	57–4

[1] Semitrailers up to 53 feet may also operate without a permit by conforming to a kingpin-to-rearmost axle distance of 38 feet. Semitrailers that are consistent with 23 CFR 658.13(g) may operate without a permit provided the distance from the kingpin to the center of the rear axle is 46 feet or less.

[2] Semitrailers up to 53 feet in length may operate without a permit by conforming to a kingpin-to-rearmost axle distance of 40 feet 6 inches. Semitrailers that are consistent with 23 CFR 658.13(g) may operate without a permit provided the distance from the kingpin to the center of the rear axle is 46 feet or less.

[3] Semitrailers up to 53 feet in length may operate without a permit by conforming to a kingpin-to-rear axle distance of 41 feet, measured to the center of the rear tandem assembly. Semitrailers that are consistent with 23 CFR 658.13(g) may operate without a permit provided the distance from the kingpin to the center of the rear axle is 46 feet or less.

[53 FR 2599, Jan. 29, 1988, as amended at 54 FR 1931, Jan. 18, 1989; 62 FR 10181, Mar. 5, 1997; 72 FR 7749, Feb. 20, 2007]

APPENDIX C TO PART 658—TRUCKS OVER 80,000 POUNDS ON THE INTERSTATE SYSTEM AND TRUCKS OVER STAA LENGTHS ON THE NATIONAL NETWORK

This appendix contains the weight and size provisions that were in effect on or before June 1, 1991 (July 6, 1991 for Alaska), for vehicles covered by 23 U.S.C. 127(d) (LCV's) and 49 U.S.C. app. 2311(j) (commercial motor vehicles (CMV's) with 2 or more cargo-carrying units). Weights and dimensions are "frozen" at the values shown here, which were in effect on June 1, 1991 (Alaska, July 6, 1991). All vehicles are listed by configuration type.

Trucks Over 80,000 Pounds on the Interstate System

In the State-by-State descriptions, CMV combinations which can also be LCV's are identified with the letters "LCV" following the type of combination vehicle. The maximum allowable gross vehicle weight is given in this appendix (in thousands of pounds indicated by a "K"), as well as information summarizing the operational conditions, routes, and legal citations. The term "Interstate System" as used herein refers to the Dwight D. Eisenhower System of Interstate and Defense Highways.

Trucks Over STAA Lengths on the National Network

Listed for each State by combination type is either:

1. The maximum cargo-carrying length (shown in feet); or

2. A notation that such vehicle is not allowed (indicated by a "NO").

CMV's are categorized as follows:

1. A CMV combination consisting of a truck tractor and two trailing units.

2. A CMV combination consisting of a truck tractor and three trailing units.

3. CMV combinations with two or more cargo-carrying units not included in descriptions 1 or 2.

In the following table the left number is the maximum cargo-carrying length measured in feet from the front of the first cargo unit to the rear of the last cargo unit. This distance is not to include length exclusive devices which have been approved by the Secretary or by any State. Devices excluded from length determination shall only include items whose function is related to the safe and efficient operation of the semitrailer or trailer. No device excluded from length determination shall be designed or used for carrying cargo. The right number is the maximum gross weight in thousands of pounds that the type of vehicle can carry when operating as an LCV on the Interstate System. For every State where there is a length or weight number in the table that follows, additional information is provided.

VEHICLE COMBINATIONS SUBJECT TO PUB. L. 102–240

State	1 Truck tractor and *2* trailing units	2 Truck tractor and *3* trailing units	3 Other
Alabama	NO	NO	NO
Alaska	95′	110′	83′
Arizona	95′ 129K	95′ 129K	(1)
Arkansas	NO	NO	NO
California	NO	NO	NO
Colorado	111′ 110K	115.5′ 110K	78′
Connecticut	NO	NO	NO
Delaware	NO	NO	NO
Dist. of Columbia	NO	NO	NO
Florida	106′ (2)	NO	NO
Georgia	NO	NO	NO
Hawaii	65′ (2)	NO	NO
Idaho	95′ 105.5K	95′ 105.5K	(1)
Illinois	NO	NO	NO
Indiana	106′ 127.4K	104.5′ 127.4K	58′
Iowa	100′ 129K	100′ 129K	78′
Kansas	109′ 120K	109′ 120K	NO
Kentucky	NO	NO	NO
Louisiana	NO	NO	NO
Maine	NO	NO	NO
Maryland	NO	NO	NO
Massachusetts	104′ 127.4K	NO	NO
Michigan	58′ 164K	No	63′
Minnesota	NO	NO	NO
Mississippi	65′ (2)	NO	NO
Missouri	110′ 120K(4)	109′ 120K	NO
Montana	93′ 137.8K	100′ 131.06K	(1)
Nebraska	95′ 95K	95′ (2)	68′
Nevada	95′ 129K	95′ 129K	98′
New Hampshire	NO	NO	NO
New Jersey	NO	NO	NO
New Mexico	86.4K(3)	NO	NO
New York	102′ 143K	NO	NO
North Carolina	NO	NO	NO
North Dakota	103′ 105.5K	100′ 105.5K	103′
Ohio	102′ 127.4K	95′ 115K	NO
Oklahoma	110′ 90K	95′ 90K	NO
Oregon	68′ 105.5K	96′ 105.5K	70′ 5″
Pennsylvania	NO	NO	NO
Puerto Rico	NO	NO	NO
Rhode Island	NO	NO	NO
South Carolina	NO	NO	NO
South Dakota	100′ 129K	100′ 129K	(1)
Tennessee	NO	NO	NO
Texas	NO	NO	NO
Utah	95′ 129K	95′ 129K	(1)
Vermont	NO	NO	NO
Virginia	NO	NO	NO
Washington	68′ 105.5K	NO	68′
West Virginia	NO	NO	NO
Wisconsin	NO	NO	NO
Wyoming	81′ 117K	NO	(1)

(1)—State submission includes multiple vehicles in this category—see individual State listings.

(2)—No maximum weight is established as this vehicle combination is not considered an "LCV" per the ISTEA definition. Florida's combination is not allowed to operate on the Interstate System, and the combinations for Hawaii, Mississippi, and Nebraska are not allowed to exceed 80,000 pounds.

(3)—No maximum cargo-carrying length is established for this combination. Because State law limits each trailing unit to not more than 28.5 feet in length, this combination is allowed to operate on all NN routes under the authority of the STAA of 1982, regardless of actual cargo-carrying length. The maximum weight listed is New Mexico's maximum allowable gross weight on the Interstate System under the grandfather authority of 23 U.S.C. 127.

(4)—These dimensions do not apply to the same combinations. The 110-foot length is limited to vehicles entering from Oklahoma, also limited to 90K gross weight. The 120K gross weight is limited to vehicles entering from Kansas, also limited to a cargo carrying length of 109 feet.

The following abbreviation convention is used throughout the narrative State-by-State descriptions for the captions OPERATIONAL CONDITIONS, ROUTES, and LEGAL CITATIONS: two letter State abbreviation, dash, "TT" for truck tractor, and 2 or 3 for two or three trailing units. For example, the phrase "Arizona truck tractor and 2 trailing units", would be noted as "AZ-TT2"; the phrase "Indiana truck tractor and 3 trailing units" would be noted as "IN-TT3", etc.

STATE: ALASKA

COMBINATION: Truck tractor and 2 trailing units

LENGTH OF THE CARGO-CARRYING UNITS: 95 feet

OPERATIONAL CONDITIONS:

WEIGHT: The combination must be in compliance with State laws and regulations. There are no highways in the State subject to Interstate System weight limits. Therefore, the ISTEA freeze as it applies to maximum weight is not applicable.

DRIVER: The driver must have a commercial driver's license with the appropriate endorsement.

VEHICLE: Combinations with an overall length greater than 75 feet, measured bumper to bumper, must display an "OVERSIZE## warning sign on the front and rear. In combinations where one cargo-carrying unit is more than 5,000 pounds heavier than the other, the heavier unit shall be placed immediately behind the power unit. Weather restrictions are imposed when hazardous conditions exist, as determined by the Alaska Department of Transportation and Public Facilities (DOT&PF) and the Alaska Department of Public Safety, Division of State Troopers. Time of day travel is not restricted.

PERMIT: None required.

ACCESS: Alaska allows reasonable access not to exceed 5 miles to reach or return from terminals and facilities for food, fuel, or rest. The most direct route must be used. The Commissioner of the Alaska DOT&PF may allow access to specific routes if it can be shown that travel frequency, necessity, and route accommodation are required.

ROUTES

	From	To
AK–1	Anchorage (Potter Weigh Station).	Palmer (Palmer-Wasilla Highway Junction).
AK–2	Fairbanks (Gaffney Road Junction).	Delta Junction (MP 1412 Alaska Highway).
AK–3	Jct. AK–1	Fairbanks (Gaffney Road Junction).

LEGAL CITATIONS:

17 AAC 25, and 35; the Administrative Permit Manual.

STATE: ALASKA

COMBINATION: Truck tractor and 3 trailing units

LENGTH OF THE CARGO-CARRYING UNITS: 110 feet

OPERATIONAL CONDITIONS:

WEIGHT and ACCESS: Same as the AK-TT2 combination.

DRIVER: The driver must have a commercial driver's license with the appropriate endorsement. Drivers of this combination must have 10 years of experience in Alaska and certified training in operation of these combinations.

VEHICLE: Individual trailer length in a three trailing unit combination shall not exceed 28.5 feet. Engine horsepower rating shall not be less than 400 horsepower.

These combinations are allowed to operate only between May 1 and September 30 of each year. Weather restrictions are imposed when hazardous conditions exist, as determined by the Alaska DOT&PF and the Department of Public Safety, Division of State Troopers. No movement is permitted if visibility is less than 1,000 feet.

PERMIT: Permits are required with specified durations of not less than 3 months or more than 18 months. There is a fee.

ROUTES

	From	To
AK–1	Anchorage (Potter Weigh Station).	Jct. AK–3.
AK–3	Jct. AK–1	Fairbanks (Gaffney Road Junction)

LEGAL CITATIONS: Same as the AK-TT2 combination.

STATE: ALASKA

COMBINATION: Truck-trailer

LENGTH OF THE CARGO-CARRYING UNITS: 83 feet

OPERATIONAL CONDITIONS:

WEIGHT, DRIVER, PERMIT, and ACCESS: Same as the AK-TT2 combination.

VEHICLE: Same as the AK-TT2 combination, except that overall combination length may not exceed 90 feet.

ROUTES: Same as the AK-TT2 combination.

LEGAL CITATIONS: Same as the AK-TT2 combination.

STATE: ARIZONA

COMBINATION: Truck tractor and 2 trailing units—LCV

LENGTH OF THE CARGO-CARRYING UNITS: 95 feet

MAXIMUM ALLOWABLE GROSS WEIGHT: 129,000 pounds

OPERATIONAL CONDITIONS:

WEIGHT: Single-axle maximum weight limit is 20,000 pounds, tandem-axle maximum weight limit is 34,000 pounds, and the gross vehicle weight limit is 129,000 pounds, subject to the Federal Bridge Formula.

DRIVER: The driver must have a commercial driver's license with the appropriate endorsement. Drivers must comply with the Federal Motor Carrier Safety Regulations of the U.S. Department of Transportation and Title 28, Arizona Revised Statutes.

VEHICLE: This vehicle must be able to operate at speeds compatible with other traffic on level roads and maintain 20 miles per hour speed on grades where operated. A heavy-duty fifth wheel is required. The kingpin must be a solid type, not a screw-out or folding type. All hitch connectors must be of a no-slack type, preferably an air-actuated ram. Axles must be those designed for the width of the body. All braking systems must comply with State and Federal requirements. A brake force limiting valve, sometimes called a "slippery road" valve, may be provided on the steering axle. Mud flaps or splash guards are required. When traveling on a smooth, paved surface, trailers must follow in the path of the towing vehicle without shifting or swerving more than 3 inches to either side when the towing vehicle is moving in a straight line.

PERMITS: Permits are required. Fees are charged. This vehicle is allowed continuous travel, however, the State may restrict or prohibit operations during periods when traffic, weather, or other safety considerations make such operations unsafe or inadvisable. All multiple-trailer combinations shall be driven in the right-hand traffic lane.

Access: Access is allowed for 20 miles from I-15 Exits 8 and 27 or 20 miles from other authorized routes.

ROUTES

	From	To
I-15	Nevada	Utah
US 89	20 miles south of Utah.	Utah
US 160	US 163	New Mexico
US 163	US 160	Utah
	LEGAL CITATIONS	
ARS 28-107	ARS 28-1009	ARS 28-1011.O
ARS 28-108.5	ARS 28-1009.01	ARS 28-1012
ARS 28-108.13	ARS 28-1011.A	ARS 28-1013
ARS 28-108.14	ARS 28-1011.C	ARS 28-1014
ARS 28-403	ARS 28-1011.F	ARS 28-1031
ARS 28-405	ARS 28-1011.K	ARS 28-1051
ARS 28-1001	ARS 28-1011.L	ARS 28-1052
ARS 28-1004.G	ARS 28-1011.M	R17-40-426
ARS 28-1008.		

STATE: ARIZONA

COMBINATION: Truck tractor and 3 trailing units—LCV

LENGTH OF THE CARGO-CARRYING UNITS: 95 feet

MAXIMUM ALLOWABLE GROSS WEIGHT: 123,000 pounds (129,000 pounds on I-15).

OPERATIONAL CONDITIONS:

VEHICLE, and ACCESS: Same as the AZ-TT2 combination.

Weight: Single-axle maximum weight limit is 20,000 pounds, tandem-axle maximum weight limit is 34,000 pounds, and the gross vehicle weight is 123,500 pounds (129,000 on I-15), subject to the Federal Bridge Formula.

DRIVER: The driver must have a commercial driver's license with the appropriate endorsement. Drivers must comply with the Federal Motor Carrier Safety Regulations of the U.S. Department of Transportation and Title 28, Arizona Revised Statutes. Drivers must be trained by an experienced driver of a three trailing unit combination. Training should be through special instructions or by traveling with the new driver until such time as the new driver is deemed adequately qualified by the trainer on the use and operation of these combinations.

PERMIT: Permits are required. Fees are charged. This vehicle is allowed continuous travel, however, the State may restrict or prohibit operations during periods when traffic, weather, or other safety considerations make such operations unsafe or inadvisable. These combinations shall not be dispatched during adverse weather conditions. All multiple-trailer combinations shall be driven in the right-hand traffic lane.

ROUTES: Same as the AZ-TT2 combination.

LEGAL CITATIONS: Same as the AZ-TT2 combination.

STATE: ARIZONA

COMBINATION: Truck-trailer

LENGTH OF THE CARGO-CARRYING UNITS: 69 feet

OPERATIONAL CONDITIONS:

WEIGHT: This combination must operate in compliance with State laws and regulations. Because it is not an LCV, it is not subject to the ISTEA freeze as it applies to maximum weight.

DRIVER, VEHICLE, PERMIT, and ACCESS: Same as the AZ-TT2 combination.

ROUTES: Same as the AZ-TT2 combination.

LEGAL CITATIONS: Same as the AZ-TT2 combination.

STATE: ARIZONA

COMBINATION: Truck-semitrailer-trailer

LENGTH OF THE CARGO-CARRYING UNITS: 98 feet

OPERATIONAL CONDITIONS:

WEIGHT: This combination must operate in compliance with State laws and regulations. Because it is not an LCV, it is not subject to the ISTEA freeze as it applies to maximum weight.

DRIVER, VEHICLE, PERMIT, and ACCESS: Same as the AZ-TT2 combination.

ROUTES: Same as the AZ-TT2 combination.

LEGAL CITATIONS: Same as the AZ-TT2 combination.

STATE: COLORADO

COMBINATION: Truck tractor and 2 trailing units—LCV

LENGTH OF THE CARGO-CARRYING UNITS: 111 feet

MAXIMUM ALLOWABLE GROSS WEIGHT: 110,000 pounds

OPERATIONAL CONDITIONS:

WEIGHT: The maximum gross weight is 110,000 pounds, subject to the formula W = 800(L + 40) where "W" equals the gross weight in pounds and "L" equals the length in feet between the centers of the first and last axles, or the gross weight determined by the Federal Bridge Formula, whichever is least. A single axle shall not exceed 20,000 pounds and a tandem axle shall not exceed 36,000 pounds.

DRIVER: The driver must have a commercial driver's license with the appropriate endorsement. The driver cannot have had any suspension of driving privileges in any State during the past 3 years where such suspension arose out of the operation of a motor vehicle used as a contract or common carrier of persons or property.

The driver must be certified by the motor carrier permit holder's safety office. The certification shall demonstrate that the driver has complied with all written requirements, and that the driver has successfully completed a company-approved road test for each type of combination vehicle operated.

VEHICLE: Vehicles shall not have fewer than six axles or more than nine axles. They shall be configured such that the shorter trailer shall be operated as the rear trailer, and the trailer with the heavier gross weight shall be operated as the front trailer. In the event that the shorter trailer is also the heavier, the load must be adjusted so that the front trailer is the longer and heavier of the two.

Vehicles shall have adequate power to maintain a minimum speed of 20 miles per hour on any grade over which the combination operates and can resume a speed of 20 miles per hour after stopping on any such grade.

Tires must conform to the standards in the Department of Public Safety's (DPS) Rules and Regulations Concerning Minimum Standards for the Operation of Commercial Motor Vehicles, at 8 CCR 1507–1 and C.R.S. 42–4–225 and 42–2–406.

Vehicles are required to have a heavy-duty fifth wheel and equal strength pick-up plates that meet the standards in the DPS Commercial Vehicle Rules. This equipment must be properly lubricated and located in a position that provides stability during normal operation, including braking. The trailers shall follow in the path of the towing vehicle without shifting or swerving more than 3 inches to either side when the towing vehicle is moving in a straight line.

Kingpins must be of a solid type and permanently fastened. Screw-out or folding type kingpins are prohibited.

Hitch connections must be of a no-slack type, preferably air-actuated ram.

Drawbar lengths shall be adequate to provide for the clearances required between the towing vehicle and the trailer(s) for turning and backing maneuvers.

Axles must be those designed for the width of the body of the trailer(s).

Braking systems must comply with the DPS Commercial Vehicle Rules and C.R.S. 42–4–220. Fast air-transmission and release valves must be provided on all trailer(s) and converter dolly axles. A brake force limiting valve, sometimes called a "slippery road" valve, may be provided on the steering axle.

PERMIT: An annual permit is required for which a fee is charged. Also, the vehicle must have an overweight permit pursuant to C.R.S. 42–4–409(11)(a)(II) (A), (B), or (C), and comply with Rule 4–15 in the rules pertaining to Extra-Legal Vehicles or Loads.

A truck tractor and two trailing units wherein at least one of the trailing units exceeds 28.5 feet in length shall not operate on the following designated highway segments during the hours of 6 a.m. to 9 a.m. and from 3 p.m. to 6 p.m., Monday through Friday, for Colorado Springs, Denver, and Pueblo. (A truck tractor with two trailing units wherein at least one of the trailing units exceeds 28.5 feet in length not operating at greater than the legal maximum weight of 80,000 pounds is subject to different hours-of-operation restrictions. Refer to rules pertaining to Extra-Legal Vehicles or Loads).

Colorado Springs: I–25 between Exit 135 (CO 83 Academy Blvd. So.) and Exit 150 (CO 83, Academy Blvd. No.).

Denver: I–25 between Exit 200 (Jct. I–225) and Exit 223 (CO 128, 120th Avenue),

I–70 between Exit 259 (CO 26/US 40) and Exit 282 (Jct. I–225),

I–76 between Exit 5 (Jct. I–25) and Exit 12 (US 85),

I–225 entire length,

I–270 entire length.

Pueblo: I–25 between Exit 94 (CO 45 Lake Ave.) and Exit 101 (US 50/CO 47).

The holder of a longer vehicle combination (LVC) permit must have an established safety program as provided in Chapter 9 of the "Colorado Department of Highways Rules and Regulations for Operation of Longer Vehicle Combinations on Designated State Highway Segments." Elements of the program include compliance with minimum safety standards at 8 CCR 1507–1, hazardous materials regulations at 8 CCR 1507–7, –8, and –9, Colorado Uniform Motor Vehicle Law, Articles 1 through 4 of Title 42, C.R.S. as amended, and Public Utility Commission regulations at 4 CCR 723–6, –8, –15, –22, and –23.

ACCESS: A vehicle shall not be operated off the designated portions of the Interstate System except to access food, fuel, repairs, and rest or to access a facility. Access to a facility shall be subject to the following conditions:

(1) The facility must:

(a) Be either a manufacturing or a distribution center, a warehouse, or truck terminal located in an area where industrial uses are permitted;

(b) Be a construction site; and

(c) Meet the following criteria:

1 vehicles are formed for transport or broken down for delivery on the premises;

2 adequate off-roadway space exists on the premises to safely maneuver the vehicles; and

3 adequate equipment is available on the premises to handle, load, and unload the vehicle, its trailers, and cargo.

(2) The facility must be located within a maximum distance of 10 miles from the point where the vehicle enters or exits the designated portions of the Interstate System. Such 10-mile distance shall be measured by the actual route(s) to be traveled to the facility, rather than by a straight line radius from the designated Interstate System to the facility;

(3) The access route(s) between the designated Interstate System and the facility must be approved in advance by the public entity (Colorado DOT, municipality, or county) having jurisdiction for the roadway(s) that make up the route(s). Where the State of Colorado has jurisdiction over the access route(s), it will consider the following safety, engineering, and other criteria in determining whether to approve the route(s):

(a) Safety of the motoring public;

(b) Geometrics of the street and roadway;

(c) Traffic volumes and patterns;

(d) Protection of State highways, roadways, and structures;

(e) Zoning and general characteristics of the route(s) to be encountered; and

(f) Other relevant criteria warranted by special circumstances of the proposed route(s).

Local entities, counties, and municipalities having jurisdiction over route(s), should consider similar criteria in determining whether to approve the proposed ingress and egress route(s); and

(4) A permit holder shall access only the facility or location authorized by the permit. If the permit authorizes more than one facility or location, then on any single trip by an LVC from the designated Interstate System the permit holder may access only one facility or location before returning to the designated Interstate System.

ROUTES

	From	To
I–25	New Mexico	Wyoming
I–70	Utah	I–70 Exit 90 Rifle
I–70	I–70 Exit 259 Golden.	Kansas
I–76	Jct. I–70	Nebraska
I–225	Jct. I–25	Jct. I–70
I–270	Jct. I–76	Jct. I–70

LEGAL CITATIONS: Vehicles must comply with all applicable statutes, such as C.R.S. 42–4–402(1), 42–4–404(1), 42–4–407(1)(c)(III)(A), 42–4–409(11)(a)(II) (A), (B) or (C). All LVC's must comply with the Extra-Legal Vehicles and Loads Rules and the Longer Vehicle Combination Rules. However, when the rules address the same subject, the LVC, since it is operating at greater than 80,000 pounds, must comply with the Extra-Legal Vehicles and Loads Rules. Such rules are: 4–1–2 and 4–1–3 concerning holiday travel restrictions, 4–1–5 concerning hours of operation restrictions, 4–8 concerning minimum distance between vehicles and 4–15 concerning maximum allowable gross weight.

STATE: COLORADO

COMBINATION: Truck tractor and 3 trailing units—LCV

LENGTH OF THE CARGO-CARRYING UNITS: 115.5 feet

MAXIMUM ALLOWABLE GROSS WEIGHT: 110,000 pounds

OPERATIONAL CONDITIONS: Same as the CO-TT2 combination.

ROUTES: Same as the CO-TT2 combination.

LEGAL CITATIONS: Same as the CO-TT2 combination.

STATE: COLORADO

COMBINATION: Truck-trailer

LENGTH OF THE CARGO-CARRYING UNITS: 78 feet

OPERATIONAL CONDITIONS:

WEIGHT: This combination must operate in compliance with State laws and regulations. Because it is not an LCV, it is not subject to the ISTEA freeze as it applies to maximum weight.

DRIVER, VEHICLE, PERMIT, and ACCESS: Same as the CO-TT2 combination.

ROUTES: Same as the CO-TT2 combination.

LEGAL CITATIONS: Same as the CO-TT2 combination.

STATE: FLORIDA

COMBINATION: Truck tractor and 2 trailing units

LENGTH OF THE CARGO-CARRYING UNITS: 106 feet

OPERATIONAL CONDITIONS: All overdimensional and weight regulations of the Florida Turnpike Authority shall apply to such units unless specifically excluded under the terms of the Tandem Trailer Permit or these regulations.

WEIGHT: This combination must operate in compliance with State laws and regulations. Because it is not an LCV, it is not subject to the ISTEA freeze as it applies to maximum weight.

DRIVER: The driver must have a commercial driver's license with the appropriate endorsement. Proposed drivers of tandem-trailer units shall be registered by the Florida Turnpike Authority prior to driving such equipment on the turnpike system. For further information, see Rule 14–62.016 FAC.

VEHICLE: A complete tandem-trailer combination shall consist of a truck tractor, first semitrailer, fifth-wheel converter dolly, and a second semitrailer. The converter dolly may be either a separate unit or an integral component of the first semitrailer. The width shall not exceed 102 inches and the height shall not exceed 13 feet 6 inches. A tractor used in the tandem-trailer operations shall be capable of hauling the maximum gross load to be transported by a permittee at a speed of not less than 40 miles per hour on all portions of the turnpike system excepting that portion of the roadway, as posted in 1988, between mileposts 234 and 238 where a minimum speed of 30 miles per hour will be permitted.

Every tandem-trailer combination shall be equipped with full air brakes or air-activated hydraulic brakes on the tractor and either air or electric brakes on the dolly and trailers.

A tractor, which will be used to haul a complete tandem-trailer combination with a total gross weight of 110,000 pounds or more, shall be equipped with tandem rear axles and driving power shall be applied to all wheels on both axles. When the above tandem-axle tractor is required, a tandem-axle dolly converter must be used.

Every tandem-trailer combination shall be equipped with emergency equipment that equals or exceeds both the equipment requirements and the performance standards cited in Chapter 316, Florida Statutes and subpart H "Emergency Equipment" of 49 CFR 393.95.

A converter (fifth-wheel) dolly used in the tandem-trailer operations may have either single or tandem axles, according to its total gross weight. In addition to the primary towbar(s), the dolly vehicle must be equipped with safety chains or cables for connecting the dolly to the lead semitrailer and must be adequate to prevent breakaway.

Lamps and Reflectors. Each tractor, trailer, and converter dolly in a tandem-trailer combination shall be equipped with electric lamps and reflectors mounted on the vehicle in accordance with Chapter 316, Florida Statutes, and subpart B "Lighting Devices, Reflectors and Electrical Equipment," of 49 CFR 393.9 through 49 CFR 393.33.

Coupling Devices. Coupling devices shall be so designed, constructed, and installed and the vehicles in a tandem-trailer combination shall equal or exceed both the equipment requirements and the performance standards established on 49 CFR 393.70, except that such devices shall be so designed and constructed as to ensure that any such combination traveling on a level, smooth paved surface will follow in the path of the towing vehicle without shifting or swerving from side to side over 2 inches to each side of the path of the vehicle when it is moving in a straight line. (For further information see Rule 14–62.002; 14–62.005; 14–62.006; 14–62.007; 14–62.008; 14–62.009; 14–62.010; 14–62.011; 14–62.012; 14–62.013; and 14–62.015, FAC)

PERMIT: Tandem-trailer units may operate on the turnpike system under a Tandem Trailer Permit issued by the Florida Turnpike Authority upon application, except as provided in subparagraph (2) below.

(1) The Florida Turnpike Authority shall provide a copy of each such permit to the Motor Carrier Compliance Office.

(2) Tandem-trailer trucks of the dimensions mandated by the STAA of 1982 and operating in compliance with Rule Chapter 14–54, FAC, and under the provisions of section 316.515, Florida Statutes shall be exempt from the provisions of this rule chapter to the extent provided in Rule 14–54.0011, FAC.

(For further information see Rules 14–62.001; 14–62.022; 14–62.023; 14–62.024; 14–62.026; 14–62.027, FAC)

ACCESS: Staging. Tandem-trailer combinations shall be made up and broken up only in special assembly (staging) areas as designated for this purpose. For further information, see Rule 14–62.017, FAC. Make-up and break-up of tandem-trailer combinations shall not be allowed on a public right-of-way unless the area is designated for such use or unless an emergency exists.

ROUTES

	From	To
Florida's Turnpike	South end Homestead Extension at US 1.	Exit 304 Wildwood.

LEGAL CITATIONS: Chapter 14–62, "Regulations Governing Tandem Combinations of Florida's Turnpike," Florida Administrative Code.

STATE: HAWAII

COMBINATION: Truck tractor and 2 trailing units

LENGTH OF CARGO CARRYING UNITS: 65 feet

OPERATIONAL CONDITIONS:

WEIGHT: This combination must operate in compliance with State laws and regulations.

DRIVER: The driver must have a commercial driver's license with the appropriate endorsement.

VEHICLE: No load may exceed the carrying capacity of the axles specified by the manufacturer and no combination vehicle shall have a total weight in excess of its designed gross combination weight limit.

PERMITS: No permits are required.

ACCESS: Designated routes off the NN.

ROUTES: All NN routes except HI–95 from H–1 to Barbers Point Harbor.

LEGAL CITATIONS: Chapter 291, Section 34, Hawaii Revised Statutes and Chapter 104 of Title 19, Administrative Rules.

STATE: IDAHO

COMBINATION: Truck tractor and 2 trailing units—LCV

LENGTH OF THE CARGO-CARRYING UNITS: 95 feet

MAXIMUM ALLOWABLE GROSS WEIGHT: 105,500 pounds

OPERATIONAL CONDITIONS:

WEIGHT: Single axle: 20,000 pounds, tandem axle: 34,000 pounds, and gross vehicle weight up to 105,500 pounds.

Axle spacing: must comply with Idaho Code 49–1001.

Trailer weights: The respective loading of any trailer shall not be substantially greater than the weight of any trailer located ahead of it in the vehicle combination. Substantially greater shall be defined as more than 4,000 pounds heavier.

DRIVER: The driver must have a commercial driver's license with the appropriate endorsement.

VEHICLE: The rules provide that all CMV's with two or more cargo-carrying units (except for truck-trailer combinations which are limited to an 85-foot combination length) are subject to calculated maximum offtracking (CMOT) limits. The CMOT formula is:

$CMOT = R - [R^2 - (A^2 + B^2 + C^2 + D^2 + E^2)]^{1/2}$

$R = 161$

A, B, C, D, E, etc. = measurements between points of articulation or pivot. Squared dimensions to stinger steer points of articulation are negative.

The power unit of LCV's and extra-length combinations shall have adequate power and traction to maintain a speed of 15 miles per hour under normal operating conditions on any up-grade over which the combination is operated.

Fifth-wheel, drawbar, and other coupling devices shall be as specified by Federal Motor Carrier Safety Regulations, section 393.70.

Every combination operated under special permit authority shall be covered by insurance meeting State and Federal requirements. Evidence of this insurance must be carried in the permitted vehicle.

PERMIT: Permits are required. Permit duration is for 1 year from the date of issuance.

ACCESS: Combinations with a CMOT limit of less than 6.5 feet may use any Interstate or designated highway system interchange for access. Combinations with a CMOT of 6.5 to 8.75 feet may use only the following Interstate System interchanges:

I–15 Exits 58 and 119.

I–84 Exits 3, 49, 50, 52, 54, 57, 95, 168, 173, 182, 208, and 211.

I–86 Exits 36, 40, 56, and 58.

ROUTES: All NN routes.

LEGAL CITATIONS: Other regulations and restrictions that must be complied with are:

Idaho Code 49–1001, –1002, –1004, –1010, and –1011.

Idaho Transportation Department Rules 39.C.01, .06, .08, .09, .10, .11, .15, and .19–.23.

STATE: IDAHO

COMBINATION: Truck tractor and 3 trailing units—LCV

LENGTH OF THE CARGO-CARRYING UNITS: 95 feet

MAXIMUM ALLOWABLE GROSS WEIGHT: 105,500 pounds

OPERATIONAL CONDITIONS: Same as the ID-TT2 combination.

ROUTES: Same as the ID-TT2 combination.

LEGAL CITATIONS: Same as the ID-TT2 combination.

STATE: IDAHO

COMBINATION: Truck-trailer

LENGTH OF THE CARGO-CARRYING UNITS: 78 feet

OPERATIONAL CONDITIONS:

WEIGHT: This combination must operate in compliance with State laws and regulations. Because it is not an LCV, it is not subject to the ISTEA freeze as it applies to maximum weight.

DRIVER, PERMIT, and ACCESS: Same as the ID-TT2 combination.

VEHICLE: Overall combination length limited to 85 feet.

ROUTES: Same as the ID-TT2 combination.

LEGAL CITATIONS: Same as the ID-TT2 combination.

STATE: IDAHO

COMBINATION: Truck-trailer-trailer, and Truck-semitrailer-trailer.

LENGTH OF THE CARGO-CARRYING UNITS: 98 feet

OPERATIONAL CONDITIONS:

WEIGHT: This combination must operate in compliance with State laws and regulations. Because it is not an LCV, it is not subject to the ISTEA freeze as it applies to maximum weight.

DRIVER, PERMIT, and ACCESS: Same as the ID-TT2 combination.

VEHICLE: Overall combination length limited to 105 feet.

ROUTES: Same as the ID-TT2 combination.

LEGAL CITATIONS: Same as the ID-TT2 combination.

STATE: INDIANA

COMBINATION: Truck tractor and 2 trailing units—LCV

LENGTH OF THE CARGO-CARRYING UNITS: 106 feet

MAXIMUM ALLOWABLE GROSS WEIGHT: 127,400 pounds

OPERATIONAL CONDITIONS:

WEIGHT: Single axle = 22,400 pounds. Axles spaced less than 40 inches between centers are considered to be single axles.

Tandem axle = 36,000 pounds. Axles spaced more than 40 inches but less than 9 feet between centers are considered to be tandem axles.

Gross vehicle weight = 90,000 pounds plus 1,070 pounds per foot for each foot of total vehicle length in excess of 60 feet with a maximum gross weight not to exceed 127,400 pounds.

DRIVER: The driver must have a commercial driver's license with the appropriate endorsement, and a Toll Road identification card. Drivers must be at least 26 years old, in good health, and with 5 years of experience driving tractor-semitrailers or tandem-trailer combinations. Experience must include driving in all four seasons.

VEHICLE: Lightest trailer to the rear. Distance between coupled trailers shall not exceed 9 feet. The combination vehicle, including coupling devices, shall be designed and constructed so as to ensure that while traveling on a level, smooth paved surface each trailing unit will follow in the path of the towing vehicle without shifting or swerving from side to side more than 3 inches. The combination vehicle must have at least five axles but not more than nine axles and except on ramps be able to achieve and maintain a speed of 45 miles per hour. Following distance is 500 feet, and passing maneuvers must be completed within 1 mile. The truck tractor must be equipped at a minimum with emergency equipment including fire extinguisher, spare fuses, tire chains, tire tread minimums, and disabled vehicle warning devices. Every dolly must be coupled with safety chain directly to the frame of the semitrailer by which it is towed. Each unit in a multi-trailer combination must be equipped at a minimum with electric lights and reflectors mounted on the vehicle.

PERMIT: A free annual tandem-trailer permit must be obtained from the Indiana DOT for loads which exceed 90,000 pounds. A multiple-trip access permit, for which a fee is charged, must also be obtained for access to points of delivery or to breakdown locations. Permission to operate can be temporarily suspended by the Indiana DOT due to weather, road conditions, holiday traffic, or other emergency conditions. Any oversize vehicle whose length exceeds 80 feet shall not be operated at a speed in excess of 45 miles per hour. Oversize loads are not to be operated at any time when wind velocity exceeds 25 miles per hour.

ACCESS: 15 miles from toll gates.

ROUTES

	From	To
I–80/90 (IN Toll Road).	Toll Road Gate 21	Ohio.
I–90 (IN Toll Road)	Illinois	Toll Road Gate 21.

LEGAL CITATIONS:

Indiana Code 9–8–1–16
Indiana Code 8–15–2
135 Indiana Administrative Code 2

STATE: INDIANA

COMBINATION: Truck tractor and 3 trailing units—LCV

LENGTH OF THE CARGO-CARRYING UNITS: 104.5 feet

MAXIMUM ALLOWABLE GROSS WEIGHT: 127,400 pounds

OPERATIONAL CONDITIONS:

WEIGHT, DRIVER, PERMIT, and ACCESS: Same as the IN-TT2 combination.

VEHICLE: Semitrailers and trailers shall not be longer than 28.5 feet, and the minimum number of axles for the combination is seven. Three trailing unit combinations must be equipped with adequate spray-suppressant mud flaps which are properly maintained.

ROUTES: Same as the IN-TT2 combination.

LEGAL CITATIONS: Same as the IN-TT2 combination.

STATE: INDIANA

COMBINATION: Combination of three or more vehicles coupled together

LENGTH OF THE CARGO CARRYING UNITS: 58 feet

OPERATIONAL CONDITIONS:

WEIGHT: This combination must operate in compliance with State laws and regulations. Because it is not an LCV, it is not subject to the ISTEA freeze as it applies to maximum weight.

DRIVER: The driver must have a commercial driver's license with the appropriate endorsement.

VEHICLE: The maximum width is 102 inches, and the maximum height is 13 feet 6 inches.

PERMIT: None required.

ACCESS: Unlimited.

ROUTES: All roads within the State.

LEGAL CITATIONS: Indiana Code 9–8–1–2.

STATE: IOWA

COMBINATION: Truck tractor and 2 trailing units—LCV.

LENGTH OF THE CARGO-CARRYING UNITS: 100 feet when entering Sioux City from South Dakota or South Dakota from Sioux City; 65 feet when entering Sioux City from Nebraska or Nebraska from Sioux City.

MAXIMUM ALLOWABLE GROSS WEIGHT: 129,000 pounds when entering Sioux City from South Dakota or South Dakota from Sioux City; 95,000 pounds when entering Sioux City from Nebraska or Nebraska from Sioux City.

OPERATIONAL CONDITIONS:

Iowa allows vehicles from South Dakota and Nebraska access to terminals which are located within the corporate limits of Sioux City and its commercial zone as shown in 49 CFR 1048.101 on November 28, 1995. These vehicles must be legal in the State from which they enter Iowa.

WEIGHT, DRIVER, VEHICLE, AND PERMIT: Same conditions which apply to a truck tractor and 2 trailing units legally operating in South Dakota or Nebraska.

ACCESS: These combinations may operate on any road within the corporate limits of Sioux City and its commercial zone as shown in 49 CFR 1048.101 on November 28, 1995, when authorized by appropriate State or local authority.

ROUTES: LCV combinations may operate on all Interstate System routes in Sioux City and its commercial zone as shown in 49 CFR 1048.101 on November 28, 1995. If subject only to the ISTEA freeze on length, they may operate on all NN routes in Sioux City and its commercial zone, as above.

LEGAL CITATIONS: Iowa Code §321.457(2)(f) (1995).

STATE: IOWA

COMBINATION: Truck tractor and 3 trailing units—LCV.

LENGTH OF CARGO-CARRYING UNITS: 100 feet when entering Sioux City from South Dakota or South Dakota from Sioux City.

MAXIMUM ALLOWABLE GROSS WEIGHT: 129,000 POUNDS when entering Sioux City from South Dakota or South Dakota from Sioux City.

OPERATIONAL CONDITIONS:

WEIGHT, DRIVER, VEHICLE, AND PERMIT: Same as the SD-TT3 combination.

ACCESS: Same as the IA-TT2 combination.

ROUTES: Same as the IA-TT2 combination.

LEGAL CITATION: Same as the IA-TT2 combination.

STATE: IOWA

COMBINATION: Truck-trailer.

LENGTH OF THE CARGO-CARRYING UNITS: 78 feet when entering Sioux City from South Dakota or South Dakota from Sioux City; 68 feet when entering Sioux City from Nebraska or Nebraska from Sioux City.

OPERATIONAL CONDITIONS:

Iowa allows vehicles from South Dakota and Nebraska access to terminals which are located within the corporate limits of Sioux City and its commercial zone, as shown in 49 CFR 1048.101 on November 28, 1995. These vehicles must be legal in the State from which they enter Iowa.

WEIGHT, DRIVER, VEHICLE, AND PERMIT: Same conditions which apply to a truck-trailer combination legally operating in Nebraska or South Dakota.

ACCESS: Same as the IA-TT2 combination.

ROUTES: Same as IA-TT2 combination.

LEGAL CITATION: Same as the IA-TT2 combination.

STATE: KANSAS

COMBINATION: Truck tractor and 2 trailing units—LCV

LENGTH OF THE CARGO-CARRYING UNITS: 109 feet

MAXIMUM ALLOWABLE GROSS WEIGHT: 120,000 pounds

OPERATIONAL CONDITIONS:

WEIGHT: Combinations consisting of a truck tractor and two trailing units must comply with the Federal Bridge Formula, with maximum weights of 20,000 pounds on a single axle and 34,000 pounds on a tandem axle, and with a maximum gross weight of 120,000 pounds.

DRIVER: The driver must have a commercial driver's license with the appropriate endorsement.

VEHICLE: Truck tractor and two trailing unit combinations must meet legal width and height with no time-of-day travel restrictions or other special requirements.

PERMIT: Permits are not required for operation on the Kansas Turnpike. A permit is required for access between the Turnpike and motor freight terminals located within a 10-mile radius of each toll booth, except at the northeastern end of the Turnpike where a 20-mile radius is allowed. Access permits are valid for 6 months.

ACCESS: Turnpike access routes include all routes between the Turnpike and a motor freight terminal located within a 10-mile radius of each toll booth, except at the northeastern end of the Turnpike where a 20-mile radius is allowed.

ROUTES

	From	To
I–35 Kansas Tpk. Authority (KTA).	Oklahoma	KTA Exit 127.
I–70 KTA	KTA Exit 182	KTA Exit 223.
I–335 KTA	KTA Exit 127	KTA Exit 177.
I–470 KTA	KTA Exit 177	KTA Exit 182.
LEGAL CITATIONS:		
Kansas Statutes Annotated (KSA)		
KSA 8–1911	KSA 68–2004	KSA 68–2019.
KSA 8–1914	KSA 68–2005	KSA 68–2048a.
KSA 68–2003.		

STATE: KANSAS

COMBINATION: Truck tractor and 3 trailing units—LCV

LENGTH OF THE CARGO-CARRYING UNITS: 109 feet

MAXIMUM ALLOWABLE GROSS WEIGHT: 120,000 pounds

OPERATIONAL CONDITIONS: The operations of triple trailing unit combinations are governed by two sets of criteria: (1) The Turnpike and Turnpike access rules, and (2) the SVC rules which apply off of the Turnpike except in the case of vehicles operating under Turnpike access authority. The Turnpike and Turnpike access rules allow a maximum combination vehicle length of 119 feet overall. The SVC rules require "Triples" to have trailers of no more than 28.5 feet maximum length or a cargo-carrying length of approximately 95 feet.

The Turnpike and Turnpike access rules have no time-of-day travel restrictions or other special requirements.

The SVC rules have several operational conditions. SVC's cannot operate on holidays or during holiday weekends. SVC's cannot be dispatched or operated during adverse weather conditions. SVC's must travel in the right lane, except for passing, and the following distance is 100 feet for every 10 miles per hour. SVC permits can include any restrictions deemed necessary, including specific routes and hours, days, and/or seasons of operation. Rules and regulations can be promulgated regarding driver qualifications, vehicle equipment, and operational standards.

WEIGHT: All triple trailing unit combinations must comply with the Federal Bridge Formula with maximum axle weights of 20,000 pounds on a single axle and 34,000 pounds on a tandem axle. The maximum gross weight is 120,000 pounds on the Turnpike and Turnpike access routes, but the SVC's have a maximum weight of 110,000 pounds.

DRIVER: A commercial driver's license with the appropriate endorsement is required under both Turnpike and SVC rules. In addition, for SVC operation drivers must have completed SVC driver training and a company road test. Drivers must also have 2 years of experience driving tractor-semitrailers and 1 year driving doubles.

VEHICLE: Vehicle requirements apply to the SVC program only. All axles, except steering axles, must have dual wheels, and all vehicles must be able to achieve and maintain a speed of 40 miles per hour on all grades. Antispray mud flaps shall be attached to the rear of each axle except the steering axle. Mud flaps shall have a surface designed to absorb and deflect excess moisture to the road surface. Drop and lift axles are prohibited. Vehicles may have a minimum of six and a maximum of nine axles. The heaviest trailers are to be placed forward. Hazardous cargo is prohibited. Convex mirrors are required on both sides of the cab. Equipment must comply with the requirements of 49 CFR 390–399.

Any SVC shall be stable at all times during normal braking and normal operation. When traveling on a level, smooth paved surface, an SVC shall follow the towing vehicle without shifting or swerving beyond the restraints of the lane of travel.

PERMIT: Same as the KS-TT2 combination on the Turnpike and Turnpike access routes. A fee per company plus a permit fee for each power unit is required for the SVC program, and the SVC permits are valid for 1 year. SVC's operated pursuant to regulation 36–1–33 under an annual permit shall be covered by insurance.

ACCESS: Turnpike access routes include all routes between the Turnpike and a motor freight terminal located within a 10-mile radius of each toll booth, except at the northeastern end of the Turnpike where a 20-mile radius is allowed. SVC access routes include all routes between the Interstate and a motor freight terminal located within 5 miles of the Interstate at Goodland.

ROUTES:

A. For vehicles subject to the Turnpike and Turnpike access rules:

	From	To
I–35 KTA	Oklahoma	KTA Exit 127.
I–70 KTA	KTA Exit 182	KTA Exit 223.
I–335 KTA	KTA Exit 127	KTA Exit 177.
I–470 KTA	KTA Exit 177	KTA Exit 182.

B. For vehicles subject to the SVC rules:

	From	To
I–70	Colorado	I–70 Exit 19 Goodland.

LEGAL CITATIONS: Same as the KS-TT2 combination, plus KSA 8–1915.

STATE: MASSACHUSETTS

COMBINATION: Truck tractor and 2 trailing units—LCV

LENGTH OF CARGO-CARRYING UNITS: 104 feet

MAXIMUM ALLOWABLE GROSS WEIGHT: 127,400 pounds

OPERATIONAL CONDITIONS:

WEIGHT: Any combination of vehicles may not exceed a maximum gross weight of 127,400 pounds. The maximum gross weight of the tractor and first semitrailer shall not exceed 71,000 pounds. The maximum gross weight of each unit of dolly and semitrailer shall not exceed 56,400 pounds. The maximum gross weight for the tractor and first semitrailer is governed by the formula 35,000 pounds plus 1,000 pounds per foot between the center of the foremost axle and the center of the rearmost axle of the semitrailer. The maximum gross weight on any one axle is 22,400 pounds, and on any tandem axle it is 36,000 pounds. Axles less than 46 inches between centers are considered to be one axle.

DRIVER: The driver must have a commercial driver's license with the appropriate endorsement and must be registered with the Massachusetts Turnpike Authority (MTA). Registration shall include all specified driving records, safety records, physical examinations, and minimum of 5 years of driving experience with tractor trailers.

VEHICLE:

(1) Brake Regulation. The brakes on any vehicle, dolly converter, or combination of vehicles used in tandem-trailer operations as a minimum shall comply with Federal Motor Carrier Safety Regulations in 49 CFR part 393. In addition, any vehicle, dolly converter or combination of vehicles used in tandem-trailer operations shall meet the requirements of the provisions of the Massachusetts Motor Vehicle Law. Tandem-trailer combinations certified on or after June 1, 1968, shall be equipped with suitable devices to accelerate application and release of the brakes of the towed vehicle.

(2) Axles. A tractor used to haul a tandem trailer combination with a gross weight of more than 110,000 pounds shall be equipped with tandem rear axles, each of which shall be engaged to bear its full share of the load on the roadway surface.

(3) Tandem Assembly. When the gross weight of the trailers vary by more than 20 percent, they shall be coupled with the heaviest trailer attached to the tractor. Coupling devices and towing devices shall comply with the Federal regulations as stated in 49 CFR part 393. When the distance between the rear of the one semitrailer and the front of the following semitrailer is 10 feet or more, the dolly shall be equipped with a device, or the trailers shall be connected along the sides with suitable material, which will indicate to other Turnpike users that the trailers are connected and are in effect one unit. The MTA shall approve the devices or connections to be used on the semitrailers that would indicate it is one unit. Coupling devices shall be so designed, constructed, and installed, and the vehicles in a tandem trailer combination shall be so designed and constructed to ensure that when traveling on a level, smooth paved surface they will follow in the path of the towing vehicle without shifting or swerving over 3 inches to each side of the path of the towing vehicle when it is moving in a straight line. A tandem

trailer unit may pass another vehicle traveling in the same direction only if the speed differential will allow the tandem trailer unit to complete the maneuver and return to the normal driving lane within a distance of 1 mile.

Each truck tractor shall be equipped with at least one spare fuse or other overload protective device, if the devices are not of a reset type, for each kind and size used. The vehicle is to carry at least one set of tire chains for at least one driving wheel on each side between October 15 and May 1 of each year. Each truck tractor shall carry a fire extinguisher which shall have an aggregate rating of 20 BC.

PERMIT: A permittee must demonstrate to the MTA that it has insurance coverage of the type and amounts required by Turnpike regulation. Both the tractor manufacturer and the permittee shall certify to the MTA, prior to the approval of a tractor, that it is capable of hauling the maximum permissible gross load to be transported by the permittee at a speed not less than 20 miles per hour on all portions of the turnpike system. The MTA may revoke or temporarily suspend any permit at will and the instructions of the MTA or Massachusetts State Police shall be complied with immediately.

ACCESS: Makeup and breakup areas. Tandem trailer units shall not leave the Turnpike right-of-way and shall be assembled and disassembled only in designated areas.

ROUTES

	From	To
I–90 Mass Turnpike.	New York State	Turnpike Exit 18 Boston.

LEGAL CITATIONS:

The MTA, Massachusetts Rules and Regulations 730, and CMR 4.00.

STATE: MICHIGAN

COMBINATION: Truck tractor and 2 trailing units—LCV

LENGTH OF CARGO-CARRYING UNITS: 58 feet

MAXIMUM ALLOWABLE GROSS WEIGHT: 164,000 pounds

OPERATIONAL CONDITIONS:

WEIGHT: The single-axle weight limit for LCV's is 18,000 pounds for axles spaced 9 feet or more apart. For axles spaced more than 3.5 but less than 9 feet apart, the single-axle weight limit is 13,000 pounds. The tandem-axle weight limit is 16,000 pounds per axle for the first tandem and 13,000 pounds per axle for all other tandems. Axles spaced less than 3.5 feet apart are limited to 9,000 pounds per axle. Maximum load per inch width of tire is 700 pounds. Maximum gross weight is determined based on axle and axle group weight limits.

When restricted seasonal loadings are in effect, load per inch width of tire and maximum axle weights are reduced as follows: Rigid pavements—525 pounds per inch of tire width, 25 percent axle weight reduction; Flexible pavements—450 pounds per inch of tire width, 35 percent axle weight reduction.

DRIVER: The driver must have a commercial driver's license with the appropriate endorsement.

VEHICLE: Truck height may not exceed 13.5 feet. There is no overall length for LCV's operating on the Interstate System when semitrailer and trailer lengths do not exceed 28.5 feet. If either the trailer or semitrailer is longer than 28.5 feet, the distance from the front of the first box to the rear of the second box may not exceed 58 feet. A combination of vehicles shall not have more than 11 axles, and the ratio of gross weight to net horsepower delivered to the clutch shall not exceed 400 to 1.

PERMIT: Permits for divisible loads of more than 80,000 pounds must conform to either Federal or grandfathered axle and bridge spacing requirements.

ACCESS: All designated State highways.

ROUTES: All Interstate routes and designated State highways.

LEGAL CITATIONS:

Michigan Public Act 300, section 257.722
Michigan Public Act 300, section 257.719

STATE: MICHIGAN

COMBINATION: Truck-trailer

LENGTH OF THE CARGO-CARRYING UNITS: 63 feet

OPERATIONAL CONDITIONS:

WEIGHT: This combination must operate in compliance with State laws and regulations. Because it is not an LCV, it is not subject to the ISTEA freeze as it applies to maximum weight.

DRIVER: The driver must have a commercial driver's license with appropriate endorsement.

VEHICLE: The overall length of this combination is limited to 70 feet. The only cargo that may be carried is saw logs, pulpwood, and tree length poles.

PERMIT: None required.

ACCESS: All NN routes.

ROUTES: All NN routes.

LEGAL CITATIONS: Michigan Public Act 300, section 257.719.

STATE: MISSISSIPPI

COMBINATION: Truck tractor and 2 trailing units

LENGTH OF THE CARGO-CARRYING UNITS: 65 feet

OPERATIONAL CONDITIONS:

WEIGHT: This combination must operate in compliance with State laws and regulations.

DRIVER: The driver must have a commercial driver's license with the appropriate endorsement.

VEHICLE: Each trailing unit may be a maximum of 30 feet long.

PERMIT: None required.

ACCESS: No restrictions, may operate Statewide.

ROUTES: All NN routes.

LEGAL CITATIONS: Section 63–5–19, Mississippi Code, Annotated, 1972.

STATE: MISSOURI

COMBINATION: Truck tractor and 2 trailing units—LCV

LENGTH OF THE CARGO-CARRYING UNITS: 110 feet

MAXIMUM ALLOWABLE GROSS WEIGHT: 120,000 pounds when entering Missouri from Kansas; 95,000 pounds when entering from Nebraska; 90,000 pounds when entering from Oklahoma.

OPERATIONAL CONDITIONS: Missouri allows vehicles from neighboring States access to terminals in Missouri which are within 20 miles of the Missouri State Line. These vehicles must be legal in the State from which they are entering Missouri.

WEIGHT, DRIVER, VEHICLE: Same conditions which apply to a truck tractor and two trailing units legally operating in Kansas, Nebraska, or Oklahoma.

PERMIT: Annual blanket overdimension permits are issued to allow a truck tractor and two trailing units legally operating in Kansas, Nebraska, or Oklahoma to move to and from terminals in Missouri which are located within a 20-mile band of the State Line for these three States. There is a permit fee per power unit. The permits carry routine permit restrictions, but do not address driver qualifications or any other restrictions not included in the rules and regulations for all permitted movement.

ACCESS: Routes as necessary to reach terminals.

ROUTES: All NN routes within a 20-mile band from the Kansas, Nebraska, and Oklahoma borders.

LEGAL CITATIONS: §304.170 and §304.200 Revised Statutes of Missouri 1990.

STATE: MISSOURI

COMBINATION: Truck tractor and 3 trailing units—LCV

LENGTH OF THE CARGO-CARRYING UNITS: 109 feet

MAXIMUM ALLOWABLE GROSS WEIGHT: 120,000 pounds when entering Missouri from Kansas; 90,000 pounds when entering from Oklahoma.

OPERATIONAL CONDITIONS: Missouri allows vehicles from neighboring States access to terminals in Missouri which are within 20 miles of the Missouri State Line. These vehicles must be legal in the State from which they are entering Missouri.

WEIGHT, DRIVER, VEHICLE: Same conditions which apply to a truck tractor and three trailing units legally operating in Kansas or Oklahoma.

PERMIT: Annual blanket overdimension permits are issued to allow a truck tractor and three trailing units legally operating in Kansas or Oklahoma, to move to and from terminals in Missouri which are located within a 20-mile band of the State Line for these two States. There is a permit fee per power unit. The permits carry routine permit restrictions, but do not address driver qualifications or any other restrictions not included in the rules and regulations for all permitted movement.

ACCESS: Routes as necessary to reach terminals.

ROUTES: All NN routes within a 20-mile band from the Kansas and Oklahoma borders.

LEGAL CITATIONS: §304.170 & §304.200 Revised Statutes of Missouri 1990.

STATE: MONTANA

COMBINATION: Truck tractor and 2 trailing units—LCV

LENGTH OF CARGO-CARRYING UNITS: 93 feet

MAXIMUM ALLOWABLE GROSS WEIGHT: 137,800 pounds for vehicles operating under the Montana/Alberta Memorandum of Understanding (MOU). For other MT-TT2 combinations, the maximum allowable gross weight is 131,060 pounds.

OPERATIONAL CONDITIONS:

WEIGHT: Except for vehicles operating under the MOU, any vehicle carrying a divisible load over 80,000 pounds must comply with the Federal Bridge Formula found in 23 U.S.C. 127.

Maximum single-axle limit: 20,000 pounds
Maximum tandem-axle limit: 34,000 pounds
Maximum gross weight limit: 131,060 pounds
Maximum weight allowed per inch of tire width is 600 pounds.

WEIGHT, MONTANA/ALBERTA MOU:
Maximum single-axle limit: 20,000 pounds

Maximum tandem-axle limit: 37,500 pounds
Maximum tridem-axle limit:
Axles spaced from 94″ to less than 118″: 46,300 pounds
Axles spaced from 118″ to less than 141″: 50,700 pounds
Axles spaced from 141″ to 146″: 52,900 pounds
Maximum gross weight:
A-Train: 118,000 pounds
B-Train (eight axle): 137,800 pounds
B-Train (seven axle): 124,600 pounds

The designation of "A-Train" or "B-Train" refers to the manner in which the two trailing units are connected.

DRIVER: The driver must have a commercial driver's license with the appropriate endorsement.

VEHICLE: No special requirements beyond compliance with Federal Motor Carrier Safety Regulations.

PERMIT: Special permit required for double trailer combinations if either trailer exceeds 28.5 feet. Permits are available on an annual or a trip basis and provide for continuous travel. Statutory reference: 61–10–124, MCA. For vehicles being operated under the Montana/Alberta MOU, operators must have paid gross vehicle weight fees for the total weight being carried. In addition, a term Restricted Route and Oversize Permit for which an annual fee is charged must be obtained. Finally, vehicle operators must secure a single-trip, overweight permit prior to each trip.

ACCESS: Access must be authorized by the Montana DOT. For vehicles operated under the Montana/Alberta MOU, access routes from I–15 into Shelby are authorized when permits are issued. For vehicles with a cargo-carrying length greater than 88 feet, but not more than 93 feet, a 2-mile access from the Interstate System is automatically granted to terminals and service areas. Access outside the 2-mile provision may be granted on a case-by-case basis by the Administrator of the Motor Carrier Services Division.

ROUTES: Combinations with a cargo-carrying length greater than 88 feet, but not more than 93 feet, are limited to the Interstate System. Combinations with a cargo-carrying length of 88 feet or less can use all NN routes except U.S. 87 from milepost 79.3 to 82.5. For vehicles being operated under the Montana/Alberta MOU, the only route available is I–15 from the border with Canada to Shelby.

LEGAL CITATION:

61–10–124 MCA ..	61–10–104 MCA ..	ARM 18.8.509(6)
61–10–107 (3) MCA.	61–10–121 MCA ..	ARM 18.8.517, 518

Montana/Alberta Memorandum of Understanding
Administrative Rules of Montana

STATE: MONTANA

COMBINATION: Truck tractor and 3 trailing units—LCV

LENGTH OF THE CARGO-CARRYING UNITS: 100 feet

MAXIMUM ALLOWABLE GROSS WEIGHT: 131,060 pounds

OPERATIONAL CONDITIONS:

WEIGHT: Any vehicle carrying a divisible load over 80,000 pounds must comply with the Federal Bridge Formula found in 23 U.S.C. 127.
Maximum single-axle limit: 20,000 pounds
Maximum tandem-axle limit: 34,000 pounds
Maximum gross weight limit: 131,060 pounds
Maximum weight allowed per inch of tire width is 600 pounds.

DRIVER: Drivers of three trailing unit combinations must be certified by the operating company. This certification includes an actual driving test and knowledge of Federal Motor Carrier Safety Regulations and State law pertaining to triple vehicle operations. Drivers are also required to have a commercial driver's license with the appropriate endorsement.

VEHICLE: The 100-foot cargo-carrying length is only with a conventional tractor within a 110-foot overall length limit. If a cabover tractor is used, the cargo length is 95 feet within a 105-foot overall length limit. Vehicles involved in three trailing unit operations must comply with the following regulations:

1. Shall maintain a minimum speed of 20 miles per hour on any grade;
2. Kingpins must be solid and permanently affixed;
3. Hitch connections must be no-slack type;
4. Drawbars shall be of minimum practical length;
5. Permanently affixed axles must be designed for the width of the trailer;
6. Anti-sail mudflaps or splash and spray suppression devices are required;
7. The heavier trailers shall be in front of lighter trailers;
8. A minimum distance of 100 feet per 10 miles per hour is required between other vehicles except when passing;
9. Operating at speeds greater than 55 miles per hour is prohibited; and
10. Vehicle and driver are subject to Federal Motor Carrier Safety Regulations.

Reference: 18.8.517 Administrative Rules of Montana.

PERMIT: Special triple vehicle permits are required for the operation of these combinations. Permits are available on an annual or trip basis. Permits are good for travel on the Interstate System only and are subject to the following conditions:

1. Travel is prohibited during adverse weather conditions;

2. Transportation of Class A explosives is prohibited; and

3. Companies operating triple combinations must have an established safety program including driver certifications.

ACCESS: Access is for 2 miles beyond the Interstate System, or further if granted by the Administrator of the Motor Carrier Services Division.

ROUTES: Interstate System routes in the State.

LEGAL CITATION: 18.8.517 Administrative Rules of Montana.

STATE: MONTANA

COMBINATION: Truck-Trailer

LENGTH OF CARGO-CARRYING UNITS: 88 feet

OPERATIONAL CONDITIONS:

WEIGHT: This combination must operate in compliance with State laws and regulations. Because it is not an LCV, it is not subject to the ISTEA freeze as it applies to maximum weight.

DRIVER, and ACCESS: Same as the MT-TT2 combination.

VEHICLE: Same as the MT-TT2 combination, except overall length limited to 95 feet.

PERMIT: Special permit required if overall length exceeds 75 feet. Special permits allow continuous travel and are available on an annual or trip basis.

ROUTES: Same as the MT-TT2 combination.

LEGAL CITATIONS: 61–10–121 and 61–10–124, MCA.

STATE: MONTANA

COMBINATION: Truck-trailer-trailer

LENGTH OF THE CARGO-CARRYING UNITS: 103 feet

WEIGHT: This combination must operate in compliance with State laws and regulations. Because it is not an LCV, it is not subject to the ISTEA freeze as it applies to maximum weight.

DRIVER, PERMIT, and ACCESS: Same as the MT-TT2 combination.

VEHICLE: The cargo-carrying unit length is 103 feet with a conventional truck within a 110-foot overall length limit, and 98 feet with a cab-over-engine truck within a 105-foot overall length limit. On two-lane highways the cargo-carrying unit length is 88 feet within a 95-foot overall length limit.

ROUTES: All NN routes except U.S. 87 between mileposts 79.3 and 82.5.

LEGAL CITATIONS:

61–10–124 MCA
61–10–121 MCA
ARM 18–8–509

STATE: NEBRASKA

COMBINATION: Truck tractor and 2 trailing units—LCV

LENGTH OF THE CARGO-CARRYING UNITS: 95 feet for combination units traveling empty. 65 feet for combination units carrying cargo, except those carrying seasonally harvested products from the field where they are harvested to storage, market, or stockpile in the field, or from stockpile to market, which may extend the length to 71.5 feet.

OPERATIONAL CONDITIONS:

WEIGHT:

Maximum weight:

Single axle = 20,000 pounds

Tandem axle = 34,000 pounds

Gross = Determined by Federal Bridge Formula B, but not to exceed 95,000 pounds.

Truck tractor and 2 trailing unit combinations with a length of cargo-carrying units of over 65 feet are required to travel empty.

DRIVER: The driver must have a commercial driver's license with the appropriate endorsement. There are no additional special qualifications where the cargo-carrying unit lengths are 65 feet or less. For cargo-carrying unit lengths over 65 feet, the driver must comply with all State and Federal requirements and must not have had any accidents while operating such vehicles.

VEHICLE: For combinations with a cargo-carrying length over 65 feet, but not over 85 feet, the semitrailer cannot exceed 48 feet in length and the full trailer cannot be less than 26 feet or more than 28 feet long. The shorter trailer must be placed to the rear. The wheel path of the trailer(s) cannot vary more than 3 inches from that of the towing vehicle.

For combinations with a cargo-carrying length greater than 85 feet, up to and including 95 feet, the trailers must be of approximately equal length.

PERMIT: A weight permit in accordance with Chapter 12 of the Nebraska Department of Roads (NDOR) Rules and Regulations is required for operating on the Interstate System with weight in excess of 80,000 pounds.

A length permit, in accordance with Chapters 8 or 11 of the NDOR Rules and Regulations, is required for two trailing unit combinations with a length of cargo-carrying units over 65 feet. Except for permits issued to carriers hauling seasonally harvested products in combinations with a cargo-carrying length greater than 65 feet but not more than 71.5 feet which may move as necessary to accommodate crop movement requirements, holders of length permits are subject to the following conditions.

Movement is prohibited on Saturdays, Sundays, and holidays; when ground wind speed exceeds 25 miles per hour; when visibility is less than 800 feet; or when steady rain, snow, sleet, ice, or other conditions cause slippery pavement. Beginning November 15 until April 16 permission to move must be obtained from the NDOR Permit Office within 3 hours of movement. Beginning April 16 until November 15 permission to move must be obtained within 3 days of the movement.

Fees are charged for all permits. Length permits for combinations carrying seasonally harvested products are valid for 30 days and are renewable but may not authorize operation for more than 150 days per year.

All permits are subject to revocation if the terms are violated.

ACCESS: Access to NN routes is not restricted for two trailing unit combinations with a cargo-carrying length of 65 feet or less, or 71.5 feet or less if involved in carrying seasonally harvested products. For two trailing unit combinations with a cargo-carrying length greater than 65 feet and not involved in carrying seasonally harvested products, access to and from I–80 is limited to designated staging areas within six miles of the route between the Wyoming State Line and Exit 440 (Nebraska Highway 50); and except for weather, emergency, and repair, cannot reenter I–80 after exiting.

ROUTES: Except for length permits issued to carriers hauling seasonally harvested products in combinations with a cargo-carrying length greater than 65 feet but not more than 71.5 feet which may use all non-Interstate NN routes, vehicles requiring length permits are restricted to Interstate 80 between the Wyoming State Line and Exit 440 (Nebraska Highway 50). Combinations not requiring length permits may use all NN routes.

LEGAL CITATIONS:

Nebraska Revised Statutes Reissued 1988

§ 39–6,179 (Double trailers under 65 feet)

§ 39–6,179.01 (Double trailers over 65 feet)

§ 39–6,180.01 (Authorized weight limits)

§ 39–6,181 (Vehicles; size; weight; load; overweight; special permits; etc.)

Nebraska Department of Roads Rules and Regulations, Title 408, Chapter 1 (Double trailers over 65 feet)

STATE: NEBRASKA

COMBINATION: Truck tractor and 3 trailing units

LENGTH OF THE CARGO-CARRYING UNITS: 95 feet

OPERATIONAL CONDITIONS:

WEIGHT: A truck tractor and three trailing unit combination is required to travel empty.

DRIVER: Same as the NE-TT2 combination.

PERMIT: A length permit, in accordance with Chapter 11 of the NDOR Rules and Regulations is required for a three trailing unit combination. Conditions of the length permit prohibit movements on Saturdays, Sundays, and holidays; when ground wind speed exceeds 25 miles per hour; and when visibility is less than 800 feet. Movement is also prohibited during steady rain, snow, sleet, ice, or other conditions causing slippery pavement. Beginning November 15 until April 16 permission to move must be obtained from the NDOR Permit Office within 3 hours of movement. Beginning April 16 until November 15 permission to move must be obtained within 3 days of the movement. A fee is charged for the annual length permit. These permits can be revoked if the terms are violated.

ACCESS: Access to and from I–80 is limited to designated staging areas within 6 miles of the route between Wyoming State Line and Exit 440 (Nebraska Route 50). Except for weather, emergency, and repair, three trailing unit combinations cannot reenter the Interstate after having exited.

VEHICLE: A three trailing unit combination must have trailers of approximately equal length and the overall vehicle length cannot exceed 105 feet.

ROUTES: I–80 from Wyoming to Exit 440 (Nebraska Highway 50).

LEGAL CITATIONS:

Neb. Rev. Stat. § 39–6.179,01 (Reissue 1988)

Nebraska Department of Roads Rules and Regulations, Title 408, Chapter 1

STATE: NEBRASKA

COMBINATION: Truck-trailer

LENGTH OF THE CARGO-CARRYING UNITS: 68 feet

OPERATIONAL CONDITIONS:

WEIGHT: This combination must operate in compliance with State laws and regulations. Because it is not an LCV, it is not subject to the ISTEA freeze as it applies to maximum weight.

DRIVER: The driver must have a commercial driver's license with the appropriate endorsement.

VEHICLE: The overall vehicle length, including load, cannot exceed 75 feet.

PERMIT: No permit is required.

ACCESS: Statewide during daylight hours only.

ROUTES: All NN routes.

LEGAL CITATIONS: Neb. Rev. Stat. §39–6,179.

STATE: NEVADA

COMBINATION: Truck tractor and 2 trailing units—LCV

LENGTH OF THE CARGO-CARRYING UNITS: 95 feet

MAXIMUM ALLOWABLE GROSS WEIGHT: 129,000 pounds

OPERATIONAL CONDITIONS:

WEIGHT: The single-axle weight limit is 20,000 pounds, the tandem-axle weight limit is 34,000 pounds, and the gross weight is subject to the Federal Bridge Formula limits, provided that two consecutive tandems with a distance of 36 feet or more between the first and last axle may carry 34,000 pounds on each tandem.

DRIVER: The driver must have a commercial driver's license with the appropriate endorsement, be at least 25 years old, and have had a medical exam within previous 24 months. Every operator must be covered by a liability insurance policy with personal injury and property damage limits meeting State requirements.

VEHICLE: No trailer may be longer than 48 feet. If one trailer is 48 feet long, the other trailer cannot exceed 42 feet. Towed vehicles must not shift or sway more than 3 inches to right or left and must track in a straight line on a level, smooth paved highway. Vehicles must be able to accelerate and operate on a level highway at speeds which are compatible with other traffic and with the speed limits and must be able to maintain a minimum of 20 miles per hour on any grade on which they may operate. All vehicles must have safety chains on converter dollies. Vehicles must carry snow chains for each drive wheel.

Vehicle operations may be suspended in adverse weather and high winds, as determined by police or the Nevada DOT.

The shortest trailer must be in the rear of a combination unless it is heavier than the longer trailer.

Brakes must comply with all State and Federal requirements for commercial vehicles including automatic braking for separation of vehicles, parking brakes, and working lights.

Vehicles must not exceed posted speed limits and cannot operate on any highway on which they cannot at all times stay on the right side of the center line. All LCV's must keep a distance of at least 500 feet from each other.

Every full-sized truck or truck tractor used in a combination of vehicles must be equipped with at least the following emergency and safety equipment:

1. One fire extinguisher which meets "Classification B" of the National Fire Protection Association.

2. One spare light bulb for every electrical lighting device used on the rear of the last vehicle in a combination of vehicles.

3. One spare fuse for each different kind and size of fuse used in every vehicle in the combination of vehicles. If the electrical system of any vehicle in the combination contains any devices for protection of electrical circuits from overloading, other than fuses and circuit breakers which can be reset, one spare of each such device must be kept as emergency and safety equipment.

4. Any flares, reflectors or red electrical lanterns which meet State or Federal law or regulation.

Before operating a combination of vehicles on a highway of this State, the owner or operator of the combination shall certify to the Nevada DOT, on a form provided by it, that all vehicles and equipment in the combination meet the requirements of and will be operated in compliance with NAC 484.300 to 484.440, inclusive.

All axles except for steering axles and axles that weigh less than 10,000 pounds must have at least four tires unless the tire width of each tire on the axles is 14 inches or greater.

PERMIT: Permits are required and a fee is charged. They may be revoked for violation of any of the provisions of the legal regulations. The State may suspend operation on roads deemed unsafe or impracticable. Permits must be carried in the vehicle along with identification devices issued by the Nevada Department of Motor Vehicles.

ACCESS: As authorized by the Nevada DOT.

ROUTES: All NN routes, except US 93 from Nevada State route 500 to Arizona.

LEGAL CITATIONS: NRS 484.400, .405(4), .425, .430, .739, 408.100–4, .100–6(a), and 706.531. Also, "Regulations for the Operation of 70 to 105 foot Combinations" (1990).

STATE: NEVADA

COMBINATION: Truck tractor and 3 trailing units—LCV

LENGTH OF THE CARGO-CARRYING UNITS: 95 feet

MAXIMUM ALLOWABLE GROSS WEIGHT: 129,000 pounds

OPERATIONAL CONDITIONS: Same as the NV-TT2 combination.

ROUTES: Same as the NV-TT2 combination.

LEGAL CITATIONS: Same as the NV-TT2 combination.

STATE: NEVADA

COMBINATION: Truck-trailer, and Truck-trailer-trailer

LENGTH OF THE CARGO-CARRYING UNITS: 98 feet

OPERATIONAL CONDITIONS:

WEIGHT: This combination must operate in compliance with State laws and regulations. Because it is not an LCV, it is not subject to the ISTEA freeze as it applies to maximum weight.

DRIVER, VEHICLE, and ACCESS: Same as the NV-TT2 combination.

PERMITS: Same as the NV-TT2 combination, except permits for Truck-trailer, or Truck-trailer-trailer combinations are only required when the overall length is 70 feet or more.

ROUTES: Same as the NV-TT2 combination.

LEGAL CITATIONS: Same as the NV-TT2 combination.

STATE: NEW MEXICO

COMBINATION: Truck tractor and 2 trailing units—LCV

LENGTH OF THE CARGO-CARRYING UNITS: Not applicable

MAXIMUM ALLOWABLE GROSS WEIGHT: 86,400 pounds

OPERATIONAL CONDITIONS: The cargo-carrying length restriction does not apply to this combination. The length of each trailing unit is limited to 28.5 feet. This describes a two trailing unit vehicle whose operation is guaranteed by the STAA of 1982 regardless of inter-unit spacing. As long as each trailing unit is 28.5 feet long or less, cargo-carrying length is not restricted. This combination is listed as a LCV because it can exceed the 80,000-pound threshold established in the Congressional definition. The 86,400-pound gross weight limit is grandfathered for New Mexico.

WEIGHT: Single axle = 21,600 pounds. Tandem axle = 34,200 pounds. Load per inch of tire width = 600 pounds. The total gross weight with load imposed on the highway by any vehicle or combination of vehicles where the distance between the first and last axles is less than 19 feet shall not exceed that given for the respective distances in the following table:

Distance in feet between first and last axles of group	Allowed load in pounds on group of axles
4	34,320
5	35,100
6	35,880
7	36,660
8	37,440
9	38,220
10	39,000
11	39,780
12	40,560
13	41,340
14	42,120
15	42,900
16	43,680
17	44,460
18	45,240

The total gross weight with load imposed on the highway by any vehicle or combination of vehicles where the distance between the first and last axles is 19 feet or more shall not exceed that given for the respective distances in the following table:

Distance in feet between first and last axles of group	Allowed load in pounds on group of axles
19	53,100
20	54,000
21	54,900
22	55,800
23	56,700
24	57,600
25	58,500
26	59,400
27	60,300
28	61,200
29	62,100
30	63,000
31	63,900
32	64,800
33	65,700
34	66,600
35	67,500
36	68,400
37	69,300
38	70,200
39	71,100
40	72,000
41	72,900
42	73,800
43	74,700
44	75,600
45	76,500
46	77,400
47	78,300

Distance in feet between first and last axles of group	Allowed load in pounds on group of axles
48	79,200
49	80,100
50	81,000
51	81,900
52	82,800
53	83,700
54	84,600
55	85,500
56 and over	86,400

The distance between the centers of the axles shall be measured to the nearest even foot. When a fraction is exactly one-half the next larger whole number shall be used.

DRIVER: The driver must have a commercial driver's license with the appropriate endorsement.

VEHICLE: No special requirements beyond normal Federal Motor Carrier or State regulations. The maximum length of the trailing units is 28.5 feet.

PERMIT: None Required.

ACCESS: STAA vehicles must be allowed reasonable access in accordance with 23 CFR 658.19.

ROUTES: All Interstate highways.

LEGAL CITATIONS:

66–7–409 NMSA 1978
66–7–410 NMSA 1978

STATE: NEW YORK

COMBINATION: Truck tractor and 2 trailing units—LCV

LENGTH OF THE CARGO-CARRYING UNITS: 102 feet

MAXIMUM ALLOWABLE GROSS WEIGHT: 143,000 pounds

OPERATIONAL CONDITIONS:

WEIGHT: The following information pertains to tandem trailer combinations with either trailer more than 28.5 feet long but not more than 48 feet long. A nine-axle combination vehicle may not exceed a total maximum gross weight of 143,000 pounds. An eight-axle combination vehicle may not exceed a total maximum gross weight of 138,400 pounds. The maximum gross weight that may be carried upon any combination of units is limited by the maximum gross weight that can be carried upon the axles as follows. For a nine-axle combination: Drive axles—36,000 pounds, axles four/five—36,000 pounds, axles six/seven—27,000 pounds, and axles eight/nine—36,000 pounds. A minimum 12-foot axle spacing between the fifth and sixth axles is also required on the nine-axle LCV. For an eight-axle combination: Drive axles—36,000 pounds, axles four/five—36,000 pounds, sixth axle—22,400 pounds, and axles seven/eight—36,000 pounds. The eight-axle LCV has no minimum axle-spacing requirements. For gross weights in excess of 138,400 pounds the combination must include a tandem-axle dolly to meet the nine-axle requirements. Maximum permissible gross weight for B-train combination is 127,000 pounds.

When the gross weight of the two trailers in a tandem combination vary more than 20 percent, the heaviest of the two must be placed in the lead position.

For tandem trailer combinations in which neither trailing unit exceeds 28.5 feet in length the following maximum allowable weights apply: for a single axle—28,000 pounds (except that steering axles may not exceed 22,400 pounds), for a tandem axle—42,500 pounds, for a tri-axle—52,500 pounds. The gross weight may not exceed 100,000 pounds or the manufacturers gross weight rating, whichever is lower.

DRIVER: For operation on highways under the jurisdiction of the New York State Thruway Authority (NYSTA), except for the full length of I–84 and that portion of I–287 from Thruway exit 8 to I–95, the driver must have a commercial driver's license with the appropriate endorsement, and hold a Tandem Trailer Driver's Permit issued by the NYSTA. In order to obtain an NYSTA driver's permit, an applicant must (1) hold a valid commercial driver's license with multiple-trailer endorsement; (2) be over 26 years old, in good health, and have at least 5 years of provable experience driving tractor-trailer combinations; and (3) meet all other application requirements with regard to driving history established by the NYSTA. Qualified drivers receive a Tandem Trailer Driver's Permit for Tandem Vehicle Operation which is valid only for the operation of the certified equipment owned by the company to which the permit is issued.

For operation on highways under the jurisdiction of the New York State DOT, cities not wholly included in one county, the full length of I–84 and that portion of I–287 from Thruway exit 8 to I–95, the driver must have a commercial driver's license with the appropriate endorsement.

VEHICLE: All vehicles must meet the requirements of applicable Federal and State statutes, rules, and regulations. Vehicles operating on highways under the jurisdiction of the NYSTA, except for the full length of I–84 and that portion of I–287 from Thruway exit 8 to I–95, must also meet the following additional requirements. The tractor manufacturer and the permittee shall certify to the NYSTA prior to the approval of the tractor that it is capable of hauling the maximum permissible gross load at a speed of not less than 20 miles per hour on all portions of the thruway system.

The brakes on any vehicle, dolly converter, or combination of vehicles shall comply with

49 CFR part 393 and, in addition, any vehicle or dolly converter shall meet the provisions of the New York State Traffic Law.

Tandem trailer operations shall be equipped, at a minimum, with emergency equipment as required by 49 CFR part 393, subpart H, as amended, tire chains from October 15 to May 1 of each year, a fire extinguisher with an aggregate rating of 20BC, and each trailer with specific lamps and reflectors.

All tractors certified by the NYSTA for use with tandem trailers will be assigned an identification number by the NYSTA which must be placed on the vehicle. The number must be at least 3 inches in height and visible to a person standing at ground level opposite the driver's position in the cab.

Axle Type. Tractors to be used for hauling 110,000 pounds or more shall be equipped with tandem rear axles, both with driving power. Tractors to be used for hauling 110,000 pounds or less may have a single drive axle. Tandem combinations using single wheel tires commonly referred to as "Super Singles" are required to use triple-axle tractors, dual-axle trailers, and dual-axle dollies.

Dollies. Every converter dolly certified on and after June 1, 1968, used to convert a semitrailer to a full trailer may have either single or tandem axles at the option of the permittee. Single-axle dollies may not utilize low profile tires. Combination vehicles with a gross weight in excess of 138,400 pounds must have a tandem-axle dolly to meet the nine-axle requirement. If the distance between two semitrailers is 10 feet or more, the dolly shall be equipped with a device or the trailers connected along the sides with suitable material to indicate they are in effect one unit. The devices or connection shall be approved by the NYSTA prior to use on a tandem trailer combination. The NYSTA tandem-trailer provisions require that converter dollies shall be coupled with one or more safety chains or cables to the frame or an extension of the frame of the motor vehicle by which it is towed. Each dolly converter must also be equipped with mud flaps. Tandem combinations using a sliding fifth wheel attached to the lead trailer, known as a "B-Train" combination, will require a separate Thruway Engineer Service approval prior to the initial tandem run. Special provisions regarding B-Trains will be reviewed at the time of the application or request for use on the Thruway.

PERMIT: For operation on highways under the jurisdiction of the New York State DOT, cities not wholly included in one county, or the following highway sections under NYSTA jurisdiction; the full length of I–84 and that portion of I–287 from Thruway exit 8 to I–95, a permit to exceed the weight limits set forth in section 385(15) of the New York State Vehicle and Traffic Law must be obtained from the State DOT, city involved, or the NYSTA. A fee is charged for the permit.

For operation on highways under the jurisdiction of the NYSTA, except for the full length of I–84 and that portion of I–287 from Thruway exit 8 to I–95, companies must file an application for a Tandem Trailer Permit with the NYSTA. Permits are issued to such companies upon meeting qualifications, including insurance, for tandem combinations over 65 feet in length. No permit fee is charged; however, Thruway tolls are charged for each use of the Thruway, and the equipment must be certified by the NYSTA annually. The annual re-certification of equipment is handled by: New York State Thruway Authority, Manager of Traffic Safety Services, P.O. Box 189, Albany, New York 12201–0189

Transportation of hazardous materials is subject to special restrictions plus 49 CFR part 397 of the Federal Motor Carrier Safety Regulations.

ACCESS: For tandem trailer combinations with either trailer more than 28.5 feet long but not more than 48 feet long, the following access is available to authorized operating routes.

I–87 (New York Thruway) Access provided at Thruway Exit 21B to or from a point 1,500 feet north of the Thruway on US 9W.

I–90 (NYSTA-Berkshire Section) access provided at:

(1) Thruway Exit B–1 to or from a point 0.8 mile north of the southern most access ramp on US 9.

(2) Thruway Exit B–3 within a 2,000-foot radius of the Thruway ramps to NY 22.

I–90 (New York Thruway) access provided at:

(1) Thruway Exit 28 within a radius of 1,500 feet of the toll booth at Fultonville, New York.

(2) Thruway Exit 32 to or from a point 0.6 mile north of the Thruway along NY 233.

(3) Thruway Exit 44 to or from a point 0.8 mile from the Thruway along NY 332 and Collett Road.

(4) Thruway Exit 52 to or from:

(a) A point 1.7 miles west and south of the Thruway via Walden Avenue and NY 240 (Harlem Road);

(b) A point 0.85 mile east and south of the Thruway via Walden Avenue and a roadway purchased by the Town of Cheektowaga from Sorrento Cheese, Inc.

(5) Thruway Exit 54 to or from a point approximately 2.5 miles east and north of the Thruway via routes NY 400 and NY 277.

(6) Thruway Exit 56 to or from a point approximately 2 miles west and south of the Thruway via NY 179 and Old Mile Strip Road.

I–190 (NYSTA—Niagara Section) access provided at:

(1) Thruway Exit N1 to or from:

(a) A point 0.8 mile west of the Thruway exit along Dingens Street.

(b) A point 0.45 mile from the Thruway exit via Dingens Street and James E. Casey Drive.

(2) Thruway Exit N5 to or from a point approximately 1.0 miles south of the Thruway via Louisiana Street and South Street.

(3) Thruway Exit N15 to or from a point 0.5 mile southeast of the Thruway via NY 325 (Sheridan Drive) and Kenmore Avenue.

(4) Thruway Exit N17 to or from:

(a) A point 1.5 miles north of the Thruway on NY 266 (River Road).

(b) A point approximately 0.4 mile south of the Thruway on NY 266 (River Road).

Tandem trailer combinations in which neither trailing unit exceeds 28.5 feet in length are restricted to the Designated Qualifying and Access Highway System.

ROUTES: For tandem trailer combinations with either trailer more than 28.5 feet long, but not more than 48 feet long, the following routes are available:

	From	To
I–87 (New York Thruway).	Bronx/Westchester County Line.	Thruway Exit 24.
I–90 (New York Thruway).	Pennsylvania.	Thruway Exit 24.
I–90 (New York Thruway Berkshire Section).	Thruway Exit B–1	Massachusetts.
I–190 (New York Thruway Niagara Section).	Thruway Exit 53 ...	Int'l Border with Canada.
NY 912M (Berkshire Connection of the New York Thruway).	Thruway Exit 21A	Thruway Exit B–1.

Tandem trailer combinations in which neither trailing unit exceeds 28.5 feet in length may operate on all NN Highways.

LEGAL CITATIONS:

Public Authorities Law—Title 9, sec. 350, et. seq. (section 361 is most relevant)

New York State Thruway Authority Rules & Regulations, sections 100.6, 100.8, and 103.13

New York State Vehicle & Traffic Law, sections 385 and 1630

STATE: NORTH DAKOTA

COMBINATION: Truck tractor and 2 trailing units—LCV

LENGTH OF THE CARGO-CARRYING UNITS: 103 feet

MAXIMUM ALLOWABLE GROSS WEIGHT: 105,500 pounds

OPERATIONAL CONDITIONS:

WEIGHT: The Gross Vehicle Weight (GVW) of any vehicle or combination of vehicles is determined by the Federal Bridge Formula, including the exception for two sets of tandems spaced 36 feet apart.

No single axle shall carry a gross weight in excess of 20,000 pounds. Axles spaced 40 inches or less apart are considered one axle. Axles spaced 8 feet or more apart are considered as individual axles. The gross weight of two individual axles may be restricted by the weight formula. Spacing between axles shall be measured from axle center to axle center.

Axles spaced over 40 inches but less than 8 feet apart shall not carry a gross weight in excess of 17,000 pounds per axle. The gross weight of three or more axles in a grouping is determined by the measurement between the extreme axle centers. During the spring breakup season or on otherwise posted highways, reductions in the above axle weights may be specified.

The weight in pounds on any one wheel shall not exceed one-half the allowable axle weight. Dual tires are considered one wheel.

The weight per inch of tire width shall not exceed 550 pounds. The width of tire shall be the manufacturer's rating.

DRIVER: The driver must have a commercial driver's license with the appropriate endorsement.

VEHICLE: The cargo length of a two trailing unit combination may not exceed 100 feet (when the power unit is a truck tractor) or 103 feet (when the power unit is a truck) when traveling on the NN or local highways designated by local authorities.

All hitches must be of a load-bearing capacity capable of bearing the weight of the towed vehicles. The towing vehicle must have a hitch commonly described as a fifth wheel or gooseneck design, or one that is attached to the frame.

The hitch on the rear of the vehicle connected to the towing vehicle must be attached to the frame of the towed vehicle. All hitches, other than a fifth wheel or gooseneck, must be of a ball and socket type with a locking device or a pintle hook.

The drawn vehicles shall be equipped with brakes and safety chains adequate to control the movement of, and to stop and hold, such vehicles. When the drawn vehicle is of a fifth wheel or gooseneck design, safety chains are not required.

In any truck or truck tractor and two trailer combination, the lighter trailer must always be operated as the rear trailer, except when the gross weight differential with the other trailer does not exceed 5,000 pounds.

The power unit shall have adequate power and traction to maintain a minimum speed of 15 miles per hour on all grades.

PERMIT: No permits are required for GVW of 80,000 pounds or less. Single-trip permits are required for GVW exceeding 80,000 pounds. Weather restrictions (37–06–04–06, NDAC), weight distribution on trailers (37–06–04, NDAC), and signing requirements (37–06–04–05, NDAC) are applicable.

Movements of LCV's are prohibited when:

1. Road surfaces, due to ice, snow, slush, or frost present a slippery condition which may be hazardous to the operation of the unit or to other highway users;

2. Wind or other conditions may cause the unit or any part thereof to swerve, whip, sway, or fail to follow substantially in the path of the towing vehicle; or

3. Visibility is reduced due to snow, ice, sleet, fog, mist, rain, dust, or smoke.

The North Dakota Highway Patrol may restrict or prohibit operations during periods when in its judgment traffic, weather, or other safety conditions make travel unsafe.

The last trailer in any combination must have a "LONG LOAD" sign mounted on the rear. It must be a minimum of 12 inches in height and 60 inches in length. The lettering must be 8 inches in height with 1-inch brush strokes. The letters must be black on a yellow background.

Legal width—8 feet 6 inches on all highways.

Legal height—13 feet 6 inches.

ACCESS: Access for vehicles with cargo-carrying length of 68 feet or more is 10 miles off the NN. Vehicles with a cargo-carrying length less than 68 feet may travel on all highways in North Dakota.

ROUTES: All NN routes.

LEGAL CITATIONS: North Dakota Century Code, section 38–12–04; North Dakota Administrative Code, article 37–06.

STATE: NORTH DAKOTA

COMBINATION: Truck tractor and 3 trailing units—LCV

LENGTH OF THE CARGO-CARRYING UNITS: 100 feet

MAXIMUM ALLOWABLE GROSS WEIGHT: 105,500 pounds

OPERATIONAL CONDITIONS:

WEIGHT, DRIVER, PERMIT, and ACCESS: Same as the ND-TT2 combination.

VEHICLE: Same as the ND-TT2 combination, and in addition, in any combination with three trailing units the lightest trailer must always be operated as the rear trailer. For the first two trailing units the lighter trailer must always be second except when the gross weight differential with the other trailer does not exceed 5,000 pounds.

ROUTES: Same as the ND-TT2 combination.

LEGAL CITATIONS: Same as the ND-TT2 combination.

STATE: NORTH DAKOTA

COMBINATION: Truck-trailer, and Truck-trailer-trailer

LENGTH OF THE CARGO-CARRYING UNITS: 103 feet

OPERATIONAL CONDITIONS:

WEIGHT: This combination must operate in compliance with State laws and regulations. Because it is not an LCV, it is not subject to the ISTEA freeze as it applies to maximum weight.

DRIVER, VEHICLE, PERMIT, and ACCESS: Same as the ND-TT2 combination.

ROUTES: Same as the ND-TT2 combination.

LEGAL CITATIONS: Same as the ND-TT2 combination.

STATE: OHIO

COMBINATION: Truck tractor and 2 trailing units—LCV

LENGTH OF THE CARGO-CARRYING UNITS: 102 feet

MAXIMUM ALLOWABLE GROSS WEIGHT: 127,400 pounds

OPERATIONAL CONDITIONS: Long double combination vehicles are only allowed on that portion of Ohio's Interstate System which is under the jurisdiction of the Ohio Turnpike Commission (OTC). These same vehicles are not allowed on any portion of the Interstate System under the jurisdiction of the Ohio DOT.

WEIGHT: The OTC has established the following provisions for operation:

Maximum Weight: Single axle = 21,000 pounds; tandem axle spaced 4 feet or less apart = 24,000 pounds; tandem axle spaced more than 4 feet but less than 8 feet apart = 34,000 pounds; gross weight for doubles 90 feet or less in length = 90,000 pounds; gross weight for doubles over 90 feet but less than 112 feet in length = 127,400 pounds.

DRIVER: The driver must have a commercial driver's license with the appropriate endorsement, be over 26 years of age, in good health, and shall have not less than 5 years of experience driving tractor-trailer or tractor-short double trailer motor vehicles. Such driving experience shall include experience throughout the four seasons. Drivers must comply with the applicable current requirements of the Federal Motor Carrier Safety Regulations, Federal Hazardous Materials Regulations, and the Economic and Safety regulations of the Ohio Public Utility Commission.

VEHICLE: Vehicles being operated under permit at night must be equipped with all lights and reflectors required by the Ohio Public Utilities Commission and the Federal Motor Carrier Safety Regulations, except that the trailer shall be equipped with two red tail lights and two red or amber stop lights mounted with one set on each side. Trailer and semitrailer length for doubles cannot exceed 48 feet, and mixed trailer length combinations are not allowed for combination vehicles over 90 feet in length. Combined cargo-carrying length, including the trailer hitch, cannot be less than 80 feet or more than 102 feet. The number of axles on a double shall be a minimum of five and a maximum of nine. A tractor used in the operation of a double shall be capable of hauling the maximum weight at a speed of not less than 40 miles per hour on all portions of the Turnpike.

PERMIT: A special permit is required if the vehicle is over 102 inches wide, 14 feet high, or 65 feet in length including overhang. Tractor-semitrailer-semitrailer combinations require a permit if over 75 feet in length, excluding an allowed 3-foot front overhang and a 4-foot rear overhang. For vehicles over 120 inches wide, 14 feet high, or 80 feet long or if any unit of the combination vehicle is over 60 feet in length, travel is restricted to daylight hours Monday through noon Saturday, except holidays and the day before and after holidays. Operators are restricted to daylight driving if the load overhang is more than 4 feet. A "Long Double Trailer Permit" issued by the OTC is required for operation of doubles in excess of 90 feet in length. Towing units and coupling devices shall have sufficient structural strength to ensure safe operation. Vehicles and coupling devices shall be so designed, constructed, and installed in a double as to ensure that any towed vehicles when traveling on a level, smooth paved surface will follow in the path of the towing vehicle without shifting or swerving more than 3 inches to either side of the path of the towing vehicle when the latter is moving in a straight line. Vehicle coupling devices and brakes shall meet the requirements of the Ohio Public Utilities Commission and Federal Motor Carrier Safety Regulations. The distance between the rearmost axle of a semitrailer and the front axle of the next semitrailer in a coupled double unit shall not exceed 12 feet 6 inches. In no event shall the distance between the semitrailers coupled in a double exceed 9 feet. Double and triple trailer combinations must be equipped with adequate, properly maintained spray-suppressant mud flaps on all axles except the steering axle. In the event that the gross weights of the trailers vary by more than 20 percent, they shall be coupled according to their gross weights with the heavier trailer forward. A minimum distance of 500 feet shall be maintained between double units and/or triple units except when overtaking and passing another vehicle. A double shall remain in the right-hand, outside lane except when passing or when emergency or work-zone conditions exist. When, in the opinion of the OTC, the weather conditions are such that operation of a double is inadvisable, the OTC will notify the permittee that travel is prohibited for a certain period of time.

Class A and B explosives; Class A poisons; and Class 1, 2, and 3 radioactive material cannot be transported in double trailer combinations. Other hazardous materials may be transported in one trailer of a double. The hazardous materials should be placed in the front trailer unless doing so will result in the second trailer weighing more than the first trailer.

ACCESS: Tandem trailer units shall not leave the Turnpike right-of-way and shall be assembled and disassembled only in designated areas located at Exits 4, 7, 10, 11, 13, 14, and 16.

ROUTES

	From	To
I–76 Ohio Turnpike	Turnpike Exit 15 ...	Pennsylvania.
I–80 Ohio Turnpike	Turnpike Exit 8A ..	Turnpike Exit 15.
I–80/90 Ohio Turnpike.	Indiana	Turnpike Exit 8A.

LEGAL CITATIONS: Statutory authority, as contained in Chapter 5537 of the Ohio Revised Code, to regulate the dimensions and weights of vehicles using the Turnpike.

STATE: OHIO

COMBINATION: Truck tractor and 3 trailing units—LCV

LENGTH OF THE CARGO–CARRYING UNITS: 95 feet

MAXIMUM ALLOWABLE GROSS WEIGHT: 115,000 pounds

OPERATIONAL CONDITIONS: Same as the OH–TT2 combination, except as follows below, and triple trailer units may operate on any "turnpike project" as defined in Ohio Revised Code (ORC) section 5537.01 and permitted by the Ohio Turnpike and Infrastructure Commission under the program authorized in ORC 5537.16 (The Ohio Turnpike Act of 1949 and as amendedand effective prior to June 1, 1991).

WEIGHT: Gross weight for triples with an overall length greater than 90 feet but not over 105 feet in length = 115,000 pounds.

DRIVER: The driver must have a commercial driver's license with the appropriate endorsement, be over 26 years of age, in good health, and shall have not less than 5 years of experience driving double trailer combination units. Such driving experience shall include experience throughout the four seasons. Each driver must have special training on triple combinations to be provided by the Permittee.

VEHICLE: Triple trailer combination vehicles are allowed to operate on the Turnpike provided the combination vehicle is at least 90 feet long but less than 105 feet long and each trailer is not more than 28.5 feet in length. The minimum number of axles on the triple shall be seven and the maximum is nine.

PERMIT: A triple trailer permit to operate on the Turnpike is required for triple trailer combinations in excess of 90 feet in length. There is an annual fee for the permit. Class A and B explosives; Class A poisons; and Class 1, 2, and 3 radioactive material cannot be transported in triple trailer combinations. Other hazardous materials may be transported in two trailers of a triple. The hazardous materials should be placed in the front two trailers unless doing so will result in the third trailer weighing more than either one of the lead trailers. In addition, under ORC 4513 .34, ODOT and local authorities are authorized to issue special permits for oversized vehicles.

ACCESS: With two exceptions, triple trailer units shall not leave the Turnpike Project. The first exception is that triple trailer combinations are allowed on State Route 21 from I–80 Exit 11 (Ohio Turnpike) to a terminal located approximately 500 feet to the north in the town of Richfield. The second exception is for a segment of State Route 7 from Ohio Turnpike Exit 16 to 1 mile south. Triple trailer units shall not leave the Turnpike project. Section 5537.01, as discussed above defines "turnpike project" as: "(B) "Project" or "turnpike project" means . . . interchanges, entrance plazas, approaches, those portions of connecting public roads that serve interchanges and are determined by the commission and the director of transportation to be necessary for the safe merging of traffic between the turnpike project and those public roads, . . ."

ROUTES

	From	To
I–76 Ohio Turnpike	Turnpike Exit 15 ...	Pennsylvania.
I–80 Ohio Turnpike	Turnpike Exit 8A ..	Turnpike Exit 15.
I–80/90 Ohio Turnpike.	Indiana	Turnpike Exit 8A.
OH–7	Turnpike Exit 16 ...	Extending 1 mile south.

LEGAL CITATIONS: Same as the OH–TT2 combination.

STATE: OKLAHOMA

COMBINATION: Truck tractor and 2 trailing units—LCV

LENGTH OF THE CARGO-CARRYING UNITS: 110 feet

MAXIMUM ALLOWABLE GROSS WEIGHT: 90,000 pounds

OPERATIONAL CONDITIONS:

WEIGHT: Single axle = 20,000 pounds; tandem axle = 34,000 pounds; gross vehicle weight = 90,000 pounds. The total weight on any group of two or more consecutive axles shall not exceed the amounts shown in Table 1.

TABLE 1—OKLAHOMA ALLOWABLE AXLE GROUP WEIGHT

Axle Spacing (ft)	Maximum load (lbs) by axle group				
	2 Axles	3 Axles	4 Axles	5 Axles	6 Axles
4	34,000				
5	34,000				
6	34,000				
7	34,000				
8	34,000	42,000			
9	39,000	42,500			
10	40,000	43,500			
11		44,000			
12		45,000	50,000		
13		45,500	50,500		
14		46,500	51,500		
15		47,000	52,000		
16		48,000	52,500	58,000	
17		48,500	53,500	58,500	
18		49,500	54,000	59,000	
19		50,000	54,500	60,000	
20		51,000	55,500	60,500	66,000
21		51,500	56,000	61,000	66,500
22		52,500	56,500	61,500	67,000
23		53,000	57,500	62,500	68,000
24		54,000	58,000	63,000	68,500
25		54,500	58,500	63,500	69,000
26		56,000	59,500	64,000	69,500
27		57,500	60,000	65,000	70,000
28		59,000	60,500	65,500	71,000
29		60,500	61,500	66,000	71,500
30		62,000	62,000	66,500	72,000
31		63,500	63,500	67,000	72,500
32		64,000	64,000	68,000	73,500
33			64,500	68,500	74,000
34			65,000	69,000	74,500
35			66,000	70,000	75,000
36			68,000	70,500	75,500
37			68,000	71,000	76,000
38			69,000	72,000	77,000
39			70,000	72,500	77,500
40			71,000	73,000	78,000
41			72,000	73,500	78,500
42			73,000	74,000	79,000
43			73,280	75,000	80,000
44			73,280	75,500	80,500
45			73,280	76,000	81,000
46			73,280	76,500	81,500
47			73,500	77,500	82,000
48			74,000	78,000	82,000
49			74,500	78,500	83,500
50			75,500	79,000	84,000
51			76,000	80,000	84,500

TABLE 1—OKLAHOMA ALLOWABLE AXLE GROUP WEIGHT—Continued

Axle Spacing (ft)	Maximum load (lbs) by axle group				
	2 Axles	3 Axles	4 Axles	5 Axles	6 Axles
52	....	....	76,500	80,500	85,000
53	....	....	77,500	81,000	86,000
54	....	....	78,000	81,500	86,500
55	....	....	78,500	82,500	87,000
56	....	....	79,500	83,000	87,500
57	....	....	80,000	83,500	88,000
58	....	....	....	84,000	89,000
59	....	....	....	85,000	89,500
60	....	....	....	85,500	90,000

DRIVER: All drivers must have a commercial driver's license with the appropriate endorsement and must meet the requirements of the Federal Motor Carrier Safety Regulations (49 CFR parts 390–397). State requirements more stringent and not in conflict with Federal requirements take precedence.

VEHICLE: All vehicles must meet the requirements of applicable Federal and State statutes, rules, and regulations. Vehicles and load shall not exceed 102 inches in width on the Interstate System and four-lane divided highways. Maximum semitrailer length is 53 feet.

Multiple trailer combinations must be stable at all times during braking and normal operation. A multiple trailer combination when traveling on a level, smooth, paved surface must follow in the path of the towing vehicle without shifting or swerving more than 3 inches to either side when the towing vehicle is moving in a straight line. Heavier trailers are to be placed to the front in multiple trailer combinations.

PERMIT: An annual special authorization permit is required for tandem trailer vehicles operating on the Interstate System having a gross weight of more than 80,000 pounds. A fee is charged for the special authorization permit.

ACCESS: Access is allowed from legally available routes (listed below) to service facilities and terminals within a 5-mile radius. Access is also authorized on two-lane roadways which connect multi-lane divided highways when such connection does not exceed 15 miles.

ROUTES: Doubles with 29-foot trailers may use any route on the NN. Doubles with at least one trailer or semitrailer over 29 feet in length are limited to the Interstate and other multi-lane divided highways listed below.

	From	To
I–35	Texas	Kansas.
I–40	Texas	Arkansas.
I–44	Texas	Missouri.
I–235	Entire length in Oklahoma City.	
I–240	Entire length in Oklahoma City.	
I–244	Entire length in Tulsa.	
I–444	Entire length in Tulsa.	
I–40 Bus	I–40 Exit 119	US 81 El Reno.
US 60	I–35 Exit 214	US 177 Ponca City.
US 62	US 69 Muskogee	OK 80 Ft. Gibson.
US 62	I–44 Exit 39A Lawton	OK 115 Cache.
US 64	Cimarron Turnpike	I–244 Tulsa.
US 64	I–35 Exit 186 Perry	US 77 Perry.
US 64	I–40 Exit 325 Roland	Arkansas.
US 69	Texas	I–44 (Will Rogers Tpk.) Exit 282.
US 70	OK 76 Wilson	I–35 Exits 31A-B Ardmore.
US 75	I–40 Exits 240A-B Henryetta	I–244 Exit 2 Tulsa.
US 75	I–44 Exits 6A-B Tulsa	Dewey.
US 77	I–35 Exit 141 Edmond	3.5 mi. W of I–35.
US 81	I–44 (Bailey Tpk.) Exit 80	South Intersection OK 7 Duncan.
US 81	OK 51 Hennessey	11.5 mi. N of US 412.
US 169	OK 51 Tulsa	OK 20 Collinsville.
US 270	Indian Nation Tpk. Exit 4	US 69 McAlester.
US 270	OK 9 Tecumseh	I–40 Exit 181.
US 271	Texas	Indian Nation Tpk. Hugo.
US 412	I–44 Exit 241 Catoosa	US 69.
US 412	OK 58 Ringwood	I–35 Exits 194A-B.
US 412	US 69 Chouteau	OK 412 B.
OK 3	I–44 Exit 123	Oklahoma/Canadian County Line.
OK 3A	OK 3 Oklahoma City	I–44 Exit 125B Oklahoma City.
OK 7	I–44 Exits 36A-B	OK 65 Pumpkin Center.
OK 7	I–35 Exit 55	US 177 Sulphur.
OK 7	South intersection US 81 Duncan	7.5 mi. E of US 81.
OK 9	I–35 Exit 108A	US 77 Norman.
OK 11	I–35 Exit 222	US 177 Blackwell.
OK 11	US 75 Tulsa	I–244 Exit 12B.
OK 33	US 77 Guthrie	I–35 Exit 157 Guthrie.
OK 51	I–35 Exit 174	US 177 Stillwater.
OK 51	I–44 Exit 231 Tulsa	Muskogee Tpk. Broken Arrow.

	From	To
OK 165	Connecting two sections of the Muskogee Turnpike at Muskogee.	
OK 165	US 64/Bus. US 64 Muskogee	Muskogee Tpk.
Cimarron Tpk	I–35 Exit 194	US 64.
Cimarron Tpk Conn	US 177 Stillwater	Cimarron Tpk.
Indian Nation Turnpike.	US 70/271 Hugo	I–40 Exits 240A-B Henryetta.
Muskogee Tpk	OK 51 Broken Arrow	US 62/OK 165 Muskogee.
Muskogee Tpk	OK 165 Muskogee	I–40 Exit 286 Webber's Falls.

LEGAL CITATIONS:

Title 47 1981 O.S. 14–101
Title 47 1990 O.S. 14–103, –109, and –116
DPS Size and Weight Permit Manual 595:30.

STATE: OKLAHOMA

COMBINATION: Truck tractor and 3 trailing units—LCV

LENGTH OF THE CARGO-CARRYING UNITS: 95 feet

MAXIMUM ALLOWABLE GROSS WEIGHT: 90,000 pounds

OPERATIONAL CONDITIONS:

WEIGHT and ACCESS: Same as the OK-TT2 combination.

DRIVER: Same as the OK-TT2 combination except that in addition, a driver of a three trailing unit combination must have had at least 2 years of experience driving tractor-trailer combinations.

VEHICLE: All vehicles must meet the requirements of applicable Federal and State statutes, rules, and regulations. Vehicle and load shall not exceed 102 inches in width on the Interstate System and other four-lane divided highways. Maximum unit length of triple trailers is 29 feet. Truck tractors pulling triple trailers must have sufficient horsepower to maintain a minimum speed of 40 miles per hour on the level and 20 miles per hour on grades under normal operation conditions. Heavy-duty fifth wheels, pick-up plates equal in strength to the fifth wheel, solid kingpins, no-slack hitch connections, mud flaps and splash guards, and full-width axles are required on triple trailer combinations. All braking systems must comply with State and Federal requirements.

Multiple trailer combinations must be stable at all times during braking and normal operation. A multiple trailer combination when traveling on a level, smooth paved surface must follow in the path of the towing vehicle without shifting or swerving more than 3 inches to either side when the towing vehicle is moving in a straight line. Heavier trailers are to be placed to the front in multiple trailer combinations.

PERMIT: An annual special combination permit is required for the operation of triple-trailer combinations on the Interstate System and other four-lane divided primary highways. This permit also authorizes such combinations to exceed 80,000 pounds on the Interstate System.

The permit holder must certify that the driver of a triple-trailer combination is qualified. Operators of triple-trailer combinations must maintain a 500-foot following distance and must drive in the right lane, except when passing or in an emergency.

Speed shall be reduced and extreme caution exercised when operating triple-trailer combinations under hazardous conditions, such as those caused by snow, wind, ice, sleet, fog, mist, rain, dust, or smoke. When conditions become sufficiently dangerous, as determined by the company or driver, operations shall be discontinued and shall not resume until the vehicle can be safely operated. The State may restrict or prohibit operations during periods when, in the State's judgment, traffic, weather, or other safety conditions make such operations unsafe or inadvisable.

Class A and B explosives; Class A poisons; Class 1, 2, and 3 radioactive material; and any other material deemed to be unduly hazardous by the U.S. Department of Transportation cannot be transported in triple-trailer combinations.

A fee is charged for the annual special authorization permit.

ROUTES: Same as the OK-TT2 combination.

LEGAL CITATIONS:

Title 47 1981 O.S. 14–101
Title 47 1990 O.S. 14–109, –116, –121
DPS Size and Weight Permit Manual 595:30.

STATE: OREGON

COMBINATION: Truck tractor and 2 trailing units—LCV

LENGTH OF THE CARGO-CARRYING UNITS: 68 feet

MAXIMUM ALLOWABLE GROSS WEIGHT: 105,500 pounds

OPERATIONAL CONDITIONS:

WEIGHT: Maximum allowable weights are as follows: single wheel—10,000 pounds, single axle—20,000 pounds, tandem axle—34,000 pounds. Gross vehicle weights over 80,000 pounds must follow the Oregon extended weight table, with a maximum of 105,500 pounds. Weight is also limited to 600 pounds per inch of tire width.

EXTENDED WEIGHT TABLE

Gross weights over 80,000 pounds are authorized only when operating under the authority of a Special Transportation Permit.

MAXIMUM ALLOWABLE WEIGHTS

1. The maximum allowable weights for single axles and tandem axles shall not exceed those specified under ORS 818.010.

2. The maximum allowable weight for groups of axles spaced at 46 feet or less apart shall not exceed those specified under ORS 818.010.

3. The maximum weights for groups of axles spaced at 47 feet or more and the gross combined weight for any combination of vehicles shall not exceed those set forth in the following table:

Axle spacing in feet	Maximum gross weight in pounds on			
	5 Axles	6 Axles	7 Axles	8 or More axles
47	77,500	81,000	81,000	81,000
48	78,000	82,000	82,000	82,000
49	78,500	83,000	83,000	83,000
50	79,000	84,000	84,000	84,000
51	80,000	84,500	85,000	85,000
52	80,500	85,000	86,000	86,000
53	81,000	86,000	87,000	87,000
54	81,500	86,500	88,000	91,000
55	82,500	87,000	89,000	92,000
56	83,000	87,500	90,000	93,000
57	83,500	88,000	91,000	94,000
58	84,000	89,000	92,000	95,000
59	85,000	89,500	93,000	96,000
60	85,500	90,000	94,000	97,000
61	86,000	90,500	95,000	98,000
62	87,000	91,000	96,000	99,000
63	87,500	92,000	97,000	100,000
64	88,000	92,500	97,500	101,000
65	88,500	93,000	98,000	102,000
66	89,000	93,500	98,500	103,000
67	90,000	94,000	99,000	104,000
68	90,000	95,000	99,500	105,000
69	90,000	95,500	100,000	105,500
70	90,000	96,000	101,000	105,500
71	90,000	96,500	101,500	105,000
72	90,000	96,500	102,000	105,500
73	90,000	96,500	102,500	105,500
74	90,000	96,500	103,000	105,500
75	90,000	96,500	104,000	105,500
76	90,000	96,500	104,500	105,500
77	90,000	96,500	105,000	105,500
78	90,000	96,500	105,500	105,500

Distance measured to nearest foot; when exactly one-half foot, take next larger number.

DRIVER: The driver must have a commercial driver's license with the appropriate endorsement.

VEHICLE: For a combination which includes a truck tractor and two trailing units, the lead trailing unit (semitrailer) may be up to 40 feet long. The second trailing unit may be up to 35 feet long. However, the primary control is the total cargo-carrying distance which has a maximum length of 68 feet. Any towed vehicles in a combination must be equipped with safety chains or cables to prevent the towbar from dropping to the ground in the event the coupling fails. The chains or cables must have sufficient strength to control the towed vehicle in the event the coupling device fails and must be attached with no more slack than necessary to permit proper turning. However, this requirement does not apply to a fifth-wheel coupling if the upper and lower halves of the fifth wheel must be manually released before they can be separated.

PERMIT: A permit is required for operation if the gross combination weight exceeds 80,000 pounds. A fee is charged. Permitted movements must have the lighter trailing unit placed to the rear, and use splash and spray devices when operating in rainy weather. Movement is not allowed when road surfaces are hazardous due to ice or snow, or when other atmospheric conditions make travel unsafe.

ACCESS: As allowed by the Oregon DOT.

ROUTES: All NN routes.

LEGAL CITATIONS: ORS 810.010, ORS 810.030 through 810.060, and ORS 818.010 through 818.235.

STATE: OREGON

COMBINATION: Truck tractor and 3 trailing units—LCV

LENGTH OF THE CARGO-CARRYING UNITS: 96 feet

MAXIMUM ALLOWABLE GROSS WEIGHT: 105,500 pounds

OPERATIONAL CONDITIONS:

WEIGHT, DRIVER, PERMIT, and ACCESS: Same as the OR-TT2 combination.

VEHICLE: Trailing units must be of reasonably uniform in length. The overall length of the combination is limited to 105 feet. Any towed vehicles in a combination must be equipped with safety chains or cables to prevent the towbar from dropping to the ground in the event the coupling fails. The chains or cables must have sufficient strength to control the towed vehicle in the event the coupling device fails and must be attached with no more slack than necessary to permit proper turning. However, this requirement does not apply to a fifth-wheel coupling if the upper and lower halves of the fifth wheel must be manually released before they can be separated.

ROUTES: The following NN routes are also open to truck tractor and three trailing unit combinations.

	From	To
I–5	California	Washington.
I–105	Entire length in the Eugene-Springfield area.	
I–205	Jct. I–5	Washington.
I–405	Entire length in Portland.	
I–82	Washington	Jct. I–84.
I–84	Jct. I–5	Idaho.
US 20	Jct OR 22/OR 126 Santiam Junction.	US 26 Vale.
US 20	East Jct OR 99E Albany.	I–5 Exit 233.
US 26	US 101 Cannon Beach Junction.	OR 126 Prineville.
US 20/26	Vale	Idaho.
US 30	US 101 Astoria	I–405 Exit 3 Portland.
US 95	Nevada	Idaho.
SPUR US 95	OR 201	Idaho.
US 97	California	Washington.
US 101	US 30 Astoria	US 26 Cannon Beach Jct.
US 101	OR 18 Otis	US 20 Newport.
US 101	Bandon	North city limit Coos Bay.
US 197	I–84 Exit 87 The Dalles.	Washington.
US 395	I–82 Exit 1 Umatilla.	I–84 Exit 188 Stanfield.
US 395	US 26 John Day	OR 140 Lakeview.
US 730	I–84 Exit 168	Washington.
OR 6	US 101 Tillamook	US 26 near Banks.
OR 8	OR 47 Forest Grove.	OR 217 Beaverton.
OR 11	Washington	Mission Cutoff near Pendleton.
OR 18	US 101 Otis	OR 99W Dayton.
OR 19	I–84 Exit 137	South 2.5 miles.
OR 22	OR 18 near Willamena.	OR 99E Salem.
OR 22	I–5 Exit 253	Jct US 20/OR 126 Santiam Jct.
OR 31	US 97 La Pine	US 395 Valley Falls.
OR 34	Jct US 20/OR 99W Corvallis.	I–5 Exit 228.
OR 35	I–84 Exit 64	Mt. Hood Hood River.
OR 39	OR 140 East of Klamath Falls.	California.
OR 58	I–5 Exit 188 Goshen.	US 97 near Chemult.
OR 62	OR 99 Medford	OR 140 White City.
OR 78	Jct US 20/ US 395 Burns.	US 95 Burns Junction.
OR 99	I–5 Exit 58 Grants Pass.	I–5 Exit 48 Rogue River.
OR 99	I–5 Exit 192 Eugene.	Jct OR 99E/ OR 99W Junction City.
OR 99E	I–5 Exit 307 Portland.	I–205 Exit 9 Oregon City.
OR 99E	I–5 Exit 233 Albany.	Tangent.
OR 99E	OR 228 Halsey	Harrisburg.
OR 99W	Jct US 20/OR 34 Corvallis.	I–5 Exit 294 Portland.
OR 126	US 20 Sisters	US 26 Prineville.
OR 138	I–5 Exit 136 Sutherlin.	East 2 miles.
OR 140	OR 62 White City	Jct US 97/OR 66 Klamath Falls.
OR 201	Jct US 20/US 26	SPUR US 95 Cairo Junction.
OR 207	I–84 Exit 182	OR 74 Lexington.
OR 207/OR 74	Jct OR 207/OR 74 Lexington.	Jct OR 207/ OR 74/OR 206 Heppner.
OR 212	I–205 Exit 12	US 26 Boring.
OR 214	I–5 Exit 271 Woodburn.	OR 99E Woodburn.
OR 217	I–5 Exit 292 Tigard	US 26 Beaverton.
OR 224	OR 99E Milwaukie	I–205 Exit 13.

LEGAL CITATIONS: Same as the OR-TT2 combination.

STATE: OREGON

COMBINATION: Truck-trailer

LENGTH OF CARGO-CARRYING UNITS: 70 feet, 5 inches.

WEIGHT: This combination must operate in compliance with State laws and regulations. Because it is not an LCV, it is not subject to the ISTEA freeze as it applies to maximum weight.

DRIVER, ACCESS, ROUTES, AND LEGAL CITATIONS: Same as OR-TT2 combination.

VEHICLE: The truck or trailer may be up to 40 feet long not to exceed 75 feet overall. The truck may have a built-in hoist to load cargo. Any towed vehicle in a combination must be equipped with safety chains or cables to prevent the towbar from dropping to the ground in the event the coupling fails. The chains or cables must have sufficient strength to control the towed vehicle in the event the coupling device fails and must be attached with no more slack than necessary to permit proper turning. However, this requirement does not apply to a fifth-wheel coupling if the upper and lower halves of the fifth wheel must be manually released before they can be separated.

PERMIT: No overlength permit required.

STATE: PENNSYLVANIA

COMBINATION: Truck tractor and 2 trailing units

LENGTH OF THE CARGO-CARRYING UNITS: 57 feet

OPERATIONAL CONDITIONS:

WEIGHT: The maximum gross weight is 100,000 pounds.

DRIVER: The driver must have a commercial driver's license with the appropriate endorsement.

VEHICLE: A semitrailer, or the trailer of a tandem trailer combination, may not be longer than 28½ feet. A tandem combination—including the truck tractor, semitrailer and trailer—which exceeds 85 feet in length is considered a Class 9 vehicle which requires a special permit to travel on the Turnpike System. In tandem combinations, the heaviest trailer shall be towed next to the truck tractor.

PERMIT: None required except for a Class 9 vehicle.

ROUTES

	From	To
I–76 Pennsylvania Turnpike Mainline.	Ohio	Turnpike Exit 75.
I–76/1–70 Pennsylvania Turnpike Mainline.	Turnpike Exit 75 ...	Turnpike Exit 161.
I–76 Pennsylvania Turnpike Mainline.	Turnpike Exit 161	Turnpike Exit 326.
1–276 Pennsylvania Turnpike Mainline.	Turnpike Exit 326	I–95 Interchange.
I–95 interchange Pennsylvania Turnpike Mainline.	I–95 Interchange ..	New Jersey.
I–476 Pennsylvania Turnpike Northeastern Extension.	Turnpike Exit 20 ...	Turnpike Exit 131.
I–376 Pennsylvania Turnpike Beaver Valley Expressway.	Turnpike Exit 15 ...	Turnpike Exit 31.
Pennsylvania Turnpike 66 Greensburg Bypass.	Turnpike Exit 0	Turnpike Exit 14.
Pennsylvania Turnpike 43 Mon/ Fayette Expressway (I–68 to Route 43).	West Virginia	Turnpike Exit M8.
Pennsylvania Turnpike 43 Mon/ Fayette Expressway (Uniontown to Brownsville).	Turnpike Exit M 15	Turnpike Exit M28.
Pennsylvania Turnpike 43 Mon/ Fayette Expressway (US–40 to PA–51).	Turnpike Exit M30	Turnpike Exit M54.
Pennsylvania Turnpike 43 Mon/ Fayette Expressway (PA–51 to I–376/Monroeville).	Turnpike Exit M54	I–376/Monroeville.
Pennsylvania Turnpike 576 Southern Beltway (I–376 to US–22).	Turnpike Exit S1 ..	Turnpike Exit S6.
Pennsylvania Turnpike 576 Southern Beltway (US–22 to I–79).	Turnpike Exit S6 ..	I–79.

ROUTES—Continued

	From	To
Pennsylvania Turnpike 576 Southern Beltway (I–79 to Mon/Fayette Expressway).	I–79	Pennsylvania Turnpike 43 Mon/Fayette Expressway.

LEGAL CITATIONS: Pennsylvania Vehicle Code, 75 Pa.C.S. §6110(a); Pennsylvania Code, 67 Pa. Code, Chapter 601.

STATE: SOUTH DAKOTA

COMBINATION: Truck tractor and 2 trailing units—LCV

LENGTH OF CARGO-CARRYING UNITS: 100 feet

MAXIMUM ALLOWABLE GROSS WEIGHT: 129,000 pounds

OPERATIONAL CONDITIONS:

WEIGHT: For all combinations, the maximum gross weight on two or more consecutive axles is limited by the Federal Bridge Formula but cannot exceed 129,000 pounds. The weight on single axles or tandem axles spaced 40 inches or less apart may not exceed 20,000 pounds. Tandem axles spaced more than 40 inches but 96 inches or less may not exceed 34,000 pounds. Two consecutive sets of tandem axles may carry a gross load of 34,000 pounds each, provided the overall distance between the first and last axles of the tandems is 36 feet or more. The weight on the steering axle may not exceed 600 pounds per inch of tire width.

For combinations with a cargo-carrying length greater than 81.5 feet the following additional regulations also apply. The weight on all axles (other than the steering axle) may not exceed 500 pounds per inch of tire width. Lift axles and belly axles are not considered load-carrying axles and will not count when determining allowable vehicle weight.

DRIVER: The driver must have a commercial driver's license with the appropriate endorsement.

VEHICLE: For all combinations, a semitrailer or trailer may neither be longer than nor weigh 3,000 pounds more than the trailer located immediately in front of it. Towbars longer than 19 feet must be flagged during daylight hours and lighted at night.

For combinations with a cargo-carrying length of 81.5 feet or less, neither trailer may exceed 45 feet, including load overhang. Vehicles may be 12 feet wide when hauling baled feed during daylight hours.

For combinations with a cargo-carrying length over 81.5 feet long, neither trailer may exceed 48 feet, including load overhang.

Loading the rear of the trailer heavier than the front is not allowed. All axles except the steering axle require dual tires. Axles spaced 8 feet or less apart must weigh within 500 pounds of each other. The trailer hitch offset may not exceed 6 feet. The maximum effective rear trailer overhang may not exceed 35 percent of the trailer's wheelbase. The power unit must have sufficient power to maintain 40 miles per hour. A "LONG LOAD" sign measuring 18 inches high by 7 feet long with black on yellow lettering 10 inches high is required on the rear. Offtracking is limited to 8.75 feet for a turning radius of 161 feet.

Offtracking Formula = $161 - [161^2 - (L_1^2 + L_2^2 + L_3^2 + L_4^2 + L_5^2 + L_6^2 + L_7^2 + L_8^2)]^{1/2}$

NOTE: L_1 through L_8 are measurements between points of articulation or vehicle pivot points. Squared dimensions to stinger steer points of articulation are negative. For two trailing unit combinations where at least one trailer is 45 feet long or longer, all the dimensions used to calculate offtracking must be written in the "Permit Restriction" area of the permit along with the offtracking value derived from the calculation.

PERMIT: For combinations with a cargo-carrying length of 81.5 feet or less, a single-trip permit is required for movement on the Interstate System if the gross vehicle weight exceeds 80,000 pounds. An annual or single-trip permit is required for hauling baled feed over 102 inches wide.

For combinations with a cargo-carrying length greater than 81.5 feet, a single-trip permit is required for all movements. Operations must be discontinued when roads are slippery due to moisture, visibility must be good, and wind conditions must not cause trailer whip or sway.

For all combinations, a fee is charged for any permit.

ACCESS: For combinations with a cargo-carrying length of 81.5 feet or less, access is Statewide off the NN unless restricted by the South Dakota DOT.

For combinations with a cargo-carrying length greater than 81.5 feet, access to operating routes must be approved by the South Dakota DOT.

ROUTES: Combinations with a cargo-carrying length of 81.5 feet or less may use all NN routes. Combinations with a cargo-carrying length over 81.5 feet, are restricted to the Interstate System and:

	From	To
US 14	W. Jct. US 14 Bypass and US 14 Brookings.	So. Jct. US 14 and US 281.
Bypass US 14	I–29 Exit 133 Brookings.	W. Jct. US 14 Bypass and US 14 Brookings.
US 85	I–90 Exit 10 Spearfish.	North Dakota.
US 281	I–90 Exit 310.	So. Jct. US 14 and US 281.
US 281	8th Ave. Aberdeen	North Dakota.
SD 50	Burleigh Street Yankton.	I–29 Exit 26.

LEGAL CITATIONS: SDCL 32–22–8.1, –38, –39, –41, –42, and –52; and Administrative Rules 70:03:01:37, :47, :48, and :60 through :70.

STATE: SOUTH DAKOTA

COMBINATION: Truck tractor and 3 trailing units—LCV

LENGTH OF CARGO-CARRYING UNITS: 100 feet

MAXIMUM ALLOWABLE GROSS WEIGHT: 129,000 pounds

OPERATIONAL CONDITIONS:

WEIGHT, DRIVER, PERMIT, and ACCESS: Same as the SD-TT2 combination.

VEHICLE: Same as the SD-TT2 combination, except trailer lengths are limited to 28.5 feet, including load overhang, and the overall length cannot exceed 110 feet, including load overhang.

ROUTES: Same as the SD-TT2 combination with a cargo-carrying length over 81.5 feet.

LEGAL CITATIONS: SDCL 32–22–14.14, –38, –39, –42, and –52; and Administrative Rules 70:03:01:60 through :70.

STATE: SOUTH DAKOTA

COMBINATION: Truck-Trailer

LENGTH OF CARGO-CARRYING UNITS: 73 feet

OPERATIONAL CONDITIONS:

WEIGHT: This combination must operate in compliance with State laws and regulations. Because it is not an LCV, it is not subject to the ISTEA freeze as it applies to maximum weight.

DRIVER, and PERMIT: Same as the SD-TT2 combination.

VEHICLE: Same as the SD-TT2 combination except that in addition, the overall length including load overhang is limited to 80 feet. Trailer length is not limited.

ACCESS: Same as the access provisions for the SD-TT2 combination with a cargo-carrying length of 81.5 feet or less.

ROUTES: Same as the route provisions for the SD-TT2 combination with a cargo-carrying length of 81.5 feet or less.

LEGAL CITATIONS: SDCL 32–22–8.1, –38, –39, –41, –42, and –52; and Administrative Rules 70:03:01:37, :47, and :48.

STATE: SOUTH DAKOTA

COMBINATION: Truck-Trailer

LENGTH OF CARGO-CARRYING UNITS: 78 feet

OPERATIONAL CONDITIONS:

WEIGHT: This combination must operate in compliance with State laws and regulations. Because it is not an LCV, it is not subject to the ISTEA freeze as it applies to maximum weight.

DRIVER, and PERMIT: Same as the SD-TT2 combination.

VEHICLE: Same as the SD-TT2 combination with a cargo-carrying length over 81.5 feet, except that in addition, the overall length is limited to 85 feet.

ACCESS: Same as the access provisions for the SD-TT2 combination with a cargo-carrying length greater than 81.5 feet.

ROUTES: Same as the route provisions for the SD-TT2 combination with a cargo-carrying length greater than 81.5 feet.

LEGAL CITATIONS: SDCL 32–22–38, –39, –42, and –52; and Administrative Rules 70:03:01:60 through :70.

STATE: UTAH

COMBINATION: Truck tractor and 2 trailing units—LCV

LENGTH OF THE CARGO-CARRYING UNITS: 95 feet

MAXIMUM ALLOWABLE GROSS WEIGHT: 129,000 pounds

OPERATIONAL CONDITIONS:

WEIGHT: Weight limits are as follows:
Single axle: 20,000 pounds
Tandem axle: 34,000 pounds
Gross weight: 129,000 pounds
Vehicles must comply with the Federal Bridge Formula

Tire loading on vehicles requiring an overweight or oversize permit shall not exceed 500 pounds per inch of tire width for tires 11 inches wide and greater, and 450 pounds per inch of tire width for tires less than 11 inches wide as designated by the tire manufacturer on the side wall of the tire. Tire loading on vehicles not requiring an overweight or oversize permit shall not exceed 600 pounds per inch of tire width as designated by the tire manufacturer on the sidewall.

DRIVER: The driver must have a commercial driver's license with the appropriate endorsement. Carriers must certify that their drivers have a safe driving record and have passed a road test administered by a qualified safety supervisor.

VEHICLE: While in transit, no trailer shall be positioned ahead of another trailer which carries an appreciably heavier load. An empty trailer shall not precede a loaded trailer. Vehicles shall be powered to operate on level terrain at speeds compatible with other traffic. They must be able to maintain a minimum speed of 20 miles per hour under normal operating conditions on any grade of 5 percent or less over which the combination is operated and be able to resume a speed of 20 miles per hour after stopping on any such grade, except in extreme weather conditions.

Oversize signs are required on vehicles in excess of 75 feet in length on two-lane highways.

A heavy-duty fifth wheel is required. All fifth wheels must be clean and lubricated with a light-duty grease prior to each trip. The fifth wheel must be located in a position which provides adequate stability. Pick-up plates must be of equal strength to the fifth wheel. The kingpin must be of a solid type and permanently fastened. Screw-out or folding-type kingpins are prohibited.

All hitch connections must be of a no-slack type, preferably a power-actuated ram. Air-actuated hitches which are isolated from the primary air transmission system are recommended.

The drawbar length should be the practical minimum consistent with the clearances required between trailers for turning and backing maneuvers.

Axles must be those designed for the width of the body.

All braking systems must comply with State and Federal requirements. In addition, fast air transmission and release valves must be provided on all semitrailer and converter-dolly axles. A brake force limiting valve, sometimes called a "slippery road" valve, may be provided on the steering axle. Anti-sail type mud flaps are recommended.

The use of single tires on any combination vehicle requiring an overweight or oversize permit shall not be allowed on single axles. A single axle is defined as one having more than 8 feet between it and the nearest axle or group of axles on the vehicle.

When traveling on a level, smooth paved surface, the trailing units must follow in the path of the towing vehicle without shifting or swerving more than 3 inches to either side when the towing vehicle is moving in a straight line. Each combination shall maintain a minimum distance of 500 feet from another commercial vehicle traveling in the same direction on the same highway. Loads shall be securely fastened to the transporter with material and devices of sufficient strength to prevent the load from becoming loose, detached, dangerously displaced, or in any manner a hazard to other highway users. The components of the load shall be reinforced or bound securely in advance of travel to prevent debris from being blown off the unit and endangering the safety of the traveling public. Any debris from the special permit vehicle deposited on the highway shall be removed by the permittee.

Bodily injury and property damage insurance is required before a special Transportation Permit will be issued.

In the event any claim arises against the State of Utah, Utah Department of Transportation, Utah Highway Patrol, or their employees from the operation granted under the permit, the permittee shall agree to indemnify and hold harmless each of them from such claim.

PERMIT: Permits must be purchased. The Utah DOT Motor Carrier Safety Division will, on submission of an LCV permit request, assign an investigator to perform an audit on the carrier, which must have an established safety program that is in compliance with the Federal Motor Carrier Safety Regulations (49 CFR parts 387–399), the Federal Hazardous Materials Regulations (49 CFR parts 171–178), and a "Satisfactory" safety rating. The request must show a travel plan for the operation of the vehicles. Permits are subject to Highway Patrol supervision and permitted vehicles may be subject to temporary delays or removed from the highways when necessary during hazardous road, weather, or traffic conditions. The permit will be cancelled without refund if violated. Expiration dates cannot be extended except for reasons beyond the control of the permittee, including adverse weather. Permits are void if defaced, modified, or obliterated. Lost or destroyed permits cannot be duplicated and are not transferable.

ACCESS: Routes approved by the Utah DOT plus local delivery destination travel on two-lane roads.

ROUTES: For combinations with a cargo-carrying length of 85 feet or less, all NN routes. Combinations with a cargo-carrying length over 85 feet are restricted to the following NN routes:

	From	To
I–15	Arizona	Idaho.
I–70	Jct. I–15	Colorado.
I–80	Nevada	Wyoming.
I–84	Idaho	Jct. I–80.
I–215	Entire length in the Salt Lake City area.	
UT–201	I–80 Exit 102 Lake Point Jct.	300 West Street, Salt Lake City.

LEGAL CITATIONS:

Utah Code 27–12–154 and –155; Utah Administrative Code, Section R–909–1.

STATE: UTAH

COMBINATION: Truck tractor and 3 trailing units—LCV

LENGTH OF THE CARGO-CARRYING UNITS: 95 feet

MAXIMUM ALLOWABLE GROSS WEIGHT: 129,000 pounds

OPERATIONAL CONDITIONS: Same as the UT-TT2 combination.

ROUTES: Same as the UT-TT2 combination with a cargo-carrying length greater than 85 feet.

LEGAL CITATIONS: Same as the UT-TT2 combination.

STATE: UTAH

COMBINATION: Truck-trailer

LENGTH OF THE CARGO-CARRYING UNITS: 88 feet

OPERATIONAL CONDITIONS:

WEIGHT: This combination must operate in compliance with State laws and regulations. Because it is not an LCV, it is not subject to the ISTEA freeze as it applies to maximum weight.

DRIVER, VEHICLE, PERMIT, and ACCESS: Same as the UT-TT2 combination.

ROUTES:

1. Truck-trailer combinations hauling bulk gasoline or LP gas: cargo-carrying length less than or equal to 78 feet, all NN routes; cargo-carrying lengths over 78 feet up to and including 88 feet, same as UT-TT2 with cargo-carrying length over 85 feet.

2. All other truck-trailer combinations: cargo-carrying length less than or equal to 70 feet, all NN routes; cargo-carrying lengths over 70 feet up to and including 78 feet, same as UT-TT2 with cargo-carrying length over 85 feet.

LEGAL CITATIONS: Same as the UT-TT2 combination.

STATE: UTAH

COMBINATION: Truck-trailer-trailer

LENGTH OF THE CARGO-CARRYING UNITS: 88 feet

OPERATIONAL CONDITIONS: Same as the Utah truck-trailer combination.

ROUTES: Same as the UT-TT2.

LEGAL CITATIONS: Same as the UT-TT2 combination.

STATE: UTAH

COMBINATION: Automobile transporter

LENGTH OF THE CARGO-CARRYING UNITS: 105 feet

OPERATIONAL CONDITIONS:

WEIGHT, DRIVER, PERMIT, and ACCESS: Same as the Utah truck-trailer combination.

VEHICLE: The cargo-carrying length of automobile transporters that carry vehicles on the power unit is the same as the overall length.

ROUTES: For automobile transporters with a cargo-carrying length of 92 feet or less, all NN routes. Automobile transporters with a cargo-carrying length over 92 feet up to and including 105 feet, same as UT-TT2 with cargo-carrying length over 85 feet.

LEGAL CITATIONS: Same as the UT-TT2 combination.

STATE: WASHINGTON

COMBINATION: Truck tractor and 2 trailing units—LCV

LENGTH OF THE CARGO-CARRYING UNITS: 68 feet

MAXIMUM ALLOWABLE GROSS WEIGHT: 105,500 pounds

OPERATIONAL CONDITIONS:

WEIGHT: Single axle limit = 20,000 pounds; tandem axle limit = 34,000 pounds; gross weight must comply with the Federal Bridge Formula.

DRIVER: The driver must have a commercial driver's license with the appropriate endorsement.

VEHICLE: Operating conditions are the same for permitted doubles as for STAA of 1982 doubles.

PERMIT: Combinations with a cargo-carrying length over 60 feet in length but not exceeding 68 feet must obtain an annual overlength permit to operate. A fee is charged.

ACCESS: All State routes except SR 410 and SR 123 in or adjacent to Mt. Rainier National Park. In addition, restrictions may be imposed by local governments having maintenance responsibilities for local highways.

ROUTES: All NN routes except SR 410 and SR 123 in the vicinity of Mt. Rainier National Park.

LEGAL CITATIONS:

RCW 46.37, 46.44.030, .037(3), .041, and .0941.

STATE: WASHINGTON

COMBINATION: Truck-trailer

LENGTH OF THE CARGO-CARRYING UNITS: 68 feet

OPERATIONAL CONDITIONS:

WEIGHT: This combination must operate in compliance with State laws and regulations. Because it is not an LCV, it is not subject to the ISTEA freeze as it applies to maximum weight.

DRIVER, PERMIT, and ACCESS: Same as the WA-TT2 combination.

VEHICLE: Overall length limited to 75 feet.

ROUTES: Same as the WA-TT2 combination.

LEGAL CITATIONS: Same as the WA-TT2 combination.

STATE: WYOMING

COMBINATION: Truck tractor and 2 trailing units—LCV

LENGTH OF THE CARGO-CARRYING UNITS: 81 feet

MAXIMUM ALLOWABLE GROSS WEIGHT: 117,000 pounds

OPERATIONAL CONDITIONS:

WEIGHT: No single axle shall carry a load in excess of 20,000 pounds. No tandem axle shall carry a load in excess of 36,000 pounds. No triple axle, consisting of three consecutive load-bearing axles that articulate from an attachment to the vehicle including a connecting mechanism to equalize the load between axles having a spacing between the first and third axle of at least 96 inches and not more than 108 inches, shall carry a load in excess of 42,500 pounds. No vehicles operated on the Interstate System shall exceed the maximum weight allowed by application of Federal Bridge Weight Formula B.

No wheel shall carry a load in excess of 10,000 pounds. No tire on a steering axle shall carry a load in excess of 750 pounds per inch of tire width and no other tire on a vehicle shall carry a load in excess of 600 pounds per inch of tire width. "Tire width" means the width stamped on the tire by the manufacturer.

Dummy axles may not be considered in the determination of allowable weights.

DRIVER: The driver must have a commercial driver's license with the appropriate endorsement.

VEHICLE: The lead semitrailer can be up to 48 feet long with the trailing unit up to 40 feet long. In a truck tractor-semitrailer-trailer combination, the heavier towed vehicle shall be directly behind the truck-tractor and the lighter towed vehicle shall be last if the weight difference between consecutive towed vehicles exceeds 5,000 pounds.

PERMITS: No permits required.

ACCESS: Unlimited access off the NN to terminals.

ROUTES: All NN routes.

LEGAL CITATIONS:

WS 31–5–1001, –1002, –1004, –1008, and WS 31–17–1–1 through 31–17–117.

STATE: WYOMING

COMBINATION: Truck-trailer

LENGTH OF THE CARGO-CARRYING UNITS: 78 feet

OPERATIONAL CONDITIONS:

WEIGHT: This combination must operate in compliance with State laws and regulations. Because it is not an LCV, it is not subject to the ISTEA freeze as it applies to maximum weight.

DRIVER, PERMIT, and ACCESS: Same as the WY-TT2 combination.

VEHICLE: No single vehicle shall exceed 60 feet in length within an overall limit of 85 feet.

ROUTES: Same as the WY-TT2 combination.

LEGAL CITATIONS:

WS 31–5–1002

STATE: WYOMING

COMBINATION: Automobile/Boat Transporter

LENGTH OF CARGO CARRYING UNITS: 85 feet

OPERATIONAL CONDITIONS:

WEIGHT: This combination must operate in compliance with State laws and regulations. Because it is not an LCV, it is not subject to the ISTEA freeze as it applies to maximum weight.

DRIVER, PERMIT, and ACCESS: Same as the WY-TT2 combination.

VEHICLE: The cargo-carrying length of automobile transporters that carry vehicles on the power unit is the same as the overall length. No single vehicle shall exceed 60 feet in length within an overall limit of 85 feet.

ROUTES: Same as the WY-TT2 combination.

LEGAL CITATIONS: Same as the WY-TT2 combination.

STATE: WYOMING

COMBINATION: Saddlemount Combination

LENGTH OF CARGO CARRYING UNITS: 85 feet

WEIGHT: This combination must operate in compliance with State laws and regulations. Because it is not an LCV, it is not subject to the ISTEA freeze as it applies to maximum weight.

DRIVER, PERMIT, and ACCESS: Same as the WY-TT2 combination.

VEHICLE: The cargo-carrying length of saddlemount combinations that carry vehicles on the power unit is the same as the overall length. No single vehicle shall exceed 60 feet in length within an overall limit of 85 feet.

No more than three saddlemounts may be used in any combination, except additional vehicles may be transported when safely loaded upon the frame of a vehicle in a properly assembled saddlemount combination.

Towed vehicles in a triple saddlemount combination shall have brakes acting on all wheels which are in contact with the roadway.

All applicable State and Federal rules on coupling devices shall be observed and complied with.

ROUTES: Same as the WY-TT2 combination.

LEGAL CITATIONS: Same as the WY-TT2 combination.

[59 FR 30422, June 13, 1994, as amended at 60 FR 15215, Mar. 22, 1995; 60 FR 16571, Mar. 31, 1995; 62 FR 10181, Mar. 5, 1997; 63 FR 70653, Dec. 22, 1998; 67 FR 15110, Mar. 29, 2002; 77 FR 32014, May 31, 2012; 83 FR 49488, Oct. 2, 2018]

Appendix D to Part 658—Devices That Are Excluded From Measurement of the Length or Width of a Commercial Motor Vehicle

The following devices are excluded from measurement of the length or width of a commercial motor vehicle, as long as they do not carry property and do not exceed the dimensional limitations included in §658.16. This list is not exhaustive.

1. All devices at the front of a semitrailer or trailer including, but not limited to, the following:

(a) A device at the front of a trailer chassis to secure containers and prevent movement in transit;

(b) A front coupler device on a semitrailer or trailer used in road and rail intermodal operations;

(c) Aerodynamic devices, air deflector;

(d) Air compressor;

(e) Certificate holder (manifest box);

(f) Door vent hardware;

(g) Electrical connector;

(h) Gladhand;

(i) Handhold;

(j) Hazardous materials placards and holders;

(k) Heater;

(l) Ladder;

(m) Non-load carrying tie-down devices on automobile transporters;

(n) Pickup plate lip;

(o) Pump offline on tank trailer;

(p) Refrigeration unit;

(q) Removable bulkhead;
(r) Removable stakes;
(s) Stabilizing jack (anti-nosedive device);
(t) Stake pockets;
(u) Step;
(v) Tarp basket;
(w) Tire carrier; and
(x) Uppercoupler.

2. Devices excluded from length measurement at the rear of a semitrailer or trailer including, but not limited to, the following:
(a) Handhold;
(b) Hazardous materials placards and holders;
(c) Ladder;
(d) Pintle hook;
(e) Removable stakes;
(f) Splash and spray suppression device;
(g) Stake pockets; and
(h) Step.

3. Devices excluded from width determination, not to exceed 3 inches from the side of the vehicle including, but not limited to, the following:
(a) Corner caps;
(b) Hazardous materials placards and holders;
(c) Lift pads for trailer on flatcar (piggyback) operation;
(d) Rain gutters;
(e) Rear and side door hinges and their protective hardware;
(f) Side marker lamps;
(g) Structural reinforcement for side doors or intermodal operation (limited to 1 inch from the side within the 3 inch maximum extension);
(h) Tarping systems for open-top trailers;
(i) Movable devices to enclose the cargo area of flatbed semitrailers or trailers, usually called tarping systems, where no component part of the system extends more than 3 inches from the sides or back of the vehicle when the vehicle is in operation. This exclusion applies to all component parts of tarping systems, including the transverse structure at the front of the vehicle to which the sliding walls and roof of the tarp mechanism are attached, provided the structure is not also intended or designed to comply with 49 CFR 393.106, which requires a headerboard strong enough to prevent cargo from penetrating or crushing the cab; the transverse structure may be up to 108 inches wide if properly centered so that neither side extends more than 3 inches beyond the structural edge of the vehicle. Also excluded from measurement are side rails running the length of the vehicle and rear doors, provided the only function of the latter, like that of the transverse structure at the front of the vehicle, is to seal the cargo area and anchor the sliding walls and roof. On the other hand, a headerboard designed to comply with 49 CFR 393.106 is load bearing and thus limited to 102 inches in width. However, the "wings" designed to close the gap between such a headerboard and the movable walls and roof of a tarping system are width exclusive, provided they are add-on pieces designed to bear only the load of the tarping system itself and are not integral parts of the load-bearing headerboard structure;
(j) Tie-down assembly on platform trailers;
(k) Wall variation from true flat; and
(l) Weevil pins and sockets on low-bed trailers.

[67 FR 15110, Mar. 29, 2002]

PART 660—SPECIAL PROGRAMS (DIRECT FEDERAL)

Subpart A—Forest Highways

Subparts B–D [Reserved]

Subpart E—Defense Access Roads

Subpart A—Forest Highways

AUTHORITY: 16 U.S.C. 1608–1610; 23 U.S.C. 101, 202, 204, and 315; 49 CFR 1.48.

SOURCE: 59 FR 30300, June 13, 1994, unless otherwise noted.

§660.101 Purpose.

The purpose of this subpart is to implement the Forest Highway (FH) Program which enhances local, regional, and national benefits of FHs funded under the public lands highway category of the coordinated Federal Lands Highway Program. As provided in 23 U.S.C. 202, 203, and 204, the program, developed in cooperation with State and local agencies, provides safe and adequate transportation access to and through National Forest System (NFS) lands for visitors, recreationists, resource users, and others which is not met by other transportation programs. Forest highways assist rural and community economic development and promote tourism and travel.

§ 660.103 Definitions.

In addition to the definitions in 23 U.S.C. 101(a), the following apply to this subpart:

Cooperator means a non-Federal public authority which has jurisdiction and maintenance responsibility for a FH.

Forest highway means a forest road under the jurisdiction of, and maintained by, a public authority and open to public travel.

Forest road means a road wholly or partly within, or adjacent to, and serving the NFS and which is necessary for the protection, administration, and utilization of the NFS and the use and development of its resources.

Jurisdiction means the legal right or authority to control, operate, regulate use of, maintain, or cause to be maintained, a transportation facility, through ownership or delegated authority. The authority to construct or maintain such a facility may be derived from fee title, easement, written authorization, or permit from a Federal agency, or some similar method.

Metropolitan Planning Organization (MPO) means that organization designated as the forum for cooperative transportation decisionmaking pursuant to the provisions of part 450 of this title.

Metropolitan Transportation Plan means the official intermodal transportation plan that is developed and adopted through the metropolitan transportation planning process for the metropolitan planning area.

National Forest System means lands and facilities administered by the Forest Service (FS), U.S. Department of Agriculture, as set forth in the Forest and Rangeland Renewable Resource Planning Act of 1974, as amended (16 U.S.C. 1601 note, 1600–1614).

Open to public travel means except during scheduled periods, extreme weather conditions, or emergencies, open to the general public for use with a standard passenger auto, without restrictive gates or prohibitive signs or regulations, other than for general traffic control or restrictions based on size, weight, or class of registration.

Public authority means a Federal, State, county, town, or township, Indian tribe, municipal or other local government or instrumentality with authority to finance, build, operate, or maintain toll or toll-free facilities.

Public lands highway means: (1) A forest road under the jurisdiction of and maintained by a public authority and open to public travel or (2) any highway through unappropriated or unreserved public lands, nontaxable Indian lands, or other Federal reservations under the jurisdiction of and maintained by a public authority and open to public travel.

Public road means any road or street under the jurisdiction of and maintained by a public authority and open to public travel.

Renewable resources means those elements within the scope of responsibilities and authorities of the FS as defined in the Forest and Rangeland Renewable Resource Planning Act of August 17, 1974 (88 Stat. 476) as amended by the National Forest Management Act of October 22, 1976 (90 Stat. 2949; 16 U.S.C. 1600–1614) such as recreation, wilderness, wildlife and fish, range, timber, land, water, and human and community development.

Resources means those renewable resources defined above, plus other nonrenewable resources such as minerals, oil, and gas which are included in the FS's planning and land management processes.

Statewide transportation plan means the official transportation plan that is: (1) Intermodal in scope, including bicycle and pedestrian features, (2) addresses at least a 20-year planning horizon, and (3) covers the entire State pursuant to the provisions of part 450 of this title.

§ 660.105 Planning and route designation.

(a) The FS will provide resource planning and related transportation information to the appropriate MPO and/or State Highway Agency (SHA) for use in developing metropolitan and statewide transportation plans pursuant to the provisions of part 450 of this title. Cooperators shall provide various planning (23 U.S.C. 134 and 135) information to the Federal Highway Administration (FHWA) for coordination with the FS.

(b) The management systems required under 23 U.S.C. 303 shall fulfill the requirement in 23 U.S.C. 204(a) regarding the establishment and implementation of pavement, bridge, and safety management systems for FHs. The results of bridge management systems and safety management systems on all FHs and results of pavement management systems for FHs on Federal-aid highways are to be provided by the SHAs for consideration in the development of programs under §660.109 of this part. The FHWA will provide appropriate pavement management results for FHs which are not Federal-aid highways.

(c) The FHWA, in consultation with the FS, the SHA, and other cooperators where appropriate, will designate FHs.

(1) The SHA and the FS will nominate forest roads for FH designation.

(2) The SHA will represent the interests of all cooperators. All other agencies shall send their proposals for FHs to the SHA.

(d) A FH will meet the following criteria:

(1) Generally, it is under the jurisdiction of a public authority and open to public travel, or a cooperator has agreed, in writing, to assume jurisdiction of the facility and to keep the road open to public travel once improvements are made.

(2) It provides a connection between adequate and safe public roads and the resources of the NFS which are essential to the local, regional, or national economy, and/or the communities, shipping points, or markets which depend upon those resources.

(3) It serves:

(i) Traffic of which a preponderance is generated by use of the NFS and its resources; or

(ii) NFS-generated traffic volumes that have a substantial impact on roadway design and construction; or

(iii) Other local needs such as schools, mail delivery, commercial supply, and access to private property within the NFS.

§660.107 Allocations.

On October 1 of each fiscal year, the FHWA will allocate 66 percent of Public Lands Highway funds, by FS Region, for FHs using values based on relative transportation needs of the NFS, after deducting such sums as deemed necessary for the administrative requirements of the FHWA and the FS; the necessary costs of FH planning studies; and the FH share of costs for approved Federal Lands Coordinated Technology Implementation Program studies.

§660.109 Program development.

(a) The FHWA will arrange and conduct a conference with the FS and the SHA to jointly select the projects which will be included in the programs for the current fiscal year and at least the next 4 years. Projects included in each year's program will be selected considering the following criteria:

(1) The development, utilization, protection, and administration of the NFS and its resources;

(2) The enhancement of economic development at the local, regional, and national level, including tourism and recreational travel;

(3) The continuity of the transportation network serving the NFS and its dependent communities;

(4) The mobility of the users of the transportation network and the goods and services provided;

(5) The improvement of the transportation network for economy of operation and maintenance and the safety of its users;

(6) The protection and enhancement of the rural environment associated with the NFS and its resources; and

(7) The results for FHs from the pavement, bridge, and safety management systems.

(b) The recommended program will be prepared and approved by the FHWA with concurrence by the FS and the SHA. Following approval, the SHA shall advise any other cooperators in the State of the projects included in the final program and shall include the approved program in the State's process for development of the Statewide

Transportation Improvement Program. For projects located in metropolitan areas, the FHWA and the SHA will work with the MPO to incorporate the approved program into the MPO's Transportation Improvement Program.

§ 660.111 Agreements.

(a) A statewide FH agreement shall be executed among the FHWA, the FS, and each SHA. This agreement shall set forth the responsibilities of each party, including that of adherence to the applicable provisions of Federal and State statutes and regulations.

(b) The design and construction of FH projects will be administered by the FHWA unless otherwise provided for in an agreement approved under this subpart.

(c) A project agreement shall be entered into between the FHWA and the cooperator involved under one or more of the following conditions:

(1) A cooperator's funds are to be made available for the project or any portion of the project;

(2) Federal funds are to be made available to a cooperator for any work;

(3) Special circumstances exist which make a project agreement necessary for payment purposes or to clarify any aspect of the project; or

(4) It is necessary to document jurisdiction and maintenance responsibility.

§ 660.112 Project development.

(a) Projects to be administered by the FHWA or the FS will be developed in accordance with FHWA procedures for the Federal Lands Highway Program. Projects to be administered by a cooperator shall be developed in accordance with Federal-aid procedures and procedures documented in the statewide agreement.

(b) The FH projects shall be designed in accordance with part 625 of this chapter or those criteria specifically approved by the FHWA for a particular project.

§ 660.113 Construction.

(a) No construction shall be undertaken on any FH project until plans, specifications, and estimates have been concurred in by the cooperator(s) and the FS, and approved in accordance with procedures contained in the statewide FH agreement.

(b) The construction of FHs will be performed by the contract method, unless construction by the FHWA, the FS, or a cooperator on its own account is warranted under 23 U.S.C. 204(e).

(c) Prior to final construction acceptance by the contracting authority, the project shall be inspected by the cooperator, the FS, and the FHWA to identify and resolve any mutual concerns.

§ 660.115 Maintenance.

The cooperator having jurisdiction over a FH shall, upon acceptance of the project in accordance with § 660.113(c), assume operation responsibilities and maintain, or cause to be maintained, any project constructed under this subpart.

§ 660.117 Funding, records and accounting.

(a) The Federal share of funding for eligible FH projects may be any amount up to and including 100 percent. A cooperator may participate in the cost of project development and construction, but participation shall not be required.

(b) Funds for FHs may be used for:

(1) Planning;

(2) Federal Lands Highway research;

(3) Preliminary and construction engineering; and

(4) Construction.

(c) Funds for FHs may be made available for the following transportation-related improvement purposes which are generally part of a transportation construction project:

(1) Transportation planning for tourism and recreational travel;

(2) Adjacent vehicular parking areas;

(3) Interpretive signage;

(4) Acquisition of necessary scenic easements and scenic or historic sites;

(5) Provisions for pedestrians and bicycles;

(6) Construction and reconstruction of roadside rest areas including sanitary and water facilities; and

(7) Other appropriate public road facilities as approved by the FHWA.

(d) Use of FH funds for right-of-way acquisition shall be subject to specific approval by the FHWA.

(e) Cooperators which administer construction of FH projects shall maintain their FH records according to 49 CFR part 18.

(f) Funds provided to the FHWA by a cooperator should be received in advance of construction procurement unless otherwise specified in a project agreement.

Subparts B–D [Reserved]

Subpart E—Defense Access Roads

AUTHORITY: 23 U.S.C. 210, 315; 49 CFR 1.48(b).

SOURCE: 49 FR 21924, May 24, 1984, unless otherwise noted.

§ 660.501 Purpose.

The purpose of this regulation is to prescribe policies and procedures governing evaluations of defense access road needs, and administration of projects financed under the defense access roads and other defense related special highway programs.

§ 660.503 Objectives.

The defense access roads program provides a means by which the Federal Government may pay its fair share of the cost of:

(a) Highway improvements needed for adequate highway service to defense and defense related installations;

(b) New highways to replace those which must be closed to permit establishment or expansion of defense installations;

(c) Repair of damage to highways caused by major military maneuvers;

(d) Repair of damages due to the activities of contractors engaged in the construction of missile sites; and

(e) Missile routes to ensure their continued ability to support the missile transporter-erector (TE) vehicle.

§ 660.505 Scope.

This regulation focuses on procedures as they apply to the defense access roads and other special highway programs of the Department of Defense (DOD).

§ 660.507 Definitions.

(a) *Defense installation.* A military reservation or installation, or defense related industry or source of raw materials.

(b) *Military Traffic Management Command (MTMC).* The military transportation agency with responsibilities assigned by the Secretary of Defense for maintaining liaison with the Federal Highway Administration (FHWA) and other agencies for the integration of defense needs into the Nation's highway program.

(c) *Certification.* The statement to the Secretary of Transportation by the Secretary of Defense (or such other official as the President may designate) that certain roads are important to the national defense.

(d) *Access road.* An existing or proposed public highway which is needed to provide essential highway transportation services to a defense installation. (This definition may include public highways through military installations only when right-of-way for such roads is dedicated to public use and the roads are maintained by civil authority.)

(e) *Replacement road.* A public road constructed to replace one closed by establishment of a new, or the expansion of an old, defense installation.

(f) *Maneuver area road.* A public road in an area delineated by official orders for field maneuvers or exercises of military forces.

(g) *Transporter-erector route.* A public road specifically designated for use by the TE vehicle for access to missile sites.

§ 660.509 General principles.

(a) State and local highway agencies are expected to assume the same responsibility for developing and maintaining adequate highways to permanent defense installations as they do for highways serving private industrial establishments or any other permanent traffic generators. The Federal Government expects that highway improvements in the vicinity of defense installations will receive due priority consideration and treatment as State and local agencies develop their programs of improvement. The FHWA will provide assistance, as requested by MTMC, to ascertain State program plans for improvements to roads serving as access to defense installations. Roads which serve permanent defense installations and which qualify under established criteria as Federal-aid routes should be included in the appropriate Federal-aid system.

(b) It is recognized that problems may arise in connection with the establishment, expansion, or operation of defense installations which create an unanticipated impact upon the long-range requirements for the development of highways in the vicinity. These problems can be resolved equitably only by Federal assistance from other than normal Federal-aid highway programs for part or all of the cost of highway improvements necessary for the functioning of the installation.

§ 660.511 Eligibility.

(a) The MTMC has the responsibility for determining the eligibility of proposed improvements for financing with defense access roads funds. The evaluation report will be furnished to MTMC for its use in making the determination of eligibility and certification of importance to the national defense. The criteria upon which MTMC will base its determination of eligibility are included in the Federal-Aid Highway Program Manual, Volume 6, Chapter 9, Section 5, Attachment 2. [1]

(b) If the project is determined to be eligible for financing either in whole or in part with defense access road funds, MTMC will certify the project as important to the national defense and will authorize expenditure of defense access road funds. The Commander, MTMC, is the only representative of the DOD officially authorized to make the certification required by section 210, title 23, U.S.C., in behalf of the Secretary of Defense.

§ 660.513 Standards.

(a) Access roads to permanent defense installations and all replacement roads shall be designed to conform to the same standards as the agency having jurisdiction is currently using for other comparable highways under similar conditions in the area. In general, where the agency having jurisdiction does not have established standards, the design shall conform to American Association of State Highway and Transportation Officials (AASHTO) standards. Should local agencies desire higher standards than are currently being used for other comparable highways under similar conditions in the area, they shall finance the increases in cost.

(b) Access roads to temporary military establishments or for service to workers temporarily engaged in construction of defense installations should be designed to the minimum standards necessary to provide service for a limited period without intolerable congestion and hazard. As a guide, widening to more than two lanes generally will not be undertaken to accommodate anticipated one-way, peak-hour traffic of less than 1,200 vehicles per hour and resurfacing or strengthening of existing pavements will be held to the minimum type having the structural integrity to carry traffic for the short period of anticipated use.

§ 660.515 Project administration.

(a) Determination of the agency best able to accomplish the location, design, and construction of the projects covered by this regulation will be made by the FHWA Division Administrator after consultation with the State and/or local highway agency within whose jurisdiction the highway lies. When an agency other than the State or local highway agency is selected to administer the project, the Division Administrator will be responsible during the life of the project for any necessary coordination between the selected agency and the State or local highway agency.

(b) Defense access road projects under the supervision of a State or local highway agency, whether on or off the Federal-aid system, shall be administered in accordance with Federal-aid procedures, as modified specifically herein or as limited by the delegations of authority to Regional and Division Administrators, unless approval of other procedures has been obtained

[1] This document is available for inspection and copying from the FHWA headquarters and field offices as prescribed by 49 CFR part 7, appendix D.

from Washington Headquarters Office of Direct Federal Programs (HDF–1).

(c) The Division Administrator shall have a firm commitment from the State or local highway agency, within whose jurisdiction the access road lies, that it will accept the responsibility for maintenance of the completed facility before authorization of acquisition of right-of-way or construction of a project.

(d) When defense access road funds are available for a pro-rata portion of the total project cost, the remaining portion of the project may be funded as a Federal-aid project if on a Federal-aid route. Defense access road funds shall not be substituted for the State's matching share of the Federal-aid portion of a project.

§660.517 Maneuver area roads.

(a) Claims by a highway agency for costs incurred to restore, to their former condition, roads damaged by maneuvers involving a military force at least equal in strength to a ground division or an air wing will be paid from funds appropriated for the maneuver and transferred to FHWA by the DOD agency. Defense access road funds may be used to reimburse the highway authority pending transfer of funds by the DOD agency.

(b) Costs incurred by State or local highway authorities while conducting a pre- or post-condition survey may be included in the claim to DOD for direct settlement or in the damage repair project as appropriate.

§660.519 Missile installations and facilities.

Should damage occur to public highways as a result of construction activities, the contractor would normally be held responsible for restoring the damages. However, should the contractor deny responsibility on the basis of contract terms, restoration is provided for under 23 U.S.C. 210(h).

(a) *Restoration under the contract.* (1) The highway agency having jurisdiction over the road shall take appropriate actions, such as load and speed restrictions, to protect the highway. When extensive damage is anticipated and the contractor under the terms of the contract is responsible, it may be necessary to require a performance bond to assure restoration.

(2) If the contractor does not properly maintain the roads when requested in writing, the highway agency having jurisdiction over the road shall perform extraordinary maintenance as necessary to keep the roads serviceable and maintain adequate supporting records of the work performed. Claims shall be presented to the contractor for this extraordinary maintenance and any other work required to restore the roads. If the contractor denies responsibility on the basis of the contract terms, the claim with the required supporting documentation shall be presented to the contracting officer for disposition and arrangement for reimbursement.

(b) *Restoration under 23 U.S.C. 210(h).* (1) To implement 23 U.S.C. 210(h), DOD must make the determination that a contractor for a missile installation or facility did not include in the bid the cost of repairing damage caused to public highways by the operation of the contractor's vehicles and equipment. The FHWA must then make the determination that the State highway agency is, or has been, unable to prevent such damage by restrictions upon the use of the highways without interference with, or delay in, the completion of the contract. If these determinations are made, the Division Administrator will be authorized by the Washington Headquarters to reimburse the highway agency for the cost of the work necessary to keep the roads in a serviceable condition.

(2) Upon receipt of a damage claim, division office representatives accompanied by representatives of the agencies that made the original condition survey will inspect the roads on which damage is claimed. The Division Administrator shall then prepare an estimate of the cost of restoring the roads to original condition as well as any documented cost for extraordinary maintenance for which reimbursement has not been received. No allowance for upgrading the roads shall be included.

PART 661—INDIAN RESERVATION ROAD BRIDGE PROGRAM

AUTHORITY: 23 U.S.C. 120(j) and (k), 202, and 315; Section 1119 of the Safe, Accountable, Flexible, Efficient Transportation Equity Act: A Legacy for Users (SAFETEA–LU) (Pub. L. 109–59, 119 Stat. 1144); and 49 CFR 1.48.

SOURCE: 73 FR 15664, Mar. 25, 2008, unless otherwise noted.

§ 661.1 What is the purpose of this regulation?

The purpose of this regulation is to prescribe policies for project selection and fund allocation procedures for administering the Indian Reservation Road Bridge Program (IRRBP).

§ 661.3 Who must comply with this regulation?

Public authorities must comply to participate in the IRRBP by applying for preliminary engineering (PE), construction, and construction engineering (CE) activities for the replacement or rehabilitation of structurally deficient and functionally obsolete Indian Reservation Road (IRR) bridges.

§ 661.5 What definitions apply to this regulation?

The following definitions apply to this regulation:

Approach roadway means the portion of the highway immediately adjacent to the bridge that affects the geometrics of the bridge, including the horizontal and vertical curves and grades required to connect the existing highway alignment to the new bridge alignment using accepted engineering practices and ensuring that all safety standards are met.

Construction engineering (CE) is the supervision, inspection, and other activities required to ensure the project construction meets the project's approved acceptance specifications, including but not limited to: additional survey staking functions considered necessary for effective control of the construction operations; testing materials incorporated into construction;

checking shop drawings; and measurements needed for the preparation of pay estimates.

Functionally obsolete (FO) is the state in which the deck geometry, load carrying capacity (comparison of the original design load to the State legal load), clearance, or approach roadway alignment no longer meets the usual criteria for the system of which it is an integral part.

Indian Reservation Road (IRR) means a public road that is located within or provides access to an Indian reservation or Indian trust land or restricted Indian land that is not subject to fee title alienation without the approval of the Federal government, or Indian and Alaska Native villages, groups, or communities in which Indians and Alaska Natives reside, whom the Secretary of the Interior has determined are eligible for services generally available to Indians under Federal laws specifically applicable to Indians.

Indian reservation road bridge means a structure located on an IRR, including supports, erected over a depression or an obstruction, such as water, a highway, or a railway, and having a track or passageway for carrying traffic or other moving loads, and having an opening measured along the center of the roadway of more than 20 feet between undercopings of abutments or spring lines of arches, or extreme ends of the openings for multiple boxes; it may also include multiple pipes, where the clear distance between openings is less than half of the smaller contiguous opening.

Life cycle cost analysis (LCCA) means a process for evaluating the total economic worth of a usable project segment by analyzing initial costs and discounted future costs, such as maintenance, user costs, reconstruction, rehabilitation, restoring, and resurfacing costs, over the life of the project segment.

National Bridge Inventory (NBI) means the aggregation of structure inventory and appraisal data collected to fulfill the requirements of the National Bridge Inspection Standards (NBIS).

Plans, specifications and estimates (PS&E) means construction drawings, compilation of provisions, and construction project cost estimates for the performance of the prescribed scope of work.

Preliminary engineering (PE) means planning, survey, design, engineering, and preconstruction activities (including archaeological, environmental, and right-of-way activities) related to a specific bridge project.

Public authority means a Federal, State, county, town, or township, Indian tribe, municipal or other local government or instrumentality with authority to finance, build, operate, or maintain toll or toll-free facilities.

Public road means any road or street under the jurisdiction of and maintained by a public authority and open to public travel.

Structurally deficient (SD) means a bridge becomes structurally deficient when it reaches the set threshold of one of the six criteria from the FHWA NBI.

Structure Inventory and Appraisal (SI&A) Sheet means the graphic representation of the data recorded and stored for each NBI record in accordance with the Recording and Coding Guide for the Structure Inventory and Appraisal of the Nation's Bridges (Report No. FHWA–PD–96–001).

Sufficiency rating (SR) means the numerical rating of a bridge based on its structural adequacy and safety, essentiality for public use, and its serviceability and functional obsolescence.

§661.7 What is the IRRBP?

The IRRBP, as established under 23 U.S.C. 202(d)(4), is a nationwide priority program for improving structurally deficient and functionally obsolete IRR bridges.

§661.9 What is the total funding available for the IRRBP?

The statute authorizes $14 million to be appropriated from the Highway Trust Fund in Fiscal Years 2005 through 2009.

§661.11 When do IRRBP funds become available?

IRRBP funds are authorized at the start of each fiscal year but are subject to Office of Management and Budget apportionment before they become available to FHWA for further distribution.

§ 661.13 How long are these funds available?

IRRBP funds for each fiscal year are available for obligation for the year authorized plus three years (a total of four years).

§ 661.15 What are the eligible activities for IRRBP funds?

(a) IRRBP funds can be used to carry out PE, construction, and CE activities of projects to replace, rehabilitate, seismically retrofit, paint, apply calcium magnesium acetate, sodium acetate/formate or other environmentally acceptable, minimally corrosive anti-icing and deicing compositions, or install scour countermeasures for structurally deficient or functionally obsolete IRR bridges, including multiple pipe culverts.

(b) If a bridge is replaced under the IRRBP, IRRBP funds can be also used for the demolition of the old bridge.

§ 661.17 What are the criteria for bridge eligibility?

(a) Bridge eligibility requires the following:

(1) Have an opening of 20 feet or more;

(2) Be located on an IRR that is included in the IRR Inventory;

(3) Be structurally deficient or functionally obsolete, and

(4) Be recorded in the NBI maintained by the FHWA.

(b) Bridges that were constructed, rehabilitated or replaced in the last 10 years, will be eligible only for seismic retrofit or installation of scour countermeasures.

§ 661.19 When is a bridge eligible for replacement?

To be eligible for replacement, the bridge must be considered structurally deficient or functionally obsolete and must be in accordance with 23 CFR part 650.409(a) for bridge replacement. After an existing bridge is replaced under the IRRBP, it must be taken completely out of service and removed from the inventory. If the original bridge is considered historic, it must still be removed from the inventory, however the Tribe is allowed to request an exemption from the BIA Division of Transportation (BIADOT) to allow the bridge to remain in place.

§ 661.21 When is a bridge eligible for rehabilitation?

To be eligible for rehabilitation, the bridge must be considered structurally deficient or functionally obsolete and must be in accordance with 23 CFR part 650.409(a) for bridge rehabilitation. A bridge eligible for rehabilitation may be replaced if the life cycle cost analysis is conducted which shows the cost for bridge rehabilitation exceeds the replacement cost.

§ 661.23 How will a bridge project be programmed for funding once eligibility has been determined?

(a) All projects will be programmed for funding after a completed application package is received and accepted by the FHWA. At that time, the project will be acknowledged as either BIA and Tribally owned, or non-BIA owned and placed in either a PE or a construction queue.

(b) All projects will be ranked and prioritized based on the following criteria:

(1) Bridge sufficiency rating (SR);

(2) Bridge status with structurally deficient (SD) having precedence over functionally obsolete (FO);

(3) Bridges on school bus routes;

(4) Detour length;

(5) Average daily traffic; and

(6) Truck average daily traffic.

(c) Queues will carryover from fiscal year to fiscal year as made necessary by the amount of annual funding made available.

§ 661.25 What does a complete application package for PE consist of and how does the project receive funding?

(a) A complete application package for PE consists of the following: the certification checklist, IRRBP transportation improvement program (TIP), project scope of work, detailed cost for PE, and SI&A sheet.

(b) For non-BIA IRR bridges, the application package must also include a tribal resolution supporting the project and identification of the required minimum 20 percent local funding match.

(c) The IRRBP projects for PE will be placed in queue and determined as eligible for funding after receipt by FHWA of a complete application package. Incomplete application packages will be disapproved and returned for revision and resubmission along with a notation providing the reason for disapproval.

(d) Funding for the approved eligible projects on the queues will be made available to the Tribes, under an FHWA/Tribal agreement, or the Secretary of the Interior upon availability of program funding at FHWA.

§661.27 What does a complete application package for construction consist of and how does the project receive funding?

(a) A complete application package for construction consists of the following: a copy of the approved PS&E, the certification checklist, SI&A sheet, and IRRBP TIP. For non-BIA IRR bridges, the application package must also include a copy of a letter from the bridge's owner approving the project and its PS&E, a tribal resolution supporting the project, and identification of the required minimum 20 percent local funding match. All environmental and archeological clearances and complete grants of public rights-of-way must be acquired prior to submittal of the construction application package.

(b) The IRRBP projects for construction will be placed in queue and determined as eligible for funding after receipt by FHWA of a complete application package. Incomplete application packages will be disapproved and returned for revision and resubmission along with a notation providing the reason for disapproval.

(c) Funding for the approved eligible projects on the queues will be made available to the Tribes, under an FHWA/Tribal agreement, or the Secretary of the Interior upon availability of program funding at FHWA.

§661.29 How does ownership impact project selection?

Since the Federal government has both a trust responsibility and owns the BIA bridges on Indian reservations, primary consideration will be given to eligible projects on BIA and Tribally owned IRR bridges. A smaller percentage of available funds will be set aside for non-BIA IRR bridges, since States and counties have access to Federal-aid and other funding to design, replace and rehabilitate their bridges and that 23 U.S.C. 204(c) requires that IRR funds be supplemental to and not in lieu of other funds apportioned to the State. The program policy will be to maximize the number of IRR bridges participating in the IRRBP in a given fiscal year regardless of ownership.

§661.31 Do IRRBP projects have to be listed on an approved IRR TIP?

Yes. All IRRBP projects must be listed on an approved IRR TIP. The approved IRR TIP will be forwarded by FHWA to the respective State for inclusion into its State TIP.

§661.33 What percentage of IRRBP funding is available for PE and construction?

Up to 15 percent of the funding made available in any fiscal year will be eligible for PE. The remaining funding in any fiscal year will be available for construction.

§661.35 What percentage of IRRBP funding is available for use on BIA and Tribally owned IRR bridges, and non-BIA owned IRR bridges?

(a) Up to 80 percent of the available funding made available for PE and construction in any fiscal year will be eligible for use on BIA and Tribally owned IRR bridges. The remaining funding in any fiscal year will be made available for PE and construction for use on non-BIA owned IRR bridges.

(b) At various times during the fiscal year, FHWA will review the projects awaiting funding and may shift funds between BIA and Tribally owned, and non-BIA owned bridge projects so as to maximize the number of projects funded and the overall effectiveness of the program.

§661.37 What are the funding limitations on individual IRRBP projects?

The following funding provisions apply in administration of the IRRBP:

(a) An IRRBP eligible BIA and Tribally owned IRR bridge is eligible for 100 percent IRRBP funding, with a $150,000 maximum limit for PE.

(b) An IRRBP eligible non-BIA owned IRR bridge is eligible for up to 80 percent IRRBP funding, with a $150,000 maximum limit for PE and $1,000,000 maximum limit for construction. The minimum 20 percent local match will need to be identified in the application package. IRR Program construction funds received by a Tribe may be used as the local match.

(c) Requests for additional funds above the referenced thresholds may be submitted along with proper justification to FHWA for consideration. The request will be considered on a case-by-case basis. There is no guarantee for the approval of the request for additional funds.

§ 661.39 How are project cost overruns funded?

(a) A request for additional IRRBP funds for cost overruns on a specific bridge project must be submitted to BIADOT and FHWA for approval. The written submission must include a justification, an explanation as to why the overrun occurred, and the amount of additional funding required with supporting cost data. If approved by FHWA, the request will be placed at the top of the appropriate queue (with a contract modification request having a higher priority than a request for additional funds for a project award) and funding may be provided if available.

(b) Project cost overruns may also be funded out of the Tribe's regular IRR Program construction funding.

§ 661.41 After a bridge project has been completed (either PE or construction) what happens with the excess or surplus funding?

Since the funding is project specific, once a bridge design or construction project has been completed under this program, any excess or surplus funding is returned to FHWA for use on additional approved deficient IRRBP projects.

§ 661.43 Can other sources of funds be used to finance a queued project in advance of receipt of IRRBP funds?

Yes. A Tribe can use other sources of funds, including IRR Program construction funds, on a project that has been approved for funding and placed on the queue and then be reimbursed when IRRBP funds become available. If IRR Program construction funds are used for this purpose, the funds must be identified on an FHWA approved IRR TIP prior to their expenditure.

§ 661.45 What happens when IRRBP funds cannot be obligated by the end of the fiscal year?

IRRBP funds provided to a project that cannot be obligated by the end of the fiscal year are to be returned to FHWA during August redistribution. The returned funds will be re-allocated to the BIA the following fiscal year after receipt and acceptance at FHWA from BIA of a formal request for the funds, which includes a justification for the amounts requested and the reason for the failure of the prior year obligation.

§ 661.47 Can bridge maintenance be performed with IRRBP funds?

No. Bridge maintenance repairs, e.g., guard rail repair, deck repairs, repair of traffic control devices, striping, cleaning scuppers, deck sweeping, snow and debris removal, etc., are not eligible uses of IRRBP funding. The Department of the Interior annual allocation for maintenance and IRR Program construction funds are eligible funding sources for bridge maintenance.

§ 661.49 Can IRRBP funds be spent on Interstate, State Highway, and Toll Road IRR bridges?

Yes. Interstate, State Highway, and Toll Road IRR bridges are eligible for funding as described in § 661.37(b).

§ 661.51 Can IRRBP funds be used for the approach roadway to a bridge?

(a) Yes, costs associated with approach roadway work, as defined in § 661.5 are eligible.

(b) Long approach fills, causeways, connecting roadways, interchanges, ramps, and other extensive earth structures, when constructed beyond an attainable touchdown point, are not eligible uses of IRRBP funds.

§661.53 What standards should be used for bridge design?

(a) Replacement—A replacement structure must meet the current geometric, construction and structural standards required for the types and volumes of projected traffic on the facility over its design life consistent with 25 CFR part 170, Subpart D, Appendix B and 23 CFR part 625.

(b) Rehabilitation—Bridges to be rehabilitated, as a minimum, should conform to the standards of 23 CFR part 625, Design Standards for Federal-aid Highways, for the class of highway on which the bridge is a part.

§661.55 How are BIA and Tribal owned IRR bridges inspected?

BIA and Tribally owned IRR bridges are inspected in accordance with 25 CFR part 170.504–170.507.

§661.57 How is a list of deficient bridges to be generated?

(a) In consultation with the BIA, a list of deficient BIA IRR bridges will be developed each fiscal year by the FHWA based on the annual April update of the NBI. The NBI is based on data from the inspection of all bridges. Likewise, a list of non-BIA IRR bridges will be obtained from the NBI. These lists would form the basis for identifying bridges that would be considered potentially eligible for participation in the IRRBP. Two separate master bridge lists (one each for BIA and non-BIA IRR bridges) will be developed and will include, at a minimum, the following:

(1) Sufficiency rating (SR);

(2) Status (structurally deficient or functionally obsolete);

(3) Average daily traffic (NBI item 29);

(4) Detour length (NBI item 19); and

(5) Truck average daily traffic (NBI item 109).

(b) These lists would be provided by the FHWA to the BIADOT for publication and notification of affected BIA regional offices, Indian Tribal governments (ITGs), and State and local governments.

(c) BIA regional offices, in consultation with ITGs, are encouraged to prioritize the design for bridges that are structurally deficient over bridges that are simply functionally obsolete, since the former is more critical structurally than the latter. Bridges that have higher average daily traffic (ADT) should be considered before those that have lower ADT. Detour length should also be a factor in selection and submittal of bridges, with those having a higher detour length being of greater concern. Lastly, bridges with higher truck ADT should take precedence over those which have lower truck ADT. Other items of note should be whether school buses use the bridge and the types of trucks that may cross the bridge and the loads imposed.

§661.59 What should be done with a deficient BIA owned IRR bridge if the Indian Tribe does not support the project?

The BIA should notify the Tribe and encourage the Tribe to develop and submit an application package to FHWA for the rehabilitation or replacement of the bridge. For safety of the motoring public, if the Tribe decides not to pursue the bridge project, the BIA shall work with the Tribe to either reduce the bridge's load rating or close the bridge, and remove it from the IRR inventory in accordance with 25 CFR part 170 (170.813).

PART 667—PERIODIC EVALUATION OF FACILITIES REPEATEDLY REQUIRING REPAIR AND RECONSTRUCTION DUE TO EMERGENCY EVENTS

AUTHORITY: Sec. 1315(b) of Pub. L. 112–141, 126 Stat. 405; 23 U.S.C. 109, 144, and 315; 49 CFR 1.85.

SOURCE: 81 FR 73267, Oct. 24, 2016, unless otherwise noted.

§667.1 Statewide evaluation.

Each State, acting through its department of transportation (State DOT), shall conduct statewide evaluations to determine if there are reasonable alternatives to roads, highways, and bridges that have required repair and reconstruction activities on two or more occasions due to emergency events. The evaluations shall be conducted in accordance with the requirements in this part.

§ 667.3 Definitions.

For purposes of this part:

Catastrophic failure means the sudden failure of a major element or segment of a road, highway, or bridge due to an external cause. The failure must not be primarily attributable to gradual and progressive deterioration or lack of proper maintenance.

Evaluation means an analysis that includes identification and consideration of any alternative that will mitigate, or partially or fully resolve, the root cause of the recurring damage, the costs of achieving the solution, and the likely duration of the solution. The evaluations shall consider the risk of recurring damage and cost of future repair under current and future environmental conditions. These considerations typically are a part of the planning and project development process.

Emergency event means a natural disaster or catastrophic failure resulting in an emergency declared by the Governor of the State or an emergency or disaster declared by the President of the United States.

Reasonable alternatives include options that could partially or fully achieve the following:

(1) Reduce the need for Federal funds to be expended on emergency repair and reconstruction activities;

(2) Better protect public safety and health and the human and natural environment; and

(3) Meet transportation needs as described in the relevant and applicable Federal, State, local, and tribal plans and programs. Relevant and applicable plans and programs include the Long-Range Statewide Transportation Plan, Statewide Transportation Improvement Plan (STIP), Metropolitan Transportation Plan(s), and Transportation Improvement Program(s) (TIP) that are developed under part 450 of this title.

Repair and reconstruction means work on a road, highway, or bridge that has one or more reconstruction elements. The term includes permanent repairs such as restoring pavement surfaces, reconstructing damaged bridges and culverts, and replacing highway appurtenances, but excludes emergency repairs as defined in 23 CFR 668.103.

Roads, highways, and bridges means a highway, as defined in 23 U.S.C. 101(a)(11), that is open to the public and eligible for financial assistance under title 23, U.S.C.; but excludes tribally owned and federally owned roads, highways, and bridges.

§ 667.5 Data time period, availability, and sources.

(a) The beginning date for every evaluation under this part shall be January 1, 1997. The end date must be no earlier than December 31 of the year preceding the date on which the evaluation is due for completion. Evaluations should cover a longer period if useful data is reasonably available. Subject to the timing provisions in § 667.7, evaluations must include any road, highway, or bridge that, on or after January 1, 1997, required repair and reconstruction on two or more occasions due to emergency events.

(b) State DOTs must use reasonable efforts to obtain the data needed for the evaluation. If the State DOT determines the necessary data for the evaluation is unavailable, the State DOT must document in the evaluation the lack of available data for that facility.

(c) A State DOT may use whatever sources and types of data it determines are useful to the evaluation. Available data sources include reports or other information required to receive emergency repair funds under title 23, other sources used to apply for Federal or nonfederal funding, and State or local records pertaining to damage sustained and/or funding sought.

§ 667.7 Timing of evaluations.

(a) Not later than November 23, 2018, the State DOT must complete the statewide evaluation for all NHS roads, highways and bridges. The State DOT shall update the evaluation after every emergency event to the extent needed to add any roads, highways, or bridges subject to this paragraph that were affected by the event. The State DOT shall review and update the entire evaluation at least every 4 years. In establishing its evaluation cycle, the State DOT should consider how the evaluation can best inform the State DOT's preparation of its asset management plan and STIP.

(b) Beginning on November 23, 2020, for all roads, highways, and bridges not included in the evaluation prepared under paragraph (a) of this section, the State DOT must prepare an evaluation that conforms with this part for the affected portion of the road, highway, or bridge prior to including any project relating to such facility in its STIP.

§ 667.9 Consideration of evaluations.

(a) The State DOT shall consider the results of an evaluation prepared under this part when developing projects. State DOTs and metropolitan planning organizations are encouraged to include consideration of the evaluations during the development of transportation plans and programs, including TIPs and STIPs, and during the environmental review process under part 771 of this title. Nothing in this section prohibits State DOTs from proceeding with emergency repairs to restore functionality of the system, or from receiving emergency repair funding under part 668 of this title.

(b) The FHWA will periodically review the State DOT's compliance under this part, including evaluation performance, consideration of evaluation results during project development, and overall results achieved. Nothing in this paragraph limits FHWA's ability to consider the results of the evaluations when relevant to an FHWA decision, including when making a planning finding under 23 U.S.C. 134(g)(8), making decisions during the environmental review process under part 771 of this title, or when approving funding. The State DOT must make evaluations required under this part available to FHWA upon request.

PART 668—EMERGENCY RELIEF PROGRAM

Subpart A—Procedures for Federal-Aid Highways

Sec.

Subpart B—Procedures for Federal Agencies for Federal Roads

AUTHORITY: 23 U.S.C. 101, 120(e), 125 and 315; 49 CFR 1.48(b).

Subpart A—Procedures for Federal-Aid Highways

SOURCE: 52 FR 21948, June 10, 1987, unless otherwise noted.

§ 668.101 Purpose.

To establish policy and provide program guidance for the administration of emergency funds for the repair or reconstruction of Federal-aid highways, which are found to have suffered serious damage by natural diasters over a wide area or serious damage from catastrophic failures. Guidance for application by Federal agencies for reconstruction of Federal roads that are not part of the Federal-aid highways is contained in 23 CFR part 668, subpart B.

[52 FR 21948, June 10, 1987, as amended at 61 FR 67212, Dec. 20, 1996]

§ 668.103 Definitions.

In addition to others contained in 23 U.S.C. 101(a), the following definitions shall apply as used in this regulation:

Applicant. The State highway agency is the applicant for Federal assistance under 23 U.S.C. 125 for State highways and local roads and streets which are a part of the Federal-aid highways.

Betterments. Added protective features, such as rebuilding of roadways at a higher elevation or the lengthening of bridges, or changes which modify the function or character of a highway facility from what existed prior to the disaster or catastrophic failure, such as additional lanes or added access control.

Catastrophic failure. The sudden failure of a major element or segment of the highway system due to an external cause. The failure must not be primarily attributable to gradual and progressive deterioration or lack of proper maintenance. The closure of a facility because of imminent danger of collapse is not in itself a sudden failure.

Emergency repairs. Those repairs including temporary traffic operations undertaken during or immediately following the disaster occurrence for the purpose of:

(1) Minimizing the extent of the damage,

(2) Protecting remaining facilities, or

(3) Restoring essential traffic.

External cause. An outside force or phenomenon which is separate from the damaged element and not primarily the result of existing conditions.

Heavy maintenance. Work usually done by highway agencies in repairing damage normally expected from seasonal and occasionally unusual natural conditions or occurrences. It includes work at a site required as a direct result of a disaster which can reasonably be accommodated by a State or local road authority's maintenance, emergency or contingency program.

Natural disaster. A sudden and unusual natural occurrence, including but not limited to intense rainfall, floods, hurricanes, tornadoes, tidal waves, landslides, volcanoes or earthquakes which cause serious damage.

Proclamation. A declaration of emergency by the Governor of the affected State.

Serious damage. Heavy, major or unusual damage to a highway which severely impairs the safety or usefulness of the highway or results in road closure. Serious damage must be beyond the scope of heavy maintenance.

State. Any one of the United States, the District of Columbia, Puerto Rico or the Virgin Islands, Guam, American Samoa or Commonwealth of the Northern Mariana Islands.

[52 FR 21948, June 10, 1987, as amended at 61 FR 67212, Dec. 20, 1996; 65 FR 25444, May 2, 2000]

§ 668.105 Policy.

(a) The Emergency Relief (ER) program is intended to aid States in repairing road facilities which have suffered widespread serious damage resulting from a natural disaster over a wide area or serious damage from a catastrophic failure.

(b) ER funds are not intended to supplant other funds for correction of preexisting, nondisaster related deficiencies.

(c) The expenditure of ER funds for emergency repair shall be in such a manner so as to reduce, to the greatest extent feasible, the cost of permanent restoration work.

(d) The approval to use available ER funds to repair or restore highways damaged by a natural disaster shall be based on the combination of the extraordinary character of the natural disturbance and the wide area of impact as well as the seriousness of the damage. Storms of unusual intensity occurring over a small area may not meet the above conditions.

(e) ER funds shall not duplicate assistance under another Federal program or compensation from insurance or any other source. Partial compensation for a loss by other sources will not preclude emergency fund assistance for the part of such loss not compensated otherwise. Any compensation for damages or insurance proceeds including interest recovered by the State or political subdivision or by a toll authority for repair of the highway facility must be used upon receipt to reduce ER fund liability on the project.

(f) Prompt and diligent efforts shall be made by the State to recover repair costs from the legally responsible parties to reduce the project costs particularly where catastrophic damages are caused by ships, barge tows, highway vehicles, or vehicles with illegal loads or where damage is increased by improperly controlled objects or events.

(g) The processing of ER requests shall be given prompt attention and shall be given priority over non-emergency work.

(h) ER projects shall be promptly constructed. Any project that has not advanced to the construction obligation stage by the end of the second fiscal year following the disaster occurrence will not be advanced unless suitable justification to warrant retention is furnished to the FHWA.

(i) Permanent repair and reconstruction work, not accomplished as emergency repairs, shall be done by the contract method unless the State Highway agency adequately demonstrates that some other method is more cost effective as described in 23 CFR 635.204.

Emergency repair work may be accomplished by the contract, negotiated contract or highway agency force account methods as determined by the Highway agency as best suited to protect the public health and safety.

(j) ER program funding is only to be used to repair highways which have been seriously damaged and is not intended to fund heavy maintenance or routine emergency repair activities which should normally be funded as contingency items in the State and local road programs. An application for ER funds in the range of $700,000 or less must be accompanied by a showing as to why the damage repair involved is considered to be beyond the scope of heavy maintenance or routine emergency repair. As a general rule, widespread nominal road damages in this range would not be considered to be of a significant nature justifying approval by the FHWA Division Administrator for ER funding.

[52 FR 21948, June 10, 1987, as amended at 61 FR 67212, Dec. 20, 1996; 65 FR 25444, May 2, 2000]

§668.107 Federal share payable.

(a) The Federal share payable on account of any repair or reconstruction provided for by funds made available under 23 U.S.C. 125 of this title on account of any project on a Federal-aid highway system, including the Interstate System, shall not exceed the Federal share payable on a project on such system as provided in 23 U.S.C. 120; except that the Federal share payable for eligible emergency repairs to minimize damage, protect facilities, or restore essential traffic accomplished within 180 days after the actual occurrence of the natural disaster or catastrophic failure may amount to 100 percent of the costs thereof.

(b) Total obligations of ER funds in any State, excluding the Virgin Islands, Guam, American Samoa or Commonwealth of the Northern Mariana Islands, for all projects (including projects on both the Federal-aid systems and those on Federal roads under 23 CFR part 668, subpart B), resulting from a single natural disaster or a single catastrophic failure, shall not exceed $100 million per disaster or catastrophic failure. The total obligations for ER projects in any fiscal year in the Virgin Islands, Guam, American Samoa and the Commonwealth of the Northern Mariana Islands shall not exceed $20 million.

[52 FR 21948, June 10, 1987, as amended at 52 FR 32540, Aug. 28, 1987; 61 FR 67212, Dec. 20, 1996; 65 FR 25444, May 2, 2000]

§668.109 Eligibility.

(a) The eligibility of all work is contingent upon approval by the FHWA Division Administrator of an application for ER and inclusion of the work in an approved program of projects.

(1) Prior FHWA approval or authorization is not required for emergency repairs and preliminary engineering (PE).

(2) Permanent repairs or restoration must have prior FHWA program approval and authorization, unless done as part of the emergency repairs.

(b) ER funds may participate in:

(1) Repair to or reconstruction of seriously damaged highway elements as necessary to restore the facility to predisaster conditions, including necessary clearance of debris and other deposits in drainage courses within the right-of way (ROW);

(2) Restoration of stream channels outside the highway ROW when:

(i) The public highway agency has responsibility for the maintenance and proper operation of the stream channel section, and

(ii) The work is necessary for satisfactory operation of the highway system involved;

(3) Actual PE and construction engineering costs on approved projects;

(4) Emergency repairs;

(5) Temporary operations, including emergency traffic services such as flagging traffic through inundated sections of highways, undertaken by the applicant during or immediately following the disaster;

(6) Betterments, only where clearly economically justified to prevent future recurring damage. Economic justification must weigh the cost of betterment against the risk of eligible recurring damage and the cost of future repair;

(7) Temporary work to maintain essential traffic, such as raising roadway grade during a period of flooding by

placing fill and temporary surface material;

(8) Raising the grades of critical Federal-aid highways faced with long-term loss of use due to basin flooding as defined by an unprecedented rise in basin water level both in magnitude and time frame. Such grade raises are not considered to be a betterment for the purpose of 23 CFR 668.109(b)(6); and

(9) Repair of toll facilities when the provisions of 23 U.S.C. 129 are met. If a toll facility does not have an executed toll agreement with the FHWA at the time of the disaster, a toll agreement may be executed after the disaster to qualify for that disaster.

(c) ER funds may not participate in:

(1) Heavy maintenance such as repair of minor damages consisting primarily of eroded shoulders, filled ditches and culverts, pavement settlement, mud and debris deposits off the traveled way, slope sloughing, slides, and slipouts in cut or fill slopes. In order to simplify the inspection and estimating process, heavy maintenance may be defined using dollar guidelines developed by the States and Divisions with Regional concurrence;

(2) Repair of surface damage caused by traffic whether or not the damage was aggravated by saturated subgrade or inundation, except ER funds may participate in:

(i) Repair of surface damage to any public road caused by traffic making repairs to Federal-aid highways.

(ii) Repair of surface damage to designated detours (which may lie on both Federal-aid and non-Federal-aid routes) caused by traffic that has been detoured from a damaged Federal-aid highway; and

(iii) Repair of surface damage to Federal-aid highways caused by vehicles responding to a disaster; provided the surface damage has occurred during the first 60 days after a disaster occurrence, unless otherwise approved by the FHWA Division Administrator.

(3) Repair of damage not directly related to, and isolated away from, the pattern of the disaster;

(4) Routine maintenance of detour routes, not related to the increased traffic volumes, such as mowing, maintaining drainage, pavement signing, snow plowing, etc.;

(5) Replacement of damaged or lost material not incorporated into the highway such as stockpiled materials or items awaiting installation;

(6) Repair or reconstruction of facilities affected by long-term, pre-existing conditions or predictable developing situations, such as, gradual, long-term rises in water levels in basins or slow moving slides, except for raising grades as noted in § 668.109(b)(8);

(7) Permanent repair or replacement of deficient bridges scheduled for replacement with other funds. A project is considered scheduled if the construction phase is included in the FHWA approved Statewide Transportation Improvement Program (STIP);

(8) Other normal maintenance and operation functions on the highway system including snow and ice removal; and

(9) Reimbursing loss of toll revenue.

(d) Replacement of a highway facility at its existing location is appropriate when it is not technically and economically feasible to repair or restore a seriously damaged element to its predisaster condition and is limited in ER reimbursement to the cost of a new facility to current design standards of comparable capacity and character to the destroyed facility. With respect to a bridge, a comparable facility is one which meets current geometric and construction standards for the type and volume of traffic it will carry during its design life. Where it is neither practical nor feasible to replace a damaged highway facility in kind at its existing location, an alternative selected through the National Environmental Policy Act (NEPA) process, if of comparable function and character to the destroyed facility, is eligible for ER reimbursement.

(e) Except as otherwise provided in paragraph (b)(6) of this section, the total cost of a project eligible for ER funding may not exceed the cost of repair or reconstruction of a comparable facility. ER funds may participate to the extent of eligible repair costs when proposed projects contain unjustified betterments or other work not eligible for ER funds.

[52 FR 21948, June 10, 1987, as amended at 61 FR 67212, Dec. 20, 1996; 65 FR 25444, May 2, 2000]

§ 668.111 Application procedures.

(a) *Notification.* As soon as possible after the disaster, the applicant shall notify the FHWA Division Administrator of its intent to apply for ER funds.

(b) *Damage survey.* As soon as practical after occurrence, the State will make a preliminary field survey, working cooperatively with the FHWA Division Administrator and other governmental agencies with jurisdiction over eligible highways. The preliminary field survey should be coordinated with the Federal Emergency Management Agency work, if applicable, to eliminate duplication of effort. The purpose of this survey is to determine the general nature and extent of damage to eligible highways.

(1) A damage survey summary report is to be prepared by the State. The purpose of the damage survey summary report is to provide a factual basis for the FHWA Division Administrator's finding that serious damage to Federal-aid highways has been caused by a natural disaster over a wide area or a catastrophe. The damage survey summary report should include by political subdivision or other generally recognized administrative or geographic boundaries, a description of the types and extent of damage to highways and a preliminary estimate of cost of restoration or reconstruction for damaged Federal-aid highways in each jurisdiction. Pictures showing the kinds and extent of damage and sketch maps detailing the damaged areas should be included, as appropriate, in the damage survey summary report.

(2) Unless very unusual circumstances prevail, the damage survey summary report should be prepared within 6 weeks following the applicant's notification.

(3) For large disasters where extensive damage to Federal-aid highways is readily evident, the FHWA Division Administrator may approve an application under § 668.111(d) prior to submission of the damage survey summary report. In these cases, an abbreviated damage survey summary report, summarizing eligible repair costs by jurisdiction, is to be prepared and submitted to the FHWA Division Administrator after the damage inspections have been completed.

(c) *Application.* Before funds can be made available, an application for ER must be made to, and approved by the FHWA Division Administrator. The application shall include:

(1) A copy of the Governor's proclamation, request for a Presidential declaration, or a Presidential declaration; and

(2) A copy of the damage survey summary report, as appropriate.

(d) *Approval of application.* The FHWA Division Administrator's approval of the application constitutes the finding of eligibility under 23 U.S.C. 125 and shall constitute approval of the application.

[65 FR 25444, May 2, 2000]

§ 668.113 Program and project procedures.

(a) Immediately after approval of an application, the FHWA Division Administrator will notify the applicant to proceed with preparation of a program which defines the work needed to restore or replace the damaged facilities. It should be submitted to the FHWA Division Administrator within 3 months of receipt of this notification. The FHWA field office will assist the applicant and other affected agencies in preparation of the program. This work may involve joint site inspections to view damage and reach tentative agreement on type of permanent corrective work to be undertaken. Program data should be kept to a minimum, but should be sufficient to identify the approved disaster or catastrophe and to permit a determination of the eligibility and propriety of proposed work. If the damage survey summary report is determined by the FHWA Division Administrator to be of sufficient detail to meet these criteria, additional program support data need not be submitted.

(b) *Project procedures.* (1) Projects for permanent repairs shall be processed in accordance with regular Federal-aid procedures. In those cases where a regular Federal-aid project in a State similar to the ER project would be handled under the project oversight exceptions found in title 23, United States Code, the ER project can be handled in a similar fashion subject to the following two conditions:

(i) Any betterment to be incorporated into the project and for which ER funding is requested must receive prior FHWA approval; and

(ii) The FHWA reserves the right to conduct final inspections on all ER projects. The FHWA Division Administrator has the discretion to undertake final inspections on ER projects as deemed appropriate.

(2) Simplified procedures, including abbreviated plans should be used where appropriate.

(3) Emergency repair meets the criteria for categorical exclusions pursuant to 23 CFR 771.117 and normally does not require any further NEPA approvals.

[52 FR 21948, June 10, 1987, as amended at 61 FR 67212, Dec. 20, 1996; 65 FR 25445, May 2, 2000]

Subpart B—Procedures for Federal Agencies for Federal Roads

§ 668.201 Purpose.

To establish policy, procedures, and program guidance for the administration of emergency relief to Federal agencies for the repair or reconstruction of Federal roads which are found to have suffered serious damage by a natural disaster over a wide area or by catastrophic failure.

[43 FR 59485, Dec. 21, 1978]

§ 668.203 Definitions.

(a) *Applicant.* Any Federal agency which submits an application for emergency relief and which has authority to repair or reconstruct Federal roads.

(b) *Betterments.* Added protective features, such as, the relocation or rebuilding of roadways at a higher elevation or the extension, replacement or raising of bridges, and added facilities not existing prior to the natural disaster or catastrophic failure such as additional lanes, upgraded surfacing, or structures.

(c) *Catastrophic failure.* The sudden failure of a major element or segment of a Federal road which is not primarily attributable to gradual and progressive deterioration or lack of proper maintenance. The closure of a facility because of imminent danger of collapse is not in itself a sudden failure.

(d) *Emergency repairs.* Those repairs, including necessary preliminary engineering (PE), construction engineering (CE), and temporary traffic operations, undertaken during or immediately after a natural disaster or catastrophic failure (1) to restore essential travel, (2) to protect remaining facilities, or (3) to minimize the extent of damage.

(e) *Federal roads.* Forest highways, forest development roads and trails, park roads and trails, parkways, public lands highways, public lands development roads and trails, and Indian reservation roads as defined under 23 U.S.C. 101(a).

(f) *Finding.* A letter or other official correspondence issued by the Direct Federal Division Engineer (DFDE) to a Federal agency giving notification that pursuant to 23 U.S.C. 125, Federal roads have (Affirmative Finding) or have not (Negative Finding) been found to have suffered serious damage as the result of (1) a natural disaster over a wide area, or (2) a catastrophic failure.

(g) *Natural disaster.* An unusual natural occurrence such as a flood, hurricane, severe storm, tidal wave, earthquake, or landslide which causes serious damage.

(h) *Permanent work.* Repair or reconstruction to pre-disaster or other allowed geometric and construction standards and related PE and CE.

(i) *Direct Federal Division Engineer.* Director of one of the Direct Federal field offices located in Vancouver, WA; Denver, CO; and Arlington, VA.

[43 FR 59485, Dec. 21, 1978, as amended at 47 FR 10529, Mar. 11, 1982]

§ 668.205 Policy.

(a) This emergency relief program is intended to pay the unusually heavy expenses in the repair and reconstruction of Federal roads resulting from damage caused by natural disasters over a wide area or catastrophic failures.

(b) Emergency relief work shall be given prompt attention and priority over non-emergency work.

(c) Permanent work shall be done by contract awarded by competitive bidding through formal advertising, where feasible.

(d) It is in the public interest to perform emergency repairs immediately and prior approval or authorization from the DFDE is not required. Emergency repairs may be performed by the method of contracting (advertised contract, negotiated contract, or force account) which the applicant or the Federal Highway Administration (FHWA) (where FHWA performs the work) determines to be most suited for this work.

(e) Emergency relief projects shall be promptly constructed. Projects not under construction by the end of the second fiscal year following the year in which the disaster occurred will be reevaluated by the DFDE and will be withdrawn from the approved program of projects unless suitable justification is provided by the applicant to warrant retention.

(f) The Finding for natural disasters will be based on both the extraordinary character of the natural disturbance and the wide area of impact. Storms of unusual intensity occurring over a small area do not meet these conditions.

(g) Diligent efforts shall be made to recover repair costs from the legally responsible parties to reduce the project costs where highway damages are caused by ships, barge tows, highway vehicles, vehicles with illegal loads, and similar improperly controlled objects or events.

(h) Emergency funds shall not duplicate assistance under another Federal program or compensation from insurance or any other source. Where other funding compensates for only part of an eligible cost, emergency relief funding can be used to pay the remaining costs.

[43 FR 59485, Dec. 21, 1978, as amended at 47 FR 10529, Mar. 11, 1982]

§668.207 Federal share payable from emergency fund.

The Federal share payable under this program is 100 percent of the cost.

[43 FR 59485, Dec. 21, 1978]

§668.209 Eligibility of work.

(a) Permanent work must have prior program approval in accordance with paragraph (a) of §668.215 unless such work is performed as emergency repairs.

(b) Emergency repairs, including permanent work performed incidental to emergency repairs, and all PE may begin immediately and do not need prior program approval. Reimbursement shall be contingent upon the work ultimately being approved in accordance with the requirements of paragraph (a) of §668.215.

(c) To qualify for emergency relief, the damaged or destroyed road or trail shall be designated as a Federal road.

(d) Replacement highway facilities are appropriate when it is not practical and economically feasible to repair or restore a damaged element to its preexisting condition. Emergency relief is limited to the cost of a new facility constructed to current design standards of comparable capacity and character to the destroyed facility. With respect to a bridge, a comparable facility is one which meets current geometric and construction standards for the type and volume of traffic it will carry during its design life.

(e) Emergency relief funds may participate to the extent of eligible repair costs when proposed projects contain betterments or other work not eligible for emergency funds.

(f) Work may include:

(1) Repair to, or reconstruction of, seriously damaged highway elements for a distance which would be within normal highway right-of-way limits, including necessary clearance of debris and other deposits in drainage courses, where such work would not be classed as heavy maintenance.

(2) Restoration of stream channels when the work is necessary for the satisfactory operation of the Federal road. The applicant must have responsibility and authority for maintenance and proper operation of stream channels restored.

(3) Betterments where clearly economically justified to prevent future recurring damage. Economic justification acceptable to the DFDE must weigh the cost of such betterments against the risk of eligible recurring damage and the cost of future repair.

(4) Actual PE and CE costs on approved projects.

(5) Emergency repairs.

[43 FR 59485, Dec. 21, 1978, as amended at 47 FR 10529, Mar. 11, 1982]

§ 668.211 Notification, damage assessment, and finding.

(a) *Notification.* During or as soon as possible after a natural disaster or catastrophic failure, each applicant will notify the DFDE of its tentative intent to apply for emergency relief and request that a Finding be made.

(b) *Acknowledgment.* The DFDE will promptly acknowledge the notification and briefly describe subsequent damage assessment, Finding, and application procedures.

(c) *Field report.* The applicant shall cooperate with the DFDE to promptly make a field survey of overall damage and in the preparation of a field report.

(d) *Finding.* Using the field report and other information deemed appropriate, the DFDE will promptly issue a Finding and if an Affirmative Finding is made, establish the date after which repair or reconstruction will be considered for emergency relief, and note the dates of the extraordinary natural occurrence or catastrophic event responsible for the damage or destruction.

(e) *Detailed site inspections.* (1) If an Affirmative Finding is made, the applicant shall cooperate with the DFDE to make a detailed inspection of each damage site.

(2) If it appears certain an Affirmative Finding will be made, the DFDE may elect to make these site inspections at the time damage is initially assessed pursuant to paragraph (c) of this section.

(f) The applicant shall make available to FHWA personnel conducting damage survey and estimate work maps depicting designated Federal roads in the affected area.

[43 FR 59485, Dec. 21, 1978, as amended at 47 FR 10529, Mar. 11, 1982]

§ 668.213 Application procedures.

(a) Based on the detailed site inspections and damage estimates prepared pursuant to paragraph (e) of § 668.211, the applicant will submit an application in the form of a letter to the DFDE which shall include a list of projects for which emergency relief is requested. The application shall be submitted within 3 months after an Affirmative Finding.

(b) The list of projects shall include emergency repairs, PE, and permanent work, and provide for each project a location, length, project number, type of damage, description of work with a separate breakdown for betterments including a justification for those intended for emergency relief funding, proposed method of construction, estimated cost, and any other information requested by the DFDE.

(c) If the initial list of projects is incomplete, a subsequent list(s) of projects shall be forwarded to the DFDE for approval consideration as soon as possible.

[43 FR 59485, Dec. 21, 1978, as amended at 47 FR 10529, Mar. 11, 1982]

§ 668.215 Programming and project procedures.

(a) The DFDE will advise the applicant in writing which projects in the application, or in any subsequent submittals pursuant to paragraph (c) of § 668.213 are approved including any approval conditions. Approved projects shall constitute the approved program of projects (program).

(b) Plans, specifications, and estimates (PS&E) shall be developed based on work identified in the approved program.

(c) The DFDE will approve PS&E's, concur in the award of contracts or the rejection of bids, determine that construction by the force account method is in the public interest, and accept completed work in accordance with interagency procedures established by the DFDE.

(d) The applicant shall notify the DFDE in writing of the semi-annual status and completion of each emergency relief project constructed by applicant forces.

[43 FR 59485, Dec. 21, 1978, as amended at 47 FR 10529, Mar. 11, 1982]

PART 669—ENFORCEMENT OF HEAVY VEHICLE USE TAX

Sec.

AUTHORITY: 23 U.S.C. 141(c) and 315; 49 CFR 1.85.

SOURCE: 51 FR 25364, July 14, 1986, unless otherwise noted.

§ 669.1 Scope and purpose.

To prescribe requirements for certification by the states that evidence of proof of payment is obtained either before vehicles subject to the Federal heavy vehicle use tax are lawfully registered or within 4 months after being lawfully registered if a suspension registration system is implemented.

§ 669.3 Policy.

It is the policy of the FHWA that each state require registrants of heavy trucks as described in 26 CFR part 41 to provide proof of payment of the vehicle use tax either before lawfully registering or within 4 months after lawfully registering such vehicles as provided for under a suspension registration system.

§ 669.5 Objective.

The objective of this regulation is to establish realistic and workable procedures for an annual certification process to provide suitable evidence that an effective program is being conducted by the states and to ensure that the states are not registering vehicles which have not been accounted for under the tax collection procedures instituted by the Internal Revenue Service (IRS).

§ 669.7 Certification requirement.

The Governor of each State, or his or her designee, shall certify to the FHWA before January 1 of each year that it is obtaining proof-of-payment of the heavy vehicle use tax as a condition of registration in accordance with 23 U.S.C. 141(c). The certification shall cover the 12-month period ending September 30, except for the certification due on January 1, 2011, which shall cover the 4-month period from June 1, 2010 to September 30, 2010.

[75 FR 43409, July 26, 2010]

§ 669.9 Certification content.

The certification shall consist of the following elements:

(a) A statement by the Governor of the state or a state official designated by the Governor, that evidence of payment of the heavy vehicle use tax is being obtained as a condition of registration for all vehicles subject to such tax. The statement shall include the inclusive dates of the period during which payment of the heavy vehicle use tax was verified as a condition of registration.

(b) The certifying statement required by paragraph (a) of this section shall be worded as follows:

I (name of certifying official), (position, title), of the State of ( ), do hereby certify that evidence of payment of the heavy vehicle use tax pursuant to section 4481 of the Internal Revenue Code of 1954, as amended, is being obtained as a condition of registration for vehicles subject to such tax in accordance with 23 U.S.C. 141(c) and applicable IRS rules. This certification is for the period ( ) to ( ).

(c) For the initial certification, submit a copy of any state law or regulation pertaining to the implementation of 23 U.S.C. 141(c); for subsequent certifications, submit a copy of any new or revised laws and regulations pertaining to the implementation of 23 U.S.C. 141(c).

[51 FR 25364, July 14, 1986, as amended at 75 FR 43409, July 26, 2010]

§ 669.11 Certification submittal.

The Governor or an official designated by the Governor, shall each year submit the certification, including the supporting material specified in § 669.9 to the FHWA Division Administrator prior to January 1.

[51 FR 25364, July 14, 1986, as amended at 75 FR 43409, July 26, 2010]

§ 669.13 Effect of failure to certify or to adequately obtain proof-of-payment.

If a State fails to certify as required by this regulation or if the Secretary of Transportation determines that a State is not adequately obtaining proof-of-payment of the heavy vehicle use tax as a condition of registration notwithstanding the State's certification, Federal-aid highway funds apportioned to the State under 23 U.S.C. 104(b)(1) for the next fiscal year shall be reduced in an amount up to 8 percent as determined by the Secretary.

[81 FR 32230, May 23, 2016]

§ 669.15 Procedure for the reduction of funds.

(a) Each fiscal year, each State determined to be in nonconformity with the requirements of this part will be advised of the funds expected to be withheld from apportionment in accordance with § 669.13 and 23 U.S.C. 141(c), as part of the advance notice of apportionments required under 23 U.S.C. 104(e), normally not later than 90 days prior to final apportionment.

(b) A State that received a notice in accordance with paragraph (a) of this section may within 30 days of its receipt of the advance notice of apportionments, submit documentation showing why it is in conformity with this Part. Documentation shall be submitted to the Federal Highway Administration, 1200 New Jersey Avenue, SE., Washington, DC 20590.

(c) Each fiscal year, each State determined to be in nonconformity with the requirements of this part and 23 U.S.C. 141(c), based on FHWA's final determination, will receive notice of the funds being withheld from apportionment pursuant to section 669.3 and 23 U.S.C. 141(c), as part of the certification of apportionments required under 23 U.S.C. 104(e), which normally occurs on October 1 of each fiscal year.

[75 FR 43409, July 26, 2010]

§ 669.17 Compliance finding.

(a) If, following the conference or review of submitted materials described in § 669.15, the Administrator concludes that the state is in compliance, the Administrator shall issue a decision which is the final decision, and the matter shall be concluded.

(b) If, following the conference or review of information submitted under § 669.15, the Administrator, with the concurrence of the Secretary, concludes that the state is in noncompliance, the Administrator shall issue a decision, which is the final decision, and the matter be concluded. The decision will be served on the Governor, or his/her designee.

§ 669.19 Reservation and reapportionment of funds.

(a) The Administrator may reserve from obligation up to 8 percent of a State's apportionment of funds under 23 U.S.C. 104(b)(1), pending a final determination.

(b) Funds withheld pursuant to a final administrative determination under this regulation shall be reapportioned to all other eligible States pursuant to the formulas of 23 U.S.C. 104(b)(1) and the apportionment factors in effect at the time of the original apportionments, unless the Secretary determines, on the basis of information submitted by the State, that the state has come into conformity with this regulation prior to the final determination. If the Secretary determines that the state has come into conformity, the withheld funds shall be released to the state subject to the availability of such funds under 23 U.S.C. 118(b).

(c) The reapportionment of funds under paragraph (b) of this section shall be stayed during the pendency of any judicial review of the final determination of nonconformity.

[51 FR 25364, July 14, 1986, as amended at 75 FR 43409, July 26, 2010; 81 FR 32230, May 23, 2016]

§ 669.21 Procedure for evaluating state compliance.

The FHWA shall periodically review the State's procedures for complying with 23 U.S.C. 141(c), including an inspection of supporting documentation and records. In those States where a branch office of the State, a local jurisdiction, or a private entity is providing services to register motor vehicles including vehicles subject to HVUT, the State shall be responsible for ensuring that these entities comply with the requirements of this part concerning the collection and retention of evidence of payment of the HVUT as a condition of registration for vehicles subject to such tax and develop adequate procedures to maintain such compliance. The State or other responsible entity shall retain a copy of the receipted IRS Schedule 1 (Form 2290), or an acceptable substitute prescribed by 26 CFR part 41 sec. 41.6001–2 for a period of 1 year for purposes of evaluating State compliance with 23 U.S.C. 141(c) by the FHWA. The State may develop a software system to maintain copies or images of this proof-of-payment.

[75 FR 43409, July 26, 2010]

SUBCHAPTER H—RIGHT-OF-WAY AND ENVIRONMENT

PART 710—RIGHT-OF-WAY AND REAL ESTATE

AUTHORITY: Secs.1302 and 1321, Pub. L. 112–141, 126 Stat. 405. Sec. 1307, Pub. L. 105–178, 112 Stat. 107; 23 U.S.C. 101(a), 107, 108, 111, 114, 133, 142(f), 156, 204, 210, 308, 315, 317, and 323; 42 U.S.C. 2000d *et seq.*, 4633, 4651–4655; 2 CFR 200.311; 49 CFR 1.48(b) and (cc), parts 21 and 24; 23 CFR 1.32.

SOURCE: 64 FR 71290, Dec. 21, 1999, unless otherwise noted.

Subpart A—General

SOURCE: 81 FR 57729, Aug. 23, 2016, unless otherwise noted.

§ 710.101 Purpose.

The primary purpose of the requirements in this part is to ensure the prudent use of Federal funds under title 23, United States Code, in the acquisition, management, and disposal of real property. In addition to the requirements of this part, other real property related provisions apply and are found at 49 CFR part 24.

§ 710.103 Applicability.

(a) This part applies whenever title 23, United States Code, grant funding is used, including when grant funds are expended or participate in project costs incurred by the State or other Title 23 grantee. This part applies to programs and projects administered by the Federal Highway Administration (FHWA) and, unless otherwise stated in this part, to all property purchased with title 23 grant funds or incorporated into a project carried out with grant funding provided under title 23, except property for which the title is vested in the United States upon project completion. Grantees are accountable to FHWA for complying with, and are responsible for ensuring their subgrantees, contractors, and other project partners comply with applicable Federal laws, including this part.

(b) The parties responsible for ROW and real estate activities, and for compliance with applicable Federal requirements, can vary by the nature of the responsibility or the underlying activity. Throughout this part, the FHWA identifies the parties subject to a particular provision through the use of terms of reference defined as set forth in § 710.105. It is important to refer to those definitions, such as "State Department of Transportation

(SDOT)," "grantee," "subgrantee," "State agency" and "acquiring agency," when applying the provisions in this part.

(c) Where title 23 funds are transferred to other Federal agencies to administer, those agencies' ROW and real estate procedures may be utilized. Additional guidance is available electronically at the FHWA Real Estate Services Web site: *http://www.fhwa.dot.gov/realestate/index.htm.*

§ 710.105 Definitions.

(a) Terms defined in 23 U.S.C. 101(a) and 49 CFR part 24 have the same meaning where used in this part, except as modified in this section.

(b) The following terms where used in this part have the following meaning:

Access rights mean the right of ingress to and egress from a property to a public way.

Acquiring agency means a State agency, other entity, or person acquiring real property for title 23, United States Code, purposes. When an acquiring agency acquires real property interests that will be incorporated into a project eligible for title 23 grant funds, the acquiring agency must comply with Federal real estate and ROW requirements applicable to the grant.

Acquisition means activities to obtain an interest in, and possession of, real property.

Damages means the loss in the value attributable to remainder property due to the severance or consequential damages, as limited by State law, that arise when only part of an owner's real property is acquired.

Disposal means the transfer by sale or other conveyance of permanent rights in excess real property, when the real property interest is not currently or in the foreseeable future needed for highway ROW or other uses eligible for funding under title 23 of the United States Code. A disposal must meet the requirements contained in § 710.403(b) of this part. The term "disposal" includes actions by a grantee, or its subgrantees, in the nature of relinquishment, abandonment, vacation, discontinuance, and disclaimer of real property or any rights therein.

Donation means the voluntary transfer of privately owned real property, by a property owner who has been informed in writing by the acquiring agency of rights and benefits available to owners under the Uniform Act and this section, for the benefit of a public transportation project without compensation or with compensation at less than fair market value.

Early acquisition means acquisition of real property interests by an acquiring agency prior to completion of the environmental review process for a proposed transportation project, as provided under 23 CFR 710.501 and 23 U.S.C. 108.

Early Acquisition Project means a project for the acquisition of real property interests prior to the completion of the environmental review process for the transportation project into which the acquired property will be incorporated, as authorized under 23 U.S.C. 108 and implemented under § 710.501 of this part. It may consist of the acquisition of real property interests in a specific parcel, a portion of a transportation corridor, or an entire transportation corridor.

Easement means an interest in real property that conveys a right to use or control a portion of an owner's property or a portion of an owner's rights in the property either temporarily or permanently.

Excess real property means a real property interest not needed currently or in the foreseeable future for transportation purposes or other uses eligible for funding under title 23, United States Code.

Federal-aid project means a project funded in whole or in part under, or requiring an FHWA approval pursuant to provisions in chapter 1 of title 23, United States Code.

Federally assisted means a project or program that receives grant funds under title 23, United States Code.

Grantee means the party that is the direct recipient of title 23 funds and is accountable to FHWA for the use of the funds and for compliance with applicable Federal requirements.

Mitigation property means real property interests acquired to mitigate for impacts of a project eligible for funding under title 23.

Option means the purchase of a right to acquire real property within an agreed-to period of time for an agreed-to amount of compensation or through an agreed-to method by which compensation will be calculated.

Person means any individual, family, partnership, corporation, or association.

Real Estate Acquisition Management Plan (RAMP) means a written document that details how a non-State department of transportation grantee, subgrantee, or design-build contractor will administer the title 23 ROW and real estate requirements for its project or program of projects. The document must be approved by the SDOT, or by the funding agency in the case of a non-SDOT grantee, before any acquisition work may begin. It must lay out in detail how the acquisition and relocation assistance programs will be accomplished and any anticipated issues that may arise during the process. If relocations are reasonably expected as part of the title 23 projects or program, the Real Estate Acquisition Management Plan (RAMP) must address relocation assistance and related procedures.

Real property or *real property interest* means any interest in land and any improvements thereto, including fee and less-than-fee interests such as: temporary and permanent easements, air or access rights, access control, options, and other contractual rights to acquire an interest in land, rights to control use or development, leases, and licenses, and any other similar action to acquire or preserve ROW for a transportation facility. As used in this part, the terms "real property" and "real property interest" are synonymous unless otherwise specified.

Relinquishment means the conveyance of a portion of a highway ROW or facility by a grantee under title 23, United States Code, or its subgrantee, to another government agency for continued transportation use. (See part 620, subpart B of this chapter.)

Right-of-way (ROW) means real property and rights therein obtained for the construction, operation, maintenance, or mitigation of a transportation or related facility funded under title 23, United States Code.

ROW manual means an operations manual that establishes a grantee's acquisition, valuation, relocation, and property management and disposal requirements and procedures, and has been approved in accordance with § 710.201(c).

ROW use agreement means real property interests, defined by an agreement, as evidenced by instruments such as a lease, license, or permit, for use of real property interests for non-highway purposes where the use is in the public interest, consistent with the continued operation, maintenance, and safety of the facility, and such use will not impair the highway or interfere with the free and safe flow of traffic (see also 23 CFR 1.23). These rights may be granted only for a specified period of time because the real property interest may be needed in the future for highway purposes or other purposes eligible for funding under title 23.

Settlement means the result of negotiations based on fair market value in which the amount of just compensation is agreed upon for the purchase of real property or an interest therein. This term includes the following:

(1) An *administrative settlement* is a settlement reached prior to filing a condemnation proceeding based on value related evidence, administrative consideration, or other factors approved by an authorized agency official.

(2) A *legal settlement* is a settlement reached by an authorized legal representative or a responsible official of the acquiring agency who has the legal power vested in him by State law, after filing a condemnation proceeding, including agreements resulting from mediation and stipulated settlements approved by the court in which the condemnation action had been filed.

(3) A *court settlement* or *court award* is any decision by a court that follows a contested trial or hearing before a jury, commission, judge, or other legal entity having the authority to establish the amount of just compensation for a taking under the laws of eminent domain.

State agency means: A department, agency, or instrumentality of a State or of a political subdivision of a State; any department, agency, or instrumentality of two or more States or of two or more political subdivisions of a

State or States; or any person who has the authority to acquire property by eminent domain, for public purposes, under State law.

State department of transportation (SDOT) means the State highway department, transportation department, or other State transportation agency or commission to which title 23, United States Code, funds are apportioned.

Stewardship/Oversight Agreement means the written agreement between the SDOT and FHWA that defines the respective roles and responsibilities of FHWA and the State for carrying out certain project review, approval, and oversight responsibilities under title 23, including those activities specified by 23 U.S.C. 106(c)(3).

Subgrantee means a government agency or legal entity that enters into an agreement with a grantee to carry out part or all of the activity funded by title 23 grant funds. A subgrantee is accountable to the grantee for the use of the funds and for compliance with applicable Federal requirements.

Temporary development restriction means the purchase of a right to temporarily control or restrict development or redevelopment of real property. This right is for an agreed to time period, defines specifically what is restricted or controlled, and is for an agreed to amount of compensation.

Transportation project means any highway project, public transportation capital project, multimodal project, or other project that requires the approval of the Secretary. As used in this part, the term "transportation project" does not include an Early Acquisition Project as defined in this section.

Uneconomic remnant means a remainder property which the acquiring agency has determined has little or no utility or value to the owner.

Uniform Act means the Uniform Relocation Assistance and Real Property Acquisition Policies Act of 1970, as amended (Pub. L. 91–646, 84 Stat. 1894; primarily codified in 42 U.S.C. 4601 *et seq.*), and the implementing regulations at 49 CFR part 24.

Subpart B—Program Administration

SOURCE: 81 FR 57729, Aug. 23, 2016, unless otherwise noted.

§710.201 Grantee and subgrantee responsibilities.

(a) *Program oversight.* States administer the Federal-aid highway program, funded under chapter 1 of title 23, United States Code, through their SDOTs. The SDOT shall have overall responsibility for the acquisition, management, and disposal of real property interests on its Federal-aid projects, including when those projects are carried out by the SDOT's subgrantees or contractors. This responsibility shall include ensuring compliance with the requirements of this part and other Federal laws, including regulations. Non-SDOT grantees of funds under title 23 must comply with the requirements under this part, except as otherwise expressly provided in this part, and are responsible for ensuring compliance by their subgrantees and contractors with the requirements of this part and other Federal laws, including regulations.

(b) *Organization.* Each grantee and subgrantee, including any other acquiring agency acting on behalf of a grantee or subgrantee, shall be adequately staffed, equipped, and organized to discharge its real property related responsibilities.

(c) *ROW manual.* (1) Every grantee must ensure that its title 23-funded projects are carried out using an FHWA-approved and up-to-date ROW manual or RAMP that is consistent with applicable Federal requirements, including the Uniform Act and this part. Each SDOT that receives funding under title 23, United States Code, shall maintain an approved and up-to-date ROW manual describing its ROW organization, policies, and procedures. Non-SDOT grantees may use one of the procedures in paragraph (d) to meet the requirements in this paragraph; however, the ROW manual options can only be used with SDOT approval and permission. The ROW manual shall describe functions and procedures for all phases of the ROW program, including appraisal and appraisal review, waiver valuation, negotiation and eminent domain, property management, relocation assistance, administrative settlements, legal settlements, and oversight of its subgrantees and contractors. The ROW manual shall also specify procedures to prevent conflict of interest and avoid fraud, waste, and abuse. The ROW manual shall be in sufficient detail and depth to guide the grantee, its employees, and others involved in acquiring, managing, and disposing of real property interests. Grantees, subgrantees, and their contractors must comply with current FHWA requirements whether or not the requirements are included in the FHWA-approved ROW manual.

(2) The SDOT's ROW manual must be developed and updated, as a minimum, to meet the following schedule:

(i) The SDOTs shall prepare and submit for approval by FHWA an up-to-date ROW Manual by no later than August 23, 2018.

(ii) Every 5 years thereafter, the chief administrative officer of the SDOT shall certify to the FHWA that the current SDOT ROW manual conforms to existing practices and contains necessary procedures to ensure compliance with Federal and State real estate law and regulation, including this part.

(iii) The SDOT shall update its ROW manual periodically to reflect changes in operations and submit the updated materials for approval by the FHWA.

(d) *ROW manual alternatives.* Non-SDOT grantees, and all subgrantees, design-build contractors, and other acquiring agencies carrying out a project funded by a grant under title 23, United States Code, must demonstrate that they will use FHWA-approved ROW procedures for acquisition and other real estate activities, and that they have the ability to comply with current FHWA requirements, including this part. This can be done through any of the following methods:

(1) Certification in writing that the acquiring agency will adopt and use the FHWA-approved SDOT ROW manual;

(2) Submission of the acquiring agency's own ROW manual to the grantee for review and determination whether it complies with Federal and State requirements, together with a certification that once the reviewing agency approves the manual, the acquiring agency will use the approved ROW manual; or

(3)(i) Submission of a RAMP setting forth the procedures the acquiring agency or design-build contractor intends to follow for a specified project or group of projects, along with a certification that if the reviewing agency approves the RAMP, the acquiring agency or design-build contractor will follow the approved RAMP for the specified program or project(s). The use of a RAMP is appropriate for a subgrantee, non-SDOT grantee, or design-build contractor if that party infrequently carries out title 23 programs or projects, the program or project is non-controversial, and the project is not complex.

(ii) Subgrantees, design-build contractors, and other acquiring agencies carrying out a project for an SDOT submit the required certification and information to the SDOT, and the SDOT will review and make a determination on behalf of FHWA. Non-SDOT grantees submit the required certification and information directly to FHWA. Non-SDOT grantees are responsible for submitting to FHWA the required certification and information for any subgrantee, contractor, and other acquiring agency carrying out a project for the non-SDOT grantee.

(e) *Record keeping.* The acquiring agency shall maintain adequate records of its acquisition and property management activities.

(1) Acquisition records, including records related to owner or tenant displacements, and property inventories of improvements acquired shall be in sufficient detail to demonstrate compliance with this part and 49 CFR part 24. These records shall be retained at least 3 years from the later of either:

(i) The date the SDOT or other grantee receives Federal reimbursement of the final payment made to each owner of a property and to each person displaced from a property; or

(ii) The date of reimbursement for early acquisitions or credit toward the State share of a project is approved based on early acquisition activities under § 710.501.

(2) Property management records shall include inventories of real property interests considered excess to project or program needs, as well as all authorized ROW use agreements for real property acquired with title 23 funds or incorporated into a program or project that received title 23 funding.

(f) *Procurement.* Contracting for all activities required in support of an SDOT's or other grantee's ROW projects or programs through the use of private consultants and other services shall conform to 2 CFR 200.317, except to the extent that the procurement is required to adhere to requirements under 23 U.S.C. 112(b)(2) and 23 CFR part 172 for engineering and design related consultant services.

(g) *Use of other public land acquisition organizations, conservation organizations, or private consultants.* The grantee may enter into written agreements with other State, county, municipal, or local public land acquisition organizations, conservation organizations, private consultants, or other persons to carry out its authorities under this part. Such organizations, firms, or persons must comply with the grantee's ROW manual or RAMP as approved in accordance with paragraphs (c) or (d) of this section. The grantee shall monitor any such real property interest acquisition activities to ensure compliance with State and Federal law, and is responsible for informing such persons of all such requirements and for imposing sanctions in cases of material noncompliance.

(h) *Assignment of FHWA approval actions to an SDOT.* The SDOT and FHWA will agree in their Stewardship/Oversight Agreement on the scope of property-related oversight and approvals under this part that will be performed directly by FHWA and those that FHWA will assign to the SDOT. This assignment provision does not apply to other grantees of title 23 funds. The content of the most recent Stewardship/Oversight Agreement shall be reflected in the FHWA-approved SDOT ROW manual. The agreement, and thus the SDOT ROW manual, will indicate which Federal-aid projects require submission of materials for FHWA review and approval. The FHWA retains responsibility for any approval action not expressly assigned to the SDOT in the Stewardship/Oversight Agreement.

§ 710.203 Title 23 funding and reimbursement.

(a) *General conditions.* Except as otherwise provided in § 710.501 for early acquisition, a State agency only may acquire real property, including mitigation property, with title 23 grant funds if the following conditions are satisfied:

(1) The project for which the real property is acquired is included in an approved Statewide Transportation Improvement Program (STIP);

(2) The grantee has executed a project agreement or other agreement recognized under title 23 reflecting the Federal funding terms and conditions for the project;

(3) Preliminary acquisition activities, including a title search, appraisal, appraisal review and waiver valuation preparation, preliminary property map preparation and preliminary relocation planning activities, limited to searching for comparable properties, identifying replacement neighborhoods and identifying available public services, can be advanced under preliminary engineering, as defined in § 646.204 of this chapter, prior to completion of the National Environmental Policy Act (NEPA) (42 U.S.C. 4321, *et seq.*) review, while other work involving contact with affected property owners for purposes of negotiation and relocation assistance must normally be deferred until after NEPA approval, except as provided in § 710.501, early acquisition; and in § 710.503 for protective buying and hardship acquisition; and

(4) Costs have been incurred in conformance with State and Federal requirements.

(b) *Direct eligible costs.* Federal funds may only participate in direct costs that are identified specifically as an authorized acquisition activity such as the costs of acquiring the real property incorporated into the final project and the associated direct costs of acquisition, except in the case of a State that has an approved indirect cost allocation plan as stated in § 710.203(d) or specifically provided by statute. Participation is provided for:

(1) *Real property acquisition.* Usual costs and disbursements associated with real property acquisition as required under the laws of the State, including the following:

(i) The cost of contracting for private acquisition services or the cost associated with the use of local public agencies;

(ii) Ordinary and reasonable costs of acquisition activities, such as, appraisal, waiver valuation development, appraisal review, cost estimates, relocation planning, ROW plan preparation, title work, and similar necessary ROW related work;

(iii) The compensation paid for the real property interest and costs normally associated with completing the purchase, such as document fees and document stamps. The costs of acquiring options and other contractual rights to acquire an interest in land, rights to control use or development, leases, ROWs, and any other similar action to acquire or preserve rights-of way for a transportation facility are eligible costs when FHWA determines such costs are actual, reasonable and necessary costs. Costs under this paragraph do not include salary and related expenses for an acquiring agency's employees (see payroll-related expenses in paragraph (b)(5) of this section);

(iv) The cost of administrative settlements in accordance with 49 CFR 24.102(i), legal settlements, court awards, and costs incidental to the condemnation process. This includes reasonable acquiring agency attorney's fees, but excludes attorney's fees for other parties except where required by State law (including an order of a court of competent jurisdiction) or approved by FHWA;

(v) The cost of minimum payments and waiver valuation amounts included in the approved ROW manual or approved RAMP; and

(vi) Ordinary and reasonable costs associated with closing, and costs of finalizing the acquisition.

(2) *Relocation assistance and payments.* Usual costs and disbursements associated with the following:

(i) Relocation assistance and payments required under 49 CFR part 24; and

(ii) Relocation assistance and payments provided under the laws of the State that may exceed the requirements of 49 CFR part 24, except for relocation assistance and payments provided to aliens not lawfully present in the United States.

(3) *Damages.* The cost of severance and/or consequential damages to remaining real property resulting from a partial acquisition, actual or constructive, of real property for a project based on elements compensable under State law.

(4) *Property management.* The net cost of managing real property prior to and during construction to provide for maintenance, protection, and the clearance and disposal of improvements until final project acceptance.

(5) *Payroll-related expenses.* Salary and related expenses (compensation for personal services) of employees of an acquiring agency for work on a project funded by a title 23 grant are eligible costs in accordance with 2 CFR part 225 (formerly OMB Circular A–87), as are salary and related expenses of a grantee's employees for work with an acquiring agency or a contractor to ensure compliance with Federal requirements on a title 23 project if the work is dedicated to a specific project and documented in accordance with 2 CFR part 225.

(6) *Property not incorporated into a project funded under title 23, United States Code.* The cost of property not incorporated into a project may be eligible for reimbursement in the following circumstances:

(i) *General.* Costs for construction material sites, property acquisitions to a logical boundary, eligible Transportation Alternatives (TA) projects, sites for disposal of hazardous materials, environmental mitigation, environmental banking activities, or last resort housing; and

(ii) *Easements and alternate access not incorporated into the ROW.* The cost of acquiring easements and alternate access points necessary for highway construction and maintenance outside the approved ROW limits for permanent or temporary use.

(7) *Uneconomic remnants.* The cost of uneconomic remnants purchased in connection with the acquisition of a

partial taking for the project as required by the Uniform Act.

(8) *Access rights.* Payment for full or partial control of access on an existing road or highway (*i.e.*, one not on a new location), based on elements compensable under applicable State law. Participation does not depend on another real property interest being acquired or on further construction of the highway facility.

(9) *Utility and railroad property.* (i) The cost to replace operating real property owned by a displaced utility or railroad and conveyed to an acquiring agency for a project, as provided in 23 CFR part 140, subpart I, Reimbursement for Railroad Work, and 23 CFR part 645, subpart A, Utility Relocations, Adjustments and Reimbursement, and 23 CFR part 646, subpart B, Railroad-Highway Projects; and

(ii) Participation in the cost of acquiring non-operating utility or railroad real property shall be in the same manner as that used in the acquisition of other privately owned property.

(c) *Withholding payment.* The FHWA may withhold payment under the conditions described in 23 CFR 1.36 for failure to comply with Federal law or regulation, State law, or under circumstances of waste, fraud, and abuse.

(d) *Indirect costs.* Indirect costs may be claimed under the provisions of 2 CFR part 225 (formerly OMB Circular A–87). Indirect costs may be included on billings after the indirect cost allocation plan has been prepared in accordance with 2 CFR part 225 and approved by FHWA, other cognizant Federal agency, or, in the case of an SDOT subgrantee without a rate approved by a cognizant Federal agency, by the SDOT. Indirect costs for an SDOT may include costs of providing program-level guidance, consultation, and oversight to other acquiring agencies and contractors where ROW activities on title 23-funded projects are performed by non-SDOT personnel.

Subpart C—Project Development

SOURCE: 81 FR 57729, Aug. 23, 2016, unless otherwise noted.

§710.301 General.

The project development process typically follows a sequence of actions and approvals in order to qualify for funding. The key steps in this process typically are planning, environmental review, project agreement/authorization, acquisition, construction advertising, and construction.

§710.303 Project authorization and agreements.

As a condition of Federal funding under title 23, the grantee shall obtain FHWA authorization in writing or electronically before proceeding with any real property acquisition using title 23 funds, including early acquisitions under §710.501(e) and hardship acquisition and protective buying under §710.503. For projects funded under chapter 1, title 23, United States Code, the grantee must prepare a project agreement in accordance with 23 CFR part 630, subpart A. Authorizations and agreements shall be based on an acceptable estimate for the cost of acquisition.

§710.305 Acquisition.

(a) *General.* The process of acquiring real property includes appraisal, appraisal review, waiver valuations, establishing estimates of just compensation, negotiations, relocation assistance, administrative and legal settlements, and court settlements and condemnations. Grantees must ensure all acquisition and related relocation assistance activities are performed in accordance with 49 CFR part 24 and this part. If a grantee does not directly own the real property interests used for a title 23 project, the grantee must have an enforceable subgrant agreement or other agreement with the owner of the ROW that permits the grantee to enforce applicable Federal requirements affecting the real property interests, including real property management requirements under subpart D of this part.

(b) *Adequacy of real property interest.* The real property interests acquired for any project funded under title 23 must be adequate to fulfill the purpose of the project. Except in the case of an Early Acquisition Project, this means adequate for the construction, operation, and maintenance of the resulting facility, and for the protection of both the facility and the traveling public.

(c) *Establishment and offer of just compensation.* The amount believed to be just compensation shall be approved by a responsible official of the acquiring agency. This shall be done in accordance with 49 CFR 24.102(d).

(d) *Description of acquisition process.* The acquiring agency shall provide persons affected by projects or acquisitions advanced under title 23 of the United States Code with a written description of its real property acquisition process under State law and this part, and of the owner's rights, privileges, and obligations. The description shall be written in clear, non-technical language and, where appropriate, be available in a language other than English in accordance with 49 CFR 24.5, 24.102(b), and 24.203.

§ 710.307 Construction advertising.

(a) The grantee must manage real property acquired for a project until it is required for construction. Except for properties acquired under the early acquisition provisions of 23 CFR 710.501(e), clearance of improvements can be scheduled during the acquisition phase of the project using sale/removal agreements, separate demolition contracts, or be included as a work item in the construction contract. The grantee shall develop ROW availability statements and certifications related to project acquisitions as described in 23 CFR 635.309.

(b) The FHWA–SDOT Stewardship/Oversight Agreement will specify SDOT responsibility for the review and approval of the ROW availability statements and certifications in accordance with applicable law. Generally, for non-National Highway System projects, the SDOT has full responsibility for determining that right-of-way is available for construction. For non-SDOT grantees, FHWA will be responsible for the review and approval.

§ 710.309 Design-build projects.

(a) In the case of a design-build project, ROW must be acquired and cleared in accordance with the Uniform Act and the FHWA-approved ROW manual or RAMP, as provided in § 710.201(c) and (d). The grantee shall submit a ROW certification in accordance with 23 CFR 635.309(p) when requesting FHWA's authorization. The grantee shall ensure that ROW is available prior to the start of physical construction on individual properties.

(b) The decision to advance a ROW segment to the construction stage shall not impair the safety or in any way be coercive in the context of 49 CFR 24.102(h) with respect to unacquired or occupied properties on the same or adjacent segments of project ROW.

(c) The grantee may choose not to allow construction to commence until all property is acquired and relocations have been completed; or, the grantee may permit the construction to be phased or segmented to allow ROW activities to be completed on individual properties or a group of properties, with ROW certifications done in a manner satisfactory to the grantee for each phase or segment.

(d) If the grantee elects to include ROW services within the design-builder's scope of work for the design-build contract, the following provisions must be addressed in the request for proposals document:

(1) The design-builder must submit written certification in its proposal that it will comply with the process and procedures in the FHWA-approved ROW manual or RAMP as provided in § 710.201(c) and (d).

(2) When relocation of displaced persons from their dwellings has not been completed, the grantee or design-builder shall establish a hold off zone around all occupied properties to ensure compliance with ROW procedures prior to starting construction activities in affected areas. The limits of this zone should be established by the grantee prior to the design-builder entering onto the property. There should be no construction-related activity within the hold off zone until the property is vacated. The design-builder must have written notification of vacancy from the grantee prior to entering the hold off zone.

(3) Contractors activities must be limited to those that the grantee determines do not have a material adverse impact on the quality of life of those in occupied properties that have been or will be acquired.

(4) The grantee will provide a ROW project manager who will serve as the first point of contact for all ROW issues.

(e) If the grantee elects to perform all ROW services relating to the design-build contract, the provisions in §710.307 will apply. The grantee will notify potential offerors of the status of all ROW issues in the request for proposal document.

Subpart D—Real Property Management

SOURCE: 81 FR 57729, Aug. 23, 2016, unless otherwise noted.

§710.401 General.

This subpart describes the grantee's responsibilities to control the use of real property acquired for a project in which Federal funds participated in any phase of the project. The grantee shall specify in its approved ROW manual or RAMP, the procedures for the maintenance, ROW use agreements, and disposal of real property interests acquired with title 23 funds. The grantee shall ensure that subgrantees, including local agencies, follow Federal requirements and approved ROW procedures as provided in §710.201(c) and (d).

§710.403 Management.

(a) As provided in §710.201(h), FHWA and SDOT may use their Stewardship/Oversight Agreement to enter into a written agreement establishing which approvals the SDOT may make on behalf of FHWA, provided FHWA may not assign to the SDOT the decision to allow any ROW use agreement or any disposal on or within the approved ROW limits of the Interstate, including any change in access control. The assignment agreement provisions in §710.201(h) and this paragraph do not apply to non-SDOT grantees.

(b) The grantee must ensure that all real property interests within the approved ROW limits or other project limits of a facility that has been funded under title 23 are devoted exclusively to the purposes of that facility and the facility is preserved free of all other public or private alternative uses, unless such non-highway alternative uses are permitted by Federal law (including regulations) or the FHWA. An alternative use, whether temporary under §710.405 or permanent as provided in §710.409, must be in the public interest, consistent with the continued operation, maintenance, and safety of the facility, and such use must not impair the highway or interfere with the free and safe flow of traffic (see also 23 CFR 1.23). Park and Ride lots are exempted from the provisions of this part. Park and Ride lots requirements are found 23 U.S.C. 137 and 23 CFR 810.106.

(c) Grantees shall specify procedures in their approved ROW manual or RAMP for determining when a real property interest is excess real property and may be disposed of in accordance with this part. These procedures must provide for coordination among relevant State organizational units that may be interested in the proposed use or disposal of the real property. Grantees also shall specify procedures in their ROW manual or RAMP for determining when a real property interest is excess and when a real property interest may be made available under a ROW use agreement for an alternative use that satisfies the requirements described in paragraph (b) of this section.

(d) Disposal actions and ROW use agreements, including leasing actions, are subject to 23 CFR part 771.

(e) Current fair market value must be charged for the use or disposal of all real property interests if those real property interests were obtained with title 23, United States Code, funding except as provided in paragraphs (e)(1) through (6) of this section. The term fair market value as used for acquisition and disposal purposes is as defined by State statute and/or State court decisions. Exceptions to the requirement for charging fair market value must be submitted to FHWA in writing and may be approved by FHWA in the following situations:

(1) When the grantee shows that an exception is in the overall public interest based on social, environmental, or

economic benefits, or is for a non-proprietary governmental use. The grantee's ROW manual or RAMP must include criteria for evaluating disposals at less than fair market value, and a method for ensuring the public will receive the benefit used to justify the less than fair market value disposal.

(2) Use by public utilities in accordance with 23 CFR part 645.

(3) Use by railroads in accordance with 23 CFR part 646.

(4) Use for bikeways and pedestrian walkways in accordance with 23 CFR part 652.

(5) Uses under 23 U.S.C. 142(f), Public Transportation. Lands and ROWs of a highway constructed using Federal-aid highway funds may be made available without charge to a publicly owned mass transit authority for public transit purposes whenever the public interest will be served, and where this can be accomplished without impairing automotive safety or future highway improvements.

(6) Use for other transportation projects eligible for assistance under title 23 of the United States Code, provided that a concession agreement, as defined in § 710.703, shall not constitute a transportation project exempt from fair market value requirements.

(f) The Federal share of net income from the use or disposal of real property interests obtained with title 23 funds shall be used by the grantee for activities eligible for funding under title 23. Where project income derived from the use or disposal of real property interests is used for subsequent title 23-eligible projects, the funds are not considered Federal financial assistance and use of the income does not cause title 23 requirements to apply.

§ 710.405 ROW use agreements.

(a) A ROW use agreement for the non-highway use of real property interests may be executed with a public entity or private party in accordance with § 710.403 and this section. Any non-highway alternative use of real property interests requires approval by FHWA, including a determination by FHWA that such occupancy, use, or reservation is in the public interest; is consistent with the continued use, operations, maintenance, and safety of the facility; and such use does not impair the highway or interfere with the free and safe flow of traffic as described in § 710.403(b). Except for Interstate Highways, where the SDOT controls the real property interest, the FHWA may assign its determination and approval responsibilities to the SDOT in their Stewardship/Oversight Agreement.

(1) This section applies to highways as defined in 23 U.S.C. 101(a) that received title 23, United States Code, financial assistance in any way.

(2) This section does not apply to the following:

(i) Uses by railroads and public utilities which cross or otherwise occupy Federal-aid highway ROW and that are governed by other sections of this title;

(ii) Relocations of railroads or utilities for which reimbursement is claimed under 23 CFR part 140, subparts E and H, 23 CFR part 645, or 23 CFR part 646, subpart B; and

(iii) Bikeways and pedestrian walkways as covered in 23 CFR part 652.

(b) Subject to the requirements in this subpart, ROW use agreements for a time-limited occupancy or use of real property interests may be approved if the grantee has acquired sufficient legal right, title, and interest in the ROW of a federally assisted highway to permit the non-highway use. A ROW use agreement must contain provisions that address the following items:

(1) Ensure the safety and integrity of the federally assisted facility;

(2) Define the term of the agreement;

(3) Identify the design and location of the non-highway use;

(4) Establish terms for revocation of the ROW use agreement and removal of improvements at no cost to the FHWA;

(5) Provide for adequate insurance to hold the grantee and the FHWA harmless;

(6) Require compliance with nondiscrimination requirements;

(7) Require grantee and FHWA approval, if not assigned to SDOT, and SDOT approval if the agreement affects a Federal-aid highway and the SDOT is not the grantee, for any significant revision in the design, construction, or operation of the non-highway use; and

(8) Grant access to the non-highway use by the grantee and FHWA, and the SDOT if the agreement affects a Federal-aid highway and the SDOT is not the grantee, for inspection, maintenance, and for activities needed for reconstruction of the highway facility.

(9) Additional terms and conditions appropriate for inclusion in ROW use agreements are described in FHWA guidance at *http://www.fhwa.dot.gov/real_estate/right-of-way/corridor_management/airspace_guidelines.cfm.* The terms and conditions listed in the guidance are not mandatory requirements.

(c) Where a proposed use requires changes in the existing highway, such changes shall be provided without cost to Federal funds unless otherwise specifically agreed to by the grantee and FHWA.

(d) Proposed uses of real property interests shall conform to the current design standards and safety criteria of FHWA for the functional classification of the highway facility in which the property is located.

(e) An individual, company, organization, or public agency desiring to use real property interests shall submit a written request to the grantee, together with an application supporting the proposal. If FHWA is the approving authority, the grantee shall forward the request, application, and the SDOT's recommendation if the proposal affects a Federal-aid highway, and the proposed ROW use agreement, together with its recommendation and any necessary supplemental information, to FHWA. The submission shall affirmatively provide for adherence to all requirements contained in this subpart and must include the following information:

(1) Identification of the party responsible for developing and operating the proposed use;

(2) A general statement of the proposed use;

(3) A description of why the proposed use would be in the public interest;

(4) Information demonstrating the proposed use would not impair the highway or interfere with the free and safe flow of traffic;

(5) The proposed design for the use of the space, including any facilities to be constructed;

(6) Maps, plans, or sketches to adequately demonstrate the relationship of the proposed project to the highway facility;

(7) Provision for vertical and horizontal access for maintenance purposes;

(8) A description of other general provisions such as the term of use, insurance requirements, design limitations, safety mandates, accessibility, and maintenance as outlined further in this section; and

(9) An adequately detailed three-dimensional presentation of the space to be used and the facility to be constructed if required by FHWA or the grantor. Maps and plans may not be required if the available real property interest is to be used for leisure activities (such as walking or biking), beautification, parking of motor vehicles, public mass transit facilities, and similar uses. In such cases, an acceptable metes and bounds description of the surface area, and appropriate plans or cross sections clearly defining the vertical use limits, may be furnished in lieu of a three-dimensional description, at the grantee's discretion.

§710.407 [Reserved]

§710.409 Disposal of excess real property.

(a) Excess real property outside or within the approved right-of-way limits or other project limits may be sold or conveyed to a public entity or to a private party in accordance with §710.403(a), (c), (d), (e), (f) and this section. Approval by FHWA is required for disposal of excess real property unless otherwise provided in this section or in the FHWA–SDOT Stewardship/Oversight Agreement.

(b) Federal, State, and local agencies shall be afforded the opportunity to acquire excess real property considered for disposal when such real property interests have potential use for parks, conservation, recreation, or related purposes, and when such a transfer is allowed by State law. When this potential exists, the grantee shall notify the appropriate agencies of its intentions to dispose of the real property interests determined to be excess.

(c) The grantee may decide to retain excess real property to restore, preserve, or improve the scenic beauty and environmental quality adjacent to the transportation facility.

(d) Where the transfer of excess real property to other agencies at less than fair market value for continued public use is clearly justified as in the public interest and approved by FHWA under § 710.403(e), the deed shall provide for reversion of the property for failure to continue public ownership and use. Where property is sold at fair market value, no reversion clause is required.

(e) No FHWA approval is required for disposal of excess real property located outside of the approved ROW limits or other project limits if Federal funds did not participate in the acquisition cost of the real property.

(f) Highway facilities in which Federal funds participated in either the ROW or construction may be relinquished to another governmental agency for continued highway use under the provisions of 23 CFR part 620, subpart B.

(g) A request for approval of a disposal must demonstrate compliance with the requirements of § 710.403(a), (c), (d), (e), (f) and this section. An individual, company, organization, or public agency requesting a grantee to approve of a disposal of excess real property within the approved ROW limits or other project limits, or to approve of a disposal of excess real property outside the ROW limits that was acquired with title 23 of the United States Code funding, shall submit a written request to the grantee, together with an application supporting the proposal. If the FHWA is the approving authority, the grantee shall forward the request, the SDOT recommendation if the proposal affects a Federal-aid highway, the application, and proposed terms and conditions, together with its recommendation and any necessary supplemental information, to FHWA. The submission shall affirmatively provide for adherence to requirements contained in this section and must include the information specified in § 710.405(e)(1) through (9).

Subpart E—Property Acquisition Alternatives

SOURCE: 81 FR 57729, Aug. 23, 2016, unless otherwise noted.

§ 710.501 Early acquisition.

(a) *General.* A State agency may initiate acquisition of real property interests for a proposed transportation project at any time it has the legal authority to do so. The State agency may undertake Early Acquisition Projects before the completion of the environmental review process for the proposed transportation project for corridor preservation, access management, or other purposes. Subject to the requirements in this section, State agencies may fund Early Acquisition Project costs entirely with State funds with no title 23 participation; use State funds initially but seek title 23 credit or reimbursement when the acquired property is incorporated into a transportation project eligible for Federal surface transportation program funds; or use the normal Federal-aid project agreement and reimbursement process to fund an Early Acquisition Project pursuant to paragraph (e) of this section. The early acquisition of a real property interest under this section shall be carried out in compliance with all requirements applicable to the acquisition of real property interests for federally assisted transportation projects.

(b) *State-funded early acquisition without Federal credit or reimbursement.* A State agency may carry out early acquisition entirely at its expense and later incorporate the acquired real property into a transportation project or program for which the State agency receives Federal financial assistance or other Federal approval under title 23 for other transportation project activities. In order to maintain eligibility for future Federal assistance on the project, early acquisition activities funded entirely without Federal participation must comply with the requirements of § 710.501(c)(1) through (5).

(c) *State-funded early acquisition eligible for future credit.* Subject to § 710.203(b) (direct eligible costs), § 710.505(b), and § 710.507 (State and local contributions), Early Acquisition

Project costs incurred by a State agency at its own expense prior to completion of the environmental review process for a proposed transportation project are eligible for use as a credit toward the non-Federal share of the total project costs if the project receives surface transportation program funds, and if the following conditions are met:

(1) The property was lawfully obtained by the State agency;

(2) The property was not land described in 23 U.S.C. 138;

(3) The property was acquired, and any relocations were carried out, in accordance with the provisions of the Uniform Act and regulations in 49 CFR part 24;

(4) The State agency complied with the requirements of title VI of the Civil Rights Act of 1964 (42 U.S.C. 2000d–2000d-4);

(5) The State agency determined, and FHWA concurred, the early acquisition did not influence the environmental review process for the proposed transportation project, including:

(i) The decision on need to construct the proposed transportation project;

(ii) The consideration of any alternatives for the proposed transportation project required by applicable law; and

(iii) The selection of the design or location for the proposed transportation project; and

(6) The property will be incorporated into the project for which surface transportation program funds are received and to which the credit will be applied.

(d) *State-funded early acquisition eligible for future reimbursement.* Early Acquisition Project costs incurred by a State agency prior to completion of the environmental review process for the transportation project are eligible for reimbursement from title 23 funds apportioned to the State once the real property interests are incorporated into a project eligible for surface transportation program funds if the State agency demonstrates, and FHWA concurs, that the terms and conditions specified in the requirements of §710.501(c)(1) through (5), and the requirements of §710.203(b) (direct eligible costs) have been met. The State agency must demonstrate that it has met the following requirements, as set forth in 23 U.S.C. 108(c)(3):

(1) Any land acquired, and relocation assistance provided, complied with the Uniform Act;

(2) The requirements of title VI of the Civil Rights Act of 1964 have been complied with;

(3) The State has a mandatory comprehensive and coordinated land use, environment, and transportation planning process under State law and the acquisition is certified by the Governor as consistent with the State plans before the acquisition;

(4) The acquisition is determined in advance by the Governor to be consistent with the State transportation planning process pursuant to 23 U.S.C. 135;

(5) The alternative for which the real property interest is acquired is selected by the State pursuant to regulations issued by the Secretary which provide for the consideration of the environmental impacts of various alternatives;

(6) Before the time that the cost incurred by a State is approved for Federal participation, environmental compliance pursuant to the National Environmental Policy Act has been completed for the project for which the real property interest was acquired by the State, and the acquisition has been approved by the Secretary under this Act, and in compliance with section 303 of title 49, section 7 of the Endangered Species Act, and all other applicable environmental laws that shall be identified by the Secretary in regulations; and

(7) Before the time that the cost incurred by a State is approved for Federal participation, the Secretary has determined that the property acquired in advance of Federal approval or authorization did not influence the environmental assessment of the project, the decision relative to the need to construct the project, or the selection of the project design or location.

(e) *Federally funded early acquisition.* The FHWA may authorize the use of funds apportioned to a State under title 23 for an Early Acquisition Project if the State agency certifies, and FHWA concurs, that all of the following conditions have been met:

(1) The State has authority to acquire the real property interest under State law; and

(2) The acquisition of the real property interest—

(i) Is for a transportation project or program eligible for funding under title 23 that will not require FHWA approval under 23 CFR 774.3;

(ii) Will not cause any significant adverse environmental impacts either as a result of the Early Acquisition Project or from cumulative effects of multiple Early Acquisition Projects carried out under this section in connection with a proposed transportation project;

(iii) Will not limit the choice of reasonable alternatives for a proposed transportation project or otherwise influence the decision of FHWA on any approval required for a proposed transportation project;

(iv) Will not prevent the lead agency from making an impartial decision as to whether to accept an alternative that is being considered in the environmental review process for a proposed transportation project;

(v) Is consistent with the State transportation planning process under 23 U.S.C. 135;

(vi) Complies with other applicable Federal laws (including regulations);

(vii) Will be acquired through negotiation, without the threat of, or use of, condemnation; and

(viii) Will not result in a reduction or elimination of benefits or assistance to a displaced person required by the Uniform Act and title VI of the Civil Rights Act of 1964 (42 U.S.C. 2000d *et seq.*).

(3) The Early Acquisition Project is included as a project in an applicable transportation improvement program under 23 U.S.C. 134 and 135 and 49 U.S.C. 5303 and 5304.

(4) The environmental review process for the Early Acquisition Project is complete and FHWA has approved the Early Acquisition Project. Pursuant to 23 U.S.C. 108(d)(4)(B), the Early Acquisition Project is deemed to have independent utility for purposes of the environmental review process under NEPA. When the Early Acquisition Project may result in a change to the use or character of the real property interest prior to the completion of the environmental review process for the proposed transportation project, the NEPA evaluation for the Early Acquisition Project must consider whether the change has the potential to cause a significant environmental impact as defined in 40 CFR 1508.27, including a significant adverse impact within the meaning of paragraph (e)(2)(ii) of this section. The Early Acquisition Project must comply with all applicable environmental laws.

(f) *Prohibited activities.* Except as provided in this paragraph, real property interests acquired under paragraph (e) of this section and pursuant to 23 U.S.C. 108(d) cannot be developed in anticipation of a transportation project until all required environmental reviews for the transportation project have been completed. For the purpose of this paragraph, "development in anticipation of a transportation project" means any activity related to demolition, site preparation, or construction that is not necessary to protect public health or safety. With prior FHWA approval, a State agency may carry out limited activities necessary for securing real property interests acquired as part of an Early Acquisition Project, such as limited clearing and demolition activity, if the activities are necessary to protect the public health or safety and are considered during the environmental review of the Early Acquisition Project.

(g) *Reimbursement.* If Federal-aid reimbursement is made for real property interests acquired early under this section and the real property interests are not subsequently incorporated into a project eligible for surface transportation funds within the time allowed by 23 U.S.C. 108 (a)(2), FHWA must offset the amount reimbursed against funds apportioned to the State.

(h) *Relocation assistance eligibility.* In the case of an Early Acquisition Project, a person is considered to be displaced when required to move from the real property as a direct result of a binding written agreement for the purchase of the real property interest(s) between the acquiring agency and the property owner. Options to purchase and similar agreements used for Early

Acquisition Projects that give the acquiring agency a right to prevent new development or to decide in the future whether to acquire the real property interest(s), but do not create an immediate commitment by the acquiring agency to acquire and do not require an owner or tenant to relocate, do not create relocation eligibility until the acquiring agency legally commits itself to acquiring the real property interest(s).

§710.503 Protective buying and hardship acquisition.

(a) *General conditions.* Prior to final environmental approval of a transportation project, the grantee may request FHWA agreement to provide reimbursement for advance acquisition of a particular parcel or a limited number of parcels, to prevent imminent development and increased costs on the preferred location (Protective Buying), or to alleviate hardship to a property owner or owners on the preferred location (Hardship Acquisition), provided the following conditions are met:

(1) The transportation project is included in the currently approved STIP;

(2) The grantee has complied with applicable public involvement requirements in 23 CFR parts 450 and 771;

(3) A determination has been completed for any property interest subject to the provisions of 23 U.S.C. 138; and

(4) Procedures of the Advisory Council on Historic Preservation are completed for properties subject to (54 U.S.C. 306108), (historic properties).

(b) *Protective buying.* The grantee must clearly demonstrate that development of the property is imminent and such development would limit future transportation choices. A significant increase in cost may be considered as an element justifying a protective purchase.

(c) *Hardship acquisitions.* The grantee must accept and concur in an owner's request for a hardship acquisition based on a property owner's written submission that—

(1) Supports the hardship acquisition by providing justification, on the basis of health, safety or financial reasons, that remaining in the property poses an undue hardship compared to other property owners; and

(2) Documents an inability to sell the property because of the impending project, at fair market value, within a time period that is typical for properties not impacted by the impending project.

(d) *Environmental decisions.* Acquisition of property under this section is subject to environmental review under part 771 of this chapter. Acquisitions under this section shall not influence the environmental review of a transportation project which would use the property, including decisions about the need to construct the transportation project or the selection of an alternative.

§710.505 Real property donations.

(a) *Donations of property being acquired.* A non-governmental owner whose real property is required for a title 23 project may donate the property. Donations may be made at any time during the development of a project subject to applicable State laws. Prior to accepting the property, the owner must be informed in writing by the acquiring agency of his/her right to receive just compensation for the property, the right to an appraisal or waiver valuation of the real property, and of all other applicable financial and non-financial assistance provided under 49 CFR part 24 and applicable State law. All donations of property received prior to the approval of the NEPA document for the project must meet the requirements specified in 23 U.S.C. 323(d).

(b) *Credit for donations.* Donations of real property may be credited to the State's matching share of the project in accordance with 23 U.S.C. 323. As required by 23 U.S.C. 323(b)(2), credit to the State's matching share for donated property shall be based on fair market value established on the earlier of the following: Either the date on which the donation becomes effective, or the date on which equitable title to the property vests in the State. The fair market value shall not include increases or decreases in value caused by the project. The grantee shall ensure sufficient documentation is developed to indicate compliance with paragraph (a) of this section and with the provisions of 23 U.S.C. 323, and to support the amount of credit applied. The total credit cannot exceed the State's pro-rata share under the project agreement to which it is applied.

(c) *Donations and conveyances in exchange for construction features or services.* A property owner may donate property in exchange for construction features or services. The value of the donation is limited to the fair market value of property donated less the cost of the construction features or services. If the value of the donated property exceeds the cost of the construction features or services, the difference may be eligible for a credit to the State's share of project costs.

§ 710.507 State and local contributions.

(a) *Credit for State and local government contributions.* If the requirements of 23 U.S.C. 323 are met, real property owned by State and local governments that is incorporated within a project receiving financial assistance from the Highway Trust Fund can be used as a credit toward the grantee or subgrantee's matching share of total project cost. A credit cannot exceed the grantee or subgrantee's matching share required by the project agreement. The grantee must ensure there is documentation supporting all credits, including the following:

(1) A certification that the State or local government acquisition satisfied the conditions in 23 CFR 710.501(c)(1) through (6); and

(2) Justification of the value of credit applied. Acquisition costs incurred by the State or local government to acquire title can be used as justification for the value of the real property.

(b) *Exemptions.* Credits are not available for real property acquired with any form of Federal financial assistance except as provided in 23 U.S.C. 120(j), or for real property already incorporated into existing ROW and used for transportation purposes.

(c) *Contributions without credit.* Property may be presented for project use with the understanding that no credit for its use is sought. In such case, the grantee shall assure that the acquisition satisfied the conditions in 23 CFR 710.501(c)(1) through (6).

§ 710.509 Functional replacement of real property in public ownership.

(a) *General.* When publicly owned real property, including land and/or facilities, is to be acquired for a project receiving grant funds under title 23, in lieu of paying the fair market value for the real property, the acquiring agency may provide compensation by functionally replacing the publicly owned real property with another facility that will provide equivalent utility.

(b) *Federal participation.* Federal-aid funds may participate in functional replacement costs only if the following conditions are met:

(1) Functional replacement is permitted under State law and the acquiring agency elects to provide it;

(2) The property in question is in public ownership and use;

(3) The replacement facility will be in public ownership and will continue the public use function of the acquired facility;

(4) The acquiring agency has informed, in writing, the public entity owning the property of its right to an estimate of just compensation based on an appraisal of fair market value and of the option to choose either just compensation or functional replacement;

(5) The FHWA concurs in the acquiring agency determination that functional replacement is in the public interest; and

(6) The real property is not owned by a utility or railroad.

(c) *Federal land transfers.* Use of this section for functional replacement of real property in Federal ownership shall be in accordance with Federal land transfer provisions in subpart F of this part.

(d) *Limits upon participation.* Federal-aid participation in the costs of functional replacement is limited to costs that are actually incurred in the replacement of the acquired land and/or facility and are—

(1) Costs for facilities that do not represent increases in capacity or betterments, except for those necessary to replace utilities, to meet legal, regulatory, or similar requirements, or to meet reasonable prevailing standards; and

(2) Costs for land to provide a site for the replacement facility.

(e) *Procedures.* When a grantee determines that payments providing for functional replacement of public facilities are allowable under State law, the grantee will incorporate within its approved ROW manual, or approved RAMP, full procedures covering review and oversight that will be applied to such cases.

§ 710.511 Transportation Alternatives.

(a) *General.* 23 U.S.C. 133(h) sets aside an amount from each State's Surface Transportation Block Grant apportionment for Transportation Alternatives (TA). The TA projects that involve the acquisition, management, and disposition of real property, and the relocation of families, individuals, and businesses, are governed by the general requirements of the Federal-aid program found in titles 23 and 49 of the CFR, except as specified in paragraph (b)(2) of this section.

(b) *Requirements.* (1) Acquisition and relocation activities for TA projects are subject to the Uniform Act.

(2) When a person or agency acquires real property for a project receiving title 23 grant funds on behalf of an acquiring agency with eminent domain authority, the requirements of the Uniform Act apply as if the acquiring agency had acquired the property itself.

(3) When, subsequent to Federal approval of property acquisition, a person or agency acquires real property for a project receiving title 23 grant funds, and there will be no use or recourse to the power of eminent domain, the limited requirements of 49 CFR 24.101(b)(2) apply.

(c) *Property management and disposal of property acquired for TA projects.* Subpart D of this part applies to the management and disposal of real property interests acquired with TA funds, including alternate uses authorized under ROW use agreements. A TA project involving acquisition of any real property interest must have a real property agreement between FHWA and the grantee that identifies the expected useful life of the TA project and establishes a pro rata formula for repayment of TAP funding by the grantee if—

(1) The acquired real property interest is used in whole or in part for purposes other than the TA project purposes for which it was acquired; or

(2) The actual TA project life is less than the expected useful life specified in the real property agreement.

Subpart F—Federal Assistance Programs

SOURCE: 81 FR 57729, Aug. 23, 2016, unless otherwise noted.

§ 710.601 Federal land transfers.

(a) The provisions of this subpart apply to any project constructed on a Federal-aid highway or under Chapter 2 of title 23, of the United States Code. When the FHWA determines that a strong Federal transportation interest exists, these provisions may also be applied to highway projects that are eligible for Federal funding under Chapters 1 and 2 of title 23, of the United States Code, and to highway-related transfers that are requested by a State in conjunction with a military base closure under the Defense Base Closure and Realignment Act of 1990 (Pub. L. 101–510, 104 Stat. 1808, as amended).

(b) Under certain conditions, real property interests owned by the United States may be transferred to a non-Federal owner for use for highway purposes. Sections 107(d) and 317 of title 23, United States Code, establish the circumstances under which such transfers may occur, and the parties eligible to receive such transfers (SDOTs and their nominees).

(c) An eligible party may file an application with FHWA, or can make application directly to the Federal land management agency if the Federal land management agency has its own authority for granting interests in land.

(d) Applications under this section shall include the following information:

(1) The purpose for which the lands are to be used;

(2) The estate or interest in the land required for the project;

(3) The Federal project number or other appropriate references;

(4) The name of the Federal agency exercising jurisdiction over the land

and identity of the installation or activity in possession of the land;

(5) A map showing the survey of the lands to be acquired;

(6) A legal description of the lands desired; and

(7) A statement of compliance with the National Environmental Policy Act of 1969 (42 U.S.C. 4321, *et seq.*) and any other applicable Federal environmental laws, including the National Historic Preservation Act (54 U.S.C. 306108), and 23 U.S.C. 138.

(e) If the FHWA concurs in the need for the transfer, the Federal land management agency will be notified and a right-of-entry requested. For projects not on the Interstate System, the Federal land management agency shall have a period of 4 months in which to designate conditions necessary for the adequate protection and utilization of the reserve or to certify that the proposed appropriation is contrary to the public interest or inconsistent with the purposes for which such land or materials have been reserved. The FHWA may extend the reply period at the timely request of the Federal land management agency for good cause.

(f) The FHWA may participate in the payment of fair market value or the functional replacement of impacted facilities under 710.509 and the reimbursement of the ordinary and reasonable direct costs of the Federal land management agency for the transfer when reimbursement is required by the Federal land management agency's governing laws as a condition of the transfer.

(g) Deeds for conveyance of real property interests owned by the United States shall be prepared by the eligible party and must be certified as being legally sufficient by an attorney licensed within the State where the real property is located. Such deeds shall contain the clauses required by FHWA and 49 CFR 21.7(a)(2). After the eligible party prepares the deed, it will submit the proposed deed with the certification to FHWA for review and execution.

(h) Following execution by FHWA, the eligible party shall record the deed in the appropriate land record office and so advise FHWA and the affected Federal land management agency.

(i) When the need for the interest acquired under this subpart no longer exists, the party that received the real property must restore the land to the condition which existed prior to the transfer, or to a condition that is acceptable to the Federal land management agency to which such property would revert, and must give notice to FHWA and to the affected Federal land management agency that such interest will immediately revert to the control of the Federal land management agency from which it was appropriated or to its assigns. Where authorized by Federal law, the Federal land management agency and such party may enter into a separate agreement to release the reversion clause and make alternative arrangements for the sale, restoration, or other disposition of the lands no longer needed.

§ 710.603 Direct Federal acquisition.

(a) The provisions of this paragraph may be applied to any real property that is not owned by the United States and is needed in connection with a project for the construction, reconstruction, or improvement of any section of the Interstate System or for a Defense Access Road project under 23 U.S.C. 210, if the SDOT is unable to acquire the required ROW or is unable to obtain possession with sufficient promptness. If the landowner tenders a right-of-entry or other right of possession document required by State law any time before FHWA makes a determination that the SDOT is unable to acquire the ROW with sufficient promptness, the SDOT is legally obligated to accept such tender and FHWA may not proceed with Federal acquisition. To enable FHWA to make the necessary findings and to proceed with the acquisition of the ROW, the SDOT's written application for Federal acquisition must include the following:

(1) Justification for the Federal acquisition of the lands or interests in lands;

(2) The date FHWA authorized the SDOT to commence ROW acquisition, the date of the project agreement, and a statement that the agreement contains the provisions required by 23 U.S.C. 111;

(3) The necessity for acquisition of the particular lands under request;

(4) A statement of the specific interests in lands to be acquired, including the proposed treatment of control of access;

(5) The SDOT's intentions with respect to the acquisition, subordination, or exclusion of outstanding interests, such as minerals and utility easements, in connection with the proposed acquisition;

(6) A statement on compliance with the provisions of parts 771 and 774 of this chapter, as applicable;

(7) Adequate legal descriptions, plats, appraisals, and title data;

(8) An outline of the negotiations that have been conducted with landowners;

(9) An agreement that the SDOT will pay its pro rata share of costs incurred in the acquisition of, or the attempt to acquire, ROW; and

(10) A statement that assures compliance with the applicable provisions of the Uniform Act.

(b) Except as provided in paragraph (a) of this section, direct Federal acquisitions from non-Federal owners for projects administered by the FHWA Office of Federal Lands Highway may be carried out in accordance with applicable Federal condemnation laws. The FHWA will proceed with such a direct Federal acquisition only when the public agency responsible for the road is unable to obtain the ROW necessary for the project. The public agency must make a written request to FHWA for the acquisition and, if the public agency is a Federal agency, the request shall include a commitment that any real property obtained will be under that agency's sole jurisdiction and control and FHWA will have no jurisdiction or control over the real property as a result of the acquisition. The FHWA may require the applicant to provide any information FHWA needs to make the required determinations or to carry out the acquisition.

(c) If the applicant for direct Federal acquisition obtains title to a parcel prior to the filing of the Declaration of Taking, it shall notify FHWA and immediately furnish the appropriate U.S. Attorney with a disclaimer together with a request that the action against the landowner be dismissed (ex parte) from the proceeding and the estimated just compensation deposited into the registry of the court for the affected parcel be withdrawn after the appropriate motions are approved by the court.

(d) When the United States obtains a court order granting possession of the real property, FHWA shall authorize the applicant for direct Federal acquisition to immediately take over supervision of the property. The authorization shall include, but need not be limited to, the following:

(1) The right to take possession of unoccupied properties;

(2) The right to give 90 days notice to owners to vacate occupied properties and the right to take possession of such properties when vacated;

(3) The right to permit continued occupancy of a property until it is required for construction and, in those instances where such occupancy is to be for a substantial period of time, the right to enter into rental agreements, as appropriate, to protect the public interest;

(4) The right to request assistance from the U.S. Attorney in obtaining physical possession where an owner declines to comply with the court order of possession;

(5) The right to clear improvements and other obstructions;

(6) Instructions that the U.S. Attorney be notified prior to actual clearing, so as to afford him an opportunity to view the lands and improvements, to obtain appropriate photographs, and to secure appraisals in connection with the preparation of the case for trial;

(7) The requirement for appropriate credits to the United States for any net salvage or net rentals obtained by the applicant for direct Federal acquisition, as in the case of ROW acquired by an SDOT for Federal-aid projects; and

(8) Instructions that the authority granted to the applicant for direct Federal acquisition is not intended to preclude the U.S. Attorney from taking action, before the applicant has made arrangements for removal, to reach a settlement with the former owner which would include provision for removal.

(e) If the Federal Government initiates condemnation proceedings against the owner of real property in a Federal court and the final judgment is that FHWA cannot acquire the real property by condemnation, or the proceeding is abandoned, the court is required by law to award such a sum to the owner of the real property that in the opinion of the court provides reimbursement for the owner's reasonable costs, disbursements, and expenses, including reasonable attorney, appraisal, and engineering fees, actually incurred because of the condemnation proceedings.

(f) As soon as practicable after the date of payment of the purchase price or the date of deposit in court of funds to satisfy the award of the compensation in a Federal condemnation, FHWA shall reimburse the owner to the extent deemed fair and reasonable, the following costs:

(1) Recording fees, transfer taxes, and similar expenses incidental to conveying such real property to the United States;

(2) Penalty costs for prepayment of any preexisting recorded mortgage entered into in good faith encumbering such real property; and

(3) The pro rata portion of real property taxes paid which are allocable to a period subsequent to the date of vesting title in the United States or the effective date of possession, whichever is the earlier.

(g) The lands or interests in lands, acquired under this section, will be conveyed to the State or the appropriate political subdivision thereof, upon agreement by the SDOT, or said subdivision to:

(1) Maintain control of access where applicable;

(2) Accept title thereto;

(3) Maintain the project constructed thereon;

(4) Abide by any conditions which may set forth in the deed; and

(5) Notify the FHWA at the appropriate time that all the conditions have been performed.

(h) The deed from the United States to the State, or to the appropriate political subdivision thereof, or in the case of a Federal applicant for a direct Federal acquisition any document designating jurisdiction, shall include the conditions required by 49 CFR part 21 and shall not include any grant of jurisdiction to FHWA. The deed shall be recorded by the grantee in the appropriate land record office, and the FHWA shall be advised of the recording date.

[81 FR 57729, Aug. 23, 2016, as amended at 83 FR 21710, May 10, 2018]

Subpart G—Concession Agreements

AUTHORITY: 23 U.S.C. 156 and 315; 23 CFR 1.32; 49 CFR 1.48.

SOURCE: 73 FR 77503, Dec. 19, 2008, unless otherwise noted.

§ 710.701 Purpose.

The purpose of this subpart is to prescribe the standards that ensure fair market value is received by a highway agency under concession agreements involving federally funded highways.

§ 710.703 Definitions.

As used in this subpart:

(a) *Best value* means the proposal offering the most overall public benefits as determined through an evaluation of the amount of the concession payment and other appropriate considerations. Such other appropriate considerations may include, but are not limited to, qualifications and experience of the concessionaire, expected quality of services to be provided, the history or track record of the concessionaire in providing the services, timelines for the delivery of services, performance standards, complexity of the services to be rendered, and revenue sharing. Such appropriate considerations may also include, but are not limited to, policy considerations that are important, but not quantifiable, such as retaining the ability to amend the concession agreement if conditions change, having a desired level of oversight over the facility, ensuring a certain level of maintenance and operations for the facility, considerations relative to the structure and amount of the toll rates, economic development impacts and considerations, or social and environmental benefits and impacts.

(b) *Concession agreement* means an agreement between a highway agency and a concessionaire under which the concessionaire is given the right to operate and collect revenues or fees for the use of a federally funded highway in return for compensation to be paid to the highway agency. A concession agreement may include, but not be limited to, obligations concerning the development, design, construction, maintenance, operation, level of service, and/or capital improvements to a facility over the term of the agreement. Concession agreement shall not include agreements between government entities, even when compensation is paid, where the primary purpose of the transaction is not commercial in nature but for the purpose of determining governmental ownership, control, jurisdiction, or responsibilities with respect to the operation of a federally funded highway. The highway agency's determination as to whether an agreement between government entities constitutes a concession agreement shall be controlling.

(c) *Concessionaire* means any private or public entity that enters into a concession agreement with a highway agency.

(d) *Fair market value* means the price at which a highway agency and concessionaire are ready and willing to enter into a concession agreement for a federally funded highway on, or as if in, the open market for a reasonable period of time and in an arm's length transaction to any willing, knowledgeable, and able buyer. For purposes of this subpart, a concession agreement based on best value shall be deemed fair market value.

(e) *Federally funded highway* means any highway (including highways, bridges, and tunnels) acquired with Federal assistance made available from the Highway Trust Fund (other than the Mass Transit Account). A highway shall be deemed to be acquired with Federal assistance if Federal assistance participated in either the purchase of any real property, or in any capital expenditures in any fixtures located on real property, within the right-of-way, including the highway and any structures located upon the property.

(f) *Highway agency* in this subpart means any SDOT or other public authority with jurisdiction over a federally funded highway.

[73 FR 77503, Dec. 19, 2008, as amended at 81 FR 57741, Aug. 23, 2016]

§710.705 Applicability.

This subpart applies to all concession agreements involving federally funded highways that are executed after January 18, 2009.

§710.707 Fair market value.

A highway agency shall receive fair market value for any concession agreement involving a federally funded highway.

§710.709 Determination of fair market value.

(a) Fair market value may be determined either on a best value basis, highest net present value of the payments to be received over the life of the agreement, or highest bid received, as may be specified by the highway agency in the request for proposals or other relevant solicitation. If best value is used, the highway agency should identify, in the relevant solicitation, the criteria to be used as well as the weight afforded to the criteria.

(b) In order to be considered fair market value, the terms of the concession agreement must be both legally binding and enforceable.

(c) Any concession agreement awarded pursuant to a competitive process with more than one bidder shall be deemed to be fair market value. Any concession agreement awarded pursuant to a competitive process with only one bidder shall be presumed to be fair market value. Such presumption may be overcome only if the highway agency determines the proposal to not be fair market value based on the highway agency's estimates. Nothing in this subpart shall be construed to require a highway agency to accept any proposal, even if the proposal is deemed fair market value. For purposes of this subsection, a competitive process shall afford all interested proposers an equal opportunity to submit a proposal for the concession agreement and shall comply with applicable State and local law.

(d) If a concession agreement is not awarded pursuant to a competitive process, the highway agency must receive fair market value, as determined by the highway agency in accordance with State law, so long as an independent third party assessment is conducted and made publicly available.

(e) Nothing in this subpart is intended to waive the requirements of part 172, part 635, and part 636 whenever any Federal-aid (including TIFIA assistance) is to be used for a project under the concession agreement.

PART 750—HIGHWAY BEAUTIFICATION

Subpart A—National Standards for Regulation by States of Outdoor Advertising Adjacent to the Interstate System Under the 1958 Bonus Program

Subpart B—National Standards for Directional and Official Signs

Subpart C [Reserved]

Subpart D—Outdoor Advertising (Acquisition of Rights of Sign and Sign Site Owners)

Subpart E—Signs Exempt From Removal in Defined Areas

Subpart F [Reserved]

Subpart G—Outdoor Advertising Control

SOURCE: 38 FR 16044, June 20, 1973, unless otherwise noted.

Subpart A—National Standards for Regulation by States of Outdoor Advertising Adjacent to the Interstate System Under the 1958 Bonus Program

AUTHORITY: Sec. 12, Pub. L. 85–381, 72 Stat. 95, as amended; 23 U.S.C. 131; delegation of authority in 49 CFR 1.48(b).

§ 750.101 Purpose.

(a) In section 12 of the Federal-Aid Highway Act of 1958, Pub. L. 85–381, 72 Stat. 95, hereinafter called the *act*, the Congress declared that:

(1) To promote the safety, convenience, and enjoyment of public travel and the free flow of interstate commerce and to protect the public investment in the National System of Interstate and Defense Highways, hereinafter called the *Interstate System*, it is in the public interest to encourage and assist the States to control the use of and to improve areas adjacent to such system by controlling the erection and maintenance of outdoor advertising signs, displays, and devices adjacent to that system.

(2) It is a national policy that the erection and maintenance of outdoor advertising signs, displays, or devices

within 660 feet of the edge of the right-of-way and visible from the main-traveled way of all portions of the Interstate System constructed upon any part of right-of-way, the entire width of which is acquired subsequent to July 1, 1956, should be regulated, consistent with national standards to be prepared and promulgated by the Secretary of Transportation.

(b) The standards in this part are hereby promulgated as provided in the act.

[38 FR 16044, June 20, 1973, as amended at 39 FR 28629, Aug. 9, 1974]

§ 750.102 Definitions.

The following terms when used in the standards in this part have the following meanings:

(a) *Acquired for right-of-way* means acquired for right-of-way for any public road by the Federal Government, a State, or a county, city, or other political subdivision of a State, by donation, dedication, purchase, condemnation, use, or otherwise. The date of acquisition shall be the date upon which title (whether fee title or a lesser interest) vested in the public for right-of-way purposes under applicable Federal or State law.

(b) *Centerline of the highway* means a line equidistant from the edges of the median separating the main-traveled ways of a divided Interstate Highway, or the centerline of the main-traveled way of a nondivided Interstate Highway.

(c) *Controlled portion of the Interstate System* means any portion which:

(1) Is constructed upon any part of right-of-way, the entire width of which is acquired for right-of-way subsequent to July 1, 1956 (a portion shall be deemed so constructed if, within such portion, no line normal or perpendicular to the centerline of the highway and extending to both edges of the right-of-way will intersect any right-of-way acquired for right-of-way on or before July 1, 1956);

(2) Lies within a State, the highway department of which has entered into an agreement with the Secretary of Transportation as provided in the act; and

(3) Is not excluded under the terms of the act which provide that agreements entered into between the Secretary of Transportation and the State highway department shall not apply to those segments of the Interstate System which traverse commercial or industrial zones within the boundaries of incorporated municipalities, as such boundaries existed on September 21, 1959, wherein the use of real property adjacent to the Interstate System is subject to municipal regulation or control, or which traverse other areas where the land use as of September 21, 1959, was clearly established by State law as industrial or commercial.

(d) *Entrance roadway* means any public road or turning roadway, including acceleration lanes, by which traffic may enter the main-traveled way of an Interstate Highway from the general road system within a State, irrespective of whether traffic may also leave the main-traveled way by such road or turning roadway.

(e) *Erect* means to construct, build, raise, assemble, place, affix, attach, create, paint, draw, or in any other way bring into being or establish.

(f) *Exit roadway* means any public road or turning roadway including deceleration lanes, by which traffic may leave the main-traveled way of an Interstate Highway to reach the general road system within a State, irrespective of whether traffic may also enter the main-traveled way by such road or turning roadway.

(g) *Informational site* means an area or site established and maintained within or adjacent to the right-of-way of a highway on the Interstate System by or under the supervision or control of a State highway department, wherein panels for the display of advertising and informational signs may be erected and maintained.

(h) *Legible* means capable of being read without visual aid by a person of normal visual acuity.

(i) *Maintain* means to allow to exist.

(j) *Main-traveled way* means the traveled way of an Interstate Highway on which through traffic is carried. In the case of a divided highway, the traveled way of each of the separated roadways for traffic in opposite directions is a main-traveled way. It does not include such facilities as frontage roads, turning roadways, or parking areas.

(k) *Protected areas* means all areas inside the boundaries of a State which are adjacent to and within 660 feet of the edge of the right-of-way of all controlled portions of the Interstate System within that State. Where a controlled portion of the Interstate System terminates at a State boundary which is not perpendicular or normal to the centerline of the highway, protected areas also means all areas inside the boundary of such State which are within 660 feet of the edge of the right-of-way of the Interstate Highway in the adjoining State.

(l) *Scenic area* means any public park or area of particular scenic beauty or historical significance designated by or pursuant to State law as a scenic area.

(m) *Sign* means any outdoor sign, display, device, figure, painting, drawing, message, placard, poster, billboard, or other thing which is designed, intended, or used to advertise or inform, any part of the advertising or informative contents of which is visible from any place on the main-traveled way of a controlled portion of the Interstate System.

(n) *State* means the District of Columbia and any State of the United States within the boundaries of which a portion of the Interstate System is located.

(o) *State law* means a State constitutional provision or statute, or an ordinance, rule, or regulation enacted or adopted by a State agency or political subdivision of a State pursuant to State constitution or statute.

(p) *Trade name* shall include brand name, trademark, distinctive symbol, or other similar device or thing used to identify particular products or services.

(q) *Traveled way* means the portion of a roadway for the movement of vehicles, exclusive of shoulders.

(r) *Turning roadway* means a connecting roadway for traffic turning between two intersection legs of an interchange.

(s) *Visible* means capable of being seen (whether or not legible) without visual aid by a person of normal visual acuity.

§ 750.103 Measurements of distance.

(a) Distance from the edge of a right-of-way shall be measured horizontally along a line normal or perpendicular to the centerline of the highway.

(b) All distances under § 750.107 (a)(2) and (b) shall be measured along the centerline of the highway between two vertical planes which are normal or perpendicular to and intersect the centerline of the highway, and which pass through the termini of the measured distance.

[38 FR 16044, June 20, 1973, as amended at 41 FR 9321, Mar. 4, 1976]

§ 750.104 Signs that may not be permitted in protected areas.

Erection or maintenance of the following signs may not be permitted in protected areas:

(a) Signs advertising activities that are illegal under State or Federal laws or regulations in effect at the location of such signs or at the location of such activities.

(b) Obsolete signs.

(c) Signs that are not clean and in good repair.

(d) Signs that are not securely affixed to a substantial structure, and

(e) Signs that are not consistent with the standards in this part.

§ 750.105 Signs that may be permitted in protected areas.

(a) Erection or maintenance of the following signs may be permitted in protected areas:

Class 1—Official signs. Directional or other official signs or notices erected and maintained by public officers or agencies pursuant to and in accordance with direction or authorization contained in State of Federal law, for the purpose of carrying out an official duty or responsibility.

Class 2—On-premise signs. Signs not prohibited by State law which are consistent with the applicable provisions of this section and § 750.108 and which advertise the sale or lease of, or activities being conducted upon, the real property where the signs are located.

Not more than one such sign advertising the sale or lease of the same property may be permitted under this class in such manner as to be visible to traffic proceeding in any one direction on any one Interstate Highway.

Not more than one such sign, visible to traffic proceeding in any one direction on any one Interstate Highway and advertising activities being conducted upon the real property where the sign is located, may be permitted under this class more than 50 feet from the advertised activity.

Class 3—Signs within 12 miles of advertised activities. Signs not prohibited by State law which are consistent with the applicable provisions of this section and §§ 750.106, 750.107, and 750.108 and which advertise activities being conducted within 12 air miles of such signs.

Class 4—Signs in the specific interest of the traveling public. Signs authorized to be erected or maintained by State law which are consistent with the applicable provisions of this section and §§ 750.106, 750.107, and 750.108 and which are designed to give information in the specific interest of the traveling public.

(b) A Class 2 or 3 sign, except a Class 2 sign not more than 50 feet from the advertised activity, that displays any trade name which refers to or identifies any service rendered or product sold, used, or otherwise handled more than 12 air miles from such sign may not be permitted unless the name of the advertised activity which is within 12 air miles of such sign is displayed as conspicuously as such trade name.

(c) Only information about public places operated by Federal, State, or local governments, natural phenomena, historic sites, areas of natural scenic beauty or naturally suited for outdoor recreation and places for camping, lodging, eating, and vehicle service and repair is deemed to be in the specific interest of the traveling public. For the purposes of the standards in this part, a trade name is deemed to be information in the specific interest of the traveling public only if it identifies or characterizes such a place or identifies vehicle service, equipment, parts, accessories, fuels, oils, or lubricants being offered for sale at such a place. Signs displaying any other trade name may not be permitted under Class 4.

(d) Notwithstanding the provisions of paragraph (b) of this section, Class 2 or Class 3 signs which also qualify as Class 4 signs may display trade names in accordance with the provisions of paragraph (c) of this section.

§ 750.106 Class 3 and 4 signs within informational sites.

(a) Informational sites for the erection and maintenance of Class 3 and 4 advertising and informational signs may be established in accordance with § 1.35 of this chapter. The location and frequency of such sites shall be as determined by agreements between the Secretary of Transportation and the State highway departments.

(b) Class 3 and 4 signs may be permitted within such informational sites in protected areas in a manner consistent with the following provisions:

(1) No sign may be permitted which is not placed upon a panel.

(2) No panel may be permitted to exceed 13 feet in height or 25 feet in length, including border and trim, but excluding supports.

(3) No sign may be permitted to exceed 12 square feet in area, and nothing on such sign may be permitted to be legible from any place on the main-traveled way or a turning roadway.

(4) Not more than one sign concerning a single activity or place may be permitted within any one informational site.

(5) Signs concerning a single activity or place may be permitted within more than one informational site, but no Class 3 sign which does not also qualify as a Class 4 sign may be permitted within any informational site more than 12 air miles from the advertised activity.

(6) No sign may be permitted which moves or has any animated or moving parts.

(7) Illumination of panels by other than white lights may not be permitted, and no sign placed on any panel may be permitted to contain, include, or be illuminated by any other lights, or any flashing, intermittent, or moving lights.

(8) No lighting may be permitted to be used in any way in connection with any panel unless it is so effectively shielded as to prevent beams or rays of light from being directed at any portion of the main-traveled way of the Interstate System, or is of such low intensity or brilliance as not to cause glare or to impair the vision of the driver of any motor vehicle, or to otherwise interfere with any driver's operation of a motor vehicle.

[23 FR 8793, Nov. 13, 1958, as amended at 35 FR 18719, Dec. 10, 1970; 41 FR 9321, Mar. 4, 1976]

§ 750.107 Class 3 and 4 signs outside informational sites.

(a) The erection or maintenance of the following signs may be permitted within protected areas, outside informational sites:

(1) Class 3 signs which are visible only to Interstate highway traffic not served by an informational site within 12 air miles of the advertised activity;

(2) Class 4 signs which are more than 12 miles from the nearest panel within an informational site serving Interstate highway traffic to which such signs are visible.

(3) Signs that qualify both as Class 3 and 4 signs may be permitted in accordance with either paragraph (a)(1) or (2) of this section.

(b) The erection or maintenance of signs permitted under paragraph (a) of this section may not be permitted in any manner inconsistent with the following:

(1) In protected areas in advance of an intersection of the main-traveled way of an Interstate highway and an exit roadway, such signs visible to Interstate highway traffic approaching such intersection may not be permitted to exceed the following number:

Distance from intersection	Number of signs
0–2 miles	0.
2–5 miles	6.
More than 5 miles	Average of one sign per mile.

The specified distances shall be measured to the nearest point of the intersection of the traveled way of the exit roadway and the main-traveled way of the Interstate highway.

(2) Subject to the other provisions of this paragraph, not more than two such signs may be permitted within any mile distance measured from any point, and no such signs may be permitted to be less than 1,000 feet apart.

(3) Such signs may not be permitted in protected areas adjacent to any Interstate highway right-of-way upon any part of the width of which is constructed an entrance or exit roadway.

(4) Such signs visible to Interstate highway traffic which is approaching or has passed an entrance roadway may not be permitted in protected areas for 1,000 feet beyond the furthest point of the intersection between the traveled way of such entrance roadway and the main-traveled way of the Interstate highway.

(5) No such signs may be permitted in scenic areas.

(6) Not more than one such sign advertising activities being conducted as a single enterprise or giving information about a single place may be permitted to be erected or maintained in such manner as to be visible to traffic moving in any one direction on any one Interstate highway.

(c) No Class 3 or 4 signs other than those permitted by this section may be permitted to be erected or maintained within protected areas, outside informational sites.

§ 750.108 General provisions.

No Class 3 or 4 signs may be permitted to be erected or maintained pursuant to § 750.107, and no Class 2 sign may be permitted to be erected or maintained, in any manner inconsistent with the following:

(a) No sign may be permitted which attempts or appears to attempt to direct the movement of traffic or which interferes with, imitates or resembles any official traffic sign, signal or device.

(b) No sign may be permitted which prevents the driver of a vehicle from having a clear and unobstructed view of official signs and approaching or merging traffic.

(c) No sign may be permitted which contains, includes, or is illuminated by any flashing, intermittent or moving light or lights.

(d) No lighting may be permitted to be used in any way in connection with any sign unless it is so effectively shielded as to prevent beams or rays of light from being directed at any portion of the main-traveled way of the Interstate System, or is of such low intensity or brilliance as not to cause glare or to impair the vision of the driver of any motor vehicle, or to otherwise interfere with any driver's operation of a motor vehicle.

(e) No sign may be permitted which moves or has any animated or moving parts.

(f) No sign may be permitted to be erected or maintained upon trees or painted or drawn upon rocks or other natural features.

(g) No sign may be permitted to exceed 20 feet in length, width or height, or 150 square feet in area, including border and trim but excluding supports, except Class 2 signs not more than 50 feet from, and advertising activities being conducted upon, the real property where the sign is located.

§ 750.109 Exclusions.

The standards in this part shall not apply to markers, signs and plaques in appreciation of sites of historical significance for the erection of which provisions are made in an agreement between a State and the Secretary of Transportation, as provided in the Act, unless such agreement expressly makes all or any part of the standards applicable.

§ 750.110 State regulations.

A State may elect to prohibit signs permissible under the standards in this part without forfeiting its rights to any benefits provided for in the act.

Subpart B—National Standards for Directional and Official Signs

AUTHORITY: 23 U.S.C. 131, 315, 49 U.S.C. 1651; 49 CFR 1.48(b).

§ 750.151 Purpose.

(a) In section 131 of title 23 U.S.C., Congress has declared that:

(1) The erection and maintenance of outdoor advertising signs, displays, and devices in areas adjacent to the Interstate System and the primary system should be controlled in order to protect the public investment in such highways, to promote safety and recreational value of public travel, and to preserve natural beauty.

(2) Directional and official signs and notices, which signs and notices shall include, but not be limited to, signs and notices pertaining to natural wonders, scenic and historical attractions, which are required or authorized by law, shall conform to national standards authorized to be promulgated by the Secretary, which standards shall contain provisions concerning the lighting, size, number and spacing of signs, and such other requirements as may be appropriate to implement the section.

(b) The standards in this part are issued as provided in section 131 of title 23 U.S.C.

[38 FR 16044, June 30, 1973, as amended at 40 FR 21934, May 20, 1975]

§ 750.152 Application.

The following standards apply to directional and official signs and notices located within six hundred and sixty (660) feet of the right-of-way of the Interstate and Federal-aid primary systems and to those located beyond six hundred and sixty (660) feet of the right-of-way of such systems, outside of urban areas, visible from the main traveled way of such systems and erected with the purpose of their message being read from such main traveled way. These standards do not apply to directional and official signs erected on the highway right-of-way.

[40 FR 21934, May 20, 1975]

§ 750.153 Definitions.

For the purpose of this part:

(a) *Sign* means an outdoor sign, light, display, device, figure, painting, drawing, message, placard, poster, billboard, or other thing which is designed, intended, or used to advertise or inform, any part of the advertising or informative contents of which is visible from any place on the main traveled way of the Interstate or Federal-aid primary highway.

(b) *Main traveled way* means the through traffic lanes of the highway, exclusive of frontage roads, auxiliary lanes, and ramps.

(c) *Interstate System* means the National System of Interstate and Defence Highways described in section 103(d) of title 23 U.S.C.

(d) *Primary system* means the Federal-aid highway system described in section 103(b) of title 23 U.S.C.

(e) *Erect* means to construct, build, raise, assemble, place, affix, attach, create, paint, draw, or in any other way bring into being or establish.

(f) *Maintain* means to allow to exist.

(g) *Scenic area* means any area of particular scenic beauty or historical significance as determined by the Federal,

State, or local officials having jurisdiction thereof, and includes interests in land which have been acquired for the restoration, preservation, and enhancement of scenic beauty.

(h) *Parkland* means any publicly owned land which is designated or used as a public park, recreation area, wildlife or waterfowl refuge or historic site.

(i) *Federal or State law* means a Federal or State constitutional provision or statute, or an ordinance, rule, or regulation enacted or adopted by a State or Federal agency or a political subdivision of a State pursuant to a Federal or State constitution or statute.

(j) *Visible* means capable of being seen (whether or not legible) without visual aid by a person of normal visual acuity.

(k) *Freeway* means a divided arterial highway for through traffic with full control of access.

(l) *Rest area* means an area or site established and maintained within or adjacent to the highway right-of-way by or under public supervision or control for the convenience of the traveling public.

(m) *Directional and official signs and notices* includes only official signs and notices, public utility signs, service club and religious notices, public service signs, and directional signs.

(n) *Official signs and notices* means signs and notices erected and maintained by public officers or public agencies within their territorial or zoning jurisdiction and pursuant to and in accordance with direction or authorization contained in Federal, State, or local law for the purposes of carrying out an official duty or responsibility. Historical markers authorized by State law and erected by State or local government agencies or nonprofit historical societies may be considered official signs.

(o) *Public utility signs* means warning signs, informational signs, notices, or markers which are customarily erected and maintained by publicly or privately owned public utilities, as essential to their operations.

(p) *Service club and religious notices* means signs and notices, whose erection is authorized by law, relating to meetings of nonprofit service clubs or charitable associations, or religious services, which signs do not exceed 8 square feet in area.

(q) *Public service signs* means signs located on school bus stop shelters, which signs:

(1) Identify the donor, sponsor, or contributor of said shelters;

(2) Contain public service messages, which shall occupy not less than 50 percent of the area of the sign;

(3) Contain no other message;

(4) Are located on schoolbus shelters which are authorized or approved by city, county, or State law, regulation, or ordinance, and at places approved by the city, county, or State agency controlling the highway involved; and

(5) May not exceed 32 square feet in area. Not more than one sign on each shelter shall face in any one direction.

(r) *Directional signs* means signs containing directional information about public places owned or operated by Federal, State, or local governments or their agencies; publicly or privately owned natural phenomena, historic, cultural, scientific, educational, and religious sites; and areas of natural scenic beauty or naturally suited for outdoor recreation, deemed to be in the interest of the traveling public.

(s) *State* means any one of the 50 States, the District of Columbia, or Puerto Rico.

(t) *Urban area* means an urbanized area or, in the case of an urbanized area encompassing more than one State, that part of the urbanized areas in each such State, or an urban place as designated by the Bureau of the Census having a population of five thousand or more and not within any urbanized area, within boundaries to be fixed by responsible State and local officials in cooperation with each other, subject to approval by the Secretary. Such boundaries shall, as a minimum, encompass the entire urban place designated by the Bureau of the Census.

[38 FR 16044, June 30, 1973, as amended at 40 FR 21934, May 20, 1975]

§ 750.154 Standards for directional signs.

The following apply only to directional signs:

(a) *General.* The following signs are prohibited:

(1) Signs advertising activities that are illegal under Federal or State laws or regulations in effect at the location of those signs or at the location of those activities.

(2) Signs located in such a manner as to obscure or otherwise interfere with the effectiveness of an official traffic sign, signal, or device, or obstruct or interfere with the driver's view of approaching, merging, or intersecting traffic.

(3) Signs which are erected or maintained upon trees or painted or drawn upon rocks or other natural features.

(4) Obsolete signs.

(5) Signs which are structurally unsafe or in disrepair.

(6) Signs which move or have any animated or moving parts.

(7) Signs located in rest areas, parklands or scenic areas.

(b) *Size*. (1) No sign shall exceed the following limits:

(i) Maximum area—150 square feet.

(ii) Maximum height—20 feet.

(iii) Maximum length—20 feet.

(2) All dimensions include border and trim, but exclude supports.

(c) *Lighting*. Signs may be illuminated, subject to the following:

(1) Signs which contain, include, or are illuminated by any flashing, intermittent, or moving light or lights are prohibited.

(2) Signs which are not effectively shielded so as to prevent beams or rays of light from being directed at any portion of the traveled way of an Interstate or primary highway or which are of such intensity or brilliance as to cause glare or to impair the vision of the driver of any motor vehicle, or which otherwise interfere with any driver's operation of a motor vehicle are prohibited.

(3) No sign may be so illuminated as to interfere with the effectiveness of or obscure an official traffic sign, device, or signal.

(d) *Spacing*. (1) Each location of a directional sign must be approved by the State highway department.

(2) No directional sign may be located within 2,000 feet of an interchange, or intersection at grade along the Interstate System or other freeways (measured along the Interstate or freeway from the nearest point of the beginning or ending of pavement widening at the exit from or entrance to the main traveled way).

(3) No directional sign may be located within 2,000 feet of a rest area, parkland, or scenic area.

(4)(i) No two directional signs facing the same direction of travel shall be spaced less than 1 mile apart;

(ii) Not more than three directional signs pertaining to the same activity and facing the same direction of travel may be erected along a single route approaching the activity;

(iii) Signs located adjacent to the Interstate System shall be within 75 air miles of the activity; and

(iv) Signs located adjacent to the primary system shall be within 50 air miles of the activity.

(e) *Message content*. The message on directional signs shall be limited to the identification of the attraction or activity and directional information useful to the traveler in locating the attraction, such as mileage, route numbers, or exit numbers. Descriptive words or phrases, and pictorial or photographic representations of the activity or its environs are prohibited.

(f) *Selection method and criteria*. (1) Privately owned activities or attractions eligible for directional signing are limited to the following: natural phenomena; scenic attractions; historic, educational, cultural, scientific, and religious sites; and outdoor recreational areas.

(2) To be eligible, privately owned attractions or activities must be nationally or regionally known, and of outstanding interest to the traveling public.

(3) Each State shall develop specific selection methods and criteria to be used in determining whether or not an activity qualifies for this type of signing. A statement as to selection methods and criteria shall be furnished to the Secretary of Transportation before the State permits the erection of any such signs under section 131(c) of title 23 U.S.C., and this part.

§ 750.155 State standards.

This part does not prohibit a State from establishing and maintaining standards which are more restrictive with respect to directional and official signs and notices along the Federal-aid highway systems than these national standards.

[38 FR 16044, June 20, 1973, as amended at 40 FR 21934, May 20, 1975]

Subpart C [Reserved]

Subpart D—Outdoor Advertising (Acquisition of Rights of Sign and Sign Site Owners)

AUTHORITY: 23 U.S.C. 131 and 315; 23 CFR 1.32 and 1.48(b).

SOURCE: 39 FR 27436, July 29, 1974, unless otherwise noted.

§ 750.301 Purpose.

To prescribe the Federal Highway Administration (FHWA) policies relating to Federal participation in the costs of acquiring the property interests necessary for removal of nonconforming advertising signs, displays and devices on the Federal-aid Primary and Interstate Systems, including toll sections on such systems, regardless of whether Federal funds participated in the construction thereof. This regulation should not be construed to authorize any additional rights in eminent domain not already existing under State law or under 23 U.S.C. 131(g).

§ 750.302 Policy.

(a) Just compensation shall be paid for the rights and interests of the sign and site owner in those outdoor advertising signs, displays, or devices which are lawfully existing under State law, in conformance with the terms of 23 U.S.C. 131.

(b)(1) Federal reimbursement will be made on the basis of 75 percent of the acquisition, removal and incidental costs legally incurred or obligated by the State.

(2) Federal funds will participate in 100 percent of the costs of removal of those signs which were removed prior to January 4, 1975, by relocation, pursuant to the provisions of 23 CFR § 750.305(a)(2), and which are required to be removed as a result of the amendments made to 23 U.S.C. 131 by the Federal-Aid Highway Amendments of 1974, Pub. L. 93–643, section 109, January 4, 1975. Such signs must have been relocated to a legal site, must have been legally maintained since the relocation, and must not have been substantially changed, as defined by the State maintenance standards, issued pursuant to 23 CFR 750.707(b).

(c) Title III of the Uniform Relocation Assistance and Real Property Acquisition Policies Act of 1970 (42 U.S.C. 4651, *et seq.*) applies except where complete conformity would defeat the purposes set forth in 42 U.S.C. 4651, would impede the expeditious implementation of the sign removal program or would increase administrative costs out of proportion to the cost of the interests being acquired or extinguished.

(d) Projects for the removal of outdoor advertising signs including hardship acquisitions should be programed and authorized in accordance with normal program procedures for right-of-way projects.

[39 FR 27436, July 29, 1974; 39 FR 30349, Aug. 22, 1974, as amended at 41 FR 31198, July 27, 1976]

§ 750.303 Definitions.

(a) *Sign.* An outdoor sign, light, display, device, figure, painting, drawing, message, placard, poster, billboard or other thing which is designed, intended of the advertising or informative contents of which is visible from any place on the main-traveled way of the Interstate or Primary Systems, whether the same be permanent or portable installation.

(b) *Lease (license, permit, agreement, contract or easement).* An agreement, oral or in writing, by which possession or use of land or interests therein is given by the owner or other person to another person for a specified purpose.

(c) *Leasehold value.* The leasehold value is the present worth of the difference between the contractual rent and the current market rent at the time of the appraisal.

(d) *Illegal sign.* One which was erected and/or maintained in violation of State law.

(e) *Nonconforming sign.* One which was lawfully erected, but which does not comply with the provisions of State law or State regulations passed at a later date or which later fails to comply with State law or State regulations due to changed conditions. Illegally erected or maintained signs are not nonconforming signs.

(f) *1966 inventory*. The record of the survey of advertising signs and junkyards compiled by the State highway department.

(g) *Abandoned sign*. One in which no one has an interest, or as defined by State law.

§750.304 State policies and procedures.

The State's written policies and operating procedures for implementing its sign removal program under State law and complying with 23 U.S.C. 131 and its proposed time schedule for sign removal and procedure for reporting its accomplishments shall be submitted to the FHWA for approval within 90 days of the date of this regulation. This statement should be supported by the State's regulations implementing its program. Revisions to the State's policies and procedures shall be submitted to the FHWA for approval. The statement should contain provisions for the review of its policies and procedure to meet changing conditions, adoption of improved procedures, and for internal review to assure compliance. The statement shall include as a minimum the following:

(a) *Project priorities*. The following order of priorities is recommended.

(1) Illegal and abandoned signs.

(2) Hardship situations.

(3) Nominal value signs.

(4) Signs in areas which have been designated as scenic under authority of State law.

(5) Product advertising on:

(i) Rural interstate highway.

(ii) Rural primary highway.

(iii) Urban areas.

(6) Nontourist-oriented directional advertising.

(7) Tourist-oriented directional advertising.

(b) *Programing*. (1) A sign removal project may consist of any group of proposed sign removals. The signs may be those belonging to one company or those located along a single route, all of the signs in a single county or other locality, hardship situations, individually or grouped, such as those involving vandalized signs, or all of a sign owner's signs in a given State or area, or any similar grouping.

(2) A project for sign removal on other than a Federal-aid primary route basis e.g., a countywide project or a project involving only signs owned by one company, should be identified as CAF–000B( ), continuing the numbering sequence which began with the sign inventory project in 1966.

(3) Where it would not interfere with the State's operations, the State should program sign removal projects to minimize disruption of business.

(c) *Valuation and review methods*—(1) *Schedules—formulas*. Schedules, formulas or other methods to simplify valuation of signs and sites are recommended for the purpose of minimizing administrative and legal expenses necessarily involved in determining just compensation by individual appraisals and litigation. They do not purport to be a basis for the determination of just compensation under eminent domain.

(2) *Appraisals*. Where appropriate, the State may use its approved appraisal report forms including those for abbreviated or short form appraisals. Where a sign or site owner does not accept the amount computed under an approved schedule, formula, or other simplified method, an appraisal shall be utilized.

(3) *Leaseholds*. When outdoor advertising signs and sign sites involve a leasehold value, the State's procedures should provide for determining value in the same manner as any other real estate leasehold that has value to the lessee.

(4) *Severance damages*. The State has the responsibility of justifying the recognition of severance damages pursuant to 23 CFR 710.304(h), and the law of the State before Federal participation will be allowed. Generally, Federal participation will not be allowed in the payment of severance damages to remaining signs, or other property of a sign company alleged to be due to the taking of certain of the company's signs. Unity of use of the separate properties, as required by applicable principles of eminent domain law, must be shown to exist before participation in severance damages will be allowed. Moreover, the value of the remaining signs or other real property

must be diminished by virtue of the taking of such signs. Payments for severance damages to economic plants or loss of business profits are not compensable. Severance damage cases must be submitted to the FHWA for prior concurrence, together with complete legal and appraisal justification for payment of these damages. To assist the FHWA in its evaluation, the following data will accompany any submission regarding severance:

(i) One copy of each appraisal in which this was analyzed. One copy of the State's review appraiser analysis and determination of market value.

(ii) A plan or map showing the location of each sign.

(iii) An opinion by the State highway department's chief legal officer that severance is appropriate in accordance with State law together with a legal opinion that, in the instant case, the damages constitute severance as opposed to consequential damage as a matter of law. The opinion shall include a determination, and the basis therefor, that the specific taking of some of an outdoor advertiser's signs constitutes a distinct economic unit, and that unity of use of the separate properties in conformity with applicable principles of eminent domain law had been satisfactorily established. A legal memorandum must be furnished citing and discussing cases and other authorities supporting the State's position.

(5) *Review of value estimates.* All estimates of value shall be reviewed by a person other than the one who made the estimate. Appraisal reports shall be reviewed and approved prior to initiation of negotiations. All other estimates shall be reviewed before the agreement becomes final.

(d) *Nominal value plan.* (1) This plan may provide for the removal costs of eligible nominal value signs and for payments up to $250 for each nonconforming sign, and up to $100 for each nonconforming sign site.

(2) The State's procedures may provide for negotiations for sign sites and sign removals to be accomplished simultaneously without prior review.

(3) Releases or agreements executed by the sign and/or site owner should include the identification of the sign, statement of ownership, price to be paid, interest acquired, and removal rights.

(4) It is not expected that salvage value will be a consideration in most acquisitions; however, the State's procedures may provide that the sign may be turned over to the sign owner, site owner, contractor, or individual as all or a part of the consideration for its removal, without any project credits.

(5) Programing and authorizations will be in accord with § 750.308 of this regulation. A detailed estimate of value of each individual sign is not necessary. The project may be programed and authorized as one project.

(e) *Sign removal.* The State's procedural statement should include provision for:

(1) Owner retention.

(2) Salvage value.

(3) State removal.

[39 FR 27436, July 29, 1974; 42 FR 30835, June 17, 1977, as amended at 50 FR 34093, Aug. 23, 1985]

§ 750.305 Federal participation.

(a) Federal funds may participate in:

(1) Payments made to a sign owner for his right, title and interest in a sign, and where applicable, his leasehold value in a sign site, and to a site owner for his right and interest in a site, which is his right to erect and maintain the existing nonconforming sign on such site.

(2) The cost of relocating a sign to the extent of the cost to acquire the sign, less salvage value if any.

(3) A duplicate payment for the site owner's interest of $2,500 or less because of a bona fide error in ownership, provided the State has followed its title search procedures as set forth in its policy and procedure submission.

(4) The cost of removal of signs, partially completed sign structures, supporting poles, abandoned signs and those which are illegal under State law within the controlled areas, provided such costs are incurred in accordance with State law. Removal may be by State personnel on a force account basis or by contract. Documentation for Federal participation in such removal projects should be in accord with the State's normal force account

and contractual reimbursement procedures. The State should maintain a record of the number of signs removed. These data should be retained in project records and reported on the periodic report required under § 750.308 of this regulation.

(5) Signs materially damaged by vandals. Federal funds shall be limited to the Federal pro-rata share of the fair market value of the sign immediately before the vandalism occurred minus the estimated cost of repairing and re-erecting the sign. If the State chooses, it may use its FHWA approved nominal value plan procedure to acquire these signs.

(6) The cost of acquiring and removing completed sign structures which have been blank or painted out beyond the period of time established by the State for normal maintenance and change of message, provided the sign owner can establish that his nonconforming use was not abandoned or discontinued, and provided such costs are incurred in accordance with State law, or regulation. The evidence considered by the State as acceptable for establishing or showing that the nonconforming use has not been abandoned or voluntarily discontinued shall be set forth in the State's policy and procedures.

(7) In the event a sign was omitted in the 1966 inventory, and the State supports a determination that the sign was in existence prior to October 22, 1965, the costs are eligible for Federal participation.

(b) Federal funds may not participate in:

(1) Cost of title certificates, title insurance, title opinion or similar evidence or proof of title in connection with the acquisition of a landowner's right to erect and maintain a sign or signs when the amount of payment to the landowner for his interest is $2,500 or less, unless required by State law. However, Federal funds may participate in the costs of securing some lesser evidence or proof of title such as searches and investigations by State highway department personnel to the extent necessary to determine ownership, affidavit of ownership by the owner, bill of sale, etc. The State's procedure for determining evidence of title should be set forth in the State's policy and procedure submission.

(2) Payments to a sign owner where the sign was erected without permission of the property owner unless the sign owner can establish his legal right to erect and maintain the sign. However, such signs may be removed by State personnel on a force account basis or by contract with Federal participation except where the sign owner reimburses the State for removal.

(3) Acquisition costs paid for abandoned or illegal signs, potential sign sites, or signs which were built during a period of time which makes them ineligible for compensation under 23 U.S.C. 131, or for rights in sites on which signs have been abandoned or illegally erected by a sign owner.

(4) The acquisition cost of supporting poles or partially completed sign structures in nonconforming areas which do not have advertising or informative content thereon unless the owner can show to the State's satisfaction he has not abandoned the structure. When the State has determined the sign structure has not been abandoned, Federal funds will participate in the acquisition of the structure, provided the cost are incurred in accordance with State law.

§ 750.306 Documentation for Federal participation.

The following information concerning each sign must be available in the State's files to be eligible for Federal participation.

(a) *Payment to sign owner.* (1) A photograph of the sign in place. Exceptions may be made in cases where in one transaction the State has acquired a number of a company's nominal value signs similar in size, condition and shape. In such cases, only a sample of representative photographs need be provided to document the type and condition of the signs.

(2) Evidence showing the sign was nonconforming as of the date of taking.

(3) Value documentation and proof of obligation of funds.

(4) Satisfactory indication of ownership of the sign and compensable interest therein (e.g., lease or other agreement with the property owner, or an

affidavit, certification, or other such evidence of ownership).

(5) Evidence that the sign falls within one of the three categories shown in § 750.302 of this regulation. The specific category should be identified.

(6) Evidence that the right, title, or interest pertaining to the sign has passed to the State, or that the sign has been removed.

(b) *Payment to the site owner.* (1) Evidence that an agreement has been reached between the State and owner.

(2) Value documentation and proof of obligation of funds.

(3) Satisfactory indication of ownership or compensable interest.

(c) In those cases where Federal funds participate in 100 percent of the cost of removal, the State file shall contain the records of the relocation made prior to January 4, 1975.

[39 FR 27436, July 29, 1974, as amended at 41 FR 31198, July 27, 1976]

§ 750.307 FHWA project approval.

Authorization to proceed with acquisitions on a sign removal project shall not be issued until such time as the State has submitted to FHWA the following:

(a) A general description of the project.

(b) The total number of signs to be acquired.

(c) The total estimated cost of the sign removal project, including a breakdown of incidental, acquisition and removal costs.

§ 750.308 Reports.

Periodic reports on site acquisitions and actual sign removals shall be submitted on FHWA Form 1424 and as prescribed.[1]

[39 FR 27436, July 29, 1974, as amended at 41 FR 9321, Mar. 4, 1976]

Subpart E—Signs Exempt From Removal in Defined Areas

AUTHORITY: 23 U.S.C. 131 and 315, 49 CFR 1.48, 23 CFR 1.32.

SOURCE: 41 FR 45827, Oct. 18, 1976, unless otherwise noted.

[1] Forms are available at FHWA Division Offices located in each State.

§ 750.501 Purpose.

This subpart sets forth the procedures pursuant to which a State may, if it desires, seek an exemption from the acquisition requirements of 23 U.S.C. 131 for signs giving directional information about goods and services in the interest of the traveling public in defined areas which would suffer substantial economic hardship if such signs were removed. This exemption may be granted pursuant to the provisions of 23 U.S.C. 131(o).

§ 750.502 Applicability.

The provisions of this subpart apply to signs adjacent to the Interstate and primary systems which are required to be controlled under 23 U.S.C. 131.

§ 750.503 Exemptions.

(a) The Federal Highway Administration (FHWA) may approve a State's request to exempt certain nonconforming signs, displays, and devices (hereinafter called signs) within a defined area from being acquired under the provisions of 23 U.S.C. 131 upon a showing that removal would work a substantial economic hardship throughout that area. A defined area is an area with clearly established geographical boundaries defined by the State which the State can evaluate as an economic entity. Neither the States nor FHWA shall rely on individual claims of economic hardship. Exempted signs must:

(1) Have been lawfully erected prior to May 5, 1976, and must continue to be lawfully maintained.

(2) Continue to provide the directional information to goods and services offered at the same enterprise in the defined area in the interest of the traveling public that was provided on May 5, 1976. Repair and maintenance of these signs shall conform with the State's approved maintenance standards as required by subpart G of this part.

(b) To obtain the exemption permitted by 23 U.S.C. 131(o), the State shall establish:

(1) Its requirements for the directional content of signs to qualify the signs as directional signs to goods and services in the defined area.

(2) A method of economic analysis clearly showing that the removal of

signs would work a substantial economic hardship throughout the defined area.

(c) In support of its request for exemption, the State shall submit to the FHWA:

(1) Its requirements and method (see § 750.503(b)).

(2) The limits of the defined area(s) requested for exemption, a listing of signs to be exempted, their location, and the name of the enterprise advertised on May 5, 1976.

(3) The application of the requirements and method to the defined areas, demonstrating that the signs provide directional information to goods and services of interest to the traveling public in the defined area, and that removal would work a substantial economic hardship in the defined area(s).

(4) A statement that signs in the defined area(s) not meeting the exemption requirements will be removed in accordance with State law.

(5) A statement that the defined area will be reviewed and evaluated at least every three (3) years to determine if an exemption is still warranted.

(d) The FHWA, upon receipt of a State's request for exemption, shall prior to approval:

(1) Review the State's requirements and methods for compliance with the provisions of 23 U.S.C. 131 and this subpart.

(2) Review the State's request and the proposed exempted area for compliance with State requirements and methods.

(e) Nothing herein shall prohibit the State from acquiring signs in the defined area at the request of the sign owner.

(f) Nothing herein shall prohibit the State from imposing or maintaining stricter requirements.

Subpart F [Reserved]

Subpart G—Outdoor Advertising Control

AUTHORITY: 23 U.S.C. 131 and 315; 49 CFR 1.48.

SOURCE: 40 FR 42844, Sept. 16, 1975, unless otherwise noted.

§ 750.701 Purpose.

This subpart prescribes the Federal Highway Administration (FHWA) policies and requirements relating to the effective control of outdoor advertising under 23 U.S.C. 131. The purpose of these policies and requirements is to assure that there is effective State control of outdoor advertising in areas adjacent to Interstate and Federal-aid primary highways. Nothing in this subpart shall be construed to prevent a State from establishing more stringent outdoor advertising control requirements along Interstate and Primary Systems than provided herein.

§ 750.702 Applicability.

The provisions of this subpart are applicable to all areas adjacent to the Federal-aid Interstate and Primary Systems, including toll sections thereof, except that within urban areas, these provisions apply only within 660 feet of the nearest edge of the right-of-way. These provisions apply regardless of whether Federal funds participated in the costs of such highways. The provisions of this subpart do not apply to the Federal-aid Secondary or Urban Highway System.

§ 750.703 Definitions.

The terms as used in this subpart are defined as follows:

(a) *Commercial and industrial zones* are those districts established by the zoning authorities as being most appropriate for commerce, industry, or trade, regardless of how labeled. They are commonly categorized as commercial, industrial, business, manufacturing, highway service or highway business (when these latter are intended for highway-oriented business), retail, trade, warehouse, and similar classifications.

(b) *Erect* means to construct, build, raise, assemble, place, affix, attach, create, paint, draw, or in any other way bring into being or establish.

(c) *Federal-aid Primary Highway* means any highway on the system designated pursuant to 23 U.S.C. 103(b).

(d) *Interstate Highway* means any highway on the system defined in and designated, pursuant to 23 U.S.C. 103(e).

(e) *Illegal sign* means one which was erected or maintained in violation of State law or local law or ordinance.

(f) *Lease* means an agreement, license, permit, or easement, oral or in writing, by which possession or use of land or interests therein is given for a specified purpose, and which is a valid contract under the laws of a State.

(g) *Maintain* means to allow to exist.

(h) *Main-traveled way* means the traveled way of a highway on which through traffic is carried. In the case of a divided highway, the traveled way of each of the separate roadways for traffic in opposite directions is a main-traveled way. It does not include such facilities as frontage roads, turning roadways, or parking areas.

(i) *Sign, display or device*, hereinafter referred to as "sign," means an outdoor advertising sign, light, display, device, figure, painting, drawing, message, placard, poster, billboard, or other thing which is designed, intended, or used to advertise or inform, any part of the advertising or informative contents of which is visible from any place on the main-traveled way of the Interstate or Primary Systems, whether the same be permanent or portable installation.

(j) *State law* means a State constitutional provision or statute, or an ordinance, rule or regulation, enacted or adopted by a State.

(k) *Unzoned area* means an area where there is no zoning in effect. It does not include areas which have a rural zoning classification or land uses established by zoning variances or special exceptions.

(l) *Unzoned commercial or industrial areas* are unzoned areas actually used for commercial or industrial purposes as defined in the agreements made between the Secretary, U.S. Department of Transportation (Secretary), and each State pursuant to 23 U.S.C. 131(d).

(m) *Urban area* is as defined in 23 U.S.C. 101(a).

(n) *Visible* means capable of being seen, wehter or not readable, without visual aid by a person of normal visual acuity.

§ 750.704 Statutory requirements.

(a) 23 U.S.C. 131 provides that signs adjacent to the Interstate and Federal-aid Primary Systems which are visible from the main-traveled way and within 660 feet of the nearest edge of the right-of-way, and those additional signs beyond 660 feet outside of urban areas which are visible from the main-traveled way and erected with the purpose of their message being read from such main-traveled way, shall be limited to the following:

(1) Directional and official signs and notice which shall conform to national standards promulgated by the Secretary in subpart B, part 750, chapter I, 23 CFR, National Standards for Directional and Official Signs;

(2) Signs advertising the sale or lease of property upon which they are located;

(3) Signs advertising activities conducted on the property on which they are located;

(4) Signs within 660 feet of the nearest edge of the right-of-way within areas adjacent to the Interstate and Federal-aid Primary Systems which are zoned industrial or commercial under the authority of State law;

(5) Signs within 660 feet of the nearest edge of the right-of-way within areas adjacent to the Interstate and Federal-aid Primary Systems which are unzoned commercial or industrial areas, which areas are determined by agreement between the State and the Secretary; and

(6) Signs lawfully in existence on October 22, 1965, which are determined to be landmark signs.

(b) 23 U.S.C. 131(d) provides that signs in § 750.704(a) (4) and (5) must comply with size, lighting, and spacing requirements, to be determined by agreement between the State and the Secretary.

(c) 23 U.S.C. 131 does not permit signs to be located within zoned or unzoned commercial or industrial areas beyond 660 feet of the right-of-way adjacent to the Interstate or Federal-aid Primary System, outside of urban areas.

(d) 23 U.S.C. 131 provides that signs not permitted under § 750.704 of this regulation must be removed by the State.

§ 750.705 Effective control.

In order to provide effective control of outdoor advertising, the State must:

(a) Prohibit the erection of new signs other than those which fall under § 750.704(a)(1) through (6);

(b) Assure that signs erected under § 750.704(a)(4) and (5) comply, at a minimum, with size, lighting, and spacing criteria contained in the agreement between the Secretary and the State;

(c) Assure that signs erected under § 750.704(a)(1) comply with the national standards contained in subpart B, part 750, chapter I, 23 CFR;

(d) Remove illegal signs expeditiously;

(e) Remove nonconforming signs with just compensation within the time period set by 23 U.S.C. 131 (subpart D, part 750, chapter I, 23 CFR, sets forth policies for the acquisition and compensation for such signs);

(f) Assure that signs erected under § 750.704(a)(6) comply with § 750.710, Landmark Signs, if landmark signs are allowed;

(g) Establish criteria for determining which signs have been erected with the purpose of their message being read from the main-traveled way of an Interstate or primary highway, except where State law makes such criteria unnecessary. Where a sign is erected with the purpose of its message being read from two or more highways, one or more of which is a controlled highway, the more stringent of applicable control requirements will apply;

(h) Develop laws, regulations, and procedures to accomplish the requirements of this subpart;

(i) Establish enforcement procedures sufficient to discover illegally erected or maintained signs shortly after such occurrence and cause their prompt removal; and

(j) Submit regulations and enforcement procedures to FHWA for approval.

[40 FR 42844, Sept. 16, 1975; 40 FR 49777, Oct. 24, 1975]

§ 750.706 Sign control in zoned and unzoned commercial and industrial areas.

The following requirements apply to signs located in zoned and unzoned commercial and industrial areas within 660 feet of the nearest edge of the right-of-way adjacent to the Interstate and Federal-aid primary highways.

(a) The State by law or regulation shall, in conformity with its agreement with the Secretary, set criteria for size, lighting, and spacing of outdoor advertising signs located in commercial or industrial zoned or unzoned areas, as defined in the agreement, adjacent to Interstate and Federal-aid primary highways. If the agreement between the Secretary and the State includes a grandfather clause, the criteria for size, lighting, and spacing will govern only those signs erected subsequent to the date specified in the agreement. The States may adopt more restrictive criteria than are presently contained in agreements with the Secretary.

(b) Agreement criteria which permit multiple sign structures to be considered as one sign for spacing purposes must limit multiple sign structures to signs which are physically contiguous, or connected by the same structure or cross-bracing, or located not more than 15 feet apart at their nearest point in the case of back-to-back or "V" type signs.

(c) Where the agreement and State law permits control by local zoning authorities, these controls may govern in lieu of the size, lighting, and spacing controls set forth in the agreement, subject to the following:

(1) The local zoning authority's controls must include the regulation of size, of lighting and of spacing of outdoor advertising signs, in all commercial and industrial zones.

(2) The regulations established by local zoning authority may be either more restrictive or less restrictive than the criteria contained in the agreement, unless State law or regulations require equivalent or more restrictive local controls.

(3) If the zoning authority has been delegated, extraterritorial, jurisdiction under State law, and exercises control of outdoor advertising in commercial and industrial zones within this extraterritorial jurisdiction, control by the zoning authority may be accepted in lieu of agreement controls in such areas.

(4) The State shall notify the FHWA in writing of those zoning jurisdictions wherein local control applies. It will not be necessary to furnish a copy of

the zoning ordinance. The State shall periodically assure itself that the size, lighting, and spacing control provisions of zoning ordinances accepted under this section are actually being enforced by the local authorities.

(5) Nothing contained herein shall relieve the State of the responsibility of limiting signs within controlled areas to commercial and industrial zones.

§ 750.707 Nonconforming signs.

(a) *General.* The provisions of § 750.707 apply to nonconforming signs which must be removed under State laws and regulations implementing 23 U.S.C. 131. These provisions also apply to nonconforming signs located in commercial and industrial areas within 660 feet of the nearest edge of the right-of-way which come under the so-called grandfather clause contained in State-Federal agreements. These provisions do not apply to conforming signs regardless of when or where they are erected.

(b) *Nonconforming signs.* A nonconforming sign is a sign which was lawfully erected but does not comply with the provisions of State law or State regulations passed at a later date or later fails to comply with State law or State regulations due to changed conditions. Changed conditions include, for example, signs lawfully in existence in commercial areas which at a later date become noncommercial, or signs lawfully erected on a secondary highway later classified as a primary highway.

(c) *Grandfather clause.* At the option of the State, the agreement may contain a grandfather clause under which criteria relative to size, lighting, and spacing of signs in zoned and unzoned commercial and industrial areas within 660 feet of the nearest edge of the right-of-way apply only to new signs to be erected after the date specified in the agreement. Any sign lawfully in existence in a commercial or industrial area on such date may remain even though it may not comply with the size, lighting, or spacing criteria. This clause only allows an individual sign at its particular location for the duration of its normal life subject to customary maintenance. Preexisting signs covered by a grandfather clause, which do not comply with the agreement criteria have the status of nonconforming signs.

(d) *Maintenance and continuance.* In order to maintain and continue a nonconforming sign, the following conditions apply:

(1) The sign must have been actually in existence at the time the applicable State law or regulations became effective as distinguished from a contemplated use such as a lease or agreement with the property owner. There are two exceptions to actual existence as follows:

(i) Where a permit or similar specific State governmental action was granted for the construction of a sign prior to the effective date of the State law or regulations and the sign owner acted in good faith and expended sums in reliance thereon. This exception shall not apply in instances where large numbers of permits were applied for and issued to a single sign owner, obviously in anticipation of the passage of a State control law.

(ii) Where the State outdoor advertising control law or the Federal-State agreement provides that signs in commercial and industrial areas may be erected within six (6) months after the effective date of the law or agreement provided a lease dated prior to such effective date was filed with the State and recorded within thirty (30) days following such effective date.

(2) There must be existing property rights in the sign affected by the State law or regulations. For example, paper signs nailed to trees, abandoned signs and the like are not protected.

(3) The sign may be sold, leased, or otherwise transferred without affecting its status, but its location may not be changed. A nonconforming sign removed as a result of a right-of-way taking or for any other reason may be relocated to a conforming area but cannot be reestablished at a new location as a nonconforming use.

(4) The sign must have been lawful on the effective date of the State law or regulations, and must continue to be lawfully maintained.

(5) The sign must remain substantially the same as it was on the effective date of the State law or regulations. Reasonable repair and maintenance of the sign, including a change of

advertising message, is not a change which would terminate nonconforming rights. Each State shall develop its own criteria to determine when customary maintenance ceases and a substantial change has occurred which would terminate nonconforming rights.

(6) The sign may continue as long as it is not destroyed, abandoned, or discontinued. If permitted by State law and reerected in kind, exception may be made for signs destroyed due to vandalism and other criminal or tortious acts.

(i) Each state shall develop criteria to define destruction, abandonment and discontinuance. These criteria may provide that a sign which for a designated period of time has obsolete advertising matter or is without advertising matter or is in need of substantial repair may constitute abandonment or discontinuance. Similarly, a sign damaged in excess of a certain percentage of its replacement cost may be considered destroyed.

(ii) Where an existing nonconforming sign ceases to display advertising matter, a reasonable period of time to replace advertising content must be established by each State. Where new content is not put on a structure within the established period, the use of the structure as a nonconforming outdoor advertising sign is terminated and shall constitute an abandonment or discontinuance. Where a State establishes a period of more than one (1) year as a reasonable period for change of message, it shall justify that period as a customary enforcement practice within the State. This established period may be waived for an involuntary discontinuance such as the closing of a highway for repair in front of the sign.

(e) *Just compensation.* The States are required to pay just compensation for the removal of nonconforming lawfully existing signs in accordance with the terms of 23 U.S.C. 131 and the provisions of subpart D, part 750, chapter I, 23 CFR. The conditions which establish a right to maintain a nonconforming sign and therefore the right to compensation must pertain at the time it is acquired or removed.

§ 750.708 Acceptance of state zoning.

(a) 23 U.S.C. 131(d) provide that signs "may be erected and maintained within 660 feet of the nearest edge of the right-of-way within areas . . . which are zoned industrial or commercial under authority of State law." Section 131(d) further provides, "The States shall have full authority under their own zoning laws to zone areas for commercial or industrial purposes, and the actions of the States in this regard will be accepted for the purposes of this Act."

(b) State and local zoning actions must be taken pursuant to the State's zoning enabling statute or constitutional authority and in accordance therewith. Action which is not a part of comprehensive zoning and is created primarily to permit outdoor advertising structures, is not recognized as zoning for outdoor advertising control purposes.

(c) Where a unit of government has not zoned in accordance with statutory authority or is not authorized to zone, the definition of an unzoned commercial or industrial area in the State-Federal agreement will apply within that political subdivision or area.

(d) A zone in which limited commercial or industrial activities are permitted as an incident to other primary land uses is not considered to be a commercial or industrial zone for outdoor advertising control purposes.

§ 750.709 On-property or on-premise advertising.

(a) A sign which consists solely of the name of the establishment or which identifies the establishment's principal or accessory products or services offered on the property is an on-property sign.

(b) When a sign consists principally of brand name or trade name advertising and the product or service advertised is only incidental to the principal activity, or if it brings rental income to the property owner, it shall be considered the business of outdoor advertising and not an on-property sign.

(c) A sale or lease sign which also advertises any product or service not conducted upon and unrelated to the business or selling or leasing the land on which the sign is located is not an on-property sign.

(d) Signs are exempt from control under 23 U.S.C. 131 if they solely advertise the sale or lease of property on which they are located or advertise activities conducted on the property on which they are located. These signs are subject to regulation (subpart A, part 750, chapter I, 23 CFR) in those States which have executed a bonus agreement, 23 U.S.C. 131(j). State laws or regulations shall contain criteria for determining exemptions. These criteria may include:

(1) A property test for determining whether a sign is located on the same property as the activity or property advertised; and

(2) A purpose test for determining whether a sign has as its sole purpose the identification of the activity located on the property or its products or services, or the sale or lease of the property on which the sign is located.

(3) The criteria must be sufficiently specific to curb attempts to improperly qualify outdoor advertising as "on-property" signs, such as signs on narrow strips of land contiguous to the advertised activity when the purpose is clearly to circumvent 23 U.S.C. 131.

§ 750.710 Landmark signs.

(a) 23 U.S.C. 131(c) permits the existence of signs lawfully in existence on October 22, 1965, determined by the State, subject to the approval of the Secretary, to be landmark signs, including signs on farm structures or natural surfaces, of historic or artistic significance, the preservation of which is consistent with the purpose of 23 U.S.C. 131.

(b) States electing to permit landmark signs under 23 U.S.C. 131(c) shall submit a one-time list to the Federal Highway Administration for approval. The list should identify each sign as being in the original 1966 inventory. In the event a sign was omitted in the 1966 inventory, the State may submit other evidence to support a determination that the sign was in existence on October 22, 1965.

(c) Reasonable maintenance, repair, and restoration of a landmark sign is permitted. Substantial change in size, lighting, or message content will terminate its exempt status.

§ 750.711 Structures which have never displayed advertising material.

Structures, including poles, which have never displayed advertising or informative content are subject to control or removal when advertising content visible from the main-traveled way is added or affixed. When this is done, an "outdoor advertising sign" has then been erected which must comply with the State law in effect on that date.

§ 750.712 Reclassification of signs.

Any sign lawfully erected after the effective date of a State outdoor advertising control law which is reclassified from legal-conforming to nonconforming and subject to removal under revised State statutes or regulations and policy pursuant to this regulation is eligible for Federal participation in just compensation payments and other eligible costs.

§ 750.713 Bonus provisions.

23 U.S.C. 131(j) specifically provides that any State which had entered into a bonus agreement before June 30, 1965, will be entitled to remain eligible to receive bonus payments provided it continues to carry out its bonus agreement. Bonus States are not exempt from the other provisions of 23 U.S.C. 131. If a State elects to comply with both programs, it must extend controls to the Primary System, and continue to carry out its bonus agreement along the Interstate System except where 23 U.S.C. 131, as amended, imposes more stringent requirements.

PART 751—JUNKYARD CONTROL AND ACQUISITION

Sec.

AUTHORITY: 23 U.S.C. 136 and 315, 42 U.S.C. 4321–4347 and 4601–4655, 23 CFR 1.32, 49 CFR 1.48, unless otherwise noted.

SOURCE: 40 FR 8551, Feb. 28, 1975, unless otherwise noted.

§ 751.1 Purpose.

Pursuant to 23 U.S.C. 136, this part prescribes Federal Highway Administration [FHWA] policies and procedures relating to the exercise of effective control by the States of junkyards in areas adjacent to the Interstate and Federal-aid primary systems. Nothing in this part shall be construed to prevent a State from establishing more stringent junkyard control requirements than provided herein.

[40 FR 12260, Mar. 18, 1975]

§ 751.3 Applicability.

The provisions of this part are applicable to all areas within 1,000 feet of the nearest edge of the right-of-way and visible from the main traveled way of all Federal-aid Primary and Interstate Systems regardless of whether Federal funds participated in the construction thereof, including toll sections of such highways. This part does not apply to the Urban System.

§ 751.5 Policy.

In carrying out the purposes of this part:

(a) Emphasis should be placed on encouraging recycling of scrap and junk where practicable, in accordance with the National Environmental Policy Act of 1969 (42 U.S.C. 4321, *et seq.*);

(b) Every effort should be made to screen nonconforming junkyards which are to continue as ongoing businesses; and

(c) Nonconforming junkyards should be relocated only as a last resort.

§ 751.7 Definitions.

For purposes of this part, the following definitions shall apply:

(a) *Junkyard*. (1) A Junkyard is an establishment or place of business which is maintained, operated or used for storing, keeping, buying, or selling junk, or for the maintenance or operation of an automobile graveyard. This definition includes scrap metal processors, auto-wrecking yards, salvage yards, scrap yards, autorecycling yards, used auto parts yards and temporary storage of automobile bodies and parts awaiting disposal as a normal part of a business operation when the business will continually have like materials located on the premises. The definition includes garbage dumps and sanitary landfills. The definition does not include litter, trash, and other debris scattered along or upon the highway, or temporary operations and outdoor storage of limited duration.

(2) An Automobile Graveyard is an establishment or place of business which is maintained, used, or operated for storing, keeping, buying, or selling wrecked, scrapped, ruined, or dismantled motor vehicles or motor vehicle parts. Ten or more such vehicles will constitute an automobile graveyard.

(3) An Illegal Junkyard is one which was established or is maintained in violation of State law.

(4) A Nonconforming Junkyard is one which was lawfully established, but which does not comply with the provisions of State law or State regulations passed at a later date or which later fails to comply with State regulations due to changed conditions. Illegally established junkyards are not nonconforming junkyards.

(b) *Junk*. Old or scrap metal, rope, rags, batteries, paper, trash, rubber, debris, waste, or junked, dismantled, or wrecked automobiles, or parts thereof.

(c) *Main traveled way*. The traveled way of a highway on which through traffic is carried. In the case of a divided highway, the traveled way of each of the separated roadways for traffic in opposite directions is a main traveled way. It does not include such facilities as frontage roads, turning roadways, or parking areas.

(d) *Industrial zones*. Those districts established by zoning authorities as being most appropriate for industry or manufacturing. A zone which simply permits certain industrial activities as an incident to the primary land use designation is not considered to be an industrial zone. The provisions of part 750, subpart G of this chapter relative to Outdoor Advertising Control shall apply insofar as industrial zones are concerned.

(e) *Unzoned industrial areas.* An area where there is no zoning in effect and which is used primarily for industrial purposes as determined by the State and approved by the FHWA. An unzoned area cannot include areas which may have a rural zoning classification or land uses established by zoning variances or special exceptions.

[40 FR 8551, Feb. 28, 1975, as amended at 41 FR 9321, Mar. 4, 1976]

§ 751.9 Effective control.

(a) In order to provide effective control of junkyards located within 1,000 feet of Interstate and Federal-aid primary highways, the State must:

(1) Require such junkyards located outside of zoned and unzoned industrial areas to be screened or located so as not to be visible from the main traveled way, or be removed from sight.

(2) Require the screening or removal of nonconforming junkyards within a reasonable time, but no later than 5 years after the date the junkyard becomes nonconforming unless Federal funds are not available in adequate amounts to participate in the cost of such screening or removal as provided in 23 U.S.C. 136(j).

(3) Prohibit the establishment of new junkyards unless they comply with the requirements of paragraph (a)(1) of this section.

(4) Expeditiously require junkyards which are illegally established or maintained to conform to the requirements of paragraph (a)(1) of this section.

(b) Sanitary landfills as described herein need not be screened to satisfy requirements of Title 23, U.S.C., but landscaping should be required when the fill has been completed and operations have ceased, unless the landfill area is to be used for immediate development purposes. A sanitary landfill, for the purposes of this part, is a method of disposing of refuse on land without creating a nuisance or hazards to public health or safety by utilizing the principles of engineering to confine the refuse to the smallest practical area, to reduce it to the smallest practical volume, and to cover it with a layer of earth at the conclusion of each day's operation or at such more frequent intervals as may be necessary.

(c) The State shall have laws, rules, and procedures sufficient to provide effective control, to discover illegally established or maintained junkyards shortly after such occurrence, and to cause the compliance or removal of same promptly in accordance with State legal procedures.

§ 751.11 Nonconforming junkyards.

Subject to the provisions of § 751.9 of this part, the following requirements for the maintenance and continuance of a nonconforming junkyard apply:

(a) The junkyard must have been actually in existence at the time the State law or regulations became effective as distinguished from a contemplated use, except where a permit or similar specific State governmental action was granted for the establishment of a junkyard prior to the effective date of the State law or regulations, and the junkyard owner acted in good faith and expended sums in reliance thereon.

(b) There must be existing property rights in the junkyard or junk affected by the State law or regulation. Abandoned junk and junkyards, worthless junk, and the like are not similarly protected.

(c) If the location of a nonconforming junkyard is changed as a result of a right-of-way taking or for any other reason, it ceases to be a nonconforming junkyard, and shall be treated as a new junkyard at a new location.

(d) The nonconforming junkyard must have been lawful on the effective date of the State law or regulations and must continue to be lawfully maintained.

(e) The nonconforming junkyard may continue as long as it is not extended, enlarged, or changed in use. Once a junkyard has been made conforming, the placement of junk so that it may be seen above or beyond a screen, or otherwise becomes visible, shall be treated the same as the establishment of a new junkyard.

(f) The nonconforming junkyard may continue as long as it is not abandoned, destroyed, or voluntarily discontinued. Each State should develop criteria to define these terms.

§751.13 Control measures.

(a) Consistent with the goals of the National Environmental Policy Act of 1969 (42 U.S.C. 4321), recycling of junk and scrap is to be encouraged to the greatest extent practicable in the implementation of the junkyard control program. Recycling should be considered in conjunction with other control measures. To facilitate recycling, junk or scrap should be moved to an automobile wrecker, or a scrap processor, or put to some other useful purpose.

(b) Every effort shall be made to screen where the junkyard is to continue as an ongoing business. Screening may be accomplished by use of natural objects, landscaping plantings, fences, and other appropriate means, including relocating inventory on site to utilize an existing natural screen or a screenable portion of the site.

(c) Where screening is used, it must, upon completion of the screening project, effectively screen the junkyard from the main traveled way of the highway on a year-round basis, and be compatible with the surroundings. Each State shall establish criteria governing the location, design, construction, maintenance, and materials used in fencing or screening.

(d) A junkyard should be relocated only when other control measures are not feasible. Junkyards should be relocated to a site not visible from the highway or to an industrial area, and should not be relocated to residential, commercial, or other areas where foreseeable environmental problems may develop.

(e) The State may develop and use other methods of operation to carry out the purposes of this directive, subject to prior FHWA approval.

§751.15 Just compensation.

(a) Just compensation shall be paid the owner for the relocation, removal, or disposal of junkyards lawfully established under State law, which are required to be removed, relocated, or disposed of pursuant to 23 U.S.C. 136.

(b) No rights to compensation accrue until a taking or removal has occurred. The conditions which establish a right to maintain and continue a nonconforming junkyard as provided in §751.11 must pertain at the time of the taking or removal in order to establish a right to just compensation.

§751.17 Federal participation.

(a) Federal funds may participate in 75 percent of the costs of control measures incurred in carrying out the provisions of this part including necessary studies for particular projects, and the employment of fee landscape architects and other qualified consultants.

(b) Where State control standards are more stringent than Federal control requirements along Interstate and primary highways, the FHWA may approve Federal participation in the costs of applying the State standards on a statewide basis. Where State standards require control of junkyards in zoned or unzoned industrial areas, Federal funds may participate only if such action will make an effective contribution to the character of the area as a whole and the cost is reasonable, but such projects should be deferred until the work in the areas where control is required has progressed well toward completion.

(c) Generally, only costs associated with the acquisition of minimal real property interests, such as easements or temporary rights of entry, necessary to accomplish the purposes of this part are eligible for Federal participation. The State may request, on a case-by-case basis, participation in costs of other interests beyond the minimum necessary, including fee title.

(d) Federal funds may participate in costs to correct the inadequacies of screening in prior control projects where the inadequacy is due to higher screening standards established in this part or due to changed conditions.

(e) Federal funds may participate in the costs of moving junk or scrap to a recycling place of business, or in the case of junk with little or no recycling potential, to a site for permanent disposal. In the latter case, reasonable land rehabilitation costs or fees connected with the use of such a disposal site are also eligible. In a case where the acquisition of a permanent disposal site by the State would be the most economical method of disposal, Federal funds may participate in the net cost (cost of acquisition less a credit after disposal) of a site obtained for this purpose.

(f) Federal funds may participate in control measure costs involved in any junkyard lawfully established or maintained under State law which is reclassified from conforming to nonconforming under revised State regulations and policy pursuant to this part.

(g) Federal funds may participate in the costs of acquisition of a dwelling in exceptional cases where such acquisition is found necessary and in the public interest, and where acquisition of the dwelling can be accomplished without resort to eminent domain.

(h) Federal funds shall not participate in:

(1) Costs associated with the control of illegal junkyards except for removal by State personnel on a force account basis or by contract, or in costs of controlling junkyards established after the effective date of the State's compliance law except where a conforming junkyard later becomes nonconforming due to changed conditions;

(2) Any costs associated with the acquisition of any dwelling or its related buildings if acquired through eminent domain in connection with the junkyard control program;

(3) Costs of acquisition of interests or rights as a measure for prohibition or control of the establishment of future junkyards;

(4) Costs of maintaining screening devices after they have been erected; or

(5) Costs of screening junk which has been or will be removed as a part of a junkyard control project.

§ 751.19 Documentation for Federal participation.

The following information concerning each eligible junkyard must be available in the States' files to be eligible for Federal participation in the costs thereof:

(a) Satisfactory evidence of ownership of the junk or junkyard or both.

(b) Value or cost documentation (including separate interests if applicable) including proof of obligation or payment of funds.

(c) Evidence that the necessary property interests have passed to the State and that the junk has been screened, relocated, removed or disposed of in accordance with the provisions of this part.

(d) If a dwelling has been acquired by condemnation, evidence that the costs involved are not included in the State's claim for participation.

[40 FR 8551, Feb. 28, 1975; 40 FR 12260, Mar. 18, 1975]

§ 751.21 Relocation assistance.

Relocation assistance benefits pursuant to 49 CFR part 24 are available for:

(a) The actual reasonable moving expenses of the junk, actual direct loss of tangible personal property and actual reasonable expenses in searching for a replacement business or, if the eligibility requirements are met, a payment in lieu of such expenses.

(b) Relocation assistance in locating a replacement business.

(c) Moving costs of personal property from a dwelling and relocation assistance in locating a replacement dwelling, provided the acquisition of the real property used for the business causes a person to vacate a dwelling.

(d) Replacement housing payments if the acquisition of the dwelling is found by FHWA to be necessary for the federally assisted junkyard control project.

[40 FR 8551, Feb. 28, 1975, as amended at 50 FR 34094, Aug. 23, 1985; 54 FR 47076, Nov. 9, 1989]

§ 751.23 Concurrent junkyard control and right-of-way projects.

The State is encouraged to coordinate junkyard control and highway right-of-way projects. Expenses incurred in furtherance of concurrent projects shall be prorated between projects.

§ 751.25 Programming and authorization.

(a) Junkyard control projects shall be programmed in accordance with the provisions of part 630, subpart A of this chapter. Such projects may include one or more junkyards.

(b) Authorization to proceed with a junkyard control project may be given when the State submits a written request to FHWA which includes the following:

(1) The zoning and validation of the legal status of each junkyard on the project;

(2) The control measures proposed for each junkyard including, where applicable, information relative to permanent disposal sites to be acquired by the State;

(3) The real property interest to be acquired in order to implement the control measures;

(4) Plans or graphic displays indicating the location of the junkyard relative to the highway, the 1,000 foot control lines, property ownership boundaries, the general location of the junk or scrap material, and any buildings, structures, or improvement involved; and

(5) Where screening is to be utilized, the type of screening, and adequately detailed plans and cross sections, or other adequate graphic displays which illustrate the relationship of the motorist, the screen, and the material to be screened at critical points of view.

[40 FR 8551, Feb. 28, 1975, as amended at 41 FR 9321, Mar. 4, 1976]

PART 752—LANDSCAPE AND ROADSIDE DEVELOPMENT

AUTHORITY: 23 U.S.C. 131, 315, 319; 42 U.S.C. 4321 *et seq.;* 49 CFR 1.48(b), unless otherwise noted.

SOURCE: 43 FR 19390, May 5, 1978, unless otherwise noted.

§ 752.1 Purpose.

The purpose of this part is to furnish guidelines and prescribe policies regarding landscaping and scenic enhancement programs, safety rest areas, and scenic overlooks under 23 U.S.C. 319; information centers and systems under 23 U.S.C. 131(i); and vending machines in safety rest areas under 23 U.S.C. 111.

[48 FR 38610, Aug. 25, 1983]

§ 752.2 Policy.

(a) Highway esthetics is a most important consideration in the Federal-aid highway program. Highways must not only blend with our natural social, and cultural environment, but also provide pleasure and satisfaction in their use.

(b) The FHWA will cooperate with State and local agencies and organizations to provide opportunities for the display of original works of art within the highway rights-of-way.

(c) The development of the roadside to include landscape development, safety rest areas, and the preservation of valuable adjacent scenic lands is a necessary component of highway development. Planning and development of the roadside should be concurrent with or closely follow that of the highway. Further, the development of travel information centers and systems is encouraged as an effective method of providing necessary information to the traveling public.

§ 752.3 Definitions.

(a) *Safety rest area.* A roadside facility safely removed from the traveled way with parking and such facilities for the motorist deemed necessary for his rest, relaxation, comfort and information needs. The term is synonymous with "rest and recreation areas."

(b) *Scenic overlook.* A roadside improvement for parking and other facilities to provide the motorist with a safe opportunity to stop and enjoy a view.

(c) *Information centers.* Facilities located at safety rest areas which provide information of interest to the traveling public.

(d) *Information systems.* Facilities located within the right-of-way which provide information of interest to the traveling public. An information system is not a sign, display or device otherwise permitted under 23 U.S.C. 131 or prohibited by any local, State or Federal law or regulation.

(e) *Landscape project.* Any action taken as part of a highway construction project or as a separate action to enhance the esthetics of a highway through the placement of plant materials consistent with a landscape design plan. Seeding undertaken for erosion control and planting vegetation for screening purposes shall not constitute a landscaping project.

[43 FR 19390, May 5, 1978, as amended at 52 FR 34638, Sept. 14, 1987]

§ 752.4 Landscape development.

(a) Landscape development, *which includes landscaping projects and other highway planting programs* within the right-of-way of all federally funded highways or on adjoining scenic lands, shall be in general comformity with accepted concepts and principles of highway landscaping and environmental design.

(b) *Landscape development* should have provisions for plant establishment periods of a duration sufficient for expected survival in the highway environment. Normal 1-year plant establishment periods may be extended to 3-year periods where survival is considered essential to their function, such as junkyard screening or urban landscaping projects.

(c) In urban areas new and major reconstructed highways and completed Interstate and expressway sections are to be landscaped as appropriate for the adjacent existing or planned environment.

(d) In rural areas new and major reconstructed highways should be landscaped as appropriate for the adjacent environment. Planning should include the opportunity for natural regeneration of native growth and the management of that growth.

(e) Landscaping projects shall include the planting of native wildflower seeds or seedlings or both, unless a waiver is granted as provided in § 752.11(b).

[43 FR 19390, May 5, 1978, as amended at 52 FR 34638, Sept. 14, 1987]

§ 752.5 Safety rest areas.

(a) Safety rest areas should provide facilities reasonably necessary for the comfort, convenience, relaxation, and information needs of the motorist. Caretakers' quarters may be provided in conjunction with a safety rest area at such locations where accommodations are deemed necessary. All facilities within the rest area are to provide full consideration and accommodation for the handicapped.

(b) The State may permit the placement of vending machines in existing or new safety rest areas located on the rights-of-way of the Interstate system for the purpose of dispensing such food, drink, or other articles as the State determines are appropriate and desirable, except that the dispensing by any means, of petroleum products or motor vehicle replacement parts shall not be allowed. Such vending machines shall be operated by the State.

(c) The State may operate the vending machines directly or may contract with a vendor for the installation, operation, and maintenance of the vending machines. In permitting the placement of vending machines the State shall give priority to vending machines which are operated through the State licensing agency designated pursuant to section 2(a)(5) of the Randolph-Sheppard Act, U.S.C. 107(a)(5).

(d) Access from the safety rest areas to adjacent publicly owned conservation and recreation areas may be permitted if access to these areas is only available through the rest area and if these areas or their usage does not adversely affect the facilities of the safety rest area.

(e) The scenic quality of the site, its accessibility and adaptability, and the availability of utilities are the prime considerations in the selection of rest area sites. A statewide safety rest area system plan should be maintained. This plan should include development priorities to ensure safety rest areas will be constructed first at locations most needed by the motorist. Proposals for safety rest areas or similar facilities on Federal-aid highways in suburban or urban areas shall be special case and must be fully justified before being authorized by the FHWA Regional Administrator.

(f) Facilities within newly constructed safety rest areas should meet the forecast needs of the design year. Expansion and modernization of older existing rest areas that do not provide adequate service should be considered.

(g) No charge to the public may be made for goods and services at safety rest areas except for telephone and articles dispensed by vending machines.

[43 FR 19390, May 5, 1978, as amended at 48 FR 38611, Aug. 25, 1983]

§ 752.6 Scenic overlooks.

Scenic overlooks shall be located and designed as appropriate to the site and the scenic view with consideration for safety, access, and convenience of the motorist. Scenic overlooks may provide facilities equivalent to those provided in safety rest area.

§ 752.7 Information centers and systems.

(a) The State may establish at existing or new safety rest areas information centers for the purpose of providing specific information to the motorist as to services, as to places of interest within the State and such other information as the State may consider desirable.

(b) The State may construct and operate the facilities, may construct and lease the operation of information facilities, or may lease the construction and operation of information facilities.

(c) Where the information center or system includes an enclosed building, the identification of the operator and all advertising must be restricted to the interior of the building. Where a facility is in the nature of a bulletin board or partial enclosure, none of the advertising, including the trade name, logo, or symbol of the operator shall be legible from the main traveled way.

(d) Subject to FHWA approval, States may establish or permit information systems within the right-of-way of federally funded highways which provide information of specific interest to the traveling public which do not visually intrude upon the main-traveled way of the highway in a manner violating 23 U.S.C. 131 and other applicable local, State, and Federal laws, rules, and regulations.

§ 752.8 Privately operated information centers and systems.

(a) Subject to the FHWA Regional Administrator's approval of the lease or agreement, the State may permit privately operated information centers and systems which conform with the standards of this directive.

(b) There shall be no violation of control of access, and no adverse effect on traffic in the main traveled way.

(c) The agreement between the State and the private operator shall provide that:

(1) The State shall have title to the information center or system upon completion of construction or termination of the lease.

(2) Advertising must be limited to matters relating to and of interest to the traveling public.

(3) Equal access must be provided at reasonable rates to all advertisers considered qualified by the State.

(4) Forty percent or more of all display areas and audible communications shall be devoted free of charge to providing information to the traveling public and public service announcements.

(5) No charge to the public may be made for goods or services except telephone and articles dispensed by vending machines.

(6) Nondiscrimination provisions must be included in accordance with the State assurance with regard to 42 U.S.C. 2000d—2000d-5 (Civil Rights Act of 1964). The private operator may not permit advertising from advertisers who do not provide their services without regard to race, color, or national origin.

(7) The center or system shall be adequately maintained and kept clean and sanitary.

(8) The State may promulgate reasonable rules and regulations on the conduct of the information center or system in the interests of the public.

(9) The State may terminate the lease or agreement for violation of its terms or for other cause.

[43 FR 19390, May 5, 1978, as amended at 48 FR 38611, Aug. 25, 1983]

§ 752.9 Scenic lands.

(a) Acquisition of interests in and improvement of strips of land or water areas adjacent to Federal-aid highways may be made as necessary for restoration, preservation, and enhancement of scenic beauty.

(b) Scenic strip interests may be acquired in urban or rural areas, combined in one or more projects, authorized separately whether or not there is or has been a Federal-aid project on the adjoining Federal-aid highway.

(c) Approval of acquisition and development of scenic strips on completed Interstate should be conditioned on a showing that the acquisition of scenic strips was considered under the Highway Beautification Program for that particular section of Interstate.

§ 752.10 Abandoned vehicles.

(a) Abandoned motor vehicles may be removed from the right-of-way and from private lands adjacent to Federal-aid highways for the restoration, preservation, or enhancement of scenic beauty as seen from the traveled way of the highway as a landscape or roadside development project.

(b) The State shall obtain permission or sufficient legal authority to go on private land to carry out this program. Where feasible, an agreement should be made with the owner that he will not in the future place junk, or allow junk to be placed, on his land so as to create an eyesore to the traveling public. The permission or authority and the agreement may be informal.

(c) The collection of abandoned motor vehicles from within the right-of-way must be a development project and not a maintenance operation. Once a State completes a development project for the removal of abandoned motor vehicles from within the highway right-of-way, it is obligated to continue the removal of future abandoned motor vehicles from within the development project limits without further participation.

§ 752.11 Federal participation.

(a) Federal-aid highway funds, but generally excluding Interstate construction funds, are available for landscape development; for the acquisition and development of safety rest areas, scenic overlooks, and scenic lands; for the development of information centers and systems; and for the removal of abandoned motor vehicles.

(b) Federal-aid highway funds may participate in any landscaping project undertaken pursuant to paragraph (a) of this section provided that at least one-quarter of one percent of funds expended for such landscaping project is used to plant native wildflower seeds or seedlings or both. The Administrator may, upon the request of a State highway agency, grant a waiver to this requirement provided the State certifies that:

(1) Native wildflowers or seedlings cannot be grown satisfactorily; or

(2) There is a scarcity of available planting areas; or

(3) The available planting areas will be used for agricultural purposes.

(c) Subject to the requirement of paragraph (b) of this section, Federal-aid highway funds may participate in plant establishment periods in or associated with landscape development.

(d) Notwithstanding the provisions of paragraph (b) of this section, Federal-aid highway funds may participate in the planting of flowering materials, including native wildflowers, donated by garden clubs and other organizations or individuals.

(e) The value of donated plant materials shall not count toward the one-quarter of one percent minimum expenditure required by paragraph (b) of this section.

(f) Federal-aid funds may not be used for assemblage, printing, or distribution of information materials; for temporary or portable information facilities; or for installation, operation, or maintenance of vending machines.

[52 FR 34638, Sept. 14, 1987]

PART 771—ENVIRONMENTAL IMPACT AND RELATED PROCEDURES

Sec.

AUTHORITY: 42 U.S.C. 4321 *et seq.*; 23 U.S.C. 106, 109, 128, 138, 139, 315, 325, 326, and 327; 49 U.S.C. 303; 49 U.S.C. 24201; 40 CFR parts 1500–1508; 49 CFR 1.81, 1.85, and 1.91; Pub. L. 109–59, 119 Stat. 1144, Sections 6002 and 6010; Pub. L. 112–141, 126 Stat. 405, Sections 1315, 1316, 1317, 1318, and 1319; and Public Law 114–94, 129 Stat. 1312, Sections 1304 and 1432.

SOURCE: 83 FR 54493, Oct. 29, 2018, unless otherwise noted.

§771.101 Purpose.

This part prescribes the policies and procedures of the Federal Highway Administration (FHWA), the Federal Railroad Administration (FRA), and the Federal Transit Administration (FTA) for implementing the National Environmental Policy Act of 1969 as amended (NEPA), and supplements the NEPA regulations of the Council on Environmental Quality (CEQ), 40 CFR parts 1500 through 1508 (CEQ regulations). Together these regulations set forth all FHWA, FRA, FTA, and U.S. Department of Transportation (DOT) requirements under NEPA for the processing of highway, public transportation, and railroad actions. This part also sets forth procedures to comply with 23 U.S.C. 109(h), 128, 138, 139, 325, 326, and 327; 49 U.S.C. 303; 49 U.S.C. 24201; and 5323(q); Public Law 112–141, 126 Stat. 405, section 1301 as applicable; and Public Law 114–94, 129 Stat. 1312, section 1304.

§771.103 [Reserved]

§771.105 Policy.

It is the policy of the Administration that:

(a) To the maximum extent practicable and consistent with Federal law, all environmental investigations, reviews, and consultations be coordinated as a single process, and compliance with all applicable environmental requirements be reflected in the environmental review document required by this part.[1]

(b) Programmatic approaches be developed for compliance with environmental requirements (including the requirements found at 23 U.S.C. 139(b)(3)), coordination among agencies and/or the public, or to otherwise enhance and accelerate project development.

(c) Alternative courses of action be evaluated and decisions be made in the best overall public interest based upon a balanced consideration of the need for safe and efficient transportation; of the social, economic, and environmental impacts of the proposed transportation improvement; and of national, State, and local environmental protection goals.

(d) Public involvement and a systematic interdisciplinary approach be essential parts of the development process for proposed actions.

(e) Measures necessary to mitigate adverse impacts be incorporated into the action. Measures necessary to mitigate adverse impacts are eligible for Federal funding when the Administration determines that:

(1) The impacts for which the mitigation is proposed actually result from the Administration action; and

(2) The proposed mitigation represents a reasonable public expenditure after considering the impacts of the action and the benefits of the proposed mitigation measures. In making this determination, the Administration will consider, among other factors, the extent to which the proposed measures would assist in complying with a Federal statute, executive order, or Administration regulation or policy.

(f) Costs incurred by the applicant for the preparation of environmental documents requested by the Administration be eligible for Federal assistance.

(g) No person, because of handicap, age, race, color, sex, or national origin, be excluded from participating in, or denied benefits of, or be subject to discrimination under any Administration

[1] FHWA, FRA, and FTA have supplementary guidance on environmental documents and procedures for their programs available on the internet at *http://www.fhwa.dot.gov*, *http://www.fra.dot.gov*, and *http://www.fta.dot.gov*, or in hardcopy by request.

program or procedural activity required by or developed pursuant to this part.

§ 771.107 Definitions.

The definitions contained in the CEQ regulations and in titles 23 and 49 of the United States Code are applicable. In addition, the following definitions apply to this part.

Action. A highway, transit, or railroad project proposed for U.S. DOT funding. It also can include activities such as joint and multiple use permits, changes in access control, or rulemakings, which may or may not involve a commitment of Federal funds.

Administration. The FHWA, FRA, or FTA, whichever is the designated Federal lead agency for the proposed action. A reference herein to the Administration means the FHWA, FRA, or FTA, or a State when the State is functioning as the FHWA, FRA, or FTA in carrying out responsibilities delegated or assigned to the State in accordance with 23 U.S.C. 325, 326, or 327, or other applicable law. A reference herein to the FHWA, FRA, or FTA means the State when the State is functioning as the FHWA, FRA, or FTA respectively in carrying out responsibilities delegated or assigned to the State in accordance with 23 U.S.C. 325, 326, or 327, or other applicable law. Nothing in this definition alters the scope of any delegation or assignment made by FHWA, FRA, or FTA.

Administration action. FHWA, FRA, or FTA approval of the applicant's request for Federal funds for construction. It also can include approval of activities, such as joint and multiple use permits, changes in access control, rulemakings, etc., that may or may not involve a commitment of Federal funds.

Applicant. Any Federal, State, local, or federally recognized Indian Tribal governmental unit that requests funding approval or other action by the Administration and that the Administration works with to conduct environmental studies and prepare environmental review documents. When another Federal agency, or the Administration itself, is implementing the action, then the lead agencies (as defined in this section) may assume the responsibilities of the applicant in this part. If there is no applicant, then the Federal lead agency will assume the responsibilities of the applicant in this part.

Environmental studies. The investigations of potential environmental impacts to determine the environmental process to be followed and to assist in the preparation of the environmental document.

Lead agencies. The Administration and any other agency designated to serve as a joint lead agency with the Administration under 23 U.S.C. 139(c)(3) or under the CEQ regulations.

Participating agency. A Federal, State, local, or federally recognized Indian Tribal governmental unit that may have an interest in the proposed project and has accepted an invitation to be a participating agency or, in the case of a Federal agency, has not declined the invitation in accordance with 23 U.S.C. 139(d)(3).

Programmatic approaches. An approach that reduces the need for project-by-project reviews, eliminates repetitive discussion of the same issue, or focuses on the actual issues ripe for analyses at each level of review, consistent with NEPA and other applicable law.

Project sponsor. The Federal, State, local, or federally recognized Indian Tribal governmental unit, or other entity, including any private or public-private entity that seeks Federal funding or an Administration action for a project. Where it is not the applicant, the project sponsor may conduct some of the activities on the applicant's behalf.

Section 4(f). Refers to 49 U.S.C. 303 and 23 U.S.C. 138 (as implemented by 23 CFR part 774).

§ 771.109 Applicability and responsibilities.

(a)(1) The provisions of this part and the CEQ regulations apply to actions where the Administration exercises sufficient control to condition the permit, project, or other approvals. Steps taken by the applicant that do not require Federal approvals, such as preparation of a regional transportation plan, are not subject to this part.

(2) This part does not apply to or alter approvals by the Administration made prior to November 28, 2018.

(3) For FHWA and FTA, environmental documents accepted or prepared after November 28, 2018 must be developed in accordance with this part.

(4) FRA will apply this part to actions initiated after November 28, 2018.

(b)(1) The project sponsor, in cooperation with the Administration, is responsible for implementing those mitigation measures stated as commitments in the environmental documents prepared pursuant to this part unless the Administration approves of their deletion or modification in writing. The FHWA will ensure that this is accomplished as a part of its stewardship and oversight responsibilities. The FRA and FTA will ensure implementation of committed mitigation measures through incorporation by reference in the grant agreement, followed by reviews of designs and construction inspections.

(2) When entering into Federal-aid project agreements pursuant to 23 U.S.C. 106, FHWA must ensure that the State highway agency constructs the project in accordance with and incorporates all committed environmental impact mitigation measures listed in approved environmental review documents.

(c) The following roles and responsibilities apply during the environmental review process:

(1) The lead agencies are responsible for managing the environmental review process and the preparation of the appropriate environmental review documents.

(2) Any State or local governmental entity applicant that is or is expected to be a direct recipient of funds under title 23, U.S. Code or chapter 53 of title 49, U.S. Code for the action, or is or is expected to be a direct recipient of financial assistance for which FRA is responsible (e.g., Subtitle V of Title 49, U.S. Code) must serve as a joint lead agency with the Administration in accordance with 23 U.S.C. 139, and may prepare environmental review documents if the Administration furnishes guidance and independently evaluates the documents.

(3) The Administration may invite other Federal, State, local, or federally recognized Indian Tribal governmental units to serve as joint lead agencies in accordance with the CEQ regulations. If the applicant is serving as a joint lead agency under 23 U.S.C. 139(c)(3), then the Administration and the applicant will decide jointly which other agencies to invite to serve as joint lead agencies.

(4) When the applicant seeks an Administration action other than the approval of funds, the Administration will determine the role of the applicant in accordance with the CEQ regulations and 23 U.S.C. 139.

(5) Regardless of its role under paragraphs (c)(2) through (c)(4) of this section, a public agency that has statewide jurisdiction (for example, a State highway agency or a State department of transportation) or a local unit of government acting through a statewide agency, that meets the requirements of section 102(2)(D) of NEPA, may prepare the EIS and other environmental review documents with the Administration furnishing guidance, participating in the preparation, and independently evaluating the document. All FHWA applicants qualify under this paragraph.

(6) Subject to paragraph (e) of this section, the role of a project sponsor that is a private institution or firm is limited to providing technical studies and commenting on environmental review documents.

(7) A participating agency must provide input during the times specified in the coordination plan under 23 U.S.C. 139(g) and within the agency's special expertise or jurisdiction. Participating agencies provide comments and concurrence on the schedule within the coordination plan.

(d) When entering into Federal-aid project agreements pursuant to 23 U.S.C. 106, the State highway agency must ensure that the project is constructed in accordance with and incorporates all committed environmental impact mitigation measures listed in approved environmental review documents unless the State requests and receives written FHWA approval to modify or delete such mitigation features.

(e) When FRA is the lead Federal agency, the project sponsor is a private entity, and there is no applicant acting as a joint-lead agency, FRA and the project sponsor may agree to use a qualified third-party contractor to prepare an EIS. Under this arrangement, a project sponsor retains a contractor to assist FRA in conducting the environmental review. FRA selects, oversees, and directs the preparation of the EIS and retains ultimate control over the contractor's work. To enter into a third-party contract, FRA, the project sponsor, and the contractor will enter into a memorandum of understanding (MOU) that outlines at a minimum the conditions and procedures to be followed in carrying out the MOU and the responsibilities of the parties to the MOU. FRA may require use of a third-party contractor for preparation of an EA at its discretion.

§ 771.111 Early coordination, public involvement, and project development.

(a)(1) Early coordination with appropriate agencies and the public aids in determining the type of environmental review documents an action requires, the scope of the document, the level of analysis, and related environmental requirements. These activities contribute to reducing or eliminating delay, duplicative processes, and conflict, including by incorporating planning outcomes that have been reviewed by agencies and Indian Tribal partners in project development.

(2)(i) The information and results produced by or in support of the transportation planning process may be incorporated into environmental review documents in accordance with 40 CFR parts 1500 through 1508, 23 CFR part 450, 23 CFR part 450 Appendix A, or 23 U.S.C. 139(f), 168, or 169, as applicable.

(ii) The planning process described in paragraph (a)(2)(i) of this section may include mitigation actions consistent with a programmatic mitigation plan developed pursuant to 23 U.S.C. 169 or from a programmatic mitigation plan developed outside of that framework.

(3) Applicants intending to apply for funds or request Administration action should notify the Administration at the time that a project concept is identified. When requested, the Administration will advise the applicant, insofar as possible, of the probable class of action (see § 771.115) and related environmental laws and requirements and of the need for specific studies and findings that would normally be developed during the environmental review process. A lead agency, in consultation with participating agencies, must develop an environmental checklist, as appropriate, to assist in resource and agency identification.

(b)(1) The Administration will identify the probable class of action as soon as sufficient information is available to identify the probable impacts of the action.

(2) For projects to be evaluated with an EIS, the Administration must respond in writing to a project sponsor's formal project notification within 45 days of receipt.

(c) When the FHWA, FRA, or FTA are jointly involved in the development of an action, or when the FHWA, FRA, or FTA act as a joint lead agency with another Federal agency, a mutually acceptable process will be established on a case-by-case basis. A project sponsor may request the Secretary to designate the lead Federal agency when project elements fall within the expertise of multiple U.S. DOT agencies.

(d) During early coordination, the lead agencies may invite other agencies that may have an interest in the action to participate. The lead agencies must, however, invite such agencies if the action is subject to the project development procedures in 23 U.S.C. 139 within 45 days from publication of the notice of intent.[2] Any such agencies with special expertise concerning the action may also be invited to become cooperating agencies. Any such agencies with jurisdiction by law concerning the action must be invited to become cooperating agencies.

(e) Other States and Federal land management entities that may be significantly affected by the action or by any of the alternatives must be notified early and their views solicited by

[2] The Administration has guidance on 23 U.S.C. 139 available at *http://www.fhwa.dot.gov* or in hard copy upon request.

the applicant in cooperation with the Administration. The Administration will provide direction to the applicant on how to approach any significant unresolved issues as early as possible during the environmental review process.

(f) Any action evaluated under NEPA as a categorical exclusion (CE), environmental assessment (EA), or environmental impact statement (EIS) must:

(1) Connect logical termini and be of sufficient length to address environmental matters on a broad scope;

(2) Have independent utility or independent significance, *i.e.*, be usable and be a reasonable expenditure even if no additional transportation improvements in the area are made; and

(3) Not restrict consideration of alternatives for other reasonably foreseeable transportation improvements.

(g) For major transportation actions, the tiering of EISs as discussed in the CEQ regulation (40 CFR 1502.20) may be appropriate. The first tier EIS would focus on broad issues such as general location, mode choice, and areawide air quality and land use implications of the major alternatives. The second tier would address site-specific details on project impacts, costs, and mitigation measures.

(h) For the Federal-aid highway program:

(1) Each State must have procedures approved by the FHWA to carry out a public involvement/public hearing program pursuant to 23 U.S.C. 128 and 139 and CEQ regulations.

(2) State public involvement/public hearing procedures must provide for:

(i) Coordination of public involvement activities and public hearings with the entire NEPA process;

(ii) Early and continuing opportunities during project development for the public to be involved in the identification of social, economic, and environmental impacts, as well as impacts associated with relocation of individuals, groups, or institutions;

(iii) One or more public hearings or the opportunity for hearing(s) to be held by the State highway agency at a convenient time and place for any Federal-aid project that requires significant amounts of right-of-way, substantially changes the layout or functions of connecting roadways or of the facility being improved, has a substantial adverse impact on abutting property, otherwise has a significant social, economic, environmental or other effect, or for which the FHWA determines that a public hearing is in the public interest;

(iv) Reasonable notice to the public of either a public hearing or the opportunity for a public hearing. Such notice will indicate the availability of explanatory information. The notice must also provide information required to comply with public involvement requirements of other laws, executive orders, and regulations;

(v) Explanation at the public hearing of the following information, as appropriate:

(A) The project's purpose, need, and consistency with the goals and objectives of any local urban planning,

(B) The project's alternatives and major design features,

(C) The social, economic, environmental, and other impacts of the project,

(D) The relocation assistance program and the right-of-way acquisition process, and

(E) The State highway agency's procedures for receiving both oral and written statements from the public;

(vi) Submission to the FHWA of a transcript of each public hearing and a certification that a required hearing or hearing opportunity was offered. The transcript will be accompanied by copies of all written statements from the public, both submitted at the public hearing or during an announced period after the public hearing;

(vii) An opportunity for public involvement in defining the purpose and need and the range of alternatives, for any action subject to the project development procedures in 23 U.S.C. 139; and

(viii) Public notice and an opportunity for public review and comment on a Section 4(f) *de minimis* impact finding, in accordance with 23 CFR 774.5(b)(2)(i).

(i) Applicants for FRA programs or the FTA capital assistance program:

(1) Achieve public participation on proposed actions through activities that engage the public, including public hearings, town meetings, and

charrettes, and seek input from the public through scoping for the environmental review process. Project milestones may be announced to the public using electronic or paper media (e.g., newsletters, note cards, or emails) pursuant to 40 CFR 1506.6. For actions requiring EISs, an early opportunity for public involvement in defining the purpose and need for the action and the range of alternatives must be provided, and a public hearing will be held during the circulation period of the draft EIS.

(2) May participate in early scoping as long as enough project information is known so the public and other agencies can participate effectively. Early scoping constitutes initiation of NEPA scoping while local planning efforts to aid in establishing the purpose and need and in evaluating alternatives and impacts are underway. Notice of early scoping must be made to the public and other agencies. If early scoping is the start of the NEPA process, the early scoping notice must include language to that effect. After development of the proposed action at the conclusion of early scoping, FRA or FTA will publish the notice of intent if it is determined at that time that the proposed action requires an EIS. The notice of intent will establish a 30-day period for comments on the purpose and need, alternatives, and the scope of the NEPA analysis.

(3) Are encouraged to post and distribute materials related to the environmental review process, including, environmental documents (e.g., EAs and EISs), environmental studies (e.g., technical reports), public meeting announcements, and meeting minutes, through publicly-accessible electronic means, including project websites. Applicants should keep these materials available to the public electronically until the project is constructed and open for operations.

(4) Should post all findings of no significant impact (FONSIs), combined final environmental impact statements (final EISs)/records of decision (RODs), and RODs on a project website until the project is constructed and open for operation.

(j) Information on the FHWA environmental process may be obtained from: FHWA Director, Office of Project Development and Environmental Review, Federal Highway Administration, Washington, DC 20590, or *www.fhwa.dot.gov*. Information on the FRA environmental process may be obtained from: FRA Chief, Environmental and Corridor Planning Division, Office of Program Delivery, Federal Railroad Administration, Washington, DC 20590, or *www.fra.dot.gov*. Information on the FTA environmental process may be obtained from: FTA Director, Office of Environmental Programs, Federal Transit Administration, Washington, DC 20590 or *www.fta.dot.gov*.

§ 771.113 Timing of Administration activities.

(a) The lead agencies, in cooperation with the applicant and project sponsor, as appropriate, will perform the work necessary to complete the environmental review process. This work includes drafting environmental documents and completing environmental studies, related engineering studies, agency coordination, public involvement, and identification of mitigation measures. Except as otherwise provided in law or in paragraph (d) of this section, final design activities, property acquisition, purchase of construction materials or rolling stock, or project construction must not proceed until the following have been completed:

(1)(i) The Administration has classified the action as a CE;

(ii) The Administration has issued a FONSI; or

(iii) The Administration has issued a combined final EIS/ROD or a final EIS and ROD;

(2) For actions proposed for FHWA funding, the Administration has received and accepted the certifications and any required public hearing transcripts required by 23 U.S.C. 128;

(3) For activities proposed for FHWA funding, the programming requirements of 23 CFR part 450, subpart B, and 23 CFR part 630, subpart A, have been met.

(b) For FHWA actions, completion of the requirements set forth in paragraphs (a)(1) and (2) of this section is considered acceptance of the general project location and concepts described in the environmental review documents unless otherwise specified by the approving official.

(c) Letters of Intent issued under the authority of 49 U.S.C. 5309(g) are used by FTA to indicate an intention to obligate future funds for multi-year capital transit projects. Letters of Intent will not be issued by FTA until the NEPA process is completed.

(d) The prohibition in paragraph (a)(1) of this section is limited by the following exceptions:

(1) Early acquisition, hardship and protective acquisitions of real property in accordance with 23 CFR part 710, subpart E for FHWA. Exceptions for the acquisitions of real property are addressed in paragraphs (c)(6) and (d)(3) of § 771.118 for FTA.

(2) The early acquisition of right-of-way for future transit use in accordance with 49 U.S.C. 5323(q) and FTA guidance.

(3) A limited exception for rolling stock is provided in 49 U.S.C. 5309(l)(6).

(4) FRA may make exceptions on a case-by-case basis for purchases of railroad components or materials that can be used for other projects or resold.

§ 771.115 Classes of actions.

There are three classes of actions that prescribe the level of documentation required in the NEPA process. A programmatic approach may be used for any class of action.

(a) *EIS (Class I).* Actions that significantly affect the environment require an EIS (40 CFR 1508.27). The following are examples of actions that normally require an EIS:

(1) A new controlled access freeway.

(2) A highway project of four or more lanes on a new location.

(3) Construction or extension of a fixed transit facility (e.g., rapid rail, light rail, commuter rail, bus rapid transit) that will not be located primarily within an existing transportation right-of-way.

(4) New construction or extension of a separate roadway for buses or high occupancy vehicles not located within an existing transportation right-of-way.

(5) New construction or extension of a separate roadway for buses not located primarily within an existing transportation right-of-way.

(6) New construction of major railroad lines or facilities (e.g., terminal passenger stations, freight transfer yards, or railroad equipment maintenance facilities) that will not be located within an existing transportation right-of-way.

(b) *CE (Class II).* Actions that do not individually or cumulatively have a significant environmental effect are excluded from the requirement to prepare an EA or EIS. A specific list of CEs normally not requiring NEPA documentation is set forth in § 771.117(c) for FHWA actions or pursuant to § 771.118(c) for FTA actions. When appropriately documented, additional projects may also qualify as CEs pursuant to § 771.117(d) for FHWA actions or pursuant to § 771.118(d) for FTA actions. FRA's CEs are listed in § 771.116.

(c) *EA (Class III).* Actions for which the Administration has not clearly established the significance of the environmental impact. All actions that are not EISs or CEs are EAs. All actions in this class require the preparation of an EA to determine the appropriate environmental document required.

§ 771.116 FRA categorical exclusions.

(a) CEs are actions that meet the definition contained in 40 CFR 1508.4, and, based on FRA's past experience with similar actions, do not involve significant environmental impacts. They are actions that do not induce significant impacts to planned growth or land use for the area; do not require the relocation of significant numbers of people; do not have a significant impact on any natural, cultural, recreational, historic or other resource; do not involve significant air, noise, or water quality impacts; do not have significant impacts on travel patterns; or do not otherwise, either individually or cumulatively, have any significant environmental impacts.

(b) Any action that normally would be classified as a CE but could involve unusual circumstances will require FRA, in cooperation with the applicant, to conduct appropriate environmental studies to determine if the CE classification is proper. Such unusual circumstances include:

(1) Significant environmental impacts;

(2) Substantial controversy on environmental grounds;

(3) Significant impact on properties protected by Section 4(f) requirements or Section 106 of the National Historic Preservation Act; or

(4) Inconsistencies with any Federal, State, or local law, requirement or administrative determination relating to the environmental aspects of the action.

(c) Actions that FRA determines fall within the following categories of FRA CEs and that meet the criteria for CEs in the CEQ regulation (40 CFR 1508.4) and paragraph (a) of this section may be designated as CEs only after FRA approval. FRA may request the applicant or project sponsor submit documentation to demonstrate that the specific conditions or criteria for these CEs are satisfied and that significant environmental effects will not result.

(1) Administrative procurements (e.g., for general supplies) and contracts for personal services, and training.

(2) Personnel actions.

(3) Planning or design activities that do not commit to a particular course of action affecting the environment.

(4) Localized geotechnical and other investigations to provide information for preliminary design and for environmental analyses and permitting purposes, such as drilling test bores for soil sampling; archeological investigations for archeology resources assessment or similar survey; and wetland surveys.

(5) Internal orders, policies, and procedures not required to be published in the FEDERAL REGISTER under the Administrative Procedure Act, 5 U.S.C. 552(a)(1).

(6) Rulemakings issued under section 17 of the Noise Control Act of 1972, 42 U.S.C. 4916.

(7) Financial assistance to an applicant where the financial assistance funds an activity that is already completed, such as refinancing outstanding debt.

(8) Hearings, meetings, or public affairs activities.

(9) Maintenance or repair of existing railroad facilities, where such activities do not change the existing character of the facility, including equipment; track and bridge structures; electrification, communication, signaling, or security facilities; stations; tunnels; maintenance-of-way and maintenance-of-equipment bases.

(10) Emergency repair or replacement, including reconstruction, restoration, or retrofitting, of an essential rail facility damaged by the occurrence of a natural disaster or catastrophic failure. Such repair or replacement may include upgrades to meet existing codes and standards as well as upgrades warranted to address conditions that have changed since the rail facility's original construction.

(11) Operating assistance to a railroad to continue existing service or to increase service to meet demand, where the assistance will not significantly alter the traffic density characteristics of existing rail service.

(12) Minor rail line additions, including construction of side tracks, passing tracks, crossovers, short connections between existing rail lines, and new tracks within existing rail yards or right-of-way, provided that such additions are not inconsistent with existing zoning, do not involve acquisition of a significant amount of right-of-way, and do not significantly alter the traffic density characteristics of the existing rail lines or rail facilities.

(13) Acquisition or transfer of real property or existing railroad facilities, including track and bridge structures; electrification, communication, signaling or security facilities; stations; and maintenance of way and maintenance of equipment bases or the right to use such real property and railroad facilities, for the purpose of conducting operations of a nature and at a level of use similar to those presently or previously existing on the subject properties or facilities.

(14) Research, development, or demonstration activities on existing railroad lines or facilities, such as advances in signal communication or train control systems, equipment, or track, provided that such activities do not require the acquisition of a significant amount of right-of-way and do not significantly alter the traffic density

characteristics of the existing rail line or facility.

(15) Promulgation of rules, the issuance of policy statements, the waiver or modification of existing regulatory requirements, or discretionary approvals that do not result in significantly increased emissions of air or water pollutants or noise.

(16) Alterations to existing facilities, locomotives, stations, and rail cars in order to make them accessible for the elderly and persons with disabilities, such as modifying doorways, adding or modifying lifts, constructing access ramps and railings, modifying restrooms, and constructing accessible platforms.

(17) The rehabilitation, reconstruction or replacement of bridges, the rehabilitation or maintenance of the rail elements of docks or piers for the purposes of intermodal transfers, and the construction of bridges, culverts, or grade separation projects that are predominantly within existing right-of-way and that do not involve extensive in-water construction activities, such as projects replacing bridge components including stringers, caps, piles, or decks, the construction of roadway overpasses to replace at-grade crossings, construction or reconstruction of approaches or embankments to bridges, or construction or replacement of short span bridges.

(18) Acquisition (including purchase or lease), rehabilitation, transfer, or maintenance of vehicles or equipment, including locomotives, passenger coachers, freight cars, trainsets, and construction, maintenance or inspection equipment, that does not significantly alter the traffic density characteristics of an existing rail line.

(19) Installation, repair and replacement of equipment and small structures designed to promote transportation safety, security, accessibility, communication or operational efficiency that take place predominantly within the existing right-of-way and do not result in a major change in traffic density on the existing rail line or facility, such as the installation, repair or replacement of surface treatments or pavement markings, small passenger shelters, passenger amenities, benches, signage, sidewalks or trails, equipment enclosures, and fencing, railroad warning devices, train control systems, signalization, electric traction equipment and structures, electronics, photonics, and communications systems and equipment, equipment mounts, towers and structures, information processing equipment, and security equipment, including surveillance and detection cameras.

(20) Environmental restoration, remediation, pollution prevention, and mitigation activities conducted in conformance with applicable laws, regulations and permit requirements, including activities such as noise mitigation, landscaping, natural resource management activities, replacement or improvement to storm water oil/water separators, installation of pollution containment systems, slope stabilization, and contaminated soil removal or remediation activities.

(21) Assembly or construction of facilities or stations that are consistent with existing land use and zoning requirements, do not result in a major change in traffic density on existing rail or highway facilities, and result in approximately less than ten acres of surface disturbance, such as storage and maintenance facilities, freight or passenger loading and unloading facilities or stations, parking facilities, passenger platforms, canopies, shelters, pedestrian overpasses or underpasses, paving, or landscaping.

(22) Track and track structure maintenance and improvements when carried out predominantly within the existing right-of-way that do not cause a substantial increase in rail traffic beyond existing or historic levels, such as stabilizing embankments, installing or reinstalling track, re-grading, replacing rail, ties, slabs and ballast, installing, maintaining, or restoring drainage ditches, cleaning ballast, constructing minor curve realignments, improving or replacing interlockings, and the installation or maintenance of ancillary equipment.

(d) Any action qualifying as a CE under §771.117 or §771.118 may be approved by FRA when the applicable requirements of those sections have been met. FRA may consult with FHWA or FTA to ensure the CE is applicable to the proposed action.

§ 771.117 FHWA categorical exclusions.

(a) CEs are actions that meet the definition contained in 40 CFR 1508.4, and, based on FHWA's past experience with similar actions, do not involve significant environmental impacts. They are actions that: Do not induce significant impacts to planned growth or land use for the area; do not require the relocation of significant numbers of people; do not have a significant impact on any natural, cultural, recreational, historic or other resource; do not involve significant air, noise, or water quality impacts; do not have significant impacts on travel patterns; or do not otherwise, either individually or cumulatively, have any significant environmental impacts.

(b) Any action that normally would be classified as a CE but could involve unusual circumstances will require the FHWA, in cooperation with the applicant, to conduct appropriate environmental studies to determine if the CE classification is proper. Such unusual circumstances include:

(1) Significant environmental impacts;

(2) Substantial controversy on environmental grounds;

(3) Significant impact on properties protected by Section 4(f) requirements or Section 106 of the National Historic Preservation Act; or

(4) Inconsistencies with any Federal, State, or local law, requirement or administrative determination relating to the environmental aspects of the action.

(c) The following actions meet the criteria for CEs in the CEQ regulations (40 CFR 1508.4) and paragraph (a) of this section and normally do not require any further NEPA approvals by the FHWA:

(1) Activities that do not involve or lead directly to construction, such as planning and research activities; grants for training; engineering to define the elements of a proposed action or alternatives so that social, economic, and environmental effects can be assessed; and Federal-aid system revisions that establish classes of highways on the Federal-aid highway system.

(2) Approval of utility installations along or across a transportation facility.

(3) Construction of bicycle and pedestrian lanes, paths, and facilities.

(4) Activities included in the State's highway safety plan under 23 U.S.C. 402.

(5) Transfer of Federal lands pursuant to 23 U.S.C. 107(d) and/or 23 U.S.C. 317 when the land transfer is in support of an action that is not otherwise subject to FHWA review under NEPA.

(6) The installation of noise barriers or alterations to existing publicly owned buildings to provide for noise reduction.

(7) Landscaping.

(8) Installation of fencing, signs, pavement markings, small passenger shelters, traffic signals, and railroad warning devices where no substantial land acquisition or traffic disruption will occur.

(9) The following actions for transportation facilities damaged by an incident resulting in an emergency declared by the Governor of the State and concurred in by the Secretary, or a disaster or emergency declared by the President pursuant to the Robert T. Stafford Act (42 U.S.C. 5121):

(i) Emergency repairs under 23 U.S.C. 125; and

(ii) The repair, reconstruction, restoration, retrofitting, or replacement of any road, highway, bridge, tunnel, or transit facility (such as a ferry dock or bus transfer station), including ancillary transportation facilities (such as pedestrian/bicycle paths and bike lanes), that is in operation or under construction when damaged and the action:

(A) Occurs within the existing right-of-way and in a manner that substantially conforms to the preexisting design, function, and location as the original (which may include upgrades to meet existing codes and standards as well as upgrades warranted to address conditions that have changed since the original construction); and

(B) Is commenced within a 2-year period beginning on the date of the declaration.

(10) Acquisition of scenic easements.

(11) Determination of payback under 23 U.S.C. 156 for property previously acquired with Federal-aid participation.

(12) Improvements to existing rest areas and truck weigh stations.

(13) Ridesharing activities.

(14) Bus and rail car rehabilitation.

(15) Alterations to facilities or vehicles in order to make them accessible for elderly and handicapped persons.

(16) Program administration, technical assistance activities, and operating assistance to transit authorities to continue existing service or increase service to meet routine changes in demand.

(17) The purchase of vehicles by the applicant where the use of these vehicles can be accommodated by existing facilities or by new facilities that themselves are within a CE.

(18) Track and railbed maintenance and improvements when carried out within the existing right-of-way.

(19) Purchase and installation of operating or maintenance equipment to be located within the transit facility and with no significant impacts off the site.

(20) Promulgation of rules, regulations, and directives.

(21) Deployment of electronics, photonics, communications, or information processing used singly or in combination, or as components of a fully integrated system, to improve the efficiency or safety of a surface transportation system or to enhance security or passenger convenience. Examples include, but are not limited to, traffic control and detector devices, lane management systems, electronic payment equipment, automatic vehicle locaters, automated passenger counters, computer-aided dispatching systems, radio communications systems, dynamic message signs, and security equipment including surveillance and detection cameras on roadways and in transit facilities and on buses.

(22) Projects, as defined in 23 U.S.C. 101, that would take place entirely within the existing operational right-of-way. Existing operational right-of-way means all real property interests acquired for the construction, operation, or mitigation of a project. This area includes the features associated with the physical footprint of the project including but not limited to the roadway, bridges, interchanges, culverts, drainage, clear zone, traffic control signage, landscaping, and any rest areas with direct access to a controlled access highway. This also includes fixed guideways, mitigation areas, areas maintained or used for safety and security of a transportation facility, parking facilities with direct access to an existing transportation facility, transportation power substations, transportation venting structures, and transportation maintenance facilities.

(23) Federally funded projects:

(i) That receive less than $5,000,000 (as adjusted annually by the Secretary to reflect any increases in the Consumer Price Index prepared by the Department of Labor, see *www.fhwa.dot.gov* or *www.fta.dot.gov*) of Federal funds; or

(ii) With a total estimated cost of not more than $30,000,000 (as adjusted annually by the Secretary to reflect any increases in the Consumer Price Index prepared by the Department of Labor, see *www.fhwa.dot.gov* or *www.fta.dot.gov*) and Federal funds comprising less than 15 percent of the total estimated project cost.

(24) Localized geotechnical and other investigation to provide information for preliminary design and for environmental analyses and permitting purposes, such as drilling test bores for soil sampling; archeological investigations for archeology resources assessment or similar survey; and wetland surveys.

(25) Environmental restoration and pollution abatement actions to minimize or mitigate the impacts of any existing transportation facility (including retrofitting and construction of stormwater treatment systems to meet Federal and State requirements under sections 401 and 402 of the Federal Water Pollution Control Act (33 U.S.C. 1341; 1342)) carried out to address water pollution or environmental degradation.

(26) Modernization of a highway by resurfacing, restoration, rehabilitation, reconstruction, adding shoulders, or adding auxiliary lanes (including

parking, weaving, turning, and climbing lanes), if the action meets the constraints in paragraph (e) of this section.

(27) Highway safety or traffic operations improvement projects, including the installation of ramp metering control devices and lighting, if the project meets the constraints in paragraph (e) of this section.

(28) Bridge rehabilitation, reconstruction, or replacement or the construction of grade separation to replace existing at-grade railroad crossings, if the actions meet the constraints in paragraph (e) of this section.

(29) Purchase, construction, replacement, or rehabilitation of ferry vessels (including improvements to ferry vessel safety, navigation, and security systems) that would not require a change in the function of the ferry terminals and can be accommodated by existing facilities or by new facilities that themselves are within a CE.

(30) Rehabilitation or reconstruction of existing ferry facilities that occupy substantially the same geographic footprint, do not result in a change in their functional use, and do not result in a substantial increase in the existing facility's capacity. Example actions include work on pedestrian and vehicle transfer structures and associated utilities, buildings, and terminals.

(d) Additional actions that meet the criteria for a CE in the CEQ regulations (40 CFR 1508.4) and paragraph (a) of this section may be designated as CEs only after Administration approval unless otherwise authorized under an executed agreement pursuant to paragraph (g) of this section. The applicant must submit documentation that demonstrates that the specific conditions or criteria for these CEs are satisfied, and that significant environmental effects will not result. Examples of such actions include but are not limited to:

(1)–(3) [Reserved]

(4) Transportation corridor fringe parking facilities.

(5) Construction of new truck weigh stations or rest areas.

(6) Approvals for disposal of excess right-of-way or for joint or limited use of right-of-way, where the proposed use does not have significant adverse impacts.

(7) Approvals for changes in access control.

(8) Construction of new bus storage and maintenance facilities in areas used predominantly for industrial or transportation purposes where such construction is not inconsistent with existing zoning and located on or near a street with adequate capacity to handle anticipated bus and support vehicle traffic.

(9) Rehabilitation or reconstruction of existing rail and bus buildings and ancillary facilities where only minor amounts of additional land are required, and there is not a substantial increase in the number of users.

(10) Construction of bus transfer facilities (an open area consisting of passenger shelters, boarding areas, kiosks and related street improvements) when located in a commercial area or other high activity center in which there is adequate street capacity for projected bus traffic.

(11) Construction of rail storage and maintenance facilities in areas used predominantly for industrial or transportation purposes where such construction is not inconsistent with existing zoning, and where there is no significant noise impact on the surrounding community.

(12) Acquisition of land for hardship or protective purposes. Hardship and protective buying will be permitted only for a particular parcel or a limited number of parcels. These types of land acquisition qualify for a CE only where the acquisition will not limit the evaluation of alternatives, including shifts in alignment for planned construction projects, which may be required in the NEPA process. No project development on such land may proceed until the NEPA process has been completed.

(i) Hardship acquisition is early acquisition of property by the applicant at the property owner's request to alleviate particular hardship to the owner, in contrast to others, because of an inability to sell his property. This is justified when the property owner can document on the basis of health, safety or financial reasons that remaining in the property poses an undue hardship compared to others.

(ii) Protective acquisition is done to prevent imminent development of a parcel that may be needed for a proposed transportation corridor or site. Documentation must clearly demonstrate that development of the land would preclude future transportation use and that such development is imminent. Advance acquisition is not permitted for the sole purpose of reducing the cost of property for a proposed project.

(13) Actions described in paragraphs (c)(26), (c)(27), and (c)(28) of this section that do not meet the constraints in paragraph (e) of this section.

(e) Actions described in (c)(26), (c)(27), and (c)(28) of this section may not be processed as CEs under paragraph (c) if they involve:

(1) An acquisition of more than a minor amount of right-of-way or that would result in any residential or non-residential displacements;

(2) An action that needs a bridge permit from the U.S. Coast Guard, or an action that does not meet the terms and conditions of a U.S. Army Corps of Engineers nationwide or general permit under section 404 of the Clean Water Act and/or section 10 of the Rivers and Harbors Act of 1899;

(3) A finding of "adverse effect" to historic properties under the National Historic Preservation Act, the use of a resource protected under 23 U.S.C. 138 or 49 U.S.C. 303 (section 4(f)) except for actions resulting in *de minimis* impacts, or a finding of "may affect, likely to adversely affect" threatened or endangered species or critical habitat under the Endangered Species Act;

(4) Construction of temporary access or the closure of existing road, bridge, or ramps that would result in major traffic disruptions;

(5) Changes in access control;

(6) A floodplain encroachment other than functionally dependent uses (e.g., bridges, wetlands) or actions that facilitate open space use (e.g., recreational trails, bicycle and pedestrian paths); or construction activities in, across or adjacent to a river component designated or proposed for inclusion in the National System of Wild and Scenic Rivers.

(f) Where a pattern emerges of granting CE status for a particular type of action, the FHWA will initiate rulemaking proposing to add this type of action to the list of categorical exclusions in paragraph (c) or (d) of this section, as appropriate.

(g) FHWA may enter into programmatic agreements with a State to allow a State DOT to make a NEPA CE certification or determination and approval on FHWA's behalf, for CEs specifically listed in paragraphs (c) and (d) of this section and that meet the criteria for a CE under 40 CFR 1508.4, and are identified in the programmatic agreement. Such agreements must be subject to the following conditions:

(1) The agreement must set forth the State DOT's responsibilities for making CE determinations, documenting the determinations, and achieving acceptable quality control and quality assurance;

(2) The agreement may not have a term of more than five years, but may be renewed;

(3) The agreement must provide for FHWA's monitoring of the State DOT's compliance with the terms of the agreement and for the State DOT's execution of any needed corrective action. FHWA must take into account the State DOT's performance when considering renewal of the programmatic CE agreement; and

(4) The agreement must include stipulations for amendment, termination, and public availability of the agreement once it has been executed.

(h) Any action qualifying as a CE under §771.116 or §771.118 may be approved by FHWA when the applicable requirements of those sections have been met. FHWA may consult with FRA or FTA to ensure the CE is applicable to the proposed action.

§771.118 FTA categorical exclusions.

(a) CEs are actions that meet the definition contained in 40 CFR 1508.4, and, based on FTA's past experience with similar actions, do not involve significant environmental impacts. They are actions that: Do not induce significant impacts to planned growth or land use for the area; do not require the relocation of significant numbers of people; do not have a significant impact on any natural, cultural, recreational, historic or other resource; do not involve significant air, noise, or water quality impacts; do not have significant impacts on travel patterns; or do not otherwise, either individually or cumulatively, have any significant environmental impacts.

(b) Any action that normally would be classified as a CE but could involve unusual circumstances will require FTA, in cooperation with the applicant, to conduct appropriate environmental studies to determine if the CE classification is proper. Such unusual circumstances include:

(1) Significant environmental impacts;

(2) Substantial controversy on environmental grounds;

(3) Significant impact on properties protected by Section 4(f) requirements or Section 106 of the National Historic Preservation Act; or

(4) Inconsistencies with any Federal, State, or local law, requirement or administrative determination relating to the environmental aspects of the action.

(c) Actions that FTA determines fall within the following categories of FTA CEs and that meet the criteria for CEs in the CEQ regulation (40 CFR 1508.4) and paragraph (a) of this section normally do not require any further NEPA approvals by FTA.

(1) Acquisition, installation, operation, evaluation, replacement, and improvement of discrete utilities and similar appurtenances (existing and new) within or adjacent to existing transportation right-of-way, such as: Utility poles, underground wiring, cables, and information systems; and power substations and utility transfer stations.

(2) Acquisition, construction, maintenance, rehabilitation, and improvement or limited expansion of standalone recreation, pedestrian, or bicycle facilities, such as: A multiuse pathway, lane, trail, or pedestrian bridge; and transit plaza amenities.

(3) Activities designed to mitigate environmental harm that cause no harm themselves or to maintain and enhance environmental quality and site aesthetics, and employ construction best management practices, such as: Noise mitigation activities; rehabilitation of public transportation buildings, structures, or facilities; retrofitting for energy or other resource conservation; and landscaping or revegetation.

(4) Planning and administrative activities that do not involve or lead directly to construction, such as: Training, technical assistance and research; promulgation of rules, regulations, directives, or program guidance; approval of project concepts; engineering; and operating assistance to transit authorities to continue existing service or increase service to meet routine demand.

(5) Activities, including repairs, replacements, and rehabilitations, designed to promote transportation safety, security, accessibility and effective communication within or adjacent to existing right-of-way, such as: The deployment of Intelligent Transportation Systems and components; installation and improvement of safety and communications equipment, including hazard elimination and mitigation; installation of passenger amenities and traffic signals; and retrofitting existing transportation vehicles, facilities or structures, or upgrading to current standards.

(6) Acquisition or transfer of an interest in real property that is not within or adjacent to recognized environmentally sensitive areas (e.g., wetlands, non-urban parks, wildlife management areas) and does not result in a substantial change in the functional use of the property or in substantial displacements, such as: Acquisition for scenic easements or historic sites for the purpose of preserving the site. This CE extends only to acquisitions and transfers that will not limit the evaluation of alternatives for future FTA-assisted projects that make use of the acquired or transferred property.

(7) Acquisition, installation, rehabilitation, replacement, and maintenance of vehicles or equipment, within or accommodated by existing facilities, that does not result in a change in functional use of the facilities, such as: equipment to be located within existing facilities and with no substantial off-site impacts; and vehicles, including buses, rail cars, trolley cars, ferry boats and people movers that can be accommodated by existing facilities or

by new facilities that qualify for a categorical exclusion.

(8) Maintenance, rehabilitation, and reconstruction of facilities that occupy substantially the same geographic footprint and do not result in a change in functional use, such as: Improvements to bridges, tunnels, storage yards, buildings, stations, and terminals; construction of platform extensions, passing track, and retaining walls; and improvements to tracks and railbeds.

(9) Assembly or construction of facilities that is consistent with existing land use and zoning requirements (including floodplain regulations) and uses primarily land disturbed for transportation use, such as: Buildings and associated structures; bus transfer stations or intermodal centers; busways and streetcar lines or other transit investments within areas of the right-of-way occupied by the physical footprint of the existing facility or otherwise maintained or used for transportation operations; and parking facilities.

(10) Development of facilities for transit and non-transit purposes, located on, above, or adjacent to existing transit facilities, that are not part of a larger transportation project and do not substantially enlarge such facilities, such as: Police facilities, daycare facilities, public service facilities, amenities, and commercial, retail, and residential development.

(11) The following actions for transportation facilities damaged by an incident resulting in an emergency declared by the Governor of the State and concurred in by the Secretary, or a disaster or emergency declared by the President pursuant to the Robert T. Stafford Act (42 U.S.C. 5121):

(i) Emergency repairs under 49 U.S.C. 5324; and

(ii) The repair, reconstruction, restoration, retrofitting, or replacement of any road, highway, bridge, tunnel, or transit facility (such as a ferry dock or bus transfer station), including ancillary transportation facilities (such as pedestrian/bicycle paths and bike lanes), that is in operation or under construction when damaged and the action:

(A) Occurs within the existing right-of-way and in a manner that substantially conforms to the preexisting design, function, and location as the original (which may include upgrades to meet existing codes and standards as well as upgrades warranted to address conditions that have changed since the original construction); and

(B) Is commenced within a 2-year period beginning on the date of the declaration.

(12) Projects, as defined in 23 U.S.C. 101, that would take place entirely within the existing operational right-of-way. Existing operational right-of-way means all real property interests acquired for the construction, operation, or mitigation of a project. This area includes the features associated with the physical footprint of the project including but not limited to the roadway, bridges, interchanges, culverts, drainage, clear zone, traffic control signage, landscaping, and any rest areas with direct access to a controlled access highway. This also includes fixed guideways, mitigation areas, areas maintained or used for safety and security of a transportation facility, parking facilities with direct access to an existing transportation facility, transportation power substations, transportation venting structures, and transportation maintenance facilities.

(13) Federally funded projects:

(i) That receive less than $5,000,000 (as adjusted annually by the Secretary to reflect any increases in the Consumer Price Index prepared by the Department of Labor, see *www.fhwa.dot.gov* or *www.fta.dot.gov*) of Federal funds; or

(ii) With a total estimated cost of not more than $30,000,000 (as adjusted annually by the Secretary to reflect any increases in the Consumer Price Index prepared by the Department of Labor, see *www.fhwa.dot.gov* or *www.fta.dot.gov*) and Federal funds comprising less than 15 percent of the total estimated project cost.

(14) Bridge removal and bridge removal related activities, such as in-channel work, disposal of materials and debris in accordance with applicable regulations, and transportation facility realignment.

(15) Preventative maintenance, including safety treatments, to culverts and channels within and adjacent to

transportation right-of-way to prevent damage to the transportation facility and adjoining property, plus any necessary channel work, such as restoring, replacing, reconstructing, and rehabilitating culverts and drainage pipes; and, expanding existing culverts and drainage pipes.

(16) Localized geotechnical and other investigations to provide information for preliminary design and for environmental analyses and permitting purposes, such as drilling test bores for soil sampling; archeological investigations for archeology resources assessment or similar survey; and wetland surveys.

(d) Additional actions that meet the criteria for a CE in the CEQ regulations (40 CFR 1508.4) and paragraph (a) of this section may be designated as CEs only after FTA approval. The applicant must submit documentation that demonstrates that the specific conditions or criteria for these CEs are satisfied and that significant environmental effects will not result. Examples of such actions include but are not limited to:

(1) Modernization of a highway by resurfacing, restoring, rehabilitating, or reconstructing shoulders or auxiliary lanes (e.g., lanes for parking, weaving, turning, climbing).

(2) Bridge replacement or the construction of grade separation to replace existing at-grade railroad crossings.

(3) Acquisition of land for hardship or protective purposes. Hardship and protective buying will be permitted only for a particular parcel or a limited number of parcels. These types of land acquisition qualify for a CE only where the acquisition will not limit the evaluation of alternatives, including shifts in alignment for planned construction projects, which may be required in the NEPA process. No project development on such land may proceed until the NEPA process has been completed.

(i) Hardship acquisition is early acquisition of property by the applicant at the property owner's request to alleviate particular hardship to the owner, in contrast to others, because of an inability to sell his property. This is justified when the property owner can document on the basis of health, safety or financial reasons that remaining in the property poses an undue hardship compared to others.

(ii) Protective acquisition is done to prevent imminent development of a parcel that may be needed for a proposed transportation corridor or site. Documentation must clearly demonstrate that development of the land would preclude future transportation use and that such development is imminent. Advance acquisition is not permitted for the sole purpose of reducing the cost of property for a proposed project.

(4) Acquisition of right-of-way. No project development on the acquired right-of-way may proceed until the NEPA process for such project development, including the consideration of alternatives, has been completed.

(5) [Reserved]

(6) Facility modernization through construction or replacement of existing components.

(7) Minor transportation facility realignment for rail safety reasons, such as improving vertical and horizontal alignment of railroad crossings, and improving sight distance at railroad crossings.

(8) Modernization or minor expansions of transit structures and facilities outside existing right-of-way, such as bridges, stations, or rail yards.

(e) Any action qualifying as a CE under § 771.116 or § 771.117 may be approved by FTA when the applicable requirements of those sections have been met. FTA may consult with FHWA or FRA to ensure the CE is applicable to the proposed action.

(f) Where a pattern emerges of granting CE status for a particular type of action, FTA will initiate rulemaking proposing to add this type of action to the appropriate list of categorical exclusions in this section.

§ 771.119 Environmental assessments.

(a)(1) The applicant must prepare an EA in consultation with the Administration for each action that is not a CE and does not clearly require the preparation of an EIS, or where the Administration concludes an EA would assist in determining the need for an EIS.

(2) When FTA or the applicant, as joint lead agency, select a contractor to prepare the EA, then the contractor

must execute an FTA conflict of interest disclosure statement. The statement must be maintained in the FTA Regional Office and with the applicant. The contractor's scope of work for the preparation of the EA should not be finalized until the early coordination activities or scoping process found in paragraph (b) of this section is completed (including FTA approval, in consultation with the applicant, of the scope of the EA content).

(3) When FRA or the applicant, as joint lead agency, select a contractor to prepare the EA, then the contractor must execute an FRA conflict of interest disclosure statement. In the absence of an applicant, FRA may require private project sponsors to provide a third-party contractor to prepare the EA as described in 771.109(e).

(b) For actions that require an EA, the applicant, in consultation with the Administration, must, at the earliest appropriate time, begin consultation with interested agencies and others to advise them of the scope of the project and to achieve the following objectives: Determine which aspects of the proposed action have potential for social, economic, or environmental impact; identify alternatives and measures that might mitigate adverse environmental impacts; and identify other environmental review and consultation requirements that should be performed concurrently with the EA. The applicant must accomplish this through early coordination activities or through a scoping process. The applicant must summarize the public involvement process and include the results of agency coordination in the EA.

(c) The Administration must approve the EA before it is made available to the public as an Administration document.

(d) The applicant does not need to circulate the EA for comment, but the document must be made available for public inspection at the applicant's office and at the appropriate Administration field offices or, for FRA at Headquarters, for 30 days and in accordance with paragraphs (e) and (f) of this section. The applicant must send the notice of availability of the EA, which briefly describes the action and its impacts, to the affected units of Federal, Tribal, State and local government. The applicant must also send notice to the State intergovernmental review contacts established under Executive Order 12372. To minimize hardcopy requests and printing costs, the Administration encourages the use of project websites or other publicly accessible electronic means to make the EA available.

(e) When a public hearing is held as part of the environmental review process for an action, the EA must be available at the public hearing and for a minimum of 15 days in advance of the public hearing. The applicant must publish a notice of the public hearing in local newspapers that announces the availability of the EA and where it may be obtained or reviewed. Any comments must be submitted in writing to the applicant or the Administration during the 30-day availability period of the EA unless the Administration determines, for good cause, that a different period is warranted. Public hearing requirements are as described in §771.111.

(f) When a public hearing is not held, the applicant must place a notice in a newspaper(s) similar to a public hearing notice and at a similar stage of development of the action, advising the public of the availability of the EA and where information concerning the action may be obtained. The notice must invite comments from all interested parties. Any comments must be submitted in writing to the applicant or the Administration during the 30-day availability period of the EA unless the Administration determines, for good cause, that a different period is warranted.

(g) If no significant impacts are identified, the applicant must furnish the Administration a copy of the revised EA, as appropriate; the public hearing transcript, where applicable; copies of any comments received and responses thereto; and recommend a FONSI. The EA should also document compliance, to the extent possible, with all applicable environmental laws and executive orders, or provide reasonable assurance that their requirements can be met.

(h) When the FHWA expects to issue a FONSI for an action described in §771.115(a), copies of the EA must be made available for public review (including the affected units of government) for a minimum of 30 days before the FHWA makes its final decision (See 40 CFR 1501.4(e)(2)). This public availability must be announced by a notice similar to a public hearing notice.

(i) If, at any point in the EA process, the Administration determines that the action is likely to have a significant impact on the environment, the preparation of an EIS will be required.

(j) If the Administration decides to apply 23 U.S.C. 139 to an action involving an EA, then the EA must be prepared in accordance with the applicable provisions of that statute.

§ 771.121 Findings of no significant impact.

(a) The Administration will review the EA, comments submitted on the EA (in writing or at a public hearing or meeting), and other supporting documentation, as appropriate. If the Administration agrees with the applicant's recommendations pursuant to § 771.119(g), it will issue a separate written FONSI incorporating by reference the EA and any other appropriate environmental documents.

(b) After the Administration issues a FONSI, a notice of availability of the FONSI must be sent by the applicant to the affected units of Federal, State and local government, and the document must be available from the applicant and the Administration upon request by the public. Notice must also be sent to the State intergovernmental review contacts established under Executive Order 12372. To minimize hardcopy requests and printing costs, the Administration encourages the use of project websites or other publicly accessible electronic means to make the FONSI available.

(c) If another Federal agency has issued a FONSI on an action that includes an element proposed for Administration funding or approval, the Administration will evaluate the other agency's EA/FONSI. If the Administration determines that this element of the project and its environmental impacts have been adequately identified and assessed and concurs in the decision to issue a FONSI, the Administration will issue its own FONSI incorporating the other agency's EA/FONSI. If environmental issues have not been adequately identified and assessed, the Administration will require appropriate environmental studies.

§ 771.123 Draft environmental impact statements.

(a) A draft EIS must be prepared when the Administration determines that the action is likely to cause significant impacts on the environment. When the applicant, after consultation with any project sponsor that is not the applicant, has notified the Administration in accordance with 23 U.S.C. 139(e), and the decision has been made by the Administration to prepare an EIS, the Administration will issue a notice of intent (40 CFR 1508.22) for publication in the FEDERAL REGISTER. Applicants are encouraged to announce the intent to prepare an EIS by appropriate means at the State or local level.

(b)(1) After publication of the notice of intent, the lead agencies, in cooperation with the applicant (if not a lead agency), will begin a scoping process that may take into account any planning work already accomplished, in accordance with 23 CFR 450.212, 450.318, 23 CFR part 450 Appendix A, or any applicable provisions of the CEQ regulations at 40 CFR parts 1500–1508. The scoping process will be used to identify the purpose and need, the range of alternatives and impacts, and the significant issues to be addressed in the EIS and to achieve the other objectives of 40 CFR 1501.7. Scoping is normally achieved through public and agency involvement procedures required by § 771.111. If a scoping meeting is to be held, it should be announced in the Administration's notice of intent and by appropriate means at the State or local level.

(2) The lead agencies must establish a coordination plan, including a schedule, within 90 days of notice of intent publication.

(c) The draft EIS must be prepared by the lead agencies, in cooperation with the applicant (if not a lead agency). The draft EIS must evaluate all reasonable alternatives to the action and document the reasons why other alternatives, which may have been considered, were eliminated from detailed study. The range of alternatives considered for further study must be used for all Federal environmental reviews and permit processes, to the maximum extent practicable and consistent with Federal law, unless the lead and participating agencies agree to modify the alternatives in order to address significant new information and circumstances or to fulfill NEPA responsibilities in a timely manner, in accordance with 23 U.S.C. 139(f)(4)(B). The draft EIS must also summarize the studies, reviews, consultations, and coordination required by environmental laws or executive orders to the extent appropriate at this stage in the environmental process.

(d) Any of the lead agencies may select a consultant to assist in the preparation of an EIS in accordance with applicable contracting procedures and with 40 CFR 1506.5(c). When FTA or the applicant, as joint lead agency, select a contractor to prepare the EIS, then the contractor must execute an FTA conflict of interest disclosure statement. The statement must be maintained in the FTA Regional Office and with the applicant. The contractor's scope of work for the preparation of the EIS will not be finalized until the early coordination activities or scoping process found in paragraph (b) of this section is completed (including FTA approval, in consultation with the applicant, of the scope of the EIS content). When FRA or the applicant, as joint lead agency, select a contractor to prepare the EIS, then the contractor must execute an FRA conflict of interest disclosure statement.

(e) The draft EIS should identify the preferred alternative to the extent practicable. If the draft EIS does not identify the preferred alternative, the Administration should provide agencies and the public with an opportunity after issuance of the draft EIS to review the impacts of the preferred alternative.

(f) At the discretion of the lead agency, the preferred alternative (or portion thereof) for a project, after being identified, may be developed to a higher level of detail than other alternatives in order to facilitate the development of mitigation measures or compliance with other legal requirements, including permitting. The development of such higher level of detail must not prevent the lead agency from making an impartial decision as to whether to accept another alternative that is being considered in the environmental review process.[3]

(g) The Administration, when satisfied that the draft EIS complies with NEPA requirements, will approve the draft EIS for circulation by signing and dating the cover sheet. The cover sheet should include a notice that after circulation of the draft EIS and consideration of the comments received, the Administration will issue a combined final EIS/ROD document unless statutory criteria or practicability considerations preclude issuance of the combined document.

(h) A lead, joint lead, or a cooperating agency must be responsible for publication and distribution of the EIS. Normally, copies will be furnished free of charge. However, with Administration concurrence, the party requesting the draft EIS may be charged a fee that is not more than the actual cost of reproducing the copy or may be directed to the nearest location where the statement may be reviewed. To minimize hardcopy requests and printing costs, the Administration encourages the use of project websites or other publicly accessible electronic means to make the draft EIS available.

(i) The applicant, on behalf of the Administration, must circulate the draft EIS for comment. The draft EIS must be made available to the public and transmitted to agencies for comment no later than the time the document is filed with the Environmental Protection Agency in accordance with 40 CFR 1506.9. The draft EIS must be transmitted to:

(1) Public officials, interest groups, and members of the public known to have an interest in the proposed action or the draft EIS;

[3] FHWA Order 6640.1A clarifies the Federal Highway Administration's (FHWA) policy regarding the permissible project related activities that may be advanced prior to the conclusion of the NEPA process.

(2) Cooperating and participating agencies. The draft EIS must also be transmitted directly to appropriate State and local agencies, and to the State intergovernmental review contacts established under Executive Order 12372; and

(3) States and Federal land management entities that may be significantly affected by the proposed action or any of the alternatives. These transmittals must be accompanied by a request that such State or entity advise the Administration in writing of any disagreement with the evaluation of impacts in the statement. The Administration will furnish the comments received to the applicant along with a written assessment of any disagreements for incorporation into the final EIS.

(j) When a public hearing on the draft EIS is held (if required by § 771.111), the draft EIS must be available at the public hearing and for a minimum of 15 days in advance of the public hearing. The availability of the draft EIS must be mentioned, and public comments requested, in any public hearing notice and at any public hearing presentation. If a public hearing on an action proposed for FHWA funding is not held, a notice must be placed in a newspaper similar to a public hearing notice advising where the draft EIS is available for review, how copies may be obtained, and where the comments should be sent.

(k) The FEDERAL REGISTER public availability notice (40 CFR 1506.10) must establish a period of not fewer than 45 days nor more than 60 days for the return of comments on the draft EIS unless a different period is established in accordance with 23 U.S.C. 139(g)(2)(A). The notice and the draft EIS transmittal letter must identify where comments are to be sent.

§ 771.124 Final environmental impact statement/record of decision document.

(a)(1) After circulation of a draft EIS and consideration of comments received, the lead agencies, in cooperation with the applicant (if not a lead agency), must combine the final EIS and ROD, to the maximum extent practicable, unless:

(i) The final EIS makes substantial changes to the proposed action that are relevant to environmental or safety concerns; or

(ii) There are significant new circumstances or information relevant to environmental concerns that bear on the proposed action or the impacts of the proposed action.

(2) When the combined final EIS/ROD is a single document, it must include the content of a final EIS presented in § 771.125 and present the basis for the decision as specified in 40 CFR 1505.2, summarize any mitigation measures that will be incorporated in the project, and document any required Section 4(f) approval in accordance with part 774 of this chapter.

(3) If the comments on the draft EIS are minor and confined to factual corrections or explanations that do not warrant additional agency response, an errata sheet may be attached to the draft statement pursuant to 23 U.S.C. 139(n)(1) and 40 CFR 1503.4(c), which together must then become the combined final EIS/ROD.

(4) A combined final EIS/ROD will be reviewed for legal sufficiency prior to issuance by the Administration.

(5) The Administration must indicate approval of the combined final EIS/ROD by signing the document. The provision on Administration's Headquarters prior concurrence in § 771.125(c) applies to the combined final EIS/ROD.

(b) The FEDERAL REGISTER public availability notice published by EPA (40 CFR 1506.10) will not establish a waiting period or a period of time for the return of comments on a combined final EIS/ROD. When filed with EPA, the combined final EIS/ROD must be available at the applicant's offices and at appropriate Administration offices. A copy should also be made available at institutions such as local government offices, libraries, and schools, as appropriate. To minimize hardcopy requests and printing costs, the Administration encourages the use of project websites or other publicly accessible electronic means to make the combined final EIS/ROD available.

§771.125 Final environmental impact statements.

(a)(1) After circulation of a draft EIS and consideration of comments received, a final EIS must be prepared by the lead agencies, in cooperation with the applicant (if not a lead agency). The final EIS must identify the preferred alternative and evaluate all reasonable alternatives considered. It must also discuss substantive comments received on the draft EIS and responses thereto, summarize public involvement, and describe the mitigation measures that are to be incorporated into the proposed action. Mitigation measures presented as commitments in the final EIS will be incorporated into the project as specified in paragraphs (b) and (d) of §771.109. The final EIS should also document compliance, to the extent possible, with all applicable environmental laws and executive orders, or provide reasonable assurance that their requirements can be met.

(2) Every reasonable effort must be made to resolve interagency disagreements on actions before processing the final EIS. If significant issues remain unresolved, the final EIS must identify those issues and the consultations and other efforts made to resolve them.

(b) The final EIS will be reviewed for legal sufficiency prior to Administration approval.

(c) The Administration will indicate approval of the EIS for an action by signing and dating the cover page. Final EISs prepared for actions in the following categories will be submitted to the Administration's Headquarters for prior concurrence:

(1) Any action for which the Administration determines that the final EIS should be reviewed at the Headquarters office. This would typically occur when the Headquarters office determines that:

(i) Additional coordination with other Federal, State or local governmental agencies is needed;

(ii) The social, economic, or environmental impacts of the action may need to be more fully explored;

(iii) The impacts of the proposed action are unusually great; (iv) major issues remain unresolved; or

(iv) The action involves national policy issues.

(2) Any action to which a Federal, State or local government agency has indicated opposition on environmental grounds (which has not been resolved to the written satisfaction of the objecting agency).

(d) Approval of the final EIS is not an Administration action as defined in §771.107 and does not commit the Administration to approve any future request for financial assistance to fund the preferred alternative.

(e) The initial publication of the final EIS must be in sufficient quantity to meet the request for copies that can be reasonably expected from agencies, organizations, and individuals. Normally, copies will be furnished free of charge. However, with Administration concurrence, the party requesting the final EIS may be charged a fee that is not more than the actual cost of reproducing the copy or may be directed to the nearest location where the statement may be reviewed.

(f) The final EIS must be transmitted to any persons, organizations, or agencies that made substantive comments on the draft EIS or requested a copy, no later than the time the document is filed with EPA. In the case of lengthy documents, the agency may provide alternative circulation processes in accordance with 40 CFR 1502.19. The applicant must also publish a notice of availability in local newspapers and make the final EIS available through the mechanism established pursuant to DOT Order 4600.13, which implements Executive Order 12372. When filed with EPA, the final EIS must be available for public review at the applicant's offices and at appropriate Administration offices. A copy should also be made available for public review at institutions such as local government offices, libraries, and schools, as appropriate. To minimize hardcopy requests and printing costs, the Administration encourages the use of project websites or other publicly accessible electronic means to make the final EIS available.

(g) The final EIS may take the form of an errata sheet pursuant to 23 U.S.C. 139(n)(1) and 40 CFR 1503.4(c).

§ 771.127 Record of decision.

(a) When the final EIS is not combined with the ROD, the Administration will complete and sign a ROD no sooner than 30 days after publication of the final EIS notice in the FEDERAL REGISTER or 90 days after publication of a notice for the draft EIS, whichever is later. The ROD will present the basis for the decision as specified in 40 CFR 1505.2, summarize any mitigation measures that will be incorporated in the project, and document any required Section 4(f) approval in accordance with part 774 of this chapter. To minimize hardcopy requests and printing costs, the Administration encourages the use of project websites or other publicly accessible electronic means to make the ROD available.

(b) If the Administration subsequently wishes to approve an alternative that was not identified as the preferred alternative but was fully evaluated in the draft EIS, combined FEIS/ROD, or final EIS, or proposes to make substantial changes to the mitigation measures or findings discussed in the ROD, a revised or amended ROD must be subject to review by those Administration offices that reviewed the final EIS under § 771.124(a) or § 771.125(c). To the extent practicable, the approved revised or amended ROD must be provided to all persons, organizations, and agencies that received a copy of the final EIS.

§ 771.129 Re-evaluations.

The Administration must determine, prior to granting any new approval related to an action or amending any previously approved aspect of an action, including mitigation commitments, whether an approved environmental document remains valid as described in this section.

(a) The applicant must prepare a written evaluation of the draft EIS, in cooperation with the Administration, if an acceptable final EIS is not submitted to the Administration within three years from the date of the draft EIS circulation. The purpose of this evaluation is to determine whether or not a supplement to the draft EIS or a new draft EIS is needed.

(b) The applicant must prepare a written evaluation of the final EIS before the Administration may grant further approvals if major steps to advance the action (e.g., authority to undertake final design, authority to acquire a significant portion of the right-of-way, or approval of the plans, specifications and estimates) have not occurred within three years after the approval of the final EIS, final EIS supplement, or the last major Administration approval or grant.

(c) After the Administration issues a combined final EIS/ROD, ROD, FONSI, or CE designation, the applicant must consult with the Administration prior to requesting any major approvals or grants to establish whether or not the approved environmental document or CE designation remains valid for the requested Administration action. These consultations will be documented when determined necessary by the Administration.

§ 771.130 Supplemental environmental impact statements.

(a) A draft EIS, final EIS, or supplemental EIS may be supplemented at any time. An EIS must be supplemented whenever the Administration determines that:

(1) Changes to the proposed action would result in significant environmental impacts that were not evaluated in the EIS; or

(2) New information or circumstances relevant to environmental concerns and bearing on the proposed action or its impacts would result in significant environmental impacts not evaluated in the EIS.

(b) However, a supplemental EIS will not be necessary where:

(1) The changes to the proposed action, new information, or new circumstances result in a lessening of adverse environmental impacts evaluated in the EIS without causing other environmental impacts that are significant and were not evaluated in the EIS; or

(2) The Administration decides to approve an alternative fully evaluated in an approved final EIS but not identified as the preferred alternative. In such a case, a revised ROD must be prepared and circulated in accordance with § 771.127(b).

(c) Where the Administration is uncertain of the significance of the new impacts, the applicant will develop appropriate environmental studies or, if the Administration deems appropriate, an EA to assess the impacts of the changes, new information, or new circumstances. If, based upon the studies, the Administration determines that a supplemental EIS is not necessary, the Administration must so indicate in the project file.

(d) A supplement is to be developed using the same process and format (*i.e.*, draft EIS, final EIS, and ROD) as an original EIS, except that scoping is not required.

(e) In some cases, an EA or supplemental EIS may be required to address issues of limited scope, such as the extent of proposed mitigation or the evaluation of location or design variations for a limited portion of the overall project. Where this is the case, the preparation of a supplemental document must not necessarily:

(1) Prevent the granting of new approvals;

(2) Require the withdrawal of previous approvals; or

(3) Require the suspension of project activities, for any activity not directly affected by the supplement. If the changes in question are of such magnitude to require a reassessment of the entire action, or more than a limited portion of the overall action, the Administration must suspend any activities that would have an adverse environmental impact or limit the choice of reasonable alternatives, until the supplemental document is completed.

§771.131 Emergency action procedures.

Responses to some emergencies and disasters are categorically excluded under §771.117 for FHWA, §771.118 for FTA, or §771.116 for FRA. Otherwise, requests for deviations from the procedures in this part because of emergency circumstances (40 CFR 1506.11) must be referred to the Administration's Headquarters for evaluation and decision after consultation with CEQ.

§771.133 Compliance with other requirements.

(a) The combined final EIS/ROD, final EIS or FONSI should document compliance with requirements of all applicable environmental laws, executive orders, and other related requirements. If full compliance is not possible by the time the combined final EIS/ROD, final EIS or FONSI is prepared, the combined final EIS/ROD, final EIS or FONSI should reflect consultation with the appropriate agencies and provide reasonable assurance that the requirements will be met. Approval of the environmental document constitutes adoption of any Administration findings and determinations that are contained therein. The FHWA's approval of an environmental document constitutes its finding of compliance with the report requirements of 23 U.S.C. 128.

(b) In consultation with the Administration and subject to Administration approval, an applicant may develop a programmatic approach for compliance with the requirements of any law, regulation, or executive order applicable to the project development process.

§771.137 International actions.

(a) The requirements of this part apply to:

(1) Administration actions significantly affecting the environment of a foreign nation not participating in the action or not otherwise involved in the action.

(2) Administration actions outside the U.S., its territories, and possessions that significantly affect natural resources of global importance designated for protection by the President or by international agreement.

(b) If communication with a foreign government concerning environmental studies or documentation is anticipated, the Administration must coordinate such communication with the Department of State through the Office of the Secretary of Transportation.

§771.139 Limitations on actions.

Notices announcing decisions by the Administration or by other Federal agencies on a transportation project may be published in the FEDERAL REGISTER indicating that such decisions are final within the meaning of 23 U.S.C. 139(*l*). Claims arising under Federal law seeking judicial review of any such decisions are time barred unless filed within 150 days after the date of publication of the limitations on claims notice by FHWA or FTA. Claims arising under Federal law seeking judicial review of any such decisions are time barred unless filed within 2 years after the date of publication of the limitations on claims notice by FRA. These time periods do not lengthen any shorter time period for seeking judicial review that otherwise is established by the Federal law under which judicial review is allowed.[5] This provision does not create any right of judicial review or place any limit on filing a claim that a person has violated the terms of a permit, license, or approval.

PART 772—PROCEDURES FOR ABATEMENT OF HIGHWAY TRAFFIC NOISE AND CONSTRUCTION NOISE

AUTHORITY: 23 U.S.C. 109(h) and (i); 42 U.S.C. 4331, 4332; sec. 339(b), Pub. L. 104–59, 109 Stat. 568, 605; 49 CFR 1.48(b).

SOURCE: 75 FR 39834, July 13, 2010, unless otherwise noted.

§ 772.1 Purpose.

To provide procedures for noise studies and noise abatement measures to help protect the public's health, welfare and livability, to supply noise abatement criteria, and to establish requirements for information to be given to local officials for use in the planning and design of highways approved pursuant to title 23 U.S.C.

§ 772.3 Noise standards.

The highway traffic noise prediction requirements, noise analyses, noise abatement criteria, and requirements for informing local officials in this regulation constitute the noise standards mandated by 23 U.S.C. 109(1). All highway projects which are developed in conformance with this regulation shall be deemed to be in accordance with the FHWA noise standards.

§ 772.5 Definitions.

Benefited receptor. The recipient of an abatement measure that receives a noise reduction at or above the minimum threshold of 5 dB(A), but not to exceed the highway agency's reasonableness design goal.

Common Noise Environment. A group of receptors within the same Activity Category in Table 1 that are exposed to similar noise sources and levels; traffic volumes, traffic mix, and speed; and topographic features. Generally, common noise environments occur between two secondary noise sources, such as interchanges, intersections, crossroads.

Date of public knowledge. The date of approval of the Categorical Exclusion (CE), the Finding of No Significant Impact (FONSI), or the Record of Decision (ROD), as defined in 23 CFR part 771.

Design year. The future year used to estimate the probable traffic volume for which a highway is designed.

Existing noise levels. The worst noise hour resulting from the combination of natural and mechanical sources and human activity usually present in a particular area.

Feasibility. The combination of acoustical and engineering factors considered in the evaluation of a noise abatement measure.

Impacted Receptor. The recipient that has a traffic noise impact.

L10. The sound level that is exceeded 10 percent of the time (the 90th percentile) for the period under consideration, with L10(h) being the hourly value of L10.

Leq. The equivalent steady-state sound level which in a stated period of

[5] The FHWA published a detailed discussion of the Department's interpretation of 23 U.S.C. 139(l), in appendix E to the 'SAFETEA-LU Environmental Review Process: Final Guidance,' dated November 15, 2006. The implementation procedures in appendix E apply only to FHWA projects. The setion 6002 guidance, including appendix E, is available at http://www.fhwa.dot.gov/, or in hard copy by request.

time contains the same acoustic energy as the time-varying sound level during the same time period, with Leq(h) being the hourly value of Leq.

Multifamily dwelling. A residential structure containing more than one residence. Each residence in a multifamily dwelling shall be counted as one receptor when determining impacted and benefited receptors.

Noise barrier. A physical obstruction that is constructed between the highway noise source and the noise sensitive receptor(s) that lowers the noise level, including stand alone noise walls, noise berms (earth or other material), and combination berm/wall systems.

Noise reduction design goal. The optimum desired dB(A) noise reduction determined from calculating the difference between future build noise levels with abatement, to future build noise levels without abatement. The noise reduction design goal shall be at least 7 dB(A), but not more than 10 dB(A).

Permitted. A definite commitment to develop land with an approved specific design of land use activities as evidenced by the issuance of a building permit.

Property owner. An individual or group of individuals that holds a title, deed, or other legal documentation of ownership of a property or a residence.

Reasonableness. The combination of social, economic, and environmental factors considered in the evaluation of a noise abatement measure.

Receptor. A discrete or representative location of a noise sensitive area(s), for any of the land uses listed in Table 1.

Residence. A dwelling unit. Either a single family residence or each dwelling unit in a multifamily dwelling.

Statement of likelihood. A statement provided in the environmental clearance document based on the feasibility and reasonableness analysis completed at the time the environmental document is being approved.

Substantial construction. The granting of a building permit, prior to right-of-way acquisition or construction approval for the highway.

Substantial noise increase. One of two types of highway traffic noise impacts. For a Type I project, an increase in noise levels of 5 to 15 dB(A) in the design year over the existing noise level.

Traffic noise impacts. Design year build condition noise levels that approach or exceed the NAC listed in Table 1 for the future build condition; or design year build condition noise levels that create a substantial noise increase over existing noise levels.

Type I project. (1) The construction of a highway on new location; or,

(2) The physical alteration of an existing highway where there is either:

(i) Substantial Horizontal Alteration. A project that halves the distance between the traffic noise source and the closest receptor between the existing condition to the future build condition; or,

(ii) Substantial Vertical Alteration. A project that removes shielding therefore exposing the line-of-sight between the receptor and the traffic noise source. This is done by either altering the vertical alignment of the highway or by altering the topography between the highway traffic noise source and the receptor; or,

(3) The addition of a through-traffic lane(s). This includes the addition of a through-traffic lane that functions as a HOV lane, High-Occupancy Toll (HOT) lane, bus lane, or truck climbing lane; or,

(4) The addition of an auxiliary lane, except for when the auxiliary lane is a turn lane; or,

(5) The addition or relocation of interchange lanes or ramps added to a quadrant to complete an existing partial interchange; or,

(6) Restriping existing pavement for the purpose of adding a through-traffic lane or an auxiliary lane; or,

(7) The addition of a new or substantial alteration of a weigh station, rest stop, ride-share lot or toll plaza.

(8) If a project is determined to be a Type I project under this definition then the entire project area as defined in the environmental document is a Type I project.

Type II project. A Federal or Federal-aid highway project for noise abatement on an existing highway. For a Type II project to be eligible for Federal-aid funding, the highway agency must develop and implement a Type II program in accordance with section 772.7(e).

Type III project. A Federal or Federal-aid highway project that does not meet the classifications of a Type I or Type II project. Type III projects do not require a noise analysis.

§ 772.7 Applicability.

(a) This regulation applies to all Federal or Federal-aid Highway Projects authorized under title 23, United States Code. Therefore, this regulation applies to any highway project or multimodal project that:

(1) Requires FHWA approval regardless of funding sources, or

(2) Is funded with Federal-aid highway funds.

(b) In order to obtain FHWA approval, the highway agency shall develop noise policies in conformance with this regulation and shall apply these policies uniformly and consistently statewide.

(c) This regulation applies to all Type I projects unless the regulation specifically indicates that a section only applies to Type II or Type III projects.

(d) The development and implementation of Type II projects are not mandatory requirements of section 109(i) of title 23, United States Code.

(e) If a highway agency chooses to participate in a Type II program, the highway agency shall develop a priority system, based on a variety of factors, to rank the projects in the program. This priority system shall be submitted to and approved by FHWA before the highway agency is allowed to use Federal-aid funds for a project in the program. The highway agency shall re-analyze the priority system on a regular interval, not to exceed 5 years.

(f) For a Type III project, a highway agency is not required to complete a noise analysis or consider abatement measures.

§ 772.9 Traffic noise prediction.

(a) Any analysis required by this subpart must use the FHWA Traffic Noise Model (TNM), which is described in "FHWA Traffic Noise Model" Report No. FHWA–PD–96–010, including Revision No. 1, dated April 14, 2004, or any other model determined by the FHWA to be consistent with the methodology of the FHWA TNM. These publications are incorporated by reference in accordance with section 552(a) of title 5, U.S.C. and part 51 of title 1, CFR, and are on file at the National Archives and Record Administration (NARA). For information on the availability of this material at NARA, call (202) 741–6030 or go to *http://www.archives.gov/federal_register/code_of_federal_regulations/ibr_locations.html*. These documents are available for copying and inspection at the Federal Highway Administration, 1200 New Jersey Avenue, SE., Washington, DC 20590, as provided in part 7 of title 49, CFR. These documents are also available on the FHWA's Traffic Noise Model Web site at the following URL: *http://www.fhwa.dot.gov/environment/noise/index.htm*.

(b) Average pavement type shall be used in the FHWA TNM for future noise level prediction unless a highway agency substantiates the use of a different pavement type for approval by the FHWA.

(c) Noise contour lines may be used for project alternative screening or for land use planning to comply with § 772.17 of this part, but shall not be used for determining highway traffic noise impacts.

(d) In predicting noise levels and assessing noise impacts, traffic characteristics that would yield the worst traffic noise impact for the design year shall be used.

§ 772.11 Analysis of traffic noise impacts.

(a) The highway agency shall determine and analyze expected traffic noise impacts.

(1) For projects on new alignments, determine traffic noise impacts by field measurements.

(2) For projects on existing alignments, predict existing and design year traffic noise impacts.

(b) In determining traffic noise impacts, a highway agency shall give primary consideration to exterior areas where frequent human use occurs.

(c) A traffic noise analysis shall be completed for:

(1) Each alternative under detailed study;

(2) Each Activity Category of the NAC listed in Table 1 that is present in the study area;

(i) *Activity Category A.* This activity category includes the exterior impact criteria for lands on which serenity and quiet are of extraordinary significance and serve an important public need, and where the preservation of those qualities is essential for the area to continue to serve its intended purpose. Highway agencies shall submit justifications to the FHWA on a case-by-case basis for approval of an Activity Category A designation.

(ii) *Activity Category B.* This activity category includes the exterior impact criteria for single-family and multi-family residences.

(iii) *Activity Category C.* This activity category includes the exterior impact criteria for a variety of land use facilities. Each highway agency shall adopt a standard practice for analyzing these land use facilities that is consistent and uniformly applied statewide.

(iv) *Activity Category D.* This activity category includes the interior impact criteria for certain land use facilities listed in Activity Category C that may have interior uses. A highway agency shall conduct an indoor analysis after a determination is made that exterior abatement measures will not be feasible and reasonable. An indoor analysis shall only be done after exhausting all outdoor analysis options. In situations where no exterior activities are to be affected by the traffic noise, or where the exterior activities are far from or physically shielded from the roadway in a manner that prevents an impact on exterior activities, the highway agency shall use Activity Category D as the basis of determining noise impacts. Each highway agency shall adopt a standard practice for analyzing these land use facilities that is consistent and uniformly applied statewide.

(v) *Activity Category E.* This activity category includes the exterior impact criteria for developed lands that are less sensitive to highway noise. Each highway agency shall adopt a standard practice for analyzing these land use facilities that is consistent and uniformly applied statewide.

(vi) *Activity Category F.* This activity category includes developed lands that are not sensitive to highway traffic noise. There is no impact criteria for the land use facilities in this activity category and no analysis of noise impacts is required.

(vii) *Activity Category G.* This activity includes undeveloped lands.

(A) A highway agency shall determine if undeveloped land is permitted for development. The milestone and its associated date for acknowledging when undeveloped land is considered permitted shall be the date of issuance of a building permit by the local jurisdiction or by the appropriate governing entity.

(B) If undeveloped land is determined to be perrmitted, then the highway agency shall assign the land to the appropriate Activity Category and analyze it in the same manner as developed lands in that Activity Category.

(C) If undeveloped land is not permitted for development by the date of public knowledge, the highway agency shall determine noise levels in accordance with 772.17(a) and document the results in the project's environmental clearance documents and noise analysis documents. Federal participation in noise abatement measures will not be considered for lands that are not permitted by the date of public knowledge.

(d) The analysis of traffic noise impacts shall include:

(1) Identification of existing activities, developed lands, and undeveloped lands, which may be affected by noise from the highway;

(2) For projects on new or existing alignments, validate predicted noise level through comparison between measured and predicted levels;

(3) Measurement of noise levels. Use an ANSI Type I or Type II integrating sound level meter;

(4) Identification of project limits to determine all traffic noise impacts for the design year for the build alternative. For Type II projects, traffic noise impacts shall be determined from current year conditions;

(e) Highway agencies shall establish an approach level to be used when determining a traffic noise impact. The approach level shall be at least 1 dB(A) less than the Noise Abatement Criteria for Activity Categories A to E listed in Table 1 to part 772;

(f) Highway agencies shall define substantial noise increase between 5 dB(A) to 15 dB(A) over existing noise levels. The substantial noise increase criterion is independent of the absolute noise level.

(g) A highway agency proposing to use Federal-aid highway funds for a Type II project shall perform a noise analysis in accordance with § 772.11 of this part in order to provide information needed to make the determination required by § 772.13(a) of this part.

§ 772.13 Analysis of noise abatement.

(a) When traffic noise impacts are identified, noise abatement shall be considered and evaluated for feasibility and reasonableness. The highway agency shall determine and analyze alternative noise abatement measures to abate identified impacts by giving weight to the benefits and costs of abatement and the overall social, economic, and environmental effects by using feasible and reasonable noise abatement measures for decision-making.

(b) In abating traffic noise impacts, a highway agency shall give primary consideration to exterior areas where frequent human use occurs.

(c) If a noise impact is identified, a highway agency shall consider abatement measures. The abatement measures listed in § 772.15(c) of this part are eligible for Federal funding.

(1) At a minimum, the highway agency shall consider noise abatement in the form of a noise barrier.

(2) If a highway agency chooses to use absorptive treatments as a functional enhancement, the highway agency shall adopt a standard practice for using absorptive treatment that is consistent and uniformly applied statewide.

(d) *Examination and evaluation of feasible and reasonable noise abatement measures for reducing the traffic noise impacts.* Each highway agency, with FHWA approval, shall develop feasibility and reasonableness factors.

(1) *Feasibility*: (i) Achievement of at least a 5 dB(A) highway traffic noise reduction at impacted receptors. The highway agency shall define, and receive FHWA approval for, the number of receptors that must achieve this reduction for the noise abatement measure to be acoustically feasible and explain the basis for this determination; and

(ii) Determination that it is possible to design and construct the noise abatement measure. Factors to consider are safety, barrier height, topography, drainage, utilities, and maintenance of the abatement measure, maintenance access to adjacent properties, and access to adjacent properties (*i.e.* arterial widening projects).

(2) *Reasonableness*:—(i) *Consideration of the viewpoints of the property owners and residents of the benefited receptors.* The highway agency shall solicit the viewpoints of all of the benefited receptors and obtain enough responses to document a decision on either desiring or not desiring the noise abatement measure. The highway agency shall define, and receive FHWA approval for, the number of receptors that are needed to constitute a decision and explain the basis for this determination.

(ii) *Cost effectiveness of the highway traffic noise abatement measures.* Each highway agency shall determine, and receive FHWA approval for, the allowable cost of abatement by determining a baseline cost reasonableness value. This determination may include the actual construction cost of noise abatement, cost per square foot of abatement, the maximum square footage of abatement/benefited receptor and either the cost/benefited receptor or cost/benefited receptor/dB(A) reduction. The highway agency shall re-analyze the allowable cost for abatement on a regular interval, not to exceed 5 years. A highway agency has the option of justifying, for FHWA approval, different cost allowances for a particular geographic area(s) within the State, however, the highway agancy must use the same cost reasonableness/construction cost ratio statewide.

(iii) *Noise reduction design goals for highway traffic noise abatement measures.* When noise abatement measure(s) are being considered, a highway agency shall achieve a noise reduction design goal. The highway agency shall define, and receive FHWA approval for, the design goal of at least 7 dB(A) but not more than 10 dB(A), and shall define the number of benefited receptors that must achieve this design goal and explain the basis for this determination.

(iv) The reasonableness factors listed in § 772.13(d)(5)(i), (ii) and (iii), must collectively be achieved in order for a noise abatement measure to be deemed reasonable. Failure to achieve § 772.13(d)(5)(i), (ii) or (iii), will result in the noise abatement measure being deemed not reasonable.

(v) In addition to the required reasonableness factors listed in § 772.13(d)(5)(i), (ii), and (iii), a highway agency has the option to also include the following reasonableness factors: Date of development, length of time receivers have been exposed to highway traffic noise impacts, exposure to higher absolute highway traffic noise levels, changes between existing and future build conditions, percentage of mixed zoning development, and use of noise compatible planning concepts by the local government. No single optional reasonableness factor can be used to determine reasonableness.

(e) Assessment of Benefited Receptors. Each highway agency shall define the threshold for the noise reduction which determines a benefited receptor as at or above the 5 dB(A), but not to exceed the highway agency's reasonableness design goal.

(f) *Abatement measure reporting*: Each highway agency shall maintain an inventory of all constructed noise abatement measures. The inventory shall include the following parameters: type of abatement; cost (overall cost, unit cost per/sq. ft.); average height; length; area; location (State, county, city, route); year of construction; average insertion loss/noise reduction as reported by the model in the noise analysis; NAC category(s) protected; material(s) used (precast concrete, berm, block, cast in place concrete, brick, metal, wood, fiberglass, combination, plastic (transparent, opaque, other); features (absorptive, reflective, surface texture); foundation (ground mounted, on structure); project type (Type I, Type II, and optional project types such as State funded, county funded, tollway/turnpike funded, other, unknown). The FHWA will collect this information, in accordance with OMB's Information Collection requirements.

(g) Before adoption of a CE, FONSI, or ROD, the highway agency shall identify:

(1) Noise abatement measures which are feasible and reasonable, and which are likely to be incorporated in the project; and

(2) Noise impacts for which no noise abatement measures are feasible and reasonable.

(3) *Documentation of highway traffic noise abatement*: The environmental document shall identify locations where noise impacts are predicted to occur, where noise abatement is feasible and reasonable, and locations with impacts that have no feasible or reasonable noise abatement alternative. For environmental clearance, this analysis shall be completed to the extent that design information on the alterative(s) under study in the environmental document is available at the time the environmental clearance document is completed. A statement of likelihood shall be included in the environmental document since feasibility and reasonableness determinations may change due to changes in project design after approval of the environmental document. The statement of likelihood shall include the preliminary location and physical description of noise abatement measures determined feasible and reasonable in the preliminary analysis. The statement of likelihood shall also indicate that final recommendations on the construction of an abatement measure(s) is determined during the completion of the project's final design and the public involvement processes.

(h) The FHWA will not approve project plans and specifications unless feasible and reasonable noise abatement measures are incorporated into the plans and specifications to reduce the noise impact on existing activities, developed lands, or undeveloped lands for which development is permitted.

(i) For design-build projects, the preliminary technical noise study shall document all considered and proposed noise abatement measures for inclusion in the NEPA document. Final design of design-build noise abatement measures shall be based on the preliminary noise abatement design developed in the technical noise analysis. Noise abatement measures shall be considered, developed, and constructed in accordance with this standard and in conformance with the provisions of 40 CFR 1506.5(c) and 23 CFR 636.109.

(j) Third party funding is not allowed on a Federal or Federal-aid Type I or Type II project if the noise abatement measure would require the additional funding from the third party to be considered feasible and/or reasonable. Third party funding is acceptable on a Federal or Federal-aid highway Type I or Type II project to make functional enhancements, such as absorptive treatment and access doors or aesthetic enhancements, to a noise abatement measure already determined feasible and reasonable.

(k) On a Type I or Type II projects, a highway agency has the option to cost average noise abatement among benefited receptors within common noise environments if no single common noise environment exceeds two times the highway agency's cost reasonableness criteria and collectively all common noise environments being averaged do not exceed the highway agency's cost reasonableness criteria.

§ 772.15 Federal participation.

(a) *Type I and Type II projects.* Federal funds may be used for noise abatement measures when:

(1) Traffic noise impacts have been identified; and

(2) Abatement measures have been determined to be feasible and reasonable pursuant to § 772.13(d) of this chapter.

(b) *For Type II projects.* (1) No funds made available out of the Highway Trust Fund may be used to construct Type II noise barriers, as defined by this regulation, if such noise barriers were not part of a project approved by the FHWA before the November 28, 1995.

(2) Federal funds are available for Type II noise barriers along lands that were developed or were under substantial construction before approval of the acquisition of the rights-of-ways for, or construction of, the existing highway.

(3) FHWA will not approve noise abatement measures for locations where such measures were previously determined not to be feasible and reasonable for a Type I project.

(c) *Noise abatement measures.* The following noise abatement measures may be considered for incorporation into a Type I or Type II project to reduce traffic noise impacts. The costs of such measures may be included in Federal-aid participating project costs with the Federal share being the same as that for the system on which the project is located.

(1) Construction of noise barriers, including acquisition of property rights, either within or outside the highway right-of-way. Landscaping is not a viable noise abatement measure.

(2) Traffic management measures including, but not limited to, traffic control devices and signing for prohibition of certain vehicle types, time-use restrictions for certain vehicle types, modified speed limits, and exclusive lane designations.

(3) Alteration of horizontal and vertical alignments.

(4) Acquisition of real property or interests therein (predominantly unimproved property) to serve as a buffer zone to preempt development which would be adversely impacted by traffic noise. This measure may be included in Type I projects only.

(5) Noise insulation of Activity Category D land use facilities listed in Table 1. Post-installation maintenance and operational costs for noise insulation are not eligible for Federal-aid funding.

§ 772.17 Information for local officials.

(a) To minimize future traffic noise impacts on currently undeveloped lands of Type I projects, a highway agency shall inform local officials within whose jurisdiction the highway project is located of:

(1) Noise compatible planning concepts;

(2) The best estimation of the future design year noise levels at various distances from the edge of the nearest travel lane of the highway improvement where the future noise levels meet the highway agency's definition of "approach" for undeveloped lands or properties within the project limits. At a minimum, identify the distance to the exterior noise abatement criteria in Table 1;

(3) Non-eligibility for Federal-aid participation for a Type II project as described in § 772.15(b).

(b) If a highway agency chooses to participate in a Type II noise program or to use the date of development as one of the factors in determining the reasonableness of a Type I noise abatement measure, the highway agency shall have a statewide outreach program to inform local officials and the public of the items in § 772.17(a)(1) through (3).

§ 772.19 Construction noise.

For all Type I and II projects, a highway agency shall:

(a) Identify land uses or activities that may be affected by noise from construction of the project. The identification is to be performed during the project development studies.

(b) Determine the measures that are needed in the plans and specifications to minimize or eliminate adverse construction noise impacts to the community. This determination shall include a weighing of the benefits achieved and the overall adverse social, economic, and environmental effects and costs of the abatement measures.

(c) Incorporate the needed abatement measures in the plans and specifications.

TABLE 1 TO PART 772—NOISE ABATEMENT CRITERIA

[Hourly A-Weighted Sound Level_decibels (dB(A)) [1]]

Activity category	Activity Leq(h)	Criteria [2] L10(h)	Evaluation location	Activity description
A	57	60	Exterior	Lands on which serenity and quiet are of extraordinary significance and serve an important public need and where the preservation of those qualities is essential if the area is to continue to serve its intended purpose.
B [3]	67	70	Exterior	Residential.
C [3]	67	70	Exterior	Active sport areas, amphitheaters, auditoriums, campgrounds, cemeteries, day care centers, hospitals, libraries, medical facilities, parks, picnic areas, places of worship, playgrounds, public meeting rooms, public or nonprofit institutional structures, radio studios, recording studios, recreation areas, Section 4(f) sites, schools, television studios, trails, and trail crossings.
D	52	55	Interior	Auditoriums, day care centers, hospitals, libraries, medical facilities, places of worship, public meeting rooms, public or nonprofit institutional structures, radio studios, recording studios, schools, and television studios.
E [3]	72	75	Exterior	Hotels, motels, offices, restaurants/bars, and other developed lands, properties or activities not included in A–D or F.
F				Agriculture, airports, bus yards, emergency services, industrial, logging, maintenance facilities, manufacturing, mining, rail yards, retail facilities, shipyards, utilities (water resources, water treatment, electrical), and warehousing.
G				Undeveloped lands that are not permitted.

[1] Either Leq(h) or L10(h) (but not both) may be used on a project.

[2] The Leq(h) and L10(h) Activity Criteria values are for impact determination only, and are not design standards for noise abatement measures.

[3] Includes undeveloped lands permitted for this activity category.

PART 773—SURFACE TRANSPORTATION PROJECT DELIVERY PROGRAM APPLICATION REQUIREMENTS AND TERMINATION

AUTHORITY: 23 U.S.C. 315 and 327; 49 CFR 1.81(a)(4)–(6); 49 CFR 1.85

SOURCE: 79 FR 55398, Sept. 16, 2014, unless otherwise noted.

§ 773.101 Purpose.

The purpose of this part is to establish the requirements for an application by a State to participate in the Surface Transportation Project Delivery Program (Program). The Program allows, under certain circumstances, the Secretary to assign and a State to assume the responsibilities under the National Environmental Policy Act of 1969 (NEPA) and for environmental review, consultation, or other action required under certain Federal environmental laws with respect to one or more highway, railroad, public transportation, or multimodal projects within the State.

§ 773.103 Definitions.

Unless otherwise specified in this part, the definitions in 23 U.S.C. 101(a) and 49 U.S.C., are applicable to this part. As used in this part:

Classes of projects means either a defined group of projects or all projects to which Federal environmental laws apply.

Federal environmental law means any Federal law, regulation, or Executive Order (E.O.) under which the Secretary of the U.S. Department of Transportation (DOT) has responsibilities for environmental review, consultation, or other action with respect to the review or approval of a highway, railroad, public transportation, or multimodal project. The Federal environmental laws for which a State may assume the responsibilities of the Secretary under this Program include the list of laws contained in Appendix A to this part.

Highway project means any undertaking that is eligible for financial assistance under title 23 U.S.C. and for which the Federal Highway Administration has primary responsibility. A highway project may include an undertaking that involves a series of contracts or phases, such as a corridor, and also may include anything that may be constructed in connection with a highway, bridge, or tunnel. The term highway project does not include any project authorized under 23 U.S.C. 202, 203, or 204 unless the State will design and construct the project.

MOU means a Memorandum of Understanding, a written agreement that complies with 23 U.S.C. 327(b)(4)(C) and (c), and this part.

NEPA means the National Environmental Policy Act of 1969 (42 U.S.C. 4321 *et seq.*).

Operating Administration means any agency established within the DOT, including the Federal Aviation Administration, Federal Highway Administration (FHWA), Federal Motor Carrier Safety Administration, Federal Railroad Administration (FRA), Federal Transit Administration (FTA), Maritime Administration, National Highway Traffic Safety Administration, Office of the Secretary of Transportation, Pipeline and Hazardous Materials Safety Administration, and Saint Lawrence Seaway Development Corporation.

Program means the "Surface Transportation Project Delivery Program" established under 23 U.S.C. 327.

Public transportation project means a capital project or operating assistance for "public transportation," as defined in chapter 53 of title 49 U.S.C.

Railroad project means any undertaking eligible for financial assistance from FRA to construct (including initial construction, reconstruction, replacement, rehabilitation, restoration, or other improvements) a railroad, as that term is defined in 49 U.S.C. 20102, including: environmental mitigation activities; an undertaking that involves a series of contracts or phases, such as a railroad corridor; and anything that may be constructed in connection with a railroad. The term railroad project does not include any undertaking in which FRA provides financial assistance to Amtrak or private entities.

State means any agency under the direct jurisdiction of the Governor of any of the 50 States or Puerto Rico, or the mayor in the District of Columbia, which is responsible for implementing highway, public transportation, or railroad projects eligible for assignment. The term "State" does not include agencies of local governments, transit authorities or commissions under their own board of directors, or State-owned corporations.

§773.105 Eligibility.

(a) *Applicants.* A State must comply with the following conditions to be eligible and to retain eligibility for the Program.

(1) For highway projects:

(i) The State must act by and through the State Department of Transportation (State DOT) established and maintained in conformity with 23 U.S.C. 302 and 23 CFR 1.3;

(ii) The State expressly consents to accept the jurisdiction of the Federal courts for compliance, discharge, and enforcement of any responsibility assumed by the State;

(iii) The State has laws in effect that authorize the State to take the actions necessary to carry out the responsibilities it is assuming;

(iv) The State has laws in effect that are comparable to the Freedom of Information Act (FOIA) (5 U.S.C. 552), including laws providing that any decision regarding the public availability of a document under those State laws is reviewable by a court of competent jurisdiction; and

(v) The State has the financial and personnel resources necessary to carry out the responsibilities it is assuming.

(2) For railroad or public transportation projects:

(i) The State must comply with paragraphs (a)(1)(ii) through (v) of this section; and

(ii) The State must have assumed the responsibilities of the Secretary under this part with respect to one or more highway projects.

(b) *Responsibilities.* Responsibilities eligible for Program assignment and State assumption include all NEPA responsibilities and all or part of the reviews, consultations, and other actions required under other environmental laws, regulations, and E.O.s. Appendix A to this part contains an example list of other environmental laws, regulations, and E.O.s that may be assigned to and assumed by the State. These may include the environmental review responsibilities for the elements of a multimodal project that are within an applicable Operating Administration's jurisdiction. The following responsibilities are ineligible for Program assignment and State assumption:

(1) Conformity determinations required under section 176 of the Clean Air Act (42 U.S.C. 7506);

(2) The Secretary's responsibilities under 23 U.S.C. 134 and 135;

(3) The Secretary's responsibilities under 49 U.S.C. 5303 and 5304;

(4) The Secretary's responsibilities for government-to-government consultation with Indian tribes;

(5) The Secretary's responsibilities for approvals that are not considered to be part of the environmental review of a project, such as project approvals, Interstate access approvals, and safety approvals; and

(6) The Secretary's responsibilities under NEPA and for reviews, consultations, and other actions required under other Federal environmental laws for actions of Operating Administrations other than FHWA, FRA, and FTA.

(c) *Projects.* Environmental reviews ineligible for assignment and State assumption under the Program include reviews for the following types of projects:

(1) Projects that cross State boundaries, and

(2) Projects adjacent to or that cross international boundaries.

(d) *Discretion retained.* Nothing in this section limits an Operating Administration's discretion to withhold approval of assignment of eligible responsibilities or projects under this Program.

§ 773.107 Pre-application requirements.

(a) *Coordination meeting.* The State must request and participate in a pre-application coordination meeting with the appropriate Division or Regional, and Headquarters office of the applicable Operating Administration(s) before soliciting public comment on its application.

(b) *Public comment.* The State must give notice of its intention to participate in the Program and must solicit public comment by publishing the complete application in accordance with the appropriate State public notice laws not later than 30 days prior to submitting its application to the appropriate Operating Administration(s). If allowed under State law, publishing a statewide notice of availability of the application rather than the application itself may satisfy the requirements of this provision so long as the complete application is made available on the internet and is reasonably available to the public for inspection. Solicitation of public comment must include solicitation of the views of other State agencies, tribal agencies, and Federal agencies that may have consultation or approval responsibilities associated with the project(s) within State boundaries.

(1) The State requesting FTA's responsibilities with respect to public transportation projects must identify and solicit public comment from potential recipients of assistance under chapter 53 of title 49 U.S.C. These comments may include requests for the Secretary to maintain the environmental review responsibilities with respect to one or more public transportation projects.

(2) The State must submit copies of all comments received as a result of the publication of the respective application(s). The State must summarize the comments received, develop responses to substantive comments, and note any revisions or actions taken in response to the public comment.

(c) *Sovereign immunity waiver.* The State must identify and complete the process required by State law for consenting and accepting exclusive Federal court jurisdiction with respect to compliance, discharge, and enforcement of any of the responsibilities being sought.

(d) *Comparable State laws.* The State must determine that it has laws that are in effect that authorize the State to take actions necessary to carry out the responsibilities the State is seeking and a public records access law that is comparable to FOIA. The State must ensure that it cures any deficiency in applicable State laws before submitting its application.

§ 773.109 Application requirements.

(a) *Highway project responsibilities.* An eligible State DOT may submit an application to FHWA to participate in the Program for one or more highway projects or classes of highway projects. The application must include:

(1) The highway projects or classes of highway projects for which the State is requesting assumption of Federal environmental review responsibilities under NEPA. The State must specifically identify in its application each highway project for which a draft environmental impact statement has been issued and for which a final environmental impact statement is pending, prior to the submission of its application;

(2) Each Federal environmental law, review, consultation, or other environmental responsibility the State seeks to assume under this Program. The State must indicate whether it proposes to phase-in the assumption of these responsibilities, *i.e.*, initially assuming only some responsibilities with a plan to assume additional responsibilities at specific future times;

(3) For each responsibility requested in paragraphs (a)(1) and (2) of this section, the State must describe how it intends to carry out these responsibilities. Such description must include:

(i) A summary of State procedures currently in place to guide the development of documents, analyses, and consultations required to fulfill the environmental review responsibilities requested. For States that have comparable State environmental review procedures, the discussion should describe the differences, if any, between the State environmental review process and the Federal environmental review process, focusing on any standard that is mandated by State law, regulation, executive order, or policy that is not applicable to the Federal environmental review. The State must submit a copy of the procedures with the application unless these are available electronically. The State may submit the procedures electronically, either through email or by providing a hyperlink;

(ii) Any changes that the State has made or will make in the management of its environmental program to provide the additional staff and training necessary for quality control and assurance, appropriate levels of analysis, adequate expertise in areas where the State is requesting responsibilities, and expertise in management of the NEPA process and reviews under other Federal environmental laws;

(iii) A discussion of how the State will conduct legal reviews for the environmental documents it produces, including legal sufficiency reviews where required by law, policy, or guidance;

(iv) A discussion of how the State will identify and address those projects that without assignment would have required FHWA Headquarters' prior concurrence of the final environmental impact statement under 23 CFR 771.125(c); and

(v) A discussion of otherwise permissible project delivery methods the State intends to pursue, and the process it will use to decide whether pursuing those project delivery methods and being responsible for the environmental review meet the objectivity and integrity requirements of NEPA.

(4) A verification of the personnel necessary to carry out the authority that the State may assume under the Program. The verification must contain the following information:

(i) A description of the staff positions, including management, that will be dedicated to fulfilling the additional functions needed to perform the assigned responsibilities;

(ii) A description of any changes to the State's organizational structure that would be necessary to provide for efficient administration of the responsibilities assumed; and

(iii) A discussion of personnel needs that may be met by the State's use of outside consultants, including legal counsel provided by the State Attorney General or private counsel;

(5) A summary of the anticipated financial resources available to meet the activities and staffing needs identified in paragraphs (a)(3) and (4) of this section, and a commitment to make adequate financial resources available to meet these needs;

(6) Certification and explanation by the State's Attorney General, or other State official legally empowered by State law to issue legal opinions that bind the State, that the State has legal authority to assume the responsibilities of the Secretary for the Federal environmental laws and projects requested, and that the State consents to exclusive Federal court jurisdiction with respect to the responsibilities the State is requesting to assume. Such consent must be broad enough to include future changes in relevant Federal policies and procedures or allow for its amendment to include such future changes;

(7) Certification by the State's Attorney General, or other State official legally empowered by State law to issue legal opinions that bind the State, that the State has laws that are comparable to FOIA, including laws that allow for any decision regarding the public availability of a document under those laws to be reviewed by a court of competent jurisdiction;

(8) Evidence that the required notice and solicitation of public comment by the State relating to participation in the Program has taken place and copies of the State's responses to the comments;

(9) A point of contact for questions regarding the application and a point of contact regarding the implementation of the Program (if different); and

(10) The State Governor's (or in the case of District of Columbia, the Mayor's) signature approving the application. For the Secretary's responsibilities with respect to highway projects, the top ranking transportation official in the State who is charged with responsibility for highway construction may sign the application instead of the Governor.

(b) *Public transportation project responsibilities.* An eligible State may submit an application to FTA to participate in the Program for one or more public transportation projects or classes of public transportation projects. The application must provide the information required by paragraphs (a)(1) through (10) of this section, but with respect to FTA's program and the public transportation project(s) at issue. In addition, the application must include:

(1) Evidence that FHWA has assigned to the State, or the State has requested assignment of the responsibilities of, FHWA with respect to one or more highway projects within the State under NEPA; and

(2) Evidence that any potential recipients of assistance under chapter 53 of title 49 U.S.C. for any public transportation project or classes of public transportation projects in the State being sought for Program assignment have received written notice of the application with adequate time to provide comments on the application.

(c) *Railroad project responsibilities.* An eligible State may submit an application to FRA to participate in the Program for one or more railroad projects or classes of railroad projects. The application must provide the information required by paragraphs (a)(1) through (10) of this section, but with respect to the railroad project(s) at issue. In addition, the application must include evidence that FHWA has assigned to the State, or the State has requested assignment of, the responsibilities of FHWA with respect to one or more highway projects within the State under NEPA.

(d) *Multimodal project responsibilities.* The Operating Administration(s) will presume that the responsibilities sought by the State include the Secretary's environmental review responsibilities for multimodal projects' elements that would otherwise fall under the Operating Administration's authority. These responsibilities include establishing appropriate relationships with the other Operating Administration(s) involved in the multimodal project, including cooperating agency, participating agency, and lead or colead agency relationships under NEPA. The State must affirmatively reject multimodal environmental review responsibilities in its application if it intends to have the responsibilities remain with the Operating Administration when a multimodal project is involved. In addition, States may:

(1) Request the Secretary's environmental review responsibilities with respect to the highway, railroad, and/or public transportation elements of one or more particular multimodal projects by submitting an application with the information required in paragraphs (a)(1) through (10) of this section, but with respect to the multimodal project(s) at issue. The application must either request highway responsibilities for the multimodal project or include evidence that FHWA has assigned to the State, or the State has requested assignment of, the responsibilities of FHWA with respect to one or more highway projects within the State under NEPA; and

(2) Request, at the same time the State applies for assignment of one of the Operating Administration's environmental review responsibilities, the general multimodal environmental review responsibilities of the other Operating Administration(s).

(e) *Electronic submissions.* Applications may be submitted electronically to the appropriate Operating Administration.

(f) *Joint application.* A State may submit joint applications for multiple Operating Administrations' responsibilities. A joint application should avoid redundancies and duplication of information to the maximum extent practicable. In its application, the State must distinguish the projects or classes of projects it seeks to assume by transportation mode. A joint application must provide all of the information required by each Operating Administration for which a State is seeking assignment. A State must submit joint applications to FHWA.

(g) *Requests for additional information.* The appropriate Operating Administration(s) may request that the State provide additional information to address any deficiencies in the application or clarifications that may be needed prior to determining that the application is complete.

§ 773.111 Application review and approval.

(a) The Operating Administration(s) must solicit public comment on the pending request and must consider comments received before rendering a decision on the State's application. Materials made available for this public review must include the State's application, a draft of the MOU, and a list of responsibilities sought by the State that the Operating Administration(s) proposes to retain. The notification may be a joint notification if two or more Operating Administrations are involved in the assignment for a project or a class of projects.

(b) If the Operating Administration(s) approves the application of a State, then the Operating Administration(s) will invite the State to execute the MOU.

(c) The Administrator for the appropriate Operating Administration will be responsible for approving the application and executing the MOU on behalf of the Operating Administration.

(d) The State's participation in the Program is effective upon full execution of the MOU. The Operating Administration's responsibilities under NEPA and any other environmental laws may not be assigned to or assumed by the State prior to execution of the MOU with the exception of renewal situations under § 773.115(g) of this part.

(e) The MOU must have a term of not more than 5 years that may be renewed pursuant to § 773.115 of this part.

(f) The State must publish the MOU and approved application on its Web site and other relevant State Web sites and make it reasonably available to the public for inspection and copying.

§ 773.113 Application amendments.

(a) After a State submits its application to the appropriate Operating Administration(s), but prior to the execution of the MOU(s), the State may amend its application at any time to request the addition or withdrawal of projects, classes of projects, or environmental review responsibilities consistent with the requirements of this part.

(1) Prior to submitting any such amendment, the State must coordinate with the appropriate Operating Administration(s) to determine if the amendment represents a substantial change in the application to such an extent that additional notice and opportunity for public comment is needed. The Operating Administration is responsible for making the final decision on whether notice and public comment is needed and whether to provide one opportunity (pursuant to § 773.107(b)) or two opportunities (pursuant to § 773.107(b) and § 773.111(a)) for public comment. The Operating Administration will make this determination based on the magnitude of the changes.

(2) If the Operating Administration determines that notice and solicitation of public comment is needed pursuant to § 773.107(b), the State must include copies of all comments received, responses to substantive comments, and note the changes, if any, that were made in response to the comments.

(b) After the execution of the MOU(s) or renewal MOU(s), a State may amend its application to the appropriate Operating Administration(s) to request additional projects, classes of projects, or more environmental review responsibilities consistent with the requirements of this part.

(1) Prior to requesting any such amendment, the State must coordinate with the appropriate Operating Administration(s) to determine if the amendment represents a substantial change in the application information to the extent that additional notice and opportunity for public comment is needed. The Operating Administration is responsible for making the final decision on whether notice and public comment are needed and whether to provide one opportunity (pursuant to § 773.107(b) or § 773.111(a)) or two opportunities (pursuant to § 773.107(b) and § 773.111(a)) for public comment. The Operating Administration will make this determination based on the magnitude of the changes.

(2) If the Operating Administration determines that notice and solicitation of public comment is required pursuant to § 773.107(b), the State must include copies of all comments received, responses to substantive comments, and note the changes, if any, that were made in response to the comments.

(3) The Operating Administration is responsible for making the final decision on whether to accept the amendment and whether an amendment to the MOU is required. Amendments do not change the expiration date of the initial or renewal MOU.

§ 773.115 Renewals.

(a) A State that intends to renew its participation in the Program must notify the appropriate Operating Administration(s) at least 12 months before the expiration of the MOU.

(b) Prior to requesting renewal, the State must coordinate with the appropriate Operating Administration(s) to determine if significant changes have occurred or new assignment responsibilities are being sought that would warrant statewide notice and opportunity for public comment prior to the State's submission of the renewal package. The Operating Administration is responsible for making the final decision on whether the State should engage in statewide notification prior to its submittal. The Operating Administration will make this determination based on the magnitude of the change(s) in the information and/or circumstances.

(c) The renewal package must:

(1) Describe changes to the information submitted in the initial Program application;

(2) Provide up-to-date certifications required in § 773.109(a)(6) and (7) of this part for the applicable Operating Administration(s), if up-to-date certifications are needed or if the necessary State laws have termination dates that would occur before the end of a renewal period;

(3) Provide evidence of the statewide public notification, if one was required under paragraph (b) of this section, and include copies of all comments received, responses to substantive comments, and note the changes, if any, that were made to the renewal package in response to the comments; and

(4) Include the State Governor's (or in the case of District of Columbia, the Mayor's) signature approving the renewal package. For the Secretary's responsibilities with respect to highway projects, the top ranking transportation official in the State who is charged with responsibility for highway construction may sign the renewal package instead of the Governor.

(d) A State must submit a renewal package no later than 180 days prior to the expiration of the MOU.

(e) The Operating Administration(s) may request that the State provide additional information to address any deficiencies in the renewal application or to provide clarifications.

(f) The Operating Administration(s) must provide FEDERAL REGISTER notification and solicit public comment on the renewal request and must consider comments received before approving the State's renewal application. Materials made available for this public review will include the State's original application, the renewal package, a draft of the renewal MOU, a list of responsibilities sought by the State that the Operating Administration proposes to retain, and auditing and monitoring reports developed as part of the Program. The notification may be a joint notification if two or more Operating Administrations are involved in the assignment for a project or a class of projects.

(g) In determining whether to approve the State's renewal request, the Operating Administration will take into account the renewal package, comments received if an opportunity for public comments was provided in accordance with paragraph (f) of this section, the auditing and monitoring reports, and the State's overall performance in the Program. If the Operating Administration(s) approves the renewal request, then the Operating Administration(s) will invite the State to execute the renewal MOU. The Administrator for the appropriate Operating Administration will be responsible for approving the application and executing the renewal MOU on behalf of the Operating Administration. The renewal MOU must have a term of not more than 5 years, and the State must publish it on the State's DOT Web site and other relevant State Web site(s).

(h) At the discretion of the Operating Administration, a State may retain temporarily its assigned and assumed responsibilities under a MOU after the expiration of the MOU, where the relevant Operating Administration(s) determines that:

(1) The State made a timely submission of a complete renewal application in accordance with the provisions of this section;

(2) The Operating Administration(s) determines that all reasonable efforts have been made to achieve a timely execution of the renewal; and

(3) The Operating Administration(s) determines that it is in the best interest of the public to grant the continuance.

§ 773.117 Termination.

(a) *Termination by the Operating Administration.* An Operating Administration(s) that approved the State's participation in the Program may terminate the State's participation if the Operating Administration(s) determines that the State is not adequately carrying out the responsibilities assigned to the State. Examples of situations where such a finding may be made include: persistent neglect of, or noncompliance with, any Federal laws, regulations, and policies; failure to address deficiencies identified during the audit or monitoring process; failure to secure or maintain adequate personnel and/or financial resources to carry out the responsibilities assumed; intentional noncompliance with the terms of the MOU(s); and persistent failure to adequately consult, coordinate, and/or take into account the concerns of other Operating Administrations, when applicable, and appropriate Federal, State, tribal, and local agencies with oversight, consulting, or coordination responsibilities under Federal environmental laws and regulations.

(1) The Operating Administration(s) may rely on the auditing and monitoring reports as sources for a finding that the State is not adequately carrying out its responsibilities. The Operating Administration(s) may also rely on information on noncompliance obtained outside the auditing and monitoring process.

(2) The Operating Administration(s) may not terminate a State's participation without providing the State with notification of the noncompliance issue that could give rise to the termination, and without affording the State an opportunity to take corrective action to address the noncompliance issue. The Operating Administration(s) must provide the State a period of no less than thirty (30) days to take the corrective actions. The Operating Administration(s) is responsible for making the final decision on whether the corrective action is satisfactory.

(b) *Termination by the State.* The State may terminate its participation at any time by notifying the Secretary no later than 90 days prior to the proposed termination date. The notice must include a draft transition plan detailing how the State will transfer the projects and responsibilities to the appropriate Operating Administration(s). Termination will not take effect until the State and the Operating Administration(s) agree, and the Operating Administration(s) approve a final transition plan. Transition plans must include:

(1) A list of projects and their status in the environmental review process that the State will return to the Operating Administration(s);

(2) A process for transferring files on pending projects;

(3) A process for notifying the public that the State will terminate its participation in the Program and a projected date upon which this termination will take effect;

(4) Points of contacts for pending projects; and

(5) Any other information required by the Operating Administration(s) to ensure the smooth transition of environmental review responsibilities and prevent disruption in the environmental reviews of projects to the maximum extent possible.

(c) *Termination by mutual agreement.* The State and the Operating Administration(s) may agree to terminate assignment on a specific date before the expiration of the MOU. Termination will not take effect until the State and the Operating Administration(s) agree, and the Operating Administration(s) approve a final transition plan. Transition plans must include the information outlined in paragraphs (b)(1)–(5) of this section.

(d) *Effect of termination of highway responsibilities.* Termination of the assignment of the Secretary's environmental review responsibilities with respect to highway projects will result in the termination of assignment of environmental responsibilities for railroad, public transportation, and multimodal projects.

APPENDIX A TO PART 773—EXAMPLE LIST OF THE SECRETARY'S ENVIRONMENTAL REVIEW RESPONSIBILITIES THAT MAY BE ASSIGNED UNDER 23 U.S.C. 327

FEDERAL PROCEDURES

NEPA, 42 U.S.C. 4321 *et seq.*

Regulations for Implementing the Procedural Provisions of NEPA at 40 CFR parts 1500–1508.

FHWA/FTA environmental regulations at 23 CFR part 771.

FRA's Procedures for Considering Environmental Impacts, 64 FR 28545, May 26, 1999 and 78 FR 2713, Jan. 14, 2013.

Clean Air Act, 42 U.S.C. 7401–7671q. Any determinations that do not involve conformity.

Efficient Environmental Reviews for Project Decisionmaking, 23 U.S.C. 139.

Noise

Noise Control Act of 1972, 42 U.S.C. 4901–4918.

Airport Noise and Capacity Act of 1990, 49 U.S.C. 47521–47534.

FHWA noise regulations at 23 CFR part 772.

Wildlife

Endangered Species Act of 1973, 16 U.S.C. 1531–1544.

Marine Mammal Protection Act, 16 U.S.C. 1361–1423h.

Anadromous Fish Conservation Act, 16 U.S.C. 757a–757f.

Fish and Wildlife Coordination Act, 16 U.S.C. 661–667d.

Migratory Bird Treaty Act, 16 U.S.C. 703–712.

Magnuson-Stevens Fishery Conservation and Management Act of 1976, as amended, 16 U.S.C. 1801–1891d.

Historic and Cultural Resources

National Historic Preservation Act of 1966, 16 U.S.C. 470 *et seq.*

Archaeological Resources Protection Act of 1979, 16 U.S.C. 470aa–470mm.

Archeological and Historic Preservation Act, 16 U.S.C. 469–469c.

Native American Graves Protection and Repatriation Act, 25 U.S.C. 3001–3013; 18 U.S.C. 1170.

Social and Economic Impacts

American Indian Religious Freedom Act, 42 U.S.C. 1996.

Farmland Protection Policy Act, 7 U.S.C. 4201–4209.

Water Resources and Wetlands

Clean Water Act, 33 U.S.C. 1251–1387.

Section 404, 33 U.S.C. 1344
Section 401, 33 U.S.C. 1341
Section 319, 33 U.S.C. 1329

Coastal Barrier Resources Act, 16 U.S.C. 3501–3510.

Coastal Zone Management Act, 16 U.S.C. 1451–1466.

Safe Drinking Water Act, 42 U.S.C. 300f—300j–26.

Rivers and Harbors Act of 1899, 33 U.S.C. 403.

Wild and Scenic Rivers Act, 16 U.S.C. 1271–1287.

Emergency Wetlands Resources Act, 16 U.S.C. 3901 and 3921.

Wetlands Mitigation, 23 U.S.C. 119(g) and 133(b)(14).

FHWA wetland and natural habitat mitigation regulations at 23 CFR part 777.

Flood Disaster Protection Act, 42 U.S.C. 4001–4130.

Parklands

Section 4(f), 49 U.S.C. 303; 23 U.S.C. 138.

FHWA/FTA Section 4(f) regulations at 23 CFR part 774.

Land and Water Conservation Fund, 16 U.S.C. 460*l*–4–460*l*–11.

Hazardous Materials

Comprehensive Environmental Response, Compensation, and Liability Act, 42 U.S.C. 9601–9675.

Superfund Amendments and Reauthorization Act of 1986, 42 U.S.C. 9671–9675.

Resource Conservation and Recovery Act, 42 U.S.C. 6901–6992k.

Executive Orders Relating to Eligible Projects

E.O. 11990, *Protection of Wetlands*

E.O. 11988, *Floodplain Management*

E.O. 12898, *Federal Actions to Address Environmental Justice in Minority Populations and Low Income Populations*

E.O. 13112, *Invasive Species*

PART 774—PARKS, RECREATION AREAS, WILDLIFE AND WATERFOWL REFUGES, AND HISTORIC SITES (SECTION 4(f))

Sec.

AUTHORITY: 23 U.S.C. 103(c), 109(h), 138, 325, 326, 327 and 204(h)(2); 49 U.S.C. 303; Section 6009 of the Safe, Accountable, Flexible, Efficient Transportation Equity Act: A Legacy for Users (Pub. L. 109–59, Aug. 10, 2005, 119 Stat. 1144); 49 CFR 1.81 and 1.91; and, Pub. L. 114–94, 129 Stat. 1312, Sections 1303 and 11502.

SOURCE: 73 FR 13395, Mar. 12, 2008, unless otherwise noted.

§774.1 Purpose.

The purpose of this part is to implement 23 U.S.C. 138 and 49 U.S.C. 303, which were originally enacted as Section 4(f) of the Department of Transportation Act of 1966 and are still commonly referred to as "Section 4(f)."

§774.3 Section 4(f) approvals.

The Administration may not approve the use, as defined in §774.17, of Section 4(f) property unless a determination is made under paragraph (a) or (b) of this section.

(a) The Administration determines that:

(1) There is no feasible and prudent avoidance alternative, as defined in §774.17, to the use of land from the property; and

(2) The action includes all possible planning, as defined in §774.17, to minimize harm to the property resulting from such use; or

(b) The Administration determines that the use of the property, including any measure(s) to minimize harm (such as any avoidance, minimization, mitigation, or enhancement measures) committed to by the applicant, will have a *de minimis* impact, as defined in §774.17, on the property.

(c) If the analysis in paragraph (a)(1) of this section concludes that there is no feasible and prudent avoidance alternative, then the Administration may approve, from among the remaining alternatives that use Section 4(f) property, only the alternative that:

(1) Causes the least overall harm in light of the statute's preservation purpose. The least overall harm is determined by balancing the following factors:

(i) The ability to mitigate adverse impacts to each Section 4(f) property (including any measures that result in benefits to the property);

(ii) The relative severity of the remaining harm, after mitigation, to the protected activities, attributes, or features that qualify each Section 4(f) property for protection;

(iii) The relative significance of each Section 4(f) property;

(iv) The views of the official(s) with jurisdiction over each Section 4(f) property;

(v) The degree to which each alternative meets the purpose and need for the project;

(vi) After reasonable mitigation, the magnitude of any adverse impacts to resources not protected by Section 4(f); and

(vii) Substantial differences in costs among the alternatives.

(2) The alternative selected must include all possible planning, as defined in §774.17, to minimize harm to Section 4(f) property.

(d) Programmatic Section 4(f) evaluations are a time-saving procedural alternative to preparing individual Section 4(f) evaluations under paragraph (a) of this section for certain minor uses of Section 4(f) property. Programmatic Section 4(f) evaluations are developed by the Administration based on experience with a specific set of conditions that includes project type, degree of use and impact, and evaluation of avoidance alternatives.[1] An approved programmatic Section 4(f) evaluation may be relied upon to cover a particular project only if the specific conditions in the programmatic evaluation are met

(1) The determination whether a programmatic Section 4(f) evaluation applies to the use of a specific Section 4(f) property shall be documented as specified in the applicable programmatic Section 4(f) evaluation.

(2) The Administration may develop additional programmatic Section 4(f) evaluations. Proposed new or revised programmatic Section 4(f) evaluations

[1] FHWA Section 4(f) Programmatic Evaluations can be found at *www.environment.fhwa.dot.gov/4f/4fnationwideevals.asp.*

will be coordinated with the Department of Interior, Department of Agriculture, and Department of Housing and Urban Development, and published in the FEDERAL REGISTER for comment prior to being finalized. New or revised programmatic Section 4(f) evaluations shall be reviewed for legal sufficiency and approved by the Headquarters Office of the Administration.

(e) The coordination requirements in § 774.5 must be completed before the Administration may make Section 4(f) approvals under this section. Requirements for the documentation and timing of Section 4(f) approvals are located in §§ 774.7 and 774.9, respectively.

[73 FR 13395, Mar. 12, 2008, as amended at 73 FR 31610, June 3, 2008; 83 FR 54506, Oct. 29, 2018]

§ 774.5 Coordination.

(a) Prior to making Section 4(f) approvals under § 774.3(a), the Section 4(f) evaluation shall be provided for coordination and comment to the official(s) with jurisdiction over the Section 4(f) resource and to the Department of the Interior, and as appropriate to the Department of Agriculture and the Department of Housing and Urban Development. The Administration shall provide a minimum of 45 days for receipt of comments. If comments are not received within 15 days after the comment deadline, the Administration may assume a lack of objection and proceed with the action.

(b) Prior to making *de minimis* impact determinations under § 774.3(b), the following coordination shall be undertaken:

(1) For historic properties:

(i) The consulting parties identified in accordance with 36 CFR part 800 must be consulted; and

(ii) The Administration must receive written concurrence from the pertinent State Historic Preservation Officer (SHPO) or Tribal Historic Preservation Officer (THPO), and from the Advisory Council on Historic Preservation (ACHP) if participating in the consultation process, in a finding of "no adverse effect" or "no historic properties affected" in accordance with 36 CFR part 800. The Administration shall inform these officials of its intent to make a *de minimis* impact determination based on their concurrence in the finding of "no adverse effect" or "no historic properties affected."

(iii) Public notice and comment, beyond that required by 36 CFR part 800, is not required.

(2) For parks, recreation areas, and wildlife and waterfowl refuges:

(i) Public notice and an opportunity for public review and comment concerning the effects on the protected activities, features, or attributes of the property must be provided. This requirement can be satisfied in conjunction with other public involvement procedures, such as a comment period provided on a NEPA document.

(ii) The Administration shall inform the official(s) with jurisdiction of its intent to make a *de minimis* impact finding. Following an opportunity for public review and comment as described in paragraph (b)(2)(i) of this section, the official(s) with jurisdiction over the Section 4(f) resource must concur in writing that the project will not adversely affect the activities, features, or attributes that make the property eligible for Section 4(f) protection. This concurrence may be combined with other comments on the project provided by the official(s).

(c) The application of a programmatic Section 4(f) evaluation to the use of a specific Section 4(f) property under § 774.3(d)(1) shall be coordinated as specified in the applicable programmatic Section 4(f) evaluation.

(d) When Federal encumbrances on Section 4(f) property are identified, coordination with the appropriate Federal agency is required to ascertain the agency's position on the proposed impact, as well as to determine if any other Federal requirements may apply to converting the Section 4(f) land to a different function. Any such requirements must be satisfied, independent of the Section 4(f) approval.

§ 774.7 Documentation.

(a) A Section 4(f) evaluation prepared under § 774.3(a) shall include sufficient supporting documentation to demonstrate why there is no feasible and prudent avoidance alternative and shall summarize the results of all possible planning to minimize harm to the Section 4(f) property.

(b) A *de minimis* impact determination under §774.3(b) shall include sufficient supporting documentation to demonstrate that the impacts, after avoidance, minimization, mitigation, or enhancement measures are taken into account, are *de minimis* as defined in §774.17; and that the coordination required in §774.5(b) has been completed.

(c) If there is no feasible and prudent avoidance alternative the Administration may approve only the alternative that causes the least overall harm in accordance with §774.3(c). This analysis must be documented in the Section 4(f) evaluation.

(d) The Administration shall review all Section 4(f) approvals under §§774.3(a) and 774.3(c) for legal sufficiency.

(e) A Section 4(f) approval may involve different levels of detail where the Section 4(f) involvement is addressed in a tiered EIS under §771.111(g) of this chapter.

(1) When the first-tier, broad-scale EIS is prepared, the detailed information necessary to complete the Section 4(f) approval may not be available at that stage in the development of the action. In such cases, the documentation should address the potential impacts that a proposed action will have on Section 4(f) property and whether those impacts could have a bearing on the decision to be made. A preliminary Section 4(f) approval may be made at this time as to whether the impacts resulting from the use of a Section 4(f) property are *de minimis* or whether there are feasible and prudent avoidance alternatives. This preliminary approval shall include all possible planning to minimize harm to the extent that the level of detail available at the first-tier EIS stage allows. It is recognized that such planning at this stage may be limited to ensuring that opportunities to minimize harm at subsequent stages in the development process have not been precluded by decisions made at the first-tier stage. This preliminary Section 4(f) approval is then incorporated into the first-tier EIS.

(2) The Section 4(f) approval will be finalized in the second-tier study. If no new Section 4(f) use, other than a *de minimis* impact, is identified in the second-tier study and if all possible planning to minimize harm has occurred, then the second-tier Section 4(f) approval may finalize the preliminary approval by reference to the first-tier documentation. Re-evaluation of the preliminary Section 4(f) approval is only needed to the extent that new or more detailed information available at the second-tier stage raises new Section 4(f) concerns not already considered.

(3) The final Section 4(f) approval may be made in the second-tier CE, EA, final EIS, ROD or FONSI.

(f) In accordance with §§771.105(a) and 771.133 of this chapter, the documentation supporting a Section 4(f) approval should be included in the EIS, EA, or for a project classified as a CE, in a separate document. If the Section 4(f) documentation cannot be included in the NEPA document, then it shall be presented in a separate document. The Section 4(f) documentation shall be developed by the applicant in cooperation with the Administration.

§774.9 Timing.

(a) The potential use of land from a Section 4(f) property shall be evaluated as early as practicable in the development of the action when alternatives to the proposed action are under study.

(b) Except as provided in paragraph (c) of this section, for actions processed with EISs the Administration will make the Section 4(f) approval either in the final EIS or in the ROD. Where the Section 4(f) approval is documented in the final EIS, the Administration will summarize the basis for its Section 4(f) approval in the ROD. Actions requiring the use of Section 4(f) property, and proposed to be processed with a FONSI or classified as a CE, shall not proceed until notification by the Administration of Section 4(f) approval.

(c) After the CE, FONSI, or ROD has been processed, a separate Section 4(f) approval will be required, except as provided in §774.13, if:

(1) A proposed modification of the alignment or design would require the use of Section 4(f) property; or

(2) The Administration determines that Section 4(f) applies to the use of a property; or

(3) A proposed modification of the alignment, design, or measures to minimize harm (after the original Section 4(f) approval) would result in a substantial increase in the amount of Section 4(f) property used, a substantial increase in the adverse impacts to Section 4(f) property, or a substantial reduction in the measures to minimize harm.

(d) A separate Section 4(f) approval required under paragraph (c) of this section will not necessarily require the preparation of a new or supplemental NEPA document. If a new or supplemental NEPA document is also required under § 771.130 of this chapter, then it should include the documentation supporting the separate Section 4(f) approval. Where a separate Section 4(f) approval is required, any activity not directly affected by the separate Section 4(f) approval can proceed during the analysis, consistent with § 771.130(f) of this chapter.

(e) Section 4(f) may apply to archeological sites discovered during construction, as set forth in § 774.11(f). In such cases, the Section 4(f) process will be expedited and any required evaluation of feasible and prudent avoidance alternatives will take account of the level of investment already made. The review process, including the consultation with other agencies, will be shortened as appropriate.

§ 774.11 Applicability.

(a) The Administration will determine the applicability of Section 4(f) in accordance with this part.

(b) When another Federal agency is the Federal lead agency for the NEPA process, the Administration shall make any required Section 4(f) approvals unless the Federal lead agency is another U.S. DOT agency.

(c) Consideration under Section 4(f) is not required when the official(s) with jurisdiction over a park, recreation area, or wildlife and waterfowl refuge determine that the property, considered in its entirety, is not significant. In the absence of such a determination, the Section 4(f) property will be presumed to be significant. The Administration will review a determination that a park, recreation area, or wildlife and waterfowl refuge is not significant to assure its reasonableness.

(d) Where Federal lands or other public land holdings (e.g., State forests) are administered under statutes permitting management for multiple uses, and, in fact, are managed for multiple uses, Section 4(f) applies only to those portions of such lands which function for, or are designated in the plans of the administering agency as being for, significant park, recreation, or wildlife and waterfowl refuge purposes. The determination of which lands so function or are so designated, and the significance of those lands, shall be made by the official(s) with jurisdiction over the Section 4(f) resource. The Administration will review this determination to assure its reasonableness.

(e) In determining the applicability of Section 4(f) to historic sites, the Administration, in cooperation with the applicant, will consult with the official(s) with jurisdiction to identify all properties on or eligible for the National Register of Historic Places (National Register). The Section 4(f) requirements apply to historic sites on or eligible for the National Register unless the Administration determines that an exception under § 774.13 applies.

(1) The Section 4(f) requirements apply only to historic sites on or eligible for the National Register unless the Administration determines that the application of Section 4(f) is otherwise appropriate.

(2) The Interstate System is not considered to be a historic site subject to Section 4(f), with the exception of those individual elements of the Interstate System formally identified by FHWA for Section 4(f) protection on the basis of national or exceptional historic significance.

(f) Section 4(f) applies to all archeological sites on or eligible for inclusion on the National Register, including those discovered during construction, except as set forth in § 774.13(b).

(g) Section 4(f) applies to those portions of federally designated Wild and Scenic Rivers that are otherwise eligible as historic sites, or that are publicly owned and function as, or are designated in a management plan as, a significant park, recreation area, or wildlife and waterfowl refuge. All other applicable requirements of the Wild and Scenic Rivers Act, 16 U.S.C. 1271–1287, must be satisfied, independent of the Section 4(f) approval.

(h) When a property formally reserved for a future transportation facility temporarily functions for park, recreation, or wildlife and waterfowl refuge purposes in the interim, the interim activity, regardless of duration, will not subject the property to Section 4(f).

(i) When a property is formally reserved for a future transportation facility before or at the same time a park, recreation area, or wildlife and waterfowl refuge is established, and concurrent or joint planning or development of the transportation facility and the Section 4(f) resource occurs, then any resulting impacts of the transportation facility will not be considered a use as defined in §774.17.

(1) Formal reservation of a property for a future transportation use can be demonstrated by a document of public record created prior to or contemporaneously with the establishment of the park, recreation area, or wildlife and waterfowl refuge. Examples of an adequate document to formally reserve a future transportation use include:

(i) A map of public record that depicts a transportation facility on the property;

(ii) A land use or zoning plan depicting a transportation facility on the property; or

(iii) A fully executed real estate instrument that references a future transportation facility on the property.

(2) Concurrent or joint planning or development can be demonstrated by a document of public record created after, contemporaneously with, or prior to the establishment of the Section 4(f) property. Examples of an adequate document to demonstrate concurrent or joint planning or development include:

(i) A document of public record that describes or depicts the designation or donation of the property for both the potential transportation facility and the Section 4(f) property; or

(ii) A map of public record, memorandum, planning document, report, or correspondence that describes or depicts action taken with respect to the property by two or more governmental agencies with jurisdiction for the potential transportation facility and the Section 4(f) property, in consultation with each other.

[73 FR 13395, Mar. 12, 2008, as amended at 83 FR 54506, Oct. 29, 2018]

§774.13 Exceptions.

The Administration has identified various exceptions to the requirement for Section 4(f) approval. These exceptions include, but are not limited to:

(a) The use of historic transportation facilities in certain circumstances:

(1) Common post-1945 concrete or steel bridges and culverts that are exempt from individual review under 54 U.S.C. 306108.

(2) Improvement of railroad or rail transit lines that are in use or were historically used for the transportation of goods or passengers, including, but not limited to, maintenance, preservation, rehabilitation, operation, modernization, reconstruction, and replacement of railroad or rail transit line elements, except for:

(i) Stations;

(ii) Bridges or tunnels on railroad lines that have been abandoned, or transit lines not in use, over which regular service has never operated, and that have not been railbanked or otherwise reserved for the transportation of goods or passengers; and

(iii) Historic sites unrelated to the railroad or rail transit lines.

(3) Maintenance, preservation, rehabilitation, operation, modernization, reconstruction, or replacement of historic transportation facilities, if the Administration concludes, as a result of the consultation under 36 CFR 800.5, that:

(i) Such work will not adversely affect the historic qualities of the facility that caused it to be on or eligible for the National Register, or this work achieves compliance with Section 106 through a program alternative under 36 CFR 800.14; and

(ii) The official(s) with jurisdiction over the Section 4(f) resource have not objected to the Administration conclusion that the proposed work does not adversely affect the historic qualities of the facility that caused it to be on or eligible for the National Register, or the Administration concludes this work achieves compliance with 54 U.S.C. 306108 (Section 106) through a program alternative under 36 CFR 800.14.

(b) Archeological sites that are on or eligible for the National Register when:

(1) The Administration concludes that the archeological resource is important chiefly because of what can be learned by data recovery and has minimal value for preservation in place. This exception applies both to situations where data recovery is undertaken and where the Administration decides, with agreement of the official(s) with jurisdiction, not to recover the resource; and

(2) The official(s) with jurisdiction over the Section 4(f) resource have been consulted and have not objected to the Administration finding in paragraph (b)(1) of this section.

(c) Designations of park and recreation lands, wildlife and waterfowl refuges, and historic sites that are made, or determinations of significance that are changed, late in the development of a proposed action. With the exception of the treatment of archeological resources in § 774.9(e), the Administration may permit a project to proceed without consideration under Section 4(f) if the property interest in the Section 4(f) land was acquired for transportation purposes prior to the designation or change in the determination of significance and if an adequate effort was made to identify properties protected by Section 4(f) prior to acquisition. However, if it is reasonably foreseeable that a property would qualify as eligible for the National Register prior to the start of construction, then the property should be treated as a historic site for the purposes of this section.

(d) Temporary occupancies of land that are so minimal as to not constitute a use within the meaning of Section 4(f). The following conditions must be satisfied:

(1) Duration must be temporary, *i.e.*, less than the time needed for construction of the project, and there should be no change in ownership of the land;

(2) Scope of the work must be minor, *i.e.*, both the nature and the magnitude of the changes to the Section 4(f) property are minimal;

(3) There are no anticipated permanent adverse physical impacts, nor will there be interference with the protected activities, features, or attributes of the property, on either a temporary or permanent basis;

(4) The land being used must be fully restored, *i.e.*, the property must be returned to a condition which is at least as good as that which existed prior to the project; and

(5) There must be documented agreement of the official(s) with jurisdiction over the Section 4(f) resource regarding the above conditions.

(e) Projects for the Federal lands transportation facilities described in 23 U.S.C. 101(a)(8).

(f) Certain trails, paths, bikeways, and sidewalks, in the following circumstances:

(1) Trail-related projects funded under the Recreational Trails Program, 23 U.S.C. 206(h)(2);

(2) National Historic Trails and the Continental Divide National Scenic Trail, designated under the National Trails System Act, 16 U.S.C. 1241–1251, with the exception of those trail segments that are historic sites as defined in § 774.17;

(3) Trails, paths, bikeways, and sidewalks that occupy a transportation facility right-of-way without limitation to any specific location within that right-of-way, so long as the continuity of the trail, path, bikeway, or sidewalk is maintained; and

(4) Trails, paths, bikeways, and sidewalks that are part of the local transportation system and which function primarily for transportation.

(g) Transportation enhancement activities, transportation alternatives projects, and mitigation activities, where:

(1) The use of the Section 4(f) property is solely for the purpose of preserving or enhancing an activity, feature, or attribute that qualifies the property for Section 4(f) protection; and

(2) The official(s) with jurisdiction over the Section 4(f) resource agrees in writing to paragraph (g)(1) of this section.

[73 FR 13395, Mar. 12, 2008, as amended at 83 FR 54507, Oct. 29, 2018]

§774.15 Constructive use determinations.

(a) A constructive use occurs when the transportation project does not incorporate land from a Section 4(f) property, but the project's proximity impacts are so severe that the protected activities, features, or attributes that qualify the property for protection under Section 4(f) are substantially impaired. Substantial impairment occurs only when the protected activities, features, or attributes of the property are substantially diminished.

(b) If the project results in a constructive use of a nearby Section 4(f) property, the Administration shall evaluate that use in accordance with §774.3(a).

(c) The Administration shall determine when there is a constructive use, but the Administration is not required to document each determination that a project would not result in a constructive use of a nearby Section 4(f) property. However, such documentation may be prepared at the discretion of the Administration.

(d) When a constructive use determination is made, it will be based upon the following:

(1) Identification of the current activities, features, or attributes of the property which qualify for protection under Section 4(f) and which may be sensitive to proximity impacts;

(2) An analysis of the proximity impacts of the proposed project on the Section 4(f) property. If any of the proximity impacts will be mitigated, only the net impact need be considered in this analysis. The analysis should also describe and consider the impacts which could reasonably be expected if the proposed project were not implemented, since such impacts should not be attributed to the proposed project; and

(3) Consultation, on the foregoing identification and analysis, with the official(s) with jurisdiction over the Section 4(f) property.

(e) The Administration has reviewed the following situations and determined that a constructive use occurs when:

(1) The projected noise level increase attributable to the project substantially interferes with the use and enjoyment of a noise-sensitive facility of a property protected by Section 4(f), such as:

(i) Hearing the performances at an outdoor amphitheater;

(ii) Sleeping in the sleeping area of a campground;

(iii) Enjoyment of a historic site where a quiet setting is a generally recognized feature or attribute of the site's significance;

(iv) Enjoyment of an urban park where serenity and quiet are significant attributes; or

(v) Viewing wildlife in an area of a wildlife and waterfowl refuge intended for such viewing.

(2) The proximity of the proposed project substantially impairs esthetic features or attributes of a property protected by Section 4(f), where such features or attributes are considered important contributing elements to the value of the property. Examples of substantial impairment to visual or esthetic qualities would be the location of a proposed transportation facility in such proximity that it obstructs or eliminates the primary views of an architecturally significant historical building, or substantially detracts from the setting of a Section 4(f) property which derives its value in substantial part due to its setting;

(3) The project results in a restriction of access which substantially diminishes the utility of a significant publicly owned park, recreation area, or a historic site;

(4) The vibration impact from construction or operation of the project substantially impairs the use of a Section 4(f) property, such as projected vibration levels that are great enough to physically damage a historic building or substantially diminish the utility of the building, unless the damage is repaired and fully restored consistent with the Secretary of the Interior's Standards for the Treatment of Historic Properties, *i.e.*, the integrity of the contributing features must be returned to a condition which is substantially similar to that which existed prior to the project; or

(5) The ecological intrusion of the project substantially diminishes the value of wildlife habitat in a wildlife and waterfowl refuge adjacent to the

project, substantially interferes with the access to a wildlife and waterfowl refuge when such access is necessary for established wildlife migration or critical life cycle processes, or substantially reduces the wildlife use of a wildlife and waterfowl refuge.

(f) The Administration has reviewed the following situations and determined that a constructive use does not occur when:

(1) Compliance with the requirements of 36 CFR 800.5 for proximity impacts of the proposed action, on a site listed on or eligible for the National Register, results in an agreement of "no historic properties affected" or "no adverse effect;"

(2) For projected noise levels:

(i) The impact of projected traffic noise levels of the proposed highway project on a noise-sensitive activity do not exceed the FHWA noise abatement criteria as contained in Table 1 in part 772 of this chapter; or

(ii) The projected operational noise levels of the proposed transit or railroad project do not exceed the noise impact criteria for a Section 4(f) activity in the FTA guidelines for transit noise and vibration impact assessment or the moderate impact criteria in the FRA guidelines for high-speed transportation noise and vibration impact assessment;

(3) The projected noise levels exceed the relevant threshold in paragraph (f)(2) of this section because of high existing noise, but the increase in the projected noise levels if the proposed project is constructed, when compared with the projected noise levels if the project is not built, is barely perceptible (3 dBA or less);

(4) There are proximity impacts to a Section 4(f) property, but a governmental agency's right-of-way acquisition or adoption of project location, or the Administration's approval of a final environmental document, established the location for the proposed transportation project before the designation, establishment, or change in the significance of the property. However, if it is reasonably foreseeable that a property would qualify as eligible for the National Register prior to the start of construction, then the property should be treated as a historic site for the purposes of this section; or

(5) Overall (combined) proximity impacts caused by a proposed project do not substantially impair the activities, features, or attributes that qualify a property for protection under Section 4(f);

(6) Proximity impacts will be mitigated to a condition equivalent to, or better than, that which would occur if the project were not built, as determined after consultation with the official(s) with jurisdiction;

(7) Change in accessibility will not substantially diminish the utilization of the Section 4(f) property; or

(8) Vibration levels from project construction activities are mitigated, through advance planning and monitoring of the activities, to levels that do not cause a substantial impairment of protected activities, features, or attributes of the Section 4(f) property.

[73 FR 13395, Mar. 12, 2008, as amended at 83 FR 54507, Oct. 29, 2018]

§ 774.17 Definitions.

The definitions contained in 23 U.S.C. 101(a) are applicable to this part. In addition, the following definitions apply:

Administration. The FHWA, FRA, or FTA, whichever is approving the transportation program or project at issue. A reference herein to the Administration means the State when the State is functioning as the FHWA, FRA, or FTA in carrying out responsibilities delegated or assigned to the State in accordance with 23 U.S.C. 325, 326, 327, or other applicable law.

All possible planning. All possible planning means that all reasonable measures identified in the Section 4(f) evaluation to minimize harm or mitigate for adverse impacts and effects must be included in the project.

(1) With regard to public parks, recreation areas, and wildlife and waterfowl refuges, the measures may include (but are not limited to): design modifications or design goals; replacement of land or facilities of comparable value and function; or monetary compensation to enhance the remaining property or to mitigate the adverse impacts of the project in other ways.

(2) With regard to historic sites, the measures normally serve to preserve

the historic activities, features, or attributes of the site as agreed by the Administration and the official(s) with jurisdiction over the Section 4(f) resource in accordance with the consultation process under 36 CFR part 800.

(3) In evaluating the reasonableness of measures to minimize harm under §774.3(a)(2), the Administration will consider the preservation purpose of the statute and:

(i) The views of the official(s) with jurisdiction over the Section 4(f) property;

(ii) Whether the cost of the measures is a reasonable public expenditure in light of the adverse impacts of the project on the Section 4(f) property and the benefits of the measure to the property, in accordance with §771.105(d) of this chapter; and

(iii) Any impacts or benefits of the measures to communities or environmental resources outside of the Section 4(f) property.

(4) All possible planning does not require analysis of feasible and prudent avoidance alternatives, since such analysis will have already occurred in the context of searching for feasible and prudent alternatives that avoid Section 4(f) properties altogether under §774.3(a)(1), or is not necessary in the case of a *de minimis* impact determination under §774.3(b).

(5) A *de minimis* impact determination under §774.3(b) subsumes the requirement for all possible planning to minimize harm by reducing the impacts on the Section 4(f) property to a *de minimis* level.

Applicant. The Federal, State, or local government authority, proposing a transportation project, that the Administration works with to conduct environmental studies and prepare environmental documents. For transportation actions implemented by the Federal government on Federal lands, the Administration or the Federal land management agency may take on the responsibilities of the applicant described herein.

CE. Refers to a categorical exclusion, which is an action with no individual or cumulative significant environmental effect pursuant to 40 CFR 1508.4 and §771.116, §771.117, or §771.118 of this chapter; unusual circumstances are taken into account in making categorical exclusion determinations.

De minimis impact. (1) For historic sites, *de minimis* impact means that the Administration has determined, in accordance with 36 CFR part 800 that no historic property is affected by the project or that the project will have "no adverse effect" on the historic property in question.

(2) For parks, recreation areas, and wildlife and waterfowl refuges, a *de minimis* impact is one that will not adversely affect the features, attributes, or activities qualifying the property for protection under Section 4(f).

EA. Refers to an Environmental Assessment, which is a document prepared pursuant to 40 CFR parts 1500–1508 and §771.119 of this title for a proposed project that is not categorically excluded but for which an EIS is not clearly required.

EIS. Refers to an Environmental Impact Statement, which is a document prepared pursuant to NEPA, 40 CFR parts 1500–1508, and §§771.123 and 771.125 of this chapter for a proposed project that is likely to cause significant impacts on the environment.

Feasible and prudent avoidance alternative. (1) A feasible and prudent avoidance alternative avoids using Section 4(f) property and does not cause other severe problems of a magnitude that substantially outweighs the importance of protecting the Section 4(f) property. In assessing the importance of protecting the Section 4(f) property, it is appropriate to consider the relative value of the resource to the preservation purpose of the statute.

(2) An alternative is not feasible if it cannot be built as a matter of sound engineering judgment.

(3) An alternative is not prudent if:

(i) It compromises the project to a degree that it is unreasonable to proceed with the project in light of its stated purpose and need;

(ii) It results in unacceptable safety or operational problems;

(iii) After reasonable mitigation, it still causes:

(A) Severe social, economic, or environmental impacts;

(B) Severe disruption to established communities;

(C) Severe disproportionate impacts to minority or low income populations; or

(D) Severe impacts to environmental resources protected under other Federal statutes;

(iv) It results in additional construction, maintenance, or operational costs of an extraordinary magnitude;

(v) It causes other unique problems or unusual factors; or

(vi) It involves multiple factors in paragraphs (3)(i) through (3)(v) of this definition, that while individually minor, cumulatively cause unique problems or impacts of extraordinary magnitude.

FONSI. Refers to a Finding of No Significant Impact prepared pursuant to 40 CFR 1508.13 and § 771.121 of this chapter.

Historic site. For purposes of this part, the term "historic site" includes any prehistoric or historic district, site, building, structure, or object included in, or eligible for inclusion in, the National Register. The term includes properties of traditional religious and cultural importance to an Indian tribe or Native Hawaiian organization that are included in, or are eligible for inclusion in, the National Register.

Official(s) with jurisdiction. (1) In the case of historic properties, the official with jurisdiction is the SHPO for the State wherein the property is located or, if the property is located on tribal land, the THPO. If the property is located on tribal land but the Indian tribe has not assumed the responsibilities of the SHPO as provided for in the National Historic Preservation Act, then a representative designated by such Indian tribe shall be recognized as an official with jurisdiction in addition to the SHPO. When the ACHP is involved in a consultation concerning a property under Section 106 of the NHPA, the ACHP is also an official with jurisdiction over that resource for purposes of this part. When the Section 4(f) property is a National Historic Landmark, the National Park Service is also an official with jurisdiction over that resource for purposes of this part.

(2) In the case of public parks, recreation areas, and wildlife and waterfowl refuges, the official(s) with jurisdiction are the official(s) of the agency or agencies that own or administer the property in question and who are empowered to represent the agency on matters related to the property.

(3) In the case of portions of Wild and Scenic Rivers to which Section 4(f) applies, the official(s) with jurisdiction are the official(s) of the Federal agency or agencies that own or administer the affected portion of the river corridor in question. For State administered, federally designated rivers (section 2(a)(ii) of the Wild and Scenic Rivers Act, 16 U.S.C. 1273(a)(ii)), the officials with jurisdiction include both the State agency designated by the respective Governor and the Secretary of the Interior.

Railroad or rail transit line elements. Railroad or rail transit line elements include the elements related to the operation of the railroad or rail transit line, such as the railbed, rails, and track; tunnels; elevated support structures and bridges; substations; signal and communication devices; maintenance facilities; and railway-highway crossings.

ROD. Refers to a record of decision prepared pursuant to 40 CFR 1505.2 and §§ 771.124 or 771.127 of this chapter.

Section 4(f) evaluation. Refers to the documentation prepared to support the granting of a Section 4(f) approval under § 774.3(a), unless preceded by the word "programmatic." A "programmatic Section 4(f) evaluation" is the documentation prepared pursuant to § 774.3(d) that authorizes subsequent project-level Section 4(f) approvals as described therein.

Section 4(f) Property. Section 4(f) property means publicly owned land of a public park, recreation area, or wildlife and waterfowl refuge of national, State, or local significance, or land of an historic site of national, State, or local significance.

Station. A station is a platform and the associated building or structure such as a depot, shelter, or canopy used by intercity or commuter rail transportation passengers for the purpose of boarding and alighting a train. A station does not include tracks, railyards, or electrification, communications or signal systems, or equipment. A platform alone is not considered a station.

Use. Except as set forth in §§774.11 and 774.13, a "use" of Section 4(f) property occurs:

(1) When land is permanently incorporated into a transportation facility;

(2) When there is a temporary occupancy of land that is adverse in terms of the statute's preservation purpose as determined by the criteria in §774.13(d); or

(3) When there is a constructive use of a Section 4(f) property as determined by the criteria in §774.15.

[73 FR 13395, Mar. 12, 2008, as amended at 83 FR 54507, Oct. 29, 2018]

PART 777—MITIGATION OF IMPACTS TO WETLANDS AND NATURAL HABITAT

AUTHORITY: 42 U.S.C. 4321 *et seq.;* 49 U.S.C. 303; 23 U.S.C. 101(a), 103, 109(h), 133(b)(1), (b)(11), and (d)(2), 138, 315; E.O. 11990; DOT Order 5660.1A; 49 CFR 1.48(b).

SOURCE: 65 FR 82924, Dec. 29, 2000, unless otherwise noted.

§777.1 Purpose.

To provide policy and procedures for the evaluation and mitigation of adverse environmental impacts to wetlands and natural habitat resulting from Federal-aid projects funded pursuant to provisions of title 23, U.S. Code. These policies and procedures shall be applied by the Federal Highway Administration (FHWA) to projects under the Federal Lands Highway Program to the extent such application is deemed appropriate by the FHWA.

§777.2 Definitions.

In addition to those contained in 23 U.S.C. 101(a), the following definitions shall apply as used in this part:

Biogeochemical transformations means those changes in chemical compounds and substances which naturally occur in ecosystems. Examples are the carbon, nitrogen, and phosphorus cycles in nature, in which these elements are incorporated from inorganic substances into organic matter and recycled on a continuing basis.

Compensatory mitigation means restoration, enhancement, creation, and under exceptional circumstances, preservation, of wetlands, wetland buffer areas, and other natural habitats, carried out to replace or compensate for the loss of wetlands or natural habitat area or functional capacity resulting from Federal-aid projects funded pursuant to provisions of title 23, U.S. Code. Compensatory mitigation usually occurs in advance of or concurrent with the impacts to be mitigated, but may occur after such impacts in special circumstances.

Mitigation bank means a site where wetlands and/or other aquatic resources or natural habitats are restored, created, enhanced, or in exceptional circumstances, preserved, expressly for the purpose of providing compensatory mitigation in advance of authorized impacts to similar resources. For purposes of the Clean Water Act, Section 404 (33 U.S.C. 1344), use of a mitigation bank can only be authorized when impacts are unavoidable.

Natural habitat means a complex of natural, primarily native or indigenous vegetation, not currently subject to cultivation or artificial landscaping, a primary purpose of which is to provide habitat for wildlife, either terrestrial or aquatic. For purposes of this part, habitat has the same meaning as natural habitat. This definition excludes rights-of-way that are acquired with Federal transportation funds specifically for highway purposes.

Net gain of wetlands means a wetland resource conservation and management principle under which, over the long term, unavoidable losses of wetlands area or functional capacity due to highway projects are offset by gains at a ratio greater than 1:1, through restoration, enhancement, preservation, or creation of wetlands or associated areas critical to the protection or conservation of wetland functions. This definition specifically excludes natural habitat, as defined in this section, other than wetlands.

On-site, in-kind mitigation means compensatory mitigation which replaces wetlands or natural habitat area or functions lost as a result of a highway project with the same or like wetland or habitat type and functions adjacent or contiguous to the site of the impact.

Practicable means available and capable of being done after taking into consideration cost, existing technology, and logistics, in light of overall project purposes.

Service area of a mitigation bank means that the service area of a wetland or natural habitat mitigation bank shall be consistent with that in the Federal Guidance for the Establishment, Use and Operation of Mitigation Banks (60 FR 58605, November 28, 1995), *i.e.*, the designated area (e.g., watershed, county) wherein a bank can be expected to provide appropriate compensation for impacts to wetlands and/or other aquatic or natural habitat resources.

Wetland or habitat enhancement means activities conducted in existing wetlands or other natural habitat to achieve specific management objectives or provide conditions which previously did not exist, and which increase one or more ecosystem functions. Enhancement may involve tradeoffs between the resource structure, function, and values; a positive change in one may result in negative effects to other functions. Examples of activities which may be carried out to enhance wetlands or natural habitats include, but are not limited to, alteration of hydrologic regime, vegetation management, erosion control, fencing, integrated pest management and control, and fertilization.

Wetland or habitat establishment period means a period of time agreed to by the FHWA, State DOT, and U.S. Army Corps of Engineers, as necessary to establish wetland or natural habitat functional capacity in a compensatory mitigation project sufficient to compensate wetlands or habitat losses due to impacts of Federal-aid highway projects. The establishment period may vary depending on the specific wetland or habitat type being developed.

Wetland or habitat functional capacity means the ability of a wetland or natural habitat to perform natural functions, such as provide wildlife habitat, support biodiversity, store surface water, or perform biogeochemical transformations, as determined by scientific functional assessment. Natural functions of wetlands include, but are not limited to, those listed by the U.S. Army Corps of Engineers at 33 CFR 320.4(b)(2)(i) through (viii).

Wetland or habitat preservation means the protection of ecologically important wetlands, other aquatic resources, or other natural habitats in perpetuity through the implementation of appropriate legal and physical mechanisms. Preservation of wetlands for compensatory mitigation purposes may include protection of upland areas adjacent to wetlands as necessary to ensure protection and/or enhancement of the aquatic ecosystem.

Wetland or habitat restoration means the reestablishment of wetlands or natural habitats on a site where they formerly existed or exist in a substantially degraded state.

Wetland or wetlands means those areas that are inundated or saturated by surface or ground water at a frequency and duration to support, and that under normal circumstances do support, a prevalence of vegetation typically adapted for life in saturated soil conditions. Wetlands generally include swamps, marshes, bogs and similar areas.

Wetlands or habitat mitigation credit means a unit of wetlands or habitat mitigation, defined either by area or a measure of functional capacity through application of scientific functional assessment. With respect to mitigation banks, this definition means the same as that in the Federal Guidance for the Establishment, Use, and Operation of Mitigation Banks.

§ 777.3 Background.

(a) Executive Order 11990 (42 FR 26961, 3 CFR, 1977 Comp., p. 121) Protection of Wetlands, and DOT Order 5660.1A,[1] Preservation of the Nation's Wetlands, emphasize the important functions and

[1] DOT Order 5660.1A is available for inspection and copying from FHWA headquarters and field offices as prescribed at 49 CFR part 7.

values inherent in the Nation's wetlands. Federal agencies are directed to avoid new construction in wetlands unless the head of the agency determines that:

(1) There is no practicable alternative to such construction, and

(2) The proposed action includes all practicable measures to minimize harm to wetlands which may result from such use.

(b) Sections 103 and 133 of title 23, U.S. Code, identify additional approaches for mitigation and management of impacts to wetlands and natural habitats which result from projects funded pursuant to title 23, U.S. Code, as eligible for participation with title 23, U.S. Code, funds.

(c) 33 CFR parts 320 through 330, Regulatory Program, U.S. Army Corps of Engineers; Section 404, Clean Water Act and 40 CFR part 230, Section 404(b)(1) Guidelines for the Specification of Disposal Sites for Dredged or Fill Material, establish requirements for the permitting of discharge of dredge or fill material in wetlands and other waters of the United States.

(d) Federal Guidance for the Establishment, Use, and Operation of Mitigation Banks presents guidance for the use of ecological mitigation banks as compensatory mitigation in the Section 404 Regulatory Program for unavoidable impacts to wetlands and other aquatic resources.

(e) Interagency Cooperation—Endangered Species Act of 1973, as amended (50 CFR part 402), presents regulations establishing interagency consultation procedures relative to impacts to species listed under the authority of the Act and their habitats as required by Section 7, Interagency Coordination, of the Endangered Species Act of 1973 (16 U.S.C. 1536).

§777.5 Federal participation.

(a) Those measures which the FHWA and a State DOT find appropriate and necessary to mitigate adverse environmental impacts to wetlands and natural habitats are eligible for Federal participation where the impacts are the result of projects funded pursuant to title 23, U.S. Code. The justification for the cost of proposed mitigation measures should be considered in the same context as any other public expenditure; that is, the proposed mitigation represents a reasonable public expenditure when weighed against other social, economic, and environmental values, and the benefit realized is commensurate with the proposed expenditure. Mitigation measures shall give like consideration to traffic needs, safety, durability, and economy of maintenance of the highway.

(b) It is FHWA policy to permit, consistent with the limits set forth in this part, the expenditure of title 23, U.S. Code, funds for activities required for the planning, design, construction, monitoring, and establishment of wetlands and natural habitat mitigation projects, and acquisition of land or interests therein.

§777.7 Evaluation of impacts.

(a) The reasonableness of the public expenditure and extent of Federal participation with title 23, U.S. Code, funds shall be directly related to:

(1) The importance of the impacted wetlands and natural habitats;

(2) The extent of highway impacts on the wetlands and natural habitats, as determined through an appropriate, interdisciplinary, impact assessment; and

(3) Actions necessary to comply with the Clean Water Act, Section 404, the Endangered Species Act of 1973, and other relevant Federal statutes.

(b) Evaluation of the importance of the impacted wetlands and natural habitats shall consider:

(1) Wetland and natural habitat functional capacity;

(2) Relative importance of these functions to the total wetland or natural habitat resource of the area;

(3) Other factors such as uniqueness, esthetics, or cultural values; and

(4) Input from the appropriate resource management agencies through interagency coordination.

(c) A determination of the highway impact should focus on both the short- and long-term affects of the project on wetland or natural habitat functional capacity, consistent with 40 CFR part 1500, 40 CFR 1502.16, 33 CFR 320.4, and the FHWA's environmental compliance regulations, found at 23 CFR part 771.

§ 777.9 Mitigation of impacts.

(a) Actions eligible for Federal funding. There are a number of actions that can be taken to minimize the impact of highway projects on wetlands or natural habitats. The following actions qualify for Federal-aid highway funding:

(1) Avoidance and minimization of impacts to wetlands or natural habitats through realignment and special design, construction features, or other measures.

(2) Compensatory mitigation alternatives, either inside or outside of the right-of-way. This includes, but is not limited to, such measures as on-site mitigation, when that alternative is determined to be the preferred approach by the appropriate regulatory agency; improvement of existing degraded or historic wetlands or natural habitats through restoration or enhancement on or off site; creation of new wetlands; and under exceptional circumstances, preservation of existing wetlands or natural habitats on or off site. Restoration of wetlands is generally preferable to enhancement or creation of new wetlands.

(3) Improvements to existing wetlands or natural habitats. Such activities may include, but are not limited to, construction or modification of water level control structures or ditches, establishment of natural vegetation, re-contouring of a site, installation or removal of irrigation, drainage, or other water distribution systems, integrated pest management, installation of fencing, monitoring, and other measures to protect, enhance, or restore the wetland or natural habitat character of a site.

(4) Mitigation banks. In accordance with all applicable Federal law (including regulations), with respect to participation in compensatory mitigation related to a project funded under title 23, U.S. Code, that has an impact on wetlands or natural habitat occurring within the service area of a mitigation bank, preference shall be given, to the maximum extent practicable, to the use of the mitigation bank, if the bank contains sufficient available credits to offset the impact and the bank is approved in accordance with the Federal Guidance for the Establishment, Use, and Operation of Mitigation Banks, or other agreement between appropriate agencies.

(b) Mitigation banking alternatives eligible for participation with Federal-aid funds including such measures as the following:

(1) Mitigation banks in which mitigation credits are purchased by State DOTs to mitigate impacts to wetlands or natural habitats due to projects funded under title 23, U.S. Code, including privately owned banks or those established with private funds to mitigate wetland or natural habitat losses.

(2) Single purpose banks established by and for the use of a State DOT with Federal-aid participation; or multipurpose publicly owned banks, established with public, non-title 23 Federal highway funds, in which credits may be purchased by highway agencies using title 23 highway funds on a per-credit basis.

(c) Contributions to statewide and regional efforts to conserve, restore, enhance and create wetlands or natural habitats. Federal-aid funds may participate in the development of statewide and regional wetlands conservation plans, including any efforts and plans authorized pursuant to the Water Resources Development Act of 1990 (Pub. L. 101–640, 104 Stat. 4604). Contributions to these efforts may occur in advance of project construction only if such efforts are consistent with all applicable requirements of Federal law and regulations and State transportation planning processes.

(d) Mitigation or restoration of historic impacts to wetlands and natural habitats caused by past highway projects funded pursuant to title 23, U.S. Code, even if there is no current federally funded highway project in the immediate vicinity. These impacts must be related to transportation projects funded under the authority of title 23, U.S. Code.

§ 777.11 Other considerations.

(a) The development of measures proposed to mitigate impacts to wetlands or natural habitats shall include consultation with appropriate State and Federal agencies.

(b) Federal-aid funds shall not participate in the replacement of wetlands or natural habitats absent sufficient assurances, such as, but not limited to, deed restrictions, fee ownership, permanent easement, or performance bond, that the area will be maintained as a wetland or natural habitat.

(c) The acquisition of proprietary interests in replacement wetlands or natural habitats as a mitigation measure may be in fee simple, by easement, or by other appropriate legally recognized instrument, such as a banking instrument legally approved by the appropriate regulatory agency. The acquisition of mitigation credits in wetland or natural habitat mitigation banks shall be accomplished through a legally recognized instrument, such as permanent easement, deed restriction, or legally approved mitigation banking instrument, which provides for the protection and permanent continuation of the wetland or natural habitat nature of the mitigation.

(d) A State DOT may acquire privately owned lands in cooperation with another public agency or third party. Such an arrangement may accomplish greater benefits than would otherwise be accomplished by the individual agency acting alone.

(e) A State DOT may transfer the title to, or enter into an agreement with, an appropriate public natural resource management agency to manage lands acquired outside the right-of-way without requiring a credit to Federal funds. Any such transfer of title or agreement shall require the continued use of the lands for the purpose for which they were acquired. In the event the purpose is no longer served, the lands and interests therein shall immediately revert to the State DOT for proper disposition.

(f) The reasonable costs of acquiring lands or interests therein to provide replacement lands with equivalent wetlands or natural habitat area or functional capacity associated with these areas are eligible for Federal participation.

(g) The objective in mitigating impacts to wetlands in the Federal-aid highway program is to implement the policy of a net gain of wetlands on a program wide basis.

(h) Certain activities to ensure the viability of compensatory mitigation wetlands or natural habitats during the period of establishment are eligible for Federal-aid participation. These include, but are not limited to, such activities as repair or adjustment of water control structures, pest control, irrigation, fencing modifications, replacement of plantings, and mitigation site monitoring. The establishment period should be specifically determined by the mitigation agreement among the mitigation planners prior to beginning any compensatory mitigation activities.

SUBCHAPTER I—PUBLIC TRANSPORTATION

PART 810—MASS TRANSIT AND SPECIAL USE HIGHWAY PROJECTS

Subpart A—General

Subpart B—Highway Public Transportation Projects and Special Use Highway Facilities

Subpart C—Making Highway Rights-of-Way Available for Mass Transit Projects

Subpart D—Federal-Aid Urban System Nonhighway Public Mass Transit Projects

AUTHORITY: 23 U.S.C. 137, 142, 149 and 315; sec. 4 of Pub. L. 97–134, 95 Stat. 1699; secs. 118, 120, and 163 of Pub. L. 97–424, 96 Stat. 2097; 49 CFR 1.48(b) and 1.51(f).

SOURCE: 50 FR 33917, Aug. 22, 1985, unless otherwise noted.

Subpart A—General

§ 810.2 Purpose.

The purpose of this regulation is to implement sections 137, 142, and 149 of title 23, U.S.C.

§ 810.4 Definitions.

(a) Except as otherwise provided terms defined in 23 U.S.C. 101(a) are used in this subpart as so defined.

(b) The following terms, where used in the regulations in this subpart have the following meanings:

(1) Exclusive or preferential high occupancy vehicle, truck, or emergency vehicle lanes-one or more lanes of a highway facility or an entire highway facility where high occupancy vehicles, trucks or emergency vehicles or any combination thereof, are given, at all times or at any regularly scheduled times, a priority or preference over some or all other vehicles moving in the general stream of mixed highway traffic. Carpool lane(s)—is any high occupancy vehicle lane which allows use by carpools.

(2) Fringe and transportation corridor parking facilities—those facilities which are intended to be used for the temporary storage of vehicles and which are located and designed so as to facilitate the safe and convenient transfer of persons traveling in such vehicles to and from high occupancy vehicles and/or public mass transportation systems including rail. The term *parking facilities* includes but is not limited to access roads, buildings, structures, equipment, improvements and interests in land.

(3) High occupancy vehicle—a bus or other motorized passenger vehicle such as a carpool or vanpool vehicle used for ridesharing purposes and occupied by a specified minimum number of persons.

(4) Highway traffic control devices—traffic control devices as defined by the currently approved "Manual on Uniform Traffic Control Devices for Streets and Highways."[1]

[1] The MUTCD is incorporated by reference at 23 CFR part 655, subpart F.

(5) Metropolitan Planning Organization—that organization designated as being responsible, together with the State, for carrying out the provisions of 23 U.S.C. 134, as required by 23 U.S.C. 104(f)(3), and capable of meeting the requirements of sections 3(e)(1), 5(1), 8 (a) and (c) and 9(e)(3)(G) of the Urban Mass Transportation Act of 1964, as amended, 49 U.S.C. 1602(e)(1), 1604(1), 1607 (a) and (c) and 1607a(e)(3)(G). This organization shall be the forum for cooperative transportation decisionmaking.

(6) Nonhighway public mass transit project—a project to develop or improve public mass transit facilities or equipment. A project need not be physically located or operated on a route designated as part of the Federal-aid urban system, but must be included in and related to a program for the development or improvement of an urban public mass transit system which includes the purchase and rehabilitation of passenger buses and rolling stock for fixed rail facilities, and the purchase, construction, reconstruction or improvement of fixed rail passenger operating facilities. Such projects may also include the construction, reconstruction or rehabilitation of passenger loading and unloading facilities for either bus or rail passengers.

(7) Passenger loading areas and facilities (including shelters)—areas and facilities located at or near passenger loading points for safety, protection, comfort, or convenience of high occupancy vehicle passengers. The term *areas and facilities* includes but is not limited to access roads, buildings, structures, equipment, improvements, and interest in land.

(8) Responsible local officials—(i) In areas under 50,000 population, the principal elected officials of general purpose local governments; or (ii) In urbanized areas, the principal elected officials of general purpose local governments acting through the Metropolitan Planning Organization.

[50 FR 33917, Aug. 22, 1985, as amended at 51 FR 16834, May 7, 1986]

§810.6 Prerequisites for projects authorized by 23 U.S.C. 137, 142, or 149.

(a) Projects in an urbanized area must be based on a continuing comprehensive transportation planning process, carried on in accordance with 23 U.S.C. 134 as prescribed in 23 CFR part 450, subpart A and included in the transportation improvement program required by 23 CFR part 450, subpart B.

(b) Except as otherwise provided by 23 CFR 450.202, projects under this subpart located outside the urbanized area boundaries should be coordinated with the appropriate local officials of the urbanized area as necessary to insure compatibility with the area's urban transportation plan.

(c) All proposed projects must be included in a program of projects approved pursuant to 23 CFR part 630, subpart A (Federal-Aid Program Approval and Authorization).

§810.8 Coordination.

The Federal Highway Administrator and the Urban Mass Transportation Administrator shall coordinate with each other on any projects involving public mass transit to facilitate project selection, approval and completion.

Subpart B—Highway Public Transportation Projects and Special Use Highway Facilities

§810.100 Purpose.

The purpose of the regulations in this subpart is to implement 23 U.S.C. 137, 142(a)(1), 142(b), and 149, which authorize various highway public mass transportation improvements and special use highway facilities as Federal-aid highway projects.

§810.102 Eligible projects.

Under this subpart the Federal Highway Administrator may approve on any Federal-aid system projects which facilitate the use of high occupancy vehicles and public mass transportation systems so as to increase the traffic capacity of the Federal-aid system for the movement of persons. Eligible projects include:

(a) Construction of exclusive or preferential high occupancy vehicle, truck, or emergency vehicle lanes, except the construction of exclusive or preferential lanes limited to use by emergency vehicles can be approved only on the Federal-aid Interstate System;

(b) Highway traffic control devices;

(c) Passenger loading areas and facilities (including shelters) that are on or serve a Federal-aid system; and

(d) Construction or designation of fringe and transportation corridor parking facilities. For parking facilities located in the central business district the Federal-aid project must be limited to space reserved exclusively for the parking of high occupancy vehicles used for carpools or vanpools.

§ 810.104 Applicability of other provisions.

(a) Projects authorized under § 810.102 shall be deemed to be highway projects for all purposes of title 23 U.S.C., and shall be subject to all regulations of title 23 CFR.

(b) Projects approved under this subpart on the Federal-aid Interstate System for exclusive or preferential high occupancy vehicle, truck, and emergency vehicle lanes are excepted from the minimum four-lane requirement of 23 U.S.C. 109(b).

(c) Exclusive or preferential lanes on the Interstate System, including approaches and directly related facilities, can be constructed with Interstate construction funds only if they were approved in the 1981 Interstate Cost Estimate.

(d) The Federal proportional share of a project approved under this subpart shall be as provided in 23 U.S.C. 120 for the class of funds involved. The Federal share for Interstate substitution projects is 85 percent except for signalization projects which may be 100 percent as provided by 23 U.S.C. 120(d). The provisions of section 120(d) title 23 U.S.C. may also be applied to regularly funded projects under § 810.102 of this subpart as follows:

(1) Signalization projects.

(2) Passenger loading area and facilities which principally serve carpools and vanpools.

(3) Fringe and transportation corridor parking facilities or portions thereof which are reserved exclusively for use by carpool and vanpool passengers and vehicles.

(e) As required by section 163 of the Surface Transportation Assistance Act of 1982, approval of Federal-aid highway funding for a physical construction or resurfacing project having a carpool lane(s) within the project limits may not be granted unless the project allows the use of the carpool lane(s) by motorcycles or it is certified by the State that such use will create a safety hazard. This requirement does not apply to high occupancy vehicle lanes which exclude carpools or to carpool lanes constructed by the State without the use of Federal-aid Highway funds. The issue of the extent of utilization of these facilities including those constructed prior to January 6, 1982 with Federal-aid Highway funds is a matter for individual determination by the State Highway Agency.

§ 810.106 Approval of fringe and transportation corridor parking facilities.

(a) In approving fringe and transportation corridor parking facilities, the Federal Highway Administrator:

(1) Shall make a determination that the proposed parking facility will benefit the Federal-aid systems by improving its traffic capacity for the movement of persons;

(2) May approve acquisition of land proximate to the right-of-way of a Federal-aid highway;

(3) May approve construction of publicly-owned parking facilities on land within the right-of-way of any Federal-aid highway, including the use of the airspace above and below the established gradeline of the highway pavement, and on land, acquired with or without Federal-aid funds which is not within the right-of-way of any Federal-aid highway but which was acquired in accordance with the Uniform Relocation Assistance and Land Acquisition Policies Act of 1970 (84 Stat. 1894, 42 U.S.C. 4601 *et seq.*);

(4) May permit the charging of fees for the use of the facility, except that the rate of the fee shall not be in excess of that required for maintenance and operation and the cost of providing shuttle service to and from the facility (including compensation to any person for operating such facility and for providing such shuttle service);

(5) Shall determine that the State, or the political subdivision thereof, where the project is to be located, or any agency or instrumentality of such State or political subdivision, has the authority and capability of constructing, maintaining, and operating the facility.

(6) Shall receive assurance from the State that the facility will remain in public ownershp as long as the facility is needed and that any change in ownership shall have prior FHWA approval;

(7) Shall enter into an agreement with the State, political subdivision, agency, or instrumentality governing the financing, maintenance, and operation of the parking facility; and

(8) Shall approve design standards for constructing the facility as developed in cooperation with the State highway agency.

(b) A State political subdivision, agency, or instrumentality thereof may contract with any person to operate any parking facility constructed under this section.

(c) In authorizing projects involving fringe and transportation corridor parking facilities, the class of Federal-aid funds (primary, secondary, or urban system) used for projects under this subpart may be either funds designated for the Federal-aid system on which the facility is located or the Federal-aid system substantially benefited. For Interstate funds to be used for such eligible projects the Federal-aid Interstate system must be the system which substantially benefits. The benefiting system is that system which would have otherwise carried the high occupancy vehicle or rail passengers to their destination. Interstate construction funds may be used only where the parking facility was approved in the 1981 Interstate Cost Estimate and is constructed in conjunction with a high occupancy vehicle lane approved in the 1981 Interstate Cost Estimate.

§810.108 Designation of existing facilities.

(a) In accordance with the provisions of 23 CFR 810.102, the Federal Highway Administrator may approve on any Federal-aid system the work necessary to designate existing parking facilities (such as at shopping centers or other public or private locations) for fringe and transportation corridor parking.

(1) Eligible activities include the acquisition of or the initial and renewal costs for leasing existing parking space, signing of and modifications to existing facilities, trail blazer signs, and passenger loading areas and facilities.

(2) The approval criteria in 23 CFR 810.106 (a)(1), (4), (5), (7) and (8) apply to these parking facilities.

(b) In accordance with the provisions of 23 CFR 810.102, the Federal Highway Administrator may approve on any Federal-aid system the work necessary to designate existing highway lanes as high occupancy vehicle lanes.

(1) Eligible activities include preliminary engineering, signing, pavement marking, traffic control devices, minor physical modifications and initial inspection or monitoring of use.

(2) Such improvements may be approved on any public road if they facilitate more efficient use of any Federal-aid highway.

(c) Interstate construction funds may be used only where the proposed projects were approved in the 1981 Interstate Cost Estimate.

Subpart C—Making Highway Rights-of-Way Available for Mass Transit Projects

§810.200 Purpose.

The purpose of this subpart is to implement 23 U.S.C. 142(g), which permits the Federal Highway Administrator to authorize a State to make available to a publicly-owned mass transit authority existing highway rights-of-way for rail or other non-highway public mass transit facilities.

§810.202 Applicability.

(a) The provisions of this subpart are applicable to the rights-of-way of all Federal-aid highways in which Federal-aid highway funds have participated or will participate in any part of the cost of the highway.

(b) The provisions of this subpart do not preclude acquisition of rights-of-way for use involving mass transit facilities under the provisions of subparts B and D of this part. Rights-of-way made available under this subpart may be used in combination with rights-of-way acquired under subparts B and D of this part.

§ 810.204 Application by mass transit authority.

A publicly-owned mass transit authority desiring to utilize land existing within the publicly acquired right-of-way of any Federal-aid highway for a rail or other nonhighway public mass transit facility may submit an application therefor to the State highway agency.

§ 810.206 Review by the State Highway Agency.

The State highway agency, after reviewing the application, may request the Federal Highway Administrator to authorize the State to make available to the publicly-owned mass transit authority the land needed for the proposed facility. A request shall be accompanied by evidence that utilization of the land for the proposed purposes will not impair future highway improvements or the safety of highway users.

§ 810.208 Action by the Federal Highway Administrator.

The Federal Highway Administrator may authorize the State to make available to the publicly-owned mass transit authority the land needed for the proposed facility, if it is determined that:

(a) The evidence submitted by the State highway agency under § 810.206 is satisfactory;

(b) The public interest will be served thereby; and

(c) The proposed action in urbanized areas is based on a continuing, comprehensive transportation planning process carried on in accordance with 23 U.S.C. 134 as described under 23 CFR part 450, subpart A.

§ 810.210 Authorization for use and occupancy by mass transit.

(a) Upon being authorized by the Federal Highway Administrator, the State shall enter into a written agreement with the publicly-owned mass transit authority relating to the use and occupancy of highway right-of-way subject to the following conditions:

(1) That any significant revision in the design, construction, or use of the facility for which the land was made available shall receive prior review and approval by the State highway agency.

(2) The use of the lands made available to the publicly-owned mass transit authority shall not be transferred to another party without the prior approval of the State highway agency.

(3) That, if the publicly-owned mass transit authority fails within a reasonable or agreed time to use the land for the purpose for which it was made available, or if it abandons the land or the facility developed, such use shall terminate. Any abandoned facility developed or under development by the publicly-owned mass transit authority which was financed all or in part with Federal funds shall be disposed of in a manner prescribed by OMB Circular A–102, Attachment N. The land shall revert to the State for its original intended highway purpose.

(b) A copy of the use and occupancy agreement and any modification under paragraphs (a) (1), (2), and (3) of this section shall be forwarded to the Federal Highway Administrator.

§ 810.212 Use without charge.

The use and occupancy of the lands made available by the State to the publicly owned transit authority may be without charge. Costs incidental to making the lands available for mass transit shall be borne by the publicly owned mass transit authority.

[81 FR 57741, Aug. 23, 2016]

Subpart D—Federal-Aid Urban System Nonhighway Public Mass Transit Projects

§ 810.300 Purpose.

The purpose of this subpart is to implement 23 U.S.C. 142(a)(2), which allows the Urban Mass Transportation Administrator, by delegation of the Secretary, to approve nonhighway public mass transit projects as Federal-aid urban system projects.

§ 810.302 Eligible projects.

(a) Eligible projects are those defined as nonhighway public mass transit projects in § 810.4 of this part subject to the limitations in paragraph (b) of this section.

(b) All projects under this subpart for the construction, reconstruction, or improvement of fixed rail facilities shall be located within the urban boundaries established under 23 U.S.C. 101(a).

§810.304 Submission of projects.

(a) An application for an urban system nonhighway public mass transit project shall be developed by a public body as defined under the UMTA Discretionary Capital Assistance Program and shall be prepared in accordance with procedures for the same Discretionary Capital Assistance program.

(b) The application shall be submitted concurrently to the State highway agency and to the UMTA Administrator. The State highway agency, if it concurs, shall submit a request to the FHWA Administrator for a reservation of apportioned Federal-aid urban system funds. The State shall include in its submission advice that such reservation of funds will not impair its ability to comply with the provisions of section 105(d) of Pub. L. 97–424 (if a State certifies it does not need forty percent of its Federal-aid urban system funds for 4R work, and the Secretary accepts such certification, the State may spend that unneeded amount for other eligible FAUS purpose, including nonhighway public mass transit projects).

§810.306 Reservation of funds.

(a) The FHWA Administrator shall review the State request, determine whether sufficient Federal-aid urban system funds are available, and notify the State highway agency and the UMTA Administrator of the reservation of funds.

(b) The apportioned funds reserved for the proposed project under paragraph (a) of this section shall remain available for obligation unless the FHWA Administrator is notified that the application has been disapproved by the UMTA Administrator, or unless the responsible local officials in whose jurisdiction the project is to be located and the State highway agency jointly request the withdrawal of the project application.

§810.308 Approval of urban system nonhighway public mass transit projects.

(a) An urban system public mass transit project may be approved by the UMTA Administrator when it is determined that:

(1) The application and project are in accordance with the current UMTA procedures relating to discretionary capital assistance grants; and

(2) Notification has been received from the FHWA Administrator that sufficient apportioned Federal-aid urban system funds are available to finance the Federal share of the cost of the proposed project.

(b) Approval of the plans, specifications, and estimates of a nonhighway public mass transit project shall be deemed to occur on the date the UMTA Administrator approves the project application. This approval which is subject to the availability of obligation authority at the time of approval, will obligate the United States to pay its proportional share of the cost of the project.

(c) Upon approval of an urban system nonhighway public mass transit project, the UMTA Administrator will execute a grant contract covering implementation of the project.

§810.310 Applicability of other provisions.

The Federal proportional share of the cost of an urban system nonhighway public mass transit project approved under this subpart shall be equal to the Federal share which would have been paid if the project were a highway project as determined under 23 U.S.C. 120(a).

SUBCHAPTER J—HIGHWAY SAFETY

PART 924—HIGHWAY SAFETY IMPROVEMENT PROGRAM

AUTHORITY: 23 U.S.C. 104(b)(3), 130, 148, 150, and 315; 49 CFR 1.85.

SOURCE: 81 FR 13739, Mar. 15, 2016, unless otherwise noted.

§ 924.1 Purpose.

The purpose of this regulation is to prescribe requirements for the development, implementation, and evaluation of a highway safety improvement program (HSIP) in each State.

§ 924.3 Definitions.

Unless otherwise specified in this part, the definitions in 23 U.S.C. 101(a) are applicable to this part. In addition, the following definitions apply:

Hazard index formula means any safety or crash prediction formula used for determining the relative risk at railway-highway crossings, taking into consideration weighted factors, and severity of crashes.

Highway means:

(1) A road, street, or parkway and all associated elements such as a right-of-way, bridge, railway-highway crossing, tunnel, drainage structure, sign, markings, guardrail, protective structure, etc.;

(2) A roadway facility as may be required by the United States Customs and Immigration Services in connection with the operation of an international bridge or tunnel; and

(3) A facility that serves pedestrians and bicyclists pursuant to 23 U.S.C. 148(e)(1)(A).

Highway Safety Improvement Program (HSIP) means a State safety program with the purpose to reduce fatalities and serious injuries on all public roads through the implementation of the provisions of 23 U.S.C. 130, 148, and 150, including the development of a data-driven Strategic Highway Safety Plan (SHSP), Railway-Highway Crossings Program, and program of highway safety improvement projects.

Highway safety improvement project means strategies, activities, or projects on a public road that are consistent with a State SHSP and that either correct or improve a hazardous road segment, location, or feature, or addresses a highway safety problem. Examples of projects are described in 23 U.S.C. 148(a).

MIRE Fundamental data elements mean the minimum subset of the roadway and traffic data elements from the FHWA's Model Inventory of Roadway Elements (MIRE) that are used to support a State's data-driven safety program.

Public railway-highway crossing means a railway-highway crossing where the roadway (including associated sidewalks, pathways, and shared use paths) is under the jurisdiction of and maintained by a public authority and open to public travel, including non-motorized users. All roadway approaches must be under the jurisdiction of a public roadway authority, and no roadway approach may be on private property.

Public road means any highway, road, or street under the jurisdiction of and maintained by a public authority and open to public travel, including non-State-owned public roads and roads on tribal land.

Reporting year means a 1-year period defined by the State, unless noted otherwise in this section. It may be the Federal fiscal year, State fiscal year, or calendar year.

Railway-highway crossing protective devices means those traffic control devices in the Manual on Uniform Traffic Control Devices (MUTCD) specified for use at such crossings; and system components associated with such traffic control devices, such as track circuit improvements and interconnections with highway traffic signals.

Road safety audit means a formal safety performance examination of an existing or future road or intersection by an independent multidisciplinary audit team for improving road safety for all users.

Safety data includes, but are not limited to, crash, roadway characteristics, and traffic data on all public roads. For railway-highway crossings, safety data also includes the characteristics of highway and train traffic, licensing, and vehicle data.

Safety stakeholder means, but is not limited to:

(1) A highway safety representative of the Governor of the State;

(2) Regional transportation planning organizations and metropolitan planning organizations, if any;

(3) Representatives of major modes of transportation;

(4) State and local traffic enforcement officials;

(5) A highway-rail grade crossing safety representative of the Governor of the State;

(6) Representatives conducting a motor carrier safety program under section 31102, 31106, or 31309 of title 49, U.S.C.;

(7) Motor vehicle administration agencies;

(8) County transportation officials;

(9) State representatives of non-motorized users; and

(10) Other Federal, State, tribal, and local safety stakeholders.

Spot safety improvement means an improvement or set of improvements that is implemented at a specific location on the basis of location-specific crash experience or other data-driven means.

Strategic highway safety plan (SHSP) means a comprehensive, multiyear, data-driven plan developed by a State department of transportation (DOT) in accordance with 23 U.S.C. 148.

Systemic safety improvement means a proven safety countermeasure(s) that is widely implemented based on high-risk roadway features that are correlated with particular severe crash types.

§924.5 Policy.

(a) Each State shall develop, implement, and evaluate on an annual basis a HSIP that has the objective to significantly reduce fatalities and serious injuries resulting from crashes on all public roads.

(b) HSIP funds shall be used for highway safety improvement projects that are consistent with the State's SHSP. HSIP funds should be used to maximize opportunities to advance highway safety improvement projects that have the greatest potential to reduce the State's roadway fatalities and serious injuries.

(c) Safety improvements should also be incorporated into projects funded by other Federal-aid programs, such as the National Highway Performance Program (NHPP) and the Surface Transportation Program (STP). Safety improvements that are provided as part of a broader Federal-aid project should be funded from the same source as the broader project.

(d) Eligibility for Federal funding of projects for traffic control devices under this part is subject to a State or local/tribal jurisdiction's substantial conformance with the National MUTCD or FHWA-approved State MUTCDs and supplements in accordance with part 655, subpart F, of this chapter.

§924.7 Program structure.

(a) The HSIP shall include:

(1) A SHSP;

(2) A Railway-Highway Crossing Program; and

(3) A program of highway safety improvement projects.

(b) The HSIP shall address all public roads in the State and include separate processes for the planning, implementation, and evaluation of the HSIP components described in paragraph (a) of this section. These processes shall be developed by the States in cooperation with the FHWA Division Administrator in accordance with this section and the requirements of 23 U.S.C. 148. Where appropriate, the processes shall be developed in consultation with other safety stakeholders and officials of the various units of local and Tribal governments.

§924.9 Planning.

(a) The HSIP planning process shall incorporate:

(1) A process for collecting and maintaining safety data on all public roads.

Roadway data shall include, at a minimum, the MIRE Fundamental Data Elements as established in § 924.17. Railway-highway crossing data shall include all fields from the U.S. DOT National Highway-Rail Crossing Inventory.

(2) A process for advancing the State's capabilities for safety data collection and analysis by improving the timeliness, accuracy, completeness, uniformity, integration, and accessibility of their safety data on all public roads.

(3) A process for updating the SHSP that identifies and analyzes highway safety problems and opportunities in accordance with 23 U.S.C.148. A SHSP update shall:

(i) Be completed no later than 5 years from the date of the previous approved version;

(ii) Be developed by the State DOT in consultation with safety stakeholders;

(iii) Provide a detailed description of the update process. The update process must be approved by the FHWA Division Administrator;

(iv) Be approved by the Governor of the State or a responsible State agency official that is delegated by the Governor;

(v) Adopt performance-based goals that:

(A) Are consistent with safety performance measures established by FHWA in accordance with 23 U.S.C. 150; and

(B) Are coordinated with other State highway safety programs;

(vi) Analyze and make effective use of safety data to address safety problems and opportunities on all public roads and for all road users;

(vii) Identify key emphasis areas and strategies that have the greatest potential to reduce highway fatalities and serious injuries and focus resources on areas of greatest need;

(viii) Address engineering, management, operations, education, enforcement, and emergency services elements of highway safety as key features when determining SHSP strategies;

(ix) Consider the results of State, regional, local, and tribal transportation and highway safety planning processes and demonstrate mutual consultation among partners in the development of transportation safety plans;

(x) Provide strategic direction for other State and local/tribal transportation plans, such as the HSIP, the Highway Safety Plan, and the Commercial Vehicle Safety Plan; and

(xi) Describe the process and potential resources for implementing strategies in the emphasis areas.

(4) A process for analyzing safety data to:

(i) Develop a program of highway safety improvement projects, in accordance with 23 U.S.C. 148(c)(2), to reduce fatalities and serious injuries on all public roads through the implementation of a comprehensive program of systemic and spot safety improvement projects.

(ii) Develop a Railway-Highway Crossings program that:

(A) Considers the relative risk of public railway-highway crossings based on a hazard index formula;

(B) Includes onsite inspection of public railway-highway crossings; and

(C) Results in a program of highway safety improvement projects at railway-highway crossings giving special emphasis to the statutory requirement that all public crossings be provided with standard signing and markings.

(5) A process for conducting engineering studies (such as road safety audits and other safety assessments or reviews) to develop highway safety improvement projects.

(6) A process for establishing priorities for implementing highway safety improvement projects that considers:

(i) The potential reduction in fatalities and serious injuries;

(ii) The cost effectiveness of the projects and the resources available; and

(iii) The priorities in the SHSP.

(b) The planning process of the HSIP may be financed with funds made available through 23 U.S.C. 104(b)(3) and 505, and, where applicable in metropolitan planning areas, 23 U.S.C. 104(d). The eligible use of the program funding categories listed for HSIP planning efforts is subject to that program's eligibility requirements and cost allocation procedures as per 2 CFR part 200.

(c) Highway safety improvement projects, including non-infrastructure safety projects, to be funded under 23 U.S.C. 104(b)(3) shall be carried out as part of the Statewide and Metropolitan Transportation Planning Process consistent with the requirements of 23 U.S.C. 134 and 135 and 23 CFR part 450.

§924.11 Implementation.

(a) The HSIP shall be implemented in accordance with the requirements of §924.9.

(b) States shall incorporate specific quantifiable and measurable anticipated improvements for the collection of MIRE fundamental data elements into their Traffic Records Strategic Plan by July 1, 2017. States shall have access to a complete collection of the MIRE fundamental data elements on all public roads by September 30, 2026.

(c) The SHSP shall include or be accompanied by actions that address how the SHSP emphasis area strategies will be implemented.

(d) Funds set-aside for the Railway-Highway Crossings Program under 23 U.S.C. 130 shall be used to implement railway-highway crossing safety projects on any public road. If a State demonstrates that it has met its needs for the installation of railway-highway crossing protective devices to the satisfaction of the FHWA Division Administrator, the State may use funds made available under 23 U.S.C. 130 for other types of highway safety improvement projects pursuant to the special rule in 23 U.S.C. 130(e)(2).

(e) Highway safety improvement projects may also be implemented with other funds apportioned under 23 U.S.C. 104(b) subject to the eligibility requirements applicable to each program.

(f) Award of contracts for highway safety improvement projects shall be in accordance with 23 CFR parts 635 and 636, where applicable, for highway construction projects, 23 CFR part 172 for engineering and design services contracts related to highway construction projects, or 2 CFR part 200 for non-highway construction projects.

(g) Except as provided in 23 U.S.C. 120 and 130, the Federal share of the cost of a highway safety improvement project carried out with funds apportioned to a State under 23 U.S.C. 104(b)(3) shall be 90 percent.

§924.13 Evaluation.

(a) The HSIP evaluation process shall include:

(1) A process to analyze and assess the results achieved by the program of highway safety improvement projects in terms of contributions to improved safety outcomes and the attainment of safety performance targets established as per 23 U.S.C. 150.

(2) An evaluation of the SHSP as part of the regularly recurring update process to:

(i) Confirm the validity of the emphasis areas and strategies based on analysis of current safety data; and

(ii) Identify issues related to the SHSP's process, implementation, and progress that should be considered during each subsequent SHSP update.

(b) The information resulting from paragraph (a)(1) of this section shall be used:

(1) To update safety data used in the planning process in accordance with §924.9;

(2) For setting priorities for highway safety improvement projects;

(3) For assessing the overall effectiveness of the HSIP; and

(4) For reporting required by §924.15.

(c) The evaluation process may be financed with funds made available under 23 U.S.C. 104(b)(3) and 505, and, for metropolitan planning areas, 23 U.S.C. 104(d). The eligible use of the program funding categories listed for HSIP evaluation efforts is subject to that program's eligibility requirements and cost allocation procedures as per 2 CFR part 200.

§924.15 Reporting.

(a) For the period of the previous reporting year, each State shall submit, via FHWA's HSIP online reporting tool, to the FHWA Division Administrator no later than August 31 of each year, the following reports related to the HSIP in accordance with 23 U.S.C. 148(h) and 130(g):

(1) A report describing the progress being made to implement the HSIP that:

(i) Describes the structure of the HSIP. This section shall:

(A) Describe how HSIP funds are administered in the State; and

(B) Provide a summary of the methodology used to develop the programs and projects being implemented under the HSIP on all public roads.

(ii) Describes the progress in implementing highway safety improvement projects. This section shall:

(A) Compare the funds programmed in the STIP for highway safety improvement projects and those obligated during the reporting year; and

(B) Provide a list of highway safety improvement projects that were obligated during the reporting year, including non-infrastructure projects. Each project listed shall identify how it relates to the State SHSP.

(iii) Describes the progress in achieving safety outcomes and performance targets. This section shall:

(A) Provide an overview of general highway safety trends. General highway safety trends shall be presented by number and rate of fatalities and serious injuries on all public roads by calendar year, and to the maximum extent practicable, shall also be presented by functional classification and roadway ownership. General highway safety trends shall also be presented for the total number of fatalities and serious injuries for non-motorized users;

(B) Document the safety performance targets established in accordance with 23 U.S.C. 150 for the following calendar year. Documentation shall also include a discussion of the basis for each established target, and how the established target supports SHSP goals. In future years, documentation shall also include a discussion of any reasons for differences in the actual outcomes and targets; and

(C) Present information related to the applicability of the special rules defined in 23 U.S.C. 148(g).

(iv) Assesses the effectiveness of the improvements. This section shall describe the effectiveness of groupings or similar types of highway safety improvement projects previously implemented under the HSIP.

(v) Is compatible with the requirements of 29 U.S.C. 794(d), Section 508 of the Rehabilitation Act.

(2) A report describing progress being made to implement railway-highway crossing improvements in accordance with 23 U.S.C. 130(g) and the effectiveness of these improvements.

(b) The preparation of the State's annual reports may be financed with funds made available through 23 U.S.C. 104(b)(3).

§ 924.17 MIRE fundamental data elements.

The MIRE fundamental data elements shall be collected on all public roads, as listed in Tables 1, 2, and 3 of this section. For the purpose of MIRE fundamental data elements applicability, the term open to public travel is consistent with 23 CFR 460.2(c).

TABLE 1—MIRE FUNDAMENTAL DATA ELEMENTS FOR NON-LOCAL (BASED ON FUNCTIONAL CLASSIFICATION) PAVED ROADS

MIRE name (MIRE No.) [1]	
Roadway segment	Intersection
Segment Identifier (12)	Unique Junction Identifier (120).
Route Number (8) [2]	Location Identifier for Road 1 Crossing Point (122).
Route/street Name (9) [2]	Location Identifier for Road 2 Crossing Point (123).
Federal Aid/Route Type (21) [2]	Intersection/Junction Geometry (126).
Rural/Urban Designation (20) [2]	Intersection/Junction Traffic Control (131).
Surface Type (23) [2]	AADT (79) [for Each Intersecting Road].
Begin Point Segment Descriptor (10) [2]	AADT Year (80) [for Each Intersecting Road].
End Point Segment Descriptor (11) [2]	
Segment Length (13) [2]	
Direction of Inventory (18)	Unique Approach Identifier (139).
Functional Class (19) [2]	
Median Type (54)	
Access Control (22) [2]	
One/Two-Way Operations (91) [2]	Interchange/Ramp.
Number of Through Lanes (31) [2]	Unique Interchange Identifier (178).
Average Annual Daily Traffic (79) [2]	Location Identifier for Roadway at Beginning Ramp Terminal (197).

TABLE 1—MIRE FUNDAMENTAL DATA ELEMENTS FOR NON-LOCAL (BASED ON FUNCTIONAL CLASSIFICATION) PAVED ROADS—Continued

MIRE name (MIRE No.)[1]	
Roadway segment	Intersection
AADT Year (80)[2]	Location Identifier for Roadway at Ending Ramp Terminal (201).
Type of Governmental Ownership (4)[2]	Ramp Length (187).
	Roadway Type at Beginning Ramp Terminal (195).
	Roadway Type at Ending Ramp Terminal (199).
	Interchange Type (182).
	Ramp AADT (191).[2]
	Year of Ramp AADT (192).[2]
	Functional Class (19).[2]
	Type of Governmental Ownership (4).[2]

[1] *Model Inventory of Roadway Elements—MIRE, Version 1.0,* Report No. FHWA–SA–10–018, October 2010, *http://safety.fhwa.dot.gov/tools/data_tools/mirereport/mirereport.pdf.*

[2] Highway Performance Monitoring System full extent elements are required on all Federal-aid highways and ramps located within grade-separated interchanges, *i.e.,* National Highway System (NHS) and all functional systems excluding rural minor collectors and locals.

TABLE 2—MIRE FUNDAMENTAL DATA ELEMENTS FOR LOCAL (BASED ON FUNCTIONAL CLASSIFICATION) PAVED ROADS

MIRE name (MIRE No.)[1]
Roadway segment:
Segment Identifier (12).
Functional Class (19).[2]
Surface Type (23).[2]
Type of Governmental Ownership (4).[2]
Number of Through Lanes (31).[2]
Average Annual Daily Traffic (79).[2]
Begin Point Segment Descriptor (10).[2]
End Point Segment Descriptor (11).[2]
Rural/Urban Designation (20).[2]

[1] *Model Inventory of Roadway Elements—MIRE, Version 1.0,* Report No. FHWA-SA-10-018, October 2010, *http://safety.fhwa.dot.gov/tools/data_tools/mirereport/mirereport.pdf.*

[2] Highway Performance Monitoring System full extent elements are required on all Federal-aid highways and ramps located within grade-separated interchanges, *i.e.,* National Highway System (NHS) and all functional systems excluding rural minor collectors and locals.

TABLE 3—MIRE FUNDAMENTAL DATA ELEMENTS FOR UNPAVED ROADS

MIRE name (MIRE No.)[1]
Roadway segment:
Segment Identifier (12).
Functional Class (19).[2]
Type of Governmental Ownership (4).[2]
Begin Point Segment Descriptor (10).[2]
End Point Segment Descriptor (11).[2]

[1] *Model Inventory of Roadway Elements—MIRE, Version 1.0,* Report No. FHWA–SA–10–018, October 2010, *http://safety.fhwa.dot.gov/tools/data_tools/mirereport/mirereport.pdf.*

[2] Highway Performance Monitoring System full extent elements are required on all Federal-aid highways and ramps located within grade-separated interchanges, *i.e.,* National Highway System (NHS) and all functional systems excluding rural minor collectors and locals.

SUBCHAPTER K—INTELLIGENT TRANSPORTATION SYSTEMS

PART 940—INTELLIGENT TRANSPORTATION SYSTEM ARCHITECTURE AND STANDARDS

AUTHORITY: 23 U.S.C. 101, 106, 109, 133, 315, and 508; sec 5206(e), Public Law 105–178, 112 Stat. 457 (23 U.S.C. 502 note); and 49 CFR 1.48.

SOURCE: 66 FR 1453, Jan. 8, 2001, unless otherwise noted.

§ 940.1 Purpose.

This regulation provides policies and procedures for implementing section 5206(e) of the Transportation Equity Act for the 21st Century (TEA–21), Public Law 105–178, 112 Stat. 457, pertaining to conformance with the National Intelligent Transportation Systems Architecture and Standards.

§ 940.3 Definitions.

Intelligent Transportation System (ITS) means electronics, communications, or information processing used singly or in combination to improve the efficiency or safety of a surface transportation system.

ITS project means any project that in whole or in part funds the acquisition of technologies or systems of technologies that provide or significantly contribute to the provision of one or more ITS user services as defined in the National ITS Architecture.

Major ITS project means any ITS project that implements part of a regional ITS initiative that is multi-jurisdictional, multi-modal, or otherwise affects regional integration of ITS systems.

National ITS Architecture (also "national architecture") means a common framework for ITS interoperability. The National ITS Architecture comprises the logical architecture and physical architecture which satisfy a defined set of user services. The National ITS Architecture is maintained by the United States Department of Transportation (DOT) and is available on the DOT web site at *http://www.its.dot.gov.*

Project level ITS architecture is a framework that identifies the institutional agreement and technical integration necessary to interface a major ITS project with other ITS projects and systems.

Region is the geographical area that identifies the boundaries of the regional ITS architecture and is defined by and based on the needs of the participating agencies and other stakeholders. In metropolitan areas, a region should be no less than the boundaries of the metropolitan planning area.

Regional ITS architecture means a regional framework for ensuring institutional agreement and technical integration for the implementation of ITS projects or groups of projects.

Systems engineering is a structured process for arriving at a final design of a system. The final design is selected from a number of alternatives that would accomplish the same objectives and considers the total life-cycle of the project including not only the technical merits of potential solutions but also the costs and relative value of alternatives.

§ 940.5 Policy.

ITS projects shall conform to the National ITS Architecture and standards in accordance with the requirements contained in this part. Conformance with the National ITS Architecture is interpreted to mean the use of the National ITS Architecture to develop a regional ITS architecture, and the subsequent adherence of all ITS projects to that regional ITS architecture. Development of the regional ITS architecture should be consistent with the transportation planning process for Statewide and Metropolitan Transportation Planning.

§ 940.7 Applicability.

(a) All ITS projects that are funded in whole or in part with the highway trust fund, including those on the National Highway System (NHS) and on non-NHS facilities, are subject to these provisions.

(b) The Secretary may authorize exceptions for:

(1) Projects designed to achieve specific research objectives outlined in the National ITS Program Plan under section 5205 of the TEA–21, or the Surface Transportation Research and Development Strategic Plan developed under 23 U.S.C. 508; or

(2) The upgrade or expansion of an ITS system in existence on the date of enactment of the TEA–21, if the Secretary determines that the upgrade or expansion:

(i) Would not adversely affect the goals or purposes of Subtitle C (Intelligent Transportation Systems Act of 1998) of the TEA–21;

(ii) Is carried out before the end of the useful life of such system; and

(iii) Is cost-effective as compared to alternatives that would meet the conformity requirement of this rule.

(c) These provisions do not apply to funds used for operations and maintenance of an ITS system in existence on June 9, 1998.

§ 940.9 Regional ITS architecture.

(a) A regional ITS architecture shall be developed to guide the development of ITS projects and programs and be consistent with ITS strategies and projects contained in applicable transportation plans. The National ITS Architecture shall be used as a resource in the development of the regional ITS architecture. The regional ITS architecture shall be on a scale commensurate with the scope of ITS investment in the region. Provision should be made to include participation from the following agencies, as appropriate, in the development of the regional ITS architecture: Highway agencies; public safety agencies (e.g., police, fire, emergency/medical); transit operators; Federal lands agencies; State motor carrier agencies; and other operating agencies necessary to fully address regional ITS integration.

(b) Any region that is currently implementing ITS projects shall have a regional ITS architecture by April 8, 2005.

(c) All other regions not currently implementing ITS projects shall have a regional ITS architecture within four years of the first ITS project for that region advancing to final design.

(d) The regional ITS architecture shall include, at a minimum, the following:

(1) A description of the region;

(2) Identification of participating agencies and other stakeholders;

(3) An operational concept that identifies the roles and responsibilities of participating agencies and stakeholders in the operation and implementation of the systems included in the regional ITS architecture;

(4) Any agreements (existing or new) required for operations, including at a minimum those affecting ITS project interoperability, utilization of ITS related standards, and the operation of the projects identified in the regional ITS architecture;

(5) System functional requirements;

(6) Interface requirements and information exchanges with planned and existing systems and subsystems (for example, subsystems and architecture flows as defined in the National ITS Architecture);

(7) Identification of ITS standards supporting regional and national interoperability; and

(8) The sequence of projects required for implementation.

(e) Existing regional ITS architectures that meet all of the requirements of paragraph (d) of this section shall be considered to satisfy the requirements of paragraph (a) of this section.

(f) The agencies and other stakeholders participating in the development of the regional ITS architecture shall develop and implement procedures and responsibilities for maintaining it, as needs evolve within the region.

[66 FR 1453, Jan. 8, 2001, as amended at 66 FR 19856, Apr. 18, 2001]

§ 940.11 Project implementation.

(a) All ITS projects funded with highway trust funds shall be based on a systems engineering analysis.

(b) The analysis should be on a scale commensurate with the project scope.

(c) The systems engineering analysis shall include, at a minimum:

(1) Identification of portions of the regional ITS architecture being implemented (or if a regional ITS architecture does not exist, the applicable portions of the National ITS Architecture);

(2) Identification of participating agencies roles and responsibilities;

(3) Requirements definitions;

(4) Analysis of alternative system configurations and technology options to meet requirements;

(5) Procurement options;

(6) Identification of applicable ITS standards and testing procedures; and

(7) Procedures and resources necessary for operations and management of the system.

(d) Upon completion of the regional ITS architecture required in §§ 940.9(b) or 940.9(c), the final design of all ITS projects funded with highway trust funds shall accommodate the interface requirements and information exchanges as specified in the regional ITS architecture. If the final design of the ITS project is inconsistent with the regional ITS architecture, then the regional ITS architecture shall be updated as provided in the process defined in § 940.9(f) to reflect the changes.

(e) Prior to the completion of the regional ITS architecture, any major ITS project funded with highway trust funds that advances to final design shall have a project level ITS architecture that is coordinated with the development of the regional ITS architecture. The final design of the major ITS project shall accommodate the interface requirements and information exchanges as specified in this project level ITS architecture. If the project final design is inconsistent with the project level ITS architecture, then the project level ITS architecture shall be updated to reflect the changes. The project level ITS architecture is based on the results of the systems engineering analysis, and includes the following:

(1) A description of the scope of the ITS project;

(2) An operational concept that identifies the roles and responsibilities of participating agencies and stakeholders in the operation and implementation of the ITS project;

(3) Functional requirements of the ITS project;

(4) Interface requirements and information exchanges between the ITS project and other planned and existing systems and subsystems; and

(5) Identification of applicable ITS standards.

(f) All ITS projects funded with highway trust funds shall use applicable ITS standards and interoperability tests that have been officially adopted through rulemaking by the DOT.

(g) Any ITS project that has advanced to final design by April 8, 2001 is exempt from the requirements of paragraphs (d) through (f) of this section.

[66 FR 1453, Jan. 8, 2001, as amended at 66 FR 19856, Apr. 18, 2001]

§ 940.13 Project administration.

(a) Prior to authorization of highway trust funds for construction or implementation of ITS projects, compliance with § 940.11 shall be demonstrated.

(b) Compliance with this part will be monitored under Federal-aid oversight procedures as provided under 23 U.S.C. 106 and 133.

PART 950—ELECTRONIC TOLL COLLECTION

AUTHORITY: 23 U.S.C. 109, 315; sec. 1604(b)(5) and (b)(6), Pub. L. 109–59, 119 Stat. 1144; 49 CFR 1.48.

SOURCE: 74 FR 51771, Oct. 8, 2009, unless otherwise noted.

§ 950.1 Purpose.

The purpose of this part is to establish interoperability requirements for toll facilities that are tolled under section 1604 of the Safe, Accountable, Flexible, Efficient Transportation Equity Act: A Legacy for Users (SAFETEA–LU) (Pub. L. 109–59; 119 Stat. 1144) that use electronic toll collection.

§ 950.3 Definitions.

As used in this part:

1604 toll program refers to any of the tolling programs authorized under section 1604 of SAFETEA–LU. These programs include the Value Pricing Pilot Program, the Express Lanes Demonstration Program, and the Interstate System Construction Toll Pilot Program.

Electronic toll collection means the ability for vehicle operators to pay tolls automatically without slowing down from normal highway speeds.

Toll agency means the relevant public or private entity or entities to which toll authority has been granted for a facility under a 1604 toll program.

§950.5 Requirement to use electronic toll collection technology.

(a) Any toll agency operating a toll facility pursuant to authority under a 1604 toll program shall use an electronic toll collection system as the method for collecting tolls from vehicle operators for the use of the facility unless the toll agency can demonstrate to the FHWA that some other method is either more economically efficient or will make the facility operate more safely. If a facility is collecting tolls pursuant to section 1604(b) of SAFETEA–LU, the toll agency shall only use electronic toll collection systems. Nothing in this subsection shall prevent a toll agency from using cash payment methods, such as toll booths, in areas that are not located in the toll facility's lanes of travel if the location and use of such methods do not create unsafe operating conditions on the toll facility.

(b) A toll agency using electronic toll collection technology must develop and implement reasonable methods to enable vehicle operators that are not enrolled in a toll collection program that is interoperable with the toll collection system of the relevant toll facility to use the facility.

(c) A toll agency using electronic toll collection technology must develop, implement, and make publicly available privacy policies to safeguard the disclosure of any data that may be collected through such technology concerning any user of a toll facility operating pursuant to authority under a 1604 toll program, but is not required to submit such policies to FHWA for approval.

§950.7 Interoperability requirements.

(a) For any toll facility operating pursuant to authority under a 1604 toll program, the toll agency shall—

(1) Identify the projected users of the facility;

(2) Identify the predominant toll collection systems likely utilized by the users of the facility; and

(3) Identify the noncash electronic technology likely to be in use within the next five years in that area.

(b) Based on the identification conducted under subsection (a), the toll agency shall receive the FHWA's concurrence that the facility's toll collection system's standards and design meet the requirements of this part.

(c) In requesting the FHWA's concurrence, the toll agency shall demonstrate to the FHWA that the selected toll collection system and technology achieves the highest reasonable degree of interoperability both with technology currently in use at other existing toll facilities and with technology likely to be in use at toll facilities within the next five years in that area. The toll agency shall explain to the FHWA how the toll collection system takes into account both the use of noncash electronic technology currently deployed within an appropriate geographic area of travel (as defined by the toll agency) and the noncash electronic technology likely to be in use within the next five years in that area. FHWA, in determining whether to concur in the toll agency's proposal, will give appropriate weight to current and future interoperability with toll facilities in that area. The facility's toll collection system design shall include the communications requirements between roadside equipment and toll transponders, as well as accounting compatibility requirements in order to ensure that users of the toll facilities are properly identified and tolls are charged to the appropriate account of the user.

(d) A toll agency that operates any toll facility pursuant to authority under a 1604 toll program must upgrade its toll collection system to meet any applicable standards and interoperability tests that have been officially adopted through rulemaking by the FHWA.

(e) With respect to facilities that are tolled pursuant to the Value Pricing Pilot Program, this part only applies if tolls are imposed on a facility after the effective date of this rule. However, such facility is subject to this part if the facility's toll collection system's method or technology used to collect tolls from vehicle operators is changed or upgraded after the effective date of the regulations in this part.

(f) Nothing in this part shall be construed as requiring the use of any particular type of electronic toll collection technology. However, any such toll collection technology must meet the interoperability requirement of this section.

§ 950.9 Enforcement.

(a) The tolling authority of any facility operating pursuant to authority under a 1604 toll program shall be suspended in the event the relevant toll agency is not in compliance with this part within six (6) months of receiving a written notice of non-compliance from FHWA. If the toll agency demonstrates that it is taking the necessary steps to come into compliance within a reasonable period of time, FHWA shall extend such tolling authority.

(b) The FHWA may take other action as may be appropriate, including action pursuant to § 1.36 of this title.

SUBCHAPTER L—FEDERAL LANDS HIGHWAYS

PART 970—NATIONAL PARK SERVICE MANAGEMENT SYSTEMS

Subpart A—Definitions

Subpart B—National Park Service Management Systems

AUTHORITY: 23 U.S.C. 204 and 315; 42 U.S.C. 7410 *et seq.;* 49 CFR 1.48.

SOURCE: 69 FR 9473, Feb. 27, 2004, unless otherwise noted.

Subpart A—Definitions

§ 970.100 Purpose.

The purpose of this subpart is to provide definitions for terms used in this part.

§ 970.102 Applicability.

The definitions in this subpart are applicable to this part, except as otherwise provided.

§ 970.104 Definitions.

Alternative transportation systems means modes of transportation other than private vehicles, including methods to improve system performance such as transportation demand management, congestion management, and intelligent transportation systems. These mechanisms help reduce the use of private vehicles and thus improve overall efficiency of transportation systems and facilities.

Elements means the components of a bridge important from a structural, user, or cost standpoint. Examples are decks, joints, bearings, girders, abutments, and piers.

Federal lands bridge management system (BMS) means a systematic process used by the Forest Service (FS), the Fish and Wildlife Service (FWS) and the National Park Service (NPS) for collecting and analyzing bridge data to make forecasts and recommendations, and provides the means by which bridge maintenance, rehabilitation, and replacement programs and policies may be efficiently and effectively considered.

Federal lands congestion management system (CMS) means a systematic process used by the NPS, the FWS and the FS for managing congestion that provides information on transportation system performance, and alternative strategies for alleviating congestion and enhancing the mobility of persons and goods to levels that meet Federal, State and local needs.

Federal Lands Highway Program (FLHP) means a federally funded program established in 23 U.S.C. 204 to address transportation needs of Federal and Indian lands.

Federal lands pavement management system (PMS) means a systematic process used by the NPS, the FWS and the FS that provides information for use in implementing cost-effective pavement reconstruction, rehabilitation, and preventive maintenance programs and policies, and that results in pavement designed to accommodate current and forecasted traffic in a safe, durable, and cost-effective manner.

Federal lands safety management system (SMS) means a systematic process used by the NPS, the FWS and the FS with the goal of reducing the number and severity of traffic accidents by ensuring that all opportunities to improve roadway safety are identified, considered, implemented, and evaluated, as appropriate, during all phases of highway planning, design, construction, operation and maintenance, by providing information for selecting and implementing effective highway safety strategies and projects.

Highway safety means the reduction of traffic accidents on public roads, including reductions in deaths, injuries, and property damage.

Intelligent transportation system (ITS) means electronics, communications, or information processing used singly or in combination to improve the efficiency and safety of a surface transportation system.

Life-cycle cost analysis means an evaluation of costs incurred over the life of a project allowing a comparative analysis between or among various alternatives. Life-cycle cost analysis promotes consideration of total cost, including maintenance and operation expenditures. Comprehensive life-cycle cost analysis includes all economic variables essential to the evaluation, including user costs such as delay, safety costs associated with maintenance and rehabilitation projects, agency capital costs, and life-cycle maintenance costs.

Metropolitan planning area means the geographic area in which the metropolitan transportation planning process required by 23 U.S.C. 134 and 49 U.S.C. 5303–5306 must be carried out.

Metropolitan planning organization (MPO) means the forum for cooperative transportation decision-making for the metropolitan planning area pursuant to 23 U.S.C. 134 and 49 U.S.C. 5303.

National Park Service transportation plan means an official NPS multimodal transportation plan that is developed through the NPS transportation planning process pursuant to 23 U.S.C. 204.

Operations means those activities associated with managing, controlling, and regulating highway and pedestrian traffic.

Park road means a public road, including a bridge built primarily for pedestrian use, but with capacity for use by emergency vehicles, that is located within, or provides access to, an area in the National Park System with title and maintenance responsibilities vested in the United States.

Park Road Program transportation improvement program (PRPTIP) means a staged, multi-year, multimodal program of NPS transportation projects in a State area. The PRPTIP is consistent with the NPS transportation plan and developed through the NPS planning processes pursuant to 23 U.S.C. 204.

Park roads and parkways program means a program that is authorized in 23 U.S.C. 204 with funds allocated to the NPS by the Federal Highway Administration (FHWA) for each fiscal year as provided in 23 U.S.C. 202(c) and 23 U.S.C. 204.

Parkway means a parkway authorized by Act of Congress on lands to which title is vested in the United States.

Secretary means the Secretary of Transportation.

Serviceability means the degree to which a bridge provides satisfactory service from the point of view of its users.

State means any one of the fifty States, the District of Columbia, or Puerto Rico.

Transportation facilities means roads, streets, bridges, parking areas, transit vehicles, and other related transportation infrastructure.

Transportation Management Area (TMA) means an urbanized area with a population over 200,000 (as determined by the latest decennial census) or other area when TMA designation is requested by the Governor and the MPO (or affected local officials), and officially designated by the Administrators of the FHWA and the Federal Transit Administration (FTA). The TMA designation applies to the entire metropolitan planning area(s).

Subpart B—National Park Service Management Systems

§ 970.200 Purpose.

The purpose of this subpart is to implement 23 U.S.C. 204, which requires the Secretary and the Secretary of each appropriate Federal land management agency, to the extent appropriate, to develop by rule safety, bridge, pavement, and congestion management systems for roads funded under the FLHP. These management systems serve to guide the National Park Service (NPS) in developing transportation plans and making resource allocation decisions for the PRPTIP.

§970.202 Applicability.

The provisions in this subpart are applicable to the NPS and the Federal Highway Administration (FHWA) that are responsible for satisfying these requirements for management systems pursuant to 23 U.S.C. 204.

§970.204 Management systems requirements.

(a) The NPS shall develop, establish and implement the management systems as described in this subpart. The NPS may tailor all management systems to meet the NPS goals, policies, and needs using professional engineering and planning judgment to determine the required nature and extent of systems coverage consistent with the intent and requirements of this rule. The management systems also shall be developed so they assist in meeting the goals and measures that were jointly developed by the FHWA and the NPS in response to the Government Performance and Results Act of 1993 (Pub. L. 103–62, 107 Stat. 285).

(b) The NPS and the FHWA shall develop an implementation plan for each of the management systems. These plans will include, but are not limited to, the following: Overall goals and policies concerning the management systems, each agency's responsibilities for developing and implementing the management systems, implementation schedule, data sources, and cost estimate. The FHWA will provide the NPS ongoing technical engineering support for the development, implementation, and maintenance of the management systems.

(c) The NPS shall develop and implement procedures for the development, establishment, implementation and operation of management systems. The procedures shall include:

(1) A process for ensuring the outputs of the management systems are considered in the development of NPS transportation plans and PRPTIPs and in making project selection decisions under 23 U.S.C. 204;

(2) A process for the analysis and coordination of all management system outputs to systematically operate, maintain, and upgrade existing transportation assets cost-effectively;

(3) A description of each management system;

(4) A process to operate and maintain the management systems and their associated databases; and

(5) A process for data collection, processing, analysis and updating for each management system.

(d) All management systems will use databases with a geographical reference system that can be used to geolocate all database information.

(e) Existing data sources may be used by the NPS to the maximum extent possible to meet the management system requirements.

(f) The NPS shall develop an appropriate means to evaluate the effectiveness of the management systems in enhancing transportation investment decision-making and improving the overall efficiency of the affected transportation systems and facilities. This evaluation is to be conducted periodically, preferably as part of the NPS planning process.

(g) The management systems shall be operated so investment decisions based on management system outputs can be considered at the national, regional, and park levels.

§970.206 Funds for establishment, development, and implementation of the systems.

The Park Roads and Parkways program funds may be used for development, establishment, and implementation of the management systems. These funds are to be administered in accordance with the procedures and requirements applicable to the funds.

§970.208 Federal lands pavement management system (PMS).

In addition to the requirements provided in §970.204, the PMS must meet the following requirements:

(a) The NPS shall have PMS coverage of all paved park roads, parkways, parking areas and other associated facilities, as appropriate, that are funded under the FLHP.

(b) The PMS may be utilized at various levels of technical complexity depending on the nature of the transportation network. These different levels may depend on mileage, functional classes, volumes, loading, usage, surface type, or other criteria the NPS deems appropriate.

(c) The PMS shall be designed to fit the NPS goals, policies, criteria, and needs using the following components, at a minimum, as a basic framework for a PMS:

(1) A database and an ongoing program for the collection and maintenance of the inventory, inspection, cost, and supplemental data needed to support the PMS. The minimum PMS database shall include:

(i) An inventory of the physical pavement features including the number of lanes, length, width, surface type, functional classification, and shoulder information;

(ii) A history of project dates and types of construction, reconstruction, rehabilitation, and preventive maintenance. If some of the inventory or historic data is difficult to establish, it may be collected when preservation or reconstruction work is performed;

(iii) Condition data that includes roughness, distress, rutting, and surface friction (as appropriate);

(iv) Traffic information including volumes and vehicle classification (as appropriate); and

(v) Data for estimating the costs of actions.

(2) A system for applying network level analytical procedures that are capable of analyzing data for all park roads, parkways and other appropriate associated facilities in the inventory or any subset. The minimum analyses shall include:

(i) A pavement condition analysis that includes roughness, distress, rutting, and surface friction (as appropriate);

(ii) A pavement performance analysis that includes present and predicted performance and an estimate of the remaining service life (performance and remaining service life to be developed with time); and

(iii) An investment analysis that:

(A) Identifies alternative strategies to improve pavement conditions;

(B) Estimates costs of any pavement improvement strategy;

(C) Determines maintenance, repair, and rehabilitation strategies for pavements using life-cycle cost analysis or a comparable procedure;

(D) Provides for short and long term budget forecasting; and

(E) Recommends optimal allocation of limited funds by developing a prioritized list of candidate projects over a predefined planning horizon (both short and long term).

(d) For any park roads, parkways and other appropriate associated facilities in the inventory or subset thereof, PMS reporting requirements shall include, but are not limited to, percentage of roads in good, fair, and poor condition.

[69 FR 9473, Feb. 27, 2004; 69 FR 16793, Mar. 31, 2004]

§ 970.210 Federal lands bridge management system (BMS).

In addition to the requirements provided in § 970.204, the BMS must meet the following requirements:

(a) The NPS shall have a BMS for the bridges which are under the NPS jurisdiction, funded under the FLHP, and required to be inventoried and inspected as prescribed by 23 U.S.C. 144.

(b) The BMS shall be designed to fit the NPS goals, policies, criteria, and needs using, as a minimum, the following components:

(1) A database and an ongoing program for the collection and maintenance of the inventory, inspection, cost, and supplemental data needed to support the BMS. The minimum BMS database shall include:

(i) Data described by the inventory section of the National Bridge Inspection Standards (23 CFR part 650, subpart C);

(ii) Data characterizing the severity and extent of deterioration of bridge elements;

(iii) Data for estimating the cost of improvement actions;

(iv) Traffic information including volumes and other pertinent information; and

(v) A history of conditions and actions taken on each bridge, excluding minor or incidental maintenance.

(2) A system for applying network level analytical procedures that are capable of analyzing data for all bridges in the inventory or any subset. The minimum analyses shall include:

(i) A prediction of performance and estimate of the remaining service life of structural and other key elements of each bridge, both with and without intervening actions; and

(ii) A recommendation for optimal allocation of limited funds through development of a prioritized list of candidate projects over predefined short and long term planning horizons.

(c) The BMS may include the capability to perform an investment analysis as appropriate, considering size of structure, traffic volume, and structural condition. The investment analysis may:

(1) Identify alternative strategies to improve bridge condition, safety and serviceability;

(2) Estimate the costs of any strategies ranging from maintenance of individual elements to full bridge replacement;

(3) Determine maintenance, repair, and rehabilitation strategies for bridge elements using life cycle cost analysis or a comparable procedure;

(4) Provide short and long term budget forecasting; and

(5) Evaluate the cultural and historical values of the structure.

(d) For any bridge in the inventory or subset thereof, BMS reporting requirements shall include, but are not limited to, percentage of non-deficient bridges.

§ 970.212 Federal lands safety management system (SMS).

In addition to the requirements provided in § 970.204, the SMS must meet the following requirements:

(a) The NPS shall have an SMS for all transportation systems serving NPS facilities, as appropriate, funded under the FLHP.

(b) The NPS shall use the SMS to ensure that safety is considered and implemented, as appropriate, in all phases of transportation system planning, design, construction, maintenance, and operations.

(c) The SMS shall be designed to fit the NPS goals, policies, criteria, and needs and shall contain the following components: (1) An ongoing program for the collection, maintenance and reporting of a data base that includes:

(i) Accident records with details for analysis such as accident type, using standard reporting descriptions (e.g., right-angle, rear-end, head-on, pedestrian-related), location, description of event, severity, weather and cause;

(ii) An inventory of safety appurtenances such as signs, delineators, and guardrails (including terminals);

(iii) Traffic information including volume, speed, and vehicle classification, as appropriate.

(iv) Accident rates by customary criteria such as location, roadway classification, and vehicle miles of travel.

(2) Development, establishment, and implementation of procedures for:

(i) Routinely maintaining and upgrading safety appurtenances including highway-rail crossing warning devices, signs, highway elements, and operational features, where appropriate;

(ii) Identifying and investigating hazardous or potentially hazardous transportation elements and systems, transit vehicles and facilities, roadway locations and features;

(iii) Establishing countermeasures and setting priorities to address identified needs.

(3) A process for communication, coordination, and cooperation among the organizations responsible for the roadway, human, and vehicle safety elements;

(d) While the SMS applies to appropriate transportation systems serving NPS facilities funded under the FLHP, the extent of system requirements (e.g., data collection, analyses, and standards) for low volume roads may be tailored to be consistent with the functional classification of the road and number and types of transit and other vehicles operated by the NPS.

§ 970.214 Federal lands congestion management system (CMS).

(a) For purposes of this section, congestion means the level at which transportation system performance is no longer acceptable due to traffic interference. For portions of the NPS transportation system outside the boundaries of TMAs, the NPS shall:

(1) Develop criteria to determine when a CMS is to be implemented for a specific transportation system; and

(2) Have CMS coverage for all transportation systems serving NPS facilities that meet minimum CMS needs criteria, as appropriate, funded through the FLHP.

(b) The NPS shall consider the results of the CMS when selecting congestion mitigation strategies that are the most time efficient and cost effective and that add value (protection/rejuvenation of resources, improved visitor experience) to the park and adjacent communities.

(c) In addition to the requirements provided in §970.204, the CMS must meet the following requirements:

(1) For those NPS transportation systems that require a CMS, in both metropolitan and non-metropolitan areas, consideration shall be given to strategies that promote alternative transportation systems, reduce private automobile travel, and best integrate private automobile travel with other transportation modes.

(2) For portions of the NPS transportation system within transportation management areas (TMAs), the NPS transportation planning process shall include a CMS that meets the requirements of this section. By agreement between the TMA and the NPS, the TMA's CMS coverage may include the transportation systems serving NPS facilities, as appropriate. Through this agreement(s), the NPS may meet the requirements of this section.

(3) If congestion exists at a NPS facility within the boundaries of a TMA, and the TMA's CMS does not provide coverage of the portions of the NPS transportation facilities experiencing congestion, the NPS shall develop a separate CMS to cover those facilities. Approaches may include the use of alternate mode studies and implementation plans as components of the CMS.

(4) A CMS will:

(i) Identify and document measures for congestion (e.g., level of service);

(ii) Identify the causes of congestion;

(iii) Include processes for evaluating the cost and effectiveness of alternative strategies;

(iv) Identify the anticipated benefits of appropriate alternative traditional and nontraditional congestion management strategies;

(v) Determine methods to monitor and evaluate the performance of the multi-modal transportation system; and

(vi) Appropriately consider strategies, or combinations of strategies for each area, such as:

(A) Transportation demand management measures;

(B) Traffic operational improvements;

(C) Public transportation improvements;

(D) ITS technologies; and

(E) Additional system capacity.

PART 971—FOREST SERVICE MANAGEMENT SYSTEMS

Subpart A—Definitions

Subpart B—Forest Highway Program Management Systems

AUTHORITY: 23 U.S.C. 204, 315; 42 U.S.C. 7410 *et seq.;* 49 CFR 1.48.

SOURCE: 69 FR 9480, Feb. 27, 2004, unless otherwise noted.

Subpart A—Definitions

§971.100 Purpose.

The purpose of this subpart is to provide definitions for terms used in this part.

§971.102 Applicability.

The definitions in this subpart are applicable to this part, except as otherwise provided.

§ 971.104 Definitions.

Alternative transportation systems means modes of transportation other than private vehicles, including methods to improve system performance such as transportation demand management, congestion management, and intelligent transportation systems. These mechanisms help reduce the use of private vehicles and thus, improve overall efficiency of transportation systems and facilities.

Elements mean the components of a bridge that are important from a structural, user, or cost standpoint. Examples are decks, joints, bearings, girders, abutments, and piers.

Federal lands bridge management system (BMS) means a systematic process used by the Forest Service (FS), the Fish and Wildlife Service (FWS), and the National Park Service (NPS) for collecting and analyzing bridge data to make forecasts and recommendations, and that provides the means by which bridge maintenance, rehabilitation, and replacement programs and policies may be efficiently and effectively considered.

Federal lands congestion management system (CMS) means a systematic process used by the FS, FWS, and NPS for managing congestion that provides information on transportation system performance, and alternative strategies for alleviating congestion and enhancing the mobility of persons and goods to levels that meet Federal, State, and local needs.

Federal Lands Highway Program (FLHP) means a federally funded program established in 23 U.S.C. 204 to address transportation needs of Federal and Indian lands.

Federal lands pavement management system (PMS) means a systematic process used by the FS, FWS, and NPS that provides information for use in implementing cost-effective pavement reconstruction, rehabilitation, and preventive maintenance programs and policies, and that results in pavement designed to accommodate current and forecasted traffic in a safe, durable, and cost-effective manner.

Federal lands safety management system (SMS) means a systematic process used by the FS, FWS, and NPS with the goal of reducing the number and severity of traffic accidents by ensuring that all opportunities to improve roadway safety are identified, considered, implemented, and evaluated as appropriate, during all phases of highway planning, design, construction, operation and maintenance, by providing information for selecting and implementing effective highway safety strategies and projects.

Forest highway (FH) means a forest road under the jurisdiction of, and maintained by, a public authority and open to public travel.

Forest Highway Program means the public lands highway funds allocated each fiscal year, as is provided in 23 U.S.C. 202, for projects that provide access to and within the National Forest system, as described in 23 U.S.C. 202(b) and 23 U.S.C. 204.

Forest Highway Program transportation improvement program (FHTIP) means a staged, multiyear, multimodal program of transportation projects in a State area consistent with the FH transportation plan and developed through the tri-party FH planning processes pursuant to 23 U.S.C. 204, and 23 CFR 660 subpart A.

Forest Service transportation plan means the official FH multimodal, transportation plan that is developed through the tri-party FH transportation planning process pursuant to 23 U.S.C. 204.

Highway safety means the reduction of traffic accidents on public roads, including reductions in deaths, injuries, and property damage.

Intelligent transportation system (ITS) means electronics, communications, or information processing, used singly or in combination, to improve the efficiency and safety of a surface transportation system.

Life-cycle cost analysis means an evaluation of costs incurred over the life of a project allowing a comparative analysis between or among various alternatives. Life-cycle cost analysis promotes consideration of total cost, including maintenance and operation expenditures. Comprehensive life-cycle cost analysis includes all economic variables essential to the evaluation including user costs such as delay, safety costs associated with maintenance and rehabilitation projects, agency capital costs, and life-cycle maintenance costs.

Metropolitan planning area means the geographic area in which the metropolitan transportation planning process, required by 23 U.S.C. 134 and 49 U.S.C. 5303–5306, must be carried out.

Metropolitan planning organization (MPO) means the forum for cooperative transportation decision-making for the metropolitan planning area pursuant to 23 U.S.C. 134 and 49 U.S.C. 5303.

National Forest System means all the lands and waters reported by the FS as being part of the National Forest System, including those generally known as National Forests and National Grasslands.

Operations means those activities associated with managing, controlling, and regulating highway traffic.

Secretary means the Secretary of Transportation.

Serviceability means the degree to which a bridge provides satisfactory service from the point of view of its users.

State means any one of the 50 States, the District of Columbia, or Puerto Rico.

Transportation facilities mean roads, streets, bridges, parking areas, transit vehicles, and other related transportation infrastructure.

Transportation Management Area (TMA) means an urbanized area with a population over 200,000 (as determined by the latest decennial census) or other area when TMA designation is requested by the Governor and the MPO (or affected local officials). It also must be officially designated by the Administrators of the Federal Highway Administration (FHWA) and the Federal Transit Administration (FTA). The TMA designation applies to the entire metropolitan planning area(s).

Tri-party means the joint, cooperative, shared partnership among the Federal Lands Highway Division (FLHD), State Department of Transportation (State DOT), and the FS to carry out the FH program.

Subpart B—Forest Highway Program Management Systems

§ 971.200 Purpose.

The purpose of this subpart is to implement 23 U.S.C. 204, which requires the Secretary and the Secretary of each appropriate Federal land management agency, to the extent appropriate, to develop by rule safety, bridge, pavement, and congestion management systems for roads funded under the FLHP.

§ 971.202 Applicability.

The provisions in this subpart are applicable to the FS, the Federal Highway Administration, and the State DOTs that are responsible for satisfying these requirements for management systems pursuant to 23 U.S.C. 204.

§ 971.204 Management systems requirements.

(a) The tri-party partnership shall develop, establish, and implement the management systems as described in this subpart. If the State has established a management system for FH that fulfills the requirements in 23 U.S.C. 303, that management system, to the extent applicable, can be used to meet the requirements of this subpart consistent with 23 CFR 660.105(b). The management systems may be tailored to meet the FH program goals, policies, and needs using professional engineering and planning judgment to determine the nature and extent of systems coverage consistent with the intent and requirements of this rule.

(b) The tri-party partnership shall develop and implement procedures for the acceptance of the existing, or the development, establishment, implementation, and operation of new management systems. The procedures shall include:

(1) A process for ensuring the output of the management systems is considered in the development of the FH program transportation plans and transportation improvement programs, and in making project selection decisions under 23 U.S.C. 204;

(2) A process for the analyses and coordination of all management systems outputs to systematically operate,

maintain, and upgrade existing transportation assets cost-effectively;

(3) A description of each management system;

(4) A process to operate and maintain the management systems and their associated databases; and

(5) A process for data collection, processing, analysis, and updating for each management system.

(c) All management systems will use databases with a common or coordinated reference system, that can be used to geolocate all database information, to ensure that data across management systems are comparable.

(d) Existing data sources may be used by the tri-party partnership to meet the management system requirements.

(e) The tri-party partnership shall develop an appropriate means to evaluate the effectiveness of the management systems in enhancing transportation investment decision-making and improving the overall efficiency of the affected transportation systems and facilities. This evaluation is to be conducted periodically, preferably as part of the FS planning process.

(f) The management systems shall be operated so investment decisions based on management system outputs can be accomplished at the State level.

§971.206 Funds for establishment, development, and implementation of the systems.

The FH program funds may be used for development, establishment, and implementation of the management systems. These funds are to be administered in accordance with the procedures and requirements applicable to the funds.

§971.208 Federal lands pavement management system (PMS).

In addition to the requirements provided in §971.204, the PMS must meet the following requirements:

(a) The tri-party partnership shall have PMS coverage of all FHs and other associated facilities, as appropriate, funded under the FLHP.

(b) The PMS may be based on the concepts described in the AASHTO's "Pavement Management Guide."[1]

(c) The PMS may be utilized at various levels of technical complexity depending on the nature of the transportation network. These different levels may depend on mileage, functional classes, volumes, loading, usage, surface type, or other criteria the tri-party partnership deems appropriate.

(d) The PMS shall be designed to fit the FH program goals, policies, criteria, and needs using the following components, at a minimum, as a basic framework for a PMS:

(1) A database and an ongoing program for the collection and maintenance of the inventory, inspection, cost, and supplemental data needed to support the PMS. The minimum PMS database shall include:

(i) An inventory of the physical pavement features including the number of lanes, length, width, surface type, functional classification, and shoulder information;

(ii) A history of project dates and types of construction, reconstruction, rehabilitation, and preventive maintenance. If some of the inventory or historic data is difficult to establish, it may be collected when preservation or reconstruction work is performed;

(iii) A condition survey that includes ride, distress, rutting, and surface friction (as appropriate);

(iv) Traffic information including volumes and vehicle classification (as appropriate); and

(v) Data for estimating the costs of actions.

(2) A system for applying network level analytical procedures that are capable of analyzing data for all FHs and other appropriate associated facilities in the inventory or any subset. The minimum analyses shall include:

[1] "Pavement Management Guide," AASHTO, 2001, is available for inspection as prescribed at 49 CFR part 7. It is also available from the American Association of State Highway and Transportation Officials (AASHTO), Publication Order Dept., P.O. Box 96716, Washington, DC 20090–6716 or online at *http://www.transportation.org/publications/bookstore.nsf*.

(i) A pavement condition analysis that includes ride, distress, rutting, and surface friction (as appropriate);

(ii) A pavement performance analysis that includes present and predicted performance and an estimate of the remaining service life. Performance and remaining service life may be developed with time; and

(iii) An investment analysis that:

(A) Identifies alternative strategies to improve pavement conditions;

(B) Estimates costs of any pavement improvement strategy;

(C) Determines maintenance, repair, and rehabilitation strategies for pavements using life cycle cost analysis or a comparable procedure;

(D) Provides for short and long term budget forecasting; and

(E) Recommends optimal allocation of limited funds by developing a prioritized list of candidate projects over a predefined planning horizon (both short and long term).

(e) For any FHs and other appropriate associated facilities in the inventory or subset thereof, PMS reporting requirements shall include, but are not limited to, percentage of roads in good, fair, and poor condition.

§971.210 Federal lands bridge management system (BMS).

In addition to the requirements provided in §971.204, the BMS must meet the following requirements:

(a) The tri-party partnership shall have a BMS for the FH bridges funded under the FLHP and required to be inventoried and inspected under 23 CFR 650, subpart C, National Bridge Inspection Standards (NBIS).

(b) The BMS may be based on the concepts described in the AASHTO's "Guidelines for Bridge Management Systems."[2]

(c) The BMS shall be designed to fit the FH program goals, policies, criteria, and needs using the following components, as a minimum, as a basic framework for a BMS:

(1) A database and an ongoing program for the collection and maintenance of the inventory, inspection, cost, and supplemental data needed to support the BMS. The minimum BMS database shall include:

(i) The inventory data required by the NBIS (23 CFR 650, subpart C);

(ii) Data characterizing the severity and extent of deterioration of bridge elements;

(iii) Data for estimating the cost of improvement actions;

(iv) Traffic information including volumes and vehicle classification (as appropriate); and

(v) A history of conditions and actions taken on each bridge, excluding minor or incidental maintenance.

(2) A system for applying network level analytical procedures at the State or local area level, as appropriate, and capable of analyzing data for all bridges in the inventory or any subset. The minimum analyses shall include:

(i) A prediction of performance and estimate of the remaining service life of structural and other key elements of each bridge, both with and without intervening actions; and

(ii) A recommendation for optimal allocation of limited funds through development of a prioritized list of candidate projects over predefined short and long-term planning horizons.

(d) The BMS may include the capability to perform an investment analysis, as appropriate, considering size of structure, traffic volume, and structural condition. The investment analysis may:

(1) Identify alternative strategies to improve bridge condition, safety, and serviceability;

(2) Estimate the costs of any strategies ranging from maintenance of individual elements to full bridge replacement;

(3) Determine maintenance, repair, and rehabilitation strategies for bridge elements using life cycle cost analysis or a comparable procedure; and

(4) Provide short and long-term budget forecasting.

[2] "Guidelines for Bridge Management Systems," AASHTO, 1993, is available for inspection as prescribed at 49 CFR part 7. It is also available from the American Association of State Highway and Transportation Officials (AASHTO), Publication Order Dept., P.O. Box 96716, Washington, DC 20090–6716 or online at *http://www.transportation.org/publications/bookstore.nsf*.

(e) For any bridge in the inventory or subset thereof, BMS reporting requirements shall include, but are not limited to, percentage of non-deficient bridges.

§971.212 Federal lands safety management system (SMS).

In addition to the requirements provided in §971.204, the SMS must meet the following requirements:

(a) The tri-party partnership shall have an SMS for transportation systems providing access to and within National Forests and Grasslands, and funded under the FLHP.

(b) The SMS may be based on the guidance in "Safety Management Systems: Good Practices for Development and Implementation."[3]

(c) The tri-party partnership shall utilize SMS to ensure that safety is considered and implemented, as appropriate, in all phases of transportation system planning, design, construction, maintenance, and operations.

(d) The SMS may be utilized at various levels of complexity depending on the nature of the facility and/or network involved.

(e) The SMS shall be designed to fit the FH program goals, policies, criteria, and needs and shall contain the following components:

(1) An ongoing program for the collection, maintenance, and reporting of a database that includes:

(i) Accident records with detail for analysis such as accident type using standard reporting descriptions (e.g., right-angle, rear-end, head-on, pedestrian-related, etc.), location, description of event, severity, weather, and cause;

(ii) An inventory of safety appurtenances such as signs, delineators, and guardrails (including terminals);

(iii) Traffic information including volume and vehicle classification (as appropriate); and

(iv) Accident rates by customary criteria such as location, roadway classification, and vehicle miles of travel.

(2) Development, establishment, and implementation of procedures for:

(i) Where appropriate, routine maintenance and upgrading of safety appurtenances including highway rail crossing safety devices, signs, highway elements, and operational features,

(ii) Identifying, investigating, and analyzing hazardous or potentially hazardous transportation system safety problems, roadway locations, and features;

(iii) Establishing countermeasures and setting priorities to correct the identified hazards and potential hazards.

(3) Identification of focal points for all contacts at State, regional, tribal, and local levels to coordinate, develop, establish, and implement the SMS among the agencies.

(f) While the SMS applies to appropriate transportation systems providing access to and within National Forests and Grasslands funded under the FLHP, the extent of system requirements (e.g., data collection, analyses, and standards) for low volume roads may be tailored to be consistent with the functional classification of the roads. However, adequate requirements should be included for each roadway to provide for effective inclusion of safety decisions in the administration of the FH program.

[69 FR 9480, Feb. 27, 2004, as amended at 74 FR 28442, June 16, 2009]

§971.214 Federal lands congestion management system (CMS).

(a) For purposes of this section, congestion means the level at which transportation system performance is no longer acceptable due to traffic interference. For portions of the FH network outside the boundaries of TMAs, the tri-party partnership shall:

(1) Develop criteria to determine when a CMS is to be implemented for a specific FH; and

(2) Have CMS coverage for the transportation systems providing access to and within National Forests, as appropriate, that meet minimum CMS criteria.

[3] "Safety Management Systems: Good Practices for Development and Implementation," FHWA and NHTSA, May 1996, may be obtained at the FHWA, Office of Safety, 1200 New Jersey Avenue, SE., Washington, DC 20590, or electronically at *http://safety.fhwa.dot.gov/media/documents.htm.* It is available for inspection and copying as prescribed at 49 CFR part 7.

(b) The tri-party partnership shall consider the results of the CMS when selecting the implementation of strategies that provide the most efficient and effective use of existing and future transportation facilities.

(c) In addition to the requirements provided in § 971.204, the CMS must meet the following requirements:

(1) For those FH transportation systems that require a CMS, in both metropolitan and non-metropolitan areas, consideration shall be given to strategies that reduce private automobile travel and improve existing transportation efficiency. Approaches may include the use of alternative mode studies and implementation plans as components of the CMS.

(2) A CMS will:

(i) Identify and document measures for congestion (e.g., level of service);

(ii) Identify the causes of congestion;

(iii) Include processes for evaluating the cost and effectiveness of alternative strategies to manage congestion;

(iv) Identify the anticipated benefits of appropriate alternative traditional and nontraditional congestion management strategies;

(v) Determine methods to monitor and evaluate the performance of the multi-modal transportation system; and

(vi) Appropriately consider the following example categories of strategies, or combinations of strategies for each area:

(A) Transportation demand management measures;

(B) Traffic operational improvements;

(C) Public transportation improvements;

(D) ITS technologies; and

(E) Additional system capacity.

PART 972—FISH AND WILDLIFE SERVICE MANAGEMENT SYSTEMS

Subpart A—Definitions

Subpart B—Fish and Wildlife Service Management Systems

AUTHORITY: 23 U.S.C. 204, 315; 42 U.S.C. 7410 *et seq.;* 49 CFR 1.48.

SOURCE: 69 FR 9487, Feb. 27, 2004, unless otherwise noted.

Subpart A—Definitions

§ 972.100 Purpose.

The purpose of this subpart is to provide definitions for terms used in this part.

§ 972.102 Applicability.

The definitions in this subpart are applicable to this part, except as otherwise provided.

§ 972.104 Definitions.

Alternative transportation systems means modes of transportation other than private vehicles, including methods to improve system performance such as transportation demand management, congestion management, and intelligent transportation systems. These mechanisms help reduce the use of private vehicles and thus improve overall efficiency of transportation systems and facilities.

Elements mean the components of a bridge important from a structural, user, or cost standpoint. Examples are decks, joints, bearings, girders, abutments, and piers.

Federal lands bridge management system (BMS) means a systematic process used by the Forest Service (FS), the Fish and Wildlife Service (FWS) and the National Park Service (NPS) for analyzing bridge data to make forecasts and recommendations, and provides the means by which bridge maintenance, rehabilitation, and replacement programs and policies may be effectively considered.

Federal lands congestion management system (CMS) means a systematic process used by the FS, FWS and NPS for managing congestion that provides information on transportation system performance and alternative strategies for alleviating congestion and enhancing the mobility of persons and goods to levels that meet Federal, State and local needs.

Federal Lands Highway Program (FLHP) means a federally funded program established in 23 U.S.C. 204 to address transportation needs of Federal and Indian lands.

Federal lands pavement management system (PMS) means a systematic process used by the FS, FWS and NPS that provides information for use in implementing cost-effective pavement reconstruction, rehabilitation, and preventive maintenance programs and policies and that results in pavement designed to accommodate current and forecasted traffic in a safe, durable, and cost-effective manner.

Federal lands safety management system (SMS) means a systematic process used by the FS, FWS and NPS with the goal of reducing the number and severity of traffic accidents by ensuring that all opportunities to improve roadway safety are identified, considered, implemented and evaluated as appropriate, during all phases of highway planning, design, construction, operation and maintenance, by providing information for selecting and implementing effective highway safety strategies and projects.

Fish and Wildlife Service transportation plan means the official Fish and Wildlife Service-wide multimodal transportation plan that is developed through the Fish and Wildlife Service transportation planning process pursuant to 23 U.S.C. 204.

Highway safety means the reduction of traffic accidents, and deaths, injuries, and property damage resulting therefrom, on public roads.

Intelligent transportation system (ITS) means electronics, communications, or information processing used singly or in combination to improve the efficiency and safety of a surface transportation system.

Life-cycle cost analysis means an evaluation of costs incurred over the life of a project allowing a comparative analysis between or among various alternatives. Life-cycle cost analysis promotes consideration of total cost, to include maintenance and operation expenditures. Comprehensive life-cycle costs analysis includes all economic variables essential to the evaluation: User costs such as delay and safety costs associated with maintenance and rehabilitation projects, agency capital cost, and life-cycle maintenance costs.

Metropolitan planning area means the geographic area in which the metropolitan transportation planning process required by 23 U.S.C. 134 and 49 U.S.C. 5303–5306 must be carried out.

Metropolitan planning organization (MPO) means the forum for cooperative transportation decision-making for the metropolitan planning area pursuant to 23 U.S.C. 134 and 49 U.S.C. 5303.

National Wildlife Refuge System (Refuge System) means all the lands and waters reported by the FWS as being part of the National Wildlife Refuge System in the annual "Report of Lands Under Control of the U.S. FWS."[1] Included in the Refuge System are those lands that are generally known as refuges, waterfowl production areas, wetland management districts, and coordination areas.

Operations means those activities associated with managing, controlling, and regulating highway traffic.

Refuge road means a public road that provides access to or is located within a unit of the National Wildlife Refuge System and for which title and maintenance responsibilities are vested in the United States Government.

Refuge Roads Program means the funds allocated each fiscal year, as described in 23 U.S.C. 202(e) and 23 U.S.C. 204(k).

---

[1] "Report of Lands under Control of the U.S. FWS," U.S. FWS, (published annually on September 30). A free copy is available from the U.S. FWS, Division of Realty, 4401 N. Fairfax Drive, Suite 622, Arlington, VA 22203; telephone: (703) 358–1713.

Refuge Roads transportation improvement program (RRTIP) means a staged, multiyear, multimodal program of transportation projects for the Refuge Roads Program consistent with the Fish and Wildlife Service transportation plan and planning processes pursuant to 23 U.S.C. 204(a) and (k).

Secretary means the Secretary of Transportation.

State means any one of the fifty States, the District of Columbia, or Puerto Rico.

Transportation facilities means roads, streets, bridges, parking areas, transit vehicles, and other related transportation infrastructure.

Transportation Management Area (TMA) means an urbanized area with a population over 200,000 (as determined by the latest decennial census) or other area when TMA designation is requested by the Governor and the MPO (or affected local officials), and officially designated by the Administrators of the Federal Highway Administration and the Federal Transit Administration. The TMA designation applies to the entire metropolitan planning area(s).

Subpart B—Fish and Wildlife Service Management Systems

§ 972.200 Purpose.

The purpose of this subpart is to implement 23 U.S.C. 204 which requires the Secretary and the Secretary of each appropriate Federal land management agency, to the extent appropriate, to develop by rule safety, bridge, pavement, and congestion management systems for roads funded under the FLHP.

§ 972.202 Applicability.

The provisions in this subpart are applicable to the Fish and Wildlife Service (FWS) and the Federal Highway Administration (FHWA) that are responsible for satisfying these requirements for management systems pursuant to 23 U.S.C. 204.

§ 972.204 Management systems requirements.

(a) The FWS shall develop, establish and implement the management systems as described in this subpart. The FWS may tailor the management systems to meet the FWS goals, policies, and needs using professional engineering and planning judgment to determine the required nature and extent of systems coverage consistent with the intent and requirements of this rule.

(b) The FWS and the FHWA shall develop an implementation plan for each of the management systems. These plans will include, but are not limited to, the following: Overall goals and policies concerning the management systems, each agency's responsibilities for developing and implementing the management systems, implementation schedule, data sources, and cost estimate. The FHWA will provide the FWS ongoing technical engineering support for the development, implementation, and maintenance of the management systems.

(c) The FWS shall develop and implement procedures for the development, establishment, implementation and operation of management systems. The procedures shall include:

(1) A process for ensuring the results of any of the management systems are considered in the development of FWS transportation plans and transportation improvement programs and in making project selection decisions under 23 U.S.C. 204;

(2) A process for the analyses and coordination of all management system outputs to systematically operate, maintain, and upgrade existing transportation assets cost-effectively;

(3) A description of each management system;

(4) A process to operate and maintain the management systems and their associated databases; and

(5) A process for data collection, processing, analysis and updating for each management system.

(d) All management systems will use databases with a geographical reference system that can be used to geolocate all database information.

(e) Existing data sources may be used by the FWS to the maximum extent possible to meet the management system requirements.

(f) The FWS shall develop an appropriate means to evaluate the effectiveness of the management systems in enhancing transportation decision-making and improving the overall efficiency of the affected federally owned transportation systems and facilities. This evaluation is to be conducted periodically, preferably as part of the comprehensive resource conservation planning process.

(g) The management systems shall be operated so investment decisions based on management system outputs can be accomplished at the regional level.

§ 972.206 Funds for establishment, development, and implementation of the systems.

The Refuge Roads program funds may be used for development, establishment, and implementation of the management systems. These funds are to be administered in accordance with the procedures and requirements applicable to the funds.

§ 972.208 Federal lands pavement management system (PMS).

In addition to the requirements provided in § 972.204, the PMS must meet the following requirements:

(a) The FWS shall, at a minimum, have PMS coverage of all paved refuge roads and other associated facilities, as appropriate, funded under the FLHP.

(b) The PMS may be based on the concepts described in the AASHTO's "Pavement Management Guide."[2]

(c) The PMS may be utilized at various levels of technical complexity depending on the nature of the pavement network. These different levels may depend on mileages, functional classes, volumes, loadings, usage, surface type, or other criteria the FWS deems appropriate.

(d) The PMS shall be designed to fit the FWS goals, policies, criteria, and needs using the following components, at a minimum, as a basic framework for a PMS:

(1) A database and an ongoing program for the collection and maintenance of the inventory, inspection, cost, and supplemental data needed to support the PMS. The minimum PMS database shall include:

(i) An inventory of the physical pavement features including the number of lanes, length, width, surface type, functional classification, and shoulder information;

(ii) A history of project dates and types of construction, reconstruction, rehabilitation, and preventive maintenance. If some of the inventory or historic data are difficult to establish, it may be collected when preservation or reconstruction work is performed;

(iii) A condition survey that includes ride, distress, rutting, and surface friction (as appropriate);

(iv) Traffic information including volumes and vehicle classification (as appropriate); and

(v) Data for estimating the costs of actions.

(2) A system for applying network level analytical procedures that are capable of analyzing data for all FWS managed transportation facilities in the inventory or any subset. The minimum analyses shall include:

(i) A pavement condition analysis that includes ride, distress, rutting, and surface friction (as appropriate);

(ii) A pavement performance analysis that includes present and predicted performance and an estimate of the remaining service life (performance and remaining service life to be developed with time); and

(iii) An investment analysis that:

(A) Identifies alternative strategies to improve pavement conditions;

(B) Estimates costs of any pavement improvement strategy;

(C) Determines maintenance, repair, and rehabilitation strategies for pavements using life-cycle cost analysis or a comparable procedure;

(D) Provides short and long term budget forecasting; and

(E) Recommends optimal allocation of limited funds by developing a prioritized list of candidate projects over a predefined planning horizon (both short and long term).

[2] "Pavement Management Guide," AASHTO, 2001, is available for inspection as prescribed at 49 CFR part 7. It is also available from the American Association of State Highway and Transportation Officials (AASHTO), Publication Order Dept., P.O. Box 96716, Washington, DC 20090–6716 or online at *http://www.transportation.org/publications/bookstore.nsf.*

(e) For any FWS managed transportation facilities in the inventory or subset thereof, PMS reporting requirements shall include, but are not limited to, percentage of roads in good, fair, and poor condition.

§ 972.210 Federal lands bridge management system (BMS).

In addition to the requirements provided in § 972.204, the BMS must meet the following requirements:

(a) The FWS shall have a BMS for bridges which are under the FWS jurisdiction, funded under the FLHP, and required to be inventoried and inspected under 23 CFR 650, subpart C, National Bridge Inspection Standards (NBIS).

(b) The BMS shall be designed to fit the FWS goals, policies, criteria, and needs using the following components, as a minimum, as a basic framework for a BMS:

(1) A database and an ongoing program for the collection and maintenance of the inventory, inspection, cost, and supplemental data needed to support the BMS. The minimum BMS database shall include:

(i) The inventory data required by the NBIS (23 CFR 650, subpart C);

(ii) Data characterizing the severity and extent of deterioration of bridge elements;

(iii) Data for estimating the cost of improvement actions;

(iv) Traffic information including volumes and vehicle classification (as appropriate); and

(v) A history of conditions and actions taken on each bridge, excluding minor or incidental maintenance.

(2) Analytical procedures that are capable of analyzing data for all bridges in the inventory or any subset. These procedures include, as appropriate, such factors as bridge condition, recommended repairs/replacement and estimated costs, prediction of the estimated remaining life of the bridge, development of a prioritized list of candidate projects over a specified planning horizon, and budget forecasting.

(c) For any bridge in the inventory or subset thereof, BMS reporting requirements shall include, but are not limited to, percentage of non-deficient bridges.

§ 972.212 Federal lands safety management system (SMS).

In addition to the requirements provided in § 972.204, the SMS must meet the following requirements:

(a) The FWS shall have an SMS for all transportation facilities serving the Refuge System, as appropriate, funded under the FLHP.

(b) The FWS SMS may be based on the guidance in "Safety Management Systems: Good Practices for Development and Implementation."[3]

(c) The FWS shall utilize the SMS to ensure that safety is considered and implemented as appropriate in all phases of transportation system planning, design, construction, maintenance, and operations.

(d) The SMS may be utilized at various levels of complexity depending on the nature of the transportation facility involved.

(e) The SMS shall be designed to fit the FWS goals, policies, criteria, and needs using, as a minimum, the following components as a basic framework for a SMS:

(1) An ongoing program for the collection, maintenance and reporting of a database that includes:

(i) Accident records with sufficient detail for analysis such as accident type using standard reporting descriptions (e.g., right-angle, rear-end, head-on, pedestrian-related, etc.), location, description of event, severity, weather and cause;

(ii) An inventory of safety appurtenances such as signs, delineators, and guardrails (including terminals);

(iii) Traffic information including volumes and vehicle classification (as appropriate); and

(iv) Accident rates by customary criteria such as location, roadway classification, and vehicle miles of travel.

(2) Development, establishment and implementation of procedures for:

[3] "Safety Management Systems: Good Practices for Development and Implementation," FHWA and NHTSA, May 1996, may be obtained at the FHWA, Office of Safety, 1200 New Jersey Avenue, SE., Washington, DC 20590, or electronically at *http://safety.fhwa.dot.gov/media/documents.htm*. It is available for inspection and copying as prescribed at 49 CFR part 7.

(i) Routinely maintaining and upgrading safety appurtenances including highway-rail crossing warning devices, signs, highway elements, and operational features where appropriate; and

(ii) Identifying and investigating hazardous or potentially hazardous transportation system safety problems, roadway locations and features, then establishing countermeasures and setting priorities to correct the identified hazards and potential hazards.

(3) A process for communication, coordination, and cooperation among the organizations responsible for the roadway, human, and vehicle safety elements; and

(4) Development and implementation of public information and education activities on safety needs, programs, and countermeasures which affect safety on the FWS transportation systems.

(f) While the SMS applies to appropriate transportation facilities serving the Refuge System funded under the FLHP, the extent of system requirements (e.g., data collection, analyses, and standards) for low volume roads may be tailored to be consistent with the functional classification of the roads. However, sufficient detail should be included for each functional classification to provide adequate information for use in making safety decisions in the RR program.

[69 FR 9487, Feb. 27, 2004, as amended at 74 FR 28442, June 16, 2009]

§972.214 Federal lands congestion management system (CMS).

(a) For purposes of this section, congestion means the level at which transportation system performance is no longer acceptable due to traffic interference. For those FWS transportation systems that require a CMS, in both metropolitan and non-metropolitan areas, consideration shall be given to strategies that reduce private automobile travel and improve existing transportation system efficiency. Approaches may include the use of alternate mode studies and implementation plans as components of the CMS. The FWS shall consider the results of the CMS when selecting the implementation of strategies that provide the most efficient and effective use of existing and future transportation facilities, and alleviate congestion.

(b) In addition to the requirements provided in §972.204, the CMS must meet the following requirements:

(1) For portions of the FWS transportation system within TMAs, the FWS transportation planning process shall include a CMS that meets the requirements of this section. By agreement between the TMA and the FWS, the TMA's CMS coverage may include the transportation facilities serving the Refuge System, as appropriate. Through this agreement(s), the FWS may meet the requirements of this section.

(2) If congestion exists at a FWS facility within the boundaries of a TMA, and the TMA's CMS does not provide coverage of the portions of the FWS transportation facilities experiencing congestion, the FWS shall develop a separate CMS to cover those facilities.

(3) For portions of the FWS transportation system outside the boundaries of TMAs, the FWS shall:

(i) Develop criteria to determine when a CMS is to be implemented for a specific transportation system; and

(ii) Have CMS coverage for all transportation facilities serving the Refuge System, as appropriate, funded through the FLHP that meet minimum CMS needs criteria.

(4) A CMS will:

(i) Identify and document measures for congestion (e.g., level of service);

(ii) Identify the causes of congestion;

(iii) Include processes for evaluating the cost and effectiveness of alternative strategies to manage congestion;

(iv) Identify the anticipated benefits of appropriate alternative traditional and nontraditional congestion management strategies;

(v) Determine methods to monitor and evaluate the performance of the multi-modal transportation system;

(vi) Appropriately consider the following example categories of strategies, or combinations of strategies for each area:

(A) Transportation demand management measures;

(B) Traffic operational improvements;

(C) Public transportation improvements;

(D) ITS technologies;

(E) Additional system capacity; and

(vii) Provide information supporting the implementation of actions.

PART 973—MANAGEMENT SYSTEMS PERTAINING TO THE BUREAU OF INDIAN AFFAIRS AND THE INDIAN RESERVATION ROADS PROGRAM

AUTHORITY: 23 U.S.C. 204, 315, 42 U.S.C. 7410 *et seq.;* 49 CFR 1.48.

SOURCE: 69 FR 9499, Feb. 27, 2004, unless otherwise noted.

Subpart A—Definitions

§ 973.100 Purpose.

The purpose of this subpart is to provide definitions for terms used in this part.

§ 973.102 Applicability.

The definitions in this subpart are applicable to this part, except as otherwise provided.

§ 973.104 Definitions.

Alternative transportation systems means modes of transportation other than private vehicles, including methods to improve system performance such as transportation demand management, congestion management, and intelligent transportation systems. These mechanisms help reduce the use of private vehicles and thus improve overall efficiency of transportation systems and facilities.

Elements means the components of a bridge important from a structural, user, or cost standpoint. Examples are decks, joints, bearings, girders, abutments, and piers.

Federal Lands Highway Program (FLHP) means a federally funded program established in 23 U.S.C. 204 to address transportation needs of Federal and Indian lands.

Indian lands bridge management system (BMS) means a systematic process used by the Bureau of Indian Affairs (BIA) or Indian Tribal Governments (ITGs) for analyzing bridge data to make forecasts and recommendations, and provides the means by which bridge maintenance, rehabilitation, and replacement programs and policies may be efficiently considered.

Indian lands congestion management system (CMS) means a systematic process used by the BIA or ITGs for managing congestion that provides information on transportation system performance and alternative strategies for alleviating congestion and enhancing the mobility of persons and goods to levels that meet Federal, State and local needs.

Indian lands pavement management system (PMS) means a systematic process used by the BIA or ITGs that provides information for use in implementing cost-effective pavement reconstruction, rehabilitation, and preventive maintenance programs and policies, and that results in pavement designed to accommodate current and forecasted traffic in a safe, durable, and cost-effective manner.

Indian lands safety management system (SMS) means a systematic process used by the BIA or ITGs with the goal of reducing the number and severity of traffic accidents by ensuring that all opportunities to improve roadway safety are identified, considered, implemented and evaluated, as appropriate, during all phases of highway planning, design, construction, operation and maintenance by providing information for selecting and implementing effective highway safety strategies and projects.

Indian reservation road (IRR) means a public road that is located within or provides access to an Indian reservation or Indian trust land or restricted Indian land that is not subject to fee title alienation without the approval of the Federal government, or Indian and Alaska Native villages, groups, or communities in which Indians and Alaskan Natives reside, whom the Secretary of the Interior has determined are eligible for services generally available to Indians under Federal laws specifically applicable to Indians.

Indian Reservation Roads (IRR) Program means a part of the FLHP established in 23 U.S.C. 204 to address the transportation needs of federally recognized ITGs.

Indian Reservation Roads transportation improvement program (IRRTIP) means a multi-year, financially constrained list by year, State, and tribe of IRR-funded projects selected by ITGs that are programmed for construction in the next 3 to 5 years.

Indian Reservation Roads transportation plan means a document setting out a tribe's long-range transportation priorities and needs. The IRR transportation plan, which can be developed by either the tribe or the BIA on behalf of that tribe, is developed through the IRR transportation planning process pursuant to 23 U.S.C. 204 and 25 CFR part 170.

Indian Tribal Government (ITG) means a duly formed governing body of an Indian or Alaska Native Tribe, Band, Nation, Pueblo, Village, or Community that the Secretary of the Interior acknowledges to exist as an Indian tribe pursuant to the Federally Recognized Indian Tribe List Act of 1994, 25 U.S.C. 479a.

Indian tribe (tribe) means any Indian tribe, nation, band, pueblo, rancheria, colony, or community, including any Alaska Native Village, or regional or village corporation as defined or established under the Alaska Native Claims Settlement Act which is federally recognized by the U.S. government for special programs and services provided by the Secretary of the Interior to Indians because of their status as Indians.

Intelligent transportation system (ITS) means electronics, communications, or information processing used singly or in combination to improve the efficiency and safety of a surface transportation system.

Life-cycle cost analysis means an evaluation of costs incurred over the life of a project allowing a comparative analysis between or among various alternatives. Life-cycle cost analysis promotes consideration of total cost, to include maintenance and operation expenditures. Comprehensive life-cycle cost analysis includes all economic variables essential to the evaluation: Safety costs associated with maintenance and rehabilitation projects, agency capital cost, and life-cycle maintenance costs.

Operations means those activities associated with managing, controlling, and regulating highway traffic.

Secretary means the Secretary of Transportation.

Serviceability means the degree to which a bridge provides satisfactory service from the point of view of its users.

State means any one of the fifty States, the District of Columbia, or Puerto Rico.

Transportation facilities means roads, streets, bridges, parking areas, transit vehicles, and other related transportation infrastructure.

Subpart B—Bureau of Indian Affairs Management Systems

§ 973.200 Purpose.

The purpose of this subpart is to implement 23 U.S.C. 204 which requires the Secretary and the Secretary of each appropriate Federal land management agency to the extent appropriate, to develop by rule safety, bridge, pavement, and congestion management systems for roads funded under the FLHP.

§ 973.202 Applicability.

The provisions in this subpart are applicable to the Bureau of Indian Affairs (BIA), the Federal Highway Administration (FHWA), and the Indian Tribal Governments (ITGs) that are responsible for satisfying these requirements for management systems pursuant to 23 U.S.C. 204.

§ 973.204 Management systems requirements.

(a) The BIA, in consultation with the tribes, shall develop, establish and implement nationwide pavement, bridge, and safety management systems for federally and tribally owned IRRs. The BIA may tailor the nationwide management systems to meet the agency's goals, policies, and needs, after considering the input from the tribes, and using professional engineering and planning judgment to determine the required nature and extent of systems coverage consistent with the intent and requirements of this rule.

(b) The BIA and the FHWA, in consultation with the tribes, shall develop an implementation plan for each of the nationwide management systems. These plans will include, but are not limited to, the following: Overall goals and policies concerning the nationwide management systems, each agency's responsibilities for developing and implementing the nationwide management systems, implementation schedule, data sources, including the need to accommodate State and local data, and cost estimate.

(c) Indian tribes may develop, establish, and implement tribal management systems under a self-determination contract or self-governance annual funding agreement. The tribe may tailor the management systems to meet its goals, policies, and needs, using professional engineering and planning judgment to determine the required nature and extent of systems coverage consistent with the intent and requirements of this rule.

(d) The BIA, in consultation with the tribes, shall develop criteria for cases in which tribal management systems are not appropriate.

(e) The BIA, in consultation with the tribes, or the tribes under a self-determination contract or self-governance annual funding agreement, may incorporate data provided by States and local governments into the nationwide or tribal management systems, as appropriate, for State and locally owned IRRs.

(f) The BIA, in consultation with the tribes, shall develop and implement procedures for the development, establishment, implementation and operation of nationwide management systems. If a tribe develops tribal management systems, the tribe shall develop and implement procedures for the development, establishment, implementation and operation of tribal management systems. The procedures shall include:

(1) A description of each management system;

(2) A process to operate and maintain the management systems and their associated databases;

(3) A process for data collection, processing, analysis and updating for each management system;

(4) A process for ensuring the results of the management systems are considered in the development of IRR transportation plans and transportation improvement programs and in making project selection decisions under 23 U.S.C. 204; and

(5) A process for the analysis and coordination of all management systems outputs to systematically operate, maintain, and upgrade existing transportation assets cost-effectively;

(g) All management systems shall use databases with a common or coordinated reference system that can be used to geolocate all database information.

(h) Existing data sources may be used by the BIA and the tribes to the maximum extent possible to meet the management system requirements.

(i) A nationwide congestion management system is not required. The BIA and the FHWA, in consultation with the tribes, shall develop criteria for determining when congestion management systems are required for BIA or tribal transportation facilities providing access to and within the Indian reservations. Either the tribes or the BIA, in consultation with the tribes, shall develop, establish and implement congestion management systems for the transportation facilities that meet the criteria.

(j) The BIA shall develop an appropriate means to evaluate the effectiveness of the nationwide management systems in enhancing transportation investment decisions and improving the overall efficiency of the affected transportation systems and facilities.

This evaluation is to be conducted periodically, preferably as part of the BIA planning process to assist the FHWA in evaluating the efficiency and effectiveness of the management systems as a component of the IRR program, and may include consultation with the tribes, as appropriate.

(k) The management systems shall be operated so investment decisions based on management system outputs can be accomplished at the BIA region and tribal level and can be utilized throughout the transportation planning process.

§973.206 Funds for establishment, development, and implementation of the systems.

The IRR program management funds may be used to accomplish nationwide management system activities. For tribal management system activities, the IRR two percent tribal transportation planning or construction funds may be used. (Refer to 23 U.S.C. 204(b) and 204(j)). These funds are to be administered in accordance with the procedures and requirements applicable to the funds.

§973.208 Indian lands pavement management system (PMS).

In addition to the requirements provided in §973.204, the PMS must meet the following requirements:

(a) The BIA shall have PMS coverage for all federally and tribally owned, paved IRRs included in the IRR inventory.

(b) Where a tribe collects data for the tribe's PMS, the tribe shall provide the data to the BIA to be used in the nationwide PMS.

(c) The nationwide and tribal PMSs may be based on the concepts described in the AASHTO's "Pavement Management Guide."[1]

(d) The nationwide and tribal PMSs may be utilized at various levels of technical complexity depending on the nature of the pavement network. These different levels may depend on mileage, functional classes, volumes, loading, usage, surface type, or other criteria the BIA and ITGs deem appropriate.

(e) A PMS shall be designed to fit the BIA's or tribes' goals, policies, criteria, and needs using the following components, at a minimum, as a basic framework for a PMS:

(1) A database and an ongoing program for the collection and maintenance of the inventory, inspection, cost, and supplemental data needed to support the PMS. The minimum PMS database shall include:

(i) An inventory of the physical pavement features including the number of lanes, length, width, surface type, functional classification, and shoulder information;

(ii) A history of project dates and types of construction, reconstruction, rehabilitation, and preventive maintenance. If some of the inventory or historic data is difficult to establish, it may be collected when preservation or reconstruction work is performed;

(iii) A condition survey that includes ride, distress, rutting, and surface friction (as appropriate);

(iv) Traffic information including volumes and vehicle classification (as appropriate); and

(v) Data for estimating the costs of actions.

(2) A system for applying network level analytical procedures that are capable of analyzing data for all federally and tribally owned IRR in the inventory or any subset. The minimum analyses shall include:

(i) A pavement condition analysis that includes ride, distress, rutting, and surface friction (as appropriate);

(ii) A pavement performance analysis that includes present and predicted performance and an estimate of the remaining service life (performance and remaining service life to be developed with time); and

(iii) An investment analysis that:

(A) Identifies alternative strategies to improve pavement conditions;

(B) Estimates costs of any pavement improvement strategy;

[1] "Pavement Management Guide," AASHTO, 2001, is available for inspection as prescribed at 49 CFR part 7. It is also available from the American Association of State Highway and Transportation Officials (AASHTO), Publication Order Dept., P.O. Box 96716, Washington, DC 20090–6716 or online at *http://www.transportation.org/publications/bookstore.nsf.*

(C) Determines maintenance, repair, and rehabilitation strategies for pavements using life cycle cost analysis or a comparable procedure;

(D) Performs short and long term budget forecasting; and

(E) Recommends optimal allocation of limited funds by developing a prioritized list of candidate projects over a predefined planning horizon (both short and long term).

(f) For any roads in the inventory or subset thereof, PMS reporting requirements shall include, but are not limited to, percentage of roads in good, fair, and poor condition.

§ 973.210 Indian lands bridge management system (BMS).

In addition to the requirements provided in § 973.204, the BMS must meet the following requirements:

(a) The BIA shall have a nationwide BMS for the federally and tribally owned IRR bridges that are funded under the FLHP and required to be inventoried and inspected under 23 CFR 650, subpart C, National Bridge Inspection Standards (NBIS).

(b) Where a tribe collects data for the tribe's BMS, the tribe shall provide the data to the BIA to be used in the nationwide BMS.

(c) The nationwide and tribal BMSs may be based on the concepts described in the AASHTO's "Guidelines for Bridge Management Systems."[2]

(d) A BMS shall be designed to fit the BIA's or tribe's goals, policies, criteria, and needs using the following components, as a minimum, as a basic framework for a BMS:

(1) A database and an ongoing program for the collection and maintenance of the inventory, inspection, cost, and supplemental data needed to support the BMS. The minimum BMS database shall include:

(i) The inventory data described by the NBIS (23 CFR part 650, subpart C);

(ii) Data characterizing the severity and extent of deterioration of bridge components;

(iii) Data for estimating the cost of improvement actions;

(iv) Traffic information including volumes and vehicle classification (as appropriate); and

(v) A history of conditions and actions taken on each bridge, excluding minor or incidental maintenance.

(2) A systematic procedure for applying network level analytical procedures that are capable of analyzing data for all bridges in the inventory or any subset. The minimum analyses shall include:

(i) A prediction of performance and estimate of the remaining service life of structural and other key elements of each bridge, both with and without intervening actions; and

(ii) A recommendation for optimal allocation of limited funds by developing a prioritized list of candidate projects over a predefined planning horizon (both short and long term).

(e) The BMS may include the capability to perform an investment analysis (as appropriate, considering size of structure, traffic volume, and structural condition). The investment analysis may include the ability to:

(1) Identify alternative strategies to improve bridge condition, safety and serviceability;

(2) Estimate the costs of any strategies ranging from maintenance of individual elements to full bridge replacement;

(3) Determine maintenance, repair, and rehabilitation strategies for bridge elements using life cycle cost analysis or a comparable procedure; and

(4) Perform short and long term budget forecasting.

(f) For any bridge in the inventory or subset thereof, BMS reporting requirements shall include, but are not limited to, percentage of non-deficient bridges.

§ 973.212 Indian lands safety management system (SMS).

In addition to the requirements provided in § 973.204, the SMS must meet the following requirements:

(a) The BIA shall have a nationwide SMS for all federally and tribally

[2] "Guidelines for Bridge Management Systems," AASHTO, 1993, is available for inspection as prescribed at 49 CFR part 7. It is also available from the American Association of State Highway and Transportation Officials (AASHTO), Publication Order Dept., P.O. Box 96716, Washington, DC 20090–6716 or online at *http://www.transportation.org/publications/bookstore.nsf*.

owned IRR and public transit facilities included in the IRR inventory.

(b) Where a tribe collects data for the tribe's SMS, the tribe shall provide the data to the BIA to be used in the nationwide SMS.

(c) The nationwide and tribal SMS may be based on the guidance in "Safety Management Systems: Good Practices for Development and Implementation."[3]

(d) The BIA and ITGs shall utilize the SMSs to ensure that safety is considered and implemented as appropriate in all phases of transportation system planning, design, construction, maintenance, and operations.

(e) The nationwide and tribal SMSs may be utilized at various levels of complexity depending on the nature of the IRR facility involved.

(f) An SMS shall be designed to fit the BIA's or ITG's goals, policies, criteria, and needs using, as a minimum, the following components as a basic framework for an SMS:

(1) A database and an ongoing program for the collection and maintenance of the inventory, inspection, cost, and supplemental data needed to support the SMS. The minimum SMS database shall include:

(i) Accident records;

(ii) An inventory of safety hardware including signs, guardrails, and lighting appurtenances (including terminals); and

(iii) Traffic information including volume and vehicle classification (as appropriate).

(2) Development, establishment and implementation of procedures for:

(i) Routinely maintaining and upgrading safety appurtenances including highway-rail crossing warning devices, signs, highway elements, and operational features where appropriate;

(ii) Routinely maintaining and upgrading safety features of transit facilities;

(iii) Identifying and investigating hazardous or potentially hazardous transportation system safety problems, roadway locations and features; and

(iv) Establishing countermeasures and setting priorities to correct the identified hazards and potential hazards.

(3) A process for communication, coordination, and cooperation among the organizations responsible for the roadway, human, and vehicle safety elements;

(4) Development and implementation of public information and education activities on safety needs, programs, and countermeasures which affect safety on the BIA's and ITG's transportation systems; and

(5) Identification of skills, resources and training needs to implement safety programs for highway and transit facilities and the development of a program to carry out necessary training.

(g) While the SMS applies to all federally and tribally owned IRRs in the IRR inventory, the extent of system requirements (e.g., data collection, analyses, and standards) for low volume roads may be tailored to be consistent with the functional classification of the roads. However, adequate requirements should be included for each BIA functional classification to provide for effective inclusion of safety decisions in the administration of transportation by the BIA and ITGs.

(h) For any transportation facilities in the IRR inventory or subset thereof, SMS reporting requirements shall include, but are not limited to, the following:

(1) Accident types such as right-angle, rear-end, left turn, head-on, sideswipe, pedestrian-related, run-off-road, fixed object, and parked vehicle;

(2) Accident severity per year measured as number of accidents with fatalities, injuries, and property damage only; and

(3) Accident rates measured as number of accidents (fatalities, injuries, and property damage only) per 100 million vehicle miles of travel, number of accidents (fatalities, injuries, and property damage only) per 1000 vehicles, or

[3] "Safety Management Systems: Good Practices for Development and Implementation," FHWA and NHTSA, May 1996, may be obtained at the FHWA, Office of Safety, 1200 New Jersey Avenue, SE., Washington, DC 20590, or electronically at *http://safety.fhwa.dot.gov/media/documents.htm.* It is available for inspection and copying as prescribed at 49 CFR part 7.

number of accidents (fatalities, injuries, and property damage only) per mile.

[69 FR 9499, Feb. 27, 2004, as amended at 74 FR 28442, June 16, 2009]

§ 973.214 Indian lands congestion management system (CMS).

(a) For purposes of this section, congestion means the level at which transportation system performance is no longer acceptable due to traffic interference. The BIA and the FHWA, in consultation with the tribes, shall develop criteria to determine when a CMS is to be implemented for a specific federally or tribally owned IRR transportation system that is experiencing congestion. Either the tribe or the BIA, in consultation with the tribe, shall consider the results of the CMS in the development of the IRR transportation plan and the IRRTIP, when selecting strategies for implementation that provide the most efficient and effective use of existing and future transportation facilities to alleviate congestion and enhance mobility.

(b) In addition to the requirements provided in § 973.204, the CMS must meet the following requirements:

(1) For those BIA or tribal transportation systems that require a CMS, consideration shall be given to strategies that reduce private automobile travel and improve existing transportation system efficiency. Approaches may include the use of alternate mode studies and implementation plans as components of the CMS.

(2) A CMS will:

(i) Identify and document measures for congestion (e.g., level of service);

(ii) Identify the causes of congestion;

(iii) Include processes for evaluating the cost and effectiveness of alternative strategies;

(iv) Identify the anticipated benefits of appropriate alternative traditional and nontraditional congestion management strategies;

(v) Determine methods to monitor and evaluate the performance of the multi-modal transportation system; and

(vi) Appropriately consider the following example categories of strategies, or combinations of strategies for each area:

(A) Transportation demand management measures;

(B) Traffic operational improvements;

(C) Public transportation improvements;

(D) ITS technologies; and

(E) Additional system capacity.

PARTS 974–999 [RESERVED]

CHAPTER II—NATIONAL HIGHWAY TRAFFIC SAFETY ADMINISTRATION AND FEDERAL HIGHWAY ADMINISTRATION, DEPARTMENT OF TRANSPORTATION

SUBCHAPTER A—PROCEDURES FOR STATE HIGHWAY SAFETY PROGRAMS

PART 1200—UNIFORM PROCEDURES FOR STATE HIGHWAY SAFETY GRANT PROGRAMS

AUTHORITY: 23 U.S.C. 402; 23 U.S.C. 405; delegation of authority at 49 CFR 1.95.

SOURCE: 78 FR 5010, Jan. 23, 2013, unless otherwise noted.

Subpart A—General

§ 1200.1 Purpose.

This part establishes uniform procedures for State highway safety programs authorized under Chapter 4, Title 23, United States Code.

§ 1200.2 Applicability.

The provisions of this part apply to highway safety programs authorized under 23 U.S.C. 402 beginning fiscal year 2014 and, except as specified in § 1200.24(a), to national priority safety programs authorized under 23 U.S.C. 405 beginning fiscal year 2013.

§ 1200.3 Definitions.

As used in this part—

Approving Official means a Regional Administrator of the National Highway Traffic Safety Administration.

Carry-forward funds means those funds that a State has not expended on projects in the fiscal year in which they were apportioned or allocated, that are being brought forward and made available for expenditure in a subsequent fiscal year.

Contract authority means the statutory language that authorizes an agency to incur an obligation without the need for a prior appropriation or further action from Congress and which, when exercised, creates a binding obligation on the United States for which Congress must make subsequent liquidating appropriations.

Fiscal year means the Federal fiscal year, consisting of the 12 months beginning each October 1 and ending the following September 30.

Governor means the Governor of any of the fifty States, Puerto Rico, the U.S. Virgin Islands, Guam, American Samoa, or the Commonwealth of the Northern Mariana Islands, the Mayor of the District of Columbia, or, for the application of this part to Indian Country as provided in 23 U.S.C. 402(h), the Secretary of the Interior.

Governor's Representative for Highway Safety means the official appointed by the Governor to implement the State's highway safety program or, for the application of this part to Indian Country as provided in 23 U.S.C. 402(h), an official of the Bureau of Indian Affairs or other Department of Interior official who is duly designated by the Secretary of the Interior to implement the Indian highway safety program.

Highway Safety Plan (HSP) means the document, coordinated with the State strategic highway safety plan as defined in 23 U.S.C. 148(a), that the State submits each fiscal year as its application for highway safety grants, which describes the strategies and projects the State plans to implement and the resources from all sources it plans to use to achieve its highway safety performance targets.

Highway safety program means the planning, strategies and performance measures, and general oversight and management of highway safety strategies and projects by the State either directly or through sub-recipients to address highway safety problems in the State. A State highway safety program is defined in the annual Highway Safety Plan and any amendments.

MAP–21 or "Moving Ahead for Progress in the 21st Century Act" means Public Law 112–141.

NHTSA means the National Highway Traffic Safety Administration.

Program area means any of the national priority safety program areas identified in 23 U.S.C. 405 or a program area identified by the State in the highway safety plan as encompassing a major highway safety problem in the State and for which documented effective or projected by analysis to be effective countermeasures have been identified.

Project means any undertaking or activity proposed or implemented with grant funds under 23 U.S.C. Chapter 4.

Project agreement means a written agreement at the State level or between the State and a subgrantee or contractor under which the State agrees to provide 23 U.S.C. Chapter 4 funds in exchange for the subgrantee's or contractor's performance of one or more undertakings or activities supporting the highway safety program.

Project number means a unique identifier assigned by a State to each project in the HSP.

Public road means any road under the jurisdiction of and maintained by a public authority and open to public travel.

Section 402 means section 402 of title 23 of the United States Code.

Section 405 means section 405 of title 23 of the United States Code.

State means, except as provided in § 1200.25(b), any of the fifty States of the United States, the District of Columbia, Puerto Rico, the U.S. Virgin Islands, Guam, American Samoa, the Commonwealth of the Northern Mariana Islands, or, for the application of this part to Indian Country as provided in 23 U.S.C. 402(h), the Secretary of the Interior.

State highway safety improvement program means the program defined in section 148(a)(11) of title 23 of the United States Code.

State strategic highway safety plan means the plan defined in section 148(a)(12) of title 23, United States Code.

§ 1200.4 State Highway Safety Agency—Authority and functions.

(a) *Policy*. In order for a State to receive grant funds under this part, the Governor shall exercise responsibility for the highway safety program through a State Highway Safety Agency that has adequate powers and is suitably equipped and organized to carry out the State's highway safety program.

(b) *Authority*. Each State Highway Safety Agency shall be authorized to—

(1) Develop and execute the Highway Safety Plan and highway safety program in the State;

(2) Obtain information about programs to improve highway safety and projects administered by other State and local agencies;

(3) Maintain or have ready access to information contained in State highway safety data systems, including crash, citation, adjudication, emergency medical services/injury surveillance, roadway and vehicle record keeping systems, and driver license data;

(4) Periodically review and comment to the Governor on the effectiveness of programs to improve highway safety in the State from all funding sources that the State plans to use for such purposes;

(5) Provide financial and technical assistance to other State agencies and political subdivisions to develop and carry out highway safety strategies and projects; and

(6) Establish and maintain adequate staffing to effectively plan, manage, and provide oversight of highway safety projects approved in the Highway Safety Plan.

(c) *Functions*. Each State Highway Safety Agency shall—

(1) Develop and prepare the Highway Safety Plan based on evaluation of highway safety data, including crash fatalities and injuries, roadway, driver and other data sources to identify safety problems within the State;

(2) Establish highway safety projects to be funded within the State under 23 U.S.C. Chapter 4 based on identified safety problems and priorities;

(3) Provide direction, information and assistance to sub-grantees concerning highway safety grants, procedures for participation, and development of projects;

(4) Encourage and assist sub-grantees to improve their highway safety planning and administration efforts;

(5) Review and approve, and evaluate the implementation and effectiveness of State and local highway safety programs and projects from all funding sources that the State plans to use under the HSP, and approve and monitor the expenditure of grant funds awarded under 23 U.S.C. Chapter 4;

(6) Assess program performance through analysis of highway safety data and data-driven performance measures;

(7) Ensure that the State highway safety program meets the requirements of 23 U.S.C. Chapter 4 and applicable Federal and State laws, including but not limited to the standards for financial management systems required under 49 CFR 18.20;

(8) Ensure that all legally required audits of the financial operations of the State Highway Safety Agency and of the use of highway safety grant funds are conducted;

(9) Track and maintain current knowledge of changes in State statute or regulation that could affect State qualification for highway safety grants or fund transfer programs; and

(10) Coordinate the Highway Safety Plan and highway safety data collection and information systems activities with other federally and non-federally supported programs relating to or affecting highway safety, including the State strategic highway safety plan as defined in 23 U.S.C. 148(a).

§ 1200.5 Due dates—Interpretation.

If any deadline or due date in this part falls on a Saturday, Sunday or Federal holiday, the applicable deadline or due date shall be the next business day.

Subpart B—Highway Safety Plan

§ 1200.10 General.

Beginning with grants authorized in fiscal year 2014, to apply for any highway safety grant under 23 U.S.C. Chapter 4, a State shall submit a Highway Safety Plan meeting the requirements of this subpart.

§ 1200.11 Contents.

Each fiscal year, the State's Highway Safety Plan shall consist of the following components:

(a) *Highway safety planning process.* (1) A brief description of the data sources and processes used by the State to identify its highway safety problems, describe its highway safety performance measures and define its performance targets, develop and select evidence-based countermeasure strategies and projects to address its problems and achieve its performance targets. In describing these data sources and processes, the State shall identify the participants in the processes (e.g., highway safety committees, program stakeholders, community and constituent groups), discuss the strategies for project selection (e.g., constituent outreach, public meetings, solicitation of proposals), and list the information and data sources consulted (e.g., *Countermeasures That Work*, Sixth Edition, 2011).

(2) A description of the efforts to coordinate and the outcomes from the coordination of the highway safety plan, data collection, and information systems with the State strategic highway safety plan (as defined in 23 U.S.C. 148(a)).

(b) *Performance plan.* A performance plan containing the following elements:

(1) A list of annual quantifiable and measurable highway safety performance targets that is data-driven, consistent with the Uniform Guidelines for Highway Safety Program and based on highway safety problems identified by the State during the planning process conducted under paragraph (a) of this section.

(2) Performance measures developed by DOT in collaboration with the Governor's Highway Safety Association and others, beginning with the MAP–21 directed "Traffic Safety Performance Measures for States and Federal Agencies" (DOT HS 811 025), which are used as a minimum in developing the performance targets identified in paragraph (b)(1) of this section. Beginning with grants awarded after fiscal year 2014, the performance measures common to the State's HSP and the State highway safety improvement program (fatalities, fatality rate, and serious injuries) shall be defined identically, as coordinated through the State strategic highway safety plan. At least one performance measure and performance target that is data driven shall be provided for each program area that enables the State to track progress, from a specific baseline, toward meeting the target (e.g., a target to "increase seat belt use from X percent in Year 1 to Y percent in Year 2," using a performance measure of "percent of restrained occupants in front outboard seating positions in passenger motor vehicles"). For each performance measure, the State shall provide:

(i) Documentation of current safety levels;

(ii) Quantifiable annual performance targets; and

(iii) Justification for each performance target that explains why the target is appropriate and data-driven.

(3) Additional performance measures, not included under paragraph (b)(2) of this section. For program areas where performance measures have not been jointly developed, a State shall develop its own performance measures and performance targets that are data-driven (e.g., distracted driving, bicycles). The State shall provide the same information as required under paragraph (b)(2) of this section.

(c) *Highway safety strategies and projects.* A description of—

(1) Each countermeasure strategy and project the State plans to implement to reach the performance targets identified in paragraph (b) of this section. At a minimum, the State shall describe one year of Section 402 and 405 countermeasure strategies and projects (which should include countermeasure strategies identified in the State strategic highway safety plan) and shall identify funds from other sources, including Federal, State, local, and private sector funds, that the State plans to use for such projects or use to achieve program area performance targets.

(2) The State's process for selecting the countermeasure strategies and projects described in paragraph (c)(1) of this section to allow the State to meet the highway safety performance targets described in paragraph (b) of this

section. At a minimum, the State shall provide an assessment of the overall traffic safety impacts of the strategies chosen and proposed or approved projects to be funded.

(3) The data and data analysis or other documentation supporting the effectiveness of proposed countermeasure strategies described in paragraph (c)(1) of this section (e.g., the State may include information on the cost effectiveness of proposed countermeasure strategies, if such information is available).

(4) The evidence-based traffic safety enforcement program to prevent traffic violations, crashes, and crash fatalities and injuries in areas most at risk for such incidents. At a minimum, the State shall provide for—

(i) An analysis of crashes, crash fatalities, and injuries in areas of highest risk;

(ii) Deployment of resources based on that analysis; and

(iii) Continuous follow-up and adjustment of the enforcement plan.

(5) The planned high visibility enforcement strategies to support national mobilizations.

(d) *Performance report.* A program-area-level report on the State's success in meeting State performance targets from the previous fiscal year's Highway Safety Plan.

(e) *Program cost summary and list of projects.* (1) HS Form 217, meeting the requirements of Appendix B, completed to reflect the State's proposed allocations of funds (including carry-forward funds) by program area. The funding level used shall be an estimate of available funding for the upcoming fiscal year based on amounts authorized for the fiscal year and projected carry-forward funds.

(2) For each program area, an accompanying list of projects that the State proposes to conduct for that fiscal year and an estimated amount of Federal funds for each such project.

(f) *Certifications and assurances.* Appendix A—Certifications and Assurances for Section 402 Grants, signed by the Governor's Representative for Highway Safety, certifying the HSP application contents and providing assurances that the State will comply with applicable laws and regulations, financial and programmatic requirements, and, in accordance with §1200.13 of this part, the special funding conditions for the Section 402 program.

(g) *Teen Traffic Safety Program.* If the State elects to include the Teen Traffic Safety Program authorized under 23 U.S.C. 402(m), a description of projects that the State will conduct as part of the Teen Traffic Safety Program—a statewide program to improve traffic safety for teen drivers—and the assurances in Appendix C, signed by the Governor's Representative for Highway Safety.

(h) *Section 405 grant application.* Application for any of the national priority safety program grants, in accordance with the requirements of subpart C, including Appendix D—Certifications and Assurances for Section 405 Grants, signed by the Governor's Representative for Highway Safety.

§1200.12 Due date for submission.

(a) Except as specified under §1200.61(a), a State shall submit its Highway Safety Plan electronically to the NHTSA regional office no later than July 1 preceding the fiscal year to which the Highway Safety Plan applies.

(b) Failure to meet this deadline may result in delayed approval and funding of a State's Section 402 grant or disqualification from receiving Section 405 grants.

§1200.13 Special funding conditions for Section 402 grants.

The State's highway safety program under Section 402 shall be subject to the following conditions, and approval under §1200.14 of this part shall be deemed to incorporate these conditions:

(a) *Planning and administration costs.* (1) Federal participation in P&A activities shall not exceed 50 percent of the total cost of such activities, or the applicable sliding scale rate in accordance with 23 U.S.C. 120. The Federal contribution for P&A activities shall not exceed 13 percent of the total funds the State receives under 23 U.S.C. 402. In accordance with 23 U.S.C. 120(i), the Federal share payable for projects in the U.S. Virgin Islands, Guam, American Samoa and the Commonwealth of the Northern Mariana Islands shall be

100 percent. The Indian Country, as defined by 23 U.S.C. 402(h), is exempt from the provisions of P&A requirements. NHTSA funds shall be used only to finance P&A activities attributable to NHTSA programs. Determinations of P&A shall be in accordance with the provisions of Appendix F.

(2) P&A tasks and related costs shall be described in the P&A module of the State's Highway Safety Plan. The State's matching share shall be determined on the basis of the total P&A costs in the module.

(b) *Automated traffic enforcement systems prohibition.* The State may not expend funds apportioned to the State under 23 U.S.C. 402 to carry out a program to purchase, operate, or maintain an automated traffic enforcement system. The term "automated traffic enforcement system" includes any camera which captures an image of a vehicle for the purposes only of red light and speed enforcement, and does not include hand held radar and other devices operated by law enforcement officers to make an on-the-scene traffic stop, issue a traffic citation, or other enforcement action at the time of the violation.

§ 1200.14 Review and approval procedures.

(a) *General.* Upon receipt and initial review of the Highway Safety Plan, NHTSA may request additional information from a State to ensure compliance with the requirements of this part. Failure to respond promptly to a request for additional information concerning the Section 402 grant application may result in delayed approval and funding of a State's Section 402 grant. Failure to respond promptly to a request for additional information concerning any of the Section 405 grant applications may result in a State's disqualification from consideration for a Section 405 grant.

(b) *Approval and disapproval of Highway Safety Plan.* Within 60 days after receipt of the Highway Safety Plan under this subpart—

(1) For Section 402 grants, the Approving Official shall issue—

(i) A letter of approval with conditions, if any, to the Governor and the Governor's Representative for Highway Safety; or

(ii)(A) A letter of disapproval to the Governor and the Governor's Representative for Highway Safety informing the State of the reasons for disapproval and requiring resubmission of the Highway Safety Plan with proposed modifications necessary for approval; and

(B) A letter of approval or disapproval upon resubmission of the Highway Safety Plan within 30 days after NHTSA receives the revised Highway Safety Plan.

(2) For Section 405 grants—

(i) The NHTSA Administrator shall notify States in writing of Section 405 grant awards and specify any conditions or limitations imposed by law on the use of funds; or

(ii) The Approving Official shall notify States in writing if a State's application does not meet the qualification requirements for any of the Section 405 grants.

§ 1200.15 Apportionment and obligation of Federal funds.

(a) Except as provided in paragraph (b) of this section, on October 1 of each fiscal year, or soon thereafter, the NHTSA Administrator shall, in writing, distribute funds available for obligation under 23 U.S.C. Chapter 4 to the States and specify any conditions or limitations imposed by law on the use of the funds.

(b) In the event that authorizations exist but no applicable appropriation act has been enacted by October 1 of a fiscal year the NHTSA Administrator may, in writing, distribute a part of the funds authorized under 23 U.S.C. Chapter 4 contract authority to the States to ensure program continuity, and in that event shall specify any conditions or limitations imposed by law on the use of the funds. Upon appropriation of grant funds, the NHTSA Administrator shall, in writing, promptly adjust the obligation limitation, and specify any conditions or limitations imposed by law on the use of the funds.

(c) Funds distributed under paragraph (a) or (b) of this section shall be available for expenditure by the States to satisfy the Federal share of expenses under the approved Highway Safety

Plan, and shall constitute a contractual obligation of the Federal Government, subject to any conditions or limitations identified in the distributing document. Such funds shall be available for expenditure by the States as provided in § 1200.41(b), after which the funds shall lapse.

(d) Notwithstanding the provisions of paragraph (c) of this section—

(1) Reimbursement of State expenses for Section 402 grant funds shall be contingent upon the submission of an updated HS Form 217 and an updated project list that includes project numbers for each project within 30 days after the beginning of the fiscal year or the date of the written approval provided under § 1200.14(b)(1) of this part, whichever is later, and approval of the updated HS Form 217 by the Approving Official.

(2) Reimbursement of State expenses for Section 405 grant funds shall be contingent upon the submission of an updated Highway Safety Plan, HS Form 217, and project list to address the grant funds awarded under subpart C, within 30 days after the beginning of the fiscal year or the date of the grant award notice provided under § 1200.14(b)(2), whichever is later, and approval of the updated Highway Safety Plan and HS Form 217 by the Approving Official. Submitting the updated Highway Safety Plan and HS Form 217 is a precondition to reimbursement of grant expenses.

(3) The updated HS Form 217 required under paragraphs (d)(1) and (d)(2) of this section shall reflect the State's allocation of grant funds made available for expenditure during the fiscal year, including carry-forward funds. Within each program area, the State shall provide a project list to be conducted during the fiscal year.

Subpart C—National Priority Safety Program Grants

§ 1200.20 General.

(a) *Scope.* This subpart establishes criteria, in accordance with 23 U.S.C. 405, for awarding grants to States that adopt and implement programs and laws to address national priorities for reducing highway deaths and injuries.

(b) *Definitions.* As used in this subpart—

Blood alcohol concentration or *BAC* means grams of alcohol per deciliter or 100 milliliters blood, or grams of alcohol per 210 liters of breath.

FARS means NHTSA's Fatality Analysis Reporting System.

Majority means greater than 50 percent.

Passenger motor vehicle means a passenger car, pickup truck, van, minivan or sport utility vehicle with a gross vehicle weight rating of less than 10,000 pounds.

Personal wireless communications device means a device through which personal wireless services (commercial mobile services, unlicensed wireless services, and common carrier wireless exchange access services) are transmitted, but does not include a global navigation satellite system receiver used for positioning, emergency notification, or navigation purposes.

Primary offense means an offense for which a law enforcement officer may stop a vehicle and issue a citation in the absence of evidence of another offense.

(c) *Eligibility.* Except as provided in § 1200.25(c), the 50 States, the District of Columbia, Puerto Rico, American Samoa, the Commonwealth of the Northern Mariana Islands, Guam and the U.S. Virgin Islands are each eligible to apply for national priority safety program grants under this subpart.

(d) *Qualification based on State statutes.* Whenever a State statute is the basis for a grant award under this subpart, such statute shall have been enacted by the application due date and be in effect and enforced, without interruption, by the beginning of and throughout the fiscal year of the grant award.

(e) *Award determinations and transfer of funds.* (1) Except as in provided § 1200.26(d), the amount of a grant award to a State in a fiscal year under this subpart shall be determined by applying the apportionment formula under 23 U.S.C. 402(c) for fiscal year 2009 to all qualifying States, in proportion to the amount each such State received under 23 U.S.C. 402(c) for fiscal year 2009, so that all available amounts are distributed to qualifying States to the maximum extent practicable.

(2) Notwithstanding paragraph (e)(1) of this section, and except as provided in § 1200.25(k), a grant awarded to a State in a fiscal year under this subpart may not exceed 10 percent of the total amount made available for that section for that fiscal year.

(3) If it is determined after review of applications that funds for a grant program under this subpart will not all be distributed, such funds shall be transferred to other programs authorized under 23 U.S.C. 402 and 405 to ensure, to the maximum extent practicable, that each State receives the maximum funding for which it qualifies.

(f) *Matching.* The Federal share of the costs of activities or programs funded using amounts from grants awarded under this subpart may not exceed 80 percent.

§ 1200.21 Occupant protection grants.

(a) *Purpose.* This section establishes criteria, in accordance with 23 U.S.C. 405(b), for awarding grants to States that adopt and implement effective occupant protection programs to reduce highway deaths and injuries resulting from individuals riding unrestrained or not properly restrained in motor vehicles.

(b) *Definitions.* As used in this section—

Child restraint means any device (including a child safety seat, booster seat used in conjunction with 3-point belts, or harness, but excluding seat belts) that is designed for use in a motor vehicle to restrain, seat, or position a child who weighs 65 pounds (30 kilograms) or less and that meets the Federal motor vehicle safety standard prescribed by the National Highway Traffic Safety Administration for child restraints.

High seat belt use rate State means a State that has an observed seat belt use rate of 90.0 percent or higher (not rounded) based on validated data from the State survey of seat belt use conducted during the previous calendar year, in accordance with the Uniform Criteria for State Observational Surveys of Seat Belt Use, 23 CFR Part 1340 (e.g., for a grant application submitted on July 1, 2014, the "previous calendar year" would be 2013).

Lower seat belt use rate State means a State that has an observed seat belt use rate below 90.0 percent (not rounded) based on validated data from the State survey of seat belt use conducted during the previous calendar year, in accordance with the Uniform Criteria for State Observational Surveys of Seat Belt Use, 23 CFR Part 1340 (e.g., for a grant application submitted on July 1, 2014, the "previous calendar year" would be 2013).

Seat belt means, with respect to open-body motor vehicles, including convertibles, an occupant restraint system consisting of a lap belt or a lap belt and a detachable shoulder belt, and with respect to other motor vehicles, an occupant restraint system consisting of integrated lap and shoulder belts.

Problem identification means the data collection and analysis process for identifying areas of the State, types of crashes, or types of populations (e.g., high-risk populations) that present specific safety or usage challenges in efforts to improve occupant protection.

(c) *Eligibility determination.* A State is eligible to apply for a grant under this section as a high seat belt use rate State or as a lower seat belt use rate State, in accordance with paragraph (d) or (e) of this section, as applicable.

(d) *Qualification criteria for a high seat belt use rate State.* To qualify for an occupant protection grant in a fiscal year, a high seat belt use rate State (as determined by NHTSA) shall submit an executed Part 1 of Appendix D and the following documentation:

(1) *Occupant protection plan.* (i) For a first fiscal year award, a copy of the State occupant protection program area plan to be included in the State HSP that describes the programs the State will implement to achieve reductions in traffic crashes, fatalities, and injuries on public roads.

(ii) For subsequent fiscal year awards, an update of the State's occupant protection plan provided in paragraph (d)(1)(i) of this section.

(2) *Participation in Click-it-or-Ticket national mobilization.* A description of the State's planned participation, and

the assurance provided in Part 1 of Appendix D, signed by the Governor's Highway Safety Representative, that the State will participate in the Click it or Ticket national mobilization during the fiscal year of the grant;

(3) *Child restraint inspection stations.* Documentation that the State has an active network of child inspection stations and/or inspection events that are—

(i) Located in areas that service the majority of the State's population and show evidence of outreach to underserved areas; and

(ii) Staffed with at least one current nationally Certified Child Passenger Safety Technician during official posted hours.

(4) *Child passenger safety technicians.* A copy of the State's plan to recruit, train and retain nationally Certified Child Passenger Safety Technicians to staff each child inspection station and inspection events located in the State.

(5) *Maintenance of effort.* The assurance provided in Part 1 of Appendix D, signed by the Governor's Highway Safety Representative, that the State shall maintain its aggregate expenditures from all State and local sources for occupant protection programs at or above the average level of such expenditure in fiscal years 2010 and 2011.

(e) *Qualification criteria for a lower seat belt use rate State.* To qualify for an occupant protection grant in a fiscal year, a lower seat belt use rate State (as determined by NHTSA) shall satisfy all the requirements of and submit all the documentation required under paragraph (d) of this section, and submit documentation demonstrating that it meets at least three of the following additional criteria:

(1) *Primary enforcement seat belt use law.* The assurance provided in Part 1 of Appendix D, signed by the Governor's Highway Safety Representative, providing legal citations to the State statute or statutes demonstrating that the State has enacted and is enforcing occupant protection laws that make a violation of the requirement to be secured in a seat belt or child restraint a primary offense.

(2) *Occupant protection laws.* The assurance provided in Part 1 of Appendix D, signed by the Governor's Highway Safety Representative, providing legal citations to State statute or statutes demonstrating that the State has enacted and is enforcing occupant protection laws that require—

(i) Each occupant riding in a passenger motor vehicle who is under eight years of age, weighs less than 65 pounds and is less than four feet, nine inches in height to be secured in an age-appropriate child restraint;

(ii) Each occupant riding in a passenger motor vehicle other than an occupant identified in paragraph (e)(2)(i) of this section to be secured in a seat belt or appropriate child restraint;

(iii) A minimum fine of $25 per unrestrained occupant for a violation of the occupant protection laws described in paragraphs (e)(2)(i) and (ii) of this section.

(iv) No exemption from coverage, except the following:

(A) Drivers, but not passengers, of postal, utility, and commercial vehicles that make frequent stops in the course of their business;

(B) Persons who are unable to wear a seat belt or child restraint because of a medical condition, provided there is written documentation from a physician;

(C) Persons who are unable to wear a seat belt or child restraint because all other seating positions are occupied by persons properly restrained in seat belts or child restraints;

(D) Emergency vehicle operators and passengers in emergency vehicles during an emergency;

(E) Persons riding in seating positions or vehicles not required by Federal Motor Vehicle Safety Standards to be equipped with seat belts;

(F) Passengers in public and livery conveyances.

(3) *Seat belt enforcement.* Documentation of the State's plan to conduct ongoing and periodic seat belt and child restraint enforcement during the fiscal year of the grant involving—

(i) At least 70 percent of the State's population as shown by the latest available Federal census; or

(ii) Law enforcement agencies responsible for seat belt enforcement in geographic areas in which at least 70 percent of the State's unrestrained passenger vehicle occupant fatalities occurred (reported in the HSP).

(4) *High risk population countermeasure programs.* Documentation that the State has implemented data-driven programs to improve seat belt and child restraint use for at least two of the following at-risk populations:

(i) Drivers on rural roadways;

(ii) Unrestrained nighttime drivers;

(iii) Teenage drivers;

(iv) Other high-risk populations identified in the occupant protection plan required under paragraph (d)(1) of this section.

(5) *Comprehensive occupant protection program.* Documentation demonstrating that the State has—

(i) Conducted a NHTSA-facilitated program assessment that evaluates the program for elements designed to increase seat belt usage in the State;

(ii) Developed a multi-year strategic plan based on input from statewide stakeholders (task force) under which the State developed—

(A) *A program management* strategy that provides leadership, training and technical assistance to other State agencies and local occupant protection programs and projects;

(B) *A program evaluation* strategy that assesses performance in achieving the State's measurable goals and objectives for increasing seat belt and child restraint usage for adults and children;

(C) *A communication and education program* strategy that has as its cornerstone the high visibility enforcement model that combines use of media, both paid and earned, and education to support enforcement efforts at the State and community level aimed at increasing seat belt use and correct usage of age appropriate child restraint systems; and

(D) *An enforcement* strategy that includes activities such as encouraging seat belt use policies for law enforcement agencies, vigorous enforcement of seat belt and child safety seat laws, and accurate reporting of occupant protection system information on police accident report forms.

(iii) designated an occupant protection coordinator; and

(iv) established a statewide occupant protection task force that includes agencies and organizations that can help develop, implement, enforce and evaluate occupant protection programs.

(6) *Occupant protection program assessment.* (i) A NHTSA-facilitated assessment of all elements of its occupant protection program within the three years prior to October 1 of the grant year; or

(ii) For the first year of the grant, the assurance provided in Part 1 of Appendix D, signed by the Governor's Representative for Highway Safety, that the State will conduct a NHTSA-facilitated assessment by September 1 of the grant year. The agency will require the return of grant funds awarded under this section if the State fails to conduct such an assessment by the deadline and will redistribute any such grant funds in accordance with §1200.20(e) to other qualifying States under this section.

(f) *Use of grant funds*—(1) *Eligible uses.* Except as provided in paragraph (f)(2) of this section, use of grant funds awarded under this section shall be limited to the following programs or purposes:

(i) To support high-visibility enforcement mobilizations, including paid media that emphasizes publicity for the program, and law enforcement;

(ii) To train occupant protection safety professionals, police officers, fire and emergency medical personnel, educators, and parents concerning all aspects of the use of child restraints and occupant protection;

(iii) To educate the public concerning the proper use and installation of child restraints, including related equipment and information systems;

(iv) To provide community child passenger safety services, including programs about proper seating positions for children and how to reduce the improper use of child restraints;

(v) To establish and maintain information systems containing data concerning occupant protection, including the collection and administration of child passenger safety and occupant protection surveys; and

(vi) To purchase and distribute child restraints to low-income families, provided that not more than five percent of the funds received in a fiscal year are used for such purpose.

(2) *Eligible uses for high seat belt use rate States.* Notwithstanding paragraph (f)(1) of this section, a State that qualifies for grant funds as a high seat belt use rate State may use up to 75 percent of such funds for any project or activity eligible for funding under 23 U.S.C. 402.

§ 1200.22 State traffic safety information system improvements grants.

(a) *Purpose.* This section establishes criteria, in accordance with 23 U.S.C. 405(c), for grants to States to develop and implement effective programs that improve the timeliness, accuracy, completeness, uniformity, integration, and accessibility of State safety data needed to identify priorities for Federal, State, and local highway and traffic safety programs, evaluate the effectiveness of such efforts, link State data systems, including traffic records and systems that contain medical, roadway, and economic data, improve the compatibility and interoperability of State data systems with national data systems and the data systems of other States, and enhance the agency's ability to observe and analyze national trends in crash occurrences, rates, outcomes, and circumstances.

(b) *Requirement for traffic records coordinating committee (TRCC)*—(1) *Structure and composition.* The State shall have a traffic records coordinating committee that—

(i) Is chartered or legally mandated;

(ii) Meets at least three times annually;

(iii) Has a multidisciplinary membership that includes owners, operators, collectors and users of traffic records and public health and injury control data systems, highway safety, highway infrastructure, law enforcement and adjudication officials, and public health, emergency medical services, injury control, driver licensing, and motor carrier agencies and organizations; and

(iv) Has a designated TRCC coordinator.

(2) *Functions.* The traffic records coordinating committee shall—

(i) Have authority to review any of the State's highway safety data and traffic records systems and any changes to such systems before the changes are implemented;

(ii) Consider and coordinate the views of organizations in the State that are involved in the collection, administration, and use of highway safety data and traffic records systems, and represent those views to outside organizations;

(iii) Review and evaluate new technologies to keep the highway safety data and traffic records system current; and

(iv) Approve annually the membership of the TRCC, the TRCC coordinator, any change to the State's multiyear Strategic Plan required under paragraph (c) of this section, and performance measures to be used to demonstrate quantitative progress in the accuracy, completeness, timeliness, uniformity, accessibility or integration of a core highway safety database.

(c) *Requirement for a state traffic records strategic plan.* The State shall have a Strategic Plan, approved by the TRCC, that—

(1) Describes specific, quantifiable and measurable improvements anticipated in the State's core safety databases, including crash, citation or adjudication, driver, emergency medical services or injury surveillance system, roadway, and vehicle databases;

(2) For any identified performance measure, uses the formats set forth in the Model Performance Measures for State Traffic Records Systems collaboratively developed by NHTSA and the Governors Highway Safety Association (GHSA);

(3) Includes a list of all recommendations from its most recent highway safety data and traffic records system assessment;

(4) Identifies which such recommendations the State intends to implement and the performance measures to be used to demonstrate quantifiable and measurable progress; and

(5) For recommendations that the State does not intend to implement, provides an explanation.

(d) *Requirement for quantitative improvement.* A State shall demonstrate quantitative improvement in the data attributes of accuracy, completeness, timeliness, uniformity, accessibility and integration in a core database by demonstrating an improved consistency within the State's record system or by achieving a higher level of compliance with a national model inventory of data elements, such as the Model Minimum Uniform Crash Criteria (MMUCC), the Model Impaired Driving Records Information System (MIDRIS), the Model Inventory of Roadway Elements (MIRE) or the National Emergency Medical Services Information System (NEMSIS).

(e) *Requirement for assessment.* The State shall have conducted or updated, within the five years prior to the application due date, an in-depth, formal assessment of its highway safety data and traffic records system accurately performed by a group knowledgeable about highway safety data and traffic records systems that complies with the procedures and methodologies outlined in NHTSA's Traffic Records Highway Safety Program Advisory (DOT HS 811 644).

(f) *Requirement for maintenance of effort.* The State shall maintain its aggregate expenditures from all State and local sources for State traffic safety information system programs at or above the average level of such expenditure in fiscal years 2010 and 2011, as provided in Part 2 of Appendix D, signed by the Governor's Highway Safety Representative.

(g) *Qualification criteria.* To qualify for a grant under this section in a fiscal year, a State shall submit an executed Part 2 of Appendix D and the following documentation:

(1) Either the TRCC charter or legal citation(s) to the statute or regulation legally mandating a TRCC with the functions required by paragraph (b)(2) of this section;

(2) Meeting schedule, all reports and data system improvement and policy guidance documents promulgated by the TRCC during the 12 months immediately preceding the grant application due date;

(3) A list of the TRCC membership and the organizations and functions they represent;

(4) The name and title of the State's Traffic Records Coordinator.

(5) A copy of the Strategic Plan required under paragraph (c) of this section, including any updates to the Strategic Plan.

(6) Either a written description of the performance measures, and all supporting data, that the State is relying on to demonstrate quantitative improvement in the preceding 12 months of the grant application due date in one or more of the significant data program attributes or the location where this information is detailed in the Strategic Plan.

(7) The certification provided in Part 2 of Appendix D, signed by the Governor's Representative for Highway Safety, that an assessment of the State's highway safety data and traffic records system was conducted or updated within the five years prior to the application due date as provided in paragraph (e) of this section.

(h) *Use of grant funds.* Grant funds awarded under this section shall be used to make quantifiable, measureable progress improvements in the accuracy, completeness, timeliness, uniformity, accessibility or integration of data in a core highway safety database.

§ 1200.23 Impaired driving countermeasures grants.

(a) *Purpose.* This section establishes criteria, in accordance with 23 U.S.C. 405(d), for awarding grants to States that adopt and implement effective programs to reduce traffic safety problems resulting from individuals driving motor vehicles while under the influence of alcohol, drugs, or the combination of alcohol and drugs or that enact alcohol ignition interlock laws.

(b) *Definitions.* As used in this section—

24–7 sobriety program means a State law or program that authorizes a State court or a State agency, as a condition of sentence, probation, parole, or work permit, to require an individual who pleads guilty to or was convicted of driving under the influence of alcohol or drugs to—

(1) Abstain totally from alcohol or drugs for a period of time; and

(2) Be subject to testing for alcohol or drugs at least twice per day by continuous transdermal alcohol monitoring via an electronic monitoring device, or by an alternative method approved by NHTSA.

Alcohol means wine, beer and distilled spirits.

Average impaired driving fatality rate means the number of fatalities in motor vehicle crashes involving a driver with a blood alcohol concentration of at least 0.08 percent for every 100,000,000 vehicle miles traveled, based on the most recently reported three calendar years of final data from the FARS.

Assessment means a NHTSA-facilitated process that employs a team of subject matter experts to conduct a comprehensive review of a specific highway safety program in a State.

Driving under the influence of alcohol, drugs, or a combination of alcohol and drugs means operating a vehicle while the alcohol and/or drug concentration in the blood or breath, as determined by chemical or other tests, equals or exceeds the level established by the State or is equivalent to the standard offense for driving under the influence of alcohol or drugs in the State.

Driving While Intoxicated (DWI) Court means a court that specializes in cases involving driving while intoxicated and abides by the Ten Guiding Principles of DWI Courts in effect on the date of the grant, as established by the National Center for DWI Courts.

Drugs means controlled substances as that term is defined under section 102(6) of the Controlled Substances Act, 21 U.S.C. 802(6).

High visibility enforcement efforts means participation in national impaired driving law enforcement campaigns organized by NHTSA, participation in impaired driving law enforcement campaigns organized by the State, or the use of sobriety checkpoints and/or saturation patrols, conducted in a highly visible manner and supported by publicity through paid or earned media.

High-range State means a State that has an average impaired driving fatality rate of 0.60 or higher.

Low-range State means a State that has an average impaired driving fatality rate of 0.30 or lower.

Mid-range State means a State that has an average impaired driving fatality rate that is higher than 0.30 and lower than 0.60.

Saturation patrol means a law enforcement activity during which enhanced levels of law enforcement are conducted in a concentrated geographic area (or areas) for the purpose of detecting drivers operating motor vehicles while impaired by alcohol and/or other drugs.

Sobriety checkpoint means a law enforcement activity during which law enforcement officials stop motor vehicles on a non-discriminatory, lawful basis for the purpose of determining whether the operators of such motor vehicles are driving while impaired by alcohol and/or other drugs.

Standard offense for driving under the influence of alcohol or drugs means the offense described in a State's law that makes it a criminal offense to operate a motor vehicle while under the influence of alcohol or drugs, but does not require a measurement of alcohol or drug content.

(c) *Eligibility determination.* A State is eligible to apply for a grant under this section as a low-range State, a mid-range State or a high-range State, in accordance with paragraphs (d), (e) or (f) of this section, as applicable. Independent of this range determination, a State may also qualify for a separate grant under this section as an ignition interlock State, as provided in paragraph (g) of this section.

(d) *Qualification criteria for a low-range State.* To qualify for an impaired driving countermeasures grant in a fiscal year, a low-range State (as determined by NHTSA) shall submit an executed Part 3 of Appendix D providing assurances, signed by the Governor's Representative for Highway Safety, that the State will—

(1) Use the funds awarded under 23 U.S.C. 405(d)(1) only for the implementation and enforcement of programs authorized in paragraph (i) of this section; and

(2) Maintain its aggregate expenditures from all State and local sources for impaired driving programs at or

above the average level of such expenditure in fiscal years 2010 and 2011, as provided in Part 3 of Appendix D.

(e) *Qualification criteria for a mid-range State.* To qualify for an impaired driving countermeasures grant in a fiscal year, a mid-range State (as determined by NHTSA) shall submit the information required in paragraph (d) of this section and the following additional documentation:

(1) *Statewide impaired driving plan.* If the State has not received a grant under this section for a previously submitted statewide impaired driving plan, the State shall submit a copy of a statewide impaired driving plan that—

(i) Has been developed within the three years prior to the application due date;

(ii) Has been approved by a statewide impaired driving task force that meets the requirements of paragraph (e)(2) of this section;

(iii) Provides a comprehensive strategy that uses data and problem identification to identify measurable goals and objectives for preventing and reducing impaired driving behavior and impaired driving crashes; and

(iv) Covers general areas that include program management and strategic planning, prevention, the criminal justice system, communication programs, alcohol and other drug misuse, and program evaluation and data.

(2) *Statewide impaired driving task force.* The State shall submit a copy of information describing its statewide impaired driving task force that—

(i) Provides the basis for the operation of the task force, including any charter or establishing documents;

(ii) Includes a schedule of all meetings held in the 12 months preceding the application due date and any reports or documents produced during that time period; and

(iii) Includes a list of membership and the organizations and functions represented and includes, at a minimum, key stakeholders from the State Highway Safety Office and the areas of law enforcement and criminal justice system (e.g., prosecution, adjudication, probation), and, as appropriate, stakeholders from the areas of driver licensing, treatment and rehabilitation, ignition interlock programs, data and traffic records, public health, and communication.

(3) *Assurances.* For the first year of the grant as a mid-range State, if the State is not able to meet the requirements of paragraph (e)(1) of this section, the State may provide the assurances provided in Part 3 of Appendix D, signed by the Governor's Representative for Highway Safety, that the State will convene a statewide impaired driving task force to develop a statewide impaired driving plan that meets the requirements of paragraph (e)(1) of this section and submit the statewide impaired driving plan by September 1 of the grant year. The agency will require the return of grant funds awarded under this section if the State fails to submit the plan by the deadline and will redistribute any such grant funds in accordance with §1200.20(e) to other qualifying States under this section.

(f) *Qualification criteria for a high-range State.* To qualify for an impaired driving countermeasures grant in a fiscal year, a high-range State (as determined by NHTSA) shall submit the information required in paragraph (d) of this section and the following additional documentation:

(1) *Impaired driving program assessment.* (i) The assurances provided in Part 3 of Appendix D, signed by the Governor's Representative for Highway Safety, providing the date of the NHTSA-facilitated assessment of the State's impaired driving program conducted within the three years prior to the application due date; or

(ii) For the first year of the grant as a high-range State, the assurances provided in Part 3 of Appendix D, signed by the Governor's Representative for Highway Safety, that the State will conduct a NHTSA-facilitated assessment by September 1 of the grant year.

(2) *Statewide impaired driving plan.* (i) *First year compliance.* For the first year of the grant as a high-range State, the assurances provided in Part 3 of Appendix D, signed by the Governor's Representative for Highway Safety, that the State will convene a statewide impaired driving task force to develop a statewide impaired driving plan, which will be submitted to NHTSA for review

and approval by September 1 of the grant year that—

(A) Meets the requirements of paragraph (e)(1) of this section;

(B) Addresses any recommendations from the assessment of the State's impaired driving program required in paragraph (f)(1) of this section;

(C) Includes a detailed plan for spending any grant funds provided for high visibility enforcement efforts; and

(D) Describes how the spending supports the State's impaired driving program and achievement of its performance goals and targets;

(ii) *Subsequent year compliance.* For subsequent years of the grant as a high-range State, the State shall submit for NHTSA review and comment a statewide impaired driving plan that meets the requirements of paragraph (f)(2)(i)(A) through (D) of this section or an update to its statewide impaired driving plan, as part of its application for a grant.

(g) *Ignition interlock State.* To qualify for a separate grant as an ignition interlock State in a fiscal year, a State shall submit the assurances in Part 3 of Appendix D, signed by the Governor's Representative for Highway Safety, providing legal citation(s) to the State statute demonstrating that the State has enacted and is enforcing a law that requires all individuals convicted of driving under the influence of alcohol or of driving while intoxicated to drive only vehicles with alcohol ignition interlocks for a period of not less than 30 days.

(h) *Award.* (1) The amount available for grants under paragraphs (d), (e) and (f) of this section shall be determined based on the total amount of eligible States for these grants and after deduction of the amount necessary to fund grants under paragraph (g) of this section.

(2) The amount available for grants under paragraph (g) of this section shall not exceed 15 percent of the total amount made available to States under this section for the fiscal year.

(i) *Use of grant funds.* (1) *Low-range States* may use grant funds awarded under this section for the following authorized programs:

(i) High visibility enforcement efforts;

(ii) Hiring a full-time or part-time impaired driving coordinator of the State's activities to address the enforcement and adjudication of laws regarding driving while impaired by alcohol;

(iii) Court support of high visibility enforcement efforts, training and education of criminal justice professionals (including law enforcement, prosecutors, judges, and probation officers) to assist such professionals in handling impaired driving cases, hiring traffic safety resource prosecutors, hiring judicial outreach liaisons, and establishing driving while intoxicated courts;

(iv) Alcohol ignition interlock programs;

(v) Improving blood-alcohol concentration testing and reporting;

(vi) Paid and earned media in support of high visibility enforcement of impaired driving laws, and conducting standardized field sobriety training, advanced roadside impaired driving evaluation training, and drug recognition expert training for law enforcement, and equipment and related expenditures used in connection with impaired driving enforcement;

(vii) Training on the use of alcohol screening and brief intervention;

(viii) Developing impaired driving information systems; and

(ix) Costs associated with a 24–7 sobriety program.

(x) Programs designed to reduce impaired driving based on problem identification.

(2) *Mid-range States* may use grant funds awarded under this section for any of the authorized uses described in paragraph (i)(1) of this section, provided that use of grant funds for programs described in paragraph (i)(1)(x) of this section requires advance approval from NHTSA.

(3) *High-range States* may use grant funds awarded under this section for high visibility enforcement efforts and any of the authorized uses described in paragraph (i)(1) of this section, provided the proposed uses are described in a statewide impaired driving plan submitted to and approved by NHTSA in accordance with paragraph (f)(2) of this section and subject to the conditions in paragraph (j) of this section.

(4) *Ignition interlock States* may use grant funds awarded under this section for any of the authorized uses described under paragraph (i)(1) of this section and for eligible activities under 23 U.S.C. 402.

(j) *Special conditions for use of funds by high-range States.* No expenses incurred or vouchers submitted by a high-range State shall be approved for reimbursement until such State submits for NHTSA review and approval a statewide impaired driving plan as provided in paragraph (f)(2) of this section. If a high-range State fails to timely provide the statewide impaired driving plan required under paragraph (f)(2) of this section, the agency will redistribute any grant funds in accordance with § 1200.20(e) to other qualifying States under this section.

§ 1200.24 Distracted driving grants.

(a) *Purpose.* This section establishes criteria, in accordance with 23 U.S.C. 405(e), for awarding grants to States that enact and enforce laws prohibiting distracted driving, beginning with fiscal year 2014 grants.

(b) *Definitions.* As used in this section—

Driving means operating a motor vehicle on a public road, including operation while temporarily stationary because of traffic, a traffic light or stop sign, or otherwise, but does not include operating a motor vehicle when the vehicle has pulled over to the side of, or off, an active roadway and has stopped in a location where it can safely remain stationary.

Texting means reading from or manually entering data into a personal wireless communications device, including doing so for the purpose of SMS texting, emailing, instant messaging, or engaging in any other form of electronic data retrieval or electronic data communication.

(c) *Qualification criteria.* To qualify for a distracted driving grant in a fiscal year, a State shall submit the assurances in Part 4 of Appendix D, signed by the Governor's Representative for Highway Safety, providing legal citations to the State statute or statutes demonstrating compliance with the following requirements:

(1) *Prohibition on texting while driving.* The statute shall—

(i) Prohibit drivers from texting through a personal wireless communications device while driving;

(ii) Make a violation of the law a primary offense; and

(iii) Establish—

(A) A minimum fine of $25 for a first violation of the law; and

(B) Increased fines for repeat violations within five years of the previous violation.

(2) *Prohibition on youth cell phone use while driving.* The statute shall—

(i) Prohibit a driver who is younger than 18 years of age from using a personal wireless communications device while driving;

(ii) Make a violation of the law a primary offense;

(iii) Require distracted driving issues to be tested as part of the State's driver's license examination; and

(iv) Establish—

(A) A minimum fine of $25 for a first violation of the law; and

(B) Increased fines for repeat violations within five years of the previous violation.

(3) *Permitted exceptions.* A State statute providing for the following exceptions, and no others, shall not be deemed out of compliance with the requirements of this section:

(i) A driver who uses a personal wireless communications device to contact emergency services;

(ii) Emergency services personnel who use a personal wireless communications device while operating an emergency services vehicle and engaged in the performance of their duties as emergency services personnel; and

(iii) An individual employed as a commercial motor vehicle driver or a school bus driver who uses a personal wireless communications device within the scope of such individual's employment if such use is permitted under the regulations promulgated pursuant to 49 U.S.C. 31136.

(d) *Use of grant funds.* (1) At least 50 percent of the grant funds awarded under this section shall be used to educate the public through advertising containing information about the dangers of texting or using a cell phone while driving, for traffic signs that notify drivers about the distracted driving law of the State, or for law enforcement costs related to the enforcement of the distracted driving law;

(2) Not more than 50 percent of the grant funds awarded under this section may be used for any eligible project or activity under 23 U.S.C. 402.

§ 1200.25 Motorcyclist safety grants.

(a) *Purpose.* This section establishes criteria, in accordance with 23 U.S.C. 405(b), for awarding grants to States that adopt and implement effective programs to reduce the number of single-vehicle and multiple-vehicle crashes involving motorcyclists.

(b) *Definitions.* As used in this section—

Impaired means alcohol-impaired or drug-impaired as defined by State law, provided that the State's legal alcohol-impairment level does not exceed .08 BAC.

Motorcycle means a motor vehicle with motive power having a seat or saddle for the use of the rider and designed to travel on not more than three wheels in contact with the ground.

Motorcyclist awareness means individual or collective awareness of the presence of motorcycles on or near roadways and of safe driving practices that avoid injury to motorcyclists.

Motorcyclist awareness program means an informational or public awareness or education program designed to enhance motorcyclist awareness that is developed by or in coordination with the designated State authority having jurisdiction over motorcyclist safety issues, which may include the State motorcycle safety administrator or a motorcycle advisory council appointed by the Governor of the State.

Motorcyclist safety training or *Motorcycle rider training* means a formal program of instruction that is approved for use in a State by the designated State authority having jurisdiction over motorcyclist safety issues, which may include the State motorcycle safety administrator or a motorcycle advisory council appointed by the governor of the State.

State means any of the 50 States, the District of Columbia, and Puerto Rico.

(c) *Eligibility.* The 50 States, the District of Columbia and Puerto Rico are eligible to apply for a motorcyclist safety grant.

(d) *Qualification criteria.* To qualify for a motorcyclist safety grant in a fiscal year, a State shall submit an executed Part 5 of Appendix D, signed by the Governor's Representative for Highway Safety, and submit documentation demonstrating compliance with at least two of the criteria in paragraphs (e) through (j) of this section.

(e) *Motorcycle rider training course.* (1) To satisfy this criterion, a State shall have an effective motorcycle rider training course that is offered throughout the State and that provides a formal program of instruction in accident avoidance and other safety-oriented operational skills to motorcyclists. The program shall—

(i) Use a training curriculum that—

(A) Is approved by the designated State authority having jurisdiction over motorcyclist safety issues;

(B) Includes a formal program of instruction in crash avoidance and other safety-oriented operational skills for both in-class and on-the-motorcycle training to motorcyclists; and

(C) May include innovative training opportunities to meet unique regional needs;

(ii) Offer at least one motorcycle rider training course either—

(A) In a majority of the State's counties or political subdivisions; or

(B) In counties or political subdivisions that account for a majority of the State's registered motorcycles;

(iii) Use motorcycle rider training instructors to teach the curriculum who are certified by the designated State authority having jurisdiction over motorcyclist safety issues or by a nationally recognized motorcycle safety organization with certification capability; and

(iv) Use quality control procedures to assess motorcycle rider training courses and instructor training courses conducted in the State.

(2) To demonstrate compliance with this criterion, the State shall submit—

(i) A copy of the official State document (e.g., law, regulation, binding policy directive, letter from the Governor) identifying the designated State authority over motorcyclist safety issues;

(ii) Document(s) demonstrating that the training curriculum is approved by the designated State authority having jurisdiction over motorcyclist safety issues and includes a formal program of instruction in crash avoidance and other safety-oriented operational skills for both in-class and on-the-motorcycle training to motorcyclists;

(iii) Either:

(A) A list of the counties or political subdivisions in the State, noting in which counties or political subdivisions and when motorcycle rider training courses were offered in the 12 months preceding the due date of the grant application, if the State seeks to qualify under this criterion by showing that it offers at least one motorcycle rider training course in a majority of counties or political subdivisions in the State; or

(B) A list of the counties or political subdivisions in the State, noting in which counties or political subdivisions and when motorcycle rider training courses were offered in the 12 months preceding the due date of the grant application and the corresponding number of registered motorcycles in each county or political subdivision according to official State motor vehicle records, if the State seeks to qualify under this criterion by showing that it offers at least one motorcycle rider training course in counties or political subdivisions that account for a majority of the State's registered motorcycles;

(iv) Document(s) demonstrating that the State uses motorcycle rider training instructors to teach the curriculum who are certified by the designated State authority having jurisdiction over motorcyclist safety issues or by a nationally recognized motorcycle safety organization with certification capability; and

(v) A brief description of the quality control procedures to assess motorcycle rider training courses and instructor training courses used in the State (e.g., conducting site visits, gathering student feedback) and the actions taken to improve the courses based on the information collected.

(f) *Motorcyclist awareness program.* (1) To satisfy this criterion, a State shall have an effective statewide program to enhance motorist awareness of the presence of motorcyclists on or near roadways and safe driving practices that avoid injuries to motorcyclists. The program shall—

(i) Be developed by, or in coordination with, the designated State authority having jurisdiction over motorcyclist safety issues;

(ii) Use State data to identify and prioritize the State's motorcyclist awareness problem areas;

(iii) Encourage collaboration among agencies and organizations responsible for, or impacted by, motorcycle safety issues; and

(iv) Incorporate a strategic communications plan that—

(A) Supports the State's overall safety policy and countermeasure program;

(B) Is designed, at a minimum, to educate motorists in those jurisdictions where the incidence of motorcycle crashes is highest or in those jurisdictions that account for a majority of the State's registered motorcycles;

(C) Includes marketing and educational efforts to enhance motorcyclist awareness; and

(D) Uses a mix of communication mechanisms to draw attention to the problem.

(2) To demonstrate compliance with this criterion, the State shall submit—

(i) A copy of the State document identifying the designated State authority having jurisdiction over motorcyclist safety issues;

(ii) A letter from the Governor's Highway Safety Representative stating that the State's motorcyclist awareness program was developed by or in coordination with the designated State authority having jurisdiction over motorcyclist safety issues;

(iii) Data used to identify and prioritize the State's motorcycle safety problem areas, including either—

(A) A list of counties or political subdivisions in the State ranked in order of the highest to lowest number of motorcycle crashes per county or political subdivision, if the State seeks to qualify under this criterion by showing that it identifies and prioritizes the State's motorcycle safety problem areas based on motorcycle crashes. Such data shall be from the most recent calendar year for which final State crash data is available, but data no older than two calendar years prior to the application due date (e.g., for a grant application submitted on July 1, 2013, a State shall provide calendar year 2012 data, if available, and may not provide data older than calendar year 2011); or

(B) A list of counties or political subdivisions in the State and the corresponding number of registered motorcycles for each county or political subdivision according to official State motor vehicle records, if the State seeks to qualify under this criterion by showing that it identifies and prioritizes the State's motorcycle safety problem areas based on motorcycle registrations;

(iv) A brief description of how the State has achieved collaboration among agencies and organizations responsible for, or impacted by, motorcycle safety issues; and

(v) A copy of the strategic communications plan showing that it—

(A) Supports the State's overall safety policy and countermeasure program;

(B) Is designed to educate motorists in those jurisdictions where the incidence of motorcycle crashes is highest (*i.e.*, the majority of counties or political subdivisions in the State with the highest numbers of motorcycle crashes) or is designed to educate motorists in those jurisdictions that account for a majority of the State's registered motorcycles (*i.e.*, the counties or political subdivisions that account for a majority of the State's registered motorcycles as evidenced by State motor vehicle records);

(C) Includes marketing and educational efforts to enhance motorcyclist awareness; and

(D) Uses a mix of communication mechanisms to draw attention to the problem (e.g., newspapers, billboard advertisements, email, posters, flyers, mini-planners, or instructor-led training sessions).

(g) *Reduction of fatalities and crashes involving motorcycles.* (1) To satisfy this criterion, a State shall demonstrate a reduction for the preceding calendar year in the number of motorcyclist fatalities and in the rate of motor vehicle crashes involving motorcycles in the State (expressed as a function of 10,000 registered motorcycle registrations), as computed by NHTSA. The State shall—

(i) Experience a reduction of at least one in the number of motorcyclist fatalities for the most recent calendar year for which final FARS data is available as compared to the final FARS data for the calendar year immediately prior to that year; and

(ii) Based on State crash data expressed as a function of 10,000 motorcycle registrations (using FHWA motorcycle registration data), experience at least a whole number reduction in the rate of crashes involving motorcycles for the most recent calendar year for which final State crash data is available, but data no older than two calendar years prior to the application due date, as compared to the calendar year immediately prior to that year.

(2) To demonstrate compliance with this criterion, the State shall submit—

(i) State data showing the total number of motor vehicle crashes involving motorcycles in the State for the most recent calendar year for which final State crash data is available, but data no older than two calendar years prior to the application due date and the same type of data for the calendar year immediately prior to that year (e.g., for a grant application submitted on July 1, 2013, the State shall submit calendar year 2012 data and 2011 data, if both data are available, and may not provide data older than calendar year 2011 and 2010, to determine the rate); and

(ii) A description of the State's methods for collecting and analyzing data submitted in paragraph (g)(2)(i) of this section, including a description of the State's efforts to make reporting of motor vehicle crashes involving motorcycles as complete as possible.

(h) *Impaired driving program.* (1) To satisfy this criterion, a State shall implement a statewide program to reduce impaired driving, including specific measures to reduce impaired motorcycle operation. The program shall—

(i) Use State data to identify and prioritize the State's impaired driving and impaired motorcycle operation problem areas; and

(ii) Include specific countermeasures to reduce impaired motorcycle operation with strategies designed to reach motorcyclists and motorists in those jurisdictions where the incidence of motorcycle crashes involving an impaired operator is highest.

(2) To demonstrate compliance with this criterion, the State shall submit—

(i) State data used to identify and prioritize the State's impaired driving and impaired motorcycle operation problem areas, including a list of counties or political subdivisions in the State ranked in order of the highest to lowest number of motorcycle crashes involving an impaired operator per county or political subdivision. Such data shall be from the most recent calendar year for which final State crash data is available, but data no older than two calendar years prior to the application due date (e.g., for a grant application submitted on July 1, 2013, a State shall provide calendar year 2012 data, if available, and may not provide data older than calendar year 2011);

(ii) A detailed description of the State's impaired driving program as implemented, including a description of each countermeasure established and proposed by the State to reduce impaired motorcycle operation, the amount of funds allotted or proposed for each countermeasure and a description of its specific strategies that are designed to reach motorcyclists and motorists in those jurisdictions where the incidence of motorcycle crashes involving an impaired operator is highest (*i.e.*, the majority of counties or political subdivisions in the State with the highest numbers of motorcycle crashes involving an impaired operator); and

(iii) The legal citation(s) to the State statute or regulation defining impairment. (A State is not eligible for a grant under this criterion if its legal alcohol-impairment level exceeds .08 BAC.)

(i) *Reduction of fatalities and accidents involving impaired motorcyclists.* (1) To satisfy this criterion, a State shall demonstrate a reduction for the preceding calendar year in the number of fatalities and in the rate of reported crashes involving alcohol-impaired and drug-impaired motorcycle operators (expressed as a function of 10,000 motorcycle registrations), as computed by NHTSA. The State shall—

(i) Experience a reduction of at least one in the number of fatalities involving alcohol-and drug-impaired motorcycle operators for the most recent calendar year for which final FARS data is available as compared to the final FARS data for the calendar year immediately prior to that year; and

(ii) Based on State crash data expressed as a function of 10,000 motorcycle registrations (using FHWA motorcycle registration data), experience at least a whole number reduction in the rate of reported crashes involving alcohol-and drug-impaired motorcycle operators for the most recent calendar year for which final State crash data is available, but data no older than two calendar years prior to the application due date, as compared to the calendar year immediately prior to that year.

(2) To demonstrate compliance with this criterion, the State shall submit—

(i) State data showing the total number of reported crashes involving alcohol- and drug-impaired motorcycle operators in the State for the most recent calendar year for which final State crash data is available, but data no older than two calendar years prior to the application due date and the same type of data for the calendar year immediately prior to that year (e.g., for a grant application submitted on July 1, 2013, the State shall submit calendar year 2012 and 2011 data, if both data are available, and may not provide data older than calendar year 2011 and 2010, to determine the rate); and

(ii) A description of the State's methods for collecting and analyzing data submitted in paragraph (i)(2)(i) of this section, including a description of the State's efforts to make reporting of crashes involving alcohol-impaired and drug-impaired motorcycle operators as complete as possible; and

(iii) The legal citation(s) to the State statute or regulation defining alcohol-impaired and drug-impairment. (A State is not eligible for a grant under this criterion if its legal alcohol-impairment level exceeds .08 BAC.)

(j) *Use of fees collected from motorcyclists for motorcycle programs.* (1) To satisfy this criterion, a State shall have a process under which all fees collected by the State from motorcyclists for the purposes of funding motorcycle training and safety programs are used for motorcycle training and safety programs. A State may qualify under this criterion as either a Law State or a Data State.

(i) A Law State is a State that has a statute or regulation requiring that all fees collected by the State from motorcyclists for the purposes of funding motorcycle training and safety programs are to be used for motorcycle training and safety programs.

(ii) A Data State is a State that does not have a statute or regulation requiring that all fees collected by the State from motorcyclists for the purposes of funding motorcycle training and safety programs are to be used for motorcycle training and safety programs but can show through data and/or documentation from official records that all fees collected by the State from motorcyclists for the purposes of funding motorcycle training and safety programs were, in fact, used for motorcycle training and safety programs, without diversion.

(2)(i) To demonstrate compliance as a Law State, the State shall submit the legal citation(s) to the statute or regulation requiring that all fees collected by the State from motorcyclists for the purposes of funding motorcycle training and safety programs are to be used for motorcycle training and safety programs and the legal citation(s) to the State's current fiscal year appropriation (or preceding fiscal year appropriation, if the State has not enacted a law at the time of the State's application) appropriating all such fees to motorcycle training and safety programs.

(ii) To demonstrate compliance as a Data State, a State shall submit data or documentation from official records from the previous State fiscal year showing that all fees collected by the State from motorcyclists for the purposes of funding motorcycle training and safety programs were, in fact, used for motorcycle training and safety programs. Such data or documentation shall show that revenues collected for the purposes of funding motorcycle training and safety programs were placed into a distinct account and expended only for motorcycle training and safety programs.

(k) *Award limitation.* A grant awarded under the procedures described in § 1200.20(e)(1) may not exceed the amount of a grant made to State for fiscal year 2003 under 23 U.S.C. 402.

(l) *Use of grant funds.* (1) *Eligible uses.* A State may use grant funds awarded under this section for motorcyclist safety training and motorcyclist awareness programs, including—

(i) Improvements to motorcyclist safety training curricula;

(ii) Improvements in program delivery of motorcycle training to both urban and rural areas, including—

(A) Procurement or repair of practice motorcycles;

(B) Instructional materials;

(C) Mobile training units; and

(D) Leasing or purchasing facilities for closed-course motorcycle skill training;

(iii) Measures designed to increase the recruitment or retention of motorcyclist safety training instructors; and

(iv) Public awareness, public service announcements, and other outreach programs to enhance driver awareness of motorcyclists, such as the "share-the-road" safety messages developed using Share-the-Road model language available on NHTSA's Web site at *http://www.trafficsafetymarketing.gov.*

(2) *Suballocation of funds.* A State that receives a grant under this section may suballocate funds from the grant to a nonprofit organization incorporated in that State to carry out grant activities under this section.

§ 1200.26 State graduated driver licensing incentive grants.

(a) *Purpose.* This section establishes criteria, in accordance with 23 U.S.C. 405(g), for awarding grants to States that adopt and implement graduated driver's licensing laws that require novice drivers younger than 21 years of age to comply with a 2-stage licensing process prior to receiving a full driver's license.

(b) *Definitions.* As used in this section—

Conviction-free means that, during the term of the permit or license covered by the program, the driver has not been convicted of any offense under State or local law relating to the use or operation of a motor vehicle, including but not limited to driving while intoxicated, reckless driving, driving without wearing a seat belt, speeding, prohibited use of a personal wireless communications device, and violation of the driving-related restrictions applicable to the stages of the graduated driver's licensing process set forth in paragraph (c) of this section, as well as misrepresentation of a driver's true age.

Driving, for purposes of paragraph (c)(2)(iii) of this section, means operating a motor vehicle on a public road, including operation while temporarily stationary because of traffic, a traffic light or stop sign, or otherwise, but does not include operating a motor vehicle when the vehicle has pulled over to the side of, or off, an active roadway and has stopped in a location where it can safely remain stationary.

Full driver's license means a license to operate a passenger motor vehicle on public roads at all times.

Licensed driver means a driver who possesses a valid full driver's license.

Novice driver means a driver who has not been issued by a State an intermediate license or full driver's license.

(c) *Qualification criteria.* (1) *General.* To qualify for a grant under this section, a State shall submit the assurances in Part 6 of Appendix D, signed by the Governor's Representative for Highway Safety, providing legal citations to the State statute or statutes demonstrating compliance with the requirements of paragraph (c)(2) of this section, and provide legal citation(s) to the statute or regulation or provide documentation demonstrating compliance with the requirements of paragraph (c)(3) of this section.

(2) *Graduated driver's licensing law.* A State's graduated driver's licensing law shall include a learner's permit stage and an intermediate stage meeting the following minimum requirements:

(i) The learner's permit stage shall—

(A) Apply to any novice driver who is younger than 21 years of age prior to the receipt by such driver from the State of any other permit or license to operate a motor vehicle;

(B) Commence only after an applicant for a leaner's permit passes vision and knowledge tests, including tests about the rules of the road, signs, and signals;

(C) Subject to paragraph (c)(2)(iii)(B), be in effect for a period of at least six months, but may not expire until the driver reaches at least 16 years of age; and

(D) Require the learner's permit holder to—

(*1*) Be accompanied and supervised by a licensed driver who is at least 21 years of age at all times while the learner's permit holder is operating a motor vehicle;

(*2*) Receive not less than 40 hours of behind-the-wheel training with a licensed driver who is at least 21 years of age;

(*3*) Complete a driver education or training course that has been certified by the State; and

(*4*) Pass a driving skills test prior to entering the intermediate stage or being issued another permit, license or endorsement.

(ii) The intermediate stage shall—

(A) Apply to any driver who has completed the learner's permit stage and who is younger than 18 years of age;

(B) Commence immediately after the expiration of the learner's permit stage;

(C) Subject to paragraph (c)(2)(iii)(B), be in effect for a period of at least six months, but may not expire until the driver reaches at least 18 years of age;

(D) Require the intermediate license holder to be accompanied and supervised by a licensed driver who is at least 21 years of age during the period of time between the hours of 10:00 p.m. and 5:00 a.m., except in case of emergency; and

(E) Prohibit the intermediate license holder from operating a motor vehicle with more than one nonfamilial passenger younger than 21 years of age unless a licensed driver who is at least 21 years of age is in the motor vehicle.

(iii) During both the learner's permit and intermediate stages, the State shall—

(A) Impose a prohibition enforced as a primary offense on use of a cellular telephone or any communications device by the driver while driving, except in case of emergency; and

(B) Require that the driver who possesses a learner's permit or intermediate license remain conviction-free for a period of not less than six consecutive months immediately prior to the expiration of that stage.

(3) *Requirement for license distinguishability.* The State learner's permit, intermediate license, and full driver's license shall be distinguishable from each other. A State may satisfy this requirement by submitting—

(i) Legal citations to the State statute or regulation requiring that the State learner's permit, intermediate license, and full driver's license be visually distinguishable:

(ii) Sample permits and licenses that contain visual features that would enable a law enforcement officer to distinguish between the State learner's permit, intermediate license, and full driver's license; or

(iii) A description of the State's system that enables law enforcement officers in the State during traffic stops to distinguish between the State learner's permit, intermediate license, and full driver's license.

(4) *Exceptions.* A State that otherwise meets the minimum requirements set forth in paragraph (c)(2) of this section will not be deemed ineligible for a grant under this section if—

(i) The State enacted a law prior to January 1, 2011, establishing a class of permit or license that allows drivers younger than 18 years of age to operate a motor vehicle—

(A) In connection with work performed on, or for the operation of, a farm owned by family members who are directly related to the applicant or licensee; or

(B) If demonstrable hardship would result from the denial of a license to the licensees or applicants, provided that the State requires the applicant or licensee to affirmatively and adequately demonstrate unique undue hardship to the individual; and

(ii) Drivers who possess only the permit or license permitted under paragraph (c)(4)(i) of this section are treated as novice drivers subject to the graduated driver's licensing requirements of paragraph (c)(2) of this section as a pre-condition of receiving any other permit, license or endorsement.

(d) *Award.* (1) *Grant Amount.* Subject to paragraph (d)(2) of this section, grant funds for a fiscal year under this section shall be allocated among States that meet the qualification criteria on the basis of the apportionment formula under 23 U.S.C. 402 for that fiscal year.

(2) *Limitation.* Amount of grant award to a State under this section may not exceed 10 percent of the total amount made available for Section 405(g) for that fiscal year.

(e) *Use of grant funds.* A State may use grant funds awarded under this section as follows:

(1) At least 25 percent of the grant funds shall be used, in connection with the State's graduated driver's licensing law that complies with the minimum requirements set forth in paragraph (c) of this section, to:

(i) Enforce the graduated driver's licensing process;

(ii) Provide training for law enforcement personnel and other relevant State agency personnel relating to the enforcement of the graduated driver's licensing process;

(iii) Publish relevant educational materials that pertain directly or indirectly to the State graduated driver's licensing law;

(iv) Carry out administrative activities to implement the State's graduated driver's licensing process; or

(v) Carry out a teen traffic safety program described in 23 U.S.C. 402(m);

(2) No more than 75 percent may be used for any eligible project or activity under 23 U.S.C. 402.

Subpart D—Administration of the Highway Safety Grants

§ 1200.30 General.

Subject to the provisions of this subpart, the requirements of 49 CFR part 18 and applicable cost principles govern the implementation and management of State highway safety programs and projects carried out under 23 U.S.C. Chapter 4. Cost principles include those referenced in 49 CFR 18.22.

§ 1200.31 Equipment.

(a) *Title.* Except as provided in paragraphs (e) and (f) of this section, title to equipment acquired under 23 U.S.C. Chapter 4 will vest upon acquisition in the State or its subgrantee, as appropriate.

(b) *Use.* All equipment shall be used for the originally authorized grant purposes for as long as needed for those purposes, as determined by the Approving Official, and neither the State nor any of its subgrantees or contractors shall encumber the title or interest while such need exists.

(c) *Management and disposition.* Subject to the requirement of paragraphs (b), (d), (e) and (f) of this section, States and their subgrantees and contractors shall manage and dispose of equipment acquired under 23 U.S.C. Chapter 4 in accordance with State laws and procedures.

(d) *Major purchases and dispositions.* Equipment with a useful life of more than one year and an acquisition cost of $5,000 or more shall be subject to the following requirements—

(1) Purchases shall receive prior written approval from the Approving Official;

(2) Dispositions shall receive prior written approval from the Approving Official unless the age of the equipment has exceeded its useful life as determined under State law and procedures.

(e) *Right to transfer title.* The Approving Official may reserve the right to transfer title to equipment acquired under 23 U.S.C. Chapter 4 to the Federal Government or to a third party when such third party is eligible under Federal statute. Any such transfer shall be subject to the following requirements:

(1) The equipment shall be identified in the grant or otherwise made known to the State in writing;

(2) The Approving Official shall issue disposition instructions within 120 calendar days after the equipment is determined to be no longer needed for highway safety purposes, in the absence of which the State shall follow the applicable procedures in 49 CFR part 18.

(f) *Federally-owned equipment.* In the event a State or its subgrantee is provided Federally-owned equipment:

(1) Title shall remain vested in the Federal Government;

(2) Management shall be in accordance with Federal rules and procedures, and an annual inventory listing shall be submitted;

(3) The State or its subgrantee shall request disposition instructions from the Approving Official when the item is no longer needed for highway safety purposes.

§ 1200.32 Changes—Approval of the Approving Official.

States shall provide documentary evidence of any reallocation of funds between program areas by submitting to the NHTSA regional office an amended HS Form 217, reflecting the changed allocation of funds and updated list of projects under each program area, as provided in § 1200.11(e), within 30 days of implementing the change. The amended HS Form 217 and list of projects is subject to the approval of the Approving Official.

§ 1200.33 Vouchers and project agreements.

(a) *General.* Each State shall submit official vouchers for expenses incurred to the Approving Official.

(b) *Content of vouchers.* At a minimum, each voucher shall provide the following information for expenses claimed in each program area:

(1) Program Area for which expenses were incurred and an itemization of project numbers and amount of Federal funds expended for each project for which reimbursement is being sought;

(2) Federal funds obligated;

(3) Amount of Federal funds allocated to local benefit (provided no less than mid-year (by March 31) and with the final voucher);

(4) Cumulative Total Cost to Date;

(5) Cumulative Federal Funds Expended;

(6) Previous Amount Claimed;

(7) Amount Claimed this Period;

(8) Matching rate (or special matching writeoff used, *i.e.*, sliding scale rate authorized under 23 U.S.C. 120).

(c) *Project agreements.* Copies of each project agreement for which expenses are being claimed under the voucher (and supporting documentation for the vouchers) shall be made promptly available for review by the Approving Official upon request. Each project agreement shall bear the project number to allow the Approving Official to match the voucher to the corresponding activity.

(d) *Submission requirements.* At a minimum, vouchers shall be submitted to the Approving Official on a quarterly basis, no later than 15 working days after the end of each quarter, except that where a State receives funds by electronic transfer at an annualized rate of one million dollars or more, vouchers shall be submitted on a monthly basis, no later than 15 working days after the end of each month. A final voucher shall be submitted to the Approving Official no later than 90 days after the end of the fiscal year, and all unexpended balances shall be carried forward to the current fiscal year.

(e) *Reimbursement.* (1) Failure to provide the information specified in paragraph (b) of this section shall result in rejection of the voucher.

(2) Failure to meet the deadlines specified in paragraph (d) of this section may result in delayed reimbursement.

(3) Vouchers that request reimbursement for projects whose project numbers or amounts claimed do not match the list of projects or exceed the estimated amount of Federal funds provided under § 1200.11(e), or exceed the allocation of funds to a program area in the HS Form 217, shall be rejected, in whole or in part, until an amended list of projects and/or estimated amount of Federal funds and an amended HS Form 217 is submitted to and approved by the Approving Official in accordance with § 1200.32.

§ 1200.34 Program income.

(a) *Definition.* Program income means gross income received by the grantee or subgrantee directly generated by a program supported activity, or earned only as a result of the grant agreement during the period of time between the effective date of the grant award and the expiration date of the grant award.

(b) *Inclusions.* Program income includes income from fees for services performed, from the use or rental of real or personal property acquired with grant funds, from the sale of commodities or items fabricated under the grant agreement, and from payments of principal and interest on loans made with grant funds.

(c) *Exclusions.* Program income does not include interest on grant funds, rebates, credits, discounts, refunds, taxes, special assessments, levies, fines, proceeds from the sale of real property or equipment, income from royalties and license fees for copyrighted material, patents, and inventions, or interest on any of these.

(d) *Use of program income.* (1) *Addition.* Program income shall ordinarily be added to the funds committed to the Highway Safety Plan. Such program income shall be used to further the objectives of the program area under which it was generated.

(2) *Cost sharing or matching.* Program income may be used to meet cost sharing or matching requirements only upon written approval of the Approving Official. Such use shall not increase the commitment of Federal funds.

§ 1200.35 Annual Report.

Within 90 days after the end of the fiscal year, each State shall submit an Annual Report describing—

(a) A general assessment of the State's progress in achieving highway safety performance measure targets identified in the Highway Safety Plan;

(b) A general description of the projects and activities funded and implemented under the Highway Safety Plan;

(c) The amount of Federal funds expended on projects from the Highway Safety Plan; and

(d) How the projects funded during the fiscal year contributed to meeting the State's highway safety targets. Where data becomes available, a State should report progress from prior year projects that have contributed to meeting current State highway safety targets.

§ 1200.36 Appeals of written decision by Approving Official.

Review of any written decision regarding the administration of the grants by an Approving Official under this subpart may be obtained by submitting a written appeal of such decision, signed by the Governor's Representative for Highway Safety, to the Approving Official. Such appeal shall be forwarded promptly to the NHTSA Associate Administrator, Regional Operations and Program Delivery. The decision of the NHTSA Associate Administrator shall be final and shall be transmitted to the Governor's Representative for Highway Safety through the cognizant Approving Official.

Subpart E—Annual Reconciliation

§ 1200.40 Expiration of the Highway Safety Plan.

(a) The State's Highway Safety Plan for a fiscal year and the State's authority to incur costs under that Highway Safety Plan shall expire on the last day of the fiscal year.

(b) Except as provided in paragraph (c) of this section, each State shall submit a final voucher which satisfies the requirements of § 1200.33 within 90 days after the expiration of the State's Highway Safety Plan as provided in paragraph (a) of this section. The final voucher constitutes the final financial reconciliation for each fiscal year.

(c) The Approving Official may extend the time period to submit a final voucher only in extraordinary circumstances. States shall submit a written request for an extension describing the extraordinary circumstances that necessitate an extension. The approval of any such request for extension shall be in writing, shall specify the new deadline for submitting the final voucher, and shall be signed by the Approving Official.

§ 1200.41 Disposition of unexpended balances.

(a) *Carry-forward balances.* Except as provided in paragraph (b) of this section, grant funds that remain unexpended at the end of a fiscal year and the expiration of a Highway Safety Plan shall be credited to the State's highway safety account for the new fiscal year, and made immediately available for use by the State, provided the following requirements are met:

(1) The State's new Highway Safety Plan has been approved by the Approving Official pursuant to § 1200.14 of this part;

(2) The State has identified Section 402 carry-forward funds by the program area from which they are removed and identified by program area the manner in which the carry-forward funds will be used under the new Highway Safety Plan.

(3) The State has identified Section 405 carry-forward funds by the national priority safety program under which they were awarded (*i.e.*, occupant protection, state traffic safety information system improvements, impaired driving, ignition interlock, distracted driving, motorcyclist safety or graduated driver licensing). These funds shall not be used for any other program.

(4) The State has submitted for approval an updated HS Form 217 for funds identified in paragraph (a)(2) or (a)(3) of this section. Reimbursement of costs is contingent upon the approval of updated Highway Safety Plan and HS Form 217.

(5) Funds carried forward from grant programs rescinded by MAP–21 shall be separately identified and shall be subject to the statutory and regulatory requirements that were in force at the time of award.

(b) *Deobligation of funds.* (1) Except as provided in paragraph (b)(2) of this section, unexpended grant funds shall not be available for expenditure beyond the period of three years after the last day of the fiscal year of apportionment or allocation.

(2) NHTSA shall notify States of any such unexpended grant funds no later than 180 days prior to the end of the period of availability specified in paragraph (b)(1) of this section and inform States of the deadline for commitment. States may commit such unexpended grant funds to a specific project by the specified deadline, and shall provide documentary evidence of that commitment, including a copy of an executed project agreement, to the Approving Official.

(3) Grant funds committed to a specific project in accordance with paragraph (b)(2) of this section shall remain committed to that project and be expended by the end of the succeeding fiscal year. The final voucher for that project shall be submitted within 90 days of the end of that fiscal year.

(4) NHTSA shall deobligate unexpended balances at the end of the time period in paragraph (b)(1) or (b)(3) of this section, whichever is applicable, and the funds shall lapse.

§ 1200.42 Post-grant adjustments.

The expiration of a Highway Safety Plan does not affect the ability of NHTSA to disallow costs and recover funds on the basis of a later audit or other review or the State's obligation to return any funds due as a result of later refunds, corrections, or other transactions.

§ 1200.43 Continuing requirements.

Notwithstanding the expiration of a Highway Safety Plan, the provisions for post-award requirements in 49 CFR part 18, including but not limited to equipment and audit, continue to apply to the grant funds authorized under 23 U.S.C. Chapter 4.

Subpart F—Non-Compliance

§ 1200.50 General.

Where a State is found to be in noncompliance with the requirements of the grant programs authorized under 23 U.S.C. Chapter 4 or with applicable law, the special conditions for high-risk grantees and the enforcement procedures of 49 CFR part 18, the sanctions procedures in § 1200.51, and any other sanctions or remedies permitted under Federal law may be applied as appropriate.

§ 1200.51 Sanctions—Reduction of apportionment.

(a) *Determination of sanctions.* (1) The Administrator shall not apportion any funds under 23 U.S.C. 402 to any State which is not implementing an approved highway safety program.

(2) If the Administrator has apportioned funds to a State and subsequently determines that the State is not implementing an approved highway safety program, the Administrator shall reduce the funds apportioned under 23 U.S.C. 402 to the State by amounts equal to not less than 20 percent, until such time as the Administrator determines that the State is implementing an approved highway safety program.

(3) The Administrator shall consider the gravity of the State's failure to implement an approved highway safety program in determining the amount of the reduction.

(4) If the Administrator determines that a State has begun implementing an approved highway safety program not later than July 31 of the fiscal year for which the funds were withheld, the Administrator shall promptly apportion to the State the funds withheld from its apportionment.

(5) If the Administrator determines that the State did not correct its failure by July 31 of the fiscal year for which the funds were withheld, the Administrator shall reapportion the withheld funds to the other States, in accordance with the formula specified in 23 U.S.C. 402(c), not later than the last day of the fiscal year.

(b) *Reconsideration of sanctions determination.* (1) In any fiscal year, if the Administrator determines that a State is not implementing an approved highway safety program in accordance with 23 U.S.C. 402 and other applicable Federal law, the Administrator shall issue to the State an advance notice, advising the State that the Administrator expects to either withhold funds from apportionment under 23 U.S.C. 402, or reduce the State's apportioned funds under 23 U.S.C. 402. The Administrator shall state the amount of the expected withholding or reduction. The advance notice will normally be sent not later than 60 days prior to final apportionment.

(2) If the Administrator issues an advance notice to a State, under paragraph (b)(1) of this section, the State may, within 30 days of its receipt of the advance notice, submit documentation demonstrating that it is implementing an approved highway safety program. Documentation shall be submitted to the NHTSA Administrator, 1200 New Jersey Avenue SE., Washington, DC 20590.

(3) If the Administrator decides, after reviewing all relevant information submitted, that the State is not implementing an approved highway safety program in accordance with 23 U.S.C. 402, the Administrator shall issue a final notice, advising the State either of the funds being withheld from apportionment under 23 U.S.C. 402, or of the amount of funds reduced from the apportionment under 23 U.S.C. 402. The final notice will normally be issued no later than September 30. The final notice of a reduction will be issued at the time of a final decision.

Subpart G—Special Provisions for Fiscal Year 2013 Highway Safety Grants and Highway Safety Grants Under Prior Authorizations

§ 1200.60 Fiscal year 2013 Section 402 grants.

Highway safety grants apportioned under 23 U.S.C. 402 for fiscal year 2013 shall be governed by the applicable implementing regulations at the time of grant award.

§ 1200.61 Fiscal year 2013 Section 405 grants.

(a) For fiscal year 2013 grants authorized under 23 U.S.C. 405(b), (c), (d), (f) and (g), a State shall submit electronically its application as provided in § 1200.11(h) to *NHTSAGrants@dot.gov* no later than March 25, 2013.

(b) If a State's application contains incomplete information, NHTSA may request additional information from the State prior to making a determination of award for each component of the Section 405 grant program. Failure to respond promptly for request of additional information may result in a State's disqualification from one or more Section 405 grants for fiscal year 2013.

(c) After reviewing applications and making award determinations, NHTSA shall, in writing, distribute funds available for obligation under Section 405 to qualifying States and specify any conditions or limitations imposed by law on the use of the funds.

(d) Grant awards are subject to the availability of funds. If there are insufficient funds to award full grant amounts to qualifying States, NHTSA may release interim amounts and release the remainder, up to the State's proportionate share of available funds, when it becomes available in the fiscal year.

(e) The administration, reconciliation and noncompliance provisions of subparts D through F of this part apply to fiscal year 2013 grants awarded to qualifying States.

§ 1200.62 Pre-2013 fiscal year grants.

Highway safety grants rescinded by MAP–21 are governed by the applicable implementing regulations at the time of grant award.

Appendix A to Part 1200—Certification and Assurances for Highway Safety Grants (23 U.S.C. Chapter 4)

State: ____________________

Fiscal Year: ________

Each fiscal year the State must sign these Certifications and Assurances that it complies with all requirements including applicable Federal statutes and regulations that are in effect during the grant period. (Requirements that also apply to subrecipients are noted under the applicable caption.)

In my capacity as the Governor's Representative for Highway Safety, I hereby provide the following certifications and assurances:

GENERAL REQUIREMENTS

To the best of my personal knowledge, the information submitted in the Highway Safety Plan in support of the State's application for Section 402 and Section 405 grants is accurate and complete. (Incomplete or incorrect information may result in the disapproval of the Highway Safety Plan.)

The Governor is the responsible official for the administration of the State highway safety program through a State highway safety agency that has adequate powers and is suitably equipped and organized (as evidenced by appropriate oversight procedures governing such areas as procurement, financial administration, and the use, management, and disposition of equipment) to carry out the program. (23 U.S.C. 402(b)(1)(A))

The State will comply with applicable statutes and regulations, including but not limited to:

- 23 U.S.C. Chapter 4—Highway Safety Act of 1966, as amended

• 49 CFR Part 18—Uniform Administrative Requirements for Grants and Cooperative Agreements to State and Local Governments

• 23 CFR Part 1200—Uniform Procedures for State Highway Safety Grant Programs

The State has submitted appropriate documentation for review to the single point of contact designated by the Governor to review Federal programs, as required by Executive Order 12372 (Intergovernmental Review of Federal Programs).

FEDERAL FUNDING ACCOUNTABILITY AND TRANSPARENCY ACT (FFATA)

The State will comply with FFATA guidance, *OMB Guidance on FFATA Subward and Executive Compensation Reporting*, August 27, 2010, (*https://www.fsrs.gov/documents/OMB_Guidance_on_FFATA_Subaward_and_Executive_Compensation_Reporting_08272010.pdf*) by reporting to FSRS.gov for each sub-grant awarded:

• Name of the entity receiving the award;

• Amount of the award;

• Information on the award including transaction type, funding agency, the North American Industry Classification System code or Catalog of Federal Domestic Assistance number (where applicable), program source;

• Location of the entity receiving the award and the primary location of performance under the award, including the city, State, congressional district, and country; and an award title descriptive of the purpose of each funding action;

• A unique identifier (DUNS);

• The names and total compensation of the five most highly compensated officers of the entity if:

(i) the entity in the preceding fiscal year received—

(I) 80 percent or more of its annual gross revenues in Federal awards;

(II) $25,000,000 or more in annual gross revenues from Federal awards; and

(ii) the public does not have access to information about the compensation of the senior executives of the entity through periodic reports filed under section 13(a) or 15(d) of the Securities Exchange Act of 1934 (15 U.S.C. 78m(a), 78o(d)) or section 6104 of the Internal Revenue Code of 1986;

• Other relevant information specified by OMB guidance.

NONDISCRIMINATION

(APPLIES TO SUBRECIPIENTS AS WELL AS STATES)

The State highway safety agency will comply with all Federal statutes and implementing regulations relating to nondiscrimination. These include but are not limited to: (a) Title VI of the Civil Rights Act of 1964 (Pub. L. 88–352), which prohibits discrimination on the basis of race, color or national origin (and 49 CFR Part 21); (b) Title IX of the Education Amendments of 1972, as amended (20 U.S.C. 1681–1683 and 1685–1686), which prohibits discrimination on the basis of sex; (c) Section 504 of the Rehabilitation Act of 1973, as amended (29 U.S.C. 794), and the Americans with Disabilities Act of 1990 (Pub. L. 101–336), as amended (42 U.S.C. 12101, *et seq.*), which prohibits discrimination on the basis of disabilities (and 49 CFR Part 27); (d) the Age Discrimination Act of 1975, as amended (42 U.S.C. 6101–6107), which prohibits discrimination on the basis of age; (e) the Civil Rights Restoration Act of 1987 (Pub. L. 100–259), which requires Federal-aid recipients and all subrecipients to prevent discrimination and ensure nondiscrimination in all of their programs and activities; (f) the Drug Abuse Office and Treatment Act of 1972 (Pub. L. 92–255), as amended, relating to nondiscrimination on the basis of drug abuse; (g) the comprehensive Alcohol Abuse and Alcoholism Prevention, Treatment and Rehabilitation Act of 1970 (Pub. L. 91–616), as amended, relating to nondiscrimination on the basis of alcohol abuse or alcoholism; (h) Sections 523 and 527 of the Public Health Service Act of 1912, as amended (42 U.S.C. 290dd–3 and 290ee–3), relating to confidentiality of alcohol and drug abuse patient records; (i) Title VIII of the Civil Rights Act of 1968, as amended (42 U.S.C. 3601, *et seq.*), relating to nondiscrimination in the sale, rental or financing of housing; (j) any other nondiscrimination provisions in the specific statute(s) under which application for Federal assistance is being made; and (k) the requirements of any other nondiscrimination statute(s) which may apply to the application.

THE DRUG-FREE WORKPLACE ACT OF 1988 (41 U.S.C. 8103)

The State will provide a drug-free workplace by:

• Publishing a statement notifying employees that the unlawful manufacture, distribution, dispensing, possession or use of a controlled substance is prohibited in the grantee's workplace and specifying the actions that will be taken against employees for violation of such prohibition;

• Establishing a drug-free awareness program to inform employees about:

○ The dangers of drug abuse in the workplace.

○ The grantee's policy of maintaining a drug-free workplace.

○ Any available drug counseling, rehabilitation, and employee assistance programs.

○ The penalties that may be imposed upon employees for drug violations occurring in the workplace.

○ Making it a requirement that each employee engaged in the performance of the

www.ingramcontent.com/pod-product-compliance
Lightning Source LLC
Chambersburg PA
CBHW060416220326
41598CB00021BA/2194

* 9 7 8 1 6 4 0 2 4 5 6 4 8 *